# Financial Accounting and Reporting

EIGHTEENTH EDITION

Barry Elliott and Jamie Elliott

## Pearson

Harlow, England • London • New York • Boston • San Francisco • Toronto • Sydney • Dubai • Singapore • Hong Kong
Tokyo • Seoul • Taipei • New Delhi • Cape Town • São Paulo • Mexico City • Madrid • Amsterdam • Munich • Paris • Milan

100 640 199

657.
3
ELL

**Pearson Education Limited**
Edinburgh Gate
Harlow CM20 2JE
United Kingdom
Tel: +44 (0)1279 623623
Web: www.pearson.com/uk

First published 1993 (print)
Second edition 1996 (print)
Third edition 1999 (print)
Fourth edition 2000 (print)
Fifth edition 2001 (print)
Sixth edition 2002 (print)
Seventh edition 2003 (print)
Eighth edition 2004 (print)
Ninth edition 2005 (print)
Tenth edition 2006 (print)
Eleventh edition 2007 (print)
Twelfth edition 2008 (print)
Thirteenth edition 2009 (print)
Fourteenth edition 2011 (print)
Fifteenth edition 2012 (print and electronic)
Sixteenth edition 2013 (print and electronic)
Seventeenth edition 2015 (print and electronic)
**Eighteenth edition 2017 (print and electronic)**

ISBN: 978-1-292-16240-9 (print)
       978-1-292-16243-0 (PDF)
       978-1-292-16242-3 (ePub)

**British Library Cataloguing-in-Publication Data**
A catalogue record for the print edition is available from the British Library

**Library of Congress Cataloging-in-Publication Data**
10 9 8 7 6 5 4 3 2 1
18 17

Front cover image: PM Images/GettyImages

Print edition typeset in 10/12 pt Ehrhardt MT Std by SPi Global
Printed and bound in Malaysia (CTP-PJB)

NOTE THAT ANY PAGE CROSS REFERENCES REFER TO THE PRINT EDITION

# Financial Accounting and Reporting

# Brief contents

**Preface**        xxi
**Publisher's acknowledgements**        xxvii

**Part 1**
**INTRODUCTION TO ACCOUNTING ON A CASH FLOW AND
ACCRUAL ACCOUNTING BASIS**        1

  1 Accounting and reporting on a cash flow basis        3
  2 Accounting and reporting on an accrual accounting basis        21

**Part 2**
**PREPARATION OF INTERNAL AND PUBLISHED FINANCIAL
STATEMENTS**        31

  3 Preparation of financial statements of comprehensive income,
    changes in equity and financial position        33
  4 Annual report: additional financial disclosures        70
  5 Statements of cash flows        102

**Part 3**
**REGULATORY FRAMEWORK – AN ATTEMPT TO ACHIEVE
UNIFORMITY**        129

  6 Financial reporting – evolution of global standards        131
  7 Concepts – evolution of an international conceptual framework        155
  8 Ethical behaviour and implications for accountants        173

**Part 4**
**INCOME AND ASSET VALUE MEASUREMENT SYSTEMS**        199

  9 Income and asset value measurement: an economist's approach        201
 10 Accounting for price-level changes        220
 11 Revenue recognition        253

**Part 5**

**STATEMENT OF FINANCIAL POSITION – EQUITY, LIABILITY AND ASSET MEASUREMENT AND DISCLOSURE**  277

12 Share capital, distributable profits and reduction of capital  279
13 Liabilities  303
14 Financial instruments  326
15 Employee benefits  359
16 Taxation in company accounts  386
17 Property, plant and equipment (PPE)  410
18 Leasing  443
19 Intangible assets  465
20 Inventories  493
21 Construction contracts  519

**Part 6**

**CONSOLIDATED ACCOUNTS**  543

22 Accounting for groups at the date of acquisition  545
23 Preparation of consolidated statements of financial position after the date of acquisition  565
24 Preparation of consolidated statements of income, changes in equity and cash flows  579
25 Accounting for associates and joint arrangements  601
26 Introduction to accounting for exchange differences  627

**Part 7**

**INTERPRETATION**  649

27 Earnings per share  651
28 Review of financial ratio analysis  677
29 Analysis of published financial statements  713
30 An introduction to digital financial reporting  755

**Part 8**

**ACCOUNTABILITY**  779

31 Corporate governance  781
32 Integrated reporting: sustainability, environmental and social  817

**Index**  853

# Contents

**Preface**                                                                    xxi
**Publisher's acknowledgements**                                               xxvii

Part I
INTRODUCTION TO ACCOUNTING ON A CASH FLOW AND
ACCRUAL ACCOUNTING BASIS                                                        I

1 **Accounting and reporting on a cash flow basis**                            3
  1.1    Introduction                                                           3
  1.2    Shareholders                                                           3
  1.3    What skills does an accountant require in respect of external reports?  4
  1.4    Managers                                                               4
  1.5    What skills does an accountant require in respect of internal reports?  5
  1.6    Procedural steps when reporting to internal users                      5
  1.7    Agency costs                                                           8
  1.8    Illustration of periodic financial statements prepared under the cash
         flow concept to disclose realised operating cash flows                 8
  1.9    Illustration of preparation of statement of financial position         13
  1.10   Treatment of non-current assets in the cash flow model                 14
  1.11   What are the characteristics of these data that make them reliable?    15
  1.12   Reports to external users                                              16
  Summary                                                                       17
  Review questions                                                              18
  Exercises                                                                     18
  Notes                                                                         20

2 **Accounting and reporting on an accrual accounting basis**                  21
  2.1    Introduction                                                           21
  2.2    Historical cost convention                                            22
  2.3    Accrual basis of accounting                                           22
  2.4    Mechanics of accrual accounting – adjusting cash receipts and payments 23
  2.5    Reformatting the statement of financial position                      24
  2.6    Accounting for the sacrifice of non-current assets                    24
  2.7    Published statement of cash flows                                     27

| | | |
|---|---|---|
| Summary | | 28 |
| Review questions | | 28 |
| Exercises | | 29 |
| Notes | | 30 |

**Part 2**
**PREPARATION OF INTERNAL AND PUBLISHED FINANCIAL STATEMENTS** 31

| | | |
|---|---|---|
| **3** | **Preparation of financial statements of comprehensive income, changes in equity and financial position** | **33** |
| 3.1 | Introduction | 33 |
| 3.2 | Preparing an internal statement of income from a trial balance | 33 |
| 3.3 | Reorganising the income and expenses into one of the formats required for publication | 36 |
| 3.4 | Format 1: classification of operating expenses and other income by function | 37 |
| 3.5 | Format 2: classification of operating expenses according to their nature | 40 |
| 3.6 | Other comprehensive income | 40 |
| 3.7 | How non-recurring or exceptional items can affect operating income | 41 |
| 3.8 | How decision-useful is the statement of comprehensive income? | 43 |
| 3.9 | Statement of changes in equity | 43 |
| 3.10 | The statement of financial position | 44 |
| 3.11 | The explanatory notes that are part of the financial statements | 45 |
| 3.12 | Has prescribing the formats meant that identical transactions are reported identically? | 48 |
| 3.13 | Fair presentation | 51 |
| 3.14 | What does an investor need in addition to the primary financial statements to make decisions? | 52 |
| | Summary | 56 |
| | Review questions | 57 |
| | Exercises | 58 |
| | Notes | 68 |
| **4** | **Annual report: additional financial disclosures** | **70** |
| 4.1 | Introduction | 70 |
| 4.2 | IAS 10 *Events after the Reporting Period* | 70 |
| 4.3 | IAS 8 *Accounting Policies, Changes in Accounting Estimates and Errors* | 73 |
| 4.4 | What do segment reports provide? | 75 |
| 4.5 | IFRS 8 *Operating Segments* | 75 |
| 4.6 | Benefits and continuing concerns following the issue of IFRS 8 | 79 |
| 4.7 | Discontinued operations – IFRS 5 *Non-current Assets Held for Sale and Discontinued Operations* | 82 |
| 4.8 | Held for sale – IFRS 5 *Non-current Assets Held for Sale and Discontinued Operations* | 83 |
| 4.9 | IAS 24 *Related Party Disclosures* | 85 |
| | Summary | 90 |
| | Review questions | 90 |
| | Exercises | 91 |
| | Notes | 101 |

**5 Statements of cash flows** 102

5.1 Introduction 102

5.2 Development of statements of cash flows 102

5.3 Applying IAS 7 (revised) Statements of Cash Flows 103

5.4 Step approach to preparation of a statement of cash flows – indirect method 106

5.5 Additional notes required by IAS 7 109

5.6 Analysing statements of cash flows 110

5.7 Approach to answering questions with time constraints 116

5.8 Preparing a statement of cash flows when no statement of income is available 118

5.9 Critique of cash flow accounting 120

Summary 120

Review questions 121

Exercises 121

Notes 128

**Part 3**
**REGULATORY FRAMEWORK – AN ATTEMPT TO ACHIEVE UNIFORMITY** 129

**6 Financial reporting – evolution of global standards** 131

6.1 Introduction 131

6.2 Why do we need financial reporting standards? 131

6.3 Why do we need standards to be mandatory? 132

6.4 Arguments in support of standards 134

6.5 Arguments against standards 135

6.6 Standard setting and enforcement by the Financial Reporting Council (FRC) in the UK 135

6.7 The International Accounting Standards Board 138

6.8 Standard setting and enforcement in the European Union (EU) 139

6.9 Standard setting and enforcement in the US 142

6.10 Advantages and disadvantages of global standards for publicly accountable entities 144

6.11 How do reporting requirements differ for non-publicly accountable entities? 145

6.12 IFRS for SMEs 146

6.13 Why have there been differences in financial reporting? 146

6.14 Move towards a conceptual framework 150

Summary 151

Review questions 151

Exercises 152

Notes 153

**7 Concepts – evolution of an international conceptual framework** 155

7.1 Introduction 155

7.2 Different countries meant different financial statements 155

7.3 Historical overview of the evolution of financial accounting theory 156

7.4    Framework for the Preparation and Presentation of Financial Statements 158
7.5    Conceptual Framework for Financial Reporting 2010                        159
7.6    Chapter 4 content                                                       163
7.7    The *Conceptual Framework for Financial Reporting* – latest developments   164
7.8    Current developments – concept of materiality                           167
Summary                                                                        169
Review questions                                                               170
Exercises                                                                      170
Notes                                                                          172

8  **Ethical behaviour and implications for accountants**                      **173**
8.1    Introduction                                                            173
8.2    The meaning of ethical behaviour                                        173
8.3    The accounting standard-setting process and ethics                     174
8.4    The IFAC *Code of Ethics for Professional Accountants*                  175
8.5    Implications of ethical values for the principles – versus rules-based
       approaches to accounting standards                                      178
8.6    Ethics in the accountant's work environment – a research report        181
8.7    Implications of unethical behaviour for stakeholders using the financial
       reports                                                                 183
8.8    The increasing role of whistle-blowing                                  188
8.9    Legal requirement to report – national and international regulation     190
8.10   Why should students learn ethics?                                       191
Summary                                                                        192
Review questions                                                               193
Exercises                                                                      195
Notes                                                                          197

Part 4
INCOME AND ASSET VALUE MEASUREMENT
SYSTEMS                                                                         199

9  **Income and asset value measurement: an economist's**
   **approach**                                                                **201**
9.1    Introduction                                                            201
9.2    Role and objective of income measurement                               201
9.3    Accountant's view of income, capital and value                         204
9.4    Critical comment on the accountant's measure                           207
9.5    Economist's view of income, capital and value                          208
9.6    Critical comment on the economist's measure                            214
9.7    Income, capital and changing price levels                              214
Summary                                                                        216
Review questions                                                               216
Exercises                                                                      217
Notes                                                                          219
Bibliography                                                                   219

## 10 Accounting for price-level changes — 220

| | | |
|---|---|---|
| 10.1 | Introduction | 220 |
| 10.2 | Review of the problems of historical cost accounting (HCA) | 220 |
| 10.3 | Inflation accounting | 221 |
| 10.4 | The concepts in principle | 221 |
| 10.5 | The four models illustrated for a company with cash purchases and sales | 222 |
| 10.6 | Critique of each model | 226 |
| 10.7 | Operating capital maintenance – a comprehensive example | 229 |
| 10.8 | Critique of CCA statements | 240 |
| 10.9 | Measurement bases | 241 |
| 10.10 | The IASB position where there is hyperinflation | 241 |
| 10.11 | Future developments | 242 |
| | Summary | 244 |
| | Review questions | 245 |
| | Exercises | 245 |
| | Notes | 252 |
| | Bibliography | 252 |

## 11 Revenue recognition — 253

| | | |
|---|---|---|
| 11.1 | Introduction | 253 |
| 11.2 | IAS 18 *Revenue* | 254 |
| 11.3 | The issues involved in developing a new standard | 255 |
| 11.4 | The challenges under both IAS 18 and IFRS 15 | 256 |
| 11.5 | IFRS 15 *Revenue from Contracts with Customers* | 257 |
| 11.6 | Five-step process to identify the amount and timing of revenue | 258 |
| 11.7 | Disclosures | 269 |
| | Summary | 270 |
| | Review questions | 270 |
| | Exercises | 272 |
| | Notes | 276 |

## Part 5
## STATEMENT OF FINANCIAL POSITION – EQUITY, LIABILITY AND ASSET MEASUREMENT AND DISCLOSURE — 277

## 12 Share capital, distributable profits and reduction of capital — 279

| | | |
|---|---|---|
| 12.1 | Introduction | 279 |
| 12.2 | Common themes | 279 |
| 12.3 | Total owners' equity: an overview | 280 |
| 12.4 | Total shareholders' funds: more detailed explanation | 281 |
| 12.5 | Accounting entries on issue of shares | 283 |
| 12.6 | Creditor protection: capital maintenance concept | 284 |
| 12.7 | Creditor protection: why capital maintenance rules are necessary | 284 |
| 12.8 | Creditor protection: how to quantify the amounts available to meet creditors' claims | 285 |
| 12.9 | Issued share capital: minimum share capital | 286 |

12.10  Distributable profits: general considerations 286
12.11  Distributable profits: how to arrive at the amount using
        relevant accounts 288
12.12  When may capital be reduced? 288
12.13  Writing off part of capital which has already been lost and is not
        represented by assets 288
12.14  Repayment of part of paid-in capital to shareholders or cancellation
        of unpaid share capital 294
12.15  Purchase of own shares 294
Summary 296
Review questions 296
Exercises 297
Notes 302

13  **Liabilities** 303
13.1   Introduction 303
13.2   Provisions – a decision tree approach to their impact on
        the statement of financial position 304
13.3   Treatment of provisions 305
13.4   The general principles that IAS 37 applies to the recognition
        of a provision 305
13.5   Management approach to measuring the amount of a provision 306
13.6   Application of criteria illustrated 308
13.7   Provisions for specific purposes 308
13.8   Contingent liabilities 311
13.9   Contingent assets 311
13.10  ED IAS 37 *Non-financial Liabilities* 312
13.11  ED/2010/1 *Measurement of Liabilities in IAS 37* 319
Summary 319
Review questions 320
Exercises 320
Notes 325

14  **Financial instruments** 326
14.1   Introduction 326
14.2   Financial instruments – the IASB's problem child 326
14.3   IAS 32 *Financial Instruments: Disclosure and Presentation* 329
14.4   IFRS 9 *Financial Instruments* 335
14.5   IFRS 7 *Financial Instruments: Disclosure* 345
Summary 351
Review questions 351
Exercises 352
Notes 358

15  **Employee benefits** 359
15.1   Introduction 359
15.2   Greater employee interest in pensions 359
15.3   Financial reporting implications 360
15.4   Types of scheme 360

15.5    Defined contribution pension schemes                                      363
15.6    Defined benefit pension schemes                                          363
15.7    IAS 19 (revised 2011) *Employee Benefits*                                364
15.8    The asset or liability for pension and other post-retirement costs       364
15.9    Changes in the pension asset or liability position                       365
15.10   Comprehensive illustration                                               368
15.11   Multi-employer plans                                                     369
15.12   Disclosures                                                              369
15.13   Other long-service benefits                                              370
15.14   Short-term benefits                                                      370
15.15   Termination benefits                                                     371
15.16   IFRS 2 *Share-based Payment*                                             372
15.17   Scope of IFRS 2                                                          373
15.18   Recognition and measurement                                             373
15.19   Equity-settled share-based payments                                     373
15.20   Cash-settled share-based payments                                       376
15.21   Transactions which may be settled in cash or shares                     377
15.22   IAS 26 *Accounting and Reporting by Retirement Benefit Plans*           377
Summary                                                                          380
Review questions                                                                 380
Exercises                                                                        381
Notes                                                                            385

**16  Taxation in company accounts**                                            **386**
16.1    Introduction                                                             386
16.2    Corporation tax                                                          386
16.3    Corporation tax systems – the theoretical background                    387
16.4    Corporation tax and dividends                                           388
16.5    Corporation tax systems – avoidance and evasion                         389
16.6    IAS 12 – accounting for current taxation                                393
16.7    Deferred tax                                                            394
16.8    A critique of deferred taxation                                         402
16.9    Value added tax (VAT)                                                   404
Summary                                                                          405
Review questions                                                                 405
Exercises                                                                        406
Notes                                                                            409

**17  Property, plant and equipment (PPE)**                                     **410**
17.1    Introduction                                                            410
17.2    PPE – concepts and the relevant IASs and IFRSs                          410
17.3    What is PPE?                                                            411
17.4    How is the cost of PPE determined?                                      412
17.5    What is depreciation?                                                   414
17.6    What are the constituents in the depreciation formula?                  415
17.7    Calculation of depreciation                                             417
17.8    Measurement subsequent to initial recognition                          421
17.9    IAS 36 *Impairment of Assets*                                          423
17.10   IFRS 5 *Non-current Assets Held for Sale and Discontinued Operations*  428

17.11  Disclosure requirements                                          429
17.12  Government grants towards the cost of PPE                         430
17.13  Investment properties                                            432
17.14  Effect of accounting policy for PPE on the interpretation of
       the financial statements                                        433
Summary                                                                 435
Review questions                                                        435
Exercises                                                               436
Notes                                                                   442

**18 Leasing**                                                          **443**
18.1   Introduction                                                     443
18.2   Need for an accounting standard on leasing                       444
18.3   Distinction between finance leases and operating leases          447
18.4   Reason for a replacement standard for IAS 17                     448
18.5   IFRS 16 *Leases* – the criteria that determine whether it's a lease  449
18.6   Leases in the financial statements of lessees                    451
18.7   Leases in the financial statements of lessors                    455
18.8   Sale and leaseback transactions                                  457
18.9   An evaluation of the new IFRS 16                                 460
Summary                                                                 460
Review questions                                                        461
Exercises                                                               462
Note                                                                    464

**19 Intangible assets**                                                **465**
19.1   Introduction                                                     465
19.2   Intangible assets defined                                        465
19.3   Accounting treatment for research and development                468
19.4   Why is research expenditure not capitalised?                     469
19.5   Capitalising development costs                                   470
19.6   Disclosure of R&D                                                471
19.7   *IFRS for SMEs*' treatment of intangible assets                  471
19.8   Internally generated and purchased goodwill                      472
19.9   The accounting treatment of goodwill                             472
19.10  Critical comment on the various methods that have
       been used to account for goodwill                                474
19.11  Negative goodwill/badwill                                        476
19.12  Brands                                                           477
19.13  Accounting for acquired brands                                   479
19.14  Intellectual capital disclosures (ICDs) in the annual report     480
19.15  Review of the implementation of IFRS 3                           481
19.16  Review of the implementation of identified intangibles under IAS 38  481
Summary                                                                 483
Review questions                                                        483
Exercises                                                               485
Notes                                                                   491

## 20 Inventories — **493**

| | | |
|---|---|---:|
| 20.1 | Introduction | 493 |
| 20.2 | Inventory defined | 493 |
| 20.3 | The impact of inventory valuation on profits | 494 |
| 20.4 | IAS 2 *Inventories* | 495 |
| 20.5 | Inventory valuation | 496 |
| 20.6 | Work in progress | 502 |
| 20.7 | Inventory control | 504 |
| 20.8 | Creative accounting | 505 |
| 20.9 | Audit of the year-end physical inventory count | 507 |
| 20.10 | Published accounts | 509 |
| 20.11 | Agricultural activity | 510 |
| | Summary | 513 |
| | Review questions | 513 |
| | Exercises | 514 |
| | Notes | 518 |

## 21 Construction contracts — **519**

| | | |
|---|---|---:|
| 21.1 | Introduction | 519 |
| 21.2 | The need to replace IAS 11 *Construction Contracts* | 519 |
| 21.3 | Identification of contract revenue under IAS 11 | 521 |
| 21.4 | Identification of contract costs under IAS 11 | 521 |
| 21.5 | IFRS 15 treatment of construction contracts | 524 |
| 21.6 | An approach when a contract can be separated into components | 526 |
| 21.7 | Accounting for a contract – an example | 527 |
| 21.8 | Illustration – loss-making contract using the step approach | 529 |
| 21.9 | Public–private partnerships (PPPs) | 531 |
| | Summary | 534 |
| | Review questions | 535 |
| | Exercises | 535 |
| | Notes | 542 |

### Part 6
## CONSOLIDATED ACCOUNTS — 543

## 22 Accounting for groups at the date of acquisition — **545**

| | | |
|---|---|---:|
| 22.1 | Introduction | 545 |
| 22.2 | Preparing consolidated accounts for a wholly owned subsidiary | 545 |
| 22.3 | IFRS 10 *Consolidated Financial Statements* | 545 |
| 22.4 | Fair values | 547 |
| 22.5 | Illustration where there is a wholly owned subsidiary | 548 |
| 22.6 | Preparing consolidated accounts when there is a partly owned subsidiary | 549 |
| 22.7 | The treatment of differences between a subsidiary's fair value and book value | 552 |
| 22.8 | The parent issues shares to acquire shares in a subsidiary | 553 |
| 22.9 | IFRS 3 *Business Combinations* treatment of goodwill at the date of acquisition | 554 |

|  | 22.10 | When may a parent company not be required to prepare consolidated accounts? | 554 |
|  | 22.11 | When may a parent company exclude or not exclude a subsidiary from a consolidation? | 555 |
|  | 22.12 | IFRS 13 *Fair Value Measurement* | 555 |
|  | 22.13 | What advantages are there for stakeholders from requiring groups to prepare consolidated accounts? | 557 |
|  | Summary | | 557 |
|  | Review questions | | 557 |
|  | Exercises | | 558 |
|  | Notes | | 564 |

| **23** | **Preparation of consolidated statements of financial position after the date of acquisition** | | **565** |
|  | 23.1 | Introduction | 565 |
|  | 23.2 | Uniform accounting policies and reporting dates | 565 |
|  | 23.3 | Pre- and post-acquisition profits/losses | 565 |
|  | 23.4 | The Bend Group – assuming there have been no inter-group transactions | 566 |
|  | 23.5 | Inter-company transactions | 568 |
|  | 23.6 | The Prose Group – assuming there have been inter-group transactions | 569 |
|  | Summary | | 571 |
|  | Review questions | | 572 |
|  | Exercises | | 572 |
|  | Notes | | 578 |

| **24** | **Preparation of consolidated statements of income, changes in equity and cash flows** | | **579** |
|  | 24.1 | Introduction | 579 |
|  | 24.2 | Eliminate inter-company transactions | 579 |
|  | 24.3 | Preparation of a consolidated statement of income – the Ante Group | 580 |
|  | 24.4 | The statement of changes in equity (SOCE) | 582 |
|  | 24.5 | Other consolidation adjustments | 582 |
|  | 24.6 | A subsidiary acquired part-way through the year | 584 |
|  | 24.7 | Published format statement of income | 586 |
|  | 24.8 | Consolidated statements of cash flows | 587 |
|  | Summary | | 589 |
|  | Review questions | | 589 |
|  | Exercises | | 590 |
|  | Notes | | 600 |

| **25** | **Accounting for associates and joint arrangements** | | **601** |
|  | 25.1 | Introduction | 601 |
|  | 25.2 | Definitions of associates and of significant influence | 601 |
|  | 25.3 | The treatment of associated companies in consolidated accounts | 602 |
|  | 25.4 | The Brill Group – group accounts with a profit-making associate | 602 |
|  | 25.5 | The Brill Group – group accounts with a loss-making associate | 605 |
|  | 25.6 | The acquisition of an associate part-way through the year | 607 |

| | | |
|---|---|---|
| 25.7 | Joint arrangements | 608 |
| 25.8 | Disclosure in the financial statements | 612 |
| 25.9 | Parent company use of the equity method in its separate financial statements | 613 |
| | Summary | 615 |
| | Review questions | 615 |
| | Exercises | 616 |
| | Notes | 626 |

**26 Introduction to accounting for exchange differences**      **627**

| | | |
|---|---|---|
| 26.1 | Introduction | 627 |
| 26.2 | How to record foreign currency transactions in a company's own books | 628 |
| 26.3 | Boil plc – a more detailed illustration | 630 |
| 26.4 | IAS 21 *Concept of Functional and Presentation Currencies* | 631 |
| 26.5 | Translating the functional currency into the presentation currency | 633 |
| 26.6 | Preparation of consolidated accounts | 633 |
| 26.7 | How to reduce the risk of translation differences | 637 |
| 26.8 | Critique of the use of presentational currency | 638 |
| 26.9 | IAS 29 *Financial Reporting in Hyperinflationary Economies* | 638 |
| | Summary | 640 |
| | Review questions | 640 |
| | Exercises | 641 |
| | Notes | 648 |

**Part 7**
**INTERPRETATION**      **649**

**27 Earnings per share**      **651**

| | | |
|---|---|---|
| 27.1 | Introduction | 651 |
| 27.2 | Why is the earnings per share figure important? | 651 |
| 27.3 | How is the EPS figure calculated? | 652 |
| 27.4 | The use to shareholders of the EPS | 653 |
| 27.5 | Illustration of the basic EPS calculation | 654 |
| 27.6 | Adjusting the number of shares used in the basic EPS calculation | 654 |
| 27.7 | Rights issues | 657 |
| 27.8 | Adjusting the earnings and number of shares used in the diluted EPS calculation | 662 |
| 27.9 | Procedure where there are several potential dilutions | 664 |
| 27.10 | Exercise of conversion rights during the financial year | 666 |
| 27.11 | Disclosure requirements of IAS 33 | 666 |
| 27.12 | The Improvement Project | 668 |
| 27.13 | The Convergence Project | 668 |
| | Summary | 669 |
| | Review questions | 669 |
| | Exercises | 670 |
| | Notes | 676 |

## 28 Review of financial ratio analysis    677

| | | |
|---|---|---|
| 28.1 | Introduction | 677 |
| 28.2 | Overview of techniques for the analysis of financial data | 678 |
| 28.3 | Ratio analysis – a case study | 679 |
| 28.4 | Introductory review | 680 |
| 28.5 | Financial statement analysis, part 1 – financial performance | 683 |
| 28.6 | Financial statement analysis, part 2 – liquidity | 690 |
| 28.7 | Financial statement analysis, part 3 – financing | 693 |
| 28.8 | Peer comparison | 695 |
| 28.9 | Report based on the analysis | 696 |
| 28.10 | Caution when using ratios for prediction | 697 |
| | Summary | 699 |
| | Review questions | 699 |
| | Exercises | 700 |
| | Note | 712 |

## 29 Analysis of published financial statements    713

| | | |
|---|---|---|
| 29.1 | Introduction | 713 |
| 29.2 | Improvement of information for shareholders | 714 |
| 29.3 | Published financial statements – their limitations for interpretation purposes | 716 |
| 29.4 | Published financial statements – additional entity-wide cash-based performance measures | 717 |
| 29.5 | Ratio thresholds to satisfy Shariah compliance | 720 |
| 29.6 | Use of ratios in restrictive loan covenants | 721 |
| 29.7 | Investor-specific ratios | 724 |
| 29.8 | Determining value | 727 |
| 29.9 | Predicting corporate failure | 732 |
| 29.10 | Professional risk assessors | 736 |
| 29.11 | Valuing shares of an unquoted company – quantitative process | 737 |
| 29.12 | Valuing shares of an unquoted company – qualitative process | 740 |
| 29.13 | Possible effect of 'Brexit' on financial statements | 742 |
| | Summary | 743 |
| | Review questions | 744 |
| | Exercises | 745 |
| | Notes | 753 |

## 30 An introduction to digital financial reporting    755

| | | |
|---|---|---|
| 30.1 | Introduction | 755 |
| 30.2 | The objectives of financial reporting | 755 |
| 30.3 | Reports and the flow of information pre-XBRL | 757 |
| 30.4 | What are HTML, XML and XBRL? | 758 |
| 30.5 | Reports and the flow of information post-XBRL | 759 |
| 30.6 | Why are companies adopting XBRL? | 760 |
| 30.7 | What are the processes followed to adopt XBRL for outputting information? | 763 |
| 30.8 | What is needed when receiving XBRL output information? | 766 |
| 30.9 | Progress of XBRL development for internal accounting | 771 |
| 30.10 | Real-time reporting | 771 |

Stakeholder interaction with XBRL data     772
Summary     773
Review questions     774
Exercises     774
Notes     775
Bibliography     776

**Part 8
ACCOUNTABILITY**     779

**31 Corporate governance**     **781**
31.1   Introduction     781
31.2   A systems perspective     781
31.3   Different jurisdictions have different governance priorities     783
31.4   Pressures on good governance behaviour vary over time     785
31.5   Types of past unethical behaviour     785
31.6   The effect on capital markets of good corporate governance     786
31.7   Risk management     787
31.8   The role of internal control, internal audit and audit committees in
corporate governance     789
31.9   External audits in corporate governance     790
31.10   Executive remuneration in the UK     796
31.11   Corporate governance, legislation and codes     800
31.12   Corporate governance – the UK experience     801
Summary     810
Review questions     811
Exercises     813
Notes     815

**32 Integrated reporting: sustainability, environmental and social**     **817**
32.1   Introduction     817
32.2   Environmental and social disasters and the adverse consequences
that can follow     818
32.3   Management accountability for environmental and social responsibility     821
32.4   Integrated reporting concepts     825
32.5   The historical context of the evolution of integrated reporting
including the drivers of this movement     828
32.6   The efforts on which integrated reporting builds     832
32.7   The contribution of accountants     837
32.8   Integrated reporting – its impact on the future development of
financial reporting and accounting     843
Review questions     844
Exercises     846
Notes     851

**Index**     853

# Preface

Our objective is to provide a balanced and comprehensive framework to enable students to acquire the requisite knowledge and skills to appraise current practice critically and to evaluate proposed changes from a theoretical base. To this end, the text contains:

- extracts from current IASs and IFRSs;
- illustrations from published accounts;
- a range of review questions;
- exercises of varying difficulty;
- extensive references.

Solutions to selected exercises marked in the text with * can be found on MyAccountingLab.

We have assumed that readers will have an understanding of financial accounting to a foundation or first-year level, although the text and exercises have been designed on the basis that a brief revision is still helpful. For the preparation of financial statements in Parts 1, 2 and 5 we have structured the chapters to assist readers who may have no accounting knowledge.

Lecturers are using the text selectively to support a range of teaching programmes for second-year and final-year undergraduate and postgraduate programmes. We have therefore attempted to provide subject coverage of sufficient breadth and depth to assist selective use.

The text has been adopted for financial accounting, reporting and analysis modules on:

- second-year undergraduate courses for Accounting, Business Studies and Combined Studies;
- final-year undergraduate courses for Accounting, Business Studies and Combined Studies;
- MBA courses;
- specialist MSc courses; and
- professional courses preparing students for professional accountancy examinations.

## Changes to the eighteenth edition

Our emphasis has been on keeping the text current and responsive to constructive comments from reviewers and lecturers.

### National accounting standards and the IASB

Since 2005 UK listed companies have followed international standards EU-IFRS for their consolidated accounts.

### Accounting standards – eighteenth edition updates

Chapters covering the following International Standards have been revised. They are as follows:

| | | |
|---|---|---|
| Chapter 3 | Preparation of financial statements | IAS 1 |
| Chapter 4 | Preparation of additional financial statements | IAS 10, IAS 24, IFRS 5 and IFRS 8 |
| Chapter 5 | Statements of cash flows | IAS 7 |
| Chapter 10 | Accounting for price-level changes | IAS 29 |
| Chapter 11 | Revenue recognition | IFRS 15 and IAS 18 |
| Chapter 13 | Liabilities | IAS 37/ED/2010/1 |
| Chapter 14 | Financial instruments | IAS 32, IFRS 7 and IFRS 9 |
| Chapter 15 | Employee benefits | IAS 19 (revised 2011), IAS 26 and IFRS 2 |
| Chapter 16 | Taxation in company accounts | IAS 12 |
| Chapter 17 | Property, plant and equipment (PPE) | IAS 16, IAS 20, IAS 23, IAS 36, IAS 40 and IFRS 5 |
| Chapter 18 | Leasing | IFRS 16 |
| Chapter 19 | Intangible assets | IAS 38 and IFRS 3 |
| Chapter 20 | Inventories | IAS 2 |
| Chapter 21 | Construction contracts | IAS 11 and IFRS 15 |
| Chapters 22–26 | Consolidation | IAS 21, IAS 28, IFRS 3, 10, 11, 12 and 13 |
| Chapter 27 | Earnings per share | IAS 33 |

## Part 1 Introduction to accounting on a cash flow and accrual accounting basis

Chapters 1 and 2 continue to cover accounting and reporting on a cash flow and accrual basis.

## Part 2 Preparation of internal and published financial statements

Chapters 3 to 5 have been revised. They cover the preparation of statements of income, changes in equity, financial position and cash flows.

## Part 3 Regulatory framework – an attempt to achieve uniformity

Chapters 6 and 7 have been revised.

## Part 4 Income and asset value measurement systems

Chapters 9 and 10 covering the economic income approach and accounting for price-level changes have been retained. Chapter 11 discusses the application of IFRS 15 and IAS 18.

## Part 5 Statement of financial position

Chapters 12–21 are core chapters which have been retained and updated as appropriate.

## Part 6 Consolidated accounts

Chapters 22–26 have been updated and revised to improve accessibility with explanations from first principles.

## Part 7 Interpretation

Chapters 28 and 29 are retained, aiming at encouraging good report writing based on the pyramid approach to ratios and an introduction to other tools and techniques for specific assignments. Chapter 30 has been revised to discuss an overview of financial reporting on the internet.

## Part 8 Accountability

Chapters 31 and 32 have been updated and continue to focus on the accountant's role in corporate governance and in the development of Integrated Reporting.

## Recent developments

We cover the issue by the IASB of IFRS 16 *Leases* and the IFRS 9 *Financial Instruments* provisions on the impairment requirements, which follow an 'expected loss' model.

In addition we discuss Integrated Reporting and relevant EU proposals, such as that the remuneration policy for company directors should also contribute to the long-term growth of the company, and SEC requirements such as the publication of pay ratios which might be adopted by the UK government.

The content of financial reports continues to be subjected to discussion with tension between preparers, stakeholders, auditors, academics and standard setters; this is mirrored in the tension that exists between theory and practice.

- Preparers favour reporting transactions on a historical cost basis, which is reliable but does not provide shareholders with relevant information to appraise past performance or to predict future earnings.
- Shareholders favour forward-looking reports relevant in estimating future dividend and capital growth and in understanding environmental and social impacts.
- Stakeholders favour quantified and narrative disclosure of environmental and social impacts and the steps taken to reduce negative impacts.
- Auditors favour reports that are verifiable so that the figures can be substantiated to avoid them being proved wrong at a later date.
- Academic accountants favour reports that reflect economic reality and are relevant in appraising management performance and in assessing the capacity of the company to adapt.

- Standard setters lean towards the academic view and favour reporting according to the commercial substance of a transaction.

In order to understand the tensions that exist, students need:

- the skill to prepare financial statements in accordance with the historical cost and current cost conventions, both of which appear in annual financial reports;

- an understanding of the main thrust of mandatory and voluntary standards;

- an understanding of the degree of flexibility available to the preparers and the impact of this on reported earnings and the figures in the statement of financial position;

- an understanding of the limitations of financial reports in portraying economic reality; and

- an exposure to source material and other published material in so far as time permits.

## Acknowledgements

Financial reporting is a dynamic area and we see it as extremely important that the text should reflect this and be kept current. Assistance has been generously given by colleagues and many others in the preparation and review of the text and assessment material. This eighteenth edition continues to be very much a result of the authors, colleagues, reviewers and Pearson editorial and production staff working as a team and we are grateful to all concerned for their assistance in achieving this.

We owe particular thanks to Charles Batchelor, formerly of FTC Kaplan, for 'Financial instruments' (Chapter 14); Ozer Erman of Kingston University for 'Share capital, distributable profits and reduction of capital' (Chapter 12); Paul Robins of the Financial Training Company for 'Leasing' (Chapter 18); Professor Garry Tibbits of the University of Western Sydney for 'Integrated Reporting' (Chapter 32); Hendrika Tibbits of the University of Western Sydney for 'An introduction to digital financial reporting' (Chapter 30); and David Towers, formerly of Keele University, for 'Taxation in company accounts' (Chapter 16).

The authors are grateful for the constructive comments received over various editions from the following reviewers who have assisted us in making improvements: Andreas Scholze of Osnabruck University; Christos Kallandranis of Regent's University London; Ian Money of The University of York; Katherine Martin of University Of Nottingham; Kathryn Heam of University of Greenwich; Svend Erik Thomsen of University of Southern Denmark; Pik Liew of Essex University; Anitha Majeed of Coventry University; Allison Wylde of London Metropolitan University; Terry Morris of Queen Mary University of London; Ajjay Mandal of London South Bank University; and Michael Jeffrey of Manchester Metropolitan University. We would also like to thank the reviewers of this new edition of the book.

Thanks are owed to Keith Brown, formerly of De Montfort University; Kenneth N. Field of the University of Leeds; David Murphy of Manchester Business School; Bahadur Najak of the University of Durham; Graham Sara of the University of Warwick; and Laura Spira of Oxford Brookes University.

Thanks are also due to the following organisations: the Financial Reporting Council, the International Accounting Standards Board, the Association of Chartered Certified Accountants, the Association of International Accountants, the Chartered Institute of Management Accountants, the Institute of Certified Public Accountants (CPA) in Ireland, the Institute of Chartered Accountants of England and Wales, the Institute of Chartered Accountants of Scotland and the Institute of Chartered Secretaries and Administrators.

We would also like to thank the authors of some of the end-of-chapter exercises. Some of these exercises have been inherited from a variety of institutions with which we have been associated, and we have unfortunately lost the identities of the originators of such material with the passage of time. We are sorry that we cannot acknowledge them by name and hope that they will excuse us for using their material.

We are indebted to Rebecca Pedley and the editorial team at Pearson Education for active support in keeping us largely to schedule and the attractively produced and presented text.

Finally we thank our wives, Di and Jacklin, for their continued good-humoured support during the period of writing and revisions, and Giles Elliott for his critical comment from the commencement of the project. We alone remain responsible for any errors and for the thoughts and views that are expressed.

*Barry and Jamie Elliott*

# Publisher's acknowledgements

We are grateful to the following for permission to reproduce copyright material:

## Figures

Figure on p. 49 from Annual Report, Inventories, http://www.astrazeneca-annualreports.com/2007/financial_statements/accounting_policies_group.asp.; Figure on p. 259 from Hewlett-Packard Company and Subsidiaries, Annual Report 2013, Note 1, pp. 86–8; Figures 30.1, 30.2, 30.3 from www.xbrl.org.au/training/NSWWorkshop.pdf

## Text

Extract on p. 54 from IFRS Practice Statement Management Commentary. International Financial Reporting Standards Foundation (IFRS / IASB). http://www.ifrs.org/Current-Projects/IASB-Projects/Management-Commentary/P.s/Management-Commentary.aspx. This publication contains copyright material of the IFRS Foundation in respect of which all rights are reserved. Reproduced by Pearson with the permission of the IFRS Foundation. No permission granted to third parties to reproduce or distribute. For full access to IFRS Standards and the work of the IFRS Foundation please visit http://eifrs.ifrs.org; Exercise on p. 67 from F1 November 2014 Question Paper, p. 10. http://www.cimaglobal.com/Documents/Student%20docs/2010%20syllabus%20docs/F1/F1%20November%202014%20Question%20Paper.pdf ; Extract on p. 88 from IAS 24 (BC 43). IAS 24 Related Party Disclosures, IASB, revised 2009 © 2014 International Accreditation Service, © Copyright IFRS Foundation; Exercises on pp. 99, 437, 438, 439, 563, 750 from Association of Chartered Certified Accountants (ACCA), We are grateful to the Association of Chartered Certified Accountants (ACCA) for permission to reproduce past examination questions. The suggested solutions in the exam answer bank have been prepared by us, unless otherwise stated.; Exercise on p. 100 from Institute of Certified Public Accountants (CPA), Professional Stage 1 Corporate Reporting Examination, August 2011), p. 9, http://www.cpaireland.ie/docs/default-source/Students/Study-Support/P1-Corporate-Reporting/august-2011.pdf?sfvrsn=0; Exercise on p. 125 from Institute of Certified Public Accountants (CPA) Professional Stage 1 Corporate Reporting Examination, April 2013; Extracts on pp. 313, 315, 316, 317 from ED IAS 37 Non-financial Liabilities, IASB, 2005. IAS © 2014 International Accreditation Service, © Copyright IFRS Foundation; Extract on p. 328 from Statement from G-20 Summit, Summit on Financial Markets and the World Economy, 15 November 2008. https://georgewbush-whitehouse.archiv. . .; Extracts on pp. 340, 347 from IFRS 9 Financial Instruments, © Copyright IFRS Foundation; Extracts on pp. 346, 348 from IAS 7 Statement of Cash Flow, © Copyright IFRS Foundation; Extract on p. 348 from Findel plc 2015 Annual Report, p. s 105–108 http://www.findel.co.uk/content/financial-reports/145-Annual-Report-and-Accounts-2015/WEB_Findel%20ra2015.pdf; Exercise on p. 382 from Dip IFR Diploma in International Financial Reporting Monday 11 December 2006, p. 10. Association of Chartered Certified Accountants (ACCA). We are grateful to the Association of Chartered Certified Accountants (ACCA) for permission to reproduce past examination questions. The suggested solutions in the exam answer bank have been prepared by us, unless otherwise stated; Extract on p. 362 from J Sainsbury plc Annual Report and Financial Statements 2014, Notes to the financial statements, p. 90. http://annualreport2014.j-sainsbury.co.uk/media/47785/notes_to_the_financial_statements.pdf, Reproduced by kind permission of Sainsbury's Supermarkets Ltd; Extract on p. 398 from Statement of Financial Accounting Standards no. 109. FAS109 Status P., FAS109 Summary. Accounting for Income Taxes February 1992. p. 31 no. 77, 78. Reproduced with permission, Copyright © 2010 by Financial Accounting Foundation; Extract on p. 403 from Conceptual Framework for Financial Reporting, IASB, 2010, OB17, © Copyright IFRS Foundation; Extract on p. 403 from Conceptual Framework for Financial Reporting, IASB, 2010, OB17, para. 4.8, © Copyright IFRS Foundation; Extract on p. 403 from Conceptual Framework for Financial Reporting, IASB, 2010, OB17, BC3.26, © Copyright IFRS Foundation; Exercises on pp. 66, 97, 99, 441, 440, 539, 575, 623, 628, 645, 674, 674, 703, 751 from Association of International Accountants (AIA), © 2012 AIA. All rights reserved; Exercise on p. 441 from Institute of Certified Public Accountants (CPA), Professional Stage 1 Corporate Reporting Examination, April 2015; Exercise on p. 489 from © First published in 2014 by The Chartered Institute of Public Finance and Accountancy (CIPFA) from CIPFA Advanced Diploma in International Public Financial Management – FINANCIAL REPORTING, p. 2; Exercise on p. 517 from ACCA DipIFR 2004. Association of Chartered Certified Accountants (ACCA). We are grateful to the Association of Chartered Certified Accountants (ACCA) for permission to reproduce past examination questions. The suggested solutions in the exam answer bank have been prepared by us, unless otherwise stated; Exercise on p. 541 from Cima F1 March 2014 Past Papers (approximate) p. 8 http://www.cimapastpapers.com/cima-f1-mrach-2014-past-papers; Exercise on p. 597 from Institute of Certified Public Accountants (ICPA), Professional I Stage I Corporate Reporting Examination, August 2014; Exercise on p. 599 from © First published in 2014 by The Chartered Institute of Public Finance and Accountancy (CIPFA) from CIPFA Advanced Diploma in International Public Financial Management – Financial Reporting, p. 7; Extract on p. 615 from IAS 28 Investments in Associates and Joint Ventures, p. 619 paragraph 30 from IAS 28, © Copyright IFRS Foundation. Used by permission © Copyright IFRS Foundation; Extract on p. 628 from IAS 21 The Effects of Changes in Foreign Exchange Rates, © Copyright IFRS Foundation; Extract on p. 633 from IAS 21 The Effects of Changes in Foreign Exchange Rates, paragraph 39, © Copyright IFRS Foundation; Exercise on p. 647 from Institute of Certified Public Accountants (CPA), Professional Stage 1 Corporate Reporting Examination, August 2013; Exercise on p. 710 from Institute of Certified Public Accountants (CPA) Professional Stage 1 Corporate Reporting Examination, April 2014; Extract on p. 796 from Vince Cable, UK Secretary of State for business and industry, in 2012, licensed under the Open Government Licence v.3.0.

### PART I

# Introduction to accounting on a cash flow and accrual accounting basis

# CHAPTER 1

# Accounting and reporting on a cash flow basis

## 1.1 Introduction

Accountants are communicators. Accountancy is the art of communicating financial information about a business entity to users such as shareholders and managers. The communication is generally in the form of financial statements that show in money terms the economic resources under the control of the management. The art lies in selecting the information that is relevant to the user and is reliable.

Shareholders require periodic information that the managers are accounting properly for the resources under their control. This information helps the shareholders to evaluate the performance of the managers. The performance measured by the accountant shows the extent to which the economic resources of the business have grown or diminished during the year.

The shareholders also require information to **predict future performance**. At present companies are not required to publish forecast financial statements on a regular basis and the shareholders use the report of past performance when making their predictions.

Managers require information in order to control the business and make investment decisions.

### Objectives

By the end of this chapter, you should be able to:

- explain the extent to which cash flow accounting satisfies the information needs of shareholders and managers;
- prepare a cash budget and operating statement of cash flows;
- explain the characteristics that make cash flow data a reliable and fair representation;
- critically discuss the use of cash flow accounting for predicting future dividends.

## 1.2 Shareholders

Shareholders are external users. As such, they are unable to obtain access to the same amount of detailed historical information as the managers, e.g. total administration costs are disclosed in the published profit and loss account, but not an analysis to show how the figure is made up. Shareholders are also unable to obtain associated information, e.g. budgeted sales and costs. Even though the shareholders own a company, their entitlement to information is restricted.

The information to which shareholders are entitled is restricted to that specified by statute, e.g. the Companies Acts, or by professional regulation, e.g. Financial Reporting Standards, or by market regulations, e.g. listing requirements. This means that there may be a tension between the **amount** of information that a shareholder would like to receive and the amount that the directors are prepared to provide. For example, shareholders might consider that forecasts of future cash flows would be helpful in predicting future dividends, but the directors might be concerned that such forecasts could help competitors or make directors open to criticism if forecasts are not met. As a result, this information is not disclosed.

There may also be a tension between the **quality** of information that shareholders would like to receive and that which directors are prepared to provide. For example, the shareholders might consider that judgements made by the directors in the valuation of long-term contracts should be fully explained, whereas the directors might prefer not to reveal this information given the high risk of error that often attaches to such estimates. In practice, companies tend to compromise: they do not reveal the judgements to the shareholders, but maintain confidence by relying on the auditor to give a clean audit report.

The financial reports presented to the shareholders are also used by other parties such as lenders and trade creditors, and they have come to be regarded as general-purpose reports. However, it may be difficult or impossible to satisfy the needs of all users. For example, users may have different timescales – shareholders may be interested in the long-term trend of earnings over three years, whereas creditors may be interested in the likelihood of receiving cash within the next three months.

The information needs of the shareholders are regarded as the primary concern. The government perceives shareholders to be important because they provide companies with their economic resources. It is shareholders' needs that take priority in deciding on the nature and detailed content of the general-purpose reports.[1]

## 1.3 What skills does an accountant require in respect of external reports?

For external reporting purposes the accountant has a twofold obligation:

- an obligation to ensure that the financial statements comply with statutory, professional and listing requirements; this requires the accountant to possess **technical expertise**;

- an obligation to ensure that the financial statements present the substance of the commercial transactions the company has entered into; this requires the accountant to have **commercial awareness**.

## 1.4 Managers

Managers are internal users. As such, they have access to detailed financial statements showing the current results, the extent to which these vary from the budgeted results and the future budgeted results. Other examples of internal users are sole traders, partners and, in a company context, directors and managers.

There is no statutory restriction on the amount of information that an internal user may receive; the only restriction would be that imposed by the company's own policy. Frequently, companies operate a 'need to know' policy and only the directors see all the financial statements; employees, for example, would be most unlikely to receive information that would assist them in claiming a salary increase – unless, of course, it happened to be a time of recession, when information would be more freely provided by management as a means of containing claims for an increase.

## 1.5 What skills does an accountant require in respect of internal reports?

For the internal user, the accountant is able to tailor his or her reports. The accountant is required to produce financial statements that are specifically relevant to the user requesting them.

The accountant needs to be skilled in identifying the information that is needed and conveying its implication and meaning to the user. The user needs to be confident that the accountant understands the user's information needs and will satisfy them in a language that is understandable. The accountant must be a skilled communicator who is able to instil confidence in the user that the information is:

● relevant to the user's needs;

● measured objectively;

● presented within a timescale that permits decisions to be made with appropriate information;

● verifiable, in that it can be confirmed that the report represents the transactions that have taken place;

● reliable, in that it is as free from bias as is possible;

● a complete picture of material items;

● a fair representation of the business transactions and events that have occurred or are being planned.

The accountant is a trained reporter of financial information. Just as for external reporting, the accountant needs commercial awareness. It is important, therefore, that he or she should not operate in isolation.

### 1.5.1 Accountants' reporting role

The accountant's role is to ensure that the information provided is useful for making decisions. For external users, the accountant achieves this by providing a general-purpose financial statement that complies with statute and is reliable. For internal users, this is done by interfacing with the user and establishing exactly what financial information is relevant to the decision that is to be made.

We now consider the steps required to provide relevant information for internal users.

## 1.6 Procedural steps when reporting to internal users

A number of user steps and accounting action steps can be identified within a financial decision model. These are shown in Figure 1.1.

Note that, although we refer to an accountant/user interface, this is not a single occurrence because the user and accountant interface at each of the user decision steps.

At **step 1,** the accountant attempts to ensure that the decision is based on the appropriate appraisal methodology. However, the accountant is providing a service to a user and, while the accountant may give guidance, the final decision about methodology rests with the user.

**Figure 1.1 General financial decision model to illustrate the user/accountant interface**

| USER | | ACCOUNTANT |
|---|---|---|
| *User step 1* | | Identify the material information |
| Identify decision and | | needed by the user |
| how it is to be made | | Measure the relevant |
| *User step 2* | | information |
| Establish with the | **USER/ACCOUNTANT** | Prepare report for user to |
| accountant the | **INTERFACE** | allow user to make decision |
| information necessary | | Provide an understandable |
| for decision making | | report to the user |
| *User step 3* | | |
| Seek relevant data | | |
| from the accountant | | |

At **step 2,** the accountant needs to establish the information necessary to support the decision that is to be made.

At **step 3,** the accountant needs to ensure that the user **understands** the full impact and financial implications of the accountant's report, taking into account the user's level of understanding and prior knowledge. This may be overlooked by the accountant, who feels that the task has been completed when the written report has been typed.

It is important to remember in following the model that the accountant is attempting to satisfy the information needs of the individual user rather than those of a 'user group'. It is tempting to divide users into groups with apparently common information needs, without recognising that a group contains individual users with different information needs. We return to this later in the chapter, but for the moment we continue by studying a situation where the directors of a company are considering a proposed capital investment project.

Let us assume that there are three companies in the retail industry: Retail A Ltd, Retail B Ltd and Retail C Ltd. The directors of each company are considering the purchase of a warehouse. We could assume initially that, because the companies are operating in the same industry and are faced with the same investment decision, they have identical information needs. However, enquiry might establish that the directors of each company have a completely different attitude to, or perception of, the primary business objective.

For example, it might be established that Retail A Ltd is a large company and under the Fisher–Hirshleifer separation theory the directors seek to maximise profits for the benefit of the equity investors; Retail B Ltd is a medium-sized company in which the directors seek to obtain a satisfactory return for the equity shareholders; and Retail C Ltd is a smaller company in which the directors seek to achieve a satisfactory return for a wider range of stakeholders, including, perhaps, the employees as well as the equity shareholders.

The accountant needs to be aware that these differences may have a significant effect on the information required. Let us consider this diagrammatically in the situation where a capital investment decision is to be made, referring particularly to user step 2: 'Establish with the accountant the information necessary for decision making'.

**Figure 1.2 Impact of different user attitudes on the information needed in relation to a capital investment proposal**

|  | USER A | USER B | USER C |
|---|---|---|---|
|  | Directors of | Directors of | Directors of |
|  | Retail A Ltd | Retail B Ltd | Retail C Ltd |
| User attitude | PROFIT MAXIMISER for SHAREHOLDERS | PROFIT SATISFICER for SHAREHOLDERS | PROFIT SATISFICER for SHAREHOLDERS/ STAFF |
| Relevant data to measure | CASH FLOWS | CASH FLOWS | CASH FLOWS |
| Appraisal method (decided on by user) | IRR | NPV | NPV |
| Appraisal criterion (decided on by user) | HIGHEST IRR | NPV but only if positive | NPV possibly even if negative |

We can see from Figure 1.2 that the accountant has identified that:

● the relevant financial data are the same for each of the users, i.e. cash flows; but

● the appraisal methods selected, i.e. internal rate of return (IRR) and net present value (NPV), are different; and

● the appraisal criteria employed by each user, i.e. higher IRR and NPV, are different.

In practice, the user is likely to use more than one appraisal method, as each has advantages and disadvantages. However, we can see that, even when dealing with a single group of apparently homogeneous users, the accountant has first to identify the information needs of the particular user. Only then is the accountant able to identify the relevant financial data and the appropriate report. It is the user's needs that are predominant.

If the accountant's view of the appropriate appraisal method or criterion differs from the user's view, the accountant might decide to report from both views. This approach affords the opportunity to improve the user's understanding and encourages good practice.

The diagrams can be combined (Figure 1.3) to illustrate the complete process. The user is assumed to be Retail A Ltd, a company that has directors who are profit maximisers.

The accountant is reactive when reporting to an internal user. We observe this characteristic in the Norman example set out in Section 1.8. Because the cash flows are identified as relevant to the user, it is these flows that the accountant will record, measure and appraise.

The accountant can also be proactive, by giving the user advice and guidance in areas where the accountant has specific expertise, such as the appraisal method that is most appropriate to the circumstances.

**Figure 1.3 User/accountant interface where the user is a profit maximiser**

| General model<br><br><br>USER | Specific<br>application for<br>Retail A Ltd<br>A PROFIT<br>MAXIMISER | | General model<br><br><br>ACCOUNTANT | Specific<br>application for<br>Retail A Ltd<br>ACCOUNTANT |
|---|---|---|---|---|
| *Step 1*<br>Decision to<br>be made | Appraise which<br>project warrants<br>capital investment | | Identify information<br>needed by the user | User decision<br>criterion is IRR |
| | | **USER/**<br>**ACCOUNTANT**<br>**INTERFACE** | Measure | Measure the project<br>cash flows |
| *Step 2*<br>Information needed | Project with the<br>highest IRR | | Prepare report | Prepare report of<br>highest IRR |
| *Step 3*<br>Seek relevant data | Report of IRR<br>project | | Provide report | Submit report of<br>project with highest<br>IRR per £ invested |

## 1.7 Agency costs[2]

The information in Figure 1.2 assumes that the directors have made their investment decision based on the assumed preferences of the shareholders. However, in real life, the directors might also be influenced by how the decision impinges on their own position. If, for example, their remuneration is a fixed salary, they might select not the investment with the highest IRR, but the one that maintains their security of employment. The result might be suboptimal investment and financing decisions based on risk aversion and over-retention. To the extent that the potential cash flows have been reduced, there will be an agency cost to the shareholders. This agency cost is an opportunity cost – the amount that was forgone because the decision making was suboptimal – and, as such, it will not be recorded in the books of account and will not appear in the financial statements.

## 1.8 Illustration of periodic financial statements prepared under the cash flow concept to disclose realised operating cash flows

In the above example of Retail A, B and C, the investment decision for the acquisition of a warehouse was based on an appraisal of cash flows. This raises the question: 'Why not continue with the cash flow concept and report the financial changes that occur after the investment has been undertaken using that same concept?'

To do this, the company will record the consequent cash flows through a number of subsequent accounting periods; report the cash flows that occur in each financial period; and produce a balance sheet at the end of each of the financial periods. For illustration we follow this procedure in Sections 1.8.1 and 1.8.2 for transactions entered into by Mr S. Norman.

### 1.8.1 Appraisal of the initial investment decision

Mr Norman is considering whether to start up a retail business by acquiring the lease of a shop for five years at a cost of £80,000.

Our first task has been set out in Figure 1.1 above. It is to establish the information that Mr Norman needs, so that we can decide what data need to be collected and measured. Let us assume that, as a result of a discussion with Mr Norman, it has been ascertained that he is a profit satisficer who is looking to achieve at least a 10% return, which represents the time value of money. This indicates that, as illustrated in Figure 1.2:

- the relevant data to be measured are **cash flows,** represented by the outflow of cash invested in the lease and the inflow of cash represented by the realised operating cash flows;
- the appropriate appraisal method is **NPV**; and
- the appraisal criterion is a **positive NPV** using the discount rate of 10%.

Let us further assume that the cash to be invested in the lease is £80,000 and that the realised operating cash flows over the life of the investment in the shop are as shown in Figure 1.4. This shows that there is a forecast of £30,000 annually for five years and a final receipt of £29,000 in 20X6 when he proposes to cease trading.

We already know that Mr Norman's investment criterion is a positive NPV using a discount factor of 10%. A calculation (Figure 1.5) shows that the investment easily satisfies that criterion.

#### Figure 1.4 Forecast of realised operating cash flows

|  | Annually years 20X1–20X5 | Cash in year 20X6 after shop closure |
|---|---|---|
|  | £ | £ |
| Receipts from |  |  |
| Customers | 400,000 | 55,000 |
| Payments to |  |  |
| Suppliers | (342,150) | (20,000) |
| Expense creditors | (21,600) | (3,000) |
| Rent | (6,250) | (3,000) |
| Total payments | (370,000) | (26,000) |
| Realised operating cash flows | 30,000 | 29,000 |

#### Figure 1.5 NPV calculation using discount tables

|  | £ | £ |
|---|---|---|
| Cost of lease |  | (80,000) |
| £30,000 annually for 5 years (30,000 × 3.79) | 113,700 |  |
| £29,000 received in year 6 (29,000 × 0.564) | 16,356 |  |
|  |  | 130,056 |
| Positive net present value |  | 50,056 |

The accountant's input does not stop there but needs to be proactive. Management will benefit from a report analysing progress at regular intervals showing if the project is on time and within budget and, if not, identifying how to get back to initial plan.

### 1.8.2 Preparation of periodic financial statements under the cash flow concept

Having **predicted** the realised operating cash flows for the purpose of making the investment decision, we can assume that the owner of the business will wish to obtain **feedback** to evaluate the correctness of the investment decision. He does this by reviewing the actual results on a regular **timely** basis and **comparing** these with the predicted forecast. Actual results should be reported quarterly, half-yearly or annually in the same format as used when making the decision in Figure 1.4. The actual results provide management with the feedback information required to audit the initial decision; it is a technique for achieving accountability. However, frequently, companies do not provide a report of actual cash flows to compare with the forecast cash flows, and fail to carry out an audit review.

In some cases, the transactions relating to the investment cannot be readily separated from other transactions, and the information necessary for the audit review of the investment cannot be made available. In other cases, the routine accounting procedures fail to collect such cash flow information because the reporting systems have not been designed to provide financial reports on a cash flow basis; rather, they have been designed to produce reports prepared on an accrual basis.

#### What would financial reports look like if they were prepared on a cash flow basis?

To illustrate cash flow period accounts, we will prepare half-yearly accounts for Mr Norman. To facilitate a comparison with the forecast that underpinned the investment decision, we will redraft the forecast annual statement on a half-yearly basis. The data for the first year given in Figure 1.4 have therefore been redrafted to provide a forecast for the half-year to 30 June, as shown in Figure 1.6.

We assume that, having applied the net present value appraisal technique to the cash flows and ascertained that the NPV was positive, Mr Norman proceeded to set up the business on 1 January 20X1. He introduced capital of £50,000, acquired a five-year lease for £80,000 and

### Figure 1.6 Forecast of realised operating cash flows

|  | Half-year to 30 June 20X1 £ |
|---|---|
| Receipts from |  |
| Customers | 165,000 |
| Payments to |  |
| Suppliers | (124,000) |
| Expense creditors | (18,000) |
| Rent | (6,250) |
| Total payments | (148,250) |
| Realised operating cash flows | 16,750 |

paid £6,250 in advance as rent to occupy the property to 31 December 20X1. He has decided to prepare financial statements at half-yearly intervals. The information given in Figure 1.7 concerns his trading for the half-year to 30 June 20X1.

Mr Norman was naturally eager to determine whether the business was achieving its forecast cash flows for the first six months of trading, so he produced the statement of realised operating cash flows (Figure 1.8) from the information provided in Figure 1.7. From this statement we can see that the business generated positive cash flows after the end of February. These are, of course, only the cash flows relating to the trading transactions.

The information in the 'Total' row of Figure 1.7 can be extracted to provide the financial statement for the six months ended 30 June 20X1, as shown in Figure 1.9.

The figure of £15,650 needs to be compared with the forecast cash flows used in the investment appraisal. This is a form of auditing. It allows the assumptions made on the initial investment decision to be confirmed. The forecast/actual comparison (based on the information in Figures 1.6 and 1.9) is set out in Figure 1.10.

**Figure 1.7 Monthly sales, purchases and expenses for six months ended 30 June 20X1**

| Month | Sales invoiced £ | Cash received £ | Purchases invoiced £ | Cash paid £ | Expenses invoiced £ | Cash paid £ |
|---|---|---|---|---|---|---|
| January | 15,000 | 7,500 | 16,000 | | 3,400 | 3,100 |
| February | 20,000 | 17,500 | 19,000 | 16,000 | 3,500 | 3,400 |
| March | 35,000 | 27,500 | 29,000 | 19,000 | 3,800 | 3,500 |
| April | 40,000 | 37,500 | 32,000 | 29,000 | 3,900 | 3,800 |
| May | 40,000 | 40,000 | 33,000 | 32,000 | 3,900 | 3,900 |
| June | 45,000 | 42,500 | 37,000 | 33,000 | 4,000 | 3,900 |
| TOTAL | 195,000 | 172,500 | 166,000 | 129,000 | 22,500 | 21,600 |

Note: The following items were included under the Expenses invoiced heading:
Expense creditors – amount
Wages – £3,100 per month paid in the month
Commission – 2% of sales invoiced payable one month in arrears

**Figure 1.8 Monthly realised operating cash flows**

| | Jan £ | Feb £ | Mar £ | Apr £ | May £ | Jun £ | Total £ |
|---|---|---|---|---|---|---|---|
| Receipts | | | | | | | |
| Customers | 7,500 | 17,500 | 27,500 | 37,500 | 40,000 | 42,500 | 172,500 |
| Less payments | | | | | | | |
| Suppliers | | 16,000 | 19,000 | 29,000 | 32,000 | 33,000 | 129,000 |
| Expense creditors | 3,100 | 3,400 | 3,500 | 3,800 | 3,900 | 3,900 | 21,600 |
| Rent | 6,250 | | | | | | 6,250 |
| Realised | (1,850) | (1,900) | 5,000 | 4,700 | 4,100 | 5,600 | 15,650 |

**Figure 1.9 Realised operating cash flows for the six months ended 30 June 20X1**

|  | £ |
|---|---|
| *Receipts from* | |
| Customers | 172,500 |
| *Payments to* | |
| Suppliers | (129,000) |
| Expense creditors | (21,600) |
| Rent | (6,250) |
|  | 156,850 |
| Realised operating cash flow | 15,650 |

**Figure 1.10 Forecast/actual comparison**

|  | | Actual £ | Forecast £ |
|---|---|---|---|
| *Receipts from* | | | |
| Customers | | 172,500 | 165,000 |
| *Payment to* | | | |
| Suppliers | (129,000) | | (124,000) |
| Expense creditors | (21,600) | | (18,000) |
| Rent | (6,250) | | (6,250) |
| Total payments | | (156,850) | (148,250) |
| Realised operating cash flow | | 15,650 | 16,750 |

### What are the characteristics of these data that make them relevant?

- The data are **objective**. There is no judgement involved in deciding the values to include in the financial statement, as each value or amount represents a verifiable cash transaction with a third party.

- The data are **consistent**. The statement incorporates the same cash flows within the periodic financial report of trading as the cash flows that were incorporated within the initial capital investment report. This permits a logical comparison and confirmation that the decision was realistic.

- The results have a **confirmatory** value by helping users confirm or correct their past assessments.

- The results have a **predictive** value, in that they provide a basis for revising the initial forecasts if necessary.

- There is **no requirement for accounting standards** or disclosure of accounting policies that are necessary to regulate accrual accounting practices, e.g. depreciation methods.

## 1.9 Illustration of preparation of statement of financial position

Although the information set out in Figure 1.10 permits us to compare and evaluate the initial decision, it does not provide a sufficiently sound basis for the following:

● assessing the stewardship over the total cash funds that have been employed within the business;

● signalling to management whether its working capital policies are appropriate.

### 1.9.1 Stewardship

To assess the stewardship over the total cash funds we need to:

(a) evaluate the effectiveness of the accounting system to make certain that all transactions are recorded;

(b) extend the cash flow statement to take account of the capital cash flows; and

(c) prepare a statement of financial position or balance sheet as at 30 June 20X1.

The additional information for (b) and (c) above is set out in Figures 1.11 and 1.12 respectively.

**Figure 1.11 Cash flow statement to calculate the net cash balance**

|  | Jan | Feb | Mar | Apr | May | Jun | Total |
|---|---|---|---|---|---|---|---|
|  | £ | £ | £ | £ | £ | £ | £ |
| Operating cash | (1,850) | (1,900) | 5,000 | 4,700 | 4,100 | 5,600 | 15,650 |
| New capital | 50,000 |  |  |  |  |  | 50,000 |
| Lease payment | (80,000) |  |  |  |  |  | (80,000) |
| Cash balance | (31,850) | (33,750) | (28,750) | (24,050) | (19,950) | (14,350) | (14,350) |

**Figure 1.12 Statement of financial position**

|  | Opening 1 Jan 20X1 £ | Closing 30 Jun 20X1 £ |
|---|---|---|
| Capital introduced | 50,000 | 50,000 |
| Net operating cash flow |  | 15,650 |
|  | 50,000 | 65,650 |
| Lease |  | 80,000 |
| Net cash balance | 50,000 | −14,350 |
|  | 50,000 | 65,650 |

The cash flow statement and statement of financial position, taken together, are a means of assessing stewardship. They identify the movement of **all** cash and derive a **net** balance figure. These statements are a normal feature of a sound system of internal control, but they have not been made available to external users.

### 1.9.2 Working capital policies

By 'working capital' we mean the current assets and current liabilities of the business. In addition to providing a means of making management accountable, cash flows are the raw data required by financial managers when making decisions on the management of working capital. One of the decisions would be to set the appropriate terms for credit policy. For example, Figure 1.11 shows that the business will have a £14,350 overdraft at 30 June 20X1. If this is not acceptable, management will review its working capital by reconsidering the credit given to customers, the credit taken from suppliers, stock-holding levels and the timing of capital cash inflows and outflows.

If, in the example, it were possible to obtain 45 days' credit from suppliers, then the creditors at 30 June would rise from £37,000 to a new total of £53,500. This increase in trade credit of £16,500 means that half of the May purchases (£33,000/2) would not be paid for until July, which would convert the overdraft of £14,350 into a positive balance of £2,150. As a new business it might not, of course, be always possible to obtain credit from all of the suppliers. In that case, other steps would be considered, such as phasing the payment for the lease of the warehouse or introducing more capital.

An interesting research report[3] identified that for small firms survival and stability were the main objectives rather than profit maximisation. This, in turn, meant that cash flow indicators and managing cash flow were seen as crucial to survival. In addition, cash flow information was perceived as important to external bodies such as banks which require detailed cash flow forecasts before considering any application for a loan. Banks such as Barclays[4] assist their customers by making a cash flow forecast tool accessible on line.

## 1.10 Treatment of non-current assets in the cash flow model

The statement of financial position in Figure 1.12 does not take into account any **unrealised** cash flows. Such flows are deemed to occur as a result of any rise or fall in the realisable value of the lease. This could rise if, for example, the annual rent payable under the lease were to be substantially lower than the rate payable under a new lease entered into on 30 June 20X1. It could also fall with the passing of time, with six months having expired by 30 June 20X1. We need to consider this further and examine the possible treatment of non-current assets in the cash flow model.

Using the cash flow approach, we require an independent verification of the realisable value of the lease at 30 June 20X1. If the lease has fallen in value, the difference between the original outlay and the net realisable figure could be treated as a negative unrealised operating cash flow.

For example, if the independent estimate was that the realisable value was £74,000, then the statement of financial position would be prepared as in Figure 1.13. The fall of £6,000 in realisable value is an unrealised cash flow and, while it does not affect the calculation of the net cash balance, it does affect the statement of financial position.

The same approach would be taken to all non-current assets and could result in there being an unrealised cash flow where there is limited resale market for an asset, even though it might be productive and have value in use by the firm that owns it.

**Figure 1.13 Statement of financial position as at 30 June 20X1 (assuming that there were unrealised operating cash flows)**

|  | £ |
|---|---|
| Capital introduced | 50,000 |
| Net operating flow: **realised** | 15,650 |
| : **unrealised** | (6,000) |
|  | 59,650 |
|  |  |
| Lease: **net realisable value** | 74,000 |
| Net cash balance | −14,350 |
|  | 59,650 |

The additional benefit of the statement of financial position, as revised, is that the owner is able clearly to identify the following:

- the operating cash inflows of £15,650 that have been realised from the business operations;
- the operating cash outflow of £6,000 that has not been realised, but has arisen as a result of investing in the lease;
- the net cash balance of −£14,350;
- the statement provides a **stewardship-oriented** report: that is, it is a means of making the management accountable for the cash within its control.

## 1.11 What are the characteristics of these data that make them reliable?

We have already discussed some characteristics of cash flow reporting which indicate that the data in the financial statements are **relevant,** e.g. their predictive and confirmatory roles. We now introduce five more characteristics of cash flow statements which indicate that the information is also **reliable,** i.e. free from bias. These are prudence, neutrality, completeness, faithful representation and substance over form.

### 1.11.1 Prudence characteristic

Revenue and profits are included in the cash flow statement only when they are realised. Realisation is deemed to occur when cash is received. In our Norman example, the £172,500 cash received from debtors represents the revenue for the half-year ended 30 June 20X1. This policy is described as prudent because it **does not anticipate** cash flows: cash flows are recorded only when they actually occur and not when they are reasonably certain to occur. This is one of the factors that distinguishes cash flow from accrual accounting.

### 1.11.2 Neutrality characteristic

Financial statements are not neutral if, by their selection or presentation of information, they influence the making of a decision in order to achieve a predetermined result or outcome. With cash flow accounting, the information is not subject to management selection criteria.

Cash flow accounting avoids the tension that can arise between prudence and neutrality because, whilst neutrality involves freedom from deliberate or systematic bias, prudence is a potentially biased concept that seeks to ensure that, under conditions of uncertainty, gains and assets are not overstated and losses and liabilities are not understated.

### 1.11.3 Completeness characteristic

The cash flows can be verified for completeness provided there are adequate internal control procedures in operation. In small and medium-sized enterprises there can be a weakness if one person, typically the owner, has control over the accounting system and is able to under-record cash receipts.

### 1.11.4 Faithful representation characteristic

Cash flows can be depended upon by users to represent faithfully what they purport to represent provided, of course, that the completeness characteristic has been satisfied.

### 1.11.5 Substance over form

Cash flow accounting does not necessarily possess this characteristic which requires that transactions should be accounted for and presented in accordance with their substance and economic reality and not merely their legal form.

## 1.12 Reports to external users

### 1.12.1 Stewardship orientation

Cash flow accounting provides objective, consistent and prudent financial information about a business's transactions. It is stewardship-oriented and offers a means of achieving accountability over cash resources and investment decisions.

### 1.12.2 Prediction orientation

External users are also interested in the ability of a company to pay dividends. It might be thought that the past and current cash flows are the best indicators of future cash flows and dividends. However, the cash flow might be misleading, in that a declining company might sell non-current assets and have a better **net cash position** than a growing company that buys non-current assets for future use. There is also no matching of cash inflows and outflows, in the sense that a benefit is matched with the sacrifice made to achieve it.

Consequently, it has been accepted accounting practice to view the income statement prepared on the accrual accounting concept as a better predictor of future cash flows to an investor than the cash flow statements that we have illustrated in this chapter.

However, the operating cash flows arising from trading and the cash flows arising from the introduction of capital and the acquisition of non-current assets can become significant to investors, e.g. they may threaten the company's ability to survive or may indicate growth.

### 1.12.3 Going concern

The Financial Reporting Council suggests in its Consultation Paper *Going Concern and Financial Reporting*[5] that directors in assessing whether a company is a going concern may prepare monthly cash flow forecasts and monthly budgets covering, as a minimum, the period up to the next statement of financial position date. The forecasts would also be supported by a detailed list of assumptions which underlie them.

### 1.12.4 Tax authorities[6]

In the UK accounts prepared on a cash flow basis have, from April 2013, been acceptable to the tax authorities for small unincorporated micro-businesses. This is seen as cutting costs and reducing the need to engage accountants. Companies are still required to determine income on an accrual accounting basis on the grounds that this better reflects economic substance in that most incorporated businesses would have inventory or work in progress, or have creditors for the supply of materials.

## Summary

To review our understanding of this chapter, we should ask ourselves the following questions.

### How useful is cash flow accounting for internal decision making?

Forecast cash flows are relevant for the appraisal of proposals for capital investment. Actual cash flows are relevant for the confirmation of the decision for capital investment.

Cash flows are relevant for the management of working capital. Financial managers might have a variety of mathematical models for the efficient use of working capital, but cash flows are the raw data upon which they work.

### How useful is cash flow accounting for making management accountable?

The cash flow statement is useful for confirming decisions and, together with the statement of financial position, provides a stewardship report. Lee states that 'Cash flow accounting appears to satisfy the need to supply owners and others with stewardship-orientated information as well as with decision-orientated information.'[7]

Lee further states that:

> By reducing judgements in this type of financial report, management can report factually on its stewardship function, whilst at the same time disclosing data of use in the decision-making process. In other words, cash flow reporting eliminates the somewhat artificial segregation of stewardship and decision-making information.

This is exactly what we saw in our Norman example – the same realised operating cash flow information was used for both the investment decision and financial reporting. However, for stewardship purposes it was necessary to extend the cash flow to include **all** cash movements and to extend the statement of financial position to include the **unrealised** cash flows.

### How useful is cash flow accounting for reporting to external users?

Cash flow information is relevant:

- as a basis for making internal management decisions in relation to both non-current assets and working capital;
- for stewardship and accountability; and
- for assessing whether a business is a going concern.

  Cash flow information is reliable and a fair representation, being:
- objective; consistent; prudent; and neutral.

However, professional accounting practice requires reports to external users to be on an accrual accounting basis. This is because the accrual accounting profit figure is a better predictor for investors of the future cash flows likely to arise from the dividends paid to them by the business, and of any capital gain on disposal of their investment.

In the next chapter, we revise the preparation of the same three statements using the **accrual accounting** model.

## REVIEW QUESTIONS

1  Explain why it is the user who should determine the information that the accountant collects, measures and reports, rather than the accountant who is the expert in financial information.

2  'Yuji Ijiri rejects decision usefulness as the main purpose of accounting and puts in its place accountability. Ijiri sees the accounting relationship as a tripartite one, involving the accountor, the accountee, and the accountant . . . the decision useful approach is heavily biased in favour of the accountee . . . with little concern for the accountor . . . in the central position Ijiri would put fairness.'[8] Discuss Ijiri's view in the context of cash flow accounting.

3  Explain the effect on the statement of financial position in Figure 1.13 if the non-current asset consisted of expenditure on industry-specific machine tools rather than a lease.

4  'It is essential that the information in financial statements has a prudent characteristic if the financial statements are to be objective.' Discuss.

5  Explain why realised cash flow might not be appropriate for investors looking to predict future dividends.

6  Discuss why it might not be sufficient for a small business person who is carrying on business as a sole trader to prepare accounts on a cash flow basis.

7  'Unrealised operating cash flows are only of use for internal management purposes and are irrelevant to investors.' Discuss.

8  'While accountants may be free from bias in the measurement of economic information, they cannot be unbiased in identifying the economic information that they consider to be relevant.' Discuss.

## EXERCISES

*Question 1

Sasha Parker is going to set up a new business on 1 January 20X1. She estimates that her first six months in business will be as follows:

(i) She will put £150,000 into a bank account for the firm on 1 January 20X1.

(ii) On 1 January 20X1 she will buy machinery £30,000, motor vehicles £24,000 and premises £75,000, paying for them immediately.

(iii) All purchases will be effected on credit. She will buy £30,000 goods on 1 January and will pay for these in February. Other purchases will be: rest of January £48,000; February, March, April, May and June £60,000 each month. Other than the £30,000 worth bought in January, all other purchases will be paid for two months after purchase.

(iv) Sales (all on credit) will be £60,000 for January and £75,000 for each month after. Customers will pay for the goods in the fourth month after purchase, i.e. £60,000 is received in May.

(v) She will make drawings of £1,200 per month.

(vi) Wages and salaries will be £2,250 per month and will be paid on the last day of each month.

(vii) General expenses will be £750 per month, payable in the month following that in which they are incurred.

(viii) Rates will be paid as follows: for the three months to 31 March 20X1 by cheque on 28 February 20X1; for the 12 months ended 31 March 20X2 by cheque on 31 July 20X1. Rates are £4,800 per annum.

(ix) She will introduce new capital of £82,500 on 1 April 20X1.

(x) Insurance covering the 12 months of 20X1 of £2,100 will be paid for by cheque on 30 June 20X1.

(xi) All receipts and payments will be by cheque.

(xii) Inventory on 30 June 20X1 will be £30,000.

(xiii) The net realisable value of the vehicles is £19,200, machinery £27,000 and premises £75,000.

Required: Cash flow accounting
(a) Draft a cash budget (includes bank) month by month for the period January to June, showing clearly the amount of bank balance or overdraft at the end of each month.
(b) Draft an operating cash flow statement for the six-month period.
(c) Assuming that Sasha Parker sought your advice as to whether she should actually set up in business, state what further information you would require.

## * Question 2

Mr Norman set up a new business on 1 January 20X8. He invested €50,000 in the new business on that date. The following information is available.

1 Gross profit was 20% of sales. Monthly sales were as follows:

| Month | Sales € |
|---|---|
| January | 15,000 |
| February | 20,000 |
| March | 35,000 |
| April | 40,000 |
| May | 40,000 |
| June | 45,000 |
| July | 50,000 |

2 50% of sales were for cash. Credit customers (50% of sales) pay in the month following the sale.

3 The supplier allowed one month's credit.

4   Monthly payments were made for rent and rates €2,200 and wages €600.

5   On 1 January 20X8 the following payments were made: €80,000 for a five-year lease of business premises and €3,500 for insurances on the premises for the year. The realisable value of the lease was estimated to be €76,000 on 30 June 20X8 and €70,000 on 31 December 20X8.

6   Staff sales commission of 2% of sales was paid in the month following the sale.

Required:

(a)   A purchases budget for each of the first six months.

(b)   A cash flow statement for the first six months.

(c)   A statement of operating cash flows and financial position as at 30 June 20X8.

(d)   Write a brief letter to the bank supporting a request for an overdraft.

## Notes

1   *Conceptual Framework For Financial Reporting* FRC, ED 2015-3, BC 1–11.
2   G. Whittred and I. Zimmer, *Financial Accounting: Incentive Effects and Economic Consequences*, Holt, Rinehart & Winston, 1992, p. 27.
3   R. Jarvis, J. Kitching, J. Curran and G. Lightfoot, *The Financial Management of Small Firms: An Alternative Perspective*, ACCA Research Report No. 49, 1996.
4   www.barclays.co.uk/BusinessBankAccounts/Helpfulformsforbusinesslending/P1242631461287
5   *Guidance on the Going Concern Basis of Accounting and Reporting on Solvency and Liquidity Risks*, FRC, October 2015, paras 5.5–5.6.
6   www.gov.uk/simpler-income-tax-cash-basis
7   T.A. Lee, *Income and Value Measurement: Theory and Practice* (3rd edition), Van Nostrand Reinhold (UK), 1985, p. 173.
8   D. Solomons, *Making Accounting Policy*, Oxford University Press, 1986, p. 79.

# CHAPTER 2

# Accounting and reporting on an accrual accounting basis

## 2.1 Introduction

The main purpose of this chapter is to extend cash flow accounting by adjusting for the effect of transactions that have not been completed by the end of an accounting period.

### Objectives

By the end of this chapter, you should be able to:

- explain the historical cost convention and accrual concept;
- adjust cash receipts and payments in accordance with IAS 18;
- account for the amount of non-current assets used during the accounting period;
- prepare a statement of income and a statement of financial position;
- reconcile cash flow accounting and accrual accounting data.

### 2.1.1 Objective of financial statements

The *Conceptual Framework for Financial Reporting*[1] states that the objective of general purpose financial statements is to provide information about the financial position, performance and cash flows of an enterprise that is useful to existing and potential investors, lenders and creditors in making economic decisions about providing resources.

#### Common information needs for decision making

The IASB recognises that all the information needs of all users cannot be met by financial statements, but it takes the view that some needs are common to all users: in particular, they have some interest in the financial position, performance and adaptability of the enterprise as a whole. This leaves open the question of which user is the primary target; the IASB states that, as investors are providers of risk capital, financial statements that meet their needs would also meet most of the needs of other users.

#### Stewardship role of financial statements

In addition to assisting in making economic decisions, financial statements also show the results of the stewardship of management: that is, the accountability of management for the resources entrusted to it. The IASB view is that users who assess the stewardship do so in order to make economic decisions, e.g. whether to hold or sell shares in a particular company or change the management.

### 2.1.2 Statements making up the financial statements published for external users

In 2007 the IASB stated[2] that a complete set of financial statements should comprise:

- a statement of financial position as at the end of the period;
- a statement of comprehensive income for the period;
- a statement of changes in equity for the period;
- a statement of cash flows for the period;
- notes comprising a summary of significant accounting policies and other explanatory information.

In this chapter we consider two of the conventions under which the statement of comprehensive income and statement of financial position are prepared: the historical cost convention and the accrual accounting concept. In Chapters 3–5 we consider each of the above statements.

## 2.2 Historical cost convention

The historical cost convention results in an appropriate measure of the economic resource that has been withdrawn or replaced.

Under it, transactions are reported at the £ amount recorded at the date the transaction occurred. Financial statements produced under this convention provide a basis for determining the outcome of agency agreements with reasonable certainty and predictability because the data are relatively objective.[3]

By this we mean that various parties who deal with the enterprise, such as lenders, will know that the figures produced in any financial statement are objective and not manipulated by subjective judgements made by the directors. For example, being confident that the revenue and expenses in the statement of income are stated at the £ amount that appears on the invoices. This means that the amount is objective and can be independently verified.

Because of this, the historical cost convention has strengths for stewardship purposes, i.e. providing an objective record of the resources that managers have had under their control. However, the price-level-adjusted figures which we discuss in Chapter 10 may well be more appropriate for decision making.

## 2.3 Accrual basis of accounting

The accrual basis dictates when transactions with third parties should be recognised and, in particular, determines the accounting periods in which they should be incorporated into the financial statements. Under this concept the cash receipts from customers and payments to creditors are replaced by revenue and expenses respectively.

Revenue and expenses are derived by adjusting the realised operating cash flows to take account of business trading activity that has occurred during the accounting period, but has not been converted into cash receipts or payments by the end of the period.

### 2.3.1 Accrual accounting is a better indicator than cash flow accounting of ability to generate cash

The IASB view is that financial statements prepared on an accrual basis inform users not only of past transactions involving the payment and receipt of cash, but also of obligations to pay cash in the future and of resources that represent cash to be received in the future, and that they provide the type of information about past transactions and other events that is most useful in making economic decisions about the future.[4]

Having briefly considered why accrual accounting may be more useful than cash flow accounting, we will briefly revise the preparation of financial statements under the accrual accounting convention.

## 2.4 Mechanics of accrual accounting – adjusting cash receipts and payments

Let us assume that the cash flows for the six months were as illustrated in Chapter 1:

Receipts £172,500, Materials purchased £129,000, Services paid for £21,600 and Rent paid £6,250.

Additional information that now has to be taken into account relating to the half year's transactions:

Invoices issued to customers but unpaid totalled £22,500; Invoices received from suppliers but unpaid totalled £21,600; Invoices for services received but unpaid totalled £900 and half of the £6,250 payment for rent relates to the following half year.

As these all relate to the current six months' business activity, the cash figures need to be adjusted in both the statement of income and statement of financial position as in Figures 2.1 and 2.2.

**Figure 2.1 Statement of income for the six months ended 30 June 20X1**

|  | Operating cash flow £ | ADJUST cash flow £ | Business activity £ |
|---|---|---|---|
| Revenue from business activity | 172,500 | 22,500 | 195,000 |
| Less: Matching expenses |  |  |  |
| Transactions for materials | 129,000 | 37,000 | 166,000 |
| Transactions for services | 21,600 | 900 | 22,500 |
| Transaction with landlord | 6,250 | (3,125) | 3,125 |
| OPERATING CASH FLOW from business activity | 15,650 |  |  |
| Transactions NOTconverted to cash or relating to a subsequent period |  | (12,275) |  |
| PROFIT from business activity |  |  | 3,375 |

**Figure 2.2 Statement of financial position adjusted to an accrual basis**

|  | £ |
|---|---|
| Capital | 50,000 |
| Net operating cash flow: **realised** | 15,650 |
| Net operating cash flow: **to be realised next period** | (12,275) |
|  | 53,375 |
| Lease | 80,000 |
| Net cash balance (refer to Figure 1.11) | (14,350) |
| Net amount of activities not converted to cash or relating to subsequent periods | (12,275) |
|  | 53,375 |

## 2.5 Reformatting the statement of financial position

The item 'net amount of activities not converted to cash or relating to subsequent periods' is the net trade receivable/trade payable balance. If we wished, the statement of financial position could be reframed into the customary statement of financial position format, where items are classified as assets or liabilities. The IASB defines assets and liabilities in its *Conceptual Framework*:

- An asset is a resource:
  - controlled by the enterprise;
  - as a result of past events;
  - from which future economic benefits are expected to flow.
- A liability is a present obligation:
  - arising from past events
  - the settlement of which is expected to result in an outflow of resources.

The reframed statement set out in Figure 2.3 is in accordance with these definitions.

## 2.6 Accounting for the sacrifice of non-current assets

The statement of income and statement of financial position have both been prepared using verifiable data that have arisen from transactions with third parties outside the business. However, in order to determine the full sacrifice of economic resources that a business has made to achieve its revenue, it is necessary also to take account of the use made of the non-current assets during the period in which the revenue arose.

### 2.6.1 Going concern assumption

For all non-current assets a decision has to be made as to the amount to be charged against the current period's profits for the use of the asset. This is where the going concern

**Figure 2.3  Reframed statement as at 30 June**

| | Reframed | |
|---|---:|---:|
| | £ | £ |
| CAPITAL | 50,000 | 50,000 |
| Net operating cash flow: **realised** | 15,650 | |
| Net operating cash flow: **to be realised** | (12,275) | |
| NET INCOME | | 3,375 |
| | 53,375 | 53,375 |
| NON-CURRENT ASSETS | 80,000 | 80,000 |
| NET CURRENT ASSETS | | |
| Net amount of activities not converted to cash | (12,275) | |
| CURRENT ASSETS | | |
| Trade receivables | | 22,500 |
| Other receivables: prepaid rent | | 3,125 |
| CURRENT LIABILITIES | | |
| Trade payables | | (37,000) |
| Other payables: service suppliers | | (900) |
| Net cash balance | (14,350) | (14,350) |
| | 53,375 | 53,375 |

assumption comes into effect by assuming that the business enterprise will continue in operational existence for the foreseeable future and not be disposed of at the end of the current period. It is for this reason that an estimate is made of the amount to be charged and we do not use the amount for which the asset could actually be sold.

### Treatment of a lease

For example, assuming that the lease could be transferred to a third party at the end of the current period for £50,000 there would be a loss of £30,000 to be charged against the current period's profit IF this action was taken. However, as the intention is to retain and continue to use the asset, the approach is to estimate how much of the cost has been used up in the current period. In our example this would be £8,000 for the half-year. The effect of this charge (referred to as amortisation) on the statements of income and position are shown in Figures 2.4 and 2.5.

### Treatment of a tangible non-current asset

If the business was using a tangible non-current asset such as a vehicle then there would be a similar approach to calculate the amount to charge (referred to as depreciation) in the statement of income. The approach is first to calculate the depreciable amount which is the cost of the vehicle less its residual value on disposal, then to estimate its useful economic life and finally to decide how much of the depreciable amount to charge to each of the years that it is in use. Depreciation is discussed in greater detail in Chapter 17.

**Figure 2.4 Statement of income for the six months ending 30 June**

| | Operating cash flow CURRENT period £ | Adjust cash flow £ | Business activity CURRENT period £ |
|---|---|---|---|
| Revenue from business activity | 172,500 | 22,500 | 195,000 |
| Less | | | |
| *Expenditure to support this activity:* | | | |
| Transactions with suppliers | 129,000 | 37,000 | 166,000 |
| Transactions with service providers | 21,600 | 900 | 22,500 |
| Transaction with landlord | 6,250 | (3,125) | 3,125 |
| OPERATING CASH FLOW from activity | 15,650 | | |
| TRANSACTIONS NOT CONVERTED TO CASH | | (12,275) | |
| INCOME from business activity | | | 3,375 |
| Allocation of non-current asset cost to this period | | | 8,000 |
| INCOME | | | (4,625) |

**Figure 2.5 Statement of financial position as at 30 June**

| | Transaction cash flows £ | Notional flows £ | Reported £ |
|---|---|---|---|
| CAPITAL | 50,000 | | 50,000 |
| Net operating cash flow: **realised** | 15,650 | | |
| Net operating cash flow: **to be realised** | (12,275) | | |
| Net income before depreciation | | 3,375 | |
| AMORTISATION | | (8,000) | |
| Net income after amortisation | | | (4,625) |
| | 53,375 | | 45,375 |
| NON-CURRENT ASSETS | 80,000 | | 80,000 |
| Less amortisation | | | (8,000) |
| Net book value | | | 72,000 |
| NET CURRENT ASSETS | | | |
| Net amount not converted to cash | (12,275) | | |
| CURRENT ASSETS | | | |
| Trade receivables | | | 22,500 |
| Other receivables – prepaid rent | | | 3,125 |
| CURRENT LIABILITIES | | | |
| Trade payables | | | (37,000) |
| Other payables: service suppliers | | | (900) |
| Net cash balance | (14,350) | | (14,350) |
| | 53,375 | | 45,375 |

### 2.6.2 Financial capital maintenance concept

The financial capital maintenance concept recognises a profit only after the original monetary investment has been maintained. This means that, as long as the cost of the assets representing the initial monetary investment is recovered against the profit, by way of a depreciation charge, the initial monetary investment is maintained.

The concept has been described in the IASC *Framework for the Preparation and Presentation of Financial Statements:*

> a profit is earned only if the financial or money amount of the net assets at the end of the period exceeds the financial or money amount of the net assets at the beginning of the period, after excluding any distributions to, and contributions from, owners during the period. Financial capital maintenance can be measured in either nominal monetary units [as we are doing in this chapter] or in units of constant purchasing power [as we will be doing in Chapter 7].

### 2.6.3 Summary of views on accrual accounting

#### Standard setters

The profit (loss) is considered to be a guide when assessing the amount, timing and uncertainty of prospective cash flows as represented by future income amounts. The IASB, the FASB in the USA and the ASB in the UK clearly stated that the accrual accounting concept was more useful in predicting future cash flows than cash flow accounting.

#### Academic researchers

Academic research provides conflicting views. In 1986, research carried out in the USA indicated that the FASB view was inconsistent with its findings and that cash flow information was a better predictor of future operating cash flows;[5] research carried out in the UK, however, indicated that accrual accounting using the historical cost convention was 'a more relevant basis for decision making than cash flow measures'.[6]

## 2.7 Published statement of cash flows

In Figure 2.3 we reframed the statement of financial position to illustrate how it would be reported when published. In Figure 2.6 we set out the statement of cash flows under the standard headings required by IAS 7 *Statement of Cash Flows*[7] to arrive at the change in cash. The required headings are cash flows from:

● Operating activities

● Investing activities

● Financing activities.

In addition to explaining how the cash has increased or decreased, a reconciliation statement is prepared to explain why there is a positive operating cash flow of £15,650 but a loss in the statement of income of £4,625.

We discuss statements of cash flow further in Chapter 5.

**Figure 2.6 Statement of cash flows in accordance with IAS 7 *Statement of Cash Flows***

|  | £ |
|---|---|
| Net cash inflow from operating activities | 15,650 |
| **Investing activities** |  |
| Payment to acquire lease | (80,000) |
| Net cash outflow before financing | (64,350) |
| **Financing activities** |  |
| Issue of capital | 50,000 |
| Decrease in cash | (14,350) |
| **Reconciliation of operating loss to net cash inflow from operating activities** | £ |
| Operating profit/loss | (4,625) |
| Amortisation charges | 8,000 |
| Increase in trade receivables | (22,500) |
| Increase in prepayments | (3,125) |
| Increase in trade payables | 37,000 |
| Increase in accruals | 900 |
|  | 15,650 |

## Summary

Accrual accounting replaces cash receipts and payments with revenue and expenses by adjusting the cash figures to take account of trading activity which has not been converted into cash.

Accrual accounting is preferred to cash accounting by the standard setters on the assumption that accrual-based financial statements give investors a better means of predicting future cash flows.

The financial statements are transaction-based, applying the historical cost accounting concept which attempts to minimise the need for personal judgements and estimates in arriving at the figures in the statements.

Under accrual-based accounting the expenses incurred are matched with the revenue earned. In the case of non-current assets, a further accounting concept has been adopted, the going concern concept, which allows an entity to allocate the cost of non-current assets over their estimated useful life.

## REVIEW QUESTIONS

1 'Cash flow accounting and accrual accounting information are both required by a potential shareholder.' Discuss.

2 'The asset measurement basis applied in accrual accounting can lead to financial difficulties when assets are due for replacement.' Discuss.

3 'Accrual accounting is preferable to cash flow accounting because the information is more relevant to all users of financial statements.' Discuss.

4 'Information contained in a statement of income and a statement of financial position prepared under accrual accounting concepts is factual and objective.' Discuss.

5 The *Conceptual Framework for Financial Reporting* identifies seven user groups: investors, employees, lenders, suppliers and other trade creditors, customers, government and the public.

Discuss which of the financial statements illustrated in Chapters 1 and 2 would be most useful to each of these seven groups if they could only receive one statement.

6 The annual financial statements of companies are used by various parties for a wide variety of purposes. Discuss which of the three statements of income, financial position and cash flows would be of most interest to (a) a loan creditor and (b) a trade creditor.

7 Discuss how amounts are reported in a statement of financial position if the accounts are not prepared on a going concern basis.

## EXERCISES

### * Question 1

Sasha Parker is going to set up a new business in Bruges on 1 January 20X1. She estimates that her first six months in business will be as follows:

(i) She will put €150,000 into the firm on 1 January 20X1.

(ii) On 1 January 20X1 she will buy machinery €30,000, motor vehicles €24,000 and premises €75,000, paying for them immediately.

(iii) All purchases will be effected on credit. She will buy €30,000 goods on 1 January and she will pay for these in February. Other purchases will be: rest of January €48,000; February, March, April, May and June €60,000 each month. Other than the €30,000 worth bought in January, all other purchases will be paid for two months after purchase, i.e. €48,000 in March.

(iv) Sales (all on credit) will be €60,000 for January and €75,000 for each month after that. Customers will pay for goods in the third month after purchase, i.e. €60,000 in April.

(v) Inventory on 30 June 20X1 will be €30,000.

(vi) Wages and salaries will be €2,250 per month and will be paid on the last day of each month.

(vii) General expenses will be €750 per month, payable in the month following that in which they are incurred.

(viii) She will introduce new capital of €75,000 on 1 June 20X1. This will be paid into the business bank account immediately.

(ix) Insurance covering the 12 months of 20X1 of €26,400 will be paid for by cheque on 30 June 20X1.

(x) Local taxes will be paid as follows: for the three months to 31 March 20X1 by cheque on 28 February 20X2, delay due to an oversight by Parker; for the 12 months ended 31 March 20X2 by cheque on 31 July 20X1. Local taxes are €8,000 per annum.

(xi) She will make drawings of €1,500 per month by cheque.

(xii) All receipts and payments are by cheque.

(xiii) Depreciate motor vehicles by 20% per annum and machinery by 10% per annum, using the straight-line depreciation method.

(xiv) She has been informed by her bank manager that he is prepared to offer an overdraft facility of €30,000 for the first year.

**Required:**

(a) Draft a cash budget (for the firm) month by month for the period January to June, showing clearly the amount of bank balance at the end of each month.

(b) Draft the projected statement of income for the first six months' trading, and a statement of financial position as at 30 June 20X1.

(c) Advise Sasha on the alternative courses of action that could be taken to cover any cash deficiency that exceeds the agreed overdraft limit.

## * Question 2

Mr Norman is going to set up a new business in Singapore on 1 January 20X8. He will invest $150,000 in the business on that date and has made the following estimates and policy decisions:

1 Forecast sales (in units) made at a selling price of $50 per unit are:

| Month | Sales units |
|---|---|
| January | 1,650 |
| February | 2,200 |
| March | 3,850 |
| April | 4,400 |
| May | 4,400 |
| June | 4,950 |
| July | 5,500 |

2 50% of sales are for cash. Credit terms are payment in the month following sale.

3 The units cost $40 each and the supplier is allowed one month's credit.

4 It is intended to hold inventory at the end of each month sufficient to cover 25% of the following month's sales.

5 Administration $8,000 and wages $17,000 are paid monthly as they arise.

6 On 1 January 20X8, the following payments will be made: $80,000 for a five-year lease of the business premises and $350 for insurance for the year.

7 Staff sales commission of 2% of sales will be paid in the month following sale.

**Required:**

(a) A purchases budget for each of the first six months.

(b) A cash flow forecast for the first six months.

(c) A budgeted statement of comprehensive income for the first six months' trading and a budgeted statement of financial position as at 30 June 20X8.

(d) Advise Mr Norman on the investment of any excess cash.

## Notes

1 *Conceptual Framework for Financial Reporting, IASB*, FRC, ED 2015–3.
2 IAS 1 *Presentation of Financial Statements*, IASB, revised 2007, para. 10.
3 M. Page, *British Accounting Review*, vol. 24(1), 1992, p. 80.
4 *Framework for the Preparation and Presentation of Financial Statements*, IASC, 1989, para. 20.
5 R.M. Bowen, D. Burgstahller and L.A. Daley, 'Evidence on the relationship between earnings and various measures of cash flow', *Accounting Review*, October 1986, pp. 713–725.
6 J.I.G. Board and J.F.S. Day, 'The information content of cash flow figures', *Accounting and Business Research*, Winter 1989, pp. 3–11.
7 IAS 7 *Statement of Cash Flows*, IASB, revised 2007.

### PART 2

# Preparation of internal and published financial statements

# Preparation of financial statements of comprehensive income, changes in equity and financial position

## 3.1 Introduction

Annual Reports consist of primary financial statements, additional disclosures and narrative.

The primary financial statements should be presented using standardised formats as prescribed by International Financial Reporting Standards:

- a statement of income;
- a statement of other comprehensive income;
- a statement of changes in equity;
- a statement of financial position;
- a statement of cash flows (covered in Chapter 5);
- explanatory notes to the accounts.

### Objectives

By the end of this chapter, you should be able to:

- understand the structure and content of published financial statements;
- prepare statements of comprehensive income, changes in equity and financial position;
- explain the nature of and reasons for notes to the accounts.

## 3.2 Preparing an internal statement of income from a trial balance

In this section we revise the steps taken to prepare an internal statement of income from a trial balance. These are to:

- identify year-end adjustments;
- calculate these adjustments;
- prepare an internal statement of income taking adjustments into account.

### 3.2.1 The trial balance of Wiggins SA

Accounts will be prepared for Wiggins SA from the trial balance set out in Figure 3.1.

**Figure 3.1 The trial balance for Wiggins SA as at 31 December 20X3**

| | €000 | €000 |
|---|---:|---:|
| Issued share capital (€1) | | 16,500 |
| Share premium | | 750 |
| Retained earnings | | 57,500 |
| 10% long-term loan (20X9) | | 63,250 |
| Bank overdraft | | 6,325 |
| Trade payables | | 30,650 |
| Depreciation – buildings | | 2,300 |
| – equipment | | 3,450 |
| – vehicles | | 9,200 |
| Freehold land | 57,500 | |
| Freehold buildings | 57,500 | |
| Equipment | 14,950 | |
| Motor vehicles | 20,700 | |
| Inventory at 1 January 20X3 | 43,125 | |
| Trade receivables | 28,750 | |
| Cash in hand | 4,600 | |
| Purchases | 258,750 | |
| Bank interest | 1,150 | |
| Dividends | 1,725 | |
| Interest on loan | 6,325 | |
| Insurance | 5,290 | |
| Salaries and wages | 20,355 | |
| Motor expenses | 9,200 | |
| Taxation that was under provided | 750 | |
| Light, power, miscellaneous | 4,255 | |
| Sales | | 345,000 |
| | 534,925 | 534,925 |

### 3.2.2 Identify the year-end adjustments

During the year cash and credit transactions are recorded by posting to the individual ledger accounts as cash is paid or received and invoices received or issued. It is only when financial statements are being prepared that adjustments are made to ensure that the statement of income includes only income and expenses related to the current financial period.

The following information relating to accruals and prepayments has not yet been taken into account in the amounts shown in the trial balance:

- Inventory valued at cost at 31 December 20X3 was €25,875,000.
- Depreciation is to be provided as follows:
  - 2% on freehold buildings using the straight-line method;
  - 10% on equipment using the reducing balance method;
  - 25% on motor vehicles using the reducing balance method.
- €2,300,000 was prepaid for light, power and miscellaneous expenses and €5,175,000 has accrued for wages.
- Freehold land was revalued on 31 December 20X3 at €77,500,000, resulting in a gain of €20,000,000.
- Assume income tax at 20% of pre-tax profit.
- 1,500 €1 shares had been issued on 1 January 20X3 at a premium of 50c each.

### 3.2.3 Calculate the year-end adjustments

In this example they relate to accrued and prepaid expenses and depreciation.

W1 Salaries and wages:

€20,355,000 + accrued €5,175,000 = €25,530,000

W2 Depreciation:

| | | |
|---|---|---|
| Buildings | 2% of €57,500,000 | €1,150,000 |
| Equipment | 10% of (€14,950,000 − €3,450,000) | €1,150,000 |
| Vehicles | 25% of (€20,700,000 − €9,200,000) | €2,875,000 |
| Total | | €5,175,000 |

W3 Light, power and miscellaneous

€4,255,000 − prepaid €2,300,000 = €1,955,000

### 3.2.4 Prepare an internal statement of income after making the year-end adjustments

By way of revision, we have set out a statement of income prepared for internal purposes in Figure 3.2. We have arranged the expenses in descending monetary value. The method for doing this is not prescribed and companies are free to organise the expenses in other ways, for example in alphabetical order.

**Figure 3.2 Statement of income of Wiggins SA for the year ended 31 December 20X3**

| | | €000 | €000 |
|---|---|---:|---:|
| Sales | | | 345,000 |
| Less: | | | |
| Opening inventory | | 43,125 | |
| Purchases | | 258,750 | |
| | | 301,875 | |
| Closing inventory | | 25,875 | |
| Cost of sales | | | 276,000 |
| Gross profit | | | 69,000 |
| Less expenses: | | | |
| Salaries and wages | W1 | 25,530 | |
| Motor expenses | | 9,200 | |
| Loan interest | | 6,325 | |
| Depreciation | W2 | 5,175 | |
| Insurance | | 5,290 | |
| Bank interest | | 1,150 | |
| Light, power and miscellaneous | W3 | 1,955 | |
| | | | 54,625 |
| Profit before tax | | | 14,375 |
| Income taxation (includes under-provision) | | | 3,625 |
| Profit after tax | | | 10,750 |
| Dividends (are disclosed in Statement of Changes in Equity in published format) | | | 1,725 |
| Retained earnings | | | 9,025 |

## 3.3 Reorganising the income and expenses into one of the formats required for publication

Public companies are required to present their statement of income in a prescribed format to assist users making inter-company comparisons. IAS 1 allows a company two choices in the way in which it analyses the expenses, and the formats[1] are as follows:

● Format 1: Vertical with costs analysed according to function, e.g. cost of sales, distribution costs and administration expenses; or

● Format 2: Vertical with costs analysed according to nature, e.g. raw materials, employee benefits expenses, operating expenses and depreciation.

Many companies use Format 1 (unless there is an industry preference or possible national requirement to use Format 2) with the costs analysed according to function. If this format is used the information regarding the nature of expenditure (e.g. raw materials, wages and depreciation) must be disclosed in a note to the accounts. The analysis of expenses classified either by the nature of the expenses or by their function within the entity is decided by whichever provides information that is reliable and more relevant.

## 3.4 Format 1: classification of operating expenses and other income by function

In order to arrive at its operating profit (a measure of profit often recognised by many companies), a company needs to classify all of the operating expenses of the business into one of four categories:

● cost of sales;
● distribution and selling costs;
● administrative expenses;
● other operating income or expense.

We comment briefly on each to explain how a company might classify its trading transactions.

### 3.4.1 Cost of sales

Expenditure classified under cost of sales will typically include direct costs, overheads, depreciation and amortisation expense and adjustments. The items that might appear under each heading are as follows:

● Direct costs: direct materials purchased; direct labour; other external charges that comprise production costs from external sources, e.g. hire charges and subcontracting costs.
● Overheads: variable and fixed production overheads.
● Depreciation and amortisation: depreciation of non-current assets used in production and impairment expense.
● Adjustments: capitalisation of own work as a non-current asset. Any amount of the costs listed above that have been incurred in the construction of non-current assets for retention by the company will not appear as an expense in the statement of comprehensive income: it will be capitalised. Any amount capitalised in this way would be treated for accounting purposes as a non-current asset and depreciated.

### 3.4.2 Distribution costs

These are costs incurred after the production of the finished article and up to and including transfer of the goods to the customer. Expenditure classified under this heading will typically include the following:

● warehousing costs associated with the operation of the premises, e.g. rent, rates, insurance, utilities, depreciation, repairs and maintenance; wage costs, e.g. gross wages and pension contributions of warehouse staff;
● promotion costs, e.g. advertising, trade shows;
● selling costs, e.g. salaries, commissions and pension contributions of sales staff; costs associated with the premises, e.g. rent, rates; cash discounts on sales; travelling and entertainment;
● transport costs, e.g. gross wages and pension contributions of transport staff, vehicle costs, e.g. running costs, maintenance and depreciation.

### 3.4.3 Administrative expenses

These are the costs of running the business that have not been classified as either cost of sales or distribution costs. Expenditure classified under this heading will typically include:

● administration, e.g. salaries, commissions, and pension contributions of administration staff;
● costs associated with the premises, e.g. rent, rates;

- amounts written off the receivables that appear in the statement of financial position under current assets;
- professional fees.

### 3.4.4 Other operating income or expense

Under this heading a company discloses material income or expenses derived from ordinary activities of the business that have not been included elsewhere. If the amounts are not material, they would not be separately disclosed but included within the other captions. Items classified under these headings may typically include the following:

- income derived from intangible assets, e.g. royalties, commissions;
- income derived from third-party use of property, plant and equipment that is surplus to the current productive needs of the company;
- income received from employees, e.g. canteen, recreation fees;
- payments for rights to use intangible assets not directly related to operations, e.g. licences.

### 3.4.5 Finance costs

In order to arrive at the profit for the period, interest received or paid on loans and bank overdraft and investment income is disclosed under the Finance cost heading.

### 3.4.6 An analysis of expenses by function

An analysis of expenses would be carried out in practice in order to classify these under their appropriate function heading. These are allocated or apportioned as appropriate. The assumptions for this exercise are shown in Figure 3.3.

### 3.4.7 Accounting for current tax

The profit reported in the statement of income is subject to taxation at a percentage rate set by government. The resulting amount is treated as an expense in the statement of income and a current liability in the statement of financial position. However, this is an estimated figure and the amount agreed with the tax authorities in the following accounting period might be higher or lower than the estimate.

#### Underprovisions

If the agreed amount should be higher, it means the company has underprovided and will be required to pay an amount higher than the liability reported in the statement of financial position – this results in a debit balance appearing in the trial balance prepared at the end of the following period. This underprovision will be added to the following year's estimated tax charged in the statement of income.

For example, if the company estimates €5,750,000 in Year 20X1 and pays €6,000,000 in 20X2 and estimates €5,220,000 in 20X2 on its 20X2 profits, then the charge in the statement of income for 20X2 will be €5,470,000 (€5,220,000 + €250,000).

#### Overprovisions

If overprovided the agreed tax payable will be lower, say €5,150,000, then the charge in 20X2 will be reduced by €600,000 (€5,750,000 − €5,150,000).

**Figure 3.3 Assumptions made in analysing the costs**

| | Total €000 | Cost of sales €000 | Distribution costs €000 | Administration expenses €000 |
|---|---|---|---|---|
| **Allocation of salaries and wages** | | | | |
| Factory staff | 12,650 | 12,650 | | |
| Sales and warehouse | 10,580 | | 10,580 | |
| Administration and accounts staff | 2,300 | | | 2,300 |
| Subtotal | 25,530 | 12,650 | 10,580 | 2,300 |
| **An analysis of depreciation** | | | | |
| Freehold buildings | 1,150 | 575 | 287.5 | 287.5 |
| Equipment | 1,150 | 575 | 287.5 | 287.5 |
| Motor vehicles (allocated) | 2,875 | | 2,875 | |
| Subtotal | 5,175 | 1,150 | 3,450 | 575 |
| Motor expenses (allocated) | 9,200 | | 9,200 | |
| **An apportionment of operating expenses on the basis of space occupied** | | | | |
| Insurance | 5,290 | 2,645 | 1,322.5 | 1,322.5 |
| Light, power and miscellaneous | 1,955 | 977.5 | 488.75 | 488.75 |
| Subtotal | 16,445 | 3,622.5 | 11,011.25 | 1,811.25 |
| TOTAL EXPENSES | 47,150 | 17,422.5 | 25,041.25 | 4,686.25 |
| Add material consumed | 276,000 | 276,000 | | |
| TOTALS for statement of income | 323,150 | 293,422.5 | 25,041.25 | 4,686.25 |

## 3.4.8 The statement of income using Format 1

Format 1 is favoured by capital markets and provides a multi-stage presentation reporting four profit measures for gross, operating, pre-tax and post-tax profit, as in Figure 3.4.

**Figure 3.4 Statement of income of Wiggins SA for the year ended 31 December 20X3**

| | €000 |
|---|---|
| Revenue | 345,000.00 |
| Cost of sales | 293,422.50 |
| Gross profit | 51,577.50 |
| Distribution costs | 25,041.25 |
| Administrative expenses | 4,686.25 |
| Operating profit | 21,850.00 |
| Finance costs | 7,475.00 |
| Profit on ordinary activities before tax | 14,375.00 |
| Income tax (2,875 + 750) | 3,625.00 |
| Profit for the year | 10,750.00 |

**Figure 3.5 Wiggins SA statement of income for the year ended 31 December 20X3**

| | €000 | €000 |
|---|---|---|
| Revenue | | 345,000 |
| Decrease in inventory | (17,250) | |
| Raw materials | (258,750) | (276,000) |
| Employee benefit expense | | |
| Salaries | | (25,530) |
| Depreciation | | (5,175) |
| Other operating expenses | | |
| Motor expenses | (9,200) | |
| Insurance | (5,290) | |
| Light, power and miscellaneous | (1,955) | (16,445) |
| | | |
| Operating profit | | 21,850 |

## 3.5 Format 2: classification of operating expenses according to their nature

Note that if Format 2 is used the expenses are classified as change in inventory, raw materials, employee benefits expense, other expenses and depreciation as in Figure 3.5. The operating profit is unchanged from that appearing in Figure 3.4 using Format 1. If this format is used, the cost of sales has to be disclosed.

This method differs in that classification by nature does not require the allocation of expenses to functions. It is a format that is seen to be appropriate to particular industries such as the airline industry where it is adopted by Air China and EasyJet.

## 3.6 Other comprehensive income

When IAS 1 was revised in 2008 the profit and loss account or 'income statement' was replaced by the statement of comprehensive income, and a new section of 'Other comprehensive income' (OCI) was added to the previous statement of income.

Other comprehensive income includes **unrealised** gains and losses resulting from changes in fair values of assets/liabilities such as changes in the fair value of intangible assets and property, plant and equipment; changes on the revaluation of equity investments; actuarial gains and losses on defined benefit plans and gains and losses from translating the financial statements of a foreign operation.

The statement was then retitled as 'Statement of Comprehensive Income'.

### 3.6.1 What is meant by comprehensive income?

Comprehensive income recognises the gains and losses, both realised **and unrealised,** that have increased or decreased the owners' equity in the business. Such gains and losses arise, for example, from the revaluation of non-current assets and from other items that are discussed later in Chapters 14 (Financial instruments) and 15 (Employee benefits). These are referred to as *Other comprehensive income.*

**Figure 3.6 Statement of comprehensive income of Wiggins SA for the year ended 31.12.20X3**

|  | €000 |
|---|---|
| Revenue | 345,000.00 |
| Cost of sales | 293,422.50 |
| Gross profit | 51,577.50 |
| Distribution costs | 25,041.25 |
| Administrative expenses | 4,686.25 |
| Operating profit | 21,850.00 |
| Finance costs | 7,475.00 |
| Profit on ordinary activities before tax | 14,375.00 |
| Income tax | 3,625.00 |
| Profit for the year | 10,750.00 |
| Other comprehensive income: |  |
|    Gains on property revaluation | 20,000.00 |
| Comprehensive income for the year | 30,750.00 |

### 3.6.2 How to report other comprehensive income

IAS 1 allows a choice. It can be presented as a separate statement or as an extension of the statement of income. In our example we have presented it as an extension of the statement of income.

In this example, there is a revaluation gain on the freehold land which needs to be added to the profit on ordinary activities for the year in order to arrive at the comprehensive income. This is shown in Figure 3.6.

### 3.6.3 Analysing other comprehensive income

Analysts consider the implication for future profits and growth. For example, it prompts questions such as:

● If there is a gain on non-current asset revaluation: what will be the cash impact on plans for replacing or increasing operating capital? What do the notes to the accounts indicate about capital commitments?

● If there is a gain or loss on foreign exchange: does it indicate a weakening or strengthening of the domestic currency? Will the translation of future overseas sales and profits result in higher or lower reported earnings per share?

## 3.7 How non-recurring or exceptional items can affect operating income

Operating income is one of the measures used by investors when attempting to predict future income. Management are, therefore, keen to highlight if the current year's operating income has been adversely affected by events that are unlikely to occur in future periods – these are referred to as 'exceptional items'. Such items are within the normal operating activities of the business but require to be separately disclosed because they are significant due to their non-recurring nature and materiality in both size and nature. A company's **quality of earnings** is important as seen in the following extract from the InterContinental Hotels Group 2015 Annual Report:

### Exceptional items

The Group discloses certain financial information both including and excluding exceptional items. The presentation of information excluding exceptional items allows a better understanding of the underlying trading performance of the Group and provides consistency with the Group's internal management reporting.

There could be a number of exceptional reasons that result in a lower profit, for example costs incurred in restructuring the business or unusually high allowances for bad debts or material write-downs of inventories to net realisable value or non-current assets to recoverable amounts.

Exceptional items are not, however, always adverse – there might, for example, have been significant gains arising from the disposal of non-current assets. The following is an extract from the John Lewis 2016 Annual Report:

|  | 2016 | 2015 |
|---|---|---|
| Operating profit before exceptional item | 399.4 | 439.8 |
| Exceptional item | 129.3 | 7.9 |
| Operating profit | 528.7 | 447.7 |

On 16 April 2015, the Group disposed of a property which was previously held for sale. The profit on disposal of £129.3m has been recorded as exceptional operating income in the period to 30 January 2016. A tax charge of £25.1m was recognised on the exceptional item.

They are a problem, however, when used to manipulate the figure for maintainable earnings, which led in 2013 to the UK's FRC issuing note PN 108 *FRC seeks consistency in the reporting of exceptional items,* which aims to discourage companies from smoothing profits by creating exceptional charges – which are then fed back in a later period as part of earnings.

### 3.7.1 Notes to the accounts

It is important to refer to information in the Notes because these items can have a material impact as seen in the Carrefour 2011 Annual Report where an operating profit is turned into an operating loss:

|  | 2011 | 2010 | % change |
|---|---|---|---|
| Total revenue | 82,764 | 81,840 | 1.1% |
| Cost of sales | (64,912) | (63,969) | 1.5% |
| Gross margin from recurring operations | 17,852 | 17,871 | (0.1)% |
| Sales, general and administrative expenses | (13,969) | (13,494) | 3.5% |
| Depreciation, amortisation and provisions | (1,701) | (1,675) | 1.6% |
| Recurring operating income | 2,182 | 2,701 | (19.2)% |
| Non-recurring income and expenses, net | (2,662) | (999) | – |
| Operating profit/(loss) | (481) | 1,703 | (128.2)% |

Non-recurring income and expenses consist mainly of gains and losses on disposal of property and equipment or intangible assets, impairment losses on property and equipment or intangible assets (including goodwill), restructuring costs and provisions for claims and litigation that are material at Group level. They are presented separately in the income statement to 'help users of the financial statements to better understand the Group's underlying operating performance and provide them with useful information to assess the earnings outlook'.

The maintainable figure to concentrate on is the Recurring operating income – in 2012 and 2013 the company reports this as remaining relatively stable at €2,124m and €2,238m respectively.

### 3.7.2 Need for consistency in presentation

In the UK the Financial Reporting Council (FRC) issued a reminder in 2013 to Boards on the need to improve the reporting of additional and exceptional items by companies and ensure consistency in their presentation to comply with the Corporate Governance Code principle that the annual report and accounts as a whole should be fair, balanced and understandable. The Financial Reporting Review Panel (FRRP) made the point that it is important that investors should be able to identify the trend in underlying, i.e. maintainable profits.

This means, for example, that where the same category of material items recurs each year and in similar amounts (for example, restructuring costs), companies should consider whether such amounts should be included as part of underlying profit. Also where significant items of expense may be subsequently reversed, they should be treated as exceptional items in the subsequent period.

### 3.7.3 Columnar format

Whilst the information could be disclosed as a note or a separate line item on the face of the statement of income, some companies emphasise the impact by preparing a three-column statement of income which is an alternative method for disclosing permitted by IAS 1.

## 3.8 How decision-useful is the statement of comprehensive income?

A key question we should ask whenever there is a proposal to present additional financial information is 'How will this be useful to users of the accounts?' There is no definitive answer, because some commentators[2] argue that there is no decision-usefulness in providing the comprehensive net income figure for investors, whereas others[3] take the opposite view. Intuitively, one might take a view that investors are interested in the total movement in equity regardless of the cause, which would lead to support for the comprehensive income figure. However, given that there is this difference of opinion and research findings, this would seem to be an area open to further empirical research to further test the decision-usefulness of each measure to analysts.

Interesting research[4] has since been carried out which supports the view that net income and comprehensive income are both decision-useful. The findings suggested that comprehensive income was more decision-relevant for assessing share returns and traditional net income more decision-relevant for setting executive bonus incentives.

## 3.9 Statement of changes in equity

This statement is designed to show the following:

- *Prior period adjustments.* The effect of any prior period adjustments is shown by adjusting the retained earnings figure brought forward (we will cover this in Chapter 4).

**Figure 3.7 Statement of changes in equity for the year ended 31 December 20X3**

| | Share capital | Share premium | Retained earnings | Revaluation surplus | Total |
|---|---|---|---|---|---|
| Balance as at 1 January 20X3 | 15,000 | — | 57,500 | | 74,750 |
| Changes in equity for 20X3 | | | | | |
| New shares issued | 1,500 | 750 | | | |
| Dividends | | | (1,725) | | (1,725) |
| Total comprehensive income for the year | | | 10,750 | 20,000 | 30,750 |
| Balance as at 31 December 20X3 | 16,500 | 750 | 66,525 | 20,000 | 103,775 |

- *Capital transactions with the owners.* This includes dividends and a reconciliation between the opening and closing equity capital, reporting any change such as increases from bonus, rights or new cash issues and decreases from any buyback of shares.
- *Transfers from revaluation reserves.* When a revalued asset is disposed of, any revaluation surplus may be transferred directly to retained earnings, or it may be left in equity under the heading 'revaluation surplus'.
- *Comprehensive income.* The comprehensive income for the period is disclosed.

The statement for Wiggins SA is shown in Figure 3.7.

Note that the statement of changes in equity is a primary statement and is required to be presented with the same prominence as the other primary statements.

## 3.10 The statement of financial position

IAS 1 specifies which items are to be included on the face of the statement of financial position. These are referred to as alpha headings (a) to (r) – for example (a) Property, plant and equipment, (b) Investment property, . . . , (g) Inventories, . . . , (k) Trade and other payables.

It does not prescribe the order and presentation that are to be followed. It would be acceptable to present the statement as assets less liabilities equalling equity, or total assets equalling total equity and liabilities.

### 3.10.1 Current/non-current classification

- The standard does not absolutely prescribe that enterprises need to split assets and liabilities into current and non-current. However, it does state that this split would need to be done if the nature of the business indicates that it is appropriate.
- If it is more relevant, a presentation could be based on liquidity and, if so, all assets and liabilities would be presented broadly in order of liquidity. However, in almost all cases it would be appropriate to split items into current and non-current and the statement in Figure 3.8 follows the headings prescribed in IAS 1.

**Figure 3.8 Wiggin SA statement of financial position as at 31.12.20X3**

|  | €000 | €000 |
|---|---|---|
| Non-current assets: |  |  |
| Property, plant and equipment (see Figure 3.10) |  | 150,525 |
|  |  |  |
| Current assets: |  |  |
| Inventory | 25,875 |  |
| Receivables | 28,750 |  |
| Cash at bank and in hand | 4,600 |  |
| Prepayments | 2,300 |  |
|  |  | 61,525 |
| Total assets |  | 212,050 |
| Equity: |  |  |
| Share capital |  | 16,500 |
| Share premium |  | 750 |
| Revaluation reserve |  | 20,000 |
| Retained earnings |  | 66,525 |
|  |  | 103,775 |
|  |  |  |
| Non-current liabilities: |  |  |
| 10% loan (20X9) |  | 63,250 |
| Current liabilities: |  |  |
| Payables | 30,650 |  |
| Provisions for income tax | 2,875 |  |
| Accruals | 5,175 |  |
| Bank overdraft | 6,325 | 45,025 |
| Total equity and liabilities |  | 212,050 |

## 3.11 The explanatory notes that are part of the financial statements

Published accounts are supported by a number of explanatory notes. These have been expanded over time to satisfy various user needs. We will comment briefly on (a) notes setting out accounting policies, (b) notes giving greater detail of the make-up of items that appear in the statement of financial position, (c) notes providing additional information to assist predicting future cash flows, and (d) notes giving information of interest to other stakeholders.

### (a) Accounting policies

Accounting policies are chosen by a company as being the most appropriate to the company's circumstances and **best able to produce a fair view**. They typically disclose the accounting policies followed for the basis of accounting, for example that the accounts have been prepared on a historical cost basis and how revenue, assets and liabilities have been reported. The policies relating to assets and liabilities will cover non-current and current items, for example the depreciation method used for non-current assets (as in Figure 3.9) and the valuation method used for inventory such as FIFO or weighted average.

**Figure 3.9 Extract from the 2016 financial statements of the Nestlé Group**

### Property, plant and equipment

Property, plant and equipment are shown on the balance sheet at their historical cost. Depreciation is provided on components that have homogeneous useful lives by using the straight-line method so as to depreciate the initial cost down to the residual value over the estimated useful lives. The residual values are 30% on head office, 20% on distribution centres for products stored at ambient temperature and nil for all other asset types.

The useful lives are as follows:

| | |
|---|---|
| Buildings | 20–35 years |
| Machinery and equipment | 10–20 years |
| Tools, furniture, information technology and sundry equipment | 3–8 years |
| Vehicles | 3–8 years |

### Land is not depreciated.

Useful lives, components and residual amounts are reviewed annually. Such a review takes into consideration the nature of the assets, their intended use and the evolution of technology.

Depreciation of property, plant and equipment is allocated to the appropriate headings of expenses by function in the statement of comprehensive income.

### How do users know the effect of changes in accounting policy?

Accounting policies are required by IAS 1 to be applied consistently from one financial period to another. It is only permissible to change an accounting policy if required by a standard or if the directors consider that a change results in financial statements that are reliable and more relevant. When a change does occur IAS 8 requires:

- the comparative figures of the previous financial period to be amended if possible;
- the disclosure of the reason for the change;
- the effect of the adjustment in the statement of comprehensive income of the period and the effect on all other periods presented with the current period financial statements.

## (b) Notes giving greater detail of the make-up of statement of financial position figures

Each of the alpha headings may have additional detail disclosed by way of a note to the accounts. For example, inventory of £25.875 million in the statement of financial position may have a note of its detailed make-up as follows:

| | £m |
|---|---|
| Raw materials | 11.225 |
| Work in progress | 1.500 |
| Finished goods | 13.150 |
| | 25.875 |

Property, plant and equipment normally have a schedule as shown in Figure 3.10. From this the net book value is read off the total column for inclusion in the statement of financial position.

**Figure 3.10 Disclosure note: Property, plant and equipment movements**

| | Freehold land | Freehold buildings | Equipment | Motor vehicles | Total |
|---|---|---|---|---|---|
| | €000 | €000 | €000 | €000 | €000 |
| **Cost/valuation** | | | | | |
| As at 1.1.20X3 | 57,500 | 57,500 | 14,950 | 20,700 | 150,650 |
| Revaluation | 20,000 | | | | 20,000 |
| Additions | | | | | |
| Disposals | | | | | |
| As at 31.12.20X3 | 77,500 | 57,500 | 14,950 | 20,700 | 170,650 |
| | | | | | |
| **Accumulated depreciation** | | | | | |
| As at 1.1.20X3 | | 2,300 | 3,450 | 9,200 | 14,950 |
| Charge for the year | | 1,150 | 1,150 | 2,875 | 5,175 |
| As at 31.12.20X3 | | 3,450 | 4,600 | 12,075 | 20,125 |
| Net book value | | | | | |
| **As at 31.12.20X3** | **77,500** | **54,050** | **10,350** | **8,625** | **150,525** |
| As at 31.12.20X2 | 57,500 | 55,200 | 11,500 | 11,500 | 135,700 |

## (c) Notes giving additional information to assist prediction of future cash flows

These are notes intended to assist in predicting future cash flows. They give information on matters such as:

- capital commitments that have been contracted for but not provided in the accounts;
- capital commitments that have been authorised but not contracted for;
- future commitments, e.g. share options that have been granted; and
- contingent liabilities, e.g. guarantees given by the company in respect of overdraft facilities arranged by subsidiary companies or customers.

In deciding upon disclosures, management have an obligation to consider whether the omission of the information is material and could influence users who base their decisions on the financial statements. The management decision would be influenced by the size or nature of the item and the characteristics of the users. They are entitled to assume that the users have a reasonable knowledge of business and accounting and a willingness to study the information with reasonable diligence.

## (d) Notes giving information that is of interest to other stakeholders

An example is information relating to staff. It is common for enterprises to provide a disclosure of the average number of employees in the period or the number of employees at the end of the period. IAS 1 does not require this information but it is likely that many businesses would provide and categorise the information, possibly following functions such as production, sales, and administration as in the following extract from the 2015 Annual Report of Wienerberger:

|  | Total (2015) | Total (2014) |
|---|---|---|
| Production | 10,696 | 10,015 |
| Administration | 1,404 | 1,315 |
| Sales | 3,713 | 3,506 |
| Total | 15,813 | 14,836 |
| Apprentices | 94 | 96 |

This shows a significant increase in staff numbers with reasons given within the report. However, the annual report is not the only source of information – there might be separate employee reports and information obtained during labour negotiations such as the ratio of short-term and long-term assets to employee numbers, the capital–labour ratios and the average revenue and net profits per employee in the company with inter-period and inter-firm comparisons. For example, in 2015 John Lewis reported profit after tax of £143.5m with staff of 93,800 compared to Tesco which reported profit after tax of £3,819m with staff of 200,966. Tesco also reports revenue per employee but there is no requirement to produce this figure and analysts would themselves need to calculate these – and questions should then perhaps be raised as to whether differing rates might mean that there is less customer satisfaction and the possibility of a fall with lower revenue or more employees.

## 3.12 Has prescribing the formats meant that identical transactions are reported identically?

That is the intention, but there are various reasons why there may still be differences. For example, let us consider some of the reasons for differences in calculating the cost of sales: (a) how inventory is valued, (b) the choice of depreciation policy, (c) management attitudes, and (d) the capability of the accounting system.

### (a) Differences arising from the choice of the inventory valuation method

Different companies may assume different physical flows when calculating the cost of direct materials used in production. This will affect the inventory valuation. One company may assume a first-in-first-out (FIFO) flow, where the cost of sales is charged for raw materials used in production as if the first items purchased were the first items used in production. Another company may use an average basis. This is illustrated in Figure 3.11 for a company that started trading on 1 January 20X1 without any opening inventory and sold 40,000 items on 31 March 20X1 for £4 per item.

**Figure 3.11 Effect on sales of using FIFO and weighted average**

| Physical flow assumption | Items | £ | FIFO £ | Average £ |
|---|---|---|---|---|
| Raw materials purchased |  |  |  |  |
| On 1 Jan 20X1 at £1 per item | 20,000 | 20,000 |  |  |
| On 1 Feb 20X1 at £2 item | 20,000 | 40,000 |  |  |
| On 1 Mar 20X1 at £3 per item | 20,000 | 60,000 |  |  |
| On 1 Mar 20X1 in inventory | 60,000 | 120,000 | 120,000 | 120,000 |
| On 31 Mar 20X1 in inventory | 20,000 |  | 60,000 | 40,000 |
| Cost of sales | 40,000 |  | 60,000 | 80,000 |

**Figure 3.12 Effect of physical inventory flow assumptions on the percentage gross profit**

|  | Items | FIFO £ | Average £ | % difference in gross profit |
|---|---|---|---|---|
| Sales | 40,000 | 160,000 | 160,000 |  |
| Cost of sales | 40,000 | 60,000 | 80,000 |  |
|  |  | 100,000 | 80,000 |  |
| Gross profit % |  | 62.5% | 50% | 25% |

Inventory valued on a FIFO basis is £60,000 with the 20,000 items in inventory valued at £3 per item, on the assumption that the purchases made on 1 January 20Xl and 1 February 20X1 were sold first. Inventory valued on an average basis is £40,000 with the 20,000 items in inventory valued at £2 per item on the assumption that sales made in March cannot be matched with a specific item.

The effect on the gross profit percentage would be as shown in Figure 3.12. This demonstrates that, even from a single difference in accounting treatment, the gross profit for the same transaction could be materially different in both absolute and percentage terms.

### How can an investor determine the effect of different assumptions?

Although companies are required to disclose their inventory valuation policy, the level of detail provided varies and we are not able to quantify the effect of different inventory valuation policies.

For example, a clear description of an accounting policy is provided by AstraZeneca. Even so, it does not allow the user to know how net realisable value was determined. Was it, for example, primarily based upon forecasted short-term demand for the product?

**AstraZeneca inventory policy (2015) Annual Report**

**Inventories**

Inventories are stated at the lower of cost or net realisable value.

The first in, first out or an average method of valuation is used.

For finished goods and work in progress, cost includes directly attributable costs and certain overhead expenses (including depreciation).

Selling expenses and certain other overhead expenses (principally central administration costs) are excluded.

Net realisable value is determined as estimated selling price less all estimated costs of completion and costs to be incurred in selling and distribution.

Write-downs of inventory occur in the general course of business and are included in cost of sales in the income statement. However, if the write-off is regarded as material it would be reported as an exceptional item.

The following illustration is an extract from the 2015 Annual Report of R & R Ice Cream plc:

| | Before exceptional items (€000) | Exceptional items (€000) | After exceptional items (€000) | Before exceptional items (€000) | Exceptional items (€000) | After exceptional items (€000) |
|---|---|---|---|---|---|---|
| Profit/(loss) before income tax | 112,538 | (69,796) | 42,742 | 75,508 | (103,122) | (27,614) |

The group incurred substantial one-off and exceptional costs in 2013 and 2014, as part of a substantial reshaping of the group's activities and financing structure. Such exceptional costs reduced substantially in 2015, since the majority of the operational restructuring was conducted in earlier years. However, there has been a smaller amount of restructuring costs that extended into 2015, though the greater part of exceptional costs in 2015 relate to aborted refinancing costs (where the group explored refinancing opportunities) and the early stage costs in relation to the potential merger.

### (b) Differences arising from the choice of depreciation method and estimates

Companies may make different choices:

- the accounting base to use, e.g. historical cost or revaluation; and
- the method that is used to calculate the charge, e.g. straight-line or reducing balance.

Companies make estimates that might differ:

- assumptions as to an asset's productive use, e.g. different estimates made as to the economic life of an asset; and
- assumptions as to the total cost to be expensed, e.g. different estimates of the residual value.

### (c) Differences arising from management attitudes

Losses might be anticipated and measured at a different rate. For example, when assessing the likelihood of the net realisable value of inventory falling below the cost figure, the management decision will be influenced by the optimism with which it views the future of the economy, the industry and the company. There could also be other influences. For example, if bonuses are based on net income, there is an incentive to overestimate the net realisable value; whereas, if management is preparing a company for a management buy-out, there is an incentive to underestimate the net realisable value in order to minimise the net profit for the period.

### (d) Differences arising from the capability of the accounting system to provide data

Accounting systems within companies differ and costs that are collected by one company may well not be collected by another company. For example, the apportionment of costs might be more detailed with different proportions being allocated or apportioned.

## 3.13 Fair presentation

IAS 1 *Presentation of Financial Statements* requires financial statements to give a **fair presentation** of the financial position, financial performance and cash flows of an enterprise. In paragraph 17 it states that:

> In virtually all circumstances, a fair presentation is achieved by compliance with applicable IFRSs. A fair presentation also requires an entity to:
>
> **(a)** select and apply accounting policies in accordance with IAS 8 *Accounting Policies, Changes in Accounting Estimates and Errors* [this is dealt with in Chapter 4];
> **(b)** present information, including accounting policies, in a manner that provides relevant, reliable, comparable and understandable information;
> **(c)** provide additional disclosures when compliance with the specific requirements in IFRSs is insufficient to enable users to understand the impact of particular transactions, other events and conditions on the entity's financial position and financial performance.

### 3.13.1 Legal opinions

In the UK we require financial statements to give a **true and fair view**. True and fair is a legal concept and can be authoritatively decided only by a court. However, the courts have never attempted to define 'true and fair'. In the UK the Accounting Standards Committee (ASC) obtained a legal opinion which included the following statement:

> Accounts will not be true and fair unless the information they contain is sufficient in quantity and quality to satisfy the reasonable expectations of the readers to whom they are addressed.

Accounting standards are an authoritative source of accounting practice.

However, an Opinion obtained by the FRC in May 2008 and again in 2013 advised that true and fair still has to be taken into consideration by preparers and auditors of financial statements whether prepared under UK company law or IFRSs. Directors have to consider whether the statements are appropriate and auditors have to exercise professional judgement when giving an audit opinion – it is not sufficient for either directors or auditors to reach a conclusion solely because the financial statements were prepared in accordance with applicable accounting standards.

### 3.13.2 Fair override

Standards are not intended to be a straitjacket and IAS 1 recognises that there may be occasions when application of an IAS/IFRS might be misleading and departure from the IAS/IFRS treatment is permitted. This is referred to as the **fair override** provision.

Although IAS 1 does not refer to true and fair or override, the FRC in a document issued in 2012 *True and Fair* concluded that preparers, those charged with governance and auditors should:

● always stand back and ensure that the accounts as a whole do give a true and fair view;
● provide additional disclosures when compliance with an accounting standard is insufficient to present a true and fair view;

- use the true and fair override where compliance with the standards does not result in the presentation of a true and fair view; and
- ensure that the consideration they give to these matters is evident in their deliberations and documentation.

Examples of the use of the IAS 1 override among European companies are very rare.

### When do companies use the fair override?

Fair override can occur for a number[5] of reasons with the most frequent being the situation where the Accounting Standards may prescribe one method, which contradicts company law and thus requires an override, for example, providing no depreciation on investment properties. Next would be where Accounting Standards may offer a choice between accounting procedures, at least one of which contradicts company law. If that particular choice is adopted, the override should be invoked, for example grants not being shown as deferred income.

### Fair override can be challenged

If a company in the UK relies on the fair override provision, it may be challenged by the Financial Reporting Review Panel and the company's decision overturned. For example, although Eurovestech had adopted an accounting policy in its 2005 and 2006 accounts not to consolidate two of its subsidiaries because its directors considered that to do so would not give a true and fair view, the FRRP decision was that this was unacceptable because the company was unable to demonstrate special circumstances warranting this treatment.

## 3.14 What does an investor need in addition to the primary financial statements to make decisions?

Investors attempt to estimate future cash flows when making an investment decision. As regards future cash flows, these are normally perceived to be influenced by past profits as reported in the statements of income and the asset base as shown by the statement of financial position.

In order to assist shareholders to predict future cash flows with an understanding of the risks involved, more information has been required by the IASB. For example:

- More quantitative information (discussed in Chapter 4):
  - financial statements are required to take account of events and information becoming available after the period-end;
  - segment reports are required;
  - disclosure is required of the impact of changes on the operation, e.g. a breakdown of turnover, costs and profits for both new and discontinued operations.
- More qualitative narrative information, including:
  - mandatory disclosures;
  - IFRS practice statement – management commentary.
- UK requirements:
  - Chairman's Statement;
  - Directors' Report;

- Disclosure: Operating and Financial Review;
- Strategic Report.

We will comment briefly on the qualitative narrative disclosures.

### 3.14.1 IFRS mandatory disclosures

When making future predictions, investors need to be able to identify that part of the net income that is likely to be maintained in the future. IAS 1 provides assistance to users in this by requiring that certain items are separately disclosed. These are items within the ordinary activities of the enterprise which are of such size, nature or incidence that their separate disclosure is required in the financial statements in order for the financial statements to show a fair view.

These items are not extraordinary and must, therefore, be presented above the tax line. It is usual to disclose the nature and amount of these items in a note to the financial statements, with no separate mention on the face of the statement of comprehensive income; however, if sufficiently material, they can be disclosed on the face of the statement.

Examples of the type of item that may give rise to separate disclosures are:

- the write-down of assets to realisable value or recoverable amount;
- the restructuring of activities of the enterprise; discontinued operations; disposals of items of property, plant and equipment and long-term investments; litigation settlements.

### 3.14.2 Subjective nature of items classified as exceptional

The items reported as exceptional require the exercise of judgement and so need to be approached with a certain amount of scepticism.

#### Exercise of judgement

Judgement is required in determining the best manner in which information is presented. IAS 1 is not prescriptive and companies may choose to present exceptional items as a line item on the face of the accounts, as a disclosure note or in columnar format.

Judgement is also required when classifying items as operating or exceptional. IAS 1 states that it would be misleading and would impair comparability if items of an operating nature were excluded from the results of operating activities. This is aimed at preventing companies from classifying operating costs as exceptional in order to improve the headline figure that is frequently used to calculate key performance indicators such as return on equity and earnings per share.

#### Exercise of scepticism

Reporting an item as exceptional may cause operating profits to be boosted, as illustrated in a 2014 S&P study *'Why Inconsistent Reporting of Exceptional Items Can Cloud Underlying Profitability'* of non-financial FTSE 100 companies which reported that 89% adjusted profits and in 73% of cases this boosted operating profits.

A similar review[6] in 2013 by the Irish Auditing and Advisory Authority found that the costs presented as exceptional exceeded the income presented as exceptional by a factor of 5:1.

Investors need to exercise scepticism and carefully scrutinise underlying earnings and exceptional items before reaching their own view of a company's performance.

### 3.14.3 IFRS Management Commentary

In December 2010 the IASB issued an IFRS Practice Statement *Management Commentary*. Management commentary is defined in the statement as:

> A narrative report that relates to financial statements that have been prepared in accordance with IFRSs. Management commentary provides users with historical explanations of the amounts presented in the financial statements, specifically the entity's financial position, financial performance and cash flows. It also provides commentary on an entity's prospects and other information not presented in the financial statements. Management commentary also serves as a basis for understanding management's objectives and its strategies for achieving those objectives.

The commentary should give management's view not only about what has happened, including both positive and negative circumstances, but also why it has happened and what the implications are for the entity's future.

Following the Practice Statement is not mandatory and the financial statements and annual report of a business can still be compliant with IFRS even if the requirements are not followed. However, it is the first document to be issued by the IASB that solely covers information that is provided by companies outside the financial statements.

The guidance does not attempt to dictate exactly how management commentary should be prepared so as to avoid the tick-box approach to compliance. Instead it indicates the information that should be included within the commentary:

(a) the nature of the business;

(b) management's objectives and its strategies for meeting those objectives;

(c) the entity's most significant resources, risks and relationships;

(d) the results of operations and prospects; and

(e) the critical performance measures and indicators that management uses to evaluate the entity's performance against stated objectives.

It will be interesting to observe the effect that this has on future annual reports.

Who presents and approves a management commentary may depend on jurisdictional requirements.

### 3.14.4 Strategic Report

In the UK the 2006 Companies Act[7] provides that from 2013 quoted companies should issue a Strategic Report to help members to assess how the directors have performed their duty of promoting the success of the company.

The report must contain a description of the company's strategy, its business model, the principal risks and uncertainties facing the company and a balanced and comprehensive analysis of the development and performance of the company's business during the financial year and its position at the end of that year.

The review must also, where appropriate, include an analysis using financial and other key performance indicators including information relating to environmental, social, employee and human rights matters.

#### Potentially useful key performance indicators

The intention is that there should not be a list of all performance measures but only those key indicators considered by the board and used in management reporting.

They might include:

- Economic measures of ability to create value (with the terms defined):
  - Return on capital employed;
  - Economic profit-type measures, i.e. post-tax profits less cost of capital;
- Market position;
- Market share;
- Development, performance and position:
  - traditional financial measures such as asset turnover rates;
  - industry-specific measures such as sales per square metre;
- Customers, employees and suppliers: how they rate the company;
- Social, environmental and community issues.

### Guidance on Strategic Report

Guidance[8] was issued by the FRC in 2014. Its objective is to ensure that relevant information that meets the needs of shareholders is presented in the Strategic Report and to encourage companies to experiment and be innovative in the drafting of their annual reports.

## 3.14.5 Chairman's Statement

This often tends to be a brief comment on the current year's performance and a view on the Outlook. For example, the following is a brief extract from Findel plc's 2015 Annual Report:

> There is considerable opportunity for our main business, Express Gifts, to continue the strong profit growth that it has delivered in recent years and its management have exciting plans to do this, although there may be near-term headwinds from the stronger US dollar on input prices. Our Education business faces significant challenges in reversing the sales decline. The new leadership team has recognised the issues and are focused on the remedial actions required, but these actions will take time and it will therefore take longer than previously anticipated to realise the potential of this business. Kitbag is already demonstrating its recovery potential, but will remain loss-making for a further year. Overall, we expect our track record of profit growth and debt reduction to continue to deliver good returns for shareholders in the coming years.

## 3.14.6 Directors' Report

The paragraph headings from Findel's 2015 Annual Report illustrate the type of information that is published. The report covered matters such as:

- reference to the Corporate Governance Report as forming part of the Directors' Report;
- reference to the Strategic Report;
- comments on Going Concern;
- comments on changes sought to the capital structure;
- activities;
- review of the year and future prospects.

### 3.14.7 Developments in meeting narrative reporting needs for the future

#### Survey findings in 2010

In 2010 the ACCA issued the results of an international survey[9] of CFOs' views on narrative reporting, '*Hitting the notes, but what's the tune?*', based on a joint survey with Deloitte of some 230 chief financial officers and other preparers in listed companies in nine countries (Australia, China, Kenya, Malaysia, Singapore, Switzerland, the UAE, the UK and the US). The major findings were that:

● the principal audiences for narrative information were shareholders and regulators;
● the most important disclosures for shareholders were the explanation of financial results and financial position, identifying the most important risks and how they were managed, an outline of future plans and prospects, a description of the business model and a description of key performance indicators (KPIs);
● the interviewees supported a reporting environment with more discretion and less regulation.

#### FRC initiatives in 2014/2015

In 2014 the FRC started *The Clear & Concise Initiative* to bring together activities from across the FRC.

In 2015 as part of this initiative it produced *Guidance on the Strategic Report* and issued a report,[10] *Clear & Concise: Developments in Narrative Reporting*, that reviewed the impact of the Strategic Report with of an analysis of recent research of quality of the strategic reports, supplemented with a detailed review of a small sample of strategic reports.

#### The need for a mature user response

The following is an extract from an ACCA paper 'Writing the narrative: the triumphs and tribulations'[11] by Afra Sajjad:

> We believe that the future of narrative reporting lies in reconciliation of competing information needs and expectations of primary users of annual reports, i.e. regulators and shareholders. This should be accompanied by nurturing of a culture of corporate reporting where integrity, probity and transparency are fundamental to reporting. Regulators also need to facilitate change in the culture of reporting by giving preparers the flexibility to use discretion and facilitate market led best practices. Shareholders . . . need also to be mature enough to encourage real transparency. If they respond with panic to disappointing news, it will inhibit the preparer's disclosure process.

## Summary

In this chapter we have revised the preparation of internal financial statements making accrual adjustments to trial balance figures.

In order to assess stewardship and management performance, there have been mandatory requirements for standardised presentation, using the two formats prescribed by International Financial Reporting Standards. The required disclosures were explained for both formats.

The importance of referring to Notes to the accounts was illustrated with discussion of exceptional items and their impact on predicting operating income.

The disclosure of accounting policies which allow shareholders to make comparisons between years by requiring companies to be consistent in the application of accounting policies or requiring disclosure if there has been a change was discussed.

The need for explanatory notes was explained and described.

The need for financial statements to give a true and fair view of the income and net assets was explained with recognition that this requires the exercise of professional judgement. Having recorded the transactions and made the normal adjustments for accruals, do the resulting financial statements give a fair presentation?

The evolving practices for narrative reporting under IASB and UK were discussed in the IFRS Practice Statement *Management Commentary*, the UK *Strategic Report* and the FRC *Clear and Concise Initiative*.

## REVIEW QUESTIONS

1  Explain the effect on income and financial position if (a) the amount of accrued expense were to be underestimated and (b) the inventory at the year-end omitted inventory held in a customs warehouse awaiting clearance.

2  Explain why two companies carrying out identical trading transactions could produce different gross profit figures.

3  Classify the following items into cost of sales, distribution costs, administrative expenses, other operating income or items to be disclosed after trading profit:

(a) Personnel department costs

(b) Computer department costs

(c) Cost accounting department costs

(d) Financial accounting department costs

(e) Bad debts

(f) Provisions for warranty claims

(g) Interest on funds borrowed to finance an increase in working capital

(h) Interest on funds borrowed to finance an increase in property, plant and equipment.

4  'We analyze a sample of UK public companies that invoked a True and Fair View (TFV) override during 1998–2000 to assess whether overrides are used opportunistically. We find overrides increase income and equity significantly, and firms with weaker performance and higher levels of debt employ overrides that are more costly . . . financial statements are not less informative than control sample.'[12]

Discuss the enquiries and action that you think an auditor should take to ensure that the financial statements give a more true and fair view than from applying standards.

5  When preparing accounts under Format 1, how would a bad debt that was materially larger than normal be disclosed?

6  'Annual accounts have been put into such a straitjacket of overemphasis on uniform disclosure that there will be a growing pressure by national bodies to introduce changes unilaterally which will again lead to diversity in the quality of disclosure. This is both healthy and necessary.' Discuss.

7  Explain the relevance to the user of accounts if expenses are classified as 'administrative expenses' rather than as 'cost of sales'.

**8** IAS 1 *Presentation of Financial Statements* requires 'other comprehensive income' items to be included in the statement of comprehensive income and it also requires a statement of changes in equity. Explain the need for publishing this information, and identify the items you would include in them.

**9** Discuss the major benefit to an investor from the UK Strategic Report.

**10** The following are three KPIs for the retail sector:[13] capital expenditure, expected return on new stores and customer satisfaction. Discuss two further KPIs that might be significant.

**11** Explain the difference between accounting policies, accounting estimates and prior period errors and how each affects the financial statements

## EXERCISES

### * Question 1

The following trial balance was extracted from the books of Old NV on 31 December 20X1.

|  | € 000 | €000 |
|---|---|---|
| Sales | | 12,050 |
| Returns outwards | | 313 |
| Provision for depreciation | | |
| Plant | | 738 |
| Vehicles | | 375 |
| Rent receivable | | 100 |
| Trade payables | | 738 |
| Debentures | | 250 |
| Issued share capital – ordinary €1 shares | | 3,125 |
| Issued share capital – preference shares (treated as equity) | | 625 |
| Share premium | | 350 |
| Retained earnings | | 875 |
| Inventory | 825 | |
| Purchases | 6,263 | |
| Returns inwards | 350 | |
| Carriage inwards | 13 | |
| Carriage outwards | 125 | |
| Salesmen's salaries | 800 | |
| Administrative wages and salaries | 738 | |
| Land | 100 | |
| Plant (includes €362,000 acquired in 20X1) | 1,562 | |
| Motor vehicles | 1,125 | |
| Goodwill | 1,062 | |
| Distribution costs | 290 | |
| Administrative expenses | 286 | |
| Directors' remuneration | 375 | |
| Trade receivables | 3,875 | |
| Cash at bank and in hand | 1,750 | |
|  | 19,539 | 19,539 |

Note of information not taken into the trial balance data:

(a) Provide for:

    (i)   An audit fee of €38,000.

    (ii)  Depreciation of plant at 20% straight-line.

    (iii)  Depreciation of vehicles at 25% reducing balance.

    (iv)  The goodwill suffered an impairment in the year of €177,000.

    (v)  Income tax of €562,000.

    (vi)  Debenture interest of €25,000.

(b) Closing inventory was valued at €1,125,000 at the lower of cost and net realisable value.

(c) Administrative expenses were prepaid by €12,000.

(d) Land was to be revalued by €50,000.

**Required:**

(a) **Prepare a statement of income for internal use for the year ended 31 December 20X1.**

(b) **Prepare a statement of comprehensive income for the year ended 31 December 20X1 and a statement of financial position as at that date in Format 1 style of presentation.**

## * Question 2

Formatone plc produced the following trial balance as at 30 June 20X6:

|  | £000 | £000 |
| --- | --- | --- |
| Land at cost | 2,160.0 | — |
| Buildings at cost | 1,080.0 | — |
| Plant and Equipment at cost | 1,728.0 | — |
| Intangible assets | 810.0 | — |
| Accum. depreciation – 30.6.20X5 |  |  |
|   Buildings | — | 432.0 |
|   Plant and equipment | — | 504.0 |
| Interim dividend paid | 108.0 |  |
| Receivables and payables | 585.0 | 532.8 |
| Cash and bank balance | 41.4 | — |
| Inventory as at 30.6.20X6 | 586.8 | — |
| Taxation | — | 14.4 |
| Deferred tax | — | 37.8 |
| Distribution cost | 529.2 | — |
| Administrative expenses | 946.8 | — |
| Retained earnings b/f | — | 891.0 |
| Sales revenue | — | 9,480.6 |
| Cost of sales | 5,909.4 | — |
| Ordinary shares of 50p each | — | 2,160.0 |
| Share premium account | — | 432.0 |
|  | 14,484.6 | 14,484.6 |

The following information is available:

(i)   A revaluation of the Land and Buildings on 1 July 20X5 resulted in an increase of £3,240,000 in the Land and £972,000 in the Buildings. This has not yet been recorded in the books.

(ii)  Depreciation:

Plant and Equipment are depreciated at 10% using the reducing balance method.

Intangible assets are to be written down by £540,000.

Buildings have an estimated life of 30 years from date of the revaluation.

(iii) Taxation

The current tax is estimated at £169,200.

There had been an overprovision in the previous year.

Deferred tax is to be increased by £27,000.

(iv) Capital

150,000 shares were issued and recorded on 1 July 20X5 for 80p each.

A further dividend of 5p per share has been declared on 30 June 20X6.

**Required:**

**Prepare for the year ended 30 June 20X6 the statement of comprehensive income, statement of changes in equity and statement of financial position.**

## * Question 3

Basalt plc is a wholesaler. The following is its trial balance as at 31 December 20X0.

| | Dr £000 | Cr £000 |
|---|---|---|
| Ordinary share capital: £1 shares | | 300 |
| Share premium | | 20 |
| General reserve | | 16 |
| Retained earnings as at 1 January 20X0 | | 55 |
| Inventory as at 1 January 20X0 | 66 | |
| Sales | | 962 |
| Purchases | 500 | |
| Administrative costs | 10 | |
| Distribution costs | 6 | |
| Plant and machinery – cost | 220 | |
| Plant and machinery – provision for depreciation | | 49 |
| Returns outwards | | 25 |
| Returns inwards | 27 | |
| Carriage inwards | 9 | |
| Warehouse wages | 101 | |
| Salesmen's salaries | 64 | |
| Administrative wages and salaries | 60 | |
| Hire of motor vehicles | 19 | |
| Directors' remuneration | 30 | |
| Rent receivable | | 7 |
| Trade receivables | 326 | |
| Cash at bank | 62 | |
| Trade payables | | 66 |
| | 1,500 | 1,500 |

The following additional information is supplied:

(i) Depreciate plant and machinery 20% on straight-line basis.

(ii) Inventory at 31 December 20X0 is £90,000.

(iii) Accrue auditors' remuneration £2,000.

(iv) Income tax for the year will be £58,000 payable October 20X1.

(v) It is estimated that 7/11 of the plant and machinery is used in connection with distribution, with the remainder for administration. The motor vehicle costs should be allocated to distribution.

Required:

Prepare a statement of income and statement of financial position in a form that complies with IAS 1. No notes to the accounts are required.

## * Question 4

HK Ltd has prepared its draft trial balance to 30 June 20X1, which is shown below.

| Trial balance at 30 June 20X1 | | |
|---|---|---|
| | $000 | $000 |
| Freehold land | 2,100 | |
| Freehold buildings (cost $4,680,000) | 4,126 | |
| Plant and machinery (cost $3,096,000) | 1,858 | |
| Fixtures and fittings (cost $864,000) | 691 | |
| Goodwill | 480 | |
| Trade receivables | 7,263 | |
| Trade payables | | 2,591 |
| Inventory | 11,794 | |
| Bank balance | 11,561 | |
| Development grant received | | 85 |
| Profit on sale of freehold land | | 536 |
| Sales | | 381,600 |
| Cost of sales | 318,979 | |
| Administration expenses | 9,000 | |
| Distribution costs | 35,100 | |
| Directors' emoluments | 562 | |
| Bad debts | 157 | |
| Auditors' remuneration | 112 | |
| Hire of plant and machinery | 2,400 | |
| Loan interest | 605 | |
| Dividends paid during the year – preference | 162 | |
| Dividends paid during the year – ordinary | 426 | |
| 9% loan | | 7,200 |
| Share capital – preference shares (treated as equity) | | 3,600 |
| Share capital – ordinary shares | | 5,400 |
| Retained earnings | | 6,364 |
| | 407,376 | 407,376 |

The following information is available:

(a) The authorised share capital is 4,000,000 9% preference shares of $1 each and 18,000,000 ordinary shares of 50c each.

(b) Provide for depreciation at the following rates:

    (i)   Plant and machinery 20% on cost

    (ii)  Fixtures and fittings 10% on cost

    (iii) Buildings 2% on cost

    Charge all depreciation to cost of sales.

(c) Provide $5,348,000 for income tax.

(d) The loan was raised during the year and there is no outstanding interest accrued at the year-end.

(e) Government grants of $85,000 have been received in respect of plant purchased during the year and are shown in the trial balance. One-fifth is to be taken into profit in the current year.

(f) During the year a fire took place at one of the company's depots, involving losses of $200,000. These losses have already been written off to cost of sales shown in the trial balance. Since the end of the financial year a settlement of $150,000 has been agreed with the company's insurers.

(g) $500,000 of the inventory is obsolete. This has a realisable value of $250,000.

(h) Acquisitions of property, plant and equipment during the year were:
Plant      $173,000          Fixtures     $144,000

(i) During the year freehold land which cost $720,000 was sold for $1,316,000.

(j) A final ordinary dividend of 3c per share is declared and was an obligation before the year-end, together with the balance of the preference dividend. Neither dividend was paid at the year-end.

(k) The goodwill has not been impaired.

(l) The land was revalued at the year-end at $2,500,000.

Required:
(a) Prepare the company's statement of comprehensive income for the year to 30 June 20X1 and a statement of financial position as at that date, complying with the relevant accounting standards in so far as the information given permits.
(All calculations to nearest $000.)
(b) Explain the usefulness of the schedule prepared in (a).

## * Question 5

Phoenix plc's trial balance at 30 June 20X7 was as follows:

|  | £000 | £000 |
|---|---|---|
| Freehold premises | 2,400 |  |
| Plant and machinery | 1,800 | 540 |
| Furniture and fittings | 620 | 360 |
| Inventory at 30 June 20X7 | 1,468 |  |
| Sales |  | 6,465 |
| Administrative expenses | 1,126 |  |
| Ordinary shares of £1 each |  | 4,500 |
| Trade investments | 365 |  |
| Revaluation reserve |  | 600 |
| Development cost | 415 |  |
| Share premium |  | 500 |
| Personal ledger balances | 947 | 566 |
| Cost of goods sold | 4,165 |  |
| Distribution costs | 669 |  |
| Overprovision for tax |  | 26 |
| Dividend received |  | 80 |
| Interim dividend paid | 200 |  |
| Retained earnings |  | 488 |
| Disposal of warehouse |  | 225 |
| Cash and bank balances | 175 |  |
|  | 14,350 | 14,350 |

The following information is available:

1  Freehold premises acquired for £1.8 million were revalued in 20X4, recognising a gain of £600,000. These include a warehouse, which cost £120,000, was revalued at £150,000 and was sold in June 20X7 for £225,000. Phoenix does not depreciate freehold premises.

2  Phoenix wishes to report plant and machinery at open market value which is estimated to be £1,960,000 on 1 July 20X6.

3  Company policy is to depreciate its assets on the straight-line method at annual rates as follows:

| | |
|---|---|
| Plant and machinery | 10% |
| Furniture and fittings | 5% |

4  Until this year the company's policy has been to capitalise development costs, to the extent permitted by relevant accounting standards. The company must now write off the development costs, including £124,000 incurred in the year, as the project no longer meets the capitalisation criteria.

5  During the year the company has issued one million shares of £1 at £1.20 each.

6  Included within administrative expenses are the following:

| | |
|---|---|
| Staff salary (including £125,000 to directors) | £468,000 |
| Directors' fees | £96,000 |
| Audit fees and expenses | £86,000 |

7  Income tax for the year is estimated at £122,000.

8  Directors propose a final dividend of 4p per share declared and an obligation, but not paid at the year-end.

**Required:**
**In respect of the year ended 30 June 20X7:**
**(a)  The statement of comprehensive income.**
**(b)  The statement of financial position as at 30 June 20X7.**
**(c)  The statement of movement of property, plant and equipment.**

## Question 6

Olive A/S, incorporated with an authorised capital consisting of one million ordinary shares of €1 each, employs 64 persons, of whom 42 work at the factory and the rest at the head office. The trial balance extracted from its books as at 30 September 20X4 is as follows:

|  | €000 | €000 |
|---|---|---|
| Land and buildings (cost €600,000) | 520 | — |
| Plant and machinery (cost €840,000) | 680 | — |
| Proceeds on disposal of plant and machinery | — | 180 |
| Fixtures and equipment (cost €120,000) | 94 | — |
| Sales | — | 3,460 |
| Carriage inwards | 162 | — |
| Share premium account | — | 150 |
| Advertising | 112 | — |
| Inventory on 1 Oct 20X3 | 211 | — |
| Heating and lighting | 80 | — |
| Prepayments | 115 | — |
| Salaries | 820 | — |
| Trade investments at cost | 248 | — |
| Dividend received (net) on 9 Sept 20X4 | — | 45 |
| Directors' emoluments | 180 | — |
| Pension cost | 100 | — |
| Audit fees and expense | 65 | — |
| Retained earnings b/f | — | 601 |
| Sales commission | 92 | — |
| Stationery | 28 | — |
| Development cost | 425 | — |
| Formation expenses | 120 | — |
| Receivables and payables | 584 | 296 |
| Interim dividend paid on 4 Mar 20X4 | 60 | — |
| 12% debentures issued on 1 Apr 20X4 | — | 500 |
| Debenture interest paid on 1 Jul 20X4 | 15 | — |
| Purchases | 925 | — |
| Income tax on year to 30 Sept 20X3 | — | 128 |
| Other administration expenses | 128 | — |
| Bad debts | 158 | — |
| Cash and bank balance | 38 | — |
| Ordinary shares of €1 fully called | — | 600 |
|  | 5,960 | 5,960 |

You are informed as follows:

(a) As at 1 October 20X3 land and buildings were revalued at €900,000. A third of the cost as well as all the valuation is regarded as attributable to the land. Directors have decided to report this asset at valuation.

(b) New fixtures were acquired on 1 January 20X4 for €40,000; a machine acquired on 1 October 20X1 for €240,000 was disposed of on 1 July 20X4 for €180,000, being replaced on the same date by another acquired for €320,000.

(c) Depreciation for the year is to be calculated on the straight-line basis as follows:

Buildings: 2% p.a.
Plant and machinery: 10% p.a.
Fixtures and equipment: 10% p.a.

(d) Inventory, including raw materials and work in progress on 30 September 20X4, has been valued at cost at €364,000.

(e) Prepayments are made up as follows:

|  | €000 |
|---|---|
| Amount paid in advance for a machine | 60 |
| Amount paid in advance for purchasing raw materials | 40 |
| Prepaid rent | 15 |
|  | €115 |

(f) In March 20X3 a customer had filed legal action claiming damages at €240,000. When accounts for the year ended 30 September 20X3 were finalised, a provision of €90,000 was made in respect of this claim. This claim was settled out of court in April 20X4 at €150,000 and the amount of the underprovision adjusted against the profit balance brought forward from previous years.

(g) The following allocations have been agreed upon:

|  | Factory | Administration |
|---|---|---|
| Depreciation of buildings | 60% | 40% |
| Salaries other than to directors | 55% | 45% |
| Heating and lighting | 80% | 20% |

(h) Pension cost of the company is calculated at 10% of the emoluments and salaries.

(i) Income tax on 20X3 profit has been agreed at €140,000 and that for 20X4 estimated at €185,000.

(j) Directors wish to write off the formation expenses as far as possible without reducing the amount of profits available for distribution.

Required:

Prepare for publication:

(a) the statement of comprehensive income of the company for the year ended 30 September 20X4,

(b) the statement of financial position as at that date along with as many notes (other than the one on accounting policy) as can be provided on the basis of the information made available, and

(c) the statement of changes in equity.

## Question 7

The following is an extract from the trial balance of Imecet at 31 October 2005:

|  | $000 | $000 |
|---|---|---|
| Property valuation | 8,000 |  |
| Factory at cost | 2,700 |  |
| Administration building at cost | 1,200 |  |
| Delivery vehicles at cost | 500 |  |
| Sales |  | 10,300 |
| Inventory at 1 November 2004 | 1,100 |  |
| Purchases | 6,350 |  |
| Factory wages | 575 |  |
| Administration expenses | 140 |  |
| Distribution costs | 370 |  |
| Interest paid (6 months to 30 April 2005) | 100 |  |
| Accumulated profit at 1 November 2004 |  | 3,701 |
| 10% loan stock |  | 2,000 |
| $1 ordinary shares (incl. issue on 1 May 2005) |  | 4,000 |
| Share premium (after issue on 1 May 2005) |  | 1,500 |
| Dividends (paid 1 June 2005) | 400 |  |
| Revaluation reserve |  | 2,500 |
| Deferred tax |  | 650 |

Other relevant information:

(i) One million $1 ordinary shares were issued 1 May 2005 at the market price of $1.75 per ordinary share.

(ii) The inventory at 31 October 2005 has been valued at $1,150,000.

(iii) A current tax provision for $350,000 is required for the period ended 31 October 2005 and the deferred tax liability at that date has been calculated to be $725,000.

(iv) The property has been further revalued at 31 October 2005 at the market price of $9,200,000.

(v) No depreciation charges have yet been recognised for the year ended 31 October 2005.

(vi) The depreciation rates are:

Factory – 5% straight-line.
Administration building – 3% straight-line.
Delivery vehicles – 25% reducing balance. The accumulated depreciation at 31 October 2004 was $10,000. No new vehicles were acquired in the year to 31 October 2005.

**Required:**
(a) **Prepare the income statement for Imecet for the year ended 31 October 2005.**
(b) **Prepare the statement of changes in equity for Imecet for the year ended 31 October 2005.**

*(The Association of International Accountants)*

## Question 8

Scott Ross, CFO of Ryan Industries PLC, is discussing the publication of the annual report with his managing director Nathan Davison. Graydon says: 'The law requires us to comply with accounting standards and at the same time to provide a true and fair view of the results and financial position. As half of the business consists of the crockery and brickmaking business which your great-great-grandmother Sasha started, and the other half is the insurance company which your father started, I am not sure that the consolidated accounts are very meaningful. It is hard to make sense of any of the ratios as you don't know what industry to compare them with. What say we also give them the comprehensive income statements and balance sheets of the two subsidiary companies as additional information, and then no one can complain that they didn't get a true and fair view?'

Nathan says: 'I don't think we should do that. The more information they have the more questions they will ask. Also they might realise we have been smoothing income by changing our level of pessimism in relation to the provisions for outstanding insurance claims. Anyway I don't want them to interfere with my business. Can't we just include a footnote, preferably a vague one, that stresses we are not comparable to insurance companies or brickmakers or crockery manufacturers because of the unique mix of our businesses? Don't raise the matter with the auditors because it will put ideas into their heads. But if it does come up we may have to charge head office costs to the two subsidiaries. You need to think up some reason why most of the charges should be passed on to the crockery operations. We don't want to show everyone how profitable that area is. I trust you will give that some thought so you will have a good answer ready.'

**Required:**
**Discuss the professional, legal and ethical implications for Ross.**

## Question 9

TYV is a manufacturing entity and produces a range of products in several factories.
TYV's trial balance at 30 September 2014 is shown below

| | Notes | $000 | $000 |
|---|---|---|---|
| Accumulated depreciation at 30 September 2013: | | | |
| Buildings | (i) | | 1,700 |
| Plant and equipment | (iv) | | 4,510 |
| Administrative expenses | | 1,820 | |
| Cash and cash equivalents | | 272 | |
| Cost of sales | | 10,200 | |
| Distribution costs | | 1,110 | |
| Equity dividend paid | | 350 | |
| Equity shares $1 each, fully paid at 30 September 2014 | | | 6,000 |
| Finance charges for new factory building | | 113 | |
| Income tax | (v) | 80 | |
| Inventory at 30 September 2014 | | 575 | |
| Land and buildings at cost at 30 September 2013 | (ii) & (iii) | 17,386 | |
| Long-term borrowings | (vi) | | 5,000 |
| Long-term borrowings loan interest | (vi) | 233 | |
| New factory building cost | | 1,014 | |
| Plant and equipment at cost at 30 September 2013 | (iv) | 7,750 | |
| Provision for deferred tax at 30 September 2013 | (v) | 625 | |
| Receipt from disposal of plant and equipment | (iv) | | 7 |
| Retained earnings at 30 September 2013 | | | 491 |
| Sales revenue | | | 19,460 |
| Share premium at 30 September 2014 | | | 850 |
| Short-term loan | (iii) | | 1,500 |
| Suspense account | (ii) | | 1,130 |
| Trade payables | | | 1,880 |
| Trade receivables | | 2,250 | |
| | | 43,153 | 43,153 |

Notes:

(i) On 1 October 2013 two of TYV's factories, factory A and factory B, were deemed obsolete and no longer suitable for TYV's use. On 1 June 2014 both factories were closed and production moved to a new facility. TYV disposed of factory B with all legal formalities completed and cash received on 31 August 2014. Factory A was not sold by the financial year-end; however at 30 September 2014 negotiations for the sale of factory A were well advanced and TYV's management expected to conclude the sale by 31 December 2014. The cost and accumulated depreciation included in land and buildings along with the fair value of each factory is shown below:

| Factory | Cost | | Depreciation | Fair value less |
|---|---|---|---|---|
| | Land | Buildings | at 30 September 2013 | cost of disposal at 30 Sept 2014 |
| A | $1,375,000 | $455,000 | $364,000 | $1,420,000 |
| B | $1,120,000 | $325,000 | $286,000 | $1,130,000 |

(ii) The suspense account is the cash received from the disposal of factory B. The only entries made in the ledgers for this item was in cash and cash equivalents and suspense account.

(iii) The cost of land included in land and buildings was $11,000,000 on 1 October 2013. TYV built the new factory on land it already owned, commencing on 1 October 2013 and completing it on 30 June 2014. To fund the project TYV raised a short-term loan on 1 October 2013, repayable on 30 September 2015.

(iv) Plant and equipment in factories A and B was relocated to the new factory, except for plant and equipment with a carrying value of $55,000 (cost $175,000) that was sold as scrap, realising $7,000. Buildings are depreciated at 2% per annum on the straight-line basis. Buildings depreciation is treated as an administrative expense. Plant and equipment is depreciated at 25% per annum using the reducing balance method and is charged to cost of sales. TYV's accounting policy for depreciation is to charge a full year in the year of acquisition and none in the year of disposal.

(v) The directors estimate the income tax charge on the year's profits at $940,000. The balance on the income tax account represents the under-provision for the previous year's tax charge. The deferred tax provision is to be reduced by $49,000.

(vi) The long-term borrowings consist of one loan issued in 2000 for 20 years at 7% interest per year. Interest is paid half yearly on 1 June and 1 December.

**Required:**
Prepare TYV's statement of profit or loss and a statement of changes in equity for the year ended 30 September 2014 and a statement of financial position at that date, in accordance with the requirements of International Financial Reporting Standards.
All workings should be to the nearest $000. Notes to the financial statements are not required but all workings must be clearly shown. Do not prepare a statement of accounting policies.

*(CIMA Financial Operations November 2014)*

## Notes

1 IAS 1 *Presentation of Financial Statements,* IASB, December 2008.
2 D. Dhaliwal, K. Subramnayam and R. Trezevant, 'Is comprehensive income superior to net income as a measure of firm performance?', *Journal of Accounting and Economics,* vol. 26(1), 1999, pp. 43–67.
3 D. Hirst and P. Hopkins, 'Comprehensive income reporting and analysts' valuation judgments', *Journal of Accounting Research,* vol. 36 (Supplement), 1998, pp. 47–74.

4 G.C. Biddles and J.-H. Choi, 'Is comprehensive income irrelevant?', 12 June 2002. Available at SSRN: http://ssrn.com/abstract=316703

5 G. Livne and M. McNichols, *An Empirical Investigation of the True and Fair Override*, LBS Accounting Subject Area Working Paper No. 031 (www.bm.ust.hk/acct/acsymp2004/Papers/Livne.pdf).

6 www.iaasa.ie/publications/IAS1/ebook/IAS1_Commentary.pdf

7 Companies Act 2006 (Strategic Report and Directors Report) Regulations 2013.

8 Guidance for Strategic Report, FRC, August 2014.

9 www.accaglobal.com/gb/en/technical-activities/technical-resources-search/2010/september/hitting-the-notes.html

10 www.frc.org.uk/Our-Work/Publications/Accounting-and-Reporting-Policy/Clear-Concise-Developments-in-Narrative-Reporti.aspx

11 www.accaglobal.com/content/dam/acca/global/PDF-technical/narrative-reporting/writing_the_narrative.pdf

12 G. Livne and M.F. McNichols, 'An empirical investigation of the true and fair override', *Journal of Business, Finance and Accounting*, pp. 1–30, January/March 2009.

13 www.pwc.com/gx/en/corporate-reporting/assets/pdfs/UK_KPI_guide.pdf

# CHAPTER 4

# Annual report: additional financial disclosures

## 4.1 Introduction

The main purpose of this chapter is to explain the additional content in an Annual Report that assists users to make informed assessments of stewardship and informed estimates of future financial performance. Investors need to be able to assess the effect on the published accounts of (a) transactions occurring after the year-end and (b) transactions occurring during the year that might not have been at arm's length. In looking at the future, investors need information on (a) the profitability of different product lines and markets and (b) the potential financial impact if any part of the business has been discontinued.

### Objectives

By the end of this chapter, you should be able to:

- make appropriate entries in the financial statements and/or disclosure in the notes to the accounts in accordance with IAS 10 *Events after the Reporting Period*;
- make appropriate entries in the financial statements in accordance with IAS 8 *Accounting Policies, Changes in Accounting Estimates and Errors*;
- identify reportable segments in accordance with IFRS 8 *Operating Segments*;
- critically discuss the benefits and continuing concerns of segmental reporting;
- explain the meaning of the term and account for 'discontinued operations' in accordance with IFRS 5 *Non-current Assets Held for Sale and Discontinued Operations*;
- prepare financial statements applying IFRS 5;
- discuss the impact of such operations on the statement of comprehensive income;
- explain the criteria laid out in IFRS 5 that need to be satisfied before an asset (or disposal group) is classified as 'held for sale';
- explain how to identify key personnel for the purposes of IAS 24 *Related Party Disclosures* and why this is considered to be important.

## 4.2 IAS 10 *Events after the Reporting Period*[1]

We have seen that transactions listed in the trial balance need to be adjusted for accruals and prepayments. They may also need to be adjusted as a result of further information becoming available after the year-end. This is covered in IAS 10.

IAS 10 requires preparers of financial statements to review events that occur after the reporting date but before the financial statements have been authorised for issue by the directors to decide whether an **adjustment** is required to be made to the financial statements or explanatory information is required to be **disclosed** by way of a note.

### 4.2.1 Adjusting events

These are events after the reporting period that provide additional evidence of conditions that existed at the period-end. Examples of such events include, but are not limited to:

- *Inventory:* After-date sales of inventory that provide additional evidence that the net realisable value of the inventory at the reporting date was lower than cost.
- *Liabilities:* Evidence received after the year-end that provides additional evidence of the appropriate measurement of a liability that existed at the reporting date, such as the settlement of a contingent liability or the calculation of bonuses for which an obligation existed at the end of the reporting period.
- *Non-current assets:* The revaluation of an asset such as a property that indicates the likelihood of impairment at the reporting date.
- The discovery of fraud or errors that show that the financial statements are incorrect.

Under IAS 10 such information becoming available after the period-end means that the financial statements themselves have to be adjusted **provided** the information becomes available before the accounts have been approved. It is important to consider the date of the period-end, the date when the financial statements are approved and the date when transactions/events occurred.

For example, consider the following scenario. Financial statements are being prepared for the year ended 31 March 20X4 and are expected to be approved in the Annual General Meeting announced for 25 June 20X4. Reviewing the audit file on 15 May, it was noted that the audit staff had identified on 29 April that stores staff had misappropriated a material amount of stock before the year-end and concealed it by reporting it as damaged. The police have been informed and are investigating. Should the financial statements be adjusted?

**Solution**: As the fraud involves a material amount occurring during the reporting period but which is only discovered after the period-end, it is classified as an adjusting event and the financial statements would require amendment.

Consideration would then be required of the accounting implications. For example, what is the impact on the cost of sales and the gross profit if closing inventory has been over-stated? Is it necessary to disclose the loss as an exceptional item? What is the likelihood of recovering recompense from the staff themselves or the company's insurers? Is any recovery an asset or contingent asset?

### 4.2.2 Non-adjusting events

These are events occurring after the reporting period that concern conditions that did not exist at the statement of financial position date. Examples would include:

- Dividends proposed. These must be disclosed in the notes [IAS 1.137]: 'the amount of dividends proposed or declared before the financial statements were authorised for issue but not recognised as a distribution to owners during the period'. The concept of a 'dividend liability' for equity shares has effectively disappeared.

- Interim dividends are not non-adjusting events, because they will have been paid during the reporting period, whereas final dividends are at the discretion of the reporting entity until approved by shareholders at a general meeting.
- An issue or redemption of shares after the reporting date, as in the following extract from the 2015 Annual Report of the InterContinental Hotels Group:

**Events after the reporting period**
In February 2016, the Board proposed a $1.5 billion return of funds to shareholders via a special dividend with share consolidation.

- Potential restructuring implications, as in the following extract from the 2013 Annual Report of Mothercare plc:

As part of the Transformation and Growth plan an in-depth organisational review was conducted to streamline the group's structure and processes. As a result of the potential restructuring a number of employees in the head office in the UK and the overseas sourcing offices are in consultation. There are likely to be additional exceptional costs of approximately £5 million in respect of the implementation of this review and these will be charged in the next financial year.

- An announcement after the reporting date of a plan to acquire another company or discontinue an operation or entering into binding agreements to sell, all of which are non-adjusting but require to be disclosed, as in the following extract from the 2014 Metrogroup Annual Report:

As part of the decision taken during the reporting period to withdraw from the whole-sale business in Denmark, METRO GROUP signed an agreement in October on the partial sale of METRO Cash & Carry Denmark to Euro Cater, a leading grocery wholesaler in Denmark and Sweden. Subject to the approval of Danish antitrust authorities, Euro Cater will take over the wholesale stores in Glostrup and Aarhus. In addition, METRO GROUP will close the remaining three wholesale stores in Denmark on 31 December 2014 and thus withdraw from the Danish market.

- The loss or other decline in value of assets due to events occurring after the reporting date.
- Entering into significant contracts, as in the following extract from the Deutz 2011 Annual Report:

On 12 January 2012, DEUTZ AG signed an agreement with the Chinese construction and agricultural equipment manufacturer Shandong Changlin Machinery Group to establish a company for the production of engines . . . . Over the medium term, the new plant will have a production capacity of around 65,000 engines . . . . At the moment, China represents the greatest area of potential growth for DEUTZ within the Asia region as a whole.

### 4.2.3 Going concern issues

Deterioration in the operating results or other major losses that occur after the period-end are basically non-adjusting events. However, if they are of such significance as to affect the going concern basis of preparation of the financial statements, then this impacts on the numbers in the financial statements, because the going concern assumption would no longer be appropriate. In this limited set of circumstances if the going concern assumption is no longer appropriate, IAS 10 requires the financial statements to be produced on a liquidation rather than going concern basis.

## 4.3 IAS 8 *Accounting Policies, Changes in Accounting Estimates and Errors*[2]

IAS 8 gives guidance when deciding whether to make a retrospective or prospective change to financial statements. A retrospective change means that the financial statements of the current and previous years will be affected. A prospective change means that accounting treatments in future years will be affected.

Let us now consider how to treat accounting policy changes, prior period adjustments and changes in accounting estimates in accordance with IAS 8.

### 4.3.1 Accounting policy changes

Accounting policies may be changed when required by a new IFRS or when management decide that it results in more relevant and reliable information being provided to users.

#### (a) When this occurs as a result of changes arising from the first application of a new IFRS

In this case there is normally a retrospective impact. For example, consider the effect on the financial statements if research costs had been capitalised by a company and a subsequent mandatory change then requires these costs to be expensed.

The research asset brought forward at the beginning of the year is treated as though it had already been expensed, which means it is eliminated and the retained earnings brought forward are reduced. The net result is that the opening assets and opening retained earnings are both reduced. Any research costs incurred in the current period will be charged to the current statement of income.

#### (b) When this occurs as a result of a change in circumstances

In this case, an entity might have applied one standard to an asset quite appropriately in one year and applied a different standard quite appropriately in the following year as its business circumstances change. For example, inventory reported under IAS 2 might be reported under IAS 16 if it is used in the construction of a capital asset. There would be no retrospective impact. The valuation would move from IAS 2 reporting at the lower of cost and net realisable value to reporting at cost/valuation less depreciation.

### 4.3.2 Prior period errors including both honest mistakes and fraud

#### Materiality

Changes are only required if the errors are material. Omissions or misstatements of items are material if they could, individually or collectively, influence the economic decisions that users make on the basis of the financial statements. Materiality depends on the size and nature of the omission or misstatement judged in the surrounding circumstances.

A decision as to their materiality depends on the entity-specific circumstances and questions would need to be asked. For example, does it change a loss to a profit? Does it avoid failing to comply with a loan covenant? Does it have the effect of increasing management's bonuses?

### Criteria

We need to be familiar with the criteria set out in the standard for prior period errors. These are as follows:

- Omissions from, and misstatements in, the entity's financial statements for one or more prior periods arising from a failure to use, or misuse of, reliable information that:
  - was available when financial statements for those periods were authorised for issue, and
  - could reasonably be expected to have been obtained and taken into account when preparing the financial statements.
- Possible scenarios:
  - Classification: current accounts payable have been classified as long-term liabilities. This might have occurred due to error or a deliberate attempt to improve the liquidity ratio – either way, the accounts payable and long-term debt must be restated;
  - Omission: trade payable invoices might have been concealed;
  - Valuation: inventory might have been overvalued by failing to record effect of obsolescence, or trade receivables overstated by failing to make adequate provision for bad debts. Expenses might have been incorrectly capitalised.

### Retained earnings restated

In each case we have to consider the effect on the retained earnings brought forward. For example, a material expense that was incorrectly capitalised would require both retained earnings and the asset to be reduced. In such a case, we would need to also consider other consequential changes such as the reversal of depreciation if that had been charged against the capital item.

## 4.3.3 Accounting estimates

Changes in methods, such as a change from straight-line depreciation to reducing balance, and changes in assumptions, such as a change in the expected economic life of an asset, do not result in any adjustment of retained earnings. These are changes being made at the end of the financial period which have a *current* and *prospective* impact in future periods.

Management should disclose, in a note to the financial statements, details of the nature of the change, and the related amounts if the change in accounting estimate has a material effect on the current period.

If criteria for treatment as a prior period error cannot be satisfied, transactions are treated as changes in accounting estimates with a prospective impact. For example, the following is an extract from the 2012 Annual Report of Imtech NV:

> The prior period errors . . . stem from accounting irregularities. These accounting irregularities resulted in an overstatement of past results, net assets by overstating receivables, work-in-progress and revenue, and understating certain costs and payables. The reversal of the respective incorrect amounts results in a negative effect in the profit and loss account . . . and a correction . . . in the balance sheets . . . .
>
> Adjustments only qualified as prior period errors when an objective determination whether the adjustment was a prior period error could be made. When this was not the case, the adjustment was accounted for as a change in estimate in 2012.

## 4.4 What do segment reports provide?

Segment reports provide a more detailed breakdown of key numbers from the financial statements. Such a breakdown potentially allows a user to:

- be more aware of the balance between the different operations and thus able to assess the quality of the entity's reported earnings, the specific risks to which the company is subject, and the areas where long-term growth may be expected;
- appreciate more thoroughly the results and financial position by permitting a better understanding of past performance and thus a better assessment of future prospects;
- be aware of the impact that changes in significant components of a business may have on the business as a whole.

The IASB requirements are set out in IFRS 8 *Operating Segments*.

## 4.5 IFRS 8 *Operating Segments*[3]

IFRS 8 applies to both separate and consolidated financial statements of entities

- whose debt or equity instruments are traded in a public market; or
- that file financial statements with a securities commission or other regulatory organisation for the purpose of issuing any class of instruments in the public market.

We will comment briefly on the following four key areas:

- identification of segments;
- identification of reportable segments;
- measurement of segment information; and
- disclosures.

### 4.5.1 Identification of segments

IFRS 8 requires the identification of operating segments on the basis of internal reports that are regularly reviewed by the entity's chief operating decision maker (CODM) in order to allocate resources to the segment and assess its performance. A segment that sells exclusively or mainly to other operating segments of the group meets the definition of an operating segment if the business is managed in that way.

#### Criteria for identifying a segment

An operating segment is a component of an entity:

(a) that engages in business activities from which it may earn revenues and incur expenses;

(b) whose operating results are regularly reviewed by the entity's chief operating decision maker, to make decisions about resources to be allocated to the segment and to assess its performance; and

(c) for which discrete financial information is available.

Not every part of the entity will necessarily be an operating segment. For example, a corporate headquarters may not earn revenues.

### Criteria for identifying the chief operating decision maker

The chief operating decision maker (CODM) may be an individual or a group of directors or others. The key identifying factors will be those of performance assessment and resource allocation. Some organisations may have overlapping sets of components for which managers are responsible, e.g. some managers may be responsible for specific geographic areas and others for products worldwide. If the CODM reviews the operating results of both sets of components, the entity determines which constitutes the operating segments using the core principles (a)–(c) above.

## 4.5.2 Identifying reportable segments

Once an operating segment has been identified, a decision has to be made as to whether it has to be reported. The segment information is required to be reported for any operating segment that meets any of the following criteria:

(a) its reported revenue, from internal and external customers, is 10% or more of the combined revenue (internal and external) of all operating segments; or

(b) the absolute measure of its reported profit or loss is 10% or more of the greater in absolute amount of (i) the combined profit of all operating segments that did not report a loss and (ii) the combined reported loss of all operating segments that reported a loss; or

(c) its assets are 10% or more of the combined assets of all operating segments.

Failure to meet any of the criteria does not, however, preclude a company from reporting a segment's results. Operating segments that do not meet any of the criteria may be disclosed voluntarily, if management think the information would be useful to users of the financial statements.

### The 75% test

If the total external revenue of the reportable operating segments is less than 75% of the entity's revenue, additional operating segments need to be identified as reportable segments (even if they don't meet the criteria in (a)–(c) above) until 75% of the entity's revenue is included.

### Combining segments

IFRS 8 includes detailed guidance on which operating segments may be combined to create a reportable segment, e.g. if they have mainly similar products, processes, customers, distribution methods and regulatory environments. Where there is an aggregation of operating segments an entity is required to disclose the judgements made by management in applying the aggregation criteria to operating segments.

Although IFRS 8 does not specify a maximum number of segments, it suggests that if the reportable segments exceed 10, the entity should consider whether a practical limit had been reached, as the disclosures may become too detailed.

**EXAMPLE ●** Varia plc is a large training and media entity with an important international component. It operates a state-of-the-art management information system which provides its directors with the information they require to plan and control the various businesses. The directors' reporting requirements are quite detailed and information is collected about the following divisions: Exam-based Training, E-Learning, Corporate Training, Print Media, Online Publishing and Cable Television. The following information is available for the year ended 31 December 2009:

| Division | Total revenue | Profit | Assets |
|---|---|---|---|
| | £m | £m | £m |
| Exam-based Training | 360 | 21 | 176 |
| E-Learning | 60 | 3 | 13 |
| Corporate Training | 125 | 5 | 84 |
| Print Media | 232 | 27 | 102 |
| Online Publishing | 124 | 2 | 31 |
| Cable TV | 73 | 5 | 39 |
| | 974 | 63 | 445 |

*Question*

Which of Varia plc's divisions are reportable segments in accordance with IFRS 8 *Operating Segments?*

*Solution*

- The revenues of Exam-based Training, Corporate Training, Print Media and Online Publishing are clearly more than 10% of total revenues and so these segments are reportable.

- All three numbers for E-Learning and Cable TV are under 10% of entity totals for revenue, profit and assets and so, unless these segments can validly be combined with others for reporting purposes, they are not reportable separately, although Varia could choose to provide separate information.

As a final check we need to establish that the combined revenues of reportable segments we have identified (£360 million + £125 million + £232 million + £124 million = £841 million) are at least 75% of the total revenues of Varia of £974 million. £841 million is 86% of £974 million so this condition is satisfied. Therefore no other segments need to be added.

### 4.5.3 Measuring segment information

IFRS 8 specifies that the amount reported for each segment should be the measures reported to the chief operating decision maker for the purposes of allocating resources and assessing performance. It does not define segment revenue, segment expense, segment result, segment assets, and segment liabilities but rather requires an explanation of how segment profit or loss and segment assets and segment liabilities are measured for each reportable segment.

Allocations and adjustments to revenues and profit should only be included in segment disclosures if they are reviewed by the CODM.

### 4.5.4 Disclosure requirements for reportable segments

The principle in IFRS 8 is that an entity should disclose 'information to enable users to evaluate the nature and financial effect of the business activities in which it engages and the economic environment in which it operates'.

IFRS 8 requires disclosure of the following segment information:

(i) Factors used to identify the entity's operating segments such as whether management organises the entity around products and services, geographical areas, regulatory environments, or a combination of factors, and whether segments have been aggregated.

(ii) Types of products and services from which each reportable segment derives its revenues.

(iii)  A measure of profit or loss for each reportable segment.

(iv)  A measure of liabilities for each reportable segment if it is regularly provided to the chief operating decision maker.

(v)  The following items if they are disclosed in the performance statement reviewed by the chief operating decision maker:
- revenues from external customers and from transactions with other operating segments
- interest revenue and interest expense
- depreciation and amortisation
- 'exceptional' items
- income tax income or expense
- other material non-cash items.

(vi)  Total assets; total amounts for additions to non-current assets if they are regularly provided to the chief operating decision maker.

(vii)  Reconciliations of profit or loss to the group totals for the entity.

(viii) Reliance on major customers. If revenues from a single external customer are 10% or more of the entity's total revenue, it must disclose that fact and the segment reporting the revenue. It need not disclose the identity of the major customer or the amount of the revenue.

### 4.5.5 Sample disclosures under IFRS 8

We consider (1) the format for disclosure of segment profits or loss, assets and liabilities, (2) the reconciliations of reportable segment revenues and assets, and (3) information about major customers.

#### (1) Format for disclosure of segment profits or loss, assets and liabilities

| | Hotels | Software | Finance | Other | Entity totals |
|---|---|---|---|---|---|
| | £m | £m | £m | £m | £m |
| **Revenue from external customers** | 800 | 2,150 | 500 | 100[a] | 3,550 |
| Intersegment revenue | — | 450 | — | — | 450 |
| Interest revenue | 125 | 250 | — | — | 375 |
| Interest expense | 95 | 180 | — | — | 275 |
| Net interest revenue[b] | — | — | 100 | — | 100 |
| Depreciation and amortisation | 30 | 155 | 110 | — | 295 |
| *Reportable segment profit* | *27* | *320* | *50* | *10* | *407* |
| Other material non-cash items – impairment of assets | 20 | — | — | — | 20 |
| *Reportable segment assets* | *700* | *1,500* | *5,700* | *200* | *8,100* |
| Expenditure for reportable segment non-current assets | 100 | 130 | 60 | — | 290 |
| *Reportable segment liabilities* | *405* | *980* | *3,000* | — | *4,385* |

Reconciliations to group totals are in **bold italics**.

Notes:

(a) Revenue from segments below the quantitative thresholds are attributed to four operating divisions. Those segments include a small electronics company, a warehouse leasing company, a retailer and an undertakers. None of these segments has ever met any of the quantitative thresholds for determining reportable segments.

(b) The finance segment derives most of its revenue from interest. Management primarily relies on net interest revenue, not the gross revenue and expense amounts, in managing that segment. Therefore, as permitted by paragraph 23, only net interest is disclosed.

### (2) Reconciliations of reportable segment revenues and assets

Reconciliations are required for every material item disclosed. The following are just sample reconciliations.

| *Revenues* | £m |
| --- | --- |
| Total revenues for reportable segments | 3,900 |
| Other revenues | 100 |
| Elimination of intersegment revenues | (450) |
| Entity's revenue | **3,550** |

| *Profit or loss* | £m |
| --- | --- |
| Total profit or loss for reportable segments | 397 |
| Other profit or loss | 10 |
| Entity profit | **407** |

| *Assets* | £m |
| --- | --- |
| Total assets for reportable segments | 7,900 |
| Other assets | 200 |
| Entity assets | **8,100** |

### (3) Information about major customers

A sample disclosure might be:

> Revenues from one customer of the software and hotels segments represent approximately £400 million of the entity's total revenue.

(Note that disclosure is not required of the customer's name or of the revenue for each operating segment.)

## 4.6 Benefits and continuing concerns following the issue of IFRS 8

### 4.6.1 The benefits of segment reporting

The majority of listed and other large entities derive their revenues and profits from a number of sources (or segments). This has implications for the investment strategy of the entity, as different segments require different amounts of investment to support their activities. Conventionally produced statements of financial position and statements of comprehensive income capture financial position and financial performance in a single column of figures.

The following is an extract from the Tesco 2011/12 Annual Report reporting on five segments within the group:

|  | Trading profit | Trading margin % | Growth % | Sales | Growth % |
|---|---|---|---|---|---|
| Group results | 3,761m | 5.8% | 1.3% | 72,035m | 7.4% |
| UK | 2,480m | 5.8% | (1.0)% | 47,355m | 6.2% |
| Asia | 737m | 6.8% | 21.5% | 11,627m | 10.4% |
| Europe | 529m | 5.3% | (0.4)% | 11,371m | 7.8% |
| US | (153m) | (24.2)% | 17.7% | 638m | 31.5% |
| Tesco Bank | 168m | 16.1% | (36.4)% | 1,044m | 13.6% |

We can see that the group is showing a trading profit growth of 1.3%. Within that, segments vary from negative growth of 36.4% to positive growth of 21.5%. Individual segments are also interesting, with sales in the US increasing by 31.5% whilst there is a trading loss.

To put the segment results into a group context we can see their relative importance to the group expressed as a percentage of the group totals as follows:

|  | Trading profit % | Sales % |
|---|---|---|
| UK | 66 | 66 |
| Asia | 20 | 16 |
| Europe | 14 | 16 |
| US | (4) | 1 |
| Tesco Bank | 4 | 1 |

The losses are a red flag to investors and the problem is addressed in the Annual Report by the Chairman, who writes as follows:

> Elsewhere, we have continued the substantial reorientation of the US business to give it the best possible opportunity to secure its future with all the potential for longer-term growth that would bring. We have announced our intention to exit from Japan. We are willing to invest for the long term but where we cannot see a profitable, scalable business earning good returns within an acceptable timescale, we prefer to pursue better opportunities. And we have slowed down the development of Tesco Bank to increase its focus on quality, service and risk management.

### 4.6.2 Concerns following the issue of IFRS 8

Despite the existence of IFRS 8, there are many concerns about the extent of segmental disclosure and its limitations must be recognised. A great deal of discretion is given to the directors concerning the **definition of each segment**. However, 'the factors which provide guidance in determining an industry segment are often the factors which lead a company's management to organise its enterprise into divisions, branches or subsidiaries'.

There is discretion concerning the **allocation of common costs** to segments on a reasonable basis. There is flexibility in the **definition of some of the items** to be disclosed (particularly net assets). These concerns have been recognised at government level and will be held under review by the European Parliament.

### European Parliament reservations

In November 2007 the European Parliament accepted the Commission's proposal to endorse IFRS 8, incorporating US Statement of Financial Accounting Standard No. 131 into EU law, which will require EU companies listed in the European Union to disclose segmental infor-mation in accordance with the 'through-the-eyes-of-management' approach.

However, it regretted[4] that the impact assessment carried out by the Commission did not sufficiently take into account the interests of users as well as the needs of small and medium-sized companies located in more than one member state and companies operating only locally. Its view was that such impact assessments must incorporate quantitative information and reflect a balancing of interests among stakeholders.

It did not accept that the convergence of accounting rules was a one-sided process where one party (the IASB) simply copies the financial reporting standards of the other party (the FASB). In particular it expressed reservations that disclosure of geographical information on the basis of IFRS 8 would be comparable to that disclosed under IAS 14.

A post-implementation review was carried out by EFRAG in 2012 (www.efrag.org).

### UK reservations

The FRRP reviewed a sample of 2009 interim accounts and 2008 annual accounts. On the basis of this review, the FRRP has highlighted situations where companies were asked to provide additional information:

- Only one operating segment is reported, but the group appears to be diverse with different businesses or with significant operations in different countries.
- The operating analysis set out in the narrative report differs from the operating segments in the financial report.
- The titles and responsibilities of the directors or executive management team imply an organisational structure which is not reflected in the operating segments.
- The commentary in the narrative report focuses on non-IFRS measures, whereas the segmental disclosures are based on IFRS amounts.

It also suggested a number of questions that directors should ask themselves when preparing segmental reports, such as:

- What are the key operating decisions made in running the business?
- Who makes the key operating decisions?
- Who are the segment managers and who do they report to?
- How are the group's activities reported in the information used by management?
- Have the reported segment amounts been reconciled to the IFRS aggregate amounts?
- Do the reported segments appear consistent with their internal reporting?

### 4.6.3 Post-implementation Review: IFRS 8 *Operating Segments*[5]

IFRS 8 was the first standard to be subjected to a post-implementation review by the IASB. The review identified different opinions among the stakeholders.

### Preparers

Standard setters, accounting firms and auditors generally supported the standard subject to suggestions for improvement.

### Investors

Views were mixed. Some were concerned that operating segments are aggregated inappropri-ately. Also there were concerns that, as the segmentation process is based on the management perspective, there is a risk that commercially sensitive information might be concealed or segments reported to conceal loss-making activities within individual segments.

Others welcome the fact that the report is audited and discloses information about how management views the business. They see added value if the segments agree with the management commentary and analyst presentations.

### Suggestions for improvement

Replace the term 'chief operating decision maker CODM' with a more common term such as key management personnel or governing body. Also, many entities present different definitions of 'operating result' or 'operating cash flow', making comparison difficult between entities. Investors would like defined line items so that they could calculate their own subtotals for operating result or cash flow.

## 4.6.4 Constraints on comparison between entities

Segment reporting is intrinsically subjective. This means that there are likely to be major differences in the way segments are determined and because costs, for instance, may be allocated differently by entities in the same industry, it is difficult to make inter-entity comparisons at the segment level and the user still has to take a great deal of responsibility for the interpretation of that information.

## 4.7 Discontinued operations – IFRS 5 *Non-current Assets Held for Sale and Discontinued Operations*[6]

IFRS 5 deals, as its name suggests, with two separate but related issues. We will first discuss the treatment of discontinued operations.

## 4.7.1 Criteria

We need to be familiar with the IFRS 5 definition of a discontinued operation. It is a component of an entity that, during the reporting period, either:

- has been disposed of (whether by sale or abandonment); or
- has been classified as held for sale, and *also*
  - represents a separate major line of business or geographical area of operations; or
  - is part of a single coordinated plan to dispose of a separate major line of business or geographical area of operations; or
  - is a subsidiary acquired exclusively with a view to resale (possibly as part of the acquisition of an existing group with a subsidiary that does not fit into the long-term plans of the acquirer).

### Defining a component

The IFRS defines a component as a part of an entity which comprises operations and cash flows that can be clearly distinguished, operationally and for financial reporting purposes, from the rest of the entity. This definition is somewhat subjective and the IASB is considering amending this definition to align it with that of an operating segment in IFRS 8 and has issued an exposure draft to this effect.

## 4.7.2 Disclosure in the statement of income

The results of discontinued operations should be separately disclosed from those of other, continuing, operations in the income statement. As a minimum, on the face of the statement, entities should show, as a single amount, the total of:

- the post-tax profit or loss of discontinued operations; and
- the post-tax gain or loss recognised on the measurement to fair value less cost to sell or on the disposal of the assets or disposal group(s) constituting the discontinued operation.

Further analysis of this amount required, either on the face of the statement of comprehensive income or in the notes:

- the revenue, expenses and pre-tax profit or loss of discontinued operations;
- the related income tax expense as required by IAS 12;
- the gain or loss recognised on the measurement to fair value less costs to sell or on the disposal of the assets or disposal group(s) constituting the discontinued operation; and
- the related income tax expense as required by IAS 12.

The following is an extract from Premier Foods' 2011 consolidated income statement:

|  | 2011 £m | 2010 £m |
|---|---|---|
| **Continuing operations** | | |
| **(Loss)/profit before taxation from continuing operations** | **(259.1)** | 28.5 |
| Taxation credit/(charge) | 29.1 | (24.4) |
| **(Loss)/profit after taxation from continuing operations** | **(230.0)** | 4.1 |
| Loss from discontinued operations | (109.0) | (103.4) |
| **Loss for the year attributable to equity shareholders of the Parent Company** | **(339.0)** | (99.3) |

There is a supporting note which details the makeup of the £109m showing the revenue, operating expenses, tax and loss on disposal.

## 4.8 Held for sale – IFRS 5 Non-current Assets Held for Sale and Discontinued Operations

Let us now discuss the treatment of assets which have been classified as held for sale.

IFRS 5 deals with the appropriate reporting of an asset (or group of assets – referred to in IFRS 5 as a 'disposal group') that management has decided to dispose of. It states that an asset (or disposal group) is classified as 'held for sale' if its carrying amount will be recovered principally through a sale transaction rather than through continuing use.

It further provides that:

- the asset or disposal group must be **available for immediate sale** in its present condition; and
- its sale must be **highly probable.**

The criteria for the sale to be highly probable are:

- The appropriate level of management must be committed to a plan to sell the asset or disposal group.

- An active programme to locate a buyer and complete the plan must have been initiated.
- The asset or disposal group must be actively marketed for sale at a price that is reasonable in relation to its current fair value.
- The sale should be expected to qualify for recognition as a completed sale within one year from the date of classification.
- Actions required to complete the plan should indicate that it is unlikely that significant changes to the plan will be made or that the plan will be withdrawn.

There is a pragmatic recognition that there may be events outside the control of the enterprise which prevent completion within one year. In such a case the 'held for sale' classification is retained, provided there is sufficient evidence that the entity remains committed to its plan to sell the asset or disposal group and has taken all reasonable steps to resolve the delay.

It is important to note that IFRS 5 specifies that this classification is appropriate for assets (or disposal groups) that are to be **sold** or distributed. The classification does not apply to assets or disposal groups that are to be **abandoned**.

### 4.8.1 IFRS 5 – implications of classification as held for sale

Assets, or disposal groups, that are classified as held for sale should be removed from their previous position in the statement of financial position and shown under a single 'held for sale' caption – usually as part of **current** assets. Any liabilities directly associated with disposal groups that are classified as held for sale should be separately presented within liabilities.

As far as disposal groups are concerned, it is acceptable to present totals on the face of the statement of financial position, with a more detailed breakdown in the notes. The following is a disclosure note from the published financial statements of Unilever for the year ended 31 December 2015:

| Assets and liabilities held for sale | 2015 £m | 2014 £m |
|---|---|---|
| *Groups held for sale* | | |
| Goodwill and intangibles | 43 | 12 |
| Property, plant and equipment | 73 | 4 |
| Inventories | 35 | 1 |
| Trade and other receivables | 3 | 1 |
| Other | 5 | 5 |
| | 159 | 23 |
| *Non-current assets held for sale* | | |
| Property, plant and equipment | 20 | 24 |
| Liabilities associated with assets held for sale | | 1 |

Depreciable assets that are classified as 'held for sale' should not be depreciated from classification date, as the classification implies that the intention of management is primarily to recover value from such assets through sale, rather than through continued use.

When assets (or disposal groups) are classified as 'held for sale', their carrying value(s) at the date of classification should be compared with the 'fair value less costs to sell' of the asset (or disposal group). If the fair value less costs to sell exceeds the carrying value, the carrying value is the amount reported as the current asset. If the transfer occurs during an accounting period, the position is reassessed at the end of the period. For example, assume that a non-current asset acquired on 1 April 2014 at a cost of £100,000 and depreciated at 10% per annum on a straight-line basis is classified as held for sale on 1 October 2016 when fair value less cost to sell was £85,000 – reassessed on 31 March 2017 as £62,000.

The fair value of £85,000 exceeded the carrying value of £75,000 (£100,000 less 2.5 years depreciation) which means that it is recorded as a current asset at its carrying value of £75,000. If the carrying value exceeds fair value less costs to sell then the excess should be treated as an impairment loss. As the fair value at 31 March 2017 was £62,000 there is an impairment of £13,000 recognised in profit or loss.

In the case of a disposal group, the impairment loss should be allocated to the specific assets in the order specified in IAS 36 *Impairment of Assets*. The treatment of impairment losses is discussed in detail in Chapter 17.

### 4.8.2 What if a non-current asset ceases to be classified as held for sale?

When a non-current asset ceases to be classified as held for sale paragraph 27 of IFRS 5 *Non-current Assets Held for Sale and Discontinued Operations* requires a new measurement basis. Paragraph 27 of IFRS 5 states:

> The entity shall measure a non-current asset that ceases to be classified as held for sale (or ceases to be included in a disposal group classified as held for sale) at the lower of:
>
> (a) its carrying amount before the asset (or disposal group) was classified as held for sale, adjusted for any depreciation, amortisation or revaluations that would have been recognised had the asset (or disposal group) not been classified as held for sale, and
>
> (b) its *recoverable amount* at the date of the subsequent decision not to sell.

## 4.9 IAS 24 *Related Party Disclosures*[7]

In the previous chapter we saw that after the financial statements have been drafted it is necessary to form a judgement as to whether or not they give a fair presentation of the entity's activities.

One of the considerations is whether there are any indications that transactions have not been carried out at arm's length. This can occur when one of the parties to the transaction is able to influence the management to enter into transactions which are not primarily in the best interest of the company. Where such a possibility exists, the person (or business) able to exert this influence is referred to in accounting terms as a 'related party'.

The users of financial statements would normally assume that the transactions of an entity have been carried out at arm's length and under terms which are in the best interests of the entity. The existence of related party relationships may mean that this assumption is not appropriate and IAS 24 therefore requires disclosure of such existence.

### 4.9.1 How to determine what is 'arm's length'

The Board of a company should consider a number of surrounding factors when determining whether a transaction has been at arm's length. These include considering:

- how the terms of the overall transaction compare with those of any comparable transactions between parties dealing on an arm's length basis in similar circumstances;
- the level of risk – how the transaction impacts on the company's financial position and performance, its ability to follow its business plan and the expected rate of return on the assets given the level of risk;
- other options – what other options were available to the company and whether any expert advice was obtained by the company.

### 4.9.2 IAS 24 disclosures required

The purpose of IAS 24 is to define the meaning of the term 'related party' and prescribe the disclosures that are appropriate for transactions with related parties (and in some cases for their mere existence). From the outset it is worth remembering that the term 'party' could refer to an individual (referred to as a person) or to another entity. IAS 24 breaks the definition down into two main sections relating to (a) persons and (b) entities. We will consider both below.

### 4.9.3 Definition of 'related party' when the party is a person

A person, or a close member of that person's family, whom we will refer to as P, is a related party to the reporting entity (RE) if:

● P has control or joint control over RE;

● P has significant influence over RE; or

● P is a member of the key management personnel of RE.

Close members of the family of P are those family members who may be expected to influence, or be influenced by, P in their dealings with RE and include:

● P's children and spouse or domestic partner; and

● children of the spouse or domestic partner; and

● dependants of P or P's spouse or domestic partner.

Key management personnel of RE are those persons having authority and responsibility for planning, directing and controlling the activities of RE, directly or indirectly, including any director (whether executive or otherwise) of RE.

#### Example: Individual as investor

Let us assume that Arthur has 60% of the shares in, and so controls, Garden Supplies Ltd and:

(a) he also has a 45% significant interest in Plant Growers Ltd. This means that in Garden Supplies Ltd's financial statements Plant Growers Ltd are a related party, and in Plant Growers Ltd's financial statements Garden Supplies Ltd are a related party; or

(b) a close member of his family (in this case his domestic partner) owns a 45% interest in Plant Growers Ltd. This means that a similar treatment would be required and the two companies are related; or

(c) Arthur still has the 60% interest in Garden Supplies Ltd but instead of having an investment in Plant Growers Ltd he is a member of Plant Growers Ltd's key management personnel. This means that a similar treatment would be required and the two companies are related.

### 4.9.4 Definition of 'related party' when the party is another entity

We have discussed the position where the related party relationship arises from an individual's relationship with two businesses. It also arises when companies are involved.

For example, let us now assume that Arthur, Garden Supplies and Plant Growers are all limited companies. We classify each company as follows:

● Arthur Ltd holds 60% of the shares and so is a parent of Garden Supplies Ltd.

● Plant Growers Ltd is an associate of Arthur Ltd because Arthur Ltd can exercise significant influence over Plant Growers Ltd.

This means that when any of the companies prepares its financial statements:

- Arthur Ltd is related to both Garden Supplies Ltd and Plant Growers Ltd.
- Garden Supplies Ltd is related to Plant Growers Ltd.
- Plant Growers Ltd is related to Garden Supplies Ltd.

### 4.9.5 Identifying related parties is not always clear

In the above examples we have clear knowledge of the relationship. However, there could be an intention to conceal the relationship, which requires ingenuity from any auditor. Steps might need to be taken such as discussions with lawyers and searching company records, referring to daily newspapers, trade magazines and phone books and, of course, using the Internet and social network sites.

The IASB has this area under review and, in its 2013 Annual Improvement Initiative, requires an entity that provides key management personnel services to be treated as a related party.

### 4.9.6 Parties deemed not to be related parties

IAS 24 emphasises that it is necessary to consider carefully the substance of each relationship to see whether or not a related party relationship exists. However, the standard highlights a number of relationships that would not normally lead to related party status:

- two entities simply because they have a director or other member of the key management personnel in common or because a member of the key management personnel of one entity has significant influence over the other entity;
- two venturers simply because they share control over a joint venture;
- providers of finance, trade unions, public utilities or government departments in the course of their normal dealings with the entity;
- a single customer, supplier, franchisor, distributor or general agent with whom an entity transacts a significant volume of business merely by virtue of the resulting economic dependence.

### 4.9.7 Disclosure of controlling relationships

IAS 24 requires that relationships between a parent and its subsidiaries be disclosed irrespective of whether there have been transactions between them. Where the entity is controlled, it should disclose:

- the name of its parent;
- the name of its ultimate controlling party (which could be an individual or another entity);
- if neither the parent nor the ultimate controlling party produces consolidated financial statements available for public use, the name of the next most senior parent that does produce such statements.

### 4.9.8 Exemption from disclosures re government-related entities

A reporting entity is exempt from the detailed disclosures referred to in Section 4.9.10 below in relation to related party transactions and outstanding balances with:

- a government that has control, joint control or significant influence over the reporting entity; and

- another entity that is a related party because the same government has control, joint control or significant influence over both parties.

If this exemption is applied, the reporting entity is nevertheless required to make the following disclosures about transactions with government-related entities:

- the name of the government and the nature of its relationship with the reporting entity;
- the following information in sufficient detail to enable users of the financial statements to understand the effect of related party transactions:
  - the nature and amount of each individually significant transaction; and
  - for other transactions that are collectively, but not individually, significant, a qualitative or quantitative indication of their extent.

The reason for the exemption is essentially pragmatic. In some jurisdictions where government control is pervasive it can be difficult to identify other government-related entities. In some circumstances the directors of the reporting entity may be genuinely unaware of the related party relationship. Therefore, the basis of conclusions to IAS 24 (BC 43) states that, in the context of the disclosures that are needed in these circumstances:

> The objective of IAS 24 is to provide disclosures necessary to draw attention to the possibility that the financial position and profit or loss may have been affected by the existence of related parties and by transactions and outstanding balances, including commitments, with such parties. To meet that objective, IAS 24 requires some disclosure when the exemption applies. Those disclosures are intended to put users on notice that related party transactions have occurred and to give an indication of their extent. The Board did not intend to require the reporting entity to identify **every** government-related entity, or to quantify in detail **every** transaction with such entities, because such a requirement would negate the exemption.

### 4.9.9 Disclosure of compensation of key management personnel

Compensation can be influenced by a person in this position. Consequently IAS 24 requires the disclosure of short-term employee benefits, post-employment benefits, other long-term benefits (e.g. accrued sabbatical leave), termination benefits, and share-based payment.

### 4.9.10 Disclosure of related party transactions

A related party transaction is a transfer of resources or obligations between a reporting entity and a related party, regardless of whether a price is charged. Where such transactions have occurred, the entity should disclose the nature of the related party relationship as well as information about those transactions and outstanding balances to enable a user to understand the potential effect of the relationship on the financial statements. As a minimum, the disclosures should include:

- the amount of the transactions;
- the amount of the outstanding balances and:
  - their terms and conditions, including whether they are secured, and the nature of the consideration to be provided in settlement; and
  - details of any guarantees given or received;
- provisions for doubtful debts related to the amount of outstanding balances; and

- the expense recognised during the period in respect of bad or doubtful debts due from related parties.

The following extract from the Unilever 2015 Annual Report is an example of the required disclosures:

### 30 Related party transactions

A related party is a person or entity that is related to the Group. These include both people and entities that have, or are subject to the influence or control of the Group.

The following related party balances existed with associate or joint venture businesses at 31 December:

Related party balances

|  | 2015 €million | 2014 €million |
|---|---|---|
| Trading and other balances due from joint ventures | 116 | 105 |

## 4.9.11 Possible impact of transactions with related parties

It is possible that there could be both beneficial and prejudicial impacts.

### Beneficial transactions with related parties

It could be that the related party is actually offering support to the business. For example, the business might have received benefits in a variety of ways ranging from financial support on favourable terms such as guarantees or low or no interest loans to the provision of goods or services at less than market rates.

### Prejudicial transactions with related parties

These can arise when the business enters into transactions on terms that would not be offered to an unrelated party. There are numerous ways that this could be arranged, such as:

- **Loans:**
  - borrowing at above market rates;
  - lending at below market rates;
  - lending with no agreement as to date for repayment;
  - lending with little prospect of being repaid;
  - lending with the intention of writing off;
  - guaranteeing debts where there is no commercial advantage to the business.
- **Assets:**
  - selling non-current assets at below market value;
  - selling goods at less than normal trade price;
  - providing services at less than normal rates;
  - transfer of know-how, or research and development transfers.
- **Trading:**
  - sales made where there is secret agreement to repurchase to inflate current period revenue;
  - sales to inflate revenue with funds advanced to the debtor to allow the debt to be paid;
  - paying for services which have not been provided.

## Summary

The published accounts of a listed company are intended to provide a report to enable shareholders to assess current-year stewardship and management performance and to predict future cash flows. Financial statements prepared from a trial balance and adjusted for accruals might require further adjustments. These arise from:

(a) events after the reporting period that provide additional evidence of conditions that existed at the period-end which might require the financial statements to be adjusted; or

(b) prior period errors that may require retrospective changes to the opening balances in the statement of financial position that could affect assets, liabilities and retained earnings.

In addition to these adjustments, in order to assist shareholders to predict future cash flows with an understanding of the risks involved, more information has been required by the IASB. This has taken two forms:

(a) more quantitative information in the accounts, e.g. segmental analysis, and the impact of changes on the operation, e.g. a breakdown of turnover, costs and profits for both new and discontinued operations; and

(b) more qualitative information, e.g. related party disclosures and events occurring after the reporting period.

## REVIEW QUESTIONS

1 Explain why non-adjusting items are not reported in the financial statements if they are of sufficient materiality to be disclosed.

2 Explain the criteria that have to be satisfied when identifying an operating segment.

3 Explain the criteria that have to be satisfied to identify a reportable segment.

4 Explain why it is necessary to identify a chief operating decision maker and describe the key identifying factors.

5 Discuss the review findings of the European Securities and Markets Authority (ESMA) in relation to the role of the chief operating decision maker.

6 A research report[8] found that users were worried about the lack of comparability among segmental disclosures of different companies following the issue of IFRS 8. Discuss:

(a) why it should have resulted in a lack of comparability;

(b) whether it is more relevant because its format and content are not closely defined;

(c) whether any of the other financial statements would be more relevant to users if they were free to format as they wished;

(d) whether inter-firm comparability is more important than inter-period comparability.

7 Explain the conditions set out in IFRS 5 for determining whether operations have been discontinued and the problems that might arise in applying them.

**8** Explain the conditions that must be satisfied if a non-current asset is to be reported in the statement of financial position as held for sale.

**9** Explain why it is important to an investor to be informed about assets held for sale.

**10** Discuss how transactions with related parties can have

    **(a)** a beneficial impact

    **(b)** a prejudicial impact

    on (i) the reported income and (ii) the financial position.

## EXERCISES

### Question 1

IAS 10 deals with events after the reporting period.

Required:
(a) Define the period covered by IAS 10.
(b) Explain when the financial statements should be adjusted.
(c) Why should non-adjusting events be disclosed?
(d) A customer made a claim for £50,000 for losses suffered by the late delivery of goods. The main part (£40,000) of the claim referred to goods due to be delivered before the year-end. Explain how this would be dealt with under IAS 10.
(e) After the year-end a substantial quantity of inventory was destroyed in a fire. The loss was not adequately covered by insurance. This event is likely to threaten the ability of the business to continue as a going concern. Discuss the matters you would consider in making a decision under IAS 10.
(f) The business entered into a favourable contract after the year-end that would see its profits increase by 15% over the next three years. Explain how this would be dealt with under IAS 10.

### Question 2

Epsilon is a listed entity. You are the financial controller of the entity and its consolidated financial statements for the year ended 30 September 2008 are being prepared. Your assistant, who has prepared the first draft of the statements, is unsure about the correct treatment of a transaction and has asked for your advice. Details of the transaction are given below.

On 31 August 2008 the directors decided to close down a business segment which did not fit into its future strategy. The closure commenced on 5 October 2008 and was due to be completed on 31 December 2008. On 6 September 2008 letters were sent to relevant employees offering voluntary redundancy or redeployment in other sectors of the business. On 13 September 2008 negotiations commenced with relevant parties with a view to terminating existing contracts of the business segment and arranging sales of its assets. Latest estimates of the financial implications of the closure are as follows:

(i) Redundancy costs will total $30 million, excluding the payment referred to in (ii) below.

(ii) The cost of redeploying and retraining staff who do not accept redundancy will total $6 million.

(iii) Plant having a net book value of $11 million at 30 September 2008 will be sold for $2 million.

(iv) The operating losses of the business segment for October, November and December 2008 are estimated at $10 million.

Your assistant is unsure of the extent to which the above transactions create liabilities that should be recognised as a closure provision in the financial statements. He is also unsure as to whether or not the results of the business segment that is being closed need to be shown separately.

**Required:**
**Explain how the decision to close down the business segment should be reported in the financial statements of Epsilon for the year ended 30 September 2008.**

## * Question 3

Epsilon is a listed entity. You are the financial controller of the entity and its consolidated financial statements for the year ended 31 March 2009 are being prepared. The board of directors is responsible for all key financial and operating decisions, including the allocation of resources.

Your assistant is preparing the first draft of the statements. He has a reasonable general accounting knowledge but is not familiar with the detailed requirements of all relevant financial reporting standards. He requires your advice and he has sent you a note as shown below.

We intend to apply IFRS 8 *Operating Segments* in this year's financial statements. I am aware that this standard has attracted a reasonable amount of critical comment since it was issued in November 2006.

The board of directors receives a monthly report on the activities of the five significant operational areas of our business. Relevant financial information relating to the five operations for the year to 31 March 2009, and in respect of our head office, is as follows:

| Operational area | Revenue for year to 31 March 2009 | Profit/(loss) for year to 31 March 2009 | Assets at 31 March 2009 |
|---|---|---|---|
| | $000 | $000 | $000 |
| A | 23,000 | 3,000 | 8,000 |
| B | 18,000 | 2,000 | 6,000 |
| C | 4,000 | (3,000) | 5,000 |
| D | 1,000 | 150 | 500 |
| E | 3,000 | 450 | 400 |
| Sub-total | 49,000 | 2,600 | 19,900 |
| Head office | Nil | Nil | 6,000 |
| Entity total | 49,000 | 2,600 | 25,900 |

I am unsure of the following matters regarding the reporting of operating segments:

● How do we decide what our operating segments should be?

● Should we report segment information relating to head office?

● Which of our operational areas should report separate information? Operational areas A, B and C exhibit very distinct economic characteristics but the economic characteristics of operational areas D and E are very similar.

● Why has IFRS 8 attracted such critical comment?

**Required:**
**Draft a reply to the questions raised by your assistant.**

## * Question 4

Filios Products plc owns a chain of hotels through which it provides three basic services: restaurant facilities, accommodation, and leisure facilities. The latest financial statements contain the following information:

### Statement of financial position of Filios Products

| | £m |
|---|---|
| **ASSETS** | |
| Non-current assets at book value | 1,663 |
| *Current assets* | |
| Inventories and receivables | 381 |
| Bank balance | 128 |
| | 509 |
| **Total Assets** | 2,172 |
| **EQUITY AND LIABILITIES** | |
| **Equity** | |
| Share capital | 800 |
| Retained earnings | 1,039 |
| | 1,839 |
| *Non-current liabilities:* | |
| Long-term borrowings | 140 |
| Current liabilities | 193 |
| **Total Equity and liabilities** | 2,172 |

### Statement of comprehensive income of Filios Products

| | £m | £m |
|---|---|---|
| Revenue | | 1,028 |
| *Less:* Cost of sales | 684 | |
| Administration expenses | 110 | |
| Distribution costs | 101 | |
| Interest charged | 14 | (909) |
| Net profit | | 119 |

The following breakdown is provided of the company's results into three divisions and head office:

| | Restaurants £m | Hotels £m | Leisure £m | Head office £m |
|---|---|---|---|---|
| Revenue | 508 | 152 | 368 | — |
| Cost of sales | 316 | 81 | 287 | — |
| Administration expenses | 43 | 14 | 38 | 15 |
| Distribution costs | 64 | 12 | 25 | — |
| Interest charged | 10 | — | — | 4 |
| Non-current assets at book value | 890 | 332 | 364 | 77 |
| Inventories and receivables | 230 | 84 | 67 | — |
| Bank balance | 73 | 15 | 28 | 12 |
| Payables | 66 | 40 | 56 | 31 |
| Long-term borrowings | 100 | — | — | 40 |

Required:

(a) Outline the nature of segmental reports and explain the reason for presenting such information in the published accounts.

(b) Prepare a segmental statement for Filios Products plc complying, so far as the information permits, with the provisions of IFRS 8 *Operating Segments* so as to show for each segment and the business as a whole:
   (i)   *revenue;*
   (ii)  *profit;*
   (iii) *net assets.*

(c) Examine the relative performance of the operating divisions of Filios Products. The examination should be based on the following accounting ratios:
   (i)   *operating profit percentage;*
   (ii)  *net asset turnover;*
   (iii) *return on net assets.*

## Question 5

The following is the draft trading and income statement of Parnell Ltd for the year ending 31 December 20X8:

|  | $m | $m |
|---|---|---|
| Revenue |  | 563 |
| Cost of sales |  | 310 |
|  |  | 253 |
| Distribution costs | 45 |  |
| Administrative expenses | 78 |  |
|  |  | 123 |
| Profit on ordinary activities before tax |  | 130 |
| Tax on profit on ordinary activities |  | 45 |
| Profit on ordinary activities after taxation – all retained |  | 85 |
| Profit brought forward at 1 January 20X8 |  | 101 |
| Profit carried forward at 31 December 20X8 |  | 186 |

You are given the following additional information, which is reflected in the above statement of comprehensive income only to the extent stated:

1  Distribution costs include a bad debt of $15 million which arose on the insolvency of a major customer. There is no prospect of recovering any of this debt. Bad debts have never been material in the past.

2  The company has traditionally consisted of a manufacturing division and a distribution division. On 31 December 20X8, the entire distribution division was sold for $50 million; its book value at the time of sale was $40 million. The profit on disposal was credited to administrative expenses. (Ignore any related income tax.)

3  During 20X8, the distribution division made sales of $100 million and had a cost of sales of $30 million. There will be no reduction in stated distribution costs or administration expenses as a result of this disposal.

4  The company owns offices which it purchased on 1 January 20X6 for $500 million, comprising $200 million for land and $300 million for buildings. No depreciation was charged in 20X6 or 20X7,

but the company now considers that such a charge should be introduced. The buildings were expected to have a life of 50 years at the date of purchase, and the company uses the straight-line basis for calculating depreciation, assuming a zero residual value. No taxation consequences result from this change.

5 During 20X8, part of the manufacturing division was restructured at a cost of $20 million to take advantage of modern production techniques. The restructuring was not fundamental and will not have a material effect on the nature and focus of the company's operations. This cost is included under administration expenses in the statement of comprehensive income.

Required:
(a) State how each of the items 1–5 above must be accounted for in order to comply with the requirements of international accounting standards.
(b) Redraft the income statement of Parnell Ltd for 20X8, taking into account the additional information so as to comply, as far as possible, with relevant standard accounting practice. Show clearly any adjustments you make. Notes to the accounts are not required. Where an IAS recommends information to be on the face of the income statement it could be recorded on the face of the statement.

## * Question 6

Springtime Ltd is a UK trading company buying and selling as wholesalers fashionable summer clothes. The following balances have been extracted from the books as at 31 March 20X4:

|  | £000 |
| --- | --- |
| Auditor's remuneration | 30 |
| Income tax based on the accounting profit: | |
| For the year to 31 March 20X4 | 3,200 |
| Overprovision for the year to 31 March 20X3 | 200 |
| Delivery expenses (including £300,000 overseas) | 1,200 |
| Dividends: final (proposed – to be paid 1 August 20X4) | 200 |
| interim (paid on 1 October 20X3) | 100 |
| Non-current assets at cost: | |
| Delivery vans | 200 |
| Office cars | 40 |
| Stores equipment | 5,000 |
| Dividend income (amount received from listed companies) | 1,200 |
| Office expenses | 800 |
| Overseas operations: closure costs of entire operations | 350 |
| Purchases | 24,000 |
| Sales (net of sales tax) | 35,000 |
| Inventory at cost: | |
| At 1 April 20X3 | 5,000 |
| At 31 March 20X4 | 6,000 |
| Storeroom costs | 1,000 |
| Wages and salaries: | |
| Delivery staff | 700 |
| Directors' emoluments | 400 |
| Office staff | 100 |
| Storeroom staff | 400 |

*Notes:*

1 Depreciation is provided at the following annual rates on a straight-line basis: delivery vans 20%; office cars 25%; stores 1%.

2 The following taxation rates may be assumed: corporate income tax 35%; personal income tax 25%.

3 The dividend income arises from investments held in non-current investments.

4 It has been decided to transfer an amount of £150,000 to the deferred taxation account.

5 The overseas operations consisted of exports. In 20X3/X4 these amounted to £5,000,000 (sales) with purchases of £4,000,000. Related costs included £100,000 in storeroom staff and £15,000 for office staff.

6 Directors' emoluments include:

| | | |
|---|---|---|
| Chairperson | 100,000 | |
| Managing director | 125,000 | |
| Finance director | 75,000 | |
| Sales director | 75,000 | |
| Export director | 25,000 | (resigned 31 December 20X3) |
| | £400,000 | |

**Required:**

(a) **Produce a statement of comprehensive income suitable for publication and complying as far as possible with generally accepted accounting practice.**

(b) **Comment on how IFRS 5 has improved the quality of information available to users of accounts.**

## Question 7

Omega prepares financial statements under International Financial Reporting Standards. In the year ended 31 March 20X7 the following transaction occurred:

Omega follows the revaluation model when measuring its property, plant and equipment. One of its properties was carried in the balance sheet at 31 March 20X6 at its market value at that date of $5 million. The depreciable amount of this property was estimated at $3.2 million at 31 March 20X6 and the estimated future economic life of the property at 31 March 20X6 was 20 years.

On 1 January 20X7 Omega decided to dispose of the property as it was surplus to requirements and began to actively seek a buyer. On 1 January 20X7 Omega estimated that the market value of the property was $5.1 million and that the costs of selling the property would be $80,000. These estimates remained appropriate at 31 March 20X7.

The property was sold on 10 June 20X7 for net proceeds of $5.15 million.

**Required:**

Explain, with relevant calculations, how the property would be treated in the financial statements of Omega for the year ended 31 March 20X7 and the year ending 31 March 20X8.

## * Question 8

The following trial balance has been extracted from the books of Hoodurz as at 31 March 2006:

|  | $000 | $000 |
|---|---|---|
| Administration expenses | 210 | |
| Ordinary share capital, $1 per share | | 600 |
| Trade receivables | 470 | |
| Bank overdraft | | 80 |
| Provision for warranty claims | | 205 |
| Distribution costs | 420 | |
| Non-current asset investments | 560 | |
| Investment income | | 75 |
| Interest paid | 10 | |
| Property, at cost | 200 | |
| Plant and equipment, at cost | 550 | |
| Plant and equipment, accumulated depreciation (at 31.3.2006) | | 220 |
| Accumulated profits (at 31.3.2005) | | 80 |
| Loans (repayable 31.12.2010) | | 100 |
| Purchases | 960 | |
| Inventories (at 31.3.2005) | 150 | |
| Trade payables | | 260 |
| Sales | | 2,010 |
| 2004/2005 final dividend paid | 65 | |
| 2005/2006 interim dividend paid | 35 | |
| | 3,630 | 3,630 |

The following information is relevant:

(i) The trial balance figures include the following amounts for a disposal group that has been classified as 'held for sale' under IFRS 5 *Non-current Assets Held for Sale and Discontinued Operations*:

|  | $000 |
|---|---|
| Plant and equipment, at cost | 150 |
| Plant and equipment, accumulated depreciation | 15 |
| Trade receivables | 70 |
| Bank overdraft | 10 |
| Trade payables | 60 |
| Sales | 370 |
| Inventories (at 31.12.2005) | 25 |
| Purchases | 200 |
| Administration expenses | 55 |
| Distribution costs | 60 |

The disposal group had no inventories at the date classified as 'held for sale'.

(ii) Inventories (excluding the disposal group) at 31.3.2006 were valued at $160,000.

(iii) The depreciation charges for the year have already been accrued.

(iv) The income tax for the year ended 31.3.2006 is estimated to be $74,000. This includes $14,000 in relation to the disposal group.

(v)  The provision for warranty claims is to be increased by $16,000. This is classified as administration expense.

(vi)  Staff bonuses totalling $20,000 for administration and $20,000 for distribution are to be accrued.

(vii)  The property was acquired during February 2006; therefore, depreciation for the year ended 31.3.2006 is immaterial. The directors have chosen to use the fair value model for such an asset. The fair value of the property at 31.3.2006 is $280,000.

**Required:**
**Prepare for Hoodurz:**

(a)  an income statement for the year ended 31 March 2006; and

(b)  a balance sheet as at 31 March 2006.

Both statements should comply as far as possible with relevant International Financial Reporting Standards. No notes to the financial statements are required nor is a statement of changes in equity, but all workings should be clearly shown.

*(The Association of International Accountants)*

## Question 9

Omega prepares financial statements under International Financial Reporting Standards. In the year ended 31 March 20X7 the following transaction occurred. On 31 December 20X6 the directors decided to dispose of a property that was surplus to requirements. They instructed selling agents to procure a suitable purchaser and advertised the property at a commercially realistic price.

The property was being measured under the revaluation model and had been revalued at $15 million on 31 March 20X6. The depreciable element of the property was estimated as $8 million at 31 March 20X6 and the useful economic life of the depreciable element was estimated as 25 years from that date. Omega depreciates its non-current assets on a monthly basis.

On 31 December 20X6 the directors estimated that the market value of the property was $16 million, and that the costs incurred in selling the property would be $500,000. The property was sold on 30 April 20X7 for $15.55 million, being the agreed selling price of $16.1 million less selling costs of $550,000. The actual selling price and costs to sell were consistent with estimated amounts as at 31 March 20X7.

The financial statements for the year ended 31 March 20X7 were authorised for issue on 15 May 20X7.

**Required:**
Show the impact of the decision to sell the property on the income statement of Omega for the year ended 31 March 20X7, and on its balance sheet as at 31 March 20X7. You should state where in the income statement and the balance sheet relevant balances will be shown. You should make appropriate references to international financial reporting standards.

## Question 10

(a)  In 20X3 Arthur is a large loan creditor of X Ltd and receives interest at 20% p.a. on this loan. He also has a 24% shareholding in X Ltd. Until 20X1 he was a director of the company and left after a disagreement. The remaining 76% of the shares are held by the remaining directors.

(b)  Brenda joined Y Ltd, an insurance broking company, on 1 January 20X0 on a low salary but high commission basis. She brought clients with her that generated 30% of the company's 20X0 revenue.

(c)  Carrie is a director and major shareholder of Z Ltd. Her husband, Donald, is employed in the company on administrative duties for which he is paid a salary of £25,000 p.a. Her daughter, Emma, is a business consultant running her own business. In 20X0 Emma carried out various consultancy exercises for the company for which she was paid £85,000.

(d) Fred is a director of V Ltd. V Ltd is a major customer of W Ltd. In 20X0 Fred also became a director of W Ltd.

**Required:**
Discuss whether parties are related in the above situations.

## * Question 11

Maxpool plc, a listed company, owned 60% of the shares in Ching Ltd. Bay plc, a listed company, owned the remaining 40% of the £1 ordinary shares in Ching Ltd. The holdings of shares were acquired on 1 January 20X0.

On 30 November 20X0 Ching Ltd sold a factory outlet site to Bay plc at a price determined by an independent surveyor.

On 1 March 20X1 Maxpool plc purchased a further 30% of the £1 ordinary shares of Ching Ltd from Bay plc and purchased 25% of the ordinary shares of Bay plc.

On 30 June 20X1 Ching Ltd sold the whole of its fleet of vehicles to Bay plc at a price determined by a vehicle auctioneer.

**Required:**
Explain the implications of the above transactions for the determination of related party relationships and disclosure of such transactions in the financial statements of (a) Maxpool Group plc, (b) Ching Ltd and (c) Bay plc for the years ending 31 December 20X0 and 31 December 20X1.

*(ACCA)*

## Question 12

Gamma is a company that manufactures power tools. Gamma was established by Mr Lee, who owns all of Gamma's shares. Mrs Lee, Mr Lee's wife, owns a controlling interest in Delta, a distributor of power tools. Delta is one of Gamma's biggest customers, accounting for 70% of Gamma's sales. Delta buys exclusively from Gamma.

Gamma's official price list is based on the policy of selling goods at cost plus 50%; however, sales to Delta are priced at normal selling price less a discount of 30% to reflect the scale of the business transacted.

Gamma's terms of sale require payment within one month, but Delta is permitted three months to pay.

Mrs Lee has decided to sell her shares in Delta and has provided a potential buyer with financial information including the following:

| | |
|---|---|
| Sales revenue for the year ended 30 September 2011 | $12.0m |
| Cost of sales | $8.0m |
| Gross profit % | 33% |
| Current assets (including bank $0.3m) | $4.0m |
| Trade payables | $3.0m |
| Other current liabilities | $0.8m |
| Current ratio | 1.1:1 (in line with the ratios reported in each of the past three years) |

The buyer conducted a due diligence investigation and discovered the relationship between Gamma and Delta. She has decided to restate the figures provided in the table above to reflect a 'worst case' scenario before arriving at a final decision concerning the purchase.

Required:
(a) Discuss the manner in which IAS 24 *Related Party Disclosures* should have alerted the potential buyer in this case.
(b) Recalculate the table of figures provided by Mrs Lee on the basis that Delta will not receive favourable terms from Gamma if Mrs Lee sells her shares, and discuss the resulting changes.

*(The Association of International Accountants)*

## * Question 13

(a) IAS 8 *Accounting Policies, Changes in Accounting Estimates and Errors* lays down criteria for the selection of accounting policies and prescribes circumstances in which an entity may change an accounting policy. The standard also deals with accounting treatment of changes in accounting policies, changes in accounting estimates and correction of prior period errors.

Required:
(i) Define an accounting policy according to IAS 8. Explain briefly the difference between an accounting policy and an accounting estimate.
(ii) Outline the accounting treatment required to record (1) a change in accounting policy, (2) a change in accounting estimate and (3) the correction of an error.

(b) The following are summaries of the draft financial statements of Sigma plc for financial year ended 31 July 2015 together with the comparative figures for 2014. During August 2015, prior to the signing off of the financial statements, it was discovered that a fraud had been taking place in the company for the previous three years.

The chief financial officer had been misappropriating monies paid to the company by its customers, the amounts instead appearing as receivables. The effect of the fraud was that amounts shown in the financial statements as receivables need to be written off as they were in fact paid. There is no prospect of recovering the money as the employee lost it gambling and is now bankrupt. The amounts were as follows for each period ending on the following dates:

31 July 2013: €14,000
31 July 2014: €16,000
31 July 2015: €20,000.

Statements of Profit or Loss and Other Comprehensive Income for year ended 31 July:

|  | 2015 | 2014 |
|---|---|---|
|  | €000 | €000 |
| Revenue | 300 | 275 |
| Cost of sales | (225) | (212) |
| Gross profit | 75 | 63 |
| Expenses | (30) | (26) |
| Profit for year | 45 | 37 |

Statements of Changes in Equity (Retained Earnings only) for year ended 31 July:

|  | 2015 | 2014 |
|---|---|---|
|  | €000 | €000 |
| Balance 1 August | 258 | 236 |
| Profit for the year | 45 | 37 |
| Dividends declared | (16) | (15) |
| Balance 31 July | 287 | 258 |

Statements of Financial Position as at 31 July:

|  | 2015 | 2014 |
|---|---|---|
|  | €000 | €000 |
| Non-current Assets | 294 | 306 |
| Net Current Assets | 143 | 102 |
|  | 437 | 408 |
| Equity Share Capital | 150 | 150 |
| Retained Earnings | 287 | 258 |
|  | 437 | 408 |

Required:

**Restate the above financial statements, including comparatives, incorporating the adjustments you deem necessary as a result of the fraud. Ignore the effect of taxation. Disclosure notes are not required.**

*(Institute of Certified Public Accountants (CPA), Professional Stage 1 Corporate Reporting Examination, August 2015)*

## Notes

1 IAS 10 *Events after the Reporting Period*, IASB, revised 2003.
2 IAS 8 *Accounting Policies, Changes in Accounting Estimates and Errors*.
3 IFRS 8 *Operating Segments*, IASB, 2006.
4 www.europarl.europa.eu/sides/getDoc.do?Type=TA&Reference=P6-TA-2007-0526&language=EN
5 Post-implementation Review, IFRS 8 *Operating Segments*, IFRS Foundation, July 2013.
6 IFRS 5 *Non-current Assets Held for Sale and Discontinued Operations*, IASB, revised 2009.
7 IAS 24 *Related Party Disclosures*, IASB, revised 2009.
8 L. Crawford, H. Extance and C. Helliar, *Operating Segments: The Usefulness of IFRS 8*, The Institute of Chartered Accountants of Scotland, 2012.

# CHAPTER 5

# Statements of cash flows

## 5.1 Introduction

The main purpose of this chapter is to explain the reasons for preparing a statement of cash flows and how to prepare a statement applying IAS 7.

### Objectives

By the end of this chapter, you should be able to:

- prepare a statement of cash flows in accordance with IAS 7;
- analyse a statement of cash flows;
- critically discuss their strengths and weaknesses.

## 5.2 Development of statements of cash flows

We saw in Chapter 3 that, at the end of an accounting period, a statement of income is prepared which explains the change in the retained earnings at the beginning and end of an accounting period. In this chapter we prepare a statement of cash flows in accordance with IAS 7 *Statements of Cash Flows.*

IAS 7 explains the changes that have occurred in the amount of liquid assets easily accessible – these are defined as cash + cash equivalents.

### 5.2.1 Statements of cash flows – their benefits

As far back as 1991 Professor John Arnold wrote in a report by the ICAEW Research Board and ICAS Research Advisory Committee *The Future Shape of Financial Reports:*[1]

little attention is paid to the reporting entity's cash or liquidity position. Cash is the lifeblood of every business entity. The report . . . advocates that companies should provide a cash flow statement . . . preferably using the direct method.

Statements of cash flows are now primary financial statements and as important as statements of comprehensive income:

The emphasis on cash flows, and the emergence of the statement of cash flows as an important financial report, does not mean that operating cash flows are a substitute for, or are more important than, net income. In order to analyse financial statements correctly we need to consider *both* operating cash flows and net income.[2]

They are now primary financial statements because the financial viability and survival prospects of any organisation rest on the ability to generate positive operating cash flows. These are necessary in order to be able to pay the interest on loans and repay the loans, finance capital expenditure to maintain or expand operating capacity, and reward the investors with an acceptable dividend policy. If there is still a positive cash flow after this, it will help to reduce the need for additional external loans or equity funding.

The message is that, independent of reported profits, if an organisation is unable to generate sufficient cash, it will eventually become insolvent and fail.

The following extract from Heath and Rosenfield's article on solvency[3] is a useful conclusion to our analysis of the benefits of cash flow statements, emphasising that they also provide a basis for predicting future performance:

> Solvency is a money or cash phenomenon. A solvent company is one with adequate cash to pay its debts; an insolvent company is one with inadequate cash . . . Any information that provides insight into the amounts, timings and certainty of a company's future cash receipts and payments is useful in evaluating solvency. Statements of past cash receipts and payments are useful for the same basic reason that statements of comprehensive income are useful in evaluating profitability: both provide a basis for predicting future performance.

## 5.3 Applying IAS 7 (revised) Statements of Cash Flows

### 5.3.1 IAS 7 format

The cash flows are analysed under three standard headings to explain the net increase/decrease in cash and cash equivalents and the effect on the opening amount of cash and cash equivalents. The headings are:

- Net cash generated by operating activities;
- Cash flows from investing activities;
- Cash flows from financing activities.

### 5.3.2 The two methods of presenting cash flows from operating activities

In the quote from *The Future Shape of Financial Reports* above, reference was made to the direct method. This preference was expressed because there are two methods, both of which are permitted by IAS 7. These are the direct method and the indirect method.

- The *direct* method reports cash inflows and outflows directly, starting with the major categories of gross cash receipts and payments. This means that cash flows such as receipts from customers and payments to suppliers are stated separately within the operating activities.
- The *indirect* method starts with the profit before tax and then adjusts this figure for non-cash items such as depreciation and changes in working capital.

### 5.3.3 Statement of cash flows illustrated using the direct method

The following shows the statement of cash flows for Tyro Bruce for the period ended 31.3.20X4.

| | £000 | £000 |
|---|---|---|
| **Cash flows from operating activities** | | |
| Cash received from customers (note (a)) | 11,740 | |
| Cash paid to suppliers and employees (note (b)) | (11,431) | |
| **Cash generated from operations** | 309 | |
| Interest paid (expense + (closing accrual − opening accrual)) | (20) | |
| Income taxes paid (expense + (closing accrual − opening accrual)) | (220) | |
| *Net cash (used in) generated by operating activities* | | 69 |
| **Cash flows from investing activities** | | |
| Purchase of property, plant and equipment | (560) | |
| Proceeds from sale of equipment | 241 | |
| *Net cash used in investing activities* | | (319) |
| **Cash flows from financing activities** | | |
| Proceeds from issue of shares at a premium | 300 | |
| Redemption of loan | (50) | |
| Dividends paid | (120) | |
| *Net cash from financing activities* | | 130 |
| **Net increase in cash and cash equivalents** | | (120) |
| **Cash and cash equivalents at beginning of period** | | 72 |
| **Cash and cash equivalents at end of period** | | (48) |

*Notes:*

(a) Cash received from customers

| | £000 |
|---|---|
| Sales | 12,000 |
| Receivables increase | (260) |
| | 11,740 |

(b) Cash paid to suppliers and employees

| | £000 |
|---|---|
| Cost of sales | 10,000 |
| Payables decreased | 140 |
| Inventory increased | 900 |
| Depreciation | (102) |
| Profit on sale | 13 |
| Distribution costs | 300 |
| Administration expenses | 180 |
| | 11,431 |

### 5.3.4 Statement of cash flows illustrated using the indirect method

The two methods provide different types of information to the users. The indirect method applies changes in working capital to net income. In our illustration, for example, the cash generated from operations would be calculated as follows:

| *Cash flows from operating activities* | *£000* |
|---|---|
| Profit before tax | 1,500 |
| Adjustments for non-cash items: | |
| Depreciation | 102 |
| Profit on sale of plant | (13) |
| Adjustments for changes in working capital: | |
| Increase in trade receivables | (260) |
| Increase in inventories | (900) |
| Decrease in trade payables | (140) |
| Interest expense (added back) | 20 |
| **Cash generated from operations** | 309 |

### 5.3.5  Appraising the use of the direct method

The direct method demonstrates more of the qualities of a true cash flow statement because it provides more information about the sources and uses of cash. This information is not available elsewhere and helps in the estimation of future cash flows.

The principal advantage of the direct method is that it shows operating cash receipts and payments. Knowledge of the specific sources of cash receipts and the purposes for which cash payments were made in past periods may be useful in assessing future cash flows. Disclosure of *cash from customers* could provide additional information about an entity's ability to convert revenues to cash.

#### When is the direct method beneficial?

One such time is when the user is attempting to predict bankruptcy or future liquidation of the company. A research study looking at the cash flow differences between failed and non-failed companies[4] established that seven cash flow variables and suggested ratios captured statistically significant differences between failed and non-failed firms as much as five years prior to failure. The study further showed that the research findings supported the use of a direct cash flow statement, and the authors commented:

> An indirect cash flow statement will not provide a number of the cash flow variables for which we found significant differences between bankrupt and non-bankrupt companies. Thus, using an indirect cash flow statement could lead to ignoring important information about creditworthiness.

The direct method is the method preferred by the standard but preparers have a choice. In the UK the indirect method is often used; in other regions (e.g. Australia) the direct method is more common. It has been proposed in a review of IAS 7 that the direct method should be mandated and the alternative removed and this is the likely requirement in a new standard to eventually replace IAS 7.

### 5.3.6  Appraising the use of the indirect method

The principal advantage of the indirect method is that it highlights the differences between operating profit and net cash flow from operating activities to provide a measure of the quality of income. Many users of financial statements believe that such reconciliation is essential to give an indication of the quality of the reporting entity's earnings. Some investors and creditors assess future cash flows by estimating future income and then allowing for accruals adjustments; thus information about past accruals adjustments may be useful to help estimate future adjustments.

### Preparer and user response

The IASB indicates that the responses to the discussion paper were mixed with the preparers tending to prefer the indirect method and the users having a mixed response. There was a view that the direct method would be improved if the movements on working capital were disclosed as supplementary information, and the indirect method would be improved if the cash from customers and payments to suppliers was disclosed as supplementary information; i.e. both are found useful.

### 5.3.7 Cash equivalents

IAS 7 recognised that companies' cash management practices vary in the amount of cash and range of short- to medium-term deposits that are held. The standard standardised the treatment of near-cash items by applying the following definition when determining whether items should be aggregated with cash in the statement of cash flows:

> Cash equivalents are short-term, highly liquid investments which are readily convertible into known amounts of cash and which are subject to an insignificant risk of changes in value.

Near-cash items are normally those that are within three months of maturity at the date of acquisition. Investments falling outside this definition are reported under the heading of 'investing activities'. In view of the variety of cash management practices and banking arrangements around the world and in order to comply with IAS 1 *Presentation of Financial Statements*, an entity discloses the policy which it adopts in determining the composition of cash and cash equivalents. The following is an extract from the Tesco 2016 Annual Report:

### Cash and cash equivalents

> Cash and cash equivalents in the Group Balance Sheet consist of cash at bank, in hand, demand deposits with banks, loans and advances to banks, certificates of deposits and other receivables together with short-term deposits with an original maturity of three months or less.

## 5.4 Step approach to preparation of a statement of cash flows – indirect method

We will now explain how to prepare a statement of cash flows for Tyro Bruce (Section 5.3.3) taking a step approach. We have shown our workings on the face of the statements of financial position and income.

**Step 1:** Calculate the differences in the statements of financial position and decide whether to report under operating, investing or financing activities or as a cash equivalent.

**Statements of financial position of Tyro Bruce as at 31.3.20X3 and 31.3.20X4**

| | 20X3 | | 20X4 | | Calculate the differences | Decide which activities to report under |
|---|---|---|---|---|---|---|
| | £000 | £000 | £000 | £000 | | |
| Non-current assets at cost | 2,520 | | 2,760 | | See PPE note | Investing/financing |
| Accumulated depreciation | 452 | 2,068 | 462 | 2,298 | for acquisitions or disposals | |
| | | | | | | |
| *Current assets* | | | | | | |
| Inventory | 800 | | 1,700 | | 900 | Operating |
| Trade receivables | 640 | | 900 | | 260 | Operating |
| Securities maturing less than 3 months at acquisition | — | | 20 | | 20 | Cash equivalent |
| Cash | 80 | | 10 | | 70 | Cash equivalent |
| | 1,520 | | 2,630 | | | |
| *Current liabilities* | | | | | | |
| Trade payables | 540 | | 400 | | 140 | Operating |
| Taxation | 190 | | 170 | | 20 | Operating |
| Overdraft | 8 | | 78 | | 70 | Cash equivalent |
| | 738 | | 648 | | | |
| Net current assets | | 782 | | 1,982 | | |
| | | 2,850 | | 4,280 | | |
| Share capital | 1,300 | | 1,400 | | 100 | Financing |
| Share premium a/c | 200 | | 400 | | 200 | Financing |
| Retained earnings | 1,150 | 2,650 | 1,150 | 2,950 | | |
| Profit for year | | — | | 1,180 | | |
| 10% loan 20×7 | | 200 | | 150 | 50 | Financing |
| | | 2,850 | | 4,280 | | |

**Step 2**: Identify any items in the statement of income for the year ended 31.3.20X4 after profit before interest and tax (PBIT) to be entered under operating, investing or financing activities.

| | £000 | £000 | |
|---|---|---|---|
| Sales | | 12,000 | |
| Cost of sales | | 10,000 | |
| Gross profit | | 2,000 | |
| Distribution costs | 300 | | |
| Administrative expenses | 180 | 480 | |
| PBIT | | 1,520 | |
| Interest expense | | (20) | Operating |
| Profit before tax | | 1,500 | Operating |
| Income tax expense | | (200) | Operating |
| Profit after tax | | 1,300 | |
| Dividend paid | | (120) | Financing |
| Retained earnings for year | | 1,180 | |

**Step 3:** Refer to the PPE schedule to identify any acquisitions, disposals and depreciation charges that affect the cash flows. The Tyro Bruce schedule showed:

| Cost | £000 |
|---|---|
| As at 31 March 20X3 | 2,520 |
| (i) Additions | 560 |
| (iii) Disposal | (320) |
| As at 31.3.20X4 | 2,760 |
| Accumulated depreciation | |
| As at 31.3.20X3 | 452 |
| (ii) Charge for year | 102 |
| (iii) Disposal | (92) |
| As at 31.3.20X4 | 462 |
| NBV as at 31.3.20X4 | 2,298 |
| NBV as at 31.3.20X3 | 2,068 |

*Note: Disposal proceeds were £241,000.*

From Step 3 we can see that there are four impacts:

(i) Additions: The cash of £560,000 paid out on additions will appear under Investing.

(ii) The depreciation charge: This is a non-cash item and the £102,000 will be added back as a non-cash item to the profit before tax in the operating activities section.

(iii) Disposal proceeds: The cash received of £241,000 from the disposal was given in the Note and will appear under Investing activities. *If the Note had provided you with the profit instead of the proceeds, then you would need to calculate the proceeds by taking the NBV and adjusting for any profit or loss. In this case it would be calculated as NBV of £228,000 (320,000 − 92,000) + the profit figure of £13,000 = £241,000.*

(iv) Profit on disposal: As the full proceeds of £241,000 are included under Investing activities there would be double counting to leave the profit of £13,000 within the profit before tax figure. It is therefore deducted as a non-cash item from PBT in the Operating activities section.

### 5.4.1 The statement of cash flows

The cash flow items can then be entered into the statement of cash flows in accordance with IAS 7.

| | | £000 |
|---|---|---|
| *Cash flows from operating activities* | | |
| Profit before tax | | 1,500 |
| Adjustments for non-cash items: | | |
| Depreciation | From Step 3 (ii) | 102 |
| Profit on sale of plant | From Step 3 (iv) | (13) |
| Adjustments for changes in working capital: | | |
| Increase in trade receivables | | (260) |
| Increase in inventories | | (900) |
| Decrease in trade payables | | (140) |
| Interest expense | | 20 |
| **Cash generated from operations** | | 309 |
| Interest paid (there are no closing or opening accruals) | | (20) |
| Income taxes paid (expense + (opening accrual − closing accrual)) | 200 + (190 − 170) | (220) |
| *Net cash (used in)/generated by operating activities* | | 69 |
| **Cash flows from investing activities** | | |
| Purchase of property, plant and equipment | From Step 3 (i) | (560) |
| Proceeds from sale of equipment | From Step 3 (iii) | 241 |
| *Net cash used in investing activities* | | (319) |
| **Cash flows from financing activities** | | |
| Proceeds from issue of shares at a premium | | 300 |
| Redemption of loan | | (50) |
| Dividends paid | | (120) |
| *Net cash from financing activities* | | 130 |
| **Net increase in cash and cash equivalents** | | (120) |
| **Cash and cash equivalents at beginning of period** | 80 − 8 | 72 |
| **Cash and cash equivalents at end of period** | (10 + 20) − 78 | (48) |

Note that interest paid and interest and dividends received could be classified either as operating cash flows or as financing (for interest paid) and investing cash flows (for receipts). Dividends paid could be presented either as financing cash flows or as operating cash flows. However, it is a requirement that whichever presentation is adopted by an enterprise should be consistently applied from year to year.

## 5.5 Additional notes required by IAS 7

As well as the presentation on the face of the cash flow statement, IAS 7 requires notes to the cash flow statement to help the user understand the information. The notes that are required are as follows.

### Major non-cash transactions

If the entity has entered into major non-cash transactions that are therefore not represented on the face of the statement of cash flows, sufficient further information to understand the transactions should be provided in a note to the financial statements. Examples of major non-cash transactions might be:

- the acquisition of assets by way of finance leases;
- the conversion of debt to equity.

### Components of cash and cash equivalents

An enterprise must disclose the components of cash and cash equivalents and reconcile these into the totals in the statement of financial position. An example of a suitable disclosure in the case of Tyro Bruce is:

|                           | 20X4  | 20X3 |
|---------------------------|-------|------|
| Cash                      | 10    | 80   |
| Securities                | 20    |      |
| Overdraft                 | (78)  | (8)  |
| Cash and cash equivalents | (48)  | 72   |

Disclosure must also be given on restrictions on the use by the group of any cash and cash equivalents held by the enterprise. These restrictions might apply if, for example, cash was held in foreign countries and could not be remitted back to the parent company.

### Segmental information

IAS 7 encourages enterprises to disclose information about operating, investing and financing cash flows for each business and geographical segment. This disclosure may be relevant. IFRS 8 does not require a cash flow by segment.

### Evaluating changes in liabilities

Under *Disclosure Initiative Amendment to IAS 7 issued in 2016* entities are required to provide disclosures that enable users of financial statements to evaluate changes in liabilities arising from financing activities, including both changes arising from cash flows and non-cash changes.

One way to fulfil the disclosure requirement is by providing a reconciliation between the opening and closing balances in the statement of financial position for liabilities arising from financing activities. The following is an illustration adapted from the *Disclosure Initiative*:

|                         | 20X1   | Cash flows | Non-cash changes Foreign exchange movement | 20X2   |
|-------------------------|--------|------------|--------------------------------------------|--------|
| Long-term borrowings    | 22,000 | (1,000)    |                                            | 21,000 |
| Short-term borrowings   | 10,000 | (500)      | 200                                        | 9,700  |
| Total liabilities from financing activities | 32,000 | (1,500) | 200 | 30,700 |

In practice there might be other disclosures relating to items such as lease liabilities and acquisitions.

## 5.6 Analysing statements of cash flows

Arranging cash flows into specific classes provides users with relevant and decision-useful information by classifying cash flows as cash generated from operations, net cash from operating activities, net cash flows from investing activities, and net cash flows from financing activities.

### Lack of a clear definition

However, this does not mean that companies will necessarily report the same transaction in the same way. Although IAS 7 requires cash flows to be reported under these headings, it does not define operating activities except to say that it includes all transactions and other events that are not defined as investing or financing activities.

### Alternative treatments

Alternative treatments for interest and dividends paid could be presented as either operating or financing cash flows. Whilst most companies choose to report the dividends as financing cash flows, when making inter-firm comparisons we need to see which alternative has been chosen. The choice can have a significant impact. If, for example, in the Tyro Bruce illustration the dividends of £120,000 were reported as an operating cash flow, then the net cash (used in)/generated by operating activities would change from an inflow of £69,000 to an outflow of £51,000.

The classifications assist users in making informed predictions about future cash flows or raising questions for further enquiry which would be difficult to make using traditional accrual-based techniques.[5]

We will briefly comment on the implication of each classification.

## 5.6.1 Cash generated from operations

Cash flow generated by operations is one of the most significant numbers calculated after taking account of any investment in working capital. It shows the cash available from ongoing operations to service loans, pay tax, reinvest in the business, repay loans and pay a dividend to shareholders.

Lenders look to the cash generated from operations to pay interest and the revenue authorities to satisfy the company's tax liability. Both of these are unavoidable – it is an indication of the safety margin, i.e. how long a business could continue to pay unavoidable costs.

There are a number of examples where the failure to meet their tax liability has led to organisations being forced into administration or liquidation. Examples include football clubs: with Portsmouth FC having been put into administration; and Bolton Wanderers threatened with administration in 2016.

In the Tyro Bruce example (Section 5.3.3) we can see that there has been a significant increase in working capital of £1,300,000 (£260,000 + £900,000 + £140,000).

The effect is to reduce the profit before tax from £1,500,000 to the £309,000 reported as cash flow from operations.

Lenders in Tyro Bruce concerned with interest cover could see that there is sufficient cash available to meet their interest charges in the current year even though there has been a significant impact from the investment in working capital.

### Interest cover

Interest cover is normally defined as the number of times the profit before interest and tax covers the interest charge: in the Tyro Bruce example this is 76 times (1,520/20). The position as disclosed in the statement of cash flows is a little weaker although, even so, the interest is still covered more than 15 times (309,000/20,000).

### Current cash debt coverage ratio

This is a liquidity ratio which shows a company's ability to meet its current debt obligations. The ratio is the result of dividing *the net cash generated by operating activities* by *the average current liabilities.*

In the Tyro example the net cash generated by operations is £69,000 and the average current liabilities are £693,000 [(738,000 + 648,000)/2] giving a ratio of 0.1:1.

### Cash debt coverage ratio

In addition to interest cover, lenders also have a longer-term view and want to be satisfied that their loan will be repaid on maturity. Failure to do so could lead to a going-concern problem for the company. One measure used is to calculate the ratio of *cash flow generated by operating activities* to *total debt* and, of more immediate interest, to *loans that are about to mature.*

The ratio can be adjusted to reflect the company's current position. For example, if there is a significant cash balance, it might be appropriate to add this on the basis that it would be available to meet the loan repayment.

In the Tyro example, the ratio is £69,000/(£693,000 + £150,000) giving a ratio of 0.08:1, which is low due to the heavy investment in working capital and payment of a dividend. If the company continued to achieve profits of £1,500,000 without a further significant investment in working capital, then the ratio is in excess of 1.5:1.

### Cash dividend coverage ratio

The ratio of cash flow from operating activities less interest paid to dividends paid indicates the ability to meet the current dividend. If the dividend rate shows a rising trend, dividends declared might be used rather than the cash flow dividend paid figure. This would give a better indication of the coverage ratio for future dividends. In our example coverage is again reduced by the heavy working capital investment.

## 5.6.2 Future cash flows from operations

We need to consider trends, the discretionary costs and the investment in working capital.

### Trends

We need to look at previous periods to identify the trend. Trends are important with investors naturally hoping to invest in a company with a rising trend. If there is a loss or a downward trend, this is a cause for concern and investors should make further enquiries to identify any proposed steps to improve the position.

This is where narrative may be helpful, such as that proposed in the IFRS Practice Statement *Management Commentary,* in the Strategic Review in the UK and in a Chairman's Statement. Reading these may give some indication as to how the company will be addressing the situation. For example, is the company planning a cost reduction programme or disposing of loss-making activities? If it is not possible to improve the trend or reverse the negative cash flow, then there could be future liquidity difficulties.

### Discretionary costs

The implication for future cash flow is that such difficulties could have an impact on future discretionary costs, e.g. the curtailment of research, marketing or advertising expenditure; on investment decisions, e.g. postponing capital expenditure; and on financing decisions, e.g. the need to raise additional equity or loan capital.

### Working capital

We can see the cash implication but would need to make further enquiries to establish the reasons for the change and the likelihood of similar cash outflow movements recurring in future years. If, for example, the increased investment in inventory resulted from an increase in turnover, then a similar increase could recur if the forecast turnover continued to increase. If, on the other hand, the increase was due to poor inventory control, then it is less likely that the increase will recur once management addresses the problem.

The cash flow statement indicates the cash **extent** of the change; additional ratios (see Chapter 28) and enquiries are required to allow us to **evaluate** the change.

## 5.6.3 Evaluating the investing activities cash flows

These arise from the acquisition and disposal of non-current assets and investments.

It is useful to consider how much of the expenditure is to replace existing non-current assets and how much is to increase capacity. One way is to relate the cash expenditure to the depreciation charge; this indicates that the cash expenditure is more than five times greater than the depreciation charge, calculated as £540,000/£102,000. This seems to indicate a possible increase in productive capacity. However, the cash flow statement does not itemise the expenditure, as the extract from the non-current asset schedule does not reveal how much was spent on plant – this information would be available in practice.

### How to inform investors how much of the capital expenditure relates to replacing existing non-current assets

There has been a criticism that it is not possible to assess how much of the investing activities cash outflow related to simply maintaining operations by replacing non-current assets that were worn out rather than to increasing existing capacity with a potential for an increase in turnover and profits. The solution proposed was that investment that is merely maintained should be shown as an operating cash flow and that the investing cash flow should be restricted to increasing capacity. The IASB doubted the reliability of such a distinction but there is a view that such an analysis provides additional information, provided the breakdown between the two types of expenditure can be reliably ascertained.

### Capital expenditure ratio

This is a ratio where the numerator is *net cash flow generated by operating activities* and the denominator is *capital expenditures*. This ratio measures the capital available for internal reinvestment and for meeting existing debt. We look for a ratio that exceeds 1.0, showing that the company has funds to maintain its operational capability and has cash towards meeting its debt repayments and dividends.

It is important to remember that this ratio is industry-specific and any comparator should be with another company that has similar capital expenditure ratio (CAPEX) requirements. The ratio would be expected to be lower for companies in growth industries as opposed to those in mature industries and more variable in cyclical industries, such as housing.

It should be recognised, however, that there is a risk if a company has significant free cash flow that its managers may be too optimistic about future performance. When they are not reliant on satisfying external funders there could be less constraint on their investment decisions. If there is negative free cash flow then the opposite applies and the business would require external finance which then means that it would be subject to any conditions imposed by the new source of finance.

### 5.6.4 Free cash flow (FCF)

This is a performance measure showing how much cash a company has for further investment after deducting from net cash generated by operating capital the amount spent on capital expenditure to maintain or expand its asset base. Many companies refer to it in their annual report with possible slight variations in definition.

For example, Colt SA in its 2015 Annual Report states:

Free cash flow is net cash generated from operating activities less net cash used to purchase non-current assets *and net finance costs paid.*

#### Reasons for reporting FCF

It is emphasised by companies for different reasons – some emphasising its use as the way that the company manages its capital. For example, the following is an extract from the Kingfisher Group's 2013 Annual Report:

The Group manages its capital by:
Continued focus on free cash flow generation; Setting the level of capital expenditure and dividend in the context of current year and *forecast free cash flow* generation; Rigorous review of capital investments and post investment reviews to drive better returns; and Monitoring the level of the Group's financial and leasehold debt in the context of Group performance and its credit rating.

The company recognises the importance of free cash flow in maintaining its credit rating:

The Group will maintain a high focus on free cash flow generation going forward to maintain its solid investment grade balance sheet, fund investment where economic returns are attractive and pay healthy dividends to shareholders.

Other companies might place their emphasis on liquidity. For example, the following is an extract from the Merck Group 2011 Annual Report:

Free cash flow and underlying free cash flow are indicators that we use internally to measure the contribution of our divisions to liquidity.

Also there might be an emphasis on operational control as illustrated in this extract from the Merck Group 2013 Annual Report:

Business free cash flow (BFCF)
Apart from EBITDA pre and sales, business free cash flow (BFCF) is the third important Group and division KPI and therefore also used for internal target agreements and individual incentive plans. It comprises the major cash-relevant items that the individual businesses can influence. . . . The introduction of business free cash flow has led to considerable improvements in cash awareness as well as reduced working capital requirements.

The amount of free cash flow will be normally positive for a mature company and negative for a younger company. It will be impacted by the investment in working capital and capital expenditure and will depend on the industry. For example, free cash flow might be high in the tobacco industry and its products industry where there is low investment in either working capital or CAPEX and low in an industry such as petroleum and gas where, although the investment in working capital is low, CAPEX is high.

#### Ratios based on FCF

These include the cash conversion ratio (CCR) and cash dividend coverage ratio (CDCR).

The cash conversion ratio (CCR) is calculated as free cash flow divided by earnings before interest, tax, depreciation and amortisation (EBITDA). It indicates the rate at which profits are being turned into cash. From the point of view of the shareholders it indicates how much of the profit could be distributed as dividends without causing liquidity or cash flow problems for the company.

The cash dividend coverage ratio (CDCR) is calculated as free cash flow divided by dividends. It indicates that the company is able to generate earnings beyond maintaining its current operational capacity.

### 5.6.5 Evaluating the financing cash flows

Additional capital of £300,000 has been raised. After repaying a loan of £50,000 and payment of a dividend of £120,000, only £130,000 was left towards a negative free cash flow with a net outflow of £250,000 (£319,000 − £69,000).

This does not allow us to assess the financing policy of the company, e.g. whether the capital was raised the optimum way. Nor does it allow us to assess whether the company would have done better to provide finance by improved control over its assets, e.g. working capital reduction.[6]

The indications are healthy in that the company is relying on earnings and equity capital to finance growth. It is low-geared and further funds could be sought, possibly from the bank or private equity, particularly if it is required for capacity building purposes.

### 5.6.6 Reconciliation of net cash flows to net debt

A net debt reconciliation is useful in that it allows investors to see how business financing has changed over the year, identifying, for example, if a significant increase in cash has been achieved only by taking on increased debt.

It is not required by IFRS but is often sought by investors. The following illustrates the notes that would be prepared for Tyro Bruce (see Section 5.4 above) if the company decided to publish a reconciliation:

|  |  |  | 20X4 |  | 20X3 |
|---|---|---|---|---|---|
| 1 | Borrowings |  | (150) |  | (200) |
|  | Overdraft | (78) |  | (8) |  |
|  | Securities | 20 |  |  |  |
|  | Cash | 10 |  | 80 |  |
|  |  |  | (48) |  | 72 |
|  |  |  | (198) |  | (128) |
| 2 | Reconcile net cash flow to movement in net debt |  |  |  |  |
|  | Decrease in cash |  | (48 + 72) | (120) |  |
|  | Change in net debt resulting from cash |  | (200 − 150) | 50 |  |
|  | Movement in net debt |  | (198 − 128) | (70) |  |
|  | Net debt at beginning of period |  |  | (128) |  |
|  | Net debt at end of period |  |  | (198) |  |
| 3 | Analysis of net debt |  |  |  |  |

|  | 20X3 | Cash flow | 20X4 |
|---|---|---|---|
| Cash at bank | 80 | (120) | 10 |
| Government securities |  |  | 20 |
| Overdraft | (8) |  | (78) |
| Debt outstanding | (200) | 50 | (150) |
| Net debt | (128) | (70) | (198) |

### 5.6.7 Voluntary disclosures

IAS 7 (paragraphs 50–52) lists additional information, supported by a management commentary that may be relevant to understanding:

● liquidity, e.g. the amount of undrawn borrowing facilities;

● future profitability, e.g. cash flow representing increases in operating capacity separate from cash flow maintaining operating capacity; and

● risk, e.g. cash flows for each reportable segment, to better understand the relationship between the entity's cash flows and each segment's cash flows.

## 5.7 Approach to answering questions with time constraints

We have explained the step approach with the explanatory detail on the statements of financial position and income. In an examination it is preferable to show the workings on the statement of cash flows itself as shown in the examination question for Riddle worked below.

The following are the statements of financial position and income for Riddle plc.

**Statements of financial position as at 31 March**

|  | 20X8 | | 20X9 | |
|---|---|---|---|---|
|  | $000 | $000 | $000 | $000 |
| *Non-current assets:* | | | | |
| Property, plant and equipment, at cost | 540 | | 720 | |
| Less accumulated depreciation | (145) | | (190) | |
|  | | 395 | | 530 |
| Investments | | 115 | | 140 |
| *Current assets:* | | | | |
| Inventory | 315 | | 418 | |
| Trade receivables | 412 | | 438 | |
| Bank | 48 | 775 | 51 | 907 |
| Total assets | | 1,285 | | 1,577 |
| *Capital and reserves:* | | | | |
| Ordinary shares | 600 | | 800 | |
| Share premium | 40 | | 55 | |
| Retained earnings | 217 | 857 | 311 | 1,166 |
| *Non-current liabilities:* | | | | |
| 12% debentures | | 250 | | 200 |
| *Current liabilities:* | | | | |
| Trade payables | 139 | | 166 | |
| Taxation | 39 | 178 | 45 | 211 |
| Total equity and liabilities | | 1,285 | | 1,577 |

**Statement of income for the year ended 31 March 20X9**

|  | $000 | $000 |
|---|---|---|
| Revenue | | 2,460 |
| Cost of sales | | 1,780 |
| Gross profit | | 680 |
| Distribution costs | (124) | |
| Administration expenses | (300) | (424) |

### Statement of income for the year ended 31 March 20X9

| | $000 | $000 |
|---|---|---|
| Operating profit | | 256 |
| Interest on debentures | | (24) |
| Profit before tax | | 232 |
| Tax | | (48) |
| Profit after tax | | 184 |

*Note*: The statement of changes in equity disclosed a dividend of $90,000.

*Teaching note*: Take an initial look at the statement of financial position and notes to check whether or not there has been any disposal of non-current assets which would give rise to a profit or loss adjustment as a non-cash adjustment to the profit after tax figure in the statement of income. In the case of Riddle there have only been acquisitions.

### Required

(a) Prepare the statement of cash flows for Riddle plc for the year ended 31 March 20X9 and show the operating cash flows using the 'indirect method'.

(b) Calculate the cash generated from operations using the 'direct method'.

### Solution

(a) Using indirect method

### Statement of cash flows for the year ended 31 March 20X9

| | | $000 | $000 |
|---|---|---|---|
| **Cash from operating activities** | | | |
| Profit before tax | Income statement | | 232 |
| Adjustments for: | | | |
| Depreciation | 190 − 145 | 45 | |
| Interest expense | | 24 | 69 |
| **Operating profit before working capital changes** | | | 301 |
| Increase in inventory | 418 − 315 | (103) | |
| Increase in trade receivables | 438 − 412 | (26) | |
| Increase in trade payables | 166 − 139 | 27 | (102) |
| **Cash generated from operations** | | | 199 |
| Interest paid | | (24) | |
| Tax paid | 39 + 48 − 45 | (42) | (66) |
| *Net cash used in operating activities* | | | 133 |
| **Cash flows from investing activities:** | | | |
| Purchase of PPE | 720 − 540 | (180) | |
| Disposal proceeds of PPE | None in question | | |
| Investments | 140 − 115 | (25) | (205) |
| **Cash flows from financing activities:** | | | |
| Share capital | 800 − 600 | 200 | |
| Share premium | 55 − 40 | 15 | |
| Debentures | 200 − 250 | (50) | |
| Dividends paid | Given in note | (90) | 75 |
| **Net increase in cash and cash equivalents** | | | 3 |
| Cash and cash equivalents at beginning of year | | | 48 |
| Cash and cash equivalents at end of year | | | 51 |

**(b)** Cash generated from operations using the direct method

|  | $000 | $000 |
|---|---|---|
| (i) Received from customers |  | 2,434 |
| (ii) Paid to suppliers | 1,856 |  |
| (iii) Paid expenses (124 + 300 − depreciation 45) | 379 | 2,235 |
| **Cash generated from operations** |  | **199** |

| (i) Received from customers |  | $000 |
|---|---|---|
| Trade receivables at beginning of year |  | 412 |
| Sales |  | 2,460 |
|  |  | 2,872 |
| Less: Trade receivables at end of year |  | 438 |
| Cash received from customers |  | 2,434 |
| (ii) Paid to suppliers |  |  |

|  | $000 | $000 |
|---|---|---|
| Trade payables at beginning of year |  | 139 |
| Cost of sales | 1,780 |  |
| Closing inventory | 418 |  |
|  | 2,198 |  |
| Less: Opening inventory | 315 | 1,883 |
|  |  | 2,022 |
| Less: Trade payables at end of year |  | 166 |
| Cash paid to trade payables |  | 1,856 |

*Teaching note*: Interest on the debentures is added back when preparing the statement using the indirect method. When using the direct method there is no need to include it within the payables calculation.

## 5.8 Preparing a statement of cash flows when no statement of income is available

Questions might be met where the statements of financial position are provided and figures have to be derived.

### 5.8.1 Flow Ltd +– an example

As an example, the following statements of financial position have been provided for Flow Ltd for the years ended 31 December 20X5 and 20X6:

|  | 20X5 | | 20X6 | |
|---|---|---|---|---|
|  | € | € | € | € |
| *Non-current assets* |  |  |  |  |
| *Tangible assets* |  |  |  |  |
| PPE at cost | 1,743,750 |  | 1,983,750 |  |
| Accumulated depreciation | 551,250 | 1,192,500 | 619,125 | 1,364,625 |
| *Current assets* |  |  |  |  |
| Inventory |  | 101,250 |  | 85,500 |
| Trade receivables |  | 252,000 |  | 274,500 |
|  |  | 1,545,750 |  | 1,724,625 |

|  | 20X5 | | 20X6 | |
|---|---|---|---|---|
|  | € | € | € | € |
| *Capital and reserves* | | | | |
| *Common shares of €1 each* | | 900,000 | | 1,350,000 |
| Share premium | | | | 30,000 |
| Retained earnings | | 387,000 | | 176,625 |
| *Current liabilities* | | | | |
| Trade payables | | 183,750 | | 159,750 |
| Bank overdraft | | 75,000 | | 8,250 |
| | | 1,545,750 | | 1,724,625 |

Notes stated that during the year ended 31 December 20X6:

1  Equipment that had cost €25,500 and with a net book value of €9,375 was sold for €6,225.

2  The company paid a dividend of €45,000.

3  A bonus issue was made at the beginning of the year of one bonus share for every three shares.

4  A new issue of 150,000 shares was made on 1 July 20X6 at a price of €1.20 for each share.

5  A dividend of €60,000 was declared but no entries had been made in the books of the company.

The requirement is to prepare a statement of cash flows for the year ended 31 December 20X6 that complies with IAS 7.

## 5.8.2 Solution to Flow Ltd

Step 1. Calculate the profit by working back from the end-of-period retained earnings.

| | |
|---|---|
| Retained earnings | 176,625 |
| Less opening retained earnings | 387,000 |
| | (210,375) |
| Add back the dividend already paid | 45,000 |
| Add back amount transferred to Capital on issue of bonus shares | 300,000 |
| | 134,625 |

Step 2. Calculate the cash flow from operating activities.

| | |
|---|---|
| Profit | 134,625 |
| Depreciation | 83,500 |
| $619,125 - 551,250 = 67,875$ | |
| $25,500 - 9,375\ \ \ = 15,625$ | |
| Loss on sale of plant | 3,150 |
| $9,375 - 6,225$ | |
| Decrease in inventory | 15,750 |
| $101,250 - 85,500$ | |
| Increase in receivables | (22,500) |
| $252,000 - 274,500$ | |
| Decrease in payables | (24,000) |
| $183,750 - 159,750$ | |
| **Cash flow from operating activities** | **190,525** |

Step 3. Statement of cash flows for the year ended 31 December 20X6 for Flow Ltd.

| | | |
|---|---:|---:|
| *Net cash inflow from operating activities* | | 190,025 |
| **Cash flows from investing activities** | | |
| Purchase of non-current assets | (265,500) | |
| (1,983,750 + 25,500 − 1,743,750) | | |
| Receipts from sale of non-current assets | 6,225 | |
| *Net cash paid on investing activities* | | (259,275) |
| **Cash flows from financing activities** | | |
| Proceeds from issue of common shares | 180,000 | |
| Dividends paid | (45,000) | |
| (could be shown as operating cash flow) | | |
| *Net cash inflow from financing activities* | | 135,000 |
| *Net increase in cash and cash equivalents* | | 66,250 |
| (75,000 − 8,250) | | |

## 5.9 Critique of cash flow accounting

IAS 7 (revised) applies uniform requirements to the format and presentation of cash flow statements. It still, however, allows companies to choose between the direct and the indirect methods, and the presentation of interest and dividend cash flows. It can be argued, therefore, that it has failed to rectify the problem of a lack of comparability between statements.

An important point is that, in its search for improved comparability, IAS 7 (revised) reduced the scope for innovation. It might be argued that standard setters should not be reducing innovation, but that there should be concerted effort to increase innovation and improve the information available to user groups. The acceptability of innovation is a fundamental issue in a climate that is becoming increasingly prescriptive.

## Summary

IAS 7 (revised) defines the format and treatment of individual items within the cash flow statement. This leads to uniformity and greater comparability between companies. However, there is still some criticism of the current IAS 7:

- There are options within IAS 7 for presentation, since either the direct or the indirect method can be used; and there are choices about the presentation of dividends and interest.

- The cash flow statement does not distinguish between discretionary and non-discretionary cash flows, which would be valuable information to users.

- There is no separate disclosure of cash flows for expansion from cash flows to maintain current capital levels. This distinction would be useful when assessing the position and performance of companies, and is not always easy to identify in the current presentation.

- The definition of cash and cash equivalents can cause problems in that companies may interpret which investments are cash equivalents differently, leading to a lack of comparability. Statements of cash flows could be improved by removing cash equivalents and concentrating solely on the movement in cash, which is the current UK practice.

## REVIEW QUESTIONS

1. Explain the entries in the statement of cash flows when a non-current asset is sold (a) at a loss and (b) at a profit.

2. Explain the two ways in which dividends received might be classified and discuss which provides the more relevant information.

3. Discuss if long-term debts are ever included with cash equivalents.

4. Discuss three ways in which free cash flow might be improved.

5. Discuss the significance of a ratio relating free cash flow to EBITDA.

6. Explain why depreciation appears in a statement of cash flows prepared applying the indirect method but not in that applying the direct method.

7. Explain the information that a user can obtain from a statement of cash flows that cannot be obtained from the current or comparative statements of financial position.

8. It is suggested that a reconciliation of net cash flows to net debt should be required by IFRS. Discuss the relevance of such a reconciliation and the suggestion that it should be a mandatory requirement.

9. Discuss the limitations of a statement of cash flows when evaluating a company's control over its working capital.

10. Discuss why the financing section of a statement of cash flows does not allow a user to assess a company's financing policy.

11. Access http://scheller.gatech.edu/centers-initiatives/financial-analysis-lab/index.html and discuss what accounts for the difference in free cash flow between the top three and bottom three industries.

## EXERCISES

### * Question 1

Direct plc provided the following information from its records for the year ended 30 September 20X9:

|  | €000 |  |
|---|---|---|
| Sales | 316,000 | |
| Cost of goods sold | 110,400 | |
| Other expenses | 72,000 | |
| Rent expense | 14,400 | |
| Dividends | 10,000 | |
| Amortisation expense – PPE | 8,000 | |
| Advertising expense | 4,800 | |
| Gain on sale of equipment | 2,520 | |
| Interest expense | 320 | |

|  | 20X9 | 20X8 |
|---|---|---|
| Accounts receivable | 13,200 | 15,200 |
| Unearned revenue | 8,000 | 9,600 |
| Inventory | 18,400 | 19,200 |
| Prepaid advertising | 0 | 400 |
| Accounts payable | 11,200 | 8,800 |
| Rent payable | 0 | 1,200 |
| Interest payable | 40 | 0 |

**Required:**

Using the direct method of presentation, prepare the cash flows from the operating activities section of the statement of cash flows for the year ended 30 September 20X9. ✓

## * Question 2

Marwell plc reported a profit after tax of €14.04m for 20X2 as follows:

|  | €m | €m |
|---|---|---|
| Revenue |  | 118.82 |
| Materials | 29.70 |  |
| Wages | 30.80 |  |
| Depreciation | 22.68 |  |
| Loss on disposal of plant | 3.78 |  |
| Profit on sale of buildings | (6.48) |  |
|  |  | 80.48 |
| Operating profit |  | 38.34 |
| Interest payable |  | 16.20 |
| Profit before tax |  | 22.14 |
| Income tax expense |  | 8.10 |
| Profit after tax |  | 14.04 |

The statements of financial position and changes in equity showed:

(i)   Inventories at the year end were €5.94m higher than the previous year.

(ii)   Trade receivables were €10.26m higher.

(iii)   Trade payables were €4.86m lower.

(iv)   Tax payable had increased by €2.7m.

(v)   Dividends totalling €18.36m had been paid during the year.

**Required:**

(a) Calculate the net cash flow from operating activities.

(b) Explain why depreciation and a loss made on disposal of a non-current asset are both treated as a source of cash.

## * Question 3

The statements of financial position of Radar plc at 30 September were as follows:

|  | 20X8 | | 20X9 | |
|---|---|---|---|---|
|  | $000 | $000 | $000 | $000 |
| *Non-current assets:* |  |  |  |  |
| Property, plant and equipment, at cost | 760 |  | 920 |  |
| Less accumulated depreciation | (288) |  | (318) |  |
|  |  | 472 |  | 602 |
| Investments |  | 186 |  | 214 |
| *Current assets:* |  |  |  |  |
| Inventory | 596 |  | 397 |  |
| Trade receivables | 332 |  | 392 |  |
| Bank | 5 | 933 | — | 789 |
| Total assets |  | 1,591 |  | 1,605 |

|  | 20X8 | | 20X9 | |
|---|---|---|---|---|
|  | $000 | $000 | $000 | $000 |
| *Capital and reserves:* | | | | |
| Ordinary shares | 350 | | 500 | |
| Share premium | 75 | | 125 | |
| Retained earnings | 137 | 562 | 294 | 919 |
| *Non-current liabilities:* | | | | |
| 12% debentures | | 400 | | 100 |
| *Current liabilities:* | | | | |
| Trade payables | 478 | | 396 | |
| Accrued expenses | 64 | | 72 | |
| Taxation | 87 | | 96 | |
| Overdraft | — | | 22 | |
|  | | 629 | | 586 |
| Total equity and liabilities | | 1,591 | | 1,605 |

The following information is available:

(i) An impairment review of the investments disclosed that there had been an impairment of $20,000.

(ii) The depreciation charge made in the statement of comprehensive income was $64,000.

(iii) Equipment costing $72,000 was sold for $54,000 which gave a profit of $16,000.

(iv) The debentures redeemed in the year were redeemed at a premium of 25%.

(v) The premium paid on the debentures was written off to the share premium account.

(vi) The income tax expense was $92,000.

(vii) A dividend of $25,000 had been paid and dividends of $17,000 had been received.

**Required:**
**Prepare a statement of cash flows for the year ended 30 September using the indirect method.**

## Question 4

Shown below are the summarised final accounts of Martel plc for the last two financial years:

Statements of financial position as at 31 December

| | 20X1 | | 20X0 | |
|---|---|---|---|---|
| | £000 | £000 | £000 | £000 |
| *Non-current assets* | | | | |
| Tangible | | | | |
| Land and buildings | 1,464 | | 1,098 | |
| Plant and machinery | 520 | | 194 | |
| Motor vehicles | 140 | | 62 | |
| | | 2,124 | | 1,354 |
| *Current assets* | | | | |
| Inventory | 504 | | 330 | |
| Trade receivables | 264 | | 132 | |
| Government securities | 40 | | — | |
| Bank | — | | 22 | |
| | 808 | | 484 | |
| *Current liabilities* | | | | |
| Trade payables | 266 | | 220 | |
| Taxation | 120 | | 50 | |
| Proposed dividend | 72 | | 40 | |
| Bank overdraft | 184 | | — | |
| | 642 | | 310 | |
| Net current assets | | 166 | | 174 |
| Total assets less current liabilities | | 2,290 | | 1,528 |
| *Non-current liabilities* | | | | |
| 9% debentures | | (432) | | (350) |
| | | 1,858 | | 1,178 |
| *Capital and reserves* | | | | |
| Ordinary shares of 50p each fully paid | | 900 | | 800 |
| Share premium account | 120 | | 70 | |
| Revaluation reserve | 360 | | — | |
| General reserve | 100 | | 50 | |
| Retained earnings | 378 | | 258 | |
| | | 958 | | 378 |
| | | 1,858 | | 1,178 |

### Summarised statement of comprehensive income for the year ending 31 December

| | 20X1 | 20X0 |
|---|---|---|
| | £000 | £000 |
| Operating profit | 479 | 215 |
| Interest paid | 52 | 30 |
| Profit before taxation | 427 | 185 |
| Tax | 149 | 65 |
| Profit after taxation | 278 | 120 |

Additional information:

1 The movement in non-current assets during the year ended 31 December 20X1 was as follows:

|  | Land and buildings £000 | Plant, etc. £000 | Motor vehicles £000 |
|---|---|---|---|
| Cost at 1 January 20X1 | 3,309 | 470 | 231 |
| Revaluation | 360 | — | — |
| Additions | 81 | 470 | 163 |
| Disposals | — | (60) | — |
| Cost at 31 December 20X1 | 3,750 | 880 | 394 |
| Depreciation at 1 January 20X1 | 2,211 | 276 | 169 |
| Disposals | — | (48) | — |
| Added for year | 75 | 132 | 85 |
| Depreciation at 31 December 20X1 | 2,286 | 360 | 254 |

The plant and machinery disposed of during the year was sold for £20,000.

2 During 20X1, a rights issue was made of one new ordinary share for every eight held at a price of £1.50.

3 A dividend of £36,000 (20X0 £30,000) was paid in 20X1. A dividend of £72,000 (20X0 £40,000) was proposed for 20X1. A transfer of £50,000 was made to the general reserve.

Required:
(a) Prepare a statement of cash flows for the year ended 31 December 20X1, in accordance with IAS 7.
(b) Prepare a report on the liquidity position of Martel plc for a shareholder who is concerned about the lack of liquid resources in the company.

## Question 5

The following information has been taken from the financial statements for Payne plc (Payne) for the year ended 31 March 2013.

**\*Statement of Profit or Loss and Other Comprehensive Income (extracts) for year ended 31 March 2013:**

|  | €000 |
|---|---|
| Profit before interest and tax | 981 |
| Finance costs | (108) |
| Profit before tax | 873 |
| Income tax expense | (305) |
| Profit for the year | 568 |
| Other comprehensive income |  |
| Revaluation surplus on property, plant and equipment | 418 |
| Total comprehensive income | 986 |

**Statements of Financial Position as at 31 March**

|  | 2013 €000 | 2012 €000 |
|---|---|---|
| ASSETS |  |  |
| Non-current assets: |  |  |
| Property, plant and equipment | 11,250 | 10,500 |
| Intangibles | 500 | 452 |
|  | 11,750 | 10,952 |
| Current assets: |  |  |
| Inventories | 840 | 1,125 |
| Trade and other receivables | 260 | 210 |
| Investments | 38 | 18 |
| Cash and cash equivalents | 5 | 30 |
|  | 1,143 | 1,383 |
| Total assets | 12,893 | 12,335 |
| EQUITY AND LIABILITIES |  |  |
| Equity: |  |  |
| Ordinary share capital | 6,000 | 5,250 |
| Share premium account | 1,800 | 1,425 |
| Revaluation surplus | 750 | 356 |
| Retained earnings | 2,011 | 3,369 |
|  | 10,561 | 10,400 |
| Non-current liabilities: |  |  |
| Preference share capital (redeemable) | 760 | 600 |
| Current liabilities: |  |  |
| Trade and other payables | 222 | 210 |
| Taxation | 600 | 525 |
| Ordinary dividend payable | 750 | 600 |
|  | 1,572 | 1,335 |
| Total equity and liabilities | 12,893 | 12,335 |

**Statement of Changes in Equity for the year ended 31 March 2013 (extract)**

|  | Retained Earnings €'000 | Revaluation Surplus €'000 |
|---|---|---|
| Balance at 1 April 2012 | 3,369 | 356 |
| Dividends declared | (1,950) |  |
| Total comprehensive income for the year | 568 | 418 |
| Transfer from revaluation surplus to retained earnings | 24 | (24) |
| Balance at 31 March 2013 | 2,011 | 750 |

* In June 2011, the IASB issued amendments to IAS 1 *Presentation of Financial Statements*. One of these proposed the adoption of the title *Statement of Profit or Loss and Other Comprehensive Income* for the performance statement. The title *Statement of Comprehensive Income* could have been used above.

The following additional information is relevant:

(i) During the year Payne issued both ordinary shares and redeemable preference shares for cash. The latter were issued at par.

(ii) Investments classified as current assets are held for the short term and are readily convertible into the stated amounts of cash on demand.

(iii) During the year, Payne sold plant and equipment with a carrying amount of €840,500 for €900,000. Total depreciation charges for the year amounted to €1,100,000. Plant costing €50,000 was purchased on credit. The amount is included within trade and other payables.

(iv) Trade and other payables include accrued interest of €5,000 as at 31 March 2013 (2012: €10,000).

(v) Intangibles relate to development costs capitalised in accordance with IAS 38 *Intangible Assets*. Costs amounting to €70,000 were capitalised during the year.

Required:

(a) Prepare a Statement of Cash Flows for Payne for the year to 31 March 2013 in accordance with IAS 7 Statement of Cash Flows.

(b) You have been provided with the following additional information in relation to Payne's trading performance for the years ended on the stated dates:

|  | 31/3/2013 | 31/3/2012 |
|---|---|---|
|  | *€000* | *€000* |
| Revenue | 3,400 | 2,800 |
| Cost of sales | (2,040) | (1,400) |
| Operating expenses | (379) | (357) |

Write a report concisely analysing the cash flow, profitability and working capital management of Payne Ltd during the year ended 31 March 2013. Your report should be supported by appropriate ratios.

*(Institute of Certified Public Accountants (CPA) Professional Stage 1*
*Corporate Reporting Examination, April 2013)*

## Question 6

The financial statements of Saturn plc have been prepared as follows:

| *Statements of financial position as at 30 June* | 20X2 | | 20X1 | |
|---|---|---|---|---|
|  | *€000* | *€000* | *€000* | *€000* |
| Non-current assets: |  |  |  |  |
| Property, plant and equipment at cost | 6,600 |  | 5,880 |  |
| Accumulated depreciation | (1,680) | 4,920 | (1,380) | 4,500 |
| Development costs |  | 540 |  | 480 |
| Investments |  | 420 |  | 300 |
| Current assets: |  |  |  |  |
| Inventory | 1,665 |  | 1,872 |  |
| Trade receivables | 1,446 |  | 1,188 |  |
| Cash | 9 | 3,120 | 42 | 3,102 |
|  |  | 9,000 |  | 8,382 |
| Equity and reserves |  |  |  |  |
| Ordinary shares of €1 each | 3,000 |  | 2,700 |  |
| Share premium account | 600 |  | 270 |  |
| Retained earnings | 3,084 | 6,684 | 2,622 | 5,592 |
| Non-current liability: |  |  |  |  |
| 7% debentures |  | — |  | 1,200 |
| Current liabilities: |  |  |  |  |
| Trade payables | 1,632 |  | 1,104 |  |
| Taxation | 507 |  | 396 |  |
| Dividend declared | 60 |  | 90 |  |
| Bank overdraft | 117 | 2,316 | — | 1,590 |
|  |  | 9,000 |  | 8,382 |

Further information:

(a) Extract from statement of income

|  | €000 |
|---|---|
| Operating profit | 1,008 |
| Dividend received | 36 |
| Premium on debentures | (120) |
| Interest paid | (144) |
| Profit before taxation | 780 |
| Income tax | (258) |
| Profit after tax | 522 |

(b) Operating expenses written off in the year include the following:

|  | €000 |
|---|---|
| Amortisation of development costs | 102 |
| Depreciation of property, plant and equipment | 318 |

(c) Equipment which had cost €240,000 was sold in the year, incurring a loss of €156,000.

(d) The debentures were redeemed at a premium of 10%.

**Required:**

(a) **Prepare a statement of cash flows for the year ended 30 June 20X2.**

(b) **Briefly explain ways in which statements of cash flows may be more useful than statements of income.**

## Notes

1 J. Arnold et al., *The Future Shape of Financial Reports*, ICAEW and ICAS, 1991.

2 G.H. Sorter, M.J. Ingberman and H.M. Maximon, *Financial Accounting: An Events and Cash Flow Approach*, McGraw-Hill, 1990.

3 L.J. Heath and P. Rosenfield, 'Solvency: the forgotten half of financial reporting', in R. Bloom and P.T. Elgers (eds), *Accounting Theory and Practice*, Harcourt Brace Jovanovich, 1987, p. 586.

4 J.M. Gahlon and R.L. Vigeland, 'Early warning signs of bankruptcy using cash flow analysis', *Journal of Commercial Lending*, December 1988, pp. 4–15.

5 J.W. Henderson and T.S. Maness, *The Financial Analyst's Deskbook*, Van Nostrand Reinhold, 1989, p. 72.

6 G. Holmes and A. Sugden, *Interpreting Company Reports and Accounts* (5th edition), Woodhead-Faulkner, 1995, p. 134.

### PART 3

# Regulatory framework – an attempt to achieve uniformity

# Financial reporting – evolution of global standards

## 6.1 Introduction

The main purpose of this chapter is to describe the movement towards global standards for publicly and non-publicly accountable entities.

> ### Objectives
>
> By the end of the chapter, you should be able to:
>
> - critically discuss the arguments for and against standards;
> - describe standard setting and enforcement in the UK, the EU and the US;
> - discuss the approach taken by the EU with the new Accounting Directive;
> - describe and comment on the IASB approach to financial reporting by small and medium-sized entities (IFRS for SMEs);
> - critically discuss the advantages and disadvantages of global standards;
> - describe the reasons for differences in financial reporting.

## 6.2 Why do we need financial reporting standards?

Standards are needed because accounting numbers are important when defining contractual entitlements. Contracting parties frequently define the rights between themselves in terms of accounting numbers.[1] For example, the remuneration of directors and managers might be expressed in terms of a salary plus a bonus based on an agreed performance measure, e.g. Johnson Matthey's 2016 Annual Report states:

> Annual Bonus – which is paid as a percentage of basic salary . . . based on consolidated underlying profit before tax (PBT) compared with the annual budget. Provides a strong incentive aligned to strategy in the short term. The annual bonus are properly reflected in stretching but achievable annual budgets.

However, there is a risk of irresponsible behaviour by directors and managers if it appears that earnings will not meet performance targets. They might be tempted to adopt measures that increase the PBT but which are not in the best interest of the shareholders.

This risk is specifically addressed in the Johnson Matthey 2016 Annual Report as shown in the following extract:

> The Committee retains the discretion in awarding annual bonuses and . . . ensures that the incentive structure for senior management does not raise environmental, social and governance risks by inadvertently motivating irresponsible behaviour.

In its 2013 Annual Report the directors commented:

> At the start of the year, the board set ambitious targets, ahead of the prevailing industry analysts' consensus, but as the year unfolded, short term performance fell below that determined when setting the budget. As a result, no executive director bonuses will be paid this year, even though underlying earnings per share fell by just 2%.

This would not, however, preclude companies from taking typical steps such as **deferring discretionary expenditure,** e.g. research, advertising or training expenditure; **deferring amortisation,** e.g. making optimistic sales projections in order to classify research as development expenditure which can be capitalised; and **reclassifying** deteriorating current assets as non-current assets to avoid the need to recognise a loss under the lower of cost and net realisable value rule applicable to current assets.

The introduction of a mandatory standard that changes management's ability to adopt such measures **affects wealth distribution** within the firm. For example, if managers are able to delay the amortisation of development expenditure, then bonuses related to profit will be higher and there will effectively have been a transfer of wealth to managers from shareholders.

## 6.3 Why do we need standards to be mandatory?

Mandatory standards are needed, therefore, to define the way in which accounting numbers are presented in financial statements, so that their measurement and presentation are less subjective. It had been thought that the accountancy profession could obtain uniformity of disclosure by persuasion but, in reality, the profession found it difficult to resist management pressures.

During the 1960s the financial sector of the UK economy lost confidence in the accountancy profession when internationally known UK-based companies were seen to have published financial data that were materially incorrect. Shareholders are normally unaware that this occurs and it tends to become public knowledge only in restricted circumstances, e.g. when a third party has a **vested interest** in revealing adverse facts following a takeover, or when a company falls into the hands of an administrator, inspector or liquidator, **whose duty it is to enquire and report** on shortcomings in the management of a company.

Two scandals which disturbed the public at the time, GEC/AEI and Pergamon Press, were both made public in the restricted circumstances referred to above, when financial reports prepared from the same basic information disclosed a materially different picture.

### 6.3.1 GEC takeover of AEI in 1967

The first calamity for the profession involved GEC Ltd in its takeover bid for AEI Ltd when the pre-takeover accounts prepared by the old AEI directors differed materially from the post-takeover accounts prepared by the new AEI directors.

Under the control of the directors of GEC the accounts of AEI were produced for 1967 showing **a loss of £4.5 million.** Unfortunately, this was from basic information that was largely the same as that used by AEI when producing its profit forecast of £10 million.

There can be two reasons for the difference between the figures produced. Either the facts have changed or the judgements made by the directors have changed. In this case, it seems there was a change in the facts to the extent of a post-acquisition closure of an AEI factory;

this explained £5 million of the £14.5 million difference between the forecast profit and the actual loss. The remaining £9.5 million arose because of differences in judgement. For example, the new directors took a different view of the value of stock and work in progress.

### 6.3.2 Pergamon Press

**Audited accounts** were produced by Pergamon Press Ltd for 1968 showing a profit of approximately £2 million.

**An independent investigation** by Price Waterhouse suggested that this profit should be reduced by 75% because of a number of unacceptable valuations, e.g. there had been a failure to reduce certain stock to the lower of cost and net realisable value, and there had been a change in policy on the capitalisation of printing costs of back issues of scientific journals – they were treated as a cost of closing stock in 1968, but not as a cost of opening stock in 1968.

### 6.3.3 Public view of the accounting profession following such cases

It had long been recognised that accountancy is not an exact science, but it had not been appreciated just how much latitude there was for companies to produce vastly different results based on the same transactions. Given that the auditors were perfectly happy to sign that those accounts showing either a £10 million profit or a £4.5 million loss were true and fair, the public felt the need for action if investors were to have any trust in the figures that were being published.

The difficulty was that each firm of accountants tended to rely on precedents within its own firm in deciding what was true and fair. In fairness, there could be consistency within an audit firm's approach but not across all firms in the profession. The auditors were also under pressure to agree to practices that the directors wanted because there were no professional mandatory standards.

This was the scenario that galvanised the City press and the investing public. An embarrassed, disturbed profession announced in 1969, via the ICAEW, that there was a majority view supporting the introduction of Statements of Standard Accounting Practice to supplement the legislation.

### 6.3.4 Does the need for standards and effective enforcement still exist in the twenty-first century?

The scandals involving GEC and Pergamon Press occurred more than 45 years ago. However, the need for the ongoing enforcement of standards for financial reporting and auditing continues unabated. We only need to look at the unfortunate events with Enron and Ahold to arrive at an answer.

#### Enron

Enron was formed in the mid-1980s and became by the end of the 1990s the seventh-largest company in revenue terms in the USA. However, this concealed the fact that it had off-balance-sheet debts and that it had overstated its profits by more than $500 million – falling into bankruptcy (the largest in US corporate history) in 2001.

#### Ahold

In 2003 Ahold, the world's third-largest grocer, reported that its earnings for the past two years were overstated by more than $500 million as a result of local managers recording promotional allowances provided by suppliers to promote their goods at a figure greater than the cash received. This may reflect on the pressure to inflate profits when there are option schemes for managers.

### Tesco

In 2014 Tesco was investigated by the FRC and Serious Fraud Office following its overstatement of profits by £250m–£325m arising from the accelerated recognition of commercial income in the form of vendor allowances.

## 6.4 Arguments in support of standards

The setting of standards has both supporters and opponents. Those who support standards have a view that they are important in giving investors confidence and encouraging informed investment. In this section we discuss credibility, discipline and comparability.

### Credibility

The accountancy profession would lose all credibility if it permitted companies experiencing similar events to produce financial reports that disclosed markedly different results simply because they could select different accounting policies. Uniformity was seen as essential if financial reports were to disclose a true and fair view. However, it has been a continuing view in the UK and IASB that standards should be based on principles and not be seen as rigid rules – they were not to replace the exercise of informed judgement in determining what constituted a true and fair view in each circumstance. The US approach has been different – its approach has been to prescribe detailed rules.

### Discipline

Directors are under pressure to maintain and improve the market valuation of their company's securities. There is a temptation, therefore, to influence any financial statistic that has an impact on the market valuation, such as the trend in the earnings per share (EPS) figure, the net asset backing for the shares or the gearing ratios which show the level of borrowing relative to the amount of equity capital put in by the shareholders.

This is an ever-present risk and the Financial Reporting Council showed awareness of the need to impose discipline when it stated in its Annual Review as far back as 1991 that the high level of company failures in the then recession, some of which were associated with **obscure financial reporting,** damaged confidence in the high standard of reporting by the majority of companies.

### Comparability

In addition to financial statements allowing investors to evaluate the management's performance, i.e. their stewardship, they should also allow investors to make predictions of future cash flows and make comparisons with other companies.

In order to be able to make valid inter-company comparisons of performance and trends, investors need relevant and reliable data that have been standardised. If companies were to continue to apply different accounting policies to identical commercial activities, innocently or with the deliberate intention of disguising bad news, then investors could be misled in making their investment decisions.

## 6.5 Arguments against standards

We have so far discussed the arguments in support of standard setting. However, there are also arguments that have been made against, such as consensus-seeking and information overload with IFRSs themselves exceeding 3,000 pages.

### Consensus-seeking

Consensus-seeking can lead to the issuing of standards that are over-influenced by those who fear that a new standard will adversely affect their statements of financial position. For example, we see retail companies, who lease many of their stores, oppose the proposal to put operating leases onto the statement of financial position rather than reporting simply the future commitment as a note to the accounts.

### Overload

Standard overload is not a new charge. It has been put forward by those who consider that:

- There are too many standard setters with differing requirements, e.g. the FRC in the UK with FRSs; the FASB in the US with the Accounting Standards Codification; the IASB with IFRSs and IFRICs; the EU with separate endorsement of IFRS giving us EU-IFRS; and the EU with its Directives and national Stock Exchange listing requirements.

- Standards are too detailed if rule-based and not sufficiently detailed if principle-based, leading to the need for yet further guidance from the standard setters. For example, further guidance has to be issued by the International Financial Reporting Interpretations Committee (IFRC) when existing IFRSs do not provide the answer.

- There are too many notes to the accounts to satisfy regulatory requirements, for example disclosing charitable donations.

- There are too many notes to the accounts put in by companies themselves. Various surveys by professional accounting firms including one by Baker Tilly in 2012[2] showed that the majority of financial directors were keen to cut 'clutter' from financial disclosures, believing that the financial statements are too long, and that key messages are being lost as a result. It was felt that existing standards lead to a checklist mentality and boiler-plate disclosures that are not material and can obscure relevant information.

- There has been no definition of a note by the standard setters. This is being addressed by EFRAG with the issue of a Discussion Paper in 2012, *Towards a Disclosure Framework for the Notes,* which proposes how notes should be defined. For example, it is proposed that relevance, for instance, should only apply to disclosures that fulfil some *specific* users' needs.

- International standards have, until 2009 with the issue of *IFRS for SMEs,* focused on the large multinational companies and failed to recognise the different users and information needs between large and smaller entities.

## 6.6 Standard setting and enforcement by the Financial Reporting Council (FRC) in the UK

The Financial Reporting Council (FRC) was set up in 1990 as an independent regulator. Under the FRC the Accounting Standards Board (ASB) issued standards and the Financial Reporting Review Panel (FRRP) reviewed compliance to encourage high-quality financial reporting.

Due to its success in doing this, the government decided, following corporate disasters such as that of Enron in the USA, to give it a more **proactive** role from 2004 onwards in the areas of corporate governance, compliance with statutes and accounting and auditing standards.

Countries experience alternating periods of favourable and unfavourable economic conditions – often described as 'boom and bust'. The FRC directs its reviews towards those sectors most likely to experience difficulties at the time. For example, it announced that its review activity in 2011/12 would focus on companies operating in niche markets, companies outside the FTSE 350, and companies providing support services with significant exposure to public spending cuts. It identified Commercial property, Insurance, Support services and Travel as priority sectors for review. It also pays particular attention to the reports and accounts of companies whose shareholders have raised concerns about governance or where there have been specific complaints.

### 6.6.1 The FRC structure

The FRC structure has evolved to meet changing needs. It was restructured in 2012 to operate as a unified regulatory body with enhanced independence. The new structure is shown in Figure 6.1.

### 6.6.2 The FRC Board

The FRC Board is supported by three committees: the Codes and Standards Committee, the Conduct Committee and the Executive Committee.

#### The Codes and Standards Committee

This will advise the FRC Board on matters relating to codes, standard setting and policy questions, through its Accounting, Actuarial and Audit & Assurance Councils. The

**Figure 6.1 FRC structure from 2012**

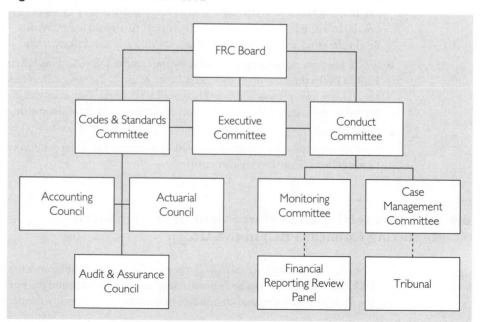

*Accounting Council* replaces the Accounting Standards Board. It reports to the Codes and Standards Committee and is responsible for providing strategic input into the work-plan of the FRC as a whole and advising on draft national and international standards to ensure that high-quality, effective standards are produced.

### The Conduct Committee

This will advise the FRC Board in matters relating to conduct to promote high-quality corporate reporting, including monitoring, oversight, investigative and disciplinary functions, through its Monitoring Committee and Case Management Committee. The *Monitoring Committee* will be concerned with the assessment and reviews of audit quality and decisions as to possible resulting sanctions and investigation leading to possible disciplinary action being taken.

### The Executive Committee

This will support the Board by advising on strategic issues and providing day-to-day oversight of the work of the FRC.

## 6.6.3 The Financial Reporting Review Panel (FRRP)

### Creative accounting

A research study[3] into companies that have been the subject of a public statement suggests that when a firm's performance comes under severe strain, even apparently well-governed firms can succumb to the pressure for creative accounting, and that good governance alone is not a sufficient condition for ensuring high-quality financial reporting. Enforcement is required.

### Risk-based proactive approach to enforcement

The FRRP has a policing role with responsibility for overseeing some 2,500 companies. Its role is to review material departures from accounting standards and, where financial statements are defective, to require the company to take appropriate remedial action. It has the right to apply to the court to make companies comply, but it prefers to deal with defects by agreement and there has never been recourse to the court.

It selects companies and documents to be examined using a proactive risk-based approach or a mixed model where a risk-based approach is combined with a rotation and/or a sampling approach – a pure rotation approach or a pure reactive approach would not be acceptable.[4]

In 2015 it reported under Areas of Future Focus that:

We are currently in a relatively mature corporate reporting environment, where UK Boards are:

generally familiar with the requirements of IFRS and can apply them appropriately in most circumstances. We spend an increasing proportion of our time evaluating the significant accounting judgements that Boards make and the quality of their conclusions, as we know that these areas are important to investors. These significant judgements involve the consideration of materiality. Boards should consider both the quantitative and qualitative aspects of materiality when making judgements. We may challenge these conclusions, particularly if we believe the Board may be using a quantitative materiality argument to achieve a particular accounting treatment, to justify giving insufficient prominence to relevant information or to avoid the transparency surrounding an error correction.

### Cooperative approach to enforcement

There were, however, reservations expressed about the quality of reporting by some smaller listed and Alternative Investment Market (AIM) quoted companies that lacked the accounting expertise of their larger listed counterparts.

The FRC is looking at how to assist smaller listed and AIM quoted companies improve their financial reports and in June 2015 published a Discussion Paper on the FRC's findings and proposals, *Improving the Quality of Reporting by Smaller Listed and AIM Quoted Companies.*[5]

This is in recognition that smaller listed and AIM quoted companies are important in generating future growth in the economy and need access to capital in order to invest and grow. The Organisation for Economic Co-operation and Development (OECD) reports that it considers small and medium-sized companies to be critical to ensuring that economic growth is sustainable and inclusive. In February 2015 the European Commission issued a Green Paper, *Building a Capital Markets Union,* which included the need for simpler reporting requirements

## 6.7 The International Accounting Standards Board

The International Accounting Standards Board (IASB) has responsibility for all technical matters including the preparation and implementation of standards. The IASB website (www.iasb.org.uk) explains that:

> The IASB is committed to developing, in the public interest, a single set of high quality, understandable and enforceable global accounting standards that require transparent and comparable information in general purpose financial statements. In addition, the IASB co-operates with national accounting standard-setters to achieve convergence in accounting standards around the world.

The IASB adopted all current IASs and began issuing its own standards, International Financial Reporting Standards (IFRSs). The body of IASs and IFRSs is referred to collectively as 'IFRS'.

As a conceptual basis to assist when drafting Standards the IASC issued a *Framework for the Preparation and Presentation of Financial Statements*[6] in 1989 (adopted by the IASB in 2001).

### 6.7.1 The Framework for the Preparation and Presentation of Financial Statements

The position was that different social, economic and legal circumstances had led to countries producing financial statements using different criteria for defining elements, recognising and measuring items appearing in the profit and loss account and balance sheet. The IASB approach was to attempt to harmonise national regulations and move towards the adoption by countries of International Standards (IFRSs). The *Framework* is being gradually revised on the issue in 2010 of the Conceptual Framework. The objective of the Conceptual Framework project is to improve financial reporting by providing the IASB with a complete and updated set of concepts to use when it develops or revises standards. It is discussed further in Chapter 7.

### Adoption by countries of IFRS

IFRS has been adopted in the EU for consolidated accounts since 2005. It is interesting to see how the other G20 countries are gradually moving towards the use of IFRS. Of these, the position with the BRICS countries is that Brazil has required individual companies to use IFRS since 2008, Russia already uses it, India is converging with IFRS, China has substantially converged national standards and South Africa has required IFRS for listed companies since 2005. Japan required mandatory compliance by 2016.

### What has been the impact of adopting IFRS

There have been numerous benefits claimed, for example:

● Multinationals see a reduction in the cost of capital and easier access to international equity markets.

● Investors see shares in companies adopting IFRS becoming more liquid and have greater confidence in earnings per share figures when making investment decisions.

● National standard setters see an advantage in the shared development of standards.

A detailed research report on the experience of converging IFRSs in China, *Does IFRS Convergence Affect Financial Reporting Quality in China?*, makes interesting reading.[7]

The report noted that there was a significant increase in the value relevance of reported earnings for the firms following mandatory adoption of IFRS-converged Chinese Accounting Standards (CAS). It also identified how access to external finance was an incentive to achieve improved quality of financial reporting, discussing the effect where companies are in the manufacturing sector, operating in less developed regions or operating under foreign ownership, in contrast to those under central government control or those that have financial problems and are tempted to manage earnings to avoid delisting.

Extant IASs and IFRSs are listed in Figure 6.2.

## 6.8 Standard setting and enforcement in the European Union (EU)[8]

A major aim of the EU has been to create a single financial market that requires access by investors to financial reports which have been prepared using common financial reporting standards. The initial steps were the issue of accounting directives – these were the Fourth Directive,[9] the Seventh Directive and the Eighth Directive which were required to be adopted by each EU country into their national laws – in the UK it is the Companies Act 2006. The existing Directives were subsumed in 2013 into a new Accounting Directive.

In the UK the requirements of the Accounting Directive were included into company law on the issue of The Companies, Partnerships and Groups (Accounts and Reports) Regulations 2015 effective from January 2016.

### 6.8.1 The new Accounting Directive[10]

There has been ongoing pressure to reduce the regulatory burden on small and medium-sized enterprises. The European Commission responded to this pressure by issuing a new Accounting Directive.

It is not a conceptual rewrite of the Directives. It aimed to address two of the major problems with the existing Directives, which were the lack of comparability arising from use of Member State Options (MSOs) and the unnecessary regulatory burden placed on SMEs.

#### The lack of comparability

The new Directive has achieved a small reduction in the number of options available to member states. It formalises fundamental accounting principles (although still with some

**Figure 6.2 Extant international standards**

| | |
|---|---|
| IAS 1 | Presentation of Financial Statements |
| IAS 2 | Inventories |
| IAS 7 | Statement of Cash Flows |
| IAS 8 | Accounting Policies, Changes in Accounting Estimates and Errors |
| IAS 10 | Events after the Reporting Period |
| IAS 11 | Construction Contracts |
| IAS 12 | Income Taxes |
| IAS 16 | Property, Plant and Equipment |
| IAS 17 | Leases |
| IAS 18 | Revenue |
| IAS 19 | Employee Benefits |
| IAS 20 | Accounting for Government Grants and Disclosure of Government Assistance |
| IAS 21 | The Effects of Changes in Foreign Exchange Rates |
| IAS 23 | Borrowing Costs |
| IAS 24 | Related Party Disclosures |
| IAS 26 | Accounting and Reporting by Retirement Benefit Plans |
| IAS 27 | Separate Financial Statements |
| IAS 28 | Investments in Associates and Joint Ventures |
| IAS 29 | Financial Reporting in Hyperinflationary Economies |
| IAS 32 | Financial Instruments: Presentation |
| IAS 33 | Earnings per Share |
| IAS 34 | Interim Financial Reporting |
| IAS 36 | Impairment of Assets |
| IAS 37 | Provisions, Contingent Liabilities and Contingent Assets |
| IAS 38 | Intangible Assets |
| IAS 39 | Financial Instruments: Recognition and Measurement |
| IAS 40 | Investment Properties |
| IAS 41 | Agriculture |
| IFRS 1 | First-time Adoption of International Financial Reporting Standards |
| IFRS 2 | Share-based Payment |
| IFRS 3 | (Revised) Business Combinations |
| IFRS 4 | Insurance Contracts |
| IFRS 5 | Non-current Assets Held for Sale and Discontinued Operations |
| IFRS 6 | Exploration for and Evaluation of Mineral Resources |
| IFRS 7 | Financial Instruments Disclosures |
| IFRS 8 | Operating Segments |
| IFRS 9 | Financial Instruments |
| IFRS 10 | Consolidated Financial Statements |
| IFRS 11 | Joint Arrangements |
| IFRS 12 | Disclosure of Interests in Other Entities |
| IFRS 13 | Fair Value Measurement |
| IFRS 14 | Regulatory Deferral Accounts |
| IFRS 15 | Revenue from Contracts with Customers |
| IFRS 16 | Leases |

Member State Options) for recognition and presentation in the financial statements. These are:

(i) There is a going concern presumption.

(ii) Accounts are to be prepared on an accrual basis.

(iii) Accounting policies and measurement bases are to be applied consistently between accounting periods.

(iv) Recognition and measurement are to be on a prudent basis, and in particular:

    (a) Items are to be measured at price or production cost.

        There is an option that allows for the revaluation of non-current assets and the use of fair values for financial and non-financial assets.

    (b) Only profits made at the balance sheet date are to be recognised.

    (c) Individual assets and liabilities are to be valued separately and set-off is not permitted.

    (d) All liabilities arising in the course of a financial year are to be recognised even if identified after the year.

    (e) All items are to be accounted for and presented in accordance with the substance of the transaction.

    (f) All negative value adjustments are to be recognised whether the result for the financial year is a profit or a loss.

(v) Materiality applies to recognition, measurement, presentation, disclosure and consolidation.

There have also been some arbitrary changes such as the requirement to write off goodwill over a period of between 5 and 10 years in exceptional cases, where the useful life of goodwill and development costs cannot be reliably estimated, and continuing options such as the option for the related costs of borrowing to be added to the cost of fixed and current assets.

### Regulatory burden on SMEs

In order to further simplify the requirements for SMEs and micro–undertakings the European Commission adopted a 'bottom-up' approach that started with the requirements for small undertakings and then added additional accounting and reporting requirements as undertakings passed the thresholds for medium and large undertakings. It has set new size thresholds for determining the category as follows:

| Undertakings | Turnover (£) | Balance sheet total (£) | Average number of employees |
|---|---|---|---|
| Micro | ≤632,000 | 316,000 | 10 |
| Small | ≤10.2m | ≤5.1m | 50 |
| Medium-sized | ≤36.0m | ≤18m | 250 |

The undertaking must be within any two of the three thresholds for two successive accounting periods. The default thresholds for small undertakings' turnover and balance sheet total are €8 million and €4 million, respectively. However, member states have the option to increase either or both of these thresholds for small undertakings up to a maximum of €12 million and €6 million, respectively.

The need for small companies to be audited has been removed.

### Progressive increase in requirements from the bottom up

The Directive starts by listing the reporting requirements applicable to a small company and then increases the disclosures required from a medium-sized and a large undertaking. A helpful summary of the requirements is provided by the Federation of European Accountants (FEE).[11]

## 6.8.2 Enforcement of standards in Europe

In 2014 ESMA issued[12] *Guidelines: Enforcement of Financial Information.* Together with European national enforcers it identifies common enforcement priorities, which for 2014 encompassed:

- preparation and presentation of consolidated financial statements and related disclosures;
- financial reporting by entities which have joint arrangements and related disclosures; and
- recognition and measurement of deferred tax assets.

### 6.8.3 The importance of enforcement

There is research evidence[13] that the cost of capital falls following the mandatory adoption of IFRS and that there is an increase in foreign equity investment. However, in addition to the standards, effective enforcement has to be in place.[14]

Even following the mandatory adoption of IFRS and enforcement of reporting standards, investors continue to take into account national considerations such as the existence of good corporate governance, the degree of shareholder protection and the level of corruption.

### 6.8.4 What might the impact be on financial reporting following Brexit?

Here we are only considering the process of financial reporting rather than the likely impact of increased volatility on individual assets and liabilities.

At the time of writing (2016), the EU influence is exerted by the issue of the Accounting Directive 2013, which has to be adopted into national law and its requirement that IFRSs should be endorsed by the EU when applied to the consolidated accounts of listed companies. In practice EU endorsement has generally been quite accepting of the IASB produced IFRSs.

Details of all endorsements can be seen on the website of the European Financial Reporting Advisory Group (EFRAG) at www.efrag.org/Endorsement.

#### Position regarding IFRSs

Departure from the EU offers the UK three choices when preparing financial statements for listed companies, namely to:

(i)   continue with EU-endorsed IFRS; or

(ii)  move to full IFRS; or

(iii) revert to UK GAAP.

It is very unlikely that the UK would decide to revert to UK GAAP given the widespread internationally of the adoption of IFRSs. It might, however, consider UK-endorsed as opposed to EU-endorsed IFRSs. This would mean that the UK profession would have the ability to adapt IFRSs to its own needs.

## 6.9 Standard setting and enforcement in the US

Reporting standards are set by the Financial Accounting Standards Board (FASB) and enforced by the Securities Exchange Commission. Since 2002 it has also been necessary to satisfy the requirements of the Sarbanes–Oxley Act (normally referred to as SOX) which was passed following the Enron disaster.

### 6.9.1 Standard setting by the FASB and other bodies

The Financial Accounting Standards Board (FASB) is responsible for setting accounting standards in the USA. The FASB is financed by a compulsory levy on public companies, which should ensure its independence. (The previous system of voluntary contributions ran the risk of major donors trying to exert undue influence on the Board.) In 2009 the FASB launched the FASB *Accounting Standards Codification* as the single source of authoritative non-governmental US Generally Accepted Accounting Principles (GAAP), combining and replacing the jumbled mix of accounting standards that have evolved over the last half-century.

## 6.9.2 Enforcement by the SEC

The Securities and Exchange Commission (SEC) is responsible for requiring the publication of financial information for the benefit of shareholders. It has the power to dictate the form and content of these reports. The largest companies whose shares are listed must register with the SEC and comply with its regulations. The SEC monitors financial reports filed in great detail and makes useful information available to the public via its website.[15] However, it is important to note that the majority of companies fall outside the SEC's jurisdiction.

## 6.9.3 SOX (the Sarbanes–Oxley Act 2002)

SOX came as a response to the failures in Enron. It is different from the UK's Code of Corporate Governance in that, rather than the comply-or-explain approach, compliance is mandatory with significant potential sanctions for individual directors where there is non-compliance.

### Prevention of fraud

The SOX objectives are to reduce the risk of fraud. It provides that

> Whoever knowingly alters, destroys, mutilates, conceals, covers up, falsifies, or makes a false entry in any record, document, or tangible object with the intent to impede, obstruct, or influence the investigation or proper administration of any matter within the jurisdiction of any department or agency of the United States . . . shall be fined under this title, imprisoned not more than 20 years, or both. (Section 802(a))

Following the Enron and other scandals, a number of weaknesses were identified which allowed the frauds to go undetected. Weaknesses included (a) the accounting profession where there was inadequate oversight and conflicts of interest, (b) company management that had poor internal controls and had been subject to weak corporate governance procedures, and (c) investors under-protected with stock analysts giving biased investment advice, the FASB which was responsible for inadequate disclosure rules, and an under-funded enforcement agency in the Securities and Exchange Commission (SEC).

### Management

CEOs of publicly traded companies are now directly responsible for ensuring that financial reports are accurate. To protect themselves CEOs rely on a sound system of internal control and management is accountable for the quality of those controls. Under SOX, management is required to certify the company's financial reports and both management and an independent accountant are required to certify the organisation's internal controls.

### Investors

SOX aimed to reduce fraud and improve investor confidence in financial reports and the capital market by seeking improvements in corporate accounting controls. In doing so it has created mandatory requirements that might have disadvantaged US companies operating in a global market where there is a comply-or-explain approach to compliance as in the UK and OECD countries.

### 6.9.4 Progress towards adoption by the USA of international standards

There has been progress since 2002 following the Norwalk Agreement on making the US standards and IFRS fully compatible and to coordinate future work programmes.

The FASB and IASB have worked together on joint projects such as Revenue Recognition and Leasing. However, there is a view[16] that the future of further convergence remains uncertain as the Boards shift attention to their own independent agendas.

It has to be recognised that there appears to be little enthusiasm for the adoption of IFRS in place of US GAAP. This is understandable when realising that the question as to whether moving to IFRS is actually in the best interests of the US securities markets generally and US investors individually is unresolved. Their decision is also influenced by their view that (a) the IASB is underfunded and too reliant on the major accountancy firms and (b) their assessment that there is neither a consistent application nor enforcement of IFRSs globally.

## 6.10 Advantages and disadvantages of global standards for publicly accountable entities

Publicly accountable entities are those whose debt or equity is publicly traded. Many are multinational and listed on a stock exchange in more than one country.

### 6.10.1 Advantages

The main advantages arising from the development of international standards are that it reduces the cost of reporting under different standards, makes it easier to raise cross-border finance, leads to a decrease in firms' costs of capital with a corresponding increase in share prices, and enables investors to compare performance. For developing countries there is also the incentive to improve accountants' technical training and expertise.

### 6.10.2 Disadvantages

#### Complexity

However, one survey[17] carried out in the UK indicated that finance directors and auditors surveyed felt that IFRSs undermined UK reporting integrity. In particular, there was little support for the further use of fair values as a basis for financial reporting, which was regarded as making the accounts less reliable with comments such as 'I think the use of fair values increases the subjective nature of the accounts and confuses unqualified users'.

There was further reference to this problem of understanding with a further comment: 'IFRS/US GAAP have generally gone too far – now nobody other than the Big 4 technical departments and the SEC know what they mean. The analyst community doesn't even bother trying to understand them – so who exactly do the IASB think they are satisfying?'

#### Impact on net profit and equity

IFRS 1 *First-time Adoption of International Financial Reporting Standards* requires companies to produce a reconciliation of their IFRS equity and profit/loss to their equity and profit/ loss reported under national GAAP.

A research report[18] prepared for the Institute of Chartered Accountants in Scotland in 2008, *The Implementation of IFRS in the UK, Italy and Ireland*, analysed the impact on net profit and equity of selected standards which showed whether the standard had caused an increase or decrease in reported net profit due to the introduction of the standard.

Their analysis showed that adopting IFRS resulted in the net profit being increased in each of the countries with the net profit under national GAAP being 66% of the IFRS figure for UK companies, 89% for Italian and 89% for Irish companies. By contrast, the equity of the average company was less under IFRS, with the equity under national GAAP being 153% higher than that under IFRS.

These are average changes and the impact on an individual company might be very different. For example, there was a dramatic effect on the headline figures for Wassenan, a Dutch company, which reported an increase of over 400% in its net income figure when the Dutch GAAP accounts were restated under IFRS. In other cases, there may be some large adjustments to individual balances, but the net effect may be less obvious.

In the short term, these changes in reported figures can have important consequences for companies' contractual obligations (e.g. they may not be able to maintain the level of liquidity required by their loan agreements) and their ability to pay dividends. There may be motivational issues to consider where staff bonuses have traditionally been based on reported accounting profit. As a result, companies may find that they need to adjust their management accounting system to align it more closely with IFRS.

### Volatility in the accounts

In most countries the use of IFRS will mean that earnings and statement of financial position values will be more volatile than in the past. This could be quite a culture shock for analysts and others used to examining trends that may have followed a fairly predictable straight line.

### Lack of familiarity

While the change to IFRS was covered in the professional and the more general press, it was not clear whether users of financial statements fully appreciated the effect of the change in accounting regulations, although surveys by KPMG[19] and PricewaterhouseCoopers[20] indicated that most analysts and investors were confident that they understood the implications of the change. A survey following the issue of *IFRS for SMEs* in 2009 indicated that, as a new standard, there was naturally a fairly widespread lack of understanding of its provisions. This has been well addressed[21] by the IASB with supporting workshops and educational material.

## 6.11 How do reporting requirements differ for non-publicly accountable entities?

The EU, national governments and standard setters have realised that there are numerous small and medium-sized businesses that do not raise funds on the stock exchange and do not prepare general-purpose financial statements for external users. Countries adopting IFRS for publicly accountable entities have, therefore, been able to issue their own national standards for non-publicly accountable entities.

In the UK companies have a statutory obligation to submit accounts annually to the shareholders and file a copy with the Registrar of Companies. In recognition of the cost implications and need for different levels of privacy, there was provision for small and medium-sized companies to file abbreviated accounts and adopt *Financial Reporting Standard for Smaller Entities* (FRSSE).[22] This standard follows the top-down approach to standard setting by reducing some of the disclosures required by standards applicable to listed companies – such as disclosing an earnings per share figure. The FRSSE was withdrawn from 1 January 2016 and replaced by either FRS 105 *The Financial Reporting Standard for the Micro-entities Regime*, or Section 1A of FRS 102 *The Financial Reporting Standard*. Whereas the UK has FRS 105, the IASB has issued the *IFRS for SMEs*.

## 6.12 IFRS for SMEs

The IASB issued *IFRS for SMEs* in July 2009. The approach follows that adopted by the ASB with FRSSE:

- some topics omitted, e.g. IAS 33 Earnings per Share, IFRS 8 Operating Segments, IAS 34 Interim Financial Reporting, IFRS 5 Assets Held for Sale and IFRS 4 Insurance Contracts;
- some additional requirements as companies adopting the IFRS will have to comply with its mandatory requirement to produce a statement of cash flows and more information as to related party transactions;
- simpler options allowed, e.g. expensing rather than capitalising borrowing cost;
- simpler recognition, e.g. allowing an amortisation (with a maximum life of 10 years) rather than an annual impairment review for goodwill;
- simpler measurement, e.g. using the historical cost-depreciation model for property, plant and equipment;
- SMEs are not prevented from adopting other options available under full IFRS and may elect to do this if they so decide.

However, in defining an SME it has moved away from the size tests towards a definition based on qualitative factors such as public accountability whereby an SME would be a business that does not have public accountability. Public accountability is implied if outside stakeholders have a high degree of investment, commercial or social interest and if the majority of stakeholders have no alternative to the external financial report for financial information.

It is intended to have a three-yearly review of the implementation of the standard and it is reasonable to expect that the IFRS will evolve based on review findings such as permitting SMEs to revalue property, plant and equipment.

### Longer-term future

This is in some doubt with the issue of the new Accounting Directive in 2013. This is designed to reduce unnecessary and disproportionate administrative costs on small companies by simplifying the preparation of financial statements and reducing the amount of information required by small companies in the notes to financial statements.

Under the Directive, small companies are only required to prepare a balance sheet, a profit and loss account and notes to meet regulatory requirements. When examining the various policy options available to replace the old Accounting Directives, the Commission examined and rejected the option to adopt the *IFRS for SMEs* at EU level as the Commission deemed that *IFRS for SMEs* did not meet the objective of reducing the administrative burden.

## 6.13 Why have there been differences in financial reporting?

Although there have been national standard-setting bodies, this has not resulted in uniform standards. A number of attempts have been made to identify reasons for differences in financial reporting.[23] The issue is far from clear but most writers agree that the following are among the main factors influencing the development of financial reporting:

- the character of the national legal system;
- the way in which industry is financed;
- the relationship of the tax and reporting systems;
- the influence and status of the accounting profession;
- the extent to which accounting theory is developed;
- accidents of history;
- language.

We will consider the effect of each of these.

### 6.13.1 The character of the national legal system

There are two major legal systems, that based on common law and that based on Roman law. It is important to recognise this because the legal systems influence the way in which behaviour in a country, including accounting and financial reporting, is regulated.

Countries with a legal system based on common law include the UK, Ireland, the USA, Australia, Canada and New Zealand. These countries rely on the application of equity to specific cases rather than a set of detailed rules to be applied in all cases. The effect in the UK, as far as financial reporting was concerned, was that there was limited legislation regulating the form and content of financial statements until the government was required to implement the EC Fourth Directive. The directive was implemented in the UK by the passing of the Companies Act 1981 and this can be seen as a watershed because it was the first time that the layout of company accounts had been prescribed by statute in the UK.

English common law heritage was accommodated within the legislation by the provision that the detailed regulations of the Act should not be applied if, in the judgement of the directors, strict adherence to the Act would result in financial statements that did not present a true and fair view.

Countries with a legal system based on Roman law include France, Germany and Japan. These countries rely on the codification of detailed rules, which are often included within their companies legislation. The result is that there is less flexibility in the preparation of financial reports in those countries. They are less inclined to look to fine distinctions to justify different reporting treatments, which is inherent in the common law approach. The existence of detailed rules or existing effective publication requirements also determines their approach to reporting standards as, for example, the reluctance in Germany to support the adoption of IFRS for SMEs.

However, it is not just that common law countries have fewer codified laws than Roman law countries. There is a fundamental difference in the way in which the reporting of commercial transactions is approached. In the common law countries there is an established practice of creative compliance. By this we mean that the spirit of the law is elusive[24] and management is more inclined to act with creative compliance in order to escape effective legal control. By creative compliance we mean that management complies with the form of the regulation but in a way that might be against its spirit, e.g. structuring leasing agreements in the most acceptable way for financial reporting purposes. This is addressed in an *ad hoc* manner with standards requiring the substance of a transaction to determine its treatment in the financial statements or revising individual standards to combat creative compliance.

### 6.13.2 The way in which industry is financed

Accountancy is the art of communicating relevant financial information about a business entity to users. One of the considerations to take into account when deciding what is relevant is the way in which the business has been financed, e.g. the information needs of equity investors will be different from those of loan creditors. This is one factor responsible for international financial reporting differences because the predominant provider of capital is different in different countries.[25] Figure 6.3 makes a simple comparison between domestic equity market capitalisation and Gross Domestic Product (GDP).[26] The higher the ratio, the greater the importance of the equity market compared with loan finance.

We see that in the USA companies have relied more heavily on individual investors to provide finance than in Europe or Japan. An active stock exchange has developed to allow shareholders to liquidate their investments. A system of financial reporting has evolved to satisfy a stewardship need where prudence and conservatism predominate, and to meet the capital market need for fair information[27] which allows interested parties to deal on an equal footing where the accruals concept and the doctrine of substance over form predominate. It is important to note that European statistics are *averages* that do not fully reflect the variation in sources of finance used between, say, the UK (where equity investment is very important) and Germany (where lending is more important). These could be important factors in the development of accounting.

We can see that the European countries have made continuing use of equity finance since 1998 rather than loan finance and this has led to a greater interest in the issue of International Financial Reporting Standards. Whereas lenders had access to management to obtain the information they sought, equity investors rely more on published information.

Since the 1990s there has been a growth globally of institutional investors, such as banks, insurance companies, retirement or pension funds, hedge funds and sovereign wealth funds.

**Figure 6.3 Domestic equity market capitalisation/gross domestic product**

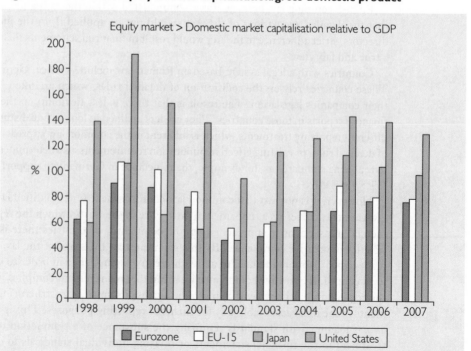

These form an ever-increasing proportion of shareholders. In theory, the information needs of these institutional investors should be the same as those of individual investors. However, in practice, they might be in a position to obtain information by direct access to management and the directors. One effect of this might be that they will become less interested in seeking disclosures in the financial statements – they will have already picked up the significant information at an informal level.

### 6.13.3 The relationship of the tax and reporting systems

In the UK separate rules have evolved for computing profit for tax and computing profit for financial reporting purposes in a number of areas. The legislation for tax purposes tends to be more prescriptive, e.g. there is a defined rate for capital allowances on fixed assets, which means that the reduction in value of fixed assets for tax purposes is decided by the government. The financial reporting environment is less prescriptive but this is compensated for by requiring greater disclosure. For example, there is no defined rate for depreciating non-current assets but there is a requirement for companies to state their depreciation accounting policy. Similar systems have evolved in the USA and the Netherlands.

However, certain countries give primacy to taxation rules and will only allow expenditure for tax purposes if it is given the same treatment in the financial accounts. In France and Germany, the tax rules effectively become the accounting rules for the accounts of individual companies, although the tax influence might be less apparent in consolidated financial statements.

This can lead to difficulties of interpretation, particularly when capital allowances, i.e. depreciation for tax purposes, are changed to secure public policy objectives such as encouraging investment in fixed assets by permitting accelerated write-off when assessing taxable profits. In fact, the depreciation charge against profit would be said by a UK accountant not to be fair, even though it could certainly be legal or correct.[28]

Depreciation has been discussed to illustrate the possibility of misinterpretation because of the different status and effect of tax rules on annual accounts. Other items that require careful consideration include inventory valuations, bad debt provisions, development expenditure and revaluation of non-current assets. There might also be public policy arrangements that are unique to a single country, e.g. the existence of special reserves to reduce taxable profits was common in Scandinavia. It has recently been suggested that level of connection between tax and financial reporting follows a predictable pattern.[29]

### 6.13.4 The influence and status of the accounting profession

The development of a capital market for dealing in shares created a need for reliable, relevant and timely financial information. Legislation was introduced in many countries requiring companies to prepare annual accounts and have them audited. This resulted in the growth of an established and respected accounting profession able to produce relevant reports and attest to their reliability by performing an audit.

In turn, the existence of a strong profession had an impact on the development of accounting regulations. It is the profession that has been responsible for the promulgation of accounting standards and recommendations in a number of countries, such as the UK, the USA, Australia, Canada and the Netherlands.

In countries where there was not the same need to provide market-sensitive information, e.g. in Eastern Europe in the 1980s, accountants were seen purely as bookkeepers and were accorded a low status. However, the position has changed rapidly and there has been a growth in the training, professionalism and contribution for both financial and management accountants as these economies have become market economies.

### 6.13.5 The extent to which accounting theory is developed

Accounting theory can influence accounting practice. Theory can be developed at both an academic and a professional level, but for it to take root it must be accepted by the profession. For example, in the UK, theories such as current purchasing power and current cost accounting first surfaced in the academic world and there were many practising accountants who regarded them then, and still regard them now, as academic.

In the Netherlands, professional accountants receive academic accountancy training as well as the vocational accountancy training that is typical in the UK. Perhaps as a result of that, there is less reluctance on the part of the profession to view academics as isolated from the real world. This might go some way to explaining why it was in the Netherlands that we saw general acceptance by the profession of the idea that for information to be relevant it needed to be based on current value accounting. Largely as a result of pressure from the Netherlands, the Fourth Directive contained provisions that allowed member states to introduce inflation accounting systems.[30]

Attempts have been made to formulate a conceptual framework for financial reporting in countries such as the UK, the USA, Canada and Australia,[31] and the International Standards Committee has also contributed to this field. One of the results has been the closer collaboration between the regulatory bodies, which might assist in reducing differences in underlying principles in the longer term.

### 6.13.6 Accidents of history

The development of accounting systems is often allied to the political history of a country. Scandals surrounding company failures, notably in the USA in the 1920s and 1930s and in the UK in the 1960s and 1980s, had a marked impact on financial reporting in those countries. In the USA the Securities and Exchange Commission was established to control listed companies, with responsibility to ensure adequate disclosure in annual accounts. Ever-increasing control over the form and content of financial statements through improvements in the accounting standard-setting process has evolved from the difficulties that arose in the UK.

International boundaries have also been crossed in the evolution of accounting. In some instances it has been a question of pooling of resources to avoid repeating work already carried out elsewhere, e.g. the Norwegians studied the report of the Dearing Committee in the UK before setting up their new accounting standard-setting system in the 1980s.[32] Other changes in nations' accounting practices have been a result of external pressure, e.g. Spain's membership of the European Community led to radical changes in accounting.[33]

### 6.13.7 Language

Language has often played an important role in the development of different methods of accounting for similar items. Certain nationalities are renowned for speaking only their own language, which has prevented them from benefiting from the wisdom of other nations. There is also the difficulty of translating concepts as well as phrases, where one country has influenced another.

## 6.14 Move towards a conceptual framework

The process of formulating standards has encouraged a constructive appraisal of the policies being proposed for individual reporting problems and has stimulated the development of a conceptual framework. For example, the standard on leasing introduced the idea in UK standards of considering the commercial substance of a transaction rather than simply the legal position.

When the ASC was set up in the 1970s there was no clear statement of accounting principles other than that accounts should be prudent, be consistent, follow accrual accounting procedures and be based on the initial assumption that the business would remain a going concern.

The immediate task was to bring some order into accounting practice. The challenge of this task is illustrated by the ASC report *A Conceptual Framework for Financial Accounting and Reporting: The Possibilities for an Agreed Structure* by R. Macve, published in 1981,[34] which considered that the possibility of an agreed body of accounting principles was remote at that time.

We will see in Chapter 7 the progress that has been made in developing a Conceptual Framework.

## Summary

It is evident from cases such as AEI/GEC, Enron and Parmalat that management cannot be permitted to have total discretion in the way in which it presents financial information in its accounts and rules are needed to ensure uniformity in the reporting of similar commercial transactions. Decisions must then be made as to the nature of the rules and how they are to be enforced.

In the UK the standard-setting bodies have tended to lean towards rules being framed as general principles and accepting the culture of voluntary compliance with explanation for any non-compliance.

Although there is a preference on the part of the standard setters to concentrate on general principles, there is growing pressure from the preparers of the accounts for more detailed illustrations and explanations as to how the standards are to be applied.

Standard setters have recognised that small and medium-sized businesses are not publicly accountable to external users and are given the opportunity to prepare financial statements under standards specifically designed to be useful and cost-effective. The new Accounting Directive now adopts a bottom-up approach with additional requirements for medium-sized and large undertakings.

The expansion in the number of multinational enterprises and transnational investments has led to a demand for a greater understanding of financial statements prepared in a range of countries. This has led to pressure for a single set of high-quality international accounting standards. IFRSs are being used increasingly for reporting to capital markets. At the same time, national standards are evolving to come into line with IFRS.

## REVIEW QUESTIONS

1 Why is it necessary for financial reporting to be subject to both (a) mandatory control and (b) statutory control?

2 Discuss how the Financial Reporting Review Panel plans its activities.

3 The increasing perception is that IFRS is overly complex and is complicating the search for appropriate forms of financial reporting for entities not covered by the EU Regulation.[35] Discuss:

(a) whether the current criteria for defining small and medium-sized companies are appropriate; and

(b) to what extent the provisions of the new Accounting Directive might alleviate the problem.

**4** 'The most favoured way to reduce information overload was to have the company filter the available information set based on users' specifications of their needs.'[36] Discuss how this can be achieved, given that users have differing needs.

**5** Research[37] has indicated that narrative reporting in annual reports is not neutral, with good news being highlighted more than is supported by the statutory accounts and more than bad news. Discuss whether mandatory or statutory regulation could enforce objectivity in narrative disclosures and who should be responsible for such enforcement.

**6** How is it possible to make shareholders aware of the significance of the exercise of judgement by directors which can turn profits of £6 million into losses of £2 million?

**7** Discuss the effect on reporting standards of the way in which industry is financed.

**8** 'Foreign equity investment increases when countries have mandatory adoption of IFRS and effective enforcement'. Discuss why this may not be required by investors in bonds.

**9** 'The existence of a strong accounting profession is more important than uniform accounting standards in providing relevant information'. Discuss.

**10** Discuss the extent to which creative compliance can have a positive influence on financial reporting standards.

**11** Access www.fee.be/images/Comparison_table_-_47_with_2013_Directive.pdf

**(a)** Identify options available for related party transactions; and

**(b)** Discuss why Member State Options are permitted by the EU.

## EXERCISES

### Question 1

Review the Accounting policies of a company in the FTSE 100 and critically discuss the extent to which it satisfies the investor requirements identified in the FRC Lab project report *Accounting Policies and Integration of Related Financial Information July 2014* (www.frc.org.uk/Our-Work/Publications/Financial-Reporting-Lab/Accounting-policies-and-integration-of-related-fin.pdf).

### Question 2

FRS 105 requires that a complete set of financial statements of a micro-entity should include the following: (a) a statement of financial position as at the reporting date with notes included at the foot of the statement; and (b) an income statement for the reporting period. (See www.frc.org.uk/Our-Work/Publications/Accounting-and-Reporting-Policy/FRS-105-The-Financial-Reporting-Standard-applicab.pdf)

**Required:**
**Critically discuss the adequacy of this requirement.**

### Question 3

Consider the interest of the tax authorities in financial reporting regulations. Explain why national tax authorities might be concerned about the transition from domestic accounting standards to IFRS in companies' Annual Reports.

## Question 4

Select an Industry sector from the FTSE 100 companies.

(i) Discuss risk factors you consider material.
(ii) Review the annual report of a company in that sector and critically comment on the coverage of risk factors.

## Question 5

(i) Critically discuss the rationale for allowing businesses in the UK a choice as to which accounting standards to apply, such as IFRS for the Group accounts and FRS 102 for UK subsidiaries.
(ii) Critically evaluate the IASB decision to move from a size criterion to a qualitative criterion in issuing *IFRS for SMEs*.

## Question 6

The FRC in its 2010 publication *Cutting Clutter in Annual Reports* observed that much immaterial information is included in an Annual Report.

**Required:**
Review an Annual Report of a company that interests you and (a) as a potential investor critically comment on information you consider immaterial and (b) as the preparer justify its inclusion.

## Notes

1 G. Whittred and I. Zimmer, *Financial Accounting Incentive Effects and Economic Consequences*, Holt, Rinehart & Winston, 1992, p. 8.
2 Baker Tilly, www.bakertilly.co.uk
3 K. Peasnell, P. Pope and S. Young, 'Breaking the rules', *Accountancy International*, February 2000, p. 76.
4 CESR, *Proposed Statement of Principles of Enforcement of Accounting Standards in Europe*, CESR02–188b Principle 13, October 2002.
5 https://frc.org.uk/Our-Work/Publications/Corporate-Reporting-Review/Coporate-Reporting-Review-Annual-Report-2013.pdf
6 IASC, *Framework for the Preparation and Presentation of Financial Statements*, 1989, adopted by IASB 2001.
7 E. Lee, M. Walker and C. Zeng, *Does IFRS Convergence Affect Financial Reporting Quality in China?*, ACCA Research Report 131. See www.accaglobal.com/content/dam/acca/global/PDF-technical/financial-reporting/rr-131-002.pdf
8 http://ec.europa.eu/internal_market/accounting/ias_en.htm#regulation
9 http://europa.eu/legislation_summaries/internal_market/business/company_law/126009_en.htm
10 EU Directive 2013/34/EU.
11 www.fee.be/images/Factsheet_New_Accounting_Directive_1401.pdf
12 www.a-tvp.si/Documents/guidelines_esma_1293en.pdf
13 S. Li, 'Does mandatory adoption of International Financial Reporting Standards in the European Union reduce the cost of equity capital?', *The Accounting Review*, vol. 85(2), 2009, pp. 607–636.
14 K.M. Shima and E.A. Gordon, 'ITFRS and the regulatory environment: the case of U.S. investor allocation choice', *Journal of Accounting and Public Policy*, vol. 30(5), 2011, pp. 481–500.
15 www.sec.gov

16 IFRS and US GAAP: similarities and differences, www.pwc.com/en_US/us/issues/ifrs-reporting/
publications/assets/ifrs-and-us-gaap-similarities-and-differences-2013.pdf

17 V. Beattie, S. Fearnley and T. Hines, 'Does IFRS undermine UK reporting integrity?', *Accountancy*,
December 2008, pp. 56–57.

18 T. Dunne, S. Fifield, G. Finningham, A. Fox, G. Hanna, C. Helliar, D. Power and M. Veneziani
'*The implementation of IFRS in the UK, Italy and Ireland*', ICAS, 2008.

19 www.kpmg.co.uk/pubs/215748.pdf

20 http://download.pwc.com/ie/pubs/ifrs_survey.pdf

21 www.ifrs.org/IFRS-for-SMEs/Pages/SME-Workshops.aspx

22 ASB, *Financial Reporting Standard for Smaller Entities*, 1997.

23 C. Nobes and R. Parker, *Comparative International Accounting* (7th edition), Pearson Education,
2002, pp. 17–33.

24 J. Freedman and M. Power, *Law and Accountancy: Conflict and Cooperation in the 1990s*, Paul Chapman
Publishing, 1992, p. 105.

25 For more detailed discussion see C. Nobes, 'Towards a general model of the reasons for international
differences in financial reporting', *Abacus*, vol. 3(2), 1998, pp. 162–187.

26 www.eurocapitalmarkets.org/files/images/equity_capGDP_col.jpg

27 C. Nobes, *Towards 1992*, Butterworths, 1989, p. 15.

28 Nobes, op. cit., p. 8.

29 C. Nobes and H.R. Schwencke, 'Modelling the links between tax and financial reporting: a longi-
tudinal examination of Norway over 30 years up to IFRS adoption', *European Accounting Review*,
vol. 15(1), 2006, pp. 63–87.

30 Nobes and Parker, op. cit., pp. 73–75.

31 See S.P. Agrawal, P.H. Jensen, A.L. Meader and K. Sellers, 'An international comparison of
conceptual frameworks of accounting', *International Journal of Accounting*, vol. 24, 1989,
pp. 237–249.

32 *Accountancy*, June 1989, p. 10.

33 See, e.g. B. Chauveau, 'The Spanish *Plan General de Contabilidad:* Agent of development and
innovation?', *European Accounting Review*, vol. 4(1), 1995, pp. 125–138.

34 www.icaew.com/N/media/Files/Events/2012/Regions/London/objectives-of-financial-reporting/
objectives-of-financial-reporting.pdf

35 S. Fearnley and T. Hines, 'How IFRS has destabilised financial reporting for UK non-listed
entities', *Journal of Financial Regulation and Compliance*, vol. 15(4), 2007, pp. 394–408.

36 V. Beattie, *Business Reporting: The Inevitable Change?*, ICAS, 1999, p. 53.

37 V. Tauringana and C. Chong, 'Neutrality of narrative discussion in annual reports of UK listed
companies', *Journal of Applied Accounting Research*, vol. 7(1), 2004, pp. 74–107.

# CHAPTER 7

# Concepts – evolution of an international conceptual framework

## 7.1 Introduction

The main purpose of this chapter is to discuss the rationale underlying financial reporting standards and concepts to apply when there are transactions for which there are no relevant standards.

### Objectives

By the end of this chapter, you should be able to:

- discuss how financial accounting theory has evolved;
- discuss the accounting principles set out in the IASB *Conceptual Framework for Financial Reporting* 2010;
- comment critically on rule-based and principles-based approaches;
- evaluate progress to date in amending the conceptual framework developed in 2010 by the IASB;
- outline the latest developments regarding disclosures and concepts of materiality.

## 7.2 Different countries meant different financial statements

In the previous chapter we discussed the evolution of national and international accounting standards. The need for standards arose initially as a means by which the accounting profession protected itself against litigation for negligence by relying on the fact that financial statements complied with the published professional standards. The standards were based on existing best practice and little thought was given to a theoretical basis.

### Reactive process

Standards were developed by individual countries and it was a reactive process. For example, in the US the Securities and Exchange Commission (SEC) was set up in 1933 to restore investor confidence in financial reporting following the Great Depression. The SEC is an enforcement agency that enforces compliance with US GAAP, which comprises often rule-based standards issued by the FASB.

There has been a similar reactive response in other countries, often reacting to major financial crises and fraud, which has undermined investor confidence in financial statements. As a result, there has been a variety of national standards with national enforcement, e.g. in the UK principles-based standards are issued by the FRC Board.

National standards varied in their quality and in the level of enforcement. This is illustrated by the following comment by the International Forum on Accountancy Development (IFAD):

**Lessons from the crisis**

. . . the Asian crisis showed that under the forces of financial globalisation it is essential for countries to improve . . . the supervision, regulation and transparency of financial systems . . . Efficiency of markets requires reliable financial information from issuers. With hindsight, it was clear that local accounting standards used to prepare financial statements did not meet international standards. Investors, both domestic and foreign, did not fully understand the weak financial position of the companies in which they were investing.

### Need for global standards

With the growth of the global economy there has been a corresponding growth in the need for global standards, so that investors around the world receive the same fair view of a company's results regardless of the legal jurisdiction in which the company is registered.

We will see in this chapter that, in addition to the realisation that global accounting standards were required, there was also growing interest in basing the standards on a conceptual framework rather than fire-fighting with pragmatic standards often dealing with an immediate problem. However, just as there have been different national standards, so there have been different conceptual frameworks.

### Development of financial accounting theory

It is interesting to take a historical overview of the evolution of the financial accounting theory underpinning standards and guiding standard setters to see how it has moved through three phases from the empirical inductive to the deductive and then to a formalised conceptual framework.

## 7.3 Historical overview of the evolution of financial accounting theory

Financial accounting practices have not evolved in a vacuum. They are dynamic responses to changing macro- and micro-conditions which may involve political, fiscal, economic and commercial changes. These can give rise to various theories as to how they should be reflected in financial statements.

For example, in response to high rates of inflation different accounting theories for the accounting treatment of changing prices that were proposed, such as proposals to:

- ignore and apply historical cost accounting; or
- adopt a modified historical cost system where tangible non-current assets are revalued, which has been the norm in the UK; or
- adopt current entry costs reflecting the operating capital maintenance concept; or
- adopt current exit costs; or
- adopt fair values.

Then, when inflation fell in many jurisdictions to levels that did not make historical cost accounting appear to misrepresent the transactions that had occurred, all alternative theories were abandoned.

It is clear from considering just the treatment of changing prices that there could be a variety of accounting treatments for similar transactions. It could be argued that, if annual financial reports are to be useful in making economic decisions, there is a need for **uniformity** or **harmonising** with all entities reporting similar transactions in similar ways and **consistency** in reporting over time within an entity.

We can see that over time there have been three approaches to achieving this: following an empirical inductive approach; or a deductive approach; and developing a conceptual framework. We will consider each of these briefly.

### 7.3.1 An empirical inductive approach

This was the approach followed by the accounting profession prior to 1970. It looked at the practices that existed and attempted to generalise from them.

This tended to be how the technical departments of accounting firms operated. By rationalising what they did, they ensured that the firm avoided clients adopting different financial reporting practices for similar transactions. The technical department's role was to advise partners and staff, i.e. it was a defensive role to avoid any potential charge from a user of the accounts that they had been misled.

Initially a technical circular was regarded as a private good and distribution was restricted to the firm's own staff. However, it then became recognised that it could benefit the firm if its practices were accepted as the industry benchmark, so that in the event of litigation it could rely on this fact.

When the technical advice ceased to be a private good, there was a perceived additional protection for the firm if their defence moved from a positive statement, i.e. this is how we always report inventories in the financial statements, to a normative statement, i.e. this is how we report and this is how all other financial reporters **ought** to report.

Consequently, there has been a growing trend since the 1980s for firms to publish rationalisations for their financial reporting practices. It has been commercially prudent for them to do so. It has also been extremely helpful to academic accountants and their students.

Typical illustrations of the result of such empirical induction are the wide acceptance of the historical cost model and various concepts such as matching and realisation that we discussed in Chapter 2 above. The early standards were produced under this regime, e.g. IAS 2, the standard on inventory valuation.

This approach has played an important role in the evolution of financial reporting practices and will continue to do so. After all, it is the preparers of the financial statements and their auditors who are first exposed to change, whether economic, political or commercial. They are the ones who have to think their way through each new problem that surfaces, for example how to measure and report financial instruments. This means that a financial reporting practice already exists by the time the problem comes to the attention of theoreticians.

This resulted in standards or reporting practices that were based on rationalising what happened in practice, i.e. it established best current practice as the norm. Under this approach there was a general disclosure standard, e.g. IAS 1 *Disclosure of Accounting Policies*, and standards for major specific items, e.g. IAS 2 *Inventories*.

It was thought that the limitations implicit in the empirical inductive approach could be overcome by the deductive approach.

### 7.3.2 A deductive approach

The deductive approach is not dependent on existing practice, which is often perceived as having been tainted because it has been determined by finance directors and auditors. However, the problem remains: from whose viewpoint is the deduction to be made?

Possible alternatives to the preparers and auditors of the accounts are economists and users. However, we saw in Chapter 6 that the economists' approach is appropriate for specific decisions such as capital investment decisions but impractical for financial reporting to stakeholders. As for users, the information they require for decisions has to be considered but their needs are so diverse that they can only be realistically satisfied in a single set of general-purpose accounts. This is why the IASB has been prompted by stakeholders to develop a conceptual framework to underpin IFRSs.

### 7.3.3 A conceptual framework approach

This was promoted in the late 1980s. It was recognised that standards were needed to ensure that financial statements provided the information that users required both to check on management's stewardship and to be able to make informed economic investment decisions.

There were a number of constraints including the requirement that they should satisfy cost/benefit criteria and the acceptance at that time that their implementation could only be achieved by consensus. Consensus was required because a proposed accounting treatment could have different financial reporting consequences, such as when finance leases were required to be reported within the assets and liabilities, so affecting ratios. It could also have direct economic consequences on entities that changed the way in which they made investment decisions.

Consensus was only achieved by permitting entities a choice from alternative accounting treatments. Currently, the IASB is required to carry out an economic impact appraisal of any proposed reporting standard. The aim, then and now, was to base standards on a sound conceptual basis.

The outcome of the wish for a conceptual framework was the publication by the IASC in 1989 of its *Framework for the Preparation and Presentation of Financial Statements.*

## 7.4 Framework for the Preparation and Presentation of Financial Statements

A *Framework* is not a reporting standard. Its main purpose is to provide the IASB with concepts to inform them when developing standards. A secondary purpose is to provide guidance to management when deciding how to report on transactions for which there is no relevant international standard.

It is concerned with general-purpose financial statements that a business enterprise prepares and presents to meet the common information needs of a wide range of users to help them make economic decisions.

The user groups include current and potential investors, employees, lenders, suppliers and other trade creditors, customers, governments and their agencies and the general public. The approach taken by the *Framework* is that it accepts that not all of the information needs of each of the user groups can be met by a single set of financial statements. There has to be a primary user group.

### The primary user group

It assumes, however, that as all users are making economic decisions, there is information in which all users have a common interest and that general-purpose financial statements should satisfy this. It further assumes that because investors are providers of risk capital to the enterprise, financial statements that meet their needs will also meet most of the general financial information needs of other users.

Typical economic decisions that are being made include:

- Assessing by stakeholders:
  - the stewardship or accountability of management;
  - when to buy, hold or sell an equity investment;
  - how much of the distributable profits to pay out as dividends;
  - the ability of the entity to pay and provide other benefits to its employees;
  - the security for amounts lent to the entity.
- Determining by regulatory authorities:
  - taxation policies;
  - how to regulate the activities of entities.

### 7.4.1 Revising the Framework for the Preparation and Presentation of Financial Statements

Just as with the convergence project, the IASB and FASB set up a joint project in 2004 to review the *Framework* in phases aiming to produce concepts relating to objectives and qualitative characteristics, elements and recognition, measurement and presentation and disclosure. There was also to be a phase aimed at reaching a converged IASB–FASB view on the secondary purpose of the framework.

The IASB and FASB worked jointly until 2010. After that date the FASB and the IASB suspended their work on the project to focus their resources on other projects. In 2012, following a public consultation that indicated that users regarded the revision of the *Framework* as a priority, the IASB revived the project as an *IASB-only comprehensive project*.

At that time the IASB resolved that:

- the conceptual framework project should focus on; elements of financial statements, measurement, reporting entity, presentation and disclosure;
- the aim should be to work towards a single discussion paper covering all these areas, rather than separate discussion papers for each area.

The idea was to add to the *Framework* that already existed. We will first discuss the current content of the *Framework* and then consider the latest state of play regarding development.

## 7.5 Conceptual Framework for Financial Reporting 2010

The *Framework* was to be produced in chapters as follows:

- Chapter 1 The objective of general purpose financial reporting
- Chapter 2 The reporting entity
- Chapter 3 Qualitative characteristics of useful financial information
- Chapter 4 The Framework (1989): this chapter containing the remaining text from the 1989 Framework and relevant paragraphs will be replaced by new chapters as the project progresses.

We comment briefly on each chapter.

### 7.5.1 Chapter 1 The objective of financial statements

This is a non-contentious chapter and is currently (in June 2016) part of the published *Framework* document. In the USA, Australia, Canada, the UK and the IASB, the approach has been the same, i.e. commencing with a consideration of the objectives of financial statements, qualitative characteristics of financial information, definition of the elements, and when these are to be recognised in the financial statements. There is a general agreement on these areas.

The fundamental objective of general-purpose financial reporting is to provide financial information about the reporting entity that is useful to present and potential equity investors, lenders and other creditors when making investment and loan decisions. Information is needed to help them assess the prospects for future cash flows which, based to an extent on the review of past performance, will assist in assessing stewardship.

#### What information should be provided to satisfy the information needs?

The *Framework* proposes that information is required on resources controlled by the entity and claims against it and changes in those resources and claims.

The information on resources and claims is provided in the statement of financial position and on changes in resources and claims in the statements of income, cash flows and changes in equity.

##### Statement of financial position

This reports the economic resources and claims. It allows us to assess:

- the financial structure, i.e. capital gearing indicating how profits will be divided between the different sources of finance;
- the ability to repay or raise new financing;
- solvency and liquidity, i.e. current and liquid ratios;
- the possibility of obtaining cash from disposal of assets without disrupting continuing business, i.e. realise readily marketable securities that might have been built up as a liquid reserve.

##### Statement of income

This reports changes in economic resources on an accrual basis. It allows us to assess financial performance defined as the return an entity obtains from the resources it controls. It provides a means to assess past management performance, how effectively resources have been utilised and the capacity to generate cash flows.

##### Statement of cash flows

This reports changes in economic resources on a cash basis free from allocation and valuation issues. It allows us to identify net cash flows from operating, investment and financing activities. It provides a means to review cash flows that had been used when making CAPEX decisions and to assess the feasibility of free cash flows to meet future capital investment requirements and the possible impact on dividend policy.

##### Statement of changes in equity

This reports changes in economic resources – other than from financial performance. It identifies increases or decreases in issued capital and distributions to shareholders.

**Do these financial statements satisfy all user needs?**

The general-purpose financial reports do not and cannot provide all of the information that existing and potential investors, lenders and other creditors need. Users other than investors need to consider information from other sources, for example general economic conditions and expectations, political events and political climate, and industry and company outlooks.

### 7.5.2 Chapter 2 The reporting entity

The chapter on the reporting entity has not yet been fully developed.

### 7.5.3 Chapter 3 Qualitative characteristics of useful financial information

This chapter and is also currently (in June 2016) part of the published *Framework* document. There are two fundamental qualitative characteristics if information is to be decision-useful and not misleading. These are **relevance** and **faithful representation**. There are also characteristics which are referred to as **enhancing**. We will now discuss each of these.

#### (i) Relevance

Relevant financial information is capable of making a difference to the decisions made by users. Financial information is capable of making a difference to decisions if it has **predictive value, confirmatory value** or both.

*Predictive value*

Financial information has predictive value if it can be used as an input to processes employed by users to predict future outcomes. It is used by users in making their own predictions.

*Confirmatory value*

Financial information has confirmatory value if it provides feedback about (confirms or changes) previous evaluations.

*Predictive and confirmatory values*

Predictive and confirmatory values are interrelated. For example, revenue information for the current year, which can be used as the basis for predicting revenues in future years, can also be compared with revenue predictions for the current year that were made in past years.

*Materiality in relation to relevance*

It is defined in IAS 8 *Accounting Policies, Changes in Accounting Estimates and Errors* as being information whose omission or misstatement could, individually or collectively, influence the economic decisions of users.

It is a matter of judgement and decided on a case-by-case basis: what may be material for one company might not be for another – £1 million is a large amount but in relation to a potential misstatement of sales by a large multinational, it is likely to be immaterial. Conversely, if it relates to a disclosure required by legislation, then a comparatively small amount of £10,000 might be seen as material, even for a large multinational, if it relates to a benefit-in-kind which has been wrongly omitted from the disclosure of directors' remuneration.[1]

There are situations in which an item will be judged material and a lower-level value set as a benchmark because of the circumstances, such as if it results in non-compliance with a bank loan or turns a profit into a loss.

### Materiality benchmarks

Materiality is entity-specific. It depends on the size of the item or error judged in the particular circumstances of its omission or misstatement. The need to exercise judgement means that the preparer needs to have a benchmark.

Many accountants and auditors have a rule of thumb,[2] assuming, for example, that if an item falls under a 5% threshold it is not material. This is to be regarded as a starting point only and exclusive reliance on this or any percentage or numerical threshold has no basis in the accounting literature or the law.

It is interesting to note the approach taken in the new enhanced audit reports where the auditors quantify the amount. For example, the following is taken from the Auditors Report in the Tesco 2015 Annual Accounts:

### Overview Materiality

Overall Group materiality for 2014/15 was £50 million, which was based on applying professional judgement, taking into consideration a number of profit based measures and the overall scale of the business. Overall Group materiality in 2013/14 was £150 million.

Their approach to balance sheet items was different as follows:

where misstatements were identified which related to the current period income statement the quantitative materiality set out in the table below (£50 million) was used to determine whether misstatements should be adjusted. For misstatements that did not impact profits and only affected the balance sheet we did not consider it appropriate to use a standard, profit based measure of materiality and our quantitative assessment had regard to whether the misstatement was above 5% of the balance sheet line to which it related and/or 1% of total assets.

### Progress on consideration of materiality in financial reports

ESMA issued a Consultation Paper, *Considerations of Materiality in Financial Reporting*, in 2011. Following the feedback it received, it referred the topic to the IASB for their further consideration. In 2014 the IASB tentatively decided to undertake a project on materiality as part of its Disclosure Initiative. The project should also develop application guidance and educational material. We will discuss these developments further later in the chapter.

## (ii) Faithful representation

Financial reports represent the effect of economic activities in words and numbers. A faithful representation would need to be complete, neutral and free from error.

### Neutral

This means that the information has not been slanted, weighted, emphasised, de-emphasised or otherwise manipulated to increase the probability that financial information will be received favourably or unfavourably by users.

### Freedom from error

Faithful representation does not mean the information is 100% accurate. 'Free from error' means there are no material errors or omissions in the description of the event or transaction and no errors in the process used to produce the reported information.

Taking the reporting of an estimate as an example, a representation of that estimate can be faithful if (a) the amount is described clearly and accurately as being an estimate and (b) the nature and limitations of the estimating process are explained and (c) no errors have been made in selecting and applying an appropriate process for developing the estimate.

### (iii) Enhancing qualities

There are other characteristics that may make the information more useful. These are:

- comparability – allowing for both inter-company and inter-period comparisons;
- verifiability – means that different knowledgeable and independent observers could broadly agree that the report provides a faithful representation of transactions;
- timeliness – information is available to decision makers in time to be capable of influencing their decisions;
- understandability – assumes that users have a reasonable knowledge of business and economic activities.

### 7.5.4 Chapter 4 The framework (1989)

This contained the remaining content of the 1989 *Framework* which was to be eventually replaced after the various phases were completed.

## 7.6 Chapter 4 Content

The content covers (a) underlying assumptions, (b) the definition, recognition and measurement of elements and (c) concepts of capital and capital maintenance.

### (a) Underlying assumptions

The underlying assumptions are that financial statements are prepared on the basis of the following.

*Accruals*
Transactions are recognised when they occur, rather than when cash or its equivalent is received or paid, and they are reported in the financial statements of the periods to which they relate. We have already seen that, in addition to cash receipts and payments, obligations to pay cash in the future and resources that represent cash to be received in the future are also reported.

*Going concern*
The financial statements presume that an enterprise will continue in operation indefinitely or, if that presumption is not valid, disclosure and a different basis of reporting are required, such as preparing the statements using the net realisable value accounting model.

*Consistency*
In order to achieve comparability, the accounting policies are followed consistently from one period to another; any change in an accounting policy is made only to achieve a fairer representation or in response to a change in IFRS requirements.

Transactions reported in the financial statements are classified into groups according to their economic characteristics. These groups are referred to as elements. These elements are **defined** and there are rules as to how they are to be **recognised** and **measured** when reported in the financial statements.

### (b) Defining elements

Assets, Liabilities, Equity, Income and Expense are defined as in Section 7.7.5 below.

### (c) Recognising elements

#### (i) Recognition in the statement of financial position

An **asset** is recognised in the statement of financial position when it is probable that the future economic benefits will flow to the enterprise and the asset has a cost or value that can be measured reliably.

A **liability** is recognised in the statement of financial position when it is probable that an outflow of resources embodying economic benefits will result from the settlement of a present obligation and the amount at which the settlement will take place can be measured reliably.

#### (ii) Recognition in the statement of income

**Income** is recognised in the statement of income when there has been an increase in an asset or a decrease of a liability has arisen that can be measured reliably.

**Expenses** are recognised when there has been a decrease in an asset or an increase of a liability has arisen that can be measured reliably.

### (d) Measurement of all the elements of financial statements

Measurement requires elements to be reported in monetary amounts. The *Framework* recognises that elements are reported using a variety of bases which include historical cost, current cost, net realisable value and present value. It does not give general guidance on the capital maintenance concept to apply but does specify a required base for particular elements on an individual IFRS basis – such as requiring inventory to be reported at the lower of cost and net realisable value.

### (e) Financial and physical concepts of capital and capital maintenance

#### Concepts of capital defined

A financial concept of capital is adopted by most entities in preparing their financial statements. Under this concept, capital is defined as the money invested in the business or as the purchasing power of the money invested in the business represented by the net assets or equity of the business.

Under a physical concept, capital is regarded as the productive capacity of the entity based on, for example, units of output per day, i.e. it looks at operating capability. These are discussed further in Chapter 10 in this volume.

## 7.7 The *Conceptual Framework for Financial Reporting* – latest developments

### 7.7.1 Summary of the approach

When the IASB restarted work on the conceptual framework project, it planned not to reconsider fundamentally the chapters describing the objective of financial reporting and the qualitative characteristics of useful financial information. However, having listened to the comments received on the Discussion Paper, the IASB issued, in May 2015, ED 2015-3, *Conceptual Framework For Financial Reporting*. The comment period for this exposure draft has now expired and the IASB is analysing the comments received from interested parties. The ED divides the *Framework* into eight chapters, which are discussed below.

### 7.7.2 Chapter 1 The objective of general purpose financial reporting

Chapter 1 is the first of two chapters that were finalised as part of the joint IASB–FASB conceptual framework project already discussed. Proposed changes to the current Chapter 1 (see Section 7.5.1 above) are very limited.

### 7.7.3 Chapter 2 Qualitative characteristics of useful financial information

This chapter – the second of the two chapters primarily derived from the existing *Framework* document (and discussed in Section 7.5.3 above) – is also subject to relatively minor changes under the exposure draft's proposals.

However, the IASB proposes to reintroduce a reference to the notion of **prudence** and states that the exercise of prudence supports neutrality. Prudence is defined as 'the exercise of caution when making judgements under conditions of uncertainty'. The chapter also proposes reintroducing a specific reference to the concept of **'substance over form'** when considering the **faithful representation** of a transaction in the financial statements.

### 7.7.4 Chapter 3 Financial statements and the reporting entity

The exposure draft states the objective of financial statements is to provide information about an entity's assets, liabilities, equity, income and expenses that is useful to the users in (a) assessing the **prospects** for future net cash inflows and (b) assessing management's **stewardship** of those resources. This chapter also sets out the **going concern** assumption.

The chapter also discusses the definition of a reporting entity and the boundary of a reporting entity. This boundary is determined by **control**, i.e. consolidation is important.

### 7.7.5 Chapter 4 The elements of financial statements

The main focus of this chapter is on the definitions of assets, liabilities and equity as well as income and expenses. The definitions are given as follows in the exposure draft:

- **Asset:** An asset is a present economic resource controlled by the entity as a result of past events. An economic resource is a right that has the potential to produce economic benefits.
- **Liability:** A liability is a present obligation of the entity to transfer an economic resource as a result of past events.
- **Equity:** Equity is the residual interest in the assets of the entity after deducting all its liabilities.
- **Income:** Income is increases in assets or decreases in liabilities that result in increases in equity, other than those relating to contributions from holders of equity claims (e.g. share issues).
- **Expenses:** Expenses are decreases in assets or increases in liabilities that result in decreases in equity, other than those relating to distributions to holders of equity claims (e.g. dividends to equity shareholders.

The IASB has decided not to consider issues relating to changes in the definitions of liabilities and equity that would address the problems that arise in classifying instruments with characteristics of both liabilities and equity. Exploring those problems has been transferred to the IASB's research project on financial instruments with the characteristics of equity.

### 7.7.6 Chapter 5 Recognition and de-recognition

The exposure draft states that only items that meet the definition of an asset, a liability or equity are to be recognised in the statement of financial position and only items that meet the definition of income or expenses are to be recognised in the statement(s) of financial performance.

**Recognition** depends on three criteria, namely, that their recognition provides users of financial statements with:

1 **relevant** information about the asset or the liability and about any income, expenses or changes in equity;

2 a **faithful representation** of the asset or the liability and of any income, expenses or changes in equity; and

3 information that results in **benefits exceeding the cost** of providing that information.

Nevertheless, the exposure draft also maintains that whether the information provided is useful to users depends on the item and the specific facts and circumstances and requires judgement and possibly varying recognition requirements between standards.

**De-recognition** requires that:

- the assets and liabilities **retained after** the transaction or other event that led to de-recognition must be presented faithfully; and

- the **change** in the entity's assets and liabilities as a result of that transaction or other event must also be presented faithfully.

### 7.7.7 Chapter 6 Measurement

This chapter is dedicated to the description of different measurement bases (historical cost and current value, fair value and value in use [for assets] or fulfilment value [for liabilities]), the information that they provide and their advantages and disadvantages. A table offers an over view of the information provided by various measurement bases. This is reproduced for assets below.

Assets

| | Historical cost measures | Current value measures | |
| --- | --- | --- | --- |
| | | Fair value (market participant assumptions) | Value in use (entity-specific assumptions) |
| Statement of financial position | Recoverable cost of the unconsumed (or uncollected) part of an asset. | Price that would be received to transfer the asset. | Present value of cash flows estimated to arise from the continuing use of the asset and from its disposal at the end of its useful life (includes present value of future costs of transfer). |

The exposure draft also sets out factors to consider when selecting a measurement basis (relevance, faithful representation, enhancing qualitative characteristics, and factors specific to initial measurement) and points out that consideration of the objective of financial reporting, the qualitative characteristics of useful financial information and the cost constraint are likely to result in the selection of different measurement bases for different assets, liabilities and items of income and expense.

Appendix A of the exposure draft supplements Chapter 6 and describes cash-flow-based measurement techniques for cases when a measure determined using a measurement basis cannot be observed. A value-in-use measure can only be determined using such a technique.

### 7.7.8 Chapter 7 Presentation and disclosure

In this chapter, the exposure draft discusses concepts that determine what information is included in the financial statements and how that information should be presented and disclosed.

The statement of comprehensive income is newly described as 'statement of financial performance'; however, the exposure draft does not specify whether this statement should consist of a single statement or two statements, it only requires that a total or sub-total for profit or loss must be provided.

Notably, the exposure draft does not *define* profit or loss, thus the question of exactly what goes into profit or loss or into other comprehensive income is still unanswered. However, the exposure draft does say that the *purpose* of the statement of profit or loss is to:

(a) depict the return that an entity has made on its economic resources during the period; and

(b) provide information that is helpful in assessing prospects for future cash flows and in assessing management's stewardship of the entity's resources.

It goes on to say that because the statement of profit or loss is the primary source of information about an entity's financial performance for the period, there is a *presumption* that all income and all expenses will be included in the statement of profit or loss. This presumption can be rebutted in some circumstances such as when excluding those income or expenses from the statement of profit or loss would enhance the relevance of the information in that statement for the period.

### 7.7.9 Chapter 8 Concepts of capital maintenance

The proposals in this chapter were taken over from the existing *Conceptual Framework* (the current Chapter 4 – discussed in Section 7.5 previously) with minor changes for consistency of terminology. The IASB states that it would consider revising the description and discussion of capital maintenance if it were to carry out a future project on accounting for high inflation. However, it also states that no such work is currently planned.

## 7.8 Current developments – concept of materiality

### 7.8.1 The issue

The concept of materiality is fundamental to financial reporting. Financial statements should provide useful financial information to the user. In order for financial information to be useful, it has to be reliable. Reliable financial information needs to present, in all *material* respects, a true and fair view of the financial performance of an entity for a reporting period and of its financial position at the end of the reporting period.

The IASB initiated a project on materiality in 2014. Its objective is to help preparers, auditors and regulators use judgement when applying the concept of materiality in order to make financial reports more meaningful.

The IASB has issued a *Practice Statement*. It is not a standard and so entities applying IFRSs are not required to comply with it unless specifically required by their jurisdiction. Furthermore, any non-compliance will not prevent an entity's financial statements from complying with IFRSs, if they otherwise do so. However, the application of the general concept of materiality is a key criterion in forming an opinion on the truth and fairness of financial statements.

### 7.8.2 The latest IASB proposals

#### Characteristics of materiality

The *Practice Statement* builds on the definition of materiality in the Exposure Draft ED/2015/3, *Conceptual Framework for Financial Reporting* (considered in Section 7.6 above), which states: 'Information is material if omitting it or misstating it could influence decisions that the primary users of general purpose financial reports make on the basis of financial information about a specific reporting entity.'

#### Presentation and disclosure in the financial statements

The *Statement* notes that in preparing the financial statements, management should consider the objective of providing information that is useful to users in assessing the prospects for future net cash inflows and in assessing its stewardship of the entity's resources. This objective provides the context for materiality judgements and may lead to different materiality assessments in different parts of the financial statements.

The IASB proposes three steps:

1 To assess what information should be presented in the primary financial statements.

2 To assess what information should be disclosed within the notes (including assessment of appropriate emphasis).

3 To review the financial statements as a whole to ensure that the financial statements are a comprehensive document with an appropriate overall mix and balance of information.

The IASB also states that an entity shall not reduce the understandability of its financial statements by obscuring material information with immaterial information or by aggregating material items that have different natures or functions, although it concedes that 'IFRS does not prohibit entities from disclosing immaterial information'.

#### Omissions and misstatements

The *Statement* notes that the materiality of identified errors or omissions needs to be assessed individually and on the basis of the financial statements as a whole. Material misstatements or omissions that offset each other still are considered material misstatements of the financial statements as such. It also states that intentionally made misstatements shall always be considered material.

#### Initial application and transition

Given the proposed practice *Statement* is not a mandatorily applicable IFRS, it does contain neither a proposed effective date nor transition guidance. The IASB also notes that the *Statement* may undergo further changes even after being finalised depending on further developments in the conceptual framework project.

## Summary

User needs have been accepted as paramount; qualitative characteristics of information have been specified; the elements of financial statements and the presentation of financial information are being revised in the IASB-only comprehensive project.

The intention remains to produce general-purpose financial statements that present a fair view. This is not achieved by detailed rules and regulations; the exercise of judgement will continue to be needed, based on a sound conceptual framework.

Judgement will be required at many levels. For example, in classifying and reporting an asset judgement is required as to (a) whether an economic resource exists, then (b) was it the result of a past event, then (c) is it controlled, then (d) what is the relevant measurement base, then (e) is it material in the context of the company or in the context of the company or group, then finally (f) should there be disclosure of the approach that had been taken when making estimates to arrive at the reported value.

Many of these judgements could be improved if there were to be more guidance from the IASB on the application of concepts and standards. It is the IASB's stated intention to provide this and additional educational material.

The question of the measurement base that should be used has yet to be settled. The IASB seems to favour choosing that which provides the most relevant information for investors making economic decisions.

The *Framework* sees the objective of financial statements as providing information about the financial position, performance and financial adaptability of an enterprise that is useful to a wide range of users for accountability and in making economic decisions. It recognises that they are limited because they largely show the financial effects of past events and do not necessarily show non-financial information.

As this material is being written, the IASB is analysing the comments made to the latest *Framework* exposure draft. Much of the comments have been broadly supportive of the IASB's approach. However, concern has been expressed by a number of respondents on the following aspects of the document:

1  The lack of discussion of the meaning of 'true and fair' – a fundamental concept in financial reporting.

2  The IASB's position regarding the concept of 'prudence' as supporting the concept of 'neutrality'. There are many examples of prudence being applied 'asymetrically' in practice, e.g. on long-term contracts with customers where losses, rather than profits, are expected.

3  The continued focus on assets and liabilities as the bedrock of identifying elements of financial statements, rather than income and expense.

4  The focus of discussion of measurement basis in the exposure draft (being solely on historical versus current cost and not considering entry versus exit values).

5  The lack of guidance on the recognition of income and expense in profit or loss rather than other comprehensive income, and on the extent to which income and expense initially recognised in other comprehensive income should be reclassified to profit or loss in a subsequent period.

6  The lack of any meaningful progress on the issue of concepts of capital and capital maintenance.

It is too early to say how the comments received may persuade the IASB to make further adjustments to the *Framework* document before it is finally published in its completed form.

## REVIEW QUESTIONS

1 'The replacement of accrual accounting with cash flow accounting would avoid the need for a conceptual framework.' Discuss.

2 'The IASB is proposing to allow the selective choice of a measurement base.' Discuss why this may or may not be preferable to adopting a single measurement base for all elements.

3 Financial accounting theory has accumulated a vast literature. A cynic might be inclined to say that the vastness of the literature is in sharp contrast to its impact on practice.

   (a) Describe the different approaches that have evolved in the development of accounting theory.

   (b) Assess their varying impacts on standard setting.

4 'Rules-based accounting adds unnecessary complexity, encourages financial engineering and does not necessarily lead to a "true and fair view" or a "fair presentation".' Discuss.

5 'Tax avoidance would not occur if there was a principle- rather than rule-based approach.' Discuss.

6 Explain what you understand by a balance sheet approach to income determination and how this is demonstrated in the definition of elements.

7 Explain how a company assesses materiality when attempting to report a true and fair view of its income.

8 'The key qualitative characteristics in the *Conceptual Framework* are relevance and faithful representation. Preparers of financial statements may face a dilemma in satisfying both criteria at once.' Discuss situations where there might be a conflict.

9 'An asset is to be defined in the *Framework* as an economic resource which an entity controls as a result of past events.' Discuss whether property, plant and equipment automatically qualify as assets.

10 'The *Conceptual Framework* regards neutrality as necessary for financial statements to provide a faithful representation of transactions. However, the view of some of the respondents to the exposure draft was that neutrality is impossible to achieve because if it is accepted that information must be relevant as a tool to influence decision making then it could not be neutral.' Discuss.

11 The concept of materiality is fundamental to financial statement preparation. Therefore the IASB's proposed *Practice Statement* on materiality should have the status of a financial reporting standard. Discuss this viewpoint.

12 Select three companies in any sector and review how the auditors have approached setting a materiality threshold in the new enhanced audit reports. Assess if there is a common approach to materiality in relation to profits and balance sheet items.

## EXERCISES

### Question 1

The following extract is from *Conceptual Framework for Financial Accounting and Reporting: Elements of Financial Statements and Their Measurement*, FASB 3, December 1976:

The benefits of achieving agreement on a conceptual framework for financial accounting and reporting manifest themselves in several ways. Among other things, a conceptual framework can (1) guide the body responsible for establishing accounting standards, (2) provide a frame of reference for resolving accounting questions in the absence of a specific promulgated standard, (3) determine bounds for judgement in preparing financial statements, (4) increase financial statement users' understanding of and confidence in financial statements, and (5) enhance comparability.

**Required:**
(a) **Define a conceptual framework.**
(b) **Critically examine why the benefits provided in the above statements are likely to flow from the development of a conceptual framework for accounting.**

## Question 2

The following extract is from 'Comments of Leonard Spacek', in R.T. Sprouse and M. Moonitz, *A Tentative Set of Broad Accounting Principles for Business Enterprises,* Accounting Research Study No. 3, AICPA, New York, 1962, reproduced in A. Belkaoui, *Accounting Theory,* Harcourt Brace Jovanovich.

A discussion of assets, liabilities, revenue and costs is premature and meaningless until the basic principles that will result in a fair presentation of the facts in the form of financial accounting and financial reporting are determined. This fairness of accounting and reporting must be for and to people, and these people represent the various segments of our society.

**Required:**
**Discuss the extent to which the IASB conceptual framework satisfies the above definition of fairness.**

## Question 3

The following is an extract from *Accountancy Age,* 25 January 2001:

A powerful and 'shadowy' group of senior partners from the seven largest firms has emerged to move closer to edging control of accounting standards from the world's accountancy regulators . . . they form the Global Steering Committee . . . The GSC has worked on plans to improve standards for the last two years after scathing criticism from investors that firms produced varying standards of audit in different countries.

**Required:**
**Discuss the effect on standard setting if control were to be edged from the world's accountancy regulators and back in the hands of the profession.**

## Question 4

The FRC in its 2009 publication *Louder than Words – Principles and Actions for Making Corporate Reports Less Complex and More Relevant* included a call for action to 'Ensure disclosure requirements are relevant and proportionate to the risks', stating that 'We would like to see a project on disclosure which investigates the characteristics of useful disclosures and the main objectives of financial reporting disclosure. . . . Ideally, we believe another organisation could constructively kick off this work with a view to providing recommendations to the relevant regulators, including the International Accounting Standards Board (IASB).'

Required:

Critically discuss how a company could determine whether any disclosure is proportionate to the risks and whether this implies that there should be fewer mandatory disclosures which lead to ever more complexity.

## Question 5

The following are criticisms made of the IASB's 2015 exposure draft proposing updates to its *Conceptual Framework*.

1 The framework does not consider the meaning of the term 'true and fair view' despite this being a fundamental characteristic discussed in International Financial Reporting Standards.

2 The identification of prudence as a fundamental concept should focus on its asymmetric application because this is current practice in a number of specific areas.

3 The discussion of measurement bases is incomplete as it does not address the issue of entry values versus exit values despite the use of such values by preparers under current practice.

4 The exposure draft provides no guidance on the issue of reclassification of gains and losses despite this matter being dealt with inconsistently in a number of existing International Financial Reporting Standards.

Required

Discuss the extent to which the above criticisms could be justified by reference to specific International Financial Reporting Standards.

## Notes

1 Tech 03/08 Guidance on materiality in Financial Reporting by UK entities, ICAEW, 2008 http://www.icaew.com/~/media/Files/Technical/technical-releases/legal-and-regulatory/ TECH-03-08-Guidance-on-Materiality-in-Financial-Reporting-by-UK-entities.pdf

2 www.sec.gov/interps/account/sab99.htm

# CHAPTER 8

# Ethical behaviour and implications for accountants

## 8.1 Introduction

The main purpose of this chapter is for you to have an awareness of the need for ethical behaviour by accountants to complement the various accounting and audit standards issued by the International Accounting Standards Board (IASB), the International Auditing and Assurance Standards Board (IAASB) and professional accounting bodies.

### Objectives

By the end of this chapter, you should be able to discuss:

● the meaning of ethical behaviour;
● the relationship of ethics to standard setting;
● the main provisions of the IFAC *Code of Ethics for Professional Accountants*;
● the implications of ethical values for the principles- versus rules-based approaches to accounting standards;
● the problem of defining principles and standards where there are cultural differences;
● the implications of unethical behaviour for stakeholders using the financial reports;
● the type of ethical issues raised for accountants in business;
● the role of whistle-blowing.

## 8.2 The meaning of ethical behaviour

Individuals in an organisation have their own ethical guidelines which may vary from person to person. These may perhaps be seen as social norms which can vary over time. For example, the relative importance of individual and societal responsibility varies over time.

### 8.2.1 Individual ethical guidelines

Individual ethical guidelines or personal ethics are the result of a varied set of influences or pressures. As an individual each of us 'enjoys' a series of ethical pressures or influences including the following:

● Parents – the first and, according to many authors, the most crucial influence on our ethical guidelines.

- Family – the family which is common in Eastern societies (aunts, uncles, grandparents and so on) can have a significant impact on personal ethics; the family which is more common in Western societies (just parent(s) and siblings) can be equally as important but is more narrowly focused.

- Social group – the ethics of our 'class' (either actual or aspirational) can be a major influence.

- Peer group – the ethics of our 'equals' (again either actual or aspirational) can be another major influence.

- Religion – ethics based in religion are more important in some cultures, e.g. Islamic societies have some detailed ethics demanded of believers as well as major guidelines for business ethics. However, even in supposedly secular cultures, individuals are influenced by religious ethics.

- Culture – this is also a very effective formulator of an individual's ethics.

- Professional – when an individual becomes part of a professional body then they are subject to the ethics of the professional body.

Given the variety of influences it is natural that there will be a variety of views on what is acceptable ethical behaviour. For example, as an accounting student, how would you handle ethical issues? Would you personally condone cheating? Would you refrain from reporting cheating in exams and assignments by friends? Would you resent other students being selfish such as by hiding library books which are very helpful for an essay? Would you resent cheating in exams by others because you do not cheat and therefore are at a disadvantage? Would that resentment be strong enough to get you to report the fact that there is cheating to the authorities even if you did not name the individuals involved?

### 8.2.2 Professional ethical guidelines

A managing director of a well-known bank described his job as deciding contentious matters for which, after extensive investigation by senior staff, there was no obvious solution. The decision was referred to him because all proposed solutions presented significant downside risks for the bank. Ethical behaviour can be similarly classified. There are matters where there are clearly morally correct answers and there are dilemmas where there are conflicting moral issues.

Professional codes of conduct tend to provide solutions to common issues which the profession has addressed many times. However, the professional code of ethics is only the starting point in the sense that it can never cover all the ethical issues an accountant will face and does not absolve accountants from dealing with other ethical dilemmas.

## 8.3 The accounting standard-setting process and ethics

Standard setters seem to view the process as similar to physics in the sense of trying to set standards with a view to achieving an objective measure of reality. However, some academics suggest that such an approach is inappropriate because the concepts of profit and value are not physical attributes but 'man-made' dimensions. For instance, for profit we measure the progress of the business but the concept of progress is a very subjective attribute which has traditionally omitted public costs such as environmental and social costs. The criterion of fairness has been seen as satisfied by preparing income statements on principles such as going concern and accrual when measuring profit and neutrality when presenting the income statement.

What if fairness is defined differently? For example, the idea of basing accounting on the criterion of fairness to all stakeholders (financiers, workers, suppliers, customers and the community) was made by Leonard Spacek[1] before the formation of the FASB. However, this view was not appreciated by the profession at that time. We now see current developments in terms of environmental and social accounting which are moves in that direction but, even so, Corporate Social Responsibility (CSR) reports are not incorporated into the financial statements prepared under IFRSs and constitute supplementary information that is not integrated into the accounting measures themselves.

### Ethics and neutrality

The accounting profession sees ethical behaviour in standard setting as ensuring that accounting is neutral. Their opponents think that neutrality is impossible and that accounting has a wide impact on society and thus to be ethical the impact on all parties affected should be taken into consideration.

The ASB and EFRAG addressed this with the issue of a Position Paper in 2012. The Paper acknowledged that accounting standards will potentially result in both micro-economic and macro-economic effects. At the micro level the standard setter should identify, analyse and take into account the effects that the new accounting standard or amendment is expected to have on investors and reporting entities. The standard setter should therefore focus on the intended micro-economic effects of the standard.

Macro-economic effects could affect the decisions of the standard setter without compromising the objective of improved financial reporting. For example, minimising adverse effects by selecting among alternatives that result in the same quality of financial reporting outcome.

The accounting profession does not address ethics at the macro level other than in pursuing neutrality, but rather focuses its attention on actions after the standards and laws are in place. The profession seeks to provide ethical standards which will increase the probability of those standards being applied in an ethical fashion at the micro level where accountants apply their individual skills.

The accounting profession through its body the International Federation of Accountants (IFAC) has developed a *Code of Ethics for Professional Accountants*.[2] That code looks at fundamental principles as well as specific issues which are frequently encountered by accountants in public practice, followed by those commonly faced by accountants in business. The intention is that the professional bodies and accounting firms 'shall not apply less stringent standards than those stated in this code' (p. 4).

## 8.4 The IFAC *Code of Ethics for Professional Accountants*

The IFAC Fundamental Principles are:

(i) 'A distinguishing mark of the accountancy profession is its acceptance of the responsibility to act in the public interest . . . ' (100.1).

(ii) 'A professional accountant shall comply with the following fundamental principles:

    (a) *Integrity* – to be straightforward and honest in all professional and business relationships.

    (b) *Objectivity* – to not allow bias, conflict of interest or undue influence of others to override professional or business judgements.

    (c) *Professional Competence and Due Care* – to maintain professional knowledge and skill at the level required to ensure that a client or employer receives competent professional services and to act diligently in accordance with applicable technical and professional standards.

(d) *Confidentiality* – to respect the confidentiality of information acquired as a result of professional and business relationships and, therefore, not disclose any such information to third parties without proper and specific authority, unless there is a legal or professional right or duty to disclose, nor use the information for the personal advantage of the professional accountant or third parties.

(e) *Professional Behaviour* – to comply with relevant laws and regulations and avoid any action that discredits the profession' (100.5).

### 8.4.1 Acting in the public interest

The first underlying statement that accountants should act in the public interest is probably more difficult to achieve than is imagined. This requires accounting professionals to stand firm against accounting standards which are not in the public interest, even when politicians and company executives may be pressing for their acceptance. Owing to the fact that, in the conduct of an audit, the auditors have mainly dealings with the management it is easy to lose sight of who the clients actually are.

For example, the expression 'audit clients' is commonly used in professional papers and academic books when they are referring to the management of the companies being audited. It immediately suggests a relationship which is biased towards management when, legally, the client may be either the shareholders as a group or specific stakeholders. Whilst it is a small but subtle distinction it could be the start of a misplaced orientation towards seeing the management as the client.

### 8.4.2 Fundamental principles

The five fundamental principles are probably uncontentious guides to professional conduct. It is the application of those guides in specific circumstances which provides the greatest challenges. The IFAC paper provides guidance in relation to public accountants covering appointments, conflicts of interest, second opinions, remuneration, marketing, acceptance of gratuities, custody of client assets, objectivity and independence. In regard to accountants in business they provide guidance in the areas of potential conflicts, preparation and reporting of information, acting with sufficient expertise, financial interests and inducements.

It is not intended to provide here all the guidance which the IFAC provides, and if students want that detail they should consult the original document.[2] This chapter will provide a flavour of the coverage relating to accountants in public practice and accountants in business.

### 8.4.3 Problems arising for accountants in practice

#### Appointments

Before accepting appointments public accountants should consider the desirability of accepting the client given the business activities involved, particularly if there are questions of their legality. They also need to consider (a) whether the current accountant of the potential client has advised of any professional reasons for not becoming involved and (b) whether they have the competency required considering the industry and their own expertise. Nor should they become involved if they already provide other services which are incompatible with being the auditor or if the size of the fees would threaten their independence. (Whilst it is not stated in the code the implication is that it is better to avoid situations which are likely to lead to difficult ethical issues.)

### Second opinions

When an accountant is asked to supply a second opinion on an accounting treatment it is likely that the opinion will be used to undermine an accountant who is trying to do the right thing. It is therefore important to ascertain that all relevant information has been provided before issuing a second opinion, and if in doubt decline the work.

### Remuneration

Remuneration must be adequate to allow the work to be done in a professional manner.

Commissions received from other parties must not be such as to make it difficult to be objective when advising your client and in any event must at least be disclosed to clients. Some accountants have addressed that by passing the commissions on to their client and charging a flat fee for the consulting.

### Marketing

Marketing should be professional and should not exaggerate or make negative comments about the work of other professionals.

### Independence

The accountant and their close relatives should not accept gifts, other than trivial ones, from clients. IFAC provides that:

> A professional accountant in public practice who provides an assurance service shall be independent of the assurance client. Independence of mind and in appearance is necessary to enable the professional accountant in public practice to express a conclusion.

Professional firms have their own criterion level as to the value of gifts that can be accepted. For example, the following is an extract from the KPMG Code of Conduct:

> Qn: I manage a reproduction center at a large KPMG office. We subcontract a significant amount of work to a local business. The owner is very friendly and recently offered to give me two free movie passes. Can I accept the passes?

> Ans: Probably. Here, the movie passes are considered a gift because the vendor is not attending the movie with you. In circumstances where it would not create the appearance of impropriety, you may accept reasonable gifts from third parties such as our vendors, provided that the value of the gift is not more than $100 and that you do not accept gifts from the same vendor more than twice in the same year.

## 8.4.4 Problems arising for accountants in business

In relation to accountants in business the major problem identified by the code seems to be the financial pressures which arise from substantial financial interests in the form of shares, options, pension plans and dependence on employment income to support themselves and their dependants. When these depend on reporting favourable performance it is difficult to withstand the pressure.

Every company naturally wants to present its results in the most favourable way possible and investors expect this and it is part of an accountant's expertise to do this. However, the ethical standards require compliance with the law and accounting standards subject to the overriding requirement for financial statements to present a fair view. Misreporting and the omission of additional significant material which would change the assessment of the financial position of the company are unacceptable.

Accountants need to avail themselves of any internal steps to report pressure to act unethically and if that fails to produce results they need to be willing to resign.

### 8.4.5 Threats to compliance with the fundamental principles

The IFAC document has identified five types of threats to compliance with their fundamental principles and they will be outlined below. The objective of outlining these potential threats is to make you sensitive to the types of situations where your ethical judgements may be clouded and where you need to take extra steps to ensure you act ethically. The statements are deliberately broad to help you handle situations not covered specifically by the guidelines. IFAC para 100.12 provides the following classification:

Threats fall into one or more of the following categories:

(a) Self-interest threat – the threat that a financial or other interest will inappropriately influence the accountant's judgment or behavior;

(b) Self-review threat – the threat that a professional accountant will not appropriately evaluate the results of a previous judgment made or service performed by another individual within the professional accountant's firm or employing organization;

(c) Advocacy threat – the threat that a professional accountant will promote a client's or employer's position to the point that the professional accountant's objectivity is compromised;

(d) Familiarity threat – the threat that due to a long or close relationship with a client or employer, a professional accountant will be too sympathetic to their interests or too accepting of their work; and

(e) Intimidation threat – the threat that a professional accountant will be deterred from acting objectively because of actual or perceived pressures.

## 8.5 Implications of ethical values for the principles – versus rules-based approaches to accounting standards

It is common in the literature for authors to quote Milton Friedman as indicating that the role of business is to focus on maximising profits, and also to cite Adam Smith as justification for not interfering in business affairs. In many cases those arguments are misinterpreting the authors.

### Societal norms

Milton Friedman recognised that what business people should do was maximise profits. He knew that without laws to give greater certainty in regard to business activities, and the creation of trust, it was not possible to have a highly efficient economy. Thus he accepted laws which facilitated business transactions and norms in society which also helped to create a cooperative environment. Thus the norms in society set the minimum standards of ethical and social activity which businesses must engage in to be acceptable to those with whom they interact.

### Equitable exchanges

Adam Smith (in *The Wealth of Nations*) did not say 'do not interfere with business'; rather, he assumed the existence of the **conditions necessary to facilitate fair and equitable**

**exchanges.** He also suggested that government should interfere to prevent monopolies but should not interfere as a result of lobbying of business groups because their normal behaviour is designed to create monopolies. He also assumed that those who did not meet ethical standards might make initial gains but would be found out and shunned. His other major book (*The Theory of Moral Sentiments*) was on morality so there is no doubt that he thought ethics were a normal and essential part of society and business.

### How does this relate to accounting standards?

The production of accounting standards is only the starting point in the application of accounting standards. We have seen that accountants can apply the standards to the letter of the law and still not achieve reporting that conveys the substance of the performance and financial state of the business. This is because businesses can structure transactions so as to avoid the application of a standard. For example, by taking liabilities off the balance sheet, such as when a company does not want to capitalise a lease, it arranges for a change in the lease terms so that it is reported as a note and not shown as a liability on the face of the accounts.

It is that type of gamesmanship which has worried accounting standard setters. The issue is whether such games are appropriate, and if they aren't, why haven't they been prevented by the ethical standards of the accountants?

### How does the accounting profession attempt to ensure that financial reports reflect the substance of a transaction?

We have seen that standards have been set in many national jurisdictions and now internationally by the IASB, in order to make financial statements fair and comparable. The number of standards varies between countries and is described as rules-based or principles-based according to the number of standardised accounting treatments.

#### Rules-based

Where there are many detailed standards as in the US, the system is described as 'rules-based' in that it attempts to specify the uniform treatment for many types of transactions. This is both a strength and a weakness in that the very use of precise standards as the only criterion leads to the types of games to get around the criteria that were mentioned earlier for lease accounting. One solution to combat this behaviour is to adopt a principles-based approach to support (or replace) the rules.

#### Principles-based

Where there are fewer standards as in the UK, the system is referred to as 'principles-based'. In the principles-based system there is greater reliance on the application of the 'true and fair' override to (a) report unusual situations and (b) address the issue of whether the accounts prepared in accordance with existing standards provide a fair picture for the decisions to be made by the various users and provide additional information where necessary.

Whilst these are positive applications the override criteria can also be misused. For example, many companies during the 'dot-com' boom around the year 2000 produced statements of **normalised** earnings. The argument was that they were in the set-up phase and many of the costs they were incurring were one-offs. To get a better understanding of the business, readers were said to need to know what an ongoing result was likely to be. So they removed set-up costs and produced **normalised** or **sustainable** earnings which suggested the company was inherently profitable. Unfortunately, many of these companies failed because those one-off costs were not one-off and had to be maintained to keep a customer base.

### Does a principles-based approach achieve true and fair reports?

The US regulators and the IASB have agreed that the principles-based approach should be adopted. However, this still leaves unanswered the question as to whether this approach can give a true and fair view to every stakeholder. Shareholders are recognised in all jurisdictions but the rights of other parties may vary according to the legal system. When, for example, do the rights of lenders become paramount? Should the accounts be tailored to suit employees when the legal system in some jurisdictions recognises that companies are not just there to support owners but have major responsibilities to recognise the preservation of employment wherever possible?

Can general-purpose accounts (whether rules-based or principles-based) ever be appropriate for the many purposes for which they are routinely used?

## 8.5.1 The problem of linking principles to accounting standards

The current conceptual framework assumes that we need to produce general-purpose financial accounts using understandability, relevance, reliability and comparability as guiding criteria. However, the individual standards do not demonstrate how those principles lead to the standards which have been produced.

## 8.5.2 The principles-based approach and ethics

The preceding discussion looked at the principle of true and fair or its equivalent from an accountant's perspective which is often seen as being achieved by following a reporting standard. However, even then there is an element of subjective judgement and it would be helpful to have an ethical concept of fairness expressed in everyday language.

### Idea of superfairness

William Baumol, a celebrated economist, provides the interesting concept of superfairness[3] which would help with this type of ethical decision. He says if you didn't know what side of the transaction you were going to be on, what would you consider to be fair? If you didn't know whether you were going to be a company executive, or an auditor, or a buyer of shares, or a seller of shares, what do you think would be a fair representation of the company's performance and financial position?

### Shift from shareholder orientation

It would, in order to avoid ambiguity, have to spell out 'fair to whom and for what purpose'. This is because at the present time society is in a process of reassessing the role of business relative to the demands by society to achieve high employment rates, to overcome environmental problems and to achieve fair treatment of all countries. Essentially this is suggesting that, given the changing orientation, consideration may have to be given to ethical criteria even if there is only a partial shift from a shareholder orientation to a balancing of competing claims in society.

Daniel Friedman (2008, p. 179)[4] says: 'The greatest challenge is to realign morals and markets so that they work together, rather than at cross purposes.' This will need a balancing act specific to the problem faced. In other words it would have to be principle driven.

## 8.5.3 The problem of defining principles and standards where there are cultural differences

Cultural differences may lead to different principles being formulated and applied. For example, the IASB has defined assets to be reported in the financial statements in such a way that human assets and social costs are not included. As regards application, an accountant in preparing accounts will always have a potential clash between what his or her employer and superior wants, what his or her profession requires and what is best from an ethical or community perspective.

This raises questions such as:

- 'What grounds are there for different accounting being applicable to different countries?'

- 'Should there be different principles if the purpose of accounting is not the same in all countries, with some countries placing, say, greater emphasis on the impact on employees or the community?'

- 'How do cultural norms and religion affect ethics in both the formulation and the interpretation of individual guidelines?'

- 'Is it correct to assume that shareholders in every country have identical information needs and apply identical ethical criteria in assessing a company's operations?'

### 8.5.4 Research into the impact of different cultural characteristics on behaviour

An interesting piece of research compared the attitudes of students in the USA and the UK to cheating and found the US students more likely to cheat.[5] The theoretical basis of the research was that different cultural characteristics, such as uncertainty avoidance or conversely the tolerance for ambiguity, lead to different attitudes to ethics.

#### Implication for multinationals

This means uniform ethical guidelines will not lead to uniform applications in multinational companies unless the corporate culture is much stronger than the country culture. This has implications for multinational businesses that want the accounts prepared in the different countries to be uniform in quality.

#### Implication for the profession

It is significant for audit firms that want their sister firms in other countries to apply the same standards to audit judgements. It is important to investment firms that are making investments throughout the world on the understanding that accounting and ethical standards mean the same things in all major security markets. It is one of the reasons that the US is reluctant to adopt IFRS as a replacement for its own US GAAP because it is not convinced that IFRSs are applied uniformly across the world.

Where there are differences in legal and cultural settings then potentially the correct accounting will also differ if a principles-based approach is adopted. Currently Western concepts dominate accounting but if the world power base shifts, either to several world centres of influence or to a new dominant world power, then principles of accounting may have to reflect that.

## 8.6 Ethics in the accountant's work environment – a research report

The Institute of Chartered Accountants in Scotland issued a discussion paper report[6] titled 'Taking ethics to heart' based on research into the application of ethics in practice. This section will discuss some of the findings of that report.

### A student's perspective

From a student's perspective one of the interesting findings was that many accountants could not remember the work on ethics which they did as students and therefore had little to draw upon to guide them when problems arose. There was agreement that students need to get more experience in dealing with case studies so as to enhance their ethical-decision-making skills. This should be reinforced throughout their careers by continuing professional development. The training should sensitise accountants so that they can easily recognise ethical situations and develop skills in resolving the dilemmas.

### A trainee's perspective

Exposure to ethical issues is usually low for junior positions, although even then there can be clear and grey issues. For example, padding an expense claim and overstating overtime are clear issues, whereas how to deal with information that has been heard in a private conversation between client staff is less clear. What if a conversation is overheard where one of the factory staff says that products which are known to be defective have been dispatched at the year-end? Would your response be different if you had been party to the conversation? Would your response be different if it had been suggested that there was a risk of injury due to the defect? Is it ethical to inform your manager or is it unethical not to inform?

### A senior's perspective

Normally exposure to ethical issues increases substantially at the manager level and continues in senior management positions. However, the significance of ethical decision making has increased with the expansion of the size of both companies and accounting practices. The impact of decisions can be more widespread and profound. Further, there has been an increase in litigation, potentially exposing the accountant to more external review. Greater numbers of accounting and auditing standards can lead to a narrower focus, making it harder for individual accountants to envisage the wider ethical dimensions and to get people to consider more than the detailed rules.

Given the likelihood of internal or external review, the emphasis that many participants in the study placed on asking 'How would this decision look to others?' seems a sensible criterion. In light of that emphasis by participants in the research it is interesting to consider the 'Resolving conflicts' section of BT PLC's document called *The Way We Work*[7] which among other things says:

> How would you explain your decision to your colleagues in different countries?
> How would you explain your decision to your family or in public?
> Does it conflict with your own or BT's commitment to integrity?

This emphasis on asking how well ethical decisions would stand public scrutiny, including scrutiny in different countries, would be particularly relevant to accountants in businesses operating across national borders.

### Ethical policies and advice

The role of the organisational setting in improving or worsening ethical decision making was given considerable attention in the ICAS report. A key starting point is having a set of ethical policies which are practical and are reinforced by the behaviour of senior management. Another support is the presence of a clearly defined process for referring difficult ethical decisions upward in the organisation.

For those in small organisations there needs to be an opportunity for those in difficult situations to seek advice about the ethical choice or the way to handle the outcomes of making an ethical stand. Most professional bodies either have senior mentors available or have organised referrals to bodies specialising in ethical issues.

The reality is that some who have taken ethical stands have lost their jobs, but some of those who haven't stood their ground have lost their reputations or their liberty.

## 8.7 Implications of unethical behaviour for stakeholders using the financial reports

One of the essential aspects of providing complete and reliable information which are taken seriously by the financial community is to have a set of rigorous internal controls. However, ultimately those controls are normally dependent on checks and balances within the system and the integrity of those with the greatest power within the system. In other words the checks and balances, such as requiring two authorisations to issue a cheque or transfer money, presume that at least one of those with authority will act diligently and will be alert to the possibility of dishonest or misguided behaviour by the other. Further, if necessary or desirable, they will take firm action to prevent any behaviour that appears suspicious. The internal control system depends on the integrity and diligence, in other words the ethical behaviour, of the majority of the staff in the organisation.

### 8.7.1 Increased cost of capital

The presence of unethical behaviour in an organisation will raise questions about the reliability of the accounts. If unethical behaviour is suspected by investors, they will probably raise the cost of capital for the individual business. If there are sufficient cases of unethical behaviour across all companies, the integrity of the whole market will be brought into question and the liquidity of the whole market is reduced. That would affect the cost of funds across the board and increase the volatility of share prices.

### 8.7.2 Hidden liabilities

A liability, particularly an environmental one, might not crystallise for a number of years, as with the James Hardie Group in Australia. The James Hardie Group was a producer of asbestos sheeting whose fibres can in the long term damage the lungs and lead to death. The challenge the company faced was the long gestation period between the exposure to the dust from the asbestos and the appearance of the symptoms of the disease. It can be up to 40 years before the victim finds out that they have a death sentence.

#### Liability transferred to a separate entity

The company reorganised so that there was a separate entity which was responsible for the liabilities and that entity was supposed to have sufficient funds to cover future liabilities as they came to light. When it was apparent that the funds set aside were grossly inadequate and that the assessment of adequacy had been based on old data rather than using the more recent data which showed an increasing rate of claims, there was widespread community outrage. As a result the James Hardie Group felt that irrespective of their legal position they had to negotiate with the state government and the unions to set aside a share of their cash flows from operations each year to help the victims.

Thus the unfair arrangements set in place came back to create the equivalent of liabilities and did considerable damage to the public image of the company. This also made some people reluctant to be associated with the company as customers or as employees. The current assessment of liability (as at 2009) is set out in a KPMG Actuarial Report.[8]

### 8.7.3 Effect of ethical collapse in an organisation

There is an increasing need to be wary of unethical behaviour by management leading to fraud.

#### Widespread awareness

Jennings (2006)[9] points out that while most of the major frauds that make the headlines tend to be attributed to a small number of individuals, there have to be many other participants who allow them to happen. For every CEO who bleeds the company through payment for major personal expenses, or through gross manipulation of accounts, or backdating of options, there have to be a considerable number of people who know what is happening but who choose not to bring it to the attention of the appropriate authorities. The appropriate authority could be the board of directors, or the auditors or regulatory authorities.

#### Signs of ethical collapse

Jennings attributes this to the culture of the organisation and suggests there are seven signs of ethical collapse in an organisation. They include pressure to maintain the numbers, suppression of dissent and bad news, iconic CEOs surrounding themselves with young executives whose careers are dependent on them, a weak board of directors, numerous conflicts of interest, innovation excess, and goodness in some areas being thought to atone for evil in others.

Others have suggested that companies with high levels of takeover activity and high leverage are often prime candidates for fraud because of the pressures to achieve the numbers. Also, if the attitude is that the sole purpose of the firm is to make money subject to compliance with the letter of the law that is also a warning sign.

#### Pressure on accountants

The ICAS report 'Taking ethics to heart' noted that it appeared that the current business and commercial environment placed an enormous pressure on accountants, wherever they work, which may result in decisions and judgements that compromise ethical standards. It noted also that increased commercial pressures on accountants may be viewed by many within the profession as heralding a disquieting new era.

The accountant working within business has a different set of problems due to his or her dual position as an employee and a professional accountant. There is a potential clash of issues where the interests of the business could be at odds with professional standards.

### 8.7.4 Auditor reaction to risk of unethical behaviour

In addition to the above items, unethical behaviour should make auditors and investors scrutinise accounts more closely. Following the experiences with companies such as Enron, the auditing standards have placed greater emphasis on auditors being sceptical. This means that if they identify instances of unethical behaviour they should ask more searching questions. Depending on the responses they get, they may need to undertake more testing to satisfy themselves of the reliability of the accounts.

### 8.7.5 Action by professional accounting bodies to assist members

The various professional bodies provide members with support such as ICAEW's Ethics Advisory Service and ICMA's confidential advice.

The type of problem raised is a good indication of the ethical issues raised for accountants in business. They include:

- requests by employers to manipulate tax returns;
- requests to produce figures to mislead shareholders;
- requests to conceal information;
- requests to manipulate overhead absorption rates to extort more income from customers (an occurrence in the defence industries);
- requests to authorise and conceal bribes to buyers and agents, a common request in some exporting businesses;
- requests to produce misleading projected figures to obtain additional finance;
- requests to conceal improper expense claims put in by senior managers;
- requests to over- or undervalue assets to avoid breaching loan covenants;
- requests to misreport figures in respect of government grants;
- requests for information which could lead to charges of 'insider dealing';
- requests to redefine bad debts as 'good' or vice versa.

For accountants in industry the message is that if your employer has a culture which is not conducive to high ethical values then a good career move would be to look for employment elsewhere. For auditors the message is that the presence of symptoms suggested above is grounds for employing greater levels of scepticism in the audit.

### 8.7.6 Action taken by governments

The Sarbanes–Oxley Act (SOX) has had a major impact on company management and auditors to address what had been seen as an inadequate oversight of the accounting profession and conflicts of interest involving the auditors.

#### Management

Following the collapse of the auditors Arthur Andersen, the introduction of SOX placed personal responsibility on the CEO and the CFO for the accounts, with serious penalties for publishing misleading accounts. This led to these officers seeking reassurance that there were adequate systems and internal controls in place. This has in turn led to complaints that management effort is being directed away from growing the business and earnings.

#### Accountants and auditors

Management and audit committees since SOX are more focused on financial reporting. SOX gave rise to a major demand by business for internal auditors to undertake this work with the focus moving to assessing financial controls, as opposed to operational processes.

As for auditors, they have to confirm that companies have adequate systems and internal controls and are required to report to the audit committee rather than management.

### 8.7.7 Action by companies – company codes of ethics

Most companies now adopt codes of ethics. They may have alternative titles such as 'our values', codes of conduct, or codes of ethics. For example, BP has a code of conduct whose coverage, which is listed below, is what one would expect of a company involved in its industry and its activities covering a large number of countries. Its Code of Conduct includes the following major categories:

- Our commitment to integrity;
- Health, safety, security and the environment;
- Employees;
- Business partners;
- Governments and communities;
- Company assets and financial integrity.

However, the challenge is to make the code an integral part of the day-to-day behaviour of the company and to be perceived as doing so by outsiders. Obviously top management have to act in ways so as to reinforce the values of the code and to eliminate existing activities which are incompatible with the new values.

BP has been criticised for behaviour inconsistent with its values but such behaviour may relate to actions taken before the adoption of the code (see Beder[10]).

Thus it is important to ensure that the corporate behaviour is consistent with the code of conduct, and that staff are rewarded for ethical behaviour and suffer penalties for non-compliance. Breaches, irrespective of whether they are in the past, are difficult to erase from the memories of society.

### Levels within codes

Stohl et al. (2009)[11] suggest that the content of codes of conduct can be divided into three levels:

- Level 1 is where there is an attempt to ensure that the company is in compliance with all the laws which impact on it in the various countries in which it operates.
- Level 2 focuses on ensuring fair and equitable relations with all parties with which the company has direct relations. In this category would be the well-publicised adverse publicity which Nike received when it was alleged that their subcontractors were exploiting child labour in countries where such treatment is legal. The adverse publicity and boycotts meant that many companies reviewed their operations and expanded their codes to cover such situations and thus moved into the second level of ethical awareness.
- Level 3 is where companies take a global perspective and recognise their responsibility to contribute to the likelihood of peace and favourable global environmental conditions. In most companies the level 1 concerns are more dominant than the level 2, and the level 2 more than the level 3. European firms are more likely than US firms to have a level 3 orientation.

## 8.7.8 Conflict between codes and targets

On the one hand we see companies developing codes of ethical conduct, whilst on the other hand we see some of these same companies developing management by objectives which set staff unachievable targets and create pressures that lead to unethical behaviour. Where this occurs there is the risk that an unhealthy corporate climate may develop, resulting in the manipulation of accounting figures and unethical behaviour.

There is a view[12] that there is a need to create an ethical climate that transcends a compliance approach to ethics and focuses instead on fostering socially harmonious relationships. An interesting article[13] proceeds to make the argument that the recent accounting scandals may be as much a reflection of a deficient corporate climate, with its concentration on setting unrealistic targets and promoting competition between the staff, as of individual moral failures of managers.

### 8.7.9 Multinationals face special problems

Modern multinational companies experience special problems in relation to ethics.

Firstly, the transactions are often extremely large, so that there are greater pressures to bend the rules so as to get the business.

Secondly, the ethical values as reflected in some of the countries may be quite different from those in the head office of the group. One company did business in a developing country where the wages paid to public officials were so low as to be insufficient to support a family even at the very modest living standards of that country. Many public officials had a second job so as to cope. Others saw it as appropriate to demand kickbacks in order for them to process any government approvals, as for them there was a strong ethical obligation to ensure their family was properly looked after, which in their opinion outweighs their obligation to the community.

Is it ethical for other nations to condemn such behaviour in the extreme cases? Should a different standard apply? What is the business to do if that is the norm in a country?

- **Decline business**
  Some may decline to do business in those countries.

- **Use intermediaries**
  Others may employ intermediaries. In the latter case, a company sells the goods to an intermediary company which then resells the goods in the problem country. The intermediary obviously has to pay fees and bribes to make the sale but that is not the concern of the multinational company! They deliberately do not ask the intermediary what they do. However, it could become a concern if a protest group identifies the questionable behaviour of the agent and decides to hold the multinational responsible.

- **Pay bribes**
  A third option is just to pay the fees and bribes. Unfortunately this reinforces the corrupt forces in the target country.

- **Risks in using intermediaries and/or paying bribes**
  The company may be held responsible by one of the countries in which they operate which has laws making it illegal to corrupt public officials in their country. The company may also be held liable by its own government.

For example, in the UK the Serious Fraud Office[14] and in the US the Department of Justice are actively investigating corrupt practices. The Serious Fraud Office made BAE Systems pay £30 million in relation to overpriced military radar sold to Tanzania whilst taking into account the implementation by the company of substantial ethical and compliance reforms. Part of the fine is being passed on to the people of Tanzania to compensate for the damage done. Ongoing investigations in 2013 include a criminal investigation into bribery and corruption at Rolls-Royce.

### 8.7.10 The support given by professional bodies in the designing of ethical codes

There are excellent support facilities available. For example, the Association of Chartered Certified Accountants' website (www.accaglobal.com) makes a toolkit available for accountants who might be involved with designing a code of ethics. The site also provides an overview which considers matters such as why ethics are important, links to other related sites, e.g. the Center for Ethics and Business at Loyola Marymount University in Los Angeles[15] with a quiz to establish one's ethical style as an ethic of justice or an ethic of care, and a toolkit from the Ethics Resource Center[16] to assist in the design of a code of ethics.

## 8.8 The increasing role of whistle-blowing

It is recognised that normally when the law or the ethical code is being broken by the company, a range of people inside and outside the company are aware of the illegal activities or have sufficient information to raise suspicions. To reduce the likelihood of illegal activity or to help identify its occurrence, a number of regulatory organisations have set up mechanisms for whistle-blowing to occur. Also a number of companies have set up their own units, often through a consulting firm, whereby employees can report illegal activities and breaches of the firm's code of ethics or any other activities which are likely to bring the company into disrepute.

### 8.8.1 Seeking advice

There are a variety of sources ranging from Public Concern at Work (PCaW) to the advice available from the professional accounting bodies themselves.

#### Public Concern at Work

There are whistle-blowing charities such as Public Concern at Work which provide confidential telephone advice, free of charge, to people who witness wrongdoing at work but are not sure whether or how to raise their concern. Since 1993, it has advised on over 10,000 actual and potential whistle-blowing concerns including tackling frauds.

It carried out a joint research project[17] in 2013 with the University of Greenwich, 'Whistle-blowing – the inside story', reviewing the story of 1,000 callers from a variety of professions including lawyers and accountants. One of the outcomes suggested that organisations seem to be better at correcting wrongdoing than at safeguarding the whistle-blower from harm.

#### Professional advice to members

All the professional bodies provide support to members. The ICAEW, for example, adopts the PCaW Guidelines and in addition has ethics advisers who can give ethics advice on the specific guidance that applies to its members. The ICAEW offers a Support Members Scheme throughout England, Wales and the Channel Islands.

### 8.8.2 Whistle-blowing – protection in the UK

In the UK the Public Interest Disclosure Act came into force in 1999 protecting whistle-blowers who raised genuine concerns about malpractice, from dismissal and victimisation in order to promote the public interest. The scope of malpractice is wide-ranging, including, e.g. the covering up of a suspected crime, a civil offence such as negligence, a miscarriage of justice, and health and safety or environmental risks.

### 8.8.3 Anonymous whistle-blowing

Whilst there is this statutory protection, and firms may well support whistle-blowers, they need to realise from the beginning that ultimately they may have to seek alternative employment.

Although the whistle-blowing policies might have been followed and the accountants protected by the provisions of the Public Interest Disclosure Act, whistle-blowing could result in a breakdown of trust making the whistle-blower's position untenable; this means that a whistle-blower might be well advised to have an alternative position in mind.

This is not to suggest they shouldn't blow the whistle. Rather it is to reflect the history of whistle-blowers.

### Reasons for reporting anonymously

People will often be reporting on activities which they have been 'forced' to do or on activities of their superior or colleagues. Given that those colleagues will not take kindly to being reported on, and are capable of making life very difficult for the informant, it is important that reports can be made anonymously. Also, even those who are not directly affected will often view whistle-blowing as letting the side down. The whistle-blower, if identified, could well be ostracised.

However, action should be taken if it exposes you to criminal prosecution or, even if not at any personal risk, it might prevent the company from becoming involved further in inappropriate behavior. Take Enron as an example where the collapse of the company and Arthur Andersen might have been avoided with the loss of many jobs if there had been earlier response to staff concerns about dubious accounting practices.

## 8.8.4 Proportionate response

In spite of the above comments it is important to keep in mind that the steps taken should reflect the seriousness of the event and that the whistle-blowing should be the final strategy rather than the first. In other words, the normal actions should be to use the internal forums such as debating issues in staff meetings or raising the issue with an immediate superior or their boss when the superior is not approachable for some reason. Nor are disagreements over business issues a reason for reporting. The motivation should be to report breaches which represent legal, moral or public interest concerns and not matters purely relating to differences of opinion on operational issues, personality differences or jealousy.

## 8.8.5 Government support

There are legal protections against victimisation, but it would be more useful if the government provided positive support such as assistance with finding other employment or, perhaps, some form of financial reward such as is available in some countries to compensate for public-spirited actions that actually lead to professional or financial hardship for the whistle-blower.

## 8.8.6 Immunity to the first party to report

In many countries the regulatory authority responsible for pursuing price fixing has authority to give immunity or favourable treatment to the first party to report the occurrence of price fixing. It may be possible for the person's lawyer to ascertain whether the item has already been reported without disclosing the identity of their client. This arrangement is in place because of the difficulty of collecting information on such activities of sufficient quality and detail to prosecute successfully.

British Airways, for example, was fined about £270m after it admitted collusion in fixing the prices of fuel surcharges. The US Department of Justice fined it $300m (£148m) for colluding on how much extra to charge on passenger and cargo flights to cover fuel costs, and the UK's Office of Fair Trading fined it £121.5m after it held illegal talks with rival Virgin Atlantic. Virgin was given immunity after it reported the collusion and was not fined.

### 8.8.7 Breach of confidentiality

Auditors are protected from the risk of liability for breach of confidence provided that:

- disclosure is made in the public interest;
- disclosure is made to a proper authority;
- there is no malice motivating the disclosure.

## 8.9 Legal requirement to report – national and international regulation

It is likely that there will be an increase in formal regulation as the search for greater transparency and ethical business behaviour continues. We comment briefly on national and international regulation relating to money laundering and bribery.

### Money laundering – overview

There are various estimates of the scale of money laundering ranging up to over 2% of global gross domestic product. Certain businesses are identified as being more prone to money laundering, e.g. import/export companies and cash businesses such as antiques and art dealers, auction houses, casinos and garages. However, the avenues are becoming more and more sophisticated with methods varying between countries, e.g. in the UK there is the increasing use of smaller non-bank institutions whereas in Spain it includes cross-border carrying of cash, money-changing at bureaux de change and investment in real estate.

### Money laundering – implications for accountants

In 2010 the Auditing Practices Board (APB) in the UK issued a revised Practice Note 12, which required auditors to take the possibility of money laundering into account when carrying out their audit and to report to the appropriate authority if they become aware of suspected laundering.

### Money laundering – the Financial Action Task Force (FATF)

The Financial Action Task Force (FATF) is an independent intergovernmental body that develops and promotes policies to protect the global financial system against money laundering and terrorist financing. Recommendations issued by the FATF define criminal justice and regulatory measures that should be implemented to counter this problem. These recommendations also include international cooperation and preventive measures to be taken by financial institutions and others such as casinos, real-estate dealers, lawyers and accountants. The recommendations are recognised as the global anti-money-laundering (AML) and counter-terrorist-financing (CTF) standard.

FATF issued a report[18] in 2009 entitled *Money Laundering through the Football Sector*. This report identified the vulnerabilities of the sector arising from transactions relating to the ownership of football clubs, the transfer market and ownership of players, betting activities and image rights, sponsorship and advertising arrangements. The report is an excellent introduction to the complex web that attracts money launderers.

## 8.10 Why should students learn ethics?

### Survival of the profession

There is debate over whether the attempts to teach ethics are worthwhile. However, this chapter is designed to raise awareness of how important ethics are to the survival of the accounting profession. Accounting is part of the system to create trust in the financial information provided. The financial markets will not operate efficiently and effectively if there is not a substantial level of trust in the system. Such trust is a delicate matter and if the accounting profession is no longer trusted then there is no role for its members to play in the system. In that event the accounting profession will vanish. It may be thought that the loss of trust is so unlikely that it need not be contemplated. But who imagined that Arthur Andersen, one of the 'Big Five' as we knew it, would vanish from the scene so quickly? As soon as the public correctly or incorrectly decided they could no longer trust Arthur Andersen, the business crashed.

### A future role for accountants in ethical assurance

The accountant within business could also be seeing a growth in the ethical policing role as internal auditors take on the role of assessing the performance of managers as to their adherence to the ethical code of the organisation. This is already partly happening as conflicts of interest are often highlighted by internal audits and comments raised on managerial practices. This is after all a traditional role for accountants, ensuring that the various codes of practice of the organisation are followed. The level of adherence to an ethical code is but another assessment for the accountant to undertake.

### Implications for training

If, as is likely, the accountant has a role in the future as 'ethical guardian', additional training will be necessary. This should be done at a very early stage, as in the US, where accountants wishing to be Certified Public Accountants (CPAs) are required to pass formal exams on ethical practices and procedures before they are allowed the privilege of working in practice. Failure in these exams prevents the prospective accountant from practising in the business environment.

In the UK, for example, ethics is central to the ACCA qualification in recognition that values, ethics and governance are themes which organisations are now embedding into company business plans, and expertise in these areas is highly sought after in today's employment market. ACCA has adopted a holistic approach to a student's ethical development through the use of 'real-life' case studies and embedding ethical issues within the exam syllabi as in Paper 1 Governance, Risk and Ethics. In addition, as part of their ethical development, students will be required to complete a two-hour online training module, developed by ACCA. This will give students exposure to a range of real-life ethical case studies and will require them to reflect on their own ethical behaviour and values. Similar initiatives are being taken by the other professional accounting bodies, with case studies available from the Association of International Accountants and The Institute of Chartered Accountants of Scotland.

### How will decisions be viewed?

Another aspect of ethical behaviour is that others will often be judging the morality of action using hindsight or whilst coming from another perspective. This is the 'how would it appear on the front page of the newspaper?' aspect. So being aware of what could happen is often part of ethical sensitivity. In other words, being able to anticipate possible outcomes or how other parties will view what you have done is a necessary part of identifying that ethical issues have to be addressed.

## What if there are competing solutions?

*Ethical behaviour involves making decisions which are as morally correct and fair as possible,* recognising that sometimes there will have to be decisions in relation to two or more competing aspects of what is morally correct which are in unresolvable conflict. One has to be sure that any trade-offs are made for the good of society and that decisions are not blatantly or subtly influenced by self-interest. They must appear fair and reasonable when reviewed subsequently by an uninvolved outsider who is not an accountant. This is because the community places their trust in professionals because they have expertise that others do not, but at the same time it is necessary to retain that trust.

## Summary

At the macro level the existence of the profession and the careers of all of us in it are dependent on the community's perception of the profession as being ethical. Students need to be very conscious of that as they will make up the profession of the future.

At a more micro level all accountants will face ethical issues during their careers, whether they recognise them or not. This chapter attempts to increase awareness of the existence of ethical questions. The simplest way to increase awareness is to ask the question:

● Who is directly or indirectly affected by this accounting decision?

Then the follow-up question is:

● If I was in their position how would I feel about the accounting decision in terms of its fairness?

By increasing awareness of the impact of decisions, including accounting decisions, on other parties, hopefully the dangers of decisions which are unfair will be recognised. By facing the implications head-on, the accountant is less likely to make wrong decisions. Also keep in mind those accountants who never set out to be unethical but by a series of small incremental decisions found themselves at the point of no return. The personal consequences of being found to be unethical can cover financial disasters, a long period of stress as civil or criminal cases wind their way through the courts, and at the extreme suicide or prison.

Another aspect of this chapter has been the attempt to highlight the vulnerability of companies to accusations of both direct and indirect unethical impacts and hence the need to be aware of trends to increasing levels of accountability.

Finally you need to be aware of the avenues for getting assistance if you find yourself under pressure to ignore ethics or to turn a blind eye to the inappropriate behaviour of others. You should be aware of built-in avenues for addressing such concerns within your own organisation. Further, you should make yourself familiar with the assistance which your professional body can provide, such as providing experienced practitioners to discuss your options and the likely advantages and disadvantages of those alternatives.

## REVIEW QUESTIONS

1 Identify two ethical issues which university students experience and where they look for guidance. How useful is that guidance?

2 The following is an extract from a *European Accounting Review*[19] article:

> On the teaching front, there is a pressing need to challenge more robustly the tenets of modern day business, and specifically accounting, education which have elevated the principles of property rights and narrow self-interest above broader values of community and ethics.

Discuss how such a challenge might impact on accounting education.

3 The International Association for Accounting Education and Research states that: 'Professional ethics should pervade the teaching of accounting' (www.iaaer.org). Discuss how this can be achieved on an undergraduate accounting degree.

4 As a trainee auditor, what ethical issues are you most likely to encounter?

5 Explain what you think are four common types of ethical issues associated with (a) auditing, (b) public practice and (c) accounting in a corporate environment.

6 Lord Borrie QC has said[20] of the Public Interest Disclosure Bill that came into force in July 1999 that the new law would encourage people to recognise and identify with the wider public interest, not just their own private position, and it will reassure them that if they act reasonably to protect the legitimate interest of others, the law will not stand idly by should they be vilified or victimised. Confidentiality should only be breached, however, if there is a statutory obligation to do so. Discuss.

7 'Confidentiality means that an accountant in business has a loyalty to the business which employs him or her which is greater than any commitment to a professional code of ethics.' Discuss.

8 An interesting ethical case arose when an employee of a Swiss bank stole records of the accounts of international investors. The records were then offered for sale to the German government on the basis that many of them would represent unreported income and thus provide evidence of tax evasion. Should the government buy the records? Provide arguments for and against.

9 Refer to the Ernst & Young Code of Conduct and discuss the questions they suggest when putting their Global Code of Conduct into action.[21]

10 Should ethics be applicable at the standard-setting level? Express and justify your own views on this as distinct from repeating the material in the chapter.

11 Discuss the role of the accounting profession in the issue of ethics.

12 'The management of a listed company has a fiduciary duty to act in the best interest of the current shareholders and it would be unethical for them to act in the interest of other parties if this did not maximise the existing earnings per share.' Discuss.

13 How might a company develop a code of ethics for its own use?

14 Outline the advantages and disadvantages of a written code of ethics.

15 In relation to the following scenarios explain why it is a breach of ethics and what steps could have been taken to avoid the issue:

(a) The son of the accountant of a company is employed during the university holiday period to undertake work associated with preparation for a visit of the auditors.

(b) A senior executive is given a first-class seat to travel to Chicago to attend an industry fair where the company is launching a new product. The executive decides to cash in the ticket and to get two economy-class tickets so her boyfriend can go with her. The company picks up the hotel bill and she reimburses the difference between what it would have cost if she went alone and the final bill. The frequent flier points were credited to her personal frequent flier account. Would it make any difference if the company was not launching a new product at the fair?

(c) You pay a sizeable account for freight on the internal shipping of product deliveries in an underdeveloped country. At morning tea the gossip is that the company is paying bribes to a general in the underdeveloped country as protection money.

(d) The credit card statement for the managing director includes payments to a casino. The managing director says it is for the entertainment of important customers.

(e) You are processing a payment for materials which have been approved for repairs and maintenance when you realise the delivery is not to one of the business addresses of the company.

16  In each of the following scenarios, outline the ethical problem and suggest ways in which the organisation may solve the problem and prevent its recurrence:

(a) A director's wife uses his company car for shopping.

(b) Groceries bought for personal use are included on a director's company credit card.

(c) A director negotiates a contract for management consultancy services but it is later revealed that her husband is a director of the management consultancy company.

(d) The director of a company hires her son for some holiday work within the company but does not mention the fact to her fellow directors.

(e) You are the accountant to a small engineering company and you have been approached by the Chairman to authorise the payment of a fee to an overseas government employee in the hope that a large contract will be awarded.

(f) Your company has had some production problems which have resulted in some electrical goods being faulty (possibly dangerous) but all production is being dispatched to customers regardless of condition.

17  In each of the following scenarios, outline the ethical or potential ethical problem and suggest ways in which it could be resolved or avoided:

(a) Your company is about to sign a contract with a repressive regime in South America for equipment which **could** have a military use. Your own government has given you no advice on this matter.

(b) Your company is in financial difficulties and a large contract has just been gained in partnership with an overseas supplier who employs children as young as seven years old on their production line. The children are the only wage earners for their families and there is no welfare available in the country where they live.

(c) You are the accountant in a large manufacturing company and you have been approached by the manufacturing director to prepare a capital investment proposal for a new production line. After your calculations the project meets **none** of the criteria necessary to allow the project to proceed but the director instructs you to change the financial forecast figures to ensure the proposal is approved.

(d) Review the last week's newspapers and select **three** examples of failures of business ethics and justify your choice of examples.

(e) The company deducts from the monthly payroll employees' compulsory contribution to their superannuation accounts. The payment to the superannuation fund, which also includes the company's matching contribution, is being made only six-monthly because the cash flow of the company is tight following rapid expansion.

18 'It has been said that football clubs are seen by criminals as the perfect vehicles for money laundering.' Discuss the reason for this view.

19 Access www.saynotoolkit.net and discuss the definition and ethical risks that an accountant in business may encounter from bid rigging, facilitation payments, intermediaries, kick-back and market manipulation.

## EXERCISES

### Question 1

You have recently qualified and set up in public practice under the name Patris Zadan. You have been approached to provide accounting services for Joe Hardiman. Joe explains that he has had a lawyer set up six businesses and he asks you to do the books and to handle tax matters. The first thing you notice is that he is running a number of laundromats which are largely financed by relatives from overseas. As the year progresses you realise those businesses are extremely profitable, given industry averages.

**Required:**
**Discuss: What do you do?**

### Question 2

Joe Withers is the chief financial officer for Withco plc responsible for negotiating bank loans. It has been the practice to obtain loans from a number of merchant banks. He has recently met Ben Billings who had been on the same undergraduate course some years earlier. They agree to meet for a game of squash and during the course of the evening Joe learns that Ben is the chief loans officer at The Swift Merchant Bank.

During the next five years Joe negotiates all of the company's loan requirements through Swift, and Ben arranges for Joe to receive substantial allocations in initial public offerings. Over that period Joe has done quite well out of taking up allocations and selling them within a few days on the market.

**Required:**
**Discuss the ethical issues.**

### Question 3

Kim Lee is a branch accountant in a multinational company Green Cocoa plc responsible for purchasing supplies from a developing country. Kim Lee is authorised to enter into contracts up to $100,000 for any single transaction. Demand in the home market is growing and Head Office are pressing for an increase in supplies. A new government official in the developing country says that Kim needs an export permit from his department and that he needs a payment to be made to his brother-in-law for consulting services if the permit is to be granted. Kim quickly checks alternative sources and finds that the normal price combined with the extra 'facilitation fee' is still much cheaper than the alternative sources of supply. Kim faces two problems, namely, whether to pay the bribe and, if so, how to record it in the accounts so it is not obvious what it is.

**Required:**
**Discuss the ethical issues.**

## Question 4

Jemma Burrett is a public practitioner. Four years earlier she had set up a family trust for a major client by the name of Simon Trent. The trust is for the benefit of Simon and his wife Marie. Marie is also a client of the practice and the practice prepares her tax returns. Subsequently Marie files for divorce. In her claim for a share of the assets she claims a third share of the business and half the other assets of the family which are listed. The assets of the family trust are not included in the list.

**Required:**
**Discuss the ethical issues raised by the case and what action the accountant should take (if any).**

## Question 5

George Longfellow is a financial controller with a listed industrial firm which has a long period of sustained growth. This has necessitated substantial use of external borrowing.

During the great financial crisis it has become harder to roll over the loans as they mature. To make matters worse sales revenues have fallen 5% for the financial year, debtors have taken longer to pay, and margins have fallen. The managing director has said that he doesn't want to report a loss for the first time in the company's history as it might scare financiers.

The finance director (FD) has told George to make every effort to get the result to come out positively. He suggests that a number of expenses should be shifted to prepayments, provisions for doubtful debts should be lowered, and new assets should not be depreciated in the year of purchase but rather should only commence depreciation in the next financial year on the argument that new assets take a while to become fully operational.

In the previous year the company had moved into a new line of business where a small number of customers paid in advance. Because these were exceptional the auditors were persuaded to allow you to avoid the need to make the systems more sophisticated to decrease revenue and to recognise a liability. After all, it was immaterial in the overall group. Fortunately, that new line of business has grown substantially in the current financial year and it was suggested that the auditors be told that the revenue in advance should not be taken out of sales because a precedent had been set the year before.

George saw this as a little bit of creative accounting and was reluctant to do what he was instructed. When he tentatively made this comment to the FD he was assured that this was only temporary to ensure the company could refinance and that next year, when the economy recovered, all the discretionary adjustments would be reversed and everyone would be happy. After all, the employment of the 20,000 people who work for the group depends upon the refinancing and it was not as if the company was not going to be prosperous in the future. The FD emphasised that the few adjustments were, after all, a win–win situation for everyone and George was threatening the livelihood of all of his colleagues – many with children and with mortgage payments to meet.

**Required:**
**Discuss who would or could benefit or lose from the finance director's proposals.**

## Notes

1 L. Spacek, 'The need for an accounting court', *The Accounting Review*, 1958, pp. 368–79.

2 IFAC, *Code of Ethics for Professional Accountants*, 2013.

3 W.J. Baumol, *Superfairness: Applications and Theory*, MIT Press, 1982.

4 D. Friedman, *Morals and Markets*, Palgrave Macmillan, 2008.

5 S.B. Salter, D.M. Guffey and J.J. McMillan, 'Truth, consequences and culture: a comparative examination of cheating and attitudes about cheating among US and UK students', *Journal of Business Ethics*, vol. 31(1), May 2001, pp. 37–50, Springer.

6 C. Helliar and J. Bebbington, 'Taking ethics to heart', ICAS, 2004, www.icas.org.uk

7 See www.btplc.com/TheWayWeWork/Businesspractice/twww_english.pdf

8 See www.ir.jameshardie.com.au/jh/asbestos_compensation.jsp

9 M.M. Jennings, *Seven Signs of Ethical Collapse: Understanding What Causes Moral Meltdowns in Organizations*, St Martin's Press, 2006.

10 S. Beder, *Beyond Petroleum*, http://www.uow.edu.au/~sharonb/bp.html

11 C. Stohl, M. Stohl and L. Popova, 'A new generation of codes of ethics', *Journal of Business Ethics*, vol. 90, 2009, pp. 607–622.

12 T. Morris, *If Aristotle Ran General Motors*, New York: Henry Holt and Company, 1997, pp. 118–145.

13 J.F. Castellano, K. Rosenweig and H.P. Roehm, 'How corporate culture impacts unethical distortion of financial numbers', *Management Accounting Quarterly*, vol. 5(4), Summer 2004.

14 See www.sfo.gov.uk

15 See www.lmu.edu/Page23070.aspx

16 See Ethics Resource Center, www.ethics.org

17 See www.pcaw.org.uk/fles/Whistleblowing%20-%20the%20inside%20story%20FINAL.pdf

18 See www.oecd.org

19 D. Owen, 'CSR after Enron: a role for the academic accounting profession?', *European Accounting Review*, vol. 14(2), 2005.

20 W. Raven, 'Social auditing', *Internal Auditor*, February 2000, p. 8.

21 See www.ey.com/Publication/vwLUAssets/Ernst-Young_Global_Code_of_Conduct/$FILE/EY_Code_of_Conduct.pdf

### PART 4

# Income and asset value measurement systems

# Income and asset value measurement: an economist's approach

## 9.1 Introduction

The main purpose of this chapter is to explain the need for income measurement, to compare the methods of measurement adopted by the accountant with those adopted by the economist, and to consider how both are being applied within the international financial reporting framework.

> ### Objectives
>
> By the end of this chapter, you should be able to:
>
> - explain the role and objective of income measurement;
> - explain the accountant's view of income, capital and value;
> - critically comment on the accountant's measure;
> - explain the economist's view of income, capital and value;
> - critically comment on the economist's measure;
> - define various capital maintenance systems.

## 9.2 Role and objective of income measurement

Although accountancy has played a part in business reporting for centuries, it is only since the Companies Act 1929 that financial reporting has become income-orientated. Prior to that Act, a statement of income was of minor importance. It was the statement of financial position that mattered, providing a list of capital, assets and liabilities that revealed the financial soundness and solvency of the business.

According to some commentators,[1] this scenario may be attributed to the sources of capital funding. Until the late 1920s, as in present-day Germany, external capital finance in the UK was mainly in the hands of bankers, other lenders and trade creditors. As the main users of published financial statements, they focused on the company's ability to pay trade creditors and the interest on loans, and to meet the scheduled dates of loan repayment: they were interested in the short-term liquidity and longer-term solvency of the entity.

Thus the statement of financial position was the prime document of interest. Perhaps in recognition of this, in the UK the statement of financial position, until recent times, tended to show liabilities on the left-hand side, thus making them the first part of the statement of financial position read.

The gradual evolution of a sophisticated investment market, embracing a range of financial institutions, together with the growth in the number of individual investors, caused a reorientation of priorities. Investor protection and investor decision-making needs started to dominate the financial reporting scene, and the revenue statement replaced the statement of financial position as the sovereign reporting document.

Consequently, attention became fixed on the statement of comprehensive income and on concepts of accounting for profit. Moreover, investor protection assumed a new meaning. It changed from simply protecting the **capital** that had **been invested** to protecting the **income information** used by investors when making an investment decision.

However, the sight of major companies experiencing severe liquidity problems over the past decade has revived interest in the statement of financial position; while its light is perhaps not of the same intensity as that of the profit and loss account, it cannot be said to be totally subordinate to its accompanying statement of income.

The main objectives of income measurement are to provide:

- a means of control in a micro- and macroeconomic sense;
- a means of prediction;
- a basis for taxation.

We consider each of these below.

### 9.2.1 Income as a means of control

#### Assessment of stewardship performance

Managers are the stewards appointed by shareholders. Income, in the sense of net income or net profit, is the crystallisation of their accountability. Maximisation of income is seen as a major aim of the entrepreneurial entity, but the capacity of the business to pursue this aim may be subject to political and social constraints in the case of large public monopolies, and private semi-monopolies such as British Telecommunications plc.

Maximisation of net income is reflected in the earnings per share (EPS) figure, which is shown on the face of the published statement of income. The importance of this figure to the shareholders is evidenced by contracts that tie directors' remuneration to growth in EPS. A rising EPS may result in an increased salary or bonus for directors and upward movement in the market price of the underlying security. The effect on the market price is indicated by another extremely important statistic, which is influenced by the statement of comprehensive income: namely, the price/earnings (PE) ratio. The PE ratio reveals the numerical relationship between the share's current market price and the last reported EPS. EPS and PE ratios are discussed in Chapters 27 and 29.

#### Actual performance versus predicted performance

This comparison enables the management and the investing public to use the lessons of the past to improve future performance. The public, as shareholders, may initiate a change in the company directorate if circumstances necessitate it. This may be one reason why management is generally loath to give a clear, quantified estimate of projected results – such an estimate is a potential measure of efficiency. The comparison of actual with projected results identifies apparent underachievement.

#### The macroeconomic concept

Good government is, of necessity, involved in managing the macroeconomic scene and as such is a user of the income measure. State policies need to be formulated concerning the allocation of economic resources and the regulation of firms and industries, as illustrated by the measures taken by Oftel and Ofwat to regulate the size of earnings by British Telecom and the water companies.

### 9.2.2 Income as a means of prediction

#### Dividend and retention policy

The profit generated for the year influences the payment of a dividend, its scale and the residual income after such dividend has been paid. Other influences are also active, including the availability of cash resources within the entity, the opportunities for further internal investment and the dividend policies of capital-competing entities with comparable shares.

However, some question the soundness of using the profit generated for the year when making a decision to invest in an enterprise. Their view is that such a practice misunderstands the nature of income data, and that the appropriate information is the prospective cash flows. They regard the use of income figures from past periods as defective because, even if the future accrual accounting income could be forecast accurately, 'it is no more than an imperfect surrogate for future cash flows'.[2]

The counter-argument is that there is considerable resistance by both managers and accountants to the publication of future operating cash flows and dividend payments.[3] This means that, in the absence of relevant information, an investor needs to rely on a surrogate. The question then arises: which is the best surrogate?

In the short term, the best surrogate is the information that is currently available, i.e. income measured according to the accrual concept. In the longer term, management will be pressed by the shareholders to provide the actual forecast data on operating cash flows and dividend distribution, or to improve the surrogate information, by for example reporting the cash earnings per share.

More fundamentally, Revsine has suggested that ideal information for investors would indicate the economic value of the business (and its assets) based on expected future cash flows. However, the Revsine suggestion itself requires information on future cash flows that it is not possible to obtain at this time.[4] Instead, he considered the use of replacement cost as a surrogate for the economic value of the business, and we return to this later in the chapter.

#### Future performance

While history is not a faultless indicator of future events and their financial results, it does have a role to play in assessing the level of future income. In this context, historic income is of assistance to existing investors, prospective investors and management.

### 9.2.3 Basis for taxation

The contemporary taxation philosophy, in spite of criticism from some economists, uses income measurement to measure the taxable capacity of a business entity.

However, the determination of income by HM Revenue and Customs is necessarily influenced by socioeconomic fiscal factors, among others, and thus accounting profit is subject to adjustment in order to achieve taxable profit. As a tax base, it has been continually eroded as the difference between accounting income and taxable income has grown.[2]

Her Majesty's Revenue and Customs in the UK has tended to disallow expenses that are particularly susceptible to management judgement. For example, a uniform capital allowance is substituted for the subjective depreciation charge that is made by management, and certain provisions that appear as a charge in the statement of income are not accepted as an expense for tax purposes until the loss crystallises, e.g. a charge to increase the doubtful debts provision may not be allowed until the debt is recognised as bad.

## 9.3 Accountant's view of income, capital and value

Variations between accountants and economists in measuring income, capital and value are caused by their different views of these measures. In this section, we introduce the accountant's view and, in Section 9.5, the economist's, in order to reconcile variations in methods of measurement.

### 9.3.1 The accountant's view

Income is an important part of accounting theory and practice, although until 1970, when a formal system of propagating standard accounting practice throughout the accountancy profession began, it received little attention in accountancy literature. The characteristics of measurement were basic and few, and tended to be of an intuitive, traditional nature, rather than being spelled out precisely and given mandatory status within the profession.

#### Accounting tradition of historical cost

The statement of income is based on the actual costs of business transactions, i.e. the costs incurred in the currency and at the price levels pertaining at the time of the transactions.

Accounting income is said to be historical income, i.e. it is an *ex post* measure because it takes place after the event. The traditional statement of income is historical in two senses: because it concerns a past period, and because it utilises historical cost, being the cost of the transactions on which it is based. It follows that the statement of financial position, being based on the residuals of transactions not yet dealt with in the statement of income, is also based on historical cost.

In practice, certain amendments may be made to historical cost in both the statement of comprehensive income and statement of financial position, but historical cost still predominates in both statements. It is justified on a number of counts which, in principle, guard against the manipulation of data.

The main characteristics of historical cost accounting are as follows:

- **Objectivity.** It is a predominantly objective system, although it does exhibit aspects of subjectivity. Its nature is generally understood and it is invariably supported by independent documentary evidence, e.g. an invoice, statement, cheque, cheque counterfoil, receipt or voucher.

- **Factual.** As a basis of fact (with exceptions such as when amended in furtherance of revaluation), it is verifiable and to that extent is beyond dispute.

- **Profit or income concept.** Profit as a concept is generally well understood in a capital market economy, even if its precise measurement may be problematic. It constitutes the difference between revenue and expenditure or, in the economic sense, between opening and closing net assets.

Unfortunately, historical cost is not without its weaknesses. It is not always objective, owing to alternative definitions of revenue and costs and the need for estimates.

For example, although inventories are valued at the lower of cost or net realisable value, the cost will differ depending upon the definition adopted, e.g. first-in-first-out, last-in-first-out or standard cost.

Estimation is needed in the case of inventory valuation, assessing possible bad debts, accruing expenses, providing for depreciation and determining the profit attributable to long-term contracts. So, although it is transaction-based, there are aspects of historical cost reporting that do not result from an independently verifiable business transaction. This means that profit is not always a unique figure.

Assets are often subjected to revaluation. In an economy of changing price levels, the historical cost system has been compromised by a perceived need to restate the carrying value of those assets that comprise a large proportion of a company's capital employed, e.g. land and buildings. This practice is controversial, not least because it is said to imply that a statement of financial position is a list of assets at market valuation, rather than a statement of unamortised costs not yet charged against revenue.

However, despite conventional accountancy income being partly the result of subjectivity, it is largely the product of the historical cost concept. A typical accounting policy specified in the published accounts of companies now reads as follows:

> The financial statements are prepared under the historical cost conventions as modified by the revaluation of certain non-current assets.

### Nature of accounting income as an *ex post* measure

Accounting income is defined in terms of the business entity. It is the excess of revenue from sales over direct and allocated indirect costs incurred in the achievement of such sales. Its measure results in a net figure. It is the numerical result of the matching and accruals concepts discussed in the preceding chapter.

Accounting income is transaction-based and therefore can be said to be factual, in as much as the revenue and costs have been realised and will be reflected in cash inflow and outflow, although not necessarily within the financial year.

Under accrual accounting, the sales for a financial period are offset by the expenses incurred in generating such sales. Objectivity is a prime characteristic of accrual accounting, but the information cannot be entirely objective because of the need to break up the ongoing performance of the business entity into calendar periods or financial years for purposes of accountability reporting. The allocation of expenses between periods requires a prudent estimate of some costs, e.g. the provision for depreciation and bad debts attributable to each period.

Accounting income is presented in the form of the conventional statement of income. This statement of income, in being based on actual transactions, is concerned with a past-defined period of time. Thus accounting profit is said to be historical income, i.e. an *ex post* measure because it is after the event.

### Nature of accounting capital

The business enterprise requires the use of non-monetary assets, e.g. buildings, plant and machinery, office equipment, motor vehicles, stock of raw materials and work in progress. Such assets are not consumed in any one accounting period, but give service over a number of periods; therefore, the unconsumed portions of each asset are carried forward from period to period and appear in the statement of financial position. This document itemises the unused asset balances at the date of the financial year-end. In addition to listing unexpired costs of non-monetary assets, the statement of financial position also displays monetary assets such as trade receivables and cash balances, together with monetary liabilities, i.e. moneys owing to trade creditors, other creditors and lenders. Funds supplied by shareholders and retained income following the distribution of dividend are also shown. Retained profits are usually added to shareholders' capital, resulting in what are known as shareholders' funds. These represent the company's equity capital.

## Statement of income as a linking statement

The net assets of the firm, i.e. that fund of unconsumed assets which exceeds moneys attributable to payables and lenders, constitutes the company's net capital, which is the same as its equity capital. Thus the statement of income of a financial period can be seen as a linking statement between that period's opening and closing statement of financial positions: in other words, income may be linked with opening and closing capital. This linking may be expressed by a formula, as follows:

$$Y_{0-1} = NA_1 - NA_0 + D_{0-1}$$

where $Y_{0-1}$ = income for the period of time $t_0$ to $t_1$; $NA_0$ = net assets of the entity at point of time $t_0$; $NA_1$ = net assets of the entity at point of time $t_1$; and $D_{0-1}$ = dividends or distribution during period $t_{0-1}$.

Less formally: $Y$ = income of financial year; $NA_0$ = net assets as shown in the statement of financial position at beginning of financial year; $NA_1$ = net assets as shown in the statement of financial position at end of financial year; and $D_{0-1}$ = dividends paid and proposed for the financial year. We can illustrate this as follows:

Income $Y_{0-1}$ for the financial year $t_{0-1}$ as compiled by the accountant was £1,200

Dividend $D_{0-1}$ for the financial year $t_{0-1}$ was £450

Net assets $NA_0$ at the beginning of the financial year were £6,000

Net assets $NA_1$ at the end of the financial year were £6,750.

The income account can be linked with opening and closing statements of financial position, namely:

$$Y_{0-1} = NA_1 - NA_0 + D_{0-1}$$
$$= £6,750 - £6,000 + £450$$
$$= £1,200 = Y_{0-1}$$

Thus $Y$ has been computed by using the opening and closing capitals for the period where capital equals net assets.

In practice, however, the accountant would compute income $Y$ by compiling a statement of income. So, of what use is this formula? For reasons to be discussed later, the economist finds use for the formula when it is amended to take account of what we call **present values**. Computed after the end of a financial year, it is the *ex post* measure of income.

## Nature of traditional accounting value

As the values of assets still in service at the end of a financial period have been based on the unconsumed costs of such assets, they are the by-product of compiling the statement of income. These values have been fixed not by direct measurement, but simply by an assessment of costs consumed in the process of generating period turnover. We can say, then, that the statement of financial position figure of net assets is a residual valuation after measuring income.

However, it is not a value in the sense of worth or market value as a buying price or selling price; it is merely a **value of unconsumed costs of assets**. This is an important point that will be encountered again later.

## 9.4 Critical comment on the accountant's measure

### 9.4.1 Virtues of the accountant's measure

As with the economist's, the accountant's measure is not without its virtues. These are invariably aspects of the historical cost concept, such as objectivity, being transaction based and being generally understood.

### 9.4.2 Faults of the accountant's measure

#### Principles of historical cost and profit realisation

The historical cost and profit realisation concepts are firmly entrenched in the transaction basis of accountancy. However, in practice, the two concepts are not free of adjustments. Because of such adjustments, some commentators argue that the system produces a heterogeneous mix of values and realised income items.[5]

For example, in the case of asset values, certain assets such as land and buildings may have a carrying figure in the statement of financial position based on a revaluation to market value, while other assets such as motor vehicles may still be based on a balance of unallocated cost. The statement of financial position thus pretends on the one hand to be a list of resultant costs pending allocation over future periods and on the other hand to be a statement of current values.

#### Prudence concept

This concept introduces caution into the recognition of assets and income for financial reporting purposes. The cardinal rule is that income should not be recorded or recognised within the system until it is realised, but unrealised losses should be recognised immediately.

However, not all unrealised profits are excluded. For example, practice is that attributable profit on long-term contracts still in progress at the financial year-end may be taken into account. As with non-current assets, rules are not applied uniformly.

#### Unrealised capital profits

Capital profits have been ignored as income until they are realised, when, in the accounting period of sale, they are acknowledged by the reporting system. This has meant that all the profit has been recognised in one financial period when, in truth, the surplus was generated over successive periods by gradual growth, albeit unrealised until disposal of the asset. Thus a portion of what are now realised profits applies to prior periods. Not all of this profit should be attributed to the period of sale. The introduction of the statement of comprehensive income has addressed this by including revaluation gains.

#### Going concern

The going concern concept is fundamental to accountancy and operates on the assumption that the business entity has an indefinite life. It is used to justify basing the periodic reports of asset values on carrying forward figures that represent unallocated costs, i.e. to justify the non-recognition of the realisable or disposal values of non-monetary assets and, in so doing, the associated unrealised profits/losses. Although the life of an entity is deemed indefinite, there is uncertainty, and accountants are reluctant to predict the future. When they are matching costs with revenue for the current accounting period, they follow the prudence concept of reasonable certainty.

In the long term, economic income and accountancy income are reconciled. The unrealised profits of the economic measure are eventually realised and, at that point, they will be recognised by the accountant's measure. In the short term, however, they give different results for each period.

### What if we cannot assume that a business will continue as a going concern?

There may be circumstances, as in the case of HMV, which in 2012 warned that, following falling sales, there was a material uncertainty on being able to continue as a going concern. The uncertainty may be reduced by showing that active steps are being taken such as introducing new sales initiatives, restructuring, cost reduction and raising additional share capital which will ensure the survival of the business. If survival is not possible, the business will prepare its accounts using net realisable values, which are discussed in the next chapter.

The key considerations for shareholders are whether there will be sufficient profits to support dividend distributions and whether they will be able to continue to dispose of their shares in the open market. The key consideration for the directors is whether there will be sufficient cash to allow the business to trade profitably. We can see all these considerations being addressed in the following extract from the 2011 Annual Report of Grontmij N.V.

> **Going concern**
> the Group faced declines in its operating results during 2011 and was unable to meet its original debt covenant ratios . . . the Company obtained a waiver . . . met the covenant levels set by the waiver . . . a deferral was granted . . . apparent that a redesign of the capital structure of the Company is required to sustain the operations of the Company in the long term . . . after a financial review by the management, it was concluded that the capital structure of the Company should consist of a committed credit facility agreement and additional equity ('the rights issue') . . . the Company reached, in principle, agreement with its major shareholders and the banks . . . as a consequence of the above, the 2011 financial statements are prepared on a going concern basis. The Company does, however, draw attention to the fact that the ability to continue as a going concern is dependent on the continuing support of its shareholders and banks . . .

## 9.5 Economist's view of income, capital and value

Let us now consider the economist's tradition of present value and the nature of economic income.

### 9.5.1 Economist's tradition of present value

Present value is a technique used in valuing a future money flow, or in measuring the money value of an existing capital stock in terms of a predicted cash flow *ad infinitum*.

Present value (PV) constitutes the nature of economic capital and, indirectly, economic income. Given the choice of receiving £100 now or £100 in one year's time, the rational person will opt to receive £100 now. This behaviour exhibits an intuitive appreciation of the fact that £100 today is worth more than £100 one year hence. Thus the mind has **discounted** the value of the future sum: £100 today is worth £100; but compared with today, i.e. **compared with present value**, a similar sum receivable in twelve months' time is worth less than £100. How much less is a matter of subjective evaluation, but compensation for the time element may be found by reference to interest: a person forgoing the spending of £1 today and spending it one year later may earn interest of, say, 10% per annum in compensation for the sacrifice undergone by deferring consumption.

So £1 today invested at 10% p.a. will be worth £1.10 one year later, £1.21 two years later, £1.331 three years later, and so on. This is the concept of compound interest. It may be calculated by the formula $(1 + r)^n$, where 1 = the sum invested; $r$ = the rate of interest; and $n$ = the number of periods of investment (in our case years). So for £1 invested at 10% p.a. for four years:

$$\begin{aligned} (1 + r)^n &= (1 + 0.10)^4 \\ &= (1.1)^4 \\ &= £1.4641 \end{aligned}$$

and for five years:

$$\begin{aligned} &= (1.1)^5 \\ &= £1.6105, \text{ and so on.} \end{aligned}$$

Notice how the **future value** increases because of the compound interest element – it **varies** over time – whereas the investment of £1 remains constant. So, conversely, the sum of £1.10 received at the end of year 1 has a PV of £1, as does £1.21 received at the end of year 2 and £1.331 at the end of year 3.

It has been found convenient to construct tables to ease the task of calculating present values. These show the cash flow, i.e. the future values, at a constant figure of £1 and allow the investment to vary. So:

$$PV = \frac{CF}{(1 + r)^n}$$

where $CF$ = anticipated cash flow; and $r$ = the discount (i.e. interest) rate. So the PV of a cash flow of £1 receivable at the end of one year at 10% p.a. is:

$$\frac{£1}{(1 + r)^2} = £0.9091$$

and of £1 at the end of two years:

$$\frac{£1}{(1 + r)^2} = £0.8264$$

and so on over successive years. The appropriate present values for years 3, 4 and 5 would be £0.7513, £0.6830, £0.6209 respectively.

£0.9091 invested today at 10% p.a. will produce £1 at the end of one year. The PV of £1 receivable at the end of two years is £0.8264 and so on.

Tables presenting data in this way are called 'PV tables', while the earlier method compiles tables usually referred to as 'compound interest tables'. Both types of table are compound interest tables; only the presentation of the data has changed.

To illustrate the ease of computation using PV tables, we can compute the PV of £6,152 receivable at the end of year 5, given a discount rate of 10%, as being £6,152 × £0.6209 = £3,820. Thus £3,820 will total £6,152 in five years given an interest rate of 10% p.a. So the PV of that cash flow of £6,152 is £3,820, because £3,820 would generate interest of £2,332 (i.e. 6,152 − 3,820) as compensation for losing use of the principal sum for five years. Future flows must be discounted to take cognisance of the time element separating cash flows. Only then are we able to compare like with like by reducing all future flows to the comparable loss of present value.

**Figure 9.1 Dissimilar cash flows**

| Cash flows | | |
|---|---|---|
| Machine A | Machine B | Receivable end of year |
| £ | £ | |
| 1,000 | 5,000 | 1 |
| 2,000 | 4,000 | 2 |
| 7,000 | 1,000 | 3 |
| 10,000 | 10,000 | |

This concept of PV has a variety of applications in accountancy and will be encountered in many different areas requiring financial measurement, comparison and decision. It originated as an economist's device within the context of economic income and economic capital models, but in accountancy it assists in the making of valid comparisons and decisions. For example, two machines may each generate an income of £10,000 over three years. However, timing of the cash flows may vary between the machines. This is illustrated in Figure 9.1.

If we simply compare the profit-generating capacity of the machines over the three-year span, each produces a total profit of £10,000. But if we pay regard to the time element of the money flows, the machines are not so equal.

However, the technique has its faults. Future money flows are invariably the subject of **estimation** and thus the actual flow experienced may show variations from forecast. Also, the element of **interest,** which is crucial to the calculation of present values, is **subjective.** It may, for instance, be taken as the average prevailing rate operating within the economy or a rate peculiar to the firm and the element of risk involved in the particular decision. In this chapter we are concerned only with PV as a tool of the economist in evaluating economic income and economic capital.

### 9.5.2 Nature of economic income

Economics is concerned with the economy in general, raising questions such as: how does it function? how is wealth created? how is income generated? why is income generated? The economy as a whole is activated by income generation. The individual is motivated to generate income because of a need to satisfy personal wants by consuming goods and services. Thus the economist becomes concerned with the individual consumer's psychological state of personal **enjoyment and satisfaction.** This creates a need to treat the economy as a **behavioural entity.**

The behavioural aspect forms a substantial part of micro- and macroeconomic thought, emanating particularly from the microeconomic. We can say that the economist's version of income measurement is microeconomics-orientated in contrast to the accountant's business entity orientation.

The origination of the economic measure of income commenced with Irving Fisher in 1930.[6] He saw income in terms of consumption, and consumption in terms of individual perception of personal enjoyment and satisfaction. His difficulty in formulating a standard measure of this personal psychological concept of income was overcome by equating this individual experience with the consumption of goods and services and assuming that the cost of such goods and services formed the measure.

Thus, he reasoned, consumption ($C$) equals income ($Y$); so $Y = C$. He excluded savings from income because savings were not consumed. There was no satisfaction derived from savings; enjoyment necessitated consumption, he argued. Money was worthless until spent; so growth of capital was ignored, but reductions in capital became part of income because such reductions had to be spent.

In Fisher's model, capital was a stock of wealth existing at a point in time, and as a stock it generated income. Eventually, he reconciled the value of capital with the value of income by employing the concept of present value. He assessed the PV of a future flow of income by **discounting** future flows using the discounted cash flow (DCF) technique. Fisher's model adopted the prevailing average market rate of interest as the discount factor.

Economists since Fisher have introduced savings as part of income. Sir John Hicks played a major role in this area.[7] He introduced the idea that income was the maximum consumption enjoyed by the individual without reducing the individual's capital stock, i.e. the amount a person could consume during a period of time that still left him or her with the same value of capital stock at the end of the period as at the beginning. Hicks also used the DCF technique in the valuation of capital.

If capital increases, the increase constitutes savings and grants the opportunity of consumption. The formula illustrating this was given in Section 9.3.1, i.e. $Y_{0-1} = NA_1 - NA_0 + D_{0-1}$.

However, in the Hicksian model, $NA_1 - NA_0$, given as £6,750 and £6,000 respectively in that section, would have been discounted to achieve present values.

The same formula may be expressed in different forms. The economist is likely to show it as $Y = C + (K_1 - K_0)$, where $C =$ consumption, having been substituted for dividend, and $K_1$ and $K_0$ have been substituted for $NA_1$ and $NA_0$ respectively.

### Hicks's income model

Hicks's income model is often spoken of as an *ex ante* model because it is usually used for the measurement of **expected** income in advance of the time period concerned. Of course, because it specifically introduces the present value concept, present values replace the statement of financial position values of net assets adopted by the accountant. Measuring income **before the event** enables the individual to estimate the level of consumption that may be achieved without depleting capital stock. Before-the-event computations of income necessitate predictions of future cash flows.

Suppose that an individual proprietor of a business anticipated that his investment in the enterprise would generate earnings over the next four years as specified in Figure 9.2. Furthermore, such earnings would be retained by the business for the financing of new equipment with a view to increasing potential output.

We will assume that the expected rate of interest on capital employed in the business is 8% p.a.

**Figure 9.2 Business cash flows for four years**

| Years | Cash inflows £ |
|-------|------------|
| 1 | 26,000 |
| 2 | 29,000 |
| 3 | 35,000 |
| 4 | 41,000 |

**Figure 9.3 Economic value at $K_0$**

| | (a) | (b) | (c) |
|---|---|---|---|
| Year | Cash flow | $DCF = \dfrac{1}{(1+r)^n}$ | $PV = (a) \times (b)$ |
| | £ | | £ |
| $K_1$ | 26,000 | $\dfrac{1}{(1.08)^1} = 0.9259$ | 24,073 |
| $K_2$ | 29,000 | $\dfrac{1}{(1.08)^2} = 0.8573$ | 24,862 |
| $K_3$ | 35,000 | $\dfrac{1}{(1.08)^3} = 0.7938$ | 27,783 |
| $K_4$ | 41,000 | $\dfrac{1}{(1.08)^4} = 0.7350$ | 30,135 |
| | 131,000 | | 106,853 |

The economic value of the business at $K_0$ (i.e. at the beginning of year 1) will be based on the discounted cash flow of the future four years. Figure 9.3 shows that $K_0$ is £106,853, calculated as the present value of anticipated earnings of £131,000 spread over a four-year term.

The economic value of the business at $K_1$ (i.e. at the end of year 1, which is the same as saying the beginning of year 2) is calculated in Figure 9.4. This shows that $K_1$ is £115,403 calculated as the present value of anticipated earnings of £131,000 spread over a four-year term.

From this information we are able to calculate $Y$ for the period $Y_1$, as in Figure 9.5. Note that $C$ (consumption) is nil because, in this exercise, dividends representing consumption have not been payable for $Y_1$. In other words, income $Y_1$ is entirely in the form of projected capital growth, i.e. savings.

By year-end $K_1$, earnings of £26,000 will have been received; in projecting the capital at $K_2$ such earnings will have been reinvested and at the beginning of year $K_2$ will have a PV of £26,000. These earnings will no longer represent a **predicted** sum because they will have been **realised** and therefore will no longer be subjected to discounting.

**Figure 9.4 Economic value at $K_1$**

| | (a) | (b) | (c) |
|---|---|---|---|
| Year | Cash flow | $DCF = \dfrac{1}{(1+r)^n}$ | $\dfrac{PV}{(a) \times (b)}$ |
| | £ | | £ |
| $K_1$ | 26,000 | 1.0000 | 26,000 |
| $K_2$ | 29,000 | $\dfrac{1}{(1+r)^1} = 0.9259$ | 26,851 |
| $K_3$ | 35,000 | $\dfrac{1}{(1+r)^2} = 0.8573$ | 30,006 |
| $K_4$ | 41,000 | $\dfrac{1}{(1+r)^3} = 0.7938$ | 32,546 |
| | 131,000 | | 115,403 |

**Figure 9.5 Calculation of Y for the period $Y_1$**

$$Y = C + (K_1 - K_0)$$
$$Y = 0 + (115,403 - 106,853)$$
$$= 0 + 8,550$$
$$= £8,550$$

The income of £8,550 represents an anticipated return of 8% p.a. on the economic capital at $K_0$ of £106,853 (8% of £106,853 is £8,548, the difference of £2 between this figure and the figure calculated above being caused by rounding).

As long as the expectations of future cash flows and the chosen interest rate do not change, then $Y_1$ will equal 8% of £106,853.

### What will the anticipated income for the year $Y_2$ amount to?

Applying the principle explained above, the anticipated income for the year $Y_2$ will equal 8% of the capital at the end of $K_1$ amounting to £115,403 = £9,233. This is demonstrated in Figure 9.6, which shows that $K_2$ is £124,636 calculated as the present value of anticipated earnings of £131,000 spread over a four-year term.

From this information we are able to calculate $Y$ for the period $Y_2$ as in Figure 9.7. Note that capital value attributable to the end of year $K_2$ is being assessed at the beginning of $K_2$. This means that the £26,000 due at the end of year $K_1$ will have been received and reinvested, earning interest of 8% p.a. Thus by the end of year $K_2$ it will be worth £28,080. The sum of £29,000 will be realised at the end of year $K_2$ so its present value at that time will be £29,000.

If the anticipated future cash flows change, the expected capital value at the successive points in time will also change. Accordingly, the actual value of capital may vary from that forecast by the *ex ante* model.

**Figure 9.6 Economic value at $K_2$**

| Year | (a)<br>Cash flow<br>£ | (b)<br>$DCF = \dfrac{1}{(1+r)^n}$<br>£ | (c)<br>$PV = (a) \times (b)$<br>£ |
|---|---|---|---|
| $K_1$ | 26,000 | 1.08 | 28,080 |
| $K_2$ | 29,000 | 1.0000 | 29,000 |
| $K_3$ | 35,000 | 0.9259 | 32,407 |
| $K_4$ | 41,000 | 0.8573 | 35,149 |
| | 131,000 | | 124,636 |

**Figure 9.7 Calculation of Y for the period $Y_2$**

$$Y = C + (K_2 - K_1)$$
$$Y = 0 + (124,636 - 115,403)$$
$$= 0 + 9,233$$
$$= £9,233$$

## 9.6 Critical comment on the economist's measure

While the income measure enables us to formulate theories regarding the behaviour of the economy, it has inherent shortcomings not only in the economic field but particularly in the accountancy sphere.

- The calculation of economic capital, hence economic income, is subjective in terms of the present value factor, often referred to as the DCF element. The factor may be based on any one of a number of factors, such as opportunity cost, the current return on the firm's existing capital employed, the contemporary interest payable on a short-term loan such as a bank overdraft, the average going rate of interest payable in the economy at large, or a rate considered justified on the basis of the risk attached to a particular investment.

- Investors are not of one mind or one outlook. For example, they possess different risk and time preferences and will therefore employ different discount factors.

- The model constitutes a compound of unrealised and realised flows, i.e. profits. Because of the unrealised element, it has not been used as a base for computing tax or for declaring a dividend.

- The projected income is dependent upon the success of a planned financial strategy. Investment plans may change, or fail to attain target.

- Windfall gains cannot be foreseen, so they cannot be accommodated in the *ex ante* model. Our prognostic cash flows may therefore vary from the actual flows generated, e.g. an unexpected price movement.

- It is difficult to construct a satisfactory, meaningful statement of financial position detailing the unused stock of net assets by determining the present values of individual assets. Income is invariably the consequence of deploying a group of assets working in unison.

## 9.7 Income, capital and changing price levels

A primary concern of income measurement to both the economist and accountant is the maintenance of the capital stock, i.e. the maintenance of capital values. The assumption is that income can only arise **after** the capital stock has been maintained at the same amount as at the beginning of the accounting period.

However, this raises the question of how we should define the capital that we are attempting to maintain. There are a number of possible definitions:

- **Money capital.** Should we concern ourselves with maintaining the fund of capital resources initially injected by the entrepreneur into the new enterprise? This is indeed one of the aims of traditional, transaction-based accountancy.

- **Potential consumption capital.** Is it this that should be maintained, i.e. the economist's present value philosophy expressed via the discounted cash flow technique?

- **Operating capacity capital.** Should maintenance of productive capacity be the rule, i.e. capital measured in terms of tangible or physical assets? This measure would utilise the current cost accounting system.

Revsine attempted to construct an analytical bridge between replacement cost accounting that maintains the operating capacity, and the economic concepts of **income** and **value,** by demonstrating that the distributable operating flow component of economic income is equal to the current operating component of replacement cost income, and that the unexpected income component of economic income is equal to the unrealisable cost savings of replacement cost income.[4] This will become clearer when the replacement cost model is dealt with in the next chapter.

- **Financial capital.** Should capital be maintained in terms of a fund of general purchasing power (sometimes called 'real' capital)? In essence, this is the consumer purchasing power (or general purchasing power) approach, but not in a strict sense, as it can be measured in a variety of ways. The basic method uses a general price index. This concept is likely to satisfy the criteria of the proprietor/shareholders of the entity. The money capital and the financial capital concepts are variations of the same theme, the former being founded on the historical cost principle and the latter applying an adjustment mechanism to take account of changing price levels.

The money capital concept has remained the foundation stone of traditional accountancy reporting, but the operating and financial capital alternatives have played a controversial secondary role over the past 25 years.

Potential consumption capital is peculiar to economics in terms of measurement of the business entity's aggregate capital, although, as discussed in Section 9.5.2, it has a major role to play as a decision-making model in financial management.

### 9.7.1 Why are these varying methods of concern?

The problem tackled by these devices is that plague of the economy known as 'changing price levels', particularly the upward spiralling referred to as **inflation**. Throughout this chapter we have assumed that there is a stable monetary unit and that income, capital and value changes over time have been in response to operational activity and the interaction of supply and demand or changes in expectations.

Following the historical cost convention, capital maintenance has involved a comparison of opening and closing capital in each accounting period. It has been assumed that the purchasing power of money has remained constant over time.

If we take into account moving price levels, particularly the fall in the purchasing power of the monetary unit due to inflation, then our measure of **income** is affected if we insist upon **maintaining capital in real terms**.

### 9.7.2 Is it necessary to maintain capital in real terms?

Undoubtedly it is necessary if we wish to prevent an erosion of the operating capacity of the entity and thus its ability to maintain real levels of income. If we do not maintain the capacity of capital to generate the current level of profit, then the income measure, being the difference between opening and closing capitals, will be overstated or overvalued. This is because the capital measure is being understated or undervalued. In other words, there is a danger of dividends being paid out of real capital rather than out of real income. It follows that, if the need to retain profits is overlooked, the physical assets will be depleted.

In accountancy there is no theoretical difficulty in measuring the impact of changing price levels. There are, however, two practical difficulties:

- A number of methods, or mixes of methods, are available and it has proved impossible to obtain consensus support for one method or compound of methods.
- There is a high element of subjectivity, which detracts from the objectivity of the information.

In the next chapter we deal with inflation and analyse the methods formulated, together with the difficulties that they in turn introduce into the financial reporting system.

## Summary

In measuring income, capital and value, the accountant's approach varies from the sister discipline of the economist, yet both are trying to achieve similar objectives.

The accountant uses a traditional transaction-based model of computing income, capital being the residual of this model.

The economist's viewpoint is anchored in a behavioural philosophy that measures capital and deduces income to be the difference between the capital at the beginning of a period and that at its end.

The objectives of income measurement are important because of the existence of a highly sophisticated capital market. These objectives involve the assessment of stewardship performance, dividend and retention policies, comparison of actual results with those predicted, assessment of future prospects, payment of taxation and disclosure of matched costs against revenue from sales.

The natures of income, capital and value must be appreciated if we are to understand and achieve measurement. The apparent conflict between the two measures can be seen as a consequence of the accountant's need for periodic reporting to shareholders. In the longer term, both methods tend to agree.

Present value as a concept is the foundation stone of the economist, while historical cost, adjusted for prudence, is that of the accountant. Present value demands a subjective discount rate and estimates that time may prove incorrect; historical cost ignores unrealised profits and in application is not always transaction based.

The economist's measure, of undoubted value in the world of micro- and macroeconomics, presents difficulty in the accountancy world of annual reports. The accountant's method, with its long track record of acceptance, ignores any generated profits, which caution and the concept of the going concern deem not to exist.

The economic trauma of changing price levels is a problem that both measures can embrace, but consensus support for a particular model of measurement has proved elusive.

## REVIEW QUESTIONS

1  What is the purpose of measuring income?

2  Explain the nature of economic income.

3  The historical cost concept has withstood the test of time. Specify the reasons for this success, together with any aspects of historical cost that you consider are detrimental in the sphere of financial reporting.

4  What is meant by present value? Does it take account of inflation?

5  Explain what you understand by an *ex ante* model.

6  Explain the principal criticisms of the economist's measure of income.

7  To an accountant, net income is essentially a historical record of the past. To an economist, net income is essentially a speculation about the future. Examine the relative merits of these two approaches for financial reporting purposes.

**8** Examine and contrast the concepts of profit that you consider to be relevant to:

(a) an economist;

(b) a speculator;

(c) a business executive;

(d) the managing director of a company;

(e) a shareholder in a private company;

(f) a shareholder in a large public company.

## EXERCISES

### * Question 1

(a) 'Measurement in financial statements', Chapter 6 of the ASB's *Statement of Principles*, was published in 1999. Among the theoretical valuation systems considered is value in use, more commonly known as economic value.

Required:
**Describe the Hicksian economic model of income and value, and assess its usefulness for financial reporting.**

(b) Jim Bowater purchased a parcel of 30,000 ordinary shares in New Technologies plc for £36,000 on 1 January 20X5. Jim, an Australian on a four-year contract in the UK, has it in mind to sell the shares at the end of 20X7, just before he leaves for Australia. Based on the company's forecast growth and dividend policy, his broker has advised him that his shares are likely to fetch only £35,000 then.

In its annual report for the year ended 31 December 20X4 the company had forecast annual dividend payouts as follows:

Year ended:  31 December 20X5, 25p per share
31 December 20X6, 20p per share
31 December 20X7, 20p per share

Required:
**Using the economic model of income:**
(i) **Compute Jim's economic income for each of the three years ending on the dates indicated above.**
(ii) **Show that Jim's economic capital will be preserved at 1 January 20X5 level. Jim's cost of capital is 20%.**

### * Question 2

(a) Describe briefly the theory underlying Hicks's economic model of income and capital. What are its practical limitations?

(b) Spock purchased a Space Invader entertainment machine at the beginning of year 1 for £1,000. He expects to receive at annual intervals the following receipts: at the end of year 1 £400; at the end of year 2 £500; at the end of year 3 £600. At the end of year 3 he expects to sell the machine for £400.

Spock could receive a return of 10% in the next best investment.

The present value of £1 receivable at the end of a period discounted at 10% is as follows:

| | |
|---|---|
| End of year 1 | £0.909 |
| End of year 2 | £0.826 |
| End of year 3 | £0.751 |

**Required:**

Calculate the ideal economic income, ignoring taxation and working to the nearest £.

Your answer should show that Spock's capital is maintained throughout the period and that his income is constant.

## Question 3

Jason commenced with £135,000 cash. He acquired an established shop on 1 January 20X1. He agreed to pay £130,000 for the fixed and current assets and the goodwill. The replacement cost of the shop premises was £100,000, stock £10,000 and debtors £4,000; the balance of the purchase price was for the goodwill. He paid legal costs of £5,000. No liabilities were taken over. Jason could have resold the business immediately for £135,000. Legal costs are to be expensed in 20X1.

Jason expected to draw £25,000 per year from the business for three years and to sell the shop at the end of 20X3 for £150,000.

At 31 December 20X1 the books showed the following tangible assets and liabilities:

| Cost to the business before any drawings by Jason: | | He estimated that the net realisable values were: | |
|---|---|---|---|
| | £ | | £ |
| Shop premises | 100,000 | | 85,000 |
| Stock | 15,500 | | 20,000 |
| Debtors | 5,200 | | 5,200 |
| Cash | 40,000 | | 40,000 |
| Creditors | 5,000 | | 5,000 |

Based on his experience of the first year's trading, he revised his estimates and expected to draw £35,000 per year for three years and sell the shop for £175,000 on 31 December 20X3. Jason's opportunity cost of capital was 20%.

**Required:**

(a) Calculate the following income figures for 20X1:
   (i) accounting income;
   (ii) income based on net realisable values;
   (iii) economic income *ex ante*;
   (iv) economic income *ex post*.
   State any assumptions made.

(b) Evaluate each of the four income figures as indicators of performance in 20X1 and as a guide to decisions about the future.

## Notes

1  T.A. Lee, *Income and Value Measurement: Theory and Practice* (3rd edition), Van Nostrand Reinhold (UK), 1985, p. 20.
2  D. Solomons, *Making Accounting Policy*, Oxford University Press, 1986, p. 132.
3  R.W. Scapens, *Accounting in an Inflationary Environment* (2nd edition), Macmillan, 1981, p. 125.
4  Ibid., p. 127.
5  T.A. Lee, *op. cit.*, pp. 52–54.
6  I. Fisher, *The Theory of Interest*, Macmillan, 1930, pp. 171–181.
7  J.R. Hicks, *Value and Capital* (2nd edition), Clarendon Press, 1946.

## Bibliography

American Institute of Certifed Public Accountants, *Objectives of Financial Statements*, Report of the Study Group, 1973. *The Corporate Report*, ASC, 1975, pp. 28–31.

N. Kaldor, 'The concept of income in economic theory', in R.H. Parker and G.C. Harcourt (eds), *Readings in the Concept and Measurement of Income*, Cambridge University Press, 1969.

T.A. Lee, 'The accounting entity concept, accounting standards and inflation accounting', *Accounting and Business Research*, Spring 1980, pp. 1–11.

J.R. Little, 'Income measurement: an introduction', *Student Newsletter*, June 1988.

D. Solomons, 'Economic and accounting concepts of income', in R.H. Parker and G.C. Harcourt (eds), *Readings in the Concept and Measurement of Income*, Cambridge University Press, 1969.

R.R. Sterling, *Theory of the Measurement of Enterprise Income*, University of Kansas Press, 1970.

# CHAPTER 10

# Accounting for price-level changes

## 10.1 Introduction

The main purpose of this chapter is to explain the impact of inflation on profit and capital measurement and the concepts that have been proposed to incorporate the effect into financial reports by adjusting the historical cost data. These concepts are periodically discussed but there is no general support for any specific concept among practitioners in the field.

### Objectives

By the end of the chapter, you should be able to:

● describe the problems of historical cost accounting (HCA);
● explain the approach taken in each of the price-level changing models;
● prepare financial statements applying each model (HCA, CPP, CCA, NRVA);
● critically comment on each model (HCA, CPP, CCA, NRVA);
● describe the approach being taken by standard setters and future developments.

## 10.2 Review of the problems of historical cost accounting (HCA)

The transaction-based historical cost concept was unchallenged in the UK until price levels started to hedge upwards at an ever-increasing pace during the 1950s and reached an annual rate of increase of 20% in the mid-1970s. The historical cost base for financial reporting witnessed growing criticism. The inherent faults of the system were discussed in Chapter 6, but inflation exacerbates the problem in the following ways:

● Profit is overstated when inflationary changes in the value of assets are ignored.

● Comparability of business entities, which is so necessary in the assessment of performance and growth, becomes distorted when assets are acquired at different times.

● The decision-making process, the formulation of plans and the setting of targets may be suboptimal if financial base data are out of date.

● Financial reports become confusing at best, misleading at worst, because revenue is mismatched with differing historical cost levels as the monetary unit becomes unstable.

● Unrealised profits arising in individual accounting periods are increased as a result of inflation.

In order to combat these serious defects, current value accounting became the subject of research and controversy as to the most appropriate method to use for financial reporting.

## 10.3 Inflation accounting

A number of versions of current value accounting (CVA) were eventually identified, but the current value postulate was said to suffer from the following disadvantages:

- It destroys the factual nature of HCA, which is transaction-based: the factual characteristic is to all intents and purposes lost as transaction-based historic values are replaced by judgemental values.
- It is not as objective as HCA because it is less verifiable from auditable documentation.
- It entails recognition of unrealised profit, a practice that is anathema to the traditionalist.
- The claimed improvement in comparability between commercial entities is a myth because of the degree of subjectivity in measuring current value by each.
- The lack of a single accepted method of computing current values compounds the subjectivity aspect. One fault-laden system is being usurped by another that is also faulty.

In spite of these criticisms, the search for a system of financial reporting devoid of the defects of HCA and capable of coping with inflation has produced a number of CVA models.

## 10.4 The concepts in principle

Several current income and value models have been proposed to replace or operate in tandem with the historical cost convention. However, in terms of basic characteristics, they may be reduced to the following three models:

- current purchasing power (CPP) or general purchasing power (GPP);
- current entry cost or replacement cost (RC);
- current exit cost or net realisable value (NRV).

We discuss each of these models below.

### 10.4.1 Current purchasing power accounting (CPPA)

The CPP model measures income and value by adopting a price index system. Movements in price levels are gauged by reference to price changes in a group of goods and services in **general** use within the economy. The aggregate price value of this **basket** of commodities-cum-services is determined at a base point in time and indexed as 100. Subsequent changes in price are compared on a regular basis with this base period price and the change recorded. For example, the price level of our chosen range of goods and services may amount to £76 on 31 March 20X1, and show changes as follows:

| | |
|---|---|
| £76 | at 31 March 20X1 |
| £79 | at 30 April 20X1 |
| £81 | at 31 May 20X1 |
| £84 | at 30 June 20X1 |

and so on.

The change in price may be indexed with 31 March as the base:

| 20X1 | Calculation | Index |
|---|---|---|
| 31 March | i.e. £76 | 100 |
| 30 April | i.e. $\dfrac{79}{76} \times 100$ | 103.9 |
| 31 May | i.e. $\dfrac{80}{76} \times 100$ | 106.6 |
| 30 June | i.e. $\dfrac{84}{76} \times 100$ | 110.5 |

In the UK, index systems similar in construction to this are known as the Retail or Consumer Price Index (RPI). The index is a barometer of fluctuating price levels covering a miscellany of goods and services as used by the average household. Thus it is a **general** price index. It is amended from time to time to take account of new commodities entering the consumer's range of choice and needs. As a model, it is unique owing to the introduction of the concept of gains and losses in **purchasing power**.

### 10.4.2 Current entry or replacement cost accounting (RCA)

The replacement cost (RC) model assesses income and value by reference to entry costs or current replacement costs of materials and other assets utilised within the business entity. The valuation attempts to replace like with like and thus takes account of the quality and condition of the existing assets. A motor vehicle, for instance, may have been purchased brand new for £25,000 with an expected life of five years, an anticipated residual value of nil and a straight-line depreciation policy. Its HCA carrying value in the statement of financial position at the end of its first year would be £25,000 less £5,000 = £20,000. However, if a similar new replacement vehicle cost £30,000 at the end of year 1, then its gross RC would be £30,000; depreciation for one year based on this sum would be £6,000 and the net RC would be £24,000. The increase of £4,000 is a holding gain and the vehicle with an HCA carrying value of £20,000 would be revalued at £24,000.

### 10.4.3 Current exit cost or net realisable value accounting (NRVA)

The net realisable value (NRV) model is based on the economist's concept of opportunity cost. It is a model that has had strong academic support, most notably in Australia from Professor Ray Chambers who referred to this approach as Continuous Contemporary Accounting (CoCoA). If an asset cost £25,000 at the beginning of year 1 and at the end of that year it had an NRV of £21,000 after meeting selling expenses, it would be carried in the NRV statement of financial position at £21,000. This amount represents the cash forgone by holding the asset, i.e. the opportunity of possessing cash of £21,000 has been sacrificed in favour of the asset. There is effectively a holding loss for the year of £25,000 less £21,000 = £4,000.

## 10.5 The four models illustrated for a company with cash purchases and sales

We will illustrate the effect on the profit and net assets of Entrepreneur Ltd.

Entrepreneur Ltd commenced business on 1 January 20X1 with a capital of £3,000 to buy and sell second-hand computers. The company purchased six computers on 1 January 20X1 for £500 each and sold three of the computers on 15 January for £900 each.

The following data are available for January 20X1:

|  | Retail Price Index | Replacement cost per computer £ | Net realisable value £ |
|---|---|---|---|
| 1 January | 100 |  |  |
| 15 January | 112 | 610 |  |
| 31 January | 130 | 700 | 900 |

The statements of income and financial position are set out in Figure 10.1 with the detailed workings in Figure 10.2.

## 10.5.1 Financial capital maintenance concept

HCA and CPP are both transaction-based models that apply the financial capital maintenance concept. This means that profit is the difference between the opening and closing net assets (expressed in HC £) or the opening and closing net assets (expressed in HC £ indexed for RPI changes) adjusted for any capital introduced or withdrawn during the month.

**Figure 10.1 Trading account for the month ended 31 January 20X1**

*Statements of income for the month ended 31 January 20X1*

|  | HCA | | CPP | | RCA | | NRVA | |
|---|---|---|---|---|---|---|---|---|
|  | £ | | CPP£ | | £ | | £ | |
| Sales | 2,700 | W1 | 3,134 | W5 | 2,700 | W1 | 2,700 | W1 |
| Opening inventory | — | | — | | — | | — | |
| Purchases | 3,000 | W2 | 3,900 | W6 | 3,000 | W2 | 3,000 | W2 |
| Closing inventory | (1,500) | W3 | (1,950) | W7 | (1,500) | W3 | (1,500) | W3 |
| COSA | na | | na | | 330 | W10 | na | |
| Cost of sales | 1,500 | | 1,950 | | 1,830 | | 1,500 | |
| Holding gain | na | | na | | na | | 1,200 | W15 |
| Profit | 1,200 | | 1,184 | | 870 | | 2,400 | |

*Statement of financial position as at 31 January 20X1*

|  | £ | | PCP£ | | £ | | £ | |
|---|---|---|---|---|---|---|---|---|
| Current assets |  | | | | | | | |
| Inventory | 1,500 | W3 | 1,950 | W7 | 2,100 | W11 | 2,700 | W14 |
| Cash | 2,700 | W4 | 2,700 | | 2,700 | | 2,700 | |
| Capital employed | 4,200 | | 4,650 | | 4,800 | | 5,400 | |
| Capital | 3,000 | | 3,900 | W8 | 3,000 | | 3,000 | |
| Holding gains |  | | | | | | | |
| On inventory consumed | na | | na | | 330 | W12 | | |
| On inventory in hand | na | | na | | 600 | W13 | | |
| Profit | 1,200 | | 1,184 | | 870 | | 2,400 | |
| Loss on monetary items | na | | (434) | W9 | na | | na | |
|  | 4,200 | | 4,650 | | 4,800 | | 5,400 | |

na = not applicable

### Figure 10.2 Workings (W)

**HCA**

| | | |
|---|---|---|
| W1 Sales | 3 × £900 = £2,700 | |
| W2 Purchases | 6 × £500 = £3,000 | |
| W3 Closing inventory | 3 × £500 = £1,500 | |
| W4 Cash | 1 January 20X1 Capital | 3,000 |
| | 1 January 20X1 Purchases | (3,000) |
| | 1 January 20X1 Balance | nil |
| | 15 January 20X1 Sales | |
| | 3 × £900 = | £2,700 |
| | 31 January 20X1 Balance | £2,700 |

**CPP**

| | | CPP£ |
|---|---|---|
| W5 Sales | £2,700 × 130/112 = | 3,134 |
| W6 Purchases | £3,000 × 130/100 = | 3,900 |
| W7 Closing inventory | £1,500 × 130/100 = | 1,950 |
| W8 Capital | £3,000 × 130/100 = | 3,900 |

W9 Balance of cash was nil until 15 January when sales generated £2,700. This sum was held until 31 January during which period cash, a monetary item, lost purchasing power. The loss of purchasing power is measured by applying the general index to the cash held: £2,700 × 130/112 − £2,700 = CPP £434.

**RCA**

W10 Additional replacement cost of inventory consumed as at the date of sale is measured as a cost of sales adjustment (COSA). COSA is calculated as follows:

| | | |
|---|---|---|
| | 3 × £610 = | 1,830 |
| *Less:* | 3 × £500 = | 1,500 |
| COSA | | £330 |

W11 Closing inventory: 3 × £700 = £2,100

W12 Holding gains on inventory consumed: as for W10 = £330

| W13 | Inventory at replacement cost | = 3 × £700 = 2,100 |
|---|---|---|
| | *Less:* inventory at cost | = 3 × £500 = 1,500 |
| | Holding gains on closing inventory | £600 |

**NRVA**

W14 Closing inventory at net realisable value = 900 × 3 = £2,700

| W15 | 3 × £900 = | 2,700 |
|---|---|---|
| | 3 × £500 = | 1,500 |
| | Holding gain | £1,200 |

### CPP adjustments

- All historical cost values are adjusted to a common index level for the month. In theory this can be the index applicable to any day of the financial period concerned. However, in practice it has been deemed preferable to use the last day of the period; thus the financial statements show the latest price level appertaining to the period.

- The application of a general price index as an adjusting factor results in the creation of an **alien** currency of **purchasing power,** which is used in place of sterling. Note, particularly, the impact on the entity's sales and capital compared with the other models. **Actual** sales shown on **invoices** will still read £2,700.

- Note the application of the concept of gain or loss on holding monetary items. In this example there is a monetary loss of CPP £434 as shown in Working 9 in Figure 10.2.

### 10.5.2 Operating capital maintenance concept

Under this concept capital is only maintained if sufficient income is retained to maintain the business entity's physical operating capacity, i.e. its ability to produce the existing level of goods or services. Profit is, therefore, the residual after increasing the cost of sales to the cost applicable at the date of sale.

- Basically, only two adjustments are involved: the additional replacement cost of inventory consumed and holding gains on closing inventories. However, in a comprehensive exercise an adjustment will be necessary regarding non-current assets and you will also encounter a gearing adjustment.

- Notice the concept of holding gains. This model introduces, in effect, unrealised profits in respect of closing inventories. The holding gain concerning inventory consumed at the time of sale has been realised and deducted from what would have been a profit of £1,200. The statement discloses profits of £870.

### 10.5.3 Capacity to adapt concept under the NRVA model

The HCA, CPP and RCA models have assumed that the business will continue as a going concern and only distribute realised profits after retaining sufficient profits to maintain either the financial or operating capital.

The NRVA concept is that a business has the capacity to realise its net assets at the end of each financial period and reinvest the proceeds and that the NRV accounts provide management with this information.

- This produces the same initial profit as HCA, namely £1,200, but a peculiarity of this system is that this realised profit is supplemented by **unrealised** profit generated by holding stocks. Under RCA accounting, such gains are shown in a separate account and are not treated as part of real income.

- This simple exercise has ignored the possibility of investment in non-current assets, thus depreciation is not involved. A reduction in the NRV of non-current assets at the end of a period compared with the beginning would be treated in a similar fashion to depreciation by being charged to the revenue account, and consequently profits would be reduced. An increase in the NRV of such assets would be included as part of the profit.

### 10.5.4 The four models compared

#### Dividend distribution

We can see from Figure 10.1 that if the business were to distribute the profit reported under HCA, CPP or NRVA the physical operating capacity of the business would be reduced and it would be paying dividends out of capital:

|  | *HCA* | *CPP* | *RCA* | *NRVA* |
|---|---|---|---|---|
| Realised profit | 1,200 | 1,184 | 870 | 1,200 |
| Unrealised profit | — | — | — | 1,200 |
| Profit for month | 1,200 | 1,184 | 870 | 2,400 |

#### Shareholder orientation

The CPP model is shareholder-oriented in that it shows whether shareholders' funds are keeping pace with inflation by maintaining their purchasing power. Only CPP changes the value of the share capital.

#### Management orientation

The RCA model is management-oriented in that it identifies holding gains which represent the amounts required to be retained in order to simply maintain the operating capital.

RCA measures the impact of inflation on the individual firm, in terms of the change in price levels of its **raw materials and assets**, i.e. inflation peculiar to the company, whereas CPP measures general inflation in the economy as a whole. CPP may be meaningless in the case of an individual company. Consider a firm that carries a constant volume of stock valued at £100 in HCA terms. Now suppose that price levels double when measured by a general price index (GPI), so that its inventory is restated to £200 in a CPP system. If, however, the cost of that **particular** inventory has risen by 500%, then under the RCA model the value of the stock should be £500.

In the mid-1970s, when the accountancy profession was debating the problem of changing price-level measurement, the general price level had climbed by some 23% over a period during which petroleum-based products had risen by 500%.

## 10.6 Critique of each model

A critique of the various models may be formulated in terms of their characteristics and peculiarities as virtues and defects in application.

### 10.6.1 HCA

This model's virtues and defects have been discussed in Chapter 6 and earlier in this chapter.

### 10.6.2 CPP

#### Virtues

- It is an **objective measure** since it is still transaction-based, as with HCA, and the possibility of subjectivity is constrained if a GPI is used that has been constructed by a central agency such as a government department. This applies in the UK, where the Retail Price Index is currently published by the Office for National Statistics.

- It is a **measure of shareholders' capital** and that capital's maintenance in terms of purchasing power units. Profit is the residual value after maintaining the money value of capital funds, taking account of changing price levels. Thus it is a measure readily understood by the shareholder/user of the accounts. It can prevent payment of a dividend out of real capital as measured by GPPA.

- It **introduces the concept of monetary items** as distinct from non-monetary items and the attendant concepts of gains and losses in holding net monetary liabilities compared with holding net monetary assets. Such gains and losses are experienced on a disturbing scale in times of inflation. They are **real** gains and losses. The **basic** RCA and NRV models do not recognise such 'surpluses' and 'deficits'.

### Defects

- It is **HCA-based but adjusted** to reflect general price movements. Thus it possesses the characteristics of HCA, good and bad, but with its values updated in the light of an arithmetic measure of general price changes. The major defect of becoming out of date is mitigated to a degree, but the impact of inflation on the entity's income and capital may be at variance with the rate of inflation affecting the economy in general.

- It may be **wrongly assumed that the CPP statement of financial position is a current value statement.** It is not a current value document because of the defects discussed above; in particular, asset values may be subject to a different rate of inflation than that reflected by the GPI.

- It **creates an alien unit of measurement** still labelled by the £ sign. Thus we have the HCA £ and the CPP £. They are different pounds: one is the *bona fide* pound, the other is a synthetic unit. This may not be fully appreciated or understood by the user when faced with the financial accounts for the recent accounting period.

- Its **concept of profit is dangerous.** It pretends to cater for changing prices, but at the same time it fails to provide for the additional costs of replacing stocks sold or additional depreciation due to the escalating replacement cost of assets. The inflation encountered by the business entity will not be the same as that encountered by the whole economy. Thus the maintenance of the CPP of shareholders' capital via this concept of profit is not the maintenance of the entity's operating capital in physical terms, i.e. its capacity to produce the same volume of goods and services. The use of CPP profit as a basis for decision making without regard to RCA profit can have disastrous consequences.

## 10.6.3 RCA

### Virtues

- Its **unit of measurement** is the monetary unit and consequently it is understood and accepted by the user of accountancy reports. In contrast, the CPP system employs an artificial unit based on arithmetic relationships, which is different and thus unfamiliar.

- It **identifies and isolates holding gains** from operating income. Thus it can prevent the inadvertent distribution of dividends in excess of operating profit. It satisfies the prudence criterion of the traditional accountant and **maintains the physical operating capacity** of the entity.

- It introduces **realistic current values** of assets in the statement of financial position, thus making the statement of financial position a 'value' statement and consequently more meaningful to the user. This contrasts sharply with the statement of financial position as a list of unallocated carrying costs in the HCA system.

### Defects

- It is a **subjective measure,** in that replacement costs are often necessarily based on estimates or assessments. It does not possess the factual characteristics of HCA. It is open to manipulation within constraints. Often it is based on index numbers which themselves may be based on a compound of prices of a mixture of similar commodities used as raw material or operating assets. This subjectivity is exacerbated in circumstances where rapid technological advance and innovation are involved in the potential new replacement asset, e.g. computers and printers.

- It **assumes replacement of assets** by being based on their replacement cost. Difficulties arise if such assets are not to be replaced by similar assets. Presumably, it will then be assumed that a replacement of equivalent value to the original will be deployed, however differently, as capital within the firm.

## 10.6.4 NRVA

### Virtues

- It is a concept readily understood by the user. The value of any item invariably has two measures – a buying price and a selling price – and the twain do not usually meet. However, when considering the value of an **existing** possession, the owner instinctively considers its 'value' to be that in potential sale, i.e. NRV.

- It **avoids the need to estimate depreciation** and, in consequence, the attendant problems of assessing lifespan and residual values. Depreciation is treated as the arithmetic difference between the NRV at the end of a financial period and the NRV at its beginning.

- It is **based on opportunity cost** and so can be said to be more meaningful. It is the **sacrificial** cost of possessing an asset, which, it can be argued, is more authentic in terms of being a true or real cost. If the asset were not possessed, its cash equivalent would exist instead and that cash would be deployed in other opportunities. Therefore, NRV = cash = opportunity = cost.

### Defects

- It is a **subjective measure** and in this respect it possesses the same major fault as RCA. It can be said to be less prudent than RCA because NRV will tend to be higher in some cases than RCA. For example, when valuing finished inventories, a profit content will be involved.

- **It is not a realistic measure** as most assets, except finished goods, are possessed in order to be utilised, not sold. Therefore, NRV is irrelevant.

- **It is not always determinable.** The assets concerned may be highly specialist and there may be no ready market by which a value can be easily assessed. Consequently, any particular value may be fictitious or erroneous, containing too high a holding gain or, indeed, too low a holding loss.

- **It violates the concept of the going concern,** which demands that the accounts are drafted on the basis that there is no intention to liquidate the entity. Admittedly, this concept was formulated with HCA in view, but the acceptance of NRV implies the possibility of a cessation of trading.

- It is less reliable and verifiable than HC.

- The statement of comprehensive income will report a more volatile profit if changes in NRV are taken to the statement of comprehensive income each year.

- The profit arising from the changes in NRV may not have been realised.

Ulster University
Belfast Campus

**Customer name: Mrs Mandeep Kaur .**
**Customer ID: B00950987**

**Items that you have checked out**

Title: Financial accounting and reporting
ID:  100640199
**Due: 08 January 2024**

Total items: 1
Account balance: £0.00
Checked out: 1
Overdue: 0
Hold requests: 0
Ready for collection: 0
13/11/2023 13:12

Thank you for using the bibliotheca SelfCheck
System.

## 10.7 Operating capital maintenance – a comprehensive example

In Figure 10.1 we considered the effect of inflation on a cash business without fixed assets, credit customers or credit suppliers. In the following example, Economica plc, we now consider the effect where there are non-current assets and credit transactions.

The HCA statements of financial position as at 31 December 20X4 and 20X5 are set out in Figure 10.3 and index numbers required to restate the non-current assets, inventory and monetary items in Figure 10.4.

### 10.7.1 Restating the opening statement of financial position to current cost

The non-current assets and inventory are restated to their current cost as at the date of the opening statement as shown in W1 and W2 below. The increase from HC to CC represents an unrealised holding gain which is debited to the asset account and credited to a reserve account called a current cost reserve, as in W3 below.

**Figure 10.3 Economica plc HCA statement of financial position**

*Statements of financial position as at 31 December on the basis of HCA*

|  | 20X5 |  | | 20X4 |
|---|---|---|---|---|
|  | £000 | £000 | £000 | £000 |
| Non-current assets: |  |  |  |  |
| Cost | 85,000 |  | 85,000 |  |
| Depreciation | 34,000 |  | 25,500 |  |
|  |  | 51,000 |  | 59,500 |
| Current assets: |  |  |  |  |
| Inventory | 25,500 |  | 17,000 |  |
| Trade receivables | 34,000 |  | 23,375 |  |
| Cash and bank | 17,000 |  | 1,875 |  |
|  | 76,500 |  | 42,250 |  |
| Current liabilities: |  |  |  |  |
| Trade payables | 25,500 |  | 17,000 |  |
| Income tax | 8,500 |  | 4,250 |  |
| Dividend declared | 5,000 |  | 4,000 |  |
|  | 39,000 |  | 25,250 |  |
| Net current assets | 37,500 |  | 17,000 |  |
| Less: 8% debentures | 11,000 |  | 11,000 |  |
|  |  | 26,500 |  | 6,000 |
|  |  | 77,500 |  | 65,500 |
| Share capital and reserves: |  |  |  |  |
| Authorised and issued £1 ordinary shares |  | 50,000 |  | 50,000 |
| Share premium |  | 1,500 |  | 1,500 |
| Retained earnings |  | 26,000 |  | 14,000 |
|  |  | 77,500 |  | 65,500 |

**Figure 10.4 Index data relating to Economica plc**

1   Index numbers as prepared by the Office for National Statistics for non-current assets:

|  |  |
|---|---|
| 1 January 20X2 | 100 |
| 1 January 20X5 | 165 |
| 1 January 20X6 | 185 |
| Average for 20X4 | 147 |
| Average for 20X5 | 167 |

2   All non-current assets were acquired on 1 January 20X2. There were no further acquisitions or disposals during the four years ended 31 December 20X5.

3   Indices as prepared by the Office for National Statistics for inventories and monetary working capital adjustments were:

|  |  |
|---|---|
| 1 October 20X4 | 115 |
| 31 December 20X4 | 125 |
| 15 November 20X4 | 120 |
| 1 October 20X5 | 140 |
| 31 December 20X5 | 150 |
| 15 November 20X5 | 145 |
| Average for 20X5 | 137.5 |

4   Three months' inventory is carried.

5   Depreciation: historical cost based on 10% p.a. straight-line with residual value of nil:

|  | £ HCA |
|---|---|
| 20X4 | 8,500,000 |
| 20X5 | 8,500,000 |

The calculations are as follows. First we shall convert the HCA statement of financial position in Figure 10.3, as at 31 December 20X4, to the CCA basis, using the index data in Figure 10.4.

The **non-monetary items,** comprising the non-current assets and inventory, are converted and the converted amounts are taken to the CC statement and the increases taken to the current cost reserve, as follows.

**(WI) Property, plant and equipment**

| | HCA £000 | | Index | | CCA £000 | Increase £000 |
|---|---|---|---|---|---|---|
| Cost | 85,000 | $\times$ | $\dfrac{165}{100}$ | $=$ | 140,250 | 55,250 |
| Depreciation | 25,500 | $\times$ | $\dfrac{165}{100}$ | $=$ | 42,075 | 16,575 |
| | 59,500 | | | | 98,175 | 38,675 |

The CCA valuation at 31 December 20X4 shows a net increase in terms of numbers of pounds sterling of £38,675,000. The £59,500,000 in the HCA statement of financial position will be replaced in the CCA statement by £98,175,000.

## (W2) Inventories

| HCA £000 | | Index | | CCA £000 | | Increase £000 |
|---|---|---|---|---|---|---|
| 17,000 | × | $\dfrac{125}{120}$ | = | 17,708 | = | 708 |

Note that Figure 10.4 specifies that three months' inventories are held. Thus on average they will have been purchased on 15 November 20X4, on the assumption that they have been acquired and consumed evenly throughout the calendar period. Hence, the index at the time of purchase would have been 120. The £17,000,000 in the HCA statement of financial position will be replaced in the CCA statement of financial position by £17,708,000.

### (W3) Current cost reserve

The total increase in CCA carrying values for non-monetary items is £39,383,000, which will be credited to CC reserves in the CC statement. It comprises £38,675,000 on the non-current assets and £708,000 on the inventory.

Note that monetary items do not change by virtue of inflation. Purchasing power will be lost or gained, but the carrying values in the CCA statement will be identical to those in its HCA counterpart. We can now compile the CCA statement as at 31 December 20X4 – this will show net assets of £104,883,000.

## 10.7.2 Adjustments that affect the profit for the year

The statement of comprehensive income for the year ended 31 December 20X5 set out in Figure 10.5 discloses a profit before interest and tax of £26,350,000. We need to deduct realised holding gains from this profit to avoid the distribution of dividends that would reduce the operating capital. These deductions are a cost of sales adjustment (COSA), a depreciation adjustment (DA) and a monetary working capital adjustment (MWCA). The accounting treatment is to debit the statement of comprehensive income and credit the current cost reserve.

The adjustments are calculated as follows.

### (W4) Cost of sales adjustment (COSA) using the average method

We will compute the cost of sales adjustment by using the average method. The average purchase price index for 20X5 is 137.5. If price increases have moved at an even pace throughout the period, this implies that consumption occurred, on average, at 30 June, the mid-point of the financial year.

| | HCA £000 | | Adjustment | | CCA £000 | | Difference £000 |
|---|---|---|---|---|---|---|---|
| Opening inventory | 17,000 | × | $\dfrac{137.5}{120}$ | = | 19,479 | = | 2,479 |
| Purchases | — | | — | | — | | — |
| | 17,000 | | | | 19,479 | | |
| Closing inventory | (25,500) | × | $\dfrac{137.5}{145}$ | = | 24,181 | = | 1,319 |
| | (8,500) | | | | (4,702) | | 3,798 |

### Figure 10.5 Economica plc HCA statement of comprehensive income

*Statement of income for the year ended 31 December 20X5, on the basis of HCA*

|  |  | 20X5 |  | 20X4 |
|---|---|---|---|---|
|  |  | £000 |  | £000 |
| Turnover |  | 42,500 |  | 38,250 |
| *Less: Cost of sales* |  | (12,070) |  | (23,025) |
| Gross profit |  | 30,430 |  | 15,225 |
| *Less: Distribution costs* | 2,460 |  | 2,210 |  |
| *Less: Administrative expenses* | 1,620 |  | 1,540 |  |
|  |  | (4,080) |  | (3,750) |
| Profit before interest and tax |  | 26,350 |  | 11,475 |
| Interest |  | (880) |  | (880) |
| Profit before tax |  | 25,470 |  | 10,595 |
| Income tax expense |  | (8,470) |  | (4,250) |
| Profit after tax |  | 17,000 |  | 6,345 |
| Dividend |  | (5,000) |  | (4,000) |
| Retentions |  | 12,000 |  | 2,345 |
| Balance b/f |  | 14,000 |  | 11,655 |
| Balance c/f |  | 26,000 |  | 14,000 |
| EPS |  | 34p |  | 13p |

The impact of price changes on the cost of sales would be an increase of £3,798,000, causing a profit decrease of like amount and a current cost reserve increase of like amount.

### (W5) Depreciation adjustment: average method

As assets are consumed throughout the year, the CCA depreciation charge should be based on average current costs.

|  | HCA £000 | Adjustment |  | CCA £000 |  | Difference £000 |
|---|---|---|---|---|---|---|
| Depreciation | 8,500 | $\times$ | $\dfrac{167}{100}$ | $=$ | 14,195 | $=$ 5,695 |

### (W6) Monetary working capital adjustment (MWCA)

The objective is to transfer from the statement of comprehensive income to CC reserve the amount by which the need for monetary working capital (MWC) has increased due to rising price levels. The change in MWC from one statement of financial position to the next will be the consequence of a combination of changes in volume and escalating price movements. Volume change may be segregated from the price change by using an average index.

|  | 20X5 | 20X4 |  | Change |
|---|---|---|---|---|
|  | £000 | £000 |  | £000 |
| Trade receivables | 34,000 | 23,375 |  |  |
| Trade payables | 25,500 | 17,000 |  |  |
| MWC | 8,500 | 6,375 | Overall change = | 2,125 |

The MWC is now adjusted by the average index for the year. This adjustment will reveal the change in volume.

$$\left(8,500 \times \frac{137.5}{150}\right) - \left(6,375 \times \frac{137.5}{125}\right)$$

$$= 7,792 - 7,012 \qquad\qquad = \text{Volume change} \qquad \underline{780}$$

So price change = $\qquad\qquad \underline{1,345}$

The profit before interest and tax will be reduced as follows:

|  | £000 | £000 |
|---|---|---|
| Profit before interest and tax |  | 26,350 |
| Less: |  |  |
| COSA (from W4) | (3,798) |  |
| DA (from W5) | (5,695) |  |
| MWCA (from W6) | (1,345) |  |
| Current cost operating adjustments |  | (10,838) |
| Current cost operating profit |  | 15,512 |

The adjustments will be credited to the current cost reserve.

### 10.7.3 Unrealised holding gains on non-monetary assets as at 31 December 20X5

The holding gains as at 31 December 20X4 were calculated in Section 10.7.1 above for non-current assets and inventory. A similar calculation is required to restate these at 20X5 current costs for the closing statement of financial position. The calculations are as in Working 7 below.

#### (W7) Non-monetary assets

(i)  Holding gain on non-current assets

|  | £000 |
|---|---|
| *Revaluation at year-end* |  |
| Non-current assets at 1 January 20X5 (as W1) at CCA revaluation | 140,250 |
| CCA value at 31 December 20X5 = $140,250 \times \dfrac{185}{165} =$ | 157,250 |
| **Revaluation holding gain for 20X5 to CC reserve in W8** | 17,000 |

This holding gain of £17,000,000 is transferred to CC reserves.

(ii) Backlog depreciation on non-current assets

|  |  |  | £000 |
|---|---|---|---|
| CCA aggregate depreciation at 31 December 20X5 for CC statement of financial position |  |  |  |

$$= \text{HCA } £34,000,000 \times \frac{185}{100} \text{ in CC Statement of financial position} \qquad \mathbf{62,900}$$

| | |
|---|---|
| *Less*: CCA aggregate depreciation at 1 January 20X5 (as per W1 and statement of financial position at 1 January 20X5) | 42,075 |
| Being CCA depreciation as revealed between opening and closing statements of financial position | 20,825 |
| But CCA depreciation charged in revenue accounts (i.e. £8,500,000 in £HCA plus additional depreciation of £5,695,000 per W5) = | 14,195 |
| **So total backlog depreciation to CC reserve in W8** | 6,630 |

| | |
|---|---|
| The CCA value of non-current assets at 31 December 20X5: | £000 |
| Gross CCA value (above) | 157,250 |
| Depreciation (above) | 62,900 |
| **Net CCA carrying value in the CC statement of financial position in W8** | 94,350 |

This £6,630,000 is backlog depreciation for 20X5. Total backlog depreciation is not expensed (i.e. charged to revenue account) as an adjustment of HCA profit, but is charged against CCA reserves. The net effect is that the CC reserve will increase by £10,370,000, i.e. £17,000,000 − £6,630,000.

(iii) Inventory valuation at year-end

| CCA valuation at 31 December 20X5 | | |
|---|---|---|
| *HCA £000* | *CCA £000* | *CCA £000* |
| = 25,500 × 150/145 = 26,379 = increase of | | 879 |
| CCA valuation at 1 January 20X5 (per W2) | | |
| = 17,000 × 125/120 = 17,708 = increase of | | 708 |
| **Inventory holding gain occurring during 20X5 to W8** | | 171 |

## 10.7.4 Current cost statement of financial position as at 31 December 20X5

The current cost statement as at 31 December 20X5 now discloses non-current assets and inventory adjusted by index to their current cost and the retained profits reduced by the current cost operating adjustments. It appears as in Working 8 below.

**(W8) Economica plc: CCA statement of financial position as at 31 December 20X5**

|  | 20X5 |  |  | 20X4 |  |
|---|---|---|---|---|---|
| *Non-current assets* | £000 | | £000 | | £000 | £000 |
| Cost | 157,250 | (W7(i)) | | 140,250 | (W1) |
| Depreciation | 62,900 | (W7(ii)) | | 42,075 | (W1) |
| | | | 94,350 (W7(ii)) | | 98,175 |
| | | | | | |
| *Current assets* | | | | | |
| Inventory | 26,379 | (W7(iii)) | | 17,708 | (W2) |
| Trade receivables | 34,000 | | | 23,375 | |
| Cash | 17,000 | | | 1,875 | |
| | 77,379 | | | 42,958 | |
| | | | | | |
| *Current liabilities* | | | | | |
| Trade payables | 25,500 | | | 17,000 | |
| Income tax | 8,500 | | | 4,250 | |
| Dividend declared | 5,000 | | | 4,000 | |
| | 39,000 | | | 25,250 | |
| Net current assets | 38,379 | | | 17,708 | |
| Less: 8% debentures | 11,000 | | | 11,000 | |
| | | | 27,379 | | 6,708 |
| | | | 121,729 | | 104,883 |
| | | | | | |
| *Financed by* | | | | | |
| Share capital: authorised | | | | | |
| and issued £1 shares | | | 50,000 | | 50,000 |
| Share premium | | | 1,500 | | 1,500 |
| CC reserve (Note 1) | | | 55,067 | | 39,383 |
| Retained profit (Note 2) | | | 15,162 | | 14,000 |
| *Shareholders' funds* | | | 121,729 | | 104,883 |

| Note 1: CC reserve | £000 | £000 |
|---|---|---|
| Opening balance | | 39,383 (W3) |
| *Holding gains* | | |
| Non-current assets | 17,000 (W7(i)) | |
| Inventory | 171 (W7(iii)) | |
| | | 17,171 |
| COSA | 3,798 (W4) | |
| MWCA | 1,345 (W6) | |
| *Less:* backlog depreciation | (6,630) (W7(ii)) | (1,487) |
| | | 55,067 |

| Note 2: Retained profit | | |
|---|---|---|
| Opening balance | | 14,000 (Figure 10.5) |
| HCA profit for 20X5 | 12,000 | |
| COSA | (3,798) (W4) | |
| Extra depreciation | (5,695) (W5) | |
| MWCA | (1,345) (W6) | |
| | | 1,162 |
| CCA profit for 20X5 | | 15,162 |

### 10.7.5 How to take the level of borrowings into account

We have assumed that the company will need to retain £10,838,000 from the current year's earnings in order to maintain the physical operating capacity of the company. However, if the business is part financed by borrowings then part of the amount required may be assumed to come from the lenders. One of the methods advocated is to make a gearing adjustment. The gearing adjustment that we illustrate here has the effect of reducing the impact of the adjustments on the profit after interest, i.e. it is based on the realised holding gains only.

The gearing adjustment will change the carrying figures of CC reserves and retained profit, but not the shareholders' funds, as the adjustment is compensating. The gearing adjustment cannot be computed before the determination of the shareholders' interest because that figure is necessary in order to complete the gearing calculation.

### (W9) Gearing adjustment

The CC operating profit of the business is quantified after making such retentions from the historical profit as are required in order to maintain the physical operating capacity of the entity. However, from a shareholder standpoint, there is no need to maintain in real terms the portion of the entity financed by loans that are fixed in monetary values. Thus, in calculating profit attributable to shareholders, that part of the CC adjustments relating to the proportion of the business financed by loans can be deducted:

$$\text{Gearing adjustment} = \frac{\text{Average net borrowings for year}}{\text{Average net borrowings for year} + \text{Average shareholders' funds for year}} \times \frac{\text{Aggregate}}{\text{adjustments}}$$

This formula is usually expressed as $\dfrac{L}{(L+S)} \times A$ where $L$ = loans (i.e. net borrowings); $S$ = shareholders' interest or funds; and $A$ = adjustments (i.e. extra depreciation + COSA + MWCA). Note that $L/(L + S)$ is often expressed as a percentage of $A$ (see example below where it is 6.31%).

### Net borrowings

This is the sum of all liabilities less current assets, excluding items included in MWC or utilised in computing COSA. In this instance it is as follows.

*Note*: in some circumstances (e.g. new issue of debentures occurring during the year) a weighted average will be used.

|  | Closing balance £000 | Opening balance £000 |
|---|---|---|
| Debentures | 11,000 | 11,000 |
| Income tax | 8,500 | 4,250 |
| Cash | (17,000) | (1,875) |
| Total net borrowings, the average of which equals $L$ | 2,500 | 13,375 |

$$\text{Average net borrowings} = \frac{2,500,00 + 13,375,000}{2} = £7,937,500$$

### Net borrowings plus shareholders' funds

| | | |
|---|---:|---:|
| Shareholders' funds in CC £ (inclusive of proposed dividends) | 126,729 | 108,883 |
| *Add*: net borrowings | 2,500 | 13,375 |
| | 129,229 | 122,258 |

Or, alternatively:

| | £000 | £000 |
|---|---:|---:|
| Non-current assets | 94,350 | 98,175 |
| Inventory | 26,379 | 17,708 |
| MWC | 8,500 | 6,375 |
| | 129,229 | 122,258 |

$$\text{Average } L + S = \frac{129,229,000 + 122,258,000}{2} = 125,743,500$$

$$\text{So gearing} = \frac{L}{L+S} \times A = \frac{7,937,500}{125,743,500} \times \frac{(\text{COSA} + \text{MWCA} + \text{extra depreciation})}{(3,798,000 + 1,345,000 + 5,695,000)}$$

$$= 6.31\% \text{ of } £10,838,000 = £683,877, \text{ say } £684,000$$

Thus the CC adjustment of £10,838,000 charged against historical profit may be reduced by £684,000 due to a gain being derived from net borrowings during a period of inflation as shown in Figure 10.6. The £684,000 is shown as a deduction from interest payable.

### Figure 10.6 Economica plc CCA statement of income

*Economica plc CCA statement of comprehensive income for year ended 31 December 20X5*
*(i.e. under the operating capital maintenance concept)*

| | | £000 |
|---|---:|---:|
| Turnover | | 42,500 |
| Cost of sales | | (12,070) |
| Gross profit | | 30,430 |
| Distribution costs | | (2,460) |
| Administrative expenses | | (1,620) |
| Historical cost operating profit | | 26,350 |
| Current cost operating adjustments (from Section 7.7.2 above) | | **(10,838)** |
| Current cost operating profit | | 15,512 |
| Interest payable | (880) | |
| Gearing adjustment | **684** | (196) |
| Current profit on ordinary activities before taxation | | 15,316 |
| Tax on profit on ordinary activities | | (8,470) |
| Current cost profit for the financial year | | 6,846 |
| Dividends declared | | (5,000) |
| Current cost profit retained | | 1,846 |
| EPS | | 13.7p |

## 10.7.6 The closing current cost statement of financial position

The closing statement with the non-current assets and inventory restated at current cost and the retained profit adjusted for current cost operating adjustments as reduced by the gearing adjustment is set out in Figure 10.7.

**Figure 10.7 Economica plc CCA statement of financial position**

Economica plc CCA statement of financial position as at 31 December 20X5

| 20X4 | | | 20X5 | |
|---|---|---|---|---|
| £000 | £000 | Non-current assets | £000 | £000 |
| 140,250 | | Property, plant and equipment | 157,250 | |
| 42,075 | | Depreciation | 62,900 | |
| | 98,175 | | | 94,350 |
| | | Current assets | | |
| 17,708 | | Inventory | 26,379 | |
| 23,375 | | Trade receivables | 34,000 | |
| 1,875 | | Cash | 17,000 | |
| 42,958 | | | 77,379 | |
| | | Current liabilities | | |
| 17,000 | | Trade payables | 25,500 | |
| | | Other payables | | |
| 4,250 | | — income tax | 8,500 | |
| 4,000 | | — dividend declared | 5,000 | |
| 25,250 | | | 39,000 | |
| | 17,708 | Net current assets | | 38,379 |
| | (11,000) | Non-current liabilities | | (11,000) |
| | 6,708 | | | 27,379 |
| | 104,883 | | | 121,729 |
| | £000 | Capital and reserves | | £000 |
| | 50,000 | Called-up share capital | | 50,000 |
| | 1,500 | Share premium account | | 1,500 |
| | 53,383 | Total of other reserves | | 70,229 |
| | 104,883 | | | 121,729 |

Analysis of 'Total of other reserves'

| | £000 | | | £000 |
|---|---|---|---|---|
| | 14,000 | Statement of income | | 15,846 |
| | 39,383 | Current cost reserve | | 54,383 |
| | 53,383 | | | 70,229 |

continued

**Figure 10.7 continued**

Movements on reserves

(a) Statement of income:    £000

Balance at 1 January 20X5    14,000 (from Figure 7.5)

Current cost retained profit    1,846 (from Figure 7.6)

Balance at 31 December 20X5    15,846

(b) Current cost reserve:

|  | Total £000 | Non-current assets £000 | Inventory £000 | MWCA £000 | Gearing £000 |
|---|---|---|---|---|---|
| Balance as at 1 January 20X5 | 39,383 | 38,675 | 708 | | |
| Movements during the year: | | | | | |
| Unrealised holding gains in year | 10,541 | 10,370 | 171 | | |
| Gearing adjustment | (684) | | | | (684) |
| MWCA | 1,345 | | | 1,345 | |
| COSA | 3,798 | | 3,798 | | |
| Balance as at 31 December 20X5 | 54,383 | 49,045 | 4,677 | 1,345 | (684) |

## 10.7.7 Real terms system

The real terms system combines both CPP and current cost concepts. This requires a calculation of total unrealised holding gains and an inflation adjustment as calculated in Workings 10 and 11 below.

**(W10) Total unrealised holding gains to be used in Figure 10.8**

[Closing statement of financial position at CC − Closing statement of financial position at HC] − [Opening statement of financial position at CC − Opening statement of financial position at HC]

$$= (£121,729,000 - £77,500,000) - (£104,883,000 - £65,500,000) = £4,846,000$$

(Working 8)    (Figure 10.3)    (Working 8)    (Figure 10.3)

**(W11) General price index numbers to be used to calculate the inflation adjustment in Figure 10.8**

General price index at 1 January 20X5 = 317.2

General price index at 31 December 20X5 = 333.2

Opening shareholders' funds at CC × percentage change in GPI during the year =

$$104,883,000 \times \frac{333.2 - 317.2}{317.2} = £5,290,435, \text{ say } £5,290,000$$

**The GPP (or CPP) real terms financial capital**

The real terms financial capital maintenance concept may be incorporated within the CCA system as in Figure 10.8 by calculating an inflation adjustment.

**Figure 10.8 Economica plc real terms statement of comprehensive income**

*Economica plc CCA statement of income under the real terms system*
*for the year ended 31 December 20X5*

|  | £000 | £000 |
|---|---:|---:|
| Historical cost profit after tax for the financial year |  | 17,000 |
| *Add*: Total unrealised holding gains arising during the year (see W10) | 4,846 |  |
| *Less*: Realised holding gains previously recognised as unrealised | none |  |
|  | 4,846 |  |
| *Less*: Inflation adjustment to CCA shareholders' funds (W11) | (5,290) |  |
| Real holding gains |  | (444) |
| *Total real gains* |  | 16,556 |
| Deduct: dividends declared |  | 5,000 |
| Amount retained |  | 11,556 |

*Real terms system: analysis of reserves*

| 20X4 |  | 20X5 |
|---:|---|---:|
| £000 |  | £000 |
| 53,383 | *Statement of income* | 64,939 |
| — | Financial capital maintenance reserve | 5,290 |
| 53,383 |  | 70,229 |

Movements on reserves

|  | Income statement | Financial capital maintenance reserve |
|---|---:|---:|
|  | £000 | £000 |
| Balances at 1 January 20X5 | 53,383 | — |
| Amount retained | 11,556 | — |
| Inflation adjustment for year |  | 5,290 |
| Balances as at 31 December 20X5 | 64,939 | 5,290 |

## 10.8 Critique of CCA statements

Considerable effort and expense are involved in compiling and publishing CCA statements. Does their usefulness justify the cost? CCA statements have the following uses:

1 The operating capital maintenance statement reveals CCA profit. Such profit has removed inflationary price increases in raw materials and other inventories, and thus is more realistic than the alternative HCA profit.

2 Significant increases in a company's buying and selling prices will give the HCA profit a holding gains content. That is, the reported HCA profit will include gains consequent upon holding inventories during a period when the cost of buying such inventories increases. Conversely, if specific inventory prices fall, HCA profit will be reduced as it takes account of losses sustained by holding inventory while its price drops. Holding gains

and losses are quite different from operating gains and losses. HCA profit does not distinguish between the two, whereas CCA profit does.

3 HCA profit might be adjusted to reflect the moving price-level syndrome:

   (a) by use of the operating capital maintenance approach, which regards only the CCA **operating** profit as the authentic result for the period and which treats any holding gain or loss as a movement on reserves;

   (b) by adoption of the real terms **financial** capital maintenance approach, which applies a general inflation measure via the RPI, combined with CCA information regarding holding gains.

   Thus the statement can reveal information to satisfy the demands of the management of the entity itself – as distinct from the shareholder/proprietor, whose awareness of inflation may centre on the **RPI**. In this way the concern of operating management can be accommodated with the different interest of the shareholder. The HCA profit would fail on both these counts.

4 CC profit is important because:

   (a) it quantifies cost of sales and depreciation after allowing for changing price levels; hence trading results, free of inflationary elements, grant a clear picture of entity activities and management performance;

   (b) resources are maintained, as a result of having eliminated the possibility of paying dividend out of real capital;

   (c) yardsticks for management performance are more comparable as a time series within the one entity and between entities, the distortion caused by moving prices having been alleviated.

## 10.9 Measurement bases

We saw in Chapter 7 that the Conceptual Framework exposure draft described different measurement bases (historical cost and current value (fair value and value in use – for assets – or fulfilment value – for liabilities), the information that they provide and their advantages and disadvantages. The factors to be considered when selecting a measurement basis (relevance, faithful representation, enhancing qualitative characteristics, and factors specific to initial measurement) mean that it is likely to result in the selection of different measurement bases for different assets, liabilities and items of income and expense.

## 10.10 The IASB position where there is hyperinflation

### 10.10.1 What do we mean by hyperinflation?

IAS 29 *Financial Reporting in Hyperinflationary Economies* states that hyperinflation occurs when money loses purchasing power at such a rate that comparison of amounts from transactions that have occurred at different times, even within the same accounting period, is misleading.

### 10.10.2 What rate indicates that hyperinflation exists?

IAS 29 does not specify an absolute rate – this is a matter of qualitative judgement – but it sets out certain pointers, such as people preferring to keep their wealth in non-monetary assets, people preferring prices to be stated in terms of an alternative stable currency rather than the domestic currency, wages and prices being linked to a price index, or the cumulative inflation rate over three years approaching 100%.

Countries where hyperinflation has been a risk include Iran, Sudan and Venezuela.

### 10.10.3 How are financial statements adjusted?

The current year financial statements, whether HCA or CCA, must be restated using the domestic measuring unit current at the statement of financial position date. The domestic statements may be adjusted using an index as in the following extract from the Diageo 2013 Annual Report:

> Since December 2009 Venezuela has been classified as a hyperinflationary economy. Hyperinflationary accounting requires the restatement of the subsidiary undertaking's income statement to current purchasing power. The index used to calculate the hyperinflationary adjustment was the Indice Nacional de Precios al Consumidor which changed from 285.5 to 398.6 in the year ended 30 June 2013.

## 10.11 Future developments

A mixed picture emerges when we try to foresee the future of changing price levels and financial reporting. The accounting profession has been reluctant to abandon the HC concept in favour of a 'valuation accounting' approach. In the UK and Australia many companies have stopped revaluing their non-current assets, with a large proportion opting instead to revert to the historical cost basis, with the two main factors influencing management's decision being cost-effectiveness and future reporting flexibility.[1]

The pragmatic approach is prevailing with each class of asset and liability being considered on an individual basis. For example, non-current assets may be reported at depreciated replacement cost if this is lower than the value in use we discussed in Chapter 6; financial assets are reported at market value (exit value in the NRV model); and current assets reported at the lower of HC and NRV. In each case the resulting changes, both realised and unrealised, in value now find their way into the financial performance statement(s).

### 10.11.1 Increasing use of fair values

A number of IFRSs now require or allow the use of fair values, e.g. IFRS 3 *Business Combinations* in which fair value is defined as 'the amount for which an asset could be exchanged or a liability settled between knowledgeable, willing parties in an arm's length transaction'. This is equivalent to the NRVA model discussed above. It is defined as an exit value rather than a cost value but like NRVA it does not imply a forced sale, i.e. it is the best value that could be obtained.

It is very possible that the number of international standards requiring or allowing fair values will increase over time and reflect the adoption on a piecemeal basis. In the meantime, efforts[2] are in hand for the FASB and IASB to arrive at a common definition of fair value which can be applied to value assets and liabilities where there is no market value available. Agreeing a definition, however, is only a part of the exercise. If analysts are to be able to compare corporate performance across borders, then it is essential that both the FASB and the IASB agree that all companies should adopt fair value accounting – this has been proving difficult.

### 10.11.2 The move to defining how to measure fair value

The IASB addressed this by issuing IFRS 13 *Fair Value Measurement* in 2011. This standard[3] does not state when fair values are to be used but applies when the decision has been made to measure at fair value so that there is uniformity in the measurement process.

#### IFRS 13 *Fair Value Measurement*

The standard (a) defines fair value, (b) sets out a framework for measuring it and (c) sets out the disclosures that are required.

#### Fair value definition

IFRS 13 defines fair value as the price that would be received to sell an asset or paid to transfer a liability in an orderly transaction between market participants at the measurement date. This means that it is a market-based measurement we would refer to as an exit price – it is not an entity-specific measurement so that the entity's intention to hold an asset or to settle a liability is not relevant when measuring fair value.

#### Fair value measurement

An entity has to identify the particular asset or liability being measured, the market in which an orderly transaction would take place and the appropriate valuation technique.

#### Fair value hierarchy

It is not always possible to obtain a directly comparable market value. The IFRS establishes, therefore, a fair value hierarchy that categorises the inputs to a valuation into three levels. It provides a framework to increase comparability but it does not remove the judgement that is required in arriving at a fair value.

Level 1 typically applies to financial investments when there are inputs such as quoted prices in an active market for identical assets or liabilities at the date the fair value is being measured.

Level 2 applies when there are not quoted prices as in Level 1 but there is observable data such as the price per square metre that had been achieved locally in an orderly market when valuing retail space.

Level 3 applies when there are no comparable observable inputs and reliance has to be on judgement using data such as discounted cash flows.

#### Judgement is required in arriving at a fair value

Judgement is required in selecting the level input appropriate to a particular asset. For example, consider Retail Properties plc:

> Retail Properties plc has a portfolio of investments linked to the retail property market which it had acquired 5 years earlier when property prices were buoyant. At the end of the current financial period it had received an offer from a private equity vulture fund of £2m to acquire the portfolio. The company has been advised that this fund had acquired similar portfolios from companies that had gone into administration – however, Retail Properties plc was solvent and under no liquidity pressure to accept this offer.

The company obtained advice from Commercial Property Valuers that from their current experience with sales in this sector the portfolio could be sold for £3m in the current market and, with the expected upturn in the retail sector, could probably realise up to £5m in 2 to 3 years' time.

There are three valuations and in determining the fair value the company has to (a) bear in mind that the fair value has to be that obtainable at the current date and (b) measured applying the IFRS 13 three hierarchy levels approach. So, taking each in turn:

Level 1 does not apply because it requires an active market such as the availability of quoted prices on a stock exchange.

Level 2 would seem to apply as there is *observable* evidence provided by commercial property valuers of the results on the sale of *similar* assets at the *current* time.

Level 3 is based on an estimated improvement of market conditions in the *future*. It is *not observable* and it is *not current* – it is not appropriate on those grounds.

The best estimate of fair value based on this analysis is the figure of £3m arrived at applying the Level 2 input which is observable and based on an orderly market – unlike the forced sale conditions that applied to the vulture fund offer.

*Note.* If there were no observable direct or indirect comparators and the Level 3 valuation used discounted cash flows, improvements in cash flows arising from action taken by the company would be acceptable provided those actions would also have been taken by any party taking over the asset. The cash flows used should reflect only the cash flows that market participants would take into account when assessing fair value. This includes both the type of cash flows (e.g. future capital expenditure) and the estimated amount of cash flows.

### How will financial statements be affected if fair values are adopted?

The financial statements will have the same virtues and defects as the NRVA model (Section 10.6.4 above). Some concerns have been raised that reported annual income will become more volatile and the profit that is reported may contain a mix of realised and unrealised profits. Supporters of the use of fair values see the statements of comprehensive income and financial position as more relevant for decision making whilst accepting that the figures might be less reliable and not as effective as a means of assessing the stewardship by the directors.

This means that in the future historical cost and realisation will be regarded as less relevant[4] and investors, analysts and management will need to come to terms with increased volatility in reported annual performance.

This is one of the reasons that narrative reports such as the Strategic Report and Management Commentary are increasingly important when investors make their predictions about future performance and position.

## Summary

The traditional HCA system reveals disturbing inadequacies in times of changing price levels, calling into question the value of financial reports using this system. Considerable resources and energy have been expended in searching for a substitute model able to counter the distortion and confusion caused by an unstable monetary unit.

Three basic models have been developed: RCA, NRVA and CPP. Each has its merits and defects; each produces a different income value and a different capital value.

In the search for more relevant decision-useful financial statements we will see the gradual replacement of historical cost figures.

The contemporary financial reporting scene continues to be dynamic.

We see value in use used as a criterion in measuring the impairment of non-current tangible and intangible assets (discussed further in Chapters 16 and 17); we see financial assets valued at fair values (discussed further in Chapter 14); we see current assets valued at lower of cost and NRV; we see the addition of a statement of comprehensive income required as a primary financial statement to report fair value adjustments.

## REVIEW QUESTIONS

1 Explain why financial reports prepared under the historical cost convention are subject to the following major limitations:

- periodic comparisons are invalidated; the depreciation charge may be understated;
- gains and losses on net monetary assets are undisclosed.

2 Explain how each of the limitations in Question 1 could be overcome.

3 Compare the operating and financial capital maintenance concepts and discuss if they are mutually exclusive.

4 Explain how the CPP model differs from the CCA model as a basis for making dividend decisions.

5 '[T]he IASB's failure to decide on a capital maintenance concept is regrettable as users have no idea as to whether total gains represent income or capital and are therefore unable to identify a meaningful "bottom line".'[5] Discuss.

6 'To be relevant to investors, the profit for the year should include both realised and unrealised gains/losses.' Discuss.

7 Discuss why there are objections to financial statements being prepared using the NRVA model.

8 Explain the criteria for determining whether hyperinflation exists.

9 'Investors benefit when unrealised changes in assets arising from fair value measurement are incorporated in the financial report even if this means that there is greater volatility in income and balance sheet ratios.' Discuss.

10 Retail plc had a portfolio linked to retail properties. Discuss the information that would be required if Level 1 and Level 2 inputs were unavailable. Explain the judgements that would be required.

## EXERCISES

### * Question 1

Raiders plc prepares accounts annually to 31 March. The following figures, prepared on a conventional historical cost basis, are included in the company's accounts to 31 March 20X5.

1 In the income statement:

|  | £000 | £000 |
|---|---|---|
| (i) Cost of goods sold: |  |  |
| Inventory at 1 April 20X4 | 9,600 |  |
| Purchases | 39,200 |  |
|  | 48,800 |  |
| Inventory at 31 March 20X5 | 11,300 | 37,500 |
| (ii) Depreciation of equipment |  | 8,640 |

2  In the statement of financial position:

|  | £000 | £000 |
|---|---|---|
| (iii)  Equipment at cost | 57,600 | |
| Less: Accumulated depreciation | 16,440 | 41,160 |
| (iv)  Inventory | | 11,300 |

The inventory held on 31 March 20X4 and 31 March 20X5 was in each case purchased evenly during the last six months of the company's accounting year.

Equipment is depreciated at a rate of 15% per annum, using the straight-line method. Equipment owned on 31 March 20X5 was purchased as follows: on 1 April 20X2 at a cost of £16 million; on 1 April 20X3 at a cost of £20 million; and on 1 April 20X4 at a cost of £21.6 million.

| | Current cost of inventory | Current cost of equipment | Retail Price Index |
|---|---|---|---|
| 1 April 20X2 | 109 | 145 | 313 |
| 1 April 20X3 | 120 | 162 | 328 |
| 30 September 20X3 | 128 | 170 | 339 |
| 31 December 20X3 | 133 | 175 | 343 |
| 31 March/1 April 20X4 | 138 | 180 | 345 |
| 30 September 20X4 | 150 | 191 | 355 |
| 31 December 20X4 | 156 | 196 | 360 |
| 31 March 20X5 | 162 | 200 | 364 |

Required:
(a) Calculate the following current cost accounting figures:
    (i)   The cost of goods sold of Raiders plc for the year ended 31 March 20X5.
    (ii)  The statement of financial position value of inventory at 31 March 20X5.
    (iii) The equipment depreciation charge for the year ended 31 March 20X5.
    (iv)  The net statement of financial position value of equipment at 31 March 20X5.
(b) Discuss the extent to which the figures you have calculated in (a) above (together with figures calculated on a similar basis for earlier years) provide information over and above that provided by the conventional historical cost statement of comprehensive income and statement of financial position figures.
(c) Outline the main reasons why the standard setters have experienced so much difficulty in their attempts to develop an accounting standard on accounting for changing prices.

## Question 2

The finance director of Toy plc has been asked by a shareholder to explain items that appear in the current cost statement of comprehensive income for the year ended 31.8.20X9 and the statement of financial position as at that date:

| | | £ | £ |
|---|---|---|---|
| Historical cost profit | | | 143,000 |
| Cost of sales adjustment | (1) | 10,000 | |
| Additional depreciation | (2) | 6,000 | |
| Monetary working capital adjustment | (3) | 2,500 | 18,500 |
| Current cost operating profit before tax | | | 124,500 |
| Gearing adjustment | (4) | | 2,600 |
| CCA operating profit | | | 127,100 |

|  |  | £ | £ |
|---|---|---|---|
| Non-current assets at gross replacement cost |  | 428,250 |  |
| Accumulated current cost depreciation | (5) | (95,650) | 332,600 |
| Net current assets |  |  | 121,400 |
| 12% debentures |  |  | (58,000) |
|  |  |  | 396,000 |
| Issued share capital |  |  | 250,000 |
| Current cost reserve | (6) |  | 75,000 |
| Retained earnings |  |  | 71,000 |
|  |  |  | 396,000 |

**Required:**

(a) Explain what each of the items numbered 1–6 represents and the purpose of each.

(b) What do you consider to be the benefits to users of providing current cost information?

## * Question 3

The statements of financial position of Parkway plc for 20X7 and 20X8 are given below, together with the income statement for the year ended 30 June 20X8.

| | Statement of financial position | | | | | |
|---|---|---|---|---|---|---|
| | | 20X8 | | | 20X7 | |
| | £000 | £000 | £000 | £000 | £000 | £000 |
| Non-current assets | Cost | Depn | NBV | Cost | Depn | NBV |
| Freehold land | 60,000 | — | 60,000 | 60,000 | — | 60,000 |
| Buildings | 40,000 | 8,000 | 32,000 | 40,000 | 7,200 | 32,800 |
| Plant and machinery | 30,000 | 16,000 | 14,000 | 30,000 | 10,000 | 20,000 |
| Vehicles | 40,000 | 20,000 | 20,000 | 40,000 | 12,000 | 28,000 |
| | 170,000 | 44,000 | 126,000 | 170,000 | 29,200 | 140,800 |
| Current assets | | | | | | |
| Inventory | | 80,000 | | | 70,000 | |
| Trade receivables | | 60,000 | | | 40,000 | |
| Short-term investments | | 50,000 | | | — | |
| Cash at bank and in hand | | 5,000 | | | 5,000 | |
| | | 195,000 | | | 115,000 | |
| Current liabilities | | | | | | |
| Trade payables | | 90,000 | | | 60,000 | |
| Bank overdraft | | 50,000 | | | 45,000 | |
| Taxation | | 28,000 | | | 15,000 | |
| Dividends declared | | 15,000 | | | 10,000 | |
| | | 183,000 | | | 130,000 | |
| Net current assets | | | 12,000 | | | (15,000) |
| | | | 138,000 | | | 125,800 |
| Financed by | | | | | | |
| ordinary share capital | | | 80,000 | | | 80,000 |
| Share premium | | | 10,000 | | | 10,000 |
| Retained profits | | | 28,000 | | | 15,800 |
| | | | 118,000 | | | 105,800 |
| Long-term loans | | | 20,000 | | | 20,000 |
| | | | 138,000 | | | 125,800 |

---

*Statement of income of Parkway plc for the year ended 30 June 20X8*

|  | £000 |
|---|---|
| Sales | 738,000 |
| Cost of sales | 620,000 |
| Gross profit | 118,000 |

*Notes*

1  The freehold land and buildings were purchased on 1 July 20X0. The company policy is to depreciate buildings over 50 years and to provide no depreciation on land.

2  Depreciation on plant and machinery and motor vehicles is provided at the rate of 20% per annum on a straight-line basis.

3  Depreciation on buildings and plant and equipment has been included in administration expenses, while that on motor vehicles is included in distribution expenses.

4  The directors of Parkway plc have provided you with the following information relating to price rises:

|  | RPI | Inventory | Land | Buildings | Plant | Vehicles |
|---|---|---|---|---|---|---|
| 1 July 20X0 | 100 | 60 | 70 | 50 | 90 | 120 |
| 1 July 20X7 | 170 | 140 | 290 | 145 | 135 | 180 |
| 30 June 20X8 | 190 | 180 | 310 | 175 | 165 | 175 |
| Average for year ending 30 June 20X8 | 180 | 160 | 300 | 163 | 145 | 177 |

**Required:**

(a) Making and stating any assumptions that are necessary, and giving reasons for those assumptions, calculate the monetary working capital adjustment for Parkway plc.

(b) Critically evaluate the usefulness of the monetary working capital adjustment.

## * Question 4

The historical cost accounts of Smith plc are as follows:

---

*Smith plc Statement of income for the year ended 31 December 20X8*

|  | £000 | £000 |
|---|---|---|
| Sales |  | 2,000 |
| Cost of sales: |  |  |
| Opening inventory 1 January 20X8 | 320 |  |
| Purchases | 1,680 |  |
|  | 2,000 |  |
| Closing inventory at 31 December 20X8 | 280 |  |
|  |  | 1,720 |
| Gross profit |  | 280 |
| Depreciation | 20 |  |
| Administration expenses | 100 |  |
|  |  | 120 |
| Net profit |  | 160 |

---

| Statement of financial position of Smith plc as at 31 December 20X8 | | |
|---|---|---|
| | 20X7 | 20X8 |
| *Non-current assets* | £000 | £000 |
| Land and buildings at cost | 1,360 | 1,360 |
| Less aggregate depreciation | (160) | (180) |
| | 1,200 | 1,180 |

| | | | |
|---|---|---|---|
| Current assets | | | |
| Inventory | 320 | 280 | |
| Trade receivables | 80 | 160 | |
| Cash at bank | 40 | 120 | |
| | 440 | 560 | |
| Trade payables | 200 | 140 | |
| | | 240 | 420 |
| | | 1,440 | 1,600 |
| Ordinary share capital | | 800 | 800 |
| Retained profit | | 640 | 800 |
| | | 1,440 | 1,600 |

*Notes*

1　Land and buildings were acquired in 20X0 with the buildings component costing £800,000 and depreciated over 40 years.
2　Share capital was issued in 20X0.
3　Closing inventories were acquired in the last quarter of the year.
4　RPI numbers were:

| | |
|---|---|
| Average for 20X0 | 120 |
| 20X7 last quarter | 216 |
| At 31 December 20X7 | 220 |
| 20X8 last quarter | 232 |
| Average for 20X8 | 228 |
| At 31 December 20X8 | 236 |

Required:
(i)　Explain the basic concept of the CPP accounting system.
(ii)　Prepare CPP accounts for Smith plc for the year ended 20X8.
　　The following steps will assist in preparing the CPP accounts:
　　(a)　Restate the statement of comprehensive income for the current year in terms of £CPP at the year-end.
　　(b)　Restate the closing statement of financial position in £CPP at year-end, but excluding monetary items, i.e. trade receivables, trade payables, cash at bank.
　　(c)　Restate the opening statement of financial position in £CPP at year-end, but including monetary items, i.e. trade receivables, trade payables and cash at bank, and showing equity as the balancing figure.
　　(d)　Compare the opening and closing equity figures derived in (b) and (c) above to arrive at the total profit/loss for the year in CPP terms. Compare this figure with the CPP profit calculated in (a) above to determine the monetary gain or monetary loss.
　　(e)　Reconcile monetary gains/loss in (d) with the increase/decrease in net monetary items during the year expressed in £CPP compared with the increase/decrease expressed in £HC.

## * Question 5

Shower Ltd was incorporated towards the end of 20X2, but it did not start trading until 20X3. Its historical cost statement of financial position at 1 January 20X3 was as follows:

|  | £ |
|---|---|
| Share capital, £1 shares | 2,000 |
| Loan (interest free) | 8,000 |
|  | £10,000 |
| Non-current assets, at cost | 6,000 |
| Inventory, at cost (4,000 units) | 4,000 |
|  | £10,000 |

A summary of Shower Limited's bank account for 20X3 is given below:

|  |  | £ | £ |
|---|---|---|---|
| 1 Jan 20X3 | Opening balance |  | nil |
| 30 Jun 20X3 | Sales (8,000 units) |  | 20,000 |
| Less |  |  |  |
| 29 Jun 20X3 | Purchase (6,000 units) | 9,000 |  |
|  | Sundry expenses | 5,000 | 14,000 |
| 31 Dec 20X3 | Closing balance |  | £6,000 |

All the company's transactions are on a cash basis.

The non-current assets are expected to last for five years and the company intends to depreciate its non-current assets on a straight-line basis. The non-current assets had a resale value of £2,000 at 31 December 20X3.

*Notes*
1  The closing inventory is 2,000 units and the inventory is sold on a first-in-first-out basis.
2  All prices remained constant from the date of incorporation to 1 January 20X3, but thereafter, various relevant price indices moved as follows:

|  |  | Specific indices | |
|---|---|---|---|
|  | General price level | Inventory | Non-current assets |
| 1 January 20X3 | 100 | 100 | 100 |
| 30 June 20X3 | 120 | 150 | 140 |
| 31 December 20X3 | 240 | 255 | 200 |

**Required:**
**Produce statements of financial position as at December 20X3 and statements of comprehensive income for the year ended on that date on the basis of:**
(i)   historical cost;
(ii)  current purchasing power (general price level);
(iii) replacement cost;
(iv) continuous contemporary accounting (NRVA).

## Question 6

Aspirations Ltd commenced trading as wholesale suppliers of office equipment on 1 January 20X1, issuing ordinary shares of £1 each at par in exchange for cash. The shares were fully paid on issue, the number issued being 1,500,000.

The following financial statements, based on the historical cost concept, were compiled for 20X1.

---

*Aspirations Ltd*

*Statement of income for the year ended 31 December 20X1*

|  | £ | £ |
|---|---|---|
| Sales |  | 868,425 |
| Purchases | 520,125 |  |
| Less: Inventory 31 December 20X1 | 24,250 |  |
| Cost of sales |  | 495,875 |
| Gross profit |  | 372,550 |
| Expenses | 95,750 |  |
| Depreciation | 25,250 |  |
|  |  | 121,000 |
| Net profit |  | 251,550 |

*Statement of financial position as at 31 December 20X1*

|  | Cost | Depreciation | |
|---|---|---|---|
|  | £ | £ | £ |
| Non-current assets |  |  |  |
| Freehold property | 650,000 | 6,500 | 643,500 |
| Office equipment | 375,000 | 18,750 | 356,250 |
|  | 1,025,000 | 25,250 | 999,750 |
| Current assets |  |  |  |
| Inventories |  | 24,250 |  |
| Trade receivables |  | 253,500 |  |
| Cash |  | 1,090,300 |  |
|  |  | 1,368,050 |  |
| Current liabilities |  | 116,250 |  |
|  |  | 1,251,800 |  |
| Non-current liabilities |  | 500,000 | 751,800 |
|  |  |  | 1,751,550 |
| Issued share capital |  |  |  |
| 1,500,000 £1 ordinary shares |  |  | 1,500,000 |
| Retained earnings |  |  | 251,550 |
|  |  |  | 1,751,550 |

---

The year 20X1 witnessed a surge of inflation and in consequence the directors became concerned about the validity of the revenue account and statement of financial position as income and capital statements.

---

*Specific index numbers reflecting replacement costs*

|  | 1 January 20X1 | 31 December 20X1 | Average for 20X1 |
|---|---|---|---|
| Inventory | 115 | 150 | 130 |
| Freehold property | 110 | 165 | 127 |
| Office equipment | 125 | 155 | 145 |
| General price index numbers | 135 | 170 | 155 |

Regarding current exit costs

Inventory is anticipated to sell at a profit of 75% of cost.

Value of assets at 31 December 20X1

|  | £ |
|---|---|
| Freehold property | 640,000 |
| Office equipment | 350,000 |

Index numbers reflecting price changes were:

Initial purchases of inventory were effected on 1 January 20X1 amounting to £34,375; the balance of purchases was evenly spread over the 12-month period. The non-current assets were acquired on 1 January 20X1 and, together with the initial inventory, were paid for in cash on that day.

**Required:**
Prepare the accounts adjusted for current values using each of the three proposed models of current value accounting: namely, the accounting methods known as replacement cost, general (or current) purchasing power and net realisable value.

## Notes

1 Ernst & Young, 'Revaluation of non-current assets', Accounting Standard, Ernst & Young, January 2002, www.ey.com/Global/gcr.nsf/Australia.
2 *SFAS 157 Fair Value Measurement*, FASB, 2006.
3 IFRS 13 *Fair Value Measurement*, IASSB, 2011.
4 A. Wilson, 'IAS: the challenge for measurement', *Accountancy*, December 2001, p. 90.
5 N. Fry and D. Bence, 'Capital or income?', *Accountancy*, April 2007, p. 81.

## Bibliography

W.T. Baxter, *Depreciation*, Sweet and Maxwell, 1971.
W.T. Baxter, *Inflation Accounting*, Philip Alan, 1984.
W.T. Baxter, *The Case for Deprival Accounting*, ICAS, 2003.
E.O. Edwards and P.W. Bell, *The Theory and Measurement of Business Income*, University of California Press, 1961.
J.R. Hicks, *Value and Capital* (2nd edition), Oxford University Press, 1975.
T.A. Lee, *Income and Value Measurement: Theory and Practice* (3rd edition), Van Nostrand Reinhold (UK), 1985, Chapter 5.
D.R. Myddleton, *On a Cloth Untrue – Inflation Accounting: The Way Forward*, Woodhead-Faulkner, 1984.
R.H. Parker and G.C. Harcourt (eds), *Readings in the Concept and Measurement of Income*, Cambridge University Press, 1969.
D. Tweedie and G. Whittington, *Capital Maintenance Concepts*, ASC, 1985.
D. Tweedie and G. Whittington, *The Debate on Inflation in Accounting*, Cambridge University Press, 1985.

# CHAPTER 11

# Revenue recognition

## 11.1 Introduction

Revenue recognition is at the core of the accounting process. A critical part of this process is to accurately identify those earnings outcomes which have been achieved during the period. The trend of earnings is important to investors, as it affects the share price, and to management, as it is often the basis for determining their bonuses.

It is in seeking to maintain an upward trend that scandals involving the manipulation of earnings have arisen on a regular basis, frequently caused by the overstatement by some companies of their revenue. The extent of such manipulation and its adverse impacts is evidenced by the considerable research undertaken in the US which has provided us with reliable statistics.

### Adverse effect on capital markets

The US Government Accountability Office[1] reports that in 2005 6.8% of listed companies had to restate earnings, and during the period July 2002 to September 2005, the restatements affected market values by $36 billion. Of those restatements, 20.1% of the restatements were in relation to revenue. Other research finds that 'investors and dealers react negatively to restatements and are more concerned with revenue recognition problems than with other financial reporting errors'.[2] In recent years the magnitudes of the restatements have typically been smaller, but this is probably just a cyclical trend.

In individual cases the differences can be critical. The US company HP took over the British company Autonomy and subsequently suffered losses as a result of the transaction. In the review of what happened, the accounting of Autonomy was subjected to scrutiny. 'In the original accounts [of Autonomy Systems Limited for 2010], audited by Deloitte, revenues were £175.6m. The restated turnover of £81.3m, signed off by HP's auditors Ernst & Young and filed on Monday at Companies House, is less than half as much.'[3] Thus correct revenue recognition is important for the effective operation of the capital markets.

### Adverse effect on staff prospects

It is not only investors who suffer. Collins et al. (2009)[4] suggest that chief financial officers of restating companies have enhanced likelihood of losing their job and find it harder to get comparable jobs subsequently.

### Harmonisation of accounting standards

In recent years the USA and IASB have attempted to harmonise their standards wherever possible. However, there has been reluctance on the part of many in the USA to give up their standard-setting authority and a belief that US standards are better. Fortunately, however, in the case of revenue recognition there has been acceptance of the need to harmonise and with it the need to agree on broad principles and to move away from their reliance on industry-specific guidelines.

In the past US accountants have been happier to have very specific guidelines, which could reflect that they operate in a more litigious environment. The harmonisation process has also been partly driven by the need to provide more guidance in relation to longer-term contracts.

This chapter will discuss the principles underlying revenue recognition and measurement, and the ethical issues arising out of attempts to circumvent the rules. The discussions will primarily be based on IFRS 15 *Revenue from Contracts with Customers,* issued jointly by the Financial Accounting Standards Board in the USA and the International Accounting Standards Board in May 2014.[5]

## Objectives

By the end of this chapter you should be able to:

- apply the principles of revenue recognition and measurement to typical accounting situations;
- understand the complexities of developing universally applicable revenue recognition standards;
- understand the importance of complying with the spirit as well as the detail of the revenue accounting standard;
- identify the situations in which there are industry-specific revenue recognition rules covered by separate standards.

## 11.2 IAS 18 Revenue

The accounting standard IAS 18 is currently in operation in accounting for (i) revenue for goods, (ii) revenue from services and (iii) interest, royalties and dividends. Each of those three categories had separate recognition criteria.

### Sale of goods

'Revenue from sale of goods shall be recognised when all of the following conditions have been satisfied:

(a) the entity has transferred to the buyer the significant risks and rewards of ownership of the goods;

(b) the entity retains neither continuing managerial involvement to the degree usually associated with ownership nor effective control over the goods sold;

(c) the amount of revenue can be measured reliably;

(d) it is probable that the economic benefits associated with the transaction will flow to the entity; and

(e) the costs incurred or to be incurred in respect of the transaction can be measured reliably.'

In practical terms this normally means most goods are invoiced as they are shipped and ownership passes and the amount of the transaction is known.

### Rendering of services

'When the outcome of a transaction involving the rendering of services can be estimated reliably, revenue associated with the transaction shall be recognised by reference to the stage of completion of the transaction at the end of the reporting period. The outcome of a transaction can be estimated reliably when all the following conditions are satisfied:

(a) the amount of revenue can be measured reliably;

(b) it is probable that the economic benefits associated with the transaction will flow to the entity;

(c) the stage of completion of the transaction at the end of the reporting period can be measured reliably; and

(d) the costs incurred for the transaction and the costs to complete the transaction can be measured reliably.'

In other words there was an attempt to measure revenue in a period if the calculation of the profit on the services could be measured with a reasonable degree of accuracy.

### Interest, royalties and dividends

These are recognised when:

(a) 'it is probable that the economic benefits associated with the transaction will flow to the entity; and

(b) the amount of the revenue can be measured reliably.'

Thus there are three separate criteria for revenue recognition. Although there are similarities it would be neater if there was one set of criteria that were applicable to all areas.

## 11.3 The issues involved in developing a new standard

Revenue broadly defined is the gross benefit arising from provision of goods and services, in the normal course of business, to external parties for which remuneration is receivable. Thus sales of non-current assets are not part of revenue. If the provision of goods or services is immediately followed by the receipt of remuneration in cash or cash equivalents (e.g. entitlement to cash from a credit card provider) then there is little controversy.

The accounting difficulties arise when:

• there is a significant probability that the full amount invoiced will not be received in full;

• gains arise from unusual or infrequent transactions with a decision required as to whether they are to be treated in revenue or kept separate;

• transactions are spread over several accounting periods so that it is not clear when the services have been provided;

• a single contract involves the supply of multiple goods and services which may not have similar patterns of delivery;

• the value of the transaction is difficult to determine because it involves payment in kind, volume discounts or the possibility of contract variations during the course of the contract;

• the application is so difficult in a particular industry that there has to be guidance to clarify the application of the general principles in that industry. This includes the construction industry where contracts may take several years, for example, road, ship and aircraft building.

**Note that:**

- the timing of revenue recognition affects the timing of transfers from inventory into cost of goods sold;

- separate standards are required as for the recognition of changes in market values of financial instruments (see Chapter 14), leases (see Chapter 18), biological assets (see Chapter 20), and the insurance, real estate and investment industries;

- all other standards which are impacted have to be modified to bring them into agreement with the revised revenue standard; and

- construction contracts are discussed in Chapter 21 but with the adoption of the new revenue standard a separate construction standard will not be necessary.

### Changes from the Exposure Draft 2010

The changes from the Exposure Draft in 2010 highlight some of the issues that had to be resolved in order to agree a revenue standard. In particular, IFRS 15 simplified the exposure draft by:

- allowing revenue to be recorded at the gross amount if it is probable the revenue will eventuate and not net of expected bad debts as was previously suggested; also

- simplifying the treatment of warranties by allowing implied interest to be ignored in contracts which are less than one year; further

- allowing as a practical expedient costs of acquiring new contracts to be written off as an expense if the contract is for less than one year; and

- making more explicit the revenue recognition in construction contracts.

These modifications highlight that the standard setters are under continued pressure from financial statement preparers to sacrifice some of the conceptual niceties in order to make the application of the standards easier.

### Effect of the standard being a joint IASB/FASB project

The other complication in developing IFRS 15 was that it was intended to be applied in the USA which is used to having much more detailed guidance in general, with many more industry guidelines. As a very litigious society, there is a philosophy in the USA that they need detailed and precise rules which they can follow. Further, there is a perception on the part of some that, if it is not covered by rules, the company is free to choose what suits it rather than trying to gauge the intent of the standard and attempting to implement that intent.

## 11.4 The challenges under both IAS 18 and IFRS 15

### A fair view

Accountants, in addition to checking that each transaction has been recorded in accordance with the accounting standards, still need to ask whether the resulting accounting statements give a fair view of the situation. In the final analysis it will be the courts that decide whether the clever ploys to get around standards, or the taking advantage of technical accounting rules, is legitimate. In *New York* v *Ernst & Young* (Part II) 451586/2010 New York State Supreme Court (Manhattan), the complainant said it was still necessary to ensure the accounts were fair. If considered unfair, they need to disclose sufficient information to rectify the situation.

### Recognising economic substance

In the case of revenue recognition, standard setters have been faced with the problem as to how to define revenue in such a way that it precludes transactions being artificially structured. Such a problem arose when Lehman Brothers in its last year entered into agreements to sell securities to a third party who agreed to sell them back after the reporting date allowing Lehman Bros to treat the transfer of securities as sales, thus increasing its revenue and reducing its leverage. So the major issue was whether the sale and the repurchase agreements should be treated as two separate transactions or as a single transaction.

This gave rise to the grey area as to whether to report according to the substance or according to the technical form. One could argue that reporting according to the technical form (i.e. applying an existing technical guideline) was the legal requirement and as a result should be reflected in the accounts – another party could argue that it was misleading and could be construed as fraudulent manipulation. Of course, it is desirable that accounting standards reduce the likelihood that such situations will arise, and following this case the SEC and FASB have issued new rules relating to sale and repurchase agreements, hoping to achieve reporting that better reflects the economic substance.

## 11.5 IFRS 15 *Revenue from Contracts with Customers*

### Effective date

The new standard will be effective for financial years commencing on or after 1 January 2017. However, if a company wishes to provide comparative figures it will need to record revenue figures for the 2016 year on a comparable basis – as well as according to the previous standard. Early adoption is allowable. Thus companies which are adopting international financial standards in the interim period may adopt the new standard immediately so as to avoid a double set of changes in a short period of time.

### Definition of revenue

There is no modification in the definition of revenues which is still:

> **Revenue** *is income arising in the course of an entity's ordinary activities whilst* **Income** *represents increases in economic benefits during the accounting period in the form of inflows or enhancements of assets or decreases in liabilities that result in increases in equity, other than those relating to contributions from equity participants.*

### 11.5.1 Transactions falling outside the IFRS 15 definition

The definition of revenue restricts it to income in the ordinary course of business through the provision of goods and services to customers. It therefore excludes:

- gains arising on the revaluation of biological assets;
- taxes collected on behalf of the government such as value added and sales tax. Thus a sale of goods on credit for £1,000 plus £125 for VAT would be recorded as:

| | | | |
|---|---|---|---|
| Dr | Accounts receivable | 1,125 | |
| Cr | Revenue | | 1,000 |
| Cr | VAT liability | | 125 |

- the effect of financing such as interest revenue or expense. Para 65 provides that 'an entity shall present the effects of financing (interest revenue or interest expense) separately from revenue from contracts with customers in the statement of comprehensive income';

● transactions dealt with under other standards such as Leasing and Insurance contracts.

However, one of the major debates in terms of developing the revenue recognition standard was how to account for uncertainty.

### 11.5.2 Revenue recognition when there is uncertainty

There are two major elements in relation to uncertainty. There may be uncertainty as to (a) the amount that will be eventually received in accordance with the terms of the contract and (b) the amount that will be received due to failure to recover the amount due.

#### (a) Uncertainty as to amount finally due under the contract

There is uncertainty if the amount is variable in that it depends on future events. The standard setters were keen to ensure that revenue reflects, as far as is practical, the level of progress whilst not being over-optimistic. Thus the criteria for determining the revenue figure where the final outcome includes an element of variability is only to report amounts which are *highly probable* of being achieved.

This means not recognising revenue in the current period that will need to be reversed in a subsequent period.

In assessing whether it is highly probable that a significant reversal in the amount of cumulative revenue recognised will not occur, the standard gives examples of factors that could increase the likelihood. The factors include:

● consideration being highly susceptible to factors outside the entity's influence such as volatility in a market, the judgement or actions of third parties, weather conditions and a high risk of obsolescence of the promised good or service;

● the uncertainty about the amount of consideration is not expected to be resolved for a long period of time;

● the entity's experience (or other evidence) with similar types of contracts is limited, or that experience (or other evidence) has limited predictive value; and

● the entity has a practice of either offering a broad range of price concessions or changing the payment terms and conditions of similar contracts in similar circumstances.

#### (b) Failure to recover the amount due

In this case the uncertainty is dealt with in the traditional manner. Revenue is recorded at the gross amount of the contract and shortfalls in collections are dealt with as bad and doubtful debt expenses.

## 11.6 Five-step process to identify the amount and timing of revenue

In order to identify the amount and timing of the recognition of revenue, the entity should go through a five-step process:

(a) identify the contract with a customer;

(b) identify the separate performance obligations in the contract;

(c) determine the transaction price;

(d) allocate the transaction price to the separate performance obligations in the contract; and

(e) recognise revenue when (or as) the entity satisfies a performance obligation.

### 11.6.1 Identify the contract with a customer (Step a)

The first step is to ascertain that there is a legal (enforceable) contract. Obviously legal rules vary across jurisdictions and industry-standard terms may form part of the agreement. Only when the full terms of the contract are ascertainable are we able to record the transaction.

Thus the terms must be specified in the contract or refer to outside references such as the price on a specified market at a specified time and date. The rights and obligations of all parties to the agreement to supply goods and/or services must be identifiable. One of those terms will be when the items are to be paid for.

The contract may relate to a single commodity or may cover a combination of goods and services. In the event of the contract involving a combination it may be necessary to untangle the elements which relate to each item so as to be able to record them as separate items.

For example, the Hewlett-Packard Company in their statement of accounting policies in their 2013 Annual Report[6] refer to agreements which cover both hardware and software and the need to identify how much of the agreed price relates to the payment for the hardware and how much refers to the provision of the software.

The second step relates to the rules for determining whether the contract has to be split into individual components.

Policy illustrated: Hewlett-Packard Company and Subsidiaries (HP)
We have discussed the various accounting policies set out in the following extracts from the Hewlett-Packard 2013 Annual Report. These highlight the application of the above:

**Accounting policies**
HP recognizes revenue when persuasive evidence of a sales arrangement exists, delivery has occurred or services are rendered, the sale price or fee is fixed or determinable, and collectability is reasonably assured.

Additionally, HP recognizes hardware revenue on sales to channel partners, including resellers. . . at the time of delivery when the channel partners have economic substance apart from HP, and HP has completed its obligations related to the sale.

HP generally recognizes revenue for its stand-alone software sales to channel partners upon receiving evidence that the software has been sold to a specific end user.

When a sales arrangement contains multiple elements, such as hardware and software products, licenses and/or services, HP allocates revenue to each element based on a selling price hierarchy. The selling price for a deliverable is based on its vendor specific objective evidence (VSOE) of selling price, if available or third party evidence ('TPE') if VSOE of selling price is not available or estimated selling price ('ESP') if neither VSOE of selling price nor TPE is available.

HP establishes VSOE of selling price using the price charged for a deliverable when sold separately and, in rare instances, using the price established by management having the relevant authority.

HP establishes TPE of selling price by evaluating largely similar and interchangeable competitor products or services in standalone sales to similarly situated customers. . .

In arrangements with multiple elements, HP determines allocation of transaction price at the inception of the arrangement based on the relative selling price of each unit of accounting. . . . .

HP limits the amount of revenue recognized for delivered element to the amount that is not contingent on the future delivery of products or services, future performance obligations or subject to customer-specified return or refund privileges.. . . .

HP reports revenue net of any required taxes collected from customers and remitted to government authorities, with the collected taxes recorded as current liabilities until remitted to the relevant government authority.. . . .[6]

The full accounting policy is much more extensive than shown in the extracts and is worthy of review.

### 11.6.2 Separate performance obligations within the same contract (Step b)

#### What is a performance obligation?

A performance obligation would include the supply of goods, the provision of services such as consulting or dry cleaning, and compensation for making available assets such as capital (interest), intellectual property (royalties), property, plant and equipment (lease payments) and software.

#### Identifying separate performance obligations

If goods or services are stand-alone products or services which can be used separately, or together with other resources reasonably available to customers and the supply company has not agreed to integrate the two products/services, then they are separate performance obligations.

A contract to supply equipment and to service it for several years in the future where the items could be bought separately from one or more companies could constitute two distinct performance obligations.

### 11.6.3 Pricing the transaction (Step c)

The third step involves the pricing of the performance obligations in the contract. In many contracts that process is relatively simple. The contract is for one item and the price is unambiguously specified in the contract. However, it is possible that the contract may be more complicated.

Where the pricing of a contract is based on events that are unknown at the time **the guiding principle is to record revenue in a manner that is unlikely to result in significant reductions in revenue in the future.** Thus the aim is to be as accurate as possible but to prohibit companies from anticipating revenue that is unlikely to be received.

Next, some common pricing arrangements such as annual refunds, performance bonuses and payments in arrears will be examined.

#### Annual refund

Dee Pharmaceutical sells to pharmacies whereby it charges the standard price and at the close of the year pays a 5% discount based on the total purchases for the year. During January Dee Pharmaceutical invoices customers €5,000,000 for goods supplied. The entry would be:

| | | | |
|---|---|---:|---:|
| Dr | Accounts receivable | 5,000,000 | |
| Cr | Sales Revenue | | 4,750,000 |
| Cr | Sales Rebate liability | | 250,000 |

(Being gross sales of €5,000,000 less the obligation to refund 5% at the end of the financial year)

### Performance bonuses

Suppose Gee Chemicals supplies chemicals to Perfection Manufacturers on the basis that it will supply 108,000 tons during the year, with shipments of 9,000 tons per month with an annual bonus of 3% on each shipment when the quality exceeds 99% purity, providing there are no late deliveries. The contract rate is £1,100 per ton.

Based on past experience, four of the months will produce a bonus and all deliveries will be on time. There are two ways of calculating the amount to record each month – (a) the most likely outcome and (b) the expected value.

#### (a) The most likely outcome approach

If we take this approach and focus on the most likely outcome, then we would calculate 9,000 tons per month at £1,100 per ton, giving £9,900,000 per month.

| | | | |
|---|---|---|---|
| Dr | Accounts receivable | 9,900,000 | |
| Cr | Sales revenue | | 9,900,000 |

(*Monthly sales based on the contract rate without recording any bonus.*)

| | | | |
|---|---|---|---|
| Dr | Accounts receivable | xxxx | |
| Cr | Sales revenue | | xxxx |

(*Recording additional revenue when bonuses are confirmed. This entry is based on the assumption that purity levels refer to the state in which they are delivered and thus depend on the outcome of testing at the customer.*)

#### (b) The expected value approach

Adopting this alternative approach we would work out the expected value based on expectations. The bonus on a month has an expected value of $(4/12) \times 3\% + (8/12) \times 0\% = 1\%$.

The 4/12 above represents the 4 months out of 12 months when they will earn a bonus and the 8/12 represents the 8 out of 12 months in which no bonus is expected.

Under this approach the monthly entry would be:

| | | | |
|---|---|---|---|
| Dr | Accounts receivable | 9,900,000 | |
| Cr | Sales revenue | | 9,999,000 |
| Dr | Bonus receivable | 99,000 | |

(*Recording expected monthly revenue including anticipated bonuses.*)

| | | | |
|---|---|---|---|
| Dr/Cr | Accounts receivable | XXX | |
| Cr | Bonus receivable | Amounts previously recorded | |
| Dr/Cr | Revenue | Over/under-recording of the revenue previously | |

(*Adjusting accounts receivable to the right amount when the size of the bonus is known, eliminating bonus receivable, and getting the revenue figure correct.*)

The choice between the two depends on what experience has shown to be the more accurate in predicting the actual outcomes and the degree to which overstatements have been associated with each approach. Adjustments downward are a problem if they are significant for the particular company.

### Treatment if payment is deferred

In a contract in which payment is not immediate on the performance of the obligation but is deferred then there is an implied financing element and the time value of money may have to be considered.

*When the interest element may be ignored*

If the timing of the delivery of the service is not specified in the contract but is instead determined by the customer, then there is not a definite financing period, so it can be ignored. Also if the total contract covers less than one year, or the gap between payment and performance is less than one year, then the standard allows the interest element to be ignored as a practical expedient.

*When the interest element must be accounted for*

The determination of an interest element assumes there are (a) pre-established times for delivery of the service and (b) payment at an agreed price. If the time value of money is relevant then the issues to consider include:

**(a)** the difference between the cash price (i.e. the price that would have been charged if the payment coincided with the performance of the obligation or occurred in accordance with normal industry terms) and the contract price;

**(b)** the interest rate in the contract; and

**(c)** the current interest rate in the market.

If interest is recognised then it is shown separately from other revenue in the statement of comprehensive income.

*Accounting treatment illustrated*

Let us assume that Heavy Goods plc entered into a contract for the sale of 10 coal trucks, at a cost of £242,000 each, which provided for deferred payment two years later. If the terms were payment on delivery, the contract price would have been £200,000 for a similar vehicle.

This would imply that each truck sold included interest of £42,000 which is at a compound interest rate of 10% per annum. If the market rate is also 10% p.a. then the recording would be:

*Year one*

| | | | |
|---|---|---|---|
| Dr | Accounts receivable | 2,420,000 | |
| Cr | Sales revenue | | 2,000,000 |
| Cr | Interest revenue | | 200,000 |
| Cr | Deferred interest | | 220,000 |

(Being the recording of the sale of 10 coal trucks and receiving 10% interest for one year)

*Year two*

| | | | |
|---|---|---|---|
| Dr | Deferred interest | 220,000 | |
| Cr | Interest revenue | | 220,000 |

(Being interest on 2,200,000 at ten percent for year two)

| | | | |
|---|---|---|---|
| Dr | Bank | 2,420,000 | |
| Cr | Accounts receivable | | 2,420,000 |

(Being settlement of the account)

However, if the market interest rate was more than 10%, that would imply that the sale price was cheaper than competitors' prices or the interest rate was discounted or both were discounted. Such cases will be discussed in the next section.

### 11.6.4 Allocate the transaction price to the separate performance obligations in the contract (Step d)

Where Step b has identified that there are two or more performance obligations under a contract it is necessary to allocate the total contract consideration (amount) across the individual performance obligations. The method that will be adopted depends on the information available.

The simplest case is where there are readily available market prices for each and every performance obligation. These prices can be used to allocate the total remuneration between the various performance obligations. The highest-quality information is external market prices for identical or very similar items sold to comparable customers in similar circumstances.

In the absence of such high-quality information, the company's own selling prices for items sold individually can be used. If the company can only get reliable or consistent information on some of the performance obligations then the residual method can be used. It must be stressed that this residual method is the last resort rather than a desirable approach.

Suppose a company sells a combination of three performance obligations X, Y and Z for £32. If the market prices of X and Y as independent items are £10 and £15 respectively then the residual of £7 is deemed to be the price of item Z. However, if the company regularly sells bundles of (X + Y) at a discount price of £24, then the residual price would be £8.

### Readily available market prices illustrated with Consensus Supplies plc

Let us illustrate the highest ranked approach whereby market prices for all performance obligations are used to allocate the contract price.

#### Consensus Supplies plc – information on contract

Let us assume that Consensus Supplies plc sells 10 printers on credit at a price of €4,000 each when the manufactured cost was €2,000 each. Let us further assume that Consensus offers its customers a combined contract for €4,800 for each printer which includes the provision of maintenance cover for two years. The cost of manufacture remains the same at €2,000 each and the cost of supplying maintenance is €250 per machine per year.

Let us also assume that customers could purchase separate maintenance cover from other suppliers for 2 years at a cost of €1,000 per printer.

#### Consensus Supplies plc – accounting for contract (ignore the financing elements to keep this introductory example simple)

The contract is for two separate performance obligations (with different timing of the services) and so the revenue has to be apportioned between the contracts and then recognised as the individual services are provided. The normal selling prices are:

| | |
|---|---:|
| Supply of printers | €40,000 |
| Supply of maintenance in Year 1 | €5,000 |
| Supply of maintenance in Year 2 | €5,000 |
| Total services provided | €50,000 |
| Combined price | €48,000 |

This shows that Consensus is selling at 48,000/50,000 or 96% of the normal price, i.e. 4% below normal selling price. Each component part of the contract is reduced by 4% as follows:

| | | |
|---|---|---:|
| Supply of printers | 40,000 × 0.96 | €38,400 |
| Supply of maintenance in Year 1 | 5,000 × 0.96 | €4,800 |
| Supply of maintenance in Year 2 | 5,000 × 0.96 | €4,800 |
| Combined price | | €48,000 |

*(This process represents Step d of the requirements which is to allocate the transaction price to the separate performance obligations in the contract.)*

The entries for a contract made in accordance with the Standard are:

| | | |
|---|---|---|
| Dr | Trade receivables | €48,000 | |
| Cr | Sales revenue (equipment sales) | | €38,400 |
| Cr | Sales revenue (maintenance) | | €4,800 |
| Cr | Revenue in advance liability | | €4,800 |

*(Being the recording of a sale and maintenance package.)*

| | | |
|---|---|---|
| Dr | Cost of goods sold (Equipment) | €20,000 | |
| Dr | Cost of goods sold (Maintenance) | €2,500 | |
| Cr | Inventory | | €20,000 |
| Cr | Bank | | €2,500 |

*(Recording costs of providing services and the outlays for wages and materials used for maintenance.)*

### Disclosure at end of Year 1

The Standard requires the company to disclose in its annual report the amount and timing of the future revenue secured by existing contracts.

A possible way of disclosing this could be as follows:

Contracts for the supply of maintenance

| | Period two | Period three |
|---|---|---|
| Prepaid amounts | £4,800 | XXX |
| Executory contracts | XXX | XXX |

Note, however, that this does not satisfy all the disclosure requirements. See paragraph 110 which says:

> The objective of the disclosure requirements is for an entity to disclose sufficient information to enable users of financial statements to understand the nature, amount, timing and uncertainty of revenue and cash flows arising from contracts with customers. To achieve that objective, an entity shall disclose qualitative and quantitative information about all of the following:
>
> **(a)** its contracts with customers. . .
>
> **(b)** the significant judgements, and changes in judgements, made. . .
>
> **(c)** any assets recognised from the costs to obtain or fulfil a contract. . .

### Accounting entries in Year 2

These would be:

| | | |
|---|---|---|
| Dr | Revenue in advance | €4,800 | |
| Cr | Sales revenue (maintenance) | | €4,800 |

*(Transferring revenue in advance to current performance.)*

| | | |
|---|---|---|
| Dr | Cost of goods sold (maintenance) | €2,500 | |
| Cr | Bank | | €2,500 |

*(Payment for materials and wages.)*

Note that in this chapter we discuss the most common and simplest approach to price allocations. In special circumstances, where specific bundles of performance obligations that represent some but not all of the obligations in the current contract, are regularly sold as a bundle at a discount, then another allocation method may be used. See paragraph 82 of the Standard if you want more details.

## 11.6.5 Recognise revenue when (or as) the entity satisfies a performance obligation (Step e)

As a performance obligation is transferred to a customer in accordance with the terms of the contract, the revenue is recognised in the books of account. The major principle is that revenue is recognised when control of an asset passes to the customer.

### Sale of goods

When the goods are delivered to the customer, normally the supplier has a right to payment for the goods, assuming they meet the contract specifications and the conditions demanded under the law (e.g. fit for its purpose). The requirement of the standard that the *revenue be recognised when the asset or service is transferred to the customer* is satisfied in that transfer of the goods is assumed to occur when control passes to customers. In the case of goods this is easy to envisage as once the customer receives the goods they are free to use the goods as they want including consuming them, using them in further manufacturing, selling them or just holding them as assets.

### Providing services

When services are transferred, the customer receives an asset such as knowledge or consumable goods, which are immediately consumed. So as soon as the customer consumes the service they clearly have taken control of the asset and thus the revenue shall be recognised.

For example, when an accounting firm gives a client advice, the client has consumed the information and the accounting firm can, therefore, record the revenue. However, if the firm is performing an audit at an agreed price and, at the firm's balance date, it has completed a third of the expected audit work, then it could not justify recording the revenue, as the client has not received the product (the audit report) and does not have control of the audit papers.

### More complex situations

If there are separate performance obligations then the agreed price has to be split, otherwise revenue is recognised for the complete transaction. Decisions may have to be made in complex situations such as when warranties, leases, long-term contracts, reservation of title, financial securities, transfers of intellectual property, equally unperformed contracts and onerous contracts are involved. We will briefly discuss each of these.

### Warranties

Let us consider a situation where goods have been supplied under a manufacturer's warranty. This means that the full performance obligation has not been completed in that there are residual obligations in the form of warranties covering faults identified in use.

We have to decide whether the warranty is part of the primary performance obligation to supply the goods in satisfactory conditions or is part of a separate performance obligation.

As the warranty is restricted to making the goods fit for their stated purpose and does not constitute an additional performance obligation, the question of splitting the agreed price into separate components does not arise. The customer clearly has control of the asset and thus the revenue is recognised but the warranty has to be accounted for in accordance with IAS 37 *Provisions, Contingent Liabilities and Contingent Assets*.

*Example where there is a manufacturer's warranty*
Let us assume that Makem Manufacturing plc has shipped 2 million units to customers during the financial year with selling prices averaging £300 per unit. Over the last ten years the warranties cost an average of £1 per unit with only minor fluctuations from year to year.

The accounting entries would be as follows:

| Dr | Accounts receivable | 600,000,000 | |
| Cr | Sales revenue | | 600,000,000 |

*(Revenue recorded at their gross sales value)*

| Dr | Warranty expenses | 2,000,000 | |
| Cr | Liability (Provision) for warranty expenses | | 2,000,000 |

*(Covering expected warranty costs)*

If the warranty covers more than is normally associated with the supply of goods and if it represents more than an insignificant amount then the possibility of the warranty giving rise to the existence of a separate performance obligation has to be considered. If it is decided that there are separate performance obligations the approach would be as taken in the Consensus example above.

## Leases

Under a lease the customer obtains control of the asset for a specified period and the benefits of use are related to the amount/period of use which can be made of the asset. This will be discussed further in the chapter on leasing.

## Long-term contracts

Longer-term contracts such as building a road may take several years to complete. In such cases if the contractor is working on the road and fails to complete, such as when the contractor goes bankrupt, then the client has possession of that which has been accomplished to date and can organise for another contractor to take over the work and to complete the project. In such cases, a contractor may have agreed with the client that it will be entitled to bill the client when major components are completed; then revenue can be recognised when those milestones are reached. Obviously there are a number of other possible scenarios depending on the detailed facts of the case. These issues will be discussed in more detail in Chapter 21.

## Reservation of title

Another sales agreement which raises questions as to whether the transaction can be recorded in the normal manner is a sale contract with a reservation of title. To reduce the likelihood of losses arising on the bankruptcy of a customer, some companies deliver goods on terms that include a specification that title to the goods does not pass until the customer has paid for them. Then if the customer gets into financial difficulties the supplier may be able to take the goods back if that is consistent with the laws of the country and provided the goods are identifiable. In the meantime the customer can deal with the goods in the normal way, such as to sell or use the asset.

### When to recognise revenue if there is reservation of title

The question is whether the initial transfer of goods to the customer should be treated as revenue in the supplier's accounts.

The relevant provision in the standard is that '*an entity shall recognise revenue when (or as) the entity satisfies a performance obligation by transferring a promised good or service (i.e. an asset) to a customer. An asset is transferred when (or as) the customer obtains control of that asset*' (para. 31).

Clearly the asset has been transferred and the customer now has control of the asset. Thus the conditions for recognising the revenue have been met. Paragraph 38 (b) says: '*If an entity retains legal title solely as protection against the customer's failure to pay, those rights of the entity would not preclude the customer from obtaining control of an asset.*'

### Financial securities

Another type of contract or combination of contracts that has been controversial in recent years has been the situation where a company sells an item, such as financial securities, and also agrees to buy them back at a later stage – such as the day after the financial reporting date. The repurchase amount would reflect the price paid for the security plus compensation for the financing cost for the holding period and the risk that the original seller will not be able undertake the repurchase at the specified date.

IFRS 15 explicitly covers sale agreements combined with a repurchase agreement or a put option. It does not matter whether the arrangement was incorporated in a single contract or there were two contracts, namely, one for the sale and the other for the repurchase if one (the sale) was executed with the understanding that the other contract (the repurchase) will also be agreed to.

IFRS 15 clearly specifies that separate contracts should be dealt with in the books as a combined contract if they are negotiated with a single commercial objective or if the amount paid in one contract depends on the consideration paid in the other contract (paragraph 17).

It also requires that revenue contracts must have commercial substance (paragraph 6). Here the sale and repurchase had a single commercial objective, which is for the initial selling company to get the financial instruments temporarily off their balance sheet and replace them with cash so as to make their balance sheet look stronger. However, no risk is being transferred as the repurchase agreement means the company temporarily holding the financial instrument gets a fixed price irrespective of what happens in the marketplace during the holding period.

### Transfers of intellectual property

Two distinct categories were identified under this heading. These categories were:

(a) Where the purchaser has the right to use the intellectual property and will pay based on the level of sales; and

(b) Where the seller transfers to the customer all or part of the ownership of the intellectual property at a point in time.

The first situation might be where a band records its own music and receives a royalty from television and radio stations as they play the records and videos. The entry would be:

Dr    Accounts receivable/Cash
Cr        Royalty revenue

The second situation might be where an entrepreneurial company develops a new drug which it has tested on mice but does not have the financial and medical connections and managerial resources to satisfy the regulatory requirements in the USA and sells its intellectual capital to a major US company. The sale of its knowledge would be a single transaction. If there was an additional undertaking to do support work for the US company that would be a separate performance obligation.

### Equally unperformed contracts

A vexed question is what to do when a company enters into a contract to be a longer-term supplier of goods. If goods have not been supplied under the contract and either of the parties can terminate the contract at any time without compensating the other party, then there is no reason to record the event. The performance obligation has not been performed, so no revenue needs to be recognised.

### Onerous contracts

After a contract has been entered into and the expected revenue has been allocated across performance obligations it may become apparent that one or more performance obligation is going to incur a loss. In such circumstances it is necessary to keep in mind two propositions; these are (a) the need to record revenue only at an amount that you are confident you will receive and (b) the need to recognise losses as soon as they are anticipated.

To estimate the amount of the anticipated loss it is necessary to ask: how can the losses be minimised? Generally the company faces two possibilities – either to complete the contract and absorb the resulting losses, or it may be able to negotiate with the customer to be released from the contract in return for payment of penalties. If both options are available the company will presumably choose the cheaper option, taking into account both direct costs and intangible costs (the negative impact on goodwill). The amount of probable losses will be based on the option chosen.

At the balance sheet date, revenue must not be overstated and any future losses need to be provided for as an onerous contract in accordance with IAS 37 *Provisions, Contingent Liabilities and Contingent Assets*. Finished goods and work in progress may also need to be reviewed to see if these need to be written down to their net realisable amount.

### 11.6.6 Modification of the terms of contracts

Sometimes the parties to a contract may modify an ongoing contract during the performance of the contract. An example of this may be when two businesses have an ongoing relationship and have negotiated a contract to formalise those ongoing transactions. It may be that the world price for the raw material that the producer uses to manufacture the goods, subject to the contract, has changed dramatically up or down. If the parties think it only fair that the contract be renegotiated then they are free to do so.

In general terms there are three types of situations involving modifications to contracts:

(a) Where the modification refers only to distinct goods or services which have not yet been supplied. In that case the future component of the contract can be treated like a new separate contract. Then the steps (a) to (e) would be applied separately to the future component to the contract.

(b) The modification may introduce another distinct performance obligation to the contract at a commercial price and will thus be separate from the previously agreed supply. Once again the additional performance obligation will be treated as if it were a new and separate contract.

(c) Where the modification relates to both previously completed performance obligations as well as to future supply. In such cases the revenue is allocated as if the new facts had been known at the commencement of the contract. That calculation will identify the extent to which revenue has previously been over- or understated and that amount will result in an immediate adjustment to revenue. In terms of the future supply those items will be recognised at the new price as the performance obligations take place.

### Illustration where the modification relates to both previously completed performance obligations as well as to future supply

Let us consider International Manufacturing which has entered into a two-year contract to make a weekly delivery of biscuits priced at £100 a box. It finds that shortly after the contract is signed and before any shipments have taken place the cost of sugar has jumped 50% because of floods in several countries which are major producers of sugar. The customer of the biscuit company, a major grocery chain, does not offer any extra remuneration because they do not know whether the sugar price increase is a short-term fluctuation or a more sustained change.

In the first four months of the new contract International Manufacturing recognised revenue of £500,000 based on the original contract price. At that point, being confident that the sugar price increase would hold for the next two years, the grocery chain agreed to a 5% increase in price from the start of the contract. International Manufacturing therefore immediately recorded an additional 5% of £500,000 or £25,000 as revenue. Future shipments were then charged at £105 per box as they were delivered.

## 11.7 Disclosures

IFRS 15 para 110 states that 'The objective of the disclosure requirements is to enable users of financial statements to understand the nature, amount, timing and uncertainty of revenue and cash flows arising from contracts with customers . . . '. This might require the revenue and assets to be disaggregated and detailed disclosures provided.

### Disaggregate revenue

In particular, the business may have a range of products and services, or items in relation to different regions of the world, which are affected by different terms and conditions, economic forces and political risks. It is therefore desirable that management disaggregate total revenue in a manner which helps analysts and investors understand current performance and to predict future performance.

### Disaggregate assets

The company has to show details of assets which arise as the result of accounting for revenue and they must be disaggregated as different levels of risk are associated with the different categories. The assets which are relevant include:

(a) Assets representing recoverable outlays in relation to obtaining contracts which relate to performance obligations in future periods;

(b) Accounts receivable representing performance obligations that have already been performed but not yet paid for; and

(c) Work in progress.

### Disclose terms and conditions

In addition, the typical terms and conditions for the various categories of revenue need to be disclosed and the associated revenue recognition policies.

### Disclose judgements

Further, any major judgements which were made in arriving at revenue figures must be disclosed, as must any changes in those judgements. In that way it is easier for outsiders to review trends in revenue.

## Summary

(a) The recognition of revenue does not occur unless there is a fully specified contract.

(b) Revenue is recognised when the performance obligation has been performed for an unrelated/independent customer.

(c) Revenue is only recognised when there is a high probability that it will be paid for.

(d) If the contract involves multiple elements or performance obligations they are separated out and accounted for individually.

(e) To divide (allocate) the contract revenue between performance obligations the company looks to the most directly relevant price information.

(f) The need to distinguish the revenue stream from amounts collected on behalf of government.

## REVIEW QUESTIONS

1  The Accounting Onion, a very good US accounting blog,[7] critically reviews the revenue recognition policy of a for-profit university and provides an extract from the policy as follows:

> Students are billed on a course-by-course basis. They are billed on the first day of attendance, and a journal entry is made to debit Accounts receivable A/R and credit deferred revenue for the amount of the billing. The A/R is ultimately adjusted by an allowance for uncollectible accounts of around 30%, and deferred revenue is recognized pro rata over the duration of the course.

> Assuming the courses (subjects) go from September to February whilst the financial year ends on 31 December, discuss whether the policy is appropriate.

2  A continuing problem in accounting is where companies use multiple contracts to circumvent the intentions of rules. Sometimes this is called 'the need for accounting to reflect substance over form'. Lehman Bros in the USA entered into a contract for sale of some securities which it agreed to buy back after balance date. What are the advantages and disadvantages of the 'substance over form' approach?

3  One of the problems faced by the standard setters was the untangling of contracts which delivered multiple performance obligations. Identify a business which supplies multiple services in one contract and identify the individual service components. Then discuss the following:

(a) whether the two service components have similar or dissimilar patterns of delivery;

(b) whether the components are sold by that business or other businesses as separate contracts or as 'stand-alone' services;

(c) the significance of the presence of other companies selling the services as individual services;

(d) the likely impact on the business if the two service components have to be recognised individually.

4  The bloggers Anthony H. Catanach Jr and J. Edward Ketz discussed in their blog Grumpy Old Accountants (www.grumpyoldaccountants.com/) on 27 August 2012 the accounting for Internet companies. The article is titled 'What is Zynga's "Real" Growth Rate?' They quote from the accounting policies of Zynga as follows: 'We recognize revenue from the sale of durable virtual goods ratably over the estimated average playing period of paying players for the applicable game'. Discuss whether the preceding policy would be an appropriate policy under IFRS 15 and whether Internet companies need their own revenue standard.

5 The ASB made a submission on the 2010 proposed revenue standard and in that submission indicated that the revenue allocation in relation to a contract which involved multiple performance obligations should reflect the normal margins of the various performance obligations. This is in contrast to the then proposed standard which allocated revenue in relation to the stand-alone prices of the various performance obligations. Discuss the merits of the two alternatives.

6 In the technology sector there has been a high proportion of problems centred on what accountants call improper 'revenue recognition' – the recording of revenue that does not exist. Discuss why the technology sector might be more likely to do this and how it would have been justified to the auditors.

7 Do the proposed/new recognition rules give primary importance to calculating income or fairly presenting the statement of financial position (balance sheet)? How do you support that conclusion?

8 Executory contracts are contracts where both sides have not yet performed their obligations. If your company has a long-term contract for the supply of raw materials to XYZ Ltd for 50,000 tons per year for five years at a selling price of €10,000 per ton and the market price has fallen to €8,000 per ton, should this be recorded as a €2,000 a ton revenue in the current period? Justify your answer.

9 During the dot-com boom two major companies with excess data transmission lines in different areas arranged a sale whereby company X transferred lines in city A to company Y which in return transferred its excess lines in city B to company X. No cash changed hands. The contract specified the agreed value of the assets transferred. Identify and explain the potential problems in accounting for such a transaction. Would it make any difference if cash had changed hands?

10 There is a company which facilitates barter exchanges. Thus the barter company may ask a restaurant to make available a number of free meals which are then effectively exchanged for other services such as a painter repainting the building in which the restaurant is located. The painter can use only some of the free meals so with the help of the barter company he exchanges the balance of the meals with a manufacturer/paint supplier for his paint needs on several projects. The paint manufacturer uses the meals in their staff training activities. The barter company which facilitates these exchanges also gets remunerated by the companies involved for its brokering activities so may also get a small quantity of meals. Discuss the recording issues for the restaurant and the barter company.

11 As soon as the authorities identify new rules, accountants for hire will attempt to find ways around the rules. Identify as many ways as you can in which the new rules can be circumvented.

12 The Australian Securities and Investment Commission (ASIC) required a company called Flight Centre to amend the way in which it recorded revenue. It had previously recorded revenue based on the gross value of the flights it had booked for customers, whereas the ASIC wanted it to record revenue based on the commissions it received. The change would have no impact on the reported profit of the company. Given the company disclosed its accounting policies and was consistent from year to year it appears no one was misled. Explain why the company would prefer the gross approach, and the regulator the net revenue approach, and whether the issue is worthy of such a debate. (Provide justification for your conclusions.)

13 Access the IASB website and critically review the various decisions made to arrive at the final IFRS on revenue recognition.

14 The traditional method for recognising revenue made no allowance for possible bad debts. The first (2010) exposure draft reduced the amount of revenue by the estimated amount of bad debts. In the second exposure draft the standard setters reverted to the traditional method of revenue recognition. Given the contribution of possible bad debts to the great financial crisis, was the reversion to the traditional method wise? Discuss.

**15** A property developer sells a building to a company which has little cash but is willing to exchange vacant land which it owns at a sought-after location. An independent valuer assesses the vacant land at £5,000,000 and on the basis of that the government charges the recipient £50,000 as land transfer taxes. Legal fees of £5,000 are incurred by the property developer. How much should be recorded as revenue and why?

**16** HP limits the amount of revenue recognised for a delivered element to the amount that is not contingent on the future delivery of products or services, future performance obligations or subject to customer-specified return or refund privileges. Discuss if this is the same as recognising revenue when it is highly probable of being achieved.

## EXERCISES

### * Question 1

Senford PLC entered into a contract to sell 3,000 telephones each with a two-year provider contract. The total cost of the contract was €120 per month payable at the end of the month. The phones were bought for cash from a supplier for €480 each and the cost of providing the telephone service is estimated at €30 a month for each phone. Senford PLC sells two-year service contracts (without supplying a phone) for €90 a month. The balance date for the company is three months after the date of the sales.

Required:
(a) Prepare all the journal entries for the current financial year that are possible from the data given. (Ignore financing costs.)
(b) Show the disclosures which will be necessary in the annual report in relation to these phone contracts.
Show your calculations.

### * Question 2

Strayway PLC sells two planes to Elliott & Elliott Budget Airlines PLC for 5 million euros each payable in two years' time on presentation of an accepted bill of exchange to be presented through Lloyds Bank. The face value of the bill is €10,000,000. Further enquiry ascertains that government bonds with two years to maturity yield 4% p.a. and Strayway borrows from their bank at 9%, and the average yield on commercial bills of exchange payable in two years' time is 8%.

Required:
Record the sale and associated transactions in the books of Strayway PLC.

### * Question 3

Penrith European Car Sales plc sells a new car with 'free' 5,000 kilometre and 20,000 kilometre services for a combined price of €41,500. The cost of the car from the manufacturer is €30,000. The two services normally cost €400 and €600 to do and are charged to casual customers at the rate of €800 and €1,200 respectively.

Required:
Record all the transactions associated with the sale.

## * Question 4

Facts:

Henry Falk subscribes to an online monthly gardening magazine and selects the option of a three-year subscription from the following options:

| | |
|---|---|
| One issue | €12 |
| Twelve issues | €120 |
| Twenty-four issues | €200 |
| Thirty-six issues | €300 |

The publisher, English Magazine Specialties plc, estimates that it will cost €60, €62 and €64 per annum respectively to supply the magazines for the respective years.

Henry duly pays by credit card as part of the subscribing process.

Show the entries in the books of the English Magazine Specialties plc.

Required:
(a) Show the entries to record the transactions associated with the sale and supply for years one, two and three. (Ignore interest for part a.)
(b) Assuming a 10% borrowing rate and a constant revenue stream show the accounting entries. Use 2% for credit card fees.
(c) Provide the disclosures which would need to be made in the annual report at the end of the first year of the contract.
(d) What other patterns of revenue recognition could be used?

## * Question 5

Assume the same facts as in Question 4(b) but add the presence of a 7.5% value added tax on the sales and a 1% transaction cost paid to the supplier of credit card transactions.

Required:
(a) Show the entries to record the transactions associated with the sale and supply for years one, two and three. (Ignore imputed interest costs.)
(b) Provide the disclosures which would need to be made in the annual report at the end of the first year of the contract.

## * Question 6

Five G Telephones enters into telephone contracts on the following terms and options:

| | |
|---|---|
| Xyz mobile phones | €1,000 |
| Basic Y phones | €200 |

Basic connection service options:

| | |
|---|---|
| A | €40 per month |
| B | €15 plus 50 cents per call |

Combined services:

Supply of Xyz and connection service €79 per month with a minimum contract period of 24 months.

Required:

Record the entries for the first month for each of the possible transactions assuming the following information:

(a) Xyz phones are purchased from a supplier for €500.
(b) Basic phones are purchased from a supplier for €120.
(c) The average user makes 100 calls a month at a variable cost of five cents per call.
(d) Ignore imputed interest.

## Question 7

Assume the facts as per Question 6 with the following additional costs:

There is a five euro cost to add a customer to the phone system and those who buy the phone outright do not default on payments for the phone or the service contract, but those who have a combined service contract default in 10% of the cases.

Required:

(a) Show the entries to record the transactions associated with the sale and supply for years one, two and three.
(b) Provide the disclosures which would need to be made in the annual report at the end of the first year of the contract.

## Question 8

Assume that in Question 3 you had also been told that cars without the inclusion of free services are typically sold by other sales outlets for €40,000.

Required:

Re-do the entries for the sale and the servicing. (Ignore interest as the timing of the servicing is not given and the amounts are modest.) Justify your answer.

## Question 9

Complete Computer Services (CCS) sells computer packages which include supply of a computer which carries the normal warranty against faulty parts plus a two-year assistance package covering problems encountered using any software sold or supplied with the computer. This package is designed for the person who lacks confidence in the use of the computer and likes to feel they have help available if they want it. The costs which CCS incurs are €600 for the purchase of the computer, €20 for normal warranty costs and €30 a year to service the assistance service component. The sales revenue is €950 being assigned as €100 for the service assistance and €850 for the computer.

Required:

Show all relevant journal entries.

## Question 10

Henry plc is a company which has established a reputation as a company which generates growth in sales from year to year and those growth prospects have been incorporated into share prices. However, the current year has been more difficult and the managing director does not want to disappoint the market. He has approached a friend with an idea he got from one of the auditors for pulling a rabbit out of the hat. The friend spends €3,000 to establish a company Dreams Come True Pty Ltd and contributes a further 2 million euros as the new company's paid-up capital. Henry plc then enters into a contract to lend 3 million euros to Dreams Come True Pty Ltd. Next, Henry plc sells a building to Dreams Come True Pty Ltd for 3 million euros for cash. A week after the end of the financial year Henry plc enters into a contract to repurchase the building from Dreams Come True for 3.5 million euros with an effective date six months into the new financial year. The managing director wants the accountant to record the building as sales revenue.

**Required:**
(a) Discuss the technical issues of the proposals.
(b) Discuss the ethical issues of the proposals.

## Question 11

Exess Steel plc specialises in steelmaking and is located in the northwest of the country. Due to an unexpected downturn in demand for its steel products it has excess coking coal. South East Steel Products plc has also been caught by the unexpected economic downturn and has an excess of steel pellets. At the steel producers annual conference the two managing directors discuss how their different auditors want them to write down the value of the excess stock because of the economic circumstances. They agree to do an exchange of the two commodities with the contracts including selling prices at the cost values in their books and a small cash payment to cover the difference between the two valuations. The two items are recorded in the books at the agreed purchase and selling prices respectively.

**Required:**
Comment critically on this proposal.

## Question 12

New Management plc is a pharmaceutical company selling to wholesalers and retail pharmacies. The new CEO was appointed at the start of the financial year and was full of enthusiasm. For the first six months her new ideas created a 10% increase in sales and then the economy crashed as the government cut spending and monetary policy was tightened. Sales dropped 20% as customers had slower sales and were required by their banks to reduce their overdrafts. A new strategy was adopted in the last two months of the year. Sales representatives were told to sell on the basis that customers would not have to pay for three months, by which time they would have sold the stock. They were also told that if sales for the month to that customer were not 5% higher than the sales for the corresponding month for the previous year, they could say to the customer, off the record of course, that they could return any unsold stock after four months. In the last two months of the financial year sales were up 10 and 11% on the respective previous corresponding periods. The first month of the new financial year recorded a 10% drop in sales.

**Required:**
Critically discuss from the point of view of (a) an investor, (b) the auditor and (c) the CEO.

## Question 13

Renee Aluminum Products plc enters into an agreement to supply Skyline Window Installers plc with standard window frames at the retail prices at the time less 40%. Renee supplies 300 windows a month at £66 each. However, the agreement provides for price increases based on Renee's increases in the cost of aluminium.

**Required:**
(a) In July Renee advises that the price will increase by 4%. Record revenue for the month of July.
(b) If in July Renee advises Skyline Windows that the price increase of 4% applies retrospectively from 1 March, what entry would be made in Renee's accounts for revenue in July?

## Notes

1 US Government Accountability Office, *Financial Restatements Update of Public Company Trends, Market Impacts and Regulatory Enforcement Activities*, GAO, 2007.
2 K.L. Anderson and T.L. Yohn, 'The Effect of 10K Restatements on Firm Value, Information Asymmetries and Investors' Reliance on Earnings', SSRN, Sept. 2002.
3 Christopher Williams, 'Autonomy profits slashed by HP accounts restatement', *The Telegraph*, 3 February 2014.
4 D. Collins, A. Masli, A.L. Reitenga and J.M. Sanchez, 'Earnings Restatements, the Sarbanes–Oxley Act and the Disciplining of Chief Financial Officers', *Journal of Accounting, Auditing and Finance*, vol. 24(1), pp. 1–34.
5 In November 2011 there was an Exposure Draft *Revenue from Contracts with Customers* and there was a staff paper *Effects of Joint IASB and FASB Redeliberations on the November 2011 Exposure Draft Revenue from Contracts with Customers* in February 2013. There were extensive consultations in arriving at the standard.
6 Hewlett-Packard Company and Subsidiaries, Annual Report 2013, Note 1, pp. 86–8.
7 http://accountingonion.com/2014/05/the-wild-west-of-nonauthoritative-gaap.html

# Statement of financial position – equity, liability and asset measurement and disclosure

# Share capital, distributable profits and reduction of capital

## 12.1 Introduction

The main purpose of this chapter is to explain the issue and reduction of capital and distributions to shareholders in the context of creditor protection.

> ### Objectives
>
> By the end of this chapter, you should be able to:
>
> - describe the reasons for the issue of shares;
> - describe the rights of different classes of shares;
> - prepare accounting entries for issue of shares;
> - explain the rules relating to distributable profits;
> - explain when capital may be reduced;
> - prepare accounting entries for reduction of capital;
> - discuss the rights of different parties on a capital reduction.

## 12.2 Common themes

Companies may be financed by equity investors, loan creditors and trade creditors. Governments have recognised that for an efficient capital market to exist the rights of each of these stakeholders need to be protected. This means that equity investors require a clear statement of their powers to appoint and remunerate directors and of their entitlement to share in residual income and net assets; loan creditors and trade creditors require assurance that the directors will not distribute funds to the equity investors before settling outstanding debts in full.

Statutory rules have, therefore, evolved which attempt a balancing act by protecting the creditors on the one hand, e.g. by restricting dividend distributions to realised profits, whilst, on the other hand, not unduly restricting the ability of companies to organise their financial affairs, e.g. by reviewing a company's right to purchase and hold treasury shares. Such rules may not be totally consistent between countries but there appear to be some common themes in much of the legislation. These are:

- Share capital can be broadly of two types, equity or preference.
- Equity shares are entitled to the residual income in the statement of comprehensive income after paying expenses, loan interest and tax.

- Equity itself is a residual figure in that the standard setters have taken the approach of defining assets and liabilities and leaving equity as the residual difference in the statement of financial position.
- Equity may consist of ordinary shares or equity elements of participating preference shares and compound instruments which include debt and equity, i.e. where there are conversion rights when there must be a split into their debt and equity elements, with each element being accounted for separately.
- Preference shareholders are not entitled (unless participating) to share in the residual income but may be entitled to a fixed or floating rate of interest on their investment.
- Distributable reserves equate to retained earnings when these have arisen from realised gains.
- Trade payables require protection to prevent an entity distributing assets to shareholders if creditors are not paid in full.
- Capital restructuring may be necessary when there are sound commercial reasons.

However, the rules are not static and there are periodic reviews in most jurisdictions, e.g. the proposal that an entity should make dividend decisions based on its ability to pay rather than on the fact that profits have been realised.

- The distributable reserves of entities are those that have arisen due to realised gains and losses (retained profits), as opposed to unrealised gains (such as revaluation reserves).
- There must be protection for trade payables to prevent an entity distributing assets to shareholders to the extent that the trade payables are not paid in full. An entity must retain net assets at least equal to its share capital and non-distributable reserves (a capital maintenance concept).
- The capital maintenance concept also applies with regard to reducing share capital, with most countries generally requiring a replacement of share capital with a non-distributable reserve if it is redeemed.

Because all countries have company legislation and these themes are common, the authors felt that, as the UK has relatively well-developed company legislation, it would be helpful to consider such legislation as illustrating a typical range of statutory provisions. We therefore now consider the constituents of total shareholders' funds (also known as total owners' equity) and the nature of distributable and non-distributable reserves. We then analyse the role of the capital maintenance concept in the protection of creditors, before discussing the effectiveness of the protection offered by the Companies Act 2006 in respect of both private and public companies.

## 12.3 Total owners' equity: an overview

Total owners' equity consists of the issued share capital stated at nominal (or par) value, non-distributable and distributable reserves. Here we comment briefly on the main constituents of total shareholders' funds. We go on to deal with them in greater detail in subsequent sections.

### 12.3.1 Right to issue shares

Companies incorporated[1] under the Companies Act 2006 are able to raise capital by the issue of shares and debentures. There are two main categories of company: private limited companies and public limited companies. Public limited companies are designated by the letters plc and have the right to issue shares and debentures to the public. Private limited companies are often family companies; they are not allowed to seek share capital by invitations to the public. The shareholders of both categories have the benefit of limited personal indemnity, i.e. their liability to creditors is limited to the amount they agreed to pay the company for the shares they bought.

### 12.3.2 Types of share

Broadly, there are two types of share: ordinary and preference.

#### Ordinary shares

Ordinary shares, often referred to as equity shares, carry the main risk and their bearers are entitled to the residual profit after the payment of any fixed interest or fixed dividend to investors who have invested on the basis of a fixed return. Distributions from the residual profit are made in the form of dividends, which are normally expressed as pence per share.

#### Preference shares

Preference shares usually have a fixed rate of dividend, which is expressed as a percentage of the nominal value of the share. The dividend is paid before any distribution to the ordinary shareholders. The specific rights attaching to a preference share can vary widely.

### 12.3.3 Non-distributable reserves

There are a number of types of **statutory** non-distributable reserve, e.g. when the paid-in capital exceeds the par value as a share premium. In addition to the statutory non-distributable reserves, a company might have restrictions on distribution within its memorandum and articles, stipulating that capital profits are non-distributable as dividends.

### 12.3.4 Distributable reserves

Distributable reserves are normally represented by the retained earnings that appear in the statement of financial position and belong to the ordinary shareholders. However, as we shall see, there may be circumstances where credits that have been made to the statement of comprehensive income are not actually distributable, usually because they do not satisfy the **realisation** concept.

Although the retained earnings in the statement of financial position contain the cumulative residual distributable profits, it is the earnings per share (EPS), based on the post-tax earnings for the year as disclosed in the profit and loss account, that influences the market valuation of the shares, applying the price/earnings ratio.

When deciding whether to issue or buy back shares, the directors will therefore probably consider the impact on the EPS figure. If the EPS increases, the share price can normally be expected also to increase.

## 12.4 Total shareholders' funds: more detailed explanation

### 12.4.1 Ordinary shares – risks and rewards

Ordinary shares (often referred to as equity shares) confer the right to:

- share proportionately in the rewards, i.e. the residual profit remaining after paying any or fixed dividends to investors who have invested on the basis of a fixed return;
- any dividends distributed from these residual profits;

- any net assets remaining after settling all creditors' claims in the event of the company ceasing to trade;

- share proportionately in the risks, i.e. lose a proportionate share of invested share capital if the company ceases to trade and there are insufficient funds to pay all the creditors and the shareholders in full.

### 12.4.2 Ordinary shares – powers

The owners of ordinary shares generally have one vote per share which can be exercised on a routine basis, e.g. at the Annual General Meeting to vote on the appointment of directors, and on an *ad hoc* basis, e.g. at an Extraordinary General Meeting to vote on a proposed capital reduction scheme.

However, there are some companies that have issued non-voting ordinary shares which may confer the right to a proportional share of the residual profits but not to vote.

Non-voting shareholders can attend and speak at the Annual General Meeting but, as they have no vote, are unable to have an influence on management if there are problems or poor performance – apart from selling their shares.

Non-voting shares are issued where typically the founders of a company wish to retain control as we can see with Facebook, LinkedIn and Google where 18% of the shares control 57% of the votes.

### 12.4.3 Methods and reasons for issuing shares

#### Methods of issuing shares

Some of the common methods of issuing shares are *offer for subscription,* where the shares are offered directly to the public; *placings,* where the shares are arranged (placed) to be bought by financial institutions; and *rights issues,* whereby the new shares are offered to the existing shareholders at a price below the market price of those shares. The rights issue might be priced significantly below the current market price but this may not mean that the shareholder is benefiting from cheap shares as the price of existing shares will be reduced, e.g. the British Telecommunications plc £5.9 billion rights issue announced in 2001 made UK corporate history in that no British company had attempted to raise so much cash from its shareholders. The offer was three BT shares for every 10 held and, to encourage take-up, the new shares were offered at a deeply discounted rate of £3 which was at a 47% discount to the share price on the day prior to the launch.

#### Reasons for issuing shares

- For future investment;
- As consideration on an acquisition, e.g. the Pfizer bid for AstraZeneca in 2014 was based on the consideration being partly funded by the issue of shares in Pfizer;
- To shareholders to avoid paying out cash from the company's funds;
- To directors and employees to avoid paying out cash in the form of salary from company funds, which is attractive to early-stage companies to preserve working capital;
- To shareholders to encourage reinvestment;
- To shareholders by way of a rights issue to shore up statements of financial position weakened in the credit crisis by reducing debt and to avoid breaching debt covenants;
- To loan creditors in exchange for debt;
- To obtain funds for future acquisitions;

- To reduce levels of debt to avoid credit rating agencies downgrading the company, which would make it difficult or more expensive to borrow;
- To overcome liquidity problems.

### 12.4.4 Types of preference shares

The following illustrate some of the ways in which specific rights can vary.

*Cumulative preference shares*
Dividends not paid in respect of any one year because of a lack of profits are accumulated for payment in some future year when distributable profits are sufficient.

*Non-cumulative preference shares*
Dividends not paid in any one year because of a lack of distributable profits are permanently forgone.

*Participating preference shares*
These shares carry the right to participate in a distribution of additional profits over and above the fixed rate of dividend after the ordinary shareholders have received an agreed percentage. The participation rights are based on a precise formula.

*Redeemable preference shares*
These shares may be redeemed by the company at an agreed future date and at an agreed price.

*Convertible preference shares*
These shares may be converted into ordinary shares at a future date on agreed terms. The conversion is usually at the preference shareholder's discretion.

There can be a mix of rights, e.g. Getronics entered into an agreement in 2005 with its cumulative preference shareholders whereby Getronics had the right in 2009 to repurchase (redeem) the shares and, if it did not redeem the shares, the cumulative preference shareholders had the right to convert into ordinary shares.

## 12.5 Accounting entries on issue of shares

### 12.5.1 Shares issued at nominal (par) value

If shares are issued at nominal value, the company simply debits the cash account with the amount received and credits the ordinary share capital or preference share capital, as appropriate, with the **nominal value** of the shares.

### 12.5.2 Shares issued at a premium

The market price of the shares of a company, which is based on the prospects of that company, is usually different from the par (nominal) value of those shares.

On receipt of consideration for the shares, the company again debits the cash account with the amount received and credits the ordinary share capital or preference share capital, as appropriate, with the **nominal value** of the shares.

Assuming that the market price exceeds the nominal value, a premium element will be credited to a share premium account. The share premium is classified as a **non-distributable**

**reserve** to indicate that it is not repayable to the shareholders who have subscribed for their shares: it remains a part of the company's permanent capital.

The accounting treatment for recording the issue of shares is straightforward. For example, the journal entries to record the issue of 1,000 £1 ordinary shares at a market price of £2.50 per share payable in instalments of:

| | | |
|---|---|---|
| on application | on 1 January 20X1 | 25p |
| on issue | on 31 January 20X1 | £1.75 including the premium |
| on first call | on 31 January 20X2 | 25p |
| on final call | on 31 January 20X4 | 25p |

would be as follows:

| 1 Jan 20X1 | Dr (£) | Cr (£) |
|---|---|---|
| Cash account | 250 | |
| Application account | | 250 |

| 31 Jan 20X1 | Dr | Cr |
|---|---|---|
| Cash account | 1,750 | |
| Issue account | | 1,750 |

| 31 Jan 20X1 | Dr | Cr |
|---|---|---|
| Application account | 250 | |
| Issue account | 1,750 | |
| Share capital account | | 500 |
| Share premium in excess of par value | | 1,500 |

The first and final call would be debited to the cash account and credited to the share capital account on receipt of the date of the calls.

## 12.6 Creditor protection: capital maintenance concept

To protect creditors, there are often rules relating to the use of the total shareholders' funds which determine how much is distributable.

As a general rule, the paid-in share capital is not repayable to the shareholders and the reserves are classified into two categories: distributable and non-distributable. The directors have discretion as to the amount of the distributable profits that they recommend for distribution as a dividend to shareholders. However, they have no discretion as to the treatment of the non-distributable funds. There may be a statutory requirement for the company to retain within the company net assets equal to the non-distributable reserves. This requirement is to safeguard the interests of creditors and is known as **capital maintenance.**

## 12.7 Creditor protection: why capital maintenance rules are necessary

It is helpful at this point to review the position of unincorporated businesses in relation to capital maintenance.

### 12.7.1 Unincorporated businesses

An unincorporated business such as a sole trader or partnership is not required to maintain any specified amount of capital within the business to safeguard the interests of its creditors. The owners are free to decide whether to introduce or withdraw capital. However, they remain personally liable for the liabilities incurred by the business, and the creditors can have recourse to the personal assets of the owners if the business assets are inadequate to meet their claims in full.

When granting credit to an unincorporated business, the creditors may well be influenced by the personal wealth and apparent standing of the owners and not merely by the assets of the business as disclosed in its financial statements. This is why in an unincorporated business there is no external reason for the capital and the profits to be kept separate.

In partnerships, there are frequently internal agreements that require each partner to maintain his or her capital at an agreed level. Such agreements are strictly a matter of contract between the owners and do not prejudice the rights of the business creditors.

Sometimes owners attempt to influence creditors unfairly, by maintaining a lifestyle in excess of what they can afford, or try to frustrate the legal rights of creditors by putting their private assets beyond their reach, e.g. by transferring their property to relatives or trusts. These subterfuges become apparent only when the creditors seek to enforce their claim against the private assets. Banks are able to protect themselves by seeking adequate security, e.g. a charge on the owners' property.

### 12.7.2 Incorporated limited liability companies

Because of limited liability, the rights of creditors against the private assets of the owners, i.e. the shareholders of the company, are restricted to any amount unpaid on their shares. Once the shareholders have paid the company for their shares, they are not personally liable for the company's debts. Creditors are restricted to making claims against the assets of the company.

Hence, the legislature considered it necessary to ensure that the shareholders did not make distributions to themselves such that the assets needed to meet creditors' claims were put beyond creditors' reach. This may be achieved by setting out statutory rules.

## 12.8 Creditor protection: how to quantify the amounts available to meet creditors' claims

Creditors are exposed to two types of risk: the business risk that a company will operate unsuccessfully and will be unable to pay them; and the risk that a company will operate successfully, but will pay its shareholders rather than its creditors.

The legislature has never intended trade creditors to be protected against ordinary business risks, e.g. the risk of the debtor company incurring either trading losses or losses that might arise from a fall in the value of the assets following changes in market conditions.

In the UK, the Companies Act 2006 requires the amount available to meet creditors' claims to be calculated by reference to the company's annual financial statements. There are two possible approaches:

- The direct approach which requires the asset side of the statement of financial position to contain assets with a realisable value sufficient to cover all outstanding liabilities.

- The indirect approach which requires the liability side of the statement of financial position to classify reserves into distributable and non-distributable reserves (i.e. respectively, available and not available to the shareholders by way of dividend distributions).

The Act follows the indirect approach by specifying capital maintenance in terms of the total shareholders' funds. However, this has not stopped certain creditors taking steps to protect themselves by following the direct approach, e.g. it is bank practice to obtain a mortgage debenture over the assets of the company. The effect of this is to disadvantage the trade creditors. The statutory restrictions preventing shareholders from reducing capital accounts on the liability side are weakened when management grants certain parties priority rights against some or all of the company's assets.

We will now consider total shareholders' funds and capital maintenance in more detail, starting with share capital. Two aspects of share capital are relevant to creditor protection: minimum capital requirements and reduction of capital.

## 12.9 Issued share capital: minimum share capital

The creditors of public companies may be protected by the requirements that there should be a minimum share capital and that capital should be reduced only under controlled conditions.

In the UK, the minimum share capital requirement for a public company is currently set at £50,000 or its euro equivalent, although this can be increased by the Secretary of State for the Department for Business, Innovation and Skills.[2] A company is not permitted to commence trading unless it has issued this amount. However, given the size of many public companies, it is questionable whether this figure is adequate.

The minimum share capital requirement refers to the nominal value of the share capital. In the UK, the law requires each class of share to have a stated nominal value. This value is used for identification and also for capital maintenance. The law ensures that a company receives an amount that is at least equal to the nominal value of the shares issued, less a controlled level of commission, by prohibiting the issue of shares at a discount and by limiting any underwriting commissions on an issue. This is intended to avoid a material discount being granted in the guise of commission. However, the requirement is concerned more with safeguarding the relative rights of existing shareholders than with protecting creditors.

There is effectively no minimum capital requirement for private companies. We can see many instances of such companies having an issued and paid-up capital of only a few £1 shares, which cannot conceivably be regarded as adequate creditor protection. The lack of adequate protection for the creditors of private companies is considered again later in the chapter.

## 12.10 Distributable profits: general considerations

We have considered capital maintenance and non-distributable reserves. However, it is not sufficient to attempt to maintain the permanent capital accounts of companies unless there are clear rules on the amount that they can distribute to their shareholders as profit. Without such rules, they may make distributions to their shareholders out of capital. The question of what can legitimately be distributed as profit is an integral part of the concept of capital maintenance in company accounts. In the UK, there are currently statutory definitions of the amount that can be distributed by private, public and investment companies.

### 12.10.1 Distributable profits: general rule for private companies

The definition of distributable profits under the Companies Act 2006 is:

> Accumulated, realised profits, so far as not previously utilised by distribution or capitalisation, less its accumulated, realised losses, as far as not previously written off in a reduction or reorganisation of capital.

This means the following:

- Unrealised profits cannot be distributed.
- There is no difference between realised revenue and realised capital profits.
- All accumulated net realised profits (i.e. realised profits less realised losses) on the statement of financial position date must be considered.

On the key question of whether a profit is realised or not, the Companies Act (paragraph 853) simply says that realised profits or realised losses are:

> such profits or losses of the company as fall to be treated as realised in accordance with principles generally accepted, at the time when the accounts are prepared, with respect to the determination for accounting purposes of realised profits or losses.

Hence, the Act does not lay down detailed rules on what is and what is not a realised profit; indeed, it does not even refer specifically to 'accounting principles'. Nevertheless, it would seem reasonable for decisions on realisation to be based on generally **accepted accounting principles** at the time, subject to the court's decision in cases of dispute.

### 12.10.2 Distributable profits: general rule for public companies

According to the Companies Act, the undistributable reserves of a public company are its share capital, share premium, capital redemption reserve and also 'the excess of accumulated unrealised profits over accumulated unrealised losses at the time of the intended distribution and . . . any reserves not allowed to be distributed under the Act or by the company's own Memorandum or Articles of Association'.

This means that, when dealing with a public company, the distributable profits have to be reduced by any net unrealised loss.

### 12.10.3 Investment companies

The Companies Act 2006 allows for the special nature of some businesses in the calculation of distributable profits. There are additional rules for investment companies in calculating their distributable profits. For a company to be classified as an investment company, it must invest its funds mainly in securities with the aim of spreading investment risk and giving its members the benefit of the results of managing its funds.

Such a company has the option of applying one of two rules in calculating its distributable profits. These are either:

- the rules that apply to public companies in general, but excluding any realised capital profits, e.g. from the disposal of investments; or
- the company's accumulated realised revenue less its accumulated realised and unrealised revenue losses, provided that its assets are at least one and a half times its liabilities both before and after such a distribution.

The reasoning behind these special rules seems to be to allow investment companies to pass the dividends they receive to their shareholders, irrespective of any changes in the values of their investments, which are subject to market fluctuations. However, the asset cover ratio of liabilities can easily be manipulated by the company simply paying creditors, whereby the ratio is improved, or borrowing, whereby it is reduced.

## 12.11 Distributable profits: how to arrive at the amount using relevant accounts

In the UK, the Companies Act 2006 stipulates that the distributable profits of a company must be based on **relevant accounts**. Relevant accounts may be prepared under either UK GAAP or EU-adopted IFRS. On occasions a new IFRS might have the effect of making a previously realised item reclassified as unrealised, which would then become undistributable. For a more detailed description on the determination of realised profits for distribution refer to the ICAEW Technical Release 02/10. These would normally be the audited annual accounts, which have been prepared according to the requirements of the Act to give a true and fair view of the company's financial affairs.

### 12.11.1 Effect of fair value accounting on decision to distribute

In the context of fair value accounting, volatility is an aspect where directors will need to consider their fiduciary duties. The fair value of financial instruments may be volatile even though such fair value is properly determined in accordance with IAS 39 *Financial Instruments: Recognition and Measurement*. Directors should consider, as a result of their fiduciary duties, whether it is prudent to distribute profits arising from changes in the fair values of financial instruments considered to be volatile, even though they may otherwise be realised profits in accordance with the technical guidance.

## 12.12 When may capital be reduced?

Once the shares have been issued and paid up, the contributed capital together with any payments in excess of par value are normally regarded as permanent. However, there might be commercially sound reasons for a company to reduce its capital and we will consider three such reasons. These are:

- writing off part of capital which has already been lost and is not represented by assets;
- repayment of part of paid-up capital to shareholders or cancellation of unpaid share capital;
- purchase of own shares.

In the UK it has been necessary for both private and public companies to obtain a court order approving a reduction of capital. In line with the wish to reduce the regulatory burden on private companies, the government legislated[3] in 2008 for private companies to be able to reduce their capital by special resolution subject to the directors signing a solvency statement to the effect that the company would remain able to meet all of its liabilities for at least a year. At the same time a reserve arising from the reduction is treated as realised and may be distributed, although it need not be and could be used for other purposes, e.g. writing off accumulated trading losses.

## 12.13 Writing off part of capital which has already been lost and is not represented by assets

This situation normally occurs when a company has accumulated trading losses which prevent it from making dividend payments under the rules relating to distributable profits. The general approach is to eliminate the debit balance on retained earnings by setting it off against the share capital and non-distributable reserves.

The following is an extract from the Findel 2015 Annual Report:

Accordingly, it is proposed that the company eliminate its accumulated deficit and create distributable reserves through a Court-approved reduction of capital to be effected by:

(i)  cancelling and extinguishing 90 pence of the amount paid up or credited as paid up on each of the issued Ordinary Shares and reducing the nominal value of each issued and authorised but unissued Ordinary Share to 10 pence, which would equate to a capital reduction of £77,798,281;

(ii)  cancelling the entire amount standing to the company's share premium account, which currently stands at £92,954,000; and

(iii)  cancelling the entire amount standing to the company's capital redemption reserve, which currently stands at £403,000;

and to credit all such amounts to the company's profit and loss account ('Capital Reduction').

Note that Findel has not only written off the accumulated deficit but created a distributable reserve – the Board stated that it had no current plans to declare dividends, but considered that the Capital Reduction would position the company more favourably to declare dividends in the future.

### 12.13.1 Accounting treatment for a capital reduction to eliminate accumulated trading losses

The accounting treatment is straightforward. A capital reduction account is opened. It is debited with the accumulated losses and credited with the amount written off the share capital and reserves.

For example, assume that the capital and reserves of Hopeful Ltd were as follows at 31 December 20X1:

|  | £ |
|---|---|
| 200,000 ordinary shares of £1 each | 200,000 |
| Retained earnings | (180,000) |

The directors estimate that the company will return to profitability in 20X2, achieving profits of £4,000 per annum thereafter. Without a capital reduction, the profits from 20X2 must be used to reduce the accumulated losses. This means that the company would be unable to pay a dividend for 45 years if it continued at that level of profitability and ignoring tax. Perhaps even more importantly, it would not be attractive for shareholders to put additional capital into the company because they would not be able to obtain any dividend for some years.

There might be statutory procedures such as the requirement for the directors to obtain a special resolution and court approval to reduce the £1 ordinary shares to ordinary shares of 10p each. Subject to satisfying such requirements, the accounting entries would be:

|  | Dr £ | Cr £ |
|---|---|---|
| Capital reduction account | 180,000 | |
| Retained earnings: | | 180,000 |
| *Transfer of debit balance* | | |
| Share capital | 180,000 | |
| Capital reduction account: | | 180,000 |
| *Reduction of share capital* | | |

### Accounting treatment for a capital reduction to eliminate accumulated trading losses and loss of value on non-current assets – losses borne by equity shareholders

Companies often take the opportunity to revalue all of their assets at the same time as they eliminate the accumulated trading losses. Any loss on revaluation is then treated in the same way as the accumulated losses and transferred to the capital reduction account.

For example, assume that the capital and reserves and assets of Hopeful Ltd were as follows at 31 December 20X1:

|  | £ | £ |
|---|---|---|
| 200,000 ordinary shares of £1 each |  | 200,000 |
| Retained earnings |  | (180,000) |
|  |  | 20,000 |
| *Non-current assets* |  |  |
| Plant and equipment |  | 15,000 |
| *Current assets* |  |  |
| Cash | 17,000 |  |
| *Current liabilities* |  |  |
| Trade payables | 12,000 |  |
| Net current assets |  | 5,000 |
|  |  | 20,000 |

The plant and equipment is revalued at £5,000 and it is resolved to reduce the share capital to ordinary shares of 5p each. The accounting entries would be:

|  | Dr | Cr |
|---|---|---|
|  | £ | £ |
| Capital reduction account | 190,000 |  |
| Statement of income |  | 180,000 |
| Plant and machinery: |  | 10,000 |
| *Transfer of accumulated losses and loss on revaluation* |  |  |
| Share capital | 190,000 |  |
| Capital reduction account: |  | 190,000 |
| *Reduction of share capital to 200,000 shares of 5p each* |  |  |

The statement of financial position after the capital reduction shows that the share capital fairly reflects the underlying asset values:

|  | £ | £ |
|---|---|---|
| 200,000 ordinary shares of 5p each |  | 10,000 |
|  |  | 10,000 |
| *Non-current assets* |  |  |
| Plant and equipment |  | 5,000 |
| *Current assets* |  |  |
| Cash | 17,000 |  |
| *Current liabilities* |  |  |
| Trade payables | 12,000 | 5,000 |
|  |  | 10,000 |

### Accounting treatment for a capital reduction to eliminate accumulated trading losses and loss of value on non-current assets – losses borne by equity and other stakeholders

In the Hopeful Ltd example above, the ordinary shareholders alone bore the losses. It might well be, however, that a reconstruction involves a compromise between shareholders and creditors, with an amendment of the rights of the latter. Such a reconstruction would be subject to any statutory requirements within the jurisdiction, e.g. the support, say, of 75% of each class of creditor whose rights are being compromised, 75% of each class of shareholder and the permission of the court. For such a reconstruction to succeed there needs to be reasonable evidence of commercial viability and that anticipated profits are sufficient to service the proposed new capital structure.

Assuming in the Hopeful Ltd example that the creditors agree to bear £5,000 of the losses, the accounting entries would be as follows:

|  | £ | £ |
|---|---|---|
| Share capital | 185,000 | |
| Creditors | 5,000 | |
| Capital reduction account: | | 190,000 |
| Reduction of share capital to 200,000 shares of 7.5p each | | |

Reconstruction schemes can be complex, but the underlying evaluation by each party will be the same. Each will assess the scheme to see how it affects their individual position.

### Trade payables

In their decision to accept £5,000 less than the book value of their debt, the trade payables of Hopeful Ltd would be influenced by their prospects of receiving payment if Hopeful were to cease trading immediately, the effect on their results without Hopeful as a continuing customer and the likelihood that they would continue to receive orders from Hopeful following reconstruction.

### Loan creditors

Loan creditors would take into account the expected value of any security they possess and a comparison of the opportunities for investing any loan capital returned in the event of liquidation with the value of their capital and interest entitlement in the reconstructed company.

### Preference shareholders

Preference shareholders would likewise compare prospects for capital and income following a liquidation of the company with prospects for income and capital from the company as a going concern following a reconstruction.

### Relative effects of the scheme

In practice, the formulation of a scheme will involve more than just the accountant, except in the case of very small companies. An advising merchant bank, major shareholders and major debenture holders will undoubtedly be concerned. Each vested interest will be asked for its opinion on specific proposals: unfavourable reactions will necessitate a rethink by the accountant. The process will continue until a consensus begins to emerge.

Each stakeholder's position needs to be considered separately. For example, any attempt to reduce the nominal value of all classes of shares and debentures on a proportionate basis would be unfair and unacceptable. This is because a reduction in the nominal values of preference shares or debentures has a different effect from a reduction in the nominal value of ordinary shares. In the former cases, the dividends and interest receivable will be reduced; in the latter case, the reduction in nominal value of the ordinary shares will have no effect on dividends as holders of ordinary shares are entitled to the residue of profit, whatever the nominal value of their shares.

Total support may well be unachievable. The objective is to maintain the company as a going concern. In attempting to achieve this, each party will continually be comparing its advantages under the scheme with its prospects in a liquidation.

### Illustration of a capital reconstruction

XYZ plc has been making trading losses, which have resulted in a substantial debit balance on the profit and loss account. The statement of financial position of XYZ plc as at 31 December 20X3 was as follows:

|  |  | £000 |
|---|---|---|
| Ordinary share capital (£1 shares) |  | 1,000 |
| Less: Accumulated losses on retained earnings | Note 1 | (800) |
|  |  | 200 |
| 10% debentures (£1) |  | 600 |
| Net assets at book value | Note 2 | 800 |

*Notes:*

1  The company is changing its product and markets and expects to make £150,000 profit before interest and tax every year from 1 January 20X4.

2  (a)  The estimated break-up or liquidation value of the assets at 31 December 20X3 was £650,000.

   (b)  The going concern value of assets at 31 December 20X3 was £700,000.

The directors are faced with a decision to liquidate or reconstruct. Having satisfied themselves that the company is returning to profitability, they propose the following reconstruction scheme:

● Write off losses and reduce asset values to £700,000.

● Cancel all existing ordinary shares and debentures.

● Issue 1,200,000 new ordinary shares of 25p each and 400,000 12.5% debentures of £1 each as follows:

  ● the existing shareholders are to be issued with 800,000 ordinary 25p shares;

  ● the existing debenture holders are to be issued with 400,000 ordinary 25p shares and the new debentures.

The stakeholders, i.e. the ordinary shareholders and debenture holders, have first to decide whether the company has a reasonable chance of achieving the estimated profit for 20X4. The company might carry out a sensitivity analysis to show the effect on dividends and interest over a range of profit levels.

Next, stakeholders must consider whether allowing the company to continue provides a better return than that available from the liquidation of the company. Assuming that it does, they assess the effect of allowing the company to continue without any reconstruction of capital and with a reconstruction of capital.

The accountant writes up the reconstruction accounts and produces a statement of financial position after the reconstruction has been effected.

The accountant will produce the following information:

*Effect of liquidating*

| | £ | Debenture holders £ | Ordinary shareholders £ |
|---|---|---|---|
| Assets realised | 650,000 | | |
| *Less*: Prior claim | (600,000) | 600,000 | |
| *Less*: Ordinary shareholders | (50,000) | | 50,000 |
| | — | 600,000 | 50,000 |

This shows that the ordinary shareholders would lose almost all of their capital, whereas the debenture holders would be in a much stronger position. This is important because it might influence the amount of inducement that the debenture holders require to accept any variation of their rights.

*Company continues without reconstruction*

| | £ | Debenture holders £ | Ordinary shareholders £ |
|---|---|---|---|
| Expected annual income: | | | |
| Expected operating profit | 150,000 | | |
| Debenture interest | (60,000) | 60,000 | |
| Less: Ordinary dividend | (90,000) | | 90,000 |
| Annual income | — | 60,000 | 90,000 |

However, as far as the ordinary shareholders are concerned, no dividend will be allowed to be paid until the debit balance of £800,000 has been eliminated, i.e. there will be no dividend for more than nine years (for simplicity the illustration ignores tax effects).

*Company continues with a reconstruction*

| | £ | Debenture holders £ | Ordinary shareholders £ |
|---|---|---|---|
| Expected annual income: | | | |
| Expected operating profit | 150,000 | | |
| *Less*: Debenture interest | (50,000) | 50,000 | |
| (12.5% on £400,000) | | | |
| *Less*: Dividend on shares | (33,000) | 33,000 | |
| *Less*: Ordinary dividend | (67,000) | | 67,000 |
| Annual income | — | 83,000 | 67,000 |

### How will debenture holders react to the scheme?

At first glance, debenture holders appear to be doing reasonably well: the £83,000 provides a return of almost 14% on the amount that they would have received in a liquidation (83,000/600,000 × 100), which exceeds the 10% currently available, and it is £23,000 more than the £60,000 currently received. However, their exposure to risk has increased because £33,000 is dependent upon the level of profits. They will consider their position in relation to the ordinary shareholders.

For the ordinary shareholders the return should be calculated on the amount that they would have received on liquidation, i.e. 134% (67,000/50,000 × 100). In addition to receiving a return of 134%, they would hold two-thirds of the share capital, which would give them control of the company.

A final consideration for the debenture holders would be their position if the company were to fail after a reconstruction. In such a case, the old debenture holders would be materially disadvantaged as their prior claim will have been reduced from £600,000 to £400,000.

### Accounting for the reconstruction

The reconstruction account will record the changes in the book values as follows:

*Reconstruction account*

| | £000 | | £000 |
|---|---|---|---|
| Retained earnings | 800 | Share capital | 1,000 |
| Assets (losses written off) | 100 | Debentures (old debentures cancelled) | 600 |
| Ordinary share capital (25p) | 300 | | |
| 12.5% debentures (new issue) | 400 | | |
| | 1,600 | | 1,600 |

The post-reconstruction statement of financial position will be as follows:

| | |
|---|---|
| Ordinary share capital (25p) | 300,000 |
| 12.5% debentures of £1 | 400,000 |
| | 700,000 |

## 12.14 Repayment of part of paid-in capital to shareholders or cancellation of unpaid share capital

This can occur when a company wishes to return liquid funds that it considers to be more than it is able to profitably employ within the business – as a result the return on equity ratio is increased. The following is an extract from the Next plc 2013 Annual Report:

> The Company has five core operational objectives . . . Underlying these operational goals is the ever present and overriding financial objective of delivering long term, sustainable growth in earnings per share.

> **One of these five objectives is to:**
> Focus on cash generation. Return funds that are not needed to develop the business to shareholders through share buybacks. This must be earnings-enhancing and in the interests of shareholders generally.

## 12.15 Purchase of own shares

This might take the form of the redemption of redeemable preference shares, the purchase of ordinary shares which are then cancelled and the purchase of ordinary shares which are not cancelled but held in treasury.

### 12.15.1 Redemption of preference shares

In the UK, when redeemable preference shares are redeemed, the company is required either to replace them with other shares or to make a transfer from distributable reserves to non-distributable reserves in order to maintain permanent capital. The accounting entries on redemption are to credit cash and debit the redeemable preference share account.

### 12.15.2 Buyback of own shares – intention to cancel

There are a number of reasons for companies buying back shares. These provide a benefit when taken as:

- a strategic measure, e.g. recognising that there is a lack of viable investment projects, i.e. expected returns being less than the company's weighted average cost of capital and so returning excess cash to shareholders to allow them to search out better growth investments;

- a defensive measure, e.g. an attempt to frustrate a hostile takeover or to reduce the power of dissident shareholders;

- a reactive measure, e.g. taking advantage of the fact that the share price is at a discount to its underlying intrinsic value or stabilising a falling share price;

- a proactive measure, e.g. creating shareholder value by reducing the number of shares in issue which increases the earnings per share, or making a distribution more tax-efficient than the payment of a cash dividend;

- a tax-efficient measure.

There is also a potential risk if the company has to borrow funds in order to make the buyback, leaving itself liable to service the debt. Where it uses free cash rather than loans it is attractive to analysts and shareholders. For example, in the BP share buyback scheme (one of the UK's largest), the chief executive, Lord Browne, said that any free cash generated from BP's assets when the oil price was above $20 a barrel would be returned to investors over the following three years.

### 12.15.3 Buyback of own shares – treasury shares

The benefits to a company holding treasury shares are that it has greater flexibility to respond to investors' attitude to gearing, e.g. reissuing the shares if the gearing is perceived to be too high. It also has the capacity to satisfy loan conversions and employee share options without the need to issue new shares which would dilute the existing shareholdings.

#### National regimes where buyback is already permitted

In Europe and the USA it has been permissible to buy back shares, known as treasury shares, and hold them for reissue. In the UK this has been permissible since 2003. There are two common accounting treatments – the cost method and the par value method. The most common method is the cost method, which provides the following.

#### On purchase

The treasury shares are debited at gross cost to a Treasury Stock account – this is deducted as a one-line entry from equity, e.g. a statement of financial position might appear as follows:

*Owners' equity section of statement of financial position*

|  | £ |
|---|---|
| Common stock, £1 par, 100,000 shares authorised, 30,000 shares issued | 30,000 |
| Paid-in capital in excess of par | 60,000 |
| Retained earnings | 165,000 |
| Treasury Stock (15,000 shares at cost) | (15,000) |
| Total owners' equity | 240,000 |

*On resale*

- If on resale the sale price is higher than the cost price, the Treasury Stock account is credited at cost price and the excess is credited to Paid-in Capital (Treasury Stock).

- If on resale the sale price is lower than the cost price, the Treasury Stock account is credited with the proceeds and the balance is debited to Paid-in Capital (Treasury Stock). If the debit is greater than the credit balance on Paid-in Capital (Treasury Stock), the difference is deducted from retained earnings. Retained earnings may be decreased but never increased as a result of Treasury Stock transactions.

## The UK experience

Treasury shares have been permitted in the UK since 2003. The regulations relating to Treasury shares are now contained in the Companies Act 2006.[4] These regulations permit companies with listed shares that purchase their own shares out of distributable profits to hold them 'in treasury' for sale at a later date or for transfer to an employees' share scheme.

There are certain restrictions whilst shares are held in treasury, namely:

- Their aggregate nominal value must not exceed 10% of the nominal value of issued share capital (if it exceeds 10% then the excess must be disposed of or cancelled).

- Rights attaching to the class of share – e.g. receiving dividends, and the right to vote – cannot be exercised by the company.

*Treasury shares – cancellation*

- Where shares are held as treasury shares, the company may at any time cancel some or all of the shares.

- If shares held as treasury shares cease to be qualifying shares, then the company must cancel the shares.

- On cancellation the amount of the company's share capital is reduced by the nominal amount of the shares cancelled.

## Summary

Creditors of companies are not expected to be protected against ordinary business risks as these are taken care of by financial markets, e.g. through the rates of interest charged on different capital instruments of different companies. However, the creditors are entitled to depend on the non-erosion of the permanent capital unless their interests are considered and protected.

The chapter also discusses the question of capital reconstructions and the need to consider the effect of any proposed reconstruction on the rights of different parties.

## REVIEW QUESTIONS

1 Discuss how the Companies Act 2006 defines distributable profits in the UK.

2 Why do companies reorganise their capital structure when they have accumulated losses?

3 What factors would a loan creditor take into account if asked to bear some of the accumulated loss?

**4** Explain a debt/equity swap and the reasons for debt/equity swaps, and discuss the effect on existing shareholders and loan creditors.

Explain why companies hold treasury shares.

**5** Discuss why a company might make a rights issue at a heavily discounted price and how equity shareholders would be affected if they did not take up the issue.

## EXERCISES

### * Question 1

The draft statement of financial position of Telin plc at 30 September 20X5 was as follows:

| | £000 | | £000 |
|---|---|---|---|
| Ordinary shares of £1 each, fully paid | 12,000 | Product development costs | 1,400 |
| 12% preference shares of £1 each, fully paid | 8,000 | Sundry assets | 32,170 |
| Share premium | 4,000 | Cash and bank | 5,450 |
| Retained (distributable) profits | 4,600 | | |
| Payables | 10,420 | | |
| | 39,020 | | 39,020 |

Preference shares of the company were originally issued at a premium of 2p per share. The directors of the company decided to redeem these shares at the end of October 20X5 at a premium of 5p per share. They also decided to write off the balances on development costs and discount on debentures.

All write-offs and other transactions are to be entered into the accounts according to the provisions of the Companies Acts and in a manner financially advantageous to the company and to its shareholders.

The following transactions took place during October 20X5:

(a) On 4 October the company issued for cash 2,400,000 10% debentures of £1 each at a discount of $2\frac{1}{2}\%$.

(b) On 6 October the balances on development costs and discount of debentures were written off.

(c) On 12 October the company issued for cash 6,000,000 ordinary shares at a premium of 10p per share. This was a specific issue to help redeem preference shares.

(d) On 29 October the company redeemed the 12% preference shares at a premium of 5p per share and included in the payments to shareholders one month's dividend for October.

(e) On 30 October the company made a bonus issue, to all ordinary shareholders, of one fully paid ordinary share for every 20 shares held.

(f) During October the company made a net profit of £275,000 from its normal trading operations. This was reflected in the cash balance at the end of the month.

Required:
(a) Write up the ledger accounts of Telin plc to record the transactions for October 20X5.
(b) Prepare the company's statement of financial position as at 31 October 20X5.
(c) Briefly explain accounting entries which arise as a result of redemption of preference shares.

## * Question 2

The following is the statement of financial position of Alpha Ltd as on 30 June 20X8:

| | £000 Cost | £000 Accumulated depreciation | £000 |
|---|---|---|---|
| Non-current assets | | | |
| Freehold property | 46 | 5 | 41 |
| Plant | 85 | 6 | 79 |
| | 131 | 11 | 120 |
| Investments | | | |
| Shares in subsidiary company | | 90 | |
| Loans | | 40 | 130 |
| Current assets | | | |
| Inventory | | 132 | |
| Trade receivables | | 106 | |
| | | 238 | |
| Current liabilities | | | |
| Trade payables | | 282 | |
| Bank overdraft | | 58 | |
| | | 340 | |
| Net current liabilities | | | (102) |
| Total assets less liabilities | | | 148 |
| Capital and reserves | | | |
| 250,000 8½% cumulative redeemable preference shares of £1 each fully paid | | | 250 |
| 100,000 ordinary shares of £1 each 75p paid | | | 75 |
| | | | 325 |
| Retained earnings | | | (177) |
| | | | 148 |

The following information is relevant:

1  There are contingent liabilities in respect of (i) a guarantee given to bankers to cover a loan of £30,000 made to the subsidiary and (ii) uncalled capital of 10p per share on the holding of 100,000 shares of £1 each in the subsidiary.

2  The arrears of preference dividend amount to £106,250.

3  The following capital reconstruction scheme, to take effect as from 1 July 20X8, has been duly approved and authorised:

   (i)   the unpaid capital on the ordinary shares to be called up;

   (ii)  the ordinary shares thereupon to be reduced to shares of 25p each fully paid up by can celling 75p per share and then each fully paid share of 25p to be subdivided into five shares of 5p each fully paid;

   (iii) the holders to surrender three of such 5p shares out of every five held for reissue as set out below;

   (iv)  the 8½% cumulative preference shares together with all arrears of dividend to be surrendered and cancelled on the basis that the holder of every 50 preference shares will pay to Alpha a sum of £30 in cash, and will be issued with:

(a)  one £40 convertible $7^3/_4$% note of £40 each, and

(b)  60 fully paid ordinary shares of 5p each (being a redistribution of shares surrendered by the ordinary shareholders and referred to in (iii) above);

(v)  the unpaid capital on the shares in the subsidiary to be called up and paid by the parent company whose guarantee to the bank should be cancelled;

(vi)  the freehold property to be revalued at £55,000;

(vii)  the adverse balance on retained earnings to be written off, £55,000 to be written off the shares in the subsidiary and the sums made available by the scheme to be used to write down the plant.

**Required:**

(a) **Prepare a capital reduction and reorganisation account.**

(b) **Prepare the statement of financial position of the company as it would appear immediately after completion of the scheme.**

## Question 3

A summary of the statement of financial position of Doxin plc, as at 31 December 20X0, is given below:

|  | £ |  | £ |
|---|---|---|---|
| 800,000 ordinary shares | 800,000 | Assets other than bank | 1,500,000 |
| of £1 each |  | (at book values) |  |
| 300,000 6% preference | 300,000 | Bank | 200,000 |
| shares of £1 each |  |  |  |
| General reserves | 200,000 |  |  |
| Payables | 400,000 |  |  |
|  | 1,700,000 |  | 1,700,000 |

During 20X1, the company:

(i)  issued 200,000 ordinary shares of £1 each at a premium of 10p per share (a specific issue to redeem preference shares);

(ii)  redeemed all preference shares at a premium of 5%. These were originally issued at 25% premium;

(iii)  issued 4,000 7% debentures of £100 each at £90;

(iv)  used share premium, if any, to issue fully paid bonus shares to members; and

(v)  made a net loss of £500,000 by end of year which affected the bank account.

**Required:**

(a) **Show the effect of each of the above items in the form of a moving statement of financial position (i.e. additions/deductions from original figures) and draft the statement of financial position of 31 December 20X1.**

(b) **Consider to what extent the interests of the creditors of the company are being protected.**

## Question 4

Discuss the advantages to a company of:

(a)  purchasing and cancelling its own shares;

(b)  purchasing and holding its own shares in treasury.

## * Question 5

Speedster Ltd commenced trading in 1986 as a wholesaler of lightweight travel accessories. The company was efficient and traded successfully until 2000 when new competitors entered the market selling at lower prices which Speedster could not match. The company has gradually slipped into losses and the bank is no longer prepared to offer overdraft facilities. The directors are considering liquidating the company and have prepared the following statement of financial position and supporting information:

| Statement of financial position | £000 | £000 |
|---|---|---|
| Non-current assets | | |
| Freehold land at cost | | 1,500 |
| Plant and equipment (NBV) | | 1,800 |
| Current assets | | |
| Inventories | 600 | |
| Trade receivables | 1,200 | |
| | 1,800 | |
| Current liabilities | | |
| Payables | 1,140 | |
| Bank overdraft (secured on the plant and equipment) | 1,320 | |
| | 2,460 | |
| Net current assets | | (660) |
| Non-current liabilities | | |
| Secured loan (secured on the land) | | (1,200) |
| | | 1,440 |
| Financed by | | |
| Ordinary shares of £1 each | | 3,000 |
| Statement of comprehensive income | | (1,560) |
| | | 1,440 |

Supporting information:

(i)   The freehold land has a market value of £960,000 if it continues in use as a warehouse. There is a possibility that planning permission could be obtained for a change of use allowing the warehouse to be converted into apartments. If planning permission were to be obtained, the company has been advised that the land would have a market value of £2,500,000.

(ii)  The net realisable values on liquidation of the other assets are:

| | |
|---|---|
| Plant and equipment | £1,200,000 |
| Inventory | £450,000 |
| Trade receivables | £1,050,000 |

(iii) An analysis of the payables indicated that there would be £300,000 owing to preferential creditors for wages, salaries and taxes.

(iv)  Liquidation costs were estimated at £200,000.

**Required:**
**Prepare a statement showing the distribution on the basis that:**
**(a) planning permission was not obtained; and**
**(b) planning permission was obtained.**

## Question 6

Delta Ltd has been developing a lightweight automated wheelchair. The research costs written off have been far greater than originally estimated and the equity and preference capital has been eroded as seen on the statement of financial position.

The following is the statement of financial position of Delta Ltd as at 31.12.20X9:

|  | £000 | £000 |
|---|---|---|
| *Intangible assets* |  |  |
| Development costs |  | 300 |
| *Non-current assets* |  |  |
| Freehold property | 800 |  |
| Plant, vehicles and equipment | 650 | 1,450 |
|  |  | 1,750 |
| *Current assets* |  |  |
| Inventory | 480 |  |
| Trade receivables | 590 |  |
| Investments | 200 |  |
|  | 1,270 |  |
| *Current liabilities* |  |  |
| Trade payables | (1,330) |  |
| Bank overdraft | (490) | (550) |
|  |  | 1,200 |
| 10% debentures (secured on freehold premises) |  | (1,000) |
| Total assets less liabilities |  | 200 |
| *Capital and reserves* |  |  |
| Ordinary shares of 50p each |  | 800 |
| 7% cumulative preference shares of £1 each |  | 500 |
| Retained earnings (debit) |  | (1,100) |
|  |  | 200 |

The finance director has prepared the following information for consideration by the board.

1 Estimated current and liquidation values were estimated as follows:

|  | Current values £000 | Liquidation values £000 |
|---|---|---|
| Capitalised development costs | 300 | — |
| Freehold property | 1,200 | 1,200 |
| Plant and equipment | 600 | 100 |
| Inventory | 480 | 300 |
| Trade receivables | 590 | 590 |
| Investments | 200 | 200 |
|  |  | 2,390 |

2 If the company were to be liquidated there would be disposal costs of £100,000.
3 The preference dividend had not been paid for five years.
4 It is estimated that the company would make profits before interest over the next five years of £150,000 rising to £400,000 by the fifth year.

5 The directors have indicated that they would consider introducing further equity capital.
6 It was the finance director's opinion that for any scheme to succeed, it should satisfy the following conditions:

(a) The shareholders and creditors should have a better benefit in capital and income terms by reconstructing rather than liquidating the company.

(b) The scheme should have a reasonable possibility of ensuring the long-term survival of the company.

(c) There should be a reasonable assurance that there will be adequate working capital.

(d) Gearing should not be permitted to become excessive.

(e) If possible, the ordinary shareholders should retain control.

**Required:**

(a) advise the unsecured creditors of the minimum that they should accept if they were to agree to a reconstruction rather than proceed to press for the company to be liquidated.

(b) Propose a possible scheme for reconstruction.

(c) Prepare the statement of financial position of the company as it would appear immediately after completion of the scheme.

## Notes

1 The Companies Act 2006.
2 Ibid., para 764.
3 Companies (Reduction of Share Capital) Order 2008.
4 The Companies Act 2006, paras 724–732.

# CHAPTER 13

# Liabilities

## 13.1 Introduction

In order for financial statements to show a true and fair view it is essential that reporting entities recognise all the liabilities that satisfy the *Framework* criteria, but **only** those liabilities that satisfy the criteria. Given that the recognition of a liability often involves a charge against profits, and the derecognition of a liability sometimes involves a credit to profits, there is the possibility that, unless this area of financial reporting is appropriately regulated, there is scope for manipulation of reporting profits when liabilities are recognised or derecognised inappropriately.

There are a number of financial reporting standards dealing with the recognition and measurement of specific liabilities that are dealt with elsewhere in this book:

- Financial liabilities (including, *inter alia*, trade payables and loans) are dealt with in IAS 39 *Financial Instruments: Recognition and Measurement* and, in the future, in IFRS 9 *Financial Instruments* (see Chapter 14).
- Pension liabilities are dealt with in IAS 19 *Employee Benefits* (see Chapter 15).
- Income tax liabilities are dealt with in IAS 12 *Income Taxes* (see Chapter 16).
- Lease liabilities are dealt with in IAS 17 *Leases* (see Chapter 18).

The above financial reporting standards deal with many types of liability but not with all liabilities. Examples of liabilities, or potential liabilities, not dealt with by the above financial reporting standards include:

- liabilities arising from legal disputes;
- liabilities arising due to corporate restructurings;
- environmental and decommissioning obligations;
- liabilities arising under contracts that have become onerous.

IAS 37 *Provisions, Contingent Liabilities and Contingent Assets* deals with the recognition, measurement and disclosure of these liabilities or potential liabilities.

### Objectives

By the end of this chapter, you should be able to:

- account for provisions, contingent liabilities and contingent assets under IAS 37;
- explain the potential change the IASB is considering in relation to provisions.

## 13.2 Provisions – a decision tree approach to their impact on the statement of financial position

The IASC (now the IASB) approved IAS 37 *Provisions, Contingent Liabilities and Contingent Assets*[1] in July 1998. The key objective of IAS 37 is to ensure that appropriate recognition criteria and measurement bases are applied and that sufficient information is disclosed in the notes to enable users to understand their nature, timing and amount.

The IAS sets out a useful decision tree, shown in Figure 13.1, for determining whether an event requires the creation of a provision, the disclosure of a contingent liability or no action.

**Figure 13.1 Decision tree**

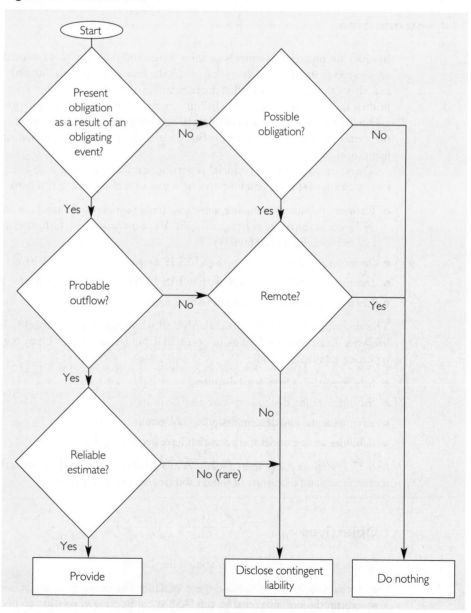

In June 2005 the IASB issued an exposure draft, IAS 37 *Non-financial Liabilities,* to revise IAS 37. A further exposure draft clarifying the proposed amendments was issued in January 2010. However, the current IASB timetable does not envisage a new accounting standard on liabilities very soon. We will now consider the current IAS 37 treatment of provisions, contingent liabilities and contingent assets.

## 13.3 Treatment of provisions

IAS 37 is mainly concerned with provisions and the distorting effect they can have on profit trends, income and capital gearing. It defines a provision as 'a liability of uncertain timing or amount'.

In particular it targets 'big-bath' provisions that companies historically have been able to make. This is a type of creative accounting that it has been tempting for directors to make in order to smooth profits without any reasonable certainty that the provision would actually be required in subsequent periods. Sir David Tweedie, the chairman of the IASB, has said:

> A main focus [of IAS 37] is 'big-bath' provisions. Those who use them sometimes pray in aid of the concept of prudence. All too often however the provision is wildly excessive and conveniently finds its way back to the statement of comprehensive income in a later period. The misleading practice needed to be stopped and [IAS 37] proposed that in future provisions should only be allowed when the company has an unavoidable obligation – an **intention** which may or may not be fulfilled will **not be enough**. Users of accounts can't be expected to be mind readers.

## 13.4 The general principles that IAS 37 applies to the recognition of a provision

The general principles are that a provision should be recognised when:[2]

**(a)** an entity has a present obligation (legal or constructive) as a result of past events;

**(b)** it is probable that a transfer of economic benefits will be required to settle the obligation;

**(c)** a reliable estimate can be made of the amount of the obligation.

Provisions by their nature relate to the future. This means that there is a need for estimation, and IAS 37 comments[3] that the use of estimates is an essential part of the preparation of financial statements and does not undermine their reliability. The IAS addresses the uncertainties arising in respect of present obligation, past event, probable transfer of economic benefits and reliable estimates when deciding whether to recognise a provision.

### Present obligation

Provisions can arise under law or because the entity has created an expectation due to its past actions that it cannot realistically avoid.

The test to be applied is whether it is more likely than not, i.e. has more than a 50% chance of occurring. For example, if involved in a disputed lawsuit, the company is required to take account of all available evidence including that of experts and of events after the reporting period to decide if there is a greater than 50% chance that the lawsuit will be decided against the company.

Where it is more likely that no present obligation exists at the period-end date, the company discloses a contingent liability, unless the possibility of a transfer of economic resources is remote.

### Past event[4]

A past event that leads to a present obligation is called an 'obligating event'. This is a new term with which to become familiar. It means that the company has no realistic alternative to settling the obligation. The IAS defines 'no alternative' as being only where the settlement of the obligation can be enforced by law or, in the case of a constructive obligation, where the event creates valid expectations in other parties that the company will discharge the obligation.

The IAS stresses that it is only those obligations arising from past events existing independently of a company's future actions that are recognised as provisions, e.g. clean-up costs for unlawful environmental damage that has occurred require a provision; environmental damage that is not unlawful but is likely to become so and involve clean-up costs will not be provided for until legislation is virtually certain to be enacted as drafted.

### Probable transfer of economic benefits[5]

The IAS defines probable as meaning that the event is more likely than not to occur. Where it is not probable, the company discloses a contingent liability unless the possibility is remote.

## 13.5 Management approach to measuring the amount of a provision

IAS 37 states[6] that the amount recognised as a provision should be the *best estimate* of the expenditure required to settle the present obligation at the period-end date.

'Best estimate' is defined as the amount that a company would rationally pay to settle the obligation or to transfer it to a third party. The estimates of outcome and financial effect are determined by the judgement of management supplemented by experience of similar transactions and reports from independent experts. Management deal with the uncertainties as to the amount to be provided in a number of ways:

- A class obligation exists:
  - where the provision involves a large population of items as with a warranty provision – statistical analysis of expected values should be used to determine the amount of the provision.
- A single obligation exists but a number of outcomes may be possible:
  - where a single obligation is measured, the individual most likely outcome may be the best estimate;
  - more than one outcome exists or the outcome is anywhere within a range; or
  - expected values may be most appropriate.

For example, a company had been using unlicensed parts in the manufacture of its products and, at the year-end, no decision had been reached by the court. The plaintiff was seeking damages of $10 million.

In the draft accounts a provision had been made of $5.85 million using expected values. This had been based on the estimate by the entity's lawyers that there was a 20% chance that the plaintiff would be unsuccessful and a 25% chance that the entity would be required to pay $10 million and a 55% chance of $7 million becoming payable to the plaintiff. The provision had been calculated as 25% of $0 + 55% of $7 million + 20% of $10 million.

The finance director, however, disagreed with this on the grounds that it was a single obligation and more likely than not there would be an outflow of funds of $7 million, and required an additional $1.15 million to be provided.

### Avoiding excessive provisions

Management must avoid creating excessive provisions based on a prudent view. Uncertainty does not justify the creation of excessive provisions.[7] If the projected costs of a particular adverse outcome are estimated on a prudent basis, that outcome should not then be deliberately treated as more probable than is realistically the case.

The measurement requirements of the current IAS 37 are somewhat imprecise and can be interpreted in more than one way. One of the objectives of the proposed amendment to IAS 37 is to remove the imprecision in the current standard. We will discuss the amendments proposed in this exposure draft in 13.10.

### Approach when time value of money is material

The IAS states[8] that 'where the effect of the time value of money is material, the amount of a provision should be the present value of the expenditures expected to be required to settle the obligation'.

Present value is arrived at by discounting the future obligation at 'a pre-tax rate (or rates) that reflect(s) current market assessments of the time value of money and the risks specific to the liability. The discount rate(s) should not reflect risks for which future cash flow estimates have been adjusted.'

If provisions are recognised at present value, a company will have to account for the unwinding of the discounting. As a simple example, assume a company is making a provision at 31 December 2010 for an expected cash outflow of €1 million on 31 December 2012. The relevant discount factor is estimated at 10%. Assume the estimated cash flows do not change and the provision is still required at 31 December 2011.

|  | €000 |
|---|---|
| Provision recognised at 31 December 2010 (€1m × 1/1.121) | 826 |
| Provision recognised at 31 December 2011 (€1m × 1/1.1) | 909 |
| Increase in the provision | 83 |

This increase in the provision is purely due to discounting for one year in 2011 as opposed to two years in 2010. This increase in the provision must be recognised as an expense in profit or loss, usually as a finance cost, although IAS 37 does not make this mandatory.

The following is an extract from the Minefinders Corporation Ltd 2011 Annual Report:

> A provision for site closure and reclamation is recorded when the Company incurs liability for costs associated with the eventual retirement of tangible long-lived assets (for example, reclamation costs). The liability for such costs exists from the time the legal or constructive obligation first arises, not when the actual expenditures are made.
>
> Such obligations are based on estimated future cash flows discounted at a rate specific to the liability. . . . The amount added to the asset is amortized in the same manner as the asset.
>
> The liability is increased in each accounting period by the amount of the implied interest inherent in the use of discounted present value methodology. . . .

## 13.6 Application of criteria illustrated

### Scenario 1

An offshore oil exploration company is required by its licence to remove the rig and restore the seabed. Management have estimated that 85% of the eventual cost will be incurred in removing the rig and 15% through the extraction of oil. The company's practice on similar projects has been to account for the decommissioning costs using the 'unit of production' method whereby the amount required for decommissioning was built up year by year, in line with production levels, to reach the amount of the expected costs by the time production ceased.

*Decision process*

1 **Is there a present obligation as a result of a past event?**
The construction of the rig has created a legal obligation under the licence to remove the rig and restore the seabed.

2 **Is there a probable transfer of economic benefits?**
This is probable.

3 **Can the amount of the outflow be reasonably estimated?**
A best estimate can be made by management based on past experience and expert advice.

4 **Conclusion**
A provision should be created of 85% of the eventual future costs of removal and restoration. This provision should be discounted if the effect of the time value of money is material. A provision for the 15% relating to restoration should be created when oil production commences.

The unit of production method is not acceptable in that the decommissioning costs relate to damage already done.

### Scenario 2

A company has a private jet costing £24 million. Air regulations required it to be overhauled every four years. An overhaul costs £1.6 million. The company policy has been to create a provision for depreciation of £2 million on a straight-line basis over 12 years and an annual provision of £400,000 to meet the cost of the required overhaul every four years.

*Decision process*

1 **Is there a present obligation as a result of a past obligating event?**
There is no present obligation. The company could avoid the cost of the overhaul by, for example, selling the aircraft.

2 **Conclusion**
No provision for cost of overhaul can be recognised. Instead of a provision being recognised, the depreciation of the aircraft takes account of the future incidence of maintenance costs, i.e. an amount equivalent to the expected maintenance costs is depreciated over four years.

## 13.7 Provisions for specific purposes

Specific purposes could include considering the treatment of future operating losses, onerous contracts, restructuring and environmental liabilities. Let us consider each of these.

### 13.7.1 A provision for future operating losses

Such losses should not be recognised if there is no obligation at the reporting date on the basis that the entity could decide to discontinue that particular business activity. However, if it is contractually unable to discontinue then it classifies the contract as an onerous contract and makes provision.

### 13.7.2 Onerous contracts

A provision should be recognised if there is an onerous contract. An onerous contract is one entered into with another party under which the unavoidable costs of fulfilling the contract exceed the revenues to be received and where the entity would have to pay compensation to the other party if the contract was not fulfilled. A typical example in times of recession is the requirement to make a payment to secure the early termination of a lease where it has been impossible to sublet the premises. This situation could arise where there has been a downturn in business and an entity seeks to reduce its annual lease payments on premises that are no longer required.

The following is an extract from the 2011 Preliminary Results of the Spirit Pub Company plc:

**Onerous lease provisions**
The Group provides for its onerous obligations under operating leases where the property is closed or vacant and for properties where rental expense is in excess of income. The estimated timings and amounts of cash flows are determined using the experience of internal and external property experts; however, any changes to the estimated method of exiting from the property could lead to changes to the level of the provision recorded.

### 13.7.3 Restructuring provisions

- **A provision for restructuring** should only be recognised when there is a commitment supported by:

  (a) a detailed formal plan for the restructuring identifying at least:

     (i)  the business or part of the business concerned;

     (ii)  the principal locations affected;

     (iii) details of the approximate number of employees who will receive compensation payments;

     (iv) the expenditure that will be undertaken; and

     (v)  when the plan will be implemented; and

  (b) a valid expectation in those affected that the business will carry out the restructuring by implementing its restructuring plans or announcing its main features to those affected by it.

- **A provision for restructuring should not be created merely on the intention to restructure.** For example, a management or board decision to restructure taken before the reporting date does not give rise to a constructive obligation at the reporting date unless the company has, before the reporting date:

  - started to implement the restructuring plan, e.g. by dismantling plant or selling assets; or

  - announced the main features of the plan with sufficient detail to raise the valid expectation of those affected that the restructuring will actually take place.

- **A provision for restructuring** should only include the direct expenditures arising from the restructuring which are necessarily entailed and not associated with the ongoing activities of the company. For example, redundancy costs would be included, but note that the following costs which relate to the future conduct of the business are not included: retraining costs, relocation costs, marketing costs, and investment in new systems and distribution networks.

### 13.7.4 Environmental liabilities and decommissioning costs

- **A provision for environmental liabilities** should be recognised at the time and to the extent that the entity becomes obliged, legally or constructively, to rectify environmental damage or to perform restorative work on the environment. This means that a provision should be set up only for the entity's costs to meet its *legal* or *constructive* obligations. It could be argued that any provision for any additional expenditure on environmental issues is a public relations decision and should be written off.

- **A provision for decommissioning costs** should be recognised to the extent that decommissioning costs relate to damage already done or goods and services already received.

Provisions for decommissioning costs often relate to non-current assets, e.g. power stations. Where a liability for decommissioning exists at the date of construction, it is recognised, normally at the present value of the expected future outflow of cash, and added to the cost of the non-current asset.

EXAMPLE • An entity constructs a nuclear power station at a cost of €20 million. The estimated useful life of the power station is 25 years. The entity has a legal obligation to decommission the power station at the end of its useful life and the estimated costs of this are €15 million in 25 years' time. A relevant annual discount factor is 5% and the present value of a payment of €15 million in 25 years' time is approximately €4.43 million.

In these circumstances a liability of €4.43 million is recognised at the completion of the construction of the facility. The debit side of this accounting entry is to property, plant and equipment, giving a total carrying amount for the power station of €24.43 million. This amount is then depreciated over 25 years which gives an annual charge (assuming straight-line depreciation with no residual value) of approximately €977,200.

The discounting of the liability is 'unwound' over the 25-year life of the power station, the annual unwinding being shown as a finance cost. The unwinding in the first year of operation is approximately €221,500 (€4.43 million × 5).

### 13.7.5 Disclosures required by IAS 37 for provisions

Specific disclosures,[9] for each material class of provision, should be given as to the amount recognised at the year-end and about any movements in the year, e.g.:

- **Increases in provisions** – any new provisions; any increases to existing provisions; and, where provisions are carried at present value, any change in value arising from the passage of time or from any movement in the discount rate.

- **Reductions in provisions** – any amounts utilised during the period. Management are required to review provisions at each reporting date and adjust to reflect the current best estimates. If it is no longer probable that a transfer of economic benefits will be required to settle the obligation, the provision should be reversed. Note, however, that only expenditure that relates to the original provision may be set against that provision.

Disclosures need not be given in cases where to do so would be seriously prejudicial to the company's interests. For example, an extract from the Technotrans 2002 Annual Report states:

A competitor filed patent proceedings in 2000, . . . the court found in favour of the plaintiff . . . paves the way for a claim for compensation which may have to be determined in further legal proceedings . . . the particulars pursuant to IAS 37.85 are not disclosed, in accordance with IAS 37.92, in order not to undermine the company's situation substantially in the ongoing legal dispute.

## 13.8 Contingent liabilities

IAS 37 deals with provisions and contingent liabilities within the same IAS because the IASB regarded all provisions as contingent as they are uncertain in timing and amount. For the purposes of the accounts, it distinguishes between provisions and contingent liabilities in that:

● Provisions are a present obligation requiring a probable transfer of economic benefits that can be reliably estimated – a provision can therefore be recognised as a liability.

● Contingent liabilities fail to satisfy these criteria, e.g. lack of a reliable estimate of the amount; not probable that there will be a transfer of economic benefits; yet to be confirmed that there is actually an obligation. A contingent liability cannot therefore be recognised in the accounts but may be disclosed by way of note to the accounts or not disclosed if an outflow of economic benefits is remote.

Where the occurrence of a contingent liability becomes sufficiently probable, it falls within the criteria for recognition as a provision as detailed above and should be accounted for accordingly and recognised as a liability in the accounts.

Where the likelihood of a contingent liability is possible but not probable and not remote, disclosure should be made, for each class of contingent liability, where practicable, of:

(a) an estimate of its financial effect, taking into account the inherent risks and uncertainties and, where material, the time value of money;

(b) an indication of the uncertainties relating to the amount or timing of any outflow; and

(c) the possibility of any reimbursement.

For example, an extract from the 2015 Manchester City Annual Report informs us that:

### 20 - Contingent liabilities
Additional transfer fees, signing on fees and loyalty bonuses of £112,918,000 (2014: £100,563,000) that will become payable upon the achievement of certain conditions contained within player and transfer contracts if they are still in the service of the Club on specific future dates are accounted for in the year in which they fall due for payment

## 13.9 Contingent assets

A contingent asset is a possible asset that arises from past events whose existence will be confirmed only by the occurrence of one or more uncertain future events not wholly within the entity's control.

Recognition as an asset is only allowed if the asset is *virtually certain*, and therefore by definition no longer contingent.

Disclosure by way of note is required if an inflow of economic benefits is *probable*. The disclosure would include a brief description of the nature of the contingent assets at the reporting date and, where practicable, an estimate of their financial effect taking into account the inherent risks and uncertainties and, where material, the time value of money.

The following is an extract from The Watford Association Football Club Limited Report and financial statements For the year ended 30th June 2015:

> At 30th June 2015 the Club had sums receivable from other clubs in respect of players, dependent upon the number of first team appearances or percentage sell-on clauses. Due to the uncertainty of receipt of these contingent assets, it is not practical to disclose the amount likely to be received. Since the year end, £30,000 has become due.

No disclosure is required where the chance of occurrence is anything less than probable. For the purposes of IAS 37, probable is defined as more likely than not, i.e. with more than a 50% chance.

## 13.10 ED IAS 37 *Non-financial Liabilities*

In June 2005, the International Accounting Standards Board (IASB) proposed amendments to IAS 37 *Provisions, Contingent Liabilities and Contingent Assets*. These strip IAS 37 of the words 'Provisions', 'Contingent' and 'Assets' and add the term 'Non-financial' to create the new title IAS 37 *Non-financial Liabilities*.[10] It is interesting to see that the new standard has been developed around the *Framework*'s definitions of an asset and a liability.

It appears that the word 'non-financial' has been added to distinguish the subject from 'financial liabilities' which are covered by IAS 32 and IAS 39. It should be noted that whilst the exposure draft remains in issue a new standard based on these proposals is not in the current IASB work-plan.

### 13.10.1 The 'old' IAS 37 *Provisions, Contingent Liabilities and Contingent Assets*

To understand the 'new' approach in ED IAS 37 *Non-financial Liabilities*, it is necessary first to look at the 'old' IAS 37. The old treatment can be represented by the following table:

| *Probability* | *Contingent liabilities* | *Contingent assets* |
|---|---|---|
| Virtually certain | Liability | Asset |
| Probable (p > 50%) | Provide | Disclose |
| Possible (p < 50%) | Disclose | No disclosure |
| Remote | No disclosure | No disclosure |

Note that contingent liabilities are those items where the probability is less than 50% (p < 50%). Where, however, the liability is probable, i.e. the probability is p > 50%, the item is classified as a provision and not a contingent liability. Normally, such a provision will be reported as the product of the value of the potential liability and its probability.

Note that the approach to contingent assets is different in that the 'prudence' concept is used which means that only virtually certain assets are reported as assets. If the probability is probable, i.e. p > 50%, then contingent assets are disclosed by way of a note to the accounts, and if the probability is p < 50% then there is no disclosure.

#### Criticisms of the 'old' IAS 37

The criticisms included the following:

- The 'old' IAS 37 was not even-handed in its treatment of contingent assets and liabilities. In ED IAS 37 the treatment of contingent assets is similar to that of contingent liabilities, and provisions are merged into the treatment of contingent liabilities.

- The division between 'probable' and 'possible' was too strict or crude (at the $p = 50\%$ level) rather than being proportional. For instance, if a television manufacturer was considering the need to provide for guarantee claims (e.g. on televisions sold with a three-year warranty), then it is probable that each television sold would have a less than 50% chance of being subject to a warranty claim and so no provision would need to be made. However, if the company sold 10,000 televisions, it is almost certain that there would be some claims which would indicate that a provison should be made. A company could validly take either treatment, but the effect on the financial statements would be different.

- If there was a single possible legal claim, then the company could decide it was 'possible' and just disclose it in the financial statements. However, a more reasonable treatment would be to assess the claim as the product of the amount likely to be paid and its probability. This latter treatment is used in the new ED IAS 37.

### 13.10.2 Approach taken by ED IAS 37 *Non-financial Liabilities*

The new proposed standard uses the term 'non-financial liabilities' which it defines as 'a liability other than a financial liability as defined in IAS 32 *Financial Instruments: Presentation*'. In considering ED IAS 37, we will look at the proposed treatment of contingent liabilities/provisions and contingent assets, starting from the *Framework*'s definitions of a liability and an asset.

#### The *Framework's* definition

The *Framework*, paragraph 91, requires a liability to be recognised as follows:

> A liability is recognised in the statement of financial position when it is probable that an outflow of resources embodying economic benefits will result from the settlement of a present obligation and the amount at which the settlement will take place can be measured reliably.

#### The ED IAS 37 approach to provisions

Considering a provision first, the old IAS 37 (paragraph 10) defines it as follows:

> A provision is distinguished from other liabilities because there is uncertainty about the timing or amount of the future expenditure required in settlement.

ED IAS 37 argues that a provision should be reported as a liability, as it satisfies the *Framework*'s definition of a liability. It makes the point that there is no reference in the *Framework* to 'uncertainty about the timing or amount of the future expenditure required in settlement'. It considers a provision to be just one form of liability which should be treated as a liability in the financial statements.

#### Will the item 'provision' no longer appear in financial statements?

One would expect that to be the result of the ED (exposure draft) classification. However, the proposed standard does not take the step of prohibiting the use of the term, as seen in the following extract (paragraph 9):

> In some jurisdictions, some classes of liabilities are described as provisions, for example those liabilities that can be measured only by using a substantial degree of estimation. Although this [draft] Standard does not use the term 'provision', it does not prescribe how entities should describe their non-financial liabilities. Therefore, entities may describe some classes of non-financial liabilities as provisions in their financial statements.

### The ED IAS 37 approach to contingent liabilities

Now considering contingent liabilities, the old IAS 37 (paragraph 10) defines these as:

**(a)** a possible obligation that arises from past events and whose existence will be confirmed only by the occurrence or non-occurrence of one or more uncertain future events not wholly within the control of the entity; or

**(b)** a present obligation that arises from past events, but is not recognised because:

  (i)  it is not probable that an outflow of resources embodying economic benefits will be required to settle the obligation; or

  (ii) the amount of the obligation cannot be measured with sufficient reliability.

This definition means that the old IAS 37 has taken the strict approach of using the term 'possible' ($p < 50\%$) when it required no liability to be recognised.

ED IAS 37 is different in that it takes a two-stage approach in considering whether 'contingent liabilities' are 'liabilities'. To illustrate this, we will take the example of a restaurant where some customers have suffered food poisoning.

*First determine whether there is a present obligation*

The restaurant's year-end is 30 June 20X6. If the food poisoning took place after 30 June 20X6, then this is not a 'present obligation' at the year-end, so it is not a liability. If the food poisoning occurred up to 30 June, then it is a 'present obligation' at the year-end, as there are possible future costs arising from the food poisoning. This is the first stage in considering whether the liability exists.

*Then determine whether a liability exists*

The second stage is to consider whether a 'liability' exists. The *Framework*'s definition of a liability says it is a liability if 'it is probable that an outflow of resources will result from the settlement of the present obligation'. So, there is a need to consider whether any payments (or other expenses) will be incurred as a result of the food poisoning. This may involve settling legal claims, other compensation or giving 'free' meals. The estimated cost of these items will be the liability (and expense) included in the financial statements.

### The rationale

ED IAS 37 explains this process as:

- the unconditional obligation (stage 1) establishes the liability; and
- the conditional obligation (stage 2) affects the amount that will be required to settle the liability.

The liability is the amount that the entity would rationally pay to settle the present obligation or to transfer it to a third party on the statement of financial position date. Often, the liability will be estimated as the product of the maximum liability and the probability of it occurring, or a decision tree will be used with a number of possible outcomes (costs) and their probability.

In many cases, the new ED IAS 37 will cover the 'possible' category for contingent liabilities and include the item as a liability (rather than as a note to the financial statements). This gives a more 'proportional' result than the previously strict line between 'probable' ($p > 50\%$) (when a liability is included in the financial statements) and 'possible' ($p < 50\%$) (when only a note is included in the financial statements and no charge is included for the liability).

### What if they cannot be measured reliably?

For other 'possible' contingent liabilities, which have not been recognised because they cannot be measured reliably, the following disclosure should be made:

- a description of the nature of the obligation;
- an explanation of why it cannot be measured reliably;
- an indication of the uncertainties relating to the amount or timing of any outflow of economic benefits; and
- the existence of any rights to reimbursement.

### What disclosure is required for maximum potential liability?

ED IAS 37 does not require disclosure of the maximum potential liability, e.g. the maximum damages if the entity loses the legal case.

## 13.10.3 Measured reliably

The *Framework*'s definition of a liability includes the condition 'and the amount at which the settlement will take place can be measured reliably'. This posed a problem when drafting ED IAS 37 because of the concern that an entity could argue that the amount of a contingent liability could not be measured reliably and that there was therefore no need to include it as a liability in the financial statements – i.e. to use this as a 'cop out' to give a 'rosier' picture in the financial statements. Whilst acknowledging that in many cases a non-financial liability cannot be measured exactly, it considered that it could (and should) be estimated. It then says that cases where the liability cannot be measured reliably are 'extremely rare'. We can see from this that the ED approach is that 'measured reliably' does not mean 'measured exactly' and that cases where the liability 'cannot be measured reliably' will be 'extremely rare'.

## 13.10.4 Contingent asset

The *Framework*, paragraph 89, requires recognition of an asset as follows:

> An Asset is recognised in the statement of financial position when it is probable that the future economic benefits will flow to the entity and the asset has a cost or value that can be measured reliably.

Note that under the old IAS 37, contingent assets included items where they were 'probable' (unlike liabilities, when this was called a 'provision'). However, probable contingent assets are not included as assets but only included in the notes to the financial statements.

### The ED IAS 37 approach

ED IAS 37 takes a similar approach to 'contingent assets' as it does to 'provisions/contingent liabilities'. It abolishes the term 'contingent asset' and replaces it with the term 'contingency'. The term contingency refers to uncertainty about the amount of the future economic benefits embodied in an asset, rather than uncertainty about whether an asset exists.

Essentially, the treatment of contingent assets is the same as that of contingent liabilities. The first stage is to consider whether an asset exists and the second stage is concerned with valuing the asset (i.e. the product of the value of the asset and its probability). A major change is to move contingent assets to IAS 38 *Intangible Assets* (and not include them in IAS 37).

The treatment of 'contingent assets' under IAS 38 is now similar to that for 'contingent liabilities/provisions'. This seems more appropriate than the former 'prudent approach' used by the old IAS 37.

### 13.10.5 Reimbursements

Under the old IAS 37 an asset could be damaged or destroyed, when the expense would be included in profit or loss (and any future costs included as a provision). If the insurance claim relating to this loss was made after the year-end, it is likely that no asset could be included in the financial statements as compensation for the loss, as the insurance claim was 'not virtually certain'. In reality, this did not reflect the true situation when the insurance claim would compensate for the loss, and there would be little or no net cost.

With the new rules under ED IAS 37, the treatment of contingent assets and contingent liabilities is the same, so an asset would be included in the statement of financial position as the insurance claim, which would offset the loss on damage or destruction of the asset. The ED position is that an asset exists because there is an unconditional right to reimbursement – the only uncertainty is to the amount that will be received. But ED IAS 37 says the liability relating to the loss (e.g. the costs of repair) must be stated separately from the asset for the reimbursement (i.e. the insurance claim) – they cannot be netted off (although they will be in profit or loss).

### 13.10.6 Constructive and legal obligations

The term 'constructive obligation' is important in determining whether a liability exists. ED IAS 37 (paragraph 10) defines it as follows:

A constructive obligation is a present obligation that arises from an entity's past actions when:

(a) by an established pattern of past practice, published policies or a sufficiently specific current statement, the entity has indicated to other parties that it will accept particular responsibilities, and

(b) as a result, the entity has created a valid expectation in those parties, that they can reasonably rely on it to discharge those responsibilities.

It also defines a legal obligation as follows:

A legal obligation is a present obligation that arises from the following:

(a) a contract (through its explicit or implicit terms)

(b) legislation, or

(c) other operating law.

A contingent liability/provision is a liability only if it is either a constructive and/or a legal obligation. Thus, an entity would not normally make a provision (recognise a liability) for the potential costs of rectifying faulty products outside their guarantee period.

### 13.10.7 Present value

ED IAS 37 says that future cash flows relating to the liability should be discounted at the pre-tax discount rate. Unwinding of the discount would still need to be recognised as an interest cost.

### 13.10.8 Subsequent measurement and derecognition

On subsequent measurement, ED IAS 37 says the carrying value of the non-financial liability should be reviewed at each reporting date. The non-financial liability should be derecognised when the obligation is settled, cancelled or expires.

### 13.10.9 Onerous contracts

If a contract becomes onerous, the entity is required to recognise a liability as the present obligation under the contract. However, if the contract becomes onerous as a result of the entity's own actions, the liability should not be recognised until it has taken the action. For example, let us assume that an entity has a non-cancellable 10-year lease on a warehouse and decides during year 7 to vacate the property. Under the old IAS 37 the present obligation arises when the entity communicates this to the lessor, whereas under ED IAS 37 the present obligation does not arise until the property is actually vacated. The contract is still onerous but there may be a later recognition.

### 13.10.10 Restructurings

ED IAS 37 says:

> An entity shall recognise a non-financial liability for a cost associated with a restructuring only when the definition of a liability has been satisfied.

There are situations where management has made a decision to restructure and the ED provides that in these cases a decision by the management of an entity to undertake a restructuring is not the requisite past event for recognition of a liability. The ED position is that an announcement is insufficient, even if there is a detailed plan, if the entity continues to be able to modify the plan. A cost associated with a restructuring is recognised as a liability on the same basis as if that cost arose independently of the restructuring. This change would, if implemented, align IAS 37 with the equivalent US standard in this area.

### 13.10.11 Other items

These include the treatment of termination costs and future operating losses where the approach is still to assess whether a liability exists. The changes to termination costs will require an amendment to IAS 19 *Employee Benefits*. In the case of termination costs, these are only recognised when a liability is incurred: e.g. the costs of closure of a factory become a liability only when the expense is incurred, and redundancy costs become a liability only when employees are informed of their redundancy. In the case of future operating losses, these are not recognised as they do not relate to a past event.

Under the new ED IAS 37, the liability arises no earlier than under the old IAS 37 and sometimes later.

### 13.10.12 Disclosure

ED IAS 37 requires the following disclosure of non-financial liabilities:

> For each class of non-financial liability, the carrying amount of the liability at the period-end together with a description of the nature of the obligation.
>
> For any class of non-financial liability with uncertainty about its estimation:
>
> (a) a reconciliation of the carrying amounts at the beginning and end of the period showing:
>
> (i) liabilities incurred;
>
> (ii) liabilities derecognised;
>
> (iii) changes in the discounted amount resulting from the passage of time and the effect of any change in the discount rate; and

(iv) other adjustments to the amount of the liability (e.g. revisions in the estimated cash flows that will be required to settle it);

(b) the expected timing of any resulting outflows of economic benefits;

(c) an indication of the uncertainties about the amount or timing of those outflows. If necessary, to provide adequate information on the major assumptions made about future events;

(d) the amount of any right to reimbursement, stating the amount of any asset that has been recognised.

If a non-financial liability is not recognised because it cannot be measured reliably, that fact should be disclosed together with:

(a) a description of the nature of the obligation;

(b) an explanation of why it cannot be measured reliably;

(c) an indication of the uncertainties relating to the amount or timing of any outflow of economic benefits; and

(d) the existence of any right to reimbursement.

## 13.10.13 Conclusion on ED IAS 37 *Non-financial Liabilities*

This proposed standard makes significant changes to the subject of 'Provisions, Contingent Liabilities and Contingent Assets', which are derived from the general principles of accounting. Its good features include:

(a) It is conceptually sound by basing changes on the *Framework*'s definitions of an asset and a liability.

(b) It is more appropriate that the treatment of provisions/contingent liabilities and contingent assets should be more 'even-handed'.

(c) It avoids the 'strict' breaks at 50% probability between 'probable' and 'possible'. It uses probability in estimating the liability down (effectively) to 0%.

(d) The definition of a constructive obligation has been more clearly defined.

(e) It overcomes the previous anomaly of not allowing reimbursements after the year-end (e.g. where there is an unsettled insurance claim at the year-end).

However, in some ways it could be argued that the proposed standard goes too far, particularly in its new terminology:

(a) The abolition of the term 'contingent liability' and not defining 'provision'. The new term 'non-financial liability' does not seem as meaningful as 'contingent liability'. It would seem better (more meaningful) to continue to use the term 'contingent liability' and make this encompass provisions (as it does for contingent assets).

(b) It would seem more appropriate to continue to include 'contingent assets' in this standard, rather than move them to 'intangible assets', as the treatment of these items is similar to that of 'contingent liabilities'.

ED IAS 37 has proved to be a controversial exposure draft where there have been significant discussions surrounding the potential changes. In addition this project could be influenced by other projects that the IASB has in development, such as on leasing and revenue recognition.

## 13.11 ED/2010/1 *Measurement of Liabilities in IAS 37*[11]

This ED is a limited re-exposure of a proposed amendment to IAS 37. It deals with only one of the measurement requirements for liabilities. The ED proposes that the non-financial liability should be measured at the amount that the entity would rationally pay to be relieved of the liability.

If the liability cannot be cancelled or transferred, the liability is measured as the present value of the resources required to fulfil the obligation. It may be that the resources required are uncertain. If so, the expected value is estimated based on the probability-weighted average of the outflows. The expected value is then increased to take into account the risk that the actual outcome might be higher, estimating the amount a third party would require to take over this risk. Where there is an obligation to undertake a service at a future date such as decommissioning plant and there is no market for such a service, it is proposed that the amount of any provision should be the cost that the entity would itself charge another party to carry out the work, including a profit margin.

If the liability can be cancelled or transferred, there is a choice available – to fulfil the obligation, to cancel the obligation or to transfer the liability. The logical choice is to choose the lower of the present value of fulfilling the obligation and the amount that would have to be paid to either cancel or transfer.

### Potential impact on ratios and transparency

A new standard that applies this measurement approach will not have an identical impact on all entities – some will have to include higher non-financial liabilities on their statement of financial position, others will have to reduce the non-financial liabilities. This means that there will be different impacts on returns on equity, gearing and debt covenants.

Given the process of establishing expected values and risk adjustments, it might be that additional narrative explanation will be required in the annual report, particularly if the non-financial liabilities are material.

### Future progress

In July 2015 the IASB issued a staff paper on a Research Project – provisions, contingent liabilities and contingent assets (IAS 37). It stated that more evidence was being gathered about the nature and extent of practical problems with IAS 37, and views on possible solutions to the problems identified.

### Summary

The *Framework* defines a liability as a present obligation arising from a past event, the settlement of which is expected to result in an outflow from the entity of economic resources. The treatment of provisions has been the subject of an ED IAS 37 which considers that a provision should be reported as a liability.

The chapter considers the approach to be taken when accounting for a variety of scenarios including the treatment of onerous contracts, future operating losses, restructuring and environmental liabilities and decommissioning costs.

Further consideration will be given by the IASB commencing in 2015.

## REVIEW QUESTIONS

**1** The Notes in the BG Group 2015 Annual Report included the following extract:

### Provisions for liabilities

Decommissioning

|  | 2015 | 2014 |
|---|---|---|
|  | £m | £m |
| As at 1 January | 4,605 | 3,662 |
| Unwinding of discount | 131 | 146 |

### Decommissioning costs

The estimated cost of decommissioning at the end of the producing lives of fields is reviewed at least annually and engineering estimates and reports are updated periodically. Provision is made for the estimated cost of decommissioning at the statement of financial position date, to the extent that current circumstances indicate BG Group will ultimately bear this cost.

Explain why the provision has been increased in 2014 and 2015 by the unwinding of discount and why these increases are for different amounts.

**2** Mining, nuclear and oil companies historically provided an amount each year over the life of an enterprise to provide for decommissioning costs. Explain why the IASB considered this to be an inappropriate treatment and how these companies would be affected by IAS 37 *Provisions, Contingent Liabilities and Contingent Assets* and ED IAS 37 *Non-financial Liabilities*.

**3** The following note appeared in the Compass-Group Annual Report:

Provisions for onerous contracts represent the liabilities in respect of short and long term leases on unoccupied properties and other contracts lasting under five years.

Discuss the criteria for assessing whether a provision may be created in these circumstances under both IAS 37 and ED IAS 37. Discuss the criteria for assessing whether a contract is onerous.

**4** One of the reasons why the IASB considered in its EDs an amendment to IAS 37 is that the criteria within that standard for the recognition of provisions are allegedly inconsistent with those in other international financial reporting standards. Discuss the extent to which you believe this statement to be true, and the improvements proposed in the 2005 and 2010 exposure drafts.

**5** Given the uncertainty inherent in the recognition of provisions or contingent liabilities, financial statements would be much more reliable if the existence of potential liabilities were disclosed, rather than being recognised under conditions of potential uncertainty. Discuss this statement.

## EXERCISES

### Question 1

(a) Provisions are particular kinds of liabilities. It therefore follows that provisions should be recognised when the definition of a liability has been met. The key requirement of a liability is a present obligation and thus this requirement is critical also in the context of the recognition of a provision. IAS 37 *Provisions, Contingent Liabilities and Contingent Assets* deals with this area.

**Required:**

(i) Explain why there was a need for detailed guidance on accounting for provisions.

(ii) Explain the circumstances under which a provision should be recognised in the financial statements according to IAS 37 *Provisions, Contingent Liabilities and Contingent Assets*.

(b) World Wide Nuclear Fuels, a public limited company, disclosed the following information in its financial statements for the year ending 30 November 20X9:

> The company purchased an oil company during the year. As part of the sale agreement, oil has to be supplied to the company's former holding company at an uneconomic rate for a period of five years. As a result, a provision for future operating losses has been set up of $135m, which relates solely to the uneconomic supply of oil. Additionally the oil company is exposed to environmental liabilities arising out of its past obligations, principally in respect of soil and ground water restoration costs, although currently there is no legal obligation to carry out the work. Liabilities for environmental costs are provided for when the group determines a formal plan of action on the closure of an inactive site. It has been decided to provide for $120m in respect of the environmental liability on the acquisition of the oil company. World Wide Nuclear Fuels has a reputation for ensuring the preservation of the environment in its business activities. The company is also facing a legal claim for $200 million from a competitor who claims they have breached a patent in one of their processes. World Wide Nuclear Fuels has obtained legal advice that the claim has little chance of success and the insurance advisers have indicated that to insure against losing the case would cost $20 million as a premium.

**Required:**

Discuss whether the provision has been accounted for correctly under IAS 37 *Provisions, Contingent Liabilities and Contingent Assets*, and whether any changes are likely to be needed under ED IAS 37.

## * Question 2

On 20 December 20X6 one of Incident plc's lorries was involved in an accident with a car. The lorry driver was responsible for the accident and the company agreed to pay for the repair to the car. The company put in a claim to its insurers on 17 January 20X7 for the cost of the claim. The company expected the claim to be settled by the insurance company except for a £250 excess on the insurance policy. The insurance company may dispute the claim and not pay out; however, the company believes that the chance of this occurring is low. The cost of repairing the car was estimated as £5,000, all of which was incurred after the year-end.

**Required:**

Explain how this item should be treated in the financial statements for the year ended 31 December 20X6 according to both IAS 37 and ED IAS 37 *Non-financial Liabilities*.

## Question 3

Plasma Ltd, a manufacturer of electrical goods, guarantees them for 12 months from the date of purchase by the customer. If a fault occurs after the guarantee period but is due to faulty manufacture or design of the product, the company repairs or replaces the product. However, the company does not make this practice widely known.

**Required:**

Explain how repairs after the guarantee period should be treated in the financial statements.

## Question 4

In 20X6 Alpha AS made the decision to close a loss-making department in 20X7. The company proposed to make a provision for the future costs of termination in the 20X6 profit or loss. Its argument was that a liability existed in 20X6 which should be recognised in 20X6. The auditor objected to recognising a liability, but agreed to recognition if it could be shown that the management decision was irrevocable.

### Required:
Discuss whether a liability exists and should be recognised in the 20X6 statement of financial position.

## * Question 5

Easy View Ltd had started business publishing training resource material in ring binder format for use in primary schools. Later it diversified into the hiring out of videos and had opened a chain of video hire shops. With the growing popularity of a mail order video/DVD supplier the video hire shops had become loss-making.

The company's year-end was 31 March and in February the financial director (FD) was asked to prepare a report for the board on the implications of closing this segment of the business.

The position at the board meeting on 10 March was as follows:

1  It was agreed that the closure should take place from 1 April 2010 to be completed by 31 May 2010.
2  The premises were freehold except for one that was on a lease with six years to run. It was in an inner-city shopping complex where many properties were empty and there was little chance of sub-letting. The annual rent was £20,000 per annum. Early termination of the lease could be negotiated for a figure of £100,000. An appropriate discount rate is 8%.
3  The office equipment and vans had a book value of £125,000 and were expected to realise £90,000, a figure tentatively suggested by a dealer who indicated that he might be able to complete by the end of April.
4  The staff had been mainly part-time and casual employees. There were 45 managers, however, who had been with the company for a number of years. These were happy to retrain to work with the training resources operation. The cost of retraining to use publishing software was estimated at £225,000.
5  Losses of £300,000 were estimated for the current year and £75,000 for the period until the closure was complete.

A week before the meeting the managing director made it clear to the FD that he wanted the segment to be treated as a discontinued operation so that the continuing operations could reflect the profitable training segment's performance.

### Required:
Draft the finance director's report to present to the MD before the meeting to clarify the financial reporting implications.

## Question 6

Suktor is an entity that prepares financial statements to 30 June each year.

On 30 April 20X1 the directors decided to discontinue the business of one of Suktor's operating divisions. They decided to cease production on 31 July 20X1, with a view to disposing of the property, plant and equipment soon after 31 August 20X1.

On 15 May 20X1 the directors made a public announcement of their intentions and offered the employees affected by the closure termination payments or alternative employment opportunities elsewhere in the group. Relevant financial details are as follows:

(a) On 30 April 20X1 the directors estimated that termination payments to employees would total $12 million and the costs of retraining employees who would remain employed by other group companies would total $1.2 million. Actual termination costs paid out on 31 May 20X1 were $12.6 million and the latest estimate of total retraining costs is $960,000.

(b) Suktor was leasing a property under an operating lease that expires on 30 September 20Y0. On 30 June 20X1 the present value of the future lease rentals (using an appropriate discount rate) was $4.56 million. On 31 August 20X1 Suktor made a payment to the lessor of $4.56 million in return for early termination of the lease. There were no rental payments made in July or August 20X1.

(c) The loss after tax of Suktor for the year ended 30 June 20X1 was $14.4 million. Suktor made further operating losses totalling $6 million for the two-month period 1 July 20X1 to 31 August 20X1.

**Required:**
**Compute the provision that is required in the financial statements of Suktor at 30 June 20X1 in respect of the decision to close.**

## * Question 7

On 1 April 20W9 Kroner began to lease an office block on a 20-year lease. The useful economic life of the office buildings was estimated at 40 years on 1 April 20W9. The supply of leasehold properties exceeded the demand on 1 April 2009 so as an incentive the lessor paid Kroner $1 million on 1 April 20W9 and allowed Kroner a rent-free period for the first two years of the lease, followed by 36 payments of $250,000, the first being due on 1 April 20X1.

Between 1 April 20W9 and 30 September 20W9 Kroner carried out alterations to the office block at a total cost of $3 million. The terms of the lease require Kroner to vacate the office block on 31 March 20Y9 and leave it in exactly the same condition as it was at the start of the lease. The directors of Kroner have consistently estimated that the cost of restoring the office block to its original condition on 31 March 20Y9 will be $2.5 million at 31 March 20Y9 prices.

An appropriately risk-adjusted discount rate for use in any discounting calculations is 6% per annum. The present value of $1 payable in $19^{1}/_{2}$ years at an annual discount rate of 6% is 32 cents.

**Required:**
**Prepare extracts from the financial statements of Kroner that show the depreciation of leasehold improvements and unwinding of discount on the restoration liability in the statement of comprehensive income for *both* of the years ended 31 March 20X0 and 20X1.**

## Question 8

Epsilon is a listed entity. You are the financial controller of the entity and its consolidated financial statements for the year ended 31 March 2009 are being prepared. The board of directors is responsible for all key financial and operating decisions, including the allocation of resources.

Your assistant is preparing the first draft of the statements. He has a reasonable general accounting knowledge but is not familiar with the detailed requirements of all relevant financial reporting standards. There is one issue on which he requires your advice and he has sent you a note as shown below:

I note that on 31 January 2009 the board of directors decided to discontinue the activities of a number of our subsidiaries. This decision was made, I believe, because these subsidiaries did not fit into the long-term plans of the group and the board did not consider it likely that the subsidiaries could be sold. This decision was communicated to the employees on 28 February 2009 and the activities of the subsidiaries affected were gradually curtailed starting on 1 May 2009, with an expected completion date of 30 September 2009. I have the following information regarding the closure programme:

(a) All the employees in affected subsidiaries were offered redundancy packages and some of the employees were offered employment in other parts of the group. These offers had to be accepted or rejected by 30 April 2009. On 31 March 2009 the directors estimated that the cost of redundancies would be $20 million and the cost of relocation of employees who accepted alternative employment would be $10 million. Following 30 April 2009 these estimates were revised to $22 million and $9 million respectively.

(b) Latest estimates are that the operating losses of the affected subsidiaries for the six months to 30 September 2009 will total $15 million.

(c) A number of the subsidiaries are leasing properties under non-cancellable operating leases. I believe that at 31 March 2009 the present value of the future lease payments relating to these properties totalled $6 million. The cost of immediate termination of these lease obligations would be $5 million.

(d) The carrying values of the freehold properties owned by the affected subsidiaries at 31 March 2008 totalled $25 million. The estimated net disposal proceeds of the properties are $29 million and all properties should realise a profit.

(e) The carrying value of the plant and equipment owned by the affected subsidiaries at 31 March 2008 was $18 million. The estimated current disposal proceeds of this plant and equipment is $2 million and its estimated value in use (including the proceeds from ultimate disposal) is $8 million.

I am unsure regarding a number of aspects of accounting for this decision by the board. Please tell me how the decision to curtail the activities of the three subsidiaries affects the financial statements.

**Required:**
**Draft a reply to the questions raised by your assistant.**

**\* Question 9**

Epsilon is a listed entity. You are the financial controller of the entity and its consolidated financial statements for the year ended 30 September 2008 are being prepared. Your assistant, who has prepared the first draft of the statements, is unsure about the correct treatment of a transaction and has asked for your advice. Details of the transaction are given below.

On 31 August 2008 the directors decided to close down a business segment which did not fit into its future strategy. The closure commenced on 5 October 2008 and was due to be completed on 31 December 2008. On 6 September 2008 letters were sent to relevant employees offering voluntary redundancy or redeployment in other sectors of the business. On 13 September 2008 negotiations commenced with relevant parties with a view to terminating existing contracts of the business segment and arranging sales of its assets. Latest estimates of the financial implications of the closure are as follows:

(i) Redundancy costs will total $30 million, excluding the payment referred to in (ii) below.

(ii) The pension plan (a defined benefit plan) will make a lump sum payment totalling $8 million to the employees who accept voluntary redundancy in termination of their rights under the plan. Epsilon will pay this amount into the plan on 31 January 2009. The actuaries have advised that the accumulated pension rights that this payment will extinguish have a present value of $7 million and this sum is unlikely to alter significantly before 31 January 2009.

(iii) The cost of redeploying and retraining staff who do not accept redundancy will total $6 million.

(iv) The business segment operates out of a leasehold property that has an unexpired lease term of 10 years from 30 September 2008. The annual lease rentals on this property are $1 million, payable on 30 September in arrears. Negotiations with the owner of the freehold indicate that the owner would accept a single payment of $5.5 million in return for early termination of the lease. There are no realistic opportunities for Epsilon to sublet this property. An appropriate rate to use in any discounting calculations is 10% per annum. The present value of an annuity of $1 receivable annually at the end of years 1 to 10 inclusive using a discount rate of 10% is $6.14.

(v) Plant having a net book value of $11 million at 30 September 2008 will be sold for $2 million.

(vi) The operating losses of the business segment for October, November and December 2008 are estimated at $10 million.

Your assistant is unsure of the extent to which the above transactions create liabilities that should be recognised as a closure provision in the financial statements. He is also unsure as to whether or not the results of the business segment that is being closed need to be shown separately.

**Required:**
Explain how the decision to close down the business segment should be reported in the financial statements of Epsilon for the year ended 30 September 2008.

## Notes

1 IAS 37 *Provisions, Contingent Liabilities and Contingent Assets*, IASC, 1998.
2 Ibid., para. 2.
3 Ibid., para. 25.
4 Ibid., para. 17.
5 Ibid., para. 23.
6 Ibid., para. 36.
7 Ibid., para. 43.
8 Ibid., para. 45.
9 Ibid., para. 84.
10 ED IAS 37 *Non-financial Liabilities*, IASB, 2005.
11 ED/2010/1 *Measurement of Liabilities in IAS 37*, IASB, 2010.

# CHAPTER 14

# Financial instruments

## 14.1 Introduction

Accounting for financial instruments has proven to be one of the most difficult and controversial areas for the IASB to provide guidance on, and the current standards are far from perfect. Following the financial crisis of 2008 the IASB began a process to replace the main existing financial instrument accounting standard IAS 39 *Financial Instruments: Recognition and Measurement,* with the issue of revised guidance on the recognition and measurement of financial instruments. A new standard, IFRS 9 *Financial Instruments,* was issued in 2009 to begin this process. When issued in 2009 IFRS 9 only covered certain aspects of the accounting for financial instruments, principally the main recognition and measurement requirements. In particular two areas were not considered, impairment of financial assets and hedging. In 2014 the final version of the standard was issued with an effective date for accounting periods beginning on or after 1 January 2018. It should be noted that at the time of writing (May 2016) the European Union had not endorsed the standard for use in Europe. The effect of this is that most companies applying IFRS are still applying IAS 39 in their current financial statements.

In this chapter we will consider the main requirements of IAS 32 *Financial Instruments: Presentation,* IFRS 9 *Financial Instruments* and IFRS 7 *Financial Instruments: Disclosure.* In considering IFRS 9 we will also review the principle differences between IFRS 9 and its predecessor, IAS 39 *Financial Instruments: Recognition and Measurement* as it provides a useful comparison to help understand why changes were felt necessary by the IASB.

### Objectives

By the end of this chapter, you should be able to:

- define what financial instruments are and be able to outline the main accounting requirements under IFRS;
- comment critically on the international accounting requirements for financial instruments and understand why they continue to prove both difficult and controversial topics in accounting;
- account for different types of common financial instrument that companies may use.

## 14.2 Financial instruments – the IASB's problem child

International accounting has had standards on financial instruments since the late 1990s and, ever since they were introduced, they have proved the most controversial requirements of IFRS. In the late 1990s, in order to make international accounting standards generally acceptable to stock exchanges, the International Accounting Standards Committee (forerunner of the International Accounting Standards Board) introduced IAS 32 and 39. These standards drew heavily on US GAAP as that was the only comprehensive regime that had guidance in this area. Even now some national accounting standards, who have not adopted international accounting standards as their local accounting regime only allow the recognition of financial instruments at cost.

Ever since their issue the guidance on financial instruments has been criticised by users, preparers, auditors and others, and has also been the only area of accounting that has caused real political problems. In the financial crisis of 2008 IAS 39 was extensively discussed and debated within the G20 and other political forums. It was suggested that the rules, particularly on fair value measurement and impairment, could have contributed to the financial crisis and this led to the rules being examined and a project by the IASB and FASB to consider the replacement of the guidance.

### 14.2.1 Rules versus principles

IAS 32 and 39 were sourced from US GAAP (although not fully consistent with US GAAP) and this led to one of the first major criticisms of the guidance, that it is too 'rules-based'. IFRS aims to be a principles-based accounting regime where the accounting standards establish good principles that underpin the accounting treatments, but not every possible situation or transaction is covered in the guidance. US GAAP, whilst still having underpinning principles, tends to have a significantly greater number of 'rules'. As a result IAS 32 and 39 have significant and detailed rules within them. IFRS 9 does address some of the concerns of IAS 39 being too rules-based. For example in the area of hedge accounting which received significant criticism, IFRS 9 follows a more principles-based approach, where, if it is the business intention to hedge, the financial statements are more likely to be able to reflect this position.

A significant difficulty with the rules-based approach can be that it does not produce financial statements that reflect the intent behind their transactions in all situations. For example, an area we will be considering in this chapter is hedge accounting. Some companies have claimed that the very strict hedge accounting requirements in IAS 39 are so difficult to comply with that they cannot reflect what they consider are genuine hedge transactions appropriately in their financial statements. The extract below is a description of a performance KPI from the 2015 Annual Report of Rolls-Royce and shows the importance of the 'underlying' performance of the business which excludes the accounting effects when not applying hedge accounting:

> We measure underlying profit before financing on a basis that shows the economic substance of the Group's hedging strategies in respect of the transactional exchange rate and commodity price movements. In particular: (a) revenues and costs denominated in US dollars and euros are presented on the basis of the exchange rates achieved during the year; (b) similar adjustments are made in respect of commodity derivatives; and (c) consequential adjustments are made to reflect the impact of exchange rates on trading assets and liabilities and long-term contracts on a consistent basis.

Rolls Royce have yet to comply with IFRS 9 and it will be interesting to see if their position changes as a result of the new guidance. It would be expected that achieving hedge accounting should, under the new regime be easier.

### 14.2.2 The 2008 financial crisis

The financial crisis that began in 2008 drew attention to the accounting for financial instruments in a way previously unseen. It was this pressure that led the IASB to start the process of revising IAS 39, something which previously had not been particularly high on the agenda. Over the period 2009 to 2014 it is fair to say that the financial instruments topic was the one that dominated the IASB agenda. The IASB was not alone in looking at financial instruments accounting. The IASB project ran concurrently and was a joint project with the US standard setter, the FASB. The IASB and FASB have ended up with differences in accounting in some areas.

One example of the pressure on the IASB to change the financial instruments requirements resulted in a position where IAS 39 was amended to allow certain reclassifications as discussed below. This was done quickly without due process, an action which the IASB felt was necessary but that drew widespread criticism.

As you read this chapter you will appreciate that financial instruments can be measured in different ways. How a company determines which measurement to use, broadly the choice being fair value or amortised cost, depends on the characteristics of the instruments and the business model of the company. Many banks in the financial crisis were caught in a position where they had loan assets measured at fair value, and the fair value of those loans was reducing significantly, with the potential for major losses needing to be recognised.

### The impact on profits of moving from fair value to amortised cost

Prior to October 2008, if a company chose to measure its financial assets or liabilities at fair value through profit or loss, it was not allowed to subsequently reclassify those loans and measure them at amortised cost. Many banks had recognised loans at fair value which, because of illiquidity in financial markets, they could not sell, but where market values were falling significantly. The losses on revaluation were all going to be charged against their profit.

The issue came to a head when the European Union identified that under US GAAP reclassification was allowed and, therefore, European banks were potentially in a worse competitive position than their American counterparts. The European Union concluded that this was unacceptable and that if IAS 39 was not altered they would 'carve out' the section of IAS 39 restricting the transfer, and effectively allow European banks to reclassify. This was perceived as a major threat by the IASB (in particular to its convergence work with US GAAP) and therefore the IASB amended IAS 39 to allow reclassification. For the first time ever an amendment was made that had not been issued as a discussion paper or exposure draft but was simply a change to the standard. This has led to significant criticism of the IASB and calls for its due process to be revisited to ensure this does not happen again.

### Political pressure on the IASB

The political interest in accounting has continued with global politicians putting pressure on the IASB to speed up its work on certain areas. In addition it has led to calls for the IASB to examine the way it operates and its governance: a number of governments are concerned that a board, on which they have no representation, can set accounting standards which have to be followed by companies in their countries. To highlight how high these issues have been on the agenda of politicians, the following are extracts from the G20 communiqué issued after the meeting on 15 November 2008:

**Strengthening Transparency and Accountability**
*Immediate Actions by March 31, 2009.*
The key global accounting standards bodies should work to enhance guidance for valuation of securities, also taking into account the valuation of complex, illiquid products, especially during times of stress.

Accounting standard setters should significantly advance their work to address weaknesses in accounting and disclosure standards for off balance sheet vehicles.

Regulators and accounting standard setters should enhance the required disclosure of complex financial instruments by firms to market participants.

With a view toward promoting financial stability, the governance of the international accounting standard setting body should be further enhanced, including by undertaking a review of its membership, in particular in order to ensure transparency, accountability, and an appropriate relationship between this independent body and the relevant authorities.

**Promoting Integrity in Financial Markets Immediate Actions by March 31, 2009.**
*Medium-term actions*
The key global accounting standards bodies should work intensively toward the objective of creating a single high-quality global standard.

Regulators, supervisors, and accounting standard setters, as appropriate, should work with each other and the private sector on an ongoing basis to ensure consistent application and enforcement of high-quality accounting standards.

The financial instruments projects of the IASB and FASB were part of the objective to achieve single high-quality global accounting standards as supported by the G20. However, differences in the final standards issued still exist.

## 14.3 IAS 32 *Financial Instruments: Disclosure and Presentation*[1]

The dynamic nature of the international financial markets has resulted in a great variety of financial instruments from traditional equity and debt instruments to derivative instruments such as futures or swaps. These instruments can be used by companies to reduce risk, but also, in some cases, can be used speculatively and increase risk. IAS 32 was introduced to highlight to users of financial statements the range of financial instruments used by an enterprise and how they affect the financial position, performance and cash flows of the enterprise.

IAS 32 only considers the areas of presentation of financial instruments; recognition and measurement are considered in IFRS 9, and disclosure is considered in IFRS 7.

### 14.3.1 Scope of the standards

IAS 32 should be applied by all enterprises and should consider all financial instruments with the exceptions[2] of

- share-based payments;
- interests in subsidiaries, associates and joint ventures;
- employers' rights and obligations under employee benefit plans; and
- rights and obligations arising under insurance contracts.

Further specific scope exemptions only for IFRS 9 and IAS 39 are highlighted later in this chapter.

### 14.3.2 Definition of terms[3]

The following are the principal definitions used when considering financial instrument accounting.

A **financial instrument** is any contract that gives rise to both a financial asset of one enterprise and a financial liability or equity instrument of another enterprise.

A **financial asset** is any asset that is:

(a) cash;

(b) a contractual right to receive cash or another financial asset from another entity;

(c) a contractual right to exchange financial instruments with another entity under conditions that are potentially favourable; or

(d) an equity instrument of another entity.

A **financial liability** is any liability that is a contractual obligation:

(a) to deliver cash or another financial asset to another entity; or

(b) to exchange financial instruments with another entity under conditions that are potentially unfavourable.

An **equity instrument** is any contract that evidences a residual interest in the assets of an entity after deducting all of its liabilities.

In addition to the basic definitions and scope, extra clarification was introduced into IAS 32 in the application of the definitions. First, a commodity-based contract (such as a commodity future) is a financial instrument if either party can settle in cash or some other financial instrument. Commodity contracts would not be financial instruments if they were expected to be settled by delivery, and this was always intended. This is commonly referred to as the 'own-use' exemption and is commonly applied by businesses to commodity contracts, so avoiding the need to account for sale and purchase contracts at fair value.

The second clarification is for the situation where an enterprise has a financial liability that can be settled with either financial assets or the enterprise's own equity shares. If the number of equity shares to be issued is variable, typically so that the enterprise always has an obligation to give shares equal to the fair value of the obligation, they are treated as a financial liability.

### 14.3.3 Presentation of instruments in the financial statements

Two main issues are addressed in the standard regarding the presentation of financial instruments. These issues are whether instruments should be classified as liabilities or equity instruments, and how compound instruments should be presented.

#### Liabilities versus equity

IAS 32 follows a substance approach[4] to the classification of instruments as liabilities or equity. If an instrument has terms such that there is an obligation on the enterprise to transfer financial assets to redeem the obligation then it is a liability instrument regardless of its legal nature. Preference shares are the main instrument where legally they may be classified as equity but in substance they should be accounted as liabilities. The common conditions on the preference share that would indicate it is to be treated as a liability instrument are as follows:

- annual dividends are compulsory and not at the discretion of directors; or
- the share provides for mandatory redemption by the issuer at a fixed or determinable amount at a future fixed or determinable date; or
- the share gives the holder the option to redeem upon the occurrence of a future event that is highly likely to occur (e.g. after the passing of a future date).

If a preference share is treated as a liability instrument, it is presented as such in the statement of financial position. Any dividends paid or payable on that share are calculated in the same way as interest and presented as a finance cost in the statement of comprehensive income. The presentation on the statement of comprehensive income could be as a separate item from other interest costs, but this is not mandatory. Any gains or losses on the redemption of financial instruments classified as liabilities are also presented in profit or loss.

*Impact on companies*

The presentation of preference shares as liabilities does not alter the cash flows or risks that the instruments give, but there is a danger that the perception of a company may change. This presentational change has the impact of reducing net assets and increasing gearing. This could be very important, for example, if a company had debt covenants on other borrowings that required the maintenance of certain ratios such as gearing or interest cover. Moving preference shares to debt and dividends to interest costs could mean the covenants are breached and other loans become repayable.

In addition, the higher gearing and reduced net assets could mean the company is perceived as more risky, and therefore result in the company being perceived to have a higher credit risk. This in turn might lead to a reduction in the company's credit rating, making obtaining future credit more difficult and expensive.

These very practical issues need to be managed by companies converting to IFRS from a local accounting regime that treats preference shares as equity or non-equity funds. Good communication with users is key to smoothing the transition.

## Compound instruments[5]

Compound instruments are financial instruments that have the characteristics of both debt and equity. A convertible loan, which gives the holder the option to convert into equity shares at some future date, is the most common example of a compound instrument. The view of the IASB is that the proceeds received by a company for these instruments are made up of two parts: (i) a debt obligation and (ii) an equity option. Following the substance of the instruments, IAS 32 requires that the two parts be presented separately, a 'split accounting' approach.

The split is made by measuring the debt part and making the equity the residual of the proceeds. This approach is in line with the definitions of liabilities and equity, where equity is treated as a residual. The debt is calculated by discounting the cash flows on the debt at a market rate of interest for similar debt without the conversion option.

The following is an extract from the 2015 Balfour Beatty Annual Report relating to convertible preference shares:

> The Company's cumulative convertible redeemable preference shares and the Group's convertible bonds are compound instruments, comprising a liability component and an equity component. The fair value of the liability components was estimated using the prevailing market interest rates at the dates of issue for similar non-convertible instruments. The difference between the proceeds of issue of the preference shares and convertible bonds and the fair value assigned to the respective liability components, representing the embedded option to convert the liability components into the Company's ordinary shares, is included in equity.

The interest expense on the liability components is calculated by applying applicable market interest rates for similar non-convertible debt prevailing at the dates of issue to the liability components of the instruments. The difference between this amount and the dividend/interest payable is included in the carrying amount of the liability component and is charged to the income statement on an accrual basis together with the dividend/interest payable.

### Illustration for compound instruments

Rohan plc issues 1,000 £100 5% convertible debentures at par on 1 January 2015. The debentures can be either converted into 50 ordinary shares per £100 of debentures, or redeemed at par at any date from 1 January 2020. Interest is paid annually in arrears on 31 December. The interest rate on similar debentures without the conversion option is 6%.

To split the proceeds the debt value must be calculated by discounting the future cash flows on the debt instrument. The value of debt is therefore:

| | |
|---|---:|
| Present value of redemption payment (discounted @ 6%) | £74,726 |
| Present value of interest (5 years) (discounted @ 6%) | £21,062 |
| Value of debt | £95,788 |
| Value of the equity proceeds: (£100,000 − £95,788) | |
| (presented as part of equity) | £4,212 |

The following is an extract from the 2011 Annual Report of Aspen Pharmacare Holdings Ltd:

For accounting purposes the preference shares have been split into an equity and a liability component. Refer to the accounting policy for detail.

| | | R million |
|---|---:|---:|
| Preference shares – equity component | | 162.0 |
| (per statement of changes in equity) | | |
| Deferred tax effect | | (8.7) |
| Net equity component | | 153.3 |
| Preference shares – liability component | | 381.3 |
| (per the statement of financial position) | | |
| Amount expensed in 2011 | | (183.2) |
| Cumulative notional interest on liability component | | |
| Opening balance | 20.1 | |
| For the year | 5.3 | 25.4 |
| | | 376.8 |

### Perpetual debt

Following a substance approach, perpetual or irredeemable debt could be argued to be an equity instrument as opposed to a debt instrument. IAS 32, however, takes the view that it is a debt instrument because the interest must be paid (as compared to dividends which are only paid if profits are available for distribution and if directors declare a dividend approved by the shareholders). The present value of all the future obligations to pay interest will equal the proceeds of the debt if discounted at a market rate. The proceeds on issue of a perpetual debt instrument are therefore a liability obligation.

## 14.3.4 Calculation of finance costs on liability instruments

The finance costs will be charged to profit or loss. The finance cost of debt is the total payments to be incurred over the lifespan of that debt less the initial carrying value. Such costs should be allocated to profit or loss over the lifetime of the debt at a constant rate of interest based on the outstanding carrying value per period. If a debt is settled before maturity, any profit or loss should be reflected immediately in profit or loss – unless the substance of the settlement transaction fails to generate any change in liabilities and assets.

### Illustration of the allocation of finance costs and the determination of carrying value

On 1 January 20X6 a company issued a debt instrument of £1,000,000 spanning a four-year term. It received from the lender £890,000, being the face value of the debt less a discount of £110,000. Interest was payable yearly in arrears at 8% per annum on the principal sum of £1,000,000. The principal sum was to be repaid on 31 December 20X9.

To determine the yearly finance costs and year-end carrying value it is necessary to compute:

- the aggregate finance cost;
- the implicit rate of interest carried by the instrument (referred to in IAS 39 as the effective yield);
- the finance charge per annum; and
- the carrying value at successive year-ends.

### Aggregate finance cost

This is the difference between the total future payments of interest plus principal, less the net proceeds received less costs of the issue, i.e. £430,000 in column (i) of Figure 14.1.

### Implicit rate of interest carried by the instrument

This can be computed by using the net present value (NPV) formula:

$$\sum_{t=1}^{t=n} \frac{A_t}{(1+r)^t} - I = 0$$

where $A$ is forecast net cash flow in year A, $t$ time (in years), $n$ the lifespan of the debt in years, $r$ the company's annual rate of discount and $I$ the initial net proceeds. Note that the application of this formula can be quite time-consuming. A reasonable method of assessment is by interpolation of the interest rate.

The aggregate formula given above may be disaggregated for calculation purposes:

$$\frac{A_1}{(1+r)} + \frac{A_2}{(1+r)^2} + \frac{A_3}{(1+r)^3} + \frac{A_4}{(1+r)^4} - I = 0$$

Using the data concerning the debt and assuming (allowing for discount and costs) an implicit constant rate of, say, 11%:

$$\Sigma = \frac{80,000}{(1.11)^1} + \frac{80,000}{(1.11)^2} + \frac{80,000}{(1.11)^3} + \frac{1,080,000}{(1.11)^4} - 890,000 = 0$$

$$= 72,072 + 64,930 + 58,495 + 711,429 - 890,000 = +16,926$$

### Figure 14.1 Allocation of finance costs and determination of carrying value

| | (i)<br>Cash flows<br>£000 | | (ii)<br>Finance charge to<br>statement of<br>comprehensive income<br>£000 | | (iii)<br>Carrying value<br>in statement of<br>financial position<br>£000 |
|---|---|---|---|---|---|
| At 1 Jan 20X6 | (890) | (1,000 – 110) | — | | 890 |
| At 31 Dec 20X6 | 80 | (8% × 1,000) | 103.2 | (11.59% × 890) | 913.2 |
| At 31 Dec 20X7 | 80 | (8% × 1,000) | 105.8 | (11.59% × 913.2) | 939.2 |
| At 31 Dec 20X8 | 80 | (8% × 1,000) | 108.8 | (11.59% × 939) | 967.8 |
| At 31 Dec 20X9 | 1,080 | (1,000 + (8% × 1,000)) | 112.2 | (11.59% × 967.8) | — |
| Net cash flow | 430 | = Cost | 430 | | |

The chosen implicit rate of 11% is too low. We now choose a higher rate, say 12%:

$$\Sigma = \frac{80,000}{(1.12)^1} + \frac{80,000}{(1.12)^2} + \frac{80,000}{(1.12)^3} + \frac{1,080,000}{(1.12)^4} - 890,000 = 0$$

$$= 71,429 + 63,776 + 56,942 + 686,360 - 890,000 = -11,493$$

This rate is too high, resulting in a negative net present value. Interpolation will enable us to arrive at an implicit rate:

$$11\% + \left[ \frac{16,926}{16,926 + 11,493} \times (12\% - 11\%) \right] = 11\% \ + 0.59\% \ = 11.59\%$$

This is a trial and error method of determining the implicit interest rate. In this example the choice of rates, 11% and 12%, constituted a change of only 1%. It would be possible to choose, say, 11% and then 14%, generating a 3% gap within which to interpolate. This wider margin would result in a less accurate implicit rate and an aggregate interest charge at variance with the desired £430,000 of column (ii). The aim is to choose interest rates as close as possible to either side of the monetary zero, so that the exact implicit rate may be computed.

The object is to determine an NPV of zero monetary units, i.e. to identify the discount rate that will enable the aggregate future discounted net flows to equate to the initial net proceeds from the debt instrument. In the above illustration, a discount (interest) rate of 11.59% enables £430,000 to be charged to profit or loss after allowing for payment of all interest, costs and repayment of the face value of the instrument.

*The finance charge per annum and the successive year-end carrying amounts*
The charge to the statement of comprehensive income and the carrying values in the statement of financial position are shown in Figure 14.1.

### 14.3.5 Offsetting financial instruments[6]

Financial assets and liabilities can only be offset and presented net if the following conditions are met:

(a) the enterprise currently has a legally enforceable right to set off the recognised amounts; and

(b) the enterprise intends either to settle on a net basis, or to realise the asset and settle the liability simultaneously.

IAS 32 emphasises the importance of the intention to settle on a net basis as well as the legal right to do so. Offsetting should only occur when the cash flows and therefore the risks associated with the financial asset and liability are offset and therefore to present them net in the statement of financial position shows a true and fair view. An example of a situation where offsetting may be appropriate would be if a company has a receivable and a payable to the same counterparty, has a legal right to offset the two, and does offset the amounts in practice when settling the cash flows.

Situations where offsetting might be considered but which would not normally be appropriate are where:

● several different financial instruments are used to emulate the features of a single financial instrument;

● financial assets and financial liabilities arise from financial instruments having the same primary risk exposure but involve different counterparties;

● financial or other assets are pledged as collateral for non-recourse financial liabilities;

- financial assets are set aside in trust by a debtor for the purpose of discharging an obligation without those assets having been accepted by the creditor in settlement of the obligation;

- obligations incurred as a result of events giving rise to losses are expected to be recovered from a third party by virtue of a claim made under an insurance policy.

## 14.4 IFRS 9 *Financial Instruments*

IFRS 9 was issued in full in July 2014, and is effective from accounting periods beginning on or after 1 January 2018. The standard is a replacement of IAS 39: *Financial Instruments: Recognition and Measurement.* The issue of a new standard on financial instruments was accelerated by the financial crisis of 2008, where the existing requirements of IAS 39 came under intense scrutiny.

### 14.4.1 Scope of the standard

IFRS 9 should be applied by all enterprises to all financial instruments except those excluded from the scope of IAS 32 (see Section 14.3.1) and the following additional instruments:

- rights and obligations under leases to which IAS 17 applies (except for embedded derivatives and the impairment and derecognition requirements);

- equity instruments of the reporting entity including options, warrants and other financial instruments that are classified as shareholders' equity;

- contracts between an acquirer and a vendor in a business combination to buy or sell or acquire at a future date. The term of the forward contract should not exceed a reasonable period normally necessary to obtain any required approvals and to complete the transaction;

- rights to payments to reimburse the entity for expenditure it is required to make to settle a liability under IAS 37;

- rights and obligations within the scope of IFRS 15 *Revenue from Contracts with Customers* that are financial instruments.

### 14.4.2 Recognition of financial instruments

#### Initial recognition

A financial asset or liability should be recognised when an entity becomes party to the contractual provisions of the instrument. This means that derivative instruments must be recognised if a contractual right or obligation exists.

#### Derecognition

Derecognition of financial assets is a complex area which has extensive rules in IFRS 9. After much debate it was decided that the IAS 39 derecognition position should be retained in IFRS 9. The derecognition rules for assets are still contentious as they can result in the same instrument being recognised in different ways in the financial statements depending on whether financial assets were previously owned. For example if an entity sold receivables, but offered the buyer a guarantee on all defaults the receivables would not be derecognised as the significant risks have not been transferred. However, if an entity simply entered into a credit guarantee without previously owning the receivables, the receivables guaranteed would not be recognised. The actual contract the entity was party to after the disposal of receivables could be identical.

**Figure 14.2 Derecognition of financial assets**

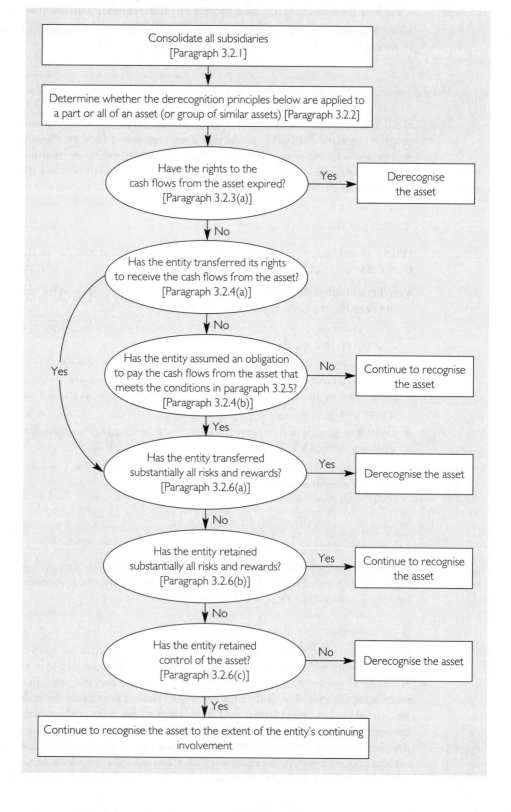

The main principle is that financial assets should only be derecognised when the entity transfers the risks and rewards that make up the asset. This could be because the benefits are realised, the rights expire or the enterprise surrenders the benefits. The flowchart in Figure 14.2 summarises the approach in the standard.

If it is not clear whether the risks and rewards have been transferred, the entity considers whether control has passed. If control has passed the entity should derecognise the asset, whereas if control is retained the asset is recognised to the extent of the entity's continuing involvement in the asset.

On derecognition any gain or loss should be recorded in profit or loss. Also any gains or losses previously recognised in reserves relating to the asset should be transferred to the profit or loss on sale.

Financial liabilities should only be derecognised when the obligation specified in the contract is discharged, is cancelled or expires.

The requirements for the derecognition of liabilities mean that it is not possible to write off liabilities unless they are discharged, cancelled or expired. In some industries this will lead to a change in business practice. For example, banks are not allowed to remove dormant accounts from their statements of financial position unless the liability has been legally extinguished.

### 14.4.3 Classification and measurement of financial instruments

Financial assets and liabilities are recognised when the entity becomes party to the contractual provisions of the instrument.

The basic initial measurement requirement for financial assets and liabilities is at fair value plus or minus transaction costs that are directly attributable to the acquisition or issue of the financial asset or financial liability. The exceptions to this are:

(i)  Trade receivables which do not have a significant financing component are measured at transaction cost; and

(ii)  For financial assets and liabilities classified as fair value through profit and loss transaction costs are expensed directly.

The subsequent measurement of financial assets and financial liabilities under IFRS 9 depends on how they are classified. There are three possible classifications depending on the characteristics of the instruments. The standard has separate guidance for the classification and subsequent measurement of financial assets and financial liabilities.

#### Financial asset classification

Financial assets classification requirements are summarised in Figure 14.3.

An entity should classify financial assets and subsequently measure financial assets at amortised cost, fair value through other comprehensive income, or fair value through profit and loss. This classification is a different approach to that previously required by IAS 39. IAS 39 had four classifications of assets, held to maturity, loans and receivables, fair value through profit and loss and available for sale. The measurement of financial assets depended on the classification and IAS39 gave some choices which are not available under IFRS 9.

Under IFRS 9 a financial asset is measured at amortised cost if both of the following conditions are met:

(a)  the financial asset is held within a business model whose objective is to hold financial assets in order to collect contractual cash flows; and

(b) the contractual terms of the financial asset give rise on specified dates to cash flows that are solely payments of principal and interest on the principal amount outstanding.

A financial asset is measured at fair value through other comprehensive income if both of the following conditions are met:

(a) the financial asset is held within a business model whose objective is achieved by both collecting contractual cash flows and selling financial assets; and

(b) the contractual terms of the financial asset give rise on specified dates to cash flows that are solely payments of principal and interest on the principal amount outstanding.

If the financial asset does not meet the conditions for recognition at amortised cost or fair value through other comprehensive income it is recognised at fair value through profit and loss. However, there are some irrevocable options that an entity can make for the measurement of financial assets:

(i) Investments in equity instruments that would otherwise be classified as fair value through profit and loss can be classified as fair value through other comprehensive income; and

(ii) Despite meeting the condition for amortised cost or fair value through other comprehensive income, an entity can choose to designate a financial asset as fair value through profit and loss if doing so eliminates or significantly reduces an 'accounting mismatch'. An accounting mismatch arises where related financial assets and liabilities are measured on different bases.

### Financial liability classification

Financial liabilities are classified and measured at amortised cost, except for:

(a) Financial liabilities at fair value through profit and loss. This includes all derivatives that are liabilities;

(b) Financial liabilities that arise when a transfer of a financial asset does not result in derecognition;

(c) Financial guarantee contracts;

(d) Commitments to provide a below-market rate interest rate loan;

(e) Contingent consideration recognised by an acquirer in a business combination to which IFRS 3 applies. After acquisition the contingent consideration is measured at fair value with changes recognised in profit and loss.

For (c) and (d) above the instrument is measured subsequent to initial recognition at the higher of:

(i) The amount of the loss allowance calculated in accordance with the impairment requirements; or

(ii) The amount initially recognised less, where appropriate, the cumulative amount of income recognised under IFRS 15.

#### Liabilities designated as at fair value through profit or loss

Prior to IFRS 9 being issued there was concern about the way that gains and losses on liabilities measured at fair value through profit and loss were presented. The fair value of a liability changes primarily due to changes in interest rates and changes in the credit position of the issuing entity. Therefore if an entity's credit risk increased (i.e. its credit rating reduced), the fair value of liabilities would fall. This is because the entity would be perceived as less able to pay its debts, meaning the debts would have a lower market value. If the entity was measuring financial liabilities at fair value through profit and loss this would result in a gain being recognised in income. There was concern that generating profits as a result of an entity's own increases in credit risk appeared counter-intuitive and potentially misleading.

As a result IFRS 9 introduced a new requirement. If a liability is designated as fair value through profit or loss the gains and losses must be presented as follows:

(a) The amount of the change in fair value that is attributable to changes in the credit risk of that liability are presented in other comprehensive income; and

(b) The remaining amount of the change in the fair value of the liability shall be presented in profit and loss.

The full gain or loss from changes in fair value is presented in the income statement if following the above treatment results in an accounting mismatch.

### Illustration of the impact of changes in fair value

Henry plc has designated financial liabilities to be measured at fair value through profit and loss. The financial liabilities are worth 100 at the start of the period and increase in fair value to 120 over the period. Over the period the credit position of Henry plc has improved which has resulted in the financial liabilities increasing in value by 5.

Henry plc would recognise the following journal to reflect the change in fair value of financial liabilities:

| | | | |
|---|---|---|---|
| Dr | Other comprehensive income | 5 | |
| Dr | Income statement | 15 | |
| Cr | Financial liabilities | | 20 |

### Amortised cost – the effective yield calculation

Amortised cost is calculated using the effective interest method on assets and liabilities.

The effective interest method is defined in IFRS 9 as:

the method that is used in the calculation of the amortised cost of a financial asset or a financial liability and in the allocation of the interest revenue or interest expense in the profit or loss over the relevant period.

The effective interest rate used in the application of the effective yield is defined as:

The rate that exactly discounts estimated future cash payments or receipts through the expected life of the financial asset or financial liability to the gross carrying amount of a financial asset or to the amortised cost of a financial liability. When calculating the effective interest rate, an entity shall estimate the expected cash flows by considering all the contractual terms of the financial instrument (for example, prepayment, extension, call and similar options) but shall not consider the expected credit losses. The calculation includes all fees and points paid or received between parties to the contract that are an integral part of the effective interest rate, transaction costs, and all other premiums or discounts. There is a presumption that the cash flows and the expected life of a group of similar financial instruments can be estimated reliably. However, in those rare cases when it is not possible to reliably estimate the cash flows or the expected life of a financial instrument (or group of financial instruments), the entity shall use the contractual cash flows over the full contractual term of the financial instrument (or group of financial instruments).

The above definitions appear complex; however, the key element is that it requires the interest rate applied to financial assets and liabilities to be constant based on the expected cash flows on the instruments.

Please note that the definition of effective yield excludes expected credit losses. Expected credit losses are taken into account in impairment calculations which are discussed in Section 14.4.5

### Illustration of the effective yield method

George plc lends £10,000 to a customer for fixed interest based on the customer paying 5% interest per annum (annually in arrears) for two years, and then 6% fixed for the remaining three years with the full £10,000 repayable at the end of the five-year term.

The tables below show the interest income over the loan period assuming:

- it is not expected that the customer will repay early (effective rate is 5.55% per annum derived from an internal rate of return calculation); and

- it is expected the customer will repay at the end of year 3 but there are no repayment penalties (effective rate is 5.3% per annum derived from an internal rate of return calculation).

The loan balance will alter as follows:

*No early repayment*

| Period | B/F | Interest income (5.55%) | Cash received | C/F |
|---|---|---|---|---|
| Year 1 | 10,000 | 555 | (500) | 10,055 |
| Year 2 | 10,055 | 558 | (500) | 10,113 |
| Year 3 | 10,113 | 561 | (600) | 10,074 |
| Year 4 | 10,074 | 559 | (600) | 10,033 |
| Year 5 | 10,033 | 557 | (10,600) | (10)* |

\* Difference due to rounding

*Early repayment*

| Period | B/F | Interest income (5.3%) | Cash received | C/F |
|---|---|---|---|---|
| Year 1 | 10,000 | 530 | (500) | 10,030 |
| Year 2 | 10,030 | 532 | (500) | 10,062 |
| Year 3 | 10,062 | 533 | (10,600) | (5)* |

\* Difference due to rounding

## 14.4.4 Embedded derivatives

Sometimes an entity will enter into a contract that includes both a derivative and a host contract, with the effect that some of the cash flows of the combined contract vary in a similar way to a stand-alone derivative.

For example, Cheng Ltd issued a £1m bond 20X1 with an interest rate of 5% redeemable in 20X6. This is referred to as the 'host contract'. If there is a condition which means that the 5% rate is related to a benchmark such as movements in the Consumer Price Index, then this is referred to as an 'embedded derivative'.

Other examples of embedded derivatives that affect the host contract cash flows include:

- contracts for the supply of commodities such as the supply of coal to coal-fired power stations where the price is related to a commodity index;

- contracts where the price of the commodity is fixed payment in a foreign currency such as the supply to the UK from South Africa where the payment is denominated in South African rand;

- leases where the rental might be related to a benchmark such as the lessee's turnover; and

- put options on an equity instrument held by an enterprise, or an equity conversion feature embedded in a debt instrument.

If the host contract for an embedded derivative is a financial asset the embedded derivative is not separated out and the entire host contract, including the embedded derivative, follows the classification and measurement basis previously discussed.

Where the host contract is not a financial asset, an embedded instrument should be separated from the host contract and accounted for as a derivative under IFRS 9 if all of the following conditions are met:

(a) the economic characteristics and risks of the embedded derivative are not closely related to the economic characteristics and risks of the host contract;

(b) a separate instrument with the same terms as the embedded derivative would meet the definition of a derivative; and

(c) the hybrid contract is not measured at fair value with changes in fair value reported in profit or loss.

If an entity is required to separate the embedded derivative from its host contract but is unable to measure the embedded derivative separately, the entire hybrid instrument should be treated as a financial instrument held at fair value through profit or loss and as a result changes in fair value should be reported through profit or loss.

### 14.4.5 Impairment of financial assets

IFRS 9 was only finally issued in full in July 2014 although the first elements of the standard were issued in 2009. The area of the standard that presented most problems for the IASB was the rules around impairment of financial assets.

Under IAS 39, the previous standard, impairment followed an 'incurred loss' model. This required that impairments were only recognised when events occurred, after the initial recognition of the financial asset, that indicated the full cash flows would not be collected, i.e. there needed to be a 'trigger event'. This was controversial as it meant that financial institutions could not provide for their expected losses over the life of loans until specific trigger events had occurred. In the financial crisis this led to significant volatility in the results of financial institutions, which, it was claimed would not have been as significant if expected losses had been provided for.

In IFRS 9 the impairment requirements follow an 'expected loss' model. This requires that impairments are considered on financial assets from the inception of the instrument and no particular trigger event is necessary.

#### Loss allowance for expected credit losses

An entity must recognise a loss allowance for expected credit losses on any of the following assets:

(i) Financial assets measured at amortised cost

(ii) Financial assets measured at fair value with gains and losses in other comprehensive income

(iii) Lease receivables

(iv) Contracts assets or a loan commitment

(v) Certain financial guarantee contracts

The general requirement is that the loss allowance is initially recognised at the amount of 12-month expected credit losses. The 12-month expected credit losses are the proportion of lifetime expected credit losses that arise from default events on a financial instrument that are possible within 12 months after the reporting date.

Expected losses continue to be measured on the basis of 12-month expected credit losses unless there is a significant deterioration in the credit quality of the receivable. If this occurs the expected loss allowance is based on the life-time expected credit losses. If subsequent to a deterioration in credit position, there is an improvement in the credit position of a company, it reverts back to basing the provision on the 12-month position.

There is a simplification in the standard for trade receivables, contract assets and lease receivables. For these assets the initial measurement can be at transaction cost and a loss allowance is always recognised for the lifetime expected credit losses. This effectively means that trade receivables always have a loss allowance for the full lifetime expected losses.

If a loss allowance is recognised on an asset measured at fair value with gains and losses in other comprehensive income, the impairment is recognised against profit or loss, but the loss allowance is recognised in other comprehensive income. As a result the value of the asset is not reduced in the statement of financial position

### Measurement of expected credit losses

The expected credit losses are measured in a way that reflects the following:

(a)  An unbiased and probability-weighted amount that is determined by evaluating a range of possible outcomes;

(b)  the time value of money; and

(c)  reasonable and supportable information that is available without undue cost or effort at the reporting date about past events, current conditions and forecasts of future economic conditions.

### Illustration of providing for expected credit losses

Manan Ltd has a portfolio of receivables recognised at amortised cost. On the first reporting date Manan estimated the 12-month expected credit losses to be 10,000. Following a significant deterioration in credit quality at the end of the second year Manan reassessed the lifetime expected credit losses to be 20,000. The actual credit loss on the portfolio was 15,000.

The accounting entries for the expected loss provision are as follows:

*Year 1*

| | | | |
|---|---|---|---|
| Dr | Profit and loss | 10,000 | |
| Cr | Expected loss allowance | | 10,000 |

*Year 2*

| | | | |
|---|---|---|---|
| Dr | Profit and loss (20,000 − 10,000) | 10,000 | |
| Cr | Expected loss allowance | | 10,000 |

*Year 3*

| | | | |
|---|---|---|---|
| Dr | Expected loss allowance | 5,000 | |
| Cr | Profit and loss | | 5,000 |

The expected loss allowance is presented offset against the value of the receivables.

### 14.4.6 Hedging

If a financial instrument has been taken out to act as a hedge, and a number of criteria within IFRS 9 are met, hedge accounting rules can be followed. The purpose of hedge accounting is to reflect the entity's risk management objectives, which otherwise may not be reflected. For example a company that engages in overseas trade may enter into a forward currency contract to buy or sell foreign currency at a fixed rate. The risk management purpose of the forward contract is to reduce foreign exchange risk on the underlying overseas trade. However, following the normal measurement rules within IFRS 9 would result in that position not being reflected:

(i) The overseas transaction would only be recognised when it occurred, and it would be measured at spot rate (as opposed to the fixed rate agreed in the forward contract); and

(ii) Gains and losses would be reflected on the forward contract before the transaction occurred as the contract would need to be measured at fair value with gains and losses in profit and loss.

In order to hedge account it is important that the risk management objective of the business is to hedge. Derivatives can be entered into for speculative purposes, and if this is the case, recognition at fair value with gains and losses in profit and loss appears appropriate. There are therefore conditions in IFRS 9 to be met to allow hedge accounting.

There are three types of hedging relationship in IFRS 9: fair value hedge, cash flow hedge and net investment hedge.

#### Fair value hedge

A fair value hedge arises when a hedging instrument is taken out as a hedge of the exposure to changes in fair value of a recognised asset or liability or an unrecognised firm commitment that will affect reported net income.

The hedge accounting requirements change the way that gains and losses on a hedged item are recognised. Any gain or loss arising on remeasuring the hedging instrument *and* the hedged item should be recognised in profit or loss in the period. Without hedge accounting the gain or loss on the hedged item would not typically be recognised in profit or loss.

An example of a fair value hedge could be protecting against interest rate changes on a fixed rate investment with a matching fixed to floating interest rate swap. This is a fair value hedge because if the interest rate changes, the fair value of the investment will be affected. The fair value change in the swap offsets this. The accounting for this arrangement as a fair value hedge would be:

(i) the interest rate swap would be recognised at fair value with gains or losses in the income statement; and

(ii) the investment would be recognised at fair value with respect to interest rate movements, and the gain or loss will be recognised in the income statement.

The gains and losses on the swap and the investment would offset in the income statement.

#### Cash flow hedge

A cash flow hedge arises when a financial instrument, typically a derivative, is taken out as a hedge of the exposure to variability in cash flows that is attributable to a particular risk associated with the recognised asset or liability, and that will affect reported net income.

A hedge of foreign exchange risk on a firm commitment may be a cash flow or a fair value hedge.

Cash flow hedge accounting changes the way that gains and losses on the hedging instrument are recognised. Assuming that the hedging instrument is a derivative the treatment without hedge accounting is to recognise the derivative as fair value through profit and loss. With hedge accounting the gain or loss on the hedging instrument is recognised directly in other comprehensive income, and reflected on the balance sheet in a separate hedge reserve. Any gains or losses recognised in other comprehensive income is included in profit or loss in the period that the hedged item affects profit or loss. If the instrument being hedged results in the recognition of a non-financial asset or liability, the gain or loss on the hedging instrument can be recognised as part of the cost of the hedged item.

### Cash flow hedge illustrated

Harvey plc directors agreed at their July 20X6 meeting to acquire additional specialist computer equipment in September 20X7 at an estimated cost of $500,000.

The company entered into a forward contract in July 20X6 to purchase $500,000 in September 20X7 and pay £260,000. At the year-end in December 20X6 the $500,000 has appreciated and has a sterling value of £276,000.

At the year-end the increase of £16,000 will be debited to a Forward Contract asset and credited to a hedge reserve.

In September 20X7 when the equipment is purchased the £16,000 will be deducted in its entirety from the Equipment carrying amount or transferred annually as a reduction of the annual depreciation charge.

### Net investment hedge

A net investment hedge arises when a hedging instrument, which commonly in this case will be a loan as opposed to a derivative, is entered into to hedge an investment in a foreign entity. The gain or loss on the hedging instrument is recognised directly in other comprehensive income to match against the gain or loss on the hedged investment. Without hedge accounting, the gain or loss on the hedging instrument would be recognised in profit or loss.

A common situation for net investment hedging arises when a foreign equity investment is financed by a foreign loan. As the entity has a foreign asset and liability when exchange rates change one makes a gain and one makes a loss. The gain or loss on the investment is recognised in other comprehensive income under IAS 21 *The Effects of Changes in Foreign Exchange Rates,* and with hedging the opposite gain or loss on the loan is also recognised in other comprehensive income.

### Conditions for hedge accounting

In order to be able to apply the hedge accounting techniques detailed above, an entity must meet a number of conditions. These conditions are designed to ensure that only genuine hedging instruments can be hedge accounted, and that the hedged positions are clearly identified and documented. Under IAS 39, the predecessor standard to IFRS 9, there was criticism that strict hedge criteria were too onerous to comply with in practice. IFRS 9 criteria detailed below are expected to make it easier to meet the conditions where hedging is part of the risk management objectives of the organisation.

The conditions are:

● the hedging relationship consists only of eligible hedging instruments and eligible hedged items;

- at the inception of the hedging relationship there is formal designation and documentation of the hedging relationship and the entity's risk management objective and strategy for undertaking the hedge. That documentation shall include identification of the hedging instrument, the hedged item, the nature of the risk being hedged and how the entity will assess whether the hedging relationship meets the hedge effectiveness requirements (including its analysis of the sources of hedge ineffectiveness and how it determines the hedge ratio);
- the hedging relationship meets all of the following hedge effectiveness requirements:
  - there is an economic relationship between the hedged item and the hedging instrument;
  - the effect of credit risk does not dominate the value changes that result from that economic relationship; and
  - the hedge ratio of the hedging relationship is the same as that resulting from the quantity of the hedged item that the entity actually hedges and the quantity of the hedging instrument that the entity actually uses to hedge that quantity of hedged item. However, that designation shall not reflect an imbalance between the weightings of the hedged item and the hedging instrument that would create hedge ineffectiveness (irrespective of whether recognised or not) that could result in an accounting outcome that would be inconsistent with the purpose of hedge accounting.

In order to comply with the conditions it is necessary to businesses to set up the appropriate processes for documenting and monitoring their hedge relationships. One aspect of the above conditions that did not exist in IAS 39 is the 'hedge ratio'. The hedge ratio is defined as 'the relationship between the quantity of the hedging instrument and the quantity of the hedged item in terms of their relative weighting'. The overall purpose of this hedge ratio is to ensure that actual hedging matches the intended risk management objectives for hedging.

If a hedge fails to meet the criteria hedge accounting may not be allowed, or a re-designation of the relationships may be necessary.

## 14.5 IFRS 7 *Financial Instruments: Disclosure*[7]

### 14.5.1 Introduction

This standard came out of the ongoing project of improvements to the accounting and disclosure requirements relating to financial instruments.

Prior to the introduction of IFRS 7 disclosures in respect of financial instruments were governed by two standards:

1 IAS 30 *Disclosures in the Financial Statements of Banks and Similar Financial Institutions;* and

2 IAS 32 *Financial Instruments: Disclosure and Presentation.*

In drafting IFRS 7, the IASB:

- reviewed existing disclosures in the two standards, and removed duplicative disclosures;
- simplified the disclosure about concentrations of risk, credit risk, liquidity risk and market risk under IAS 32; and
- transferred disclosure requirements from IAS 32.

Since the original issue of the standard there have been multiple changes to refine and improve the disclosures in respect of financial instruments.

## 14.5.2 Main requirements

The standard applies to all entities, regardless of the nature and value of financial instruments held. However, the extent of the disclosures required will depend on the extent of the entity's use of financial instruments and its exposure to risk.

The standard requires disclosure of the following. These disclosure standards effectively provide the principles that underpin the financial instrument disclosure requirements:

- the significance of financial instruments for the entity's financial position and performance (many of these disclosures were previously in IAS 32); and

- the nature and extent of risks arising from financial instruments to which the entity is exposed during the period and at the end of the reporting period, and how the entity manages those risks.

In addition to the principles above there is extensive detailed guidance in the standard of the disclosures necessary. The disclosures are a mixture of both qualitative and quantitative disclosures. The qualitative disclosures describe management's objectives, policies and processes for managing those risks. The quantitative disclosures provide information about the extent to which the entity is exposed to risk, based on the information provided internally to the entity's key management personnel.

For the disclosure of the significance of financial instruments for the entity's financial position and performance, a key aspect will be to clearly link the statement of financial position and the statement of comprehensive income to the classifications in IAS 39 or IFRS 9. The detailed requirements from IFRS 7 in this respect are as follows:

8    The carrying amounts of each of the following categories, as defined in IAS 39, shall be disclosed either on the face of the statement of financial position or in the notes:

(a) financial assets at fair value through profit or loss, showing separately (i) those designated as such upon initial recognition and (ii) those classified as held for trading in accordance with IAS 39;

(b) held-to-maturity investments;

(c) loans and receivables;

(d) available-for-sale financial assets;

(e) financial liabilities at fair value through profit or loss, showing separately (i) those designated as such upon initial recognition and (ii) those classified as held for trading in accordance with IAS 39; and

(f) financial liabilities measured at amortised cost.

20   An entity shall disclose the following items of income, expense, gains or losses either on the face of the financial statements or in the notes:

(a) net gains or net losses on:

(i) financial assets or financial liabilities at fair value through profit or loss, showing separately those on financial assets or financial liabilities designated as such upon initial recognition, and those on financial assets or financial liabilities that are classified as held for trading in accordance with IAS 39;

(ii) available-for-sale financial assets, showing separately the amount of gain or loss recognised directly in equity during the period and the amount removed from equity and recognised in profit or loss for the period;

(iii) held-to-maturity investments;

(iv) loans and receivables; and

(v) financial liabilities measured at amortised cost;

(b) total interest income and total interest expense (calculated using the effective interest method) for financial assets or financial liabilities that are not at fair value through profit or loss;

(c) fee income and expense (other than amounts included in determining the effective interest rate) arising from:

(i) financial assets or financial liabilities that are not at fair value through profit or loss; and

(ii) trust and other fiduciary activities that result in the holding or investing of assets on behalf of individuals, trusts, retirement benefit plans, and other institutions;

(d) interest income on impaired financial assets accrued in accordance with paragraph AG93 of IAS 39; and

(e) the amount of any impairment loss for each class of financial asset.

The disclosures above, together with further detailed disclosures in the standard provide the explanation of the position and performance of financial instruments. The above requirements of the standard reference IAS 39. As a result of the issue of IFRS 9 there are consequential amendments to a number of standards, including IFRS 7. The amendments in IFRS 7 are to bring the standard's references and terminology into line with IFRS 9, they are not intended to change the fundamental principles on which IFRS 7 is based. For example in IFRS 9 there is an amendment to IFRS 7, paragraph 8 as follows:

8   The carrying amounts of each of the following categories, as specified in IFRS 9, shall be disclosed either in the statement of financial position or in the notes:

(a) financial assets measured at fair value through profit or loss, showing separately (i) those designated as such upon initial recognition or subsequently in accordance with paragraph 6.7.1 of IFRS 9 and (ii) those mandatorily measured at fair value through profit or loss in accordance with IFRS 9.

(b)–(d) [deleted]

(e) financial liabilities at fair value through profit or loss, showing separately (i) those designated as such upon initial recognition or subsequently in accordance with paragraph 6.7.1 of IFRS 9 and (ii) those that meet the definition of held for trading in IFRS 9.

(f) financial assets measured at amortised cost.

(g) financial liabilities measured at amortised cost.

(h) financial assets measured at fair value through other comprehensive income, showing separately (i) financial assets that are measured at fair value through other comprehensive income in accordance with paragraph 4.1.2A of IFRS 9; and (ii) investments in equity instruments designated as such upon initial recognition in accordance with paragraph 5.7.5 of IFRS 9.

For the purposes of this text the references provided in IFRS 7 refer to IAS 39 as that is the standard references currently published. When IFRS 9 becomes mandatory in 2018,

IFRS 7 will be revised, and for those early adopters IFRS 9 already provides the necessary amendments.

IFRS 7 also requires disclosure of the risks that financial instruments give to entities. The requirement for qualitative disclosure about risk is as follows:

33  For each type of risk arising from financial instruments, an entity shall disclose:

    **(a)** the exposures to risk and how they arise;

    **(b)** its objectives, policies and processes for managing the risk and the methods used to measure the risk; and

    **(c)** any changes in (a) or (b) from the previous period.

The requirement for quantitative disclosure is as follows:

34  For each type of risk arising from financial instruments, an entity shall disclose:

    **(a)** summary quantitative data about its exposure to that risk at the end of the reporting period. This disclosure shall be based on the information provided internally to key management personnel of the entity (as defined in IAS 24 *Related Party Disclosures*), for example the entity's board of directors or chief executive officer.

    **(b)** the disclosures required by paragraphs 36–42, to the extent not provided in accordance with (a).

    **(c)** concentrations of risk if not apparent from the disclosures made in accordance with (a) and (b).

EXAMPLE • Extracts from the disclosures given by Findel plc in 2015 compliant with IFRS 7:

### FINANCIAL INSTRUMENTS

The group holds and uses financial instruments to finance its operations and to manage its interest rate and liquidity risks. The group primarily finances its operations using share capital and borrowings. The main risks arising from the group's financial instruments are credit, interest rate, foreign currency and liquidity risk. The board reviews and agrees the policies for managing each of these risks on an annual basis. A full description of the group's approach to managing these risks is set out on pages 19 and 20. The group does not engage in trading or speculative activities using derivative financial instruments. A Group offset arrangement exists for cash balances to take advantage of the most rewarding short-term investment opportunities.

### Capital risk management

The group manages its capital to ensure that the group will be able to continue as a going concern while maximising the return to stakeholders through the optimisation of the net debt and equity balance. The board of directors reviews the capital structure of the group regularly considering both the costs and risks associated with each class of capital. The capital structure of the group consists of:

|  | 2015 £000 | 2014 £000 |
|---|---|---|
| **Net debt** |  |  |
| Borrowings (note 15) | 245,021 | 231,223 |
| Cash at bank and in hand (note 17) | (38,470) | (24,270) |
|  | 206,551 | 206,953 |

## Equity

| | | |
|---|---:|---:|
| Share capital (note 24) | 126,442 | 125,942 |
| Capital reserves (note 25) | 93,857 | 93,857 |
| Translation reserve (note 26) | 760 | 505 |
| Hedging reserve (note 27) | (42) | – |
| Accumulated losses (note 28) | (137,807) | (108,656) |
| | 82,710 | 111,648 |
| Gearing (being net debt divided by equity above) | 2.50 | 1.85 |

### Externally imposed capital requirement

*Revolving credit facility*

The group is subject to three financial covenants based on debt based ratios (Interest Cover, Net Debt: EBITDA and Free Cash Flow). These covenants are tested quarterly against pre-agreed limits which change in accordance with the seasonal working capital requirements of the group's businesses.

*Securitisation facility*

The group is subject to a number of covenants in relation to the quality of receivables securitised, of which the principal measures are the collection ratio, the default ratio, the excess spread ratio and the dilution ratio. The covenants are tested monthly against pre-agreed targets, testing for compliance on a three-month rolling basis.

### Significant accounting policies

Details of the significant accounting policies and methods adopted, including the criteria for recognition, the basis of measurement and the basis on which income and expenses are recognised, in respect of each class of financial asset, financial liability and equity instrument are disclosed in note 1 to the financial statements.

### Financial risk management objectives

The group's financial risks include market risk (including currency risk and interest risk), credit risk, liquidity risk and cash flow interest rate risk. The group seeks to minimise the effects of these risks by using derivative financial instruments to manage its exposure. There was an interest rate cap in place at 27 March 2015 with a fair value of £nil. No derivative financial instruments were held at 28 March 2014. The use of financial derivatives is governed by the group's policies approved by the board of directors. The group does not enter into or trade financial instruments, including derivative financial instruments, for speculative purposes.

### Market risk

The group's activities expose it primarily to the financial risks of changes in foreign currency exchange rates and interest rates. The group enters into a variety of derivative financial instruments to manage its exposure to interest rate and foreign currency risk, including:

- forward foreign exchange contracts to hedge the exchange rate risk arising on the purchase of inventory principally in US dollars; and
- interest rate caps to mitigate the risk of rising interest rates.

### Foreign currency risk management

The group undertakes certain transactions denominated in foreign currencies. Hence, exposures to exchange rate fluctuations arise. Exchange rate exposures are managed utilising forward foreign exchange contracts.

### Foreign currency sensitivity analysis

A significant proportion of products sold through the group's Home Shopping and Educational Supplies divisions are procured through the group's Far East buying office. The currency of purchase for these goods is principally the US dollar, with a proportion being in Hong Kong dollars . . . details the group's sensitivity to a 10% increase and decrease in the Sterling against the relevant foreign currencies. 10% represents management's assessment of the reasonably possible change in foreign exchange rates.

### Interest rate risk management

The group is exposed to interest rate risk as the group borrows funds at floating interest rates. The risk is managed by the group by the use of interest rate cap contracts when considered necessary. There was an interest rate cap in place at 27 March 2015 with a fair value of £nil. Hedging activities are evaluated regularly to align with interest rate views and defined risk appetite; ensuring hedging strategies are applied, by either positioning the balance sheet or protecting interest expense through different interest rate cycles.

### Credit risk management

Credit risk refers to the risk that a counterparty will default on its contractual obligations resulting in financial loss to the group. The group's credit risk is primarily attributable to its trade receivables. The amounts presented in the balance sheet are net of allowances for doubtful receivables. An allowance for impairment is made when there is an identified loss event which, based on previous experience, is evidence of a reduction in the recoverability of the cash flows. A more detailed commentary of the group's exposure to credit risk within its trade receivables, and the procedures employed to manage this risk, is set out in note 16.

The group does not have any significant credit risk exposure to any single counterparty or any group of counterparties having similar characteristics. The group defines counterparties as having similar characteristics if they are connected entities. Concentration of credit did not exceed 5% of gross monetary assets at any time during the year. The credit risk on liquid funds and derivative financial instruments is limited because the counterparties are banks with high credit-ratings assigned by international credit-rating agencies.

The carrying amount of financial assets recorded in the financial statements, which is net of impairment losses, represents the directors' best estimate of the group's maximum exposure to credit risk without taking account of the value of any collateral obtained.

### Liquidity risk management

Ultimate responsibility for liquidity risk management rests with the board of directors, which has built an appropriate liquidity risk management framework for the management of the group's short-, medium- and long-term funding and liquidity management requirements. The group manages liquidity risk by maintaining adequate reserves, banking facilities and reserve borrowing facilities by continuously monitoring forecast and actual cash flows and matching the maturity profiles of financial assets and liabilities. Included in note 19 is a description of additional undrawn facilities that the group has at its disposal to further reduce liquidity risk.

[These are extracts from the disclosures; full disclosures including quantitative disclosures and fair value disclosures can be seen in Findel plc 2015 Annual Report.]

## Summary

This chapter has given some insight into the difficulties and complexities of accounting for financial instruments and the ongoing debate on this topic, highlighted by the financial crisis that began in 2008. The approach of the IASB is to adhere to the principles contained in the *Framework* but to also issue guidance that is robust enough to prevent manipulation and abuse. Whether the IASB has achieved this is open to debate.

The developments in IFRS 9 should, in theory at least, require companies to reflect their business intentions in the use of financial instruments more so than previously under IAS 39. This is seen in the classification and measurement requirements where entities classification is dependent on the business model, and also in hedging requirements where the risk management objectives of the organisation are key in determining whether hedge accounting should be applied.

In other areas, in particular impairment, there is concern that IFRS 9 could lead to more manipulation of results. The IASB resisted for many years the move to an expected loss model for impairment concerned that it could result in more earnings smoothing by financial institutions. Over time it will be interesting to see if the IFRS 9 requirements result in this.

As can be seen, there is much to applaud in the IFRS 9 requirements as a potential improvement over IAS 39, but it is unlikely that IFRS 9 will be the end of the debate on financial instruments. Even as this text is being written, the IASB is looking to how to address financial instruments held by insurance companies, where the requirements of IFRS 9 are proving difficult to apply.

In addition to giving an insight into the requirements of the standards, our aim has been that you should be able to calculate the debt/equity split on compound instruments, the finance cost on liability instruments, and classify and account for the different classifications of financial assets and liabilities.

## REVIEW QUESTIONS

1 Explain what is meant by the term 'split accounting' when applied to convertible debt or convertible preference shares and the rationale for splitting.

2 Discuss the implications for a business if a substance approach is used for the reporting of convertible loans.

3 Explain how a gain or loss on a forward contract is dealt with in the accounts if the contract is entered into before the period-end but does not close out until post year-end.

4 Explain how redeemable preference shares, perpetual debt, loans and equity investments are measured and presented in the financial statements.

5 The authors[8] contend that the use of current valuations can present an inaccurate view of a firm's true financial status. When assets are illiquid, current value represents only a guess. When assets participate in an economic 'bubble', current value is invariably unsustainable. Accounting standards, the authors conclude, should be flexible enough to fairly assess value in these circumstances. Discuss the alternatives that standard setters could permit in order to fairly assess values in an illiquid market.

6 Explain the difference between a cash flow hedge and a fair value hedge. Does the nature of the hedging instrument (e.g. forward contract, interest rate swap, option) influence the hedging model being used?

7 'Disclosure of the estimated fair values of financial instruments is better than adjusting the values in the financial statements with the resulting volatility that affects earnings and gearing ratios.' Discuss.

8 Companies were permitted in 2008 to reclassify financial instruments that were initially designated as at fair value through profit. Critically discuss the reasons for the standard setters changing the existing standard.

9 'If financial liabilities can be recognised at fair value all gains and losses arising should be reflected in profit or loss.' Discuss.

10 'The only true way for balance sheets to be meaningful to users would be for all financial assets and liabilities to be measured at fair value with gains and losses recognised in profit or loss.' Discuss.

## EXERCISES

### * Question 1

On 1 April year 1, a deep discount bond was issued by DDB AG. It had a face value of £2.5 million and covered a five-year term. The lenders were granted a discount of 5%. The coupon rate was 10% on the principal sum of £2.5 million, payable annually in arrears. The principal sum was repayable in cash on 31 March Year 5. Issuing costs amounted to £150,000.

**Required:**
**Compute the finance charge per annum and the carrying value of the loan to be reported in each year's profit or loss and statement of financial position respectively.**

### * Question 2

Fairclough plc borrowed €10 million from a bank on 1 January 2011. Fees of €100,000 were charged by the bank which were paid by Fairclough plc at inception of the loan. The terms of the loan are:

*Interest*
- Interest of 6% until 31 December 2013
- Interest dropping to 5% from 31 December 2013 to 31 December 2015

*Repayment schedule*

- Repayment of €5 million on 31 December 2013
- Repayment of €5 million on 31 December 2015

Interest is paid annually in arrears.

The effective yield on the loan is 6.07%.

**Required:**
(a) What is the total finance cost on the loan over the five-year period?
(b) What will be reflected as a liability in the financial statements for each 31 December year-end and what interest costs will be recognised in the statement of comprehensive income?

## * Question 3

Isabelle Limited borrows £100,000 from a bank on the following terms:

(i) arrangement fees of £2,000 are charged by the bank and deducted from the initial proceeds on the loan;

(ii) interest is payable at 5% for the first three years of the loan and then increases to 7% for the remaining two years of the loan;

(iii) the full balance of £100,000 is repaid at the end of year 5.

**Required:**
(a) What interest should be recognised in the statement of comprehensive income for each year of the loan?
(b) If Isabelle Limited repaid the loan after three years for £100,000, what gain or loss would be recognised in the statement of comprehensive income?

## * Question 4

On 1 January 2009 Henry Ltd issued a convertible debenture for €200 million carrying a coupon interest rate of 5%. The debenture is convertible at the option of the holders into 10 ordinary shares for each €100 of debenture stock on 31 December 2013. Henry Ltd considered borrowing the €200 million through a conventional debenture that repaid in cash; however, the interest rate that could be obtained was estimated at 7%, therefore Henry Ltd decided on the issue of the convertible.

**Required:**
Show how the convertible bond issue will be recognised on 1 January 2009 and determine the interest charges that are expected in the statement of comprehensive income over the life of the convertible bond.

## Question 5

On 1 October year 1, RPS plc issued one million £1 5% redeemable preference shares. The shares were issued at a discount of £50,000 and are due to be redeemed on 30 September Year 5. Dividends are paid on 30 September each year.

**Required:**
Show the accounting treatment of the preference shares throughout the lifespan of the instrument calculating the finance cost to be charged to profit or loss in each period.

## * Question 6

Milner Ltd issues a 6% cumulative preference share for €1 million that is repayable in cash at par 10 years after issue. The only condition on the dividends is that if the directors declare an ordinary dividend the preference dividend (and any arrears of preference dividend) must be paid first. Arrears of dividend do not need to be paid on redemption of the instrument.

**Required:**
**Explain how this preference share should be accounted for over its life.**

## Question 7

Creasy plc needs to raise €20 million and is considering two different instruments that could be issued:

(i)   A 7% debenture with a par value of €20 million, repayable at par in five years. Interest is paid annually in arrears.

(ii)   A 5% convertible debenture with a par value of €20 million, repayable at par in five years or convertible into 5 million €1 shares. Interest is paid annually in arrears.

**Required:**
**Comment on the effect on the statement of comprehensive income and the statement of financial position of issuing these different instruments.**

## * Question 8

On 1 October 20X1, Little Raven plc issued 50,000 debentures, with a par value of £100 each, to investors at £80 each. The debentures are redeemable at par on 30 September 20X6 and have a coupon rate of 6%, which was significantly below the market rate of interest for such debentures issued at par. In accounting for these debentures to date, Little Raven plc has simply accounted for the cash flows involved, namely:

● On issue: debenture 'liability' included in the statement of financial position at £4,000,000.

● Statements of comprehensive income: interest charged in years ended 30 September 20X2, 20X3 and 20X4 (published accounts) and 30 September 20X5 (draft accounts) – £300,000 each year (being 6% of £5,000,000).

The new finance director, who sees the likelihood that further similar debenture issues will be made, considers that the accounting policy adopted to date is not appropriate. He has asked you to suggest a more appropriate treatment.
Little Raven plc intends to acquire subsidiaries in 20X6.

Statements of comprehensive income for the years ended 30 September 20X4 and 20X5 are as follows:

|  | Y/e 30 Sept 20X5 (Draft) £000 | Y/e 30 Sept 20X4 (Actual) £000 |
| --- | --- | --- |
| Turnover | 6,700 | 6,300 |
| Cost of sales | (3,025) | (2,900) |
| Gross profit | 3,675 | 3,400 |
| Overheads | (600) | (550) |
| Interest payable – debenture | (300) | (300) |
| – others | (75) | (50) |
| Profit for the financial year | 2,700 | 2,500 |
| Retained earnings brought forward | 4,300 | 1,800 |
| Retained earnings carried forward | 7,000 | 4,300 |

Extracts from the statement of financial position are:

|  | At 30 Sept 20X5 (Draft) £000 | At 30 Sept 20X4 (Actual) £000 |
|---|---|---|
| Share capital | 2,250 | 2,250 |
| Share premium | 550 | 550 |
| Retained earnings | 7,000 | 4,300 |
|  | 9,800 | 7,100 |
| 6% debentures | 4,000 | 4,000 |
|  | 13,800 | 11,100 |

Required:

(a) Outline the considerations involved in deciding how to account for the issue, the interest cost and the carrying value in respect of debenture issues such as that made by Little Raven plc. Consider the alternative treatments in respect of the statement of comprehensive income and refer briefly to the appropriate statement of financial position disclosures for the debentures. Conclude in terms of the requirements of IAS 32 (on accounting for financial instruments) in this regard.

(b) Detail an alternative set of entries in the books of Little Raven plc for the issue of the debentures and subsequently; under this alternative the discount on the issue should be dealt with under the requirements of IAS 32. The constant rate of interest for the allocation of interest cost is given to you as 11.476%. Draw up a revised statement of comprehensive income for the year ended 30 September 20X5, together with comparatives, taking account of the alternative accounting treatment.

## * Question 9

George plc will need to adopt IFRS 9 from accounting periods beginning on or after 1 January 2018. George has three different instruments whose accounting George is concerned will change as a result of the adoption of the standard. The three instruments are:

1 An investment in 15% of the ordinary shares of Joshua Ltd, a private company.

2 An investment of €40,000 in 6% debentures redeemable on 30 June 2021. The debentures were acquired at their face value of €40,000 on 1 July 2016 and pay interest half-yearly in arrears on 31 December and 30 June each year. George intends to hold the debentures to collect the interest and principal payments.

3 An interest rate swap taken out to swap floating-rate interest on an outstanding loan to fixed-rate interest. Since taking out the swap the loan has been repaid; however, George plc decided to retain the swap as it was 'in the money' at 1 January 2016. The fair value of the swap was a €10,000 asset on 1 January 2016.

Required:
Explain how the above instruments should be presented and measured in George's financial statements under IFRS 9.

## Question 10

On 1 January 2009 Hazell plc borrows €5 million on terms with interest of 3% fixed for the period to 31 December 2009, going to variable rate thereafter (at inception the variable rate is 6%). The loan is repayable at Hazell plc's option between 31 December 2011 and 31 December 2013.

Initially Hazell plc estimates that the loan will be repaid on 31 December 2011; however, at 31 December 2010 Hazell plc revises this estimate and assumes the loan will only be repaid on 31 December 2013.

Assume that the variable rate remains at 6% throughout the period and that interest is paid annually in arrears.

Required:
(a) Determine the total expected finance costs and effective yield on the loan at 1 January 2009.
(b) Show the impact of the loan on the statement of comprehensive income and statement of financial position for periods ended 31 December 2009 and 31 December 2010.

## Question 11

Baudvin Ltd has an equity investment that cost €1 million on 1 January 2008. The investment is classified as an available-for-sale investment under IAS 39. The value of the investment at each period-end is:

| | |
|---|---|
| 31 December 2008 | €950,000 |
| 31 December 2009 | €1,030,000 |
| 31 December 2010 | €1,080,000 |

Required:
Show what should be reflected for the investment in Baudvin Ltd's financial statements for each period from 31 December 2008 to 2011. Explain how the treatment would differ under IFRS 9

## * Question 12

A company borrows on a floating-rate loan, but wishes to hedge against interest variations so swaps the interest for fixed rate. The swap should be perfectly effective and has zero fair value at inception. Interest rates increase and therefore the swap becomes a financial asset to the company at fair value of £5 million.

Required:
Describe the impact on the financial statements for the following situations:
(a) The swap is accounted for under IFRS 9, but is not designated as a hedge.
(b) The swap is accounted for under IFRS 9, and is designated as a hedge.

## Question 13

Charles plc is applying IAS 32 and IFRS 9 for the first time this year and is uncertain about the application of the standard. Charles plc's balance sheet is as follows:

| | £000 | Financial asset/liability | In scope IAS 32/ IFRS 9 | Category |
|---|---|---|---|---|
| **Non-current assets** | | | | |
| Goodwill | 2,000 | | | |
| Intangible | 3,000 | | | |
| Tangible | 6,000 | | | |
| Investments | | | | |
| Corporate bond | 1,500 | | | |
| Equity trade investments | 900 | | | |
| | 13,400 | | | |
| **Current assets** | | | | |
| Inventory | 800 | | | |
| Receivables | 700 | | | |
| Prepayments | 300 | | | |
| Forward contracts (note 1) | 250 | | | |
| Equity investments held for future sale | 1,200 | | | |
| | 3,250 | | | |

Current liabilities

| | |
|---|---|
| Trade creditors | (3,500) |
| Lease creditor | (800) |
| Income tax | (1,000) |
| Forward contracts (note 1) | (500) |
| | (5,800) |

Non-current liabilities

| | |
|---|---|
| Bank loan | (5,000) |
| Convertible debt | (1,800) |
| Deferred tax | (500) |
| Pension liability | (900) |
| | (8,200) |
| Net assets | 2,650 |

*Note*

The forward contracts have been revalued to fair value in the balance sheet. They do not qualify as hedging instruments.

Required:

Complete the above balance sheet and consider under IAS 39:

(a) Which items on the balance sheet are financial assets/liabilities?
(b) Are the balances within the scope of IAS 32 and IFRS 9?
(c) How they should be classified under IAS 32 and IFRS 9:

    FVP&L    Fair value through profit and loss
    AC    Amortised cost
    FVOCI    Fair value through other comprehensive income

Assume that the company includes items in 'fair value through profit and loss' only when required to do so, and its business model is to collect contractual cash flows from receivables.

* **Question 14**

Tan plc has the following assets originated on 1 January 2016:

(i) A loan receivable generated from lending £100,000 to a customer of the company. The loan carries interest at 7% per annum payable in arrears and is classified at amortised cost. The 12-month expected credit losses on the loan are 2% of the principal amount.

(ii) A loan receivable Tan plc acquired has classified as fair value with gains and losses in other comprehensive income. The investment is recognised at £150,000, but Tan plc expects 12-month expected credit losses to be 2% of the amount recognised.

By 31 December 2016 the 12-month expected credit losses have increased to 2½% but the credit position of the assets is not assumed to have significantly deteriorated.

Requirement

Show the journal entries for the creation of the loss allowance under IFRS 9 at 1 January 2016, and the movement in the loss allowance at 31 December 2016.

## Question 15

At the start of the year Cornish plc entered into a number of financial instruments and is considering how to classify these instruments under IFRS 9. The instruments are as follows:

(a) Investment in listed 3% government bonds for €2 million. Cornish acquired the bonds when they were issued at their nominal value of €2 million. By the year-end, 31 December 2010, interest rates had fallen and the bonds had a market value of €2,025,000.

(b) Investment in shares in Schaenzler plc, a listed company, for €1,300,000. At 31 December 2010 the investment had fallen in value and was estimated to be worth only €1,200,000.

(c) Cornish plc borrowed €5 million at floating rate in the year and to hedge the interest rate took out an interest rate swap (floating to fixed) on the loan. The swap cost nothing to enter into but by 31 December 2010 because interest rates had fallen it had a fair value (liability) of €50,000. Cornish plc does not use hedge accounting.

**Required:**
**Discuss how the investments could be classified and measured under IFRS 9.**

## Question 16

Procter Limited, a UK private company has the following financial assets and liabilities in the accounts:

(i) An equity investment in Milner plc, a UK listed company. Procter recognises the investment as an 'available for sale' investment under IAS 39 *Financial Instruments; Recognition and Measurement.*

(ii) An investment in government bonds that are classified as 'held to maturity'. The bonds only pay interest and principal and Procter Ltd expects to hold the bonds until maturity.

(iii) A financial liability that Procter Ltd unusually measures at fair value through profit and loss. The liability is measured at fair value because Procter has a documented management policy to manage the liability at fair value.

**Required:**
**Discuss how the measurement of the above instruments may change under IFRS 9** *Financial Instruments.*

## Question 17

The approach in IAS 39 to the impairment of financial assets was flawed because it did not allow financial institutions to recognise the true losses they expected on loans at the time they had made the loans. How does the final version of IFRS 9 address this?

**Discuss.**

## Notes

1 IAS 32 *Financial Instruments: Disclosure and Presentation*, IASC, revised 1998.
2 IAS 32 *Financial Instruments: Presentation*, IASC, 2005, para. 4.
3 Ibid., para. 11.
4 Ibid., para. 16.
5 Ibid., para. 28.
6 Ibid., para. 42.
7 IFRS 7 *Financial Instruments: Disclosure*, IASB, 2005.
8 S. Fearnley and S. Sunder, 'Bring back prudence', *Accountancy*, vol. 140 (1370), 2007, pp. 76–77.

# CHAPTER 15

# Employee benefits

## 15.1 Introduction

In this chapter we consider the application of IAS 19 *Employee Benefits*.[1] IAS 19 is concerned with the determination of the cost of retirement benefits in the financial statements of **employers** having retirement benefit plans (sometimes referred to as 'pension schemes', 'superannuation schemes' or 'retirement benefit schemes'). The requirements of IFRS 2 *Share-based Payment* will also be considered here. Even though IFRS 2 covers share-based payments for almost any good or service a company can receive, in practice it is employee service that is most commonly rewarded with share-based payments. We also consider the disclosure requirements of IAS 26 *Accounting and Reporting by Retirement Benefit Plans*.[2]

### Objectives

By the end of this chapter, you should be able to:

● critically comment on the approaches to pension accounting used under international accounting standards;
● understand the nature of different types of pension plan and account for the different types of pension plan that companies may have;
● explain the accounting treatment for other long-term and short-term employee benefit costs;
● understand and account for share-based payments that are made by companies to their employees;
● outline the required approach of pension schemes to presenting their financial position and performance.

## 15.2 Greater employee interest in pensions

The percentages of pensioners and public pension expenditure are increasing.

|  | % of population over 60 | | Public pensions as % of GDP |
| --- | --- | --- | --- |
|  | *2000* | *2040* | *2040* |
|  | *%* | *% (projected)* | *% (projected)* |
| Germany | 24 | 33 | 18 |
| Italy | 24 | 37 | 21 |
| Japan | 23 | 34 | 15 |
| UK | 21 | 30 | 5 |
| US | 17 | 29 | 7 |

This has led to gloomy projections that countries could even be bankrupted by the increasing demand for state pensions. In an attempt to avert what governments see as a national disaster, there have been increasing efforts to encourage private funding of pensions.

As people become more and more aware of the possible failure of governments to provide adequate basic state pensions, they recognise the advisability of making their own provision for their old age. This has raised their expectation that their employers should offer a pension scheme and other post-retirement benefits. These have increased, particularly in Ireland, the UK and the USA, and what used to be a 'fringe benefit' for only certain categories of staff has been broadened across the workforce. This growth in private pension schemes has been encouraged by various governments with favourable tax treatment of both employers' and employees' contributions to pension schemes, and requirements for companies to contribute to pension funds of employees. In the UK, for example, the government now requires employers to make contributions into private pension plans for employees through a process of auto-enrolment.

## 15.3 Financial reporting implications

The provision of pensions for employees as part of an overall remuneration package has led to the related costs being a material part of the accounts. The very nature of such arrangements means that the commitment is a long-term one that may well involve estimates. The way the related costs are allocated between accounting periods and are reported in the financial statements needs careful consideration to ensure that a fair view of the position is shown.

Over time there has been a shift of view on the way that pension costs should be accounted for, and the principle on which the accounting is based. The first accounting standards on pensions (for example IAS 19 prior to its revision in 1998) required that pension costs should be matched against the period of the employee's service so as to create an even charge for pensions against profit. However, this approach could result in the statement of financial position being misleading. The more recent approach is to make the statement of financial position more sensible, but perhaps accept greater variation in the pension cost in the statement of comprehensive income. The new view is the one endorsed by the current IAS 19 (issued in June 2011) and was the method used in the previous versions of IAS 19 issued since 1998.

Before examining the detail of how IAS 19 (2011) requires pensions and other long-term benefits to be accounted for, we need to consider the types of pension scheme that are commonly used.

## 15.4 Types of scheme

### 15.4.1 *Ex gratia* arrangements

These are not schemes at all but are circumstances where an employer agrees to grant a pension to be paid for out of the resources of the firm. Consequently these are arrangements where pensions have not been funded but decisions are made on an *ad hoc* or case-by-case basis, sometimes arising out of custom or practice. No contractual obligation to grant or pay a pension exists, although a constructive obligation may exist which would need to be provided for in accordance with IAS 37 *Provisions, Contingent Liabilities and Contingent Assets*.

## 15.4.2 Defined contribution schemes

These are schemes in which the employer undertakes to make certain contributions each year, usually a stated percentage of salary. These contributions are usually supplemented by contributions from the employee. The money is then invested and, on retirement, the employee gains the pension benefits that can be purchased from the resulting funds.

Such schemes have uncertain future benefits but fixed, predetermined costs. In recent years, due to the fixed cost to the company and the resulting low risk to the employer for providing a pension, these schemes have become increasingly popular, and for new pension schemes opened by employers, are now, almost always, the scheme of choice. They are also popular with employees who regularly change employers, since the funds accrued within the schemes are relatively easy to transfer.

The contributions may be paid into a wide variety of plans, e.g. government plans to ensure state pensions are supplemented (these may be optional or compulsory), or schemes operated by insurance companies.

The following is an extract from the 2015 Annual Report of Sainsburys plc:

**Pensions**
The Group operates various defined benefit and defined contribution pension schemes for its employees. A defined benefit scheme is a pension plan that defines an amount of pension benefit that an employee will receive on retirement. A defined contribution scheme is a pension plan under which the Group pays fixed contributions into a separate entity.

Payments to defined contribution pension schemes are charged as an expense as they fall due. Any contributions unpaid at the balance sheet date are included as an accrual as at that date. The Group has no further payment obligations once the contributions have been paid.

## 15.4.3 Defined benefit schemes

Under these schemes the employees will, on retirement, receive a pension based on the length of service and salary, usually final salary or an average of the last few (usually three) years' salary.

These schemes have become less popular when new schemes are formed because the cost to employers is uncertain and more risky, and there are greater regulatory requirements including, for example, a need to have pension trustees who can have considerable power over the level of contribution required. Three key factors contributing to the increased costs to employers are:

- the increased life expectancy for retired employees in many countries, meaning that benefits are payable for a longer period;
- the sustained low interest rate environment in many countries. This is relevant because lower interest rates lead to lower discount rates, so liabilities that are discounted are measured at higher amounts in financial statements; and
- returns on investments in many countries not meeting historic levels and expectations – meaning that the return on investments made by pension schemes is adversely affected.

Whilst the benefits to the employee are not certain, they are more predictable than under a defined contribution scheme. The cost to the employer, however, is uncertain as the employer will need to vary the contributions to the scheme to ensure it is adequately funded to meet the pension liabilities when employees eventually retire.

The following is an extract from the accounting policies in the 2015 Annual Report of AstraZeneca:

### Employee Benefits

The Group accounts for pensions and other employee benefits (principally healthcare) under IAS 19 'Employee Benefits' issued in 2011. In respect of defined benefit plans, obligations are measured at discounted present value while plan assets are measured at fair value.

The operating and financing costs of such plans are recognised separately in profit; current service costs are spread systematically over the lives of employees and financing costs are recognised in full in the periods in which they arise. Remeasurements of the net defined pension liability, including actuarial gains and losses, are recognised immediately in other comprehensive income.

Where the calculation results in a surplus to the Group, the recognised asset is limited to the present value of any available future refunds from the plan or reductions in future contributions to the plan. Payments to defined contribution plans are recognised in profit as they fall due.

The accounting policy is quite complex to apply and we will illustrate the detailed calculations involved below.

### 15.4.4 Equity compensation plans

IAS 19 does not specify recognition or measurement requirements for equity compensation plans such as shares or share options issued to employees at less than fair value. The valuation of share options has proved an extremely contentious topic and we will consider the issues that have arisen. IFRS 2 *Share-based Payment* covers these plans.[3]

The following is an extract from the accounting policies in the 2015 Annual Report of Sainsburys plc:

### Share-based compensation

The Group provides benefits to employees (including Directors) of the Group in the form of equity-settled and cash-settled share-based payment transactions, whereby employees render services in exchange for shares, rights over shares or the value of those shares in cash terms.

For equity-settled share-based payments the fair value of the employee services rendered is determined by reference to the fair value of the shares awarded or options granted, excluding the impact of any non-market vesting conditions. All share options are valued using an option-pricing model (Black–Scholes or Monte Carlo). This fair value is charged to the income statement over the vesting period of the share-based payment scheme.

For cash-settled share-based payments the fair value of the employee services rendered is determined at each balance sheet date and the charge recognised through the income statement over the vesting period of the share-based payment scheme, with the corresponding increase in accruals.

The value of the charge is adjusted in the income statement over the remainder of the vesting period to reflect expected and actual levels of options vesting, with the corresponding adjustments made in equity and accruals.

The grant by the Company of options over its equity instruments to the employees of subsidiary undertakings in the Group is treated as a capital contribution. The fair value of employee services received, measured by reference to the grant date fair value, is recognised over the vesting period as an increase to investment in subsidiary undertakings, with a corresponding credit to equity.

## 15.5 Defined contribution pension schemes

Defined contribution schemes (otherwise known as money purchase schemes) have not presented any major accounting problems. The cost of providing the pension, usually a percentage of salary, is recorded as a remuneration expense in the statement of comprehensive income in the period in which it is due. Assets or liabilities may exist for the pension contributions if the company has not paid the amount due for the period. If a contribution was payable more than 12 months after the reporting date for services rendered in the current period, the liability should be recorded at its discounted amount (using a discount rate based on the market rate for high-quality corporate bonds).

Disclosure is required of the pension contribution charged to the statement of comprehensive income for the period.

### Illustration of Andrew plc defined contribution pension scheme costs

Andrew Ltd has payroll costs of £2.7 million for the year ended 30 June 2016. Andrew Ltd pays pension contributions of 5% of salary, but for convenience paid £10,000 per month standard contribution with any shortfall to be made up in the July 2016 contribution.

*Statement of comprehensive income charge*
The pension cost is £2,700,000 × 5% = £135,000.

*Statement of financial position*
The amount paid over the period is £120,000 and therefore an accrual of £15,000 will be made in the statement of financial position at 30 June 2016.

## 15.6 Defined benefit pension schemes

### 15.6.1 The fundamental accounting issue

A problem that arises in accounting for defined benefit schemes that does not arise when accounting for defined contribution schemes is the much greater uncertainty of required contributions to meet the actual benefit payable. There is no guarantee, even after the contributing company has contributed the expected required amount, that the assets of the scheme will be sufficient to settle the likely future liabilities. Therefore the contributing company may have to provide additional contributions to finance a shortfall and these need to be provided for. Conversely, the contributions paid could exceed the amount required to meet future pension obligations allowing the employer to get re-imbursements, or more likely, future reductions in contributions.

### 15.6.2 Efforts to arrive at a solution

In order to assess the likely level of exposure for contributing companies, it is necessary to look at the work of the actuaries – specialists who advise on the funding of the scheme and its overall financial position. The actuaries will assess the financial position of the scheme on a regular basis and identify whether the liabilities of the scheme (to pay future benefits already earned out of past service) are covered by the market value of the assets into which contributions are invested until required to pay benefits. These actuarial assessments result in the identification of deficits or surpluses for such schemes.

Prior to 1998 the international accounting standard in this area focused on the charge to profit and loss for retirement benefits. The charge was typically split into two elements:

- The regular cost – a long-term estimate largely consistent with the contributions made.

- Variations from the regular cost – recognising the actuarial deficit or surplus over the remaining working lives of employees.

At each actuarial valuation these calculations would be updated and adjustments recognised in the financial statements.

Differences between the charge to profit and loss and the contributions paid in the period were recognised as liabilities or assets on the statement of financial position. This approach led to a number of problems. Two key problems were:

- The figure in the statement of financial position was difficult to explain.

- The charge to profit and loss depended, *inter alia*, on the frequency of the actuarial assessments.

It was in order to address these issues that a fundamentally different approach was advocated in IAS 19 (revised), first published in 1998 and last revised in 2011.

## 15.7 IAS 19 (revised 2011) *Employee Benefits*

After a relatively long discussion and exposure period IAS 19 (revised 1998) was issued in 1998 and redefined how all employee benefits were to be accounted for.

IAS 19 follows an 'asset or liability' approach to accounting for the pension scheme contributions by the employer and, therefore, it defines how the statement of financial position asset or liability should be built up. The statement of comprehensive income charge is effectively the movement in the asset or liability. The pension fund must be valued sufficiently regularly so that the statement of financial position asset or liability is kept up to date. The valuation would normally be done by a qualified actuary and is based on actuarial assumptions.

In June 2011 the IASB issued an amended IAS 19 which makes changes to the recognition, measurement and presentation of pension liabilities for periods beginning on or after 1 January 2013. The changes did not alter the fundamental principle that pension accounting should reflect a supportable asset or liability on the statement of financial position.

## 15.8 The asset or liability for pension and other post-retirement costs

The asset or liability for pension costs is made up from the following amounts:

**(a)** the present value of the defined benefit obligation at the period-end date;

**(b)** minus the fair value at the period-end date of plan assets (if any) out of which the obligations are to be settled directly.

If this calculation comes out with a negative amount, the company should recognise a pension asset in the statement of financial position. There is a limit on the amount of the asset, known as the 'asset ceiling', if the asset calculated above is greater than the total of:

**(i)** any unrecognised actuarial losses and past service cost; plus

**(ii)** the present value of any future refunds from the scheme or reductions in future contributions.

The two elements making up the defined benefit pension asset or liability can now be considered.

### 15.8.1 Obligations of the fund

The pension fund obligation must be calculated using the 'projected unit credit method'. This method of allocating pension costs builds up the pension liability each year for an extra year of service and a reversal of discounting. Discounting of the liability is done using the market yields on high-quality corporate bonds with similar currency and duration.

The Grado illustration below shows how the obligation to pay pension accumulates over the working life of an employee.

#### Grado illustration

A lump sum benefit is payable on termination of service and equal to 1% of final salary for each year of service. The salary in year 1 is £10,000 and is assumed to increase at 7% (compound) each year. The discount rate used is 10%. The following table shows how an obligation (in £) builds up for an employee who is expected to leave at the end of year 5. For simplicity, this example ignores the additional adjustment needed to reflect the probability that the employee may leave service at an earlier or a later date.

| Year | 1 | 2 | 3 | 4 | 5 |
|---|---|---|---|---|---|
| Benefit attributed to prior years | 0 | 131 | 262 | 393 | 524 |
| Benefit attributed to current year (1% of final salary)* | 131 | 131 | 131 | 131 | 131 |
| Benefit attributed to current and prior years | 131 | 262 | 393 | 524 | 655 |
| Opening obligation (present value of benefit attributed to prior years) | — | 89 | 196 | 324 | 476 |
| Interest at 10% | — | 9 | 20 | 33 | 48 |
| Current service cost (present value of benefit attributed to current year) | 89 | 98 | 108 | 119 | 131 |
| Closing obligation (present value of benefit attributed to current and prior years)** | 89 | 196 | 324 | 476 | 655 |

\* Final salary is £10,000 × $(1.07)^4$ = £13,100.
\*\* Discounting the benefit attributable to current and prior years at 10%.

### 15.8.2 Fair value of plan assets

This is usually the market value of the assets of the plan (or the estimated value if no immediate market value exists). The plan assets exclude unpaid contributions due from the reporting enterprise to the fund.

## 15.9 Changes in the pension asset or liability position

The pension asset or liability changes from one period to the next for a number of possible reasons. IAS 19 requires that interest and service costs are recognised in the income statement, whereas remeasurement gains or losses are recognised in other comprehensive income. The possible items to be recognised are as follows:

*Income statement recognition*

(a) current service cost;

(b) interest cost;

(c) past service cost and the effect of any curtailments or settlements.

*Remeasurements*

**(d)** actuarial gains and losses;

**(e)** the difference in the actual and expected return on plan assets.

Each of the items above is discussed in more detail below.

The items above are all the things that cause the statement of financial position asset or liability for pensions to alter, and the statement of comprehensive income is consequently based on the movement in the liability. Because of the inclusion of actuarial gains and losses and past service costs in comprehensive income, the total comprehensive income is liable to fluctuate much more than the charge made under the original IAS 19.

### 15.9.1 Current service cost

The current service cost represents the cost of providing pension benefits to employees for the current period. This cost would not be expected to fluctuate significantly from period to period but is influenced by actuarial assumptions.

### 15.9.2 Interest cost

The interest cost reflects the unwinding of the effect of discounting on the pension asset or liability. The interest cost is calculated by applying the discount rate on high-quality corporate bonds to the pension asset or liability. The effect of this is that if a pension is in an asset position interest income is recognised, and if it is a liability, interest cost is recognised.

This area was one of the key changes to IAS 19 (2011) compared to the previous versions. Prior to 2011 an interest cost was calculated on the pension obligations and an expected return was calculated on the pension assets. These were based on different rates. The two amounts were then offset and presented as a net finance cost or income in the income statement. The impact of this approach was that it was possible net interest income was recognised when the pension was in a liability position, due to the assumption the expected return on plan assets being greater than the discount rate on pension obligations.

### 15.9.3 Past service costs and the effect of curtailments and settlements

Past service costs are costs that arise for a pension scheme as a result of amendments to the scheme, or when a business introduces a plan. They are the extra liability (or asset) in respect of previous years' service by employees. Note, however, that past service costs can only arise if actuarial assumptions did not take into account the reason why they occurred. Typically they would include:

● estimates of benefit improvements as a result of actuarial gains (if the company proposes to give the gains to the employees);

● the effect of plan amendments that increase or reduce benefits for past service.

A curtailment of a pension scheme occurs when a company is committed to making a material reduction in the number of employees in a scheme or when the employees will receive no benefit for a substantial part of their future service. A settlement occurs when an enterprise enters into a transaction that eliminates any further liability from arising under the fund.

#### Accounting treatment

Past service costs and the effect of curtailments and settlements should only be recognised after the pension asset or liability has been recognised at up-to-date fair value for the assets and using current actuarial assumptions. Following the revaluation the past service cost or gain or loss on settlement or curtailment is recognised at the earlier of the following dates:

**(a)** when the plan amendment or curtailment occurs; and

**(b)** when the entity recognises related restructuring costs or termination benefits.

The gain or loss is recognised in profit and loss.

## 15.9.4 Actuarial gains and losses

Actuarial gains or losses result from either changes in the present value of the defined benefit obligation or changes in the market value of the plan assets. They arise from experience adjustments which are differences between actuarial assumptions and actual experience, or due to the effect of changes in actuarial assumptions. Typical reasons for the gains or losses would be:

- unexpectedly low or high rates of employee turnover;
- the effect of changes in the discount rate;
- changes in life expectancy assumptions.

### Accounting treatment

In the version of IAS 19 issued in 2004 there was a choice of accounting treatment for actuarial gains and losses. One approach followed a '10% corridor' and required recognition of gains and losses in the profit or loss, whereas other alternatives made no use of the corridor and required gains and losses to be recognised immediately, either in profit and loss or in other comprehensive income.

With the issue of IAS 19 (2011) there was a significant change in the accounting for actuarial gains and losses. The new standard defines them as 'remeasurements' and requires them to be recognised in full in other comprehensive income. The recognition in the income statement and the use of the 10% corridor have been abolished. IAS 19 (2011) has transition rules that allowed the effect of the change to be spread over a maximum of five years.

This change in accounting significantly impacted on the reported pension position of some businesses. For example, British Airways plc had, at 31 December 2012, prior to the new standard taking effect, £2.188bn of unrecognised actuarial losses following the 10% corridor approach and total equity of £2.758 billion. When British Airways restated their financial statements in 2013 for the effects of IAS 19 (2011), total equity at 31 December 2012 reduced by £1.69 billion, a reduction in equity of 61%.

## 15.9.5 Differences in actual and expected return on plan assets

The effect of remeasuring the pension assets is recognised in other comprehensive income together with the actuarial gains and losses. Prior to the issue of IAS 19 (2011) actuaries would estimate the expected return on plan assets and this would be included within net interest income or expense. Any differences between the actual and expected return were included within actuarial gains and losses.

With the introduction of the new standard the overall pension asset or liability generates interest income or expense using a rate on high-quality corporate bonds. To the extent that the actual return on plan assets differs from this the effect is treated as a remeasurement. In effect it is still very similar to an actuarial gain or loss and has the same accounting impact.

## 15.10 Comprehensive illustration

The following comprehensive illustration demonstrates how a pension liability and statement of comprehensive income statement charge is calculated under IAS 19 (2011). The example does not include the effect of curtailments or settlements.

### Illustration

The following information is given about a funded defined benefit plan. To keep the computations simple, all transactions are assumed to occur at the year-end. The present value of the obligation and the market value of the plan assets were both 1,000 at 1 January 20X1.

|  | 20X1 | 20X2 | 20X3 |
|---|---|---|---|
| Rate on high-quality corporate bonds at start of year | 10% | 9% | 8% |
| Current service cost | 160 | 140 | 150 |
| Benefits paid | 150 | 180 | 190 |
| Contributions paid | 90 | 100 | 110 |
| Present value of obligations at 31 December | 1,100 | 1,380 | 1,455 |
| Market value of plan assets at 31 December | 1,190 | 1,372 | 1,188 |

In 20X2 the plan was amended to provide additional benefits with effect from 1 January 20X2. The present value as at 1 January 20X2 of additional benefits for employee service before 1 January 20X2 was 50.

*Required:*

**Show how the pension scheme would be shown in the accounts for 20X1, 20X2 and 20X3.**

### Solution

*Step 1 Change in the net pension obligation*

|  | 20X1 | 20X2 | 20X3 |
|---|---|---|---|
| Present value of obligation, 1 January | — | (90) | 8 |
| Net interest cost at 10%, 9%, 8% | — | (8) | 1 |
| Current service cost | 160 | 140 | 150 |
| Past service cost | — | 50 | — |
| Contributions paid | (90) | (100) | (110) |
| *Actuarial (gain) loss on obligation (balancing figure)* * | (160) | 16 | 218 |
| Present value of the obligation (asset), 31 December | (90) | 8 | 267 |

* In this example we do not distinguish between actuarial gains and losses and differences in the actual and expected return on plan assets.

*Step 2 Calculate the impact on the statement of comprehensive income*

|  | 20X1 | 20X2 | 20X3 |
|---|---|---|---|
| Operating costs: |  |  |  |
|   Current service cost | 160 | 140 | 150 |
|   Past service cost |  | 50 |  |
| Net interest cost | — | (8) | 1 |
| *Profit and loss charge* | 160 | 182 | 151 |
| Other comprehensive income: |  |  |  |
|   Actuarial gains (losses) | 160 | (16) | (218) |

*Step 3 Calculate the statement of financial position*

|  | 20X1 | 20X2 | 20X3 |
|---|---|---|---|
| Present value of pension obligation, 31 December | 1,100 | 1,380 | 1,455 |
| Fair value of plan assets, 31 December | (1,190) | (1,372) | (1,188) |
| *Liability (asset) recognised* | *(90)* | *8* | *267* |

## 15.11 Multi-employer plans

A multi-employer plan is a defined contribution or defined benefit plan that:

(a) pools the assets contributed by various enterprises that are not under common control; and

(b) uses those assets to provide benefits to employees of more than one enterprise, on the basis that contribution and benefit levels are determined without regard to the identity of the enterprise that employs the employees concerned.

An enterprise should account for a multi-employer defined benefit plan as follows:

● it should account for its share of the defined benefit obligation, plan assets and costs associated with the plan in the same way as for any defined benefit plan; or

● if insufficient information is available to use defined benefit accounting, it should:

    ● account for the plan as if it were a defined contribution plan; and

    ● give extra disclosures.

A group pension plan is not a multi-employer plan and therefore the treatment above is not available. However, a similar exemption exists for group schemes whereby it is not necessary to split the pension liability between the contributing entities. The exemption is available when different companies in a group contribute to the same group pension scheme and it is not practicable to split the pension scheme between the contributing companies. Instead, the contributing individual entities can account for the scheme by recognising only their contributions to the plan. This means that the defined benefit accounting is only necessary in the consolidated accounts and not in the individual company accounts of all companies in the group. It is necessary, however, to recognise the full group defined benefit accounting in at least one entity in the group. The requirements for full defined benefit accounting are included in the individual sponsor company financial statements.

The requirement to reflect the group pension position in the individual sponsor entity can be a concern, particularly for example in the UK, where this treatment, for a significant pension liability, could impact on the ability of the individual sponsor entity to pay dividends.

## 15.12 Disclosures

The major disclosure requirements of the standard require entities to present information that:

(a) explains the characteristics of its defined benefit plans and risks associated with them;

(b) identifies and explains the amounts in its financial statements rising from its defined benefit plans; and

(c) describes how its defined benefit plans may affect the amount, timing and uncertainty of the entity's future cash flows.

## 15.13 Other long-service benefits

So far in this chapter we have considered the accounting for post-retirement costs for both defined contribution and defined benefit pension schemes. As well as pensions, IAS 19 (2011) considers other forms of long-service benefit paid to employees. These other forms of long-service benefit include:

(a) long-term compensated absences such as long-service or sabbatical leave;

(b) jubilee or other long-service benefits;

(c) long-term disability benefits;

(d) profit-sharing and bonuses payable 12 months or more after the end of the period in which the employees render the related service; and

(e) deferred compensation paid 12 months or more after the end of the period in which it is earned.

The measurement of these other long-service benefits is not usually as complex or uncertain as it is for post-retirement benefits and therefore a more simplified method of accounting is used for them. For other long-service benefits any remeasurement gains and losses are recognised immediately in profit or loss.

This means that the statement of financial position liability for other long-service benefits is just the present value of the future benefit obligation less the fair value of any assets that the benefit will be settled from directly.

The profit or loss charge for these benefits is therefore the total of:

(a) current and past service cost;

(b) net interest income or cost;

(c) remeasurement gains and losses.

## 15.14 Short-term benefits

In addition to pension and other long-term benefits considered earlier, IAS 19 gives accounting rules for short-term employee benefits.

Short-term employee benefits include items such as:

● wages, salaries and social security contributions;

● short-term compensated absences (such as paid annual leave and paid sick leave) where the absences are expected to occur within 12 months after the end of the period in which the employees render the related employee service;

● profit-sharing and bonuses payable within 12 months after the end of the period in which the employees render the related service; and

● non-monetary benefits (such as medical care, housing or cars) for current employees.

All short-term employee benefits should be recognised at an undiscounted amount:

● as a liability (after deducting any payments already made); and

● as an expense (unless another international standard allows capitalisation as an asset).

If the payments already made exceed the undiscounted amount of the benefits, an asset should be recognised only if it will lead to a future reduction in payments or a cash refund.

### Compensated absences

The expected cost of short-term compensated absences should be recognised:

(a) in the case of accumulating absences, when the employees render service that increases their entitlement to future compensated absences; and

(b) in the case of non-accumulating compensated absences, when the absences occur.

Accumulating absences occur when the employees can carry forward unused absence from one period to the next. They are recognised when the employee renders services, regardless of whether the benefit is vesting (the employee would get a cash alternative if they left employment) or non-vesting. The measurement of the obligation reflects the likelihood of employees leaving in a non-vesting scheme.

It is common practice for leave entitlement to be an accumulating absence (perhaps restricted to a certain number of days) but for sick pay entitlement to be non-accumulating.

### Profit-sharing and bonus plans

The expected cost of a profit-sharing or bonus plan should be recognised only when:

(a) the enterprise has a present legal or constructive obligation to make such payments as a result of past events; and

(b) a reliable estimate of the obligation can be made.

## 15.15 Termination benefits

These benefits are treated separately from other employee benefits in IAS 19 (revised) because the event that gives rise to the obligation to pay is the termination of employment as opposed to the service of the employee.

The accounting treatment for termination benefits is consistent with the requirements of IAS 37 and the rules concern when the obligation should be provided for and the measurement of the obligation.

### Recognition

Termination benefits can be recognised as a liability at the earlier of:

(a) when the entity can no longer withdraw the offer of those benefits; and

(b) when the entity recognises costs for a restructuring that is within the scope of IAS 37 and involves the payment of termination benefits. The standard provides guidance for the point at which an entity can no longer withdraw the offer of the benefits. In cases where it is the employee's decision to accept an offer, for example in a voluntary redundancy scheme, it is the point where the employee has accepted the offer.

### Measurement

If the termination benefits are to be paid more than 12 months after the period-end date, they should be discounted, using the market yield on good-quality corporate bonds as the discount rate. Prudence should also be exercised in the case of an offer made to encourage voluntary redundancy, as provision should only be based on the number of employees expected to accept the offer.

## 15.16 IFRS 2 *Share-based Payment*[3]

Share awards, either directly through shares or through options, are very common ways of rewarding employee performance. These awards align the interests of the employees with those of the shareholders and, as such, are aimed at motivating the employees to perform in the way that benefits the shareholders. In particular, there is a belief that they will motivate the employees towards looking at the long-term success of the business as opposed to focusing solely on short-term profits. They have additional benefits also to the company and employees, for example in relation to cash and tax. If employees are rewarded in shares or options, the company will not need to pay out cash to reward the employees, and in a start-up situation where cash flow is very limited this can be very beneficial. Many 'dot-com' companies initially rewarded their staff in shares for this reason. There can also be tax benefits to employees with shares in some tax regimes which give an incentive to employees to accept share awards.

Whilst commercially share-based payments have many benefits, the accounting world has struggled in finding a suitable way to account for them. IAS 19 only covered disclosure requirements for share-based payments and had no requirements for the recognition and measurement of the payments when it was issued. The result of this was that companies could give very valuable rewards to their employees in the form of shares or options that did not result in the recognition of any charge against profit. The IASB addressed this by issuing, in February 2004, IFRS 2 *Share-based Payment*, which is designed to cover all aspects of accounting for share-based payments.

### 15.16.1 Should an expense be recognised?

Historically there has been some debate about whether a charge should be recognised in the statement of comprehensive income for share-based payments. One view is that the reward is given to employees in their capacity as shareholders and, as a result, it is not an employee benefit cost. Also supporters of the 'no-charge' view claimed that to make a charge would be a double hit to earnings per share in that it would reduce profits and increase the number of shares, which they felt was unreasonable.

Supporters of a charge pointed to opposite arguments that claimed having no charge underestimated the reward given to employees and therefore overstated profit. The impact of this was to give a misleading view of the profitability of the company. Also, making a charge gave comparability between companies that rewarded their staff in different ways. Comparability is one of the key principles of financial reporting.

For many years these arguments were not resolved and no standard was in issue, but the IASB eventually decided that a charge is appropriate and issued IFRS 2. In drawing up IFRS 2 a number of obstacles had to be overcome and decisions had to be made, for example:

● What should the value of the charge be – fair value or intrinsic value?

● At what point should the charge be measured – grant date, vesting date or exercise date?

● How should the charge be spread over a number of periods?

● If the charge is made to the statement of comprehensive income, where is the opposite entry to be made?

● What exemptions should be given from the standard?

IFRS 2 has answered these questions, and when introduced it made substantial changes to the profit recognised by many companies. In the UK, for example, the share-based payments charge for many businesses was one of their most significant changes to profit on adopting IFRS.

## 15.17 Scope of IFRS 2

IFRS 2 is a comprehensive standard that covers all aspects of share-based payments. Specifically IFRS 2 covers:

- equity-settled share-based payment transactions, in which the entity receives goods or services as consideration for equity instruments issued;
- cash-settled share-based payment transactions, in which the entity receives goods or services by incurring liabilities to the supplier of those goods or services for amounts that are based on the price of the entity's shares or other equity instruments; and
- transactions in which the entity receives goods or services and either the entity or the supplier of those goods or services may choose whether the transaction is settled in cash (based on the price of the entity's shares or other equity instruments) or by issuing equity instruments.

There are no exemptions from the provisions of the IFRS except for:

(a) acquisitions of goods or other non-financial assets as part of a business combination; and

(b) acquisitions of goods or services under derivative contracts where the contract is expected to be settled by delivery as opposed to being settled net in cash.

## 15.18 Recognition and measurement

The general principles of recognition and measurement of share-based payment charges are as follows:

- Entities should recognise the goods or services acquired in a share-based payment transaction over the period the goods or services are received.
- The entity should recognise an increase in equity if the share-based payment is equity-settled and a liability if the payment is a cash-settled payment transaction.
- The share-based payment should be measured at fair value.

## 15.19 Equity-settled share-based payments

For equity-settled share-based payment transactions, the entity shall measure the goods and services received, and the corresponding increase in equity:

- **directly** at the fair value of the goods and services received, unless that fair value cannot be estimated reliably;
- **indirectly,** by reference to the fair value of the equity instruments granted, if the entity cannot estimate reliably the fair value of the goods and services received.

For transactions with employees, the entity shall measure the fair value of services received by reference to the fair value of the equity instruments granted, because typically it is not possible to estimate reliably the fair value of the services received.

In transactions with employees the IASB has decided that it is appropriate to value the benefit at the fair value of the instruments granted at their *grant date*. The IASB could have picked a number of different dates at which the options could have been valued:

- grant date – the date on which the options are given to the employees;

- vesting date – the date on which the options become unconditional to the employees; or

- exercise date – the date on which the employees exercise their options.

The IASB opted for the grant date as it was felt that the grant of options was the reward to the employees, and not the exercise of the options. This means that after the grant date any movements in the share price, whether upwards or downwards, do not influence the charge to the financial statements.

### Employee options

In order to establish the fair value of an option at grant date the market price could be used (if the option is traded on a market), but it is much more likely that an option pricing model will need to be used. Examples of option pricing models that are possible include:

- *Black–Scholes.* An option pricing model used for options with a fixed exercise date that does not require adjustment for the inability of employees to exercise options during the vesting period.

- *Binomial model.* An option pricing model used for options with a variable exercise date that will need adjustment for the inability of employees to exercise options during the vesting period.

Disclosures are required of the principal assumptions used in applying the option pricing model.

IFRS 2 does not recommend any one pricing model but insists that whichever model is chosen a number of factors affecting the fair value of the option such as exercise price, market price, time to maturity and volatility of the share price must be taken into account. In practice the Black–Scholes model is probably most commonly used; however, many companies vary the model to some extent to ensure it fits with the precise terms of their options.

Once the fair value of the option has been established at the grant date it is charged to profit or loss over the vesting period. The vesting period is the period in which the employees are required to satisfy non-market vesting conditions, for example service conditions, that allow them to exercise their options. We consider the impact of market vesting conditions later in this chapter.

EXAMPLE ● Employees were granted options to acquire 100,000 shares at $20 per share if still in employment at the end of the financial year. The market value of an option was $1.50 per share. All employees exercised their option at the year-end and the company received $2,000,000. There will be a charge in the income statement of $150,000. Although the company has not transferred cash, it has transferred value to the employees. IFRS 2 requires the charge to be measured as the market value of the option, i.e. $1.50 per share.

However, it is more usual for options to be exercised over longer periods. In this case, the charge is spread over the vesting period by calculating a revised cumulative charge each year, and then apportioning that over the vesting period with catch-up adjustments made to amend previous under- or over-charges to profit or loss. The illustration below shows how this approach works.

When calculating the charge in profit or loss the likelihood of options being forfeited due to non-market price conditions (e.g. because the employees leave in the conditional period) should be adjusted for. For non-market conditions the charge is amended each year to reflect any changes in estimates of the numbers expected to vest.

The charge cannot be adjusted, however, for market price conditions. If, for example, the share price falls and therefore the options will not be exercised due to the exercise price being higher than the market price, no adjustment can be made. This means that if options are 'underwater', the statement of comprehensive income will still be recognising a charge for those options.

The charge is made to the statement of comprehensive income but there was some debate about how the credit entry should be made. The credit entry must be made either as a liability or as an entry to equity, and the IASB has decided that it should be an entry to equity. The logic for not including a liability is that the future issue of shares is not an 'obligation to transfer economic benefits' and therefore does not meet the definition of a liability. When the shares are issued it will increase the equity of the company and be a contribution from an owner.

Even though the standard specifies that the credit entry is to equity, it does not specify which item in equity is to be used. In practice it seems acceptable either to use a separate reserve or to make the entry to retained earnings. If a separate reserve is used at the exercise date the reserve will commonly be transferred to retained earnings. Whether the reserve is included within the proceeds of a share issue is not covered under IFRS and would be ultimately a matter for company law in the entities legal jurisdiction.

### Illustration of option accounting

Alpha Ltd issued share options to staff on 1 January 20X0, details of which are as follows:

| | |
|---|---|
| Number of staff | 1,000 |
| Number of options to each staff member | 500 |
| Vesting period | 3 years |
| Fair value at grant date (per option) | £3 |
| Expected employee turnover (per annum) | 5% |

In the 31 December 20X1 financial statements, the company revised its estimate of employee turnover to 8% per annum for the three-year vesting period.

In the 31 December 20X2 financial statements, the actual employee turnover had averaged 6% per annum for the three-year vesting period.

Options vest as long as the staff remain with the company for the three-year period.

The charge for share-based payments under IFRS 2 would be as follows:

*Year ended 31 December 20X0*

In this period the charge would be based on the original terms of the share option issue. The total value of the option award at fair value at the grant date is:

| | £000 |
|---|---|
| 1,000 staff $\times$ 500 options $\times$ £3 $\times$ (0.95 $\times$ 0.95 $\times$ 0.95) | 1,286 |

The charge to the statement of comprehensive income for the period is therefore:

| | |
|---|---|
| £1,286 ÷ 3 | 429 |

*Year ended 31 December 20X1*

In this year the expected employee turnover has risen to 8% per annum. The estimate of the effect of the increase is taken into account. Amended total expected share option award at grant date:

| | £000 | £000 |
|---|---|---|
| 1,000 staff $\times$ 500 options $\times$ £3 $\times$ (0.92 $\times$ 0.92 $\times$ 0.92) | | 1,168 |

The charge to the statement of comprehensive income is therefore

| | | |
|---|---|---|
| £1,168 $\times$ $^2/_3$ | 779 | |
| *Less*: recognised to date | (429) | |
| | | 350 |

*Year ended 31 December 20X2*

The actual number of options that vest is now known. The actual value of the option award that vests at the grant date is:

|  | £000 | £000 |
|---|---|---|
| 1,000 staff × 500 options × £3 × (0.94 × 0.94 × 0.94) |  | 1,246 |

The charge to the statement of comprehensive income is therefore:

| | | |
|---|---|---|
| Total value over the vesting period | 1,246 | |
| *Less*: recognised to date | (779) | |
| | | 467 |

### Re-priced options

If an entity re-prices its options, for instance in the event of a falling share price, the incremental fair value should be spread over the remaining vesting period. The incremental fair value per option is the difference between the fair value of the option immediately before re-pricing and the fair value of the re-priced option.

### Market-related vesting conditions

We have already seen that most vesting conditions (e.g. the requirement for employees to remain employed over the vesting period) are adjusted for by estimating the number of options that are likely to vest. Where the vesting condition is a market-related condition, e.g. the share price must exceed a target amount or perform to a specified standard relative to other listed securities, the condition is adjusted in computing the fair value of the option at grant date using an appropriate model. Given that the condition is taken into account in this way, it is ignored when considering the likely vesting of the option to avoid double-counting. This means that, where such conditions exist, it is at least theoretically possible for there to be a charge to profit and loss for an equity-settled share-based payment where the options do not actually vest.

## 15.20 Cash-settled share-based payments

Cash-settled share-based payments result in the recognition of a liability. The entity measures the goods or services acquired and the liability incurred at fair value. Until the liability is settled, the entity remeasures the fair value of the liability at each reporting date, with any changes in fair value recognised in profit or loss.

For example, an entity might grant share appreciation rights to employees as part of their pay package, whereby the employees will become entitled to a future cash payment (rather than an equity instrument), based on the increase in the entity's share price from a specified level over a specified period.

The entity recognises the services received, and a liability to pay for those services, as the employees render service. For example, some share appreciation rights vest immediately, and the employees are therefore not required to complete a specified period of service to become entitled to the cash payment. In the absence of evidence to the contrary, the entity presumes that the services rendered by the employees in exchange for the share appreciation rights have been received. Thus, the entity recognises immediately the services received and a liability to pay for them. If the share appreciation rights do not vest until the employees have completed a specified period of service, the entity recognises the services received, and a liability to pay for them, as the employees render service during that period.

The liability is measured, initially and at each reporting date until settled, at the fair value of the share appreciation rights, by applying an option pricing model, taking into account the terms and conditions on which the share appreciation rights were granted, and the extent to which the employees have rendered service to date. The entity remeasures the fair value of the liability at each reporting date until settled.

Disclosure is required of the difference between the amount that would be charged to the statement of comprehensive income if the share appreciation rights are paid out in cash as opposed to being paid out with shares.

## 15.21 Transactions which may be settled in cash or shares

Some share-based payment transactions can be settled in either cash or shares with the settlement option being with the supplier of the goods or services and/or with the entity.

The accounting treatment is dependent upon which counterparty has the choice of settlement.

### Supplier/employee choice

If the supplier of the goods or services, or the employee in the case of options granted to employees, has the choice over settlement method, the entity has issued a compound instrument. The entity has an obligation to pay out cash (as the supplier can take this choice), but also has issued an equity option, as the supplier may decide to take equity to settle the transaction. The entity therefore recognises both a liability and an equity component.

The fair value of the equity option is the difference between the fair value of the offer of the cash alternative and the fair value of the offer of the equity payment. In many cases these are the same value, in which case the equity option has no value.

Once the split has been determined, each part is accounted for in the same way as other cash-settled or equity-settled transactions.

If cash is paid in settlement, any equity option recognised may be transferred to a different category in equity. If equity is issued, the liability is transferred to equity as the consideration for the equity instruments issued.

### Entity choice

For a share-based payment transaction in which an entity may choose whether to settle in cash or by issuing equity instruments, the entity determines whether it has a present obligation to settle in cash and account for the share-based payment transaction accordingly. The entity has a present obligation to settle in cash if the choice of settlement in equity instruments is not substantive, or if the entity has a past practice or a stated policy of settling in cash.

If such an obligation exists, the entity accounts for the transaction in accordance with the requirements applying to cash-settled share-based payment transactions.

If no such obligation exists, the entity accounts for the transaction in accordance with the requirements applying to equity-settled transactions.

## 15.22 IAS 26 *Accounting and Reporting by Retirement Benefit Plans*[4]

This standard provides complementary guidance in addition to IAS 19 (2011) regarding the way that the pension fund should account and report on the contributions it receives and the obligations it has to pay pensions. The standard mainly contains the presentation and disclosure requirements of the schemes as opposed to the accounting methods that they should adopt.

### 15.22.1 Defined contribution plans

The report prepared by a defined contribution plan should contain a statement of net assets available for benefits and a description of the funding policy.

With a defined contribution plan it is not normally necessary to involve an actuary, since the pension paid at the end is purely dependent on the amount of fund built up for the employee. The obligation of the employer is usually discharged by the employer paying the agreed contributions into the plan. The main purpose of the report of the plan is to provide information on the performance of the investments, and this is normally achieved by including the following statements:

(a) a description of the significant activities for the period and the effect of any changes relating to the plan, its membership and its terms and conditions;

(b) statements reporting on the transactions and investment performance for the period and the financial position of the plan at the end of the period; and

(c) a description of the investment policies.

### 15.22.2 Defined benefit plans

Under a defined benefit plan (as opposed to a defined contribution plan) there is a need to provide more information, as the plan must be sufficiently funded to provide the agreed pension benefits at the retirement of the employees. The objective of reporting by the defined benefit plan is to periodically present information about the accumulation of resources and plan benefits over time that will highlight an excess or shortfall in assets.

The report that is required should contain[4] either:

(a) a statement that shows:

    (i) the net assets available for benefits;

    (ii) the actuarial present value of promised retirement benefits, distinguishing between vested benefits and non-vested benefits; and

    (iii) the resulting excess or deficit; or

(b) a statement of net assets available for benefits, including either:

    (i) a note disclosing the actuarial present value of promised retirement benefits, distinguishing between vested benefits and non-vested benefits; or

    (ii) a reference to this information in an accompanying report.

The most recent actuarial valuation report should be used as a basis for the above disclosures and the date of the valuation should be disclosed. IAS 26 does not specify how often actuarial valuations should be done but suggests that most countries require a triennial valuation.

When the fund is preparing the report and using the actuarial present value of the future obligations, the present value could be based on either projected salary levels or current salary levels. Whichever basis has been used should be disclosed. The effect of any significant changes in actuarial assumptions should also be disclosed.

#### Report format

IAS 26 proposes three different report formats that will fulfil the content requirements detailed above. These formats are:

(a) A report that includes a statement that shows the net assets available for benefits, the actuarial present value of promised retirement benefits, and the resulting excess or deficit.

The report of the plan also contains statements of changes in net assets available for benefits and changes in the actuarial present value of promised retirement benefits. The report may include a separate actuary's report supporting the actuarial present value of promised retirement benefits.

(b) A report that includes a statement of net assets available for benefits and a statement of changes in net assets available for benefits. The actuarial present value of the promised retirement benefits is disclosed in a note to the statements. The report may also include a report from an actuary supporting the actuarial value of the promised retirement benefits.

(c) A report that includes a statement of net assets available for benefits and a statement of changes in net assets available for benefits with the actuarial present value of promised retirement benefits contained in a separate actuarial report.

In each format a trustees' report in the nature of a management or directors' report and an investment report may also accompany the statements.

### 15.22.3 All plans – disclosure requirements

For all plans, whether defined contribution or defined benefit, some common valuation and disclosure requirements exist.

#### Valuation

The investments held by retirement benefit plans should be carried at fair value. In most cases the investments will be marketable securities and the fair value is the market value. If it is impossible to determine the fair value of an investment, disclosure should be made of the reason why fair value is not used.

Market values are used for the investments because the market value is felt to be the most appropriate value at the report date and the best indication of the performance of the investments over the period.

#### Disclosure

In addition to the specific reports detailed above for defined contribution and defined benefit plans, the report should also contain:

(a) a statement of net assets available for benefits disclosing:
- assets at the end of the period suitably classified;
- the basis of valuation of assets;
- details of any single investment exceeding either 5% of the net assets available for benefits or 5% of any class or type of security;
- details of any investment in the employer;
- liabilities other than the actuarial present value of promised retirement benefits;

(b) a statement of changes in net assets for benefits showing the following:
- employer contributions;
- employee contributions;
- investment income such as interest or dividends;
- other income;
- benefits paid or payable;

- administrative expenses;
- other expenses;
- taxes on income;
- profits or losses on disposal of investment and changes in value of investments;
- transfers from and to other plans;

(c) a summary of significant accounting policies; and

(d) a description of the plan and the effect of any changes in the plan during the period.

## Summary

Accounting for employee benefits has always been a difficult problem with different views as to the appropriate methods.

The different types of pension scheme and the associated risks add to the difficulties in terms of accounting. The accounting treatment for these benefits has recently changed, the current view being that the asset or liability position takes priority over the profit or loss charge. However, one consequence of giving the statement of financial position priority is that this change to the statement of comprehensive income can be much more volatile and this is considered by some to be undesirable.

An interesting more recent development is the option to use 'other comprehensive income' to record remeasurements, i.e. for actuarial gains and losses, rather than taking them to profit or loss.

IFRS 2 is the first serious attempt of the IASB to deal with accounting for share-based payments. It requires companies to recognise that a charge should be made for share-based payments and, in line with other recent standards such as financial instruments, it requires that charge to be recognised at fair value. There has been criticism of the standard in that it brings significant estimation into assessing the amount of charges to profit; however, overall the standard has been relatively well received with companies and with users of the financial statements.

## REVIEW QUESTIONS

1 Outline the differences between a defined benefit and a defined contribution pension scheme.

2 If a defined contribution pension scheme provided a pension that was 6% of salary each year, the company had a payroll cost of €5 million, and the company paid €200,000 in the year, what would be the statement of comprehensive income charge and the statement of financial position liability at the year-end?

3 'The approach taken in IAS 19 before its 1998 revision was to match an even pension cost against the period the employees provided service. This follows the accruals principle and is therefore fundamentally correct.' Discuss.

4 Under the revised IAS 19 (2011) what amount of actuarial gains and losses should be recognised in profit or loss?

5 In a dissenting view on the issue of IAS 19 (2011), Mr Yamada states that 'the return on high quality corporate bonds would be arbitrary and would not be a faithful representation of the return that investors require or expect from each type of asset'. Discuss.

6 What is the required accounting treatment for a past service cost in a defined benefit pension scheme?

7 What distinguishes a termination benefit from the other benefits considered in IAS 19 (2011)?

8 'The issue of shares by companies, even to employees, should not result in a charge against profits. The contribution in terms of service that employees give to earn their rewards are contributions as owners and not as employees and when owners buy shares for cash there is no charge to profit.' Discuss.

9 Briefly summarise the required accounting if a company gives its staff a cash bonus directly linked to the share price.

10 Explain what distinguishes the different types of share-based payment: equity-settled, cash-settled and equity with a cash alternative.

## EXERCISES

### * Question 1

Donna, Inc. operates a defined benefit pension scheme for staff. The pension scheme has been operating for a number of years but not following IAS 19. The finance director is unsure of which accounting policy to adopt under IAS 19 because he has heard very conflicting stories. He went to one presentation in 2010 that referred to a '10% corridor' approach to actuarial gains and losses, recognising them in profit or loss, but went to another presentation in 2012 that said actuarial gains and losses should be recognised in other comprehensive income.

The pension scheme had a market value of assets of £3.2 million and a present value of obligations of £3.5 million on 1 January 2013. There were no actuarial gains and losses brought forward into 2013.

The details relevant to the pension are as follows (in £000):

|  | 2013 | 2014 | 2015 |
| --- | --- | --- | --- |
| Discount rate at start of year | 6% | 5% | 4% |
| Expected rate of return on plan assets at start of year | 10% | 9% | 8% |
| Current service cost | 150 | 160 | 170 |
| Benefits paid | 140 | 150 | 130 |
| Contributions paid | 120 | 120 | 130 |
| Present value of obligations at 31 December | 3,600 | 3,500 | 3,200 |
| Market value of plan assets at 31 December | 3,400 | 3,600 | 3,600 |

**Required:**
(a) Advise the finance director of why the presentations from 2010 and 2012 gave different treatments of actuarial gains and losses
(b) Show how the pension scheme would be presented in the financial statements for the period 2013–2015 under IAS 19 (2011).

### * Question 2

The following information (in £m) relates to the defined benefit scheme of Basil plc for the year ended 31 December 20X7:

Fair value of plan assets at 1 January 20X7 £3,150 and at 31 December 20X7 £3,386; contributions £26; current service cost £80; benefits paid £85; past service cost £150; present value of the obligation at 1 January 20X7 £3,750 and at 31 December 20X7 £4,192.

The discount rate was 7% at 31 December 20X6 and 8% at 31 December 20X7.

**Required:**
Show the amounts that will be recognised in the statement of comprehensive income and statement of financial position for Basil plc for the year ended 31 December 20X7 under IAS 19 (2011) and the movement in the net liability.

## * Question 3

The following information is available for the year ended 31 March 20X6 (values in $m):

Present value of scheme liabilities at 1 April 20X5 $1,007; fair value of plan assets at 1 April 20X5 $844; benefits paid $44; contributions paid by employers $16; current service costs $28; past service costs $1; actuarial gains on assets $31; actuarial losses on liabilities $10; net interest cost $15.

**Required:**
(a) Calculate the net liability to be recognised in the statement of financial position.
(b) Show the amounts recognised in the statement of comprehensive income.

## * Question 4

On 1 October 2005 Omega granted 50 employees options to purchase 500 shares in the entity. The options vest on 1 October 2007 for those employees who remain employed by the entity until that date. The options allow the employees to purchase the shares for $10 per share. The market price of the shares was $10 on 1 October 2005 and $10.50 on 1 October 2006. The market value of the options was $2 on 1 October 2005 and $2.60 on 1 October 2006. On 1 October 2005 the directors estimated that 5% of the relevant employees would leave in each of the years ended 30 September 2006 and 2007 respectively. It turned out that 4% of the relevant employees left in the year ended 30 September 2006 and the directors now believe that a further 4% will leave in the year ended 30 September 2007.

**Required:**
Show the amounts that will appear in the balance sheet of Omega as at 30 September 2006 in respect of the share options, and the amounts that will appear in the income statement for the year ended 30 September 2006.

You should state where in the balance sheet and where in the income statement the relevant amounts will be presented. Where necessary you should justify your treatment with reference to appropriate international financial reporting standards.

*(Dip IFR December 2006)*

## * Question 5

On 1 January 20X1 a company obtained a contract in order to keep its factory in work but had obtained it on a very tight profit margin. Liquidity was a problem and there was no prospect of offering staff a cash bonus. Instead, the company granted its 80 production employees share options for 1,000 shares each at £10 per share. There was a condition that they would only vest if they still remained in employment at 31 December 20X2. The options were then exercisable during the year ended 31 December 20X3. Each option had an estimated fair value of £6.50 at the grant date.

At 31 December 20X1:

- The fair value of each option was £7.50.
- Four employees had left.
- It was estimated that 16 of the staff would have left by 31 December 20X2.
- The share price had increased from £9 on 1 January 20X1 to £9.90.

**Required:**
Calculate the charge to the income statement for the year ended 31 December 20X1.

### * Question 6

C plc wants to reward its directors for their service to the company and has designed a bonus package with two different elements as follows. The directors are informed of the scheme and granted any options on 1 January 20X7.

1 Share options over 300,000 shares that can be exercised on 31 December 20Y0. These options are granted at an exercise price of €4 each, the share price of C plc on 1 January 20X7. Conditions of the options are that the directors remain with the company, and the company must achieve an average increase in profit of at least 10% per year, for the years ending 31 December 20X7 to 31 December 20X9. C plc obtained a valuation on 1 January 20X7 of the options which gave them a fair value of €3.

   No directors were expected to leave the company but, surprisingly, on 30 November 20X9 a director with 30,000 options did leave the company and therefore forfeited his options. At the 31 December 20X7 and 20X8 year-ends C plc estimated that they would achieve the profit targets (they said 80% sure) and by 31 December 20X9 the profit target had been achieved.

   By 31 December 20Y0 the share price had risen to €12, giving the directors who exercised their options an €8 profit per share on exercise.

2 The directors were offered a cash bonus payable on 31 December 20X8 based on the share price of the company. Each of the five directors was granted a €5,000 bonus for each €1 rise in the share price or proportion thereof by 31 December 20X8.

   On 1 January 20X7 the estimated fair value of the bonus was €75,000; this had increased to €85,000 by 31 December 20X7, and the share price on 31 December 20X8 was €8 per share.

**Required:**
Show the accounting entries required in the years ending 31 December 20X7, 20X8 and 20X9 for the directors' options and bonus above.

### Question 7

Kathryn plc, a listed company, provides a defined benefit pension for its staff, the details of which are given below.

As at 30 April 2013, actuaries valued the company's pension scheme and estimated that the scheme had assets of £10.5 million and obligations of £10.2 million (using the valuation methods prescribed in IAS 19).

The actuaries made assumptions in their valuation that the obligations were discounted using an appropriate corporate bond rate of 10%. The actuaries estimated the current service cost at £600,000. The actuaries informed the company that pensions to retired directors would be £800,000 during the year, and the company should contribute £700,000 to the scheme.

At 30 April 2014 the actuaries again valued the pension fund and estimated the assets to be worth £10.7 million, and the obligations of the fund to be £10.9 million.

*Assume that contributions and benefits are paid on the last day of each year.*

Required:

(a) Explain the reasons why IAS 19 was revised in 1998, moving from an actuarial income-driven approach to a market-based asset- and liability-driven approach. Support your answer by referring to the *Framework* principles.

(b) Show the extracts from the statement of comprehensive income and statement of financial position of Kathryn plc in respect of the information above for the year ended 30 April 2014. You do not need to show notes to the accounts.

## * Question 8

Oberon prepares financial statements to 31 March each year. Oberon makes contributions to a defined benefit post-employment benefit plan for its employees. Relevant data is as follows:

(a) At 1 April 20X0 the plan obligation was €35 million and the fair value of the plan assets was €30 million.

(b) The actuary advised that the current service cost for the year ended 31 March 20X1 was €4 million. Oberon paid contributions of €3.6 million to the plan on 31 March 20X1. These were the only contributions paid in the year.

(c) The appropriate annual interest rate was 6% on 1 April 20X0 and 5.5% on 31 March 20X1.

(d) The plan paid out benefits totalling €2 million to retired members on 31 March 20X1.

(e) At 31 March 20X1 the plan obligation was €41.5 million and the fair value of the plan assets was €32.5 million.

Required:

Compute the amounts that will appear in the statement of comprehensive income of Oberon for the year ended 31 March 20X1 and the statement of financial position at 31 March 20X1 in respect of the post-employment benefit plan. You should indicate where in each statement the relevant amounts will be presented.

## * Question 9

On 1 April 20W9 Oliver granted share options to 20 senior executives. The options are due to vest on 31 March 20X2 provided the senior executives remain with the company for the period between 1 April 20W9 and 31 March 20X2. The number of options vesting to each director depends on the cumulative profits over the three-year period from 1 April 20W9 to 31 March 20X2:

● 10,000 options per director if the cumulative profits are between €5 million and €10 million;

● 15,000 options per director if the cumulative profits are more than €10 million.

On 1 April 20W9 and 31 March 20X0 the best estimate of the cumulative profits for the three-year period ending on 31 March 20X2 was €8 million. However, following very successful results in the year ended 31 March 20X1 the latest estimate of the cumulative profits in the relevant three-year period is €14 million.

On 1 April 20W9 it was estimated that all 20 senior executives would remain with Oliver for the three-year period but on 31 December 20W9 one senior executive left unexpectedly. None of the other executives have since left and none are expected to leave before 31 March 20X2.

A further condition for vesting of the options is that the share price of Oliver should be at least €12 on 31 March 20X2. The share price of Oliver over the last two years has changed as follows:

- €10 on 1 April 20W9;
- €11.75 on 31 March 20X0;
- €11.25 on 31 March 20X1.

On 1 April 20W9 the fair value of the share options granted by Oliver was €4.80 per option. This had increased to €5.50 by 31 March 20X0 and €6.50 by 31 March 20X1.

**Required:**
**Produce extracts, with supporting explanations, from the statements of financial position at 31 March 20X0 and 20X1 and from the statements of comprehensive income for the years ended 31 March 20X0 and 20X1 that show how the granting of the share options will be reflected in the financial statements of Oliver. Ignore deferred tax.**

## Question 10

A plc issues 50,000 share options to its employees on 1 January 2008 which the employees can only exercise if they remain with the company until 31 December 2010. The options have a fair value of £5 each on 1 January 2008.

It is expected that the holders of options over 8,000 shares will leave A plc before 31 December 2010.

In March 2008 adverse press comments regarding A plc's environmental policies and a downturn in the stock market cause the share price to fall significantly to below the exercise price on the options. The share price is not expected to recover in the foreseeable future.

**Required:**
**What charge should A plc recognise for share options in the financial statements for the year ended 31 December 2008?**

## Notes

1  IAS 19 *Employee Benefits*, IASB, amended 2011.
2  IAS 26 *Accounting and Reporting by Retirement Benefit Plans*, IASC, reformatted 1994.
3  IFRS 2 *Share-based Payment*, IASB, amended 2013.
4  IAS 26 *Accounting and Reporting by Retirement Benefit Plans*, IASC, reformatted 1994.

# CHAPTER 16

# Taxation in company accounts

## 16.1 Introduction

The main purpose of this chapter is to explain the corporation tax system and the accounting treatment of deferred tax.

### Objectives

By the end of this chapter, you should be able to:

- discuss the theoretical background to corporation tax systems;
- critically discuss tax avoidance and tax evasion;
- prepare deferred tax calculations;
- critically discuss deferred tax provisions.

## 16.2 Corporation tax

Limited companies, and indeed all corporate bodies, are treated for tax purposes as being legally separate from their proprietors. Thus, a limited company is itself liable to pay tax on its profits. This tax is known as **corporation tax**. The shareholders are accountable for tax only on the income they receive by way of any dividends distributed by the company. If the shareholder is an individual, then **income tax** becomes due on their dividend income received.

This is in contrast to the position in a partnership, where each partner is individually liable for the tax on their share of the pre-tax profit that has been allocated. A partner is taxed on the profit and not simply on drawings. Note that this is different from the treatment of an employee who is charged tax on the amount of salary that is paid.

In this chapter we consider the different types of company taxation and their accounting treatment. The International Accounting Standard that applies specifically to taxation is IAS 12 *Income Taxes*. The standard was last revised by the IASB in 2012. Those UK unquoted companies that choose not to follow international standards will follow FRSs 100–102 from 2015 (with earlier adoption allowed).

Corporation tax is calculated under rules set by Parliament each year in the Finance Act. The Finance Act may alter the existing rules; it also sets the rate of tax payable. Because of this annual review of the rules, circumstances may change year by year, which makes comparability difficult and forecasting uncertain.

The reason for the need to adjust accounting profits for tax purposes is that although the tax payable is based on the accounting profits as disclosed in the statement of income, the tax rules may differ from the accounting rules which apply prudence to income recognition. For example, the tax rules may not accept that all the expenses which are recognised by the accountant under the IASB's *Framework for the Preparation and Presentation of Financial Statements* and the IAS 1 *Presentation of Financial Statements* accrual concept are deductible when arriving at the taxable profit. An example of this might be a bonus, payable to an employee (based on profits), which is payable in arrears but which is deducted from accounting profit as an accrual under IAS 1. This expense is allowed in calculating taxable profit on a cash basis only when it is paid in order to ensure that one taxpayer does not reduce his potential tax liability before another becomes liable to tax on the income received.

The accounting profit may therefore be lower or higher than the taxable profit. For example, the formation expenses of a company, which are the costs of establishing it on incorporation, must be written off in its first accounting period; the rules of corporation tax, however, state that these are a capital expense and cannot be deducted from the profit for tax purposes. This means that more tax will be assessed as payable than one would assume from an inspection of the published statement of income.

Similarly, although most businesses would consider that entertaining customers and other business associates was a normal commercial trading expense, it is not allowed as a deduction for tax purposes.

A more complicated situation arises in the case of depreciation. Because the directors have the choice of method of depreciation to use, the legislators have decided to require all companies to use the same method when calculating taxable profits. If one thinks about this, then it would seem to be the equitable practice. Each company is allowed to deduct a uniform percentage from its profits in respect of the depreciation that has arisen from the wear and tear and diminution in value of non-current assets.

The substituted depreciation that the tax rules allow is known as a **capital allowance**. The capital allowance is calculated in the same way as depreciation; the only difference is that the rates are those set out in the Finance Acts.

## 16.3 Corporation tax systems – the theoretical background

It might be useful to explain that there are three possible systems of company taxation: classical, imputation and partial imputation.[1] These systems differ solely in their tax treatment of the relationship between the limited company and those shareholders who have invested in it.

### 16.3.1 The classical system

In the classical system, a company pays tax on its profits, and then the shareholders suffer a second and separate tax liability when their share of the profits is distributed to them. In effect, the dividend income of the shareholder is regarded as a second and separate source of income from that of the profits of the company. The payment of a dividend creates an additional tax liability which falls directly on the shareholders. It could be argued that this double taxation is inequitable when compared to the taxation system on unincorporated bodies where the rate of taxation suffered overall remains the same whether or not profits are withdrawn from the business. It is suggested that this classical system discourages the distribution of profits to shareholders, since the second tranche of taxation (the tax on dividend income of the shareholders) only becomes payable on payment of the dividend, although some argue that the effect of the burden of double taxation on the economy is less serious than it might seem.[2]

It is also suggested that under this system companies have an incentive to avoid tax as any savings achieved in this way increases the after-tax profits available for dividends.

It is in some countries where the company income tax rates are low such as Ireland and Switzerland that there are classical company income tax systems where dividends are taxed at shareholder's marginal tax rate without credit for company income tax paid.

### 16.3.2 The imputation system

In an imputation system, the dividend is regarded merely as a flow of the profits on each sale to the individual shareholders, as there is considered to be merely one source of income which could be either retained in the company or distributed to the shareholders. It is certainly correct that the payment of a dividend results from the flow of moneys into the company from trading profits, and that the choice between retaining profits to fund future growth and the payment of a dividend to investing shareholders is merely a strategic choice unrelated to a view as to the nature of taxable profits.

In an imputation system the total of the tax paid by the company and by the shareholder is unaffected by the payment of dividends, and the tax paid by the company is treated as if it were also a payment of the individual shareholders' liabilities on dividends received. It is this principle of the flow of net profits from particular sales to individual shareholders that has justified the repayment of tax to shareholders with low incomes or to non-taxable shareholders of tax paid by the limited company, even though that tax credit has represented a reduction in the overall tax revenue of the state because the tax credit repaid also represented a payment of the company's own corporation tax liability. If the dividend had not been distributed to such a low-income or non-taxable shareholder who was entitled to repayment, the tax revenue collected would have been higher overall.

Australia and New Zealand alone of the OECD countries have a full imputation system where a tax credit is given to shareholders for the full corporate tax. One of the benefits seen is that Australian companies with largely resident shareholders have less incentive to avoid or defer company income tax, so reducing the need for anti-avoidance rules.

### 16.3.3 The partial imputation system

In a partial imputation system only part of the underlying corporation tax paid is treated as a tax credit. Canada and the United Kingdom operate a partial imputation system where shareholders receive a tax credit for only a portion of the corporate tax. The UK modified its imputation system in 1999, so that a low-income or non-taxable shareholder (such as a charity) could no longer recover any tax credit. Other countries such as France and Germany have moved away from the imputation system.

### 16.3.4 Common basis

All three systems are based on the taxation of profits earned as shown under the same basic principles used in the preparation of financial statements.

## 16.4 Corporation tax and dividends

A company pays corporation tax on its income. When that company pays a dividend to its shareholders it is distributing some of its taxed income among the proprietors. In an imputation system the tax paid by the company is 'imputed' to the shareholders who therefore receive a dividend which has already been taxed.

This means that, from the paying company's point of view, the concept of gross dividends does not exist. From the paying company's point of view, the amount of dividend paid shown in the statement of income will equal the cash that the company will have paid.

However, from the shareholder's point of view, the cash received from the company is treated as a net payment after deduction of tax. The shareholders will have received, with the cash dividend, a note of a tax credit, which is regarded as equal to basic rate income tax on the total of the dividend plus the tax credit. For example:

| | |
|---|---:|
| Dividend being the cash paid by the company to the shareholders and disclosed in the company's statement of income | 360 |
| Imputed tax credit of 1/9 of dividend paid (being the rate from 6 April 1999) | 40 |
| Gross dividend received by the shareholder | 400 |

The imputed tax credit calculation (as shown above) has been based on a basic tax rate of 10% for dividends paid, being the basic rate of income tax on dividend income from 6 April 1999. This means that an individual shareholder who only pays basic rate income tax has no further liability in that the assumption is that the basic rate tax has been paid by the company. A non-taxpayer (including charities and pension funds) cannot obtain a repayment of tax.

Although a company pays corporation tax on its income, when that company pays a dividend to its shareholders it is still considered to be distributing some of its taxed income among the proprietors. In this system the tax payable by the company is 'imputed' to the shareholders who therefore receive a dividend which has already been taxed.

The essential point is that the dividend-paying company makes absolutely no deduction from the dividend, **nor is any payment made by the company to HM Revenue and Customs**. The addition of 1/9 of the dividend paid as an imputed tax credit is purely nominal. A tax credit of 1/9 of the dividend will be deemed to be attached to that dividend (in effect an income tax rate of 10%). That credit is notional in that no payment of the 10% will be made to HM Revenue and Customs. The payment of taxation is not associated with dividends.

Large companies (those with taxable profits of over £1,500,000) pay their corporation tax liability in quarterly instalments starting within the year of account, rather than paying their corporation tax liability nine months thereafter. The payment of taxation is not associated with the payment of dividends. Smaller companies pay their corporation tax nine months after the year-end.

## 16.5 Corporation tax systems – avoidance and evasion

'Avoidance' means reducing your tax liability legally. In the UK and other countries there has been much discussion and public comment on companies and wealthy individuals minimising the tax they pay, sometimes by artificial tax avoidance schemes. There has been public criticism of the very small UK Corporation Tax paid by some large international companies with significant activities in the UK.

'Evasion' means avoiding tax illegally, i.e. breaking the law.

In attempting to combat evasion and artificial avoidance schemes tax legislation has become increasingly complex – its very complexity providing the opportunity to design yet more ingenious mechanisms to reduce the tax liability.

In the UK the government has passed the Targeted Anti Avoidance Rules (TAARs) and a General Anti Abuse Rule (GAAR). TAARs aim to prevent tax avoidance in specific areas of the legislation whereas the GAAR is targeted at flagrant abusive and artificial schemes. A number of other jurisdictions such as Australia and Canada also have a general anti-avoidance rule.

In 2010 the UK Government asked Graham Aaronson QC to set up a committee to seek ways of preventing major tax avoidance. This committee is called the GAAR Study and it reported in 2011. Its conclusions[3] were:

- there should not be a general anti-avoidance rule; but
- it would be beneficial to introduce a rule targeted at **abusive arrangements.**

Following this, the UK Government introduced legislation into the Finance Act 2013 which aimed to cover abusive arrangements.

Governments have to follow the same basic principles of management as individuals. To spend money, there has to be a source of funds. The sources of funds are borrowing and income. With governments, the source of income is taxation. As with individuals, there is a practical limit as to how much they can borrow; to spend for the benefit of the populace, taxation has to be collected. In a democracy, the tax system is set up to ensure that the more prosperous tend to pay a greater proportion of their income in order to fund the needs of the poorer; this is called a progressive system. As Franklin Roosevelt, the American politician, stated, 'taxes, after all, are the dues that we pay for the privileges of membership in an organized society'.[4] Corporation tax on company profits represents 6% of the taxation collected by HM Revenue and Customs in the UK from taxes on income and wages.

It appears to be a general rule that taxpayers do not enjoy paying taxation (despite the fact that they may well understand the theory underpinning the collection of taxation). This fact of human nature applies just as much to company directors handling company resources as it does to individuals. Every extra pound paid in taxation by a company reduces the resources available for retention for funding future growth or paying dividends.

### 16.5.1 Tax evasion

Politicians often complain about tax evasion. Evasion is the illegal (and immoral) manipulation of business affairs to escape taxation. An example could be the directors of a family-owned company taking cash sales for their own expenditure. Another example might be the payment of a low salary (below the threshold of income tax) to a family member not working in the company, thus reducing profits in an attempt to reduce corporation tax. It is easy to understand the illegality and immorality of such practices. Increasingly the distinction between tax avoidance and tax evasion has been blurred.[5] When politicians complain of tax evasion, they tend not to distinguish between evasion and avoidance.

### 16.5.2 Tax avoidance

Tax avoidance could initially be defined as a manipulation of one's affairs, within the law, so as to reduce liability; indeed, as it is legal, it can be argued that it is not immoral. There is a well-established tradition within the UK that 'every man is entitled if he can to order his affairs so that the tax attaching under the appropriate Acts is less than it otherwise would be'.[6]

Indeed the government deliberately sets up special provisions to reduce taxes in order to encourage certain behaviours. The more that employers and employees save for employee retirement, the less social security benefits will be paid out in the future. Thus both companies and individuals obtain full relief against taxation for pension contributions. Another example might be increased tax depreciation (capital allowances) on capital investment, in order to increase industrial investment and improve productivity within the UK economy.

The use of such provisions, as intended by the legislators, is not criticised by anyone, and might better be termed 'tax planning'. The problem area lies between the proper use of such tax planning, and illegal activities. This 'grey area' could best be called 'tax avoidance'. The Institute for Fiscal Studies has stated:

> We think it is impossible to define the expression 'tax avoidance' in any truly satisfactory manner. People routinely alter their behaviour to reduce or defer their taxation liabilities. In doing so, commentators regard some actions as legitimate tax planning and others as tax avoidance. We have regarded tax avoidance (in contra-indication to legitimate . . . tax planning) as action taken to reduce or defer tax liabilities in a way Parliament plainly did not intend.[7]

The law tends to define tax avoidance as an artificial element in the manipulation of one's affairs, within the law, so as to reduce liability.[8]

### 16.5.3 The problem of distinguishing between avoidance and evasion

The problem lies in distinguishing clearly between legal avoidance and illegal evasion. It can be difficult for accountants to walk the careful line between helping clients (in tax avoidance) and colluding with them against HM Revenue and Customs.[9]

When clients seek advice, accountants have to be careful to ensure that they have integrity in all professional and business relationships. Integrity implies not merely honesty but fair dealing and truthfulness. 'In all dealings relating to the tax authorities, a member must act honestly and do nothing that might mislead the authorities.'[10]

As an example to illustrate the problems that could arise, a client company has carried out a transaction to avoid taxation, but failed to minute the details as discussed at a directors' meeting. If the accountant were to correct this act of omission in arrears, this would be a move from tax avoidance towards tax evasion. Another example of such a move from tax avoidance to tax evasion might be where an accountant in informing HM Revenue and Customs of a tax-avoiding transaction fails to detail aspects of the transaction which might show it in a disadvantageous light.

Companies can move profit centres from high-taxation countries to low-taxation countries by setting up subsidiaries therein. These areas, known in extreme cases as 'tax havens', are disliked by governments.

**Tax havens** are countries with very low or zero tax rates on some or all forms of income. They could be classified into two groups:

1 the zero-rate and low-tax havens;

2 the tax havens that impose tax at normal rates but grant preferential treatment to certain activities.

The use of zero-rate and low-tax havens could be considered a form of tax avoidance, although sometimes they are used by tax evaders for their lack of regulation.

A similar problem has arisen in the use of charitable donations where tax relief is allowed to the donor and is a legitimate avoidance to encourage donations, except that the system has been manipulated as a form of tax evasion. This is an international problem and an OECD *Report on Abuse of Charities for Money-laundering and Tax Evasion* issued in 2009 stated that 'Tax evasion and tax fraud through the abuse of charities is a serious and increasing risk in many countries although its impact is variable. Some countries estimate that the abuse of charities costs their treasury many hundreds of millions of dollars and is becoming more prevalent'.[11]

### 16.5.4 Countering tax avoidance

An interesting discussion paper, *Countering Tax Avoidance in the UK: Which Way Forward?*, was published by the IFS in 2009.[12] It recognises that there is a difficulty in defining what constitutes avoidance.

It is a grey area and possibly not capable of a precise definition. Revenue authorities may often appear to consider tax avoidance to occur where it is sought to reduce the tax burden of individuals, businesses and other entities below the level envisaged by the government; the problem is, however, that the envisaged level is usually unclear.

In the public eye there is a view that certain types of avoidance are unacceptable. This leaves open the question, however, as to what is acceptable. What is acceptable to a taxpayer might be unacceptable to the tax collector. In principle, what is acceptable should be clear from the government as the body responsible for the raising of taxes. In practice it is incredibly difficult to cover all schemes through legislation. Detailed legislation, for instance, to indicate what is acceptable risks becoming more and more complex. This leads to the possibility for schemes to be designed which reflect the legal position but not the commercial substance. It is a similar problem to that faced by standard setters who have adopted the substance over form approach in areas such as accounting for leases.

Adopting a fuzzy approach rather than detailed legislation might appear to give the tax collector greater ability to counteract avoidance, but there is a downside – multinational companies might decide that there is too much uncertainty and base themselves in another jurisdiction.

### 16.5.5 International approaches

The discussion paper considers the approaches taken to counteracting avoidance in countries such as the UK and the Netherlands. It sets out that the Netherlands, for example, has both a case-based and a practical approach to avoidance.

The **case-based** concept is known as '*fraus legis*'. *Fraus legis* means that the person has acted contrary to the intention of the law even though they have complied with the letter of the law. In order for it to apply, the avoidance of tax must be the only or paramount motive for the transaction and there must be a conflict with the intention and purpose of the law. Once applied, the judges may decide to ignore the tax avoidance transaction or replace it with other transactions if that would better fit with the purpose of the law.

The **practical approach** is to manage the taxpayer relationship. Since 2005, the Dutch tax authorities have entered into 'enforcement covenants' with certain multinationals. Currently, more than 40 have concluded these agreements. The Dutch tax authorities agree to reduce their supervision of the taxpayer's affairs and in return the taxpayer agrees to report tax risks. The taxpayer must be recognised as compliant for this option to be offered to them. The taxpayer effectively agrees to abide by not only the letter of the law but also its spirit and has to be seen to be paying a fair share of tax. A multinational with its tax burden reduced to nil would not be viewed as suitable for this approach.

#### The EU approach

The EU is concerned about Base Erosion Profit Shifting and proposed in 2016 that all large multinationals publicly reveal aggregated earnings data for each EU country they operate in and how much they earn outside the EU and, in addition, provide detailed aggregated data for non-EU tax havens. This recognises that there is a public demand for more transparency and fairness. It does, of course, have some interesting political dimensions – for instance the EU proposal that there should be a list of jurisdictions that do not respect good governance raises the questions of how to regard the US state of Delaware where there are loose company registration rules.

## 16.6 IAS 12 – accounting for current taxation

The essence of IAS 12 is that it requires an enterprise to account for the tax consequences of transactions and other events in the same way that it accounts for the transactions and other events themselves. Thus, for transactions and other events recognised in the statement of comprehensive income, any related tax effects are also recognised in the statement of comprehensive income.

The details of how IAS 12 requires an enterprise to account for the tax consequences of transactions and other events follow below.

### Statement of comprehensive income disclosure

The standard (paragraph 77) states that the tax expense related to profit or loss from ordinary activities should be presented on the face of the statement of comprehensive income. It also provides that the major components of the tax expense should be disclosed separately. These separate components of the tax expense may include (paragraph 80):

(a) current tax expense for the period of account;

(b) any adjustments recognised in the current period of account for prior periods (such as where the charge in a past year was underprovided);

(c) the amount of any benefit arising from a previously unrecognised tax loss, tax credit or temporary difference of a prior period that is used to reduce the current tax expense; and

(d) the amount of tax expense (income) relating to those changes in accounting policies and fundamental errors which are included in the determination of net profit or loss for the period in accordance with the allowed alternative treatment in IAS 8 *Net Profit or Loss for the Period, Fundamental Errors and Changes in Accounting Policies.*

### Statement of financial position disclosure

The standard states that current tax for current and prior periods should, to the extent unpaid, be recognised as a liability. If the amount already paid in respect of current and prior periods exceeds the amount due for those periods, the excess should be recognised as an asset.

### The treatment of tax losses

As regards losses for tax purposes, the standard states that the benefit relating to a tax loss that can be carried back to recover current tax of a previous period should be recognised as an asset. Tax assets and tax liabilities should be presented separately from other assets and liabilities in the statement of financial position. An enterprise should offset (paragraph 71) current tax assets and current tax liabilities if, and only if, the enterprise:

(a) has a legally enforceable right to set off the recognised amounts; and

(b) intends either to settle on a net basis, or to realise the asset and settle the liability simultaneously.

The standard provides (paragraph 81) that the following should also be disclosed separately:

(a) tax expense (income) relating to extraordinary items recognised during the period;

(b) an explanation of the relationship between tax expense (income) and accounting profit in either or both of the following forms:

    (i) a numerical reconciliation between tax expense (income) and the product of accounting profit multiplied by the applicable tax rate(s), disclosing also the basis on which the applicable tax rate(s) is/are computed; or

(ii) a numerical reconciliation between the average effective tax rate and the applicable tax rate, disclosing also the basis on which the applicable tax rate is computed; and

(c) an explanation of changes in the applicable tax rate(s) compared to the previous accounting period.

### The relationship between tax expense and accounting profit

The following example is an explanation of the relationship between tax expense (income) and accounting profit:

*Current Tax Expense*

|  | X5 | X6 |
|---|---|---|
| Accounting profit | 8,775 | 8,740 |
| *Add* |  |  |
| Depreciation for accounting purposes | 4,800 | 8,250 |
| Charitable donations | 500 | 350 |
| Fine for environmental pollution | 700 | — |
| Product development costs | 250 | 250 |
| Health care benefits payable | 2,000 | 1,000 |
|  | 17,025 | 18,590 |
| *Deduct* |  |  |
| Depreciation for tax purposes | (8,100) | (11,850) |
| Taxable profit | 8,925 | 6,740 |
| Current tax expense at 40% | 3,570 |  |
| Current tax expense at 35% |  | 2,359 |

## 16.7 Deferred tax

### 16.7.1 IAS 12 – background to deferred taxation[13]

The profit on which tax is paid may differ from that shown in the published statement of income. This is caused by two separate factors.

#### Permanent differences

One factor that we looked at above is that certain items of expenditure may not be legitimate deductions from profit for tax purposes under the tax legislation. These differences are referred to as permanent differences because they will not be allowed at a different time and will be permanently disallowed, even in future accounting periods.

#### Timing differences

Another factor is that there are some other expenses that are legitimate deductions in arriving at the taxable profit which are allowed as a deduction for tax purposes at a later date. These might be simply timing differences in that tax relief and charges to the statement of income occur in different accounting periods. The accounting profit is prepared on an accruals basis but the taxable profit might require certain of the items to be dealt with on a cash basis. Examples of this might include bonuses payable to senior management, properly included in the financial statements under the accruals concept but not eligible for tax relief until actually paid some considerable time later, thus giving tax relief in a later period.

## Temporary differences[13]

The original IAS 12 allowed an enterprise to account for deferred tax using the statement of comprehensive income liability method which focused on timing differences. IAS 12 (revised) requires the statement of financial position liability method, which focuses on temporary differences, to be used. Timing differences are differences between taxable profit and accounting profit that originate in one period and reverse in one or more subsequent periods. Temporary differences are differences between the tax base of an asset or liability and its carrying amount in the statement of financial position. The tax base of an asset or liability is the amount attributed to that asset or liability for tax purposes. All timing differences are temporary differences.

The most significant temporary difference is depreciation. The depreciation charge made in the financial statements must be added back in the tax calculations and replaced by the official tax allowance for such an expense. The substituted expense calculated in accordance with the tax rules is rarely the same amount as the depreciation charge computed in accordance with IAS 16 *Property, Plant and Equipment*.

## Capital investment incentive effect

It is common for legislation to provide for higher rates of tax depreciation than are used for accounting purposes, for it is believed that the consequent deferral of taxation liabilities serves as an incentive to capital investment (this incentive is not forbidden by European Union law or the OECD rules). The classic effect of this is for tax to be payable on a lower figure than the accounting profit in the earlier years of an asset's life because the tax allowances usually exceed depreciation in those years. In later accounting periods, the tax allowances will be lower than the depreciation charges and the taxable profit will then be higher than the accounting profit that appears in the published statement of income.

## Deferred tax provisions

The process whereby the company pays tax on a profit that is lower than the reported profit in the early years and on a profit that is higher than reported profit in later years is known as reversal. Given the knowledge that, ultimately, these timing differences will reverse, the accruals concept requires that consideration be given to making provision for the future liability in those early years in which the tax payable is calculated on a lower figure. The provision that is made is known as a deferred tax provision.

## Alternative methods for calculating deferred tax provisions

As you might expect, there has been a history of disagreement within the accounting profession over the method to use to calculate the provision. There have been, historically, two methods of calculating the provision for this future liability – the deferral method and the liability method.

### The deferral method

The deferral method, which used to be favoured in the USA, involves the calculation each year of the tax effects of the timing differences that have arisen in that year. The tax effect is then debited or credited to the statement of income as part of the tax charge; the double entry is effected by making an entry to the deferred tax account. This deferral method of calculating the tax effect ignores the effect of changing tax rates on the timing differences that arose in earlier periods. This means that the total provision may consist of differences calculated at the rate of tax in force in the year when the entry was made to the provision.

### The liability method

The liability method requires the calculation of the total amount of potential liability each year at current rates of tax, increasing or reducing the provision accordingly. This means that the company keeps a record of the timing differences and then recalculates at the end of each new accounting period using the rate of corporation tax in force as at the date of the current statement of financial position.

To illustrate the two methods we will take the example of a single asset, costing £10,000, depreciated at 10% using the straight-line method, but subject to a tax allowance of 25% on the reducing balance method. The workings are shown in Figure 16.1. This shows that, if there were no other adjustments, for the first four years the profits subject to tax would be lower than those shown in the accounts, but afterwards the situation would reverse.

### Charge to statement of comprehensive income under the deferral method

The deferral method would charge to the statement of income each year the variation multiplied by the current tax rate, e.g. 20X5 at 25% on £1,500 giving £375.00, and 20X8 at 24% on £55 giving £13.20. This is in accordance with the accruals concept which matches the tax expense against the income that gave rise to it. Under this method the deferred tax provision will be credited with £375 in 20X6 and this amount will not be altered in 20X8 when the tax rate changes to 24%. In the example, the calculation for the five years would be as in Figure 16.2.

### Charge to statement of comprehensive income under the liability method

The liability method would make a charge so that the total balance on deferred tax equalled the cumulative variation multiplied by the current tax rate. The intention is that the statement of financial position liability should be stated at a figure which represents the tax effect as at the end of each new accounting period. This means that there would be an adjustment made in 20X8 to recalculate the tax effect of the timing difference that was provided for in earlier years. For example, the provision for 20X6 would be recalculated at 24%, giving a figure of £360 instead of the £375 that was calculated and charged in 20X6. The decrease in the expected liability will be reflected in the amount charged against the statement of income in 20X6. The £15 will in effect be credited to the 20X6 profit statement.

### Figure 16.1 Deferred tax provision using deferral method

| | | Accounts (depreciation) £ | Tax (allowances) £ | Difference (temporary) £ | Tax (rate) |
|---|---|---|---|---|---|
| 01.01.20X5 | Cost of asset | 10,000 | 10,000 | | |
| 31.12.20X5 | Depn/tax allowance | 1,000 | 2,500 | 1,500 | 25% |
| | | 9,000 | 7,500 | 1,500 | |
| 31.12.20X6 | Depn/tax allowance | 1,000 | 1,875 | 875 | 25% |
| | | 8,000 | 5,625 | 2,375 | |
| 31.12.20X7 | Depn/tax allowance | 1,000 | 1,406 | 406 | 25% |
| | | 7,000 | 4,219 | 2,781 | |
| 31.12.20X8 | Depn/tax allowance | 1,000 | 1,055 | 55 | 24% |
| | | 6,000 | 3,164 | 2,836 | |
| 31.12.20X9 | Depn/tax allowance | 1,000 | 791 | (209) | 24% |
| | | 5,000 | 2,373 | 2,627 | |

**Figure 16.2 Summary of deferred tax provision using the deferral method**

| Year ended | Timing difference £ | Basic rate % | Deferred tax charge in year £ | Deferred tax provision (deferral method) £ |
|---|---|---|---|---|
| 31.12.20X5 | 1,500 | 25% | 375.00 | 375.00 |
| 31.12.20X6 | 875 | 25% | 218.75 | 593.75 |
| 31.12.20X7 | 406 | 25% | 101.50 | 695.25 |
| 31.12.20X8 | 55 | 24% | 13.20 | 708.45 |
| 31.12.20X9 | (209) | 24% | (50.16) | 658.29 |

The effect on the charge to the 20X9 profit statement (Figures 16.2 and 16.3) is that there will be a charge of £13.20 using the deferral method and a **credit** of £14.61 using the liability method. The £14.61 is the reduction in the amount provided from £695.25 at the end of 20X8 to the £680.64 that is required at the end of 20X9.

### World trend towards the liability method

There has been a move in national standards away from the deferral method towards the liability method, which is a change of emphasis from the statement of comprehensive income to the statement of financial position because the deferred tax liability is shown at current rates of tax in the liability method. This is in accordance with the IASB's conceptual framework which requires that all items in the statement of financial position, other than shareholders' equity, must be either assets or liabilities as defined in the framework. Deferred tax as it is calculated under the traditional deferral method is not in fact a calculation of a liability, but is better characterised as deferred income or expenditure. This is illustrated by the fact that the sum calculated under the deferral method is not recalculated to take account of changes in the rate of tax charged, whereas it is recalculated under the liability method.

The world trend towards using the liability method also results in a change from accounting only for timing differences to accounting for temporary differences.

### Temporary versus timing: conceptual difference

These temporary differences are defined in the IASB standard as 'differences between the carrying amount of an asset or liability in the statement of financial position and its tax base'.[13]

**Figure 16.3 Deferral tax provision using the liability method**

| Year ended | Temporary difference £ | Basic rate | Deferred tax charge in year £ | Deferred tax provision (deferral method) £ | Rate in 20X9 | Deferred tax provision (liability method) £ |
|---|---|---|---|---|---|---|
| 31.12.20X6 | 1,500 | 25% | 375.00 | 375.00 | 24% | 360.00 |
| 31.12.20X7 | 875 | 25% | 218.75 | 593.75 | 24% | 210.00 |
| 31.12.20X8 | 406 | 25% | 101.50 | 695.25 | 24% | 97.44 |
| 31.12.20X9 | 55 | 24% | 13.20 | 708.45 | 24% | 13.20 |
| | | | | 708.45 | | 680.64 |

The conceptual difference between these two views is that under the liability method provision is made for only the future reversal of these timing differences, whereas the temporary difference approach provides for the tax that would be payable if the company were to be liquidated at statement of financial position values (i.e. if the company were to sell all assets at statement of financial position values).

The US standard SFAS 109 argues the theoretical basis for these temporary differences to be accounted for on the following grounds:

> A government levies taxes on net taxable income. Temporary differences will become taxable amounts in future years, thereby increasing taxable income and taxes payable, upon recovery or settlement of the recognized and reported amounts of an enterprise's assets or liabilities . . . A contention that those temporary differences will never result in taxable amounts . . . would contradict the accounting assumption inherent in the statement of financial position that the reported amounts of assets and liabilities will be recovered and settled, respectively; thereby making that statement internally inconsistent.[14]

A consequence of accepting this conceptual argument in IAS 12 is that provision must also be made for the potential taxation effects of asset revaluations.

### 16.7.2 IAS 12 – deferred taxation

The standard requires that the financial statements are prepared using the liability method described above (which is sometimes known as the statement of financial position liability method).

An example of how deferred taxation operates follows.

EXAMPLE ● An asset which cost £150 has a carrying amount of £100. Cumulative depreciation for tax purposes is £90 and the tax rate is 25% as shown in Figure 16.4.

The tax base of the asset is £60 (cost of £150 less cumulative tax depreciation of £90). To recover the carrying amount of £100, the enterprise must earn taxable income of £100, but will only be able to deduct tax depreciation of £60. Consequently, the enterprise will pay taxes of £10 (£40 at 25%) when it recovers the carrying amount of the asset. The difference between the carrying amount of £100 and the tax base of £60 is a taxable temporary difference of £40. Therefore, the enterprise recognises a deferred tax liability of £10 (£40 at 25%) representing the income taxes that it will pay when it recovers the carrying amount of the asset as shown in Figure 16.5.

#### The accounting treatment over the life of an asset

The following example illustrates the accounting treatment over the life of an asset.

EXAMPLE ● An enterprise buys equipment for £10,000 and depreciates it on a straight-line basis over its expected useful life of five years. For tax purposes, the equipment is depreciated

#### Figure 16.4 Cumulative depreciation

|  | In accounts | For tax |
|---|---|---|
| Cost | 150 | 150 |
| Depreciation | 50 | 90 |
| Carrying amount | 100 | 60 |

**Figure 16.5 Deferred tax liability**

| Income to recover | |
|---|---|
| Carrying amount | £100 |
| Carrying amount for tax | £60 |
| Temporary difference | £40 |
| Tax rate | 25% |
| Deferred tax | £10 |

at 25% per annum on a straight-line basis. Tax losses may be carried back against taxable profit of the previous five years. In year 0, the enterprise's taxable profit was £0. The tax rate is 40%. The enterprise will recover the carrying amount of the equipment by using it to manufacture goods for resale. Therefore, the enterprise's current tax computation is as follows:

| Year | 1 | 2 | 3 | 4 | 5 |
|---|---|---|---|---|---|
| Taxable income (£) | 2,000 | 2,000 | 2,000 | 2,000 | 2,000 |
| Depreciation for tax purposes | 2,500 | 2,500 | 2,500 | 2,500 | 0 |
| Tax profit (loss) | (500) | (500) | (500) | (500) | 2,000 |
| Current tax expense (income) at 40% | (200) | (200) | (200) | (200) | 800 |

The enterprise recognises a current tax asset at the end of years 1 to 4 because it recovers the benefit of the tax loss against the taxable profit of year 0.

The temporary differences associated with the equipment and the resulting deferred tax asset and liability and deferred tax expense and income are as follows:

| Year | 1 | 2 | 3 | 4 | 5 |
|---|---|---|---|---|---|
| Carrying amount (£) | 8,000 | 6,000 | 4,000 | 2,000 | 0 |
| Tax base | 7,500 | 5,000 | 2,500 | 0 | 0 |
| Taxable temporary difference | 500 | 1,000 | 1,500 | 2,000 | 0 |
| Opening deferred tax liability | 0 | 200 | 400 | 600 | 800 |
| Deferred tax expense (income) | 200 | 200 | 200 | 200 | (800) |
| Closing deferred tax liability | 200 | 400 | 600 | 800 | 0 |

The enterprise recognises the deferred tax liability in years 1 to 4 because the reversal of the taxable temporary difference will create taxable income in subsequent years. The enterprise's statement of comprehensive income is as follows:

| Year | 1 | 2 | 3 | 4 | 5 |
|---|---|---|---|---|---|
| Income (£) | 2,000 | 2,000 | 2,000 | 2,000 | 2,000 |
| Depreciation | 2,000 | 2,000 | 2,000 | 2,000 | 2,000 |
| Profit before tax | 0 | 0 | 0 | 0 | 0 |
| Current tax expense (income) | (200) | (200) | (200) | (200) | 800 |
| Deferred tax expense (income) | 200 | 200 | 200 | 200 | (800) |
| Total tax expense (income) | 0 | 0 | 0 | 0 | 0 |
| Net profit for the period | 0 | 0 | 0 | 0 | 0 |

Further examples of items that could give rise to temporary differences are:

● Retirement benefit costs may be deducted in determining accounting profit as service is provided by the employee, but deducted in determining taxable profit either when contributions are paid to a fund by the enterprise or when retirement benefits are paid by the enterprise. A temporary difference exists between the carrying amount of the liability (in the financial statements) and its tax base (the carrying amount of the liability for tax purposes); the tax base of the liability is usually nil.

● Research costs are recognised as an expense in determining accounting profit in the period in which they are incurred but may not be permitted as a deduction in determining taxable profit (tax loss) until a later period. The difference between the tax base (the carrying amount of the liability for tax purposes) of the research costs, being the amount the taxation authorities will permit as a deduction in future periods, and the carrying amount of nil is a deductible temporary difference that results in a deferred tax asset.

### Treatment of asset revaluations

The original IAS 12 permitted, but did not require, an enterprise to recognise a deferred tax liability in respect of asset revaluations. If such assets were sold at the revalued sum then a profit would arise that could be subject to tax. IAS 12 as currently written requires an enterprise to recognise a deferred tax liability in respect of asset revaluations.

REVALUATION EXAMPLE ● At 31.12.20X1 the company had reported its land and buildings within non-current assets at the following values:

|  | €000 |
|---|---|
| Land | 500 |
| Buildings | 1,200 |

On 1 January 20X2, the land was revalued to €700,000 and its buildings to €1,800,000. At that date the building had a remaining life of 25 years.

**Required:** Assuming that the Corporation Tax on capital gains is 30%, state the balances on the respective accounts at 1 January 20X2 following the revaluation.

**Solution:**
The land will be revalued to €700,000 with a capital gain of €200,000.

This gain will be credited €140,000 to a revaluation reserve (70% of €200,000) and €60,000 (30%) to deferred tax.

The building will be revalued to €1,800,000 with a capital gain of €600,000.

This gain will be credited €420,000 to a revaluation reserve (70%) and €180,000 to deferred tax (30%).

So, deferred tax will increase by €240,000 and the revaluation reserve by €560,000.

The revaluation of €800,000 and the transfer to deferred tax of €240,000 will appear in 'Other Comprehensive Income'. In the statement of financial position the revaluation reserve will be included under 'other components of equity' and deferred tax will be under 'non-current liabilities'.

Such a deferred tax liability on a revalued asset might not arise for many years, for there might be no intention to sell the asset. Many would argue that IAS 12 should allow for such timing differences by discounting the deferred liability (for a sum due many years in advance is certainly recognised in the business community as a lesser liability than the sum due immediately, for the sum could be invested and produce income until the liability would become due; this is termed the time value of money). The standard does not allow such discounting.[15]

Indeed, it could be argued that in reality most businesses tend to have a policy of continuous asset replacement, with the effect that any deferred liability will be further deferred by these future acquisitions, so that the deferred tax liability would only become payable on a future cessation of trade. Not only does the standard preclude discounting, it also does not permit any account being made for future acquisitions by making a partial provision for the deferred tax.

### Deferred tax asset

Except for deferred tax assets arising from taxation, deferred tax assets normally arise where:

(i) certain cash income is received in the accounting period, but not credited to the income statement until a future period such as lease premiums and rent received in advance; and

(ii) certain expenses are incurred in the current period but not paid until a future accounting period such as where a director's or employee's bonus is charged in the income statement before the year-end but not paid until after the year end.

#### Unused tax losses

A deferred tax asset should be recognised for the carry-forward of unused tax losses and unused tax credits to the extent that it is probable that future taxable profit will be available against which the unused tax losses and unused tax credits can be utilised. This is reported as in Figure 16.6 with an extract from the Bayer Group 2013 Annual Report.

At each statement of financial position date, an enterprise should reassess unrecognised deferred tax assets. The enterprise recognises a previously unrecognised deferred tax asset to the extent that it has become probable that future taxable profit will allow the deferred tax asset to be recovered. For example, an improvement in trading conditions may make it more probable that the enterprise will be able to generate sufficient taxable profit in the future for the deferred tax asset to be recovered.

### Figure 16.6 Extract from Bayer Group 2013 Annual Report

14. taxes

The breakdown of tax expenses by origin was as follows:

| | 2012 | | 2013 | |
| --- | --- | --- | --- | --- |
| | | Of which income taxes | | Of which income taxes |
| | € million | € million | € million | € million |
| **Taxes paid or accrued** | | | | |
| Income taxes | | | | |
| Germany | (534) | | (795) | |
| other countries | (1,026) | | (849) | |
| Other taxes | | | | |
| Germany | (28) | | (43) | |
| other countries | (235) | | (188) | |
| | **(1,823)** | **(1,560)** | **(1,875)** | **(1,644)** |
| **Deferred taxes** | | | | |
| from temporary differences | 782 | | 569 | |
| from tax loss carryforwards and tax credits | 55 | | 54 | |
| | **837** | **837** | **623** | **623** |
| **Total** | **(986)** | **(723)** | **(1,252)** | **(1,021)** |

The Financial Reporting Review Panel in its 2012 Annual Report stated that:

As reported last year, the Panel continued to have to remind a number of companies with a record of losses of the need to recognise a deferred tax asset for the carry forward of unused tax losses and credits only to the extent that it is probable that future taxable profit will be available against which the temporary differences can be utilised. When a company has a history of losses, in the absence of sufficient taxable temporary differences 'convincing other evidence' is required to support the company's judgement that it is probable that future taxable profits will be available against which the tax losses can be utilised. The Panel sought undertakings that, in future, as required by the standard the deferred tax asset should be quantified and the nature of the evidence supporting its recognition disclosed.

The carrying amount of a deferred tax asset has to be reviewed at the end of each reporting period and reduced to the extent that it is no longer probable that sufficient taxable profit will be available to allow the benefit of the asset to be utilised. However, any such reduction can be reversed later if it becomes probable that sufficient taxable profit will be available.

## 16.8 A critique of deferred taxation

It could be argued that deferred tax is not a legal liability until it accrues. The consequence of this argument would be that deferred tax should not appear in the financial statements, and financial statements should:

- present the tax expense for the year equal to the amount of income taxes that has been levied based on the income tax return for the year;
- accrue as a receivable any income refunds that are due from taxing authorities or as a payable any unpaid current or past income taxes;
- disclose in the notes to the financial statements differences between the income tax bases of assets and liabilities and the amounts at which they appear in the statement of financial position.

The argument is that the process of accounting for deferred tax is confusing what **did** happen to a company, i.e. the agreed tax payable for the year, and what **did not** happen to the company, which is the tax that would have been payable if the adjustments required by the tax law for timing differences had not occurred. It is felt that the investor should be provided with details of the tax charge levied on the profits for the year and an explanation of factors that might lead to a different rate of tax charge appearing in future financial statements.

The argument against adjusting the tax charge for deferred tax and the creation of a deferred tax provision holds that shareholders are accustomed to giving consideration to many other imponderables concerning the amount, timing and uncertainty of future cash receipts and payments, and the treatment of tax should be considered in the same way. This view has received support from others,[16] who have held that tax attaches to taxable income and not to the reported accounting income and that there is no legal requirement for the tax to bear any relationship to the reported accounting income. Indeed it has been argued that 'deferred tax means income smoothing'.[17]

The creation of a charge in the statement of income for a deferred tax liability has an impact on the EPS in the year in which it arises and when it reverses. However, it is suggested that the arguments for and against deferred taxation accounting must be based solely on the theory underpinning accounting, and be unaffected by commercial considerations.

### Accrual accounting assumption

It is also suggested that the above arguments against the use of deferred tax accounting are unconvincing if one considers the IASB's underlying assumption about accrual accounting, as stated in the *Framework:*

> Accrual accounting depicts the effects of transactions and other events and circumstances on a reporting entity's economic resources and claims in the periods in which those effects occur, even if the resulting cash receipts and payments occur in a different period. This is important because information about a reporting entity's economic resources and claims and changes in its economic resources and claims during a period provides a better basis for assessing the entity's past and future performance than information solely about cash receipts and payments during that period.[18]

This underlying assumption confirms that deferred tax accounting makes the fullest possible use of accrual accounting.

Pursuing this argument further, the *Framework* states:

> The future economic benefit embodied in an asset is the potential to contribute, directly or indirectly, to the flow of cash and cash equivalents to the enterprise. The potential may be a productive one that is part of the operating activities of the enterprise.[19]

If a statement of financial position includes current market valuations based on this view of an asset, it is difficult to argue logically that the implicit taxation arising on this future economic benefit should not be provided for at the same time. The previous argument for excluding the deferred tax liability cannot therefore be considered persuasive on this basis.

On the other hand, it is stated in the *Framework* that 'An essential characteristic of a liability is that the enterprise has a present obligation'.[20] One could argue solely from these words that deferred tax is not a liability, but this conflicts with the argument based on the definition of an asset; consequently when considered in context this does not provide a sustainable argument against a deferred tax provision. The fact is that accounting practice has moved definitively towards making such a provision for deferred taxation.

### Substance over form assumption

The legal argument that deferred tax is not a legal liability until it accrues runs counter to the criterion of substance over form which gives weight to the economic aspects of the event rather than the strict legal aspects. The *Framework* states:

> **Substance Over Form**
> Substance over form is not considered a separate component of faithful representation because it would be redundant. Faithful representation means that financial information represents the substance of an economic phenomenon rather than merely representing its legal form. Representing a legal form that differs from the economic substance of the underlying economic phenomenon could not result in a faithful representation.[21]

It is an interesting fact that substance over form has achieved a growing importance since the 1980s and the legal arguments are receiving less recognition. Investments are made on economic criteria, investors make their choices on the basis of anticipated cash flows, and such flows would be subject to the effects of deferred taxation.

## 16.9 Value added tax (VAT)

VAT is one other tax that affects most companies and for which there is an accounting standard (SSAP 5 *Accounting for Value Added Tax*), which was established on its introduction. This standard was issued in 1974 when the introduction of value added tax was imminent and there was considerable worry within the business community on its accounting treatment. We can now look back, having lived with VAT for well over three decades, and wonder, perhaps, why an SSAP was needed. VAT is essentially a tax on consumers collected by traders and is accounted for in a similar way to PAYE income tax, which is a tax on employees collected by employers.

IFRS 15 makes clear that the same principles are followed:

> The amount of consideration to which an entity expects to be entitled in exchange for transferring promised goods or services to a customer, excluding amounts collected on behalf of third parties.[22]

### 16.9.1 The effects of the standard

The effects of the standard vary depending on the status of the accounting entity under the VAT legislation. The term 'trader' appears in the legislation and is the terminology for a business entity. The 'traders' or companies, as we would normally refer to them, are classified under the following headings:

#### (a) Registered trader

For a registered trader, accounts should only include figures net of VAT. This means that the VAT on the sales will be deducted from the invoice amount. The VAT will be payable to the government and the net amount of the sales invoice will appear in the statement of income in arriving at the sales turnover figure. The VAT on purchases will be deducted from the purchase invoice. The VAT will then be reclaimed from the government and the net amount of the purchases invoice will appear in the statement of income in arriving at the purchases figure.

The only exception to the use of amounts net of VAT is when the input tax is not recoverable, e.g. on entertaining and on 'private' motor cars.

#### (b) Non-registered or exempt trader

For a company that is classified as non-registered or exempt, the VAT that it has to pay on its purchases and expenses is not reclaimable from the government. Because the company cannot recover the VAT, it means that the expense that appears in the statement of income must be inclusive of VAT. It is treated as part of each item of expenditure and the costs treated accordingly. It will be included, where relevant, with each item of expense (including capital expenditure) rather than being shown as a separate item.

#### (c) Partially exempt trader

An entity which is partially exempt can only recover a proportion of input VAT, and the proportion of non-recoverable VAT should be treated as part of the costs on the same lines as with an exempt trader. The VAT rules are complex but, for the purpose of understanding the figures that appear in published accounts of public companies, treatment as a registered trader would normally apply

## Summary

Corporation tax is charged on the taxable profit of a company after adjusting the accounting profit for non-allowable deductions and temporary differences.

The imputation system means that dividends are reported at the amount of cash paid out by the company and a credit is allowed on the dividend received by the shareholder.

Deferred tax is provided for under IAS 12 reflecting the amount that is expected to be settled as a liability. The requirement to make such a provision is supported by the *Framework for the Preparation and Presentation of Financial Statements*.

Tax avoidance and tax evasion have been perceived by the public as being unfair and governments have internationally attempted to combat the problem through legislation, case law and encouraging positive consumer reaction to put pressure on companies not appearing to pay a fair amount of tax nationally.

## REVIEW QUESTIONS

1 Why does the charge to taxation in a company's accounts not equal the profit multiplied by the current rate of corporation tax?

2 Deferred tax accounting may be seen as an income-smoothing device which distorts the true and fair view. Explain the impact of deferred tax on reported income and justify its continued use.

3 Distinguish between (a) the deferral and (b) the liability methods of company deferred tax.

4 'If a deferred liability or asset is not expected to crystallise they should at least be discounted.' Discuss.

5 'The effective tax rate of all companies should be published and any with a rate below the average for the sector should be subjected to consumer or government commercial pressure to make additional payments.' Discuss.

6 Discuss the problems in distinguishing tax evasion from tax avoidance.

7 Discuss whether there is a socially responsible right amount of tax for a company to pay and who is to determine what is socially responsible.

8 'A tax adviser has a duty of care to a client to legally minimise a company's tax bill and would be professionally negligent not to do so.' Discuss.

9 'A company justified paying little tax on the grounds that it invested funds more effectively than government by creating employment. It further argued that this view was supported when it appears that governments lack the technical skills to control expenditure effectively.' Discuss.

10 The Financial Reporting Review Panel (FRRP) in its 2012 Annual Report stated that: 'Several companies had to be reminded that current and deferred tax liabilities and assets are to be measured using the tax rates that have been enacted or substantively enacted by the end of the reporting period'. Discuss why this is necessary.

**11** The following is an extract from the Tesco plc 2016 Annual Report

**Unrecognised deferred tax assets**

Deferred tax assets in relation to continuing operations have not been recognised in respect of the following items:

|  | 2016 | 2015 |
|---|---|---|
|  | £m | £m |
| Deductible temporary | 11 | 29 |
| differences | 163 | 97 |
| Tax losses | 249 | 66 |
|  | 412 | 163 |

Discuss reasons for not recognising the £412m as an asset.

**12** Reconciliation of effective tax charge

Tesco plc reported a tax rate on its accounting profit of 20.1% and an effective tax rate of 33.2% in its 2016 Annual Report. Discuss three possible reasons for this difference.

**13** A judge ruled in 1929 that 'No man in this country is under the smallest obligation, moral or other, so as to arrange his legal relations to his business or to his property as to enable the Inland Revenue to put the largest possible shovel into his stores'. Discuss the extent to which this approach is permitted in the UK and any impact on an accountant advising a client.

## EXERCISES

### Question 1

In your capacity as chief assistant to the financial controller, your managing director has asked you to explain to him the differences between tax planning, tax avoidance and tax evasion.

He has also asked you to explain to him your feelings as a professional accountant about these topics.

**Required:**
**Write some notes to assist you in answering these questions.**

### * Question 2

A non-current asset (a machine) was purchased by Adjourn plc on 1 July 20X2 at a cost of £25,000.

The company prepares its annual accounts to 31 March in each year. The policy of the company is to depreciate such assets at the rate of 15% straight line (with depreciation being charged *pro rata* on a time-apportionment basis in the year of purchase). The company was granted capital allowances at 25% per annum on the reducing balance method (such capital allowances are apportioned *pro rata* on a time-apportionment basis in the year of purchase).

The rate of corporation tax has been as follows:

Year ended     31 Mar 20X3 20%
31 Mar 20X4 30%
31 Mar 20X5 20%
31 Mar 20X6 19%
31 Mar 20X7 19%

Required:
(a) Calculate the deferred tax provision using both the deferred method and the liability method.
(b) Explain why the liability method is considered by commentators to place the emphasis on the statement of financial position, whereas the deferred method is considered to place the emphasis on the statement of income.

## * Question 3

The following information is given in respect of Unambitious plc:

(a) Non-current assets consist entirely of plant and machinery. The net book value of these assets as at 30 June 2010 is £100,000 in excess of their tax written-down value.

(b) The provision for deferred tax (all of which relates to fixed asset timing differences) as at 30 June 2010 was £21,000.

(c) The company's capital expenditure forecasts indicate that capital allowances and depreciation in future years will be:

| Year ended 30 June | Depreciation charge for year | Capital allowances for year |
|---|---|---|
| £ | £ | £ |
| 2011 | 12,000 | 53,000 |
| 2012 | 14,000 | 49,000 |
| 2013 | 20,000 | 36,000 |
| 2014 | 40,000 | 32,000 |
| 2015 | 44,000 | 32,000 |
| 2016 | 46,000 | 36,000 |

For the following years, capital allowances are likely to continue to be in excess of depreciation for the foreseeable future.

(d) Corporation tax is to be taken at 21%.

Required:
Calculate the deferred tax charges or credits for the next six years, commencing with the year ended 30 June 2011, in accordance with the provisions of IAS 12.

## Question 4

The move from the preparation of accounts under UK GAAP to the users of IFRS by United Kingdom quoted companies for years beginning 1 January 2005 had an effect on the level of profits reported. How will those profits arising from the change in accounting standards be treated for taxation purposes?

## Question 5

Discuss the arguments for and against discounting the deferred tax charge.

## Question 6

Austin Mitchell MP proposed an Early Day Motion in the House of Commons on 17 May 2005 as follows:

That this House urges the Government to clamp down on artificial tax avoidance schemes and end the . . . tax avoidance loop-holes that enable millionaires and numerous companies trading in the UK to avoid UK taxes; and further urges the Government to . . . so that transactions lacking normal commercial substance and solely entered into for the purpose of tax avoidance are ignored for tax purposes, thereby providing certainty, fairness and clarity, which the UK's taxation system requires to prevent abusive tax avoidance, to protect the interests of ordinary citizens who are committed to making their contribution to society, to avoid an unnecessary burden of tax on individual taxpayers and to ensure that companies pay fair taxes on profits generated in this country.

Required:
(a) The Motion refers to tax avoidance. In your opinion, does the Early Day Motion tend to confuse the boundaries between tax avoidance and tax evasion?
(b) The Motion refers to nullifying the effects of tax avoidance to protect the interests of ordinary citizens who are making their contribution to society, to avoid an unnecessary burden of tax on individual taxpayers. If ordinary citizens require such protection, would it be possible to argue that even if tax avoidance were legal, it might well be immoral?

## Question 7

Hanson Products Ltd is a newly formed company. The company commenced trading on 1 January 20X1 when it purchased an item of plant and equipment for $240,000. The plant and equipment has an expected life of five years with zero residual value, and will be depreciated on a straight-line basis on cost over that period. The company's profits before depreciation (of the plant) are expected to be $1 million each year.

Tax allowances for plant are a 40% initial allowance with an annual 25% writing-down allowance on tax written-down value in subsequent years. The company will have a life of five years and, on closure, any unused tax allowances will be allowed as a deduction from the final year's taxable profit.

The rate of corporation tax is 20%. The company does not provide for deferred taxation.

Required:
(a) For each of the years from 20X1 to 20X5, calculate:
    (i)   the capital allowances,
    (ii)  the taxable profit,
    (iii) the tax payable on the year's profit.
(b) Discuss the advantages and disadvantages of not providing for deferred taxation.

## Question 8

The accountant of Hanson Products Ltd has asked you how your answer to Question 7 above would be affected using the following two methods of calculating deferred taxation.

Required:
(a) For each of the years from 20X1 to 20X5, calculate the deferred tax balance if:
    (i)  full provision is made for deferred tax in accordance with IAS 12 *Income Taxes*,
    (ii) the company decided to calculate the deferred tax balance using a discount rate of 5%.
(b) Discuss the advantages and disadvantages of discounting deferred tax balances. Use the following table of discount factors:

| Year | Discount factor |
|------|-----------------|
| 1    | 0.9524          |
| 2    | 0.9070          |
| 3    | 0.8638          |
| 4    | 0.8227          |
| 5    | 0.7835          |

## Question 9

The following information relates to Deferred plc:

● EBITDA (earnings before interest, tax, depreciation and amortisation) for year ended 31.12.20X1 is £300,000

● No interest payable in 20X1

● No amortisation

● Equipment cost £100,000 at 1.1.20X1

    ● Depreciation rate is 10% straight line

    ● Nil scrap value

● Tax rate is 20%

● Capital allowance is 25% on reducing balance basis.

Required:

Calculate:

(a) deferred tax;

(b) statement of income entries;

(c) statement of financial position entries.

## Notes

1 OECD, *Theoretical and Empirical Aspects of Corporate Taxation*, Paris, 1974; van den Temple, *Corporation Tax and Individual Income Tax in the EEC*, EEC Commission, Brussels, 1974.

2 G.H. Partington and R.H. Chenhall, *Dividends, Distortion and Double Taxation*, Abacus, June 1983.

3 G. Aaronson 'GAAR Study', Chatered Instiutue of Taxation, November 2011.

4 Franklin D. Roosevelt, 1936 Speech at Worcester, Mass., 1936. Roosevelt Museum.

5 *Countering Tax Avoidance in the UK: Which Way Forward?*, A Report for the Tax Law Review Committee, The Institute for Fiscal Studies, 2009, para. 4.2.

6 L.J. Tomlin, in *Duke of Westminster* v *CIR*, HL 1935, 19 TC 490.

7 *Tax Avoidance*, A Report for the Tax Law Review Committee, The Institute for Fiscal Studies, 1997, para. 7.

8 *WT Ramsay Ltd* v *CIR*, HL 1981, 54 TC 101; [1981] STC 174; [1981] 2 WLR 449; [1981] 1 All ER 865.

9 Robert Maas, *Beware Tax Avoidance Drifting into Evasion*, Taxline, Tax Planning 2003–2004, Institute of Chartered Accountants in England & Wales.

10 *Professional Conduct in Relation to Taxation*, Ethical Statement 1.308, Institute of Chartered Accountants in England & Wales, para. 2.13 (this is similar to the statements issued by the other accounting bodies).

11 www.oecd.org/tax/exchangeofinformation/42232037.pdf

12 www.ifs.org.uk/comms/dp7.pdf

13 IAS 12 *Income Taxes*, IASB, revised 2000, para. 5.

14 SFAS 109, *Accounting for Income Taxes*, FASB, 1992, extracts therefrom.

15 IAS 12 *Income Taxes*, IASB, revised 2000, para. 54.

16 R.J. Chambers, *Tax Allocation and Financial Reporting*, Abacus, 1968.

17 Prof. D.R. Middleton, letter to the Editor, *The Financial Times*, 29 September 1994.

18 *Conceptual Framework for Financial Reporting*, IASB, 2010, OB17.

19 Ibid., para. 4.8.

20 Ibid., para 4.15.

21 Ibid., BC3.26.

22 IFRS 15 *Revenue from Contracts with Customers*, IASB, 2014, Appendix A.

# Property, plant and equipment (PPE)

## 17.1 Introduction

The main purpose of this chapter is to explain how to determine the initial carrying value of PPE and to explain and account for the normal movements in PPE that occur during an accounting period.

### Objectives

By the end of this chapter, you should be able to:

- explain the meaning of PPE and determine its initial carrying value;
- account for subsequent expenditure on PPE that has already been recognised;
- explain the meaning of depreciation and compute the depreciation charge for a period;
- account for PPE measured under the revaluation model;
- explain the meaning of impairment;
- compute and account for an impairment loss;
- explain the criteria that must be satisfied before an asset is classified as held for sale and account for such assets;
- explain the accounting treatment of government grants for the purchase of PPE;
- identify an investment property and explain the alternative accounting treatment of such properties;
- explain the impact of alternative methods of accounting for PPE on key accounting ratios.

## 17.2 PPE – concepts and the relevant IASs and IFRSs

For PPE the accounting treatment is based on the accruals or matching concepts, under which expenditure is capitalised until it is charged as depreciation against revenue in the periods in which benefit is gained from its use. Thus, if an item is purchased that has an economic life of two years, so that it will be used over two accounting periods to help earn profit for the entity, then the cost of that asset should be apportioned in some way between the two accounting periods.

However, this does not take into account the problems surrounding PPE accounting and depreciation, which have so far given rise to six relevant international accounting standards. We will consider these problems in this chapter and cover the following questions.

### IAS 16 and IAS 23

- What is PPE (IAS 16)?
- How is the cost of PPE determined (IAS 16 and IAS 23)?
- How is depreciation of PPE computed (IAS 16)?
- What are the regulations regarding carrying PPE at revalued amounts (IAS 16)?

### Other relevant international accounting standards and pronouncements

- How should grants receivable towards the purchase of PPE be dealt with (IAS 20)?
- Are there ever circumstances in which PPE should not be depreciated (IAS 40)?
- What is impairment and how does this affect the carrying value of PPE (IAS 36)?
- What are the key changes made by the IASB concerning the disposal of non-current assets (IFRS 5)?

## 17.3  What is PPE?

IAS 16 *Property, Plant and Equipment*[1] defines PPE as tangible assets that are:

**(a)** held by an entity for use in the production or supply of goods and services, for rental to others, or for administrative purposes; and

**(b)** expected to be used during more than one period.

It is clear from the definition that PPE will normally be included in the non-current assets section of the statement of financial position.

### 17.3.1  Problems that may arise

Problems may arise in relation to the interpretation of the definition and in relation to the application of the materiality concept.

The definitions give rise to some areas of practical difficulty. For example, an asset that has previously been held for use in the production or supply of goods or services but is now going to be sold should, under the provisions of IFRS 5, be classified separately on the statement of financial position as an asset 'held for sale'.

Differing accounting treatments arise if there are different assessments of materiality. This may result in the same expenditure being reported as an asset in the statement of financial position of one company and as an expense in the statement of comprehensive income of another company. In the accounts of a self-employed carpenter, a kit of hand tools that, with careful maintenance, will last many years will, quite rightly, be shown as PPE. Similar assets used by the maintenance department in a large factory will, in all probability, be treated as 'loose tools' and written off as acquired.

Many entities have *de minimis* policies, whereby only items exceeding a certain value are treated as PPE; items below the cut-off amount will be expensed through the statement of comprehensive income.

For example, the Volkswagen AG 2015 Annual Report stated in its accounting policies:

> Low-value assets are written off and derecognized in full in the year they are acquired. In addition, certain items of operating and office equipment with individual purchase costs of up to €1,500 are treated as disposals when their standard useful life has expired.

## 17.4 How is the cost of PPE determined?

### 17.4.1 Components of cost[2]

According to IAS 16, the cost of an item of PPE comprises its purchase price, including import duties and non-refundable purchase taxes, plus any directly attributable costs of bringing the asset to working condition for its intended use. Examples of such directly attributable costs include:

(a) the costs of site preparation;

(b) initial delivery and handling costs;

(c) installation costs;

(d) professional fees such as for architects and engineers;

(e) the estimated cost of dismantling and removing the asset and restoring the site, to the extent that it is recognised as a provision under IAS 37 *Provisions, Contingent Liabilities and Contingent Assets*.

Administration and other general overhead costs are not a component of the cost of PPE unless they can be directly attributed to the acquisition of the asset or bringing it to its working condition. Similarly, start-up and similar pre-production costs do not form part of the cost of an asset unless they are necessary to bring the asset to its working condition.

### 17.4.2 Self-constructed assets[3]

The cost of a self-constructed asset is determined using the same principles as for an acquired asset. If the asset is made available for sale by the entity in the normal course of business then the cost of the asset is usually the same as the cost of producing the asset for sale. This cost would usually be determined under the principles set out in IAS 2 *Inventories*.

The normal profit that an enterprise would make if selling the self-constructed asset would not be recognised in 'cost' if the asset were retained within the entity. Following similar principles, where one group company constructs an asset that is used as PPE by another group company, any profit on sale is eliminated in determining the initial carrying value of the asset in the consolidated accounts (this will also clearly affect the calculation of depreciation).

If an item of PPE is exchanged in whole or in part for a dissimilar item of PPE then the cost of such an item is the fair value of the asset received. This is equivalent to the fair value of the asset given up, adjusted for any cash or cash equivalents transferred or received.

### 17.4.3 Capitalisation of borrowing costs

Where an asset takes a substantial period of time to get ready for its intended use or sale then the entity may incur significant borrowing costs in the preparation period. Under the accruals basis of accounting there is an argument that such costs should be included as a directly attributable cost of construction. IAS 23 *Borrowing Costs* was issued to deal with this issue.

IAS 23 states that borrowing costs that are directly attributable to the acquisition, construction or production of a 'qualifying asset' should be included in the cost of that asset.[4] A 'qualifying asset' is one that necessarily takes a substantial period of time to get ready for its intended use or sale.

Borrowing costs that would have been avoided if the expenditure on the qualifying asset had not been undertaken are eligible for capitalisation under IAS 23. Where the funds are borrowed specifically for the purpose of obtaining a qualifying asset, the borrowing costs that are eligible for capitalisation are those incurred on the borrowing during the period less any investment income on the temporary investment of those borrowings. Where the funds are borrowed generally and used for the purpose of obtaining a qualifying asset, the entity should use a capitalisation rate to determine the borrowing costs that may be capitalised. This rate should be the weighted average of the borrowing costs applicable to the entity, other than borrowings made specifically for the purpose of obtaining a qualifying asset. Capitalisation should commence when:

- expenditures for the asset are being incurred;
- borrowing costs are being incurred;
- activities that are necessary to prepare the asset for its intended use or sale are in progress.

When substantially all the activities necessary to prepare the qualifying asset for its intended use or sale are complete, capitalisation should cease.

### Borrowing costs for SMEs

IAS 23 *Borrowing Costs* requires borrowing costs directly attributable to the acquisition, construction or production of a qualifying asset (including some inventories) to be capitalised as part of the cost of the asset. For cost–benefit reasons, the IFRS for SMEs requires such costs to be charged to expense.

### IFRS for SMEs

All borrowing costs are charged to expense when incurred. Borrowing costs are not capitalised.

## 17.4.4 Subsequent expenditure

Subsequent expenditure relating to an item of PPE that has already been recognised should normally be recognised as an expense in the period in which it is incurred. The exception to this general rule is where it is probable that future economic benefits in excess of the originally assessed standard of performance of the existing asset will, as a result of the expenditure, flow to the entity. In these circumstances, the expenditure should be added to the carrying value of the existing asset. Examples of expenditure that might fall to be treated in this way include:

- modification of an item of plant to extend its useful life, including an increase in its capacity;
- upgrading machine parts to achieve a substantial improvement in the quality of output;
- adoption of new production processes enabling a substantial reduction in previously assessed operating costs.

Conversely, expenditure that restores, rather than increases, the originally assessed standard of performance of an asset is written off as an expense in the period incurred.

Some assets have components that require replacement at regular intervals. Two examples of such components would be the lining of a furnace and the roof of a building. IAS 16 states[5] that, provided such components have readily ascertainable costs, they should be accounted for as separate assets because they have useful lives different from the items of PPE to which they relate. This means that when such components are replaced they are accounted for as an asset disposal and acquisition of a new asset.

## 17.5 What is depreciation?

IAS 16 defines depreciation as the systematic allocation of the depreciable amount of an asset over its life. The depreciable amount is the cost of an asset or other amount substituted for cost in the financial statements, less its residual value.

Note that this definition places an emphasis on the consumption in a particular accounting period rather than an average over the asset's life. We will consider two aspects of the definition: the measure of wearing out; and the useful economic life.

### 17.5.1 Allocation of depreciable amount

Depreciation is a measure of wearing out that is calculated annually and charged as an expense against profits. Under the 'matching concept', the depreciable amount of the asset is allocated over its productive life.

It is important to make clear what depreciation is *not*:

● It is not 'saving up for a new one'; it is not setting funds aside for the replacement of the existing asset at the end of its life; it is the matching of cost to revenue. The effect is to reduce the profit available for distribution, but this is not accompanied by the setting aside of cash of an equal amount to ensure that liquid funds are available at the end of the asset's life.

● It is not 'a way of showing the real value of assets on the statement of financial position' by reducing the cost figure to a realisable value.

We emphasise what depreciation is *not* because both of these ideas are commonly held by non-accountant users of accounts; it is as well to realise these possible misconceptions when interpreting accounts for non-accountants.

Depreciation is currently conceived as a charge for funds **already expended,** and thus it cannot be considered as the setting aside of funds to meet future expenditure. If we consider it in terms of capital maintenance, then we can see that it results in the maintenance of the initial invested monetary capital of the company. It is concerned with the allocation of that expenditure over a period of time, without having regard for the **value** of the asset at any intermediate period of its life.

Where an asset has been revalued the depreciation is based on the revalued amount. This is because the revalued amount has replaced cost (less residual value) as the depreciable amount.

### 17.5.2 Useful life

IAS 16 defines this as:

(a) the period of time over which an asset is expected to be used by an entity; or

(b) the number of production or similar units expected to be obtained from the asset by an entity.[1]

The IAS 16 definition is based on the premise that almost all assets have a finite useful economic life. This may be true in principle, but it is incredibly difficult in real life to arrive at an average economic life that can be applied to even a single class of assets, e.g. plant. This is evidenced by the accounting policy in the AkzoNobel 2015 Annual Report which states:

Depreciation is calculated using the straight-line method based on the estimated useful life. In the majority of cases the useful life of plant, equipment and machinery is ten years, and for buildings ranges from 20 to 30 years. Land is not depreciated. In the majority of cases residual value is assumed to be insignificant. Depreciation methods, lives and residual values are reassessed annually.

In addition to the practical difficulty of estimating economic lives, there are also exceptions where nil depreciation is charged. Two common exceptions found in the accounts of UK companies relate to freehold land and certain types of property.

### 17.5.3 Freehold land

Freehold land (but not the buildings thereon) is considered to have an infinite life unless it is held simply for the extraction of minerals, etc. Thus land held for the purpose of, say, mining coal or quarrying gravel will be dealt with for accounting purposes as a coal or gravel deposit. Consequently, although the land may have an infinite life, the deposits will have an economic life only as long as they can be profitably extracted. If the cost of extraction exceeds the potential profit from extraction and sale, the economic life of the quarry has ended. When assessing depreciation for a commercial company, we are concerned only with these private costs and benefits, and not with public costs and benefits which might lead to the quarry being kept open.

The following extract from the Goldfields 2015 Annual Report illustrates accounting policies for land and mining assets.

**Land**
Land is shown at cost and is not depreciated.

**Amortisation and depreciation of mining assets**
Amortisation is determined to give a fair and systematic charge in the statement of comprehensive income taking into account the nature of a particular ore body and the method of mining that ore body. To achieve this the following calculation methods are used:

Mining assets, including mine development and infrastructure costs, mine plant facilities and evaluation costs, are amortised over the lives of the mines using the units-of-production method, based on estimated proved and probable ore reserves above infrastructure.

Certain mining plant and equipment included in mine development and infrastructure is depreciated on a straight-line basis over their estimated useful lives

Few jurisdictions have comprehensive accounting standards for extractive activities. IFRS 6 *Exploration for and Evaluation of Mineral Resources* is an interim measure pending a more comprehensive view by the IASB in future. IFRS 6 allows an entity to develop an accounting policy for exploration and evaluation assets without considering the consistency of the policy with the IASB framework. This may mean that for an interim period accounting policies might permit the recognition of both current and non-current assets that do not meet the criteria laid down in the IASB *Framework*. This is considered by some commentators to be unduly permissive. Indeed, about the only firm requirement IFRS 6 can be said to contain is the requirement to test exploration and evaluation assets for impairment whenever a change in facts and circumstances suggests that impairment exists.

## 17.6 What are the constituents in the depreciation formula?

In order to calculate depreciation it is necessary to determine three factors:

1 Cost (or revalued amount if the company is following a revaluation policy)

2 Economic life

3 Residual value.

A simple example is the calculation of the depreciation charge for a company that has acquired an asset on 1 January 20X1 for £1,000 with an estimated economic life of four years and an estimated residual value of £200. Applying a straight-line depreciation policy, the charge would be £200 per year using the formula of:

$$\frac{\text{Cost} - \text{estimated residual value}}{\text{Estimated economic life}} = \frac{£1,000 - £200}{4} = £200 \text{ per annum}$$

We can see that the charge of £200 is influenced in all cases by the definition of cost, the estimate of the residual value, the estimate of the economic life, and the management decision on depreciation policy.

In addition, if the asset were to be revalued at the end of the second year to £900, then the depreciation for 20X3 and 20X4 would be recalculated using the revised valuation figure. Assuming that the residual value remained unchanged, the depreciation for 20X3 would be:

$$\frac{\text{Revalued asset} - \text{estimated residual value}}{\text{Estimated economic life}} = \frac{£900 - £200}{2} = £350 \text{ per annum}$$

### 17.6.1 How is the useful life of an asset determined?

The IAS 16 definition of useful life is given in Section 17.5.2 above. This is not necessarily the total life expectancy of the asset. Most assets become less economically and technologically efficient as they grow older. For this reason, assets may well cease to have an economic life long before their working life is over. It is the responsibility of the preparers of accounts to estimate the economic life of all assets.

It is conventional for entities to consider the economic lives of assets by class or category, e.g. buildings, plant, office equipment, or motor vehicles. However, this is not necessarily appropriate, since the level of activity demanded by different users may differ. For example, compare two motor cars owned by a business: one is used by the national sales manager, covering 100,000 miles per annum visiting clients; the other is used by the accountant to drive from home to work and occasionally the bank, covering perhaps one-tenth of the mileage.

In practice, the useful economic life would be determined by reference to factors such as repair costs, the cost and availability of replacements, and the comparative cash flows of existing and alternative assets. The problem of optimal replacement lives is a normal financial management problem; its significance in financial reporting is that the assumptions used within the financial management decision may provide evidence of the expected economic life.

### 17.6.2 Other factors affecting the useful life figure

We can see that there are technical factors affecting the estimated economic life figure. In addition, other factors have prompted companies to set estimated lives that have no relationship to the active productive life of the asset. One such factor is the wish of management to take into account the effect of inflation. This led some companies to reduce the estimated economic life, so that a higher charge was made against profits during the early period of the asset's life to compensate for the inflationary effect on the cost of replacement. The total charge will be the same, but the timing is advanced. This does not result in the retention of funds necessary to replace; but it does reflect the fact that there is at present no coherent policy for dealing with inflation in the published accounts – consequently, companies resort to *ad hoc* measures that frustrate efforts to make accounts uniform and comparable. *Ad hoc* measures such as these have prompted changes in the standards.

### 17.6.3 Residual value

IAS 16 defines residual value as the net amount which an entity expects to obtain for an asset at the end of its useful life after deducting the expected costs of disposal. Where PPE is carried at cost, the residual value is initially estimated at the date of acquisition. In subsequent periods the estimate of residual value is revised, the revision being based on conditions prevailing at each statement of financial position date. Such revisions have an effect on future depreciation charges.

Besides inflation, residual values can be affected by changes in technology and market conditions. For example, during the period 1980–90 the cost of small business computers fell dramatically in both real and monetary terms, with a considerable impact on the residual (or second-hand) value of existing equipment.

## 17.7 Calculation of depreciation

Having determined the key factors in the computation, we are left with the problem of how to allocate that cost between accounting periods. For example, with an asset having an economic life of five years:

|  | £ |
|---|---|
| Asset cost | 11,000 |
| Estimated residual value (no significant change anticipated over useful economic life) | 1,000 |
| Depreciable amount | 10,000 |

How should the depreciable amount be charged to the statement of comprehensive income over the five years? IAS 16 tells us that it should be allocated on a systematic basis and the depreciation method used should reflect as fairly as possible the pattern in which the asset's economic benefits are consumed. The two most popular methods are **straight-line,** in which the depreciation is charged evenly over the useful life, and **diminishing balance,** where depreciation is calculated annually on the net written-down amount. In the case above, the calculations would be as in Figure 17.1.

Note that, although the diminishing balance is generally expressed in terms of a percentage, this percentage is arrived at by inserting the economic life into the formula as $n$; the 38% reflects the expected economic life of five years. As we change the life, so we change the percentage that is applied. The normal rate applied to vehicles is 25% diminishing balance; if we apply that to the cost and residual value in our example, we can see that we would be assuming an economic life of eight years. It is a useful test when using reducing balance percentages to refer back to the underlying assumptions.

We can see that the end result is the same. Thus, £10,000 has been charged against income, but with a dramatically different pattern of statement of comprehensive income charges. The charge for straight-line depreciation in the first year is less than half that for reducing balance.

### 17.7.1 Arguments in favour of the straight-line method

The method is simple to calculate. However, in these days of calculators and computers this seems a particularly facile argument, particularly when one considers the materiality of the figures.

**Figure 17.1 Effect of different depreciation methods**

| | Straight-line (£2,000) £ | Diminishing balance (38%) £ | Difference £ |
|---|---|---|---|
| Cost | 11,000 | 11,000 | |
| Depreciation for year 1 | 2,000 | 4,180 | 2,180 |
| Net book value (NBV) | 9,000 | 6,820 | |
| Depreciation for year 2 | 2,000 | 2,592 | 592 |
| NBV | 7,000 | 4,228 | |
| Depreciation for year 3 | 2,000 | 1,606 | (394) |
| NBV | 5,000 | 2,622 | |
| Depreciation for year 4 | 2,000 | 996 | (1,004) |
| NBV | 3,000 | 1,626 | |
| Depreciation for year 5 | 2,000 | 618 | (1,382) |
| Residual value | 1,000 | 1,008 | |

The diminishing balance formula was $1 - \sqrt[n]{(\text{Residual value/Cost})}$

### 17.7.2 Arguments in favour of the diminishing balance method

First, the charge reflects the efficiency and maintenance costs of the asset. When new, an asset is operating at its maximum efficiency, which falls as it nears the end of its life. This may be countered by the comment that in year 1 there may be 'teething troubles' with new equipment, which, while probably covered by a supplier's guarantee, will hamper efficiency.

Secondly, the pattern of diminishing balance depreciation gives a net book amount that approximates to second-hand values. For example, with motor cars the initial fall in value is very high.

### 17.7.3 Other methods of depreciating

Besides straight-line and diminishing balance, there are a number of other methods of depreciating, such as the sum of the units method, the machine-hour method and the annuity method. We will consider these briefly.

#### Sum of the units method

A compromise between straight-line and reducing balance that is popular in the USA is the sum of the units method. The calculation based on the information in Figure 17.1 is now shown in Figure 17.2. This has the advantage that, unlike diminishing balance, it is simple to obtain the exact residual amount (zero if appropriate), while giving the pattern of high initial charge shown by the diminishing balance approach.

#### Machine-hour method

The machine-hour system is based on an estimate of the asset's service potential. The economic life is measured not in accounting periods but in working hours, and the depreciation is allocated in the proportion of the actual hours worked to the potential total hours available.

**Figure 17.2 Sum of the units method**

|  |  | £ |
|---|---|---|
| Cost |  | 11,000 |
| Depreciation for year 1 | £10,000 × 5/15 | 3,333 |
| Net book value (NBV) |  | 7,667 |
| Depreciation for year 2 | £10,000 × 4/15 | 2,667 |
| NBV |  | 5,000 |
| Depreciation for year 3 | £10,000 × 3/15 | 2,000 |
| NBV |  | 3,000 |
| Depreciation for year 4 | £10,000 × 2/15 | 1,333 |
| NBV |  | 1,667 |
| Depreciation for year 5 | £10,000 × 1/15 | 667 |
| Residual value |  | 1,000 |

This method is commonly employed in aviation, where aircraft are depreciated on the basis of flying hours.

### Annuity method

With the annuity method, the asset, or rather the amount of capital representing the asset, is regarded as being capable of earning a fixed rate of interest. The sacrifice incurred in using the asset within the business is therefore twofold: the loss arising from the exhaustion of the service potential of the asset; and the interest forgone by using the funds invested in the business to purchase the non-current asset. With the help of annuity tables, a calculation shows what equal amounts of depreciation, written off over the estimated life of the asset, will reduce the book value to nil, after debiting interest to the asset account on the diminishing amount of funds that are assumed to be invested in the business at that time, as represented by the value of the asset.

Figure 17.3 contains an illustration based on the treatment of a five-year lease which cost the company a premium of £10,000 on 1 January year 1. It shows how the total depreciation charge is computed. Each year the charge for depreciation in the statement of comprehensive income is the equivalent annual amount that is required to repay the investment over the

**Figure 17.3 Annuity method**

| Year | Opening written-down value £ | Notional interest (10%) £ | Annual payment £ | Net movement £ | Closing written-down value £ |
|---|---|---|---|---|---|
| 1 | 10,000 | 1,000 | (2,638) | (1,638) | 8,362 |
| 2 | 8,362 | 836 | (2,638) | (1,802) | 6,560 |
| 3 | 6,560 | 656 | (2,638) | (1,982) | 4,578 |
| 4 | 4,578 | 458 | (2,638) | (2,180) | 2,398 |
| 5 | 2,398 | 240 | (2,638) | (2,398) | Nil |

five-year period at a rate of interest of 10% less the notional interest available on the remainder of the invested funds.

An extract from the annuity tables to obtain the annual equivalent factor for year 5 and assuming a rate of interest of 10% would show:

| Year | Annuity $A_n^{-1}$ |
|------|--------------------|
| 1    | 1.1000             |
| 2    | 0.5762             |
| 3    | 0.4021             |
| 4    | 0.3155             |
| 5    | 0.2638             |

Therefore, at a rate of interest of 10% five annual payments to repay an investor of £10,000 would each be £2,638.

A variation of this system involves the investment of a sum equal to the net charge in fixed interest securities or an endowment policy, so as to build up a fund that will generate cash to replace the asset at the end of its life.

This last system has significant weaknesses. It is based on the misconception that depreciation is 'saving up for a new one', whereas in reality depreciation is charging against profits funds already expended. It is also dangerous in a time of inflation, since it may lead management not to maintain the capital of the entity adequately, in which case they may not be able to replace the assets at their new (inflated) prices.

The annuity method, with its increasing net charge to income, does tend to take inflationary factors into account, but it must be noted that the *total* net profit and loss charge only adds up to the cost of the asset.

### 17.7.4 Which method should be used?

The answer to this seemingly simple question is 'it depends'. On the matter of depreciation IAS 16 is designed primarily to force a fair charge for the use of assets into the statement of comprehensive income each year, so that the earnings reflect a true and fair view.

Straight-line is most suitable for assets such as leases which have a definite fixed life. It is also considered most appropriate for assets with a short working life, although with motor cars the diminishing balance method is sometimes employed to match second-hand values. Extraction industries (mining, oil wells, quarries, etc.) sometimes employ a variation on the machine-hour system, where depreciation is based on the amount extracted as a proportion of the estimated reserves.

Despite the theoretical attractiveness of other methods the straight-line method is, by a long way, the one in most common use by entities that prepare financial statements in accordance with IFRSs. Reasons for this are essentially pragmatic:

● It is the most straightforward to compute.

● In the light of the three additional subjective factors – cost (or revalued amount), residual value and useful life – that need to be estimated, any imperfections in the charge for depreciation caused by the choice of the straight-line method are not likely to be significant.

● It conforms to the accounting treatment adopted by peers. For example, one group reported that it currently used the reducing balance method but, as peer companies used the straight-line method, it decided to change and adopt that policy.

## 17.8 Measurement subsequent to initial recognition

### 17.8.1 Choice of models

An entity needs to choose either the cost or the revaluation model as its accounting policy for an entire class of PPE. The cost model (definitely the most common) results in an asset being carried at cost less accumulated depreciation and any accumulated impairment losses.

### 17.8.2 The revaluation model

Under the revaluation model the asset is carried at revalued amount, being its fair value at the date of the revaluation less any subsequent accumulated depreciation and subsequent accumulated impairment losses. The fair value of an asset is defined in IAS 16 as 'the amount for which an asset could be exchanged between knowledgeable and willing parties in an arm's length transaction'. Thus fair value is basically market value. If a market value is not available, perhaps in the case of partly used specialised plant and equipment that is rarely bought and sold other than as new, then IAS 16 requires that revaluation be based on depreciated replacement cost. Note that the fair value falls within the scope of IFRS 13.

EXAMPLE ● An entity purchased an item of plant for £12,000 on 1 January 20X1. The plant was depreciated on a straight-line basis over its useful economic life, which was estimated at six years. On 1 January 20X3 the entity decided to revalue its plant. No fair value was available for the item of plant that had been purchased for £12,000 on 1 January 20X1 but the replacement cost of the plant at 1 January 20X3 was £21,000.

The carrying value of the plant immediately before the revaluation would have been:

● Cost £12,000
● Accumulated depreciation £4,000 [(£12,000/6) × 2]
● Written-down value £8,000.

Under the principles of IAS 16 the revalued amount would be £14,000 (£21,000 × 4/6). This amount would be reflected in the financial statements by either:

● showing a revised gross figure of £14,000 and reversing out all the accumulated depreciation charged to date so as to give a carrying value of £14,000; or

● restating both the gross figure and the accumulated depreciation by the proportionate change in replacement cost. This would give a gross figure of £21,000, with accumulated depreciation restated at £7,000 to once again give a net carrying value of £14,000.

### 17.8.3 Detailed requirements regarding revaluations

The frequency of revaluations depends upon the movements in the fair values of those items of PPE being revalued. In jurisdictions where the rate of price changes is very significant revaluations may be necessary on an annual basis. In other jurisdictions revaluations every three or five years may well be sufficient.

Where an item of PPE is revalued, the entire class of PPE to which that asset belongs should be revalued.[6] A class of PPE is a grouping of assets of a similar nature and use in an entity's operations. Examples would include:

● land;
● land and buildings;
● machinery.

This is an important provision because without it entities would be able to select which assets they revalued on the basis of best advantage to the financial statements. Revaluations will usually increase the carrying values of assets and equity and leave borrowings unchanged. Therefore gearing (or leverage) ratios will be reduced. It is important that, if the revaluation route is chosen, assets are revalued on a rational basis.

The following is an extract from the financial statements of Coil SA, a company incorporated in Belgium that prepares financial statements in euros in accordance with international accounting standards: 'Items of PPE are stated at historical cost modified by revaluation and are depreciated using the straight-line method over their estimated useful lives.'

### 17.8.4 Accounting for revaluations

When the carrying amount of an asset is increased as a result of a revaluation, the increase should be credited directly to other comprehensive income, being shown in equity under the heading of revaluation surplus. The only exception is where the gain reverses a revaluation decrease previously recognised as an expense **relating to the same asset.**

This means that, in the example we considered under Section 17.8.2 above, the revaluation would lead to a credit of £6,000 (£14,000 − £8,000) to other comprehensive income.

If, however, the carrying amount of an asset is decreased as a result of a revaluation, the decrease should be recognised as an expense. The only exception is where that asset had previously been revalued. In those circumstances the loss on revaluation is charged against the revaluation surplus to the extent that the revaluation surplus contains an amount **relating to the same asset.**

EXAMPLE 1 ● REVALUED BUT NOT SOLD  An entity buys freehold land for £100,000 in year 1. The land is revalued to £150,000 in year 3 and £90,000 in year 5. The land is not depreciated.

- In year 3 a surplus of £50,000 (£150,000 − £100,000) is reported as other comprehensive income and included in equity under the heading 'revaluation surplus'.
- In year 5 a deficit of £60,000 (£90,000 − £150,000) arises on the second revaluation. £50,000 of this deficit is deducted from the revaluation surplus and £10,000 is charged as an expense.
- It is worth noting that £10,000 is the amount by which the year 5 carrying amount is lower than the original cost of the land.

EXAMPLE 2 ● REVALUED AND THEN SOLD WITH THE REVALUATION SURPLUS REALISED AT TIME OF SALE  Where an asset that has been revalued is sold, the revaluation surplus becomes realised.[7] It may be transferred to retained earnings when this happens but this transfer is not made through the statement of comprehensive income.

Continuing with our example in Section 17.8.2, let us assume that:

- the plant was sold on 1 January 20X5 for £5,000; and
- the carrying amount of the asset in the financial statements immediately before the sale was £7,000 [£14,000 − (2 × £3,500)].

This means that a loss on sale of £2,000 would be taken to the statement of comprehensive income, and the revaluation surplus of £6,000 would be transferred to retained earnings.

EXAMPLE 3 ● REVALUED AND THEN SOLD WITH THE EXCESS DEPRECIATION RECOGNISED EACH YEAR  IAS 16 allows for the possibility that the revaluation surplus is transferred to retained earnings as the asset is depreciated. To turn once again to our example, we see that:

- the revaluation on 1 January 20X3 increased the annual depreciation charge from £2,000 (£12,000/6) to £3,500 (£21,000/6);

- following revaluation an amount equivalent to the 'excess depreciation' may be transferred from the revaluation surplus to retained earnings as the asset is depreciated. This would lead in our example to a transfer of £1,500 each year; and

- if this occurs then the revaluation surplus that is transferred to retained earnings on sale is £3,000 [£6,000 − (2 × £1,500)].

### 17.8.5 IFRS for SMEs

The IFRS for SMEs was amended in 2015 to allow the use of the revaluation model.

## 17.9 IAS 36 *Impairment of Assets*

### 17.9.1 IAS 36 approach

IAS 36 sets out the principles and methodology for accounting for impairments of non-current assets and goodwill. Where possible, individual non-current assets should be individually tested for impairment. However, where cash flows do not arise from the use of a single non-current asset, impairment is measured for the smallest group of assets which generates income that is largely independent of the company's other income streams. This smallest group is referred to as a cash-generating unit (CGU).

Impairment of an asset, or CGU (if assets are grouped), occurs when the carrying amount of an asset or CGU is greater than its recoverable amount, where:

- the carrying amount is the depreciated historical cost (or depreciated revalued amount);

- the recoverable amount is the higher of the net selling price and the value in use, where:

  - the net selling price is the amount at which an asset could be disposed of, less any direct selling costs;

  - and the value in use is the present value of the future cash flows obtainable as a result of an asset's continued use, including those resulting from its ultimate disposal.

When impairment occurs, a **revised carrying amount** is calculated for the statement of financial position as follows:

It is not always necessary to go through the potentially time-consuming process of computing the value in use of an asset. If the net selling price can be shown to be higher than the existing carrying value then the asset cannot possibly be impaired and no further action is necessary. However, this is not always the case for non-current assets and a number of assets (e.g. goodwill) cannot be sold, so several value in use computations are inevitable.

The revised carrying amount is then depreciated over the remaining useful economic life.

### 17.9.2 Dividing activities into CGUs

In order to carry out an impairment review it is necessary to decide how to divide activities into CGUs. There is no single answer to this – it is extremely judgemental, e.g. if the company has multi-retail sites, the cost of preparing detailed cash flow forecasts for each site could favour grouping.

The risk of grouping is that poorly performing operations might be concealed within a CGU and it would be necessary to consider whether there were any commercial reasons for breaking a CGU into smaller constituents, e.g. if a location was experiencing its own unique difficulties such as local competition or inability to obtain planning permission to expand to a more profitable size.

### 17.9.3 Indications of impairment

A review for impairment is required when there is an indication that an impairment has actually occurred. The following are indicators of impairment:

- External indicators:
  - a fall in the market value of the asset;
  - material adverse changes in regulatory environment;
  - material adverse changes in markets;
  - material long-term increases in market rates of return used for discounting.
- Internal indicators:
  - material changes in operations;
  - major reorganisation;
  - loss of key personnel;
  - loss or net cash outflow from operating activities if this is expected to continue or is a continuation of a loss-making situation.

If there is such an indication, it is necessary to determine the depreciated historical cost of a single asset, or the net assets employed if a CGU, and compare this with the net realisable value and value in use.

AkzoNobel stated in its 2015 Annual Report:

We assess the carrying value of intangible assets and property, plant and equipment whenever events or changes in circumstances indicate that the carrying value of an asset may not be recoverable. In addition, for goodwill and other intangible assets with an indefinite useful life, the carrying value is reviewed annually in the fourth quarter. If the carrying value of an asset or its cash-generating unit exceeds its estimated recoverable amount, an impairment loss is recognized in the statement of income.

The assessment for impairment is performed at the lowest level of assets generating largely independent cash inflows. For goodwill and other intangible assets with an indefinite life, we have determined this to be at business unit level (one level below segment).

Except for goodwill, we reverse impairment losses in the statement of income if and to the extent we have identified a change in estimates used to determine the recoverable amount.

### 17.9.4 Value in use calculation

Value in use is arrived at by estimating and discounting the income stream. The **income streams**:

- are likely to follow the way in which management monitors and makes decisions about continuing or closing the different lines of business;
- may often be identified by reference to major products or services;
- should be based on reasonable and supportable assumptions;

- should be consistent with the most up-to-date budgets and plans that have been formally approved by management, or if they are for a period beyond that covered by formal budgets and plans should, unless there are exceptional circumstances, assume a steady or declining growth rate;[8]
- should be projected cash flows unadjusted for risk, discounted at a rate of return expected from a similarly risky investment, or should be projected risk-adjusted pre-tax cash flows discounted at a risk-free rate.

The **discount rate** should be:

- calculated on a pre-tax basis;
- an estimate of the rate that the market would expect on an equally risky investment excluding the effects of any risk for which the cash flows have been adjusted:[9]
  - increased to reflect the way the market would assess the specific risks associated with the projected cash flows;
  - reduced to a risk-free rate if the cash flows have been adjusted for risk.

The following illustration is from the Roche Holdings, Inc. 2014 Annual Report:

> When the recoverable amount of an asset, being the higher of its net selling price and its value in use, is less than the carrying amount, then the carrying amount is reduced to its recoverable amount. This reduction is reported in the income statement as an impairment loss. Value in use is calculated using estimated cash flows, generally over a five-year period, with extrapolating projections for subsequent years. These are discounted using an appropriate long-term pre-tax interest rate. When an impairment arises, the useful life of the asset in question is reviewed and, if necessary, the future depreciation/amortisation charge is accelerated.

### 17.9.5 Treatment of impairment losses

If the carrying value exceeds the higher of net selling price and value in use, then an impairment loss has occurred. The accounting treatment of such a loss is as follows.

#### Asset not previously revalued

An impairment loss should be recognised in the statement of comprehensive income in the year in which the impairment arises.

#### Asset previously revalued

An impairment loss on a revalued asset is effectively treated as a revaluation deficit. As we have already seen, this means that the decrease should be recognised as an expense. The only exception is where that asset had previously been revalued. In those circumstances the loss on revaluation is charged against the revaluation surplus to the extent that the revaluation surplus contains an amount **relating to the same asset.**

#### Allocation of impairment losses

Where an impairment loss arises, the loss should ideally be set against the specific asset to which it relates. Where the loss cannot be identified as relating to a specific asset, it should be apportioned within the CGU to reduce the most subjective values first, as follows:

- first, to reduce any goodwill within the CGU;
- then to the unit's other assets, allocated on a *pro rata* basis;

- with the proviso that no individual asset should be reduced below the higher of:
- its net selling price (if determinable);
- its value in use (if determinable);
- zero.

The following is an example showing the allocation of an impairment loss.

EXAMPLE ● A cash-generating unit contains the following assets:

|  | £ |
|---|---|
| Goodwill | 70,000 |
| Intangible assets | 10,000 |
| PPE | 100,000 |
| Inventory | 40,000 |
| Receivables | 30,000 |
|  | 250,000 |

The unit is reviewed for impairment due to the existence of indicators and the recoverable amount is estimated at £150,000. The PPE includes a property with a carrying amount of £60,000 and a market value of £75,000. The net realisable value of the inventory is greater than its carrying values and none of the receivables is considered doubtful.

The table below shows the allocation of the impairment loss:

|  | Pre-impairment £ | Impairment £ | Post-impairment £ |
|---|---|---|---|
| Goodwill | 70,000 | (70,000) | Nil |
| Intangible assets | 10,000 | (6,000) | 4,000 |
| PPE | 100,000 | (24,000) | 76,000 |
| Inventory | 40,000 | Nil | 40,000 |
| Receivables | 30,000 | Nil | 30,000 |
|  | 250,000 | (100,000) | 150,000 |

*Notes to table:*

1  The impairment loss is first allocated against goodwill. After this has been done £30,000 (£100,000 − £70,000) remains to be allocated.

2  No impairment loss can be allocated to the property, inventory or receivables because these assets have a recoverable amount that is higher than their carrying value.

3  The remaining impairment loss is allocated pro rata to the intangible assets (carrying amount £10,000) and the plant (carrying amount £40,000 (£100,000 − £60,000)).

### Restoration of past impairment losses

Past impairment losses in respect of an asset other than goodwill may be restored where the recoverable amount increases due to an improvement in economic conditions or a change in use of the asset. Such a restoration should be reflected in the statement of comprehensive income to the extent of the original impairment previously charged to the statement of comprehensive income, adjusting for depreciation which would have been charged otherwise in the intervening period.

## 17.9.6 Illustration of data required for an impairment review

Pronto SA has a product line producing wooden models of athletes for export. The carrying amount of the net assets employed on the line as at 31 December 20X3 was £114,500. The scrap value of the net assets at 31 December 20X6 is estimated to be £5,000.

There is an indication that the export market will be adversely affected in 20X6 by competition from plastic toy manufacturers. This means that the net assets employed to produce this product might have been impaired.

The finance director estimated the net realisable value of the net assets at 31 December 20X3 to be £70,000. The value in use is now calculated to check if it is higher or lower than £70,000. If it is higher it will be compared with the carrying amount to see if impairment has occurred; if it is lower the net realisable value will be compared with the carrying amount.

Pronto SA has prepared budgets for the years ended 31 December 20X4, 20X5 and 20X6. The assumptions underlying the budgets are as follows:

**Unit costs and revenue:**

| | £ |
|---|---|
| Selling price | 10.00 |
| Buying-in cost | (4.00) |
| Production cost: material, labour, overhead | (0.75) |
| Head office overheads apportioned | (0.25) |
| Cash inflow per model | 5.00 |

**Estimated sales volumes:**

| | 20X3 | 20X4 | 20X5 | 20X6 |
|---|---|---|---|---|
| Estimated at 31 December 20X2 | 6,000 | 8,000 | 11,000 | 14,000 |
| Revised estimate at 31 December 20X3 | — | 8,000 | 11,000 | 4,000 |

**Determining the discount rate to be used:**

| | 20X4 | 20X5 | 20X6 |
|---|---|---|---|
| Rate obtainable elsewhere at same level of risk | 10% | 10% | 10% |

The discount factors to be applied to each year are then calculated using cost of capital discount rates as follows:

| 20X4 | $1/1.1$ | $= 0.909$ |
|---|---|---|
| 20X5 | $1/(1.1)^2$ | $= 0.826$ |
| 20X6 | $1/(1.1)^3$ | $= 0.751$ |

### 17.9.7 Illustrating calculation of value in use

Before calculating value in use, it is necessary to ensure that the assumptions underlying the budgets are reasonable, e.g. is the selling price likely to be affected by competition in 20X6 in addition to loss of market? Is the selling price in 20X5 likely to be affected? Is the estimate of scrap value reasonably accurate? How sensitive is value in use to the scrap value? Is it valid to assume that the cash flows will occur at year-ends? How accurate is the cost of capital? Will components making up the income stream, e.g. sales, materials, labour, be subject to different rates of inflation?

Assuming that no adjustment is required to the budgeted figures provided above, the estimated income streams are discounted using the normal DCF approach as follows:

| | 20X4 | 20X5 | 20X6 |
|---|---|---|---|
| Sales (models) | 8,000 | 11,000 | 4,000 |
| Income per model | £5 | £5 | £5 |
| Income stream (£) | 40,000 | 55,000 | 20,000 |
| Estimated scrap proceeds | | | 5,000 |
| Cash flows to be discounted | 40,000 | 55,000 | 25,000 |
| Discounted (using cost of capital factors) | 0.909 | 0.826 | 0.751 |
| Present value | 36,360 | 45,430 | 18,775 |

**Value in use = £100,565**

### 17.9.8 Illustration determining the *revised* carrying amount

If the carrying amount at the statement of financial position date exceeds net realisable value and value in use, it is revised to an amount which is the higher of net realisable value and value in use. For Pronto SA:

|  | £ |
|---|---|
| Carrying amount as at 31 December 20X3 | 114,500 |
| Net realisable value | 70,000 |
| Value in use | 100,565 |
| **Revised carrying amount** | **100,565** |

## 17.10 IFRS 5 *Non-current Assets Held for Sale and Discontinued Operations*

IFRS 5 sets out requirements for the classification, measurement and presentation of non-current assets held for sale. The requirements which replaced IAS 35 *Discontinuing Operations* were discussed in Chapter 4. The IFRS is the result of the joint short-term project to resolve differences between IFRSs and US GAAP.

### Classification as 'held for sale'

The IFRS (paragraph 6) classifies a non-current asset as 'held for sale' if its carrying amount will be recovered principally through a sale transaction rather than through continuing use. The criteria for classification as 'held for sale' are:

● the asset must be available for immediate sale in its present condition; and

● its sale must be *highly probable*.

The criteria for a sale to be highly probable are:

● the appropriate level of management must be committed to a plan to sell the asset;

● an active programme to locate a buyer and complete the plan must have been initiated;

● the asset must be actively marketed for sale at a price that is reasonable in relation to its current fair value;

● the sale should be expected to qualify for recognition as a completed sale within one year from the date of classification unless the delay is caused by events or circumstances beyond the entity's control and there is sufficient evidence that the entity remains committed to its plan to sell the asset; and

● actions required to complete the plan should indicate that it is unlikely that significant changes to the plan will be made or that the plan will be withdrawn.

### Measurement and presentation of assets held for sale

The IFRS requires that assets 'held for sale' should:

● be measured at the lower of carrying amount and *fair value* less costs to sell;

● not continue to be depreciated; and

● be presented separately on the face of the statement of financial position.

The following additional disclosures are required in the notes in the period in which a non-current asset has been either classified as held for sale or sold:

● a description of the non-current asset;

- a description of the facts and circumstances of the sale;
- the expected manner and timing of that disposal;
- the gain or loss if not separately presented on the face of the statement of comprehensive income; and
- the caption in the statement of comprehensive income that includes that gain or loss.

### 17.10.1 IFRS for SMEs

The IFRS does not require separate presentation in the statement of financial position of 'non-current assets held for sale'. However, if an entity has plans to discontinue or restructure the operation to which an asset belongs and has plans to dispose of an asset before the previously expected date, then this is to be treated as an indication that an asset may be impaired and in such a case an impairment test is required.

## 17.11 Disclosure requirements

For each class of PPE the financial statements need to disclose:

- the measurement bases used for determining the gross carrying amount;
- the depreciation methods used;
- the useful lives or the depreciation rates used;
- the gross carrying amount and the accumulated depreciation (aggregated with accumulated impairment losses) at the beginning and end of the period;
- a reconciliation of the carrying amount at the beginning and end of the period.

The style employed by J Sainsbury Plc in its 2015 accounts is almost universally employed for this:

**Property, plant and equipment**

|  | *Group Land and buildings £m* | *Group Fixtures and equipment £m* | *Group Total £m* |
|---|---|---|---|
| **Cost** |  |  |  |
| At 16 March 2014 | 9,652 | 5,049 | 14,701 |
| Acquisition of subsidiary | 5 |  | 5 |
| Additions | 475 | 485 | 960 |
| Disposals | (110) | (608) | (718) |
| Transfer to assets held for sale | (90) | (4) | (94) |
| **At 14 March 2015** | **9,932** | **4,922** | **14,854** |
| Accumulated depreciation and impairment |  |  |  |
| At 16 March 2014 | 1,774 | 3,047 | 4,821 |
| Depreciation expense for the year | 158 | 387 | 545 |
| Impairment | 412 | 128 | 540 |
| Disposals | (86) | (604) | (690) |
| Transfer to assets held for sale | (9) | (1) | (10) |
| **At 14 March 2015** | **2,249** | **2,957** | **5,206** |
| **Net book value at 14 March 2015** | **7,683** | **1,965** | **9,648** |

Additionally the financial statements should disclose:

- the existence and amounts of restrictions on title, and PPE pledged as security for liabilities;
- the accounting policy for the estimated costs of restoring the site of items of PPE;
- the amount of expenditures on account of PPE in the course of construction; and
- the amount of commitments for the acquisition of PPE.

## 17.12 Government grants towards the cost of PPE

The accounting treatment of government grants is covered by IAS 20. The basis of the standard is the accruals concept, which requires the matching of cost and revenue so as to recognise both in the statements of comprehensive income of the periods to which they relate. This should, of course, be tempered with the prudence concept, which requires that revenue is not anticipated. Therefore, in the light of the complex conditions usually attached to grants, credit should not be taken until receipt is assured.

Similarly, there may be a right to recover the grant wholly or partially in the event of a breach of conditions, and on that basis these conditions should be regularly reviewed and, if necessary, provision made.

Should the tax treatment of a grant differ from the accounting treatment, the effect of this would be accounted for in accordance with IAS 12 *Income Taxes*.

### IAS 20

Government grants should be recognised in the statement of comprehensive income so as to match the expenditure towards which they are intended to contribute. If this is retrospective, they should be recognised in the period in which they became receivable.

Grants in respect of PPE should be recognised over the useful economic lives of those assets, thus matching the depreciation or amortisation.

IAS 20 outlines two acceptable methods of presenting grants relating to assets in the statement of financial position:

(a) The first method sets up the grant as deferred income, which is recognised as income on a systematic and rational basis over the useful life of the asset.

> EXAMPLE ● An entity purchased a machine for £60,000 and received a grant of £20,000 towards its purchase. The machine is depreciated over four years.
>
> The 'deferred income method' would result in an initial carrying amount for the machine of £60,000 and a deferred income credit of £20,000. In the first year of use of the plant the depreciation charge would be £15,000. £5,000 of the deferred income would be recognised as a credit in the statement of comprehensive income, making the net charge £10,000. At the end of the first year the carrying amount of the plant would be £45,000 and the deferred income included in the statement of financial position would be £15,000.
>
> The following is an extract from the 2015 Go-Ahead Annual Report:
>
> **Government grants**
> Government grants are recognised at their fair value where there is reasonable assurance that the grant will be received and all attaching conditions will be complied with. When the grant relates to an expense item, it is recognised in the income statement over the period necessary to match on a systematic basis to the costs that it is intended to compensate. *Where the grant relates to a non-current asset, value is credited to a deferred*

*income account and is released to the income statement over the expected useful life of the relevant asset.*

(b) The second method deducts the grant in arriving at the carrying amount of the relevant asset. If we were to apply this method to the above example then the initial carrying amount of the asset would be £40,000. The depreciation charged in the first year would be £10,000. This is the same as the net charge to income under the 'deferred credit' method. The closing carrying amount of the plant would be £30,000. This is of course the carrying amount under the 'deferred income method' (£45,000) less the closing deferred income under the 'deferred income method' (£15,000).

The following extract is from the 2015 Annual Report of A & J Muklow plc:

### Capital grants

Capital grants received relating to the building or refurbishing of investment properties are deducted from the cost of the relevant property. Revenue grants are deducted from the related expenditure.

### 17.12.1 Arguments in favour of each approach

#### The capital approach

Supporters of the capital approach argue that (a) government grants are a means of financing and should therefore be reported as such in the statement of financial position rather than be recognised in profit or loss to offset the items of expense which they finance, and (b) it is inappropriate to recognise government grants in profit or loss, because they are not earned but represent an incentive provided by government without related costs.

#### The income approach

Supporters of this approach argue that (a) government grants are receipts from a source other than shareholders which should not, therefore, be recognised directly in equity but should be recognised in profit or loss in appropriate periods, and (b) they are not without cost in that the entity earns them through its compliance with their conditions. Their preferred treatment is, therefore, to recognise in profit or loss over the periods in which the entity recognises as expenses the related costs for which the grant was intended to compensate.

### 17.12.2 IASB future action

The IASB is currently considering drafting an amended standard on government grants. Among the reasons for the Board amending IAS 20 were the following:

● The recognition requirements of IAS 20 often result in accounting that is inconsistent with the *Framework*, in particular the recognition of a deferred credit when the entity has no liability, e.g. the following is an extract from the Annual Report of SSL International plc (now part of Reckitt Benckiser):

### Grant income

Capital grants are shown in other creditors within the statement of financial position and released to match the depreciation charge on associated assets.

● IAS 20 contains numerous options. Apart from reducing the comparability of financial statements, the options in IAS 20 can result in understatement of the assets controlled by the entity and do not provide the most relevant information to users of financial statements.

In due course there is the prospect of the IASB issuing a revised standard which requires entities to recognise grants as income as soon as their receipt becomes unconditional. This is consistent with the specific requirements for the recognition of grants relating to agricultural activity laid down in IAS 41 *Agriculture*. This matter is discussed in more detail in Chapter 20.

### IFRS for SMEs

Government grants are measured at the fair value of the asset received or receivable and treated as income when the proceeds are receivable if there are no future performance conditions attached. If there are performance conditions, the grant is recognised in profit or loss when the conditions are satisfied.

## 17.13 Investment properties

While IAS 16 requires all PPE to be subjected to a systematic depreciation charge, this may be considered inappropriate for properties held as assets but not employed in the normal activities of the entity, rather being held as investments. For such properties a more relevant treatment is to take account of the current market value of the property. The accounting treatment is set out in IAS 40 *Investment Property*.

Such properties may be held either as a main activity (e.g. by a property investment company) or by a company whose main activity is not the holding of such properties. In each case the accounting treatment is similar.

### Definition of an investment property[10]

For the purposes of the statement, an investment property is property held (by the owner or by the lessee under a finance lease) to earn rentals or capital appreciation or both.

Investment property does **not** include:

(a) property held for use in the production or supply of goods or services or for administrative purposes (dealt with in IAS 16);

(b) property held for sale in the ordinary course of business (dealt with in IAS 2);

(c) an interest held by a lessee under an operating lease, even if the interest was a long-term interest acquired in exchange for a large upfront payment (dealt with in IAS 17);

(d) forests and similar regenerative natural resources (dealt with in IAS 41 *Agriculture*); and

(e) mineral rights, the exploration for and development of minerals, oil, natural gas and similar non-regenerative natural resources (dealt with in IFRS 6).

### Accounting models

Under IAS 40, an entity must choose either:

● a fair value model: investment property should be measured at fair value and changes in fair value should be recognised in the statement of comprehensive income; or

● a cost model (the same as the benchmark treatment in IAS 16 *Property, Plant and Equipment*): investment property should be measured at depreciated cost (less any accumulated impairment losses). An entity that chooses the cost model should disclose the fair value of its investment property.

An entity should apply the model chosen to all its investment property. A change from one model to the other model should be made only if the change will result in a more appropriate presentation. The standard states that this is highly unlikely to be the case for a change from the fair value model to the cost model.

In exceptional cases, there is clear evidence when an entity that has chosen the fair value model first acquires an investment property (or when an existing property first becomes investment property following the completion of construction or development, or after a change in use) that the entity will not be able to determine the fair value of the investment property reliably on a continuing basis. In such cases, the entity measures that investment property using the benchmark treatment in IAS 16 until the disposal of the investment property. The residual value of the investment property should be assumed to be zero. The entity measures all its other investment property at fair value.

## 17.14 Effect of accounting policy for PPE on the interpretation of the financial statements

A number of difficulties exist when we attempt to carry out inter-firm comparisons using the external information that is available to a shareholder.

### 17.14.1 Effect of inflation on the carrying value of the asset

The most serious difficulty is the effect of inflation, which makes the charges based on historical cost inadequate. Companies have followed various practices to take account of inflation. None of these is as effective as an acceptable surrogate for index adjustment using specific asset indices on a systematic annual basis: this is the only way to ensure uniformity and comparability of the cost/valuation figure upon which the depreciation charge is based.

The method that is currently allowable under IAS 16 is to revalue the assets. This is a partial answer, but it results in lack of comparability of ratios such as gearing or leverage.

### 17.14.2 Effect of revaluation on ratios

The rules of double entry require that when an asset is revalued the 'profit' (or, exceptionally, 'loss') must be credited somewhere. As it is not a 'realised' profit, it would not be appropriate to credit the statement of comprehensive income, so a 'revaluation reserve' must be created. As the asset is depreciated, this reserve may be realised to income; similarly, when an asset is ultimately disposed of, any residue relevant to that asset may be taken into income.

One significant by-product of revaluing assets is the effect on gearing. The revaluation reserve, while not distributable, forms part of the shareholders' funds and thus improves the debt/equity ratio. Care must therefore be taken in looking at the revaluation policies and reserves when comparing the gearing or leverage of companies.

The problem is compounded because the carrying value may be amended at random periods and on a selective category of asset.

### 17.14.3 Choice of depreciation method

There are a number of acceptable depreciation methods that may give rise to very different patterns of debits against the profits of individual years.

### 17.14.4 Inherent imprecision in estimating economic life

One of the greatest difficulties with depreciation is that it is inherently imprecise. The amount of depreciation depends on the estimate of the economic life of assets, which is affected not only by the durability and workload of the asset, but also by external factors beyond the control of management. Such factors may be technological, commercial or economic. Here are some examples:

- the production by a competitor of a new product rendering yours obsolete, e.g. watches with battery-powered movements replacing those with mechanical movements;
- the production by a competitor of a product at a price lower than your production costs, e.g. imported goods from countries where costs are lower;
- changes in the economic climate which reduce demand for your product.

This means that the interpreter of accounts must pay particular attention to depreciation policies, looking closely at the market where the entity's business operates. However, this understanding is not helped by the lack of requirement to disclose specific rates of depreciation and the basis of computation of residual values. Without such information, the potential effects of differences between policies adopted by competing entities cannot be accurately assessed.

### 17.14.5 Mixed values in the statement of financial position

The effect of depreciation on the statement of financial position is also some cause for concern. The net book amount shown for non-current assets is the result of deducting accumulated depreciation from cost (or valuation); it is not intended to be (although many non-accountants assume it is) an estimate of the value of the underlying assets. The valuation of a business based on the statement of financial position is extremely difficult.

### 17.14.6 IFRS for SMEs

This IFRS differs from IAS 16 in that:

- PPE is reported at historical cost less depreciation and less any impairment of the carrying amount. The revaluation model is now permitted.
- A review of the useful life, residual value or depreciation rate is only carried out if there is a significant change in the asset or how it is used. Any adjustment is a change in estimate.
- Assets held for sale are not reported separately, although the fact that an asset is held for sale might be an indication that there has been an impairment.
- Most investment property is treated in the same way as PPE. However, if the fair value of investment property can be measured reliably without excessive cost then the fair value model applies with changes being through profit or loss.
- Separate significant components should be depreciated separately if there are significantly different patterns of consumption of economic benefits.

### 17.14.7 Different policies may be applied within the same sector

Inter-company comparisons are even more difficult. Two entities following the historical cost convention may own identical assets, which, as they were purchased at different times, may well appear as dramatically different figures in the accounts. This is particularly true of interests in land and buildings.

### 17.14.8 Effect on the return on capital employed

There is an effect not only on the net asset value, but also on the return on capital employed. To make a fair assessment of return on capital it is necessary to know the current replacement cost of the underlying assets, but, under present conventions, up-to-date valuations are required only for investment properties.

### 17.14.9 Effect on EPS

IAS 16 is concerned to ensure that the earnings of an entity reflect a fair charge for the use of the assets by the enterprise. This should ensure an accurate calculation of earnings per share. But there is a weakness here. If assets have increased in value without revaluations, then depreciation will be based on the historical cost.

## Summary

Before IAS 16 there were significant problems in relation to the accounting treatment of PPE such as the determination of a cost figure and the adjustment for inflation; companies providing nil depreciation on certain types of asset; and revaluations being made selectively and not kept current.

With IAS 16 the IASB has made the accounts more consistent and comparable. This standard has resolved some of these problems, principally requiring companies to provide for depreciation and if they have a policy of revaluation to keep such valuations reasonably current and applied to all assets within a class, i.e. removing the ability to cherry-pick which assets to revalue.

However, certain difficulties remain for the user of the accounts in that there are different management policies on the method of depreciation, which can have a major impact on the profit for the year; subjective assessments of economic life that may be reviewed each year with an impact on profits; and inconsistencies such as the presence of modified historical costs and historical costs in the same statement of financial position. In addition, with pure historical cost accounting, where non-current asset carrying values are based on original cost, no pretence is made that non-current asset net book amounts have any relevance to current values. The investor is expected to know that the depreciation charge is arithmetical in character and will not wholly provide the finance for tomorrow's assets or ensure maintenance of the business's operational base. To give recognition to these factors requires the investor to grapple with the effects of lost purchasing power through inflation; the effect of changes in supply and demand on replacement prices; technological change and its implication for the company's competitiveness; and external factors such as exchange rates. To calculate the effect of these variables necessitates not only considerable mental agility, but also far more information than is contained in a set of accounts. This is an area that needs to be revisited by the standard setters.

## REVIEW QUESTIONS

1 Define PPE and explain how materiality affects the concept of PPE.

2 Define depreciation. Explain what assets need not be depreciated and list the main methods of calculating depreciation.

**3** What is meant by the phrases 'useful life' and 'residual value'?

**4** Define 'cost' in connection with PPE.

**5** What effect does revaluing assets have on gearing (or leverage)?

**6** How should grants received towards expenditure on PPE be treated?

**7** Define an investment property and explain its treatment in financial statements.

**8** 'Depreciation should mean that a company has sufficient resources to replace assets at the end of their economic lives.' Discuss.

## EXERCISES

### * Question 1

Simple SA has just purchased a roasting/salting machine to produce roasted walnuts. The finance director asks for your advice on how the company should calculate the depreciation on this machine. Details are as follows:

| | |
|---|---|
| Cost of machine | SF800,000 |
| Residual value | SF104,000 |
| Estimated life | 4 years |
| Annual profits | SF2,000,000 |
| Annual turnover from machine | SF850,000 |

Required:
(a) Calculate the annual depreciation charge using the straight-line method and the reducing balance method. Assume that an annual rate of 40% is applicable for the reducing balance method.
(b) Comment upon the validity of each method, taking into account the type of business and the effect each method has on annual profits. Are there any other methods which would be more applicable?

### * Question 2

(a) Discuss why IAS 40 *Investment Property* was produced.
(b) Universal Entrepreneurs plc has the following items on its PPE list:
  (i) £1,000,000 – the right to extract sandstone from a particular quarry. Geologists predict that extraction at the present rate may be continued for 10 years.
  (ii) £5,000,000 – a freehold property, let to a subsidiary on a full repairing lease negotiated on arm's-length terms for 15 years. The building is a new one, erected on a greenfield site at a cost of £4,000,000.
  (iii) A fleet of motor cars used by company employees. These have been purchased under a contract which provides a guaranteed part exchange value of 60% of cost after two years' use.
  (iv) A company helicopter with an estimated life of 150,000 flying hours.
  (v) A 19-year lease on a property let out at arm's-length rent to another company.

Required:
Advise the company on the depreciation policy it ought to adopt for each of the above assets.

(c) The company is considering revaluing its interests in land and buildings, which comprise freehold and leasehold properties, all used by the company or its subsidiaries.

Required:

**Discuss the consequences of this on the depreciation policy of the company and any special instructions that need to be given to the valuer.**

## * Question 3

You have been given the task, by one of the partners of the firm of accountants for which you work, of assisting in the preparation of a trend statement for a client, Mercury.

Mercury has been in existence for four years. Figures for the three preceding years are known but those for the fourth year need to be calculated. Unfortunately, the supporting workings for the preceding years' figures cannot be found and the client's own ledger accounts and workings are not available.

One item in particular, plant, is causing difficulty and the following figures have been given to you:

| 12 months ended 31 March | 20X6 | 20X7 | 20X8 | 20X9 |
|---|---|---|---|---|
| | £ | £ | £ | £ |
| (A) Plant at cost | 80,000 | 80,000 | 90,000 | ? |
| (B) Accumulated depreciation | (16,000) | (28,800) | (28,080) | ? |
| (C) Net (written down) value | 64,000 | 51,200 | 61,920 | ? |

The only other information available is that disposals have taken place at the beginning of the financial years concerned:

| | Date of | | Original | Sales |
|---|---|---|---|---|
| | Disposal | Original acquisition | cost | Proceeds |
| | 12 months ended 31 March | | £ | £ |
| First disposal | 20X8 | 20X6 | 15,000 | 8,000 |
| Second disposal | 20X8 | 20X6 | 30,000 | 21,000 |

Plant sold was replaced on the same day by new plant. The cost of the plant which replaced the first disposal is not known but the replacement for the second disposal is known to have cost £50,000.

Required:
(a) Identify the method of providing for depreciation on plant employed by the client, stating how you have arrived at your conclusion.
(b) Show how the figures shown at line (B) for each of the years ended 31 March 20X6, 20X7 and 20X8 were calculated. Extend your workings to cover the year ended 31 March 20X9.
(c) Produce the figures that should be included in the blank spaces on the trend statement at lines (A), (B) and (C) for the year ended 31 March 20X9.
(d) Calculate the profit or loss arising on each of the two disposals.

## Question 4

In the year to 31 December 20X9, Amy bought a new machine and made the following payments in relation to it:

| | £ | £ |
|---|---|---|
| Cost as per supplier's list | 12,000 | |
| Less: Agreed discount | 1,000 | 11,000 |
| Delivery charge | | 100 |
| Erection charge | | 200 |
| Maintenance charge | | 300 |
| Additional component to increase capacity | | 400 |
| Replacement parts | | 250 |

Required:
(a) State and justify the cost figure which should be used as the basis for depreciation.
(b) What does depreciation do, and why is it necessary?
(c) Briefly explain, without numerical illustration, how the straight-line and diminishing balance methods of depreciation work. What different assumptions does each method make?
(d) Explain the term 'objectivity' as used by accountants. To what extent is depreciation objective?
(e) It is common practice in published accounts in Germany to use the diminishing balance method for PPE in the early years of an asset's life, and then to change to the straight-line method as soon as this would give a higher annual charge. What do you think of this practice? Refer to relevant accounting conventions in your answer.

*(ACCA)*

## * Question 5

The finance director of Small Machine Parts Ltd is considering the acquisition of a lease of a small work-shop in a warehouse complex that is being redeveloped by City Redevelopers Ltd at a steady rate over a number of years. City Redevelopers are granting such leases for five years on payment of a premium of £20,000.

The accountant has obtained estimates of the likely maintenance costs and disposal value of the lease during its five-year life. He has produced the following table and suggested to the finance director that the annual average cost should be used in the financial accounts to represent the depreciation charge in the profit and loss account.

Table prepared to calculate the annual average cost

| Years of life | 1 | 2 | 3 | 4 | 5 |
|---|---|---|---|---|---|
|  | £ | £ | £ | £ | £ |
| Purchase price | 20,000 | 20,000 | 20,000 | 20,000 | 20,000 |
| Maintenance/repairs |  |  |  |  |  |
| Year 2 |  | 1,000 | 1,000 | 1,000 | 1,000 |
| 3 |  |  | 1,500 | 1,500 | 1,500 |
| 4 |  |  |  | 1,850 | 1,850 |
| 5 |  |  |  |  | 2,000 |
|  | 20,000 | 21,000 | 22,500 | 24,350 | 26,350 |
| Resale value | 11,500 | 10,000 | 8,010 | 5,350 | 350 |
| Net cost | 8,500 | 11,000 | 14,490 | 19,000 | 26,000 |
| Annual average cost | 8,500 | 5,500 | 4,830 | 4,750 | 5,200 |

The finance director, however, was considering whether to calculate the depreciation chargeable using the annuity method with interest at 15%.

Required:
(a) Calculate the entries that would appear in the statement of comprehensive income of Small Machine Parts Ltd for each of the five years of the life of the lease for the amortisation charge, the interest element in the depreciation charge and the income from secondary assets using the *annuity method*. Calculate the net profit for each of the five years assuming that the operating cash flow is estimated to be £25,000 per year.
(b) Discuss briefly which of the two methods you would recommend. The present value at 15% of £1 per annum for five years is £3.35214. The present value at 15% of £1 received at the end of year 5 is £0.49717. Ignore taxation.

*(ACCA)*

## Question 6

(a) IAS 16 *Property, Plant and Equipment* requires that where there has been a permanent diminution in the value of property, plant and equipment, the carrying amount should be written down to the recoverable amount. The phrase 'recoverable amount' is defined in IAS 16 as 'the amount which the entity expects to recover from the future use of an asset, including its residual value on disposal'. The issues of how one identifies an impaired asset, the measurement of an asset when impairment has occurred and the recognition of impairment losses were not adequately dealt with by the standard. As a result the International Accounting Standards Committee issued IAS 36 *Impairment of Assets* in order to address the above issues.

Required:

(i) Describe the circumstances which indicate that an impairment loss relating to an asset may have occurred.

(ii) Explain how IAS 36 deals with the recognition and measurement of the *impairment of assets* .

(b) AB, a public limited company, has decided to comply with IAS 36 *Impairment of Assets*. The following information is relevant to the impairment review:

(i) Certain items of machinery appeared to have suffered a permanent diminution in value. The inventory produced by the machines was being sold below its cost and this occurrence had affected the value of the productive machinery. The carrying value at historical cost of these machines is $290,000 and their net selling price is estimated at $120,000. The anticipated net cash inflows from the machines are now $100,000 per annum for the next three years. A market discount rate of 10% per annum is to be used in any present value computations.

(ii) AB acquired a car taxi business on 1 January 20X1 for $230,000. The values of the assets of the business at that date based on net selling prices were as follows:

|  | $000 |
|---|---|
| Vehicles (12 vehicles) | 120 |
| Intangible assets (taxi licence) | 30 |
| Trade receivables | 10 |
| Cash | 50 |
| Trade payables | (20) |
|  | 190 |

On 1 February 20X1, the taxi company had three of its vehicles stolen. The net selling value of these vehicles was $30,000 and because of non-disclosure of certain risks to the insurance company, the vehicles were uninsured. As a result of this event, AB wishes to recognise an impairment loss of $45,000 (inclusive of the loss of the stolen vehicles) due to the decline in the value in use of the cash generating unit, that is the taxi business. On 1 March 20X1 a rival taxi company commenced business in the same area. It is anticipated that the business revenue of AB will be reduced by 25%, leading to a decline in the present value in use of the business, which is calculated at $150,000. The net selling value of the taxi licence has fallen to $25,000 as a result of the rival taxi operator. The net selling values of the other assets have remained the same as at 1 January 20X1 throughout the period.

Required:

Describe how AB should treat the above impairments of assets in its financial statements.

(In part (b) (ii) you should show the treatment of the impairment loss at 1 February 20X1 and 1 March 20X1.)

*(ACCA)*

## * Question 7

Infinite Leisure Group owns and operates a number of pubs and clubs across Europe and South East Asia. Since inception the group has made exclusive use of the cost model for the purpose of its annual financial reporting. This has led to a number of shareholders expressing concern about what they see as a consequent lack of clarity and quality in the group's financial statements.

The CEO does not support use of the alternative to the cost model (the revaluation model), believing it produces volatile information. However, she is open to persuasion and so, as an example of the impact of a revaluation policy, has asked you to carry out an analysis (using data concerning 'Sooz' – one of the group's nightclubs sold during the year to 31 October 2006) to show the impact the revaluation model would have had on the group's financial statements had the model been adopted from the day the club was acquired.

The following extract has been taken from the company's asset register:

Outlet: 'Sooz'

**Acquisition data**

| | |
|---|---|
| Date acquired | 1 November 2001 |
| Total cost | €10.24m |
| Cost components: | |
| Plant and equipment | |
| Cost | €0.24m |
| Economic life | 6 years |
| Residual value | nil |
| Property | |
| Buildings | |
| Cost | €7.0m |
| Economic life | 50 years |
| Land | |
| Cost | €3.0m |

**Updates**

1 November 2003: Replacement cost of plant and equipment €0.42m. No fair value available (mainly specialised audio-visual equipment). No change to economic life. Property revaluation €13m (land €4m, buildings €9m). Future economic life as at 1 November 2003 50 years.

**Disposal**

| | |
|---|---|
| Date committed to a plan to sell | January 2006 |
| Date sold | June 2006 |
| Net sale price | €9.1m |
| Sale price components: | |
| Plant and equipment | €0.1m |
| Property | €9.0m |

Note: the Group accounts for property and for plant and equipment as separate non-current assets in its statement of financial position using straight-line depreciation.

**Required:**

**Prepare an analysis to show the impact on Infinite Leisure's financial statements for each year the 'Sooz' nightclub was owned had the revaluation model been in place from the day the nightclub was acquired.**

*(The Association of International Accountants)*

## Question 8

The Blissopia Leisure Group consists of three divisions: Blissopia 1, which operates mainstream bars; Blissopia 2, which operates large restaurants; and Blissopia 3, which operates one hotel – the Eden.

Divisions 1 and 2 have been trading very successfully and there are no indications of any potential impairment. It is a different matter with the Eden, however. The Eden is a 'boutique' hotel and was acquired on 1 November 2006 for $6.90m. The fair value (using net selling price) of the hotel's net assets at that date and their carrying value at the year-end were as follows:

|  | Fair value 1.11.06 $m | Carrying value 31.10.07 $m |
|---|---|---|
| Land and buildings | 3.61 | 3.18 |
| Plant and equipment | 0.90 | 0.81 |
| Cash | 1.40 | 1.12 |
| Vehicles | 0.10 | 0.09 |
| Trade receivables | 0.34 | 0.37 |
| Trade payables | (0.60) | (0.74) |
|  | 5.75 | 4.83 |

The following facts were discovered following an impairment review as at 31 October 2007:

(i) During August 2007, a rival hotel commenced trading in the same location as the Eden. The Blissopia Leisure Group expects hotel revenues to be significantly affected and has calculated the value-in-use of the Eden to be $3.52m.

(ii) The company owning the rival hotel has offered to buy the Eden (including all of the above net assets) for $4m. Selling costs would be approximately $50,000.

(iii) One of the hotel vehicles was severely damaged in an accident whilst being used by an employee to carry shopping home from a supermarket. The vehicle's carrying value at 31 October 2007 was $30,000 and insurers have indicated that as it was being used for an uninsured purpose the loss is not covered by insurance. The vehicle was subsequently scrapped.

(iv) A corporate client, owing $40,000, has recently gone into liquidation. Lawyers have estimated that the company will receive only 25% of the amount outstanding.

**Required:**
**Prepare a memo for the directors of the Blissopia Leisure Group explaining how the group should account for the impairment to the Eden Hotel's assets as at 31 October 2007.**

*(The Association of International Accountants)*

## Question 9

International Financial Reporting Standards (IFRS) support the use of fair values when reporting the values of assets wherever practical. This involves periodic remeasurements of assets and the consequent recognition of gains and losses in the financial statements. There are several methods of recognising gains and losses on remeasurement of assets required by IFRS.

**Required:**
**(a) Advise how IFRS require gains or losses on remeasurement to be dealt with in the financial statements in the case of each of the following assets. The calculation of such gains or losses is not necessary, merely their accounting treatment. Your answer should indicate clearly where in the performance statement each component of gain or loss should appear.**

    (i)   Property, plant & equipment held under the revaluation model of IAS 16.

    (ii)  Investment property held under the fair value model of IAS 40.

    (iii) Financial assets held at fair value under IFRS 9. (4 marks)

(b) In each case (i) and (ii) below, outline briefly the appropriate accounting treatment and show the journal entries in the financial statements of Williamson plc (Williamson) for year ended 31 March 2015, resulting from recording the events described. Any entry affecting the performance statement must be clearly classified as either 'profit or loss' or 'other comprehensive income'. Williamson adopts the revaluation model of IAS 16 *Property, Plant & Equipment* and the fair value model of IAS 40 Investment Property. Williamson chooses to recognise any fair value gains or losses arising on its equity investments in 'other comprehensive income' as permitted by IFRS 9 Financial Instruments.

    (i)   Williamson owns a piece of property it purchased on 1 April 2012 for €3.5 million. The land component of the property was estimated to be €1 million at the date of purchase. The useful economic life of the building on this land was estimated to be 25 years on 1 April 2012. The property was used as the corporate headquarters for two years from that date. On 1 April 2014, the company moved its headquarters to another building and leased the entire property for five years to an unrelated tenant on an arms' length basis in order to benefit from the rental income and future capital appreciation. The fair value of the property on 1 April 2014 was €4.1 million (land component €1.9 million), and on 31 March 2015, €4.8 million (land component €2.1 million). The estimate of useful economic life remained unchanged throughout the period. Land and buildings are considered to be two separate assets by the directors of Williamson.

    (ii)  Williamson holds a portfolio of equity investments the value of which was correctly recorded at €12 million on 1 April 2014. During the year ended 31 March 2015, the company received dividends of €0.75 million. Further equity investments were purchased at a cost of €1.6 million. Shares were disposed of during the year for proceeds of €1.1 million. These shares had cost €0.4 million a number of years earlier but had been valued at €0.9 million on 1 April 2014. The fair value of the financial assets held on 31 March 2015 was €14 million.

*(Institute of Certified Public Accountants (CPA), Professional Stage 1
Corporate Reporting Examination, April 2015)*

## Notes

1  IAS 16 *Property, Plant and Equipment*, IASB, revised 2004, para. 6.

2  Ibid., para. 16.

3  Ibid., para. 22.

4  IAS 23 *Borrowing Costs*, IASB, revised 2007, para. 8.

5  IAS 16 *Property, Plant and Equipment*, IASB, revised 2004, para. 18.

6  Ibid., para. 29.

7  Ibid., para. 41.

8  IAS 36 *Impairment of Assets*, IASB, 2004, para. 33.

9  Ibid., paras 55–56.

10  IAS 40 *Investment Property*, IASB, 2004.

# CHAPTER 18

# Leasing

## 18.1 Introduction

A *lease* is an agreement whereby the lessor (the legal owner of an asset) conveys to the lessee (the user of the asset) the right to use an asset for an agreed period of time in return for a payment or series of payments. An alternative method of obtaining the use of an asset is to purchase the asset outright. Unless the lessee has surplus cash the asset purchase must be financed in some way, either by a share issue or (more likely) by borrowing. From a legal perspective, the two methods of obtaining asset use (leasing or outright purchase) are completely different. In the case of leasing, no asset is owned by the lessee so (from a legal perspective) no asset is recognised by the lessee. Clearly the opposite is true in the case of outright purchase of an asset. In the case of outright purchase the purchaser will recognise the asset it legally owns plus (in many cases) an associated liability.

One of the fundamental characteristics of useful financial information is that it faithfully represents the transactions reported within it. Another way of saying this is that useful financial information should reflect the economic substance of transactions. Where this 'economic substance' differs from the legal form then the economic substance will prevail. We will see in this chapter that the issue of 'substance over form' is a key factor when we consider the financial reporting of leasing transactions in the financial statements of both lessor and lessee.

### Objectives

By the end of this chapter, you should be able to:

- evaluate the 'substance over form' issue identified in the introduction and so identify why an accounting standard on leasing is necessary;
- distinguish between finance leases and operating leases as made in IAS 17 *Leases*;
- critically discuss why a replacement standard for IAS 17 was necessary;
- explain how a lease is identified in IFRS 16 *Leases* – issued in January 2016;
- account for leases in the financial statements of lessees under IFRS 16;
- account for leases in the financial statements of lessors under IFRS 16;
- account for sale and leaseback transactions in the financial statements of both the seller/lessee and the buyer/lessor;
- discuss the economic impact of IFRS 16 on the extent to which leasing is used as a means of asset procurement.

## 18.2 Need for an accounting standard on leasing

In the introduction we explained that where an entity needed the use of an asset leasing was an alternative to outright purchase. The two options have very different legal consequences and also (if accounted for in accordance with their legal form) different impacts on the financial statements.

EXAMPLE ● The summarised statement of financial position of an entity at the start of its accounting period (all accounting periods in this example are of one year's duration) is as follows:

|  | $000 |
| --- | --- |
| Non-current assets | 60,000 |
| Current assets | 40,000 |
|  | 100,000 |
| Equity | 40,000 |
| Non-current liabilities (loans) | 40,000 |
| Current liabilities (no loans included) | 20,000 |
|  | 100,000 |

Suppose the entity needs to obtain the use of an item of plant that would cost $40 million to purchase outright. The estimated useful economic life of the plant is five years, with no estimated residual value. The entity has no surplus cash to finance the purchase and it has two options available:

● To finance the purchase with a five-year loan carrying an annual finance cost of 5%. The loan is repayable in five annual amounts of $9,240,000, payable at the end of each of the next five years.

● To lease the asset on a five-year lease with annual rentals of $9,240,000, payable in arrears. The lease has no escape clauses.

In order to help us with some of the figures we are going to demonstrate, it would be good to show the profile of the loan over the five-year term:

| Period | Opening balance | Finance cost (5%) | Rental | Closing balance |
| --- | --- | --- | --- | --- |
|  | $000 | $000 | $000 | $000 |
| 1 | 40,000 | 2,000 | (9,240) | 32,760 |
| 2 | 32,760 | 1,638 | (9,240) | 25,158 |
| 3 | 25,158 | 1,258 | (9,240) | 17,176 |
| 4 | 17,176 | 859 | (9,240) | 8,795 |
| 5 | 8,795 | 440 | (9,240) | (5) |
|  |  |  |  | (a rounding difference) |

This means that the loan balances at the beginning and end of period 1 will be as follows:

| | Start of period | End of period | Comment |
| --- | --- | --- | --- |
| | $000 | $000 | |
| Current | 7,240 | 7,602 | The amount by which the overall loan balance reduces in the following period (32,760 − 25,158) |
| Non-current | 32,760 | 25,158 | |
| Total | 40,000 | 32,760 | The overall loan balance |

### Impact on gearing ratio

Let's compare the impact on the statement of financial position under the purchase option and the lease option, assuming the lease option is accounted for according to its legal form, i.e. no asset or liability recognised:

|  | Lease option | Purchase option | Comment |
|---|---|---|---|
|  | $000 | $000 |  |
| Non–current assets | 60,000 | 100,000 |  |
| Current assets | 40,000 | 40,000 |  |
|  | 100,000 | 140,000 |  |
| Equity | 40,000 | 40,000 |  |
| Non–current liabilities (loans) | 40,000 | 72,760 | Including the non-current portion of the loan (32,760) |
| Current liabilities | 20,000 | 27,240 | Including the current portion of the loan (7,240) |
|  | 100,000 | 140,000 |  |
| Gearing ratio (loans/loans + equity) | 50% | 67% |  |

The two options show a significantly different gearing ratio – the 'purchase option' showing a significantly higher (and probably less acceptable) ratio.

### Statements of financial performance and position assuming asset was leased

Let's further assume that the summarised statement of profit or loss of the entity (there is no other comprehensive income) for the period immediately following the acquisition of the asset (and assuming for the moment the asset is leased and the associated asset and any liability is not recognised) is as follows:

|  | $000 |  |
|---|---|---|
| Revenue | 80,000 |  |
| Operating costs | (68,000) | Includes the lease payment of $9.24m |
| Operating profit | 12,000 |  |
| Finance costs | (2,000) |  |
| Pre-tax profit | 10,000 |  |
| Tax | (2,000) |  |
| Post-tax profit | 8,000 |  |

Assuming also that no additional shares had been issued during the period, then the statement of financial position at the end of the period would appear as:

|  | $000 |  |
|---|---|---|
| Non–current assets | 66,000 |  |
| Current assets | 44,000 |  |
|  | 110,000 |  |
| Equity | 48,000 |  |
| Non-current liabilities (loans) | 40,000 |  |
| Current liabilities | 22,000 | Includes the tax liability |
|  | 110,000 |  |

## Compare financial statements under both lease and purchase options

Let's compare the profit or loss for the period and the closing statement of financial position under the leasing option and the purchase option. We'll start with the statements of profit or loss:

| | Lease option $000 | Purchase option $000 | Comment |
|---|---|---|---|
| Revenue | 80,000 | 80,000 | |
| Operating costs | (68,000) | (66,760) | Rental of $9.24 million not included but depreciation of $8 million added in |
| Operating profit | 12,000 | 13,240 | |
| Finance costs | (2,000) | (4,000) | Includes interest of 5% on additional $40 million loan |
| Pre-tax profit | 10,000 | 9,240 | |
| Tax | (2,000) | (1,848) | Assumes changed treatment is allowed for tax purposes |
| Post-tax profit | 8,000 | 7,392 | |

We now proceed to a comparison of the statements of financial position:

| | Lease option $000 | Purchase option $000 | Comment |
|---|---|---|---|
| Non-current assets | 66,000 | 98,000 | Includes asset purchased for $40m at the **start** of the year less 20% depreciation |
| Current assets | 44,000 | 44,000 | |
| | 110,000 | 142,000 | |
| Equity | 48,000 | 47,392 | |
| Non-current liabilities (loans) | 40,000 | 65,158 | Includes the non-current portion of the loan (25,158) |
| Current liabilities | 22,000 | 29,450 | Reduced by the slightly lower tax charge (152) but includes the current portion of the loan (7,602) |
| | 110,000 | 142,000 | |

## Impact on return on capital employed

As a final step, let's compare some accounting ratios under the two options for the period immediately following the acquisition of the asset. This is done in the following table:

| | Lease option | Purchase option | Comment |
|---|---|---|---|
| Closing equity ($000) | 48,000 | 47,392 | |
| Closing loans ($000) | 40,000 | 72,760 | Includes both current and non-current elements of the loan (32,760) |
| Closing capital employed ($000) | 88,000 | 120,152 | |
| Closing gearing ratio | 45% | 61% | Measuring gearing as loans expressed as a percentage of capital employed (Loans plus equity) |
| Operating profit ($000) | 12,000 | 13,240 | |
| Return on capital employed | 14% | 11% | Measuring return on capital employed as operating profit expressed as a percentage of capital employed |

This example shows that under the leasing option we report lower borrowing ratios and higher returns on capital. Both those factors would be regarded as indicating a superior performance when compared to the purchase option.

The argument could of course be made that the two scenarios are different. However, when you analyse the underlying commercial effect of the two options they are basically identical; under both options the entity is given the use of an asset for its entire useful economic life and under both options identical payments are made at the end of each accounting period. It would, therefore, be misleading to users for the two options to be reported differently under scenarios such as the one we have illustrated in the above example.

This is the reason, therefore, why it was necessary to develop an accounting standard which ensured that the financial reporting of lease arrangements adequately met the needs of users by appropriately recognising assets and liabilities associated with leasing transactions.

## 18.3 Distinction between finance leases and operating leases

In the previous section we reviewed an example in which the commercial effect of leasing an asset was essentially exactly the same as purchasing the asset outright with the aid of a loan. In such circumstances it does seem reasonable that the two arrangements should be accounted for in the same manner. However, in other types of leasing arrangements the economic effect of leasing is arguably very different to outright purchase.

The approach initially adopted by the International Accounting Standards Committee in IAS 17 *Leases* was to distinguish between two types of lease. Leases (such as the one illustrated in the example in Section 18.2) that represented in substance an outright purchase of the asset by the lessee financed by a loan from the lessor were classified as *finance leases*. All other leases were classified as *operating leases*. Specifically, the distinction was made in IAS 17 as follows:

- **Finance lease:** a lease that transfers substantially all the risks and rewards of ownership of an asset. Title may or may not eventually be transferred.

- **Operating lease:** a lease other than a finance lease.
  NB: we will see later that, where relevant, the classification of leases into finance and operating in IFRS 16 – the successor standard to IAS 17 – is virtually identical to that in IAS 17.

- The classification criteria we have just mentioned – risks and rewards of ownership – are basically subjective.

### IASB guidance

In order to aid application of the criteria by users. IAS 17 included some guidance material. IAS 17 included examples of situations that, individually or in combination would normally lead to a lease being classified as a finance lease (these examples are essentially replicated in IFRS 16 – the successor standard). These were:

(a) the lease transfers ownership of the asset to the lessee by the end of the lease term;

(b) the lessee has the option to purchase the asset at a price that is expected to be sufficiently lower than the fair value at the date the option becomes exercisable for it to be reasonably certain, at the inception of the lease, that the option will be exercised;

(c) the lease term is for the major part of the economic life of the asset even if title is not transferred;

(d) at the inception of the lease the present value of the minimum lease payments amounts to at least substantially all of the fair value of the leased asset; and

(e) the leased assets are of such a specialised nature that only the lessee can use them without major modifications.

## 18.4 Reason for a replacement standard for IAS 17

In the last two sections we have seen the following:

- Key financial ratios, such as return on capital employed and gearing, indicate a more favourable position for lessees when recognizing leased assets and associated liabilities in the statement of financial position compared with non-recognition of such assets and liabilities (in accordance with the strict legal form).

- The distinction made in IAS 17 between operating leases (where no assets or liabilities were recognized by the lessee) and finance leases (where they were) was based on criteria that were inherently subjective (whether or not the 'risks and rewards of ownership' were effectively transferred from the lessor to the lessee). This made the classification problematic for preparers of financial statements.

Given the above two factors there was a clear incentive for preparers of lessee's financial statements to 'argue' that leases should be classified as operating rather than finance in order to enable lease assets and liabilities to be left out of the financial statements and so improve performance. In the introduction to IFRS 16 (the replacement standard for IAS 17) the IASB stated that the significance of the missing information varied by industry and region and between companies. However, for many companies, the effect on reported assets and financial leverage was substantial.

For example, it estimated that the long-term liabilities of the heaviest users of off-balance-sheet leases were understated by: 27% in Africa/Middle East; 32% in Asia/Pacific; 26% in Europe; 45% in Latin America and 22% in North America.

Its estimate was based on a sample of 1,022 listed companies reporting under IFRS or US GAAP. These companies each have estimated off-balance-sheet leases of more than US$300 million, calculated on a discounted basis. The percentages represent estimated off-balance-sheet leases (discounted) compared to long-term liabilities reported on the balance sheet, by region.

The absence of information about leases on the balance sheet meant that investors and analysts did not have a complete picture of the financial position of a company, and were unable to properly compare companies that borrow to buy assets with those that lease assets, without making adjustments.

Accordingly, the International Accounting Standards Board (IASB) and the US national standard-setter, the Financial Accounting Standards Board (FASB), initiated a joint project to develop a new approach to lease accounting that requires a lessee to recognise assets and liabilities for the rights and obligations created by leases. This approach will result in a more faithful representation of a lessee's assets and liabilities and, together with enhanced disclosures, will provide greater transparency of a lessee's financial leverage and capital employed.

The approach taken in IFRS 16 is to define a lease based upon economic substance rather than legal form. In other words, a contract does not need to be legally established as a lease for the contract to be regarded as a lease for accounting purposes.

This new standard – IFRS 16 *Leases* – will be discussed in the sections that follow.

## 18.5 IFRS 16 *Leases* – the criteria that determine whether it's a lease

### 18.5.1 Lease definition in IFRS 16

IFRS 16 defines a lease as 'A contract, or part of a contract, that conveys the right to use an asset for a period of time in exchange for consideration'. In order for such a contract to exist, IFRS 16 states that the customer (user of the 'identified asset') needs to have the right to:

● Obtain substantially all of the economic benefits from the use of the asset; and

● The right to direct the use of the asset.

### 18.5.2 An 'identified asset'

An essential feature of a lease is that there is an 'identified asset'. This normally takes place through the asset being specified in a contract, or part of a contract. For the asset to be 'identified' the supplier of the asset must not have the right to substitute the asset throughout its period of use.

#### Right to substitute

This 'right to substitute' only exists if, at the inception of the contract:

● the supplier has the practical ability to substitute alternative assets throughout the period of use; and

● the supplier would benefit economically from the exercise of its right to substitute the asset.

The fact that the supplier of the asset has the right or the obligation to substitute the asset when a repair is necessary does not preclude the asset from being an 'identified asset'.

### 18.5.3 The right to obtain economic benefits from use

IFRS 16 states that a customer can potentially obtain economic benefits from the use of an asset in many ways, including using an asset directly or by sub-leasing the asset. If there is any restriction on the right of the customer to use the asset, the customer should assess this condition with reference to the economic benefits obtainable from using the asset within the defined scope for the use of the asset.

### 18.5.4 The right to direct the use of the asset

IFRS 16 states that a customer has the right to direct the use of an identified asset if either:

● the customer has the right to direct how and for what purpose the asset is used throughout its period of use; or

● the relevant decisions about use are pre-determined and the customer has the right to operate the asset throughout the period of use without the supplier having the right to change these operating instructions

EXAMPLE • Based on one of the illustrative examples in IFRS 16

### Part (a): The contract terms

A customer (C) enters into a contract with a ship owner (S) for the transportation of cargo from Rotterdam to Sydney on a specified ship. The ship is explicitly specified in the contract and S does not have substitution rights. The cargo will occupy substantially all of the capacity of the ship. The contract specifies the cargo to be transported on the ship and the dates of pickup and delivery.

S operates and maintains the ship and is responsible for the safe passage of the cargo on board the ship. C is prohibited from hiring another operator for the ship or operating the ship itself during the term of the contract.

*Question is: Does this contract contain a lease?*

Let us consider if it satisfies the criteria:

- There **is** an identified asset:
  - the ship is explicitly specified in the contract, and
  - S does not have the right to substitute that specified ship.
- C **does** have the right to:
  - obtain substantially all of the economic benefits from use of the ship over the period of use. Its cargo will occupy substantially all of the capacity of the ship, thereby preventing other parties from obtaining economic benefits from use of the ship.
- However, C does **not** have the **right** to:
  - **control** the use of the ship because it does not have the right to direct its use; and
  - **direct** how and for what purpose the ship is used.

DECISION: This contract does **not** contain a lease.

*Basis for the decision*

- How and for what purpose the ship will be used (i.e. the transportation of specified cargo from Rotterdam to Sydney within a specified timeframe) is predetermined in the contract.
- C has no right to change how and for what purpose the ship is used during the period of use.
- C has no other decision-making rights about the use of the ship during the period of use (for example, it does not have the right to operate the ship).
- C has only the same rights regarding the use of the ship as if it were one of many customers transporting cargo on the ship.

### Part (b)

C enters into a contract with S for the use of an explicitly specified ship for a five-year period and S does not have substitution rights. C decides what cargo will be transported, and whether, when and to which ports the ship will sail, throughout the five-year period of use, subject to *restrictions* specified in the contract. Those restrictions prevent C from sailing the ship into waters at a high risk of piracy or carrying hazardous materials as cargo. S operates and maintains the ship and is responsible for the safe passage of the cargo on board the ship. C is prohibited from operating the ship itself during the term of the contract.

*Question is: Does this contract contain a lease?*

- There **is** an identified asset:
    - the ship is explicitly specified in the contract, and
    - S does not have the right to substitute that specified ship.
- C **does** have the right to:
    - obtain substantially all of the economic benefits from use of the ship over the five-year period of use.
- C does have the right to:
    - **control** the use of the ship throughout the five-year period;
    - the exclusive use of the ship throughout the period of use; and
    - **direct** the use of the ship because C directs how and for what purpose the ship is used.

*How is the decision affected by the restrictions?*

The contractual restrictions about where the ship can sail and the cargo to be transported by the ship define the scope of C's right to use the ship. These are **protective rights** that protect S's investment in the ship and S's personnel and do not give S the right to substitute or determine how the ship is used.

DECISION: The contract **does** contain a lease.

*Basis for the decision*

- C has the right to use the ship for five years.
- Within the scope of its right of use, it is C that:
    - makes the relevant decisions about how and for what purpose the ship is used throughout the five-year period of use because it decides whether, where and when the ship sails, as well as the cargo it will transport; and
    - has the right to change these decisions throughout the five-year period of use.
- Although the operation and maintenance of the ship are essential to its efficient use, S's decisions in this regard do not give it the right to direct how and for what purpose the ship is used. Instead, S's decisions are dependent upon Cs decisions about how and for what purpose the ship is used.

## 18.6 Leases in the financial statements of lessees

### 18.6.1 Problems with the previous approach

The 'IAS 17 treatment' of leased assets in the financial statements of lessees was entirely dependent on the extremely subjective classification of the lease agreement as operating or finance. It was entirely possible that two leasing agreements that were essentially the same in nature were accounted for differently by two entities depending on their respective perception of the risks and rewards inherent in the arrangement.

IAS 17 was also criticised for possible inconsistencies with the IASB's *Conceptual Framework*. The *Framework*'s definition of a liability is an obligation to transfer economic benefits as a result of past events. As operating leases are often non-cancellable there is a strong argument that operating lease commitments in those circumstances do meet the definition of a liability. However, no liability was required to be recognised in the lessee's financial statements.

### 18.6.2 The IFRS 16 solution to the perceived problems

With a very few exceptions (see Section 18.6.5 for further details) IFRS 16 basically abolishes the distinction between an operating lease and a finance lease in the books of lessees. Lessees will recognise a **right of use asset** and **an associated liability** at the inception of the lease. The initial measurement of the asset and liability will be similar to the basis previously used for finance leases in IAS 17:

IFRS 16 basically requires that the 'right of use asset' should initially be measured at the present value of the minimum lease payments. The discount rate used to determine present value should be the rate of interest implicit in the lease. This is basically identical to the old IAS 17 approach for finance leases.

However, the 'right of use asset' would also include the following amounts, where relevant:

- Any payments made to the lessor at, or before, the commencement date of the lease, less any lease incentives received.

- Any initial direct costs incurred by the lessee.

- An estimate of any costs to be incurred by the lessee in dismantling and removing the underlying asset, or restoring the site on which it is located if obligations are recognised under IAS 37 *Provisions, Contingent Liabilities and Contingent Assets.*

- The right of use asset is subsequently depreciated in accordance with IAS 16 *Property, Plant and Equipment* (assuming it is a tangible asset).

The lease liability is effectively treated as a financial liability which is measured at amortised cost, using the rate of interest implicit in the lease as the effective interest rate.

### 18.6.3 A numerical example (based on one of the IFRS 16 Illustrative examples)

A lessee enters into a 10-year lease of a floor of a building, with an option to extend for a further five years. Lease payments are £50,000 per year during the initial term and £55,000 per year during the optional period, all payable at the beginning of each year.

To obtain the lease, the lessee incurred initial direct costs of £20,000 of which £15,000 relates to a payment to a former tenant occupying that floor of the building and £5,000 relates to a commission paid to the property agent that arranged the lease. As an incentive to the lessee for entering into the lease, the lessor agreed to reimburse to the lessee the agent's commission of £5,000.

At the commencement date the lessee:

- concluded that it is not reasonably certain to exercise the option to extend the lease and, therefore, determined that the lease term is 10 years;

- calculates the interest rate implicit in the lease at 5% per annum;

- makes the lease payment for the first year, incurs initial direct costs, receives lease incentives from the lessor;

- calculates the lease liability to be £355,400 being the present value of the remaining nine payments of £50,000, discounted at the interest rate of 5% per annum; and

- makes the following accounting entries:

|  | DR £ | CR £ |
|---|---|---|
| Cash (up front rental payment) |  | 50,000 |
| Lease liability (present value of future lease payments |  | 355,400 |
| Right of use asset | 405,400 |  |
| Cash (initial direct costs) |  | 20,000 |
| Right of use asset | 20,000 |  |
| Cash (lease incentive) | 5,000 |  |
| Right of use asset |  | 5,000 |

The carrying amount of the right of use asset after these entries is £420,400 (£405,400 + £20,000 − £5,000) and consequently the annual depreciation charge will be £42,040 (£420,400 × 1/10).

The lease liability will be measured using amortised cost principles. In order to help us with the example in the following section, we will measure the lease liability up to and including the end of year 6. This is done in the following table (note that in the case of year 1 the opening liability includes the up-front payment and so it is £405,400 (£355,400 + £50,000):

| Year | Balance b/fwd £ | Rental £ | Balance in period £ | Finance Cost (5%) £ | Balance c/fwd £ |
|---|---|---|---|---|---|
| 1 | 405,400 | (50,000) | 355,400 | 17,770 | 373,170 |
| 2 | 373,170 | (50,000) | 323,170 | 16,159 | 339,329 |
| 3 | 339,329 | (50,000) | 289,329 | 14,466 | 303,795 |
| 4 | 303,795 | (50,000) | 253,795 | 12,690 | 266,485 |
| 5 | 266,485 | (50,000) | 216,485 | 10,824 | 227,309 |
| 6 | 227,309 | (50,000) | 177,309 | 8,865 | 186,174 |

The carrying value of the right of use asset at the end of year 6 will be £168,160 (£420,400 − 6 × £42,040).

The lease liability at the end of year 6 is £186,174.

### 18.6.4 Lease modifications

A lessee should remeasure the lease liability by discounting the revised lease payments using a revised discount rate, if either:

(a) there is a change in the lease term, or

(b) there is a change in the assessment of an option to purchase the underlying asset, assessed considering relevant events and circumstances in the context of a purchase option.

In both cases, the lessee should:

• revise its estimate of the present value of the future lease payments using the revised implicit interest rate;

• adjust the lease liability; and

• make a corresponding adjustment to the right of use asset.

The only exception here is if the adjustment would reduce the right of use asset to a negative carrying amount. In such circumstances, the right of use asset would be reduced to a carrying amount of nil and any further adjustment would be recognised in profit or loss.

### Illustration where option to extend is exercised

Let us continue the example we started in Section 18.6.3 above with the addition of the following information at the end of year 6 of the original lease:

- At the end of year 6 the lessee acquires a new business and requires additional office space. This creates an incentive for the lessee to exercise its option to extend the lease for a further five years after the end of the primary lease term at the revised rental of £55,000.

The impact of this reassessment is to increase the remaining lease term to nine years (four years left of the primary lease term plus the five year option term). The revised rate of interest implicit in the lease is 6% per annum.

#### Lease liability is remeasured

The lease liability at the end of year 6 will now be the present value of four annual payments in advance of £50,000 plus the present value of five subsequent annual payments in advance of £55,000.

The present value of the four annual payments of £50,000 using an annual discount rate of 6% would be £183,650 [£50,000 + (£50,000 × 2.673)].

Similarly, the present value of the five annual payments of £55,000 starting in four years, would be £194,495 [£55,000 + (£55,000 × 3.465) (the present value of four payments of £1 in arrears at an annual discount rate of 6%)] × 0.792 (the present value of £1 payable in four years' time at an annual discount rate of 6%).

So the total revised lease liability would be remeasured to £378,145 (£183,650 + £194,495).

As the liability at the end of year six was £186,174, the increase will be £191,971 (£378,145 − £186,174).

The right of use asset will be increased by the same amount and so will be carried at a revised amount of £360,131 (£168,160 + £191,971). Assuming an even consumption of economic benefits future deprecation charges will be on a straight-line basis over a nine-year period and will be £40,015 (£360,131 × 1/9)

The change in the revised lease liability going forward will be as follows:

| Year | Balance b/fwd £ | Rental £ | Balance in period £ | Finance cost (6%) £ | Balance c/fwd £ |
|------|------|------|------|------|------|
| 7 | 378,145 | (50,000) | 328,145 | 19,689 | 347,834 |
| 8 | 347,834 | (50,000) | 297,834 | 17,870 | 315,704 |
| 9 | 315,704 | (50,000) | 265,704 | 15,942 | 281,646 |
| 10 | 281,646 | (50,000) | 231,646 | 13,899 | 245,545 |
| 11 | 245,545 | (55,000) | 190,545 | 11,433 | 201,978 |
| 12 | 201,978 | (55,000) | 146,978 | 8,819 | 155,797 |
| 13 | 155,797 | (55,000) | 100,797 | 6,048 | 106,845 |
| 14 | 106,845 | (55,000) | 51,845 | 3,111 | 54,956 |
| 15 | 54,956 | (55,000) | (44) | 44 | Nil |

The amount of 44 is a rounding difference.

### 18.6.5 A simplified approach for short-term or low-value leases

A short-term lease is a lease that, at the date of commencement, has a term of 12 months or less. Lessees can elect to treat short-term leases by recognising the lease rentals as an expense over the lease term rather than recognising a 'right of use asset' and a lease liability. The election needs to be made for relevant leased assets on a 'class-by-class' basis. For this purpose, a class of underlying asset is a grouping of underlying assets of a similar nature and use in an entity's operations.

This effectively allows lessees to continue to treat short-term leases as they would have treated operating leases under the old IAS 17 leasing standard. Note that a lease that contains a purchase option cannot be a short-term lease.

A similar election – *on a lease-by-lease basis* – can be made in respect of 'low-value assets'.

The assessment of whether an underlying asset is of low value is performed on an absolute basis. Leases of low-value assets qualify for the simplified accounting treatment explained above regardless of whether those leases are material to the lessee. The assessment is not affected by the size, nature or circumstances of the lessee. Accordingly, different lessees are expected to reach the same conclusions about whether a particular underlying asset is of low value.

An underlying asset can be of low value only if:

(a) the lessee can benefit from use of the underlying asset on its own or together with other resources that are readily available to the lessee; and

(b) the underlying asset is not highly dependent on, or highly interrelated with, other assets.

A lease of an underlying asset does not qualify as a lease of a low-value asset if the nature of the asset is such that, when new, the asset is typically not of low value. For example, leases of cars would not qualify as leases of low-value assets because a new car would typically not be of low value.

Examples of low-value underlying assets can include tablet and personal computers, small items of office furniture and telephones.

## 18.7 Leases in the financial statements of lessors

### 18.7.1 Introduction

Accounting for leases in the financial statements of lessors is essentially unchanged from IAS 17 and the distinction between finance and operating leases is still highly relevant. We have already discussed this distinction in Section 18.3 of this chapter.

### 18.7.2 Finance leases in the books of the lessor

The lessor does not recognise the leased asset as property, plant and equipment but instead recognises a lease receivable equal to the present value of the minimum lease payments plus any expected residual value at the end of the lease that is not guaranteed by the lessee (in many finance leases this latter amount is nil). Given that the discount rate to compute present value is the rate of interest implicit in the lease this measure captures any initial direct costs incurred by the lessor.

## Example where the lessor purchases the assets that is leased

Assume a lessor has purchased an item of plant for £60,000 and leased it to a lessee on a five-year finance lease. Annual lease rentals, payable in arrears, were £15,000. The life of the plant was estimated at five years and there was no estimated residual value at the end of the five-year period. The lessor incurred direct cost of £2,000 in arranging the lease.

The rate of interest implicit in the lease is the discount rate that must be applied to the lease payments to make their present value equal (£60,000 + £2,000). By trial and error, this percentage can be computed as approximately 6.7%. The reader may wish to confirm that, at a discount rate of 6.7%, the present value of five payments of £15,000 in arrears is approximately £62,000 (the fair value of the asset plus the initial direct costs of the lessor. Therefore, assuming the lessor has purchased the asset for leasing on to the lessee, the lessor makes the following accounting entry:

Credit: Cash £62,000 (£60,000 + £2,000)

Debit: Net investment in finance leases (shown as a lease receivable)

Over the five-year lease term the net investment in the finance lease is increased by the finance lease income (which is taken to profit or loss) and reduced by the lease rentals received, as shown in the following table:

| Year | Balance b/fwd £ | Finance income (6.7%) £ | Rental £ | Balance c/fwd £ |
|------|-----------------|-------------------------|----------|-----------------|
| 1 | 62,000 | 4,154 | (15,000) | 51,154 |
| 2 | 51,154 | 3,427 | (15,000) | 39,581 |
| 3 | 39,581 | 2,652 | (15,000) | 27,233 |
| 4 | 27,233 | 1,825 | (15,000) | 14,058 |
| 5 | 14,058 | 942 | (15,000) | Nil |

## Example where lessor manufactures the asset that is leased

The above example assumes the asset was purchased by the lessor for leasing on to the lessee. If the lessor has manufactured the asset then at the inception of the lease the lessor recognises a selling profit based on the fair value of the asset at the date of the lease or, if lower, the present value of the minimum lease payments.

Suppose, in the previous example, that the lessor had manufactured the leased asset at a total manufacturing cost of £48,000. The lessor would make the following accounting entries at the commencement of the finance lease:

| | Debit £ | Credit £ | Comment |
|---|---------|----------|---------|
| Revenue | | 60,000 | Recording the 'sale' of the asset at the lower of its fair value (£60,000) and the present value of the minimum lease payments (£62,000) |
| Net investment in finance lease | 60,000 | | |
| Inventory | | 48,000 | Recording a cost of sale of £48,000 and therefore a gross profit of £12,000 (£60,000 − £48,000) |
| Cost of sales | 48,000 | | |
| Cash | | 2,000 | Recording the initial direct costs of establishing the lease as part of the net investment in finance leases |
| Net investment in finance lease | 2,000 | | |

The remainder of the accounting is as shown in the example above.

### 18.7.3 Operating leases in the books of the lessor

Where the lease is an operating lease the relevant asset is recorded as property, plant and equipment by the lessor. Lease rentals are recognised as income over the lease term, normally on a straight-line basis.

EXAMPLE • A property company lets out two floors of an office block on a three-year operating lease. The lessee made an up-front payment of £120,000 followed by three annual payments of £70,000, payable in arrears.

The property would remain as property, plant and equipment of the lessor. The total lease rentals of £330,000 (£120,000 + 3 × £70,000) would be recognised as lease income over the three-year period at an amount of £110,000 each year. In year one, the lessor would make the following accounting entry:

Debit: Cash £190,000 (£120,000 + £70,000)

Credit: Profit or loss £110,000

Credit: Deferred income £80,000

In each of years two and three the lessor would make the following accounting entry:

Debit: Cash £70,000

Debit: Deferred income £40,000 (£80,000 × $^1/_2$)

Credit: Profit or loss £110,000

## 18.8 Sale and leaseback transactions

### 18.8.1 Introduction

The treatment of sale and leaseback transactions depends on whether or not the 'sale' constitutes the satisfaction of a relevant performance obligation under IFRS 15 *Revenue from Contracts with Customers*. The relevant performance obligation would be the effective 'transfer' of the asset to the lessor by the previous owner (now the lessee).

### 18.8.2 Transaction constituting a sale

If the transaction does constitute a 'sale' under IFRS 15 then the treatment is as follows:

● The seller-lessee shall measure the right-of-use asset arising from the leaseback at the proportion of the previous carrying amount of the asset that relates to the right of use retained by the seller-lessee. Accordingly, the seller-lessee shall recognise only the amount of any gain or loss that relates to the rights transferred to the buyer-lessor.

● The buyer-lessor shall account for the purchase of the asset applying applicable Standards, and for the lease applying the lessor accounting requirements in IFRS 16.

If the fair value of the consideration for the sale of an asset does not equal the fair value of the asset, or if the payments for the lease are not at market rates, an entity shall make the following adjustments to measure the sale proceeds at fair value:

● any below-market terms shall be accounted for as a prepayment of lease payments; and

● any above-market terms shall be accounted for as additional financing provided by the buyer-lessor to the seller-lessee.

The entity shall measure any potential adjustment required by the above process on the basis of the more readily determinable of:

- the difference between the fair value of the consideration for the sale and the fair value of the asset; and
- the difference between the present value of the contractual payments for the lease and the present value of payments for the lease at market rates.

### 18.8.3 A numerical example (based on one of the IFRS 16 Illustrative examples)

Entity A sells a building to entity B for cash of £2,000,000. The terms and conditions of the transaction are such that the transfer of the building by A satisfies the requirements for determining when a performance obligation is satisfied in IFRS 15 *Revenue from Contracts with Customers,* i.e. it can be recognised as a sale.

Accordingly, A and B account for the transaction as a sale and leaseback with A entering into a contract with B for the right to use the building for 18 years, with annual payments of £120,000 payable at the end of each year.

Immediately before the transaction, the building is carried at a cost of £1,000,000 and its fair value at the date of sale is £1,800,000. The amount of the excess sale price of £200,000 (£2,000,000 − £1,800,000) is recognised as additional financing provided by B to A.

Because the consideration for the sale of the building is not at fair value, A and B make adjustments to measure the sale proceeds at fair value. The annual interest rate implicit in the lease is 4.5%. The present value of the annual payments (18 payments of £120,000, discounted at 4.5%) amounts to £1,459,200. This is made up of the £200,000 additional financing and £1,259,200 (£1,459,200 − £200,000), which relates to the lease (as adjusted for the fair value difference already identified.

The annual payment that would be required to be made for 18 times in arrears to repay additional financing of £200,000 when the rate of interest is 4.5% per annum would be £16,447 (£120,000 × £200,000/£1,459,200). Therefore the residual would be regarded as a 'lease rental' at an amount of £103,553 (£120,000 − £16,447).

Given the IFRS 15 treatment as a 'sale' B would almost certainly regard the lease of the building as an operating lease.

#### Accounting by A

At the commencement date, A measures the right-of-use asset and the gain on sale.

*Right of use asset*
A measures the right-of-use asset arising from the leaseback of the building at the proportion of the previous carrying amount of the building that relates to the right of use retained by A. This is calculated as £699,555 (£1,000,000 (the carrying amount of the building) ÷ £1,800,000 (the fair value of the building) × £1,259,200 (the discounted lease payments for the 18-year right-of-use asset).

*Gain on sale*
A recognises as a gain on sale only the amount that relates to the rights transferred to B. This gain is £240,355 computed as follows:

The overall gain on sale of building (based on fair value since the financing component is being recognised separately) amounts to £800,000 (£1,800,000 − £1,000,000).

A portion of this 'gain' relates to the continued right of A to use the asset and this portion (£559,645) is not recognised. It can be computed as follows:

[£1,259,200 (the present value of the payments for the use of the asset)/ £1,800,000 (the fair value of the asset in total)] × £800,000 = £559,645

This means that of the £800,000 gain on sale only £240,355 is recognised.

### Accounting entries

Overall, on the sale and leaseback A would make the following accounting entry:

Debit: Cash £2,000,000

Debit: Right-of-use asset £699,555

Credit: Building £1,000,000

Credit: Financial liability £1,459,200 (£1,259,200 + £200,000)

Credit: Gain on rights transferred £240,355

## Accounting by B

At the commencement date, B accounts for the transaction as follows:

Debit: Building £1,800,000 (recognising the acquired building at fair value)

Financial asset £200,000 (the 'financing' element of the transaction)

Credit: Cash £2,000,000

Going forward, B will account for the lease by treating £103,553 (see above for a derivation of this figure) of the annual payments of £120,000 as lease payments. The remaining £16,447 (£120,000 − £103,553) of annual payments received from A are accounted for as payments received to settle the financial asset of £200,000 and interest revenue. The split is illustrated below (the first five years only for illustrative purposes):

| Year | Balance b/fwd £ | Finance income (4.5%) £ | Rental £ | Balance c/fwd £ |
|---|---|---|---|---|
| 1 | 200,000 | 9,000 | (16,447) | 192,553 |
| 2 | 51,154 | 3,427 | (16,447) | 39,581 |
| 3 | 39,581 | 2,652 | (16,447) | 27,233 |
| 4 | 27,233 | 1,825 | (16,447) | 14,058 |
| 5 | 14,058 | 942 | (16,447) | Nil |

## 18.8.4 Transaction not constituting a 'sale'

In these circumstances the seller does not 'transfer' the asset and continues to recognise it. The 'sales proceeds' are recognised as a financial liability and accounted for by applying IFRS 9 *Financial Instruments*. This is similar, but not identical to, the treatment of sale and lease-backs that resulted in a finance lease under IAS 17. The difference from IAS 17 is that the leased asset is not automatically recognised at fair value at the date of 'sale', with the 'profit' deferred and recognised over the lease term.

In the same circumstances, the buyer recognises a financial asset equal to the 'sales proceeds'. This is identical to the IAS 17 treatment of sale and leasebacks that resulted in a finance lease in the books of lessors.

## 18.9 An evaluation of the new IFRS 16

The requirements of IFRS 16 will have significant impacts on key accounting ratios of lessees as the recognition of leased assets and lease liabilities on the statement of financial position will reduce return on capital employed and increase gearing.

New industry norms will be established and it is too early to say whether the requirements of IFRS 16 will affect the popularity of leasing. The commercial need for finance still remains, of course, so in the opinion of this writer there is no reason to suppose that the leasing industry will be adversely affected. It may well be, though, that short-term leases become more popular, given that they are likely to be treated as currently under IAS 17.

## Summary

In its *Effects Analysis*[1] the IFRS outlined the need for change stating that, in 2005, the US Securities and Exchange Commission (SEC) estimated that US public companies may have approximately US$1.25 trillion of off-balance-sheet leases.

Under IAS 17 there were concerns about the lack of transparency of information about lease obligations and the objective was that a customer (lessee) leasing assets should recognise assets and liabilities arising from those leases. Although at the start of a lease a lessee obtained the right to use an asset for a period of time and, if payments are made over time, incurs a liability to make lease payments, most leasing transactions were not reported on a lessee's balance sheet.

For many companies, the effect on reported assets and financial leverage was substantial with some industries such as airlines and retailers significantly affected. The absence of information about leases on the balance sheet meant that investors and analysts were not able to properly compare companies that borrow to buy assets with those that lease assets, without making adjustments. IFRS 16 is expected to change the balance sheet, income statement and cash flow statement for companies with material off-balance-sheet leases.

Applying IFRS 16, a company is required for all leases, except leases of low-value assets, to:

(a) recognise lease assets and lease liabilities in the balance sheet, initially measured at the present value of unavoidable future lease payments;

(b) recognise depreciation of lease assets and interest on lease liabilities in the income statement over the lease term; and

(c) separate the total amount of cash paid into a principal portion (presented within financing activities) and interest (typically presented within either operating or financing activities) in the cash flow statement.

# REVIEW QUESTIONS

**1** 'Can the legal position on leases be ignored now that substance over form is used for financial reporting?' Discuss.

**2 (a)** Consider the importance of decisions over the categorisation of lease transactions into operating leases or finance leases when carrying out financial ratio analysis. What ratios might be affected if a finance lease is structured to fit the operating lease classification? How has IFRS 16 affected your discussion?

**(b)** Discuss the effects of requiring lessees on recognise virtually all leasing obligations as liabilities. For which industries might this classification have a significant impact on the financial ratios?

**3** State the factors that indicate that a lease is a finance lease under IFRS 16 and the extent to which this distinction is still relevant.

**4** The favourite off-balance-sheet financing trick used to be leasing. Use any illustrative numerical examples you may wish to:

**(a)** Define the term 'off-balance-sheet financing' and state why it is popular with companies.

**(b)** Illustrate what is meant by the above term in the context of leases and discuss the accounting treatments and disclosures required by IFRS 16 which have limited the usefulness of leasing as an off-balance-sheet financing technique.

**(c)** Suggest two other off-balance-sheet financing techniques and discuss the effect that each technique has on statement of financial position assets and liabilities, and on the income statement.

**5** The Tesco 2014 Annual Report included the following accounting policy:

Assets held under finance leases are recognised as assets of the Group at their fair value or, if lower, at the present value of the minimum lease payments, each determined at the inception of the lease. The corresponding liability is included in the Group Balance Sheet as a finance lease obligation. Lease payments are apportioned between finance charges and a reduction of the lease obligations so as to achieve a constant rate of interest on the remaining balance of the liability. Finance charges are charged to the Group Income Statement. Rentals payable under operating leases are charged to the Group Income Statement on a straight-line basis over the term of the lease.

Rental income from operating leases is recognised on a straight-line basis over the term of the lease.

**(a)** Explain the meaning of 'minimum lease payments and fair value'.

**(b)** Explain why fair value might be higher than the discounted minimum lease payments.

**(c)** Explain why the aim is to arrive at a constant rate of interest.

**6** Given that the details of operating lease commitments were required to be disclosed in the notes to the accounts under IAS 17, discuss why it was necessary to issue a new standard which incorporates these into the statement of financial position when sophisticated investors already do such adjustments themselves?

**7** Companies sometimes get special prices from suppliers if they undertake to purchase specified commodities from the supplier over a designated future period. These supply arrangements do not have to be recorded as assets and liabilities. However, in future leases will give rise to recording of assets and liabilities. Discuss why the transactions are to be treated differently.

**8** Access the IFRS *Effects Analysis* (www.ifrs.org/Current-Projects/IASB-Projects/Leases/Documents/IFRS_16_effects_analysis.pdf) and discuss their decision relating to changes to lessor accounting.

## EXERCISES

### * Question 1

On 1 January 20X8, Grabbit plc entered into an agreement to lease a widgeting machine for general use in the business. The agreement, which may not be terminated by either party to it, runs for six years and provides for Grabbit to make an annual rental payment of £92,500 on 31 December each year. The cost of the machine to the lessor was £350,000, and it has no residual value. The machine has a useful economic life of eight years and Grabbit depreciates its property, plant and equipment using the straight-line method.

Required:

(a) Show how Grabbit plc will account for the above transaction in its statement of financial position at 31 December 20X8, and in its statement of comprehensive income for the year then ended, as required by IFRS 16. The rate of interest implicit in the lease is 15%.

(b) Explain why the standard setters considered accounting for leases to be an area in need of standardisation and discuss the rationale behind the approach adopted in the standard.

(c) The lessor has suggested that the lease could be drawn up with a minimum payment period of one year and an option to renew. The lessor alleges that this would mean the lease could be kept 'off balance sheet'. Discuss this suggestion.

### * Question 2

(a) When accounting for leases, accountants prefer to overlook legal form in favour of commercial substance.

Required:
Discuss the above statement in the light of the requirements of IFRS 16 *Leases*.

(b) State briefly how you would distinguish between a finance lease and an operating lease and the extent to which it is relevant following the issue of IFRS 16.

(c) Smarty plc prepares financial statements to 31 March each year. On 1 October 20X7 it leased machinery from Hirer on the following terms:

(i) a lease rental of £50,000 is payable half-yearly for five years
(ii) the rate of interest implicit in the lease is reliably computed at 4% per *half-year*
(iii) on completion of the primary period Smarty has an option to lease the asset for a further two years at a rental of £25,000, payable half-yearly in arrears. At the start of the lease it was considered unlikely that Smarty would exercise this option.
(iv) the estimated useful economic life of the machinery at the inception of the lease was 12 years

Required:

(1) Compute the carrying value of the 'right of use asset' in the statement of financial position of Smarty at 31 March 20X8 and 31 March 20X9.

(2) Compute the finance cost of Smarty for the years ended 31 March 20X8 and 31 March 20X9.

(3) Compute the lease liability that will be included in the statement of financial position of Smarty at 31 March 20X8 and 31 March 20X9. In both cases show the split into the current and non-current portions.

## * Question 3

On 1 April 20Y1 Smarty (see question 2) reassessed its future strategy and concluded that it would take up the option to lease the machine for a further two years from 1 October 20Y2. This was regarded as a modification to the original lease and Smarty re-computed the rate of interest implicit in the lease at 3% per half year.

### Required:
(a) Show how the modification would be reflected in the financial statements of Smarty for the year ended 31 March 20Y2, providing relevant extracts as in Question 2.
(b) Hirer prepares financial statements to 30 September each year. Show how the lease would be accounted for by Hirer throughout its duration. You may assume that Hirer consistently retains the risks and rewards of ownership of the leased asset.

## Question 4

Bertie prepares financial statements to 31 December each year. On 1 January 20X1 Bertie purchased a machine for £200,000 and immediately leased the machine to Carter. The lease term was five years – equal to the expected useful life of the asset. Bertie estimated that the residual value of the asset at the end of the lease would be £2,000, and incurred initial direct costs of £1,500 in arranging the lease. Carter agreed to pay rentals of £50,000 per annum in arrears to lease the asset from Bertie.

### Required:
(a) Compute the rate of interest implicit in the lease by Bertie to Carter.
(b) Show how the arrangement will be reported in the financial statements of Bertie for the year ended 31 December 20X1. You should show the split of any relevant assets into their current and non-current portions.

## Question 5

Delta owned two assets which were sold on 1 April 20X1 – the first day of Delta's accounting period. Both assets were sold for their fair value. Details of the sales are as follows:

### Asset 1
Asset 1 was sold for £500,000 and leased back on a five-year lease. The carrying amount of the asset at the date of sale was £360,000 and its estimated future economic life was ten years. The terms of the lease were that Delta would make five annual payments of £60,000 for the use of the asset. This transaction qualifies as a sale of the asset by Delta under the provisions of IFRS 15 *Revenue from Contracts with Customers.*

### Asset 2
Asset 2 was sold for £600,000 and leased back on a ten-year lease. The carrying amount of the asset at the date of sale was £540,000 and its estimated future economic life was ten years. The terms of the lease were that Delta would make ten annual payments of £77,700 for the use of the asset. This transaction does not qualify as a sale of the asset by Delta under the provisions of IFRS 15 *Revenue from Contracts with Customers.*

### Required:
Describe how both these assets and transactions would be reported under IFRS 16 in the financial statements of Delta for the year ended 31 March 20X2. The implicit rate of interest in both leases is 5% per annum.

## Question 6

Under a contract between a customer, Charlie (C) and a freight carrier Solutions Ltd (S), S provides C with 10 rail cars for five years. The cars, which are owned by S, are specified in the contract. C determines when, where and which goods are to be transported using the cars. When the cars are not in use, they are kept at C's premises. C can use the cars for another purposes (for example, storage) if it so chooses. If a particular car needs to be serviced or repaired, S is required to substitute a car of the same type. Otherwise, and other than on default by C, S cannot retrieve the cars during the five-year period.

The contract also requires S to provide an engine and a driver when requested by C. S keeps the engines at its premises and provides instructions to the driver detailing C's requests to transport goods. S can choose to use any one of a number of engines to fulfil each of C's requests, and one engine could be used to transport not only C's goods, but also the goods of other customers (i.e. if other customers require the transportation of goods to destinations close to the destination requested by C and within a similar timeframe, S can choose to attach up to 100 rail cars to the engine.

**Required:**

**Advise Charlie if there is a lease in the contract under IFRS 16 in regard to the cars and the engines.**

*(Question based on one of the illustrative examples in IFRS 16)*

## Note

1 www.ifrs.org/Current-Projects/IASB-Projects/Leases/Documents/IFRS_16_effects_analysis. pdf (January 2016).

# CHAPTER 19

# Intangible assets

## 19.1 Introduction

The statement of financial position or balance sheet has traditionally reported tangible non-current assets and working capital. In order to protect future economic benefits, i.e. profits, companies have paid for legal or contractual intangible assets such as patents and copyright. As these were evidenced by a payment, they satisfied the accounting definition of an asset with a measurable cost and probable future economic benefit.

As business has become more complex, future economic benefits have become more reliant on internally generated intellectual capital that does not satisfy all the criteria for inclusion as an asset in the statement of financial position. For example, expenditure on a skilled workforce, training, research, and the development of a loyal customer base are all charged as an expense in the statement of income.

There are two adverse results that may arise from this: (a) the current year's profits are reduced by the charge and the company may be at risk in the short term from a predatory takeover; and (b) there is a mismatch between the market value of a company and the book value of its net assets.

The main purpose of this chapter is to consider the approach taken by IAS 38 *Intangible Assets*[1] and IFRS 3 *Business Combinations*[2] to the accounting treatment of intangible assets.

### Objectives

By the end of this chapter, you should be able to:

- define and explain how to account for:
  - legally enforceable intangibles and internally generated intangibles;
  - research and development (R&D);
  - goodwill;
  - brands; and
  - emissions trading certificates;
- account for development costs;
- comment critically on the IASB requirements in IAS 38 and IFRS 3.

## 19.2 Intangible assets defined

Intangible assets are identifiable non-monetary assets that cannot be seen, touched or physically measured but are identifiable as a separate asset.

### 19.2.1 Criteria for recognition as an asset in the statement of financial position

IAS 38 *Intangible Assets* states that an asset is recognised in respect of an intangible item if the asset is characterised by the following properties:

- The asset is identifiable.

- The standard states that for an intangible asset to exist (or be identifiable) it must either be separable or arise from contractual or other legal rights (such as a patent), whether or not the asset can be separately disposed of (such as goodwill).

- The asset is controlled by the entity.
  Control is one of the central features of the *Framework* definition of an asset. Control is said to exist if the entity has the power to obtain the future economic benefits flowing from the underlying resource and to restrict the access of others to those benefits. *It is failing to satisfy the control criterion that prevents the skills of the workforce being recognised as an asset in the statement of financial position.*

- The asset gives future economic benefits.
  Again, it is inherent in the *Framework* definition of an asset that the potential future economic benefits can be identified with reasonable certainty.

If the identifiability and control tests are satisfied then IAS 38 allows recognition of an intangible asset if:

- it is **probable** that the expected future economic benefits that are attributable to the asset will flow to the entity; and

- the cost of the asset can be **measured reliably**.

Application of these criteria means that the costs associated with most internally generated intangible assets are expensed to the statement of income. An exception is development costs, **provided** these meet additional recognition criteria required by the standard.

### 19.2.2 Examples of intangible assets to be recognised and reported

Examples of intangible assets that should be recognised and reported in the statement of financial position are set out in IAS 38.[3] They include:

- **Marketing-related** intangible assets which are used primarily in the marketing or promotion of products or services such as trademarks, newspaper mastheads, Internet domain names and non-compete agreements.

- **Technology-related** intangible assets which arise from contractual rights to use technology (patented and unpatented), databases, formulae, designs, software, processes and recipes.

- **Customer- or supplier-related** intangible assets which arise from relationships with or knowledge of customers or suppliers such as licensing, royalty and standstill agreements, servicing contracts and use rights such as airport landing slots and customer lists.

- **Artistic-related** intangible assets which arise from the right to benefits such as royalties from artistic works such as plays, books, films and music, and from non-contractual copyright protection.

### 19.2.3 Recognition criteria illustrated

Devon Cheeses Ltd decided to diversify into the production of vegetarian organic sausages. The project team produced a list of cost headings for the acquisition of:

(a) recipes from an international chef;

(b) a licence to use a specialised computer-controlled oven;

(c) registration of a trade name 'The Organo One'; and

(d) training courses for management in sausage making.

Their auditors were asked for advice on the possibility of capitalising all costs arising in respect of the above. The advice received was that the cost of recipes, the licence and the trade name registration could be capitalised, since:

● they were identifiable arising from contractual rights;

● Devon Cheeses Ltd controlled the future economic benefits;

● the costs could be measured reliably;

● it was probable that there would be future economic benefits; and

● the trade name was a defensive intangible that protected the receipt of the future economic benefits.

The training courses would improve management expertise but failed the control criterion and should be expensed.

### 19.2.4 Accounting treatment of recognised intangible assets at year-ends

The accounting treatment depends on whether the asset has a finite or an indefinite life.

#### Recognising intangible assets with a finite life

IAS 38 states that recognised intangible non-current assets should be reported at cost less accumulated amortisation or, as when a parent acquires a subsidiary with intangible assets, fair value less accumulated amortisation.

#### Amortisation of intangible assets with a finite life

The asset should be amortised on a systematic basis over its estimated useful economic life. This is very similar to the treatment of property, plant and equipment under IAS 16 in that it is frequently on a straight-line basis as for patents with a finite legal life. The following extract is from the Bayer Group 2015 Annual Report:

> Intangible assets are recognised at the cost of acquisition or generation . . . Those with a determinable useful life are amortised accordingly on a straight-line basis over a period of up to 30 years, except where their actual depletion demands a different amortisation pattern.

#### An acceptable basis for amortisation

Amortisation is to be based on the expected pattern of consumption of the future economic benefits of an asset. A clarification[4] issued by the IASB in 2014 advised that the use of revenue-based methods to calculate the depreciation of an asset is not appropriate because revenue generated by an activity that includes the use of an asset generally reflects factors other than the consumption of the economic benefits embodied in the asset.

### Impairment of intangible assets with a finite life

Intangible assets are also tested for impairment where there is a triggering event. The following Accounting Policy extract from the SABMiller 2016 Annual Report explains the amortisation and impairment policy for intangibles with finite lives:

> Intangible assets are stated at cost less accumulated amortisation on a straight-line basis (if applicable) and impairment losses . . . Amortisation is included within net operating expenses in the income statement . . . Intangible assets with finite lives are amortised over their estimated useful economic lives, and only tested for impairment where there is a triggering event.

### Amortisation of intangible assets with an indefinite life

Where the estimated useful economic life is indefinite there is no amortisation but the asset is subject to annual impairment reviews under IAS 36.

### 19.2.5 Disclosure of intangible assets under IAS 38

IAS 38 requires the disclosure of the following for each type of intangible asset:[5]

- whether useful lives are indefinite or finite;
- the amortisation methods used for intangible assets with finite useful lives;
- the gross carrying amount and accumulated amortisation at the beginning and end of the period;
- increases or decreases resulting from revaluations and from impairment losses recognised or reversed directly in equity (IAS 36 *Impairment of Assets*); and
- for R&D, disclosure in the financial statements of the charge for research and development in the period.[6]

Where an intangible asset is assessed as having an indefinite useful life, the carrying value of the asset must be stated[7] along with the reasons for supporting the assessment of an indefinite life.

## 19.3 Accounting treatment for research and development

Under IAS 38 *Intangible Assets*, research expenditure **must be expensed** whereas development expenditure **must be capitalised** provided a strict set of criteria is met. In this section we will consider R&D activities, why research expenditure is written off and the tests for capitalising development expenditure.

### 19.3.1 Research activities

IAS 38 states[8] 'expenditure on research shall be recognised as an expense when it is incurred'. This means that it cannot be included as an intangible asset in the statement of financial position. The standard gives examples of research activities[9] as:

- activities aimed at obtaining new knowledge;
- the search for, evaluation and final selection of, applications of research findings or other knowledge;

- the search for alternatives for materials, devices, products, processes, systems and services; and

- the formulation, design, evaluation and final selection of possible alternatives for new or improved materials, devices, products, processes, systems or services.

Normally, research expenditure is not related directly to any of the company's products or processes. For instance, development of a high-temperature material which could be used in any aero engine would be 'research', but development of a honeycomb for a particular engine would be 'development'.

Whilst it is in the research phase, the IAS position[10] is that an entity cannot demonstrate that an intangible asset exists that will generate probable future economic benefits. It is this inability that justifies the IAS requirement for research expenditure not to be capitalised but to be charged as an expense when it is incurred.

### 19.3.2 Development activities

Expenditure on development is recognised[11] as an asset if the entity can demonstrate that the expenditure will generate probable future economic benefits. The standard gives examples of development activities:[12]

(a) the design, construction and testing of pre-production and pre-use prototypes and models;

(b) the design of tools, jigs, moulds and dies involving new technology;

(c) the design, construction and operation of a pilot plant that is not of a scale economically feasible for commercial production; and

(d) the design, construction and testing of a chosen alternative for new or improved materials, devices, products, processes, systems or services.

## 19.4 Why is research expenditure not capitalised?

Many readers will think of research not as a cost but as a strategic investment which is essential to remain competitive in world markets. Indeed, this was the view[13] taken by the House of Lords Select Committee on Science and Technology, stating that 'R&D has to be regarded as an investment which leads to growth, not a cost'.

It is reported[14] that global R&D spending is in excess of 1.7% of GDP, taking place particularly in the advanced technical industries such as pharmaceuticals, where a sustained high level of R&D investment is required. The regulators, however, do not consider that the expenditure can be classified as an asset for financial reporting purposes.

### Why do the regulators not regard research expenditure as an asset?

The IASC in its *Framework for the Preparation and Presentation of Financial Statements*[15] defines an asset as a resource that is controlled by the enterprise, as a result of past events and from which future economic benefits are expected to flow.

Research is controlled by the enterprise and results from past events but there is no reasonable certainty that the intended economic benefits will be achieved. Because of this uncertainty, the accounting profession has traditionally considered it more prudent to write off the investment in research as a cost rather than report it as an asset in the statement of financial position.

### The importance to investors of disclosure

It might be thought that this is concealing an asset from investors, but in research on the reactions of both analysts[16] and accountants[17] to R&D expenditure, B. Nixon found that: 'Two important dimensions of the corporate reporting accountants' perspective emerge: first, disclosure is seen as more important than the accounting treatment of R&D expenditure and, second, the financial statements are not viewed as the primary channel of communication for information on R&D.'

This highlights the importance of reading carefully the narrative in financial reports. An interesting study in Singapore[18] examined the impact of annual report disclosures on analysts' forecasts for a sample of firms listed on the Stock Exchange of Singapore (SES) and showed that the level of disclosure affected the accuracy of earnings forecasts among analysts and also led to greater analyst interest in the firm.

### Management attitudes to capitalising research expenditure

Management might prefer in general to be able to capitalise research expenditure but there could be circumstances where writing off might be preferred. For example, directors might be pleased to take the expense in a year when they know its impact rather than carry it forward. They are aware of profit levels in the year in which the expenditure arises and could, perhaps, find it embarrassing to take the charge in a subsequent year when profits were lower or the company even reported a trading loss.

Development expenditure, on the other hand, has more probability of achieving future economic benefits and the regulators, therefore, require such expenditure to be capitalised.

## 19.5 Capitalising development costs

### 19.5.1 Conditions to be satisfied

The relevant paragraph of IAS 38[19] says an intangible asset for development expenditure must be recognised if and only if an entity can demonstrate **all** of the following:

(a) the technical feasibility of completing the intangible asset so that it will be available for use or sale;

(b) the intention to complete the intangible asset and use or sell it;

(c) its ability to use or sell the intangible asset;

(d) how the intangible asset will generate probable future economic benefits;

(e) the availability of adequate technical, financial and other resources to complete the development and to use or sell the intangible asset;

(f) its ability to measure reliably the expenditure attributable to the intangible asset during its development.

It is important to note that if the answers to all the conditions (a) to (f) above are 'Yes' then the entity *must* capitalise the development expenditure subject to reviewing for impairment.

### 19.5.2 What costs can be included?

The costs that can be included in development expenditure are similar to those used in determining the cost of inventory (IAS 2 *Inventories*).

It is important to note that only expenditure incurred after the project satisfies the IAS 38 criteria can be capitalised – all expenditure incurred prior to this date must be written off as an expense in the statement of income. Experience tends to indicate that people who develop products are notoriously optimistic. In practice, they encounter many more problems than they imagined and the cost is much greater than estimates. This means that the development project may well be approaching completion before future development costs can be estimated reliably.

At the year-ends development costs are usually amortised over the sales of the product (i.e. the charge in 20X5 would be: 20X5 sales/total estimated sales × capitalised development expenditure) with straight-line as the default.

Whilst development cost can be capitalised there is a requirement in the new EU Accounting Directive that, where the costs of development have not been completely written off, there can be no distribution of profits unless the amount of the reserves available for distribution and profits brought forward is at least equal to that of the costs not written off.

## 19.6 Disclosure of R&D

R&D is important to many manufacturing companies, such as pharmaceutical companies and car and defence manufacturers. Disclosure is required of the aggregate amount of research and development expenditure recognised as an expense during the period.[4] Normally, this total expenditure will be:

(a) research expenditure;

(b) development expenditure amortised;

(c) development expenditure not capitalised; and

(d) impairment of capitalised development expenditure.

Under IAS 38 more companies may capitalise development expenditure. Management view of the probability of making future profits from the sale of the product is a critical element in making a decision. The following is the R&D policy extract from the Rolls-Royce Annual Report for the year ended 31 December 2015:

> Research and development
> In accordance with IAS 38 Intangible Assets, expenditure incurred on research and development is distinguished as relating either to a research phase or to a development phase.
> All research phase expenditure is charged to the income statement. Development expenditure is capitalised as an internally generated intangible asset only if it meets strict criteria, relating in particular to technical feasibility and generation of future economic benefits. . . . the Group considers that it is not possible to distinguish reliably between research and development activities until relatively late in the programme.
> Expenditure capitalised is amortised on a straight-line basis over its useful economic life, up to a maximum of 15 years from the entry into service of the product.

## 19.7 *IFRS for SMEs'* treatment of intangible assets

### Internally generated intangible assets

The IFRS provides that internally generated intangible assets are not recognised. This means that both research and development costs are expensed.

### Separately purchased intangible assets

The IFRS provides the following:

- Such assets should be amortised over the asset's useful life; and if the useful life cannot be estimated, then a 10-year useful life is presumed.
- If there is a significant change in the asset or how it is used, then the useful life, residual value and depreciation rate are reviewed.
- Impairment testing is carried out where there are impairment indications.
- The revaluation of intangible assets is prohibited.

## 19.8 Internally generated and purchased goodwill

IFRS 3 *Business Combinations* defines goodwill[20] as: 'future economic benefits arising from assets that are not capable of being individually identified and separately recognised'. The definition effectively affirms that the value of a business as a whole is more than the sum of the accountable and identifiable net assets. Goodwill can be internally generated through the normal operations of an existing business or purchased as a result of a business combination.

### 19.8.1 Internally generated goodwill

Internally generated goodwill falls within the scope of IAS 38 *Intangible Assets* which states that 'Internally Generated Goodwill (or "self-generated goodwill") shall not be recognised as an asset'. If companies were allowed to include internally generated goodwill as an asset in the statement of financial position, it would boost total assets and produce a more favourable view of the statement of financial position, for example by reducing the gearing ratio.

### 19.8.2 Purchased goodwill

#### How goodwill is calculated

The key distinction between internally generated goodwill and purchased goodwill is that purchased goodwill has an identifiable 'cost', being the difference between the fair value of the total consideration that was paid to acquire a business and the fair value of the identifiable net assets acquired. This is the initial cost reported in the statement of financial position.

Companies reporting under IFRS are required to disclose the nature of the intangible assets comprising goodwill and explain why they cannot be valued separately.

## 19.9 The accounting treatment of goodwill

Now that we have a definition of goodwill, we need to consider how to account for it in subsequent years. One might have reasonably thought that a simple requirement to amortise the cost over its estimated useful life would have been sufficient. This has been far from the case. Over the past 40 years, there have been a number of approaches to accounting for purchased goodwill, including:

(a) writing off the cost of the goodwill directly to reserves in the year of acquisition;

(b) reporting goodwill at cost in the statement of financial position (this was attractive to management as there was no charge against profits in any year);

(c) reporting goodwill at cost, amortising over its expected life; and

(d) reporting goodwill at cost, but checking it annually for impairment.

The last (d) is now the treatment required by IFRS 3.

### 19.9.1 The current IFRS 3 treatment

IFRS 3 prohibits the amortisation of goodwill. It treats goodwill as if it has an indefinite life with the amount reviewed annually for impairment. If the carrying value is greater than the recoverable value of the goodwill, the difference is written off.

Whereas goodwill amortisation gave rise to an annual charge, impairment losses will arise at irregular intervals. This means that the profit for the year will become more volatile. This is why companies and analysts rely more on the EBITDA (earnings before interest, tax, depreciation and amortisation) when assessing a company's performance, assuming that this is a better indication of maintainable profits.

This is illustrated by the following extract from the 2015 Vodafone Annual Report which shows the volatile effect of impairment charges on maintainable profits:

|  | 2015 £m | 2014 £m | 2013 £m |
|---|---|---|---|
|  | 42,227 | 38,346 | 38,041 |
| Gross profit | 11,345 | 10,404 | 11,474 |
| Impairment losses | – | (6,600) | (7,700) |
| Operating profit (loss) | 1,967 | (3,913) | (2,202) |

This illustrates the volatility when impairment charges are included when calculating operating profit or loss with a pre-impairment profit reporting a profit decrease in 2015 instead of a significant increase.

### 19.9.2 Identifying intangible assets to reduce the amount of goodwill

Because goodwill is reviewed annually for impairment under IFRS 3 and other intangible assets are mainly amortised annually under IAS 38, standard setters wanted companies to identify any intangible assets that were acquired on an acquisition of another company and not to include them within a global figure of goodwill.

This has two effects: (a) there is greater transparency and control over assets by identifying the asset that the parent acquired; and (b) intangible assets are amortised rather than being reviewed annually for impairment, so reducing the volatility in the reported operating profits.

The following is an extract from the Intel 2015 Annual Report relating to intangible assets:

| (In millions) | Gross Assets | Accumulated Amortisation | Net |
|---|---|---|---|
| Acquisition-related developed technology | $2,928 | $(2,276) | $652 |
| Acquisition-related customer relationships | 1,738 | 1,219 | 519 |
| Acquisition-related trade names | 59 | (55) | 4 |
| Licensed technology and patents | 3,017 | (1,200) | 1,817 |
| Identified intangible assets subject to amortization | 7,742 | (4,750) | 2,992 |
| Acquisition-related trade names | 767 | — | 767 |
| Other intangible assets | 174 | — | 174 |
| Identified intangible assets not subject to amortization | 941 | — | 941 |
| Total identified intangible assets | $8,683 | $(4,750) | $3,933 |

The notes to the accounts relating to amortisation include:

The estimated useful life ranges for substantially all identified intangible assets that are subject to amortization as of 28 December 28 2015, were as follows:

| (In Years) | Estimated Useful Life |
|---|---|
| Acquisition-related developed technology | 3–9 |
| Acquisition-related customer relationships | 5–11 |
| Acquisition-related trade names | 5–8 |
| Licensed technology and patents | 2–17 |

Greater transparency in relation to the make-up of the goodwill figure should be achieved following the amendment in July 2009 to IFRS 3 which provides that if an intangible asset can be separately identified then it can be measured reliably, as the two conditions are inter-dependent. This will place further pressure on companies to properly consider the nature and value of any intangible assets they acquire.

However, there is a concern that shareholders might lose sight of the outcome of the acquisition – investors can see if there is a single figure for goodwill which has to be written down if it becomes impaired. This makes it easier to hold management to account for the decision to make the acquisition.

## 19.10 Critical comment on the various methods that have been used to account for goodwill

Let us consider briefly the alternative accounting treatments.

### (a) Reporting goodwill unchanged at cost

It is (probably) wrong to keep goodwill unchanged in the statement of financial position, as its value will decline with time. Its value may be *maintained* by further expenditure, e.g. continued advertising, but this expenditure is essentially creating 'internally generated good-will' which is not allowed to be capitalised.

### (b) Writing off the cost of the goodwill directly to reserves in the year of acquisition

A buyer pays for goodwill on the basis that future profits will be improved. It is wrong, therefore, to write it off in the year of acquisition against previous years in the reserves. The loss in value of the goodwill does not occur at the time of acquisition but occurs over a longer period. The goodwill is losing value over its life, and this loss in value should be charged to the statement of comprehensive income each year. Making the charge direct to reserves stops this charge from appearing in the future income statements.

### (c) Amortising the goodwill over its expected useful life

Amortising goodwill over its life could achieve a matching under the accrual concept with a charge in the statement of comprehensive income. However, there are problems (i) in deter-mining the life of the goodwill and (ii) in choosing an appropriate method for amortising.

#### (i) What is the life of the goodwill?

Companies wishing to minimise the amortisation charge could make a high estimate of the economic life of the goodwill and auditors have to be vigilant in checking the company's justification. The range of lives can vary widely. For example, goodwill paid to acquire a business in the fashion industry could be quite short compared to that paid to acquire an established business with a loyal customer base.

### (ii) The method for amortising

Straight-line amortisation is the simplest method. However, as the benefits are likely to be greater in earlier years than in later ones, amortisation could use the reducing balance method. One might think intuitively that amortisation based on the percentage of actual sales to expected total sales would reasonably match the cost consumed with the revenue – however, it is not an acceptable method under IFRS.

It could be argued that amortising goodwill is equivalent to depreciating tangible fixed assets as prescribed by IAS 16 *Property, Plant and Equipment* and that the amortisation approach appears to be the best way of treating goodwill in the statement of financial position and statement of comprehensive income. This is effectively following a 'statement of comprehensive income' approach to 'expense' (e.g. depreciation) with the expense charged over the life of the asset or in relation to the profits obtained from the acquisition.

There are difficulties but these should not prevent us from using this method. After all, accountants have to make many judgements when valuing items in the statement of financial position, such as assessing the life of property, plant and equipment, the value of inventory and bad debt provisions.

### (d) An annual impairment check

IFRS 3 introduced a new treatment for purchased goodwill when it arises from a business combination (i.e. the purchase of a company which becomes a subsidiary). It assumes that goodwill has an indefinite economic life, which means that it is not possible to make a realistic estimate of its economic life and a charge should be made to the statement of income only when it becomes impaired.

This is called a 'statement of financial position' approach to accounting, as the charge is made only when the value (in the statement of financial position) falls below its original cost.

The IFRS 3 treatment is consistent with the *Framework*,[21] which says: 'Expenses are recognised in the statement of comprehensive income when a decrease in future economic benefits related to a decrease in an asset or an increase of a liability has arisen that can be measured reliably.'

### Criticism of the 'statement of financial position' approach

However, there has been much criticism of the 'statement of financial position' approach of the *Framework*.

For example, if a company purchased specialised plant which had a resale value of 5% of its cost, then it could be argued that the depreciation charge should be 95% of its cost immediately after it comes into use. This is not sensible, as the purpose of buying the plant is to produce a product, so the depreciation charge should be over the life of the product.

Alternatively, if the 'future economic benefit' approach was used to value the plant, there would be no depreciation until the future economic benefit was less than its original cost. So, initial sales would incur no depreciation charge, but later sales would have an increased charge.

This example shows the weakness of using impairment and the 'statement of financial position' approach for charging goodwill to the statement of comprehensive income – the charge occurs at the wrong time. The charge should be made earlier when sales, selling prices and profits are high, not when the product becomes out of date and sales and profits are falling.

### Why the impairment charge occurs at the wrong time

Although the IFRS 3 treatment of impairment appears to be correct according to the *Framework*, it could be argued that the impairment approach is not correct, as the charge occurs at the wrong time (i.e. when there is a loss in value, rather than when profits are being made), it is very difficult to estimate the future economic benefit of the goodwill and those estimates are likely to be over-optimistic.

In addition, it means that the treatment of goodwill for IFRS 3 transactions is different from the treatment in IAS 38 *Intangible Assets*. This shows the inconsistency of the standards – they should use a single treatment, either IAS 38 amortisation or IFRS 3 impairment.

### 19.10.1 Why has the IFRS 3 treatment of goodwill differed from the treatment of intangible assets in IAS 38?

The answer is probably related to the convergence of International Accounting Standards to US accounting standards, and pressure from listed companies.

#### Convergence pressure

In issuing recent International Standards, the IASB has not only aimed to produce 'worldwide' standards but also standards which are acceptable to US standard setters. The IASB wanted their standards to be acceptable for listing on the New York Stock Exchange (NYSE), so there was strong pressure on the IASB to make their standards similar to US standards. The equivalent US standard to IFRS 3 uses impairment of goodwill as the charge against profits (rather than amortisation). Thus, IFRS 3 uses the same method and it prohibits amortisation.

#### Commercial pressure

A further pressure for impairment rather than amortisation comes from listed companies. Essentially, listed companies want to maximise their reported profit, and amortisation reduces profit. For most of the time, companies can argue that the future economic benefit of the goodwill is greater than its original cost (or carrying value if it has been previously impaired), and thus avoid a charge to the statement of comprehensive income. Also, companies could argue that the 'impairment charge' is an unexpected event and charge it as an exceptional item.

In the UK, many companies publicise their profit before exceptional items and impairment to highlight maintainable profits.

The new EU Accounting Directive provides that in exceptional cases where the useful life of goodwill and development costs cannot be reliably estimated, such assets shall be written off within a maximum period set by the member state – that maximum period to be not shorter than five years and not longer than 10 years. IFRS takes precedence over the Directive.

## 19.11 Negative goodwill/badwill

Negative goodwill/badwill arises when the amount paid is less than the fair value of the net assets acquired. IFRS 3 says the acquirer should:

**(a)** reassess the identification and measurement of the acquiree's identifiable assets, liabilities and contingent liabilities and the measurement of the cost of the combination in case the assets have been undervalued or the liabilities overstated; and

**(b)** recognise immediately in the statement of comprehensive income any excess remaining after that reassessment.

The immediate crediting of badwill to the statement of comprehensive income seems difficult to justify when, as in many situations, the reason why the consideration is less than the value of the net identifiable assets is that there are expected to be future losses or redundancy payments. Whilst the redundancy payments could be included in the 'contingent liabilities' at the date of acquisition, standard setters are very reluctant to allow a provision to be made for future losses (this has been prohibited in recent accounting standards). This means that the only option is to say the badwill should be credited to the statement of comprehensive income at the date of acquisition. This results in the group profit being inflated when a subsidiary with badwill is acquired.

In some ways, it would be better to credit the badwill to the statement of comprehensive income over the years the losses are expected. However, the 'provision for future losses' (i.e. the badwill) does not fit in very well with the *Framework*'s definition of a liability as being recognised 'when it is probable that an outflow of resources embodying economic benefits will result from the settlement of a present obligation and the amount at which the settlement will take place can be measured reliably'. It is questionable whether future losses are a 'present obligation' and whether they can be 'measured reliably', so it is very unlikely that future losses can be included as a liability in the statement of financial position.

## 19.12 Brands

We have discussed intangible assets and goodwill above but brands deserve a separate consideration because of their major significance in some companies. For example, the following information appears in the 2015 Diageo annual report:

|                                  | £m    | £m    |
|----------------------------------|-------|-------|
| Total equity (i.e. net assets)   |       | 9,256 |
| Intangible assets:               |       |       |
| Brands                           | 7,320 |       |

We can see that brands alone are 79% of total equity. It is interesting to take a look at the global importance of brands within sectors.

### 19.12.1 The importance of brands to particular sectors

It is interesting to note that certain sectors have high global brand valuations. For example, the Best Global Brands Report 2015[22] showed electronics (Apple $170,276m), Internet services (Google $120,314m), beverages (Coca-Cola $78,423m) and business services (Microsoft $67,670m). Even the hundredth exceeded $4,000 million (Lenovo $4,114m).

This indicates the importance of investors having as much information as possible to assess management's stewardship of brands. If this cannot be reported on the face of the statement of financial position then there is an argument for having an additional statement to assist shareholders, including the information that the directors consider when managing brands.

### 19.12.2 Justifications for reporting all brands as assets

We now consider some other justifications that have been put forward for the inclusion of brands as a separate asset in the statement of financial position.

### Reduce equity depletion

For acquisitive companies it could be attributed to the accounting treatment required for measuring and reporting goodwill. The London Business School carried out research into the 'brands phenomenon' and found that 'a major aim of brand valuation has been to repair or pre-empt equity depletion caused by UK goodwill accounting rules'.[23]

### Strengthen the statement of financial position

Non-acquisitive companies do not incur costs for acquiring goodwill, so their reserves are not eroded by writing off purchased goodwill. However, these companies may have incurred promotional costs in creating home-grown brands and it would strengthen the statement of financial position if they were permitted to include a valuation of these brands.

### Effect on equity shareholders' funds

Immediate goodwill write-off results in a fall in net tangible assets as disclosed by the statement of financial position, even though the market capitalisation of the company increases. One way to maintain the asset base and avoid such a depletion of companies' reserves is to divide the purchased goodwill into two parts: the amount attributable to brands and the remaining amount attributable to pure goodwill.

### Effect on borrowing powers

The borrowing powers of public companies may be expressed in terms of multiples of net assets. In Articles of Association there may be strict rules regarding the multiple that a company must not exceed. In addition, borrowing agreements and Stock Exchange listing agreements are generally dependent on net assets.

### Effect on ratios

Immediate goodwill write-off distorts the gearing ratios, but the inclusion of brands as intangible assets minimises this distortion by providing a more realistic value for shareholders' funds.

### Effect on management decisions

Including brands on the statement of financial position should lead to more informed and improved management decision making. As brands represent one of the most important assets of a company, management should be aware of the success or failure of each individual brand. Knowledge about the performance of brands ensures that management reacts accordingly to maintain or improve competitive advantage.

*Effect on management decisions where brands are not capitalised*
Whether or not a brand is capitalised, management does take its existence into account when making decisions affecting a company's gearing ratios. For example, in 2007 the Hugo Boss management in explaining its thinking about the advisability of making a Special Dividend payment[24] recognised that one effect was to reduce the book value of equity and increase the gearing ratio, but commented:

> The book value of the equity capital of the HUGO BOSS Group will be reduced by the special dividend. However this perception does not take into consideration that the originally created market value 'HUGO BOSS' is not reflected in the book value of the equity capital. This does not therefore mirror the strong economic position of HUGO BOSS fully.

The implication is that the existence of brand value is recognised by the market and leads to a more sustainable market valuation.

There is also evidence[25] that companies with valuable brand names are not including these in their statements of financial position and are not, therefore, taking account of the assets for insurance purposes.

The above are the justifications for recognising internally generated brands as assets. However, IAS 38 prohibits[26] this by saying: 'Internally generated brands, mastheads, publishing titles, customer lists and items similar in substance shall not be recognised as intangible assets.'

## 19.13 Accounting for acquired brands

Acquired brands require to be valued. In 2009, the International Valuation Standards Council issued an Exposure Draft, *Valuation of Intangible Assets for IFRS Reporting Purposes,*[27] which considers the need to define more clearly terms used within IFRSs such as 'active' and 'inactive' markets.

A decision is then made in respect of each brand as to whether it should be treated in the financial statements as having a finite or an infinite life. The following is an extract from the accounting policies of WPP in their 2015 Annual Report:

> Corporate brand names . . . acquired as part of acquisitions of business are capitalised separately from goodwill as intangible assets . . . amortisation is provided at rates calculated to write off the cost less estimated residual value of each asset on a straight-line basis over its estimated useful life as follows:
>
> Brand names (with finite lives) – 10–20 years; Customer-related intangibles – 3–10 years; Other proprietary tools – 3–10 years; Other (including capitalised computer software) – 3–5 years.
>
> Certain corporate brands of the Group are considered to have an indefinite economic life because of the institutional nature of the corporate brand names, their proven ability to maintain market leadership and profitable operations over long periods of time and the Group's commitment to develop and enhance their value. The carrying value of these intangible assets is reviewed at least annually for impairment and adjusted to the recoverable amount if required.

### 19.13.1 How effective have IFRS 3 and IAS 38 been?

There is still a temptation for companies to treat the excess paid on acquiring a subsidiary as goodwill. If it is treated as goodwill, then there has been no requirement to make an annual amortisation charge. If any part of the excess is attributed to an intangible, then this has to be amortised.

The position in the UK is that the FRRP will be policing the allocation of any excess on acquisitions to ensure that there is appropriate effort to attribute to intangible asset categories if that is the economic reality.

However, even so, the information is limited in that only acquired brands can be reported on the statement of financial position, which gives an incomplete picture of an entity's value. Even with acquired brands, their value can only remain the same or be revised downward following an impairment review. This means that there is no record of any added value that might have been achieved by the new owners to allow shareholders to assess the current stewardship.

## 19.14 Intellectual capital disclosures (ICDs) in the annual report

The problem of valuing for financial reporting purposes has meant that investors need to look outside the annual report for information which tends to be predominately narrative. This is highlighted in an ICAEW Research Report[28], which comments:

> A wide range of media were used to report ICDs, with the annual report accounting for less than a third of total ICDs across all reporting media . . . examination of ICDs in annual reports was not a good proxy for overall ICD practices in the sample studied . . . disclosures are overwhelmingly narrative. Previous studies have tended to indicate that monetary expression of IC elements in corporate reports is a relatively rare practice (see, for example, Beattie and Thompson, 2010).[29] This current study of UK ICR practices reinforces this observation.

The report also referred to the fact that preparers of reports did not see that the annual report was the appropriate place to be providing stakeholders with new information on intellectual capital – the annual report being seen as having a confirmatory role in relation to information that was already in the public domain.

### 19.14.1 The downside of not recognising ICDs in the statement of financial position

There is a common saying 'out of sight – out of mind' that could well be applied to ICDs that are not quantified and reported in the financial statements.

The focus of management's attention may be the physical assets that are reported with a concentration on return on total assets, return on capital employed and return on equity – all of which fail to include the ICDs within the denominator.

The focus of investors' attention may be on assessing the risks attached to achieving maintainable profits. This risk might well be overestimated if there is not an observable asset 'ICD' reported in the financial statements which leads to an increase in the cost of capital.

Investors may be unaware of a failure to achieve the optimum return on ICDs if they are not reported. For example, is the company commercially exploiting its ICDs by, for example, licensing its intellectual property?[30]

Lenders have tended to lend against assets with longer-term debts secured on non-current assets and short-term finance secured by factoring and invoice discounting. There is less confidence and more scepticism in lending against intellectual property. This is seen in SMEs where lenders tend to look for a guarantee supported by a tangible asset in addition to lending on the basis of ICDs. In an increasingly technological world, this is a severe disadvantage to SMEs.

Recognising and reporting ICDs remains an unsolved challenge.

### 19.14.2 Can internally generated intangibles continue to be unseen?

When a company acquires net assets in another company and pays more than their fair value the difference is treated as goodwill. This is a figure that is evidenced by a payment in the open market, so we know this is an arm's length valuation.

This total figure for goodwill is, for financial report purposes, disaggregated if possible into identifiable intangibles. The IASB view is that if they can be recognised they can be valued as a subset of the total market evidenced figure.

It would seem that companies do not consider that their market value is undervalued by the omission of an 'intellectual property' asset provided they keep investors and analysts up-to-date with developments. A contrary approach could be taken by companies that see an economic value in valuing and reporting in acquisition situations, e.g. payment to acquire customer lists.

## 19.15 Review of the implementation of IFRS 3

In 2014 the IASB issued a Request for Information (RFI). The RFI is part of a post-implementation review and is the second being reviewed under its new review programme (the first reviewed IFRS 8). Its purpose is to seek comments from stakeholders to identify whether IFRS 3 *Business Combinations* provides information that is useful to users of financial statements; whether there are areas of IFRS 3 that are difficult to implement and may prevent the consistent implementation of the standard; and whether unexpected costs have arisen in connection with applying or enforcing the standard.

There are nine questions to which answers are requested – only one relates to this chapter, namely:

Does the separate recognition of intangible assets and accounting for negative goodwill (badwill) provide useful information?

### Report and Feedback Statement

In June 2015 there was a *Report and Feedback Statement*,[36] which reported opposing views as to the separate recognition of intangible assets. Some investors support the current practice of identifying additional intangible assets (for example, brands, customer relationships, etc.) separately from goodwill because it provides an insight on why an entity purchased another entity and provides critical information on the fundamental drivers of value in an acquired business. Other investors do not agree because they think it is highly subjective and their view is that these intangible assets should only be recognised if there is a market for them.

As a possible next step it states that research will be undertaken to possibly consider whether particular intangible assets (for example, customer relationships) should be subsumed into goodwill and what additional guidance could be given to assist in the identification of customer relationship intangible assets and their associated measurement.

## 19.16 Review of the implementation of identified intangibles under IAS 38

We saw in Section 19.9.2 the following in the Intel 2015 Annual Report relating to identified intangible assets subject to amortisation:

Acquisition-related customer relationships          1,738          1,219          519

This item appears in the balance sheet of Intel but not in the balance sheet of the company from which the customer relationships had been purchased. On acquisition intangibles are valued at fair value using one of three IFRS 13 approaches. These are:

● the **market** approach using observable market prices or market transactions – this might be difficult to apply to many of the intangible assets such as brands which are company-specific; or
● the **income** approach which is based on relief from cost (say of a trademark) or the present value of excess earnings over an agreed number of years or the present value of incremental cash flows – this is the most appropriate approach for the majority of intangible assets; or
● the **cost** approach which attaches a value which is no higher than replacement cost.

### Treatment of unrealised profits/gains

It is clear that the relationships are capable of being valued and the principal reason for omitting them from the balance sheet is the fact that they have been unrealised.

This is now at odds with the treatment of other assets which have been revalued and the difference between their carrying value and fair value included in Other comprehensive income and carried through into Total equity.

Is it time that the balance sheet reported *Other comprehensive equity* and *Other comprehensive asset* entries with each class of asset disclosed at carrying value and fair value?

Taking human capital as an example, this value would have been built up over time and the expenditure charged against profits – not as an identified charge but subsumed within the cost of recruitment and training.

It would be useful for users to have the asset and equity identified and revalued each year. If human capital improved the asset would increase – if it deteriorated then the asset would be reduced.

### 19.16.1 How might human resources be valued each year?

One approach might be that taken by Infosys Technologies (www.infosys.com) which became the first software company to value its human resources in India. The company stated in its 2011 Annual Report:

> A fundamental dichotomy in accounting practices is between human and non-human capital. As a standard practice, non-human capital is considered as assets and reported in the financial statements, whereas human capital is mostly ignored by accountants. The definition of wealth as a source of income inevitably leads to the recognition of human capital as one of the several forms of wealth such as money, securities and physical capital.
>
> We have used the Lev & Schwartz model to compute the value of human resources. The evaluation is based on the present value of future earnings of employees and on the following assumptions:

(a) Employee compensation includes all direct and indirect benefits earned both in India and overseas

(b) The incremental earnings based on group/age have been considered

(c) The future earnings have been discounted at the cost of capital of 11.21% (previous year 10.60%).

It produced the following analysis:

|  | 2011 | 2010 |
|---|---|---|
| Total income[1] | 27,501 | 22,742 |
| Total employee cost[1] | 14,856 | 12,093 |
| Value-added | 25,031 | 20,935 |
| Net profit[1] | 6,823 | 6,219 |
| Ratios |  |  |
| Value of human resources per employee | 1.03 | 1.00 |
| Total income/human resources value (ratio) | 0.20 | 0.20 |
| Employee cost/human resources value (%) | 11.0 | 10.7 |
| Value-added/human resources value (ratio) | 0.19 | 0.18 |
| Return on human resources value (%) | 5.1 | 5.5 |

[1]*As per IFRS (audited) financial statements*

## Summary

Intangible assets have grown in importance with the rise of the new economy. This has been principally driven by information and knowledge. It has been identified by the Organisation for Economic Co-operation and Development (OECD) as explaining the increased prominence of intellectual capital as a business and research topic.[31]

Since the industrial revolution, the following chain of events is observable:[32]

(a) Capital and labour were brought together and the factors of production became localised and accessible.

(b) Firms pushed to increase volumes of production to meet the demands of growing markets.

(c) Firms began to build intangibles like brand equity and reputation (goodwill) in order to create a competitive advantage in markets where new entrants limited the profit-making potential of a strategy of mass production.

(d) Firms invested heavily in information technology to increase the quality of products and improve the speed with which those products could be brought to market.

(e) Firms invested heavily in human capital with staff development and customer loyalty creation.

At each stage of this corporate evolution non-current tangible assets became less important, in relative terms, compared with intangible assets in determining a company's success. Accounting and financial reporting practices, however, have remained largely unchanged. Expenditure on intellectual capital (except for development costs) is expensed, net assets are understated and book values of the assets bear little relationship to market values.

This makes it more important for stakeholders to refer to non-financial disclosures in the annual reports and elsewhere. As with all information, more detailed explanations about intellectual capital investment should see a fall in the cost of capital and encourage management to provide more, as found in a research study.[33]

IAS 38 requires development costs to be recognised if they satisfy strict criteria. IFRS 3 requires purchased goodwill to be reviewed annually for impairment and not amortised. There is now a case for recognising internally generated intangible assets such as human capital and customer relationships.

## REVIEW QUESTIONS

1 Why do standard setters consider it necessary to distinguish between research and development expenditure, and how does this distinction affect the accounting treatment?

2 Discuss the suggestion that the requirement for companies to write off research investment rather than showing it as an asset exposes companies to short-term pressure from acquisitive companies that are damaging to the country's interest.

3 Discuss why the market value of a business may increase to reflect the analysts' assessment of future growth but the asset(s) responsible for the growth may not appear in the statement of financial position.

**4** Discuss the advantages and disadvantages of the proposal that there should be a separate category of asset in the statement of financial position clearly identified as 'research investment – outcome uncertain'.

**5** IFRS 3 has introduced a new concept into accounting for purchased goodwill – annual impairment testing, rather than amortisation. Consider the effect of a change from amortisation of goodwill (in IAS 22) to impairment testing and no amortisation in IFRS 3, and in particular:

- the effect on the financial statements;
- the effect on financial performance ratios;
- the effect on the annual impairment or amortisation charge and its timing;
- which method gives the fairest charge over time for the value of the goodwill when a business is acquired;
- whether impairment testing with no amortisation complies with the IASC's *Framework for the Preparation and Presentation of Financial Statements*;
- why there has been a change from amortisation to impairment testing – is this pandering to pressure from the US FASB and/or listed companies?

**6** Discuss reasons for the undervaluing of intangibles and subsuming within goodwill.

**7** One goodwill impairment indicator is the loss of key personnel. Discuss two further possible indicators.

**8** There has been a requirement for companies to disaggregate the amount paid for goodwill into other intangible assets. This has led to the valuation of certain of the relational intellectual capital items such as customer lists. Recent research[34] indicates that there is a variety of structural, human and relational capital components which are considered by a representative cross-section of preparers to be significantly more important than others and these key components should be a focus for future research. The researchers raise the need to investigate whether a set of industry-specific standardised metrics can be developed and their disclosure regulated and recommend that IASB include the intangibles project on its active agenda.

Discuss the argument that potentially the future of the accounting profession and its role as the key reporting function could depend on addressing this issue effectively.

**9** Critically evaluate the basis of the following assertion: 'I am sceptical that the impairment test will work reliably in practice, given the complexity and subjectivity that lie within the calculations.'[34]

**10** Access the annual report of a company (such as WPP plc) in which there is a large amount of goodwill and discuss the effect on earnings if goodwill is required to be amortised over a period of between 5 and 10 years. Discuss how this would affect headline profit.

**11** Prior to IFRS 3 some countries permitted goodwill to be written off to equity. Discuss the reason why this was a permitted option and consider whether it is preferable to the estimated amortisation approach.

**12** Discuss, after considering the approach taken by Infosys in valuing, whether investors would benefit from having human capital included as an asset in the statement of financial position.

## EXERCISES

### Question 1

IAS 38 *Intangible Assets* was issued primarily in order to identify the criteria that need to be present before expenditure on intangible items can be recognised as an asset. The standard also prescribes the subsequent accounting treatment of intangible assets that satisfy the recognition criteria and are recognised in the statement of financial position.

Required:

(a) Explain the criteria that need to be satisfied before expenditure on intangible items can be recognised in the statement of financial position as intangible assets.

(b) Explain how the criteria outlined in (a) are applied to the recognition of separately purchased intangible assets, intangible assets acquired in a business combination, and internally generated intangible assets. You should give an example of each category discussed.

(c) Explain the subsequent accounting treatment of intangible assets that satisfy the recognition criteria of IAS 38.

Iota prepares financial statements to 30 September each year. During the year ended 30 September 20X6 Iota (which has a number of subsidiaries) engaged in the following transactions:

1  On 1 April 20X6 Iota purchased all the equity capital of Kappa, and Kappa became a subsidiary from that date. Kappa sells a branded product that has a well-known name and the directors of Iota have obtained evidence that the fair value of this name is $20 million and that it has a useful economic life that is expected to be indefinite. The value of the brand name is not included in the statement of financial position of Kappa, as the directors of Kappa do not consider that it satisfies the recognition criteria of IAS 38 for internally developed intangible assets. However, the directors of Kappa have taken legal steps to ensure that no other entities can use the brand name.

2  On 1 October 20X4 Iota began a project that sought to develop a more efficient method of organising its production. Costs of $10 million were incurred in the year to 30 September 20X5 and debited to the statement of comprehensive income in that year. In the current year the results of the project were extremely encouraging and on 1 April 20X6 the directors of Iota were able to demonstrate that the project would generate substantial economic benefits for the group from 31 March 20X7 onwards as its technical feasibility and commercial viability were clearly evident. Throughout the year to 30 September 20X6 Iota spent $500,000 per month on the project.

Required:

(d) Explain how both of the above transactions should be recognised in the financial statements of Iota for the year ending 30 September 20X6. You should quantify the amounts recognised and make reference to relevant provisions of IAS 38 wherever possible.

### Question 2

Environmental Engineering plc is engaged in the development of an environmentally friendly personal transport vehicle. This will run on an electric motor powered by solar cells, supplemented by passenger effort in the form of pedal assistance.

At the end of the current accounting period, the following costs have been attributed to the project:

(a) A grant of £500,000 to the Polytechnic of the South Coast Faculty of Solar Engineering to encourage research.

(b) Costs of £1,200,000 expended on the development of the necessary solar cells prior to the decision to incorporate them in a vehicle.

(c) Costs of £5,000,000 expended on designing the vehicle and its motors, and the planned promotional and advertising campaign for its launch on the market in 12 months' time.

**Required:**

(i) Explain, with reasons, which of the above items could be considered for treatment as deferred development expenditure, quoting any relevant International Accounting Standard.

(ii) Set out the criteria under which any items can be so treated.

(iii) Advise on the accounting treatment that will be afforded to any such items after the product has been launched.

## * Question 3

As chief accountant at Italin NV, you have been given the following information by the director of research:

---

*Project Luca*

|  | €000 |
|---|---|
| Costs to date (pure research 25%, applied research 75%) | 200 |
| Costs to develop product (to be incurred in the year to 30 September 20X1) | 300 |
| Expected future sales per annum for 20X2–20X7 | 1,000 |
| Fixed assets purchased in 20X1 for the project: |  |
| Cost | 2,500 |
| Estimated useful life | 7 years |
| Residual value | 400 |
| (These assets will be disposed of at their residual value at the end of their estimated useful lives.) |  |

---

The board of directors considers that this project is similar to the other projects that the company undertakes, and is confident of a successful outcome. The company has enough finances to complete the development and enough capacity to produce the new product.

**Required:**

(a) Prepare a report for the board outlining the principles involved in accounting for research and development and showing what accounting entries will be made in the company's accounts for each of the years ending 30 September 20X1–20X7 inclusive.

(b) Indicate what factors need to be taken into account when assessing each research and development project for accounting purposes, and what disclosure is needed for research and development in the company's published accounts.

## * Question 4

Oxlag plc, a manufacturer of pharmaceutical products, has the following research and development projects on hand at 31 January 20X2:

(A) A general survey into the long-term effects of its sleeping pill Chalcedon upon human resistance to infections. At the year-end the research is still at a basic stage and no worthwhile results with any particular applications have been obtained.

(B) A development for Meebach NV in which the company will produce market research data relating to Meebach's range of drugs.

(C) An enhancement of an existing drug, Euboia, which will enable additional uses to be made of the drug and which will consequently boost sales. This project was completed successfully on 30 April 20X2, with the expectation that all future sales of the enhanced drug would greatly exceed the costs of the new development.

(D) A scientific enquiry with the aim of identifying new strains of antibiotics for future use. Several possible substances have been identified, but research is not sufficiently advanced to permit patents and copyrights to be obtained at the present time.

The following costs have been brought forward at 1 February 20X1:

| Project | A £000 | B £000 | C £000 | D £000 |
|---|---|---|---|---|
| Specialised laboratory | | | | |
| Cost | — | — | 500 | — |
| Depreciation | — | — | 25 | — |
| Specialised equipment | | | | |
| Cost | — | — | 75 | 50 |
| Depreciation | — | — | 15 | 10 |
| Capitalised development costs | — | — | 200 | — |
| Market research costs | — | 250 | — | — |

The following costs were incurred during the year:

| Project | A £000 | B £000 | C £000 | D £000 |
|---|---|---|---|---|
| Research costs | 25 | — | 265 | 78 |
| Market research costs | — | 75 | — | — |
| Specialised equipment cost | 50 | — | — | 50 |

Depreciation on specialised laboratories and special equipment is provided by the straight-line method and the assets have an estimated useful life of 25 and five years respectively. A full year's depreciation is provided on assets purchased during the year.

Required:

(a) Write up the research and development, fixed asset and market research accounts to reflect the above transactions in the year ended 31 January 20X2.

(b) Calculate the amount to be charged as research costs in the statement of comprehensive income of Oxlag plc for the year ended 31 January 20X2.

(c) State on what basis the company should amortise any capitalised development costs and what disclosures the company should make in respect of amounts written off in the year to 31 January 20X3.

(d) Calculate the amounts to be disclosed in the statement of financial position in respect of fixed assets, deferred development costs and work in progress.

(e) State what disclosures you would make in the accounts for the year ended 31 January 20X2 in respect of the new improved drug developed under project C, assuming sales begin on 1 May 20X2, and show strong growth to the date of signing the accounts, 14 July 20X2, with the expectation that the new drug will provide 25% of the company's pre-tax profits in the year to 31 January 20X3.

## Question 5

Ross Neale is the divisional accountant for the Research and Development division of Critical Pharmaceuticals PLC. He is discussing the third-quarter results with Tina Snedden who is the manager of the division. The conversation focuses on the fact that whilst they have already fully committed the development capital expenditure budget for the year, the annual expense budget for research is well underspent because of the staff shortages which occurred in the last quarter. Tina mentions that she is under pressure to meet or exceed her expense budgets this year as the industry is renegotiating prescription costs this year and doesn't want to be seen to be too profitable.

Ross suggests that there are several strategies they could employ, namely:

(a) Several of the subcontractors have us as their largest customer and so we could ask them to describe the services in the fourth quarter, which are essentially development cost, as research costs.

(b) We could ask them to charge us in advance for research work that will be required in the first quarter of next year without mentioning that it is an advance in documentation. That would be good for them as it would improve their cash flow and it would guarantee that they would get the work next year.

(c) We could ask some of the subcontractors on development projects to charge us in the first quarter of next year and we could hold out to them that we would give them some better-priced projects next year to compensate them for the interest incurred as a result of the delayed payment.

**Required:**
Discuss the advantages and disadvantages of adopting these strategies.

## Question 6

### The brands debate

Under IAS 22, the depletion of equity reserves caused by the accounting treatment for purchased goodwill resulted in some companies capitalising brands on their statements of financial position. This practice was started by Rank Hovis McDougall (RHM) – a company which has since been taken over. Martin Moorhouse, the group chief accountant at RHM, claimed that putting brands on the statement of financial position forced a company to look to their value as well as to profits. It served as a reminder to management of the value of the assets for which they were responsible and that at the end of the day those companies which were prepared to recognise brands on the statement of financial position could be better and stronger for it.[35]

There were many opponents to the capitalisation of brands. A London Business School research study found that brand accounting involves too many risks and uncertainties and too much subjective judgement. In short, the conclusion was that 'the present flexible position, far from being neutral, is potentially corrosive to the whole basis of financial reporting and that to allow brands – whether acquired or homegrown – to continue to be included in the statement of financial position would be highly unwise'.[36]

**Required:**
Consider the arguments for and against brand accounting. In particular, consider the issues of brand valuation; the separability of brands; purchased versus home-grown brands; and the maintenance/ substitution argument.

## Question 7

Brands plc is preparing its accounts for the year ended 31 October 20X8 and the following information is available relating to various intangible assets acquired on the acquisition of Countrywide plc:

(a) A milk quota of 2,000,000 litres at 30p per litre. There is an active market trading in milk and other quotas.

(b) A government licence to experiment with the use of hormones to increase the cream content of milk had been granted to Countrywide shortly before the acquisition by Brands plc. No fee had been required. This is the first licence to be granted by the government and was one of the reasons why Brands acquired Countrywide. The licence is not transferable but the directors estimate that it has a value to the company based on discounted cash flows for a five-year period of £1 million.

(c) A full-cream yoghurt sold under the brand name 'Naughty but Nice' was valued by the directors at £2 million. Further enquiry established that a similar brand name had been recently sold for £1.5 million.

**Required:**

Explain how each of the above items would be treated in the consolidated financial statements using IAS 38.

## Question 8

James Bright has just taken up the position of managing director following the unsatisfactory achievements of the previous incumbent. James arrives as the accounts for the previous year are being finalised. James wants the previous performance to look poor so that whatever he achieves will look good in comparison. He knows that if he can write off more expenses in the previous year, he will have lower expenses in his first year and possibly a lower asset base. He gives directions to the accountants to write off as many bad debts as possible and to make sure accruals can be as high as they can get past the auditors. Further, he wants all brand name assets reviewed using assumptions that the sales levels achieved during the economic downturn are only going to improve slightly over the foreseeable future. Also he mentions that the cost of capital has risen over the period of the financial crisis so the projected benefits are to be discounted at a higher rate, preferably at a much higher rate than that used in the previous reviews!

**Required:**

Discuss the accountant's professional responsibility and any ethical questions arising in this case.

## Question 9

The following list of balances has been extracted from the records of Cowgale company as at 31 October 2011, the end of Cowgale's most recent financial year:

|  | Note | £ |
| --- | --- | --- |
| Draft profit before tax for the year ended 31 October 2011 |  | 3,820 |
| Cash at bank and in hand |  | 290 |
| Bank loans repayable within 1 year |  | 170 |
| Allowance for receivables, as at 1 November 2010 | 1 | 40 |
| Corporation tax (credit balance) | 2 | 110 |
| Debentures, repayable in October 2015 |  | 500 |
| Debentures, repayable in October 2012 |  | 300 |
| Deferred tax | 3 | 240 |
| Development expenditure | 4 | 470 |
| Dividends paid | 5 | 240 |
| Goodwill, at cost | 6 | 480 |
| Inventory, as at 31 October 2011 |  | 520 |
| Land, at valuation | 7 | 800 |
| Buildings, at valuation | 7 | 2,200 |
| Equipment, at cost | 7 | 1,410 |
| Accumulated depreciation, as at 1 November 2010 |  |  |
| Buildings | 7 | 400 |
| Equipment | 7 | 780 |

| | | |
|---|---|---|
| Proceeds from sale of non-current assets | 7 | 440 |
| Investment properties | 8 | 1,330 |
| Ordinary shares of 25 pence | 9 | 1,000 |
| Retained earnings, as at 1 November 2010 | | 240 |
| Share premium | | 640 |
| Other receivables | 10 | 280 |
| Trade and Other Payables | | 680 |
| Revaluation reserve | | 240 |
| Trade and Other Receivables | 1 | 1,580 |

The following additional information is available:

1 Following an impairment review of receivables as at 31 October 2011 specific invoices totalling £320,000 are to be written off, but no allowance for doubtful debts is to be made on trade receivables as at 31 October 2011.

2 The balance on the corporation tax account represents an over provision for corporation tax for the financial year ended 31 October 2011. Corporation tax payable for the year ended 31 October 2011 has been estimated at £600,000.

3 The balance on the deferred tax account is to be adjusted for corporation tax of £135,000 payable on taxable temporary differences arising during the year ended 31 October 2011.

There were no reversing temporary differences during the year.

4 The balance on development expenditure as at 31 October 2011 comprises:

- £120,000 spent during the year on the initial training of staff for a proposed customer call centre in an overseas country with low labour costs. Following social unrest and increasing political instability in that country, Cowgale decided in September 2011 not to proceed any further with this project.

- £350,000 spent during the year to make the company's packaging process cheaper, more efficient and more environmentally responsible. Cowgale expects to incur further development costs of £107,000 but is on target to introduce the new packaging process in January 2012. The new process will significantly cut costs, increase output and will recover all its development costs.

5 During the year ended 31 October 2011 Cowgale paid the final dividend of 3 pence per share for the year ended 31 October 2010 and an interim dividend of 3 pence per share for the year ended 31 October 2011. The directors of Cowgale will be proposing a final dividend of 4 pence per share at its annual general meeting which will be held in January 2012 and the shareholders are expected to approve the proposal.

6 The goodwill arose on 1 November 2010 when Cowgale purchased and absorbed another business as a going concern. The economic life of the goodwill was estimated as 20 years from 1 November 2010. The directors have been advised that the fair value of the goodwill was £350,000 as at 31 October 2011.

7 The proceeds on sale of non-current assets account records £440,000 cash received from the sale of tangible non-current assets during the year ended 31 October 2011. The £440,000 was also debited to bank account but no other entries in connection with the disposals have been made. The carrying values of the assets sold during the year were:

| | |
|---|---|
| Land | £100,000 |
| Buildings | £290,000 (£360,000 gross revaluation and £70,000 accumulated depreciation) |
| Equipment | £140,000 (£290,000 cost and £150,000 accumulated depreciation) |

Cowgale uses the revaluation model for land and buildings and the revaluation reserve includes £90,000 of revaluation surpluses relating to the land and buildings sold during the year.

Cowgale's depreciation policies are:

| Land | no depreciation |
| Buildings | 5% straight-line, full-year basis |
| Equipment | 30% reducing balance, full-year basis |

Depreciation for the year ended 31 October 2011 is still to be charged on all assets in use at the end of the financial year.

8 Cowgale uses the fair value model for investment properties. The market value of the company's investment properties was estimated at £1,400,000 as at 31 October 2011.

9 Cowgale used the share premium account to finance a bonus issue of 1 for 4 shares on 31 October 2011. This has not yet been recorded in the accounts. The bonus shares will qualify for all dividends paid after 31 October 2011.

10 The Other Receivables balance represents the excess of value added tax on inputs (purchases) over value added tax on outputs (sales) for the last quarter of the financial year.

11 Cowgale vacated some office property it was leasing on 1 August 2011 in order to rationalise its administration procedures. Under the lease agreement Cowgale was committed as at 31 October 2011 to making further payments totalling £108,000 on the lease until 31 July 2012. Cowgale is allowed to sublease the premises but this has proved difficult because of redevelopment plans for the area and a local recession. The only offer that Cowgale has received has been from a charity which wants to rent the offices for four months for a total of £22,000. Cowgale has decided to accept this offer. The lease is being accounted for as an operating lease.

**Required:**

(a) **Prepare the Statement of Financial Position of Cowgale as at 31 October 2011.**

(b) **Prepare a calculation of retained earnings as at 31 October 2011 starting with the draft profit before tax of £3,820,000 for the year ended 31 October 2011 and using the additional information in notes 1 to 11 above.**

*(CIPFA Advanced Diploma in International Public Financial Management FINANCIAL REPORTING Specimen examination)*

## Notes

1  IAS 38 *Intangible Assets*, IASC, revised March 2004.
2  IFRS 3 *Business Combinations*, IASB, revised 2008.
3  IAS 38 *Intangible Assets*, IASC, revised March 2004, para. 119.
4  Clarification of Acceptable Methods of Depreciation and Amortisation (Amendments to IAS 16 and IAS 38), IASB, 2014.
5  IAS 38 *Intangible Assets*, IASC, revised March 2004, para. 118.
6  Ibid., para. 126.
7  Ibid., para. 122.
8  Ibid., para. 54.
9  Ibid., para. 56.
10  Ibid., para. 55.
11  Ibid., para. 58.
12  Ibid., para. 59.

13 B. Nixon and A. Lonie, 'Accounting for R&D: the need for change', *Accountancy*, February 1990, p. 91; B. Nixon, 'R&D disclosure: SSAP 13 and after', *Accountancy*, February 1991, pp. 72–73.

14 www.rdmag.com/Featured-Articles/2011/12/2012-Global-RD-Funding-Forecast-RD-Spending-Growth-Continues-While-Globalization-Accelerates/

15 IASC, *Framework for the Preparation and Presentation of Financial Statements*, IASB, April 2001, para. 49.

16 A. Goodacre and J. McGrath, 'An experimental study of analysts' reactions to corporate R&D expenditure', *British Accounting Review*, vol. 29, 1997, pp. 155–179.

17 B. Nixon, 'The accounting treatment of research and development expenditure: views of UK company accountants', *European Accounting Review*, vol. 6(2), 1997, pp. 265–277.

18 Li Li Eng and Hong Kiat Teo, 'The relation between annual report disclosures, analysts' earnings forecast and analysts following: evidence from Singapore', *Pacific Accounting Review*, vol. 11 (1/2), 1999, pp. 219–239.

19 IAS 38 *Intangible Assets*, IASC, revised March 2004, para. 57.

20 IFRS 3 *Business Combinations*, IASB, 2004, para. 51.

21 IASC, *Framework for the Preparation and Presentation of Financial Statements*, IASB, April 2001, para. 94.

22 www.interbrand.com/best_global_brands.aspx

23 P. Barwise, C. Higson, A. Likierman and P. Marsh, *Accounting for Brands*, ICAEW, June 1989; M. Cooper and A. Carey, 'Brand valuation in the balance', *Accountancy*, June 1989.

24 http://group.hugoboss.com/en/faq_special_dividend.htm

25 M. Gerry, 'Companies ignore value of brands', *Accountancy Age*, March 2000, p. 4.

26 IAS 38 *Intangible Assets*, IASC, revised March 2004, para. 63.

27 www.ivsc.org

28 J. Unerman, J. Guthrie and M. Striukova, *UK Reporting of Intellectual Capital*, ICAEW, 2007, www.icaew.co.uk

29 V. Beattie and S.J. Thompson, *Intellectual Capital Reporting: Academic Utopia or Corporate Reality in a Brave New World?*, 2010, www.icas.org.uk

30 www.ipo.gov.uk/ipresearch-bankingip.pdf

31 OECD, *Final Report: Measuring and Reporting Intellectual Capital: Experience, Issues and Prospects*, Paris: OECD, 2000.

32 J. Guthrie and R. Petty, 'Knowledge management: the information revolution has created the need for a codified system of gathering and controlling knowledge', *Company Secretary*, vol. 9(1), January 1999, pp. 38–41; R. Tissen et al., *Value-Based Knowledge Management*, Longman Nederland BV, 1998, pp. 25–44.

33 M. Mangena, R. Pike and J. Li, *Intellectual Capital Disclosure Practices and Effects on the Cost of Equity Capital: UK Evidence*, ICAS, 2010.

34 V. Beattie and S.J. Thomson, *Intellectual Capital Reporting: Academic Utopia or Corporate Reality in a Brave New World?*, ICAS, 2010, www.icas.org.uk/site/cms/contentviewarticle.asp?article=6837

35 M. Moorhouse, 'Brands debate: wake up to the real world', *Accountancy*, July 1990, p. 30.

36 www.ifrs.org/Current-Projects/IASB-Projects/PIR/PIR-IFRS-3/Documents/PIR_IFRS%203-Business-Combinations_FBS_WEBSITE.pdf

# CHAPTER 20

# Inventories

## 20.1 Introduction

The main purpose of this chapter is to explain the accounting principles involved in the valuation of inventory and biological assets.

### Objectives

By the end of this chapter, you should be able to:

- define inventory in accordance with IAS 2;
- explain why valuation has been controversial;
- explain the impact of inventory valuation on profits;
- describe acceptable valuation methods;
- describe procedure for ascertaining cost;
- calculate inventory value;
- explain how inventory could be used for creative accounting;
- explain IAS 41 provisions relating to agricultural activity;
- calculate biological value.

## 20.2 Inventory defined

IAS 2 *Inventories* defines inventories as assets:

(a) held for sale in the ordinary course of business;

(b) in the process of production for such sale;

(c) in the form of materials or supplies to be consumed in the production process or in the rendering of services.[1]

The valuation of inventory involves:

(a) the establishment of physical existence and ownership;

(b) the determination of unit costs;

(c) the calculation of provisions to reduce cost to net realisable value, if necessary.[2]

The resulting evaluation is then disclosed in the financial statements.

These definitions appear to be very precise. We shall see, however, that although IAS 2 was introduced to bring some uniformity into financial statements, there are many areas where professional judgement must be exercised. Sometimes this may distort the financial statements to such an extent that we must question whether they do represent a 'true and fair' view.

## 20.3 The impact of inventory valuation on profits

The valuation of inventory has impacts on both:

- the statement of income as the earnings per share (EPS) figure is based on the profit after tax. The EPS is then used to calculate the price earnings (PE) ratio; and
- the statement of financial position as the net asset backing for shares and the current ratio are affected.

### A small change in inventory valuation may have a material impact on profit

Figure 20.1 presents information relating to Rolls-Royce. It shows that the inventory is material in relation to pre-tax profits. In relation to the profits we can see that an error of 5% in the 2015 inventory values would potentially cause the pre-tax profit to be turned into a loss for the year. As inventory is usually a multiple rather than a fraction of profit, inventory errors may have a disproportionate effect on the accounts.

### Income smoothing

This is achieved by adjusting the inventory valuation of the closing inventory to increase or decrease the profit for the year. There will be an opposite impact on the profits of the following year – the current year's increase in profit will be the following year's decrease Figure 20.2 illustrates the point. Simply by increasing the value of inventory in year 1 by £10,000, profit (and current assets) is increased by a similar amount. Even if the closing inventory value is the same (£15,000) in year 2, such manipulation allows profit to be 'smoothed' and £10,000 profit switched from year 2 to year 1.

### Management attitude when estimating need to reduce inventory to net realisable value

According to normal accrual accounting principles, profit is determined by matching costs with related revenues. If it is unlikely that the revenue will in fact be received, prudence dictates that the irrecoverable amount should be written off immediately against current revenue and the inventory stated at net realisable value. If profits are falling or less than forecast it could be a temptation for management to estimate a lower figure for inventory deterioration or obsolescence. Likewise, if profits are rising and there is an expected fall in the following year, management might be inclined to overestimate the provision required.

### Figure 20.1  Rolls-Royce Holdings plc

|  | 2015 | Inventory reduced by 5% | Effect |
|---|---|---|---|
| Profit for year | £84m | (£10m) | Loss for the year |
| Inventories | £2,367m | £2,249m | |

**Figure 20.2 Inventory values manipulated to smooth income**

|  | | Year 1 | Year 1<br>_With inventory inflated_ |
|---|---|---|---|
| Sales | | 100,000 | 100,000 |
| Opening inventory | — | | — |
| Purchases | 65,000 | | 65,000 |
| Less: Closing inventory | 5,000 | | 15,000 |
| COST OF SALES | | 60,000 | 50,000 |
| PROFIT | | 40,000 | 50,000 |

|  | | Year 2 | Year 2<br>_With inventory inflated_ |
|---|---|---|---|
| Sales | | 150,000 | 150,000 |
| Opening inventory | 5,000 | | 15,000 |
| Purchases | 100,000 | | 100,000 |
| | 105,000 | | 115,000 |
| Less: Closing inventory | 15,000 | | 15,000 |
| COST OF SALES | | 90,000 | 100,000 |
| PROFIT | | 60,000 | 50,000 |

Such circumstances tend to come to light with a change of management and it was considered important that a definitive statement of accounting practice should be issued in an attempt to standardise treatment. This is now set out in IAS 2 with the aim of making inventory valuation consistent, comparable between periods and comparable between companies in the same industry.

## 20.4 IAS 2 _Inventories_

No area of accounting has produced wider differences in practice than the computation of the amount at which inventory is stated in financial accounts. An accounting standard on the subject needs to define the practices, to narrow the differences and variations in those practices and to ensure adequate disclosure in the accounts.

IAS 2 requires that the amount at which inventory is stated in periodic financial statements should be the total of the lower of cost and net realisable value of the separate items of inventory or of groups of similar items. The standard also emphasises the need to match costs against revenue, and it aims, like other standards, to achieve greater uniformity in the measurement of income as well as improving the disclosure of inventory valuation methods. To an extent, IAS 2 relies on management to choose the most appropriate method of inventory valuation for the production processes used and the company's environment.

Various methods of valuation are theoretically available, including FIFO, LIFO and weighted average or any similar method (see below). In selecting the most suitable method, management must exercise judgement to ensure that the methods chosen provide the fairest practical approximation to cost. IAS 2 does not allow the use of LIFO because it often results in inventory being stated in the statement of financial position at amounts that bear little relation to recent cost levels.

At the end of the day, even though there is an International Accounting Standard in existence, the valuation of inventory can provide areas of subjectivity and choice to management. We will return to this theme many times in the following sections of this chapter.

## 20.5 Inventory valuation

The valuation rule outlined in IAS 2 is difficult to apply because of uncertainties about what is meant by cost (with some methods approved by IAS 2 and others not) and what is meant by net realisable value.

### 20.5.1 Methods acceptable under IAS 2

The acceptable methods of inventory valuation include FIFO, AVCO and standard cost.

#### First-in-first-out (FIFO)

Inventory is valued at the most recent 'cost', since the cost of oldest inventory is charged out first, whether or not this accords with the actual physical flow. FIFO is illustrated in Figure 20.3.

#### Average cost (AVCO)

Inventory is valued at a 'weighted average cost', i.e. the unit cost is weighted by the number of items carried at each 'cost', as shown in Figure 20.4. This is popular in organisations holding a large volume of inventory at fluctuating 'costs'. The practical problem of actually recording and calculating the weighted average cost has been overcome by the use of sophisticated computer software.

The following is an extract from the J Sainsbury plc 2013 Annual Report:

**Inventories**
Inventories . . . are valued on a weighted average cost basis and carried at the lower of cost and net realisable value. Net realisable value represents the estimated selling price less all estimated costs of completion and costs to be incurred in marketing, selling and

**Figure 20.3 First-in-first-out method (FIFO)**

| Date | Receipts | | | Issues | | | Balance | | |
|---|---|---|---|---|---|---|---|---|---|
| | Quantity | Rate | £ | Quantity | Rate | £ | Quantity | Rate | £ |
| January | 10 | 15 | 150 | | | | 10 | | 150 |
| February | | | | 8 | 15 | 120 | 2 | | 30 |
| March | 10 | 17 | 170 | | | | 12 | | 200 |
| April | 20 | 20 | 400 | | | | 32 | | 600 |
| May | | | | 2 | 15 | 30 | | | |
| | | | | 10 | 17 | 170 | | | |
| | | | | 12 | 20 | 240 | | | |
| | | | | Cost of goods sold | | 560 | | | |
| | | | | Inventory | | | 8 | 20 | 160 |

**Figure 20.4 Average cost method (AVCO)**

| | Receipts | | | | Issues | | | | Balance | | |
|---|---|---|---|---|---|---|---|---|---|---|---|
| Date | Quantity | Rate | £ | | Quantity | Rate | £ | | Quantity | Rate | £ |
| January | 10 | 15 | 150 | | | | | | 10 | | 150 |
| February | | | | | 8 | 15 | 120 | | 2 | | 30 |
| March | 10 | 17 | 170 | | | | | | 12 | | 200 |
| April | 20 | 20 | 400 | | | | | | 32 | | 600 |
| May | | | | | 24 | 18.75 | 450 | | | | 600 |
| | | | | | Cost of goods sold | | 570 | | | | |
| | | | | | Inventory | | | | 8 | 18.75 | 150 |

distribution. Cost includes all direct expenditure and other appropriate attributable costs incurred in bringing inventories to their present location and condition.

## Standard cost

A standard cost valuation is acceptable only if it approximates to actual cost. This means that variances need to be reviewed to see if they affect the standard cost and for inventory evaluation as seen in the following extract from the Noranda Aluminium Holding Corp 2015 Annual Report:

> Inventories in our Flat-Rolled Products segment, our Bauxite segment and our Alumina segment are valued using a standard costing system, which gives rise to cost variances. Variances are capitalized to inventory in proportion to the quantity of inventory remaining at period end to quantities produced during the period. Variances are recorded such that ending inventory reflects actual costs on a year-to-date basis.

## Retail method

IAS 2 recognises that an acceptable method of arriving at cost is the use of selling price, less an estimated profit margin. This method is only acceptable if it can be demonstrated that it gives a reasonable approximation of the actual cost.

The following is an extract from the Shoprite Holdings Ltd 2015 Annual Financial Statements:

> Valuation of inventory: Trading inventories are valued by use of the retail inventory method as an approximation of weighted average cost.
>
> Significant judgment is required in the application thereof, specifically as far as it relates to gross margin percentages, accrual rates for rebates and settlement discounts and shrinkage rates applied.
>
> The retail method approximates the weighted average cost and is determined by reducing the sales value of the inventory by the appropriate percentage gross margin. The percentage used takes into account inventory that has been marked down below original selling price. An average percentage per retail department is used.

Care has to be taken in determining the appropriate percentage write-down. For example, one company, Stein Mart Inc., had to restate its accounts in 2012, having identified that a practice that had been in place for more than ten years was incorrect. It had been accounting for certain markdowns as promotional (temporary) rather than permanent – as a result its inventories were overstated by approximately $3 million.

IAS 2 does not recommend any specific method. This is a decision for each organisation based upon sound professional advice and the organisation's unique operating conditions.

### 20.5.2 Methods rejected by IAS 2

Methods rejected by IAS 2 include LIFO and (by implication) replacement cost.

#### Last-in-first-out (LIFO)

The cost of the inventory most recently received is charged out first at the most recent 'cost'. The practical upshot is that the inventory value is based upon an 'old cost', which may bear little relationship to the current 'cost'. Where LIFO is used companies reconcile the LIFO valuation to the FIFO valuation. LIFO is illustrated in Figure 20.5.

US companies commonly use the LIFO method, as illustrated by this extract from the Deere and Company 2015 Annual Report:

#### Inventories

Most inventories owned by Deere & Company and its U.S. equipment subsidiaries are valued at cost, on the 'last–in, first–out' (LIFO) basis. . . . If all inventories had been valued on a FIFO basis, estimated inventories . . . would have been in millions of

|  | 2015 | 2014 |
|---|---|---|
| Total FIFO value ....................................................... | 5,243 | 5,738 |
| Less adjustment to LIFO value ................................ | 1,426 | 1,528 |
| Inventories .............................................................. | $3,817 | $4,210 |

Although LIFO does not have IAS 2 approval, it is still used in practice. For example, LIFO is commonly used by UK companies with US subsidiaries, since LIFO is the main method of inventory valuation in the USA.

#### Replacement cost

The inventory is valued at the current cost of the individual item (i.e. the cost to the organisation of replacing the item) rather than the actual cost at the time of manufacture or purchase.

#### Figure 20.5 Last-in-first-out method (LIFO)

| | Receipts | | | Issues | | | Balance | | |
|---|---|---|---|---|---|---|---|---|---|
| Date | Quantity | Rate | £ | Quantity | Rate | £ | Quantity | Rate | £ |
| January | 10 | 15 | 150 | | | | 10 | | 150 |
| February | | | | 8 | 15 | 120 | 2 | | 30 |
| March | 10 | 17 | 170 | | | | 12 | | 200 |
| April | 20 | 20 | 400 | | | | 32 | | 600 |
| May | | | | 20 | 20 | 400 | | | |
| | | | | 4 | 17 | 68 | | | |
| | | | | Cost of goods sold | | 588 | | | |
| | | | | Inventory | | | 8 | | 132 |

May closing balance = [(2 × 15) + (6 × 17)]

The value may be reported as additional information as in the following extract from the A.M. Castle & Co 2015 Annual Report:

> The current replacement cost of inventories at the Company's Plastics segment which are accounted for under the LIFO method exceeded book value by $2,462 and $2,682 at December 31, 2015 and 2014, respectively.

The use of replacement cost is not specifically prohibited by IAS 2 but is out of line with the basic principle underpinning the standard, which is to value inventory at the actual costs incurred in its purchase or production. The IASC *Framework for the Preparation and Presentation of Financial Statements* describes historical cost and current cost as two distinct measurement bases, and where a historical cost measurement base is used for assets and liabilities the use of replacement cost is inconsistent.

### 20.5.3 Procedure to ascertain cost

Having decided upon the accounting policy of the company, there remains the problem of ascertaining the cost. In a retail environment, the 'cost' is the price the organisation had to pay to acquire the goods, and it is readily established by reference to the purchase invoice from the supplier. However, in a manufacturing organisation the concept of cost is not as simple. Should we use prime cost, or production cost, or total cost? IAS 2 attempts to help by defining cost as 'all costs of purchase, costs of conversion and other costs incurred in bringing the inventories to their present location and condition'.

In a manufacturing organisation each expenditure is taken to include three constituents: direct materials, direct labour and appropriate overhead.

#### Direct materials

These include not only the costs of raw materials and component parts, but also the costs of insurance, handling (special packaging) and any import duties. An additional problem is waste and scrap. For instance, if a process inputs 100 tonnes at £45 per tonne, yet outputs only 90 tonnes, the output's inventory value **must** be £4,500 (£45 × 100) and not £4,050 (90 × £45). (This assumes the 10 tonnes loss is a normal, regular part of the process.) An adjustment may be made for the residual value of the scrap/waste material, if any. The treatment of component parts will be the same, provided they form part of the finished product.

#### Direct labour

This is the cost of the actual production in the form of gross pay and those incidental costs of employing the direct workers (employer's national insurance contributions, additional pension contributions, etc.). The labour costs will be spread over the goods' production.

#### Appropriate overhead

It is here that the major difficulties arise in calculating the true cost of the product for inventory valuation purposes. Normal practice is to classify overheads into five types and decide whether to include them in inventory. The five types are as follows:

- Direct overheads – subcontract work, royalties.
- Indirect overheads – the cost of running the factory and supporting the direct workers, and the depreciation of capital items used in production.
- Administration overheads – the office costs and salaries of senior management.

- Selling and distribution overheads – advertising, delivery costs, packaging, salaries of sales personnel, and depreciation of capital items used in the sales function.
- Finance overheads – the cost of borrowing and servicing debt.

We will look at each of these in turn, to demonstrate the difficulties that the accountant experiences.

Regular, routine direct overhead will be included in the inventory valuation. Special sub-contract work would form part of the inventory value where it is readily identifiable to individual units of inventory such as in a customised car manufacturer making 20 cars a month.

**Indirect overheads.** These always form part of the inventory valuation, as such expenses are incurred in support of production. They include factory rent and rates, factory power and depreciation of plant and machinery; in fact, any indirect factory-related cost, including the warehouse costs of storing completed goods, will be included in the value of inventory.

**Administration overheads.** This overhead is in respect of the whole business, so only that portion easily identifiable to production should form part of the inventory valuation. For instance, the costs of the personnel or wages department could be apportioned to production on a head-count basis and that element would be included in the inventory valuation. Any production-specific administration costs (welfare costs, canteen costs, etc.) would also be included in the inventory valuation. If the expense cannot be identified as forming part of the production function, it will not form part of the inventory valuation.

**Selling and distribution overheads.** These costs will not normally be included in the inventory valuation as they are incurred after production has taken place. However, if the goods are on a 'sale or return' basis and are on the premises of the customer but remain the supplier's property, the delivery and packing costs will be included in the inventory value of goods held on a customer's premises.

**Finance overheads.** Normally these overheads would never be included within the inventory valuation because they are not normally identifiable with production. In a job-costing context, however, it might be possible to use some of this overhead in inventory valuation. Let us take the case of an engineering firm being requested to produce a turbine engine, which requires parts/components to be imported. It is logical for the financial charges for these imports (e.g. exchange fees or fees for letters of credit) to be included in the inventory valuation.

Thus it can be seen that the identification of the overheads to be included in inventory valuation is far from straightforward. In many cases it depends upon the judgement of the accountant and the unique operating conditions of the organisation.

In addition to the problem of deciding **whether** the five types of overhead should be included, there is the problem of deciding **how much** of the total overhead to include in the inventory valuation at the year-end. IAS 2 stipulates the use of 'normal activity' when making this decision on overheads. The vast majority of overheads are 'fixed', i.e. do not vary with activity, and it is customary to share these out over a normal or expected output.

The following is an extract from the Agrana Group 2014/15 Annual Report:

### Inventories

Inventories are measured at the lower of cost of purchase and/or conversion and net selling price. The weighted average formula is used. In accordance with IAS 2, the conversion costs of unfinished and finished products include – in addition to directly attributable unit costs – reasonable proportions of the necessary material costs and production overheads inclusive of depreciation of manufacturing plant (*based on the assumption of normal capacity utilisation*) as well as production-related administrative costs [our italics]. . . . If this expected output [based on normal capacity utilisation] is not reached, it is not acceptable to allow the actual production to bear the full overhead for inventory purposes.

A numerical example will illustrate this:

| | |
|---|---|
| Overhead for the year | £200,000 |
| Planned activity | 10,000 units |
| Closing inventory | 3,000 units |
| Direct costs | £2 per unit |
| Actual activity | 6,000 units |

*Inventory value based on actual activity*

| | | |
|---|---|---|
| Direct costs | 3,000 × £2 | £6,000 |
| Overhead | 3,000 × £200,000 / 6,000 | £100,000 |
| Closing inventory value | | £106,000 |

*Inventory value based on planned or normal activity*

| | | |
|---|---|---|
| Direct cost | 3,000 × £2 | £6,000 |
| Overhead | 3,000 × £200,000 / 10,000 | £60,000 |
| Closing inventory value | | £66,000 |

Comparing the value of inventory based upon actual activity with the value based upon planned or normal activity, we have a £40,000 difference. This could be regarded as increasing the current year's profit by carrying forward expenditure of £40,000 to set against the following year's profit.

The problem occurs because of the organisation's failure to meet expected output level (6,000 actual versus 10,000 planned). By adopting the **actual activity basis**, the organisation makes a profit out of failure. This cannot be an acceptable position when evaluating performance. Therefore, IAS 2 stipulates **the planned or normal activity model** for inventory valuation. The failure to meet planned output could be due to a variety of sources (e.g. strikes, poor weather, industrial conditions); the cause, however, is classed as abnormal or non-routine, and all such costs should be excluded from the valuation of inventory.

### 20.5.4 What is meant by net realisable value?

IAS 2 requires inventory to be stated at the lower of cost and net realisable value. In arriving at net realisable value a deduction is made from realisable value for any additional expense expected for repackaging, advertising, delivery and, where necessary, repairing damaged inventory prior to sale.

The following is an extract from the Next PLC 2015 Annual Report:

Inventories (stocks) are valued at the lower of standard cost or net realisable value. Net realisable value is based on estimated selling prices less further costs to be incurred to disposal.

Prudence dictates that net realisable value will be used if it is lower than the 'cost' of the inventory (however that may be calculated). These occasions will vary among organisations, but can be summarised as follows:

● There is a permanent fall in the market price of inventory. Short-term fluctuations should not cause net realisable value to be implemented.

- The organisation is attempting to dispose of high inventory levels or excessively priced inventory to improve its liquidity position (acid test ratio) or reduce its inventory holding costs. Such high inventory volumes or values are primarily a result of poor management decision making.

- The inventory is physically deteriorating or is of an age where the market is reluctant to accept it. This is a common feature of the food industry, especially with the use of 'sell by' dates in the retail environment.

- Inventory suffers obsolescence through some unplanned development. (Good management should never be surprised by obsolescence.) This development could be technical in nature, or due to the development of different marketing concepts within the organisation or a change in market needs.

- The management could decide to sell the goods at 'below cost' for sound marketing reasons. The concept of a 'loss leader' is well known in supermarkets, but organisations also sell below cost when trying to penetrate a new market or as a defence mechanism when attacked.

Such decisions are important and the change to net realisable value should not be undertaken without considerable forethought and planning. Obsolescence should be a decision based upon sound market intelligence and not a managerial 'whim'. The auditors of companies always examine such decisions to ensure they were made for sound business reasons. The opportunities for fraud in such 'price-cutting' operations validate this level of external control.

For example, goods costing £1,000 had been flood damaged and were not covered by insurance. It was estimated that if £200 were spent on cleaning the goods could be sold for £550 giving a NRV for inventory of £350.

A numerical example will demonstrate this concept:

| Item | Cost (£) | Net realisable value (£) | Inventory value (£) |
|------|------|------|------|
| 1 No. 876 | 7,000 | 9,000 | 7,000 |
| 2 No. 997 | 12,000 | 12,500 | 12,000 |
| 3 No. 1822 | 8,000 | 4,000 | 4,000 |
| 4 No. 2076 | 14,000 | 8,000 | 8,000 |
| 5 No. 4732 | 27,000 | 33,000 | 27,000 |
| | (a) 68,000 | (b) 66,500 | (c) 58,000 |

The inventory value chosen for the accounts is (c) £58,000, although each item is assessed individually.

## 20.6 Work in progress

Inventory classified as work in progress (WIP) is mainly found in manufacturing organisations and is simply the production that has not been completed by the end of the accounting period.

The valuation of WIP must follow the same IAS 2 rules and be the lower of cost and net realisable value. We again face the difficulty of deciding what to include in cost. The three basic classes of cost – direct materials, direct labour and appropriate overhead – will still form the basis of ascertaining cost.

### 20.6.1 Direct materials

It is necessary to decide what proportion of the total materials have been used in WIP. The proportion will vary with different types of organisation, as the following two examples illustrate:

● If the item is complex or materially significant (e.g. a custom-made car or a piece of specialised machinery), the WIP calculation will be based on actual recorded materials and components used to date.

● If, however, we are dealing with mass production, it may not be possible to identify each individual item within WIP. In such cases, the accountant will make a judgement and define the WIP as being $x\%$ complete in regard to raw materials and components. For example, a drill manufacturer with 1 million tools per week in WIP may decide that in respect of raw materials they are 100% complete; WIP then gets the full materials cost of one million tools.

In both cases **consistency** is vital so that, however WIP is valued, the same method will always be used.

### 20.6.2 Direct labour

Again, it is necessary to decide how much direct labour the items in WIP have actually used. As with direct materials, there are two broad approaches:

● Where the item of WIP is complex or materially significant, the actual time 'booked' or recorded will form part of the WIP valuation.

● In a mass production situation, such precision may not be possible and an accounting judgement may have to be made as to the average percentage completion in respect of direct labour. In the example of the drill manufacturer, it could be that, on average, WIP is 80% complete in respect of direct labour.

### 20.6.3 Appropriate overhead

The same two approaches as for direct labour can be adopted:

● With a complex or materially significant item, it should be possible to allocate the overhead actually incurred. This could be an actual charge (e.g. subcontract work) or an application of the appropriate overhead recovery rate (ORR). For example, if we use a direct labour hour recovery rate and we have an ORR of £10 per direct labour hour and the recorded labour time on the WIP item is 12 hours, then the overhead charge for WIP purposes is £120.

EXAMPLE • A custom-car company making sports cars has the following costs in respect of No. 821/C, an unfinished car, at the end of the month:

| | |
|---|---|
| Materials charged to job 821/C | £2,100 |
| Labour 120 hours @ £4 | £480 |
| Overhead £22/DLH × 120 hours | £2,640 |
| WIP value of 821/C | £5,220 |

This is an accurate WIP value provided *all* the costs have been accurately recorded and charged. The amount of accounting work involved is not great as the information is required by a normal job cost system. An added advantage is that the figure can be formally audited and proven.

- With mass production items, the accountant must either use a budgeted overhead recovery rate approach or simply decide that, in respect of overheads, WIP is $y$% complete.

EXAMPLE • A company produces drills. The costs of a completed drill are:

|  | £ |
|---|---|
| Direct materials | 2.00 |
| Direct labour | 6.00 |
| Appropriate overhead | 10.00 |
| Total cost | 18.00 (for finished goods inventory value purposes) |

Assuming that the company accountant takes the view that for WIP purposes the following applies:

| Direct material | 100% complete |
|---|---|
| Direct labour | 80% complete |
| Appropriate overhead | 30% complete |

then, for one WIP drill:

| Direct material | £2.00 × 100% = £2.00 |
|---|---|
| Direct labour | £6.00 × 80% = £4.80 |
| Appropriate overhead | £10.00 × 30% = £3.00 |
| WIP value | £9.80 |

If the company has 100,000 drills in WIP, the value is:

$$100,000 \times £9.80 = £980,000$$

This is a very simplistic view, but the principle can be adapted to cover more complex issues. For instance, there could be 200 different types of drill, but the same calculation can be done on each. Of course, sophisticated software makes the accountant's job mechanically easier.

This technique is particularly useful in processing industries, such as petroleum, brewing, dairy products or paint manufacture, where it might be impossible to identify WIP items precisely. The approach must be consistent and the role of the auditor in validating such practices is paramount.

## 20.7 Inventory control

Inventory shrinkage can occur for a number of reasons ranging from criminal activity to internal administrative errors. For example, the following statistics were collected in the US in 2012:[3]

| Sources of Inventory Shrinkage in Retail | Percent |
|---|---|
| Employee Theft | 40.9% |
| Shoplifting | 33.1% |
| Administrative Error | 15.3% |
| Vendor Fraud | 5.9% |
| Unknown | 7.4% |

Management are responsible for internal control but auditors become involved in reporting and advising on internal control procedures – in the case of employee theft, for example, advising on the installation of sales audit and loss prevention software and procedures for authorisation of employee purchases and all documents that allow goods to leave the premises. The final decision on action, however, lies with the management.

Errors can occur at the year-end inventory count when physical inventory is checked against book inventory. A major cause of discrepancy between physical and book inventory is the 'cut-off' date. In matching sales with cost of sales, it may be difficult to identify exactly into which period of account certain inventory movements should be placed, especially when the annual inventory count lasts many days or occurs at a date other than the last day of the financial year. It is customary to make an adjustment to the inventory figure. In many cases the auditor will be present at the inventory count to observe that there are effective systems being followed.

In practice, errors may continue unidentified for a number of years,[4] particularly if there is a paper-based system in operation. This was evident when T.J. Hughes reduced its profit for the year ended 31 January 2001 by £2.5–3 million from a forecast £8 million when stock discrepancies came to light following the implementation of a new stock management system.

## 20.8 Creative accounting

No area of accounting provides more opportunities for subjectivity and creative accounting than the valuation of inventory. This is illustrated by the report *Fraudulent Financial Reporting: 1987–1997 – An Analysis of U.S. Public Companies* prepared by the Committee of Sponsoring Organizations of the Treadway Commission.[5] This report, which was based on the detailed analysis of approximately 200 cases of fraudulent financial reporting, identified that the fraud often involved the overstatement of revenues and assets with inventory fraud featuring frequently – assets were overstated by understating allowances for receivables, overstating the value of inventory and other tangible assets, and recording assets that did not exist.

This section summarises some of the major methods employed.

### 20.8.1 Year-end manipulations

There are a number of stratagems companies have followed to reduce the cost of goods sold by inflating the inventory figure. These include the following.

#### Manipulating cut-off procedures

A major cause of discrepancy between physical and book inventory is the 'cut-off' date. In matching sales with cost of sales, it may be difficult to identify exactly into which period of account certain inventory movements should be placed, especially when the annual inventory count lasts many days or occurs at a date other than the last day of the financial year. It is customary to make an adjustment to the inventory figure, as shown in Figure 20.6.

**Figure 20.6 Adjusted inventory figure**

|  | £ |
|---|---|
| Inventory on 7 January 20X1 | XXX |
| *Less:* Purchases | (XXX) |
| *Add:* Cost of sales | XXX |
| Inventory at 31 December 20X0 | XXX |

Goods may be taken into inventory but the purchase invoices are not recorded or sales recorded and goods are still in the warehouse. An accurate record is required of movements between the inventory count date and the financial year-end.

The authors of *Fraudulent Financial Reporting: 1987–1997 – An Analysis of U.S. Public Companies* found that over half the frauds involved overstating revenues by recording revenues prematurely or fictitiously and that such overstatement tended to occur right at the end of the year – hence the need for adequate cut-off procedures. This was illustrated by Ahold's experience in the USA where subsidiary companies took credit for bulk discounts allowed by suppliers before inventory was actually received.

### Fictitious transfers to overseas locations

Year-end inventory is inflated by recording fictitious transfers of non-existent inventory, e.g. it was alleged by the SEC that certain officers of the Miniscribe Corporation had increased the company's inventory by recording fictitious transfers of non-existent inventory from a Colorado location to overseas locations where physical inventory counting would be more difficult for the auditors to verify or the goods are described as being 'in transit'.[6]

### Inaccurate inventory records

Where inventory records are poorly maintained it has been possible for senior management to fail to record material shrinkage due to loss and theft, as in the matter of Rite Aid Corporation.[7]

### Journal adjustments

In addition to suppressing purchase invoices, making fictitious transfers and failing to write off obsolete inventory or recognise inventory losses, the senior management may simply reduce the cost of goods sold by adjusting journal entries. Auditors pay particular attention to journal adjustments, questioning whether there have been significant adjusting entries that have increased the inventory balance and whether there have been material reversing entries made to the inventory account after the close of an accounting period.

## 20.8.2 Net realisable value (NRV)

Although the determination of net realisable value is dealt with extensively in the appendix to IAS 2, the extent to which provisions can be made to reduce cost to NRV is highly subjective and open to manipulation. A provision is an effective smoothing device and allows overcautious write-downs to be made in profitable years and consequent write-backs in unprofitable ones.

## 20.8.3 Overheads

The treatment of overheads has been dealt with extensively above and is probably the area that gives the greatest scope for manipulation. Including overhead in the inventory valuation has the effect of deferring the overhead's impact and so boosting profits. IAS 2 allows expenses incidental to the acquisition or production cost of an asset to be included in its cost. We have seen that this includes not only directly attributable production overheads, but also those which are indirectly attributable to production and interest on borrowed capital. IAS 2 provides guidelines on the classification of overheads to achieve an appropriate allocation, but in practice it is difficult to make these distinctions and auditors may find it difficult to challenge management on such matters.

The statement suggests that the allocation of overheads included in the valuation needs to be based on the company's normal level of activity. The cost of unused capacity should be written off in the current year. The auditor will insist that allocation should be based on normal activity levels, because if the company underproduces, the overhead per unit increases and can therefore lead to higher year-end values. The creative accountant will be looking for ways to manipulate these year-end values, so that in bad times costs are carried forward to more profitable accounting periods.

### 20.8.4 Other methods of creative accounting

#### Over- or understated quantities

A simple manipulation is to show more or less inventory than actually exists. If the commodity is messy and indistinguishable, the auditor may not have either the expertise or the will to verify measurements taken by the client's own employees. This lack of auditor measuring knowledge and involvement allowed one of the biggest frauds ever, which became known as 'the great salad oil swindle'.[8]

#### Understated obsolete inventory

Another obvious ploy is to include, in the inventory valuation, obsolete or 'dead' inventory. Of course, such inventory should be written off. However, management may be 'optimistic' that it can be sold, particularly in times of economic recession. In high-tech industries, unrealistic values may be placed on inventory that in times of rapid development becomes obsolete quickly.

#### Lack of marketability

This is a problem that investors need to be constantly aware of, particularly when a company experiences a downturn in demand but a pressure to maintain the semblance of growth. An example is provided by Lexmark[9] which was alleged to have made highly positive statements regarding strong sales and growth for its printers although there was intense competition in the industry – the company reported quarter after quarter of strong financial growth, whereas the actual position appeared to be very different with unmarketable inventory in excess of $25 million to be written down in the fourth quarter of fiscal year 2001. The share price of a company that conceals this type of information is maintained and allows insiders to offload their shareholding on an unsuspecting investing public.

## 20.9 Audit of the year-end physical inventory count

The problems of accounting for inventory are highlighted at the company's year-end. This is when the closing inventory figure to be shown in both the statement of comprehensive income and the statement of financial position is calculated. In practice, the company will assess the final inventory figure by physically counting all inventory held by the company for trade. The year-end inventory count is therefore an important accounting procedure, one in which the auditors are especially interested.

The auditor generally attends the inventory count to verify both the physical quantities and the procedure of collating those quantities. At the inventory count, values are rarely assigned to inventory items, so the problems facing the auditor relate to the identification of inventory items, their ownership, and their physical condition.

### 20.9.1 Identification of inventory items

The auditor will visit many companies in the course of a year and will spend a considerable time looking at accounting records. However, it is important for the auditor also to become familiar with each company's products by visiting the shop floor or production facilities during the audit. This makes identification of individual inventory items easier at the year-end. Distinguishing between two similar items can be crucial where there are large differences in value. For example, steel-coated brass rods look identical to steel rods, but their value to the company will be very different. It is important that they are not confused at inventory count because, once recorded on the inventory sheets, values are assigned, production carries on, and the error cannot be traced.

### 20.9.2 Physical condition of inventory items

Inventory in premium condition has a higher value than damaged inventory. The auditor must ensure that the condition of inventory is recorded at inventory count, so that the correct value is assigned to it. Items that are damaged or have been in inventory for a long period will be written down to their net realisable value (which may be nil) as long as adequate details are given by the inventory counter. Once again, this is a problem of identification, so the auditor must be able to distinguish between, for instance, rolls of first quality and faulty fabric. Similarly, items that have been in inventory for several inventory counts may have little value, and further enquiries about their status should be made at the time of inventory count.

### 20.9.3 Adjustment if inventory is taken after the year-end date

If inventory is counted after the year-end then an adjustment will need to be made to add back the cost of items sold and deduct the cost of purchases made after the year-end that have been taken into stock.

For example, assume that after the year-end, sales of £100,000 at cost plus 25% were made and dispatched and purchases of £45,000 were made and received. Inventory would be increased by £100,000 × 20/100 = £80,000 and reduced by £45,000.

### 20.9.4 Adjustment if errors are discovered

Typical errors could include:

- Sales invoices raised and posted but goods are awaiting dispatch – these should be excluded from the year-end inventory.
- Purchase invoices received and posted without waiting for the goods received note – the purchases figure should be reduced.
- Errors on pricing items or casting inventory sheets – these should be corrected when identified.
- Consumable stock might have been included – this should be taken out of inventory. The cost of sales will be higher, gross profit lower and the consumables expense reduced with no effect on the net profit.
- Omitting stock held by third parties on approval or consignment – these would need to be taken into closing inventory at cost.

## 20.10 Published accounts

Disclosure requirements in IAS 2 have already been indicated. The standard requires the accounting policies that have been applied to be stated and applied consistently from year to year. Inventory should be sub-classified in the statement of financial position or in the notes to the financial statements so as to indicate the amounts held in each of the main categories in the standard statement of financial position formats. But will the ultimate user of those financial statements be confident that the information disclosed is reliable, relevant and useful? We have already indicated many areas of subjectivity and creative accounting, but are such possibilities material?

In 1982 Westwick and Shaw examined the accounts of 125 companies with respect to inventory valuation and its likely impact on reported profit.[10] The results showed that the effect on profit before tax of a 1% error in closing inventory valuation ranged from a low of 0.18% to a high of 25.9% (in one case) with a median of 2.26%. The industries most vulnerable to such errors were household goods, textiles, mechanical engineering, contracting and construction.

Clearly, the existence of such variations has repercussions for such measures as ROCE, EPS and the current ratio. The research also showed that, in a sample of audit managers, 85% were of the opinion that the difference between a pessimistic and an optimistic valuation of the same inventory could be more than 6%.

IAS 2 has since been strengthened and these results may not be so indicative of the present situation. However, using the same principle, let us take a random selection of eight companies' recent annual accounts, apply a 5% increase in the closing inventory valuation and calculate the effect on EPS (taxation is simply taken at 35% on the change in inventory).

Figure 20.7 shows that, in absolute terms, the difference in pre-tax profits could be as much as £57.7 million and the percentage change ranges from 2.7% to 24.3%. Of particular note is the change in EPS, which tends to be the major market indicator of performance. In the case of the electrical retailer (company 1), a 5% error in inventory valuation could affect

**Figure 20.7 Impact of a 5% change in closing inventory**

| Company: | 1 | 2 | 3 | 4 | 5 | 6 | 7 | 8 |
|---|---|---|---|---|---|---|---|---|
| | £m | £m | £m | £m | £m | £m | £m | £m |
| Actual inventory | 390.0 | 428.0 | 1,154.0 | 509.0 | 509.0 | 280.0 | 360.0 | 232.0 |
| Actual pre-tax profit | 80.1 | 105.6 | 479.0 | 252.5 | 358.4 | 186.3 | 518.2 | 436.2 |
| Change in pre-tax profit | 19.5 | 21.4 | 57.7 | 25.2 | 25.5 | 14.0 | 18.0 | 11.6 |
| *Impact of a 5% change in closing inventory (%)* | | | | | | | | |
| (i)  Pre-tax profit | 24.3 | 20.3 | 12.0 | 10.0 | 7.1 | 7.5 | 3.5 | 2.7 |
| (ii)  Earnings per share | 27.0 | 25.0 | 12.0 | 9.3 | 8.4 | 6.9 | 3.4 | 3.4 |

Key to companies:
1  Electrical retailer
2  Textile, etc., manufacturer
3  Brewing, public houses, etc.
4  Retailer – diversified
5  Pharmaceutical and retail chemist
6  Industrial paints and fibres
7  Food retailer
8  Food retailer

EPS by as much as 27%. The inventory of such a company could well be vulnerable to such factors as changes in fashion, technology and economic recession.

## 20.11 Agricultural activity

### 20.11.1 The overall problem

Agricultural activity is subject to special considerations and so is governed by a separate IFRS, namely IAS 41. IAS 41 defines agricultural activity as 'the management by an entity of the biological transformation of biological assets for sale, into agricultural produce or into additional biological assets'. A biological asset is a living animal or plant.

The basic problem is that biological assets, and the produce derived from them (referred to in IAS 41 as 'agricultural produce'), cannot be measured using the cost-based concepts that form the bedrock of IAS 2 and IAS 16. This is because biological assets, such as cattle, for example, are not usually purchased; they are born and develop into their current state. Therefore different accounting methods are necessary.

### 20.11.2 The recognition and measurement of biological assets and agricultural produce

IAS 41 states that an entity should recognise a biological asset or agricultural produce when:

● the entity controls the asset as a result of a past event;
● it is probable that future economic benefits associated with the asset will flow to the entity;
● the fair value or cost of the asset can be measured reliably.

Rather than the usual cost-based concepts of measurement that are used for assets, IAS 41 states that assets of this type should be measured at their fair value less estimated costs of sale. The only (fairly rare) exception to this general measurement principle is if the asset's fair value cannot be estimated reliably. In such circumstances a biological asset is measured at cost (if available). Research[11] indicates that the adoption of fair value is avoided in countries such as France where there is a culture of conservatism, which means that they rebut the presumption that fair values can be determined with reliability to justify the use of historical cost. It also means that they are able to avoid the onerous valuation requirements of the standard.

The following is an extract from the 2015 Holmen AB annual report:

**Biological assets**
The Group divides all its forest assets for accounting purposes into growing forests, which are recognised as biological assets at fair value, and land, which is stated at acquisition cost. Any changes in the fair value of the growing forests are recognised in the income statement. Holmen's assessment is that there are no relevant market prices available that can be used to value forest holdings as extensive as Holmen's. Valuation is therefore carried out by estimating the present value of expected future cash flows (after deduction of selling costs) from the growing forests.

### 20.11.3 An illustrative example

A farmer owned a dairy herd. At the start of the period the herd contained 100 animals that were two years old and 50 newly born calves. At the end of the period a further 30 calves had been born. None of the herd died during the period. Relevant fair value details were as follows:

|  | Start of period $ | End of period $ |
|---|---|---|
| Newly born calves | 50 | 55 |
| One-year-old animals | 60 | 65 |
| Two-year-old animals | 70 | 75 |
| Three-year-old animals | 75 | 80 |

The change in the fair value of the herd is $3,400, made up as follows:

Fair value at end of the year = $(100 \times \$80) = (50 \times \$65) = (30 \times \$55) = \$12,900$
Fair value at start of the year = $(100 \times \$70) = (50 \times \$50)$ $= \$9,500$

IAS 41 requires that the change in the fair value of the herd be reconciled as follows:

|  | $ |
|---|---|
| Price change – opening newly born calves: 50 ($55 − $50) | 250 |
| Physical change of opening newly born calves: 50 ($65 − $55) | 500 |
| Price change of opening two-year-old animals: 100 ($75 − $70) | 500 |
| Physical change of opening two-year-old animals: 100 ($80 − $75) | 500 |
| Due to birth of new calves: 30 × $55 | 1,650 |
| Total change | 3,400 |

The costs incurred in maintaining the herd would all be charged in the statement of comprehensive income in the relevant period.

### 20.11.4 Agricultural produce

Examples of agricultural produce would be milk from a dairy herd or crops from a cornfield. Such produce is sold by a farmer in the ordinary course of business and is inventory. The initial carrying value of the inventory at the point of 'harvest' is its fair value less costs to sell at that date. Agricultural entities then apply IAS 2 to the inventory using the initial carrying value as 'cost'.

### 20.11.5 Land

Despite its importance in agricultural activity, IAS 41 does not apply to agricultural land, which is accounted for in accordance with IAS 16. Where biological assets are physically attached to land (e.g. crops in a field) then it is often possible to compute the fair value of the biological assets by computing the fair value of the combined asset and deducting the fair value of the land alone.

### 20.11.6 Minerals

The standard does not apply to the measurement of inventories of producers of agricultural and forest products, agricultural produce after harvest, and minerals and mineral products, to the extent that they are measured at net realisable value in accordance with well-established industry practices.

### 20.11.7 Government grants relating to biological assets

As mentioned in Chapter 17 such grants are not subject to IAS 20 – the general standard on this subject. Under IAS 41 the IASB view is more consistent with the principles of the *Framework* than the provisions of IAS 20. Under IAS 41 grants are recognised as income when the entity becomes entitled to receive it. This removes the fairly dubious credit balance 'Deferred income' that arises under the IAS 20 approach and does not appear to satisfy the *Framework* definition of a liability.

### 20.11.8 Fair value or historic cost option?

An interesting research project[10] carrying out an empirical investigation of the implications of IAS 41 for the harmonisation of farm accounting practices in Australia, France and the UK found that agricultural entities in all three countries are using a variety of valuation methods under IAS 41 and that there is a lack of comparability of disclosure practices. It was their view that IAS 41 has failed to enhance the international comparability of accounting practices in the agricultural sector. The following problems have been identified.

#### Valuation method

The researchers found that although historical cost is the most common valuation basis for biological assets, a variety of proxies for fair value are used, such as net present value, independent/external valuation, net realisable value and market price, both within and across countries.

#### National characteristics impact on choice of method

Some countries may be more conservative and private than others. These characteristics and attitudes existed pre-IFRS[12] and do not change merely because the IASB has produced IFRSs.

#### Fair national or fair global value?

In the European Union IAS 41 requires biological assets to be valued by reference to artificial and highly subsidised or politically mediated market prices. This allows European farmers to export to developing countries at prices which are substantially below production costs.

#### Cost–benefit considerations

Small and medium-sized companies consider that the cost of compliance is too high and this has been recognised by the IASB which provide that, for biological assets, the fair value through profit or loss model is required only when fair value is readily determinable without undue cost or effort. If fair value is not used SMEs follow the cost–depreciation–impairment model.

## Summary

IAS 2 defines inventory and the methods of arriving at cost that are acceptable.

Valuation methods used must result in a reasonable approximation to actual cost.

Inventory manipulation can have a material impact on reported profits and balance sheet ratios to achieve a higher or lower profit in the current reporting period.

Auditors have an involvement in advising on internal controls to protect physical inventory, ensure that proper physical counts are made at the year-end and appropriate methods and procedures are in place to determine cost and net realisable value.

Although legal requirements and IAS 2 have improved the reporting requirements, many areas of subjective judgement can have substantial effects on the reporting of financial information.

## REVIEW QUESTIONS

1 Discuss the extent to which individual judgements might affect inventory valuation, e.g. changing the basis of overhead absorption.

2 Discuss the acceptability of the LIFO and replacement cost methods of inventory valuation and why the IASB has not permitted all methods to be used.

3 Explain the criteria to be applied when selecting the method to be used for allocating administrative costs.

4 Discuss the effect on work in progress and finished goods valuation if the net realisable value of the raw material is lower than cost at the statement of financial position date.

5 Discuss why the accurate valuation of inventory is so crucial if the financial statements are to show a true and fair view.

6 The following is an extract from the Anheuser-Busch InBev 2015 Annual Report:

### Inventories

Inventories are valued at the lower of cost and net realizable value.

The cost of finished products and work in progress comprises raw materials, other production materials, direct labor, other direct cost and an allocation of fixed and variable overhead based on normal operating capacity.

Discuss the possible effects on profits if the company did not use normal operating activity.

7 It has been suggested that 'Given national characteristics it will be impossible to ensure that financial statements that comply with IFRSs will ever be comparable.' Discuss whether auditors can make this change.

**8** The following is an extract from the 2013 Annual Report of SIPEF NV:

> Because of the inherent uncertainty associated with the valuation at fair value of the biological assets due to the volatility of the prices of the agricultural produce and the absence of a liquid market, their carrying value may differ from their realisable value.

Given the inherent uncertainty in applying IAS 41, discuss whether the pre-IAS 41 practice of value at historical cost is preferable for the statement of financial position.

## EXERCISES

### Question 1

Sunhats Ltd manufactures patent hats. It carries inventory of these and sells to wholesalers and retailers via a number of salespeople. The following expenses are charged in the profit and loss account:

*Wages of:*      Storemen and factory foremen

*Salaries of:*      Production manager, personnel officer, buyer, salespeople, sales manager, accountant, company secretary

*Other:*      Directors' fees, rent and rates, electric power, repairs, depreciation, carriage outwards, advertising, bad debts, interest on bank overdraft, development expenditure for new types of hat.

**Required:**
**Which of these expenses can reasonably be included in the valuation of inventory?**

### * Question 2

Purchases of a certain product during July were:

| July | | |
|---|---|---|
| | 1 | 100 units @ £10.00 |
| | 12 | 100 units @ £9.80 |
| | 15 | 50 units @ £9.60 |
| | 20 | 100 units @ £9.40 |

Units sold during the month were:

| July | | |
|---|---|---|
| | 10 | 80 units |
| | 14 | 100 units |
| | 30 | 90 units |

**Required:**
**Assuming no opening inventories:**
**(a) Determine the cost of goods sold for July under three different valuation methods.**
**(b) Discuss the advantages and/or disadvantages of each of these methods.**
**(c) A physical inventory count revealed a shortage of five units. Show how you would bring this into account.**

## * Question 3

Alpha Ltd makes one standard article. You have been given the following information:

1 The inventory sheets at the year-end show the following items:

| Raw materials: | Finished goods: |
| --- | --- |
| 100 tons of steel: | 100 finished units: |
| Cost £140 per ton | Cost of materials £50 per unit |
| Present price £130 per ton | Labour cost £150 per unit |
| | Selling price £500 per unit |
| | |
| *40 semi-finished units* | *10 damaged finished units:* |
| Cost of materials £50 per unit | Cost to rectify the damage £200 per unit |
| Labour cost to date £100 per unit | Selling price £500 per unit (when rectified) |
| Selling price £500 per unit (completed) | |

2 Manufacturing overheads are 100% of labour cost.

Selling and distribution expenses are £60 per unit (mainly salespeople's commission and freight charges).

**Required:**
From the information in notes 1 and 2, state the amounts to be included in the statement of financial position of Alpha Ltd in respect of inventory. State also the principles you have applied.

## * Question 4

Beta Ltd commenced business on 1 January and is making up its first year's accounts. The company uses standard costs. The company owns a variety of raw materials and components for use in its manufacturing business. The accounting records show the following:

| | Standard cost of purchases | Adverse (favourable) variances Price variance | Usage variance |
| --- | --- | --- | --- |
| | £ | £ | £ |
| July | 10,000 | 800 | (400) |
| August | 12,000 | 1,100 | 100 |
| September | 9,000 | 700 | (300) |
| October | 8,000 | 900 | 200 |
| November | 12,000 | 1,000 | 300 |
| December | 10,000 | 800 | (200) |
| Cumulative figures for whole year | 110,000 | 8,700 | (600) |

Raw materials control account balance at year-end is £30,000 (at standard cost).

**Required:**
The company's draft statement of financial position includes 'Inventories, at the lower of cost and net realisable value £80,000'. This includes raw materials £30,000: do you consider this to be acceptable? If so, why? If not, state what you consider to be an acceptable figure.
(*Note:* for the purpose of this exercise, you may assume that the raw materials will realise more than cost.)

## * Question 5

Uptodate plc's financial year ended on 31 March 20X8. Inventory taken on 7 April 20X8 amounted to £200,000. The following information needs to be taken into account:

(i) Purchases made during the seven days to 7 April amounted to £40,000. Invoices had not been received and only 20% had been delivered by 7 April. These had been taken into inventory.

(ii) Purchases of £10,000, which had been ordered but not paid for before the year-end, had been received before 31 March. However, as the invoices had not been received by 31 March they have not been included in the inventory.

(iii) Purchases of £5,000, which had been ordered and paid for before the year-end, had not been received by 31 March.

(iv) Purchases of £12,000, ordered and paid for by the year-end, were in a bonded warehouse awaiting customs clearance at 31 March. These were eventually delivered to the company on 9 April.

**Required:**
**Calculate the revised year-end inventory as at 31 March 20X8.**

## Question 6

Hasty plc's financial year ended on 31 March 20X8. Inventory taken on 7 April 20X8 amounted to £100,000. The following information needs to be taken into account:

(i) Sales invoices totalling £9,000 were raised during the seven days after the year-end. £1,500 of this had not been dispatched by 7 April. The company policy was to add 20% to cost.

(ii) Sales returns received on 6 April totalled £600.

(iii) Goods with an invoice value of £6,000 had been sent to customers on approval in February 20X8. £3,600 had been returned in March 20X8. The company policy was to add 20% to cost and not to process the invoice until customers gave notice of purchasing.

(iv) Goods bought in to satisfy a one-off customer order at £575 had been sent on approval in November 20X7 on a pro forma invoice for £850. These had been taken into inventory at the pro forma price.

**Required:**
**Calculate revised inventory as at 31 March 20X8.**

## Question 7

The statement of income of Bottom, a manufacturing company, for the year ending 31 January 20X2 is as follows:

|                          | $000      |
| ------------------------ | --------- |
| Revenue                  | 75,000    |
| Cost of sales            | (38,000)  |
| Gross profit             | 37,000    |
| Other operating expenses | (9,000)   |
| Profit from operations   | 28,000    |
| Investment income        |           |
| Finance cost             | (4,000)   |
| Profit before tax        | 24,000    |
| Income tax expense       | (7,000)   |
| Net profit for the period | 17,000   |

Note – accounting policies

Bottom has used the LIFO method of inventory valuation but the directors wish to assess the implications of using the FIFO method. Relevant details of the inventories of Bottom are as follows:

| Date | Inventory valuation under: | |
| --- | --- | --- |
| | FIFO | LIFO |
| | $000 | $000 |
| 1 February 20X1 | 9,500 | 9,000 |
| 31 January 20X2 | 10,200 | 9,300 |

**Required:**
Redraft the statement of income of Bottom using the FIFO method of inventory valuation and explain how the change would need to be recognised in the published financial statements, if implemented.

## * Question 8

Agriculture is a key business activity in many parts of the world, particularly in developing countries. Following extensive discussions with, and funding from, the World Bank, the International Accounting Standards Committee (IASC) developed an accounting standard relating to agricultural activity. IAS 41 *Agriculture* was published in 2001 to apply to accounting periods beginning on or after 1 January 2003.

Sigma prepares financial statements to 30 September each year. On 1 October 2003 Sigma carried out the following transactions:

- Purchased a large piece of land for $20 million.
- Purchased 10,000 dairy cows (average age at 1 October 2003, two years) for $1 million.
- Received a grant of $400,000 towards the acquisition of the cows. This grant was non-returnable.

During the year ending 30 September 2004 Sigma incurred the following costs:

- $500,000 to maintain the condition of the animals (food and protection).
- $300,000 in breeding fees to a local farmer.

On 1 April 2004, 5,000 calves were born. There were no other changes in the number of animals during the year ended 30 September 2004. At 30 September 2004, Sigma had 10,000 litres of unsold milk in inventory. The milk was sold shortly after the year-end at market prices.

Information regarding fair values is as follows:

| Item | Fair value less point-of-sale costs | | |
| --- | --- | --- | --- |
| | 1 October 2003 | 1 April 2004 | 30 September 2004 |
| | $ m | $ m | $ m |
| Land | 20 | 22 | 24 |
| New-born calves (per calf) | 20 | 21 | 22 |
| Six-month-old calves (per calf) | 23 | 24 | 25 |
| Two-year-old cows (per cow) | 90 | 92 | 94 |
| Three-year-old cows (per cow) | 93 | 95 | 97 |
| Milk (per litre) | 0.6 | 0.55 | 0.55 |

**Required:**
(a) Discuss how the IAS 41 requirements regarding the recognition and measurement of biological assets and agricultural produce are consistent with the IASC Framework for the Preparation *and Presentation of Financial Statements*.

(b) Prepare extracts from the statement of comprehensive income and the statement of financial position that show how the transactions entered into by Sigma in respect of the purchase and maintenance of the dairy herd would be reflected in the financial statements of the entity for the year ended 30 September 2004. You do not need to prepare a reconciliation of changes in the carrying amount of biological assets.

*(ACCA DipIFR 2004)*

## Notes

1 IAS 2 *Inventories,* IASB, revised 2004.
2 'A guide to accounting standards – valuation of inventory and work-in-progress', *Accountants Digest,* Summer 1984.
3 http://soccrim.clas.ufl.edu/files/nrssfinalreport2012.pdf
4 M. Perry, 'Valuation problems force FD to quit', *Accountancy Age,* 15 March 2001, p. 2.
5 The report appears on www.coso.org/index.htm
6 See www.sec.gov/litigation/admin/34-41729.htm
7 See www.sec.gov/litigation/admin/34-46099.htm
8 E. Woolf, 'Auditing the stocks – part II', *Accountancy,* May 1976, pp. 108–110.
9 See http://securities.stanford.edu/1022/LXK01-01/
10 C. Westwick and D. Shaw, 'Subjectivity and reported profit', *Accountancy,* June 1982, pp. 129–131.
11 C. Elad and K. Herbohn, *Implementing Fair Value Accounting in the Agricultural Sector,* ICAS Research Report, 2011, www.icas.org.uk/site/cms/download/res/elad_Exec_Summary_Feb_2011.pdf
12 C. Nobes, 'Different versions of IFRS practice', in C. Nobes and R. Parker (eds), *Comparative International Accounting* (10th edition), FT Prentice Hall, 2008, pp. 145–156.

# CHAPTER 21

# Construction contracts

## 21.1 Introduction

Construction contracts have been given special attention because of the size, duration and special challenges which arise in accounting for them. In this chapter we will be addressing the issues involved in supplying services which are of long duration and thus raise issues of whether revenue should be recognised continuously or whether the contract should be viewed as a series of smaller service provisions (such as a multi-level building which could be viewed as supplying one completed level after another) or whether the completion of the total contract is the delivery of the contracted service. In addition to the accounting for the revenue recognition there are a number of issues relating to the valuation of the work in progress.

The basic principles which apply to revenue recognition both currently and in the future, are applied in construction contracts. So in essence this chapter can be seen as illustrating the application of the revenue standards in a complex business situation together with the application of impairment accounting (see Chapter 17) in arriving at the valuation of the resulting assets. Both these issues will be addressed in this chapter.

We also explain the basic accounting for contracts of public–private partnerships, which have become increasingly popular for undertaking major infrastructure construction and operations.

### Objectives

By the end of this chapter, you should be:

- aware of some of the historical developments in the accounting for construction contracts such that you understand how to read accounts involving construction activities following IAS 11;
- able to prepare construction accounts in accordance with IFRS 15 revenue recognition rules and to record assets arising from construction contracts;
- understanding accounting for public–private partnerships.

## 21.2 The need to replace IAS 11 *Construction Contracts*[1]

Pre-2011 it had been considered that construction contracts were of such complexity that they warranted a separate standard (IAS 11 *Construction Contracts*) and the general rules for revenue recognition set out in IAS 18 *Revenue*[2] were specially excluded. In their place IAS

11 established a separate set of rules under which revenue is recognised progressively as the item is built, matching expenses, writing off unrecoverable costs and identifying those costs to be carried forward as assets which are expected to be recovered in the future.

However, the presence of two different sets of rules in relation to revenue recognition has not sat comfortably with the idea of having a coherent set of standards. Also IAS 11 was thought to contain insufficient guidance where the construction contract was complex.

Accordingly the IASB and the FASB have produced a joint revenue recognition standard IFRS 15 which includes the rules which will in the future govern accounting for construction contracts. IFRS 15 will be effective for annual periods beginning on or after 1 January 2017 with the option for earlier adoption. Once a company adopts IFRS 15 the old IAS 11 *Construction Costs* will be superseded and will no longer be applicable. Until then IAS 11 is still operational.

### 21.2.1 IAS 11 *Construction Contracts*

IAS 11 *Construction Contracts* defines a construction contract as:

> A contract specifically negotiated for the construction of an asset or a combination of assets that are closely inter-related or inter-dependent in terms of their design, technology and function or their ultimate purpose or use.

Some construction contracts are **fixed-price contracts**, where the contractor agrees to a fixed contract price. However, where the contract extends over a longer period it is quite normal for such fixed-price contracts to include escalation clauses. An escalation clause essentially means that when specified events beyond the control of the contractor (such as union wage rates or prices of specified material, such as iron reinforcing used in the construction) increase then the price of the contract is amended according to a previously agreed formula to allow the contractor to recover all or part of the cost increases. Thus escalation clauses are a device for sharing or transferring specified risks associated with the contract.

Other construction contracts are **cost-plus contracts**, where the contractor is reimbursed for allowable costs, plus a percentage of these costs or alternatively a fixed fee is added to the allowable costs. This type of contract would be appropriate where the amount of materials or labour needed is unclear as may be the case in an innovative project.

Some examples of construction contracts would involve building ships, aeroplanes, buildings, dams, highways and bridges.

Construction contracts are normally assessed and accounted for individually. However, in certain circumstances construction contracts may be combined or segmented. Combination or segmentation is appropriate when:

- a group of contracts is negotiated as a single package and the contracts are performed together in a continuous sequence (combination); and

- separate proposals have been submitted for each asset and the costs and revenues of each asset can readily be identified (segmentation).

A key accounting issue is when the revenues and costs (and therefore net income) under a construction contract should be recognised. There are two major possibilities:

- Only recognise net income when the contract is complete – the *completed contracts method*.

- Recognise a proportion of net income over the period of the contract – this is currently achieved using the *percentage of completion method*.

IAS 11 requires the latter approach, provided the overall contract result can be predicted with reasonable certainty. If that is not the case then the completed contract method is used.

## 21.3 Identification of contract revenue under IAS 11

Contract revenue should comprise:

(a) the initial amount of revenue agreed in the contract; and

(b) variations in contract work, claims and incentives payments, to the extent that:

  (i) it is probable that they will result in revenue;

  (ii) they are capable of being reliably measured.

Variations to the initially agreed contract price occur due to events such as:

● cost escalation clauses;

● claims for additional revenue by the contractor due to customer-caused delays or changes in the specification or design;

● incentive payments when specified performance standards are met or exceeded;

● penalty clauses representing agreed damages caused by failure to complete by the contracted date.

Incentive payments might apply to a toll road where early completion would allow additional revenue to be collected by the owner of the road. Penalty clauses might apply to a construction contract because the client would incur additional costs as a result of delays such as temporary storage expenses if they cannot move into the new factory at the agreed handover date. Penalties are a way of ensuring the client can plan ahead for the transfer of their business to the new premises at an agreed date, confident that the contractor will do everything in their power to complete on time.

The same recognition rules apply to variations as apply to the original recognition, namely the probability of occurrence is high and the amount can be predicted with reasonable certainty.

## 21.4 Identification of contract costs under IAS 11

IAS 11 classifies costs that can be identified with contracts under four headings:

● Costs that directly relate to the specific contract, such as:

  ● site labour;

  ● cost of materials;

  ● depreciation of plant and equipment used on the contract;

  ● costs of moving plant and materials to and from the contract site;

  ● costs of hiring plant and equipment;

  ● costs of design and technical assistance that are directly related to the contract;

  ● the estimated costs of rectification and guarantee work;[3]

  ● claims from third parties.

- Costs that are attributable to contract activity in general and can be allocated to specific contracts, such as:

  - insurance;

  - costs of design and technical assistance that are not directly related to a specific contract;

  - construction overheads.

  *Note:* Costs of this nature need to be allocated on a systematic and rational basis, based on the normal level of construction activity.

- The construction contract itself may specify costs which can be recovered under the contract and those of course can be charged to the contract.

- Pre-contract bid costs of obtaining a contract.

- Pre-contract bid costs

An interesting area is the cost of tendering. This may seem an insignificant cost but in relation to major complex contracts these costs may amount to many millions of pounds.

*The standard says these may be charged to the contract if at the time it is probable that the tender will be successful.* That is a difficult criterion to satisfy. Generally if a contractor is bidding for a contract against other bidders the costs of bidding would only be included in contract costs once the bidder had been selected or had received preferred bidder status. If as a result of the uncertainties involved the cost of tendering is written off in one financial year, and if the contract is awarded in the next financial year, it is **not** possible to write back the tendering expenses of the previous period as an asset. If an asset is established it has to be amortised over the period of the contract.

The following is an extract from the Balfour Beatty 2015 Annual Report:

### 2.8 Pre-contract bid costs and recovery

Pre-contract costs are expensed as incurred until it is virtually certain that a contract will be awarded, from which time further pre-contract costs are recognised as an asset and charged as an expense over the period of the contract. Amounts recovered in respect of pre-contract costs that have been written-off are deferred and amortised over the life of the contract.

### 21.4.1 Examples of recognition of revenue and statement of financial position

#### (i) Recognition of revenue

Johnson Matthey in their 2016 accounts, which follow IAS 11, state that their accounting policy is:

### Long term contracts

Where the outcome of a long term contract can be estimated reliably, revenue and costs are recognized *by reference to the stage of completion.* This is measured by the proportion that contract costs incurred to date bear to the estimated total contract costs.

Where the outcome of a long term contract cannot be estimated reliably, contract revenue is recognized to the extent of contract costs incurred that it is probable will be recoverable. Contract costs are recognized as expenses in the period in which they are incurred.

When it is probable that the total contract costs will exceed total contract revenue, the expected loss is recognized as an expense immediately.

Note the following interesting issues:

(a) revenue and expenses are recognised on the basis of stage of completion;

(b) when there is uncertainty regarding the ability of the contract to make a profit overall then the costs incurred that probably won't be recovered are immediately written off as an expense.

### (ii) Recognition of revenue when there have been variations

Balfour Beatty in their 2015 annual accounts report their accounting policy as:

> Revenue in respect of variations to contracts, claims and incentive payments is recognised when it is probable it will be agreed by the client. Revenue in respect of claims is recognised when negotiations have reached an advanced stage such that it is probable that the client will accept the claim and the probable amount can be measured reliably.

The difficulties in finalising the contract revenue, given the variations for escalation allowances and modifications to contracts and rectification of claimed deficiencies, are outlined.

### (iii) Statement of financial position

The statement of financial position presentation for construction contracts should show as an asset – *Gross amounts due from customers* – the following net amount:

● total costs incurred to date;

● plus attributable profits (or less foreseeable losses);

● less any progress billings to the customer.

Where for any contract the above amount is negative, it should be shown as a liability – *Gross amounts due to customers*.

Advances – amounts received by the contractor before the related work is performed – should be shown as a liability – effectively a payment on account by the customer.

An extract from the Lend Lease Group 2013 accounts illustrates the above:

| b. Construction Work in Progress | 2013 | 2012 |
|---|---|---|
| Construction work in progress comprises: | A$m | A$m |
| Contract costs incurred to date | 66,411.3 | 64,388.9 |
| Profit recognised to date | 3,143.2 | 3,095.6 |
| | 69,554.5 | 67,484.5 |
| *Less:* Progress billings received and receivable on contracts | (69,726.3) | (67,780.4) |
| **Net construction work in progress** | (171.8) | (295.9) |
| Costs in excess of billings – inventories | 612.0 | 505.8 |
| Billings in excess of costs – trade payables | (783.8) | (801.7) |
| | (171.8) | (295.9) |

## 21.5 IFRS 15 treatment of construction contracts[5]

When companies adopt IFRS 15 for revenue recognition then automatically they follow that standard for construction contracts and hence IAS 11 is no longer applicable. Some of the important provisions of the proposed new revenue rules include the requirement to:

- recognise revenue when control passes;
- account for onerous performance obligations as soon as they become apparent so as to be consistent with rules relating to asset recognition and impairment; and
- disclose information to allow report readers to assess the risks and rewards likely to be associated with ongoing contracts.

The main differences relate to the timing of revenue recognition. In many other respects the accounting is the same as under IAS 11.

### Recognise revenue when control passes

We discussed in Chapter 8 on revenue recognition the fact that recognition is dependent on the transfer of control rather than transfer of legal title. This will also apply to construction contracts. However, the fact that construction contracts often extend over several years and are not easily subdivided into parts makes the issue of importance to companies involved in substantial contracts. If the *revenue recognition* rules change as proposed, then it is likely that *construction* contracts will be altered in the future to more clearly specify when 'control' of components of the construction contracts pass to the clients. This illustrates that accounting standards are not neutral but are likely to alter how business is done.

### Construction over a long time

With construction contracts which take a long time to complete, the identification of when control passes can be complex. Generally these contracts fall under what the standard calls 'performance obligations satisfied over time'. Two relevant types of contracts are provided in paragraph 35:

- the entity's performance *creates* or enhances an asset (for example work in progress) that the customer controls as the asset is created or enhanced . . . ; and
- the entity's performance *does not create* an asset with an alternative use to the entity . . . and the entity has an enforceable right to payment for performance completed to date.

Whilst these conditions depend on the factual and legal situations of each case a typical example of the former would be the construction of houses in a property development where the developer owns the land and sells the houses as they are completed. An example of the latter could be the construction of a motorway which is on government land and hence cannot be diverted to other customers.

An example of an alternative use asset might be the production of a boat which is of a general category such that it could be readily sold in the open market (e.g. a leisure boat). However, if the boat was designed to very specific needs of a particular client and therefore would not be ideal for other potential customers then such a boat would not have an alternative use.

As stated before, it is difficult to generalise and each case has to be assessed on its own facts when the contract commences. One of those facts is the contractual document. If in doubt one has to go back to the basic principal – when does control pass? Additional guidance appears in Appendix B to the standard.

*Determining the amount of the contract earned*

For items where control passes over time the producer has to determine what part of the contract amount has been earned for the accounting period and the amount to show as assets at the closing date. There are two ways of measuring the amount of revenue earned, namely the output approach and the input approach.

*The output method*

The output method in many ways appears to be a good way to measure progress, provided reliable information is available at a reasonable cost. In some types of work the contract provides for an independent expert such as an architect to periodically certify the amount of work which has been completed. In such circumstances the certification will either state the contract amount which has been earned or the percentage of the contract which has been completed. Another variant of the output method might be that when certain milestones have been met (say the concrete has been laid in a contract to build a road) an engineer may certify that the work is of the appropriate quality and that the milestone has been met. This is often linked to progress payments with the expert certifying the amount to be paid or allowing that amount to be determined such as when the payment is the work to the milestone less a retention amount to cover future contingencies or future remedial work.

*The input method*

When the conditions for use of the output method are not met then the input method can be used. The input method measures the rate of progress in terms of the costs incurred to date as a proportion of the total expected costs to complete the contract. As some costs such as inefficiencies or costs to correct errors do not generate revenue or convey value to the customer they should be written off immediately as an expense and are not considered in measuring the rate of progress. The percentage of necessary costs compared to the most recent assessment of the total cost to complete the project approximates the proportion of the revenue which will be deemed earned.

The accounting does not appear to substantially alter previous requirements. The main difference is when to recognise revenue and that includes the requirement to only recognise revenue when it is probable that the entity will be entitled to the consideration.

*Onerous contracts*

Consistent with that realistic but cautious approach the standard accounts for onerous contracts as soon as it becomes apparent that the contract will not be profitable. In other words, when it becomes apparent that the contract will *not* be profitable the first step will be to recognise that some, or all, of the previously recognised contract work in progress has been impaired and needs to be written off. The impairment is recorded as an expense. When that asset has been extinguished, it is necessary to create a liability to reflect the present value of obligations which are still to be incurred but that will not be recovered through the contract price. This is not a new provision.

## Disclosure

The disclosure requirement is explained in the proposed guidance:

> 110 The objective of the disclosure requirements is for an entity to disclose sufficient information to enable users of financial statements to understand the nature, amount, timing, and uncertainty of revenue and cash flows arising from contracts with customers.

To achieve that objective, an entity shall disclose qualitative and quantitative information about all of the following:

(a) its contracts with customers . . . ;

(b) the significant judgments, and changes in judgments, made in applying this Standard to those contacts . . . ; and

(c) any assets recognized from the costs to obtain or fulfil a contract with a customer . . . '

## 21.6 An approach when a contract can be separated into components

To keep track of the construction contracts the accounting has many similarities with job costing where costs are accumulated by job and, if there are distinct components of the job, then separate records may be required for each component as a basis for invoicing.

For example, if you are constructing a shopping centre and you want to complete it in stages so that the landlord can have the first stage operational whilst the second stage is still under construction, you may need two 'jobs' in the books. Care will need to be taken to ensure the expenses are charged to the right stage with subjective decisions such as how to allocate the costs for preparing the land and installing the services. Then when the first stage is complete you may finalise the profit calculation for the first stage. You will have to keep track of the revenue earned to that stage being the contract price for stage one adjusted for contract variations. You will have in the job costing the expenses which relate to stage one. That will enable you to calculate the profit to that stage.

If the contract is not going according to plan you will have to recognise the losses you expect to make on the total contract by forecasting further costs to complete the contract and comparing it with the expected revenue. The total revenue would be the contract price plus allowances which can be invoiced under the escalation clauses plus any revenue arising from agreed variations to the original contract.

So from the above we have to keep track of:

(a) total costs incurred on the contract to date;

(b) the amount of revenue recognised in the accounts to date;

(c) the costs incurred in relation to the revenue which has been recognised;

(d) the amount of the profit or loss recorded on the contract so far;

(e) the amount invoiced to the customer so far; and

(f) the amount unpaid by the customer.

## 21.7 Accounting for a contract – an example

### First year of contract

ABC has two construction contracts (Contract A and Contract B) outstanding at the end of its financial year, 30 June 20X0. Details for Contract A are as follows:

|  | Contract A £000 |
| --- | --- |
| Total contract price | 25,000 |
| Cost incurred to date | 5,500 |
| Anticipated future costs | 14,500 |
| Progress billing | — |
| Agreed price for the component completed | 7,000 |

#### Step one: Review the anticipated overall position for the contract

|  | Contract A £000 |
| --- | --- |
| *Total expected cost to complete the contract:* | |
| Costs to date | 5,500 |
| Anticipated future costs | 14,500 |
| Expected total cost | 20,000 |
| Contract price | 25,000 |
| Forecast profit on the contract | 5,000 |

Since the contract is expected to be profitable overall, the profit on the component completed to date of £7,000,000 − 5,500,000 or £1,500,000 can be fully realised. If on the other hand the forecast total cost was greater than the revenue, then the anticipated cost overrun would need to be recorded as an expense/loss in the current period.

#### Step two: The statement of comprehensive income

|  | Contract A £000 | £000 |
| --- | --- | --- |
| Revenue | | 7,000 |
| *Less:* | | |
| Cost incurred to date | 5,500 | |
| Allowance for future losses | — | |
| Total expenses | | 5,500 |
| Net income | | 1,500 |

#### Step three: The statement of financial position entries

As the statement of financial position is a cumulative statement all figures have to be prepared on that basis.

|  | Contract A £000 |
| --- | --- |
| Costs incurred to date | 5,500 |
| *Add:* profits to date | 1,500 |
| *Less:* recognised losses to date | — |
| Gross work done for the customer | 7,000 |
| *Less:* amount billed to the customer | — |
| Gross amount due from customers | 7,000 |

Note: it is assumed that an identifiable phase of the contract had been completed for which the contract specifies the appropriate revenue is £7,000,000.

If the amount of revenue had not been given in the question then the amount of the revenue has to calculated. Suppose that the conditions have been satisfied for the output method to be used and that revenue is to be based on an independent architect's estimate of the proportion of the contract that has been completed. For example, assuming that the architect said the contract was 28% complete then the revenue to be recognised would be that proportion of the total contract price of £25,000,000 or 25,000,000 × 0.28 equals £7,000,000.

If there was no independent certified percentage of completion then the input method has to be used. In that event the completion percentage would be estimated by dividing the expenses incurred to date (£5,500,000) by the anticipated total cost to complete the project (£20,000,000) to give 27.5% and the revenue recognised at 0.275 × £25,000,000 (the total contract price) i.e. £6,875,000.

The new standard stresses satisfaction of performance obligations. One way in which this can be satisfied is for the company to create or enhance an asset that the customer controls as the creation or enhancement takes place. Alternatively completion of part of the work is associated with an enforceable right to payment, and there is no reason to expect the whole project is not going to be completed in compliance with the contract terms, then the service obligation will be seen to be accomplished. Under this alternative the approach the treatment may be similar to the method applied under IAS 11 but the conditions for its application are different.

### Year two of the contract

Details of the transactions for Contract A for the year ended 30 June 20X1 are outlined below.

|  | Contract A £000 |
|---|---|
| Total contract price | 25,000 |
| Costs incurred to date | 14,000 |
| Anticipated future costs to complete the contract | 6,000 |
| Certified revenue for work completed to date | 15,000 |
| Progress billings | 12,000 |
| Cash received for items invoiced | 12,000 |
| Advance payments | 4,000 |

#### Step one: Review the anticipated overall result for the contract

|  | Contract A £000 |
|---|---|
| Costs incurred to date | 14,000 |
| Anticipated future costs to complete | 6,000 |
| Total expected costs | 20,000 |
| Contract price | 25,000 |
| Anticipated profit | 5,000 |

Since the project is expected to be profitable there is no requirement to make accruals for losses.

*Step two: Prepare the relevant part of the comprehensive income statement*

|  | £000 | £000 |
|---|---|---|
| Total revenue for stages one and two | | 15,000 |
| Less revenue already recognised | | 7,000 |
| Revenue for the period | | 8,000 |
| Less expenses: | | |
| Additional expenses incurred in the period (14,000 − 5,500) | 8,500 | |
| Additional anticipated loss accrual | — | |
| Total expenses | | 8,500 |
| Loss for the year | | (500) |

*Step three: Prepare the statement of financial position entries*

|  | Contract A £000 |
|---|---|
| Costs incurred to date | 14,000 |
| *Add:* recognised profits | 1,500 |
| *Less:* recognised losses | (500) |
| Work performed for the customer | 15,000 |
| *Less:* progress billings | 12,000 |
| Gross amount due from customers and included in work in progress | 3,000 |

Also there would be a liability for £4,000 revenue paid in advance.

## 21.8 Illustration – loss-making contract using the step approach

### First year of contract

The terms of Contract B specify that 50% of the contract price is due on completion of stage one and 50% on completion of stage two. The details as at 30 June 20X1 are as follows:

|  | Contract B £000 |
|---|---|
| Total contract price | 20,000 |
| Costs incurred to date | 13,000 |
| Anticipated future costs | 11,000 |
| Progress billings | 10,000 |
| Advance payments | nil |

At 30 June 20X0 the project had been signed but no work had been done, so no revenue or profit would be recorded. Thus it would only appear in the accounts in the notes when the company discloses the amount of future work contracted for.

*Step one: Review the expected overall position of the contract as at 30 June 20X1*

|  | Contract B £000 |
|---|---|
| Costs incurred to date | 13,000 |
| Anticipated future costs | 11,000 |
| Forecast contract cost | 24,000 |
| Contract price (revenue) | 20,000 |
| Anticipated Loss on contract | (4,000) |

This loss has to be recognised at 30 June 20X1.

*Step two: Prepare the relevant part of the comprehensive income statement*

|  | Contract B | |
|---|---:|---:|
|  | £000 | £000 |
| Revenue earned to date (£20,000,000 × 13,000/24,000) |  | 10,833 |
| *Less:* revenue previously recognised |  | nil |
| Revenue earned in the period |  | 10,833 |
| Costs incurred to date | 13,000 |  |
| *Less:* costs previously recorded as an expense | nil |  |
|  | (13,000) |  |
| (Anticipated loss in future periods: Rev 9,167 − 11,000 expense) | (1,833) |  |
| Total expenses for the period |  | (14,833) |
| Loss on Contract B for the period |  | (4,000) |

The total loss has to be recorded as soon as it is recognised, so the loss of 4,000 for the period is consistent with that. The anticipated revenue in the future was the total of 20,000 for the contract less 10,833 recognised in this period. 11,000 was the forecast additional expenses to complete, giving a difference of negative 1,833.

*Step three: Prepare the statement of financial position entries*

The entries in the statement of financial position represent the cumulative position.

|  | Contract B |
|---|---:|
|  | £000 |
| Costs incurred to date | 13,000 |
| *Add:* profits recognised to date | nil |
| *Less:* losses recognised to date | (4,000) |
| Work performed to date at cost or net realisable value | 9,000 |
| *Less:* billings to date | (10,000) |
| Liability for anticipated expenses in excess of future billings in the next period | (1,000) |

Recap:

1  First calculate whether the contract is anticipated to be profitable overall. This is done by subtracting from the total revenue under the contract the anticipated total expenses for the contract (that is the expenses already incurred combined with the additional expenses needed to complete the contract). If there is a loss the total of that loss has to be recognised immediately.

2  Do the profit and loss calculation. Use of the appropriate method to calculate the revenue for the period. Deduct the expenses related to the project for the period. If losses are anticipated in future periods the expenses have to be increased by that amount.

3  Prepare the work in progress account which is like a debtor's account for work which has not been billed to a customer yet. It is shown as total expenses to date plus profits less losses which gives a work in progress valued at selling price. Then you deduct from that any billings made to date, leaving the balance of work done valued at selling price which has not been billed (invoiced) to customers.

4  The accounts receivable balance is calculated by taking the opening balance adding any additional amounts billed to the customers during the year less any cash received.

## 21.9 Public–private partnerships (PPPs)

PPPs have become a common government policy whereby public bodies enter into contracts with private companies which have included contracts for the building and management of transport infrastructure, prisons, schools and hospitals.

There are inherent risks in any project and the intention is that the government, through a PPP arrangement, should transfer some or all of such risks to private contractors. For this to work equitably there needs to be an incentive for the private contractors to be able to make a reasonable profit provided they are efficient whilst ensuring that the providers, users of the service, taxpayers and employees also receive a fair share of the benefits of the PPP.

The European PPP Expertise Centre (epec) states that: 'In 2013, **the aggregate value** of PPP transactions which reached financial close in the **European market**[4] totaled **EUR 16.3 billion,** a 27% increase over 2012 (EUR 12.8 billion).' They further indicate that two major UK projects were included in those figures, namely the Thameslink rolling stock (€1.9 billion) and the Royal Liverpool Hospital (€509 million).

### Improved public services

It has been recognised that where such contracts satisfy a value for money test it makes economic sense to transfer some or all of the risks to a private contractor. In this way it has been possible to deliver significantly improved public services with:

- increases in the quality and quantity of investment, e.g. by the private contractor raising equity and loan capital in the market rather than relying simply on government funding;

- tighter control of contracts during the construction stage to avoid cost and time over runs, e.g. completing construction contracts within budget and within the agreed time – this is evidenced in a report from the National Audit Office[6] which indicates that the majority are completed on time and within budget; and

- more efficient management of the facilities after construction, e.g. maintaining the buildings, security, catering and cleaning of an approved standard for a specified number of years.

### PPP defined

There is no clear definition of a PPP. It can take a number of forms, e.g. in the form of the improved use of existing public assets under the Wider Markets Initiative (WMI) or contracts for the construction of new infrastructure projects and services provided under a Private Finance Initiative (PFI).

### The Wider Markets Initiative (WMI)[7]

The WMI encourages public-sector bodies to become more entrepreneurial and to undertake commercial services based on the physical assets and knowledge assets (e.g. patents, databases) they own in order to make the most effective use of public assets. WMI does not relate to the use of surplus assets – the intention would be to dispose of these. However, wanting to become more entrepreneurial leads to the need to collaborate with private enterprises which have the necessary expertise.

### Private Finance Initiative (PFI)

The PFI has been described[8] as a form of public–private partnership (PPP) that:

> differs from privatisation in that the public sector retains a substantial role in PFI projects, either as the main purchaser of services or as an essential enabler of the project

. . . differs from contracting out in that the private sector provides the capital asset as well as the services . . . differs from other PPPs in that the private sector contractor also arranges finance for the project.

In its 2004 Government Review the HM Treasury stated[9] that:

> The Private Finance Initiative is a small but important part of the Government's strategy for delivering high quality public services. In assessing where PFI is appropriate, the Government's approach is based on its commitment to efficiency, equity and accountability and on the Prime Minister's principles of public sector reform. PFI is only used where it can meet these requirements and deliver clear value for money without sacrificing the terms and conditions of staff. Where these conditions are met, PFI delivers a number of important benefits.
>
> By requiring the private sector to put its own capital at risk and to deliver clear levels of service to the public over the long term, PFI helps to deliver high quality public services and ensure that public assets are delivered on time and to budget.

The PFI has meant that more capital projects have or will be undertaken for a given level of public expenditure, and public-service capital projects have been brought on stream earlier. However, it has to be recognised that this increased level of activity must be paid for by higher public expenditure in the future or by additional fees for services paid by the public. The aim is to offset some of those costs by additional income or better efficiency.

Thus the stream of contracted revenue payments to the private sector restricts the options which the current and future governments will have. PFI projects have committed governments to payments to private-sector contractors between 2000/01 and 2025/26 of more than £100 billion. Some of these contracts may be for long periods of time such as 30 years.

Briefly, then, PFI allows the public sector to enter into a contract (known as a concession) with the private sector to provide quality services on a long-term basis, typically 25 to 30 years, so as to take advantage of private-sector management skills working under contracts where private-sector finance is at risk. The private sector has the incentive to operate efficiently and effectively if the service requirements are comprehensive and reflect public needs appropriately, and the future risks associated with the project are fairly shared by the two parties.

### How does PFI operate?

In principle, private-sector companies accept the responsibility for the design; raise the finance; undertake the construction, maintenance and possibly the operation of assets for the delivery of public services. In return for this the public sector pays for the project by making annual payments that cover all the costs plus a return on the investment through performance payments which include incentives for being efficient.

In practice the construction company and other parties such as the maintenance companies become shareholders in a project company set up specifically to tender for a concession.

● The project company enters into the contract (the 'concession') with the public sector; then enters into two principal subcontracts with:
  ● a construction company to build the project assets; and
  ● a facilities management company to maintain the asset – this is normally for a period of 5 or so years, after which time it is re-negotiated.

*Note*: the project company will pass down to the constructor and maintenance subcontractors any penalties or income deductions that arise as a result of their mismanagement.

- The project company raises a mixture of:
  - equity and subordinated debt from the principal private promoters, i.e. the construction company and the maintenance company; and
  - long-term debt.

  *Note*: the long-term debt may be up to 90% of the finance required on the basis that it is cheaper to use debt rather than equity. The loan would typically be obtained from banks and would be without recourse to the shareholders of the project company. As there is no recourse to the shareholders, lenders need to be satisfied that there is a reliable income stream coming to the project company from the public sector, i.e. the lender needs to be confident that the project company can satisfy the contractual terms agreed with the public sector.

  The subordinated debt made available to the project company by the promoters will be subordinated to the claims of the long-term lenders in that they will only be repaid after the long-term lenders.

- The project company receives regular payments, usually over a 25- to 30-year period, from the public sector once the construction has been completed to cover the interest and construction, operating and maintenance costs.

  *Note*: such payments may be conditional on a specified level of performance and the private-sector partners need to have carried out detailed investigation of past practice for accommodation-type projects and/or detailed economic forecasting for throughput projects.

  If, for example, it is an accommodation-type project (e.g. prisons, hospitals and schools) then payment is subject to the buildings being available in an appropriate clean and decorated condition – if not, income deductions can result.

  If it is a throughput project (e.g. roads, water) with payment made on the basis of throughput such as number of vehicles or litres of water, then payment would be at a fixed rate per unit of throughput and the accuracy of the forecast usage has a significant impact on future income.

- The project company makes interest and dividend payments to the principal promoters.
- Finally, the project company returns the infrastructure assets in agreed condition to the public sector at the end of the 25- to 30-year contractual period.

This can be shown graphically as in Figure 21.1.

### Profit and cash flow profile for the shareholders

Over a typical 30-year contract the profit and cash flow profiles would follow different growth patterns.

#### Profit profile

No profits are received as dividends during construction. Before completion the depreciation and loan interest charges can result in losses in the early years. As the loans are reduced the interest charge falls and profits then grow steadily to the end of the concession.

#### Cash flow

As far as the shareholders are concerned, cash flow is negative in the early years with the introduction of equity finance and subordinated loans. Cash begins to flow in when receipts commence from the public sector and interest payments commence to be made on the

**Figure 21.1 The operation of PFI**

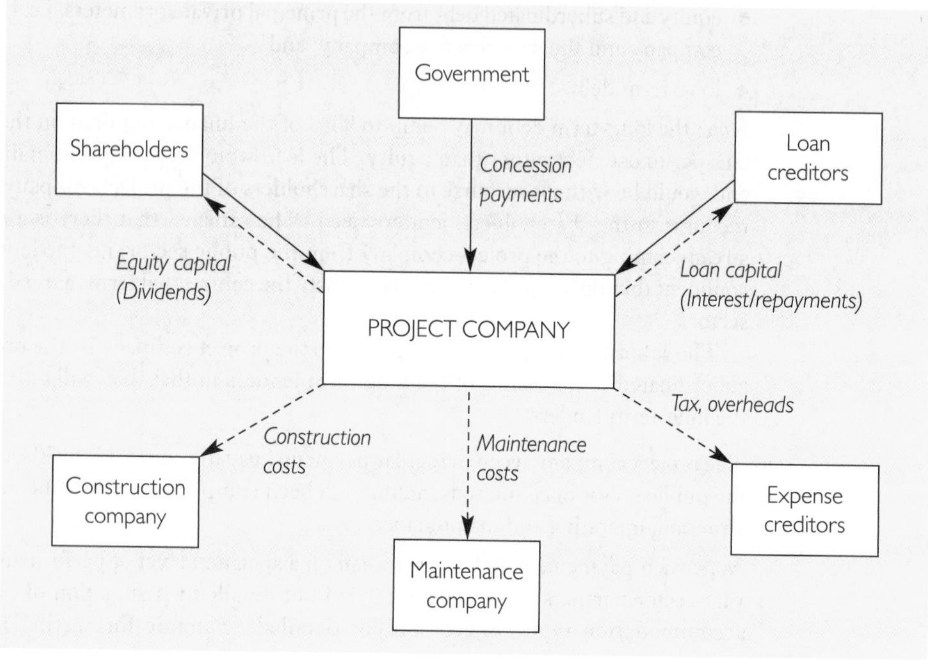

subordinated loans, say from year 5, and dividend payments start to be made to the equity shareholders, say from year 15.

## Summary

Long-term contracts are those that cannot be completed within the current financial year. This means that a decision has to be made as to whether or not to include any profit before the contract is actually completed. The view taken by the standard setters pre-2011 is that contract revenue and costs should be recognised under IAS 11 using the percentage of completion method.

There is a proviso that revenue and costs can only be recognised when the amounts are capable of independent verification and the contract has reached a reasonable stage of completion. Although profits are primarily attributed to the financial periods in which the work is carried out, there is a requirement that any foreseeable losses should be recognised immediately in the statement of comprehensive income of the current financial period and not apportioned over the life of the contract.

IAS 11 is to be superseded by IFRS 15 and application of the new standard is required for annual periods beginning on or after 1 January 2017, but early adoption is permitted under IFRS. Under IFRS 15 revenue is recognised when the service has been rendered, control has passed and the results are measurable.

## REVIEW QUESTIONS

1 Discuss the relative merits of recognising revenue under the percentage of completion method and the passing of control as major thresholds are met.

2 'Profit on a contract is not realised until completion of the contract.' Discuss.

3 'The use of the passing of control criteria for recognition of revenue will result in less comparability as companies can then manage their earnings.' Discuss.

4 'Profit on a contract that is not complete should be treated as an unrealised holding gain.' Discuss.

5 Discuss what information should be disclosed in the annual report in relation to construction costs in order for it to be useful to report users.

6 The Treasury states that 'Talk of PFI liabilities with a present value of £110 million is wrong. Adding up PFI unitary payments and pretending they present a threat to the public finances is like adding up electricity, gas, cleaning and food bills for the next 30 years.' Discuss.

7 'The operator of an asset in a PFI contract should recognise the tangible assets on its balance sheet.' Discuss.

8 'If the current financial reporting of transactions is well understood by users it is confusing to require a change when none is sought by the users.' Discuss.

## EXERCISES

Solutions for exercises marked with an asterisk (*) are accessible in MyAccountingLab.

### * Question 1

MACTAR has a series of contracts to resurface sections of motorways. The scale of the contract means several years' work and each motorway section is regarded as a separate contract.

| M1 | €m |
| --- | --- |
| Contract | 3.0 |
| Costs to date | 2.1 |
| Estimated cost to complete | 0.3 |
| Progress billings applied for to date | 1.75 |
| Payments received to date | 1.5 |
| M6 | €m |
| Contract sum | 2.0 |
| Costs to date | 0.3 |
| Estimated cost to complete | 1.1 |
| Progress billings applied for to date | 0.1 |
| Payments received to date | — |
| M62 | €m |
| Contract sum | 2.5 |
| Costs to date | 2.3 |
| Estimated costs to complete | 0.8 |
| Certified value of sections completed to date | 50% of contract |
| Progress billings applied for to date | 1.0 |
| Payments received to date | 0.75 |

The M62 contract has had major difficulties due to difficult terrain, and the contract only allows for a 10% increase in contract sum for such events.

**Required:**
From the information above, calculate for each contract the amount of profit (or loss) you would show for the year and show how these contracts would appear in the statement of financial position with all appropriate notes.

## * Question 2

At 31 October 20X9, Lytax Ltd was engaged in the following five long-term contracts. In each contract Lytax was building cold storage warehouses on five sites where the land was owned by the customer. Details are given below:

|  | 1 | 2 | 3 | 4 | 5 |
|---|---|---|---|---|---|
|  | £000 | £000 | £000 | £000 | £000 |
| Contract price | 1,100 | 950 | 1,400 | 1,300 | 1,200 |
| *At 31 October* |  |  |  |  |  |
| Cumulative costs incurred | 664 | 535 | 810 | 640 | 1,070 |
| Estimated further costs to completion | 106 | 75 | 680 | 800 | 165 |
| Estimated cost of post-completion guarantee rectification work | 30 | 10 | 45 | 20 | 5 |
| Cumulative costs incurred transferred to cost of sales | 580 | 470 | 646 | 525 | 900 |
| *Progress billings:* |  |  |  |  |  |
| Cumulative receipts | 615 | 680 | 615 | 385 | 722 |
| Invoiced |  |  |  |  |  |
| – awaiting receipt | 60 | 40 | 25 | 200 | 34 |
| – retained by customer | 75 | 80 | 60 | 65 | 84 |

It is not expected that any customers will default on their payments.

Up to 31 October 20X8, the following amounts have been included in the revenue and cost of sales figures:

|  | 1 | 2 | 3 | 4 | 5 |
|---|---|---|---|---|---|
|  | £000 | £000 | £000 | £000 | £000 |
| Cumulative revenue | 560 | 340 | 517 | 400 | 610 |
| Cumulative costs incurred transferred to cost of sales | 460 | 245 | 517 | 400 | 610 |
| Foreseeable loss transferred to cost of sales | — | — | — | 70 | — |

It is the accounting policy of Lytax Ltd to arrive at contract revenue by adjusting contract cost of sales (including foreseeable losses) by the amount of contract profit or loss to be regarded as recognised, separately for each contract.

**Required:**
Show how these items will appear in the statement of financial position of Lytax Ltd with all appropriate notes. Show all workings in tabular form.

## * Question 3

During its financial year ended 30 June 20X7 Beavers, an engineering company, has worked on several contracts. Information relating to one for Dam Ltd which is being constructed to a specific customer design is given below:

| *Contract X201* | |
|---|---|
| Date commenced | 1 July 20X6 |
| Original estimate of completion date | 30 September 20X7 |
| Contract price | £240,000 |
| Proportion of work certified as satisfactorily completed (and invoiced) up to 30 June 20X7 | £180,000 |
| Progress payments from Dam Ltd | £150,000 |
| *Costs up to 30 June 20X7* | |
| Wages | £91,000 |
| Materials sent to site | £36,000 |
| Other contract costs | £18,000 |
| Proportion of Head Office costs | £6,000 |
| Plant and equipment transferred to the site (at book value on 1 July 20X6) | £9,000 |

The plant and equipment is expected to have a book value of about £1,000 when the contract is completed.

| | |
|---|---|
| *Inventory of materials at site 30 June 20X7* | £3,000 |
| Expected additional costs to complete the contract: | |
| Wages | £10,000 |
| Materials (including stock at 30 June 20X7) | £12,000 |
| Other (including Head Office costs) | £8,000 |

At 30 June 20X7 it is estimated that work to a cost value of £19,000 has been completed, but not included in the certifications as the customer did not have control of that work which was performed off-site.

If the contract is completed one month earlier than originally scheduled, an extra £10,000 will be paid to the contractors. At the end of June 20X7 there seemed to be a 'good chance' that this would happen. Assume the output method is appropriate.

### Required:
(a) Show the account for the contract in the books of Beavers up to 30 June 20X7 (including any transfer to the statement of comprehensive income which you think is appropriate).
(b) Show the statement of financial position entries.
(c) Calculate the profit (or loss) to be recognised in the 20X6–X7 accounts.

## Question 4

Newbild SA commenced work on the construction of a block of flats on 1 July 20X0.

During the period ended 31 March 20X1 contract expenditure was as follows:

| | € |
|---|---|
| Materials issued from stores | 13,407 |
| Materials delivered direct to site | 73,078 |
| Wages | 39,498 |
| Administration expenses | 3,742 |
| Site expenses | 4,693 |

On 31 March 20X1 there were outstanding amounts for wages €396 and site expenses €122, and the stock of materials on site amounted to €5,467.

*The following information is also relevant:*

1   On 1 July 20X0 plant was purchased for exclusive use on site at a cost of €15,320. It was estimated that it would be used for two years after which it would have a residual value of €5,000.

2   By 31 March 20X1 Newbild SA had received €114,580, being the amount of work certified by the architects at 31 March 20X1 on completion and handover of the show flat, less a 15% retention.

3   The total contract price is €780,000. The company estimates that additional costs to complete the project will be €490,000. From costing records it is estimated that the costs of rectification and guarantee work will be 2.5% of the contract price.

**Required:**

(a) **Prepare the contract account for the period, together with a statement showing your calculation of the net income to be taken to the company's statement of comprehensive income on 31 March 20X1. Assume for the purpose of the question that the contract is sufficiently advanced to allow for the taking of profit.**

(b) **Give the values which you think should be included in the figures of revenue and cost of sales, in the statement of comprehensive income, and those to be included in net amounts due to or from the customer in the statement of financial position in respect of this contract.**

## * Question 5

Quickbuild Ltd entered into a two-year contract on 1 January 20X7 at a contract price of £250,000. The estimated cost of the contract was £150,000. At the end of the first year the following information was available:

● contract costs incurred totalled £70,000;

● inventories still unused at the contract site totalled £10,000;

● progress payments received totalled £60,000;

● other non-contract inventories totalled £185,000.

Invoices issued £65,000.

The problem is to be considered under two different scenarios:

   Case A where the accounting is to be performed under the percentage of completion method as required under IAS 11.
   Case B where the accounting is done under the milestone method and the customer gains control of 40% of the facility at the end of the first year.

**Required:**

(a) **Calculate the statement of comprehensive income entries for the contract revenue and the contract costs for each case.**

(b) **Calculate entries in the statement of financial position for the amounts due from construction contracts and inventories for each case.**

## Question 6

During 2006, Jack Matelot set up a company, JTM, to construct and refurbish marinas in various ports around Europe. The company's first accounting period ended on 31 October 2006 and during that period JTM won a contract to refurbish a small marina in St Malo, France. During the year ended 31 October 2007, the company won a further two contracts in Barcelona, Spain and Faro, Portugal. The following extract has been taken from the company's contract notes as at 31 October 2007:

| Contract: | Barcelona | Faro | St Malo |
|---|---|---|---|
| | €m | €m | €m |
| Contract value | 12.24 | 10.00 | 15.00 |
| Work certified as available to clients: | | | |
| To 31 October 2006 | — | — | 6.00 |
| Year to 31 October 2007 | 6.50 | 0.50 | 3.00 |
| To date | 6.50 | 0.50 | 9.00 |
| Payments received: | | | |
| To 31 October 2006 | — | — | 5.75 |
| Year to 31 October 2007 | 3.76 | — | 1.75 |
| To date | 3.76 | — | 7.50 |
| Invoices sent to client: | | | |
| To 31 October 2006 | — | — | 6.00 |
| Year to 31 October 2007 | 5.00 | 0.50 | 2.76 |
| To date | 5.00 | 0.50 | 8.76 |
| Costs incurred: | | | |
| To 31 October 2006 | — | — | 6.56 |
| Year to 31 October 2007 | 11.50 | 1.50 | 3.94 |
| To date | 11.50 | 1.50 | 10.50 |
| Estimated costs to complete: | | | |
| As at 31 October 2006 | | | 5.44 |
| As at 31 October 2007 | 4.00 | 5.50 | 1.50 |

*Notes:*

Barcelona: Experiencing difficulties. Although JTM does not anticipate any cost increases, the client has offered to increase contract value by €0.76m as compensation.

Faro: No problems.

St Malo: Work has slowed down during 2007. However, company feels it can continue profitably.

The company uses the value of work certified to estimate the percentage completion of each contract.

**Required:**

(a) For each contract, calculate the profit or loss attributable to the year ended 31 October 2007 and show how it would be recognised in the company's balance sheet at that date. (Show your workings clearly.)

(b) As JTM's 2007 accounts were being prepared, it became evident that the St Malo contract had slowed down due to a dispute with a neighbouring marina which claimed that the JTM refurbishment had damaged part of its quayside. The company has been told that the cost of repairing the damage would be €150,000. Jack Matelot believes it is a fair estimate and, in the interests of completing the contract on time, has decided to settle the claim. He is not unduly concerned about the amount involved as such eventualities are adequately covered by insurance.

Required:

How should this event be dealt with in the 2007 accounts?

(c) During 2007, Jack Matelot had two major worries: (i) the operating performance of JTM had not been as good as expected; and (ii) the planned disposal of surplus property (to finance the agreed acquisition of a competitor, MoriceMarinas, and the payment of a dividend) had not been successful. As a result of these circumstances, Jack had been warning shareholders not to expect a dividend for 2007. However, during November 2007, the property was unexpectedly disposed of for €5m; which enabled the payment of a 2007 dividend of €1m and the acquisition of MoriceMarinas for €4m.

Required:

How should the above events be dealt with in the 2007 accounts?

*(The Association of International Accountants)*

## Question 7

Backwater Construction Company is reviewing a major contract which is in serious difficulty. The contract price is €10,000,000. The project involves the construction of four buildings of equal size and complexity. The first building has been completed and costs to date are €3,000,000. The second building is expected to be completed after one more year, the third building after two years and the final building after three years. The relevant discount rate is 10% p.a.

Required:

**Prepare the entries to record the revenue for the year just completed, to record the expenses incurred, and adjust assets (if any) and liabilities (if any) at the balance date.**

## Question 8

Norwik Construction plc is a large construction company involved in multiple large contracts around the world. One contract to build three stadiums is being undertaken by the Australasian division. Each stadium has an individual contract price. Jim Norwik who is the great-grandson of the founder is in charge of that division. He is concerned that the first stadium is costing more than is included in the tender estimates. Rather than recognise an immediate loss on the contract, he orders his subordinates to charge some of the materials for stadium one to stadium two which seems to be on target.

Required:

**Discuss the consequences of Jim Norwik's actions for Norwik Construction plc and the likely impact on the behaviour of Jim Norwik's subordinates.**

## Question 9

Boldwin Construction has entered into a contract with Spears Retailers to construct a new department store on Spears land. The contract sum is £45 million. At 30 June 20X1 the situation is as follows:

(a) the contract is 30% complete;

(b) expenses to date on the contract are £15 million;

(c) additional expenses to complete the contract are estimated at £25 million;

(d) billings during the year £5 million;

(e) payments received from Spears Retailers £4 million.

Required:
(a) Show the profit entries and the resulting assets in the statement of financial position.
(b) Repeat the work in (a) assuming the cost to complete is estimated at £32 million.
(c) If the project is finished by June 20X2 and the additional cost to complete was £23 million, bill-ings for the year £26 million, and cash received £25 million, show the relevant entries in the comprehensive income statement and financial position statement, assuming first scenario (a) occurred, and then repeat the exercise under scenario (b).

## Question 10

The trial balance for LPO at 31 December 2013 was as follows:

|  | Notes | $000 | $000 |
|---|---|---|---|
| Long-term loans (repayable 2020) | (xi) |  | 900 |
| Administrative expenses |  | 455 |  |
| Cash received from construction contract client | (vi) |  | 2,000 |
| Cash and cash equivalents |  | 215 |  |
| Construction contract work in progress | (vi) | 1,875 |  |
| Distribution costs |  | 230 |  |
| Equity dividend paid | (x) | 360 |  |
| Inventory purchases |  | 1,425 |  |
| Inventory at 1 January 2013 | (i) | 420 |  |
| Land and buildings at cost | (iv) | 2,500 |  |
| Equity shares $1 each, fully paid at 31 December 2013 | (ix) |  | 1,500 |
| Plant and equipment at cost | (ii) | 1,055 |  |
| Provision for deferred tax | (iii) |  | 200 |
| Provision for buildings depreciation at 1 January 2013 | (iv) |  | 225 |
| Provision for plant and equipment depreciation at 1 January 2013 | (v) |  | 400 |
| Retained earnings at 1 January 2013 |  |  | 370 |
| Sales revenue |  |  | 3,010 |
| Share premium at 31 December 2013 | (ix) |  | 250 |
| Trade payables |  |  | 145 |
| Trade receivables | (vii) | 330 |  |
| Short-term investments |  | 135 |  |
|  |  | 9,000 | 9,000 |

Notes:

(i) Closing inventory at 31 December 2013 was $562,000.

(ii) On 31 December 2013, LPO disposed of some obsolete plant and equipment for $3,000. The plant and equipment had originally cost $46,000 and had a carrying value of $5,000. The purchaser has not yet paid for the plant and equipment and LPO has not made any entries in its financial records for this disposal.

(iii) The income tax due for the year ended 31 December 2013 is estimated at $160,000.
The deferred tax provision is to be increased by $31,000.

(iv) Depreciation is charged on buildings using the straight line method at 3% per annum.
The cost of land included in land and buildings is $900,000. Buildings depreciation is treated as an administrative expense.

(v) Plant and equipment is depreciated using the reducing balance method at 30%.
Depreciation of plant and equipment is regarded as a cost of sales.

(vi) At 31 December 2013, LPO had a construction contract in progress:

| | |
|---|---|
| Contract length | 3 years |
| Date commenced | 1 January 2013 |
| Fixed contract price | $5,500,000 |
| Contract detail for year ended 31 December 2013: | $000 |
| Construction contract work in progress | 1,875 |
| Estimated cost to complete | 2,700 |
| Cash received on account from construction contract client during the year | 2,000 |

LPO uses the cost of work completed as a proportion of total cost to recognise attributable profit for the year.

(vii) On 1 February 2014, LPO was informed that one of its customers, ZZ, had ceased trading. The liquidators advised LPO that it was very unlikely to receive payment of any of the $36,000 due from ZZ at 31 January 2014.

(viii) On 1 July 2013 one of LPO's customers started litigation against LPO, claiming damages of $30,000. LPO has been advised that the claim will probably succeed.

(ix) On 1 July 2013 LPO issued 50,000 new equity shares at a premium of 20%. All cash was received and is included in the trial balance.

(x) During the year LPO paid a final dividend of $240,000 in respect of the year ended 31 December 2012. This was in addition to the interim dividend paid on 31 July 2013 for the year ended 31 December 2013.

(xi) The long-term loans incur interest at 6% a year and this was not paid until 6 January 2014.

**Required:**
Prepare LPO's statement of profit or loss and other comprehensive income and statement of changes in equity for the year to 31 December 2013 AND the statement of financial position at that date in accordance with the requirements of International Financial Reporting Standards.

Notes to the financial statements are not required, but all workings must be clearly shown. Do not prepare a statement of accounting policies.

*(CIMA Financial Operations March 2014)*

## Notes

1 IAS 11 *Construction Contracts*, IASB, 1995.
2 IAS 18 *Revenue*, IASB, revised 2005.
3 It is common in construction work for architects to certify the amount which the contractor is entitled to as various milestones are reached. The amount payable is often the amount earned less a percentage withheld until the contract is completed and all problems resolved. If resolution does not occur the customer can use the money withheld to get a third party to rectify the remaining mistakes.
4 European PPP Expertise Centre, *Market Update*, Review of the European PPP Market in 2013. Europe for this purpose is defined as EU-28, the countries of the Western Balkans and Turkey.
5 IFRS 15 *Revenue from Contracts with Customers*, IASB, 2014.
6 National Audit Office, PFI: Construction Performance Feb. 2003, www.nao.org.uk/publications/nao_reports/02-03/0203371.pdf
7 *Selling Government Services into Wider Markets, Policy and Guidance Notes*, Enterprise and Growth Unit, HM Treasury July 1998, www.hmtreasury.gov.uk/mediastore/otherfiles/
8 Research Paper 01/0117 *Private Finance Initiative*, G. Allen, Economic Policy and Statistics Section, House of Commons, December 2001.
9 See www.hm-treasury.gov.uk/documents/public_private_partnerships/ppp_index.cfm?ptr=29

### PART 6

# Consolidated accounts

# Accounting for groups at the date of acquisition

## 22.1 Introduction

The main purpose of this chapter is to explain how to prepare consolidated financial statements at the date of acquisition and the IFRS 10 and 13 requirements.

### Objectives

By the end of this chapter, you should be able to:

- prepare consolidated accounts at the date of acquisition:
  - for a wholly owned subsidiary;
  - for a partly owned subsidiary with non-controlling interests, calculating goodwill under the two options available in IFRS 3;
  - where the fair value of a subsidiary's net assets are more or less than their book values;
- explain IFRS 10, IFRS 3 and IFRS 13 provisions;
- discuss the usefulness of group accounts to stakeholders.

## 22.2 Preparing consolidated accounts for a wholly owned subsidiary

When a company acquires the shares of another company it records the cost as an Investment. If the shares acquired give it control over the acquired company, then the acquirer is referred to as a parent or holding company and the acquired company as a subsidiary.

The shareholders of the parent company want to know how well the directors of their company have managed all of the net assets which they control. This information is provided by the preparation of consolidated accounts which aggregates the assets and liabilities of both companies. In doing this it replaces the Investment in subsidiary in the parent's accounts with the fair value of the assets and liabilities of the subsidiary.

The parent may well have had to pay a premium over and above the fair value of the net assets in order to obtain control – this is referred to as Goodwill.

## 22.3 IFRS 10 *Consolidated Financial Statements*

IFRS 10 *Consolidated Financial Statements* which defines a group and how to determine control and also requires the use of fair values for a subsidiary.

### 22.3.1 IFRS 10 definition of a group

One of IASB's main objectives had been to develop a consistent basis for determining when a company consolidates the financial statements of another company to prepare group accounts. For this, it has stated that control should be the determining factor.

Under IFRS 10 *Consolidated Financial Statements,* a group exists where one enterprise (the parent) controls, either directly or indirectly, another enterprise (the subsidiary). A group consists of a parent and its subsidiaries.

### 22.3.2 IFRS 10 definition of control

Under IFRS 10 an investor is a parent[1] when it is exposed, or has rights, to variable returns from its involvement with the investee and has the ability to affect those returns through its power over the investee.

An investor controls[2] an investee if and only if the investor satisfies all of the following requirements:

- exposure, or rights, to variable returns whether positive or negative from its involvement with the investee;
- power over the investee whereby the investor has existing rights that give it the ability to direct those activities that significantly affect the investee's returns;
- the ability to use its power over the investee to affect the amount of the investor's returns.

The following is an extract from the 2015 Linde AG annual report:

**Scope of consolidation**

The Group financial statements comprise Linde AG and all the companies over which Linde AG is able to exercise control as defined by IFRS 10.

#### What if the shares acquired are less than 50%?

Even in this situation, it may still be possible to identify an acquirer when one of the combining enterprises, as a result of the business combination, acquires:

(a) power over more than one-half of the voting rights of the other enterprise by virtue of an agreement with other investors;

(b) power to govern the financial and operating policies of the other enterprise under a statute or an agreement;

(c) power to appoint or remove the majority of the members of the board of directors; or

(d) power to cast the majority of votes at a meeting of the board of directors.

#### What if the parent holds options or potential voting rights?

IFRS 10 provides that if those options give the entity control then this could result in an entity being consolidated. For example, if the investee's management always followed the wishes of the option holder, this may be viewed as having control. The following is an extract from the BMW 2015 Annual Report:

Subsidiaries are those enterprises which, either directly or indirectly, are under the uniform control of the management of BMWAG or in which BMWAG, either directly or indirectly – holds the majority of the voting rights – has the right to appoint or remove the majority of the members of the Board of Management or equivalent governing body, and in which BMWAG is at the same time (directly or indirectly) a shareholder – has control (directly or indirectly) over another enterprise on the basis of a control agreement or a provision in the statutes of that enterprise.

### What if a company has significant voting rights in comparison to other shareholders?

If an investor is so powerful through their voting rights compared to others, for example one investor has 40% while the other 60% is widely dispersed between unconnected investors, this can also give control and result in the investee being consolidated. Both of these areas will require directors to exercise judgement in determining whether control exists.

### 22.3.3 Requirement to use fair values

When one company acquires a controlling interest in another and the combination is treated as an acquisition, the assets and liabilities of the subsidiary are recorded in the acquirer's consolidated statement of financial position at their fair value.

On consolidation, if the acquirer has acquired less than 100% of the ordinary shares, any differences (positive or negative) between the fair values of the net assets and their book value are recognised in full and the parent and non-controlling interests are credited or debited with their respective percentage interests.

## 22.4 Fair values

The **fair value** of the consideration paid to acquire an investment in a subsidiary is set against the **fair value** of the identifiable net assets in the subsidiary at the date of acquisition.

### Fair value of the consideration

Consideration may be in the form of shares in the acquiring company. If these are quoted then the fair value is the market price of the shares. If the shares are not quoted on an exchange, then they would need to be valued – for the purposes of this chapter the value is given (how to value unquoted shares is discussed in Chapter 29).

Consideration may also be in cash or a combination of shares and cash. If the cash element is deferred for more than a year the consideration is discounted to its present value. The difference is reported as an accrued finance charge.

Under IFRS3, acquisition costs (such as legal, accounting and valuation fees) must be expensed and cannot be capitalised.

If there is contingent consideration it will be accounted for as a provision under IAS37 and, if it falls to be paid more than one year later, it will be necessary to review the amount and treat any changes as an error in accordance with IAS 8 *Accounting Policies, Accounting Estimates and Errors.*

### Fair value of the net assets

The starting point is the book values in the subsidiary's statement of financial position. These are required to be re-stated at fair values when incorporating into the consolidated accounts. First, each asset and liability is reviewed. For example, land may be revalued to market value, raw materials to replacement price, finished goods to selling price less estimated profit, loans may be revalued if there has been a change in interest rates that impacts on their value. In addition to the assets and liabilities in the accounts, it is also necessary to estimate a fair value for any contingent liabilities – if unable to value then they are disclosed.

If the investment is greater than the share of net assets then the difference is regarded as the purchase of goodwill – see the Rose Group example below

## 22.5 Illustration where there is a wholly owned subsidiary

The **fair value** of the parent company's investment in a subsidiary is set against the **fair value** of the identifiable net assets in the subsidiary at the date of acquisition. If the investment is greater than the share of net assets then the difference is regarded as the purchase of goodwill – see the Rose Group example below.

EXAMPLE • THE ROSE GROUP ON 1 January 20X0 Rose plc acquired 100% of the 10,000 £1 ordinary voting shares in Tulip plc for £1.50 per share in cash and so gained control. We are assuming for this example that the fair value of Tulip's net assets at that date was the same as their book value. The individual and group statements of financial position immediately after the acquisition were as in the following schedule:

| | Rose plc £ | Tulip plc £ | Adjustments Dr | Cr | Group £ | |
|---|---|---|---|---|---|---|
| Non-current assets | 20,000 | 11,000 | | | 31,000 | Step 2 |
| Investment in Tulip | 15,000 | — | | 10,000 (a) | — | |
| | | | | 4,000 (b) | 1,000 | Step 1 |
| Net current assets | 8,000 | 3,000 | | | 11,000 | |
| Net assets | 43,000 | 14,000 | | | 43,000 | |
| Share capital | 16,000 | 10,000 | 10,000 (a) | | 16,000 | Step 3 |
| Retained earnings | 27,000 | 4,000 | 4,000 (b) | | 27,000 | Step 3 |
| | 43,000 | 14,000 | 14,000 | 14,000 | 43,000 | |

(a) and (b) identify the entries in the calculations below.

### Step 1: First we calculate the goodwill

Goodwill arises if Rose has to pay the Tulip shareholders more than the book value of the net assets in order to acquire control over those net assets.

| | | £ | £ |
|---|---|---|---|
| The parent company's investment | | | 15,000 |
| *Less:* The parent's share of | | | |
| (a) the subsidiary's share capital | (100% × 10,000) | 10,000 | |
| (b) the subsidiary's retained earnings | (100% × 4,000) | 4,000 | 14,000 |
| Goodwill reported in statement of financial position | | | 1,000 |

### Step 2: Aggregate the assets and liabilities

Having cancelled the investment in Tulip against the share capital and reserves acquired, we then add together the assets and liabilities of the two companies including any goodwill:

| | | £ |
|---|---|---|
| Non-current assets other than goodwill | (20,000 + 11,000) | 31,000 |
| Goodwill (as calculated in Step 1) | | 1,000 |
| Net current assets | (8,000 + 3,000) | 11,000 |
| | | 43,000 |

Note that the total of the net assets in the consolidated account is the same as the net assets in the individual statement of financial position except that Rose's investment in Tulip has been replaced by Tulip's net assets of £14,000 **plus** the previously unrecorded £1,000 goodwill.

**Step 3: Calculate the consolidated share capital and reserves**

This is the final step.

|  | £ |
|---|---|
| Share capital (parent company only) | 16,000 |
| Retained earnings (parent company only) | **27,000** |
|  | 43,000 |

Note that in a consolidated statement of financial position we only **ever** include the parent's share capital because, as we have seen above, the subsidiary's share capital has been cancelled as in Step 1 above.

## 22.6 Preparing consolidated accounts when there is a partly owned subsidiary

A parent company does not need to purchase all the shares of another company to gain control. The holders of any shares not acquired by the parent are collectively referred to as a **non-controlling interest**. They are part-owners of the subsidiary. However, although the parent does not **own** all the net assets of the acquired company, it does **control** them and the parent company directors are accountable for their use.

Indeed, one of the main purposes of preparing group accounts is to show how effectively the directors have used this power to control. Therefore, all of the net assets of the subsidiary will be included in the group statement of financial position and the non-controlling interest will be shown as partly financing those net assets.

### How is a non-controlling interest measured?

IFRS 3[3] allows for two different methods of measuring the non-controlling interest in the statement of financial position:

- **Method** 1 requires the non-controlling interest to be measured as the *proportionate share of the net assets* of the subsidiary at the date of acquisition. At each subsequent reporting date the non-controlling interest is measured as its percentage share of the subsidiary's net assets.

- **Method** 2 requires the non-controlling interest to be measured at *fair value* at the date of acquisition. Using fair value rather than a percentage of book value means that there could be a difference for goodwill. At each subsequent reporting date the non-controlling interest is measured as the share of the net assets of the subsidiary, plus any goodwill.

### 22.6.1 Illustration where there is a partly owned subsidiary using Method 1

We will continue with our Rose Group example on the basis that it acquired less than 100% of Tulip's shares.

On 1 January 20X0 Rose plc acquired 80% of the 10,000 £1 ordinary shares in Tulip plc for £1.50 per share in cash and so gained control. The fair value of Tulip's net assets at that date was the same as their book value.

The consolidation schedule is as follows:

| | Rose | Tulip | Adjustment | | Group | |
|---|---|---|---|---|---|---|
| | | | Dr | Cr | | |
| | £ | £ | £ | £ | £ | |
| Non-current assets | 20,000 | 11,000 | | | 31,000 | Step 3 |
| Investment in Tulip | 12,000 | — | | 8,000 (a) | — | |
| | | | | 3,200 (b) | | |
| Goodwill | — | — | | | 800 | Step 1 |
| Net current assets | **11,000** | **3,000** | | | **14,000** | Step 3 |
| Net assets | 43,000 | 14,000 | | | 45,800 | |
| Share capital | 16,000 | 10,000 | 8,000 (a) | | | Step 4 |
| | | | **2,000 (c)** | | 16,000 | |
| Retained earnings | **27,000** | **4,000** | 3,200 (b) | | | Step 4 |
| | | | **800 (d)** | | 27,000 | |
| | 43,000 | 14,000 | | | 43,000 | |
| Non-controlling interest | | — | | 2,000 (c) | | Step 2 |
| | | | | 800 (d) | **2,800** | |
| | 43,000 | 14,000 | 14,000 | 14,000 | 45,800 | |

(a), (b), (c) and (d) identify the entries in the calculations below.

### Step 1: Calculate goodwill

| | | | £ | £ |
|---|---|---|---|---|
| The parent company's investment in Tulip | | | | 12,000 |
| *Less:* (a) parent's share of Tulip's share capital | (80% × 10,000) | | 8,000 | |
| (b) parent's share of the retained earnings | (80% × 4,000) | | **3,200** | |
| Goodwill | | | | **11,200** |
| | | | | 800 |

### Step 2: Calculate the non-controlling interest in Tulip

| | | |
|---|---|---|
| (c) Non-controlling interest in the share capital | (20% × 10,000) | 2,000 |
| (d) Non-controlling interest in the retained earnings | (20% × 4,000) | **800** |
| Representing the non-controlling interest in Tulip's net assets | | 2,800 |

In the published consolidated accounts the non-controlling interest will be shown as a separate item in the equity of the group as follows:

| | |
|---|---|
| Share capital | 16,000 |
| Retained earnings | **27,000** |
| Rose shareholders' share of equity | 43,000 |
| Non-controlling interest | **2,800** |
| Total equity | 45,800 |

This recognises that the non-controlling shareholders are part of the ownership of the group rather than a liability.

### Step 3: Aggregate the assets and liabilities of the parent and subsidiary

| | | £ |
|---|---|---|
| Non-current assets other than goodwill | (20,000 + 11,000) | 31,000 |
| Goodwill (as calculated in Step 1) | | 800 |
| Net current assets | (11,000 + 3,000) | **14,000** |
| | | 45,800 |

### Step 4: Calculate the consolidated share capital and reserves

|  | £ |
|---|---|
| Share capital (*parent company only*) | 16,000 |
| Retained earnings (*parent company only*) | **27,000** |
|  | 43,000 |

Note it is only the parent's share capital that is **ever** reported in the group accounts. As for the retained earnings, it is only the earnings that arise **after** the date when the parent obtains control that are reported as part of the group retained earnings – this is dealt with further in the next chapter.

## 22.6.2 Illustration where there is a partly owned subsidiary using Method 2

Let us now consider the impact on the previous example of using Method 2 to measure the non-controlling interest. In order to use this method, we need to know the fair value of the non-controlling interest in the subsidiary at the date of acquisition. Let us assume in this case that the fair value of a share in Tulip is £1.45, giving a value for the 2,000 shares of £2,900.

*Two figures are different in the consolidated accounts if this method is used.* The use of Method 2 affects two figures – goodwill and the non-controlling interest. Whereas under Method 1 the goodwill represented the cost of Rose obtaining control, under Method 2 we also credit the non-controlling interest with its own goodwill. It is computed as follows:

|  |  | £ |
|---|---|---|
| Fair value of non-controlling interest at date of acquisition |  | 2,900 |
| 20% of the net assets at the date of acquisition | (£14,000) | **(2,800)** |
| Attributable goodwill |  | 100 |

The consolidated statement of financial position would now be as follows:

|  |  | £ |
|---|---|---|
| Non-current assets other than goodwill |  | 31,000 |
| Goodwill | (£800 + £100) | 900 |
| Net current assets |  | **14,000** |
|  |  | 45,900 |
| Share capital |  | 16,000 |
| Retained earnings |  | 27,000 |
| Non-controlling interest | (£2,800 + £100) | **2,900** |
|  |  | 45,900 |

### How to determine the value of a share not acquired by the parent

Note that we assumed that the fair value of the non-controlling interest at the date of acquisition was £2,900. If Tulip's shares are quoted then the fair value estimate would be based on the share price prior to a bid. This price could be different from that paid by Rose on the assumption that in seeking to obtain control it would probably have paid more than the current share price. In exercises or exam questions the total figure might be given (as in this example) or a price per share might be given.

In the Rose example the goodwill relating to the parent (Rose's) shareholding of 80% is £800, i.e. 10p per share. The goodwill relating to the non-controlling interest in 2,000 shares, however, based on a £2,900 valuation is £100, i.e. 5p per share.

## 22.7 The treatment of differences between a subsidiary's fair value and book value

In our examples so far we have assumed that the book value of the net assets in the subsidiary is equal to their fair value. In practice, book value rarely equals fair value and it is necessary to revalue the group's share of the assets and liabilities of the subsidiary prior to consolidation.

The following is an extract from the BMW 2015 Annual Report:

### Consolidation principles

The equity of subsidiaries is consolidated in accordance with IFRS 3 (Business Combinations). IFRS 3 requires that all business combinations are accounted for using the acquisition method, whereby identifiable assets and liabilities acquired are measured at their fair value at acquisition date. An excess of acquisition cost over the Group's share of the net fair value of identifiable assets, liabilities and contingent liabilities is recognised as goodwill in a separate balance sheet line item and allocated to the relevant cash-generating unit (CGU).

The following is an extract from the EnBW 2015 Annual Report:

### Basis of consolidation

Non-controlling interests are measured at the proportionate share of fair value of assets identified and liabilities assumed.

Note that, when consolidating, the **parent** company's assets and liabilities remain **unchanged** at book value – it is only the subsidiary's that are adjusted for the purpose of the consolidated accounts.

For example, let us assume that the fair value of Tulip's non-current assets was £600 above their book value at £11,600. If Rose owned 100% of Tulip, then the Rose shareholders would have the benefit of the £600 and the goodwill would be reduced from £800 to £200. However, as Tulip is part-financed by non-controlling shareholders, they are entitled to their 20% share of the £600 as seen in the following schedule:

| | Rose | Tulip | Group | Dr | Cr | Group fair value | |
|---|---|---|---|---|---|---|---|
| | £ | £ | £ | | | £ | |
| Non–current assets | 20,000 | 11,000 | 31,000 | 600 | | 31,600 | Step 3 |
| Goodwill | — | — | 800 | | 480 | 320 | Step 1 |
| Investment in Tulip | 12,000 | — | — | | | — | |
| Net current assets | 11,000 | 3,000 | 14,000 | | | 14,000 | |
| Net assets | 43,000 | 14,000 | 45,800 | | | 45,920 | |
| Share capital | 16,000 | 10,000 | 16,000 | | | 16,000 | |
| Retained earnings | 27,000 | 4,000 | 27,000 | | | 27,000 | |
| | 43,000 | 14,000 | 43,000 | | | 43,000 | |
| Non-controlling interest | — | — | 2,800 | | 120 | 2,920 | Step 2 |
| | 43,000 | 14,000 | 45,800 | | | 45,920 | |

**Step 1: Goodwill is adjusted when fair value exceeds book value**

As goodwill is the difference between the consideration and the net assets
acquired, any increase in the net assets will mean that the difference is lower.

|  |  |  | £ |
|---|---|---|---|
| The parent company's investment in Tulip |  |  | 12,000 |
| Less: The parent's share of the subsidiary's share capital | (80% × 10,000) | 8,000 |  |
| The parent's share of retained earnings | (80% × 4,000) | 3,200 |  |
| The parent's share of the revaluation | (80% × 600) | 480 | 11,680 |
| Goodwill |  |  | 320 |

\* This is equivalent to the share of net assets, 80% × (11,000 + 3,000 + 600).

**Step 2: Non-controlling interest adjusted for fair value in excess of book value**

| | | |
|---|---|---|
| Non-controlling interest in share capital of Tulip | (20% × 10,000) | 2,000 |
| Non-controlling interest in retained earnings of Tulip | (20% × 4,000) | 800 |
| Revaluation to fair value of the subsidiary's assets | (20% × 600) | 120 |
| | | 2,920 |

**Step 3: Aggregate the parent's non-current assets which remain at book value and the subsidiary's which have been restated to fair value**

The non-current assets would be reported as £31,600 (20,000 + 11,000 + 600). Remember
that the revaluation of the subsidiary's assets is only necessary for the consolidated accounts.
No entries need be made in the individual accounts of the subsidiary or its books of account.
The preparation of consolidated accounts is *a separate exercise* that in no way affects the
records of the individual companies.

## 22.8 The parent issues shares to acquire shares in a subsidiary

Shares in another company can be purchased with cash or through an exchange of shares. In
the former case, the cash will be reduced and exchanged for another asset called 'investment
in the subsidiary company'. If there is an exchange of shares, there will be an increase in the
parents' share capital and often in the share premium.

Let us assume that Rose issued its own shares to 80% of the Tulip shareholders who
wanted £1.50 for each share, totalling £12,000. Rose would in this case have to set a value of
its own shares that was acceptable to the Tulip shareholders.

For illustration purposes, let us assume that the Rose shares were valued at £2.50 each and
4,800 were issued (£12,000/£2.50). The consolidation schedule would show that Rose's cash
had not been reduced but the share capital and share premium had increased as follows:

| | | Rose £ | Tulip £ | Group £ |
|---|---|---|---|---|
| Non-current assets | | 20,000 | 11,600 | 31,600 |
| Investment in Tulip | | 12,000 | — | — |
| Goodwill | | — | — | 320 |
| Net current assets | 11,000 + 12,000* | 23,000 | 3,000 | 26,000 |
| Net assets | | 55,000 | 14,000 | 57,920 |

(continued)

|  |  | Rose £ | Tulip £ | Group £ |
|---|---|---|---|---|
| Share capital | 16,000 + 4,800 at par | 20,800 | 10,000 | 20,800 |
| Share premium | 4,800 × £1.50 | 7,200 |  | 7,200 |
| Retained earnings |  | 27,000 | 4,000 | 27,000 |
| Parent company's equity |  | 55,000 | 14,000 | 55,000 |
| Non-controlling interest |  | — | — | 2,920 |
|  |  | 55,000 | 14,000 | 57,920 |

* This is showing cash at £23,000 which was the position before we assumed that the shares in Tulip had been acquired for cash.

Note that there is no effect on the accounts of the acquired company as the payment of cash or exchange of shares is with the subsidiary company's individual shareholders, not the company itself.

## 22.9 IFRS 3 *Business Combinations* treatment of goodwill at the date of acquisition

Any differences between the fair values of the net assets and the consideration paid to acquire them is treated as positive goodwill or a bargain purchase (also referred to as badwill or negative goodwill) and dealt with in accordance with IFRS 3 *Business Combinations*.

### The treatment of positive goodwill

Positive purchased goodwill, where the investment exceeds the total of the net assets acquired, should be recognised as an asset with no amortisation. In subsequent years goodwill must be subject to impairment tests in accordance with IAS 36 *Impairment of Assets*. These tests will be annual, or more frequently if circumstances indicate that the goodwill might be impaired.[4] Once recognised, an impairment loss for goodwill may not be reversed in a subsequent period, which helps in preventing the manipulation of period profits.

### The treatment of a bargain purchase

The acquiring company does not always pay more than the fair value of the identifiable net assets. Paying less (sometimes referred to as negative goodwill) can arise[5] when:

(a) there have been errors measuring the fair value of either the cost of the combination or the acquiree's identifiable assets, liabilities or contingent liabilities; or

(b) future costs such as losses have been taken into account; or

(c) there has been a bargain purchase.

Where a parent pays less than the fair value of the net assets, IFRS 3 requires it to review the fair value exercise to ensure that no asset has been overstated or liability understated. Assuming this review reveals no errors, then the resulting difference is recognised immediately in the statement of income.

## 22.10 When may a parent company not be required to prepare consolidated accounts?

It may not be necessary for a parent company to prepare consolidated accounts if the parent is itself a wholly owned subsidiary and the ultimate parent produces consolidated financial statements available for public use that comply with International Financial Reporting Standards (IFRSs).[6]

If the parent company is a partially owned subsidiary of another entity, then, if its other owners have been informed and do not object, the parent company need not present consolidated financial statements; nor if its debt or equity instruments are not traded in a public foreign or domestic market.

## 22.11 When may a parent company exclude or not exclude a subsidiary from a consolidation?

### 22.11.1 Exclusion permitted

Subsidiaries may be excluded if they are immaterial or there are substantial rights exercisable by non-controlling interests.

#### Materiality

Exclusion is permissible on grounds of non-materiality[6] as the International Accounting Standards are not intended to apply to immaterial items.

For example, Linde AG states in its 2015 Annual Report:

> Non-consolidated subsidiaries, when taken together, are immaterial from the Groups point of view in terms of total assets, revenue and profit or loss for the year and do not have a significant impact on the net assets, financial position and results of operations of the Group. For that reason, they are not included in the consolidated financial statements

#### Substantial rights exercisable by the non-controlling interest

Exclusion might also be appropriate where there are substantial rights exercisable by a non-controlling interest as seen in the following extract from the Mitsubishi Logistics Corporation 2013 Annual Report:

> The company holds 51% of the voting rights in MICLTL Logistics Company Ltd, however, the other shareholder's agreement is necessary to decide important policies of finance and trade. Therefore, the Company does not treat MICLTL as a subsidiary.

### 22.11.2 Exclusion not permitted

Exclusion on the grounds that a subsidiary's activities are dissimilar from those of the others within a group is not permitted.[7] This is because information is required under IFRS 8 *Operating Segments* on the different activities of subsidiaries, and users of accounts can, therefore, make appropriate adjustments for their own purposes if required.

## 22.12 IFRS 13 *Fair Value Measurement*

IFRS 13 *Fair Value Measurement*[8] defines fair value as the price that would be received to sell an asset or paid to transfer a liability in an orderly transaction between market participants at the measurement date. The detailed guidance for determining fair value is also set out in IFRS 3.

The main provisions are that as from the date of acquisition, an acquirer should:

(a) incorporate into the statement of income the results of operations of the acquiree; and

(b) recognise in the statement of financial position the identifiable assets, liabilities and contingent liabilities of the acquiree and any goodwill or negative goodwill arising on the acquisition.

The identifiable assets, liabilities and contingent liabilities acquired that are recognised should be those of the acquiree that existed at the date of acquisition.

### Treatment of future liabilities

Liabilities should not be recognised at the date of acquisition if they result from the acquirer's intentions or actions. Therefore liabilities for terminating or reducing the activities of the acquiree should **only** be recognised where the acquiree has, at the acquisition date, an existing liability for restructuring recognised in accordance with IAS 37 *Provisions, Contingent Liabilities and Contingent Assets*.

### Treatment of future losses

Liabilities should also not be recognised for future losses[9] or other costs expected to be incurred as a result of the acquisition, whether they relate to the acquirer or the acquiree.

### Treatment of contingent liabilities

Under IFRS 3 only those contingent liabilities assumed in a business combination that are a **present** obligation and can be measured reliably are recognised. If not recognised then they are disclosed in the same way as other contingent liabilities.

### Treatment of intangible assets

There is a requirement to identify both tangible and intangible assets that are acquired. For example, fair values would be attached to intangibles such as brands and customer lists if these can be measured reliably. If it is not possible to measure them reliably, then the goodwill would be reported at a higher figure, as in the following extract from the AstraZeneca 2015 Annual Report:

> **Business Combinations and Goodwill**
> On the acquisition of a business, fair values are attributed to the identifiable assets and liabilities and contingent liabilities unless the fair value cannot be measured reliably in which case the value is subsumed into goodwill.

### Why revalue net assets?

The reason why all the net assets, including the intangible assets that did not appear in the subsidiary's statement of financial position must be identified and fair-valued at the date of acquisition is to prevent distortion of EPS in periods following the acquisition. For example, we have seen in Chapter 19 that intangible assets are required to be amortised with an annual charge against profits, whereas goodwill is not subject to an annual amortisation charge but is reviewed for impairment. Subsuming intangible assets into the goodwill figure means that a regular amortisation charge is avoided. This reason for valuing the intangible assets would not apply if goodwill were to be amortised as it had been in the UK prior to 2008.

## 22.13 What advantages are there for stakeholders from requiring groups to prepare consolidated accounts?

Advantages include investor protection, help in predicting future earnings per share and means to assess management performance.

(a) **Investor protection:** Consolidation prevents the publication of misleading accounts by such means as inflating the sales through selling to another member of a group.

(b) **Prediction:** Consolidation provides a more meaningful EPS figure. Consolidated accounts show the full earnings on a parent company's investment while the parent's individual accounts only show the dividend received from the subsidiaries.

(c) **Accountability:** Consolidation provides a better measurement of the performance of a parent company's directors as the total earnings of a group can be compared with its total assets in arriving at a group's return on capital employed (ROCE).

It is important to remember that the ROCE prepared from the consolidated financial statements is regarded by management as a ratio that is an important measure of performance and one to be maximised. For example, Northgate plc reported in its 2013 Annual Report:

Return on capital employed (ROCE) – In a capital intensive business, ROCE is a more important measure of performance than profitability alone, as low margin business returns low value to shareholders . . . ROCE is maximised through a combination of managing utilisation, hire rates, vehicle holding costs and improvements in operational efficiency.

### Summary

When one company acquires a controlling interest in another and the combination is treated as an acquisition, the investment in the subsidiary is recorded in the acquirer's statement of financial position at the fair value of the investment.

On consolidation, if the consideration exceeds the fair value of the net assets it is referred to as goodwill and appears as an asset in the statement of financial position. If the consideration is less than the fair value of the net assets it is regarded as a bargain purchase and it will be taken to profit in accordance with IFRS 3.

On consolidation, if the acquirer has acquired less than 100% of the equity shares, any differences between the fair values of the assets or liabilities and their face value are recognised in full and the parent and non-controlling interests credited or debited with their respective percentage interests.

### REVIEW QUESTIONS

1 Explain how negative goodwill (bargain purchase) may arise and its accounting treatment.

2 Explain how the fair value is calculated for:
   ● tangible non-current assets
   ● inventories
   ● monetary assets.

3 Explain why only the net assets of the subsidiary and not those of the parent are adjusted to fair value at the date of acquisition for the purpose of consolidated accounts.

4 The 2013 Annual Report of Bayer AG states:

> Subsidiaries that do not have a material impact on the Group's net worth, financial position or earnings, either individually or in aggregate, are accounted for at cost of acquisition less any impairment losses.

Discuss what criteria might have applied in determining that a subsidiary does not have a material impact.

5 Parent plc acquired Son plc at the beginning of the year. At the end of the year there were intangible assets reported in the consolidated accounts for the value of a domain name and customer lists. These assets did not appear in either Parent or Son's statements of financial position.

Discuss why these assets only appeared in the consolidated accounts.

6 In each of the following cases you are required to give your opinion, with reasons, on whether or not there is a parent/subsidiary under IFRS 3. Suggest other information, if any, that might be helpful in making a decision.

(a) Tin acquired 15% of the equity voting shares and 90% of the non-voting preferred shares of Copper. Copper has no other category of shares. The directors of Tin are also the directors of Copper, there is a common head office with shared administration departments and the functions of Copper are mainly the provision of marketing and transport facilities for Tin. Another company, Iron, holds 55% of the equity voting shares of Copper but has never used its voting power to interfere with the decisions of the directors.

(b) Hat plc owns 60% of the voting equity shares in Glove plc and 25% of the voting equity shares in Shoe plc. Glove owns 30% of the voting equity shares in Shoe plc and has the right to appoint a majority of the directors.

(c) Morton plc has 30% of the voting equity shares of Berry plc and also has a verbal agreement with other shareholders, who own 40% of the shares, that those shareholders will vote according to the wishes of Morton.

(d) Bean plc acquired 30% of the shares of Pea plc several years ago with the intention of acquiring influence over the operating and financial policies of that company. Pea sells 80% of its output to Bean. While Bean has a veto over the operating and financial decisions of Pea's board of directors it has only used this veto on one occasion, four years ago, to prevent that company from supplying one of Bean's competitors.

## EXERCISES

### Questions 1–5

Required in each case:
Prepare the statements of financial position of Parent Ltd and the consolidated statement of financial position as at 1 January 20X7 after each transaction, using for each question the statements of financial position of Parent Ltd and Daughter Ltd as at 1 January 20X7 which were as follows:

|                              | Parent Ltd | Daughter Ltd |
|------------------------------|-----------:|-------------:|
|                              | £          | £            |
| Ordinary shares of £1 each   | 40,500     | 9,000        |
| Retained earnings            | 4,500      | 1,800        |
|                              | 45,000     | 10,800       |
| Cash                         | 20,000     | 2,000        |
| Other net assets             | 25,000     | 8,800        |
|                              | 45,000     | 10,800       |

**\* Question 1**

(a) Assume that on 1 January 20X7 Parent Ltd acquired all the ordinary shares in Daughter Ltd for £10,800 cash. The fair value of the net assets in Daughter Ltd was their book value.

(b) The purchase consideration was satisfied by the issue of 5,400 new ordinary shares in Parent Ltd. The fair value of a £1 ordinary share in Parent Ltd was £2. The fair value of the net assets in Daughter Ltd was their book value.

**Required: see above.**

**\* Question 2**

(a) On 1 January 20X7 Parent Ltd acquired all the ordinary shares in Daughter Ltd for £16,200 cash. The fair value of the net assets in Daughter Ltd was their book value.

(b) The purchase consideration was satisfied by the issue of 5,400 new ordinary shares in Parent Ltd. The fair value of a £1 ordinary share in Parent Ltd was £3. The fair value of the net assets in Daughter Ltd was their book value.

**Required: see above.**

**\* Question 3**

(a) On 1 January 20X7 Parent Ltd acquired all the ordinary shares in Daughter Ltd for £16,200 cash. The fair value of the net assets in Daughter Ltd was £12,000.

(b) The purchase consideration was satisfied by the issue of 5,400 new ordinary shares in Parent Ltd. The fair value of a £1 ordinary share in Parent Ltd was £3. The fair value of the net assets in Daughter Ltd was £12,000.

**Required: see above.**

**\* Question 4**

On 1 January 20X7 Parent Ltd acquired all the ordinary shares in Daughter Ltd for £6,000 cash. The fair value of the net assets in Daughter Ltd was their book value.

**Required: see above.**

**Question 5**

On 1 January 20X7 Parent Ltd acquired 75% of the ordinary shares in Daughter Ltd for £9,000 cash. The fair value of the net assets in Daughter Ltd was their book value. Assume in each case that the non-controlling interest is measured using Method 1.

**Required: see above.**

## * Question 6

Rouge plc acquired 100% of the common shares of Noir plc on 1 January 20X0 and gained control. At that date the statements of financial position of the two companies were as follows:

|  | Rouge € million | Noir € million |
|---|---|---|
| **ASSETS** | | |
| Non-current assets | | |
| Property, plant and equipment | 100 | 60 |
| Investment in Noir | 132 | |
| Current assets | 80 | 70 |
| Total assets | 312 | 130 |
| **EQUITY AND LIABILITIES** | | |
| Ordinary €1 shares | 200 | 60 |
| Retained earnings | 52 | 40 |
|  | 252 | 100 |
| Current liabilities | 60 | 30 |
| Total equity and liabilities | 312 | 130 |

*Note:* The fair values are the same as the book values.

**Required:**

**Prepare a consolidated statement of financial position for Rouge plc as at 1 January 20X0.**

## Question 7

Ham plc acquired 100% of the common shares of Burg plc on 1 January 20X0 and gained control. At that date the statements of financial position of the two companies were as follows:

|  | Ham €000 | Burg €000 |
|---|---|---|
| **ASSETS** | | |
| Non-current assets | | |
| Property, plant and equipment | 250 | 100 |
| Investment in Burg | 90 | |
| Current assets | 100 | 70 |
| Total assets | 440 | 170 |
| **EQUITY AND LIABILITIES** | | |
| Capital and reserves | | |
| €1 shares | 200 | 100 |
| Retained earnings | 160 | 10 |
|  | 360 | 110 |
| Current liabilities | 80 | 60 |
| Total equity and liabilities | 440 | 170 |

*Notes:*

1 The fair value is the same as the book value.

2 €15,000 of the negative goodwill (badwill) arises because the net assets have been acquired at below their fair value and the remainder covers expected losses of €3,000 in the year ended 31/12/20X0 and €2,000 in the following year.

Required:

(a) Prepare a consolidated statement of financial position for Ham plc as at 1 January 20X0.

(b) Explain how the negative goodwill (badwill) will be treated.

## Question 8

Set out below is the summarised statement of financial position of Berlin plc at 1 January 20X0.

|  | £000 |
|---|---|
| **ASSETS** | |
| Non-current assets | |
| Property, plant and equipment | 250 |
| Current assets | 150 |
| Total assets | 400 |
| **EQUITY AND LIABILITIES** | |
| Capital and reserves | |
| Share capital (£5 shares) | 200 |
| Retained earnings | 80 |
| | 280 |
| Current liabilities | 120 |
| Total equity and liabilities | 400 |

On 1/1/20X0 Berlin acquired 100% of the shares of Hanover for £100,000 and gained control.

Required:

Prepare the statement of financial position of Berlin immediately after the acquisition if:

(a) Berlin acquired the shares for cash.

(b) Berlin issued 10,000 shares of £5 (market value £10).

## Question 9

Bleu plc acquired 80% of the shares of Verte plc on 1 January 20X0 and gained control. At that date the statements of financial position of the two companies were as follows:

|  | Bleu £m | Verte £m |
|---|---|---|
| **ASSETS** | | |
| *Non-current assets* | | |
| Property, plant and equipment | 150 | 120 |
| Investment in Verte | 210 | |
| Current assets | 108 | 105 |
| Total assets | 468 | 225 |
| **EQUITY AND LIABILITIES** | | |
| *Capital and reserves* | | |
| Share capital (£1 shares) | 300 | 120 |
| Retained earnings | 78 | 60 |
| | 378 | 180 |
| Current liabilities | 90 | 45 |
| Total equity and liabilities | 468 | 225 |

*Note:* The fair values are the same as the book values.

**Required:**

**Prepare a consolidated statement of financial position for Bleu plc as at 1 January 20X0. Non-controlling interests are measured using Method 1.**

## Question 10

Base plc acquired 60% of the common shares of Ball plc on 1 January 20X0 and gained control. At that date the statements of financial position of the two companies were as follows:

|  | Base | Ball |
|---|---|---|
|  | £000 | £000 |
| **ASSETS** |  |  |
| Non-current assets |  |  |
| Property, plant and equipment | 250 | 100 |
| Investment in Ball | 90 |  |
| Current assets | 100 | 70 |
| Total assets | 440 | 170 |
| **EQUITY AND LIABILITIES** |  |  |
| Capital and reserves |  |  |
| Share capital | 200 | 80 |
| Share premium |  | 20 |
| Retained earnings | 160 | 10 |
|  | 360 | 110 |
| Current liabilities | 80 | 60 |
| Total equity and liabilities | 440 | 170 |

*Note:* The fair value of the property, plant and equipment in Ball at 1/1/20X0 was £120,000. The fair value of the non-controlling interest in Ball at 1/1/20X0 was £55,000. The 'fair value method' should be used to measure the non-controlling interest.

**Required:**

**Prepare a consolidated statement of financial position for Base as at 1 January 20X0.**

## Question 11

Applying the principles of control in IFRS 10 *Consolidated Financial Statements,* as described in Section 22.3.2 of this chapter, you are required to consider whether certain investments of Austin plc are subsidiaries.

Austin plc has investments in a number of companies, and the company's accountant has asked your advice on whether certain of these companies should be treated as subsidiaries under IFRS 10 *Consolidated Financial Statements.*

**(a)** Austin plc owns 45% of the voting shares of Bond Ltd.

**(b)** Austin plc owns 60% of the voting shares of Bradford Ltd and Bradford Ltd owns 30% of the voting shares of Derby Ltd. Recently, Austin plc purchased 70% of the voting shares of Coventry Ltd. Coventry Ltd owns 30% of the voting shares of Derby Ltd. The accountant believes Derby Ltd is not a subsidiary of Austin, as Austin effectively owns only 39% of the shares of Derby − 60% × 30% = 18% through Bradford and 70% × 30% = 21% through Coventry.

**(c)** Recently, Austin plc purchased 60% of the ordinary shares of Norwich plc.

Prior to the purchase, Norwich plc had in issue 6,000,000 'A' shares of £1 each. Each 'A' share carries a single vote. These shares were owned equally by each of the directors of Norwich plc. For the purchase, the directors of Norwich plc sold 2,000,000 'A' shares to Austin plc, and Norwich plc issued 4,000,000 'B' shares of £1 each to Austin plc. 'B' shares do not carry a vote.

**Required:**

Consider and, where appropriate, discuss whether the following companies are subsidiaries of Austin plc:

(a) Bond Ltd

(b) Derby Ltd

(c) Norwich plc.

## Question 12

(a) On 1 October 2012, Paradigm acquired 75% of Strata's equity shares by means of a share exchange of two new shares in Paradigm for every five acquired shares in Strata. In addition, Paradigm issued to the shareholders of Strata a $100 10% loan note for every 1,000 shares it acquired in Strata. Paradigm has not recorded any of the purchase consideration, although it does have other 10% loan notes already in issue.

The market value of Paradigm's shares at 1 October 2012 was $2 each.

The summarised statements of financial position of the two companies as at 31 March 2013 are:

|  | Paradigm | Strata |
|---|---|---|
| *Assets* | *$000* | *$000* |
| Non-current assets Property, plant and equipment | 47,400 | 25,500 |
| Financial asset: equity investments (notes (i) and (iv)) | 7,500 | 3,200 |
|  | 54,900 | 28,700 |
| *Current assets* |  |  |
| Inventory (note (ii)) | 20,400 | 8,400 |
| Trade receivables (note (iii)) | 14,800 | 9,000 |
| Bank | 2,100 | nil |
| Total assets | 92,200 | 46,100 |
| *Equity and liabilities* |  |  |
| Equity |  |  |
| Equity shares of $1 each | 40,000 | 20,000 |
| Retained earnings/(losses) – at 1 April 2012 | 19,200 | (4,000) |
| – for year ended 31 March 2013 | 7,400 | 8,000 |
|  | 66,600 | 24,000 |
| *Non-current liabilities* |  |  |
| 10% loan notes | 8,000 | nil |
| Current liabilities |  |  |
| Trade payables (note (iii)) | 17,600 | 13,000 |
| Bank overdraft nil 9,100 |  |  |
| Total equity and liabilities | 92,200 | 46,100 |

The following information is relevant:

(i) At the date of acquisition, Strata produced a draft statement of profit or loss which showed it had made a net loss after tax of $2 million at that date. Paradigm accepted this figure as the basis for calculating the pre- and post-acquisition split of Strata's profit for the year ended 31 March 2013.

Also at the date of acquisition, Paradigm conducted a fair value exercise on Strata's net assets which were equal to their carrying amounts (including Strata's financial asset equity investments) with the exception of an item of plant which had a fair value of $3 million below its carrying amount. The plant had a remaining economic life of three years at 1 October 2012.

Paradigm's policy is to value the non-controlling interest at fair value at the date of acquisition. For this purpose, a share price for Strata of $1.20 each is representative of the fair value of the shares held by the non-controlling interest.

(ii) Each month since acquisition, Paradigm's sales to Strata were consistently $4.6 million. Paradigm had marked these up by 15% on cost. Strata had one month's supply ($4.6 million) of these goods in inventory at 31 March 2013. Paradigm's normal mark-up (to third party customers) is 40%.

(iii) Strata's current account balance with Paradigm at 31 March 2013 was $2.8 million, which did not agree with Paradigm's equivalent receivable due to a payment of $900,000 made by Strata on 28 March 2013, which was not received by Paradigm until 3 April 2013.

(iv) The financial asset equity investments of Paradigm and Strata are carried at their fair values as at 1 April 2012. As at 31 March 2013, these had fair values of $7.1 million and $3.9 million respectively.

(v) There were no impairment losses within the group during the year ended 31 March 2013.

**Required:**

**Prepare the consolidated statement of financial position for Paradigm as at 31 March 2013.**

**(b)** Paradigm has a strategy of buying struggling businesses, reversing their decline and then selling them on at a profit within a short period of time. Paradigm is hoping to do this with Strata.

**Required:**

**As an adviser to a prospective purchaser of Strata, explain any concerns you would raise about basing an investment decision on the information available in Paradigm's consolidated financial statements and Strata's entity financial statements.**

*(ACCA Financial Reporting June 2013)*

## Notes

1 IFRS 10 *Consolidated Financial Statements*, IASB, 2011, B 92-93.
2 Ibid., para. 7.
3 IFRS 3 *Business Combinations*, 2008, B 44.
4 IAS 36 *Impairment of Assets*, IASB, revised 2004, para. 34.
5 IFRS 3 *Business Combinations*, 2008, B 34.
6 IFRS 10 *Consolidated Financial Statements*, IASB, 2011.
7 Ibid., paras 5, 6 and 8.
8 IFRS 13 *Fair Value Measurement*, IASB, 2011, Appendix A.
9 IFRS 10 *Consolidated Financial Settlements*, IASB, 2011, B 92-93.

# CHAPTER 23

# Preparation of consolidated statements of financial position after the date of acquisition

## 23.1 Introduction

The main purpose of this chapter is to prepare consolidated financial statements after a period of trading.

> ### Objectives
>
> By the end of this chapter, you should be able to:
>
> - explain uniform accounting policies;
> - account for the pre- and post-acquisition profits of a subsidiary;
> - eliminate inter-company balances and deal with reconciling items;
> - account for unrealised profits on inter-company transactions;
> - calculate group retained earnings;
> - prepare consolidated statements of financial position.

## 23.2 Uniform accounting policies and reporting dates

Consolidated financial statements are required to adopt uniform accounting policies on a consistent basis in accordance with IFRS 10 *Consolidated Financial Statements*. The following is an extract from the 2015 Annual Report of Munksjo AB:

> Accounting policies for subsidiaries are changed where necessary to ensure consistent application of the Group's policies.

If this is not practicable then disclosure must be made of that together with details of the items involved.[1]

The financial statements of the parent and subsidiaries used in the consolidated accounts are usually drawn up to the same date but IFRS 10 continues to allow up to three months' difference providing that appropriate adjustments are made for significant transactions outside the common period.[2]

## 23.3 Pre- and post-acquisition profits/losses

### Pre-acquisition profits

Any profits or losses of a subsidiary made **before** the date of acquisition are referred to as **pre-acquisition profits/losses** in the consolidated financial statements. These are represented by the retained earnings that existed in the subsidiary as at the date of acquisition and, as we have seen in Chapter 22, they are taken into account when calculating the goodwill.

It is important to remember that the calculation of the initial goodwill as at the date of acquisition is unchanged in subsequent accounting periods. The goodwill only changes in subsequent accounting periods if there should be an impairment charge or amortisation charge if that should be the regulatory requirement in the local jurisdiction.

### Post-acquisition profits

Any profits or losses made **after** the date of acquisition are referred to as **post-acquisition profits/losses**. Because these will have arisen whilst the subsidiary was under the control of the parent company, they will be included in the group consolidated statement of income and so will be included in the retained earnings figure in the statement of financial position. The following example for the Bend Group illustrates the approach for dealing with pre- and post-acquisition profits.

## 23.4 The Bend Group – assuming there have been no inter-group transactions

On 1 January 20X1 Bend plc acquired 80% of the 10,000 £1 ordinary shares in Stretch plc for £1.50 per share in cash which gave it control.

- Investment in the subsidiary cost £12,000.
- The retained earnings of Stretch plc were £4,000.
- The fair value of the non-current assets in Stretch plc was £600 above book value.
- The fair value of the non-controlling interest at the date of acquisition was £2,950 and Method 2 has been adopted.

Remember that in the subsidiary's own accounts the assets may be either left at book values or restated at their fair values. If restated at fair values, they will then become subject to the requirements of IAS 16 *Property, Plant and Equipment*[3] which states that revaluations should be made with sufficient regularity that the statement of financial position figure is not materially different from the fair value at that date. This is one reason why the fair value adjustment is usually treated simply as a consolidation adjustment each year.

At 31 December 20X1 the closing statements of financial position of Bend plc and Stretch plc together with the group accounts were as follows:

|  | Bend £ | Stretch £ | Group £ |  |
|---|---|---|---|---|
| ASSETS |  |  |  |  |
| Non-current assets | 26,000 | 12,000 | 38,600 | Step 3 |
| Goodwill | — | — | 350 | Step 1 |
| Investment in Stretch | 12,000 | — | — |  |
| Net current assets | 13,000 | 4,000 | 17,000 | Step 3 |
| Net assets | 51,000 | 16,000 | 55,950 |  |
| EQUITY |  |  |  |  |
| Share capital | 16,000 | 10,000 | 16,000 | Step 4 |
| Retained earnings | 35,000 | 6,000 | 36,600 | Step 4 |
|  | 51,000 | 16,000 | 52,600 |  |
| Non-controlling interest | — | — | 3,350 | Step 2 |
|  | 51,000 | 16,000 | 55,950 |  |

*Step 1: Goodwill calculated as at 1 January 20X1*

|  | £ | £ |
|---|---|---|
| *Goodwill on Bend's 80% shareholding in Stretch* | | |
| The cost of the parent company's investment in Stretch | | 12,000 |
| *Less:* | | |
| (a) Bend's share of Stretch share capital: | | |
| 80%  × share capital of Stretch (80%  × 10,000) | 8,000 | |
| (b) Pre-acquisition profit | | |
| Bend's share of Stretch's retained earnings: | | |
| 80%  × retained earnings as at 1 January 20X1 (80%  × 4,000) | 3,200 | |
| (c) Fair value adjustment | | |
| Bend's share of any change in the book values: | | |
| 80%  × revaluation of fixed assets at 1 January 20X1 (80%  × 600) | 480 | |
| | | 11,680 |
| Goodwill attributable to the parent company shareholders | | 320 |
| *Goodwill on non-controlling interest's 20% shareholding in Stretch* | | |
| Fair value of non-controlling interest at date of acquisition | | 2,950 |
| 20% of net assets at date of acquisition (10,000 + 4,000 + 600) | | (2,920) |
| Goodwill attributable to the non-controlling interest | | 30 |
| Total goodwill of parent and non-controlling interest (£320 + £30) | | £350 |

*Step 2: Non-controlling interest in the net assets of subsidiary calculated as at 31.12.20X1*

|  | £ |
|---|---|
| (a) Subsidiary share capital | |
| Non-controlling interest in the share capital of Stretch (20%  × 10,000) | 2,000 |
| (b) Total retained earnings as at 31.12.20X1 | |
| Non-controlling interest in retained earnings of Stretch (20%  × 6,000) | 1,200 |
| (c) Fair value adjustment of subsidiary's non-current assets | |
| Non-controlling interest in fair value increase (20%  × 600) | 120 |
| Non-controlling interest in the net assets of Stretch as at 31.12.20X1 | 3,320 |
| Non-controlling interest in goodwill | 30 |
| Reported in the statement of financial position as at 31 December 20X1 | 3,350 |

*Step 3: Add together the assets and liabilities of the parent and subsidiary for the group*

|  | *Parent* | | *Subsidiary* | *Group* |
|---|---|---|---|---|
|  | £ | | £ | £ |
| Non-current tangible assets | 26,000 | + | (12,000 + revaluation 600) | 38,600 |
| Goodwill as calculated in Step 1 | | | | 350 |
| Net current assets | 13,000 | + | 4,000 | 17,000 |
| Total | | | | 55,950 |

*Step 4: Calculate the consolidated share capital and reserves for the group accounts*

|  |  |  | £ | £ |
|---|---|---|---|---|
| Share capital | Parent only | | | 16,000 |
| Retained earnings | Parent | | 35,000 | |
| | Bend's share of | | | |
| | post-acquisition | | | |
| | retained earnings | (80% of (6,000 − 4,000)) | 1,600 | 36,600 |
| Total | | | | 52,600 |

*Notes:*

1 The separation of the retained earnings into pre- and post-acquisition is only of relevance to the parent with the pre-acquisition (£4,000) used when calculating the goodwill and the post-acquisition (£2,000) reported as part of the group earnings.

2 The non-controlling shareholders are entitled to their percentage share of the closing net assets. The pre-acquisition and post-acquisition division is irrelevant to the non-controlling interests – they are entitled to their percentage share of the **total** retained earnings at the date the consolidated statement of financial position is prepared.

## 23.5 Inter-company transactions

In the Bend example we assumed that there had been no inter-company transactions. In most groups, however, there are inter-company transactions that take place. On consolidation IFRS 10 requires[4] all inter-company transactions to be eliminated. So, if goods have been sold by Many plc, the parent, for £1,500 to Few plc, a subsidiary, the sales that had been reported in Many's statement of income and the cost of sales reported in Few's statement of income would both be eliminated. This is accomplished by a consolidation journal entry:

|  | Dr | Cr |
|---|---|---|
| Sales | 1,500 | |
| Cost of sales | | 1,500 |
| *Eliminating intra-group sales* | | |

**Note** that no entries are made in the individual company's accounts and the elimination is simply to ensure that the consolidated sales and cost of sales only include transactions with non-group parties.

### 23.5.1 Adjustment when inter-company sales include a profit loading

Where sales have been made between two companies within the group, it is only necessary to provide for an unrealised profit from intra-group sales to the extent that the goods are still in the inventories of the group at the date of the statement of financial position.

We will illustrate the accounting treatment where there is unrealised profit with the Many Group example.

Let us assume that Many plc has bought £1,000 worth of goods for resale and sold them to Few plc for £1,500, making a profit of £500 in Many's own accounts.

We have already seen that one of the consolidated journal entries would be to debit sales £1,500 and credit cost of sales £1,500, whether or not the goods had been sold on to a third party.

If at the year-end Few plc still has these goods in inventory, the group has not yet made a sale to a third party and the £500 profit is therefore 'unrealised'. It must be removed from the consolidated statement of financial position by:

- reducing the retained earnings of Many by £500; and
- reducing the inventories of Few by £500.

The £500 is called a 'provision for unrealised profit'.

If the sale is made by a subsidiary to the parent and there are non-controlling interests, these will be debited with their 'proportion of the unrealised profit'.

### 23.5.2 Eliminating inter-company current account balances

If the sale were made for cash, then the cash in the seller would have increased and the cash in the buyer would have decreased. On consolidation no adjustment is, therefore, required. However, if the invoice has not been settled, there would be an account receivable in the seller's and an account payable in the buyer's statement of financial position. These must be eliminated by cancelling each.

In our Many Group example, the £1,500 would be cancelled.

#### Reconciling inter-company balances

In practice, temporary differences may arise for such items as cash or inventory in transit that are recorded in one company's books but of which the other company is not yet aware. If so, this is reconciled on consolidation for cash in transit, debit Cash and credit Accounts receivable and for inventory in transit, debit Inventory and credit Accounts payable.

If Few had sent cash of £400 to Many in part settlement of the £1,500 owing but it had not been recorded in the books of Many at the period-end date, the Many accounts would show £1,500 owing, whereas the Few accounts would show £1,100 owing and the cash balance reduced by the £500. On consolidation the Accounts receivable would be reduced to £1,100 and the cash increased by £400. The Account receivable and payable balances are both £1,100 and would be cancelled.

### 23.5.3 Inter-company dividends payable/receivable

If the subsidiary company has declared a dividend before the year-end, it will appear in the current liabilities of the subsidiary company and in the current assets of the parent company. It needs to be cancelled by set-off.

If the subsidiary is wholly owned by the parent the whole amount will be cancelled. If, however, there is a non-controlling interest in the subsidiary, the non-cancelled amount of the dividend payable in the subsidiary's statement of financial position will be the amount payable to the non-controlling interest and will be reported as part of the non-controlling interest in the consolidated statement of financial position.

Where a final dividend has not been declared by the year-end date there is no liability under IAS 10 *Events after the Reporting Period Date* and no liability will be reported.

Companies include a reference to these adjustments in their accounting policies, as seen in the following extract from the 2015 Annual Report of Munksjo AB:

> **Transaction eliminated on consolidation**
>
> Intra-Group receivables and liabilities, income or expenses and unrealised gains or losses arising from intra-Group transactions between Group companies are eliminated in full when preparing the consolidated accounts.

The Prose Group example that follows incorporates the main points dealt with so far on the preparation of a consolidated statement of financial position.

## 23.6 The Prose Group – assuming there have been inter-group transactions

On 1 January 20X1 Prose plc acquired 80% of the equity shares in Verse plc for £21,100 to gain control and 10% of the 5% loans for £900. The retained earnings as at 1 January 20X1 were £4,000. The fair value of the land in Verse was £1,000 above book value.

During the year Prose sold some of its inventory to Verse for £3,000, which represented cost plus a markup of 25%. Half of these goods are still in the inventory of Verse at 31/12/20X1.

The consolidated statement of financial position as at 31 December 20X1 is shown below with supporting notes. Note that depreciation is not charged on land and Method 1 is used to compute the non-controlling interest.

| | Prose £ | Verse £ | Adjustments Dr | Group Cr | £ | |
|---|---|---|---|---|---|---|
| **ASSETS** | | | | | | |
| Non-current assets | 25,920 | 33,400 | 1,000 | | 60,320 | |
| Investment in Verse/goodwill | 22,000 | — | | 21,500 | 500 | Step 1 |
| *Current assets* | | | | | | |
| Inventories | 9,600 | 4,000 | | 300 | 13,300 | Step 3 |
| Verse current account | 8,000 | | | 8,000 | — | Step 2 |
| Loan interest receivable | 35 | | | 35 | — | Step 2 |
| Other current assets | 3,965 | 13,350 | | | 17,315 | |
| Total assets | 69,520 | 50,750 | | | 91,435 | |
| **EQUITY and LIABILITIES** | | | | | | |
| Equity share capital | 24,000 | 21,000 | 21,000 | | 24,000 | |
| Retained earnings | 30,000 | 8,500 | 5,200 | | 33,300 | Step 5 |
| Non-controlling interest | — | — | | 6,100 | 6,100 | Step 4 |
| *Non-current liabilities* | | | | | | |
| 5% loan 2017/18 | 5,000 | 7,000 | 700 | | 11,300 | Step 2 |
| *Current liabilities* | | | | | | |
| Prose current account | | 8,000 | 8,000 | | — | |
| Loan interest payable | | 350 | 35 | | 315 | |
| Other current liabilities | 10,520 | 5,900 | | | 16,420 | |
| | 69,520 | 50,750 | 35,935 | 35,935 | 91,435 | |

## Step 1: Calculation of goodwill

(Note that this calculation will be the same as when calculated at the date of acquisition)

| | | £ | £ |
|---|---|---|---|
| Cost of investment in shares and loan | | | 22,000 |
| *Less:* | | | |
| 1 80% × equity shares of Verse | (80% × 21,000) | 16,800 | |
| 2 80% × retained earnings balance at 1.1.20X1 | (80% × 4,000) | 3,200 | |
| 3 80% × fair value increase at 1.1.20X1 | (80% × 1,000) | 800 | |
| 4 10% × loans of Verse | (10% × 7,000) | 700 | 21,500 |
| 5 Goodwill in statement of financial position | | | 500 |

## Step 2: Inter-company elimination by set-off of inter-company balances

1 The current accounts of £8,000 between the two companies are cancelled. Note that the accounts are equal, which indicates that there are no items such as goods in transit or cash in transit which would have required a reconciliation.

2 The loan interest receivable by Prose is cancelled with £35 (10% of £350) of the loan interest payable by Verse, leaving £315 (90% of £350) payable to outsiders. This is not part of the non-controlling interest as loan holders have no ownership rights in the company.

3 The loan of £700 in Prose's accounts is set off against the £7,000 in Verse's accounts, leaving 6,300 owing to non-group members.

### Step 3: Unrealised profit in inventory

| | |
|---|---:|
| Markup on the inter-company sales (£3,000 × 20%) | £600 |
| Half the goods are still in inventories at the year-end. | |
| Unrealised profit | £300 |

### Step 4: Calculation of non-controlling interest as at 31/12/20X1

Note that the non-controlling interest is calculated as at the year-end while goodwill is calculated at the date of acquisition.

| | | £ |
|---|---|---:|
| Non-controlling interest in the equity shares of Verse | (20% × 21,000) | 4,200 |
| Non-controlling interest in the retained earnings of Verse | (20% × 8,500) | 1,700 |
| Non-controlling interest in the fair value increase | (20% × 1,000) | 200 |
| Statement of financial position figure | | 6,100 |

### Step 5: Calculation of consolidated share capital and reserves for the group accounts

| | £ | £ |
|---|---:|---:|
| *Share capital:* | | |
| Equity share capital (parent company's only) | | 24,000 |
| Retained earnings (parent company's) | 30,000 | |
| *Less:* Provision for unrealised profit | (300) | 29,700 |
| Parent's share of the post-acquisition profit of the subsidiary | | |
| (80% × 8,500) | 6,800 | |
| *Less:* 80% of pre-acquisition profits (80% × 4,000) | (3,200) | 3,600 |
| Retained earnings in the consolidated statement of financial position | | 33,300 |

## Summary

When consolidated accounts are prepared after the subsidiary has traded with other members of the group, the goodwill calculation remains as at the date of the acquisition but all inter-company transactions and unrealised profits arising from inter-company transactions must be eliminated.

## REVIEW QUESTIONS

**1** An accounting policy states that all inter-company transactions, receivables, liabilities and unrealised profits, as well as intra-group profit distributions, are eliminated.

(a) Discuss three examples of inter-company (also referred to as intra-group) transactions.

(b) Explain what is meant by 'are eliminated'.

(c) Explain what effect there could be on the reported group profit if inter-company transactions were not eliminated.

**2** Explain why the non-controlling interest is not affected by the pre- and post-acquisition division.

**3** Explain why pre-acquisition profits of a subsidiary are treated differently from post-acquisition profits when consolidating.

**4** Explain the effect of a provision for unrealised profit on a non-controlling interest:

(a) where the sale was made by the parent to the subsidiary; and

(b) where the sale was made by the subsidiary to the parent.

**5** A consolidated journal adjustment set off the dividend receivable reported in the parent's statement of financial position against the dividend declared by the subsidiary. Explain why this may not fully eliminate the dividend that is reported in the group statement of financial position.

**6** Explain reasons why the current accounts in the parent and subsidiary may not agree. If not, how could the two accounts be set off?

## EXERCISES

**\* Question 1**

Sweden acquired 100% of the equity shares of Oslo on 1 March 20X1 and gained control. At that date the balances on the reserves of Oslo were as follows:

|  |  |
|---|---|
| Revaluation reserve | Kr10 million |
| Retained earnings | Kr70 million |

The statements of financial position of the two companies at 31/12/20X1 were as follows:

| | Sweden Krm | Oslo Krm |
|---|---|---|
| **ASSETS** | | |
| *Non-current assets* | | |
| Property, plant and equipment | 264 | 120 |
| Investment in Oslo | 200 | |
| Current assets | 160 | 140 |
| Total assets | 624 | 260 |
| **EQUITY AND LIABILITIES** | | |
| Kr10 shares | 400 | 110 |
| Retained earnings | 104 | 80 |
| Revaluation reserve | 20 | 10 |
| | 524 | 200 |
| Current liabilities | 100 | 60 |
| Total equity and liabilities | 624 | 260 |

*Notes:*

1  The fair values were the same as the book values on 1/3/20X1.
2  There have been no movements on share capital since 1/3/20X1.
3  20% of the goodwill is to be written off as an impairment loss.
4  Method 1 is to be used to compute the non-controlling interest.

**Required:**
**Prepare a consolidated statement of financial position for Sweden as at 31 December 20X1.**

## * Question 2

Summer plc acquired 60% of the equity shares of Winter Ltd on 30 September 20X1 and gained control. At the date of acquisition, the balance of retained earnings of Winter was €35,000.

At 31 December 20X1 the statements of financial position of the two companies were as follows:

| | Summer €000 | Winter €000 |
|---|---|---|
| **ASSETS** | | |
| *Non-current assets* | | |
| Property, plant and equipment | 200 | 200 |
| Investment in Winter | 141 | |
| Current assets | 100 | 140 |
| Total assets | 441 | 340 |
| **EQUITY AND LIABILITIES** | | |
| Equity shares | 200 | 180 |
| Retained earnings | 161 | 40 |
| | 361 | 220 |
| Current liabilities | 80 | 120 |
| Total equity and liabilities | 441 | 340 |

*Notes:*

1  The fair value of the non-controlling interest at the date of acquisition was £92,000. The non-controlling interest is to be measured using Method 2. The fair values of the identifiable net assets of Winter at the date of acquisition were the same as their book values.

2  There have been no movements on share capital since 30/9/20X1.

**Required:**

**Prepare a consolidated statement of financial position for Summer plc as at 31 December 20X1.**

## Question 3

On 30 September 20X0 Gold plc acquired 75% of the equity shares, 30% of the preferred shares and 20% of the bonds in Silver plc and gained control. The balance of retained earnings on 30 September 20X0 was £16,000. The fair value of the land owned by Silver was £3,000 above book value. No adjustment has so far been made for this revaluation.

The statements of financial position of Gold and Silver at 31 December 20X1 were as follows:

|  | Gold £ | Silver £ |
|---|---|---|
| **ASSETS** | | |
| Property, plant and equipment (including land) | 82,300 | 108,550 |
| Investment in Silver | 46,000 | — |
| *Current assets* | | |
| Inventory | 23,200 | 10,000 |
| Silver current account | 20,000 | |
| Bond interest receivable | 175 | |
| Other current assets | 5,000 | 7,500 |
| Total assets | 176,675 | 126,050 |
| **EQUITY AND LIABILITIES** | | |
| Equity share capital | 60,000 | 27,600 |
| Preferred shares | 10,000 | 20,000 |
| Retained earnings | 75,000 | 21,200 |
| | 145,000 | 68,800 |
| Non-current liabilities – bonds | 12,500 | 17,500 |
| *Current liabilities* | | |
| Gold current account | | 20,000 |
| Bond interest payable | 625 | 875 |
| Other current liabilities | 18,550 | 18,875 |
| Total equity and liabilities | 176,675 | 126,050 |

*Notes:*

1 The recoverable amount for purposes of calculating the impairment of goodwill is £50,040.

2 During the year Gold sold some of its inventory to Silver for £3,000, which represented cost plus a markup of 25%. Half of these goods are still in the inventory of Silver at 31.12.20X1.

3 There is no depreciation of land.

4 There has been no movement on share capital since the acquisition.

5 Method 1 is to be used to compute the non-controlling interest.

**Required:**
**Prepare a consolidated statement of financial position as at 31 December 20X1.**

## Question 4

Prop and Flap have produced the following statements of financial position as at 31 October 2008:

| | Prop $m | Prop $m | Flap $m | Flap $m |
|---|---|---|---|---|
| **ASSETS** | | | | |
| *Non-current assets* | | | | |
| Plant and equipment | | 2,100 | | 480 |
| Investments | | 800 | | |
| *Current assets* | | | | |
| Inventories | 880 | | 280 | |
| Receivables | 580 | | 420 | |
| Cash and cash equivalents | 400 | | 8 | |
| | | 1,860 | | 708 |
| Total assets | | 4,760 | | 1,188 |
| **EQUITY and LIABILITIES** | | | | |
| Equity share capital | | 2,400 | | 680 |
| Retained earnings | | 860 | | 200 |
| | | 3,260 | | 880 |
| *Non-current liabilities* | | | | |
| Long-term borrowing | | 400 | | |
| *Current liabilities* | | | | |
| Payables | 1,100 | | 228 | |
| Bank overdraft | — | | 80 | |
| | | 1,100 | | 308 |
| Total equity and liabilities | | 4,760 | | 1,188 |

The following information is relevant to the preparation of the financial statements of the Prop Group:

1 Prop acquired 80% of the issued ordinary share capital of Flap many years ago when the retained earnings of Flap were $72 million. Consideration transferred was $800 million. Flap has performed well since acquisition and so far there has been no impairment to goodwill.

2 At the date of acquisition the plant and equipment of Flap was revalued upwards by $40 million, although this revaluation was not recorded in the accounts of Flap. Depreciation would have been $32 million greater had it been based on the revalued figure.

3 Flap buys goods from Prop upon which Prop earns a margin of 20%. At 31 October 2008 Flap's inventories include $180 million goods purchased from Prop.

4 At 31 October 2008 Prop has receivables of $140 million owed by Flap and payables of $60 million owed to Flap.

5 The market price of the non-controlling interest shares just before Flap's acquisition by Prop was $1.30. It is the group's policy to value the non-controlling interest at fair value.

Required:

Prepare the Prop Group consolidated statement of financial position as at 31 October 2008.

*(Association of International Accountants)*

## Question 5

On 1 January 20X0 Hill plc purchased 70% of the ordinary shares of Valley plc for £1.3 million. The fair value of the non-controlling interest at that date was £0.5 million. At the date of acquisition, Valley's retained earnings were £0.4 million.

The statements of financial position of Hill and Valley at 31 December 20X0 were:

|  | Hill | Valley |
|---|---|---|
|  | £000 | £000 |
| *Capital and reserves* |  |  |
| Share capital | 5,000 | 1,000 |
| Retained earnings | 3,500 | 200 |
|  | 8,500 | 1,200 |
| Net assets | 8,500 | 1,200 |

Because of Valley's loss in 20X0, the directors of Hill decided to write down the value of goodwill by £0.3 million. The directors of Hill propose to use Method 2 to calculate goodwill in the consolidated statement of financial position. The goodwill is to be written down in proportion to the respective hold-ings of Valley's shares by Hill and the non-controlling interest.

Required:

(a) Calculate the goodwill of Valley relating to Hill plc and the non-controlling interest.

(b) Show how the goodwill will be written down at 31 December 20X0, for both Hill plc and the non-controlling interest.

(c) Comment on your answer to part (b).

## Question 6

The following accounts are the consolidated statement of financial position and parent company statement of financial position for Alpha Ltd as at 30 June 20X2:

|  | Consolidated statement of financial position | | Parent company statement of financial position | |
| --- | --- | --- | --- | --- |
|  | £ | £ | £ | £ |
| Ordinary shares |  | 140,000 |  | 140,000 |
| Capital reserve |  | 92,400 |  | 92,400 |
| Retained earnings |  | 79,884 |  | 35,280 |
| Non-controlling interest |  | 12,329 |  | — |
|  |  | 324,613 |  | 267,680 |
| **Non-current assets** |  |  |  |  |
| Property |  | 127,400 |  | 84,000 |
| Plant and equipment |  | 62,720 |  | 50,400 |
| Goodwill |  | 85,680 |  |  |
| Investment in subsidiary (50,400 shares) |  |  |  | 151,200 |
| **Current assets** |  |  |  |  |
| Inventory | 121,604 |  | 71,120 |  |
| Trade receivables | 70,429 |  | 51,800 |  |
| Cash at bank | 24,360 |  | — |  |
|  | 216,393 |  | 122,920 |  |
| **Current liabilities** |  |  |  |  |
| Trade payables | 140,420 |  | 80,920 |  |
| Income tax | 27,160 |  | 20,720 |  |
| Bank overdraft | — |  | 39,200 |  |
|  | 167,580 |  | 140,840 |  |
| Working capital |  | 48,813 |  | (17,920) |
|  |  | 324,613 |  | 267,680 |

*Notes:*

1 There was only one subsidiary, called Beta Ltd.

2 There were no capital reserves in the subsidiary.

3 Alpha produced inventory for sale to the subsidiary at a cost of £3,360 in May 20X2. The inventory was invoiced to the subsidiary at £4,200 and was still on hand at the subsidiary's warehouse on 30 June 20X2. The invoice had not been settled at 30 June 20X2.

4 The retained earnings of the subsidiary had a credit balance of £16,800 at the date of acquisition. No fair value adjustments were necessary.

5 There was a right of set-off between overdrafts and bank balances.

6 The parent owns 90% of the subsidiary.

**Required:**
Prepare the statement of financial position as at 30 June 20X2 of the subsidiary company from the information given above. The non-controlling interest is measured using Method 1.

## Notes

1 IFRS 10 *Consolidated Financial Statements*, IASB, 2011, para. 19.
2 Ibid., B 92–93.
3 IAS 16 *Property, Plant and Equipment*, IASB, revised 2003, para. 31.
4 IFRS 10 *Consolidated Financial Statements*, IASB, 2011, B 86.

# CHAPTER 24

# Preparation of consolidated statements of income, changes in equity and cash flows

## 24.1 Introduction

The main purpose of this chapter is to explain how to prepare a consolidated statement of income.

### Objectives

By the end of this chapter, you should be able to:

- eliminate inter-company transactions;
- prepare a consolidated statement of income;
- attribute income to the non-controlling shareholders;
- prepare a consolidated statement of changes in equity;
- prepare a consolidated statement of income when a subsidiary is acquired partway through a year;
- prepare a consolidated statement of cash flows.

## 24.2 Eliminate inter-company transactions

Many business combinations occur because the acquirer seeks closer links with the acquired company. There are many examples of this, such as a clothing manufacturer in Europe acquiring a denim supplier in Hong Kong with inter-company purchases and sales following the acquisition.

### Inter-company sales

When the consolidated statement of income is prepared the inter-company sales are eliminated. This avoids the possibility that the group could inflate its revenue merely by group companies selling to each other. The sales and purchases both need to be reduced by the invoiced amount of the inter-company sales. This is achieved in the consolidation process by reducing the aggregate sales and aggregate cost of sales figures.

### Unrealised profit

In the previous chapter we treated any unrealised profit by reducing the inventory figure and reducing the retained earnings figure. The retained earnings figure would have incorporated the retained earnings balance from the statement of income, i.e. the adjustment for the unrealised profit would have already been reported in the statement of income.

In the consolidation process the unrealised profit is added to the cost of sales to achieve the reduction in group gross profit.

### Dividends and interest

Having set off the sales and cost of sales and adjusted for any unrealised profit, further adjustments may be required[1] to establish the profit before tax earned by the group as a whole. This requires us to eliminate any dividends (and interest if any) that have been credited in the parent's statement of income for amounts paid or payable to the parent by the subsidiaries.

If this were not done, there would be double-counting because we would be including in the consolidated statement of income the subsidiary's profit from operations and again as dividends and interest received/receivable by the parent.

### Group profits before tax

We can see, therefore, that group profit before tax is arrived at after setting-off inter-company sales against the cost of sales, adding the unrealised profit to the cost of sales figure, and eliminating any dividends or interest received or receivable from a subsidiary.

We will illustrate this in the following Ante Group example.

## 24.3 Preparation of a consolidated statement of income – the Ante Group

The following information is available:

At the date of acquisition on 1 January 20X3:
Ante plc acquired 75% of the ordinary shares in Post plc. (*This shows that Ante had control.*) At that date the retained earnings of Post were £30,000. (*These are pre-acquisition profits and should not be included in the group profit for the year.*)

At the end of 20X3:
The retained earnings of Ante were £69,336 and the retained earnings of Post were £54,000.

During the year ended 31 December 20X4:
Ante had sold Post goods at their cost price of £9,000 plus a markup of one-third. These were the only inter-company sales. (*This indicates that the group sales and cost of sales require reducing.*)

At the end of the financial year on 31 December 20X4:
Half of these goods were still in the inventory at the end of the year. (*There is unrealised profit to be removed from the group gross profit by adding the unrealised amount to the cost of sales figure.*)

Dividends paid in 20X4 by group companies were as follows:

|  | Ante | Post |
|---|---|---|
| On ordinary shares | £40,000 | £5,000 |

Set out below are the individual statements of income of Ante and Post together with the consolidated statement of income for the year ended 31 December 20X4 with explanatory notes.

*Statements of comprehensive income for the year ended 31 December 20X4*

|  | Ante | Post | Consolidated |  |
| --- | --- | --- | --- | --- |
|  | £ | £ | £ |  |
| Sales | 200,000 | 120,000 | 308,000 | Note 1 |
| Cost of sales | 60,000 | 60,000 | 109,500 | Notes 1 and 2 |
| Gross profit | 140,000 | 60,000 | 198,500 |  |
| Expenses | 59,082 | 40,000 | 99,082 | Note 3 |
| Profit from operations | 80,918 | 20,000 | 99,418 |  |
| Dividends received – ordinary shares | 3,750 | — | — |  |
| Profit before tax | 84,668 | 20,000 | 99,418 | Note 4 |
| Income tax expense | 14,004 | 6,000 | 20,004 | Note 5 |
| Profit for the period | 70,664 | 14,000 | 79,414 |  |
| *Attributable to:* |  |  |  |  |
| Ordinary shareholders of Ante (balance) |  |  | 75,914 |  |
| Non-controlling shareholders in Post |  |  | 3,500 | Note 6 |
|  |  |  | 79,414 |  |

*Notes:*

1  Eliminate inter-company sales on consolidation
   Cancel the inter-company sales of £12,000 (£9,000 × $1^{1}/_{3}$) by

   (i)   reducing the sales of Ante from £200,000 to £188,000; and

   (ii)  reducing the cost of sales of Post by the same amount from £60,000 to £48,000.
        *(Remember that the same amount is deducted from both sales and cost of sales – a sale to one party is the amount of the purchase by the other party.)*

   (iii) Group sales are £188,000 + £120,000 = £308,000.

   (iv)  Group cost of sales (before any adjustment for unrealised profit) is
        £60,000 + £48,000 = £108,000.

2  Eliminate unrealised profit on inter-company goods still in closing inventory

   (i)   Ante had sold the goods to Post at a markup of £3,000.

   (ii)  Half of the goods remain in the inventory of Post at the year-end.

   (iii) From the group's view there is an unrealised profit of half of the markup, i.e. £1,500.
        Therefore:

        ● deduct £1,500 from the gross profit of Ante by adding this amount to the cost of sales;

        ● reduce the inventories in the consolidated statement of financial position by the amount of the provision (as explained in the previous chapter).

   (iv)  Cost of sales has been increased from £108,000 to £109,500.

3  Aggregate expenses
   In this example we do not have any inter-company transactions such as Head Office management fees that need to be set off. No adjustment is, therefore, required to the parent or subsidiary total figures.

4 Profit before tax, accounting for the inter-company dividends

The ordinary dividend of £3,750 received by Ante is an inter-company item that does not appear in the group profit before tax.

5 Aggregate the taxation figures

No adjustment is required to the parent or subsidiary total figures.

6 Allocation of profit to equity holders and non-controlling interest

Adjustment is required[2] to establish how much of the profit after tax is attributable to equity holders of the parent. The amount is that remaining after deducting the non-controlling interest's percentage of the subsidiary's after-tax figure, i.e. 25% of £14,000 = £3,500.

## 24.4 The statement of changes in equity (SOCE)[3]

In practice the opening figures for the SOCE would be available from the 20X3 group accounts. It is not uncommon in an examination context to require you to calculate the opening figure for the group SOCE. The calculation is as follows:

*Opening balance for the Ante group*

|  | £ |
|---|---|
| Ante's retained earnings at the start of the year | 69,336 |
| Group share of Post's post-acquisition earnings (75% × (54,000 − 30,000)) | 18,000 |
|  | 87,336 |

*Opening balance for the non-controlling interest*

| | | |
|---|---|---|
| Total retained earnings as at 31.12.20X3 | 25% of 54,000 | 13,500 |

We can then complete the group SOCE as follows:

|  | Ante | Non-controlling interest | Total |
|---|---|---|---|
|  | £ | £ | £ |
| Opening balance | 87,336 | 13,500 | 100,836 |
| Income for the period | 75,914 | 3,500 | 79,414 |
| Dividends paid | (40,000) | (1,250) | (41,250) |
| Closing balance | 123,250 | 15,750 | 139,000 |

### Dividends paid

In the Ante column the dividends paid are those of the parent only. The parent company's share of Post's dividend cancels out with the parent company's investment income. The non-controlling share is £5,000 minus the £3,750 paid to the parent. This is the amount dealt with in their column.

## 24.5 Other consolidation adjustments

In the above example we dealt with adjustments for intra-group sale of goods, unrealised profit on inventories and dividends received from a subsidiary. There are other adjustments that often appear in examinations relating to depreciation and dividends paid by a subsidiary out of pre-acquisition profits.

## 24.5.1 Depreciation adjustment when fair value is higher than book value

If the fair value of depreciable non-current assets is different from their book value, it is necessary to adjust the depreciation that has been charged in the subsidiary's books.

For example, assume that the parent acquired a non-current asset from a subsidiary which had a book value of £100,000 that was being depreciated by the subsidiary on a straight-line basis over five years and the scrap value was nil. The annual charge in the subsidiary's statement of income would be £20,000.

If the fair value on acquisition was £150,000, the charge in the consolidated statement of income should be based on the £150,000, i.e. £30,000 (£150,000/5) with the depreciation increased by £10,000. If there is no information as to the type of non-current asset, the £10,000 would be added to the cost of sales figure. If the type of asset is identified, for example as delivery vehicles, then the adjustment would be made to the appropriate expense, e.g. distribution costs.

## 24.5.2 Depreciation adjustment when transfer has been at cost plus a profit loading

Let us consider Digdeep plc, a civil engineering company that has a subsidiary, Heavylift plc, that manufactures digging equipment. Assume that at the beginning of the financial year Heavylift sold equipment costing £80,000 to Digdeep for £100,000. It is Digdeep's depreciation policy to depreciate at 5% using the straight-line method with nil scrap value.

On consolidation, the following adjustments are required:

(i) Revenue is reduced by £20,000 and the asset is reduced by £20,000 to bring the asset back to its cost of £80,000.

| | | |
|---|---|---|
| Dr: Revenue | £20,000 | |
| Cr: Asset | | £20,000 |

(ii) Revenue is then reduced by £80,000 and cost of sales reduced by £80,000 to eliminate the inter-company sale.

| | | |
|---|---|---|
| Dr: Revenue | £80,000 | |
| Cr: Cost of sales | | £80,000 |

(iii) Depreciation needs to be based on the cost of £80,000. The depreciation charge was £5,000 (5% of £100,000); it should be £4,000 (5% of £80,000) so the adjustment is:

| | | |
|---|---|---|
| Dr: Accumulated depreciation | £1,000 | |
| Cr: Depreciation in the statement of income | | £1,000 |

## 24.5.3 Dividends or interest paid by the subsidiary out of pre-acquisition profits

When a parent acquires the net assets of a subsidiary it is paying for all of the assets including the cash. If the subsidiary then pays part of this to the parent as a dividend it is in effect transferring an asset that the parent had already paid for. The dividend received by the parent is not, therefore, income but a return of part of the purchase price. It is credited by the parent to the investment in subsidiary account. This is illustrated in the Bow plc example below.

### Illustration of a dividend paid out of pre-acquisition profits

Bow plc acquired 75% of the shares in Tie plc on 1 January 20X4 for £80,000 when the balance of the retained earnings of Tie was £40,000. On 10 January 20X4 Bow received a dividend of £3,000 from Tie out of the profits for the year ended 31/12/20X3. The draft summarised statements of income for the year ended 31/12/20X4 were as follows:

|  | Bow £ | Tie £ | Consolidated £ |
|---|---|---|---|
| Gross profit | 130,000 | 70,000 | 200,000 |
| Expenses | 50,000 | 40,000 | 90,000 |
| Profit from operations | 80,000 | 30,000 | 110,000 |
| Dividends received from Tie (see note) | 3,000 | — | — |
| Profit before tax | 83,000 | 30,000 | 110,000 |
| Income tax expense | 24,000 | 6,000 | 30,000 |
| Profit for the period | 59,000 | 24,000 | 80,000 |

*Note:*

The treatment is incorrect. The £3,000 dividend received from Tie is not income and must not therefore appear in Bow's statement of income. The correct treatment is to deduct it from the investment in Tie, which will then become £77,000 (80,000 − 3,000) with a debit to dividends received and a credit to the Investment in Tie.

## 24.5.4 Goodwill

We know that there is no amortisation charge for goodwill. However, if there has been any impairment then this would appear as an expense in the group column of the consolidated statement of income.

For example, if in our Ante example above you were informed that the goodwill on acquisition was £10,000 and that it had been impaired by £2,000, the consolidated statement of income would have an entry in the group column and appear as follows:

|  | Ante £ | Post £ | Consolidated £ |  |
|---|---|---|---|---|
| Sales | 200,000 | 120,000 | 308,000 | Note 1 |
| Cost of sales | 60,000 | 60,000 | 109,500 | Notes 1/2 |
| Gross profit | 140,000 | 60,000 | 198,500 |  |
| Expenses | 59,082 | 40,000 | 99,082 | Note 3 |
| Goodwill impairment |  |  | 2,000 |  |
| Profit from operations | 80,918 | 20,000 | 97,418 |  |

## 24.6 A subsidiary acquired part-way through the year

It would be attractive for a company whose results had not been as good as expected to acquire a profitable subsidiary at the end of the year and take its current year's profit into the group accounts. However, this is window dressing and it is not permitted. The group can only bring in a subsidiary's profits from the date of the acquisition when it assumed control. The Tight plc example below illustrates the approach.

## 24.6.1 Illustration of a subsidiary acquired part-way through the year – Tight plc

The following information is available:

At the date of acquisition on 30 September 20X1
Tight acquired 75% of the shares and 20% of the 5% long-term loans in Loose. The book value and fair value were the same amount.

During the year
There have been no inter-company sales. If there had been then normal set-off would apply. All income and expenses are deemed to accrue evenly through the year and the dividend received may be apportioned to pre- and post-acquisition on a time basis.

At the end of the financial year
The Tight Group prepares its accounts as at 31 December each year.

Set out below are the individual statements of income of Tight and Loose together with the consolidated statement of income for the year ended 31 December 20X1.

| | Tight £ | Loose £ | Time-apportion | £ | Consolidated £ |
|---|---|---|---|---|---|
| Revenue | 200,000 | 120,000 | 3/12 | 30,000 | 230,000 |
| Cost of sales | 60,000 | 60,000 | 3/12 | 15,000 | 75,000 |
| Gross profit | 140,000 | 60,000 | 3/12 | 15,000 | 155,000 |
| Expenses | 59,082 | 30,000 | 3/12 | 7,500 | 66,582 |
| Interest paid on 5% loans | | 10,000 | | 2,500 | 2,000 |
| Interest received on Loose loans | 2,000 | | Set off | | NIL |
| | 82,918 | 20,000 | | | 86,418 |
| Dividends received | 3,600 | NIL | Set off | | NIL |
| Profit before tax | 86,518 | 20,000 | | | 86,418 |
| Income tax expense | 14,004 | 6,000 | 3/12 | 1,500 | 15,504 |
| Profit for the period after tax | 72,514 | 14,000 | | 3,500 | 70,914 |
| *Attributable to:* | | | | | |
| Ordinary shareholders of Tight (balance) | | | | | 70,039 |
| Non-controlling shareholders in Loose | | | | | 875 |
| | | | | | 70,914 |

*Notes:*

1  Time-apportion and aggregate the revenue, cost of sales, expenses and income tax
   Group items include a full year for the parent company and three months for the subsidiary (1 October to 31 December).

2  Account for inter-company interest.
   Inter-company expense items need to be eliminated or cancelled by set-off against the interest paid by Loose. Interest is an expense which is normally deemed to accrue evenly over the year and is to be apportioned on a time basis.

   (i)  It has been assumed that interest is paid annually in arrears. This means that the interest received by Tight has to be apportioned on a time basis: $^9/_{12} \times £2,000 = £1,500$ is treated as being pre-acquisition. It is therefore deducted from the cost of the investment in Loose.

(ii) The remainder (£500) is cancelled with £500 of the post-acquisition element of the interest paid by Loose. The interest paid figure in the consolidated financial statements will be the post-acquisition interest less the inter-company elimination, which represents the amount payable to the holders of 80% of the loan capital.

(iii) The interest of £10,000 paid by Loose to its loan creditors is time-apportioned with £7,500 being pre-acquisition. The post-acquisition amount of £2,500 includes £500 that was included in the £2,000 reported by Tight in its statement of income. This is cancelled, leaving £2,000 which was paid to the 80% non-group loan creditors.

3 Account for inter-company dividends

| | |
|---|---|
| Amount received by Tight = | £3,600 |
| The dividend received by Tight is apportioned on a time basis, and the pre-acquisition element is credited to the cost of investment in Tight, i.e. $^9/_{12} \times £3,600 =$ | (£2,700) |
| The post-acquisition element is cancelled | (£900) |
| Amount credited to consolidated statement of income | NIL |

4 Calculate the share of post-acquisition consolidated profits belonging to the non-controlling interest

As only the post-acquisition proportion of the subsidiary's profit after tax has been included in the consolidated statement of income, the amount deducted as the non-controlling interest in the profit after tax is also time-apportioned, i.e. 25% of £3,500 = £875.

## 24.7 Published format statement of income

The statement of comprehensive income follows the classification of expenses by function as illustrated in IAS 1:

| | £ |
|---|---|
| Revenue | 230,000 |
| Cost of sales | 75,000 |
| Gross profit | 155,000 |
| Distribution costs | 42,562 |
| Administrative expense | 24,020 |
| | 66,582 |
| | 88,418 |
| Finance cost | 2,000 |
| | 86,418 |
| Income tax expense | 15,504 |
| Profit for the period | 70,914 |
| *Attributable to:* | |
| Equity holders of the parent | 70,039 |
| Non-controlling interest | 875 |
| | 70,914 |

## 24.8 Consolidated statements of cash flows

Statements of cash flows are explained in Chapter 5 for a single company. A consolidated statement of cash flows differs from that for a single company in two respects:

(a) there are additional items such as dividends paid to non-controlling interests; and

(b) adjustments may be required to the actual amounts to reflect the assets and liabilities brought in by the subsidiary which did not arise from cash movements.

### 24.8.1 Adjustments to changes between opening and closing statements of financial position

Adjustments are required if the closing statement of financial position items have been increased or reduced as a result of non-cash movements. Such movements occur if there has been a purchase of a subsidiary to reflect the fact that the assets and liabilities from the new subsidiary have not necessarily resulted from cash flows. The following illustrates such adjustments in relation to a subsidiary acquired at the end of the financial year where the net assets of the subsidiary were as follows:

| *Net assets acquired* | *£000* | *Effect in consolidated statement of cash flows* |
|---|---|---|
| Working capital: | | |
| Inventory | 10 | Reduce inventory increase |
| Trade payables | (12) | Reduce trade payables increase |
| Non-current assets: | | |
| Vehicles | 20 | Reduce capital expenditure |
| Cash/bank: | | |
| Cash | 5 | Reduce amount paid to acquire subsidiary in investing section |
| Net assets acquired | 23 | |

Let us assume that the consideration for the acquisition was as follows:

| | | |
|---|---|---|
| Shares | 10 | Reduce share cash inflow |
| Share premium | 10 | Reduce share cash inflow |
| Cash | 3 | Payment to acquire subsidiary in investing section |
| | 23 | |

The consolidated statement of cash flows can then be prepared using the indirect method.

## Statement of cash flows using the indirect method

| | | £000 | £000 |
|---|---|---:|---:|
| *Cash flows from operating activities* | | | |
| Net profit before tax | | 500 | |
| Adjustments for: | | | |
| Depreciation | | 102 | |
| Operating profit before working capital changes | | 602 | |
| Increase in inventories | (400) | | |
| *Less:* **Inventory brought in on acquisition** | 10 | (390) | |
| Decrease in trade payables | (40) | | |
| *Add:* **Trade payables brought in on acquisition** | (12) | (52) | |
| Cash generated from operations | | 160 | |
| Income taxes paid (200 + 190 − 170) | | (220) | |
| Net cash from operating activities | | | (60) |
| Cash flows from investing activities | | | |
| Purchase of property, plant and equipment | (563) | | |
| *Less:* **Vehicles brought in on acquisition** | 20 | (543) | |
| Payment to acquire subsidiary | | (3) | |
| Cash acquired with subsidiary | | 5 | |
| Net cash used in investing activities | | | (541) |
| Cash flows from financing activities | | | |
| Proceeds from issuance of share capital | 300 | | |
| *Less:* **Shares issued on acquisition not for cash** | (20) | 280 | |
| Dividends paid (from statement of income) | | (120) | |
| Net cash from financing activities | | | 160 |
| Net decrease in cash and cash equivalents | | | (441) |
| Cash and cash equivalents at the beginning of the period | | | 72 |
| Cash and cash equivalents at the end of the period | | | (369) |

Supplemental disclosure of acquisition

| | £ |
|---|---:|
| Total purchase consideration | 23,000 |
| Portion of purchase consideration discharged by means of cash or cash equivalents | 3,000 |
| Amount of cash and cash equivalents in the subsidiary acquired | 5,000 |

## Summary

The retained earnings of the subsidiary brought forward are divided into pre-acquisition profits and post-acquisition profits – the group share of the former are used in the good-will calculation, and the share of the latter are brought into the consolidated shareholders' equity.

Revenue and cost of sales are adjusted in order to eliminate intra-group sales and unrealised profits.

Finance expenses and income are adjusted to eliminate inter-company payments of interest and dividends.

The non-controlling interest in the profit after tax of the subsidiary is deducted to arrive at the profit for the year attributable to the equity holders of the parent.

If a subsidiary is acquired during a financial year, the items in its statement of income require apportioning. In the illustration in the text we assumed that trading was evenly spread throughout the year – in practice you would need to consider any seasonal patterns that would make this assumption unrealistic, remembering that the important consideration is that the group accounts should only be credited with profits arising whilst the subsidiary was under the parent's control.

## REVIEW QUESTIONS

1 Explain why the dividends deducted from the group in the statement of changes in equity are only those of the parent company.

2 Explain two ways in which unrealised profits might arise from transactions between companies in a group and why it is important to remove them.

3 Explain why it is necessary to apportion a subsidiary's profit or loss if acquired part-way through a financial year.

4 Explain why dividends paid by a subsidiary to a parent company are eliminated on consolidation.

5 Give four examples of inter-company income and expense transactions that will need to be eliminated on consolidation and explain why each is necessary.

6 A shareholder was concerned that following an acquisition the profit from operations of the parent and subsidiary were less than the aggregate of the individual profit from operations figures. She was concerned that the acquisition, which the directors had supported as improving earnings per share, appeared to have reduced the combined profits. She wanted to know where the profits had gone. Give an explanation to the shareholder.

7 Explain how a management charge made by a parent company would be dealt with on consolidation.

8 Explain how the impairment of goodwill is dealt with on consolidation.

9 Explain why unrealised profits on inventory purchased from another member of the group is added to the cost of sales when it is not a cost.

10 Explain why differences between the opening and closing statements of financial position are adjusted when preparing a consolidated statement of cash flows when a subsidiary is acquired.

# EXERCISES

## * Question 1

Hyson plc acquired 75% of the shares in Green plc on 1 January 20X0 for £6 million when Green plc's accumulated profits were £4.5 million. At acquisition, the fair value of Green's non-current assets were £1.2 million in excess of their carrying value. The remaining life of these non-current assets is six years.

The summarised statements of comprehensive income for the year ended 31.12.20X0 were as follows:

|  | Hyson £000 | Green £000 |
|---|---|---|
| Revenue | 23,500 | 6,400 |
| Cost of sales | 16,400 | 4,700 |
| Gross profit | 7,100 | 1,700 |
| Expenses | 4,650 | 1,240 |
| Profit before tax | 2,450 | 460 |
| Income tax expense | 740 | 140 |
| Profit for the period | 1,710 | 320 |

There were no inter-company transactions. Depreciation of non-current assets is charged to cost of sales.

**Required:**
Prepare a consolidated statement of comprehensive income for the year ended 31 December 20X0.

## * Question 2

Forest plc acquired 80% of the ordinary shares of Bulwell plc some years ago. At acquisition, the fair values of the assets of Bulwell plc were the same as their carrying value. Bulwell plc manufacture plant and equipment.

On 1 January 20X3, Bulwell sold an item of plant and equipment to Forest plc for $2 million. Forest plc depreciate plant and equipment at 10% per annum on cost, and charge this expense to cost of sales. Bulwell plc made a gross profit of 30% on the sale of the plant and equipment to Forest plc.

The income statements of Forest and Bulwell for the year ended 31 December 20X3 are:

|  | Forest $000 | Bulwell $000 |
|---|---|---|
| Revenue | 21,300 | 8,600 |
| Cost of sales | 14,900 | 6,020 |
| Gross profit | 6,400 | 2,580 |
| Other operating expenses | 3,700 | 1,750 |
| Profit before tax | 2,700 | 830 |
| Taxation | 820 | 250 |
| Profit after tax | 1,880 | 580 |

**Required:**
Prepare an income statement for the Forest plc group for the year ended 31 December 20X3.

## * Question 3

Bill plc acquired 80% of the common shares and 10% of the preferred shares in Ben plc on 31 December three years ago when Ben's retained profits were €45,000. During the year Bill sold Ben goods for €8,000 plus a markup of 50%. Half of these goods were still in stock at the end of the year. There was goodwill impairment loss of €3,000. Non-controlling interests are measured using Method 1.

The statements of comprehensive income of the two companies for the year ended 31 December 20X1 were as follows:

|  | Bill | Ben |
|---|---|---|
|  | € | € |
| Revenue | 300,000 | 180,000 |
| Cost of sales | 90,000 | 90,000 |
| Gross profit | 210,000 | 90,000 |
| Expenses | 88,623 | 60,000 |
|  | 121,377 | 30,000 |
| Dividends received – common shares | 6,000 | — |
| Dividends received – preferred shares | 450 | — |
| Profit before tax | 127,827 | 30,000 |
| Income tax expense | 21,006 | 9,000 |
| Profit for the period | 106,821 | 21,000 |

### Required:
Prepare a consolidated statement of comprehensive income for the year ended 31 December 20X1.

## * Question 4

Morn Ltd acquired 90% of the shares in Eve Ltd on 1 January 20X1 for £90,000 when Eve Ltd's accumulated profits were £50,000. On 10 January 20X1 Morn Ltd received a dividend of £10,800 from Eve Ltd out of the profits for the year ended 31/12/20X0. On 31/12/20X1 Morn increased its non-current assets by £30,000 on revaluation. The summarised statements of comprehensive income for the year ended 31/12/20X1 were as follows:

|  | Morn | Eve |
|---|---|---|
|  | £ | £ |
| Gross profit | 360,000 | 180,000 |
| Expenses | 120,000 | 110,000 |
|  | 240,000 | 70,000 |
| Dividends received from Eve Ltd | 10,800 | — |
| Profit before tax | 250,800 | 70,000 |
| Income tax expense | 69,000 | 18,000 |
| Profit for the period | 181,800 | 52,000 |

There were no inter-company transactions, other than the dividend. There was no goodwill.

### Required:
Prepare a consolidated statement of comprehensive income for the year ended 31 December 20X1.

## * Question 5

River plc acquired 90% of the common shares and 10% of the 5% bonds in Pool Ltd on 31 March 20X1. All income and expenses are deemed to accrue evenly through the year. On 31 January 20X1 River sold Pool goods for £6,000 plus a markup of one-third. 75% of these goods were still in stock at the end of the year. There was a goodwill impairment loss of £4,000. On 31/12/20X1 River increased its non-current assets by £15,000 on revaluation. Non-controlling interests are measured using Method 1. Set out below are the individual statements of comprehensive income of River and Pool:

### Statements of comprehensive income for the year ended 31 December 20X1

|  | River £ | Pool £ |
|---|---|---|
| Net turnover | 100,000 | 60,000 |
| Cost of sales | 30,000 | 30,000 |
| Gross profit | 70,000 | 30,000 |
| Expenses | 20,541 | 15,000 |
| Interest payable on 5% bonds |  | 5,000 |
| Interest receivable on Pool Ltd bonds | 500 |  |
|  | 49,959 | 10,000 |
| Dividends received | 2,160 | NIL |
| Profit before tax | 52,119 | 10,000 |
| Income tax expense | 7,002 | 3,000 |
| Profit for the period | 45,117 | 7,000 |

Required:

Prepare a consolidated statement of comprehensive income for the year ended 31 December 20X1.

## Question 6

The statements of financial position of Mars plc and Jupiter plc at 31 December 20X2 are as follows:

|  | Mars £ | Jupiter £ |
|---|---|---|
| **ASSETS** | | |
| Non-current assets at cost | 550,000 | 225,000 |
| Depreciation | 220,000 | 67,500 |
|  | 330,000 | 157,500 |
| Investment in Jupiter | 187,500 | |
| *Current assets* | | |
| Inventories | 225,000 | 67,500 |
| Trade receivables | 180,000 | 90,000 |
| Current account – Jupiter | 22,500 | |
| Bank | 36,000 | 18,000 |
|  | 463,500 | 175,500 |
| **Total assets** | **981,000** | **333,000** |
| **EQUITY AND LIABILITIES** | | |
| *Capital and reserves* | | |
| £1 common shares | 196,000 | 90,000 |
| General reserve | 245,000 | 31,500 |
| Retained earnings | 225,000 | 135,000 |
|  | 666,000 | 256,500 |
| *Current liabilities* | | |
| Trade payables | 283,500 | 40,500 |
| Taxation | 31,500 | 13,500 |
| Current account – Mars | | 22,500 |
|  | 315,000 | 76,500 |
| **Total equity and liabilities** | **981,000** | **333,000** |

### Statements of comprehensive income for the year ended 31 December 20X2

|  | £ | £ |
|---|---|---|
| Sales | 1,440,000 | 270,000 |
| Cost of sales | 1,045,000 | 135,000 |
| Gross profit | 395,000 | 135,000 |
| Expenses | 123,500 | 90,000 |
| Dividends received from Jupiter | 9,000 | NIL |
| Profit before tax | 280,500 | 45,000 |
| Income tax expense | 31,500 | 13,500 |
| Profit for the period | 249,000 | 31,500 |
| Dividends paid | 180,000 | 11,250 |
|  | 69,000 | 20,250 |
| Retained earnings brought forward from previous years | 156,000 | 114,750 |
|  | 225,000 | 135,000 |

Mars acquired 80% of the shares in Jupiter on 1 January 20X0 when Jupiter's retained earnings were £80,000 and the balance on Jupiter's general reserve was £18,000. Non-controlling interests are measured using Method 1. During the year Mars sold Jupiter goods for £18,000 which represented cost plus 50%. Half of these goods were still in stock at the end of the year.

During the year Mars and Jupiter paid dividends of £180,000 and £11,250 respectively. The opening balances of retained earnings for the two companies were £156,000 and £114,750 respectively.

**Required:**

**Prepare a consolidated statement of income for the year ended 31/12/20X2, a statement of financial position as at that date, and a consolidated statement of changes in equity. Also prepare the retained earnings columns of the consolidated statement of changes in equity for the year.**

## Question 7

The statements of financial position of Red Ltd and Pink Ltd at 31 December 20X2 are as follows:

|  | Red $ | Pink $ |
|---|---|---|
| **ASSETS** | | |
| Non-current assets | 225,000 | 100,000 |
| Depreciation | 80,000 | 30,000 |
|  | 145,000 | 70,000 |
| Investment in Pink Ltd | 110,000 | |
| *Current assets* | | |
| Inventories | 100,000 | 30,000 |
| Trade receivables | 80,000 | 40,000 |
| Current account – Pink Ltd | 10,000 | |
| Bank | 16,000 | 8,000 |
|  | 206,000 | 78,000 |
| **Total assets** | **461,000** | **148,000** |
| **EQUITY AND LIABILITIES** | | |
| Capital and reserves | | |
| $1 common shares | 176,000 | 40,000 |
| General reserve | 20,000 | 14,000 |
| Revaluation reserve | 25,000 | |
| Retained earnings | 100,000 | 60,000 |
|  | 321,000 | 114,000 |
| Current liabilities | | |
| Trade payables | 125,996 | 18,000 |
| Taxation payable | 14,004 | 6,000 |
| Current account – Red Ltd | | 10,000 |
|  | 140,000 | 34,000 |
| **Total equity and liabilities** | **461,000** | **148,000** |

**Statements of comprehensive income for the year ended 31 December 20X2**

|  | $ | $ |
|---|---|---|
| Sales | 200,000 | 120,000 |
| Cost of sales | 60,000 | 60,000 |
| Gross profit | 140,000 | 60,000 |
| Expenses | 59,082 | 40,000 |
| Dividends received | 3,750 | NIL |
| Profit before tax | 84,668 | 20,000 |
| Income tax expense | 14,004 | 6,000 |
|  | 70,664 | 14,000 |
| Surplus on revaluation | 25,000 | — |
| Total comprehensive income | 95,664 | 14,000 |

Red Ltd acquired 75% of the shares in Pink Ltd on 1 January 20X0 when Pink Ltd's retained earnings were $30,000 and the balance on Pink's general reserve was $8,000. The fair value of the non-controlling interest at the date was £32,000. Non-controlling interests are to be measured using Method 2.

On 31 December 20X2 Red revalued its non-current assets. The revaluation surplus of £25,000 was credited to the revaluation reserve.

During the year Pink sold Red goods for $9,000 plus a markup of one-third. Half of these goods were still in inventory at the end of the year. Goodwill suffered an impairment loss of 20%.

**Required:**
**Prepare a consolidated statement of comprehensive income for the year ended 31/12/20X2 and a statement of financial position as at that date.**

## Question 8

H Ltd has one subsidiary, S Ltd. The company has held a controlling interest for several years. The latest financial statements for the two companies and the consolidated financial statements for the H Group are as shown below:

**Statements of comprehensive income for the year ended 30 September 20X4**

|  | H Ltd | S Ltd | H Group |
|---|---|---|---|
|  | €000 | €000 | €000 |
| Turnover | 4,000 | 2,200 | 5,700 |
| Cost of sales | (1,100) | (960) | (1,605) |
|  | 2,900 | 1,240 | 4,095 |
| Administration | (420) | (130) | (550) |
| Distribution | (170) | (95) | (265) |
| Dividends received | 180 | — | — |
| Profit before tax | 2,490 | 1,015 | 3,280 |
| Income tax | (620) | (335) | (955) |
| Profit after tax | 1,870 | 680 | 2,325 |
| *Attributable to:* |  |  |  |
| Equity shareholders of H Ltd |  |  | 2,155 |
| Non-controlling shareholders in S Ltd |  |  | 170 |
|  |  |  | 2,325 |

## Statements of financial position at 30 September 20X4

|  | H Ltd €000 | €000 | S Ltd €000 | €000 | H Group €000 | €000 |
|---|---|---|---|---|---|---|
| Non-current assets: |  |  |  |  |  |  |
| Tangible | 7,053 |  | 2,196 |  | 9,249 |  |
| Investment in S Ltd | 1,700 | 8,753 | — | 2,196 | — | 9,249 |
| Current assets: |  |  |  |  |  |  |
| Inventory | 410 |  | 420 |  | 785 |  |
| Receivables | 535 |  | 220 |  | 595 |  |
| Bank | 27 | 972 | 19 | 659 | 46 | 1,426 |
| Current liabilities: |  |  |  |  |  |  |
| Payables | (300) |  | (260) |  | (355) |  |
| Dividend to non-controlling interest | — |  | — |  | (45) |  |
| Taxation | (605) | (905) | (375) | (635) | (980) | (1,380) |
|  |  | 8,820 |  | 2,220 |  | 9,295 |

|  | H Ltd £000 | S Ltd £000 | H Group £000 |
|---|---|---|---|
| Share capital | 4,500 | 760 | 4,500 |
| Retained earnings | 4,320 | 1,460 | 4,240 |
|  | 8,820 | 2,220 | 8,740 |
| Non-controlling interest | — | — | 555 |
|  | 8,820 | 2,220 | 9,295 |

Goodwill of €410,000 was written off at the date of acquisition following an impairment review.

Required:

(a) Calculate the percentage of S Ltd which is owned by H Ltd.

(b) Calculate the value of sales made between the two companies during the year.

(c) Calculate the amount of unrealised profit which had been included in the inventory figure as a result of inter-company trading and which had to be cancelled on consolidation.

(d) Calculate the value of inter-company receivables and payables cancelled on consolidation.

(e) Calculate the balance on S Ltd's retained earnings when H Ltd acquired its stake in the company. Non-controlling interests are measured using Method 1.

(CIMA)

## Question 9

Rumpus plc is a public listed manufacturing company. Its summarised consolidated financial statements for the year ended 31 March 2014 (and 2013 comparatives where relevant) are as follows:

### Rumpus plc: Consolidated Statement of Profit or Loss and Other Comprehensive Income for the year ended 31 March 2014:

|  | € million |
|---|---:|
| Revenue | 310 |
| Cost of sales | (270) |
| Gross profit | 40 |
| Distribution costs | (10) |
| Administrative expense | (29) |
| Share of profit for year from associate | 14 |
| Finance costs | (6) |
| Profit (loss) before taxation | 9 |
| Income tax expense | (3) |
| **Profit for the year** | **6** |
| Other comprehensive income (net of tax) | |
| Items that will not be reclassified to profit or loss: | |
| Revaluation gains on group property | 13 |
| Share of revaluations gains from associate's property | 4 |
| | 17 |
| Total comprehensive income for the year | 23 |
| Profit for the year attributable to: | |
| Owners of the parent | 5 |
| Non-controlling interest | 1 |
| | 6 |
| Total comprehensive income for the year attributable to: | |
| Owners of the parent | 22 |
| Non-controlling interest | 1 |
| | 23 |

### Rumpus plc: Consolidated Statements of Financial Position as at 31 March:

|  | 2014 € million | 2013 € million |
|---|---:|---:|
| Non-current assets: | | |
| Property, plant and equipment | 290 | 245 |
| Goodwill | 6 | — |
| Investments in associates | 64 | 40 |
| | 360 | 285 |
| Current assets: | | |
| Inventory and work-in-progress | 22 | 19 |
| Trade receivables | 42 | 28 |
| Cash & cash equivalents | 18 | 1 |
| | 82 | 48 |
| **Total assets** | **442** | **333** |
| Equity: | | |
| Equity shares of €1 each | 160 | 106 |

| | 2014 | 2013 |
|---|---|---|
| | *€ million* | *€ million* |
| Share premium | 39 | ---- |
| Revaluation reserve | 62 | 45 |
| Retained earnings | 68 | 65 |
| | 329 | 216 |
| Non-controlling interests | 23 | 14 |
| | 352 | 230 |
| Non-current liabilities: | | |
| 12% debentures 2016 | 50 | 50 |
| Long-term provisions | 12 | 7 |
| | 62 | 57 |
| Current liabilities: | | |
| Trade payables | 23 | 33 |
| Current tax payable | 5 | 13 |
| | 28 | 46 |
| **Total equity and liabilities** | **442** | **333** |

The following additional information is available:

(i) The group acquired an 80% interest in Sacker plc during the year on the following terms:

- Cost of purchase of 80% of the equity shares of Sacker plc was €45 million.
- The agreed payment for the purchase was settled by issuing 25 million equity shares valued at €35 million plus cash of €10 million.
- The non-controlling interest was fair-valued at €11 million on the acquisition date.
- The net assets of Sacker plc at the acquisition date consisted entirely of the following:
  - property plant & equipment €33 million;
  - inventory €8 million;
  - cash €6 million.

    Sacker plc was correctly accounted for and fully consolidated in the above financial statements.

(ii) No disposals of non-current assets took place during the year.

(iii) Depreciation charged to cost of sales during the year amounted to €41 million.

(iv) The group purchased an interest in an associate company for cash of €13 million during the year.

(v) Equity dividends were paid during the year out of retained earnings.

(vi) Goodwill was tested for impairment at the reporting date. An impairment loss was recognised and charged to expenses.

**Required:**

(a) Prepare a consolidated statement of cash flows for year ended 31 March 2014 in accordance with IAS 7.

(b) Evaluate the liquidity position of Rumpus plc as portrayed by the above financial statements and the statement of cash flows you have prepared.

*(Institute of Certified Public Accountants (ICPA), Professional I Stage I Corporate Reporting Examination, August 2014)*

## Question 10

The following are the summarised financial statements of two companies, Peel and Caval, for the financial year ended 31 October 2011.

### Income Statements for the year ended 31 October 2011

|  | Peel £m | Caval £m |
|---|---|---|
| Revenue | 125 | 95 |
| Cost of sales | (69) | (43) |
| Gross profit | 56 | 52 |
| Operating expenses | (22) | (23) |
| Investment income | 21 | 5 |
| Interest receivable | 4 | 3 |
| Finance charges | (5) | (3) |
| Net profit before taxation | 54 | 34 |
| Taxation | (15) | (10) |
| Profit for the year | 39 | 24 |

### Statements of Financial Position as at 31 October 2011

|  | Peel | Caval |
|---|---|---|
| ASSETS |  |  |
| Non-current assets | £m | £m |
| Tangible assets, net book value | 290 | 290 |
| Investments, at cost | 265 | 13 |
|  | 555 | 303 |
| Current assets | 133 | 47 |
| Total assets | 688 | 350 |
| EQUITY and LIABILITIES |  |  |
| Equity |  |  |
| Ordinary shares of £1 | 300 | 180 |
| Retained earnings | 232 | 80 |
|  | 532 | 260 |
| Non-current liabilities | 100 | 66 |
| Current liabilities | 56 | 24 |
| Total equity and liabilities | 688 | 350 |

The following information is available:

(i) Peel purchased 90% of the ordinary shares in Caval for £240m on 1 November 2010 when the reserves of Caval were £76m. Each ordinary share in Caval carries one vote and there are no voting rights other than those attaching to the ordinary shares. Caval has not issued any additional shares since its acquisition by Peel.

(ii) Peel made a long-term loan of £23m to Caval during the year ended 31 October 2011. Caval made interest payments of £3m on this loan and there was no interest outstanding as at 31 October 2011.

(iii) During the year ended 31 October 2011 Peel made sales totalling £40m to Caval. The goods sold to Caval had cost Peel £24m and 75% had been resold by Caval by 31 October 2011. As at 31 October 2011 Caval had invoices totalling £10m payable to Peel which were unpaid.

(iv) Dividends paid by the companies during the year ended 31 October 2011 were Peel £30m and Caval £20m.

Required:

Prepare in so far as the above information permits:

(a) The consolidated statement of comprehensive income of Peel for the year ended 31 October 2011.

(b) The consolidated statement of financial position of Peel as at 31 October 2011.

Note: enter all figures correct to the nearest £m and provide full supportive workings.

*(CIPFA Financial Reporting 2014 Specimen Paper)*

## Notes

1 IFRS 10 *Consolidated Financial Statements*, IASB, 2011, B 86.

2 *Ibid.*, B 94, B 89.

3 IAS 1 *Presentation of Financial Statements*, IASB, revised 2007, Implementation Guidance.

# CHAPTER 25

# Accounting for associates and joint arrangements

## 25.1 Introduction

The previous three chapters have focused on the need for consolidated financial statements where an investor has control over an entity. In those circumstances line-by-line consolidation is appropriate. Where the size of an investment is not sufficient to give sole control, but where the investment gives the investor significant influence or joint control, then a modified form of accounting is appropriate. We will consider this issue further in this chapter.

### Objectives

By the end of this chapter, you should be able to:

- define an associate;
- incorporate a profit-making associate into the consolidated financial statements using the equity method;
- incorporate a loss-making associate into the consolidated financial statements using the equity method;
- define and describe a joint operation and a joint venture and prepare financial statements incorporating interests in joint ventures;
- explain disclosure requirements.

## 25.2 Definitions of associates and of significant influence

**An associate** is an entity over which the investor has significant influence and which is neither a subsidiary nor a joint venture of the investor.[1] **Significant influence** is the power to participate in the financial and operating policy decisions of the investee but is not control over these policies.[2]

Significant influence will be assumed in situations where one company has 20% or more of the voting power in another company, unless it can be shown that there is no such influence. Unless it can be shown to the contrary, a holding of less than 20% will be assumed insufficient for associate status. The circumstances of each case must be considered.[2]

IAS 28 *Investments in Associates and Joint Ventures* suggests that one or more of the following might be evidence of an associate:

(a) representation on the board of directors or equivalent governing body of the investee;

(b) participation in policy-making processes;

(c) material transactions between the investor and the investee;

(d) interchange of managerial personnel; or

(e) provision of essential technical information.[3]

## 25.3 The treatment of associated companies in consolidated accounts

Associated companies will be shown in consolidated accounts under the equity method, unless the investment meets the criteria of a disposal group held for sale under IFRS 5 *Non-current Assets Held for Sale and Discontinued Operations*. If this is the case it will be accounted for under IFRS 5 at the lower of carrying value and fair value less costs to sell.

The equity method is a method of accounting whereby:

● The investment is reported in the consolidated statement of financial position in the non-current asset section.[4] It is reported initially at cost adjusted, at the end of each financial year, for the post-acquisition change in the investor's share of the net assets of the investee.[5]

● In the consolidated statement of comprehensive income, income from associates is reported after profit from operations together with finance costs and finance expenses.[6] The income reflects the investor's share of the post-tax results of operations of the investee.[5]

## 25.4 The Brill Group – group accounts with a profit-making associate

Brill plc was the parent of the Brill Group which consisted of Brill and a single subsidiary, Bream plc. On 1 January 20X0 Brill acquired 20% of the ordinary shares in Cod Ltd for £20,000. At that date the retained earnings of Cod were £22,500 and the general reserve was £6,000.

Set out below are the consolidated accounts of Brill and its subsidiary Bream and the individual accounts of the associated company, Cod, together with the consolidated group accounts.

### 25.4.1 Consolidated statement of financial position

Statements of financial position of the Brill Group (parent plus subsidiary already consolidated) and Cod (an associate company) as at 31 December 20X2 are as follows:

| | Brill and subsidiary | Cod | Group | |
|---|---|---|---|---|
| | £ | £ | £ | |
| *Non-current assets* | | | | |
| Property, plant and equipment | 172,500 | 59,250 | 172,500 | |
| Goodwill on consolidation | 13,400 | | 13,400 | |
| Investment in Cod | 20,000 | | 23,600 | Note 1 |
| *Current assets* | | | | |
| Inventories | 132,440 | 27,000 | 132,440 | |
| Trade receivables | 151,050 | 27,000 | 151,050 | |
| Current account – Cod | 2,250 | | 2,250 | Note 2 |
| Bank | 36,200 | 4,500 | 36,200 | |
| Total assets | 527,840 | 117,750 | 531,440 | |
| *Current liabilities* | | | | |
| Trade payables | 110,250 | 25,500 | 110,250 | |
| Taxation | 27,750 | 6,000 | 27,750 | |
| Current account – Brill | | 2,250 | | |
| | 138,000 | 33,750 | 138,000 | |
| **Total net assets** | 389,840 | 84,000 | 393,440 | |
| **EQUITY** | | | | |
| £1 ordinary shares | 187,500 | 37,500 | 187,500 | |
| General reserve | 24,900 | 9,000 | 25,500 | Note 3 |
| Retained earnings | 145,940 | 37,500 | 148,940 | Note 4 |
| | 358,340 | 84,000 | 361,940 | |
| Non-controlling interest | 31,500 | — | 31,500 | Note 5 |
| | 389,840 | 84,000 | 393,440 | |

*Notes:*

1  **Investment in associate**

| | | £ | £ |
|---|---|---|---|
| Initial cost of the 20% holding | | | 20,000 |
| Share of post-acquisition reserves of Cod: | | | |
| Retained earnings 20% $\times$ (37,500 − 22,500) | | 3,000 | |
| General reserve 20% $\times$ (9,000 − 6,000) | | 600 | 3,600 |
| | | | 23,600 |

Note that (a) unlike subsidiaries the assets and liabilities are not joined line-by-line with those of the companies in the group; (b) where necessary the investment in the associate is tested for impairment under IAS 28;[7] and (c) goodwill is not reported separately and is only calculated initially to establish a figure when considering possible impairment.

2  **The Cod current account** is received from outside the group and must therefore continue to be shown as receivable by the group. *It is not cancelled.*

3   **General reserve consists of:**

|  |  | £ |
|---|---|---|
| Parent's general reserve |  | 24,900 |
| General reserve of Cod: |  |  |
| The group share of the post-acquisition general reserve, |  |  |
| i.e. 20% × (9,000 − 6,000) |  | 600 |
| Consolidated general reserve |  | **25,500** |

4   **Retained earnings consist of:**

|  | £ |
|---|---|
| Brill group's retained earnings | 145,940 |
| Retained earnings of Cod: |  |
| The group share of the post-acquisition retained profits, |  |
| i.e. 20% × (37,500 − 22,500) | 3,000 |
| Consolidated retained earnings | **148,940** |

5   **Non-controlling interest**

Note that there is no non-controlling interest in Cod. Only the group share of Cod's net assets has been brought into the total net assets above (see Note 1). This is unlike the consolidation of a subsidiary when all of the subsidiary's assets and liabilities are aggregated into the consolidation.

### 25.4.2 Consolidated statement of income

Statements of income for the year ended 31 December 20X2 are as follows:

|  | Brill and subsidiary £ | Cod £ | Group £ |  |
|---|---|---|---|---|
| Sales | 329,000 | 75,000 | 329,000 |  |
| Cost of sales | 114,060 | 30,000 | 114,060 |  |
| Gross profit | 214,940 | 45,000 | 214,940 |  |
| Expenses | 107,700 | 22,500 | 107,700 |  |
| Profit from operations | 107,240 | 22,500 | 107,240 |  |
| Dividends received | 1,200 | — | NIL | Note 1 |
| Share of associate's **post-tax** profit | — | — | 3,300 | Note 2 |
| Profit before tax | 108,440 | 22,500 | 110,540 |  |
| Income tax expense | 27,750 | 6,000 | 27,750 |  |
| Profit for the period | 80,690 | 16,500 | 82,790 |  |

*Notes:*

1   **Dividend received from Cod** is not shown because the share of Cod's profits (before dividend) has been included in the group account (see Note 2). To include the dividend as well would be double-counting.

2   **Share of Cod's profit after tax** = 20% × £16,500 = £3,300

As in the statement of financial position, there is no need to account for a non-controlling interest in Cod. This is because the consolidated statement of income only included the group share of Cod's profits.

There are no additional complications in the statement of changes in equity. The group retained earnings column will include the group share of Cod's post-acquisition retained earnings. There will be no additional column for a non-controlling interest in Cod.

### 25.4.3 The treatment of unrealised profits

It is never appropriate in the case of associated companies to remove 100% of any unrealised profit on inter-company transactions because only the group's share of the associate's profit and net assets are shown in the group accounts. For example, let us assume that Brill had purchased goods from Cod during the year at an agreed markup of £10,000, and a quarter of the goods were held by Brill in inventory at the year-end.

The Brill Group will provide for 20% of £2,500 (i.e. £500) by reducing the group share of the associate's profit in the statement of income and reducing the investment in the associate reported in the statement of financial position.

If the sale had been made by Brill, the cost of sales would be increased by £500 and the investment in the associate would be reduced by £500.

## 25.5 The Brill Group – group accounts with a loss-making associate

The treatment of losses in and impairment of an associate are described below.

### Losses

Losses in an associate are normally treated the same way as profits. The group statement of income will show a loss after tax of the associate, and the statement of financial position will continue to show the associate at cost plus its share of post-acquisition profits or less its share of post-acquisition losses.

If the losses were such that they exceeded the carrying amount of the investment in the associate, the investment would be reduced to zero. After that point, additional losses are recognised by a provision (liability) only to the extent that the investor has incurred legal or constructive obligations or made payments on behalf of the associate.

If the associate subsequently reports profits, the investor resumes recognising its share of those profits only after its share of the profits equals the share of losses not recognised.[8]

### Impairment

IAS 36 *Impairment of Assets* says (paragraph 9): 'An entity shall assess at the end of each reporting period whether there is any indication that an asset may be impaired. If any such indication exists [*such as making losses or small profits*], the entity shall estimate the recoverable amount of the asset.'

Brill and its subsidiary have a loss-making associate, Herring, which is 20% owned by Brill. On 1 January 20X0 Brill acquired 20% of the ordinary shares in Herring for £20,000. At that date the retained earnings of Herring were £22,500 and the general reserve was £6,000. For the year ended 31 December 20X2, Herring's loss after tax was £18,500.

Because of the losses incurred by Herring, Brill has carried out an impairment test on the value of the investment in the associate. The recoverable amount of a 20% shareholding in Herring at 31 December 20X2 is £10,000.

## Statements of financial position of the Brill Group and Herring as at 31 December 20X2

| | Brill group £ | Herring £ | Group £ | |
|---|---|---|---|---|
| *Non-current assets* | | | | |
| Property, plant and equipment | 172,500 | 59,250 | 172,500 | |
| Goodwill on consolidation | 13,400 | | 13,400 | |
| Investment in Herring | 20,000 | | 10,000 | Note 1 |
| *Current assets* | | | | |
| Inventories | 132,440 | 10,500 | 132,440 | |
| Trade receivables | 151,050 | 12,000 | 151,050 | |
| Current account – Herring | 2,250 | | 2,250 | Note 2 |
| Bank | 36,200 | 500 | 36,200 | |
| | 527,840 | 82,250 | 517,840 | |
| *Current liabilities* | | | | |
| Trade payables | 110,250 | 25,500 | 110,250 | |
| Taxation | 27,750 | — | 27,750 | |
| Current account – Herring | | 2,250 | | |
| | 138,000 | 27,750 | 138,000 | |
| Total net assets | 389,840 | 54,500 | 379,840 | |
| **EQUITY** | | | | |
| £1 ordinary shares | 187,500 | 37,500 | 187,500 | |
| General reserve | 24,900 | 7,000 | 25,100 | Note 3 |
| Retained earnings | 145,940 | 10,000 | 135,740 | Note 4 |
| | 358,340 | 54,500 | 348,340 | |
| Non-controlling interest | 31,500 | — | 31,500 | |
| | 389,840 | 54,500 | 379,840 | |

*Notes:*

1 **Investment in associate**

| | £ | £ |
|---|---|---|
| Initial cost of 20% holding | | 20,000 |
| Share of post-acquisition reserves of Herring | | |
| 20% × (10,000 − 22,500) (retained earnings) | (2,500) | |
| 20% × (7,000 − 6,000) (general reserves) | 200 | (2,300) |
| Carrying value (before impairment) | | 17,700 |
| Impairment (write down to recoverable amount) | | (7,700) |
| Value in statement of financial position | | 10,000 |

The post-acquisition loss of £12,500 gives a loss of £2,500 in the group financial statements. As the carrying value (before impairment) is higher than the recoverable amount of £10,000, the value of the associate in Brill's statement of financial position is reduced to £10,000.

2 **The Herring current account remains at £2,250.**

3 **General reserve consists of:**

| | £ |
|---|---|
| Parent's general reserve | 24,900 |
| General reserve of Herring: | |
| The group share of the post-acquisition general reserve, i.e. 20% × (7,000 − 6,000) | 200 |
| Consolidated general reserve | 25,100 |

4 **Retained earnings consist of:**

| | £ |
|---|---|
| Parent's retained earnings | 145,940 |
| Retained earnings of Herring: | |
| The group share of the post-acquisition retained earnings, | |
| i.e. 20% × (10,000 − 22,500) | (2,500) |
| Impairment of investment in associate (see Note 1) | (7,700) |
| Consolidated general reserve | 135,740 |

**Statements of income for the year ended 31 December 20X2**

| | Brill group £ | Herring £ | Group £ | |
|---|---|---|---|---|
| Sales | 329,000 | 75,000 | 329,000 | |
| Cost of sales | 114,060 | 66,000 | 114,060 | |
| Gross profit | 214,940 | 9,000 | 214,940 | |
| Expenses | 107,700 | 27,500 | 107,700 | |
| Profit/(loss) from operations | 107,240 | (18,500) | 107,240 | |
| Share of associate's after-tax loss | | | (3,700) | Note 1 |
| Impairment of investment in associate | | | (7,700) | Note 2 |
| Profit before tax | 107,240 | (18,500) | 95,840 | |
| Income tax expense | 27,750 | — | 27,750 | |
| Profit/(loss) for the period | 79,490 | (18,500) | 68,090 | |

*Notes:*

1 Share of associate's loss after tax = 20% × (18,500) = (3,700).

2 Impairment of investment in associate: this figure comes from the investment in associate in the statement of financial position. It reduces the carrying value of £17,700 to its recoverable amount of £10,000.

## 25.6 The acquisition of an associate part-way through the year

In order to match the cost (the investment) with the benefit (share of the associate's net assets), the associate's profit will only be taken into account from the date of acquiring the holding in the associate. The associate's profit at the date of acquisition represents part of the net assets that are being acquired at that date. The Puff example below is an illustration of the accounting treatment. The adjustment for unrealised profit is made against the group's share of the associate's profit and investment in the associate.

### 25.6.1 The Puff Group

**At date of acquisition on 31 March 20X4 of shares in the associate:**

● Puff plc acquired 30% of the shares in Blow plc.

● At that date the retained earnings of Blow were £61,500.

**During the year:**

● On 1/10/20X4 Blow sold Puff goods for £15,000, which was cost plus 25%.

● All income and expenditure for the year in Blow's statement of comprehensive income accrued evenly throughout the year.

**At end of financial year on 31 December 20X4:**

- 75% of the goods sold to Puff by Blow were still in inventory.

Set out below are the consolidated statement of income of Puff and its subsidiaries and the individual statement of income of an associated company, Blow, together with the consolidated group statement of income.

| | Puff and subsidiaries | Blow | Group accounts | |
|---|---|---|---|---|
| | £ | £ | £ | |
| Revenue | 225,000 | 112,500 | 225,000 | Note 1 |
| Cost of sales | 75,000 | 56,250 | 75,000 | Note 2 |
| Gross profit | 150,000 | 56,250 | 150,000 | |
| Expenses | 89,850 | 30,000 | 89,850 | |
| | 60,150 | 26,250 | 60,150 | |
| Dividends received from associate | 1,350 | NIL | NIL | Note 3 |
| Share of associate's profit | — | — | 3,713 | Note 4 |
| Profit before taxation | 61,500 | 26,250 | 63,863 | |
| Income tax for the period | 15,000 | 6,750 | 15,000 | |
| Profit for the period | 46,500 | 19,500 | 48,863 | |

*Notes:*

1 The revenue, cost of sales and all other income and expenses of the associated company are not added on a line-by-line basis with those of the parent company and its subsidiaries. The group's share of the profit after taxation of the associate is shown as one figure (see Note 4) and added to the remainder of the group's profit before taxation.

2 The group accounts 'cost of sales' figure has not been adjusted for unrealised profit, as this has been deducted from the share of the associate's profit.

3 The dividend received of £1,350 is eliminated, being replaced by the group share of its underlying profits.

4 Share of profits after tax of the associate:

| | £ |
|---|---|
| Profit after tax | 19,500 |
| Apportion for 9 months ($^9/_{12} \times 19,500$) | 14,625 |
| *Less:* Unrealised profit ($^{25}/_{125} \times 15,000$) $\times$ 75% | 2,250 |
| | 12,375 |
| Group share (30% $\times$ 12,375) | 3,713 |

5 There is no share of the associated company's retained earnings brought forward because the shares in the associate were purchased during the year.

## 25.7 Joint arrangements

IFRS 11 *Joint Arrangements* was issued by the IASB in 2011. Under this standard, joint arrangements are classified as either *joint operations* or *joint ventures* depending upon the parties' rights and obligations.

### Joint control[9]

Notice that both joint operations and joint ventures require that there should be joint control.

Joint control exists where there is a contractually agreed sharing of control of an arrangement under which decisions require the *unanimous* consent of the parties sharing control.

This may be by implicit agreement such as when two parties establish an arrangement in which each has 50% of the voting rights and the contractual arrangement between them specifies that at least 51% of the voting rights are required to make decisions, which results in joint control.

This does not mean the unanimous consent of *all* parties but of those who *collectively control* an arrangement, as illustrated in the following example.[10]

EXAMPLE ● Assume that three parties establish an arrangement: A has 50% of the voting rights in the arrangement, B has 30% and C has 20%. The contractual arrangement between A, B and C specifies that at least 75% of the voting rights are required to make decisions. Even though A can block any decision, it does not control the arrangement because it needs the agreement of B. The terms of their contractual arrangement requiring at least 75% of the voting rights to make decisions about the relevant activities imply that A and B have joint control of the arrangement, because decisions about the relevant activities of the arrangement cannot be made without both A and B agreeing.

### Joint operations[11]

This is where the parties, called joint operators, have joint control of the arrangement which gives rights to the assets and obligations for the liabilities. It is the existence of rights and obligations that is critical to determining whether a joint operation exists as opposed to the legal structure of the joint venture. In the predecessor standard, IAS 31, a joint operation could only exist where no new entity was formed.

There may be situations where the ownership rights have been varied by contract. For example, the contractual arrangement might provide for the allocation of revenues and expenses on the basis of the relative performance of each party to the joint arrangement, such as when companies control and finance an oil pipeline equally but pay according to the amount of their throughput. In other instances, the parties might have agreed to share the profit or loss on the basis of a specified proportion such as the parties' ownership interest in the arrangement. These contractual arrangements would not prevent the arrangement from being a joint operation so long as the parties have rights to the assets and obligations for the liabilities.

### Joint ventures[12]

This is where the parties, called joint venturers, have joint control of the arrangement which gives rights to the *net* assets of the arrangement. Typically in a joint venture the venturers take a share of the overall profit or loss earned by the joint venture as opposed to taking a share of the output of the venture.

## 25.7.1 Consolidated financial statements

### Joint operations

IFRS 11 says:[13]

A joint operator shall recognise in relation to its interest in a joint operation:

(a) its assets, including its share of any assets held jointly;

(b) its liabilities, including its share of any liabilities incurred jointly;

(c) its revenue from the sale of its share of the output arising from the joint operation;

(d) its share of the revenue from the sale of the output by the joint operation; and

(e) its expenses, including its share of any expenses incurred jointly.

As there are no numerical examples in the standard, it is not clear how the assets, liabilities, revenue and expenses of the joint operation will be shown in the financial statements of each contributor to the joint venture.

The following example suggests how the joint operation would be shown in the financial statements of Sherwood plc.

EXAMPLE • The joint operators are Sherwood plc and Arnold plc. Sherwood provides the land and buildings for the joint operation, and Sherwood and Arnold have provided equal cash sums to set up the joint venture. The profit is allocated equally between Sherwood and Arnold, after a payment to Sherwood of 5% of the carrying value of the land and buildings. On liquidation of the joint operation, the land and buildings will be returned to Sherwood, and the remaining assets and liabilities split equally between Sherwood and Arnold.

Sherwood's statement of financial position will include all the value of the land and buildings, and half the value of all the other assets and liabilities. It appears that these figures will be combined with the other assets and liabilities of Sherwood and not shown separately.

On the income statement, the joint operation's revenue will be included with other revenue. It would be helpful to the users of the financial statements if the revenue of the joint operation was shown separately.

On expenses, the standard is not clear whether they will be shown separately (in total) or combined with the other individual expense items of Sherwood. It may be shown as a separate figure (in total) as this would be helpful to the users of the financial statements. The rent on the land and buildings (of 5% of their carrying value) is likely to be shown separately in the income statement.

Joint operations can be very complex and require detailed analysis to identify the specific rights and obligations. Already audit firms are considering the practical implication of applying the standard and the possible restatement of prior years' financial statements if accounting policy and treatment changes.

### Joint ventures

A joint venturer recognises[14] its interest in a joint venture as an investment which is accounted for using the equity method in accordance with IAS 28 *Investments in Associates and Joint Ventures.*

### What if a party participates but does not have joint control?

If it is a joint operation the party would include its interest in the assets and liabilities. If a joint venture, the treatment then depends on the extent of influence that can be exerted. If it is significant then it is accounted for as an associate in accordance with IAS 28. If it is not significant then it is accounted for accordance with IFRS 9 *Financial Instruments.*

## 25.7.2 Determining whether we are dealing with a joint operation or a joint venture

The following is a helpful extract from www.kpmg.com:

An entity determines the type of joint arrangement by considering the structure, the legal form, the contractual arrangement and other facts and circumstances.

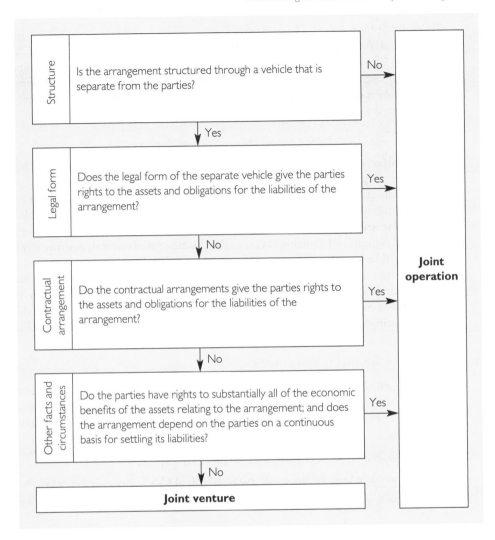

### 25.7.3 The accounting treatment required where the investment is a subsidiary, associate or joint operation

To illustrate the accounting treatments, we will take a parent company, Pete, which has an investment in another company, Sid.

#### Subsidiary – IFRS 10 *Consolidated Financial Statements applies*

If Pete owns more than 50% of the shares of Sid then Pete is presumed to have control of Sid. Sid is, therefore, classified as a subsidiary and the Pete group accounts will include all Sid's assets and liabilities as Pete has *control* over *all* of Sid's assets and liabilities.

#### Associate – IAS 28 *Investments in Associates and Joint Ventures applies*

If Pete owns between 20% and 50% of Sid's shares, then it is presumed that Pete is able to exercise significant influence and Sid will be classified as an associated company. In the Pete group accounts the investment in Sid is shown as a single figure in non-current assets. It will be reported at Pete's share of Sid's net assets at the date of acquisition plus goodwill plus post-acquisition profits.

### Joint venture

If Sid is a joint venture, then Sid is treated like an associated company of Pete. Even if Pete owns more than 50% of the shares in Sid, it would be treated like an associated company (using equity accounting) rather than a subsidiary. The reason for this is that one of the requirements of a joint venture is that decisions must be with the agreement of all the parties to the joint venture so that Pete does not have control of Sid. Thus Sid cannot be a subsidiary.

### Joint operation – IFRS 11 *Joint Arrangements* applies

The definition of a joint operation in IFRS 11 (para. 15) says that the parties that have joint control have rights to the assets and obligations for the liabilities.

So, in the example above, Pete will include in its statement of financial position the assets and liabilities of Sid over which it has the rights. So, if Pete purchased Sid's building, then the building will be included in Pete's statement of financial position. After allocating all Sid's assets and liabilities attributable to Pete in Pete's statement of financial position, any residual amount will be included in current assets and current liabilities.

In the statement of income Pete will include its share of the revenue and expenses of Sid over which it has rights. So, if £1 million of Sid's revenue is wholly attributable to Pete and £2 million of Sid's revenue over which Pete has a 40% share, the revenue of Sid which Pete will include in its financial statements would be £1.8 million (£1 million + 40% of £2 million).

## 25.7.4 Separate financial statements

The accounting for joint arrangements in an entity's separate financial statements depends on the involvement of the entity in that joint arrangement and the type of the joint arrangement.[15] For example, if the entity is a joint operator or joint venturer, it accounts for its interest in

- a joint operation in accordance with Section 25.7.1 above;
- a joint venture in accordance with paragraph 10 of IAS 27 *Separate Financial Statements*.

## 25.8 Disclosure in the financial statements

IFRS 12 *Disclosure of Interests in Other Entities* was issued by the IASB in 2011 to bring 'off-balance-sheet finance' onto the financial statements and to enable[16] users of financial statements to evaluate:

(a) the nature of, and risks associated with, its interests in other entities; and

(b) the effects of those interests on its financial position, financial performance and cash flows.

In terms of this chapter, there is a general requirement to disclose information about significant judgements and assumptions made when determining control, joint control, significant influence and classification of joint arrangements. In relation to interest in subsidiaries and joint arrangements, there are specific disclosure requirements.

### Interests in subsidiaries disclosures

An entity shall disclose information that enables[17] users of its consolidated financial statements to:

(a) understand the composition of the group and the interest that non-controlling interests have in the group's activities and cash flows; and

(b) evaluate the nature and extent of significant restrictions on its ability to access or use assets, and settle liabilities, of the group; the nature of, and changes in, the risks associated with its interests in consolidated structured entities; the consequences of changes in its ownership interest in a subsidiary that do not result in a loss of control; and the consequences of losing control of a subsidiary during the reporting period.

### Interests in joint arrangements and associates disclosures

An entity shall disclose information that enables[18] users of its financial statements to evaluate:

(a) the nature, extent and financial effects of its interests in joint arrangements and associates; and

(b) the nature of, and changes in, the risks associated with its interests in joint ventures and associates.

## 25.9 Parent company use of the equity method in its separate financial statements

In December 2013, IASB issued Exposure Draft ED/2013/10 which proposes to amend IAS 27 *Separate Financial Statements* so that an entity can use the equity method to account for investments in subsidiaries, joint ventures and associates in its separate financial statements.

IAS 27 (2011) required entities to account for investments in subsidiaries, joint ventures and associates either:

(a) at cost, or

(b) in accordance with IFRS 9 *Financial Instruments.*

This proposed amendment would allow the entity to use equity accounting to account for such investments.

Essentially, both IAS 28 *Investments in Associates* and, for joint ventures, IFRS 11 *Joint Arrangements* require equity accounting to be used for these arrangements.

Allowing subsidiaries to use equity accounting is a new alternative. Using equity accounting will reduce disclosure of the subsidiary:

(a) in the statement of financial position, a single figure in non-current assets of the cost plus share of profit since acquisition less any impairment (or share of net assets plus goodwill less impairment) (note: the two methods produce the same figure);

(b) in the statement of income, the share of the profit of the subsidiary after tax.

This means that there is far less disclosure in the parent company's financial statements. This reduces the work of the preparer of the financial statements but provides less information to the user.

Where the parent company elects not to prepare consolidated financial statements and instead prepares separate financial statements, it must disclose:

(a) the fact the financial statements are separate financial statements and that the exemption from consolidation has been used;

**(b)** a list of significant investments in subsidiaries, joint ventures and associates, including:

    (i)   the name of those investees;

    (ii)  the principal place of business of those investees;

    (iii) the proportion of ownership interest held in those investees;

**(c)** a description of the method used to account for the investments.

The option to use equity accounting (rather than cost or treating it as an investment) provides more useful information to shareholders as it gives the share of profit for the year and a measure of the value of the subsidiary/associated company/joint venture.

Comments on the Exposure Draft ED/2013/10 were favourable and the IASB published 'Equity method in Separate Financial Statements' amending IAS 27.

### 25.9.1 Critique of Equity Method in Separate Financial Statements

#### For associates and joint ventures

The permission to use equity accounting will produce the same figures and disclosure as are required by IAS 28 *Investments in Associates* and, for joint ventures, IFRS 11 *Joint Arrangements*. This is certainly much better than valuing them at cost, and, where these investments are to be held for the long term, it is more relevant information (and less subject to fluctuation) than using IFRS 7 *Financial Instruments*.

#### For subsidiaries

It is much easier for the preparer of the financial statements to include the subsidiary using the equity method, as all that is required is:

    (i)   for the income statement, the share of the profit after tax;

    (ii)  for the statement of financial position, the cost plus the share of profit since acquisition.

However, for the user/investor significantly less information is provided than a full consolidation. This would be acceptable if the subsidiary is small compared with the parent company (or the parent company and other subsidiaries). Compared with full consolidation, the reduced information will give the same profit (after tax) in the income statement and the same value of equity in the statement of financial position.

This is ignoring, however, the definition of a subsidiary which is that the parent company has **control** – so the subsidiary's results should be combined with those of the parent company. This is not what happens when the proposed amendment to IAS 27 is applied (essentially, only the parent company's detailed results are included in the separate financial statements).

Thus, applying the equity method to the parent's financial statements could well produce misleading financial statements, particularly when the subsidiary is a significant part of the group's activities (separate financial statements would suggest the group is much smaller than it is, and it would hide any risks associated with the subsidiary).

In conclusion, unless the subsidiary is immaterial, it is apparent that the user's needs are not satisfied by the reduced disclosure of IAS 27, and these reduced financial statements could be misleading. The separate financial statements may reduce the work of the preparer of the financial statements, but there is a greater loss to the user of the financial statement. Thus, the parent company should continue to consolidate the subsidiary, and not be permitted to reduce the subsidiary's disclosure solely to that required by equity accounting.

## Summary

Associates and joint ventures are accounted for under IAS 28 (revised 2011) using the equity method whereby there is a single-line entry in the statement of financial position carried initially at cost and the balance adjusted annually for the investor's share of the associate's current year's profit or loss. For joint venture entities, IAS 31 (now superseded by IFRS 11) permitted alternative treatments with investors able to adopt the equity accounting method or proportionate consolidation. Proportionate consolidation is no longer permitted. Joint operations are accounted for in accordance with with IFRS 11.

## REVIEW QUESTIONS

**1** Why are associated companies accounted for under the equity method rather than consolidated?

**2** IAS 28, paragraph 17, states:

> The recognition of income on the basis of distributions received may not be an adequate measure of the income earned by an investor on an investment in an associate.

Explain why this may be so.

**3** How does the treatment of inter-company unrealised profit differ between subsidiaries and associated companies?

**4** The result of including goodwill by valuing the non-controlling shares at their market price using

> Method 2 is to value the non-controlling shares on a different basis to valuing an equity investment in an associate. Discuss whether there should be a uniform approach to both.

**5** Where an associate has made losses, IAS 28, paragraph 30, states:

> After the investor's interest is reduced to zero, additional losses are provided for, and a liability is recognised, only to the extent that the investor has incurred legal or constructive obligations or made payments on behalf of the associate. If the associate subsequently reports profits, the investor resumes recognising its share of those profits only after its share of the profits equals the share of losses not recognised.

Explain why profits are recognised only after its share of the profits equals the share of losses not recognised.

**6** The following is an extract from the notes to the 2013 consolidated financial statements of the Chugoku Electric Power Company, Incorporated:

> For the year ended March 31, 2013, 10 affiliated companies were stated at cost without applying the equity method.

Discuss:

**(a)** why these affiliated companies are being reported at cost;

**(b)** the effect on the consolidated retained earnings if they had been reported using the equity method.

**7** Explain the difference between a joint operation and a joint venture.

**8** Explain the approach to determining whether an arrangement is a joint operation or a joint venture.

## EXERCISES

### * Question 1

The statements of income for Continent plc, Island Ltd and River Ltd for the year ended 31 December 20X9 were as follows:

|  | Continent plc € | Island Ltd € | River Ltd € |
|---|---|---|---|
| Revenue | 825,000 | 220,000 | 82,500 |
| Cost of sales | (616,000) | (55,000) | (8,250) |
| Gross profit | 209,000 | 165,000 | 74,250 |
| Administration costs | (33,495) | (18,700) | (3,850) |
| Distribution costs | (11,000) | (14,300) | (2,750) |
| Dividends receivable from Island and River | 4,620 |  |  |
| Profit before tax | 169,125 | (132,000) | 67,650 |
| Income tax | (55,000) | (33,000) | (11,000) |
| Profit after tax | 114,125 | 99,000 | 56,650 |

Continent plc acquired 80% of Island Ltd for €27,500 on 1 January 20X3, when Island Ltd's retained earnings were €22,000 and share capital was €5,500. During the year, Island Ltd sold goods costing €2,750 to Continent plc for €3,850. At the year-end, 10% of these goods were still in Continent plc's inventory.

Continent plc acquired 40% of River Ltd for €100,000 on 1 January 20X5, when River Ltd's share capital and reserves totalled €41,250 (share capital consisted of 11,000 50c shares). During the year River Ltd sold goods costing €1,650 to Continent plc for €2,200. At the year-end, 50% of these goods were still in Continent plc's inventory.

Goodwill in Island Ltd had suffered impairment charges in previous years totalling €2,200 and goodwill in River Ltd impairment charges totalling €7,700. Impairment has continued during 2009, reducing the goodwill in Island by €550 and the goodwill in River by €3,850.

Continent plc includes in its revenue management fees of €5,500 charged to Island Ltd and €2,750 charged to River Ltd. Both companies treat the charge as an administration cost.

Non-controlling interests are measured using Method 1.

### Required:
Prepare Continent plc's consolidated statement of income for the year ended 31 December 20X9.

## Question 2

The statements of comprehensive income for Highway plc, Road Ltd and Lane Ltd for the year ended 31 December 20X9 were as follows:

|  | Highway plc $ | Road Ltd $ | Lane Ltd $ |
|---|---|---|---|
| Revenue | 184,000 | 152,000 | 80,000 |
| Cost of sales | (48,000) | (24,000) | (16,000) |
| Gross profit | 136,000 | 128,000 | 64,000 |
| Administration costs | (13,680) | (11,200) | (20,800) |
| Distribution costs | (11,200) | (17,600) | (8,000) |
| Dividends receivable from Road | 2,480 |  |  |
| Profit before tax | 113,600 | 99,200 | 35,200 |
| Income tax | (32,000) | (8,000) | (4,800) |
| Profit for the period | 81,600 | 91,200 | 30,400 |

Highway plc acquired 80% of Road Ltd for $160,000 on 1.1.20X6 when Road Ltd's share capital was $64,000 and reserves were $16,000.

Highway plc acquired 30% of Lane Ltd for $40,000 on 1.1.20X7 when Lane Ltd's share capital was $8,000 and reserves were $8,000.

Goodwill of Road Ltd had suffered impairment charges of $14,400 in previous years and $4,800 was to be charged in the current year. Goodwill of Lane Ltd had suffered impairment charges of $3,520 in previous years and $1,760 was to be charged in the current year.

During the year Road Ltd sold goods to Highway plc for $8,000. These goods had cost Road Ltd $1,600. 50% were still in Highway's inventory at the year-end.

During the year Lane Ltd sold goods to Highway plc for $6,400. These goods had cost Lane Ltd $3,200. 50% were still in Highway's inventory at the year-end.

Highway's revenue included management fees of 5% of Road and Lane's turnover. Both of those companies have treated the charge as an administration cost.

Non-controlling interests are measured using Method 1.

**Required:**
**Prepare Highway's consolidated statement of comprehensive income for the year ended 31.12.20X9.**

## * Question 3

The following are the financial statements of the parent company Alpha plc, a subsidiary company Beta and an associate company Gamma.

### Statements of financial position as at 31 December 20X9

|  | Alpha £ | Beta £ | Gamma £ |
|---|---|---|---|
| **ASSETS** |  |  |  |
| *Non-current assets* |  |  |  |
| Land at cost | 540,000 | 256,500 | 202,500 |
| Investment in Beta | 216,000 |  |  |
| Investment in Gamma | 156,600 |  |  |
| *Current assets* |  |  |  |
| Inventories | 162,000 | 54,000 | 135,000 |
| Trade receivables | 108,000 | 72,900 | 91,800 |
| Dividend receivable from Beta | 10,800 |  |  |
| Dividend receivable from Gamma | 1,620 |  |  |
| Current account – Beta | 10,800 |  |  |
| Current account – Gamma | 13,500 |  |  |
| Cash | 237,600 | 62,100 | 67,500 |
| **Total current assets** | 544,320 | 189,000 | 294,300 |
| **Total assets** | 1,456,920 | 445,500 | 496,800 |
| **EQUITY AND LIABILITIES** |  |  |  |
| £1 shares | 540,000 | 67,500 | 27,000 |
| Retained earnings | 769,500 | 329,400 | 391,500 |
|  | 1,309,500 | 396,900 | 418,500 |
| *Current liabilities* |  |  |  |
| Trade payables | 93,420 | 24,300 | 59,400 |
| Dividends payable | 54,000 | 13,500 | 5,400 |
| Current account – Alpha | — | 10,800 | 13,500 |
| **Total equity and liabilities** | 1,456,920 | 445,500 | 496,800 |

On 1 January 20X5 Alpha plc acquired 80% of Beta plc for £216,000 when Beta plc's share capital and reserves were £81,000, and 30% of Gamma Ltd for £156,600 when Gamma Ltd's share capital and reserves were £40,500. The fair value of the land at the date of acquisition was £337,500 in Beta plc and £270,000 in Gamma Ltd. Both companies have kept land at cost in their statement of financial position. All other assets are recorded at fair value. There have been no further share issues or purchases of land since the date of acquisition.

At the year-end, Alpha plc has inventory acquired from Beta plc and Gamma Ltd. Beta plc had invoiced the inventory to Alpha plc for £54,000 – the cost to Beta plc had been £40,500. Gamma Ltd had invoiced Alpha plc for £13,500 – the cost to Gamma Ltd had been £8,100. Goodwill has been impaired by £52,650. The whole of the impairment relates to Beta.

Non-controlling interests are measured using Method 1.

**Required:**
**Prepare Alpha plc's consolidated statement of financial position as at 31.12.20X9.**

## Question 4

The following are the statements of financial position of Garden plc, its subsidiary Rose Ltd and its associate Petal Ltd:

### Statements of financial position as at 31 December 20X9

|  | Garden £ | Rose £ | Petal £ |
|---|---|---|---|
| **ASSETS** |  |  |  |
| *Non-current assets* |  |  |  |
| Land at cost | 240,000 |  | 84,000 |
| Land at valuation |  | 180,000 |  |
| Investment in Rose | 300,000 |  |  |
| Investment in Petal | 72,000 |  |  |
| Investments | 18,000 |  |  |
| *Current assets* |  |  |  |
| Inventories | 15,000 | 99,000 | 5,400 |
| Trade receivables | 33,000 | 98,400 | 1,200 |
| Current account – Rose | 18,000 |  |  |
| Current account – Petal | 2,400 |  |  |
| Cash | 6,600 | 67,200 | 300 |
| **Total current assets** | 75,000 | 264,600 | 6,900 |
| **Total assets** | 705,000 | 444,600 | 90,900 |
| **EQUITY AND LIABILITIES** |  |  |  |
| £1 shares | 300,000 | 120,000 | 30,000 |
| Revaluation reserve |  | 90,000 |  |
| Retained earnings | 270,000 | 216,000 | 57,600 |
|  | 570,000 | 426,000 | 87,600 |
| *Current liabilities* |  |  |  |
| Trade payables | 135,000 | 3,600 | 900 |
| Current account – Garden | — | 15,000 | 2,400 |
| **Total equity and liabilities** | 705,000 | 444,600 | 90,900 |

On 1 January 20X3 Garden plc acquired 75% of Rose Ltd for £300,000 when Rose's share capital and reserves were £252,000. Prior to the acquisition, the net book value of Rose's non-current assets was £90,000. Rose revalued its non-current assets immediately prior to the acquisition to fair value and included the revaluation in its statement of financial position.

On 1 January 20X5 Garden acquired 20% of Petal Ltd for £72,000 when the fair value of Petal's net assets were £42,000.

Goodwill has been impaired in Rose by £77,700 and in Petal by £31,800.

At the year-end, Garden plc has inventory acquired from Rose and Petal. Rose had invoiced the inventory to Garden for £6,000 – the cost to Rose had been £1,200. Petal had invoiced Garden for £3,000 – the cost to Petal had been £1,800.

Non-controlling interests are measured using Method 1.

**Required:**
**Prepare Garden plc's consolidated statement of financial position as at 31.12.20X9.**

## * Question 5

The following are the financial statements of the parent company Swish plc, a subsidiary company Broom and an associate company Handle.

### Statements of financial position as at 31 December 20X3

|  | Swish £ | Broom £ | Handle £ |
|---|---|---|---|
| **ASSETS** | | | |
| *Non-current assets* | | | |
| Property, plant and equipment at cost | 320,000 | 180,000 | 100,000 |
| Depreciation | 200,000 | 70,000 | 21,000 |
|  | 120,000 | 110,000 | 79,000 |
| Investment in Broom | 140,000 | | |
| Investment in Handle | 40,000 | | |
| *Current assets* | | | |
| Inventories | 120,000 | 60,000 | 36,000 |
| Trade receivables | 130,000 | 70,000 | 36,000 |
| Current account – Broom | 15,000 | | |
| Current account – Handle | 3,000 | | |
| Bank | 24,000 | 7,000 | 6,000 |
| **Total current assets** | 292,000 | 137,000 | 78,000 |
| **Total assets** | 592,000 | 247,000 | 157,000 |
| **EQUITY AND LIABILITIES** | | | |
| £1 ordinary shares | 250,000 | 60,000 | 50,000 |
| General reserve | 30,000 | 20,000 | 12,000 |
| Retained earnings | 150,000 | 120,000 | 50,000 |
|  | 430,000 | 200,000 | 112,000 |
| *Current liabilities* | | | |
| Trade payables | 132,000 | 25,000 | 34,000 |
| Taxation payable | 30,000 | 7,000 | 8,000 |
| Current account – Swish | | 15,000 | 3,000 |
| **Total equity and liabilities** | 592,000 | 247,000 | 157,000 |

### Statement of income for the year ended 31 December 20X3

|  | £ | £ | £ |
|---|---|---|---|
| Sales | 300,000 | 160,000 | 100,000 |
| Cost of sales | 90,000 | 80,000 | 40,000 |
| Gross profit | 210,000 | 80,000 | 60,000 |
| Expenses | 95,000 | 50,000 | 30,000 |
| Dividends received from Broom and Handle | 11,000 | NIL | NIL |
| Profit before tax | 126,000 | 30,000 | 30,000 |
| Income tax expense | 30,000 | 7,000 | 8,000 |
| Profit for the period | 96,000 | 23,000 | 22,000 |
| Dividend paid (shown in equity) | 40,000 | 10,000 | 8,000 |

Swish acquired 90% of the shares in Broom on 1 January 20X1 when the balance on the retained earnings of Broom was £60,000 and the balance on the general reserve of Broom was £16,000. Swish also acquired 25% of the shares in Handle on 1 January 20X2 when the balance on Handle's accumulated retained profits was £30,000 and the general reserve £8,000.

During the year Swish sold Broom goods for £16,000, which included a markup of one-third. 80% of these goods were still in inventory at the end of the year.

**Required:**
(a) Prepare a consolidated statement of income, including the associated company Handle's results, for the year ended 31 December 20X3.
(b) Prepare a consolidated statement of financial position as at 31 December 20X3. The group policy is to measure non-controlling interests using Method 1.

## Question 6

Set out below are the financial statements of Ant Co., its subsidiary Bug Co. and an associated company Nit Co. for the accounting year-end 31 December 20X9.

### Statements of financial position as at 31 December 20X9

|  | Ant $ | Bug $ | Nit $ |
|---|---|---|---|
| **ASSETS** | | | |
| *Non-current assets* | | | |
| Property, plant and equipment at cost | 240,000 | 135,000 | 75,000 |
| Depreciation | 150,000 | 52,500 | 15,750 |
|  | 90,000 | 82,500 | 59,250 |
| Investment in Bug | 90,000 | | |
| Investment in Nit | 30,000 | | |
| *Current assets* | | | |
| Inventories | 105,000 | 45,000 | 27,000 |
| Trade receivables | 98,250 | 52,500 | 27,000 |
| Current account – Bug | 11,250 | | |
| Current account – Nit | 2,250 | | |
| Bank | 17,250 | 5,250 | 4,500 |
| **Total current assets** | 234,000 | 102,750 | 58,500 |
| **Total assets** | 444,000 | 185,250 | 117,750 |
| **EQUITY AND LIABILITIES** | | | |
| $1 ordinary shares | 187,500 | 45,000 | 37,500 |
| General reserve | 22,500 | 15,000 | 9,000 |
| Retained earnings | 112,500 | 90,000 | 37,500 |
|  | 322,500 | 150,000 | 84,000 |
| *Current liabilities* | | | |
| Trade payables | 99,000 | 18,750 | 25,500 |
| Taxation payable | 22,500 | 5,250 | 6,000 |
| Current account – Ant | | 11,250 | 2,250 |
| **Total equity and liabilities** | 444,000 | 185,250 | 117,750 |

### Statements of comprehensive income for the year ended 31 December 20X9

|  | Ant | Bug | Nit |
|---|---|---|---|
|  | $ | $ | $ |
| Sales | 225,000 | 120,000 | 75,000 |
| Cost of sales | 67,500 | 60,000 | 30,000 |
| Gross profit | 157,500 | 60,000 | 45,000 |
| Expenses | 70,500 | 37,500 | 30,000 |
| Dividends received | 7,500 | NIL | 7,500 |
| Profit before tax | 94,500 | 22,500 | 22,500 |
| Taxation | 22,500 | 5,250 | 6,000 |
| Profit for the year | 72,000 | 17,250 | 16,500 |
| Dividends paid in year | 30,000 | 7,500 | 6,000 |

Ant Co. acquired 80% of the shares in Bug Co. on 1 January 20X7 when the balance on the retained earnings of Bug Co. was $45,000 and the balance on the general reserve of Bug Co. was $12,000. The fair value of the non-controlling interest in Bug on 1 January 20X7 was $21,000. Group policy is to measure non-controlling interests using Method 2. Ant Co. also acquired 25% of the shares in Nit Co. on 1 January 20X8 when the balance on Nit's retained earnings was $22,500 and the general reserve $6,000.

During the year Ant Co. sold Bug Co. goods for $12,000, which included a markup of one-third. 90% of these goods were still in inventory at the end of the year.

Required:

(a) Prepare a consolidated statement of income for the year ending 31/12/20X9, including the associated company Nit's results.

(b) Prepare a consolidated statement of financial position at 31/12/20X9, including the associated company.

## * Question 7

Epsilon acquired 40% of Zeta when Zeta's retained earnings were $50,000, 25% of Kappa when Kappa's retained earnings were $40,000, and 25% of Lambda when Lambda's retained earnings were $50,000.

The four companies' statements of financial position as at 31 October 2011 were as follows:

| | Epsilon $000 | Zeta $000 | Kappa $000 | Lambda $000 |
|---|---|---|---|---|
| **ASSETS** | | | | |
| Non-current assets | 1,900 | 170 | 140 | 160 |
| Investment in Zeta | 100 | | | |
| Investment in Kappa | 55 | | | |
| Investment in Lambda | 60 | | | |
| | 2,115 | 170 | 140 | 160 |
| Current assets: | | | | |
| Inventory | 8 | 6 | 12 | 11 |
| Trade receivables | 12 | 5 | 4 | 7 |
| Bank | 5 | 4 | 3 | 2 |
| | 25 | 15 | 19 | 20 |
| **Total assets** | 2,140 | 185 | 159 | 180 |
| **LIABILITIES** | | | | |
| Equity: | | | | |
| Share capital | 500 | 50 | 60 | 70 |
| Reserves | 1,563 | 124 | 91 | 98 |
| | 2,063 | 174 | 151 | 168 |
| Non-current liabilities | 50 | | | |
| Current liabilities: | | | | |
| Trade payables | 27 | 11 | 8 | 12 |
| | 2,140 | 185 | 159 | 180 |

Epsilon is entitled to appoint three members of Zeta's board. Zeta's articles state that the board of directors is restricted to five members and that board decisions are binding whenever a simple majority of the directors agree.

Epsilon used its voting rights to secure a place on Kappa's board for one of its own directors. This director has access to internal management reports and can exert some influence on decision making within the company.

Epsilon does not have a representative on the board of Lambda. The directors of Epsilon attempted to secure a place on the board, but were rebuffed by Ms Strong, who owns 75% of the shares. Ms Strong takes a very direct role in the management of Lambda.

### Required:
(a) Discuss how each of Epsilon shareholdings should be accounted for in the Epsilon group's consolidated financial statements.
(b) Prepare a consolidated statement of financial position for the Epsilon Group as at 31 October 2011.

*(The Association of International Accountants)*

## Question 8

This question concerns an associated company making a loss and possible impairment of goodwill.

Hyson plc acquired a 30% interest in the ordinary shares of Green plc on 1 January 20X3 when Green's general reserve was £25,000 and its retained earnings were £40,000.

In the year ended 31 December 20X8 Green made a loss after tax of £65,000 because of a recession in its principal sales market.

The statements of financial position of Hyson plc and Green plc at 31 December 20X8 are as follows:

|  | Hyson £ | Green £ |
|---|---|---|
| **ASSETS** |  |  |
| Non-current assets: |  |  |
| Property, plant and equipment | 650,000 | 230,000 |
| Depreciation | (310,000) | (105,000) |
|  | 340,000 | 125,000 |
| Investment in Green | 90,000 |  |
| Current assets: |  |  |
| Inventories | 145,000 | 64,000 |
| Trade receivables | 180,000 | 85,000 |
| Current account – Green | 5,000 |  |
| Bank | 25,000 | 3,000 |
| **Total current assets** | 355,000 | 152,000 |
| **Total assets** | 785,000 | 277,000 |
| **EQUITY AND LIABILITIES** |  |  |
| £1 ordinary shares | 300,000 | 200,000 |
| General reserve | 60,000 | 30,000 |
| Retained earnings | 225,000 | (57,000) |
|  | 585,000 | 173,000 |
| Current liabilities: |  |  |
| Trade payables | 163,000 | 99,000 |
| Taxation payable | 37,000 | — |
| Current account – Hyson | — | 5,000 |
| **Total equity and liabilities** | 785,000 | 277,000 |

The statements of income of Hyson and Green for the year ended 31 December 20X8 are:

|  | £ | £ |
|---|---|---|
| Sales | 1,045,000 | 350,000 |
| Cost of sales | 683,000 | 320,000 |
| Gross profit | 362,000 | 30,000 |
| Distribution expenses | 42,000 | 20,000 |
| Administration expenses | 152,000 | 75,000 |
| Profit/(loss) before tax | 168,000 | (65,000) |
| Income tax expense | 33,000 | — |
| Profit for the period | 135,000 | (65,000) |
| Dividend paid (shown in equity) | 40,000 | — |

Because of the losses of Green in 20X8, the recoverable amount of a 30% interest in Green is £40,000 at 31 December 20X8.

**Required:**
(a) Prepare a consolidated statement of financial position of Hyson plc as at 31 December 20X8.
(b) Prepare a consolidated statement of income of Hyson plc, including the associated company Green, for the year ended 31 December 20X8.
(c) State the changes to your answers in (a) and (b) above if the recoverable amount of a 30% interest in Green was £65,000.

## Question 9

Arnold plc and Bunny plc agreed to establish a Joint Operation, Carlton, which started trading on 1 January 20X1. Carlton is an unincorporated business, which is financed and managed by Arnold and Bunny.

Arnold agreed to provide land at an agreed price of £1,000,000 and plant at £600,000. In addition, Arnold and Bunny provided £200,000 in cash for working capital.

It was agreed that, on consolidation, the land and plant would remain in the statement of financial position of Arnold. All other assets and liabilities (except cash at the bank) of the joint operation would be divided equally between the partners. Cash at the bank would be divided so the capital of each partner was equal to their respective assets less liabilities.

The trial balance of the Joint Operation at 31 December 20X1 is given below:

|  | £000 | £000 |
|---|---|---|
| Sales |  | 1,500 |
| Purchases | 700 |  |
| Direct wages | 500 |  |
| Land | 1,000 |  |
| Plant | 600 |  |
| Trade receivables | 400 |  |
| Trade payables |  | 300 |
| Office expenses | 80 |  |
| Heat, light & telephone | 70 |  |
| Motor & travelling expenses | 60 |  |
| Advertising & marketing | 46 |  |
| Finance costs | 30 |  |
| Capital – Arnold |  | 1,800 |
| Capital – Bunny |  | 200 |
| Bank balance | 314 |  |
|  | 3,800 | 3,800 |

The value of inventory at 31 December 20X1 was £200,000. No depreciation is to be charged on the land. Plant is to be depreciated at 5% per annum on cost.
Profit for the year is to be distributed to the partners:

(i)   5% per annum on capital; then
(ii)  the remaining profit is to be divided equally between Arnold and Bunny.

**Required:**
For the year ended 31 December 20X1, prepare an income statement and statement of financial position of the Joint Operation at the year-end.

## Notes

1 IAS 28 *Investments in Associates and Joint Ventures,* IASB, revised 2011, para. 3.
2 Ibid., para. 5.
3 Ibid., para. 8.
4 Ibid., para. 15.
5 Ibid., para. 10.
6 IAS 1 *Presentation of Financial Statements,* IASB, revised 2003, Implementation Guidance.
7 IAS 28 *Investments in Associates and Joint Ventures,* IASB, revised 2011, para. 40.
8 Ibid., para. 30.
9 Ibid., para. 7.
10 IFRS 11 *Joint Arrangements,* IASB, 2011, B8.
11 Ibid., para. 15.
12 Ibid., para. 16.
13 Ibid., para. 20.
14 Ibid., paras 24–25.
15 Ibid., para. 26.
16 IFRS 12 *Disclosure of Interest in Other Entities,* IASB, 2011, para. 1.
17 Ibid., para. 10.
18 Ibid., para. 20.

# CHAPTER 26

# Introduction to accounting for exchange differences

## 26.1 Introduction

The increasing globalisation of business means that it is becoming more and more common for companies to enter into transactions that have to be paid for in a foreign currency.

When currency fluctuations occur the exchange rate will have changed between the date the goods or services have been invoiced and the date that payment is made. The difference impacts on cash flows and will be reported as a realised exchange gain or loss in the statement of income.

In this chapter we also consider how to prepare consolidated accounts when there is a foreign subsidiary that maintains its own accounts in the local currency which is different from that of its parent. IAS 21 refers to the local currency as the **functional** currency and the parent's currency as the **presentation** currency. The restatement of the functional currency into the presentation is referred to as translation. Any difference on exchange arising on translation has not been realised and is reported as other comprehensive income.

### Objectives

By the end of this chapter, you should be able to:

- account for foreign transactions where differences arise on actual cash inflows and outflows resulting in realised gains or losses;
- translate the financial statements of foreign subsidiaries into the parent company's currency and report any exchange differences under other comprehensive income;
- explain the criteria when determining 'functional' and 'presentation' currency;
- prepare consolidated financial statements to include subsidiaries whose financial statements prepared using the local functional currency have to be translated into a different presentation currency on consolidation;
- explain the characteristics of a hyperinflationary economy and restatement of the functional currency financial statements.

## 26.2 How to record foreign currency transactions in a company's own books

We will comment briefly on the IAS 21 provisions relating to (i) how a foreign currency transaction is defined, (ii) the amount entered into the company's accounting records on entering into a transaction, (iii) the accounting treatment of exchange differences when the transaction is settled within the current accounting period, (iv) the accounting treatment when settlement occurs in the next accounting period, (v) the accounting treatment when settlement occurs in an accounting period beyond the next, and (vi) hedging the amount payable.

### 26.2.1 Defining foreign transactions

IAS 21 *The Effects of Changes in Foreign Exchange Rates* defines foreign transactions as follows:[1]

A foreign transaction is a transaction which is denominated in or requires settlement in a foreign currency, including transactions arising when an entity:

(a) buys or sells goods or services whose price is denominated in a foreign currency;

(b) borrows or lends funds when the amounts payable or receivable are denominated in a foreign currency;

(c) otherwise acquires or disposes of assets, or incurs or settles liabilities, denominated in a foreign currency.

### 26.2.2 The amount recorded on entering into a transaction

On initial recognition,[2] transactions are entered in the books at the spot currency exchange rate at the transaction date.

For example, let us assume that Brie SA buys vintage cheese from a UK company, Cheddar Ltd, on 1 October 20X1 for £100,000 when the exchange rate was £1 = €1.20. This will be recorded by Brie as Purchases €120,000 and Trade payable (Cheddar) at €120,000.

Where it is more practical an average rate may be used for a period to translate the month's purchases (it will be inappropriate where exchange rates fluctuate significantly).

### 26.2.3 The accounting treatment of exchange differences when the transaction is settled within the current accounting period

Amounts paid or received in settlement of foreign currency monetary items during an accounting period are translated at the date of settlement, and any exchange difference is taken to the statement of income as a realised gain or loss.

For example, if the rate at the date of payment on 31 October 20X1 was £1 = €1.22, then Brie would pay €122,000 to obtain the sterling amount of £100,000. The exchange difference of €2,000 (€122,000 − €120,000) is debited to the statement of income as an operating expense. If the rate had changed to £1 = €1.18 then there would have been an operating income of €2,000.

The following is an extract from the accounting policies in Nemetschek's 2011 report:

**Currency translation**

Exchange rate differences arising on the settlement of monetary items at rates different from those at which they were initially recorded during the period, are recognized as other operating income or other operating expenses in the period in which they arise.

### 26.2.4 The accounting treatment of exchange differences at the year-end when settlement is to occur in the next accounting period

The treatment depends on the ledger balances outstanding. For instance:

- Monetary balances are retranslated at the closing rate as at the date of the statement of financial position.
- Non-monetary items such as property, plant, equipment and inventory reported at historical cost remain translated at their original transaction rate.
- Non-monetary items at fair value are translated at the rate on the date the fair value was determined.[3]

Continuing with our Brie example on accounting for inventory, there are the following possibilities.

#### Inventory has been sold but the account payable is still outstanding

Assuming that all of the cheese had been sold but Cheddar had still not been paid, then there is no inventory to consider, only the amount payable to Cheddar. This balance is required to be translated at the closing rate. If the closing rate is £1 = €1.24 then the liability to Cheddar would be restated at €124,000 and there would be a resulting exchange loss of €4,000 which is reported in the statement of income.

#### Inventory has still not been sold and the account payable is still outstanding

If the cheese had not been sold and was still held as inventory, it is required to be reported at the rate as at the date of the initial transaction and not the closing rate, i.e. reported in the statement of financial position as €120,000 – the cost as at 1 October 20X1, the date of purchase. The account payable would still be reported at €124,000.

#### Inventory has still not been sold but net realisable value is lower than cost

If enquiry established that the cheese had deteriorated and the net realisable value was 50% of cost, then this would be translated at the closing rate as €62,000 (£50,000 × 1.24) and a loss reported of €58,000.

### 26.2.5 The accounting treatment of exchange differences when settlement occurs in a yet later accounting period

If a monetary item remains unpaid beyond the next accounting period then it will need to be retranslated at the closing rate as at the end of that period.

Let us assume the following:

- Brie has translated the €120,000 due to Cheddar as €124,000 and recognised an operating loss of €4,000 in the year ended 31 December 20X1.
- Brie has reached an agreement with Cheddar that the cheese needs a further period to mature and settlement in full is to be on 1 January 20X3.
- The exchange rate is £1 = €1.23 on 31 December 20X2.

At 31 December 20X2 Brie would report that there was €123,000 owing and there would be an operating gain reported in the 20X2 statement of income of €1,000 (€124,000 − €123,000). If the exchange rate had weakened to a rate higher than £1 = €1.24 there would have been a further operating loss reported in 20X2.

### 26.2.6 Hedging a foreign currency transaction to crystallise the amount of any exchange difference

A company might enter into a hedging transaction under IAS 39 or IFRS 9 *Financial Instruments*. The intention is to neutralise the exchange risk so that the company knows exactly how much a transaction will cost when settlement is required at a later date. This can be achieved in a number of ways such as entering into a forward contract or an options contract.

For example, let us continue with our Brie example and assume that the euro is weakening and Brie's finance director wants to fix the exact amount it is required to pay in euros on 31 October 20X1 to settle the debt currently recorded as €120,000. His worry is that the end-of-month rate might be £1 = €1.30 which would result in an operating loss of €10,000. In order to take away the uncertainty, Brie enters into a forward contract to buy £100,000 at the end of the month at a rate of say €1.25. This means that there is a known loss of €5,000 as opposed to the risk of a potential loss of up to €10,000.

## 26.3 Boil plc – a more detailed illustration

Let us assume the following transactions were entered into by Boil plc, a UK company that buys and sells catering equipment in New Zealand, during the year ended 31 December 20X4:

| | |
|---|---|
| 1/11 | Buys goods for $30,000 on credit from Napier Ltd |
| 15/11 | Sells goods for $40,000 on credit to Wellington Ltd |
| 15/11 | Pays Napier Ltd $20,000 on account for the goods purchased |
| 10/12 | Receives $25,000 on account from Wellington Ltd in payment for the goods sold |
| 10/12 | Buys machinery for $80,000 from Auckland Ltd on credit |
| 22/12 | Pays Auckland Ltd $80,000 for the machinery |

Boil's functional currency is sterling and the New Zealand companies' functional currency is NZ$.

The exchange rates at the relevant dates were:

| | | | | | |
|---|---|---|---|---|---|
| 1/11 | £1 = $2.00 | 15/11 | £1 = $2.20 | 10/12 | £1 = $2.40 |
| 22/12 | £1 = $2.50 | 31/12 | £1 = $2.60 | | |

(Assume that Boil plc buys foreign currency to pay for goods and non-current assets on the day of settlement and immediately converts into sterling any currency received from sales.)

### Translating monetary accounts

We need to calculate any exchange differences on monetary accounts that are to be reported in the statement of income which arise on changes between the date of the initial transaction and the rate on the date of its settlement or the statement of financial position date, whichever is the earlier. Profits or losses on exchange differences will arise on the following monetary accounts:

| | |
|---|---|
| Napier Ltd | Trade payables |
| Wellington Ltd | Trade receivable |
| Auckland Ltd | Payable for machinery |

The profit or loss on foreign exchange in these cases will be as follows:

| **Napier** *Payable* | | | **Wellington** *Receivable* | | | **Auckland** *Payable* | | |
|---|---|---|---|---|---|---|---|---|
| NZ$ | Rate | £ | NZ$ | Rate | £ | NZ$ | Rate | £ |

(i) Record using the exchange rate on the date of transaction:
$30,000 @ 2.00 = 15,000 \quad 40,000 @ 2.20 = (18,182) \quad 80,000 @ 2.40 = 33,333$

(ii) Record using the exchange rate at the settlement date:
$20,000 @ 2.20 = (9,091) \quad 25,000 @ 2.40 = 10,417 \quad 80,000 @ 2.50 = \underline{(32,000)}$

(iii) Retranslate and record using the closing exchange rate as at the year-end:
$10,000 @ 2.60 = \underline{(3,846)} \quad 15,000 @ 2.60 = \underline{5,769}$

(iv) Calculate any gain (loss) on exchange:

$$2,063 \qquad\qquad (1,996) \qquad\qquad 1,333$$

The exchange gains of £2,063 and £1,333 and exchange loss of £1,996 have been realised and are reported in the statement of income as operating income and operating expense.

### Accounting treatment of other balances

All other balances, i.e. purchases and sales in the statement of income and machinery (non-monetary), will be translated on the day of the initial transaction and no profit or loss on foreign exchange will arise. These balances will therefore appear in the financial statements as follows:

| | |
|---|---|
| Purchases | $30,000/2.00 = £15,000 |
| Sales | $40,000/2.20 = £18,182 |
| Machinery | $80,000/2.40 = £33,333 |

## 26.4 IAS 21 Concept of Functional and Presentation Currencies

All companies have a functional and a presentation currency. In a group with foreign subsidiaries these currencies often differ.

Many groups consist of a parent with a number of foreign subsidiaries that prepare their accounts in the local currency, their functional currency. At the year-end each set of foreign subsidiary accounts is translated into the currency of the parent, the presentation currency or presentational currency.

### 26.4.1 The functional currency

The functional currency is the currency of the primary economic environment in which the entity operates. For example, the following extract is from the Rio Tinto 2015 financial statements:

> The functional currency for each entity in the Group ... is the currency of the primary economic environment in which that entity operates. For many entities, this is the currency of the country in which they are located.

#### Factors to consider when determining the functional currency for an individual company

IAS 21 sets out the factors which a reporting entity (a company preparing financial statements) will consider in determining its functional currency.[1] These are:

● the currency that mainly influences sales prices for goods and services;

● the currency that mainly influences labour, materials and other costs of providing goods and services; and

- the currency in which funds from financing activities are generated and the currency in which the receipts from operating activities are usually retained, which also provide evidence of an entity's functional currency.[4]

If the functional currency is not obvious from the above, then managers have to make a judgement as to which currency most represents the economic effects of its transactions.

### Factors a parent considers when deciding with a subsidiary on the subsidiary's functional currency

In making its decision the following factors will be considered:[5]

(a) Whether the activities of the foreign operation are carried out as an extension of the reporting entity (the parent), rather than being carried out with a significant degree of autonomy. An example of the former is when the foreign operation only sells goods imported from the parent and remits the proceeds to it. An example of the latter is when the operation accumulates cash and other monetary items, incurs expenses, generates income and arranges borrowings, all substantially in its local currency.

(b) Whether transactions with the parent are a high or low proportion of the foreign operation's activities.

(c) Whether cash flows from the activities of the foreign operation directly affect the cash flows of the parent and are readily available for remittance to it.

(d) Whether cash flows from the activities of the foreign operation are sufficient to service existing and normally expected debt obligations without funds being made available by the parent.

If the functional currency of the foreign operation is the same as that of the parent, there will of course be no need for translation and the consolidation will be just as for any other subsidiary.

### 26.4.2 The presentation currency[6]

The **presentation currency** is the currency a parent chooses for its financial statements. The parent is entitled to present its group accounts in any currency, so that in some cases the parent's presentation currency may differ from its own functional currency. There are various reasons for this, such as the principal or potential investors tending to function in a country with a different currency. For example, a parent whose functional currency is the euro might decide to raise finance in the US and so translates its euro financial statements into US$.

The following is an extract from a Press Announcement in 2010 by Tullow Oil plc:

#### Change in presentation currency

Tullow Oil plc ('the Company', together with its subsidiaries, 'the Group') will present its results in US dollars with effect from 1 January 2010. The Group has decided it is appropriate to change the presentational currency from Sterling as the majority of the Group's activities are in Africa where oil revenues and costs are dollar denominated.

## 26.5 Translating the functional currency into the presentation currency

Whenever the presentational currency is different from the functional currency, it is necessary to translate the financial statements into the presentational currency. In this situation there is no impact on cash flows and so there is no realised exchange gain or loss to be reported in the statement of income.

Any gain or loss will, therefore, be reported as other comprehensive income. The translation rules used in this situation are set out in paragraph 39 of IAS 21 as follows:

(a) assets and liabilities . . . shall be translated at the closing rate at the date of the statement of financial position;

(b) income and expenses . . . shall be translated at exchange rates at the dates of the transactions [or average rate if this is a reasonable approximation]; and

(c) all resulting exchange differences shall be recognised as a separate component of equity.

The following is an extract from Nemetschek AG's 2015 annual report:

**Currency translation**
The group's consolidated financial statements are prepared in Euros, which is the group's presentation currency.

*Functional currency policy*
Each entity in the group determines its own functional currency. That is the currency of the primarily economic environment in which the company operates. Items included in the financial statements of each entity are measured using the functional currency. Transactions in foreign currencies are initially recorded at the functional currency rate ruling on the date of the transaction.

Monetary assets and liabilities denominated in foreign currencies are retranslated at the functional currency spot rate of exchange ruling at the balance sheet date. Foreign exchange differences are recorded in profit or loss . . .

Non-monetary items that are measured in terms of historical cost in a foreign currency are translated using the exchange rate as of the date of the initial transaction. Non-monetary items measured at fair value in a foreign currency are translated using the exchange rates at the date when the fair value is determined.

*Group policy re subsidiaries*
Assets and liabilities of foreign companies are translated to the Euro at the closing rate (incl. goodwill). Income and expenses are translated at the average exchange rate. Any resulting exchange differences are recognised separately in equity.

## 26.6 Preparation of consolidated accounts

The consolidated accounts are prepared for the Pau Group from the following data.
On 1 January 20X1 Pau Inc. acquired 80% of the ordinary shares of a Brazilian company Briona for $18m when Briona's retained earnings were R$2m and the share premium was R$7m. Briona's financial statements have been audited in their functional currency of

Brazilian reals and comply with IAS 21. The summarised statements of income and financial position as at 31 December 20X1 were as follows:

### Statements of income for the year ended 31 December 20X1

| | US$000 | Pau US$000 | R$000 | Briona R$000 |
|---|---|---|---|---|
| Sales | | 200,000 | | 80,000 |
| Opening inventories | 20,000 | | 10,000 | |
| Purchases | 130,000 | | 60,000 | |
| Closing inventories | (40,000) | | (30,000) | |
| Cost of sales | | 110,000 | | 40,000 |
| Gross profit | | 90,000 | | 40,000 |
| Other expenses | | (15,000) | | (14,000) |
| Interest paid | | | | (1,000) |
| Total expenses | | (15,000) | | (15,000) |
| Profit before taxation | | 75,000 | | 25,000 |
| Taxation | | (15,000) | | (5,000) |
| Profit after taxation | | 60,000 | | 20,000 |

### Statement of financial position as at 31 December 20X1

| | US$000 | R$000 |
|---|---|---|
| Non-current assets | 70,000 | 30,000 |
| Investment in Briona | 18,000 | |
| *Current assets* | | |
| Inventories | 40,000 | 30,000 |
| Trade receivables | 27,000 | 25,000 |
| Cash | 2,000 | 1,000 |
| Total current assets | 69,000 | 56,000 |
| *Current liabilities* | | |
| Trade payables | 35,000 | 12,000 |
| Taxation | 15,000 | 5,000 |
| Total current liabilities | 50,000 | 17,000 |
| Debentures | | 6,000 |
| Total assets less liabilities | 107,000 | 63,000 |
| Share capital | 20,000 | 34,000 |
| Share premium | | 7,000 |
| Retained earnings | 87,000 | 22,000 |
| | 107,000 | 63,000 |

The following information is also available:

(i) The opening inventory was acquired when the exchange rate was US$1 = R$2.0 and the closing inventory when the rate was US$1 = R$2.4.

(ii) Exchange rates were as follows:

| | |
|---|---|
| At 1 January 20X1 | US$1 = R$2.0 |
| Average for the year ending 31 December 20X4 | US$1 = R$2.25 |
| At 31 December 20X1 | US$1 = R$2.5 |

Required:

(a) Prepare a consolidated statement of income.

(b) Prepare a consolidated statement of financial position:

    (i) Show the goodwill calculation.

    (ii) Show the non-controlling interest calculation.

    (iii) Complete with retained earnings as a balancing figure.

(c) Reconcile the retained earnings figure showing exchange gains and losses.

## 26.6.1 Pau Group draft consolidated accounts

### (a) Statement of income

| | Pau US$000 | Briona R$000 | Rate | Briona US$000 | Pau Group US$000 |
|---|---|---|---|---|---|
| Sales | 200,000 | 80,000 | 2.25 | 35,555.6 | 235,555.6 |
| Opening inventories | 20,000 | 10,000 | 2.0 | 5,000.0 | 25,000.0 |
| Purchases | 130,000 | 60,000 | 2.25 | 26,666.7 | 156,666.7 |
| Closing inventories | −40,000 | −30,000 | 2.4 | −12,500.0 | −52,500.0 |
| Cost of sales | 110,000 | 40,000 | | 19,166.7 | 129,166.7 |
| Gross profit | 90,000 | 40,000 | | 16,388.9 | 106,388.9 |
| Other expenses | −15,000 | −14,000 | 2.25 | −6,222.2 | −21,222.2 |
| Interest paid | | −1,000 | 2.25 | −444.4 | −444.4 |
| Total expenses | 15,000 | 15,000 | | 6,666.7 | 21,666.7 |
| Profit before tax | 75,000 | 25,000 | | 9,722.2 | 84,722.2 |
| Income tax | −15,000 | −5,000 | 2.5 | −2,000.0 | −17,000.0 |
| Profit after tax | 60,000 | 20,000 | | 7,722.2 | 67,722.2 |

### (b) Statement of financial position

| | Pau US$000 | Briona R$000 | Rate | Briona US$000 | | Pau Group US$000 |
|---|---|---|---|---|---|---|
| Non-current assets | 70,000 | 30,000 | 2.5 | 12,000 | | 82,000 |
| Investment in Briona | 18,000 | | | | Goodwill (b1) | 640 |
| *Current assets* | | | | | | |
| Inventories | 40,000 | 30,000 | 2.5 | 12,000 | | 52,000 |
| Trade receivables | 27,000 | 25,000 | 2.5 | 10,000 | | 37,000 |
| Cash | 2,000 | 1,000 | 2.5 | 400 | | 2,400 |
| | 69,000 | 56,000 | | 22,400 | | 91,400 |
| *Current liabilities* | | | | | | |
| Trade payables | 35,000 | 12,000 | 2.5 | 4,800 | | 39,800 |
| Taxation | 15,000 | 5,000 | 2.5 | 2,000 | | 17,000 |
| Total current liabilities | 50,000 | 17,000 | | 6,800 | | 56,800 |
| Debentures | | 6,000 | 2.5 | 2,400 | | 2,400 |
| Total assets less liabilities | 107,000 | 63,000 | | 25,200 | | 114,840 |
| Share capital | 20,000 | 34,000 | 2.5 | 13,600 | | 20,000 |
| Share premium | | 7,000 | 2.5 | 2,800 | | |
| Retained earnings | 87,000 | 22,000 | 2.5 | 8,800 | (b3) | 89,800 |
| | 107,000 | 63,000 | | 25,200 | | 109,800 |
| Non-controlling interest | | | | | (b2) | 5,040 |
| | 107,000 | 63,000 | | 25,200 | | 114,840 |

### (b1) Goodwill

| | R$000 | R$000 | Rate at 1.1.20X1 | US$000 |
|---|---|---|---|---|
| Cost | | 36,000 | | |
| Share capital | 34,000 | | | |
| Share premium | 7,000 | | | |
| Retained earnings | 2,000 | | | |
| | 43,000 × 80% | 34,400 | | |
| Goodwill | | 1,600 | 2.0 | 800 |
| Required to restate at year-end: | | | | |
| Goodwill | | 1,600 | **2.5** | 640 |

### (b2) Non-controlling interest (NCI) at 31.12.20X1

| | R$000 | Rate | US$000 | US$000 |
|---|---|---|---|---|
| Share capital | 34,000 | 2.5 | 13,600 | |
| Share premium | 7,000 | 2.5 | 2,800 | |
| Retained earnings | 22,000 | 2.5 | 8,800 | |
| | | | 25,200 × 20% | 5,040 |

(b3)  The consolidated statement of financial position could be completed by inserting a balancing figure of US$89,800 for the retained earnings made up of Pau's retained earnings of £87,000 and Briona's post-acquisition profit of £2,800. This can be proved as follows:

**(c) Subsidiary post-acquisition profit included in the $89,800 group retained earnings**

| | R$000 | Rate | US$000 | US$000 Parent | US$000 NCI |
|---|---|---|---|---|---|
| Retained profit per Income Statement | | | 7,722.2 | 6,177.8 | 1,544.4 |
| At closing rate | 20,000 | 2.5 | 8,000 | | |
| **Gain on exchange** | | | 277.8 | 222.2 | 55.6 |
| *Loss on opening shareholders' funds* | | | | | |
| Share capital | 34,000 | | | | |
| Share premium | 7,000 | | | | |
| Retained earnings | 2,000 | | | | |
| | | Opening rate | | | |
| | 43,000 | 2.0 | 21,500 | | |
| | | Closing rate | | | |
| | | 2.5 | 17,200 | | |
| **Loss** | | | − 4,300 | (3,440) | (860) |
| Loss on goodwill | | Opening rate | | | |
| Goodwill | 1,600 | 2.0 | 800 | | |
| | | Closing rate | | | |
| | | 2.5 | 640 | | |
| **Loss** | | | − 160 | (160) | |
| **Post-acquisition profit of Briona attributable to Pau** | | | | 2,800 | |
| **Post-acquisition profit attributable to NCI** | | | | | 740 |
| Opening NCI (43,000 × 20%/2.0) | | | | | 4,300 |
| Closing NCI (63,000 × 20%/2.5) | | | | | 5,040 |

| | US$000 |
|---|---|
| Group retained profit at 31.12.20X1 | |
| Pau | 87,000 |
| Briona post-acquisition (above) | 2,800 |
| Group retained profit | 89,800 |

Note that there is no post-acquisition share premium, as the subsidiary's balance at acquisition and at 31.12.20X1 is the same at R$7m.

## 26.7 How to reduce the risk of translation differences

We have seen that when a parent invests in a foreign subsidiary it is required at each year-end to translate the assets and liabilities from the subsidiary's functional currency into that of the parent.

For example, let us assume that a UK parent has spent $10m on acquiring a US trading subsidiary and at the year-end the net assets of the US subsidiary are also $10m.

On consolidation by the UK parent, the $10m net assets of the US subsidiary are translated into sterling for inclusion in the consolidated statement of financial position. At each year-end the sterling value of any foreign exchange differences are taken to reserves. This means that the group's consolidated shareholders' funds will fluctuate up and down as exchange rates move.

The parent is able to reduce the extent of such fluctuations by hedging the translation risk. It normally does so by acquiring a matching foreign exchange liability. One way is to take on a debt such as a $10m loan.

Assuming that the opening exchange rate is £1 = $2 and the closing rate is £1 == $2.5, without hedging there would be an exchange loss on holding the net assets of £1,000. If the same amount is borrowed there would be an exchange gain on holding the debt of £1,000 ($10m at 2.0 less $10m at 2.5).

In practice, it may be difficult for the parent to borrow as much as $10m unless it gave a guarantee to the lender. By borrowing all its investment in its subsidiary in dollars, the parent would minimise its exchange gains and losses in its subsidiary. In this example, the dollar depreciates against the pound and there is a loss (without hedging). If the dollar appreciated against the pound, there would be a gain (without hedging).

## 26.8 Critique of the use of presentational currency

Multinational companies may have subsidiaries in many different countries, each of which may report by choice or legal requirement internally in their local currency. With globalisation, reporting the group in a presentation currency assists the efficiency of international capital markets, particularly where a group raises funds in more than one market. Although each subsidiary might be controlled through financial statements prepared in the local currency, realism requires the use of a single presentation currency.

## 26.9 IAS 29 *Financial Reporting in Hyperinflationary Economies*[7]

IAS 29 applies where an entity's functional currency is that of a hyperinflationary economy. Its objective is to give guidance on (a) determining when an economy is hyperinflationary, and (b) restating financial statements to make them meaningful.

### 26.9.1 Determining when an economy is hyperinflationary

There is no precise criterion, although there is a view that there is hyperinflation when the cumulative inflation rate over three years exceeds 100%. The IAS 29 approach is to leave it as a matter of judgement, based on indicators (IAS 29.3) such as:

- the general population preferring to keep its wealth in non-monetary assets or in a relatively stable foreign currency, with amounts of local currency held being immediately invested to maintain purchasing power;
- the general population regarding monetary amounts not in terms of the local currency but in terms of a relatively stable foreign currency in which prices may be quoted;
- sales and purchases on credit taking place at prices that compensate for the expected loss of purchasing power during the credit period, even if the period is short;
- interest rates, wages and prices being linked to a price index; and
- the cumulative inflation rate over three years approaching, or exceeding, 100%.

### 26.9.2 How to restate financial statements

Having decided that hyperinflation has occurred, the standard requires the financial statements (and corresponding figures for previous periods) of an entity with a functional currency that is hyperinflationary to be restated for the changes in the general pricing power of the functional currency using the measuring unit current at the year-end date.

### 26.9.3 Restatement treatment of statements of income and financial position

#### The statement of comprehensive income

All items in the statement of comprehensive income are expressed in terms of the measuring unit current at the end of the reporting period. All amounts need to be restated by applying the change in the general price index from the dates when the items of income and expenses were initially recorded in the financial statements.

#### The statement of financial position

Amounts not already expressed in terms of the measuring unit current at the end of the reporting period are restated by applying a general price index.

##### Monetary items

● Monetary items are not restated because they are already expressed in terms of the monetary unit.

● Inventory also as it has been written down to net realisable value under IAS 2.

##### Non-monetary items

Non-monetary items are restated from the date of acquisition if they are historical cost financial statements or from date of valuation if any asset has been reported at valuation.

If they are current cost financial statements then there is no restatement because they are already expressed in the unit of measurement current at the end of the reporting period.

### 26.9.4 Disclosures

The following disclosures are required:

(a) the fact that the financial statements and the corresponding figures for previous periods have been restated in terms of the measuring unit current at the end of the reporting period;

(b) whether the financial statements are based on a historical cost approach or a current cost approach; and

(c) the price index that has been used and the level of the price index at the end of the reporting period and the movement in the index during the current and the previous reporting periods.

## Summary

When accounts are prepared in the functional currency, exchange differences arising on the settlement of monetary items or on translating monetary items at rates that are different from those which applied on initial recognition (i.e. settled in a later accounting period) are recognised in profit or loss in the period in which they arise.

When functional currency financial statements are translated into a different presentation currency, assets and liabilities are translated at closing rate, income and expenses are translated at the rate as at the date of the transactions (an average may be practical if appropriate), and resulting exchange gains are recognised in other comprehensive income.

## REVIEW QUESTIONS

1 Discuss the desirability or otherwise of isolating profits or losses caused by exchange differences from other profit or losses in financial statements.

2 Explain the term functional currency and describe the factors an entity should take into account when determining which is the functional currency.

3 Explain why exchange differences are treated differently in financial statements prepared in a functional currency and those prepared in a presentation currency.

4 Discuss why a company that is not part of a group might decide to translate its financial statements into a presentation currency.

5 Explain why exchange differences might appear in other comprehensive income.

6 How does the treatment of changes in foreign exchange rates relate to the prudence and accruals concepts?

7 It was reported[8] that 'Belarus' cumulative inflation index will exceed 100%, which means that IAS 29 is likely to be applicable to Belarus up to 2014 . . . does not expect any significant microeconomic consequences of Belarus' qualifying as a country with hyperinflationary economy, except for the significant deterioration in financial performance indicators of banks and enterprises applying IFRS.'

Discuss what financial performance indicators might be adversely affected by applying IAS 29.

## EXERCISES

### Question 1

Fry Ltd has the following foreign currency transactions in the year to 31/12/20X0:

| | |
|---|---|
| 15/11 | Buys goods for $40,000 on credit from Texas Inc. |
| 15/11 | Sells goods for $60,000 on credit to Alamos Inc. |
| 20/11 | Pays Texas Inc. $40,000 for the goods purchased |
| 20/11 | Receives $30,000 on account from Alamos Inc. in payment for the goods sold |
| 20/11 | Buys machinery for $100,000 from Chicago Inc. on credit |
| 20/11 | Borrows $90,000 from an American bank |
| 21/12 | Pays Chicago Inc. $80,000 for the machinery |

The exchange rates at the relevant dates were:

| | |
|---|---|
| 15/11 | £1 = $2.60 |
| 20/11 | £1 = $2.40 |
| 21/12 | £1 = $2.30 |
| 31/12 | £1 = $2.10 |

**Required:**
Calculate the profit or loss to be reported in the financial statements of Fry Ltd at 31/12/20X0.

### * Question 2

On 1 January 20X1 Fibre plc acquired 80% of the ordinary shares of a Singaporean company, Fastlink Ltd, for £6m when Fastlink's retained earnings were $15.5m and the share premium was $0.8m. Fastlink's financial statements have been prepared in their functional currency of Singapore dollars and comply with IAS 21. The summarised statements of income and financial position as at 31 December 20X1 were as follows:

**Statements of income for the year ended 31 December 20X1**

| | Fibre | Fastlink |
|---|---|---|
| | £000 | $000 |
| Sales | 200,000 | 50,000 |
| Opening inventories | 20,000 | 8,000 |
| Purchases | 130,000 | 30,000 |
| Closing inventories | (40,000) | (6,000) |
| Cost of sales | 110,000 | 32,000 |
| Gross profit | 90,000 | 18,000 |
| Expenses | (15,000) | (6,500) |
| Profit before taxation | 75,000 | 11,500 |
| Taxation | (15,000) | (3,000) |
| Profit after taxation | 60,000 | 8,500 |

**Statement of financial position as at 31 December 20X1**

|  | £000 | $000 |
|---|---|---|
| Non-current assets | 90,000 | 25,000 |
| Investment in Fastlink | 6,000 | |
| *Current assets:* | | |
| Inventories | 40,000 | 6,000 |
| Trade receivables | 27,000 | 5,000 |
| Cash | 2,000 | 4,000 |
| Total current assets | 69,000 | 15,000 |
| *Current liabilities:* | | |
| Trade payables | 35,000 | 11,000 |
| Taxation | 15,000 | 3,000 |
| Total current liabilities | 50,000 | 14,000 |
| Total assets less liabilities | 115,000 | 26,000 |
| Share capital | 20,000 | 1,200 |
| Share premium | | 800 |
| Retained earnings | 95,000 | 24,000 |
| | 115,000 | 26,000 |

The following information is also available:

(i)   The opening inventory was acquired when the exchange rate was £1 = $2.6 and the closing inventory when the rate was £1 = $2.2.

(ii)  Exchange rates were as follows:

| At 1 January 20X1 | £1 = $2.5 |
|---|---|
| Average for the year ending 31 December 20X4 | £1 = $2.25 |
| At 31 December 20X1 | £1 = $2.0 |

**Required:**

(a) Prepare a consolidated statement of income.

(b) Prepare a consolidated statement of financial position:
   (i)   Show the goodwill calculation.
   (ii)  Show the non-controlling interest calculation.
   (iii) Complete with retained earnings as a balancing figure.

(c) Reconcile the retained earnings figure showing exchange gains and losses.

## Question 3

On 1 January 20X0 Walpole Ltd acquired 90% of the ordinary shares of a French subsidiary Paris SA. At that date the balance on the retained earnings of Paris SA was €10,000. The non-controlling interest in Paris was measured as a percentage of identifiable net assets. No shares have been issued by Paris since acquisition. Paris SA's dividend was paid on 31 December 20X2. The summarised statements of comprehensive income and statements of financial position of Walpole Ltd and Paris SA at 31 December 20X2 were as follows:

## Statements of comprehensive income for the year ended 31 December 20X2

|  | Walpole Ltd £000 | Paris SA £000 |
|---|---|---|
| Sales | 317,200 | 200,000 |
| Opening inventories | 50,000 | 22,000 |
| Purchases | 180,000 | 90,000 |
| Closing inventories | 60,000 | 12,000 |
| Cost of sales | 170,000 | 100,000 |
| Gross profit | 147,200 | 100,000 |
| Dividend received from Paris SA | 1,800 | NIL |
| Depreciation | 30,000 | 30,000 |
| Other expenses | 15,000 | 7,000 |
| Interest paid | 6,000 | 3,000 |
| Total expenses | 51,000 | 40,000 |
| Profit before taxation | 98,000 | 60,000 |
| Taxation | 21,000 | 15,000 |
| Profit after taxation | 77,000 | 45,000 |
| Dividend paid | 20,000 | 10,000 |

## Statement of financial position as at 31 December 20X2

|  | Walpole Ltd £000 | Paris SA £000 |
|---|---|---|
| Non-current assets | 94,950 | 150,000 |
| Investment in Paris SA | 41,050 |  |
| *Current assets:* |  |  |
| Inventories | 60,000 | 12,000 |
| Trade receivables | 59,600 | 40,000 |
| Paris SA | 2,400 |  |
| Cash | 11,000 | 11,000 |
| Total current assets | 133,000 | 63,000 |
| *Current liabilities:* |  |  |
| Trade payables | 45,000 | 18,000 |
| Walpole Ltd |  | 12,000 |
| Taxation | 21,000 | 15,000 |
| Total current liabilities | 66,000 | 45,000 |
| Debentures | 40,000 | 10,000 |
| Total assets less liabilities | 163,000 | 158,000 |
| Share capital | 80,000 | 60,000 |
| Share premium | 6,000 | 20,000 |
| Revaluation reserve | 10,000 | 12,000 |
| Retained earnings | 67,000 | 66,000 |
|  | 163,000 | 158,000 |

The following information is also available:

(i) The revaluation reserve in Paris SA arose from the revaluation of non-current assets on 1/1/20X2.

(ii) No impairment of goodwill has occurred since acquisition.

(iii) Exchange rates were as follows:

| | |
|---|---|
| At 1 January 20X0 | £1 = €2 |
| Average for the year ending 31 December 20X2 | £1 = €4 |
| At 31 December 20X1/1 January 20X2 | £1 = €3 |
| At 31 December 20X2 | £1 = €5 |

**Required:**
Assuming that the functional currency of Paris SA is the euro, prepare the consolidated accounts for the Walpole group at 31 December 20X2.

## * Question 4

(a) According to IAS 21 *The Effects of Changes in Foreign Exchange Rates*, how should a company decide what its functional currency is?

(b) Until recently Eufonion, a UK limited liability company, reported using the euro (€) as its functional currency. However, on 1 November 2007 the company decided that its functional currency should now be the dollar ($).

The summarised balance sheet of Eufonion as at 31 October 2008 in € million was as follows:

| | | €m |
|---|---|---|
| **ASSETS** | | |
| Non-current assets | | 420 |
| *Current assets* | | |
| Inventories | 26 | |
| Trade and other receivables | 42 | |
| Cash and cash equivalents | 8 | |
| | | 76 |
| Total assets | | 496 |
| **EQUITY AND LIABILITIES** | | |
| *Equity* | | |
| Share capital | | 200 |
| Retained earnings | | 107 |
| | | 307 |
| Non-current liabilities | 85 | |
| *Current liabilities* | | |
| Trade and other payables | 63 | |
| Current taxation | 41 | |
| | 104 | |
| Total liabilities | | 189 |
| Total equity and liabilities | | 496 |

Non-current liabilities includes a loan of $70 million which was raised in dollars ($) and translated at the closing rate of $1 = €0.72425.

Trade receivables include an amount of $20 million invoiced in dollars ($) to an American customer which has been translated at the closing rate of $1 = €0.72425.

All items of property, plant and equipment were purchased in euros (€) except for plant which was purchased in British pounds (£) in 2007 and which cost £150 million. This was translated at the exchange rate of £1 = €1.46015 as at the date of purchase. The carrying value of the equipment was £90 million as at 31 October 2008.

**Required:**
Translate the balance sheet of Eufonion as at 31 October 2008 into dollars ($m), the company's new functional currency.

(c) The directors of Eufonion (as in (b) above) are now considering using the British pound (£) as the company's presentation currency for the financial statements for the year ended 31 October 2009.

**Required:**
Advise the directors how they should translate the company's income statement for the year ended 31 October 2009 and its balance sheet as at 31 October 2009 into the new presentation currency.

(d) Discuss whether or not a reporting entity should be allowed to present its financial statements in a currency which is different from its functional currency.

*(The Association of International Accountants)*

## Question 5

Helvatia GmbH is a Swiss company which is a wholly owned subsidiary of Corolli, a UK company. Helvatia GmbH was formed on 1 November 2005 to purchase and manage a property in Zürich in Switzerland. The reporting and functional currency of Helvatia GmbH is the Swiss franc (CHF).

As a financial accountant in Corolli you are converting the financial statements of Helvatia GmbH into £ sterling in order to be consolidated with the results of Corolli which reports in £s.

The following are the summarised income statements and balance sheet (in thousands of Swiss francs) of Helvatia GmbH:

**Helvatia GmbH income statement and retained earnings for the year ended 31 October 2007**

|  | CHF (000) |
|---|---|
| Revenue | 8,800 |
| Depreciation | (1,370) |
| Other operating expenses | (1,900) |
| Net income | 5,530 |
| Retained earnings at 1 November 2006 | 3,760 |
|  | 9,290 |
| Dividends paid | (1,000) |
| Retained earnings at 31 October 2007 | 8,290 |

## Helvatia GmbH balance sheet as at 31 October

|  | 2007 CHF (000) | 2006 CHF (000) |
|---|---|---|
| **ASSETS** | | |
| *Non-current assets* | | |
| Land | 6,300 | 3,300 |
| Buildings | 12,330 | 13,700 |
| | 18,630 | 17,000 |
| *Current assets* | | |
| Receivables | 550 | 1,550 |
| Cash | 5,610 | 610 |
| | 6,160 | 2,160 |
| | 24,790 | 19,160 |
| **LIABILITIES AND EQUITY** | | |
| *Non-current liabilities* | | |
| Mortgage loan | 10,800 | 10,000 |
| *Current liabilities* | | |
| Payables | 700 | 400 |
| Equity | | |
| Issued share capital | 5,000 | 5,000 |
| Retained earnings | 8,290 13,290 | 3,760 8,760 |
| | 24,790 | 19,160 |

The following exchange rates are available:

| | 1 Swiss franc = £ |
|---|---|
| At 1 November 2005 | 0.40 |
| At 1 November 2006 | 0.55 |
| At 30 November 2006 | 0.53 |
| At 31 January 2007 | 0.53 |
| At 31 October 2007 | 0.45 |
| Weighted average for the year ended 31 October 2007 | 0.50 |

The non-current assets and mortgage loan of Helvatia GmbH as at 31 October 2006 all date from 1 November 2005. Helvatia GmbH purchased additional land and increased the mortgage loan on 31 January 2007. There were no other purchases of non-current assets. Land is not depreciated but the building is depreciated at 10% a year using the reducing balance method. Helvatia GmbH's dividends were paid on 31 January 2007.

The sterling equivalent of Helvatia GmbH's retained earnings as at 31 October 2006 was £1,222,000.

**Required:**

Prepare the following statements for Helvatia GmbH in £000 sterling:
(a) A summarised income statement for the year ended 31 October 2007.
(b) A summarised balance sheet as at 31 October 2007.
(c) A statement of cash flows for the year ended 31 October 2007 using the indirect method. Additional notes are not required.

*(The Association of International Accountants)*

## Question 6

The following Statements of Comprehensive Income relate to Rooster plc (Rooster) and its investee companies, Houseton plc (Houseton) and Kelson plc (Kelson). Kelson is based in New Jersey, USA. It produces, sells and is managed autonomously in the USA. Accordingly, its financial statements are presented in dollars.

### Statements of profit or loss and other comprehensive income for year ended 31 July 2013

| | Rooster plc € million | Houseton plc € million | Kelson plc US$ million |
|---|---|---|---|
| Revenue | 2,640 | 450 | 600 |
| Cost of sales | (1,230) | (120) | (270) |
| Gross profit | 1,410 | 330 | 330 |
| Operating expenses | (270) | (120) | (180) |
| Finance costs | (60) | (30) | (20) |
| Other income | 20 | | |
| Investment income | 40 | | |
| Profit before taxation | 1,140 | 180 | 130 |
| Taxation | (275) | (24) | (40) |
| Profit for the year | 865 | 156 | 90 |
| Other comprehensive income: | | | |
| Gains on revaluation of property | 290 | 45 | 10 |
| Total comprehensive income for the year | 1,155 | 201 | 100 |

The following additional information is provided:

(i) Rooster purchased a 60% holding in Kelson on 1 August 2012 for an immediate cash payment of US$510 million.
On that date, the fair values of the net assets of Kelson totalled US$750 million, which was the same as their carrying values in the books of Kelson. The 40% non-controlling interest had a fair value of US$300 million on 1 August 2012. No impairment of goodwill had occurred by 31 July 2013.

(ii) Rooster purchased a 70% holding in the equity of Houseton on 1 December 2012. The purchase price was €650 million paid in cash. Goodwill arising on acquisition was calculated at €140 million using the fair value method.
On 31 July 2013, impairment losses against consolidated goodwill amounting to €20 million needed to be recognised.

(iii) On 1 December 2012, the fair value of certain plant & equipment held by Houseton was €24 million in excess of its carrying value. This plant & equipment had a useful economic life of 4 years from the date of acquisition. The revised values have not been incorporated into the books of Houseton and depreciation was accounted for based on the carrying values.

(iv) During the three months ended 31 July 2013, Houseton sold goods to Rooster for €24 million. These goods were sold at a mark-up on cost of 60%. One third of the goods remained in the inventory of Rooster at 31 July 2013.

(v) Houseton declared a dividend of €50 million during the year from post-acquisition profits. Rooster has recognised its share of this dividend within 'investment income'.

(vi)  The US\$ / € exchange rate was as follows during the relevant period:

| Date | US\$ per €1 |
|---|---|
| 1 August 2012 | 1.35 |
| 31 July 2013 | 1.25 |
| Average for period | 1.28 |

Required:

(a)  Calculate (i) the goodwill arising on the acquisition of Kelson for inclusion in the group accounts at the date of acquisition; and (ii) the goodwill figure to be reported in the group accounts at 31 July 2013. Explain clearly the accounting treatment of any difference between the two figures.

(b)  Prepare a consolidated Statement of Profit or Loss and Other Comprehensive Income for the Rooster Group for year ended 31 July 2013 in accordance with IFRS. Your answer should show clearly the amount of any exchange gains or losses recognised during the period.

(c)  Explain what is meant by the 'functional currency' of an entity? Discuss briefly the guidance offered by IAS 21 to assist in determining an entity's functional currency.

*(Institute of Certified Public Accountants (CPA), Professional Stage 1 Corporate Reporting Examination, August 2013)*

## Notes

1  IAS 21 *The Effects of Changes in Foreign Exchange Rates*, IASB, revised 2003, para. 20.
2  Ibid., para. 21.
3  Ibid., para. 23.
4  Ibid., para. 10.
5  Ibid., para. 11.
6  Ibid., para. 38.
7  IAS 29 *Financial Reporting in Hyperinflationary Economies*, IASB, 1989.
8  www.prime-tass.by/english/News/show.asp?id=96939

PART **7**

# Interpretation

# CHAPTER 27

# Earnings per share

## 27.1 Introduction

The main purpose of this chapter is to understand the importance of earnings per share (EPS) and the PE ratio as a measure of the financial performance of a company (or 'an enterprise'). This chapter will enable you to calculate the EPS according to IAS 33 for both the current year and prior years, when there is an issue of shares in the year. Also, it will enable you to understand and calculate the diluted earnings per share, for future changes in share capital arising from exercising of share options and conversion of other financial instruments into shares.

### Objectives

By the end of this chapter, you should be able to:

- define earnings per share and the PE ratio;
- comment critically on alternative EPS figures;
- calculate the basic earnings per share;
- calculate the diluted earnings per share.

## 27.2 Why is the earnings per share figure important?

One of the most widely publicised ratios for a public company is the price/earnings or PE ratio. The PE ratio is significant because, by combining it with a forecast of company earnings, analysts can decide whether the shares are currently over- or undervalued.[1]

The ratio is published daily in the financial press and is widely employed by those making investment decisions. The following is a typical extract:

### Breweries, Pubs and Restaurants

| Company | Price 31/10/12 | PE ratio |
|---------|---------------|----------|
| Company A | 283 | 8.9 |
| Company B | 471 | 11.0 |
| Company C | 705 | 17.0 |

The PE ratio is calculated by dividing the market price of a share by the earnings that the company generated for that share. Alternatively, the PE figure may be seen as a multiple of the earnings per share, where the multiple represents the number of years' earnings required to recoup the price paid for the share. For example, it would take a shareholder in Company B 11 years to recoup her outlay if all earnings were to be distributed, whereas it would take a shareholder in Company A almost nine years to recoup his outlay, and one in Company C 17 years.

### 27.2.1 What factors affect the PE ratio?

The PE ratio for a company will reflect investors' confidence and hopes about the international scene, the national economy and the industry sector, as well as about the current year's performance of the company as disclosed in its financial report. It is difficult to interpret a PE ratio in isolation without a certain amount of information about the company, its competitors and the industry within which it operates.

For example, a **high PE ratio** might reflect investor confidence in the existing management team: people are willing to pay a high multiple for expected earnings because of the underlying strength of the company. Conversely, it might also reflect lack of investor confidence in the existing management, but an anticipation of a takeover bid which will result in transfer of the company assets to another company with better prospects of achieving growth in earnings than has the existing team.

A **low PE ratio** might indicate a lack of confidence in the current management or a feeling that even a new management might find problems that are not easily surmounted. For example, there might be extremely high gearing, with little prospect of organic growth in earnings or new capital inputs from rights issues to reduce it.

These reasons for a difference in the PE ratios of companies, even though they are in the same industry, are market-based and not simply a function of earnings. However, both the current earnings per share figure and the individual shareholder's expectation of future growth relative to that of other companies also have an impact on the share price.

## 27.3 How is the EPS figure calculated?

Because of the importance attached to the PE ratio, it is essential that there be a consistent approach to the calculation of the EPS figure. IAS 33 *Earnings per Share*[2] was issued in 1998 for this purpose. A revised version of the standard was issued in 2003.

The EPS figure is of major interest to shareholders not only because of its use in the PE ratio calculation, but also because it is used in the earnings yield percentage calculation. It is a more acceptable basis for comparing performance than figures such as dividend yield percentage because it is not affected by the distribution policy of the directors. The formula is:

$$EPS = \frac{Earnings}{Weighted\ number\ of\ ordinary\ shares}$$

The standard defines two EPS figures for disclosure, namely,

- basic EPS based on ordinary shares currently in issue; and
- diluted EPS based on ordinary shares currently in issue plus potential ordinary shares.

### 27.3.1 Basic EPS

Basic EPS (BEPS) is defined in IAS 33 as follows:[3]

- Basic earnings per share is calculated by dividing the net profit or loss for the period attributable to ordinary shareholders by the weighted average number of ordinary shares outstanding during the period.

For the purpose of the BEPS definition:

- **Net profit** is the profit for the period attributable to the parent entity after deduction of preference dividends (assuming preference shares are equity instruments).[4]

- The **weighted average number of ordinary shares** should be adjusted for events, other than the conversion of potential ordinary shares, that have changed the number of ordinary shares outstanding, without a corresponding change in resources.[5]

- An **ordinary share** is an equity instrument that is subordinate to all other classes of equity instruments.[6]

Earnings per share is calculated on the overall profit attributable to ordinary shareholders but also on the profit from continuing operations if this is different from the overall profit for the period.

### 27.3.2 Diluted EPS

**Diluted EPS** is defined as follows:

- For the purpose of calculating diluted earnings per share, the net profit attributable to ordinary shareholders and the weighted average number of shares outstanding should be *adjusted for the effects of all dilutive potential ordinary* shares.[7]

This means that *both* the earnings *and* the number of shares used *may* need to be adjusted from the amounts that appear in the profit and loss account and statement of financial position.

- **Dilutive** means that earnings in the future may be spread over a larger number of ordinary shares.

- **Potential ordinary shares** are financial instruments that may entitle the holders to ordinary shares.

## 27.4 The use to shareholders of the EPS

Shareholders use the reported EPS to estimate future growth which will affect the future share price. It is an important measure of growth over time. There are, however, limitations in its use as a performance measure and for inter-company comparison.

### 27.4.1 How does a shareholder estimate future growth in the EPS?

The current EPS figure allows a shareholder to assess the wealth-creating abilities of a company. It recognises that the effect of earnings is to add to the individual wealth of shareholders in two ways: first, by the payment of a dividend which transfers cash from the company's control to the shareholder; and, secondly, by retaining earnings in the company for reinvestment, so that there may be increased earnings in the future.

The important thing when attempting to arrive at an estimate is to review the statement of comprehensive income of the current period and identify the earnings that can reasonably be expected to continue. In accounting terminology, you should identify the **maintainable post-tax earnings** that arise in the **ordinary course of business.**

Companies are required to make this easy for the shareholder by disclosing separately, by way of note, any unusual items and by analysing the profit and loss on trading between discontinuing and continuing activities.

Shareholders can use this information to estimate for themselves the maintainable post-tax earnings, assuming that there is no change in the company's trading activities. Clearly, in a dynamic business environment it is extremely unlikely that there will be no change in the current business activities. The shareholder needs to refer to any information on capital commitments which appear as a note to the accounts and also to the chairman's statement and any coverage in the financial press. This additional information is used to adjust the existing maintainable earnings figure.

### 27.4.2 Limitations of EPS as a performance measure

EPS is thought to have a significant impact on the market share price. However, there are limitations to its use as a performance measure.

The limitations affecting the use of EPS as an inter-period performance measure include the following:

- It is based on historical earnings. Management might have made decisions in the past to encourage current earnings growth at the expense of future growth, e.g. by reducing the amount spent on capital investment and research and development. Growth in the EPS cannot be relied on as a predictor of the rate of growth in the future.

- EPS does not take inflation into account. Real growth might be materially different from the apparent growth.

The limitations affecting inter-company comparisons include the following:

- The earnings are affected by management's choice of accounting policies, e.g. whether non-current assets have been revalued or interest has been capitalised.

- EPS is affected by the capital structure, e.g. changes in number of shares by making bonus issues.

However, the **rate of growth** of EPS is important and this may be compared between different companies and over time within the same company.

## 27.5 Illustration of the basic EPS calculation

Assume that Watts plc had post-tax profits for 20X1 of £1,250,000 and an issued share capital of £1,500,000 comprising 1,000,000 ordinary shares of 50p each and 1,000,000 £1 10% preference shares that are classified as equity. The basic EPS (BEPS) for 20X1 is calculated at £1.15 as follows:

|                                                             | £000    |
| ----------------------------------------------------------- | ------- |
| Profit on ordinary activities after tax                     | 1,250   |
| Less preference dividend                                    | (100)   |
| Profit for the period attributable to ordinary shareholders | 1,150   |

BEPS = £1,150,000/1,000,000 shares = **£1.15**

Note that it is the *number* of issued shares that is used in the calculation and *not the nominal value* of the shares. The market value of a share is not required for the BEPS calculation.

## 27.6 Adjusting the number of shares used in the basic EPS calculation

The earnings per share is frequently used by shareholders and directors to demonstrate the growth in a company's performance over time. Care is required to ensure that the number of shares is stated consistently to avoid distortions arising from changes in the capital structure that have changed the number of shares outstanding without a corresponding change in resources during the whole or part of a year. Such changes occur with (a) bonus issues and share splits; (b) new issues and buybacks at full market price during the year; and (c) the bonus element of a rights issue.

We will consider the appropriate treatment for each of these capital structure changes in order to ensure that EPS is comparable between accounting periods.

### 27.6.1 Bonus issues

A bonus issue, or capitalisation issue as it is also called, arises when a company capitalises reserves to give existing shareholders more shares. In effect, a simple transfer is made from reserves to issued share capital. In real terms, neither the shareholder nor the company is giving or receiving any immediate financial benefit. The process indicates that the reserves will not be available for distribution, but will remain invested in the physical assets of the company. There are, however, more shares.

#### Treatment in current year

In the Watts plc example, assume that the company increased its shares in issue in 20X1 by the issue of another 1 million shares and achieved identical earnings in 20X1 as in 20X0. The EPS reported for 20X1 would be immediately halved from £1.15 to £0.575. Clearly, this does not provide a useful comparison of performance between the two years.

#### Restatement of previous year's BEPS

The solution is to restate the EPS for 20X0 that appears in the 20X1 accounts, using the number of shares in issue at 31.12.20X1, i.e. £1,150,000/2,000,000 shares = BEPS of £0.575.

### 27.6.2 Share splits

When the market value of a share becomes high some companies decide to increase the number of shares held by each shareholder by changing the nominal value of each share. The effect is to reduce the market price per share but for each shareholder to hold the same total value. A share split would be treated in the same way as a bonus issue.

For example, if Watts plc split the 1,000,000 shares of 50p each into 2,000,000 shares of 25p each, the 20X1 BEPS would be calculated using 2,000,000 shares. It would seem that the BEPS had halved in 20X1. This is misleading and the 20X0 BEPS is therefore restated using 2,000,000 shares. The total market capitalisation of Watts plc would remain unchanged. For example, if, prior to the split, each share had a market value of £4 and the company had a total market capitalisation of £4,000,000, after the split each share would have a market price of £2 and the company market capitalisation would remain unchanged at £4,000,000.

A split is frequently taken as a sign that the board is confident of improved future performance, plus the fact that the fall in the share price makes the shares become more attractive to smaller investors means that the share price might rise above £4 due to the increased demand.

The following is an extract relating to Starbucks:

18 March 2015 Shareholders of record as of March 30, 2015 will receive one additional share for each share held on the record date. The new shares will be payable on April 8, 2015. Starbucks common stock will begin trading on a split-adjusted basis on April 9, 2015. This is the sixth two-for-one split of the company's common stock since its initial public offering in 1992 . . .

This split is a direct reflection of the past seven years of increasing shareholder value, enhancing the liquidity of our shares, and building an attractive share price. It also takes place at a time when Starbucks shareholders are experiencing an all-time high in value as we continue to deliver world-class customer service and, in turn, record profits and revenue.

### Effect on ratios of a share split

Those ratios that are expressed as 'per share' are restated in proportion to the split as with the earnings, dividends and asset per share ratios. For example, if the earnings per share are 50c before a two-for-one split, this will be restated as 25c per share.

### Reverse share split

The board might decide to recommend a reverse if the share price is considered too low. There are different reasons for a company making this decision. For example:

● it might be to avoid the shares appearing to be low-quality following poor results, or

● it might be to satisfy listing requirements for a minimum share price in order to avoid being delisted, or

● it might be to make the shares more attractive to institutional investors who might avoid low price shares.

Just as with a share split, the market capitalisation is unchanged. The ratio tends to be significantly higher than for a share split with 1 for 10 or higher being the norm. For example, if there were 5 million shares with a market value of 80c and there was a reverse split of one share for twenty currently held, the share price would increase to €16; however, the market capitalisation would remain at €4m.

## 27.6.3 New issue at full market value

Selling more shares to raise additional capital should generate additional earnings. In this situation we have a real change in the company's capital and there is no need to adjust any comparative figures. However, a problem arises in the year in which the issue took place. Unless the issue occurred on the first day of the financial year, the new funds would have been *available to generate profits* for only a part of the year. It would therefore be misleading to calculate the EPS figure by dividing the earnings generated during the year by the number of shares in issue at the end of the year. The method adopted to counter this is to use a time-weighted average for the number of shares.

For example, let us assume in the Watts example that the following information is available:

|  | No. of shares |
|---|---|
| Shares (nominal value 50p) in issue at 1 January 20X1 | 1,000,000 |
| Shares issued for cash at market price on 30 September 20X1 | 500,000 |

The time-weighted number of shares for EPS calculation at 31 December 20X1 will be:

|  | No. of shares |
|---|---|
| Shares in issue for 9 months to date of issue (1,000,000 × 9/12) | 750,000 |
| Shares in issue for 3 months from date of issue (1,500,000 × 3/12) | 375,000 |
| Time-weighted shares for use in BEPS calculation EPS for 20X1 | 1,125,000 |

will be £1,150,000/1,125,000 shares = **£1.02**

### 27.6.4 Buybacks at market value

Companies are prompted to buy back their own shares when there is a fall in the stock market. The main arguments that companies advance for purchasing their own shares are:

● to reduce the cost of capital when equity costs more than debt;

● the shares are undervalued;

● to return surplus cash to shareholders; and

● to increase the apparent rate of growth in BEPS.

The following is an extract from the 2012 Vodafone Group plc Annual Report:

Our business is highly cash generative and in the last four years we have returned over 30% of our market capitalisation to shareholders in the form of dividends and share buybacks, while still investing around £6 billion a year in our networks and infrastructure.

**Earnings per share**
Adjusted earnings per share was 14.91 pence, a decline of 11.0% year-on-year, reflecting the loss of our 44% interest in SFR and Polkomtel's profits, the loss of interest income from investment disposals and mark-to-market items charged through finance costs, *partially offset by a reduction in shares arising from the Group's share buyback programme.*

Shares bought back by the company are included in the basic EPS calculation time-apportioned from the beginning of the year to the date of buyback.

For example, let us assume in the Watts example that the following information is available:

|  | No. of shares |
|---|---|
| Shares (50p nominal value) in issue at 1 January 20X1 | 1,000,000 |
| Shares bought back on 31 May 20X1 | 240,000 |
| Profit attributable to ordinary shares | £1,150,000 |

The time-weighted number of shares for EPS calculation at 31 December 20X1 will be:

| | | | |
|---|---|---|---|
| 1.1.20X1 | Shares in issue for 5 months to date of buyback | (1,000,000 × 5/12) | 416,667 |
| 31.5.20X1 | Number of shares bought back by company | (240,000) | |
| 31.12.20X1 | Opening capital less shares bought back | (760,000 × 7/12) | 443,333 |
| | Time-weighted shares for use in BEPS calculation | | 860,000 |

BEPS for 20X1 will be £1,150,000/860,000 shares $=$ **£1.34**

Note that the effect of this buyback has been to increase the BEPS for 20X1 from £1.15 as calculated in Section 27.5 above. This is a mechanism for management to lift the BEPS and achieve EPS growth.

## 27.7 Rights issues

A rights issue involves giving existing shareholders 'the right' to buy a set number of additional shares at a price below the fair value which is normally the current market price. A rights issue has two characteristics, being both an issue for cash and, because the price is below fair value, a bonus issue. Consequently the rules for *both* a cash issue *and* a bonus issue need to be applied in calculating the weighted average number of shares for the basic EPS calculation.

This is an area where students frequently find difficulty with Step 1 and we will illustrate the rationale without accounting terminology.

The following four steps are required:

Step 1: Calculate the average price of shares before and after a rights issue to identify the amount of the bonus the company has granted.

Step 2: Calculate the weighted average number of shares for the current year.

Step 3: Calculate the BEPS for the current year.

Step 4: Adjust the previous year's BEPS for the bonus element of the rights issue.

### Step 1: Calculate the average price of shares before and after a rights issue to identify the amount of the bonus the company has granted

Assume that Mr Radmand purchased two 50p shares at a market price of £4 each in Watts plc on 1 January 20X1 and that on 2 January 20X1 the company offered a 1:2 rights issue (i.e. one new share for every two shares held) at £3.25 per share.

If Mr Radmand had bought at the market price, the position would simply have been:

|  | | £ |
|---|---|---|
| Two shares at market price of £4 each on 1 January 20X1 | = | 8.00 |
| One share at market price of £4 on 2 January 20X1 | = | 4.00 |
| Total cost of three shares as at 2 January 20X1 | | 12.00 |
| Average cost per share unchanged at | | 4.00 |

However, this did not happen. Mr Radmand paid only £3.25 for the new share. This meant that the total cost of three shares to him was:

|  | | £ |
|---|---|---|
| Two shares at market price of £4 each on 1 January 20X1 | = | 8.00 |
| One share at discounted price of £3.25 on 2 January 20X1 | = | 3.25 |
| Total cost of three shares | = | 11.25 |
| Average cost per share (£11.25/3 shares) | = | 3.75 |

The rights issue has had the effect of reducing the cost per share of each of the three shares held by Mr Radmand on 2 January 20X1 by £0.25 per share.

The accounting terms applied are:

● The average cost per share after the rights issue (£3.75) is *the theoretical ex-rights value*.

● The amount by which the average cost of each share is reduced (£0.25) is *the bonus element*.

In accounting terminology, Step 1 is described as follows:

Step 1: *Theoretical ex-rights calculation.* The bonus element is ascertained by calculating the theoretical ex-rights value, i.e. the £0.25 is ascertained by calculating the £3.75 and deducting it from £4 pre-rights market price.

In accounting terminology, this means that existing shareholders get an element of bonus per share (£0.25) at the same time as the company receives additional capital (£3.25 per new share). The bonus element may be quantified by the calculation of a **theoretical ex-rights price** (£3.75 ), which is compared with the last market price (£4.00) prior to the issue; the difference is a bonus. The theoretical ex-rights price is calculated as follows:

|  |  | £ |
|---|---|---|
| Two shares at fair value of £4 each prior to rights issue | = | 8.00 |
| One share at discounted rights issue price of £3.25 each | = | 3.25 |
| Three shares at fair value after issue (i.e. ex–rights) | = | 11.25 |
| Theoretical ex–rights price (£11.25/3 shares) | = | 3.75 |
| Bonus element (fair value £4 less £3.75) | = | 0.25 |

Note that for the calculation of the number of shares and the time-weighted number of shares for a bonus issue, share split and issue at full market price per share, the market price per share is not relevant. The position for a rights issue is different and the market price becomes a relevant factor in calculating the number of bonus shares.

### Step 2: Calculate the weighted average number of shares for the current year

Assume that Watts plc made a rights issue of one share for every two shares held on 1 January 20X1. There would be no need to calculate a weighted average number of shares. The total used in the BEPS calculation would be as follows:

|  |  | No. of shares |
|---|---|---|
| Shares to date of rights issue: |  |  |
| 1,000,000 shares held for a full year | = | 1,000,000 |
| Shares from date of rights issue: |  |  |
| 500,000 shares held for a full year | = | 500,000 |
| Total shares for BEPS calculation |  | 1,500,000 |

However, if a rights issue is made part-way through the year, a time-apportionment is required. For example, if we assume that a rights issue is made on 30 September 20X1, the time-weighted number of shares is calculated as follows:

|  |  | No. of shares |
|---|---|---|
| Shares to date of rights issue: |  |  |
| 1,000,000 shares held for a full year | = | 1,000,000 |
| Shares from date of rights issue: |  |  |
| 500,000 shares held for 3 months (500,000 × 3/12) | = | 125,000 |
| Weighted average number of shares |  | 1,125,000 |

Note, however, that the 1,125,000 has not taken account of the fact that the new shares had been issued at less than market price and that the company had effectively granted the existing shareholders a bonus. We saw above that when there has been a bonus issue the number of shares used in the BEPS is increased. We need, therefore, to calculate the number of bonus shares that would have been issued to achieve the reduction in market price from £4.00 to £3.75 per share. This is calculated as follows:

| Total market capitalisation 1,000,000 shares @ £4.00 per share | = £4,000,000 |
|---|---|
| Number of shares that would reduce the market price to £3.75 | = £4,000,000/£3.75 |
|  | = 1,066,667 shares |
| Number of shares prior to issue | = 1,000,000 |
| Bonus shares deemed to be issued to existing shareholders | = 66,667 |
| Bonus shares for period of 9 months to date of issue (66,667 × 9/12) = | 50,000 |

The bonus shares for the nine months are added to the existing shares and the time-apportioned new shares as follows:

**Figure 27.1 Formula approach to calculating weighted average number of shares**

|  | | | | | | No. of shares |
|---|---|---|---|---|---|---|
| Shares to date of rights issue: | | | | | | |
| No. of shares | × | Increase by bonus fraction | × | Time adjustment | | |
| 1,000,000 | | | × | 9/12 | = | 750,000 |
| Bonus: | | ((1,000,000 × 4/3.75) − 1,000,000) | × | 9/12 | = | 50,000 |
| Shares from date of issue: | | | | | | |
| 1,500,000 | × | | × | 3/12 | = | 375,000 |
| Weighted average number of shares | | | | | | 1,175,000 |

|  |  | No. of shares |
|---|---|---|
| Shares to date of rights issue: | | |
| 1,000,000 shares held for a full year | = | 1,000,000 |
| Shares from date of rights issue: | | |
| 500,000 shares held for 3 months (500,000 × 3/12) | = | 125,000 |
| Weighted average number of shares | | 1,125,000 |
| Bonus shares: | | |
| 66,667 shares held for 9 months (66,667 × 9/12) | = | 50,000 |
| | | 1,175,000 |

The same figure of 1,175,000 can be derived from the following approach using the relationship between the market price of £4.00 and the theoretical ex-rights price of £3.75 to calculate the number of bonus shares.

The relationship between the actual cum-rights price and theoretical ex-rights price is shown by the bonus fraction:

$$\frac{\text{Actual cum-rights share price}}{\text{Theoretical ex-rights share price}}$$

This fraction is applied to the number of shares before the rights issue to adjust them for the impact of the bonus element of the rights issue. This is shown in Figure 27.1.

**Step 3: Calculate the BEPS for the current year**

The BEPS for 20X1 is then calculated as £1,150,000/1,175,000 shares = £0.979.

**Step 4: Adjust the previous year's BEPS for the bonus element of the rights issue**

The 20X0 BEPS of £1.15 needs to be restated, i.e. reduced to ensure comparability with 20X1.

In Step 2 above we calculated that the company had made a bonus issue of 66,667 shares to existing shareholders. In recalculating the BEPS for 20X0 the shares should be increased by 66,667 to 1,066,667. The restated BEPS for 20X0 is as follows:

Earnings/restated number of shares
£1,150,000/1,066,667 = £1.078125

Assuming that the earnings for 20X0 and 20X1 were £1,150,000 in each year, the 20X0 BEPS figures will be reported as follows:

As reported in the 20X0 accounts as at 31.12.20X0 = £1,150,000/1,000,000 = £1.15

As restated in the 20X1 accounts as at 31.12.20X1 = £1,150,000/1,066,667 = £1.08

The same result is obtained using the bonus element approach by reducing the 20X0 BEPS as follows by multiplying it by the reciprocal of the bonus fraction:

$$\frac{\text{Theoretical ex-rights fair value per share}}{\text{Fair value per share immediately before the exercise of rights}} = \frac{£3.75}{£4.00}$$

As restated in the 20X1 accounts as at 31.12.20X1 = £1.15 × (3.75/4.00) = **£1.08.**

### 27.7.1 Would the BEPS for the current and previous years be the same if the company had made a separate full market price issue and a separate bonus issue?

This section is included to demonstrate that the BEPS is the same, i.e. £1.08, if we approach the calculation on the assumption that there was a full price issue followed by a bonus issue. This will demonstrate that the BEPS is the same as that calculated using theoretical ex-rights. There are five steps, as follows.

### Step 1: Calculate the number of full value and bonus shares in the company's share capital

| | No. of shares |
|---|---|
| Shares in issue *before* bonus | 1,000,000 |
| Rights issue at full market price | |
| (500,000 shares × £3.25 issue price/£4 full market price) | 406,250 |
| | 1,406,250 |
| Total number of bonus shares | 93,750 |
| Total shares | 1,500,000 |

### Step 2: Allocate the total bonus shares to the 1,000,000 original shares

(Note that the previous year will be restated using the proportion of original shares: original shares + bonus shares allocated to these original 1,000,000 shares.)

| | | No. of shares |
|---|---|---|
| Shares in issue before bonus | | 1,000,000 |
| Bonus issue applicable to pre-rights: | | |
| 93,750 bonus shares × (1,000,000/1,406,250) = 66,667 × 9/12 | = 50,000 | |
| Bonus issue applicable to post-rights: | | |
| 93,750 bonus shares × (1,000,000/1,406,250) = 66,667 × 3/12 | = 16,667 | |
| Total bonus shares allocated to existing 1,000,000 shares | | 66,667 |
| Total original holding plus bonus shares allocated to that holding | | 1,066,667 |

### Step 3: Time-weight the rights issue and allocate bonus shares to rights shares

Rights issue at full market price:

| | | |
|---|---|---|
| 500,000 shares × (£3.25 issue price/£4 full market price) | = | 101,563 |
| × 406,250 × 3/12 | | |

Bonus issue applicable to rights issue:

| | | |
|---|---|---|
| 93,750 bonus shares × (406,250/1,406,250) × 27,083 × 3/12 | = | 6,770 |
| Weighted average ordinary shares (includes shares from Steps 2 and 3) | | 1,175,000 |

### Step 4: BEPS calculation for 20X1

Calculate the BEPS using the post-tax profit and weighted average ordinary shares, as follows:

$$20\text{X1 BEPS} = \frac{£1,150,000}{1,175,000} = £0.979$$

### Step 5: BEPS restated for 20X0

There were 93,750 bonus shares issued in 20X1. The 20X0 BEPS needs to be reduced, therefore, by the same proportion as applied to the 1,000,000 ordinary shares in 20X1, i.e. 1,000,000:1,066,667:

$$20\text{X0 BEPS} \times \text{bonus adjustment} = \text{restated 20X0 BPES}$$

$$= £1.15 \times (1,000,000/1,066,667) = £1.08.$$

This approach illustrates the rationale for the time-weighted average and the restatement of the previous year's BEPS. The adjustment using the theoretical ex-rights approach produces the same result and is simpler to apply but the rationale is not obvious.

## 27.8 Adjusting the earnings and number of shares used in the diluted EPS calculation

We will consider briefly what dilution means and the circumstances which require the weighted average number of shares and the net profit attributable to ordinary shareholders used to calculate BEPS to be adjusted.

### 27.8.1 What is dilution?

In a modern corporate structure, a number of classes of person such as the holders of convertible bonds, the holders of convertible preference shares, members of share option schemes and share warrant holders may be entitled as at the date of the statement of financial position to become equity shareholders at a future date.

If these people exercise their entitlements at a future date, the EPS would be reduced. In accounting terminology, the EPS will have been *diluted*. The effect on future share price could be significant. Assuming that the share price is a multiple of the EPS figure, any reduction in the figure could have serious implications for the existing shareholders; they need to be aware of the potential effect on the EPS figure of any changes in the way the capital of the company is or will be constituted. This is shown by calculating and disclosing both the basic and 'diluted EPS' figures.

IAS 33 therefore requires a diluted EPS figure to be reported using as the denominator potential ordinary shares that are dilutive, i.e. would decrease net profit per share or increase net loss from continuing operations.[8]

### 27.8.2 Circumstances in which the number of shares used for BEPS is increased

The holders of convertible bonds, the holders of convertible preference shares, members of share option schemes and the holders of share warrants will each be entitled to receive ordinary shares from the company at some future date. Such additional shares, referred to as potential ordinary shares, *may* need to be added to the basic weighted average number *if they are dilutive*. It is important to note that if a company has potential ordinary shares they are not automatically included in the fully diluted EPS calculation. There is a test to apply to see if such shares actually are dilutive – this is discussed further in Section 27.9 below.

### 27.8.3 Circumstances in which the earnings used for BEPS are increased

The earnings are increased to take account of the post-tax effects of amounts recognised in the period relating to dilutive potential ordinary shares that will no longer be incurred on their conversion to ordinary shares, e.g. the loan interest payable on convertible loans will no longer be a charge after conversion and earnings will be increased by the post-tax amount of such interest.

### 27.8.4 Procedure where there are share warrants and options

Where options, warrants or other arrangements exist which involve the issue of shares below their fair value (i.e. at a price lower than the average for the period) then the impact is calculated by notionally splitting the potential issue into shares issued at fair value and shares issued at no value for no consideration.[9] Since shares issued at fair value are not dilutive, that number is ignored, but the number of shares at no value is employed to calculate the dilution. The calculation is illustrated here for Watts plc.

Assume that Watts plc had at 31 December 20X1:

- an issued capital of 1,000,000 ordinary shares of 50p each nominal value;
- profit attributable to shareholders of £1,150,000;
- an average market price per share of £4; and
- share options in existence 500,000 shares issuable in 20X2 at £3.25 per share.

The computation of basic and diluted EPS is as follows:

|  | Per share | Earnings | Shares |
|---|---|---|---|
| Profit attributable to shareholders |  | £1,150,000 |  |
| Weighted average shares during 20X1 |  |  | 1,000,000 |
| *Basic EPS (£1,150,000/1,000,000)* | 1.15 |  |  |
| Number of shares under option |  |  | 500,000 |
| Number that would have been issued at fair value |  |  | (406,250) |
| (500,000 × £3.25/£4) |  |  |  |
| Adjusted earnings and number of shares |  | £1,150,000 | 1,093,750 |
| *Diluted EPS (£1,150,000/1,093,750)* | 1.05 |  |  |

### 27.8.5 Procedure where there are convertible bonds or convertible preference shares

The post-tax profit should be adjusted[10] for:

- any dividends on dilutive potential ordinary shares that have been deducted in arriving at the net profit attributable to ordinary shareholders;
- interest recognised in the period for the dilutive potential ordinary shares; and
- any other changes in income or expense that would result from the conversion of the dilutive potential ordinary shares, e.g. the reduction of interest expense related to convertible bonds results in a higher post-tax profit but this could lead to a consequential increase in expense if there were a non-discretionary employee profit-sharing plan.

### 27.8.6 Convertible preference shares calculation

Assume that Watts plc had at 31 December 20X1:

- an issued capital of 1,000,000 ordinary shares of 50p each nominal value;
- profit attributable to ordinary shareholders of £1,150,000;
- convertible 8% preference shares of £1 each totalling £1,000,000, convertible at one ordinary share for every five convertible preference shares.

The computation of basic and diluted EPS for convertible bonds is as follows:

| | Per share | Earnings | Shares |
|---|---|---|---|
| Post-tax net profit for 20X1 (after interest) | | £1,150,000 | |
| Weighted average shares during 20X1 | | | 1,000,000 |
| Basic EPS (£1,150,000/1,000,000) | £1.15 | | |
| Number of shares resulting from conversion | | | 200,000 |
| Add back the preference dividend paid in 20X1 | | 80,000 | |
| Adjusted earnings and number of shares | | 1,230,000 | 1,200,000 |
| Diluted EPS (£1,230,000/1,200,000) | £1.025 | | |

### 27.8.7 Convertible bonds calculation

Assume that Watts plc had at 31 December 20X1:

- an issued capital of 1,000,000 ordinary shares of 50p each nominal value;
- profit attributable to ordinary shareholders of £1,150,000;
- convertible 10% loan of £1,000,000;
- an average market price per share of £4;

and the convertible loan is convertible into 250,000 ordinary shares of 50p each.

The computation of basic and diluted EPS for convertible bonds is as follows:

| | Per share | Earnings | Shares |
|---|---|---|---|
| Post-tax net profit for 20X1 (after interest) | | £1,150,000 | |
| Weighted average shares during 20X1 | | | 1,000,000 |
| Basic EPS (£1,150,000/1,000,000) | £1.15 | | |
| Number of shares resulting from conversion | | | 250,000 |
| Interest expense on convertible loan | | 100,000 | |
| Tax liability relating to interest expense, assuming the firm's marginal tax rate is 40% | | (20,000) | |
| Adjusted earnings and number of shares | | 1,230,000 | 1,250,000 |
| Diluted EPS (£1,230,000/1,250,000) | £0.98 | | |

## 27.9 Procedure where there are several potential dilutions

Where there are several potential dilutions the calculation must be done in progressive stages starting with the most dilutive and ending with the least.[11] Any potential 'antidilutive' issues (i.e. potential issues that would increase earnings per share) are ignored.

Assume that Watts plc had at 31 December 20X1:

- an issued capital of 1,000,000 ordinary shares of 50p each nominal value;
- profit attributable to ordinary shareholders of £1,150,000;

- an average market price per share of £4;
- share options in existence of 500,000 shares exercisable in year 20X2 at £3.25 per share;
- a convertible 10% loan of £1,000,000 convertible in year 20X2 into 250,000 ordinary shares of 50p each; and
- convertible 8% preference shares of £1 each totalling £1,000,000 convertible in year 20X4 at one ordinary share for every 40 preference shares.

There are two steps in arriving at the diluted EPS, namely:

Step 1: Determine the increase in earnings attributable to ordinary shareholders on conversion of potential ordinary shares.

Step 2: Determine the potential ordinary shares to include in the computation of diluted earnings per share.

### Step 1: Determine the increase in earnings attributable to ordinary shareholders on conversion of potential ordinary shares

|  | Increase in earnings | Increase in number of ordinary shares | Earnings per incremental share |
|---|---|---|---|
| *Options* |  |  |  |
| Increase in earnings |  |  |  |
| Incremental shares issued for no consideration |  |  |  |
| 500,000 × (£4 − 3.25)/£4 | NIL | 93,750 | NIL |
| *Convertible preference shares* |  |  |  |
| Increase in net profit 8% of £1,000,000 | 80,000 |  |  |
| Incremental shares 1,000,000/40 |  | 25,000 | 3.20 |
| *10% convertible bond* |  |  |  |
| Increase in net profit £1,000,000 × 0.10 × (60%) (assuming a marginal tax rate of 40%) | 60,000 |  |  |
| Incremental shares 1,000,000/4 |  | 250,000 | 0.24 |

### Step 2: Determine the potential ordinary shares to include in the computation of diluted earnings per share

|  | Net profit attributable to continuing operations | Ordinary shares | Per share |
|---|---|---|---|
| As reported for BEPS | 1,150,000 | 1,000,000 | 1.15 |
| Options | — | 93,750 |  |
|  | 1,150,000 | 1,093,750 | 1.05 dilutive |
| 10% convertible bonds | 60,000 | 250,000 |  |
|  | 1,210,000 | 1,343,750 | 0.90 dilutive |
| Convertible preference shares | 80,000 | 25,000 |  |
|  | 1,290,000 | 1,368,750 | 0.94 antidilutive |

Since the diluted earnings per share is increased when taking the convertible preference shares into account (from 90p to 94p), the convertible preference shares are antidilutive and are ignored in the calculation of diluted earnings per share. The lowest figure is selected and the diluted EPS will, therefore, be disclosed as 90p.

## 27.10 Exercise of conversion rights during the financial year

Shares actually issued will be in accordance with the terms of conversion and will be included in the BEPS calculation on a time-apportioned basis from the date of conversion to the end of the financial year.

### 27.10.1 Calculation of BEPS assuming that convertible loan has been converted and options exercised during the financial year

This is illustrated for the calculation for the year 20X2 accounts of Watts plc as follows. Assume that Watts plc had at 31 December 20X2:

- an issued capital of 1,000,000 ordinary shares of 50p each as at 1 January 20X2;
- a convertible 10% loan of £1,000,000 **converted** on 1 January 20X2 into 250,000 ordinary shares of 50p each; and
- share options for 500,000 ordinary shares of 50p each **exercised** on 1 January 20X2.

The weighted average number of shares for BEPS is calculated as follows:

|  | Net profit attributable to continuing operations | Ordinary shares | Per share |
|---|---|---|---|
| As reported for BEPS | 1,150,000 | 1,000,000 | 1.15 |
| Options | — | 93,750 | |
| | 1,150,000 | 1,093,750 | 1.05 |
| 10% convertible bonds | 60,000 | 250,000 | |
| | 1,210,000 | 1,343,750 | 0.90 |
| Convertible preference shares | 80,000 | 25,000 | |
| | 1,290,000 | 1,368,750 | 0.94 |

## 27.11 Disclosure requirements of IAS 33

The standard[12] requires the following disclosures. For the current year:

- Companies should disclose the basic and diluted EPS figures for profit or loss from continuing operations and for profit or loss with equal prominence, whether positive or negative, on the face of the statement of comprehensive income for each class of ordinary share that has a different right to share in the profit for the period.
- The amounts used as the numerators in calculating basic and diluted earnings per share, and a reconciliation of those amounts to the net profit or loss for the period.
- The weighted average number of shares used as the denominator in calculating the basic and diluted earnings per share and a reconciliation of these denominators to each other.

For the previous year (if there has been a bonus issue, rights issue or share split):

- BEPS and diluted EPS should be adjusted retrospectively.

### 27.11.1 Alternative EPS figures

Alternative EPS figures are permitted to be reported in the Annual Report by IAS 33. It is not, however, to be given greater prominence than the basic and diluted EPS figures and can only be disclosed in the notes and not on the face of the statement of comprehensive income. The adjusted earnings figure must be reconciled to the earnings reported in the statement of comprehensive income and the same weighted average number of shares must be used.

The intention is that investors are presented with an EPS figure based on sustainable or permanent earnings unaffected by exceptional and non-recurring items. The IASB does not provide a definition of permitted adjustments and it an opportunity for management to highlight or customise the earnings. The adjustments should lead to less volatility in the earnings used for the EPS figure and improve the market value of the shares.

The following is an extract from the Cello Group 2015 Annual Report:

**11 EARNINGS PER SHARE**

|  | Year ended 31 December 2014 £000 | Year ended 31 December 2015 £000 |
|---|---|---|
| Profit attributable to owners of the parent | 3,042 | 2,283 |
| Adjustments to earnings: |  |  |
| Restructuring costs | 694 | 534 |
| Charge for VAT payable and related costs | 1,301 | 2,109 |
| Start-up losses | 1,037 | 446 |
| Acquisition costs | – | 106 |
| Amortisation of intangible assets | 445 | 965 |
| Acquisition-related employee remuneration expenses | 1,591 | 1,200 |
| Share-based payments charge | 204 | 212 |
| Tax thereon | (907) | (976) |
| Headline earnings for the year | 7,407 | 6,879 |
|  |  |  |
| Basic earnings per share | 3.54p | 2.70p |
| Diluted earnings per share | 3.44p | 2.63p |

In addition to basic and diluted earnings per share, headline earnings per share, which is a non- GAAP measure, has also been presented.

| *Headline earnings per share* |  |  |
|---|---|---|
| Headline basic earnings per share | 8.61p | 8.14p |
| Headline diluted earnings per share | 8.39p | 7.93p |

Headline earnings per share is calculated using headline post-tax earnings for the year, which excludes the effect of restructuring costs, start-up losses, amortisation of intangibles, impairment charges, acquisition accounting adjustments, share option charges, fair value gains and losses on derivative financial instruments and other exceptional costs.

### Earnings defined

Whilst disclosure and calculation of headline earnings is not an IFRS requirement, the South African Institute of Chartered Accountants issued a Circular[13] to its members at the request of the Johannesburg Stock Exchange (JSE), providing detailed guidance on whether an adjustment is permitted. The JSE Listings Requirements require the calculation of headline earnings and disclosure of a detailed reconciliation of headline earnings to the earnings used in the calculation of the IAS 33 basic earnings per share. The aim is to achieve uniform treatment across all listed companies.

### Research into reasons why companies publish an alternative EPS

The initial approach was to exclude non-recurring items and provide investors with a more informative alternative figure.

An interesting 2013 research paper[14] suggested that the choice to disclose an alternative EPS figure is positively related to firms where the vesting of executive share options (ESOs) is contingent on the achievement of growth in EPS.

## 27.11.2 IAS 33 disclosure requirements

If an enterprise discloses an additional EPS figure using a reported component of net profit other than net profit for the period attributable to ordinary shareholders, IAS 33 requires that:

● it must still use the weighted average number of shares determined in accordance with IAS 33;

● if the net profit figure used is not a line item in the statement of comprehensive income, then a reconciliation should be provided between the figure and a line item which is reported in the statement of comprehensive income; and

● the additional EPS figures cannot be disclosed on the face of the statement of comprehensive income.

## 27.12 The Improvement Project

IAS 33 was one of the IASs revised by the IASB as part of its Improvement Project. The objective of the revised standard was to continue to prescribe the principles for the determination and presentation of earnings per share so as to improve comparisons between different entities and different reporting periods. The Board's main objective when revising was to provide additional guidance on selected complex issues such as the effects of contingently issuable shares and purchased put and call options. However, the Board did not reconsider the fundamental approach to the determination and presentation of earnings per share contained in the original IAS 33.

## 27.13 The Convergence Project

The earnings used as the numerator and the number of shares used as the denominator are both calculated differently under IAS 33 and the US SFAS 128 *Earnings per Share* and so produce different EPS figures.

In 2008, as part of the Convergence Project, the IASB and FASB issued an Exposure Draft which aimed to achieve some convergence in the calculation of the denominator of earnings per share. They are, in the meanwhile, conducting a joint project on financial statement presentation. When they have completed that project and their joint project on liabilities and equity, they may consider whether to conduct a more fundamental review of the method for determining EPS which would look at an agreed approach to determining earnings and number of shares to be used in both the basic and diluted EPS calculation.

# Summary

The increased globalisation of stock market transactions places an increasing level of importance on international comparisons. The EPS figure is regarded as a key figure with a widely held belief that management performance could be assessed by the comparative growth rate in this figure. This has meant that the earnings available for distribution, which was the base for calculating EPS, became significant. Management action has been directed towards increasing this figure: sometimes by healthy organic growth; sometimes by buying in earnings by acquisition; sometimes by cosmetic manipulation, e.g. structuring transactions so that all or part of the cost bypassed the statement of comprehensive income; and at other times by the selective exercise of judgement, e.g. underestimating provisions. Regulation by the IASB has been necessary.

IAS 33 permits the inclusion of an EPS figure calculated in a different way, provided that there is a reconciliation of the two figures. Analysts have expressed the view that EPS should be calculated to show the future maintainable earnings and in the UK have arrived at a formula designed to exclude the effects of unusual events and of activities discontinued during the period.

## REVIEW QUESTIONS

1  Explain: (i) basic earnings per share; (ii) diluted earnings per share; (iii) potential ordinary shares; and (iv) limitation of EPS as a performance measure.

2  In connection with IAS 33 *Earnings per Share*:

(a) Define the profit used to calculate basic and diluted EPS.

(b) Explain the relationship between EPS and the price/earnings (PE) ratio. Why may the PE ratio be considered important as a stock market indicator?

3  Would the following items justify the calculation of a separate EPS figure under IAS 33?

(a) A charge of £1,500 million that appeared in the accounts, described as additional provisions relating to exposure to countries experiencing payment difficulties.

(b) Costs of £14 million that appeared in the accounts, described as redundancy and other non-recurring costs.

(c) Costs of £62.1 million that appeared in the accounts, described as cost of rationalisation and withdrawal from business activities.

(d) The following items that appeared in the accounts:

(i)  Profit on sale of property £80m

(ii)  Reorganisation costs £35m

(iii)  Disposal and discontinuance of hotels £659m.

4  Explain the adjustments made to earnings when reporting an underlying or headline EPS figure and discuss why this is more relevant than an EPS calculated in accordance with IAS 33.

**5** The following note appeared in the 2013 Annual Report of Mercer International Inc.:

Net income (loss) per share attributable to common shareholders:

|  | 2013 | 2012 | 2011 |
|---|---|---|---|
| Basic | $(0.47) | $(0.28) | $1.39 |
| Diluted | $(0.47) | $(0.28) | $1.24 |

The calculation of diluted net income (loss) per share attributable to common shareholders does not assume the exercise of any instruments that would have an anti-dilutive effect on net income (loss) per share.

Explain what is meant by antidilutive.

**6** Why are issues at full market value treated differently from rights issues?

**7** Explain why companies buy back shares and the effect that this has on the earnings per share figure.

**8** Explain reverse share splits and the effect that this has on a company's market capitalisation.

**9** Discuss the limitations of an IAS 33 calculated EPS figure for performance reporting.

**10** Discuss the limitations of EPS as a criterion for setting executive remuneration targets.

## EXERCISES

### Question 1

Alpha plc had an issued share capital of 2,000,000 ordinary shares at 1 January 20X1. The nominal value was 25p and the market value £1 per share. On 30 September 20X1 the company made a rights issue of 1 for 4 at a price of 80p per share. The post-tax earnings were £4.5m and £5m for 20X0 and 20X1 respectively.

Required:
(a) Calculate the basic earnings per share.
(b) Restate the basic earnings per share for 20X0.

### * Question 2

Beta Ltd had the following changes during 20X1:

| 1 January | 1,000,000 shares of 50c each |
|---|---|
| 31 March | 500,000 shares of 50c each issued at full market price of $5 per share |
| 30 April | Bonus issue made of 1 for 2 |
| 31 August | 1,000,000 shares of 50c each issued at full market price of $5.50 per share |
| 31 October | Rights issue of 1 for 3. Rights price was $2.40 and market value was $5.60 per share. |

Required:
Calculate the time-weighted average number of shares for the basic earnings per share denominator. Note that adjustments will be required for time, the bonus issue and the bonus element of the rights issue.

* Question 3

The computation and publication of earnings per share (EPS) figures by listed companies are governed by IAS 33 *Earnings per Share*.

### Nottingham Industries plc
### Statement of comprehensive income for the year ended 31 March 20X6
### (extract from draft unaudited accounts)

|  |  | £000 |
|---|---|---|
| Profit on ordinary activities before taxation | (Note 2) | 1,000 |
| Tax on profit on ordinary activities | (Note 3) | (420) |
| Profit on ordinary activities after taxation |  | 580 |

*Notes:*

1  Called-up share capital of Nottingham Industries plc:
   In issue at 1 April 20X5:
   16,000,000 ordinary shares of 25p each
   1,000,000 10% cumulative preference shares of £1 each classified as equity
   1 July 20X5: Bonus issue of ordinary shares, 1 for 5.
   1 October 20X5: Market purchase of 500,000 of own ordinary shares at a price of £1.00 per share.

2  In the draft accounts for the year ended 31 March 20X6, 'profit on ordinary activities before taxation' is arrived at after charging or crediting the following items:

   (i)  accelerated depreciation on fixed assets, £80,000;

   (ii)  book gain on disposal of a major operation, £120,000.

3  Profit after tax included a write-back of deferred taxation (accounted for by the liability method) in consequence of a reduction in the rate of corporation tax from 45% in the financial year 20X4 to 40% in the financial year 20X5.

4  The following were charged:

   (i)  Provision for bad debts arising on the failure of a major customer, £150,000. Other bad debts have been written off or provided for in the ordinary way.

   (ii)  Provision for loss through expropriation of the business of an overseas subsidiary by a foreign government, £400,000.

5  In the published accounts for the year ended 31 March 20X5, basic EPS was shown as 2.2p; fully diluted EPS was the same figure.

6  Dividends paid totalled £479,000.

**Required:**
(a) On the basis of the facts given, compute the basic EPS figures for 20X6 and restate the basic EPS figure for 20X5, stating your reasons for your treatment of items that may affect the amount of EPS in the current year.
(b) Compute the diluted earnings per share for 20X6 assuming that on 1 January 20X6 executives of Nottingham plc were granted options to take up a total of 200,000 unissued ordinary shares at a price of £1.00 per share: no options had been exercised at 31 March 20X6. The average fair value of the shares during the year was £1.10.
(c) Give your opinion as to the usefulness (to the user of financial statements) of the EPS figures that you have computed.

## * Question 4

The following information relates to Simrin plc for the year ended 31 December 20X0:

| | £ |
|---|---:|
| Turnover | 700,000 |
| Operating costs | 476,000 |
| Trading profit | 224,000 |
| Net interest payable | 2,000 |
| | 222,000 |
| Exceptional charges | 77,000 |
| | 145,000 |
| Tax on ordinary activities | 66,000 |
| Profit after tax | 79,000 |

Simrin plc had 100,000 ordinary shares of £1 each in issue throughout the year. Simrin plc has in issue warrants entitling the holders to subscribe for a total of 50,000 shares in the company. The warrants may be exercised after 31 December 20X5 at a price of £1.10 per share. The average fair value of shares was £1.28. The company had paid an ordinary dividend of £15,000 and a preference dividend of £9,000 on preference shares classified as equity.

Required:
(a) Calculate the basic EPS for Simrin plc for the year ended 31 December 20X0, in accordance with best accounting practice.
(b) Calculate the diluted EPS figure, to be disclosed in the statutory accounts of Simrin plc in respect of the year ended 31 December 20X0.
(c) Briefly comment on the need to disclose a diluted EPS figure and on the relevance of this figure to the shareholders.
(d) In the past, the single most important indicator of financial performance has been earnings per share. In what way has the profession attempted to destroy any reliance on a single figure to measure and predict a company's earnings, and how successful has this attempt been?

## * Question 5

Gamma plc had an issued share capital at 1 April 20X0 of:

- £200,000 made up of 20p shares; and
- 50,000 £1 convertible preference shares classified as equity receiving a dividend of £2.50 per share. These shares were convertible in 20X6 on the basis of one ordinary share for one preference share.

There was also loan capital of:

- £250,000 10% convertible loans. The loan was convertible in 20X9 on the basis of 500 shares for each £1,000 of loan, and the tax rate was 40%.

Earnings for the year ended 31 March 20X1 were £5,000,000 after tax.

Required:
(a) Calculate the diluted EPS for 20X1.
(b) Calculate the diluted EPS assuming that the convertible preference shares were receiving a dividend of £6 per share instead of £2.50.

## Question 6

Delta NV has share capital of €1m in shares of €0.25 each. At 31 May 20X9 shares had a market value of €1.1 each. On 1 June 20X9 the company makes a rights issue of one share for every four held at €0.6 per share. Its profits were €500,000 in 20X9 and €440,000 in 20X8. The year-end is 30 November.

Required:
Calculate
(a) the theoretical ex-rights price;
(b) the bonus issue factor;
(c) the basic earnings per share for 20X8;
(d) the basic earnings per share for 20X9.

## Question 7

The following information is available for X Ltd for the year ended 31 May 20X1:

| | |
|---|---:|
| Net profit after tax and minority interest | £18,160,000 |
| Ordinary shares of £1 (fully paid) | £40,000,000 |
| Average fair value for year of ordinary shares | £1.50 |

*Notes:*

1  Share options have been granted to directors giving them the right to subscribe for ordinary shares between 20X1 and 20X3 at £1.20 per share. The options outstanding at 31 May 20X1 were 2,000,000 in number.

2  The company has £20 million of 6% convertible loan stock in issue. The terms of conversion of the loan stock per £200 nominal value of loan stock at the date of issue were:

| Conversion date | No. of shares |
|---|---|
| 31 May 20X0 | 24 |
| 31 May 20X1 | 23 |
| 31 May 20X2 | 22 |

No loan stock has as yet been converted. The loan stock had been issued at a discount of 1%.

3  There are 1,600,000 convertible preference shares in issue classified as equity. The cumulative dividend is 10p per share and each preference share can convert into two ordinary shares. The preference shares can be converted in 20X2.

4  Assume a corporation tax rate of 33% when calculating the effect on income of converting the convertible loan stock.

Required:
(a) Calculate the diluted EPS according to IAS 33.
(b) Discuss why there is a need to disclose diluted earnings per share.

## Question 8

(a) The issued share capital of Manfred, a quoted company, on 1 November 2004 consisted of 36,000,000 ordinary shares of 75 cents each. On 1 May 2005 the company made a rights issue of 1 for 6 at $1.46 per share. The market value of Manfred's ordinary shares was $1.66 before announcing the rights issue. Tax is charged at 30% of profits.

Manfred reported a profit after taxation of $4.2 million for the year ended 31 October 2005 and $3.6 million for the year ended 31 October 2004. The published figure for earnings per share for the year ended 31 October 2004 was 10 cents per share.

**Required:**

**Calculate Manfred's earnings per share for the year ended 31 October 2005 and the comparative figure for the year ended 31 October 2004.**

(b) Brachly, a publicly quoted company, has 15,000,000 ordinary shares of 40 cents each in issue throughout its financial year ended 31 October 2005. There are also:

- 1,000,000 8.5% convertible preference shares of $1 each in issue classified as equity. Each preference share is convertible into 1.5 ordinary shares.

- $2,000,000 12.5% convertible loan notes. Each $1 loan note is convertible into two ordinary shares.

- Options granted to the company's senior management giving them the right to subscribe for 600,000 ordinary shares at a cost of 75 cents each.

The statement of comprehensive income of Brachly for the year ended 31 October 2005 reports a net profit after tax of $9,285,000 and preference dividends paid of $85,000. Tax on profits is 30%. The average market price of Brachly's ordinary shares was 84 cents for the year ended 31 October 2005.

**Required:**

**Calculate Brachly's basic and diluted earnings per share figures for the year ended 31 October 2005.**

*(The Association of International Accountants)*

## Question 10

The following trial balance relates to Amethyst as at 31 March 2015:

|  | $000 | $000 |
|---|---|---|
| Revenue |  | 818,000 |
| Cost of sales | 583,000 |  |
| Distribution costs | 89,000 |  |
| Administrative expenses | 91,000 |  |
| Investment Income |  | 1,000 |
| Loan stock interest paid | 600 |  |
| Overdraft interest | 100 |  |
| Equity shares of $1 each at 31 March 2015 |  | 110,000 |
| Share premium at 31 March 2015 |  | 5,000 |
| Retained earnings at 1 April 2014 |  | 40,950 |
| Freehold land buildings at cost 1 April 2014 | 200,000 |  |
| (Land cost $50m) |  |  |
| Plant and equipment at 1 April 2014 | 120,000 |  |
| Accumulated depreciation at 1 April 2014 |  |  |
| Buildings |  | 75,000 |
| Plant and equipment |  | 40,000 |

|  | $000 | $000 |
|---|---|---|
| Inventory at 31 March 2015 | 44,000 | |
| Trade receivables | 17,000 | |
| Bank | | 7,500 |
| Trade payables | | 25,000 |
| Current tax | 2,750 | |
| Deferred tax | | 5,000 |
| 6% $1 Loan stock (2020) | | 20,000 |
| | 1,147,450 | 1,147,450 |

The following information is relevant:

1  After the year end stock take it was discovered that goods worth $4 million, which were stored in a temporary holding facility, had been accidently omitted from the stock count.

2  Amethyst previously held its land and buildings under the cost model basis. On 1 April 2014 the directors decided to adopt the policy of revaluation and obtained an external valuation of $160 million (of which $60 million related to land). The property had a total estimated useful life of 50 years at the date of acquisition and a remaining life of 25 years at the date of the revaluation. The directors decided to make the transfer from the revaluation reserve to retained earnings each year in respect of the excess depreciation.

3  Deferred tax on the revaluation is to be provided for at a tax rate of 20%.

4  Depreciation for the year is to be provided for. Depreciation on plant and equipment is charged to cost of sales on a 15% reducing balance basis. Depreciation on buildings is charged to administrative expenses.

5  On 1 January 2015 the company made a 1:10 rights issue at $1.50 per share and this was correctly accounted for and included in the trial balance above. Share issue costs of $1 million were incurred and posted to administrative expenses.

6  The share price immediately before the rights issue was $1.80 per share. Earnings per share in the year ended 31 March 2014 was $2.53.

7  Loan stock interest paid represents the interim interest paid on 30 September 2014.

8  A provision for income tax of $10 million is required at the year end. The balance on the current tax account represents the under/overprovision of tax for the year ended 31 March 2014. The deferred tax liability in the trial balance relates to the taxable temporary differences on plant and equipment. As at 31 March 2015 the deferred tax liability arising on these items has increased to $10 million (excluding the effect of the revaluation in note 2).

Required:
(a) Prepare the statement of profit or loss and other comprehensive income for the year ended 31 March 2015.
(b) Prepare the statement of changes in equity for the year ended 31 March 2015.
(c) Prepare the statement of financial position for the year ended 31 March 2015.
(d) Calculate the earnings per share for the year ended 31 March 2015 and the restated figure for the year ended 31 March 2014.

*(The Association of International Accountants)*

## Notes

1 J. Day, 'The use of annual reports by UK investment analysts', *Accounting Business Research*, Autumn 1986, pp. 295–307.
2 IAS 33 *Earnings per Share*, IASB, 2003.
3 Ibid., para. 10.
4 Ibid., para. 12.
5 Ibid., para. 26.
6 Ibid., para. 5.
7 Ibid., para. 31.
8 Ibid., para. 31.
9 Ibid., para. 45.
10 Ibid., para. 33.
11 Ibid., para. 44.
12 Ibid., paras 66 and 70.
13 www.jse.co.za/content/jsecircularitems/circular_2_2013_headline_earnings.pdf
14 C. Grey, K. Stathopoulos and M. Walker, 'The impact of executive pay on the disclosure of alternative earnings per share figures', *International Review of Financial Analysis*, vol. 29, September 2013, pp. 227–36.

# CHAPTER 28

# Review of financial ratio analysis

## 28.1 Introduction

The key objective of financial statements is to provide useful financial information to the stakeholders, or 'users' – those with legitimate rights to such information. Different users have different information needs, for example:

- Existing and potential equity investors will be primarily interested in the profitability of an entity but will also require reassurance that the entity's liquidity (ability to generate cash) is such that it can continue in operational existence for the foreseeable future as a going concern.

- Lenders (both short- and long-term) will be primarily interested in the ability of the entity to generate the cash that is required to repay them and will focus on liquidity issues.

- Management will be concerned with both profitability (to satisfy the legitimate needs of the investors to whom they are accountable) and liquidity (to satisfy the legitimate needs of the lenders and suppliers to receive repayment of the amounts owed to them).

A financial analyst needs to be able to extract useful information from financial data, whether this is produced internally as detailed statements for the benefit of management or published externally for the benefit of external stakeholders, primarily the equity investors. The purpose of this chapter is to provide a framework for the analysis of financial data in order to write a report.

### Objectives

By the end of this chapter, you should be able to:

- appreciate the potential of ratio analysis as an analytical tool;
- carry out an initial overview of financial statements;
- discuss the relationship between the return on capital employed and supporting accounting ratios through the 'pyramid of ratios';
- analyse the financial statements of a single entity;
- draft a report based on an inter-period and inter-firm comparison;
- explain the limitations of comparisons based on ratios.

## 28.2 Overview of techniques for the analysis of financial data

### 28.2.1 The 'golden rule of analysis'

This might be described as 'identify your yardstick of comparison'. Analysis without comparison is meaningless. For example, if you were simply told that an entity generated revenue of £10 million and made a profit of £900,000 it would be difficult or impossible to assess whether that was 'good' or 'bad' without reference to factors such as:

- the previous year's revenues and profits;
- the budgeted revenues and profits;
- the revenues and profits of competitors in the same industry; and
- the underlying expectations of the analyst based on their knowledge of relevant internal and external factors.

If we are making an inter-firm comparison for management purposes care has to be taken to select a company that is in the same industry.

Whilst it is possible to compare the return on investment that is obtainable in different industries when deciding whether to invest, it would be extremely difficult to compare management ratios in different industries looking at, say, how well managers are controlling the cash cycle. For example, the cash cycle of a retail company where customers generally pay on receipt of goods is completely different from that of a construction company. We need to be sure, as far as possible, that we are making a valid comparison.

### 28.2.2 The benefits of ratio analysis

The use of accounting ratios for analysis purposes has a number of important benefits for analysts:

- Ratios allow comparison with peers through inter-firm comparison schemes and comparison with industry averages so that possible strengths and weaknesses can be identified.
- Through the pyramid approach it is possible to carry out a structured analysis of financial performance and financial position by drilling down to identify ratios in ever greater detail, building up to the return on capital employed.
- It enables, for certain ratios, the comparison of entities of different sizes. For example, it is very difficult to compare the absolute profits of two entities without an appreciation of how 'large' one entity is relative to another. However, it might be perfectly legitimate to compare the ratio of profit to revenue of two entities of very different sizes in the same industry.

### 28.2.3 Ratio analysis – some notes of caution

In order to evaluate a ratio, it is customary to make a comparison with that of the previous year or with the industry average. However, remember to check if:

- The same accounting policies have been applied; for example, have non-current assets been reported using the same measurement bases (i.e. at depreciated cost or revalued amounts in both cases)?
  *Inter-firm comparison schemes overcome this problem by requiring all member companies to report using uniform defined ratios.*

- Note has been taken of different commercial practices. For example, some retail entities lease their properties on operating leases whilst others purchase them. *Accounting ratios that use assets as their denominator will be affected.*

- The ratios have been defined in the same way. This is important when comparing ratios from different companies' Annual Reports – check to see if the company has defined its ratios.

## 28.3 Ratio analysis – a case study

Vertigo plc is a family company which deals in building materials and garden supplies. It has been managed by non-family members since the principal shareholder/managing director retired from active management at the end of 20X6 on health grounds. Let us assume that you are a trainee in an accounting firm that has been approached by a client who is a family member for a report on the company's financial position and financial performance following a fall in profit available for dividend and a request by the management for an injection of more capital.

We will use the financial statements of Vertigo (see below) to illustrate the technique.

### 28.3.1 Financial statements for the case study

Vertigo plc: statement of income for year ended 31 December

|  | 20X9 | | 20X8 | |
|---|---|---|---|---|
|  | £000 | £000 | £000 | £000 |
| Revenues |  | 3,461 |  | 3,296 |
| Opening inventory | 398 |  | 253 |  |
| Purchases | 2,623 |  | 2,385 |  |
| Closing inventory | (563) |  | (398) |  |
| Cost of goods sold |  | (2,458) |  | (2,240) |
| Gross profit |  | 1,003 |  | 1,056 |
| *Distribution costs:* |  |  |  |  |
| Depreciation | 187 |  | 239 |  |
| Irrecoverable debts | 17 |  | 32 |  |
| Advertising | 24 |  | 94 |  |
|  |  | (228) |  | (365) |
| *Administrative expenses:* |  |  |  |  |
| Rent | 60 |  | 60 |  |
| Salaries and wages | 362 |  | 316 |  |
| Miscellaneous expenses | 177 |  | 159 |  |
|  |  | (599) |  | (535) |
| Operating profit |  | 176 |  | 156 |
| Dividend received |  | — |  | 51 |
| Finance costs |  | (60) |  | (53) |
| Profit before tax |  | 116 |  | 154 |
| Income tax expense |  | (25) |  | (39) |
| Profit after taxation |  | 91 |  | 115 |

Vertigo plc: statement of financial position at 31 December

|  | 20X9 £000 | 20X8 £000 |
|---|---|---|
| **ASSETS** | | |
| *Non-current assets:* | | |
| Machinery | 2,100 | 2,240 |
| Motor vehicles | 394 | 441 |
| Investments | 340 | 340 |
| | 2,834 | 3,021 |
| *Current assets:* | | |
| Inventory | 563 | 398 |
| Trade receivables | 1,181 | 912 |
| Cash and cash equivalents | 9 | 11 |
| | 1,753 | 1,321 |
| | 4,587 | 4,342 |
| **EQUITY AND LIABILITIES** | | |
| *Equity:* | | |
| Ordinary shares of 50p each | 3,000 | 3,000 |
| Retained earnings | 353 | 262 |
| | 3,353 | 3,262 |
| *Non-current liabilities:* | | |
| Long-term borrowings (repayable in 8 years) | 600 | 600 |
| *Current liabilities:* | | |
| Trade payables | 498 | 398 |
| Accrued expenses | 15 | 12 |
| Taxation | 24 | 29 |
| Short-term borrowings | 97 | 41 |
| | 634 | 480 |
| | 4,587 | 4,342 |

## 28.4 Introductory review

Before embarking on detailed ratio analysis, an analyst (whether an internal or an external user of the financial statements) would carry out a review to gain an overall impression of:

(a) the external trading conditions for the building materials sector, for example, refer to subscription sources such as the Markit/CIPS Purchasing Managers' Index (PMI) indices; and

(b) the financial statements as a whole.

We will illustrate one approach using common-sized statements for Vertigo before proceeding to consider more detailed ratios and the preparation of a report.

### Overall impressions from initial review

Common-sized statements are a useful aid when making an initial review of a company's financial structure, such as seeing the percentage of cash to current assets, and cost structures such as the percentage of sales revenue that goes on administration.

## 28.4.1 The company's financial structure

Our first thought might be to gain an impression of the financial structure of a company.

### Vertical analysis – common-sized statement

The vertical analysis approach highlights the structure of the statement of financial position by presenting non-current assets, working capital, debt and equity as a percentage of debt plus equity. It allows us to form a view on the financing of the business, in particular the extent to which a business is reliant on debt to finance its non-current assets. In times of recession this is of particular interest and is described as indicating the strength of the financial position.

|  | 20X8 £000 | 20X8 % | 20X9 £000 | 20X9 % |
|---|---|---|---|---|
| Non-current assets | 3,021 | 69.6 | 2,834 | 61.8 |
| Current assets | 1,321 | 30.4 | 1,753 | 38.2 |
| Total | 4,342 | 100 | 4,587 | 100 |
| Equity | 3,262 | 75.1 | 3,353 | 73.1 |
| Debt | 600 | 13.8 | 600 | 13.1 |
| Current liabilities | 480 | 11.1 | 634 | 13.8 |
| Total | 4,342 | 100 | 4,587 | 100 |

This indicates that the financial strength is maintained in terms of the amount of debt compared to the amount of capital put in by the shareholders.

However, the non-current assets have fallen and the fall appears to be due to the depreciation charge. We need to assess whether this lack of investment in non-current assets is likely to be a concern for the future and to check if the management has identified and quantified future capital expenditure commitments.

### Horizontal analysis – common-sized statement

A horizontal analysis looks at the percentage change that has occurred. We could calculate the percentage change for every asset and liability, but it is more helpful in Vertigo to concentrate on the area that seems to require closer investigation, i.e. current assets and liabilities. The analysis is as follows:

|  | 20X8 £000 | 20X9 £000 | Percentage change |
|---|---|---|---|
| *Current assets:* | | | |
| Inventory | 398 | 563 | +41.5 |
| Trade receivables | 912 | 1,181 | +29.5 |
| Cash and cash equivalents | 11 | 9 | −18.2 |
| Trade payables | 398 | 498 | +25.1 |
| Accrued expenses | 12 | 15 | +25.0 |
| Taxation | 29 | 24 | −17.2 |
| Bank overdraft | 41 | 97 | +136.6 |

Inventories and (to a lesser extent) trade receivables have risen significantly when we consider that sales have increased by only 5%.

This raises questions in our mind. For example, is it possibly because greater quantities of inventory are expected to be required in anticipation of growth in future sales? Alternatively, is the inventory slow-moving with the possibility that net realisable value is lower than cost?

Trade payables have increased significantly. This could be due to poor cash flow putting pressure on liquidity (short-term borrowings have increased by around £50,000 and there has been no additional long-term equity or loan finance).

The common-sized analysis of the financial position has given us questions to have in our minds when carrying out a more detailed analysis. The next step would be to extract detailed turnover ratios for inventory, trade receivables and payables and ascertain the terms and limit of the overdraft. Before doing that we carry out a similar common-sized exercise to form a view of a company's cost structure.

## 28.4.2 The company's cost structure

Again, both a vertical and horizontal analysis is helpful.

### Vertical analysis – common-sized statement

An overview is obtained by restating by function into a vertical common-sized statement format as follows:

|  | 20X8 £000 | 20X8 % | 20X9 £000 | 20X9 % |
|---|---|---|---|---|
| Sales | 3,296 | 100.0 | 3,461 | 100.0 |
| Cost of sales | 2,240 | 68.0 | 2,458 | 71.0 |
| Total gross profit | 1,056 | 32.0 | 1,003 | 29.0 |
| Distribution costs | 365 | 11.1 | 228 | 6.6 |
| Administration expenses | 588 | 17.8 | 659 | 19.0 |
| Net profit before tax | 103 | 3.1 | 116 | 3.4 |

We can see that there has been a change in the cost structure with a fall in the gross profit from 32% to 29% compensated for by a significant fall in the distribution costs.

### Horizontal analysis – common-sized statement

An overview is obtained by calculating the percentage change as follows:

|  | 20X8 £000 | 20X9 £000 | Percentage change |
|---|---|---|---|
| Sales | 3,296 | 3,461 | +5.0 |
| Cost of sales | 2,240 | 2,458 | +9.7 |
| Total gross profit | 1,056 | 1,003 | −5.0 |
| Distribution costs | 365 | 228 | −37.5 |
| Administration expenses | 588 | 659 | +12.1 |
| Net profit before tax and dividend income | 103 | 116 | +12.6 |

Our initial observations are as follows:

- Revenues have risen slightly but gross profits have fallen. We need to establish the reasons for this.

- Other operating expenses (distribution costs and administrative expenses) have fallen significantly. This appears in the main to be caused by the reduction in depreciation charges and advertising expenditure.

- No income has been received from the financial asset in the period. This may be due to timing issues (given that dividend income is basically recognised only when received). However, we would need to carry out further investigations here.

We can now go on to a more detailed analysis.

## 28.5 Financial statement analysis, part I – financial performance

### Return on investment

If the analysis is being performed exclusively for the shareholders then an appropriate ROI measure might be 'Return on equity (ROE)'. This ratio would be calculated as:

$$\frac{\text{Profit attributable to the shareholders}}{\text{Equity}}$$

For Vertigo, ROE would be

|  | 20X9 | 20X8 |
|---|---|---|
| Profit after tax | 91 | 115 |
| Equity | 3,353 | 3,262 |
| So ROE equals | 2.7% | 3.5% |

This shows a fall of more than 20%.

### Return on capital employed

If the analysis is of the overall performance of the entity (however it is financed) then the appropriate ratio is 'Return on Capital Employed (ROCE)'. Management would be likely to consider this to be the best measure of ROI, as it shows the return on the assets under their control without any effect from the rates of tax and interest which operational management might regard as outside their control.

This ratio would be calculated as:

$$\frac{\text{Profit before interest and tax (PBIT)}}{\text{Capital employed (CE) (equity } + \text{ borrowings)}}$$

*Definitions of ratios vary*

It should be remembered that there is no 'accounting standard' that governs the exact composition of this ratio and care needs to be taken when making inter-firm comparisons. For example, capital employed might be defined as:

(a) total assets, also expressed as equity plus long-term loans plus current liabilities; or

(b) net assets, also expressed as equity plus long-term loans. Even here, though, care is needed – if a company maintains a high level of relatively permanent overdraft it might be added to the long-term loans.

For the purposes of this analysis, we will take 'borrowings' to be long-term borrowings only. Therefore our ROCE would be as follows:

|  | 20X9 | 20X8 |
|---|---|---|
| Profit before interest and tax | 116 ± 60 | 154 ± 53 |
| Capital employed | 3,353 + 600 | 3,262 + 600 |
| So ROCE equals | 4.4% | 5.4% |

Our initial conclusion would be that Vertigo is less profitable in 20X9 than it was in 20X8. We would need to investigate further to establish the reasons for this. In looking for a reason for the fall from 5.4% to 4.4% we propose to follow the pyramid approach.

**Figure 28.1 Pyramid for return on capital employed**

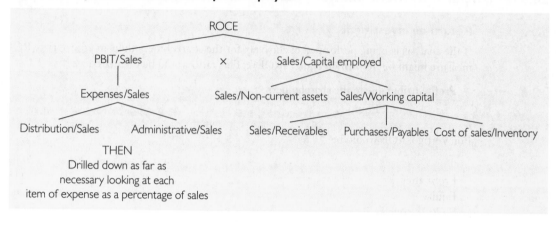

### 28.5.1 The Du Pont pyramid approach

In this approach we start at the top of the pyramid with the return on capital employed and systematically analyse those ratios that impact on the profit and those that impact on the assets employed in the business. This approach is also the basis for a number of inter-firm comparison schemes.

Diagrammatically the pyramid is shown in Figure 28.1. We can see the pyramid starts with the following relationship:

$$\frac{\text{Profit before interest and tax}}{\text{Capital employed}} = \frac{\text{Profit before interest and tax}}{\text{Revenue}} = \frac{\text{Revenue}}{\text{Capital employed}}$$

This is often expressed as:

$$\text{ROCE} = \text{Profit margin} \times \text{Asset turnover}$$

This shows us that the two key components of the return on capital employed are '**margin**' (PBIT/Revenue) and '**volume**' (Revenue/Capital employed). It is to these two aspects that we now turn.

### 28.5.2 Margin and expense analysis

The first 'margin ratio' we compute is the 'net profit margin'. This is simply:

$$\frac{\text{'Profit' (PBIT as used the ROCE ratio)}}{\text{Revenue}}$$

For Vertigo, the profit margins for 20X9 and 20X8 are:

|  | 20X9 | 20X8 |
|---|---|---|
| Profit | 176 | 207 |
| Revenue | 3,461 | 3,296 |
| So profit margin equals | 5.1% | 6.3% |

This shows us that one of the reasons for the decline in ROCE is a decline in the profit margin. For our report we 'drill down' into the detail and investigate further why the margin has reduced. Is it because the gross profit has fallen or is it due to expenses?

### Gross profit

One possibility is that the relationship between our revenues and our cost of sales has altered, so it is instructive to compute the gross profit margin. This ratio is computed as:

$$\frac{\text{Gross profit}}{\text{Revenue}}$$

For Vertigo, the gross profit margins for 20X9 and 20X8 are:

|  | 20X9 | 20X8 |
|---|---|---|
| Gross profit | 1,003 | 1,056 |
| Revenue | 3,461 | 3,296 |
| So profit margin equals | 29.0% | 32.0% |

Clearly the reduction in gross margin is not a good thing and internal analysts would almost certainly call for further investigation. We do not have the data here to perform more detailed checks.

Remember, however, that in answering any interpretation question it is always important to identify the further questions you would ask and the further information you would request, giving your reasons. For example, questions would be asked as to whether there has been:

- a change in the sales mix, with a greater proportion of lower-margin items being sold this year than last year;
- a change to maintain sales volume at the expense of the profit margin;
- discounting or longer-running sales;
- a rise in raw material costs that could not be passed on to customers in the form of increased sales prices; or
- a rise in the employment costs of production workers that could not be passed on to customers in the form of increased sales prices. This is unlikely to be the reason for the change in the gross margin here, given that cost of sales appears to include purchases, rather than production costs. Apparently Vertigo is a retail organisation rather than a manufacturing organisation – unless, perhaps, it is involved in also constructing any of the building products such as conservatories and garden studios.

### Operating expenses – administrative expenses

We could also compute:

|  | 20X9 | 20X8 |
|---|---|---|
| Administrative expenses | 599 | 535 |
| Revenues | 3,461 | 3,296 |
| Ratio | 17.3% | 16.2% |

This ratio reveals a slightly less satisfactory position in 20X9 compared with 20X8. The information we have shows us that a key factor behind the increase is the rise in salary costs of approximately 15%. This seems excessive given that revenues have grown by only 5%.

## Operating expenses – distribution costs

A further part of the analysis of the profit margin is to investigate the relationship between other operating expenses and revenues. For Vertigo, this would involve computing:

|                     | 20X9  | 20X8  |
| ------------------- | ----- | ----- |
| Distribution costs  | 228   | 365   |
| Revenues            | 3,461 | 3,296 |
| Ratio               | 6.6%  | 11.1% |

Clearly, for Vertigo, the adverse movement in the gross profit margin is at least partly mitigated by a reduction of the percentage of distribution costs to revenues. Given the information we have for Vertigo (not necessarily available to an external analyst), we can see that there has been a significant reduction in depreciation (all of which has been charged to this expense heading) and advertising costs.

We would at this stage drill down further, in the same way as when designing audit tests, to target areas of significant change.

|                          | 20X8 £000 | 20X9 £000 | Percentage change |
| ------------------------ | --------- | --------- | ----------------- |
| Sales revenue            | 3,296     | 3,461     | +5.0              |
| Inventory – opening      | 253       | 398       |                   |
| Purchases                | 2,385     | 2,623     | +10.0             |
| Inventory – closing      | (398)     | (563)     | +41.5             |
| Cost of goods sold       | (2,240)   | (2,458)   | +9.7              |
| Gross profit             | 1,056     | 1,003     | −5.0              |
| *Distribution costs:*    |           |           |                   |
| Depreciation             | 239       | 187       | −21.8             |
| Bad debts                | 32        | 17        | −46.9             |
| Advertising              | 94        | 24        | −74.5             |
| *Administrative expenses:* |         |           |                   |
| Rent                     | 60        | 60        | —                 |
| Salaries and wages       | 316       | 362       | +14.6             |
| Miscellaneous expenses   | 159       | 177       | +11.3             |
| Operating profit         | 156       | 176       | +12.8             |

It is interesting to see that discretionary costs in the form of advertising have been reduced by 74.5%. However, if the advertising had been maintained at 20X8 levels the operating profit would be reduced by £70,000 to £106,000, which would have shown a fall from the previous year of 32% rather than an increase of 12.8%.

This is where it is important to look at trends, in particular from 1 January 20X6 which was the last year when the previous Managing Director had been in control. There should be further enquiry to establish (a) the normal level over the previous three years – whether there was heavier advertising in 20X8 to achieve the 5% increase in sales in the light of the company's intention to attempt to obtain further investment in 20X9; (b) whether the reduction is likely to have an adverse effect on future sales; (c) what the company's reason was for reduced spending; and (d) the necessity or otherwise to return to a higher level in future years. This is more of commercial relevance to the client who is already concerned about the fall in profits than audit relevance.

### 28.5.3 Volume analysis – asset turnover

The basic 'volume ratio' is:

$$\frac{\text{Revenue}}{\text{Capital employed}}$$

This ratio is commonly referred to as the *asset turnover ratio*. For Vertigo, this ratio is:

|  | 20X9 | 20X8 |
|---|---|---|
| Revenue | 3,461 | 3,296 |
| Capital employed | 3,953 | 3,862 |
| Asset turnover | 87.6% | 85.3% |
| Turnover expressed as a multiple | 0.876× | 0.853× |

This shows us that the asset turnover has in fact slightly improved in 20X9 compared with 20X8. Therefore an overall conclusion we can make is that the decline in ROCE is due to a declining margin rather than a decline in the utilisation of assets. Using our formula we can now see that:

ROCE (4.4%) = profit margin (5.1%) × asset turnover (0.876)

Although the asset turnover rate has improved, we still need to analyse the reasons for the change, because the change can have resulted from changes in sales or any of the non-current and current assets.

#### Non-current asset turnover

The non-current asset turnover is:

$$\frac{\text{Revenue}}{\text{Non-current assets}}$$

For Vertigo, this ratio is:

|  | 20X9 | 20X8 |
|---|---|---|
| Revenue | 3,461 | 3,296 |
| Non-current assets | 2,834 | 3,021 |
| Non-current asset turnover | 122.1% | 109.1% |
| Turnover expressed as a multiple | 1.22× | 1.09× |

From a profitability point of view, this is an improvement. However, we should remember that there has been no investment in non-current assets this year and, after depreciation, the asset turnover would appear to have improved simply because the written-down value of the non-current assets is lower.

An increasing ratio is not always an improving ratio and might not always be good for the long-term health of the business. For example, if we had made an investment in non-current assets this year we would have quite possibly replaced older, fully depreciated, assets with newer assets that have higher net book values. This might be good for the long term but in the short term the fall in the rate of turnover of non-current assets would have a negative impact on the ROCE.

New, growth companies are likely to have a fall in the rate of non-current asset turnover as they expand. We must take care that our use of ratios does not take us into 'short-term thinking'.

### Asset turnover – working capital

When we analyse net current assets (or 'working capital') we generally do this by an individual focus on the three key components of inventory, trade receivables and trade payables.

#### Inventory turnover

The ratio we use to assess the effectiveness of our inventory management is the 'inventory days ratio'. This would normally be computed as:

$$\frac{\text{Closing inventory} \times 365}{\text{Cost of sales}}$$

The rationale behind the ratio is that we are effectively dividing closing inventory by 'one day's usage' to give us a hypothetical period for how long it will take us to sell the inventory. Whilst this analysis can be useful, we need to sound two notes of caution:

● We are relating the closing inventory to the average 'usage' in the previous year. The closing inventory will of course be used next year and so a more 'realistic' figure would be to base it on next year's projected usage, but of course this often is not available to the analyst.

● With this (and other) ratios we are comparing a 'point of time' figure (closing inventory) with a 'period' figure (cost of sales).

To a certain extent, both of the above factors are at least partly mitigated by the fact that, when using ratio analysis, we are comparing one ratio with another, and if the above factors apply to both the ratio and its comparative, to a certain extent the above 'defects' can cancel each other out.

That said, our inventory days ratio will be:

|  | 20X9 | 20X8 |
|---|---|---|
| Closing inventory × 365 | 563 × 365 | 398 × 365 |
| Cost of sales | 2,458 | 2,240 |
| Inventory days | 84 days | 65 days |
| Turnover expressed as a multiple | 4.4× | 5.6× |

Inventory is not being turned over as quickly in 20X9. This is not a positive sign. Not only does it affect the profitability of Vertigo but it also affects its liquidity, as we will see in the next section.

#### Trade receivables

The second key component of working capital is trade receivables. The equivalent ratio for trade receivables is:

$$\frac{\text{Trade receivable} \times 365}{\text{Revenue}}$$

For Vertigo, this ratio would be

|  | 20X9 | 20X8 |
|---|---|---|
| Trade receivables × 365 | 1,181 × 365 | 912 × 365 |
| Sales | 3,461 | 3,296 |
| Trade receivables days | 125 days | 101 days |
| Turnover expressed as a multiple | 2.9× | 3.6× |

It appears that Vertigo is collecting its cash from its customers less quickly in 20X9 than was the case in 20X8. This has a negative impact on profitability as the working capital cycle is lengthened when customers take longer to pay. This in turn has a negative impact on liquidity.

Late payment is a serious problem and a study in 2012 by the Clydesdale Bank and Yorkshire Bank in the UK reported that 10% of businesses say closing or seriously scaling back operations would have to be looked at if customers took more than 90 days to pay invoices. This poses a problem for management who need to tighten up their systems and controls and introduce procedures such as agreeing payment terms and conditions upfront or using incentives for early payment. Vertigo's management need to review their current procedures.

### Trade payables

The third key component of working capital is trade payables. The equivalent ratio for trade payables is:

$$\frac{\text{Trade payables} \times 365}{\text{Credit purchases}}$$

For Vertigo, this ratio would be

|  | 20X9 | 20X8 |
|---|---|---|
| Trade payables $\times$ 365 | $498 \times 365$ | $398 \times 365$ |
| Credit purchases | 2,623 | 2,385 |
| Trade payables days | 69 days | 61 days |
| Turnover expressed as a multiple | 5.3$\times$ | 6.0$\times$ |

It appears that Vertigo is taking slightly longer to pay its suppliers in 20X9 than in 20X8. Given the way we have computed the profitability ratios (capital employed is total assets less current liabilities) this will actually improve the asset turnover and hence the ROCE. Given that our suppliers effectively provide us with interest-free finance there is, in a sense, a liquidity benefit in extending the credit we take from our suppliers.

However, this can also be indicative of liquidity problems that make it difficult for us to settle our debts as they fall due and, if we allow the level of our trade payables to get too high, it could lead to problems with future supplies and ultimately could lead to the entity being wound up. Overall the 'real' level of trade payables of Vertigo is probably not a major concern but management will need to monitor this going forward.

It should be noted that, whilst the trade payables ratio can be calculated from the accounts of Vertigo, those accounts are more detailed than the information available in the published financial statements. Credit purchases would not normally be available from the published financial statements. In practice external analysts would use cost of sales as a 'proxy' for credit purchases. As stated before, whilst this practice clearly isn't strictly correct, the fact that interpretation involves a comparison of ratios means that, if used consistently, this slightly contrived ratio can be used as a means of comparing the payment policies of a single entity over time or two comparable entities over a corresponding period.

### The cash cycle

The cash cycle, also referred to as the cash conversion cycle, measures the number of days it takes to acquire and sell inventory and convert sales into cash. It measures how effective managers are in managing this process.

For Vertigo the cash cycle is:

$$\text{Accounts Receivable days} + \text{Inventory days} - \text{Accounts Payable days} = \text{Cash Cycle}$$
$$125 \qquad + \qquad 84 \qquad - \qquad 69 \qquad = \quad 140 \text{ days}$$

This means it takes Vertigo 140 days from the time the company acquires inventory from its suppliers, completes the sale of the inventory to its customers and collects the cash from accounts receivable.

The 140 days can be regarded as the length of time the company needs to have cash to cover the cash cycle or, thinking defensively, to cover its operating expenses. The means that the management of the cash cycle is critical to the cash flow and profitability of the company.

### High working capital turnover rate

As with all ratios, a high rate does not always indicate that it is acceptable. For example, a high turnover rate can indicate overtrading, i.e. the sales volume is excessive in relation to the equity investment in the business. A high turnover might be an indication that the business relies too much on credit granted by suppliers or the bank instead of providing an adequate margin of operating funds.

## 28.6 Financial statement analysis, part 2 – liquidity

Liquidity is the lifeblood of any business. The ultimate price for poor liquidity is insolvency and therefore internal managers cannot ignore it. External users who have lent or who are thinking about lending money to the entity, whether on a short-term or a long-term basis, will almost certainly be more concerned with liquidity than with profitability.

Analysts can consider the liquidity of an entity in two ways. The first is through ratio analysis. We discussed in the previous section the fact that investment in working capital, as revealed when calculating changes in inventory days, trade receivables days and trade payables days, had an impact on liquidity.

However, there are also other ratios that are commonly used to assess liquidity. These include the current ratio, the quick ratio and cash flow ratios.

### 28.6.1 The current ratio

This ratio is simply the ratio of current assets to current liabilities. In the case of Vertigo, this ratio would be:

|                            | 20X9  | 20X8  |
| -------------------------- | ----- | ----- |
| Current assets             | 1,753 | 1,321 |
| Current liabilities        | 634   | 480   |
| So current ratio equals    | 2.76  | 2.75  |

The rationale behind the ratio is that the current assets are a short-term source of cash for the entity, whilst the current liabilities are the amounts that need settling reasonably quickly.

It is very difficult to give a general level for this ratio which analysts would regard as 'satisfactory' because different entities vary so much in their working capital cycles. In most cases you would expect this ratio to be well in excess of 1 for analysts to feel comfortable. However, entities that can generate cash easily are often able to operate with current ratios well below 1.

Consider a food retailer: food retailers have little if any trade receivables, since they sell to their customers for cash. Their inventory levels necessarily have to be quite low, since their products are often perishable. However, their trade payables days would be just as large as for any manufacturing entity and, if they reinvest the cash they generate quickly, their current ratios are often less than 1/2:1. This does not mean they have liquidity problems, however!

Rather, therefore, than identifying an absolute level at which the current ratio should be, it is probably better to monitor whether or not there has been a significant change from one period to another and compare with the industry average or peer group. Comparing it with the previous year we can see that it is virtually unchanged – this does not mean, however, that it is acceptable. We would need to look further at the trend over the past four years and also at competitors' current ratios.

An increase in the current ratio beyond the company's own normal range may arise for a number of reasons, some beneficial, others unwelcome.

### Beneficial reasons

These include:

- A build-up of inventory in order to support increased sales following an advertising campaign or increasing popular demand as for, say, a PlayStation. Management action will be to establish from a cash budget that the company will not experience liquidity problems from holding such inventory, e.g. there may be sufficient cash in hand or from operations, short-term loans, extended credit or bank overdraft facilities.

- A permanent expansion of the business which will require continuing higher levels of inventory. Management action will be to consider existing cash resources or future cash flows from operations or arrange additional long-term finance, e.g. equity or long-term borrowings to finance the increased working capital.

### Unwelcome reasons

These include:

- Operating losses may have eroded the working capital base. Management action will vary according to the underlying problem, e.g. disposing of underperforming segments, arranging a sale of non-current assets or inviting a takeover.

- Inefficient control over working capital, e.g. poor inventory or accounts receivable control allowing a build-up of slow-moving inventories or doubtful trade receivables.

- Adverse trading conditions, e.g. inventory becoming obsolete or introduction of new models by competitors.

### 28.6.2 The quick ratio

Another ratio that is used for liquidity assessment purposes is the quick ratio (also known as the acid test ratio). This ratio is:

$$\frac{\text{Current assets } - \text{ inventory}}{\text{Current liablities}}$$

The rationale for using the quick ratio is that entities cannot regard their inventory as a short-term source of cash because of the time it takes to realise cash through its sale. Whether this is true depends on the nature of the entity. This would certainly be true for entities in the construction sector, but for many entities in the retail sector, particularly those entities that sell their goods directly to the general public for cash, the current ratio would be a better measure of liquidity.

For Vertigo, the quick ratio would be:

|  | 20X9 | 20X8 |
|---|---|---|
| Current assets − inventory | 1,753 − 563 | 1,321 − 398 |
| Current liabilities | 634 | 480 |
| So quick ratio equals | 1.88 | 1.92 |

There has been a small decline in this ratio given the higher trade payables levels but the decline is not significant.

### 28.6.3 Cash flow ratios

Even if a statement of cash flows is not provided in a question it is worth preparing and analysing one. If we prepared such a statement for Vertigo for the year ended 31 December 20X9 we would get the following:

|  | £000 | £000 |
|---|---|---|
| Profit before tax | 116 |  |
| Finance costs | 60 |  |
| Depreciation | 187 |  |
| Increase in inventory | (165) |  |
| Increase in trade receivables | (269) |  |
| Increase in trade payables | 100 |  |
| Increase in accrued expenses | 3 |  |
| Cash generated from operations |  | 32 |
| Interest paid |  | (60) |
| Tax paid |  | (30) |
| Reduction in cash and cash equivalents |  | (58) |
| Cash and cash equivalents, 1 January 20X9 (11 − 41) |  | (30) |
| Cash and cash equivalents, 31 December 20X9 (9 − 97) |  | (88) |

This statement shows that the entity is struggling to generate cash from its operations. This is mainly due to the increased levels of working capital; all three components have increased in real terms as we have already seen.

This increase has absorbed significant amounts of cash such that cash from operating activities is negative. There has been no investment in non-current assets or additional equity or loan capital raised, and cash flow fails to cover the current year's interest and any dividend payments.

#### Interest cover

The lenders would be interested in their interest cover, i.e. the number of times that their interest could be paid out of cash generated by the operations. In this case, the interest cover is $32/60 = 0.53$ times. Notice that this is far worse than the interest cover based on the statement of income which indicates that there is adequate cover at 2.93 times (176/60).

#### Servicing future debt

As we have already seen, the entity has not purchased any non-current assets this year but sooner or later they may have to. Their borrowing levels are not currently excessive (see Section 28.7 below) but their ability to service additional debt is questionable. Based on this, it would appear that consideration may need to be given to raising further long-term finance if future expansion of the business is envisaged.

### 28.6.4 The cash ratio

This is a more conservative ratio than the quick ratio as it shows the ratio of cash and cash equivalents to current liabilities. Suppliers are able to see whether these are enough to settle the amount owed to them. In this case, of course, it is a negative figure.

It is certainly not a problem that faces Vertigo but there are companies sitting on hoards of cash to meet cyclical demands or because they are nervous about investing in the uncertain economic climate or they are unable to find investment opportunities. We see major companies like Apple, therefore, setting aside US$10 billion for stock buybacks.

## 28.7 Financial statement analysis, part 3 – financing

One of the key issues for analysts is the way a business is financed. Of particular concern is the relationship between borrowings (debt finance) and equity finance. Because most equity investors are risk-averse, the return required by the providers of debt finance is lower than that required by equity investors as they would normally have fixed or floating security. However, management must balance the benefit of 'cheaper' debt finance against the fact that the greater the proportion of finance provided through borrowings the greater the risk for both as measured by the gearing ratio.

### 28.7.1 The gearing ratio

There are a number of ways in which the gearing ratio can be computed but the two most common are:

$$\frac{\text{Debt finance}}{\text{Debt finance} + \text{equity finance}}$$

and

$$\frac{\text{Debt finance}}{\text{Equity finance}}$$

Both these ratios will increase as the proportion of debt finance gets greater. We will use the former ratio to illustrate the gearing of Vertigo:

|  | 20X9 | 20X8 |
|---|---|---|
| Debt finance (long-term only) | 600 | 600 |
| Debt finance + equity finance | 600 + 3,353 | 600 + 3,262 |
| So gearing ratio equals | 15.2% | 15.5% |

Gearing is relatively stable, the only fluctuation being caused by the retention of 20X9 profits increasing equity whilst long-term borrowings stay static. It is difficult to generalise, but this is a relatively low gearing ratio – ratios of less than one-third would normally be regarded as 'low' and gearing would normally only be regarded as 'high' when it exceeded 50%. There would appear to be plenty of scope for Vertigo to obtain more debt finance subject to being able to produce forecasts showing its ability to service the debt.

### 28.7.2 How should a potential investor decide on an acceptable level of gearing?

This is initially influenced by the political and economic climate of the time. We have seen that prior to the credit crisis arising in 2007 high gearing was not seen by many as risky and there was a general feeling that borrowing was good, leverage was respectable, and capital gains were inevitable. This might have reduced the importance of questions that would normally have been asked, such as the following.

#### Asset values

- Are the values in the statement of financial position reasonably current? If much lower than current then the gearing ratio may be significantly overstated.

#### Gearing ratios

- Is the gearing ratio constant or has it increased over time with heavier borrowing? If higher:
  - further borrowing might be difficult;
  - it might indicate that there has been investment that will lead to higher profits, so details are needed as to how the funds borrowed have been used.
- What covenants are in place and what is the risk that they might be breached? A breach could lead to a company having to renegotiate finance at a higher interest rate or even go into administration or liquidation.
- How does the gearing compare to other companies in the same sector?

#### Use of funds

- If gearing has increased, what were the funds used for? Was it to:
  - restructure debt following inability to meet current repayment terms?
  - finance new maintenance/expansion capital expenditure?
  - improve liquid ratios?

#### Interest commitment

- How variable is the rate of interest that is being charged on the borrowings? If rates are falling then equity shareholders benefit, but if rates rise then expenses are higher.
- How many times does the earnings before tax cover the interest? A highly geared company is more at risk if the business cycle moves into recession because the company has to continue to service the debts even if sales fall substantially.
- How many times does the cash flow from operations currently cover the interest? This is a useful ratio if profits are not converted into cash, e.g. they might be reinvested in working capital.

#### Cash flows

- How variable is the company's cash flow from operations? A company with a stable cash flow is less at risk, so the trend is important.
- What is the likely effect of contingent liabilities if they crystallise on the cash flows and debt ratio? Could it have a significant adverse impact?

**A company's attitude to leverage may vary over time**

This is often dependent on the availability of finance and the possibility of profitable capital investment. If there is uncertainty about either then there will an unwillingness to lend and an unwillingness to borrow.

## 28.8 Peer comparison

We have so far prepared internal ratios for two years making our comparison with 20X8. We have now selected comparative ratios from a competitor and set out some comparative ratios where Vertigo's ratios seem too high or too low:

|                       | 20X9    | 20X8    | 20X7    | 20X6    | 20X5    |
|-----------------------|---------|---------|---------|---------|---------|
| *Asset turnover ratio:* |       |         |         |         |         |
| Vertigo               | 0.88    | 0.85    |         |         |         |
| Competitor*           | 2.77    | 2.10    | 1.96    | 1.59    | 1.43    |
| *Inventory turnover:* |         |         |         |         |         |
| Vertigo               | 84 days | 65 days |         |         |         |
| Competitor            | 58 days | 70 days | 62 days | 80 days | 87 days |

\* For illustration, the competitor comparisons were ratios reported in the Everest Industries 2012 Annual Report.

|                       | 20X9    | 20X8    | 20X7    | 20X6    | 20X5    |
|-----------------------|---------|---------|---------|---------|---------|
| *Profit before interest and tax margin:* |  |  |  |  |  |
| Vertigo               | 5.1%    | 6.3%    |         |         |         |
| Competitor            | 7.9%    | 6.41%   | 7.2%    | 6.9%    | 4.38%   |
| *Debt/equity ratio:*  |         |         |         |         |         |
| Vertigo               | 0.15    | 0.15    |         |         |         |
| Competitor            | 0.28    | 0.53    | 0.69    | 1.13    | 0.94    |
| *Current ratio:*      |         |         |         |         |         |
| Vertigo               | 2.76    | 2.75    |         |         |         |
| Competitor            | 0.86    | 1.33    | 1.07    | 0.90    | 0.89    |
| *Quick ratio:*        |         |         |         |         |         |
| Vertigo               | 1.88    | 1.92    |         |         |         |
| Competitor            | 0.66    | 0.63    | 0.70    | 0.67    | 0.70    |

Looking at the profit before interest and tax, it is interesting to see that the competitor has had a rising trend over the five years with alternating positive and negative changes but the overall trend is up. An examination of the past five years' figures for Vertigo would be helpful in identifying its trend.

The inventory turnover has risen in 20X9 for Vertigo but it is interesting to see that again the trend with the competitor is falling with uneven positive and negative changes over the five years. The competitor has clearly addressed the level of inventory held in the last year. This could well indicate that a target of 70 days for Vertigo should be achievable.

The debt/equity ratio is steady at 0.15 in Vertigo. This is almost half of the gearing in the competitor where the gearing has fallen year on year to less threatening levels.

The asset turnover, however, paints a different picture with the competitor turning over its assets three times faster than Vertigo. This would seem to indicate that Vertigo needs to work its assets more effectively and aim at increasing its sales. A 5% increase in sales compares with a 22% increase in the competitor's sales.

The current ratio and quick ratio are more than double those of the competitor whose trend figures show that it is operating on levels of less than 1:1 for both ratios.

Note that it is important to obtain a comparator from the same industry and size, as far as possible.

## 28.9 Report based on the analysis

A report based on the above analysis might read as follows:

Report:

From:

To:

Date:

**Subject: Financial Performance of Vertigo Ltd**

### Profitability

Vertigo's profitability has declined compared with 20X8, with the ROCE declining from 5.4% in 20X8 to 4.4% in 20X9. This decline is mainly due to a reduction in the profit margin (see Appendix). The reduction is a combination of three factors:

- A reduction in the gross margin. Reasons for this need to be investigated further.
- An increase in administrative expenses. This is mainly caused by a 15% rise in salary costs which is a little surprising given the rise in revenue is only 5%.
- The reduction in the profit margin is slightly mitigated by a fall in distribution costs. The key reason for this is a significant reduction (almost 75%) in advertising expenditure. This reduction might be beneficial for profitability in the short term, but as a long-term measure this may be unwise.

### Liquidity

Liquidity ratios are conservative but seem excessive when compared to the current and quick ratios of the competitor (see Appendix).

The cash generated from operations is very low given the level of profits and this amount does not cover the interest and tax payments made in the year. During 20X9 the cash balances declined by £88,000. A key reason for the disappointing cash flow is the significant increase in working capital, particularly inventory and trade receivables.

The reason for the increase in the inventory turnover needs to be discussed further with management. As far as the impact on cash is concerned, if inventory is brought back to the 65 days turnover level, the increase of £165,000 would be reduced by more than £120,000 – more than enough to pay off the existing short-term borrowings. An improvement to 70 days would be sufficient to clear all short-term borrowings.

Further investigation of the management of receivables is required, particularly in the present credit climate.

The overall rise in working capital is mitigated to a certain extent by a rise in trade payables. This needs to be carefully monitored to ensure that the credit status of Vertigo is not compromised.

### Financial position

As stated above, overall liquidity ratios are unchanged in both years but the management of the working capital needs to be addressed. There has been no investment in non-current assets during 20X9 and the shareholders have not received a dividend. Both these factors may be due to a cash shortage and Vertigo would appear to require additional long-term finance. Compared to the competitor the gearing is low which, on the basis of the current level of borrowing, would allow Vertigo to seek additional debt finance.

### Conclusion

Profits are under pressure. Although revenues are continuing to rise there appears to be a decline in the gross margin which needs investigating further.

As far as the possibility of an improvement in profitability is concerned, there is concern that the asset turnover is low and sales are increasing but at a slower rate than the competitor's. There has at the same time been a significant reduction in advertising spend, which seems strange in a competitive environment and with the slow rate of sales growth.

It is noted that there has been no investment in non-current assets in 20X9. It is not clear without further enquiry whether the current level of non-current assets can sustain an increase in sales. If not, the need for further capital expenditure could not be provided by the current level of operating cash-flow.

Further attention urgently needs to be paid to working capital management.

As far as obtaining additional loan or equity capital, profitability needs to be addressed. The ROE is low at 2.7% and operating cash is insufficient to fully cover interest payments. The more positive aspect is that, given an improvement in profitability, it would appear possible to obtain this through issuing more debt as gearing levels are fairly low.

To support a request for additional funding a feasible three-year forecast would be required and we would be pleased to assist with this if so instructed.

**Appendix – detailed ratios** (not reproduced here as computed earlier)

Subscription sources are available for inter-firm ratios such as *RMA Annual Statement Studies* (Risk Management Association).[1]

## 28.10 Caution when using ratios for prediction

At the beginning of the chapter we mentioned the importance of taking an overview which influenced your expectations as to, say, the level of sales or profits that could be expected.

The same approach has to be taken when interpreting the ratios. This involves considering external and internal factors that could help explain current ratios and what might be predicted from them.

### 28.10.1 External factors

There are a number of external factors that need to be considered when interpreting ratios bearing in mind the economic context within which a business has been and will be operating. Consider, for example, assuming that Vertigo is a retail company:

● Have the retail sales been adversely or positively affected by growth of Internet sales?

● Has there been a change in fashion or downturn in the market?

● Will this mean inventory write-downs? Discounted sales?

- Have wage costs gone up (or will they be going up) following legislation for equal pay for women, fairer pay for part-time staff and legislation for maternity and paternity leave?

- Have credit sales been affected by less being spent on non-essential items?

- Has the company had to respond to pressure to pay small suppliers on time?

- Has there been a change in the sales mix that has impacted (or will impact) on sales or profits?

- Is property leased and, if so, are any rent reviews due? Are there any onerous covenants on the leases?

### 28.10.2 Internal factors

There are internal factors to consider:

- Ratios need to be interpreted in conjunction with reading the narrative and notes in the annual reports. The narrative could be helpful in explaining changes in the ratios, e.g. whether an inventory build-up is in anticipation of sales or a fall in demand. The notes could be helpful in corroborating the narrative, e.g. if the narrative explains that the increase in inventory is due to anticipated further production and sales, check whether the non-current assets have increased or whether there is a note about future capital expenditure.

- Ratios might be distorted because they are based on period-end figures. The end-of-year figures are static and might not be a fair reflection of normal relationships such as when a business is seasonal, e.g. an arable farm might have no inventory until the harvest and a toy manufacturer might have little inventory after supplying wholesalers in the lead-up to Christmas. Any ratios based on the inventory figure such as inventory turnover could be misleading if calculated at, say, a 31 December year-end.

- The use of norms can be misleading, e.g. the current ratio of 2:1 might be totally inappropriate for an entity like Asda which does not have long inventory turnover periods and, as its sales are for cash, it would not produce trade receivable collection period ratios.

- Factors that could invalidate inter-firm comparisons, such as:

  - use of different measurement bases with non-current assets reported at historical cost or revaluation and revaluations carried out at different dates;

  - use of different commercial practices, e.g. factoring trade receivables so that cash is increased – a perfectly normal transaction but one that could cause the comparative ratio of days' credit allowed to be significantly reduced;

  - applying different accounting practice, e.g. adopting different depreciation methods such as straight-line and reducing balance; adopting different inventory valuation methods such as FIFO and weighted average; or assuming different degrees of optimism or pessimism when making judgement-based adjustments to non-current and current assets;

  - having different definitions for ratios, e.g. the numerator for ROCE could be operating profit, profit before interest, profit before interest and tax (PBIT), earnings before interest, tax, depreciation and amortisation (EBITDA), profit after tax, etc.; the denominator for ROCE could be total assets, total assets less intangibles, net assets, average total assets, etc.

### 28.10.3 Degree of scepticism

This depends on the role of the person using the ratios. For example, a financial controller/FD preparing a report to the Board would have local knowledge of the company's business activities. In the Vertigo circumstances a reporting accountant, and to a lesser extent an external auditor, might not have this local knowledge and their starting point would be to form an overall impression followed by a more detailed analysis.

In expressing an opinion they might need to be more investigative and consider:

● Whether there is a risk of window dressing to improve sales, e.g. dispatching goods at the end of the period knowing them to be defective so that they appear in the current year's sales and accepting that they will be returned later in the next period.

● Whether liabilities have been omitted to improve the quick ratio, e.g. simply by suppressing purchase invoices at the year-end.

● Whether liabilities have been omitted to improve gearing, e.g. by the use of off-balance-sheet finance such as structuring the terms of a lease to ensure that it is treated as an operating lease and not a finance lease and special-purpose enterprises to keep debts off the statement of financial position.

● Whether there has been full disclosure in the notes of, say, contingent liabilities, which could result in ratios not being accurate predictors of future earnings and solvency.

## Summary

Ratios are an aid in interpreting financial performance and liquidity. Comparison with prior periods and competitor/industry averages can provide a business with an indication of its relative performance – has it improved and how does it compare to its competitors? In this chapter we have followed a common-sized approach to the initial overview and the pyramid approach to calculating the ratios for two years to provide a basis for a report.

A comparison was made with a competitor's ratios for those areas that required further investigation. In practice it would be helpful to have data for 3–5 years in order to review trends. Reference was then made to the need to be cautious when using the ratios for prediction – remembering that at all times there needs to be a degree of scepticism when interpreting the ratios.

## REVIEW QUESTIONS

**1** State and express two ratios that can be used to analyse each of the following:

   (i)  profitability;

   (ii)  liquidity;

   (iii)  management control.

**2** Discuss the importance of the disclosure of exceptional items to the users of the annual report in addition to the operating profit.

3  Explain how a reader of the accounts might be able to assess whether the non-current asset base is being maintained.

4  Explain in what circumstances an increase in the revenue to current assets might be an indication of a possible problem.

5  Explain in what circumstances a decrease in the rate of non-current asset turnover might be a positive indicator.

6  Discuss why an increasing current ratio might not be an indicator of better working capital management.

7  The management of Alpha Ltd calculates ROCE using profit before interest and tax as a percentage of net closing assets. Discuss how this definition might be improved.

8  The asset turnover rate has increased by 50% over the previous year. Explain the questions you would have in mind and what other ratios you would review.

9  The current ratio has doubled since the previous year. Explain the questions that you would have in mind when reviewing the accounts.

10  Explain the problems a creditor might have when assessing the creditworthiness of a subsidiary entity.

11  You ascertain that inventories and (to a lesser extent) trade receivables have risen significantly when you consider that sales have increased by only 5%. Discuss the questions that you ask and the possible impact of each answer on the ratios.

12  Access the annual reports of two companies in the same industry and identify (a) the ratios that they report in common, (b) how these have been defined, and (c) why some ratios are not common to both.

13  A company has a very high rate of inventory turnover. Discuss circumstances when this might be of concern to management.

14  The ratio of current liabilities to net worth (equity + retained earnings) was 75%. Discuss how this would be viewed by suppliers and management.

15  The ratio of non-current assets to net worth was 75%. Discuss the risk that this poses for a company.

## EXERCISES

### Question 1

Flash Fashions plc has had a difficult nine months and the management team is discussing strategy for the final quarter.

In the last nine months the company has survived by cutting production, reducing staff and reducing overheads wherever possible. However, the share market, whilst recognising that sales across the industry have been poor, has worried about the financial strength of the business and as a result the share price has fallen 40%.

The company is desperate to increase sales. It has been recognised that the high fixed costs of the factory are not being fully absorbed by the lower volumes which are costed at standard cost. If sales and production can be increased then more factory costs will be absorbed and increased sales volume will raise staff morale and make analysts think the firm is entering a turnaround phase.

The company decides to drop prices by 15% for the next two months and to change the terms of sale so that property does not pass until the clothes are paid for. This is purely a reflection of the tough economic conditions and the need to protect the firm against customer insolvency. Further, it is decided that if sales have not increased enough by the end of the two months, the company representatives will be advised to ship goods to customers on the understanding that they will be invoiced but if they don't sell the goods in two months they can return them. Volume discounts will be stressed to keep the stock moving.

These actions are intended to increase sales, increase profitability, justify higher stocks, and ensure that more overheads are transferred out of the profit statement into stocks.

For the purposes of annual reporting it was decided not to spell out sales growth in financial figure terms in the managing director's report but rather to focus on units shipped in graphs using scales (possibly log scales) designed to make the fall look less dramatic. Also comparisons will be made against industry volumes as the fashion industry has been more affected by economic conditions than the economy as a whole.

To make the ratios look better, the company will enter into an agreement on the last week of the year with a so-called 'two-dollar company' called Upstart Ltd owned by Colleen Livingston, friend of the managing director of Flash Fashions, Sue Cotton. Upstart Ltd will sign a contract to buy a property for £30 million from Flash Fashions and will also sign promissory notes payable over the next three quarters for £10 million each. The auditors will not be told, but Flash Fashions will enter into an agreement to buy back the property for £31 million any time after the start of the third month in the new financial year.

**Required:**
**Critically discuss each of the proposed strategies.**

## * Question 2

Relationships plc
**You are informed that the non-current assets totalled €350,000, current liabilities €156,000, the opening retained earnings totalled €103,000, the administration expenses totalled €92,680 and that the available ratios were the current ratio 1.5, the acid test ratio 0.75, the trade receivables collection period was six weeks, the gross profit was 20% and the net assets turned over 1.4 times.**

**Required:**
**Prepare the Relationships plc statement of financial position from the above information.**

## * Question 3

The major shareholder/director of Esrever Ltd has obtained average data for the industry as a whole. He wishes to see what the forecast results and position of Esrever Ltd would be if in the ensuing year its performance were to match the industry averages.

At 1 July 20X0, actual figures for Esrever Ltd included:

|  | £ |
|---|---|
| Land and buildings (at written-down value) | 132,000 |
| Fixtures, fittings and equipment (at written-down value) | 96,750 |
| Inventory | 22,040 |
| 12% loan (repayable in 20X5) | 50,000 |
| Ordinary share capital (50p shares) | 100,000 |

For the year ended 30 June 20X1 the following forecast information is available:

1 Depreciation of non-current assets (on reducing balance)

| Land and buildings | 2% |
|---|---|
| Fixtures, fittings and equipment | 20% |

2 Net current assets will be financed by a bank overdraft to the extent necessary.

3 At 30 June 20X0 total assets minus current liabilities will be £231,808.

4 Profit after tax for the year will be 23.32% of gross profit and 11.16% of total assets minus all external liabilities, both long-term and short-term.

5 Tax will be at an effective rate of 20% of profit before tax.

6 Cost of sales will be 68% of turnover (excluding VAT).

7 Closing inventory will represent 61.9 days' average cost of sales (excluding VAT).

8 Any difference between total expenses and the aggregate of expenses ascertained from this given information will represent credit purchases and other credit expenses, in each case excluding VAT input tax.

9 A dividend of 2.5p per share will be proposed.

10 The collection period for the VAT-exclusive amount of trade receivables will be an average of 42.6 days of the annual turnover. All the company's supplies are subject to VAT output tax at 15%.

11 The payment period for the VAT-exclusive amount of trade payables (purchases and other credit expenses) will be an average of 29.7 days. All these items are subject to (reclaimable) VAT input tax at 15%. This VAT rate has been increased to 17.5% and may be subject to future changes, but for the purpose of this question the theory and workings remain the same irrespective of the rate.

12 Payables, other than trade payables, will comprise tax due, proposed dividends and VAT payable equal to one-quarter of the net amount due for the year.

13 Calculations are based on a year of 365 days.

### Required:
Construct a forecast statement of comprehensive income for Esrever Ltd for the year ended 30 June 20X1 and a forecast statement of financial position at that date in as much detail as possible. (All calculations should be made to the nearest £1.)

## * Question 4

Saddam Ltd is considering the possibility of diversifying its operations and has identified three firms in the same industrial sector as potential takeover targets. The following information in respect of the companies has been extracted from their most recent financial statements.

|  | Ali Ltd | Baba Ltd | Camel Ltd |
|---|---|---|---|
| ROCE before tax % | 22.1 | 23.7 | 25.0 |
| Net profit % | 12.0 | 12.5 | 3.75 |
| Asset turnover ratio | 1.45 | 1.16 | 3.73 |
| Gross profit % | 20.0 | 25.0 | 10.0 |
| Sales/non-current assets | 4.8 | 2.2 | 11.6 |
| Sales/current assets | 2.1 | 5.2 | 5.5 |
| Current ratio | 3.75 | 1.4 | 1.5 |
| Acid test ratio | 2.25 | 0.4 | 0.9 |
| Average number of weeks' receivables outstanding | 5.6 | 6.0 | 4.8 |
| Average number of weeks' inventory held | 12.0 | 19.2 | 4.0 |
| Ordinary dividend % | 10.0 | 15.0 | 30.0 |
| Dividend cover | 4.3 | 5.0 | 1.0 |

Required:

(a) Prepare a report for the directors of Saddam Ltd, assessing the performance of the three companies from the information provided and identifying areas which you consider require further investigation before a final decision is made.

(b) Discuss briefly why a firm's statement of financial position is unlikely to show the true market value of the business.

## Question 5

You work for Euroc, a limited liability company, which seeks growth through acquisitions. You are a member of a team that is investigating the possible purchase of Choggerell, a limited liability company that manufactures a product complementary to the products currently being sold by Euroc.

Your team leader wants you to prepare a report for the team evaluating the recent performance of Choggerell and the quality of its management, and has given you the following financial information which has been derived from the financial statements of Choggerell for the three years ended 31 March 2006, 2007 and 2008.

| Financial year ended 31 March | 2006 | 2007 | 2008 |
|---|---|---|---|
| Revenue (€ million) | 2,243 | 2,355 | 2,237 |
| Cash and cash equivalents (€ million) | −50 | 81 | −97 |
| Return on equity | 13% | 22% | 19% |
| Sales revenue to total assets | 2.66 | 2.66 | 2.01 |
| Cost of sales to sales revenue | 85% | 82% | 79% |
| Operating expenses to sales revenue | 11% | 12% | 15% |
| Net income to sales revenue | 2.6% | 4.3% | 4.2% |
| Current/Working capital ratio (to 1) | 1.12 | 1.44 | 1.06 |
| Acid test ratio (to 1) | 0.80 | 1.03 | 0.74 |
| Inventory turnover (months) | 0.6 | 0.7 | 1.0 |
| Credit to customers (months) | 1.3 | 1.5 | 1.7 |
| Credit from suppliers (months) | 1.5 | 1.5 | 2.0 |
| Net assets per share (cents per share) | 0.86 | 0.2 | 0.97 |
| Dividend per share (cents per share) | 10.0 | 14.0 | 14.0 |
| Earnings per share (cents per share) | 11.5 | 20.1 | 18.7 |

Required:

Use the above information to prepare a report for your team leader which:

(a) reviews the performance of Choggerell as evidenced by the above ratios;

(b) makes recommendations as to how the overall performance of Choggerell could be improved; and

(c) indicates any limitations in your analysis.

*(The Association of International Accountants)*

## Question 6

Liz Collier runs a small delicatessen. Her profits in recent years have remained steady at around £21,000 per annum. This type of business generally earns a uniform rate of net profit on sales of 20%.

Recently, Liz has found that this level of profitability is insufficient to enable her to maintain her desired lifestyle. She is considering three options to improve her profitability.

**Option 1**    Liz will borrow £10,000 from her bank at an interest rate of 10% per annum, payable at the end of each financial year. The whole capital sum will be repaid to the bank at the end of the second year. The money will be used to hire the services of a marketing agency for two years. It is anticipated that turnover will increase by 40% as a result of the additional advertising.

**Option 2**    Liz will form a partnership with Joan Mercer, who also runs a local delicatessen. Joan's net profits have remained at £12,000 per annum since she started in business five years ago. The sales of each shop in the combined business are expected to increase by 20% in the first year and then remain steady. The costs of the amalgamation will amount to £6,870, which will be written off in the first year. The partnership agreement will allow each partner a partnership salary of 2% of the revised turnover of their own shop. Remaining profits will be shared in the ratio of Liz 3/5, Joan 2/5.

**Option 3**    Liz will reduce her present sales by 80% and take up a franchise to sell Nickson's Munchy Sausage. The franchise will cost £80,000. This amount will be borrowed from her bank. The annual interest rate will be 10% flat rate based on the amount borrowed. Sales of Munchy Sausage yield a net profit to sales percentage of 30%. Sales are expected to be £50,000 in the first year, but should increase annually at a rate of 15% for the following three years then remain constant.

Required:

(a) Prepare a financial statement for Liz comparing the results of each option for each of the next two years.

(b) Advise Liz which option may be the best to choose.

(c) Discuss any other factors that Liz should consider under each of the options.

## Question 7

Chelsea plc has embarked on a programme of growth through acquisitions and has identified Kensington Ltd and Wimbledon Ltd as companies in the same industrial sector, as potential targets.

Using recent financial statements of both Kensington and Wimbledon and further information obtained from a trade association, Chelsea plc has managed to build up the following comparability table:

|  | Kensington | Wimbledon | Industrial average |
|---|---|---|---|
| *Profitability ratios* |  |  |  |
| ROCE before tax % | 22 | 28 | 20 |
| Return on equity % | 18 | 22 | 15 |
| Net profit margin % | 11 | 5 | 7 |
| Gross profit ratio % | 25 | 12 | 20 |
| *Activity ratios* |  |  |  |
| Total assets turnover = times | 1.5 | 4.0 | 2.5 |
| Non-current asset turnover = times | 2.3 | 12.0 | 5.1 |
| Receivables collection period in weeks | 8.0 | 5.1 | 6.5 |
| Inventory holding period in weeks | 21.0 | 4.0 | 13.0 |
| *Liquidity ratios* |  |  |  |
| Current ratio | 1.8 | 1.7 | 2.8 |
| Acid test | 0.5 | 0.9 | 1.3 |
| Debt–equity ratio % | 80.0 | 20.0 | 65.0 |

**Required:**

(a) Prepare a performance report for the two companies for consideration by the directors of Chelsea plc indicating which of the two companies you consider to be a better acquisition.

(b) Indicate what further information is needed before a final decision can be made.

## Question 8

The Housing Department of Chaldon District Council has invited tenders for re-roofing 80 houses on an estate. Chaldon Direct Services (CDS) is one of the Council's direct services organisations and it has submitted a tender for this contract, as have several contractors from the private sector.

The Council has been able to narrow the choice of contractor to the four tenderers who have submitted the lowest bids, as follows:

|  | £ |
|---|---|
| Nutfield & Sons | 398,600 |
| Chaldon Direct Services | 401,850 |
| Tandridge Tilers Ltd | 402,300 |
| Redhill Roofing Contractors plc | 406,500 |

The tender evaluation process requires that the three private tenderers be appraised on the basis of financial soundness and quality of work. These tenderers were required to provide their latest final accounts (year ended 31 March 20X4) for this appraisal; details are as follows:

| | Nutfield & Sons | Tandridge Tilers Ltd | Redhill Roofing Contractors plc |
|---|---|---|---|
| Profit and loss account for year ended 31 March 20X4 | | | |
| | £ | £ | £ |
| Revenue | 611,600 | 1,741,200 | 3,080,400 |
| Direct costs | (410,000) | (1,190,600) | (1,734,800) |
| Other operating costs | (165,000) | (211,800) | (811,200) |
| Interest | — | (85,000) | (96,000) |
| Net profit before taxation | 36,600 | 253,800 | 438,400 |
| Statement of financial position as at 31 March 20X4 | | | |
| | £ | £ | £ |
| Non-current assets (net book value) | 55,400 | 1,542,400 | 2,906,800 |
| Inventories and work in progress | 26,700 | 149,000 | 449,200 |
| Receivables | 69,300 | 130,800 | 240,600 |
| Bank | (11,000) | 10,400 | (6,200) |
| Payables | (92,600) | (140,600) | (279,600) |
| Dividend declared | — | (91,800) | (70,000) |
| Loan | — | (800,000) | (1,200,000) |
| | 47,800 | 800,200 | 2,040,800 |
| Capital | 47,800 | — | — |
| Ordinary shares @ £1 each | — | 250,000 | 1,000,000 |
| Reserves | — | 550,200 | 1,040,800 |
| | 47,800 | 800,200 | 2,040,800 |

Nutfield & Sons employ a workforce of six operatives and have been used by the Council for four small maintenance contracts worth between £60,000 and £75,000 which they have completed to an appropriate standard. Tandridge Tilers Ltd have been employed by the Council on a contract for the replacement of flat roofs on a block of flats, but there have been numerous complaints about the standard of the work. Redhill Roofing Contractors plc is a company which has not been employed by the Council in the past and, as much of its work has been carried out elsewhere, its quality of work is not known.

CDS has been suffering from the effects of increasing competition in recent years and achieved a return on capital employed of only 3.5% in the previous financial year. CDS's manager has successfully renegotiated more beneficial service-level agreements with the Council's central support departments with effect from 1 April 20X4. CDS has also reviewed its non-current asset base which has resulted in the disposal of a depot which was surplus to requirements and in the rationalisation of vehicles and plant. The consequence of this is that CDS's average capital employed for 20X4/X5 is likely to be some 15% lower than in 20X3/X4.

A further analysis of the tender bids is provided below:

| | Nutfield & Sons | Chaldon Direct Services | Tandridge Tilers Ltd |
|---|---|---|---|
| | £ | £ | £ |
| Labour | | 234,000 | 251,400 |
| Materials | 140,000 | 100,000 | 80,000 |
| Overheads (including profit) | 24,600 | 50,450 | 18,700 |

The Council's Client Services Committee can reject tenders on financial and/or quality grounds. However, each tender has to be appraised on these criteria and reasons for acceptance or rejection must be justified in the appraisal process.

**Required:**

In your capacity as accountant responsible for reporting to the Client Services Committee, draft a report to the Committee evaluating the tender bids and recommending to whom the contract should be awarded.

## Question 9

The statements of financial position, cash flows, income and movements of non-current assets of Dragon plc for the year ended 30 September 20X6 are set out below:

(i)  *Statement of financial position*

|  | 20X5 | | 20X6 | |
| --- | --- | --- | --- | --- |
|  | £000 | £000 | £000 | £000 |
| Tangible non-current assets |  | 1,200 |  | 1,160 |
| Freehold land and buildings, at cost |  | 700 |  | 1,700 |
| Plant and equipment, at net book value |  | 1,900 |  | 2,860 |
| *Current assets:* |  |  |  |  |
| Inventory | 715 |  | 1,020 |  |
| Trade receivables | 590 |  | 826 |  |
| Short-term investments | 52 |  | — |  |
| Cash at bank and in hand | 15 |  | 47 |  |
|  | 1,372 |  | 1,893 |  |
| *Current liabilities:* |  |  |  |  |
| Trade payables | 520 |  | 940 |  |
| Taxation payable | 130 |  | 45 |  |
| Dividends payable | 90 |  | 105 |  |
|  | 740 |  | 1,090 |  |
| Net current assets |  | 632 |  | 803 |
|  |  | 2,532 |  | 3,663 |
| *Long-term liability and provisions:* |  |  |  |  |
| 8% debentures, 20X9 |  | 500 |  | 1,500 |
| Provisions for deferred tax |  | 100 |  | 180 |
|  |  | 1,932 |  | 1,983 |
| Capital and reserves |  | 1,400 |  | 1,400 |
| Ordinary shares of £1 each |  |  |  |  |
| Share premium account |  | 250 |  | 250 |
| Retained earnings |  | 282 |  | 333 |
|  |  | 1,932 |  | 1,983 |

(ii)  *Statement of income (extract) for the year ended 30 September 20X6*

| | | |
|---|---:|---:|
| EBITDA | | 1,161 |
| Depreciation | | 660 |
| Operating profit | | 501 |
| Interest payable: debentures | | 150 |
| Profit before taxation | | 351 |
| Income tax | | 125 |
| Profit attributable to shareholders | | 226 |
| Dividends: paid | 70 | |
|        : proposed | 105 | 175 |
| Retained earnings for year | | 51 |
| Retained earnings brought forward | | 282 |
| Retained earnings carried forward | | 333 |

(iii)  *Statement of cash flows*

| | | |
|---|---:|---:|
| Net cash flow from operating activities | | 1,033 |
| Interest paid | (150) | |
| Income taxes paid | (130) | (280) |
| *Net cash from operating activities:* | | 753 |
| Cash flows from investing activities | | |
| Purchase of property, plant and equipment | (1,620) | |
| *Net cash used in investing activities:* | | (1,620) |
| Cash flows from financing activities | | |
| Proceeds from sale of short-term investments | 59 | |
| Proceeds from long-term borrowings | 1,000 | |
| Dividends paid | (160) | |
| *Net cash from financing activities:* | | 899 |
| Net increase in cash and cash equivalents | | 32 |
| Cash and cash equivalents at the beginning of the period | | 15 |
| Cash and cash equivalents at the end of the period | | 47 |

(iv)  *Tangible non-current assets (or PPE)*

The movements in the year were as follows:

| | Freehold land and buildings £000 | Plant and machinery £000 | Total £000 |
|---|---:|---:|---:|
| **Cost:** | | | |
| At 1 October 20X5 | 2,000 | 1,600 | 3,600 |
| Additions | — | 1,620 | 1,620 |
| **At 30 September 20X6** | 2,000 | 3,220 | 5,220 |
| **Depreciation:** | | | |
| At 1 October 20X5 | 800 | 900 | 1,700 |
| Charge during the year | 40 | 620 | 660 |
| **At 30 September 20X6** | 840 | 1,520 | 2,360 |
| **Net book value:** | | | |
| Beginning of year | 1,200 | 700 | 1,900 |
| **End of year** | 1,160 | 1,700 | 2,860 |

You are also provided with the following information:

(i)   There was a debenture issue on 1 October 20X5 with interest payable on 30 September each year.

(ii)   An interim dividend of £70,000 was paid on 1 July 20X6.

(iii)   The short-term investment was sold for £59,000 on 1 October 20X5.

(iv)   Business activity increased significantly to meet increased consumer demand.

### Required:
**(a)  Prepare a reconciliation of operating profit to net cash inflow from operating activities.**
**(b)  Discuss the financial developments at Dragon plc during the financial year ended 30 September 20X6 with particular regard to its financial position at the year-end and prospects for the following financial year, supported by appropriate financial ratios.**

## * Question 10

Amalgamated Engineering plc makes specialised machinery for several industries. In recent years, the company has faced severe competition from overseas businesses, and its sales volume has hardly changed. The company has recently applied for an increase in its bank overdraft limit from £750,000 to £1,500,000. The bank manager has asked you, as the bank's credit analyst, to look at the company's application.

You have the following information:

(i)   *Statements of financial position as at 31 December 20X5 and 20X6*

|  | 20X5 | | 20X6 | |
|---|---|---|---|---|
|  | £000 | £000 | £000 | £000 |
| *Tangible non-current assets:* | | | | |
| Freehold land and buildings, at cost | | 1,800 | | 1,800 |
| Plant and equipment, at net book value | | 3,150 | | 3,300 |
| | | 4,950 | | 5,100 |
| *Current assets:* | | | | |
| Inventory | 1,125 | | 1,500 | |
| Trade receivables | 825 | | 1,125 | |
| Short-term investments | 300 | | — | |
| | 2,250 | | 2,625 | |
| *Current liabilities:* | | | | |
| Bank overdraft | 225 | | 675 | |
| Trade payables | 300 | | 375 | |
| Taxation payable | 375 | | 300 | |
| Dividends payable | 225 | | 225 | |
| | 1,125 | | 1,575 | |
| Net current assets | | 1,125 | | 1,050 |
| | | 6,075 | | 6,150 |
| Long-term liability | | | | |
| 8% debentures, 20X9 | | 1,500 | | 1,500 |
| | | 4,575 | | 4,650 |
| *Capital and reserves:* | | | | |
| Ordinary shares of £1 each | | 2,250 | | 2,250 |
| Share premium account | | 750 | | 750 |
| Retained earnings | | 1,575 | | 1,650 |
| | | 4,575 | | 4,650 |

(ii) *Statements of comprehensive income for the years ended 31 December 20X5 and 20X6*

|  | 20X5 | | 20X6 | |
|---|---|---|---|---|
|  | £000 | £000 | £000 | £000 |
| Revenue |  | 6,300 |  | 6,600 |
| Cost of sales: materials | 1,500 |  | 1,575 |  |
| : labour | 2,160 |  | 2,280 |  |
| : production: overheads | 750 |  | 825 |  |
|  |  | 4,410 |  | 4,680 |
|  |  | 1,890 |  | 1,920 |
| Administrative expenses |  | 1,020 |  | 1,125 |
| Operating profit |  | 870 |  | 795 |
| Investment income |  | 15 |  |  |
|  |  | 885 |  | 795 |
| Interest payable: debentures | 120 |  | 120 |  |
| : bank overdraft | 15 |  | 75 |  |
|  |  | 135 |  | 195 |
| Profit before taxation |  | 750 |  | 600 |
| Taxation |  | 375 |  | 300 |
| Profit attributable to shareholders |  | 375 |  | 300 |
| Dividends |  | 225 |  | 225 |
| Retained earnings for year |  | 150 |  | 75 |

(iii) The general price level rose on average by 10% between 20X5 and 20X6. Average wages also rose by 10% during this period.

(iv) The debenture stock is secured by a fixed charge over the freehold land and buildings, which have recently been valued at £3,000,000. The bank overdraft is unsecured.

(v) Additions to plant and equipment in 20X6 amounted to £450,000: depreciation provided in that year was £300,000.

### Required:

(a) Prepare a statement of cash flows for the year ended 31 December 20X6.

(b) Calculate appropriate ratios to use as a basis for a report to the bank manager.

(c) Draft the outline of a report for the bank manager, highlighting key areas you feel should be the subject of further investigation. Mention any additional information you need, and where appropriate refer to the limitations of conventional historical cost accounts.

(d) On receiving the draft report the bank manager advised that he also required the following three cash-based ratios:

(i) Debt service coverage ratio defined as EBITDA/annual debt repayments and interest.

(ii) Cash flow from operations to current liabilities.

(iii) Cash recovery rate defined as ((cash flow from operations proceeds from sale of non-current assets)/average gross assets) × 100.

The director has asked you to explain why the bank manager has requested this additional information given that he has already been supplied with profit-based ratios.

### Question 11

Drucker plc is a public listed wholesaler. Its summarised financial statements for the year ended 31 December 2013 (and 2012 comparatives) are as follows:

**Statements of profit or loss and other comprehensive income for the years ended 31 December**

|  | 2013 | 2012 |
|---|---|---|
|  | € million | € million |
| Revenue | 275 | 200 |
| Cost of sales | (200) | (100) |
| Gross profit | 75 | 100 |
| Operating costs | (36) | (30) |
| Investment income | - | 2 |
| Gains on revaluation of investments held at fair value through P/L | (5) | 10 |
| Finance costs | (5) | (5) |
| Profit (loss) before taxation | 29 | 77 |
| Income tax expense | (4) | (15) |
| Profit for the year | 25 | 62 |
| Other comprehensive income | | |
| (Amounts that will not be reclassified to profit or loss) | | |
| Revaluation losses on property plant & equipment | (45) | — |
| Total comprehensive income (loss) for the year | (20) | 62 |

Statements of Financial Position as at 31 December:

|  | 2013 | 2012 |
|---|---|---|
|  | € million | € million |
| *Assets* | | |
| Non-current assets: | | |
| Property, plant and equipment | 215 | 245 |
| Investments at fair value through profit or loss | 35 | 40 |
|  | 250 | 285 |
| *Current assets* | | |
| Inventory | 40 | 19 |
| Trade receivables | 52 | 28 |
| Bank | — | 10 |
|  | 92 | 57 |
| Total assets | 342 | 342 |
| Equity and liabilities | | |
| Equity: | | |
| Equity shares of €1 each | 120 | 120 |
| Revaluation reserve | 10 | 55 |
| Retained earnings | 90 | 65 |
|  | 220 | 240 |
| *Non-current liabilities:* | | |
| Bank loan | 50 | 50 |
| Current liabilities: | | |
| Trade payables | 50 | 39 |
| Bank overdraft | 20 | — |
| Current tax payable | 2 | 13 |
|  | 72 | 52 |
| *Total equity and liabilities* | 342 | 342 |

You are a newly recruited accountant working for Drucker plc. The draft financial statements for year ended 31 December 2013 have just been produced. Your managing director, Tom Kirby, has asked you to explain to him what the above financial statements mean for the company's performance for the year 2013 and its financial position at 31 December 2013. He makes you aware of the following points and opinions:

(i)   Drucker plc has traditionally been very profitable, but in recent years has been finding it difficult to keep up its sales level due to the effects of internet sales. Basically it finds more customers are buying directly online from suppliers and cutting out the middleman, which includes Drucker as a whole-saler. To counteract this, on 1 January 2013, Drucker launched a strategy of cutting its prices in the hope that this would generate additional sales volume and profits.

(ii)   To support the new strategy and allow faster movement of goods, a new product movement and control system was commissioned and installed on 1 January 2013 at a cost of €40 million. This is being depreciated over a five-year useful economic life. The old system was disposed of for nil consideration on the same date, but had been carried at €15 million at the date of disposal. The loss was taken to Cost of Sales, as is depreciation. No other non-current assets were acquired or dis-posed of in either of the two years.

(iii)   Tom expresses the opinion that this strategy has not failed so far, as the total on the statement of financial position has remained the same from year to year. This proves (he claims) the company has retained its book value and therefore has not suffered any deterioration in performance from 2012 to 2013.

(iv)   The share price has declined from €2.80 per share on 31 December 2012 to €1.60 per share on 31 December 2013. Tom does not understand the reasons for this.

(v)   Tom is aware that there are valuable tools for analysing profitability, liquidity and efficiency. How-ever, he has no knowledge of how to calculate or interpret these.

Required:
(a) Calculate at least eight suitable ratios for each financial year in order to assist in addressing the issues raised by the managing director.
(b) Discuss Tom's assertion in point (iii) above that the new strategy has not failed because the company has retained its book value.
(c) Analyse and discuss the financial performance and position of Drucker plc as portrayed by the financial statements above and the additional information provided. Pay particular attention to the issues raised by Tom and their impact on the performance and position of the company.
(d) Identify the limitations of your analysis.

*(Institute of Certified Public Accountants (CPA) Professional Stage 1 Corporate Reporting Examination, April 2014)*

## Note

1  www.rmahq.org/

# CHAPTER 29

# Analysis of published financial statements

## 29.1 Introduction

In Chapter 28 we considered the way in which we could 'make the numbers talk' from a set of published financial statements. We explained the importance of taking a 'helicopter perspective' initially and identifying key issues before focusing on specific areas of detail. We showed how powerful ratio analysis could be used as an analytical tool provided the ratios were interpreted appropriately. A particularly important issue was the need to differentiate between changes to ratios that were caused by operational and business factors and changes caused by accounting policies and accounting estimates.

When we are interpreting the financial statements of an entity a key issue is the amount of financial information actually available. If we are performing an analysis on behalf of management, or a controlling shareholder, then the amount of financial information available to us is likely to be sufficient to perform any analysis we consider appropriate. On the other hand, where we are performing an analysis from a purely external perspective there will be a limit to the amount of information available to us, because published financial statements generally contain only the information that is required by the appropriate regulatory framework.

### Objectives

By the end of this chapter, you should be able to:

- discuss steps taken to improve information for shareholders;
- critically discuss the limitations of published financial data as a source of useful information for interpretation purposes;
- consider the disclosure of business risk in financial statements;
- discuss additional entity-wide cash-based performance measures;
- explain the use of ratios in determining whether a company is Shariah-compliant;
- explain the use of ratios in debt covenants;
- critically discuss various scoring systems for predicting corporate failure;
- critically discuss remuneration performance criteria;
- critically discuss the role of credit rating agencies;
- calculate the value of unquoted investments.

## 29.2 Improvement of information for shareholders

There have been a number of discussion papers, reports and voluntary code provisions from professional firms and regulators making recommendations on how to provide additional information to allow investors to form a view as to the business's future prospects by (a) making financial information more understandable and easier to analyse and (b) improving the reliability of the historical financial data. This would help ensure the equal treatment of all investors and improve accountability for stewardship.

### 29.2.1 Making financial information more understandable

There has been a view that users should bring a reasonable level of understanding when reading an annual report. This view could be supported when transactions were relatively simple. It no longer applies when even professional accountants comment that the only people who understand some of the disclosures are the technical staff of the regulator and the professional accounting firms.

#### Statutory measures

Users need the financial information to be made more accessible. This is being achieved in part by initiatives such as the Strategic Report in the UK with the requirement to publish information on the past year, including a fair review of the company's business, a description of the principal risks and uncertainties facing the company, and a balanced and comprehensive analysis of the performance of the company's business during the financial year.

As regards the future, a description of the company's strategy, a description of the company's business model and the main trends and factors likely to affect the future development, performance and position of the company's business are also required.

#### Need to understand volatility

There is a need on the part of investors to understand the volatility that can arise as a result of a company's strategy, such as recognising the short- and medium-term impact on earnings of R&D investment. There has been a view that investors are unhappy with an uneven profit trend and that companies have responded by smoothing earnings from year to year to maintain investor confidence.

An ICAEW report[1] produced in 1999 *No Surprises: The Case for Better Risk Reporting* recognised the need for management to disclose their strategies and how they managed risk whilst stating that the intention was not to encourage profit-smoothing but rather a better management of risk and a better understanding by investors of volatility.

### 29.2.2 Disclosure of business risk

Listed companies in the UK are now required to describe 'business risks' in their annual financial statements.

To illustrate how this is disclosed, the business risks have been taken from the Civil Aero Engine division of Rolls-Royce Holdings plc. Rolls-Royce is best known for producing motor cars. However, this activity is now undertaken by a subsidiary of the German motor manufacturer, BMW, where Rolls-Royce cars are produced under licence at Goodwood, near Chichester in the South of England.

The principal activity of Rolls-Royce Holdings plc is the manufacture and servicing of Civil aero engines. Other activities include military aero engines, nuclear, marine and 'power systems'.

Civil aero engines are 'jet engines' (gas turbine engines) for aircraft. This division's turnover is just over 50% of the total turnover of the Group. The two main activities are production of new aero engines (47% of turnover) and servicing & repair of the engines in service (53%).

The annual financial statements for 2015 state the business risks as:

1 If we experience a major product failure in service, then this could result in a loss of life and critical damage to our reputation

2 If an external event or severe economic downturn significantly reduces air travel, then our financial performance may be impacted

3 If our airframe customers significantly delay their production rates, then our financial performance may be impacted

4 If we fail to achieve cost reductions at the necessary pace, then our ability to invest in future programmes and technology may be reduced

5 If we suffer a major disruption in our supply chain, then our delivery schedules may be delayed, damaging our financial performance and reputation

6 If there are significant changes to the regulatory environment for the airline industry, then our market position may be impacted

The problem with this disclosure is that it doesn't quantify the risk (it is likely/unlikely to happen), and the financial consequences. Any attempt to assess the level of risk requires a reader to have detailed industry knowledge.

For instance, in item 1, a 'major product failure' could be overcome by different handling of the engine. For instance, an aircraft with a Rolls-Royce engine crashed just short of the runway at London Airport, because of loss of power on both engines. This was due to icing of the fuel at the front of an oil cooler, which blocked the flow of fuel to the engines. Short-term, this was overcome by periodically accelerating the engines during descent to avoid build-up of the ice. Longer term, a change was made to the oil cooler.

However, a major failure could result in the withdrawal of all aircraft with that engine from service. It could take time to identify the fault and produce revised components. There also could be damages claims from aircraft manufacturers, airlines and passengers.

On items 2 and 6, this will equally affect manufacturers of similar aero engines. The 'servicing' of aero engines is likely to be more stable than demand for new manufactured ones.

Item 3 is 'possible', such as when Boeing started to manufacture aircraft from 'composites' (e.g. carbon fibre) rather than aluminium. 'New technology' is likely to increase the risk of delays compared with using existing technology.

Item 4, 'cost reductions', will range from little success in cost reductions to having substantial reductions in costs.

Item 5, 'major disruption in supply chain' looks unlikely.

The list of 'risks' gives the impression that aero engines is a mature business. However, there may be significant technical developments by competitors which Rolls-Royce may either not be able to match or it would take them a long time to make them successful and reliable.

Including 'business risks' can be helpful. In the case of Rolls-Royce (and probably many other companies), it tends to state obvious risks, but does not quantify them (how likely are they and how significant is the potential financial risk). It also fails to mention other risks that could be significant.

## 29.2.3 Improving the reliability of financial information

Investors rely on the fact that annual reports are audited and so present a fair view of a company's financial performance and position. However, accounting scandals, such as in Enron,

Satyam and the SEC probe in 2012 into the auditing of Chinese companies, have led to a feeling that auditors are not protecting their interests. The profession is aware of this view and of the existence of an expectation gap between what investors expect from an audit and what can reasonably be delivered. This is discussed further in Chapter 31.

### Reliability of narrative information in the Annual Report

The following is an indication of the work carried out by an auditor.

- Other information contained in the Annual Report is read and considered as to whether it is consistent with the audited financial statements.

- The other information comprises only the Directors' Report, the unaudited part of the Directors' Remuneration Report, the Chairman's Statement, the Operating and Financial Review, the Strategic Report and the Corporate Governance Statement.

- The implications for the audit report are considered if there is an awareness of any apparent misstatements or material inconsistencies with the financial statements.

- The responsibilities of the auditor do not extend to any other information.

## 29.3 Published financial statements – their limitations for interpretation purposes

Assuming that the financial statements have been audited and present a fair view, there remain limitations such as lack of detail and the impact of unaudited information when attempting to analyse the statements.

### 29.3.1 Limitation 1 – Lack of detail

This limitation is due to the amount that corporate entities are required to disclose by the appropriate regulatory framework. Only that information that is required to be disclosed would be subject to objective external scrutiny through audit and that information is strictly limited. For example:

- When analysing the profitability of a corporate entity, whether gross or net profit, the extent to which expenses can be broken down into categories is strictly limited. Most current frameworks require the disclosure of cost of sales and other operating expenses but do not require further analysis. Therefore, when, say, the gross margin shows a variation (either from one period to another for single-entity comparison or between entities) we cannot further investigate the components of gross margin because the published financial statements do not provide the required detail.

- Most frameworks require analysis of expenses into a number of headings but do not prescribe exactly where certain expenses (e.g. advertising) would fit. This means that when we compare the gross margin of one corporate entity with that of another we may not be comparing like with like, because one may have treated advertising as part of cost of sales and another may have treated equivalent costs as other operating expenses and the amount could be significant.

- Lack of detailed information prevents the computation of certain useful ratios in their 'purest' from. For example, one of the ratios we discussed in Chapter 28 was 'payables days' – trade payables as a number of days' credit purchases. If we tried to compute this ratio from the published financial statements we would have a problem – credit purchases are not required to be disclosed in the published financial statements of corporate entities in most regulatory frameworks. It is possible to use cost of sales as a proxy for credit purchases. However, this 'contrived' ratio is not as useful as the ratio would be were credit purchases to be available.

### Limitation 2 – The impact of unaudited information

There is a varying amount of information relating to areas such as strategy, risk and KPIs and an ongoing move for improvement. For example, an interesting report issued by the FRC in 1999, *Rising to the Challenge: A Review of Narrative Reporting by UK Listed Companies,*[2] found the following:

- For KPIs, the best companies linked KPIs to strategy and provided an explanation of each measure along with some targets, reconciliations, graphical illustrations of year-on-year comparatives and tables to link KPIs to strategy and targets or future intentions. However, many reports still featured an isolated KPI table with no accompanying discussion or link to the remainder of the document.

- For principal risks, best-practice reports provided some context for the risk, indicating whether it was increasing or decreasing, and provided some idea of the impact of a risk crystallising, supported by numbers. However, users would find it difficult to assess risk where there was too little detail or too many risks identified that obscured those which were important.

## 29.4 Published financial statements – additional entity-wide cash-based performance measures

When making inter-firm comparisons there is the problem that accrual accounting requires a number of subjective judgements to be made such as the non-cash adjustments for depreciation, amortisation and impairment. Inter-firm comparison schemes overcome this by requiring member companies to restate their results using uniform policies such as restating non-current assets at current values and applying uniform depreciation policies.

External analysts are unable to achieve this and have, therefore, developed additional performance measures which are becoming more frequently met in published financial statements. However, there are concerns that they are not mandatory or uniformly defined. This is being addressed by a number of bodies including the International Federation of Accountants (IFAC) with its exposure draft for an International Good Practice Guidance on *Developing and Reporting Supplementary Financial Measures – Definition, Principles, and Disclosures,* the European Securities and Markets Authority (ESMA) with its draft *Guidelines on Alternative Performance Measures* and the IASB which has indicated an intention to research the presentation and disclosure of non-IFRS financial information as part of its *Disclosure Initiative project.*

The position then at present is that management defines the additional performance measures that they report which they consider best assist users to understand how these are used by management in making business decisions.

We discuss some of these measures below.

### 29.4.1 EBITDA

EBITDA is fairly widely used by external analysts. It stands for 'earnings before interest, tax, depreciation and amortisation'.

EBITDA more closely reflects the cash effect of earnings by adding back depreciation and amortisation charges to the operating profit. The figure can be derived by adding back the depreciation and amortisation that is disclosed in the statement of cash flows.

By taking earnings before depreciation and amortisation we eliminate differences due to different ages of plant and equipment when making inter-period comparisons of performance and also differences arising from the use of different depreciation methods when making inter-firm comparisons. By taking earnings before interest it shows how much is available to pay interest.

Note that there is no standard definition – for example some companies define it as earnings before interest, depreciation, tax, amortisation, *impairment* and *exceptional items.*

EBITDA shows an approximation to the cash impact of earnings. It differs from the cash flow from operations reported in the statement of cash flows in that it is before adjustment for working capital changes.

## Comparing segment performance

EBITDA information is useful where an entity has a number of segments. It allows performance to be compared by calculating the EBITDA for each segment which provides a figure that is independent of the age structure of the non-current assets.

For example, the following is an extract from the Vodafone 2015 Annual Report:

| | EBITDA £m | EBITDA margin % |
|---|---|---|
| **31 March 2015** | | |
| Germany | 2,670 | 31.5 |
| Italy | 1,537 | 33.1 |
| Spain | 783 | 21.4 |
| UK | 1,360 | 21.2 |
| Other Europe | 1,574 | 31.4 |
| **Europe** | **7,924** | **28.2** |

Interestingly, the company states that it uses EBITDA as an operating performance measure which is reviewed by the Chief Executive to assess internal performance in conjunction with EBITDA margin, which is an alternative sales margin figure.

## 29.4.2 Other 'EBITDA-based' ratios commonly produced

The use of EBITDA in annual reports of listed companies is becoming more frequent. For instance, Vodafone's 2015 Annual Report mentions EBITDA 166 times. However, fewer companies are using 'other EBITDA-based ratios'. These other EBITA-based ratios include the following.

### EV (Enterprise value)/EBITDA

EV is the market capitalisation of equity plus debt, non-controlling interest and preference shares less total cash equivalents

### Net debt/EBITDA

This ratio shows the number of years that it would take to 'pay off' the debt.

### Debt service coverage ratio

This is defined as EBITDA/annual debt repayments and interest

### EBITDA/Interest

This shows the number of times interest is covered. Most companies use the more familiar ratio, Profit before interest/Interest

### EBITDAR

This is a variant of EBITDA. It stands for 'earnings before interest, tax, depreciation, amortisation and **rental expense**'.

Adding this rental expense back allegedly makes performance comparisons between entities with different proportions of assets leased under operating leases more valid. It also removes the subjectivity introduced by lease classification as operating or finance.

The following is an extract from the J Sainsbury plc 2015 Annual Report:

| Key financial ratios | 2015 | 2014 |
|---|---|---|
| **Adjusted net debt to EBITDAR**[1] | **4.1 times** | 3.9 times |
| **Interest cover**[2] | **7.4 times** | 8.2 times |
| **Fixed charge cover**[3] | **2.9 times** | 3.1 times |
| **Gearing**[4] | **42.3%** | 39.7% |
| **Gearing excluding pension deficit**[5] | **37.9%** | 35.7% |

1. Net debt of £2,343 million plus capitalised lease obligations of £5,417 million (5.5 per cent discount rate), divided by Group underlying EBITDAR of £1,890 million.
2. Underlying profit before interest and tax divided by underlying net finance costs.
3. Group underlying EBITDAR divided by net rent and underlying net finance costs.
4. Net debt divided by net assets.
5. Net debt divided by net assets, excluding pension deficit.

EBITDAR in supermarket companies such as Sainsbury and Tesco refers to *rent*. It may also be defined differently, for example, as *restructuring*. In the aviation industry it is the key earnings-oriented operational performance indicator, referring to the profit before interest, taxes, depreciation, amortisation and leasing costs for aircraft. EBITDAR is generally recognised and used by the aviation industry and investors and analysts as the ratio used for measuring operational success.

### EBITDARM

EBITDARM stands for 'earnings before interest, tax, depreciation, amortisation, rental expense and management fees'. The rationale behind this measure is that management fees are extracted from different entities in different proportions.

Management charges may not always be totally representative of the services provided. Therefore management fees might sometimes be a form of profit extraction rather than a genuine expense and adding them back once again facilitates inter-entity comparison.

## 29.4.3 Evaluating the use of EBITDA

EBITDA is often used when valuing a company. It helps when comparing the performance of companies which may have differently geared capital structures, depreciation policies and tax rates.

However, it is not a substitute for cash flow in that it does not take into account changes in working capital that may be significant in a fast-growing company, material finance charges that may exist in a highly leveraged company and potential cash required by a capital-intensive company.

It needs to be used in conjunction with other ratios. For example, in reviewing a highly leveraged company the debt service coverage ratio and EBITDA/Interest would be considered. In reviewing a capital-intensive company reference would be made to Free cash flow discussed in Chapter 5. In assessing dividend potential the Free cash flow to Equity would be considered by calculating the cash after interest, taxes and reinvestment have been paid.

## 29.5 Ratio thresholds to satisfy Shariah compliance

In addition to considering the range of cash-based earnings ratios, investors might also require a company to satisfy certain threshold ratios *before* making an investment. An example is seen with the ratios relevant for shariah compliance.

Shariah law is a regulatory system that is derived from the Islamic religion. Islam commands followers to avoid consumption of alcohol and pork and so adherents avoid investments in those industries. There is screening to check that (a) business activities are not prohibited and (b) certain of the financial ratios do not exceed specified limits.

This use of ratios is included because of the growing importance of investment in shariah-compliant companies. Islamic banking is gaining popularity all over the world. Global Islamic finance assets reached a record $1.7 trillion in 2014, with industry to top $3.4 trillion by 2018.

There are a number of shariah indices including the Dow Jones Islamic Indexes, the FTSE Global Islamic Index Series, the FTSE SGX Shariah Index Series, the FTSE DIFX Shariah Index Series and the FTSE Bursa Malaysia Index Series. The indices include companies such as Google Inc., TOTAL SA, BP plc, Exxon Mobil Corporation, Petroleo Brasileiro, Novartis AG, Roche Holding, GlaxoSmithKline plc, BHP Billiton Ltd, Siemens AG, Samsung Electronics, International Business Machines Corporation, Nestlé SA, and Coca-Cola.

Investors interested in establishing whether an entity is shariah-compliant are assisted by the service provided by various Islamic indices where the constituent companies have been screened to confirm that they are shariah-compliant with reference to the nature of the business and debt ratios.

The indices are compiled after:

● screening companies to confirm that their business activities are not prohibited (or fall within the 5% permitted threshold);

● calculating three financial ratios based on total assets; and

● calculating a dividend adjustment factor which results in more relevant benchmarks, as they reflect the total return to an Islamic portfolio net of dividend purification.

Details are provided below.

### 29.5.1 Screening

Shariah investment principles do not allow investment in entities which are directly active in, or derive more than 5% of their revenue (cumulatively) from, the following activities ('prohibited activities'):

● Alcohol: distillers, vintners and producers of alcoholic beverages, including producers of beer and malt liquors, owners and operators of bars and pubs.

● Tobacco: cigarettes and other tobacco products manufacturers and retailers.

● Pork-related products: companies involved in the manufacture and retail of pork products.

- Conventional financial services: an extensive range including commercial banks, investment banks, insurance companies, consumer finance such as credit cards, and leasing.
- Defence/weapons: manufacturers of military aerospace and defence equipment, parts or products, including defence electronics and space equipment.
- Gambling/casinos: owners and operators of casinos and gaming facilities, including companies providing lottery and betting services.
- Music: producers and distributors of music, owners and operators of radio broadcasting systems.
- Hotels: owners and operators of hotels.

### Key ratios

Shariah investment principles do not allow investment in companies deriving significant income from interest or companies that have excessive leverage. MSCI Barra uses the following three financial ratios to screen for these companies:

- total debt over total assets;
- sum of an entity's cash and interest-bearing securities over total assets;
- sum of an entity's accounts receivables and cash over total assets.

None of the financial ratios may exceed 33.33%.

### Dividend adjustment (or 'purification')

If an entity does derive part of its total income from interest income and/or from prohibited activities, shariah investment principles state that this proportion must be deducted from the dividend paid out to shareholders and given to charity.

Dividend purification may be calculated by dividing prohibited income (including interest income) by total income and multiplying by the dividend received. An alternative is to divide total prohibited income (including interest income) by the number of shares issued at the end of the period and multiply by the number of shares held. MSCI Barra applies a 'dividend adjustment factor' to all reinvested dividends.

The 'dividend adjustment factor' is defined as:

$$\frac{\text{Total earnings} - (\text{Income from prohibited activities} + \text{Interest income})}{\text{Total earnings}}$$

In this formula, total earnings are defined as gross income, and interest income is defined as operating and non-operating interest.

## 29.6 Use of ratios in restrictive loan covenants

Whereas the shariah compliance criteria apply *before* making a financial commitment, frequently lenders set specific threshold ratios that a company must comply with when making a loan in order to limit the lender's risk – these are described as affirmative or negative debt covenants.

When a corporate entity borrows, the borrowing agreement often includes a provision which requires that specified accounting ratios such as gearing (relationship between debt and equity) of the entity be kept below a certain level. The loan agreement would of course have to specify exactly how any ratio is computed for this purpose.

The existence of a debt covenant or covenants has a number of potential implications for an entity and for analysts:

● An entity with a debt covenant that is close to its limit will be unable to raise funds by borrowing, so it will need to raise any required funds by an equity issue. Given the attitude of investors to risk, the return required by equity shareholders in a highly geared entity will be higher than that of an entity in which the gearing is lower. This will affect the overall amount of funding an entity can raise.

● Where a ratio of an entity subject to a debt covenant approaches the limit set out in the covenant, there is an inevitable temptation for the preparers to ensure the ratio is kept within the limit, leading to a potential temptation to misstate the financial statements.

The potential existence of a debt covenant is a factor that should be borne in mind by external analysts. The problem is that the existence of such debt covenants is not normally a required disclosure by relevant regulatory frameworks. Therefore a concerned analyst would need to attempt to obtain this information from the management of the entity. The success or otherwise of this attempt will depend on the bargaining power of the analyst.

### 29.6.1 Affirmative and negative covenants

Lenders may require borrowers to do certain things by affirmative covenants or refrain from doing certain things by negative covenants.

Affirmative covenants may, for example, include requiring the borrower to:

● provide quarterly and annual financial statements;
● remain within certain ratios whilst ensuring that each agreed ratio is not so restrictive that it impairs normal operations:
  ● maintain a current ratio of not less than an agreed ratio – say 1.6 to 1;
  ● maintain a ratio of total liabilities to tangible net worth at an agreed rate – say no greater than 2.5 to 1;
  ● maintain tangible net worth in excess of an agreed amount – say £1 million;
● maintain adequate insurance.

Negative covenants may, for example, include requiring the borrower *not* to:

● grant any other charges over the company's assets;
● repay loans from related parties without prior approval;
● change the group structure by acquisitions, mergers or divestment without prior agreement.

### 29.6.2 What happens if a company is in breach of its debt covenants?

Borrowers will normally have prepared forecasts to assure themselves and the lenders that compliance is reasonably feasible. Such forecasts will also normally include the worst-case scenario, e.g. taking account of seasonal fluctuations that may trigger temporary violations with higher borrowing required to cover higher levels of inventory and trade receivables.

If any violation has occurred, the lender has a range of options, such as:

● amending the covenant, e.g. accepting a lower current ratio; or
● granting a waiver period when the terms of the covenant are not applied; or

- renegotiating the credit facility and restructuring the finance, as in the following extract from the 2009 Annual Report of Sunshine Holdings 3 Ltd:

> The Group faces more restrictive financial covenants . . . the directors believe it is likely that the Group will not meet the financial covenants required under the first lien credit agreement.

### Directors' report

> While the directors fully expect to resolve the covenant issues with a restructuring and/ or amendment to the facility agreements, these circumstances represent a material uncertainty regarding the Group's going concern status . . . the directors have a reasonable expectation that the Group will satisfactorily conclude its covenant issues and will have adequate resources to continue in operational existence for the foreseeable future. Therefore the accounts have been prepared on a going concern basis.

In addition, companies may increase their equity capital, possibly by a rights issue as the current shareholders have a greater incentive to provide additional capital than new investors.

For example, it was reported in 2012 that Lonmin planned a $800m rights issue to avoid possibly breaching its covenants.

In times of recession a typical reaction is for companies to take steps to reduce their operating costs, align production with reduced demand, tightly control their working capital and reduce discretionary capital expenditure.

## 29.6.3 Risk of aggressive earnings management

In 2001, before the collapse of Enron, there was a consensus amongst respondents to the UK Auditing Practices Board Consultation Paper *Aggressive Earnings Management* that aggressive earnings management was a significant threat and actions should be taken to diminish it.

### Reasons for earnings management

It was considered that aggressive earnings management could occur to increase earnings in order to avoid losses, to meet profit forecasts, to ensure compliance with loan covenants and when directors' and managements' remuneration were linked to earnings. It could also occur to reduce earnings to reduce tax liabilities or to allow profits to be smoothed.

In 2004, as a part of the *Information for Better Markets* initiative, the Audit and Assurance Faculty commissioned a survey.[3] This showed that the vulnerability of corporate reporting to manipulation is perceived as being always with us but at a lower level following the greater awareness and scrutiny by non-executive directors and audit committees.

### Sector variations

The analysts interviewed in the survey believed the potential for aggressive earnings management varied from sector to sector, e.g. in the older, more established sectors followed by the same analysts for a number of years, they believed that company management would find it hard to disguise anything aggressive even if they wanted to. However, this was not true of newer sectors (e.g. IT) where the business models may be loss-making initially and imperfectly understood.

### Levels of confidence

Whilst analysts and journalists tend to have low confidence in the reported earnings where there are pressures to manipulate, there is a research report[4] which paints a rather more optimistic picture. This report aimed to assess the level of confidence investors had in different sources of company information, including audited financial information, when making investment decisions. As far as audited financial information was concerned, the levels of confidence in UK audited financial information amongst UK and US investors remained very high, with 87% of UK respondents having either a 'great deal' or a 'fair amount' of confidence in UK audited financial information.

### Need for scepticism

The auditing profession continues to respond to the need to contain aggressive earnings management. This is not easy because it requires a detailed understanding not only of the business but also of the process management follows when making its estimates. ISA 540 Revised, *Auditing Accounting Estimates, including Fair Value Accounting Estimates, and Related Disclosures*, requires auditors to exercise greater rigour and scepticism and to be particularly aware of the cumulative effect of estimates which in themselves fall within a normal range but which, taken together, are misleading.

### 29.6.4 Audit implications when there is a breach of a debt covenant

Auditors are required to bring a healthy scepticism to their work. This applies particularly at times such as when there is a potential debt covenant breach. There may then well be a temptation to manipulate to avoid reporting a breach. This will depend on the specific covenant. For example, if the current ratio is likely to fall below the agreed figure, management might be more optimistic when setting inventory obsolescence and accounts receivable provisions and assessing the probability of contingent liabilities crystallising.

### 29.6.5 Impact on share price

If there is a risk of bank covenants being breached, there can be a significant adverse effect on the share price. For example, it was reported in 2012 that Lonmin's share price dropped sharply by 4.6%, a new 52-week low for the company, following the announcement that it may be in the breach of its covenants with its financial lenders.

However, both the company and the lender might prefer to keep potential breaches private unless there is a risk that enforced disclosure is imminent.

## 29.7 Investor-specific ratios

The analysis we carried out in Chapter 28 (and the additional performance measures we discussed in Section 29.4 above) was done from the perspective of the performance and position of the entity. In this section we will focus on additional ratios and measures that have as their focus the position of the shareholders of the entity. Some of these measures are 'financial statement measures' and others are 'market-based measures'.

### 29.7.1 Return on equity

We discussed ROE in Chapter 28 so this section is included as a brief reminder. In Chapter 28 we stated that a primary entity profitability measure is 'Return on equity', i.e. 'Profit'/Capital employed. Where the focus is on the equity shareholders the applicable ratio is ROE where the numerator is the post-tax profit.

If capital employed is funded by sources other than equity, then there is a financial leverage impact on the ROCE when calculating the ROE to reflect the potential benefit to equity shareholders of the company borrowing and investing at a higher rate.

As far as the equity shareholders are concerned, it might appear that the higher the financial leverage the better. However:

- If borrowings are high, it might be difficult to obtain additional loans to take advantage of new opportunities. For example, HSBC raised £12.5 billion in 2009 by a rights issue on the basis that this would give the bank a competitive advantage over its rivals by restoring its position as having the strongest statement of financial position, i.e. high borrowings limit a company's flexibility.

- Interest has to be paid even in bad years with the risk that loan creditors could put the company into administration if interest is not paid.

The relationship is illustrated using data from the financial statements of Vertigo plc for the year ended 31 December 20X9 presented in Section 28.3.1:

|  | £000 |
|---|---|
| Total assets | 4,587 |
| Equity | 3,353 |
| Pre-tax profit | 116 |
| Tax | 25 |
| Sales | 3,461 |

The effect of leverage on ROE is:

$$\text{Pre-tax margin (3.35\%)} \times \text{Asset turnover (0.755)} = \text{Return on assets (2.53\%)}$$
$$(116/3,461) \qquad (3,461/4,587)$$

$$\text{Return on assets (2.53\%)} \times \text{Leverage (1.37)} \times (1 - \text{tax rate}) (0.785) = \text{ROE (2.72)}$$
$$(4,587/3,353) \qquad (1 - 0.215)$$

The effect of leverage on EPS (assuming 3 million shares in issue) is:

$$\text{ROE (2.72)} \times \text{Book value (1.12)} = \text{EPS (3.05)}$$
$$(3,353/3,000)$$

## 29.7.2 Price/earnings (PE) ratio

The PE ratio is computed as:

$$\frac{\text{Market value of a share}}{\text{Earnings per share}}$$

The PE ratio is a market-based measure and a high ratio indicates that investors are relatively confident in the maintainability and quality of the earnings of the entity. Entities in certain sectors (e.g. the retail sector) tend to have higher PE ratios than those in other sectors (e.g. the construction sector). Higher PE ratios imply a greater level of market confidence, which usually means that (given the attitude an average investor takes to risk) the entity with a higher PE ratio operates in a sector which is less cyclical.

We will see in Section 29.11 that competitor or industry PE ratios (or their reciprocal, the earnings yield) are used as a base for valuing shares in unquoted companies – comparators being obtained from trade association schemes or sites such as http://biz.yahoo.com/p/industries.html.

### Earnings yield

This is the reciprocal of the PE ratio. For example, a PE ratio of 10 becomes an earnings yield of 10% (1/10 × 100).

## 29.7.3 Earnings per share (EPS)

EPS is computed as:

$$\frac{\text{Profit attributable to the ordinary (equity) shareholders}}{\text{Weighted average number of ordinary shares in issue during the period}}$$

The detailed calculation of basic and diluted EPS was dealt with in Chapter 27.

EPS could be said to be a more reliable indicator of the true trend in profitability than the actual profit numbers because the denominator of the fraction factors in any change in the issued capital during the period. The fact that the weighted average number is used removes the potential inconsistency that arises when dividing a 'period' number like profit by a 'point of time' number like the number of shares.

### How EPS might be manipulated

The appropriateness of EPS as a performance measure can be influenced by the subjectivity of the directors when preparing the financial statements. For example, their remuneration may be based on the growth in EPS. Looking at calculation of the EPS of 3.05 (rounded) we can see that it is affected by:

- the number of shares in issue which can be changed by issuing bonus shares, share splits and reverse share splits;
- the profit which can be manipulated by adjusting accrued liabilities, depreciation, amortisation and impairment charges.

Simply buying back one-sixth of the shares can lift the EPS by more than 10%.

## 29.7.4 Dividend cover

Dividend cover is computed as:

$$\frac{\text{Profit for the period}}{\text{Dividends paid}} \quad \text{or} \quad \frac{\text{EPS}}{\text{Dividend per share}}$$

Dividend cover is a measure of the vulnerability of the dividend to a fall in profits. The legality of a dividend payment is normally based on cumulative profits rather than the profits for a single period, but in practice an entity would wish the dividend declared for a particular period to be 'covered' by profits made in that period. Therefore this ratio is seen as a measure of the 'security' of the dividend.

An issue with this ratio is whether a high dividend cover is good or bad. In one sense, a shareholder might be content with a high dividend cover, because this would mean that profits could potentially fall quite significantly without the dividend necessarily falling, and retained earnings are being employed profitably within the company. Alternatively, a shareholder might feel disgruntled that the dividend itself is not higher. Therefore conclusions about whether a change in dividend cover is 'good' or 'bad' need to be made with caution – the trend and inter-firm comparators from the same industry need to be looked at. For example, some companies may target the rate of dividend cover as a key performance indicator as shown in the following extract from the Morrisons 2011 Annual Report:

> Our aim is that dividend cover will be the same as the average for the European food retail sector. Our dividend cover is 2.4 times, in line with the European food retail sector average. This has resulted in dividend growth of 17%.

### 29.7.5 Dividend yield

Dividend yield is computed as:

$$\frac{\text{Dividend per share}}{\text{Market value of a share}} \text{ (expressed as a percentage)}$$

This ratio measures the 'effective' current investment by the shareholder in the entity, because by deciding to keep the share rather than dispose of it the shareholder is forgoing an amount that would be available were the shareholder to make a disposal decision.

This ratio is a 'market-based' ratio, because it is influenced by the share price of the entity. We need to interpret any 'market-based' ratio with caution. In this case a high dividend yield could mean that the shareholder is receiving a very healthy dividend (which would be very positive) or that the share price was very low (which would clearly not be a desirable position either for the entity or for the shareholder).

Indeed, in times of disappointing prices on securities markets, dividend yields often tend to be very high because entities are reluctant to cut their dividends for fear the share price will fall even further. A combination of a static dividend and falling share prices leads inevitably to a rise in dividend yields. This would become more apparent if dividend growth were considered in addition to dividend yield.

## 29.8 Determining value

There are three aspects to consider. One is to assess from an entity viewpoint whether adequate returns (EVA) are being generated, the other is to assess from a shareholder's viewpoint the total shareholder return (TSR), and the third is how either is used in setting directors' remuneration.

### 29.8.1 Economic value added (EVA)

Value is created when the return on a company's economic capital employed is greater than the cost of that capital. This is expressed as EVA which is the profit that a company earns less the cost of capital.

Companies are increasingly becoming aware that investors need to be confident that the company can achieve growth, and that communication of a positive EVA is the key. This is why companies are using the annual report to provide shareholders and potential shareholders with a measure of the company's performance that will give them confidence to maintain or make an investment in the company. This is the view expressed in the 2009 Annual Report of Geveke NV Amsterdam:

> A positive EVA indicates that over a specific period economic value has been created. Net operating profit after tax is then greater than the cost of finance (i.e. the company's weighted average cost of capital). Research has shown that a substantial part of the long-term movement in share price is explained by the development of EVA. The concept of EVA can be a very good method of performance measurement and monitoring of decisions. It is for this reason that it is being incorporated into corporate strategy worldwide.

## 29.8.2 Formula for calculating economic value added

The formula applied by Geveke is as follows:

> EVA measures economic value achieved over a specific period. It is equal to net operating profit after tax (NOPAT), corrected for the cost of capital employed (the sum of interest bearing liabilities and shareholders' equity). The cost of capital employed is the required yield (R) times capital employed (CE).

In the form of a formula: $NOPAT - (R \times CE) = EVA$

We will illustrate the formula for Alpha NV, which has the following data (in euros):

|  | 31 March 20X6 | 31 March 20X7 | 31 March 20X9 |
|---|---|---|---|
| NOPAT | 10m | 11m | 12.5m |
| Weighted average cost of capital (WACC) | 12% | 11.5% | 11% |
| Capital employed | 70m | 77m | 96m |

The EVA is:

|  | Percentage change |
|---|---|
| 31 March 20X6: EVA = 10m − (12% of 70m) = 1.6m | — |
| 31 March 20X7 EVA = 11m − (11.5% of 77m) = 2.145m | 34% |
| 31 March 20X8: EVA = 12.5m − (11% of 96m) = 1.94m | (10%) |

*The formula allows weight to be given to the capital employed to generate operating profit.* The percentage change is an important management tool in that the annual increase is seen as the created value rather than the absolute level, i.e. the 34% is the key figure rather than the 2.145 million. Further enquiry is necessary to assess how well Alpha NV will employ the EVA in future periods.

It is useful to calculate rate of change over time. However, as for all inter-company comparisons of ratios, it is necessary to identify how the WACC and capital employed have been defined. This may vary from company to company.

### WACC calculation

This figure depends on the capital structure.

For example, in its 2015 Annual Report, Lufthansa set a gearing target of 50% and calculated its WACC as 5.9% based on a cost of debt 3.4% (after tax) and cost of equity 8.4%.

Its cost of equity was arrived at as risk-free market interest rate of 2.6% + (market risk premium of 5.2% × Beta factor of 1.1).

Using this figure of 5.9%, Lufthansa's EVA was €323m (described in its accounts as EACC – earnings after cost of capital employed) being EBIT of €1,696m less cost of average capital employed €1,073m.

It is interesting to note that from 2016 the company will base variable Executive Board remuneration in part on EACC.

### Capital employed definition

The norm is to exclude non-interest-bearing liabilities including current liabilities when determining net total assets. However, there are variations in the treatment of intangible assets, e.g. goodwill may be excluded from the net assets.

### 29.8.3 Achieving increases in EVA

EVA can be improved in three ways: by increasing NOPAT, reducing WACC and/or improving the utilisation of capital employed.

- Increasing NOPAT: this is achieved by optimising strategic choices by comparing the cash flows arising from different strategic opportunities, e.g. appraising geographic and product segmental information, cost reduction programmes, appraising acquisitions and divestments.
- Reducing WACC: this is achieved by reviewing the manner in which a company is financed, e.g. determining a favourable gearing ratio and reducing the perceived risk factor by a favourable spread of products and markets.
- Improving the utilisation of capital employed: this is achieved by consideration of activity ratios, e.g. non–current asset turnover, working capital ratio.

### 29.8.4 Management attitude to use of EVA

One study[5] identified a number of companies that used value-based measures at head office level, but retained traditional profit measures in their divisions. The use of EVA is becoming more frequent when determining Executive Board remuneration, as with Siemens in its 2014 Annual Report:

> ... in setting the target for the variable compensation (bonus) for those Managing Board members with responsibilities for Sector portfolios, the Supervisory Board set economic value added (EVA) as a Sector-specific target.

#### Turning EVA into a comparative ratio

EVA momentum[6] relates the change in the EVA £ value to the previous period's sales. The formula is:

$$\text{EVA momentum} = \frac{\text{EVA}^{\text{Period 2}} - \text{EVA}^{\text{Period 1}}}{\text{Revenue}^{\text{Period 1}}}$$

Companies are now being ranked by EVA momentum and it is reported[7] that because it is based on the change in EVA rather than the level, EVA momentum captures profitability performance where it matters most – at the margin. Companies that are losing money but cut their losses dramatically score well on EVA momentum. In contrast, even extremely profitable companies can score poorly on this performance measure if their economic profits are static or declining. As a result, EVA momentum is a great measure for spotting turning points in performance.

### 29.8.5 Total shareholder return approach

#### Shareholder value (SV)

It has been a long-standing practice for analysts to arrive at shareholder value of a share by calculating the internal rate of return (IRR %) on an investment from the dividend stream and realisable value of the investment at date of disposal, i.e. taking account of dividends received and capital gains. However, it is not a generic measure in that the calculation is specific to each shareholder. The reason for this is that the dividends received will depend on the length of period the shares are held and the capital gain achieved will depend on the share price at the date of disposal – and, as we know, the share price can move significantly even over a week.

For example, consider the SV for each of the three shareholders, Miss Rapid, Mr Medium and Miss Undecided, who each invested £10,000 on 1 January 20X6 in Spacemobile Ltd which pays a dividend of £500 on these shares on 31 December each year. Miss Rapid sold her shares on 31 December 20X7. Mr Medium sold his on 31 December 20X9, whereas Miss Undecided could not decide what to do with her shares. The SV for each shareholder is as follows:

| Shareholder | Date acquired | Investment at cost | Dividends amount (total) | Date of disposal | Sale proceeds | IRR % |
|---|---|---|---|---|---|---|
| Miss Rapid | 1.1.20X6 | 10,000 | 1,000 | 31.12.20X7 | 11,000 | 10%* |
| Mr Medium | 1.1.20X6 | 10,000 | 2,000 | 31.12.20X9 | 15,000 | 15% |
| Miss Undecided | 1.1.20X6 | 10,000 | 2,000 | Undecided | | |

\* $(500 \times .9091) + (11,500 \times .8265) - 10,000 = 0$

We can see that Miss Rapid achieved a shareholder value of 10% on her shares and Mr Medium, by holding until 31.12.20X9, achieved an increased capital gain raising the SV to 15%. We do not have the information as to how Miss Rapid invested from 1.1.20X8 and so we cannot evaluate her decision – it depends on the subsequent investment and the economic value added by that new company.

### 29.8.6 Total shareholder return

Miss Undecided has a notional SV at 31.12.20X9 of 15% as calculated for Mr Medium. However, this has not been realised and, if the share price changed the following day, the SV would be different. The notional 15% calculated for Miss Undecided is referred to as the total shareholder return (TSR) – it takes into account market expectation on the assumption that share prices reflect all available information but it is dependent on the assumption made about the length of the period the shares are held.

### 29.8.7 Performance-based remuneration using EVA and TSR

#### EVA and managers' performance

In some organisations EVA has been used as a basis for determining bonus payments made to managers. There is some evidence that managers rewarded under such a scheme do perform better than those operating under more traditional schemes. However, research[8] indicated that this occurs when managers understand the concept of EVA and that it is not universally appropriate as other factors need to be taken into account such as the area of the firm in which a manager is employed. The following is an extract from the ThyssenKrupp 2009 Annual Report:

> This management and controlling system is linked to the bonus system in such a way that the amount of the performance-related remuneration is determined by the achieved EVA.

However, there is a risk that this approach can encourage short-termism by focusing on annual targets.

### TSR and managers' performance

TSR has been used for performance monitoring, as a criterion for performance-based remuneration and to satisfy statutory requirements.

#### Performance monitoring

TSR has been used by companies to monitor their performance by comparing their own TSR with that of comparator companies. It is also used to set strategic targets. For example, Unilever set itself a TSR target in the top third of a reference group of 21 international consumer goods companies. Unilever calculates the TSR over a three-year rolling period which it considers 'sensitive enough to reflect changes but long enough to smooth out short-term volatility'.

#### Statutory requirement

The Directors' Report Regulations 2002 now require a line graph to be prepared showing such a comparison. Marks & Spencer Group's 2012 Annual Report contained the following:

> **Total shareholder return performance graph**
> The graph illustrates the performance of the Company against the FTSE 100 over the past five years. The FTSE 100 has been chosen as it is a recognised broad equity market index of which the Company has been a member throughout the period.

Management and investors assess a company's performance based on the use of ratios described in Chapter 28 and earlier in the present chapter. This follows the pyramid approach of starting with the ROE and drilling down to identify possible causes of change.

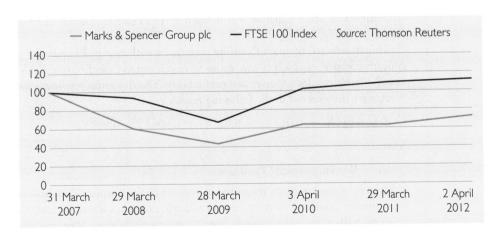

## 29.9 Predicting corporate failure

The models that attempt to predict corporate failure combine selected ratios to produce a single-figure score. There are a number of such models and we will discuss a selection.

In the preceding chapter we extolled the virtues of ratio analysis for the interpretation of financial statements. However, ratio analysis is an excellent indicator only when applied properly. Unfortunately, a number of limitations impede its proper application. How do we know which ratios to select for the analysis of company accounts? Which ratios can be combined to produce an informative end-result? How should individual ratios be ranked to give the user an overall picture of company performance? How reliable are all the ratios – can users place more reliance on some ratios than others? We will consider which ratios have been selected to produce Z-scores and H-scores.

Z-score analysis can be employed to overcome some of the limitations of traditional ratio analysis. It evaluates corporate stability and, more importantly, predicts potential instances of corporate failure. All the forecasts and predictions are based on publicly available financial statements.[9] The aim is to identify potential failures so that 'the appropriate action to reverse the process [of failure] can be taken before it is too late'.[10]

### 29.9.1 What are Z-scores?

Inman[11] describes what Z-scores are designed for:

> Z-scores attempt to replace various independent and often unreliable and misleading historical ratios and subjective rule-of-thumb tests with scientifically analysed ratios which can reliably predict future events by identifying benchmarks above which 'all's well' and below which there is imminent danger.

Z-scores provide a single-value score to describe the combination of a number of key characteristics of a company. Some of the most important predictive ratios are weighted according to perceived importance and then summed to give the single Z-score. This is then evaluated against the identified benchmark.

The two best-known Z-scores are Altman's Z-score and Taffler's Z-score.

#### Altman's Z-score

The original Z-score equation was devised by Professor E. Altman in 1968 and developed further in 1977.[12]

Altman selected 66 manufacturing companies with an equal number of failed and going concern companies. Twenty-two ratios were calculated from five categories – leverage, solvency, liquidity, sales turnover and profitability. The five ratios providing the best predictive value were then set out in the following equation:

$$Z = 0.012X_1 + 0.014X_2 + 0.033X_3 + 0.006X_4 + 0.999X_5$$

where:

$X_1$ = Working capital/Total assets

(Liquid assets are being measured in relation to the business's size and this may be seen as a better predictor than the current and acid test ratios which measure the interrelationships within working capital. For $X_1$ the more relative Working capital, the more liquidity.)

$X_2$ = Retained earnings/Total assets

(In early years the proportion of retained earnings used to finance the total asset base may be quite low and the length of time the business has been in existence has been seen as a factor in insolvency. In later years the more earnings that are retained the more funds that could be available to pay creditors. $X_2$ also acts as an indication of a company's dividend policy – a high dividend payout reduces the retained earnings with impact on solvency and creditors' position.)

$X_3$ = Earnings before interest and tax (EBIT)/Total assets

(Adequate operating profit is fundamental to the survival of a business.)

$X_4$ = Market capitalisation/Book value of debt

(This is an attempt to include market expectations which may be an early warning as to possible future problems. Solvency is less likely to be threatened if shareholders' interest is relatively high in relation to the total debt.)

$X_5$ = Sales/Total assets

(This indicates how assets are being used. If efficient, then profits available to meet interest payments are more likely. It is a measure that might have been more appropriate when Altman was researching companies within the manufacturing sector. It is a relationship that varies widely between manufacturing sectors and even more so within knowledge-based companies.)

It can be seen from the weighting (0.999) that $X_5$ is the most important ratio.

Altman identified two benchmarks. Companies scoring over 3.0 are unlikely to fail and should be considered safe, while companies scoring under 1.8 are very likely to fail. The value of 3.0 has since been revised down to 2.7.[13] Z-scores between 2.7 and 1.8 fall into the grey area. The 1968 work is claimed to be able to distinguish between successes and failures up to two or three years before the event. The 1977 work claims an improved prediction period of up to five years before the event.

### The Zeta model

This was a model developed by Altman and Zeta Services, Inc. in 1977. It is the same as the Z-score for identifying corporate failure one year ahead but it is more accurate in identifying potential failure in the period two to five years ahead. The model is based on the following variables:

$X_1$ return on assets: earnings before interest and tax/total assets;
$X_2$ stability of earnings: normalised return on assets around a five- to ten-year trend;
$X_3$ interest cover: earnings before interest and tax/total interest;
$X_4$ cumulative profitability: retained earnings/total assets;
$X_5$ liquidity: the current ratio;
$X_6$ capitalisation: equity/total market value;
$X_7$ size: total tangible assets.

Zeta is available as a subscription service and the coefficients have not been published.

### Taffler's Z-score

The exact definition of Taffler's Z-score[10, 14] is unpublished, but the following components form the equation:

$$Z = c_0 + c_1X_1 + c_2X_2 + c_3X_3 + c_4X_4$$

where:

$X_1$ = Profit before tax/Current assets (53%)

$X_2$ = Current assets/Current liabilities (13%)

$X_3$ = Current liabilities/Total assets (18%)

$X_4$ = No credit interval = Length of time which the company can continue to finance its operations using its own assets with no revenue inflow (16%)

In the equation, $c_0$ to $c_4$ are the coefficients, and the percentages in brackets represent the ratios' contributions to the power of the model.

The benchmark used to detect success or failure is 0.2. Companies scoring above 0.2 are unlikely to fail, while companies scoring less than 0.2 demonstrate the same symptoms as companies that have failed in the past.

### PAS-score: performance analysis score

Taffler adapted the Z-score technique to develop the PAS-score. The PAS-score evaluates company performance relative to other companies in the industry and incorporates changes in the economy.

The PAS-score ranks all company Z-scores in percentile terms, measuring relative performance on a scale of 0 to 100. A PAS-score of $X$ means that $100 - X\%$ of the companies have scored higher Z-scores. So, a PAS-score of 80 means that only 20% of the companies in the comparison have achieved higher Z-scores.

The PAS-score details the relative performance trend of a company over time. Any downward trends should be investigated immediately and the management should take appropriate action.

### SMEs and failure prediction

The effectiveness of applying a failure prediction model is not restricted to large companies. This is illustrated by research[15] conducted in New Zealand where such a model was applied to 185 SMEs and found to be useful. As with all models, it is also helpful to refer to other supplementary information that may be available, e.g. other credit reports, credit managers' assessments and trade magazines.

## 29.9.2 H-scores

An H-score is produced by Company Watch to determine overall financial health. The H-score is an enhancement of the Z-score technique in giving more emphasis to the strength of the statement of financial position. The Company Watch system calculates a score ranging from 0 to 100 with below 25 being in the danger zone. It takes into account profit management, asset management and funding management using seven factors: profit from the statement of income; three factors from the asset side of the statement of financial position, namely current asset cover, inventory and trade receivables management and liquidity; and three factors from the liability side of the statement of financial position, namely equity base, debt dependence and current funding.

The factors are taken from published financial statements, which makes the approach taken by the IASB to bring off-balance-sheet transactions onto the statement of financial position particularly important.

The ability to chart each factor against the sector average and to 25 level criteria over a five-year period means that it is valuable for a range of user needs, from trade creditors considering extending or continuing to allow credit to potential lenders and equity investors and the big four accounting firms in reviewing audit risk. The model also has the ability to process 'what-ifs'.

It appears to be a robust, useful and exciting tool for all user groups. It is not simply a tool for measuring risk. It can also be used by investors to identify companies whose share price might have fallen but which might be financially strong with the possibility of the share price recovering – it can indicate 'buy' situations. It is also used by leading firms of accountants for the purpose of targeting companies in need of turnaround. Further information appears on the company's website at www.companywatch.net which includes additional examples.

### 29.9.3 The A-score model

This is a qualitative model which concentrates on non-financial signs of failure.[16] This method sets out to quantify different judgemental factors.

#### Management defects and strategic mistakes

The whole basis of the analysis is that financial difficulties are the direct result of management defects and strategic mistakes which can be evidenced by symptoms. A weighting is then attached to individual defects and mistakes.

For example, in looking at management defects a weighting system might be applied such as:

| | Weight |
|---|---|
| *Defects in operational management:* | |
| The chief executive is an autocrat | 8 |
| The chief executive is also the chairman | 4 |
| The board is unbalanced, e.g. too few with finance experience | 2 |
| *Defects in financial management:* | |
| There are no budgets for budgetary control | 3 |
| Weak finance director | 3 |
| There is a poor response to change, e.g. out-of-date plant, old-fashioned products, poor marketing | 15 |

To calculate a company A-score, different scores are allocated to each defect, mistake and symptom according to their importance. Then this score is compared with the benchmark values. If companies achieve an overall score of over 25, or a defect score of over 10, or a mistakes score of over 15, then the company is demonstrating typical signs leading up to failure. Generally, companies not at risk will score below 18, and companies which are at risk will score well over 25.

#### Symptoms

With an adverse A-score, symptoms of failure will start to arise. These are directly attributable to preceding management mistakes. Typical symptoms are financial signs (e.g. poor ratios, poor Z-scores); creative accounting (management might attempt to 'disguise' signs of failure in the accounts); non-financial signs (e.g. investment decisions delayed; market share drops); and terminal signs (when the financial collapse of the company is imminent).

It is interesting to see the weighting given to the chief executive being an autocrat, which is supported by the experience in failures such as Worldcom in 2002 with the following comment:[17]

> **'Autocratic style'**
> Worldcom pursued an aggressive strategy under Ebbers . . . In 1998, Ebbers cemented his reputation when Worldcom purchased MCI for $40bn – the largest acquisition in corporate history at that time . . . But according to one journalist in Mississippi who followed Worldcom from its inception, the seeds of the disaster were sown from the start by Ebbers' aggressive autocratic management style.

However, there are also limitations to participative management which could lead to slow reaction to change in a fast-moving environment.[18]

### 29.9.4 Failure prediction combining cash flow and accrual data

There is a continuing interest in identifying variables which have the ability to predict the likelihood of corporate failure – particularly if this only requires a small number of variables. One study[19] indicated that a parsimonious model that included only three financial variables, namely a cash flow, a profitability and a financial leverage variable, was accurate in 83% of the cases in predicting corporate failure one year ahead.

## 29.10 Professional risk assessors

Credit agencies such as Standard & Poor and Moody's Investor Services assist investors, lenders and trade creditors by providing a credit rating service. Companies are given a rating that can range from AAA for companies with a strong capacity to meet their financial commitments down to D for companies that have been unable to make contractual payments or have filed for bankruptcy, with more than 10 ratings in between, e.g. BBB for companies that have adequate capacity but which are vulnerable to internal or external economic changes.

### 29.10.1 How are ratings set?

The credit agencies take a broad range of internal company and external factors into account. Internal company factors may include:

- an appraisal of the financial reports to determine:
  - trading performance, e.g. return on equity (ROE) and return on assets (ROA); earnings volatility; how well a company has coped with business cycles and severe competition;
  - cash flow adequacy, e.g. EBITDA interest cover; EBIT interest cover; free operating cash flow;
  - capital structure, e.g. gearing ratio; any off-balance-sheet financing;
- a consideration of the notes to the accounts to determine possible adverse implications, e.g. contingent liabilities, whether the company is fixed-capital- or working-capital-intensive or has heavy capital investment commitments;
- meetings and discussions with management;
- monitoring expectation, e.g. against quarterly reports, company press releases, profit warnings;
- monitoring changes in company strategy, e.g. changes to funding structure with company buyback of shares, new divestment or acquisition plans and implications for any debt covenants.

However, experience with companies such as Enron makes it clear that off-balance-sheet transactions can make appraisal difficult even for professional agencies if companies continue to avoid transparency in their reporting.

External factors may include:

- growth prospects, e.g. trends in industry sector; technology possible changes; peer comparison;

- competitors, e.g. the major domestic and foreign competitors; product differentiation; barriers to entry;

- keeping a watching brief on macroeconomic factors, e.g. environmental statutory levies, tax changes, political changes such as restrictions on the supply of oil, foreign currency risks.

### 29.10.2 Regulation of credit rating agencies

Since the credit crisis there has been severe criticism that credit rating agencies had not been independent when rating financial products. The agencies have been self-regulated but this has been totally inadequate in curtailing conflicts of interest. The conflicts have arisen because they were actively involved in the design of products (collateralised debt obligations) to which they then gave an 'objective' credit rating which did not clearly reflect the true risks associated with investing in them. This conflict of interest was compounded by the fact that (a) agency staff were free to join a company after rating its products, and (b) the companies issuing the products paid their fees.

The following swingeing comments were made by the ACCA:[20]

> *Regulation of credit agencies*
> It's a joke that an industry with such influence, particularly during the current volatile economic climate, is self-regulated and only subject to a toothless voluntary code of conduct.
>
> The mere fact that credit rating agencies are paid by the companies they rate puts their independence in jeopardy . . . greater transparency is required . . . We have to strike the right balance when regulating the market between protecting and over-burdening. A range of measures is necessary to bring about transparency in the ratings process . . . Regulation would be part of the solution, but it can't be used in isolation . . . This is a perfect example for when an international set of regulations and other measures are imperative to regain trust in financial markets and avoid further credit crunched victims.

This has led to a call for both Europe and the US to regulate the agencies.

### European Commission Agency Regulation[20]

In November 2008, the European Commission adopted a proposal for a Regulation on Credit Rating Agencies, which would require agencies to have procedures in place to ensure that:

- ratings are not affected by conflicts of interest;

- credit rating agencies have a high standard for the quality of the rating methodology and the ratings; and

- credit rating agencies act in a transparent manner.

The intention is that the agencies would remain responsible for the content of the ratings.

In 2014 the Commission adopted a report on the feasibility of a network of smaller credit rating agencies to facilitate their growth to become more competitive market players.

## 29.11 Valuing shares of an unquoted company – quantitative process

The valuation of shares brings together a number of different financial accounting procedures that we have covered in previous chapters. The assumptions may be highly subjective, but there is a standard approach. This involves the following:

- Estimate the maintainable income flow based on earnings defined in accordance with the IIMR guidelines, as described in Chapter 27. Normally the profits of the past five years are used, adjusted for any known or expected future changes.

- Estimate an appropriate dividend yield, as described in Section 29.7.5, if valuing a non-controlling holding.

- Estimate an appropriate PE or earnings yield if valuing a majority holding. In the UK there is now a Valuation Index[21] focused on SMEs which is the result of UK200's Corporate Finance members providing key data on actual transactions involving the purchase or sale of real businesses (in the form of asset or share deals) over the past five years. The average PE ratio at November 2011 stood at 6.0 and the ratio of deal value to EBITDA had increased from 4.6 to 4.9 times. Average deal size in the last two years continued to be just under £3m.

- Make a decision on any adjustment to the required yields. For example, the shares in the unquoted company might not be as marketable as those in the comparative quoted companies and the required yield would therefore be increased to reflect this lack of marketability; or the statement of financial position might not be as strong with lower current/acid test ratios or higher gearing, which would also lead to an increase in the required yield.

- Calculate the economic capital value, as described in Chapter 6, by applying the required yield to the income flow.

- Compare the resulting value with the net realisable value (NRV), as described in Chapter 7, when deciding what action to take based on the economic value.

EXAMPLE · The Doughnut Ltd is an unlisted company engaged in the baking of doughnuts. The statement of financial position of the Doughnut Ltd as at 31 December 20X9 showed:

|  | £000 | £000 |
|---|---|---|
| Freehold land | | 100 |
| Non-current assets at cost | 240 | |
| Accumulated depreciation | 40 | |
| | | 200 |
| Current assets | 80 | |
| Current liabilities | (60) | |
| | | 20 |
| | | 320 |
| Share capital in £1 shares | | 300 |
| Retained earnings | | 20 |
| | | 320 |
| *Estimated net realisable values:* | | |
| Freehold land | | 180 |
| Plant and equipment | | 120 |
| Current assets | | 70 |

The company achieved the following profit after tax (adjusted to reflect maintainable earnings) for the past five years ended 31 December:

|  | 20X5 | 20X6 | 20X7 | 20X8 | 20X9 |
|---|---|---|---|---|---|
| Maintainable earnings (£000) | 36 | 40 | 44 | 38 | 42 |
| Dividend payout history: Dividends | 10% | 10% | 12% | 12% | 12% |

Current yields for comparative quoted companies as at 31 December 20X9:

|  | Earnings yield % | Dividend yield % |
|---|---|---|
| Ace Bakers plc | 14 | 8 |
| Busi-Bake plc | 10 | 8 |
| Hard-to-beat plc | 13 | 8 |

### Acquiring a majority holding

You are required to value a holding of 250,000 shares for a shareholder, Mr Quick, who makes a practice of buying shares for sale within three years.

Now, the 250,000 shares represent an 83% holding. This is a majority holding and the steps to value it are as follows:

1 Calculate average maintainable earnings (in £000):

$$\frac{36,000 + 40,000 + 44,000 + 38,000 + 42,000}{5} = £40,000$$

2 Estimate an appropriate earnings yield:

$$\frac{14\% + 10\% + 13\%}{3} = 12.3\%$$

3 Adjust the rate for lack of marketability by, say, 3% and for the lower current ratio (of 1.3:1) by, say, 2%. Both these adjustments are subjective and would be a matter of negotiation between the parties.

| | |
|---|---|
| Required yield | =12.3 |
| Lack of marketability weighting | = 3.0 |
| Statement of financial position weakness | = 2.0 |
| Required earnings yield | =17.3 |

The adjustments depend on the actual circumstances. For instance, there might be negotiation over the use of the average of £40,000 with differing views on growth and, if Mr Quick were intending to hold the shares as a long-term investment, there might be less need to increase the required return for lack of marketability.

4 Calculate share value:

$$(£40,000 \times 100/17.3)/300,000 = 77p$$

5 Compare with the net realisable values on the basis that the company was to be liquidated:

| | £ |
|---|---|
| Net realisable values = 70,000 + 120,000 + 180,000 = | 370,000 |
| *Less:* Current liabilities | 60,000 |
| | 310,000 |
| Net asset value per share = £310,000/300,000 = | £1.03 |

The comparison indicates that, on the information we have been given, Mr Quick is paying less than the net realisable value, but the difference may not be enough to justify acquiring the shares in order to asset strip and liquidate the company to make an immediate capital gain.

### Acquiring a minority holding

Let us extend our illustration by assuming that, if Mr Quick acquires control, it is intended to replace the non-current assets at a cost of £20,000 per year out of retained earnings. One of the remaining minority shareholders, Ms Croissant, wishes to dispose of shares and is in discussion with Mr Small who has £10,000 to invest. You are required to calculate for Mr Small how many shares he should aim to acquire from Ms Croissant.

There are two significant changes: the cash available for distribution as dividends will be reduced by £20,000 per year, which is used to replace non-current assets; and Mr Small is acquiring only a minority holding, which means that the appropriate valuation method is the **dividend yield** rather than the **earnings yield**.

The share value will be calculated as follows:

1  Estimate income flow:

|  | £ |
|---|---|
| Maintainable earnings | 40,000 |
| Less: CAPEX | 20,000 |
| Cash available for distribution | 20,000 |

Note that we are here calculating not distributable profits, but the available cash flow.

2  Required dividend yield:

|  | % |
|---|---|
| Average dividend yield | 8.0 |
| Lack of negotiability, say | 2.0 |
| Financial risk, say | 1.5 |
|  | 11.5 |

3  Share value:

$$\frac{£20,000}{300,000} \times \frac{100}{11.5} = 58p$$

At this price it would be possible for Mr Small to acquire (£10,000/58p) = 17,241 shares.

## 29.12 Valuing shares of an unquoted company – qualitative process

In the section above we illustrated how to value shares using the capitalisation of earnings and capitalisation of dividends methods. However, share valuation is an extremely subjective exercise.

A company's future cash flows may be affected by a number of factors. These may occur as a result of a change of control, action within the company (e.g. management change, revenue investment) or external events (e.g. change in the rate of inflation, change in competitive pressures).

- **Change of control:**
  - Aer Lingus said the offer in 2012 of €1.30 (£1.02) per share by Ryanair was 31% below the €1.87 cash per share based on the company's cash balance of €1bn.
  - Ryanair in its offer document said it would grow jobs at Aer Lingus and raise the flag carrier's passenger numbers from 9.5 million a year to 14 million, by cutting Aer Lingus ticket prices and improving the productivity of Aer Lingus staff in order to hold down costs and maintain profit margins.

- **Management change** often heralds a significant change in a company's share price. For example, car and bike parts retailer Halfords' share price jumped after the company appointed a new Chief Executive Officer in October 2012 following the abrupt departure of David Wild in the summer, as it revealed that full-year profits would be at the top end of guidance after a strong second quarter.

- **Revenue investment** refers to discretionary revenue expenditure, such as charges to the income statement for research and development, training and advertising. It also relates to expenditure on costs such as amount of office space provided and travel expense allowed. Where in the recession there had been a reduction in face-to-face meetings and an increase in video- and web-conferencing, there is ongoing pressure to maintain this process into the future.

- **Changes in the rate of inflation** can affect the required yield. If, for example, it is expected that inflation will fall, this might mean that past percentage yields will be higher than the percentage yield that is likely to be available in the future.

- **Change in competitive pressures** can affect future sales. For example, increased foreign competition could mean that past maintainable earnings are not achievable in the future and the historic average level might need to be reduced.

These are a few of the internal and external factors that can affect the valuation of a share. The factors that are relevant to a particular company may be industry-wide (e.g. change in rate of inflation), sector-wide (e.g. change in competitive pressure) or company-specific (e.g. loss of key managers or employees).

If the company supports the acquisition of the shares, the valuer will be able to gain access to relevant internal information. For example, details of research and development expenditure may be available analysed by type of technology involved, by product line, by project and by location, and distinguishing internal from externally acquired R&D.

If the acquisition is being considered without the company's knowledge or support, the valuer will rely more heavily on information gained from public sources, e.g. statutory and voluntary disclosures in the annual accounts and industry information such as trade journals. Information on areas such as R&D may be provided in the OFR (Operating and Financial Review or Strategic Report), but probably in an aggregated form, constrained by management concerns about use by potential competitors.[22]

There is an increasing wealth of financial and narrative disclosures to assist investors in making their investment decisions. There are external data such as the various multivariate Z-scores and H-scores and professional credit agency ratings; and there is greater internal disclosure of financial data such as TSR and EVA data indicating how well companies have managed value in comparison with a peer group and of narrative information such as the IFRS Practice Statement *Management Commentary*. It is also easier to access companies' financial data through the Web.

### Literature search of qualitative factors which can lead to improved or reduced valuations

There is an interesting research report[23] investigating the nature of SME intangible assets in which the researchers have reported the following:

- **Factors identified in the literature as enhancing achieved price**: transportable business with a transferable customer base; non-cancellable service agreements and beneficial contractual arrangements; unexploited property situations; synergistic and cost-saving benefits; under-exploited brands and products; customer base providing cross-selling opportunities; competitor elimination, increased market share; complementary product or service range; market entry – a quick way of overcoming entry barriers; buy into new technology; access to distribution channels; and non-competition agreements.

● **Factors identified in the literature as diminishing achieved price:** confused accounts; poor housekeeping, doubtful debts, under-utilised equipment, outstanding litigation, etc.; over-dependence upon owner and key individuals; over-dependence on a small number of customers; unrelated side activities; poor or out-of-date company image; long-term contracts about to finish; poor liquidity; poor performance; minority and 'messy' ownership structures; inability to substantiate ownership of assets; and uncertainties surrounding liabilities.

Not all of these satisfy the criteria for recognition in annual financial statements.

## 29.13 Possible effect of 'Brexit' on financial statements

We have seen in Chapters 28 and 29 that ratio analysis is used to assess past performance and the strength of the statement of financial position with a view to (a) satisfying that there is appropriate stewardship over the assets under the management's control and (b) making predictions about the future performance and financial health of a company.

'Brexit' (the word coined in the UK media to describe the UK's 2016 referendum vote to leave the EU and consequences thereof) does not mean that we have to change our use of the pyramid of ratios when analysing financial statements. Our approach and interpretation is, however, coloured by the increased uncertainty that Brexit has created.

### Effect of uncertainty

One of the major effects of Brexit from the viewpoint of all stakeholders has been that it has created a higher level of uncertainty that affects both the income statement and the statement of position. Investors and analysts will, therefore, need to be aware of any potential industry-wide effects and the risks that arise from these.

**(a) Income statement**

    (i) Revenue – the effect depends on the industry, with varying opportunities and threats. In the tourist industry, for example, foreign holidays might be adversely affected by any fall in the rates of exchange, which could in turn lead to possible pressure on the cash flow and even the collapse of a tour company. On the other hand, the UK hospitality sector might well benefit from the opportunity for increased local demand and increased overseas visitors enjoying the benefit of any fall in sterling.

    (ii) Costs – again the effect depends on the industry – airlines and transport might be adversely affected by possible increases in any costs denominated in US dollars.

### Audit implications

Auditors will be considering how risks, such as a lower profit, might impact on company behaviour where, say, remuneration and bonuses are based on earnings growth or there is the risk of breaching loan covenants.

Particular attention will need to be paid to all discretionary expenses and the possible future impact if these are reduced – what effect is likely, for instance, from any reduction in advertising, marketing or supplier inducements? Costs that are based on management's subjective estimation will also need to be viewed carefully – has the percentage wastage rate in a retail organisation, for instance, suddenly been forecast to be at a lower rate?

Of course, it is not all negative, and it may well be that new trade deals lead to lower costs with alternative sources of supply becoming available.

### (a) Statement of financial position

(i) Assets – intangible, tangible non-current and current assets will all need to be reviewed carefully to identify any specific adverse changes that might arise from Brexit.

Longer-term economic changes that might arise following the referendum vote to leave the EU could trigger a company's need to test its finite-lived intangibles such as goodwill, customer relationships and royalty agreements for impairment.

How, for example, is goodwill affected if it has arisen on the acquisition of a financial services company if EU passporting (where, by using a UK licence as a European passport, foreign financial firms can offer their financial services throughout the EEA) should be no longer available?

(ii) Liabilities – if financial difficulties arise due to Brexit there might be a need to restructure debt at a different interest rate to strengthen the balance sheet or avoid breaching loan covenants.

### Narrative

Given the uncertainty it is increasingly important to read the narrative in the Annual Report – the Strategic Report, the Chairman's Statement, the enhanced auditor's report and explanations if there has been changes in, say, accounting policies or levels of exceptional items.

Auditors have always had to approach an audit with a degree of scepticism – following Brexit, this has become even more so.

## Summary

This chapter has introduced a number of additional analytical techniques to complement the pyramid approach to ratio analysis discussed in the previous chapter.

The increasing use of 'non-GAAP' cash-based ratios was discussed to reduce the effect of subjective judgements. The use of ratio thresholds was discussed in determining shariah compliance and in setting debt covenants.

The calculation of EVA and TSR was explained, statuary disclosures in the UK were illustrated and their use in the context of performance-related remuneration was discussed. In addition, this chapter has described the use of ratios in the valuation of unquoted shares.

All users of financial statements (both internal and external users) should be prepared to utilise any or all of the interpretive techniques suggested in this chapter and the preceding one. These techniques help to evaluate the financial health and performance of a company. Users should approach these financial indicators with real curiosity – any unexplained or unanswered questions arising from this analysis should form the basis of a more detailed examination of the company accounts.

## REVIEW QUESTIONS

**1** It has been suggested that the growth in profits can be achieved by accounting sleight of hand rather than genuine economic growth. Consider how 'accounting sleight of hand' can be used to report increased profits and discuss what measures can be taken to mitigate against the possibility of this happening.

**2** Explain how the use of debt can improve returns to equity shareholders in good years and increase their losses in poor years.

**3** Telecomsabroad plc has a dividend payout ratio of 95%. Discuss why using the ratio of free cash flow to dividend might influence your assessment of dividend growth.

**4** Discuss the difficulties when attempting to identify comparator companies for benchmarking as, for example, when selecting a TSR peer group.

**5** The Unilever annual review stated:

Total Shareholder Return (TSR) is a concept used to compare the performance of different companies' stocks and shares over time. It combines share price appreciation and dividends paid to show the total return to the shareholder. The absolute size of the TSR will vary with stock markets, but the relative position is a reflection of the market perception of overall performance relative to a reference group. The Company calculates the TSR over a three-year rolling period . . . Unilever has set itself a TSR target in the top third of a reference group of 21 . . . companies.

Discuss (a) why a three-year rolling period has been chosen, and (b) the criteria you consider appropriate for selecting the reference group of companies.

**6** Discuss Z-score analysis with particular reference to Altman's Z-score and Taffler's Z-score. In particular:

(i) What are the benefits of Z-score analysis?

(ii) What criticisms can be levelled at Z-score analysis?

**7** Identify the two most significant variables in the Altman's and Taffler's Z-scores and discuss why each variable might have been selected.

**8** Discuss three situations when management might be under pressure to adopt an aggressive earnings management approach.

**9** Explain how and why EVA is calculated.

**10** Discuss the advantages and disadvantages of all companies adopting the ratio criteria required to be shariah-compliant.

**11** Describe the measures taken to reduce the risk that credit rating agencies can mislead investors.

**12** The following is an extract from the Bayer AG 2012 Annual Report:

The value-based indicators aid management's decision-making, especially regarding strategic portfolio optimization and the allocation of resources for acquisitions and capital expenditures. The focus at the operational level is on the key drivers of enterprise value: growth (sales), cost efficiency

(EBITDA) and capital efficiency (working capital, capital expenditures), since these directly affect value creation.

Discuss (a) why and how EBITDA is used as a driver for cost efficiency, and (b) how capital efficiency is determined in relation to working capital and capital expenditures.

**13** Discuss how the following might be used by a shareholder and by the management:

(i) The ratio of dividends plus share price movement to the opening share price.

(ii) Accounting profit less an additional charge for the use of equity capital.

**14** The finance director was investigating a potential acquisition. As part of the exercise she gave your colleague the current value of total assets, the post-tax operating income, the economic life of the assets and the scrap value of the assets with a request to calculate the cash flow return on investment (CFROI) for the company. Your colleague has asked you to explain to him (a) how this is done or where he could find further information about this on the Web, and (b) how the CFROI will be used.

**15** Hard Times Ltd has been just about breaking even. It has recently identified a new project which will improve its ROC. Discuss whether entering into the project will always be to the advantage of the shareholders considering WACC.

**16** There are differences of opinion as to whether alternative performance measures (APMs) should be prescribed by the IASB or whether they should remain as defined by management. Discuss arguments for and against prescription.

## EXERCISES

### * Question 1

Belt plc and Braces plc were in the same industry. The following information appeared in their 20X9 accounts:

|  | Belt | Braces |
|---|---|---|
|  | €m | €m |
| Revenue | 200 | 300 |
| Total operating expenses | 180 | 275 |
| Average total assets during 20X9 | 150 | 125 |

Required:
(a) Calculate the following ratios for each company and show the numerical relationship between them:
  (i) Their rate of return on the average total assets.
  (ii) The net profit percentages.
  (iii) The ratio of revenue to average total assets.
(b) Comment on the relative performance of the two companies.
(c) State any additional information you would require as:
  (i) A potential shareholder.
  (ii) A potential loan creditor.

## * Question 2

Quickserve plc is a food wholesale company. Its financial statements for the years ended 31 December 20X8 and 20X9 are as follows:

### Statements of income

|  | 20X9 | 20X8 |
|---|---|---|
|  | £000 | £000 |
| Sales revenue | 12,000 | 15,000 |
| Gross profit | 3,000 | 3,900 |
| Distribution costs | 500 | 600 |
| Administrative expenses | 1,500 | 1,000 |
| Operating profit | 1,000 | 2,300 |
| Interest receivable | 80 | 100 |
| Interest payable | (400) | (350) |
| Profit before taxation | 680 | 2,050 |
| Income taxation | 240 | 720 |
| Profit after taxation | 440 | 1,330 |
| Dividends in SOCE | 800 | 600 |

### Statements of financial position

|  | 20X9 | 20X8 |
|---|---|---|
|  | £000 | £000 |
| *Non-current assets:* |  |  |
| Intangible assets | 200 | — |
| Tangible assets | 4,000 | 7,000 |
| Investments | 600 | 800 |
|  | 4,800 | 7,800 |
| *Current assets:* |  |  |
| Inventory | 250 | 300 |
| Trade receivables | 1,750 | 2,500 |
| Cash & bank | 1,500 | 200 |
|  | 3,500 | 3,000 |
| Total assets | 8,300 | 10,800 |
| *Equity and reserves:* |  |  |
| Ordinary shares of 10p each | 1,000 | 1,000 |
| Share premium account | 1,000 | 1,000 |
| Revaluation reserve | 1,110 | 1,750 |
| Retained earnings | 3,190 | 3,550 |
|  | 6,300 | 7,300 |
| Debentures | 1,000 | 2,000 |
| Current liabilities | 1,000 | 1,500 |
|  | 8,300 | 10,800 |

### Required:

(a) Describe the concerns of the following users and how reading an annual report might help satisfy these concerns:
  (i) employees;
  (ii) bankers;
  (iii) shareholders.

(b) Calculate relevant ratios for Quickserve and suggest how each of the above user groups might react to these.

## * Question 3

The following are the accounts of Bouncy plc, a company that manufactures playground equipment, for the year ended 30 November 20X6.

### Statements of comprehensive income for years ended 30 November

|  | 20X6 | 20X5 |
|---|---|---|
|  | £000 | £000 |
| Profit before interest and tax | 2,200 | 1,570 |
| Interest expense | 170 | 150 |
| Profit before tax | 2,030 | 1,420 |
| Taxation | 730 | 520 |
| Profit after tax | 1,300 | 900 |
| Dividends paid in SOCE | 250 | 250 |

### Statements of financial position as at 30 November 20X6

|  | 20X6 | 20X5 |
|---|---|---|
|  | £000 | £000 |
| Non-current assets (written-down value) | 6,350 | 5,600 |
| Current assets |  |  |
| Inventories | 2,100 | 2,070 |
| Receivables | 1,710 | 1,540 |
| Total assets | 10,160 | 9,210 |
| Creditors: amounts due within one year |  |  |
| Trade payables | 1,040 | 1,130 |
| Taxation | 550 | 450 |
| Bank overdraft | 370 | 480 |
| Total assets less current liabilities | 8,200 | 7,150 |
| Creditors: amounts due after more than one year |  |  |
| 10% debentures 20X7/20X8 | 1,500 | 1,500 |
|  | 6,700 | 5,650 |
| Capital and reserves |  |  |
| Share capital: ordinary shares of 50p fully paid up | 3,000 | 3,000 |
| Share premium | 750 | 750 |
| Retained earnings | 2,950 | 1,900 |
|  | 6,700 | 5,650 |

The directors are considering two schemes to raise £6,000,000 in order to repay the debentures and finance expansion estimated to increase profit before interest and tax by £900,000. It is proposed to make a dividend of 6p per share whether funds are raised by equity or loan. The two schemes are:

1 an issue of 13% debentures redeemable in 30 years;

2 a rights issue at £1.50 per share. The current market price is £1.80 per share (20X5: £1.50; 20X4: £1.20).

Assume a corporation tax rate of 40%.

### Required:
(a) Calculate the return on equity and any three investment ratios of interest to a potential investor.
(b) Calculate three ratios of interest to a potential long-term lender.

(c) Report briefly on the performance and state of the business from the viewpoint of a potential shareholder and lender using the ratios calculated above and explain any weaknesses in these ratios.

(d) Advise management which scheme they should adopt on the basis of your analysis above and explain what other information may need to be considered when making the decision.

## Question 4

Sally Gorden seeks your assistance to decide whether she should invest in Ruby plc or Sapphire plc. Both companies are quoted on the London Stock Exchange. Their shares were listed on 20 June 20X4 as Ruby 110p and Sapphire 120p.

The performance of these two companies during the year ended 30 June 20X4 is summarised as follows:

|  | Ruby plc £000 | Sapphire plc £000 |
|---|---|---|
| Operating profit | 588 | 445 |
| Interest and similar charges | (144) | (60) |
|  | 444 | 385 |
| Taxation | (164) | (145) |
| Profit after taxation | 280 | 240 |
| Interim dividend paid | (30) | — |
| Preference dividend paid | (90) | — |
| Ordinary dividend paid | (60) | (160) |

The companies have been financed on 30 June 20X4 as follows:

|  | Ruby plc £000 | Sapphire plc £000 |
|---|---|---|
| Ordinary shares of 50p each | 1,000 | 1,500 |
| 15% preference shares of £1 each | 600 | — |
| Share premium account | 60 | — |
| Retained earnings | 250 | 450 |
| 17% debentures | 800 | — |
| 12% debentures | — | 500 |
|  | 2,710 | 2,450 |

On 1 October 20X3 Ruby plc issued 500,000 ordinary shares of 50p each at a premium of 20%. On 1 April 20X4 Sapphire plc made a 1 for 2 bonus issue. Apart from these, there has been no change in the issued capital of either company during the year.

### Required:
(a) Calculate the earnings per share (EPS) of each company.
(b) Determine the price/earnings ratio (PE) of each company.
(c) Based on the PE ratio alone, which company's shares would you recommend to Sally?
(d) On the basis of appropriate accounting ratios (which should be calculated), identify three other matters Sally should take account of before she makes her choice.
(e) Describe the advantages and disadvantages of gearing.

## * Question 5

Growth plc made a cash offer for all of the ordinary shares of Beta Ltd on 30 September 20X9 at £2.75 per share. Beta's accounts for the year ended 31 March 20X9 showed:

|  | £000 |
|---|---|
| Profit for the year after tax | 750 |
| Dividends paid | 250 |

### Statement of financial position as at 31 March 20X9

|  |  | £000 |
|---|---|---|
| Buildings | | 1,600 |
| Other tangible non-current assets | | 1,400 |
| | | 3,000 |
| Current assets | 2,000 | |
| Current liabilities | 1,400 | |
| | | 600 |
| | | 3,600 |
| £1 ordinary shares | | 2,500 |
| Retained earnings | | 1,100 |
| | | 3,600 |

Additional information:

(i) The half yearly profits to 30 September 20X9 show an increase of 25% over those of the corresponding period in 20X8. The directors are confident that this pattern will continue, or increase even further.

(ii) The Beta directors hold 90% of the ordinary shares.

(iii) The following valuations are available:

*Realisable values*

|  | £000 |
|---|---|
| Buildings | 2,500 |
| Other non-current assets | 700 |
| Current assets | 2,500 |

*Net replacement values*

|  | £000 |
|---|---|
| Buildings | 2,600 |
| Other non-current assets | 1,800 |
| Current assets | 2,200 |

(iv) Shares in quoted companies in the same sector have a PE ratio of 10. Beta Ltd is an unquoted company.

(v) One of the shareholders is a bank manager who advises the directors to press for a better price.

(vi) The extra risk for unquoted companies is 25% in this sector.

**Required:**
(a) Calculate valuations for the Beta ordinary shares using four different bases of valuation.
(b) Draft a report highlighting the limitations of each basis and advise the directors whether the offer is reasonable.

## Question 6

R. Johnson inherited 810,000 £1 ordinary shares in Johnson Products Ltd on the death of his uncle in 20X5. His uncle had been the founder of the company and managing director until his death. The remainder of the issued shares were held in small lots by employees and friends, with no one holding more than 4%.

R. Johnson is planning to emigrate and is considering disposing of his shareholding. He has had approaches from three parties, who are:

1  A competitor – Sonar Products Ltd. Sonar Products Ltd considers that Johnson Products Ltd would complement its own business and is interested in acquiring all of the 810,000 shares. Sonar Products Ltd currently achieves a post-tax return of 12.5% on capital employed.

2  Senior employees. Twenty employees are interested in making a management buyout with each acquiring 40,500 shares from R. Johnson. They have obtained financial backing, in principle, from the company's bankers.

3  A financial conglomerate – Divest plc. Divest plc is a company that has extensive experience of acquiring control of a company and breaking it up to show a profit on the transaction. It is its policy to seek a pre-tax return of 20% from such an exercise.

The company has prepared draft accounts for the year ended 30 April 20X9. The following information is available.

(a) Past earnings and distributions:

| Year ended 30 April | Profit/(Loss) after tax | Gross dividends declared |
|---|---|---|
| | £ | % |
| 20X5 | 79,400 | 6 |
| 20X6 | (27,600) | — |
| 20X7 | 56,500 | 4 |
| 20X8 | 88,300 | 5 |
| 20X9 | 97,200 | 6 |

(b) Statement of financial position of Johnson Products Ltd as at 30 April 20X9:

| | £000 | £000 |
|---|---|---|
| Non-current assets | | |
| Land at cost | | 376 |
| Premises at cost | 724 | |
| Aggregate depreciation | 216 | |
| | | 508 |
| Equipment at cost | 649 | |
| Aggregate depreciation | 353 | |
| | | 296 |
| Current assets | | |
| Inventories | 141 | |
| Receivables | 278 | |
| Cash at bank | 70 | |
| | 489 | |
| Payables due within one year | (335) | |

|  | £000 | £000 |
|---|---|---|
| Net current assets |  | 154 |
| Non-current liabilities |  | (158) |
|  |  | 1,176 |
| *Represented by:* |  |  |
| £1 ordinary shares |  | 1,080 |
| Retained earnings |  | 96 |
|  |  | 1,176 |

(c) Information on the nearest comparable listed companies in the same industry:

| Company | Profit after tax for 20X9 £000 | Retention % | Gross dividend yield % |
|---|---|---|---|
| Eastron plc | 280 | 25 | 15 |
| Westron plc | 168 | 16 | 10.5 |
| Northron plc | 243 | 20 | 13.4 |

Profit after tax in each of the companies has been growing by approximately 8% per annum for the past five years.

(d) The following is an estimate of the net realisable values of Johnson Products Ltd's assets as at 30 April 20X9:

|  | £000 |
|---|---|
| Land | 480 |
| Premises | 630 |
| Equipment | 150 |
| Receivables | 168 |
| Inventories | 98 |

**Required:**

(a) As accountant for R. Johnson, advise him of the amount that could be offered for his shareholding with a reasonable chance of being acceptable to the seller, based on the information given in the question, by each of the following:
  (i) Sonar Products Ltd;
  (ii) the 20 employees;
  (iii) Divest plc.

(b) As accountant for Sonar Products Ltd, estimate the maximum amount that could be offered by Sonar Products Ltd for the shares held by R. Johnson.

(c) As accountant for Sonar Products Ltd, state the principal matters you would consider in determining the future maintainable earnings of Johnson Products Ltd and explain their relevance.

*(ACCA)*

## Question 7

Harry is about to start negotiations to purchase a controlling interest in NX, an unquoted limited liability company. The following is the statement of financial position of NX as at 30 June 2006, the end of the company's most recent financial year.

*NX*
*Statement of financial position as at 30 June 2006*

| ASSETS | $ |
|---|---|
| Non-current assets | 3,369,520 |
| *Current assets* | |
| Inventories, at cost | 476,000 |
| Trade and other receivables | 642,970 |
| Cash and cash equivalents | 132,800 |
| | 1,251,770 |
| *Total assets* | 4,621,290 |
| LIABILITIES AND EQUITY | |
| Non-current liabilities | |
| 8% loan note | 260,000 |
| | 260,000 |
| *Current liabilities* | |
| Trade and other payables | 467,700 |
| Current tax payable | 414,700 |
| | 882,400 |
| *Equity* | |
| Ordinary shares, 40 cent shares | 2,000,000 |
| 5% preferred shares of $1 | 200,000 |
| Retained profits | 1,278,890 |
| | 3,478,890 |
| Total liabilities | 1,142,400 |
| *Total liabilities and equity* | 4,621,290 |

The non-current assets of NX comprise:

| | Cost | Depreciation | Net |
|---|---|---|---|
| | $ | $ | $ |
| Property | 2,137,500 | 262,500 | 1,875,000 |
| Equipment | 1,611,855 | 515,355 | 1,096,500 |
| Motor vehicles | 696,535 | 298,515 | 398,020 |
| | 4,445,890 | 1,076,370 | 3,369,520 |

NX has grown rapidly since its formation in 2000 by Albert Bell and Candy Dale who are currently directors of the company and who each own half of the company's issued share capital. The company was formed to exploit knowledge developed by Albert Bell. This knowledge is protected by a number of patents and trademarks owned by the company. Candy Dale's expertise was in marketing and she was largely responsible for developing the company's customer base. Figures for turnover and profit after tax taken from the statements of comprehensive income of the company for the past three years are:

| | Turnover | Profit after tax |
|---|---|---|
| | $ | $ |
| Profit for 2004 | 8,218,500 | 1,031,000 |
| Profit for 2005 | 10,273,100 | 1,288,720 |
| Profit for 2006 | 11,414,600 | 991,320 |

NX's property has recently been valued at $3,000,000 and it is estimated that the equipment and motor vehicles could be sold for a total of $1,568,426. The net realisable values of inventory and receivables are estimated at $400,000 and $580,000 respectively. It is estimated that the costs of selling off the company's assets would be $101,000.

The 8% loan note is repayable at a premium of 30% on 31 December 2006 and is secured on the company's property. It is anticipated that it will be possible to repay the loan note by issuing a new loan note bearing interest at 11% repayable in 2012.

As directors of the company, Albert Bell and Candy Dale receive annual remuneration of $99,000 and £74,000 respectively. Both would cease their relationship with NX because they wish to set up another company together. Harry would appoint a general manager at an annual salary of $120,000 to replace Albert Bell and Candy Dale.

Investors in quoted companies similar to NX are currently earning a dividend yield of 6% and the average PE ratio for the sector is currently 11. NX has been paying a dividend of 7% on its common stock for the past two years.

Ownership of the issued common stock and preferred shares is shared equally between Albert Bell and Candy Dale.

Harry wishes to purchase a controlling interest in NX.

**Required:**
(a) On the basis of the information given, prepare calculations of the values of a preferred share and an ordinary share in NX on each of the following bases:
  (i)   net realisable values;
  (ii)  future maintainable earnings.
(b) Advise Harry on other factors which he should be considering in calculating the total amount he may have to pay to acquire a controlling interest in NX.

*(The Association of International Accountants)*

## Question 8

Briefly state:

(i)   the case for segmental reporting;

(ii)  the case against segmental reporting.

## Question 9

Discuss the following issues with regard to financial reporting for risk:

(a) How can a company identify and prioritise its key risks?

(b) What actions can a company take to manage the risks identified in (a)?

(c) How can a company measure risk?

## Notes

1  *No Surprises: The Case for Better Risk Reporting,* ICAEW, 1999.
2  www.frc.org.uk/Our-Work/Publications/ASB/Rising-to-the-Challenge/Full-results-of-a-Review-of-Narrative-Reporting-by.aspx

3  J. Collier, *Aggressive Earnings Management: Is It Still a Significant Threat?*, ICAEW, October 2004.

4  Alpa A. Virdi, *Investors' Confidence in Audited Financial Information*, Research Report, ICAEW, December 2004.

5  C. Minchington and G. Francis, 'Shareholder value', *Management Quarterly*, Part 6, January 2000.

6  www.evadimensions.com

7  www3.cfo.com/article/2011/11/benchmarking_top-and-bottom-25-eva-momentum-ranking-of-large-companies

8  J. Stern, 'Management: its mission and its measure', *Director*, October 1994, pp. 42–44.

9  C. Pratten, *Company Failure*, Financial Reporting and Auditing Group, ICAEW, 1991, pp. 43–5.

10  R.J. Taffler, 'Forecasting company failure in the UK using discriminant analysis and financial ratio data', *Journal of the Royal Statistical Society*, Series A, vol. 145, part 3, 1982, pp. 342–358.

11  M.L. Inman, 'Altman's Z-formula prediction', *Management Accounting*, November 1982, pp. 37–39.

12  E.I. Altman, 'Financial ratios, discriminant analysis and the prediction of corporate bankruptcy', *Journal of Finance*, vol. 23(4), 1968, pp. 589–609.

13  M.L. Inman, 'Z-scores and the going concern review', *ACCA Students' Newsletter*, August 1991, pp. 8–13.

14  R.J. Taffler, 'Z-scores: an approach to the recession', *Accountancy*, July 1991, pp. 95–97.

15  K. Van Peursem and M. Pratt, 'Failure prediction in New Zealand SMEs: measuring signs of trouble', *International Journal of Business Performance Management (IJBPM)*, vol. 8 (2/3), 2006.

16  J. Argenti, 'Predicting corporate failure', *Accountants Digest*, no. 138, Summer 1983, pp. 18–21.

17  http://news.bbc.co.uk/l/hi/business/4352553.stm

18  www.managementstudyguide.com/limitations-of-participitative-management.htm

19  www.accaglobal.com/databases/pressandpolicy/unitedkingdom/3107831

20  http://ec.europa.eu/internal_market/consultations/docs/securities_agencies/consultation-cra-framework_en.pdf

21  www.uk200group.co.uk/Members/SpecialistGroups/SpecialistPanels/CorporateFinance/Sp_Valuations/Sp_Valuations_Home.aspx

22  W.A. Nixon and C.J. McNair, 'A measure of R&D', *Accountancy*, October 1994, p. 138.

23  C. Martin and J. Hartley, *SME Intangible Assets*, Certified Accountants Research Report 93, London, 2006.

# CHAPTER 30

# An introduction to digital financial reporting

## 30.1 Introduction

The main objective of this chapter is to explain the developments in the way that investors and analysts obtain published financial reports and analyse the data.

### Objectives

By the end of this chapter, you should be able to:

- discuss the comparative requirements for financial statements that are both useful for assessing stewardship and decision-useful;
- explain the facilities that assist users to analyse the financial data;
- understand the reason for the development of a business reporting language;
- explain the benefits of tagging in XML and XBRL code data for financial reporting;
- understand why companies should adopt XBRL;
- list the processes a company needs to take to adopt XBRL.

## 30.2 The objectives of financial reporting

There are two objectives of financial reporting. These are that the statements should (a) provide the means for investors to assess the management's stewardship of the company's resources and (b) provide data that is decision-useful.

### 30.2.1 Stewardship

Stewardship is backward-looking. It relies on historical information. It requires this information to be reliable and complete. This historical information has been traditionally in the form of hard copy and this is now supplemented or replaced by reporting on the Internet.

#### Hard copy

This is provided for:

- annual reports which have been:
  - prepared in accordance with IFRSs, EU *Revised Transparency Directive 2013*[1] or national accounting standards;

- audited; and
- published within 4 months of the period end;
- half-yearly condensed financial statements:
  - prepared in accordance with IAS 34 *Interim Financial Reports* or national standards such as the *Disclosure and Transparency Rules* of the UK's Financial Conduct Authority;
  - not audited but reviewed by an auditor in accordance with the *International Standard on Review Engagements;* and
  - published within 2 months of the period end;
- quarterly reports or interim management statements:

  - not audited and published with a caveat such as:[2]

  *This announcement contains forward looking statements which are made in good faith based on the information available at the time of its approval. It is believed that the expectations reflected in these statements are reasonable but they may be affected by a number of risks and uncertainties that are inherent in any forward looking statement which could cause actual results to differ materially from those currently anticipated. Nothing in this document should be regarded as a profits forecast.*

  - The above caveat has legal implications which can vary from country to country.

### PDF files

At an individual company level we find that most companies have a website to communicate all types of information to interested parties including financial information. Stakeholders or other interested parties can then download this information for their own particular use. Most of the financial information is in the format of PDF files created by a software program called Adobe® Acrobat®. This program is used for the conversion of all their documents, which make up the financial information contained within the annual general reports, into one document, a PDF file, for publication on the Internet. This PDF file can be formatted to include encryption and digital signatures to ensure that the document cannot be changed.

In order for the user to be able to read the PDF files, a special software program called Adobe Reader® needs to be downloaded from the Adobe website www.adobe.com.

### 30.2.2 Decision-usefulness

Investors have been assisted in their decision making by access to:

- commercial databases where selected financial reports have been formatted by each database into a standardised format;
- individual company sites where the company provides data in downloadable format. For example, an increasing number of companies such as BP, BMW, Colgate, Dell, Lloyds TSB and Vodacom, have been providing their annual report in a multi-year downloadable Excel format as well as in PDF. Vodacom, for example provides a choice of PDF, Excel or URL formats.

  However, because companies have different items in their financial reports, it is not possible to make a line-by-line comparison. The user needs to synchronise items and to do this needs to be conversant with the accounting definition of each individual item; and
- individual company reports where the information has been described uniformly and tagged as achieved with eXtensible Business Reporting Language (XBRL).

### Commercial databases

Various financial databases have been developed to assist in ratio analysis and the appraisal of inter-period and inter-company performance. This allows subscribers to select peer groups and search across a variety of variables. Students having access to such databases at their own institution may carry out a range of assignments and projects such as selecting companies suitable for takeover based on stated criteria such as ROCE, % sales and % earnings growth.

Financial databases that might be available to students include:

- Fame (Forecasting Analysis & Modeling Environment)
  This database provides detailed, financial, descriptive and ownership information about many public and private companies in the UK and Ireland. Free trials are available for this software.[3] Access through a University Library is also possible.[4]

- Amadeus
  This database provides company information for both Western and Eastern Europe, with a focus on private company information and company financials in a standard format so that you can compare companies across borders.

- Compustat
  These bases provide academic researchers with historical fundamental and market data in a standardised format that allows comparison across companies, industries and business cycles.

- Datastream
  This database providing current/historical financial data for international companies/indices and bond data.

- PI NAVIGATOR

  This database provides the ability to download non-rekeyed financial statements from original PDFs into Excel and locate comparable reports from multiple companies.

For some of the abovementioned data bases access is possible via University's Libraries and students are advised to contact the relevant Librarian.

The fast developing world of Apps for Mobile communication devices also provides products that allow the investor to keep track of their portfolios and business segment interests.[5]

### XBRL

We will now discuss reports and the flow of information possible with the use of XBRL. We will see that information in this format could put the investor in the same position as management itself. This moves on from quarterly reporting towards continuous reporting. Whilst this might be technologically possible an investor would not have the same contextual understanding of the information with an awareness of the probability of change.

Its current strength lies in the possibility it provides of peer review across any of the elements in the statement of income, financial position and cash flows.

## 30.3 Reports and the flow of information pre-XBRL

The information flow from an organisation reporting to stakeholders and regulatory bodies and banks is considerable. The information required is not the same for each of the external parties and so one report is not appropriate.

A typical flow is set out in Figure 30.1 demonstrating how information is collated from Operational Data Stores and coded to the General Ledger (GL) using the chart of accounts

**Figure 30.1 Today: a convoluted information supply chain**

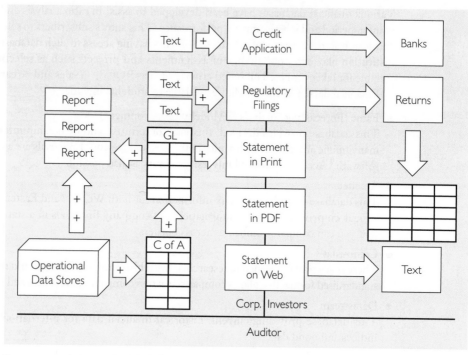

*Source:* www.xbrl.org.au/training/NSWWorkshop.pdf

(C of A). Once the data have been captured in the individual GL accounts, statements of comprehensive income, financial position and cash flows can be produced for shareholders and for statutory filing. In addition, separate reports are produced for a variety of other stakeholders such as the tax authorities, stock exchanges, banks and loan creditors.

The reports can be in different formats such as printed statements for internal management and audit use, hard-copy annual reports for investors, and summary or full reports on a company's home web page in PDF or HTML format, now that this is mandatory (as in the US) or encouraged. This is a very costly process which has led to the development of a special business reporting language called eXtensible Business Reporting Language or **XBRL**, which is based on XML.

## 30.4 What are HTML, XML and XBRL?

XBRL is based upon the eXtensible Markup Language or XML. XML itself is an extension of Hyper Text Markup Language (HTML), which controls the format and display of web pages. We will briefly comment on each.

### HTML

HTML is extensively used in website creation for the purposes of display. For example, the following text using HTML would have tags that describe the format and placement of the text:

**Assets $50,000**
**Liabilities $25,000**
```
<p><b>Assets $50,000</b></p>
<p><b>Liabilities $25,000</b></p>
```
where <p> instructs the item to be printed on the screen (and also where on the screen or in what format) and <b> instructs the item to be displayed in bold print. The </p> denotes the end of the commands and instructs the data to be 'printed' on the computer screen.

### XML

XML is a language developed by the World Wide Web Consortium.[6] It goes one step further by allowing for 'tags' to be created which convey identification and meaning of the data within the tags. Thus instead of looking simply at format and presentation, the XML code looks for the text displayed within the code. For example, the user can design the tags used in XML as follows:

**Assets $50,000** in this example of XML would be written as:
```
<Assets>$50,000</Assets>
```
and similarly for **Liabilities $25,000** the XML code would be:
```
<Liabilities>$25,000</Liabilities>
```
The computer program reading the XML code would thus know that the value found of $50,000 within the tags relates to Assets.

### XBRL

XBRL has taken XML one step further and designed 'tags' based upon the common financial language used. For example, the terms ASSETS and LIABILITIES are common terms used in financial reports even though the calculations or valuations and the definitions used in different accounting standards may be dependent on those accounting standards applicable to the company.

## 30.4.1 Advantages of XBRL

Using XBRL means that it is easier for direct system-to-system information-sharing between a company and its stakeholders and allows for improved analytical capacity. The numeric data in the financial statements of all companies filing their annual reports will be uniformly defined and presented and available for analysis, e.g. downloaded into Excel and other analytical software. According to XBRL International the Core Capabilities are:

> Creating *digital*, unambiguous, *accurate* and reusable versions of financial statements is one of the core capabilities of the XBRL standard.[7]

XBRL International emphasise that **Flexibility** is one of its main capabilities as it gives the organisation the means to create reusable reports with specific inclusions for their business case or business segmentation.

## 30.5 Reports and the flow of information post-XBRL

When XBRL is used, (a) information flows from an organisation to stakeholders are much simpler as seen in Figure 30.2, and (b) it is possible for stakeholders to receive information that can be understood by computer software and allow them to analyse the data obtained, as seen in Figure 30.3.

**Figure 30.2 With XBRL: multiple outlets from a single specification**

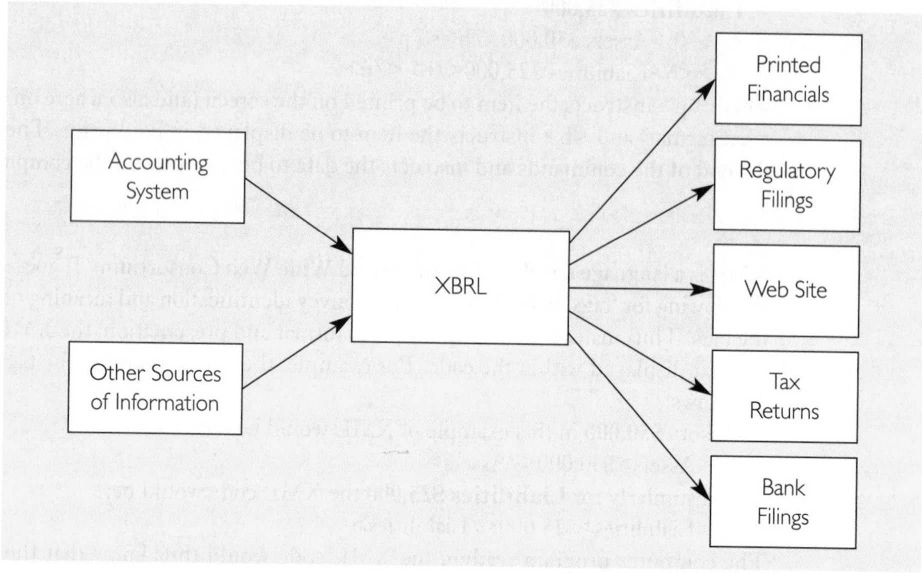

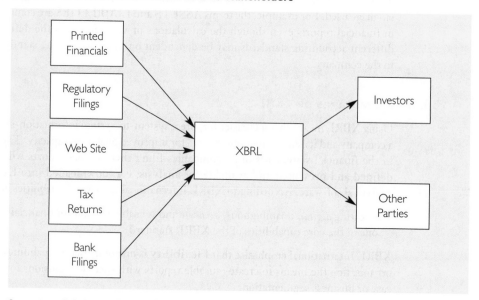

*Source:* http://xbrl.org.au/training/NSWWorkshop.pdf

**Figure 30.3 XBRL: information flow to stakeholders**

*Source:* http://xbrl.org.au/training/NSWWorkshop.pdf

## 30.6 Why are companies adopting XBRL?

We will consider briefly the influence of regulatory requirements, commercial benefits and the views of stakeholders.

### 30.6.1 Regulatory requirements

One of the driving forces has been the pressure from national regulatory bodies for companies to file corporate tax returns, stock exchange and corporate statutory financial statements in XBRL format. In some countries there are specific requirements for financial statements filing.

#### US regulatory requirements

The US Securities and Exchange Commission (SEC) has required[8] public and foreign companies with a float over $5 billion that prepare financial statements based on US GAAP to lodge their reports in XBRL since 2009. This requirement resulted in approximate 500 Companies filing their reports using XBRL in that year.

Foreign companies using IFRS have been required to lodge their financial reports since 2011.

#### UK regulatory requirements

UK companies filing accounts online at Companies House have been required since 2011 to use Inline XBRL (iXBRL). iXBRL is a specific form of XBRL that focuses on the human-readable format.

The usage of iXBrl in the UK is quite high: 97% of electronic submissions consisted of this form of XBRL whilst the other 3% used XBRL. For an example of the differences between XBRL and iXBRL visit http://download.companieshouse.gov.uk/en_accounts-data.html.

Companies House makes data freely available in the form of Monthly Data files from previous financial years as well as daily files containing the Instance documents. The user can download these files for their own purposes. When the file is opened, the financial data can be viewed. To view the XBRL source, right-click and select 'source'.

The files are in Zip format (condensed file format) and the file extension includes the company's ID number and the date on which it was received by the Companies House.

For a sample of both XBRL and iXBRL data visit http://download.companieshouse.gov.uk/en_accountsdata.html (see under 'Additional Information').

HM Revenue and Customs (HMRC) have required companies with a turnover of more than £100,000 to lodge online since 2010.

#### Singaporean regulatory requirements

Singapore's Accounting Corporate Regulatory Authority (ACRA),[9] the regulating authority for businesses incorporated in Singapore, has been receiving company reports for most incorporated commercial companies in XBRL format since 2007.

#### Australia

The Australian government uses XBRL as part of its 'Standard Business Reporting' focus with the greatest use being for the Australian Taxation Office (ATO). The ATO uses it not only for yearly taxation returns but also for 'Business Activity Statements' (BAS) and for the submissions of wage and salary deductions. In total there were about 8.1 million transactions relating to business-to-business transactions and about 1.2 million roll-over transactions for superannuation (retirement/pension) funds. The ATO estimated that the use of SBR would have saved Australian businesses about AUD400 million last year.[10]

However, progress with Annual Financial report submission to the Australian Stock Exchange (ASX) or to the Australian Securities and Investment Commission (ASIC) is slow.

Australian companies have been able to lodge their financial reports using XBRL together with a paper or PDF lodging. A perusal of both their websites revealed that most of the submissions are lodged using PDF formats. This is despite the announcement in May 2015[11] that companies may lodge their financial reports using XBRL or iXBRL and no longer need to lodge it in PDF format.

The Australian Prudential Authority (APRA), the regulator for the banking, insurance, etc. industry, also requires reports to be lodged using XBRL/SBR.[12] APRA requires organisations to lodge their submissions using its own software D2A (direct to Apra)[13]

### 30.6.2 Global perspective and use of XBRL

Table 30.1 lists a variety of uses of XBRL in a global perspective. For example, the use of XBRL in Germany goes far beyond the corporate level into a wide variety of private, public or governmental organisations.

**Table 30.1 XBRL uses worldwide**

| Country | Taxonomy | Collection agency | Data | Filing volume |
|---|---|---|---|---|
| USA | US GAAP | SEC interactive data | Public | 7000 public companies |
| Indonesia | Sharia | Bank Indonesia Islamic Banking Regulatory Reporting System | Private | 571 filing entities |
| Belgium | Belgian | National Bank of Belgium | Freely available | 400,000 companies |
| Denmark | Danish | Danish Business Authority | Public | 210,000 companies |
| United Arab Emirates | IFRS | ESCA Securities Filings Emirates Securities and Commodities Authority | Available for a fee | 250 companies |
| USA | | FFIEC Call Reports (Federal Financial Institution Examination Council | Closed filings | 6900 filers |
| UK | UK iXBRL | HMRC Corporate Tax Returns | Private | ~2.2 million filers |
| UK | UK iXBRL | Companies House Financial Statement Filing | Public | ~1.5 million filers |
| Germany | German | German E. Bilanz, Ministry of Finance | Private | ~1,35 million filers* |
| Japan | Japan iXBRL | JFSA (Japan Financial Services Agency) | Public | ~4,500 companies and 3,500 investment funds |

*Note that Germany has a wide variety of taxonomies for different types of industries in private, public and governmental organisations.

*Source:* Compiled from sources of XBRL international www.xbrl.org/the-standard/why/who-else-uses-xbrl/on 16/05/20116

### 30.6.3 Commercial benefit

The main benefit is that companies can easily generate tailored reports from a single data set and the data can be readily accessed at a lower cost by regulators, auditors, credit rating agencies, investors and research institutions.

Taxonomies can be adapted to reflect the needs of the organisation and new elements can be defined within an existing taxonomy. This makes the use of XBRL more flexible and allows for flexible reports.

This can also lead to an undesirable side effect; that of reporting using Non GAAP reporting. This can result in the publication of data that is not entirely reflective of the true financial position of the organisation. The IASB chair, Hans Hoogevorst, referred to this in his speech at the Korean Accounting association.[14]

Non GAAP disclosures such as an adjusted EPS figure are often used to illustrate and supplement financial information but these can also be misleading. The proliferation of potentially misleading Non GAAP disclosures has been commented upon in 2016 by the SEC.[15]

A study in the UK[16] found that over half investors used Non IFRS reporting figures in their analysis and that some preferred to use both IFRS and Non IFRS in their analysis.

### 30.6.4 The views of stakeholders

A report in 2009, *XBRL: The Views of Stakeholders,*[17] concluded that, overall, there is considerable lack of knowledge of XBRL within UK business. Some of its policy recommendations were that HMRC, Companies House, professional bodies such as ACCA, and IT specialists should publicise the business case for XBRL more widely with the provision of 'hands-on', user-focused sessions that highlight the interoperability and flexibility of XBRL.

The view in a subsequent research paper in the *British Accounting Review*[18] was that XBRL in the UK is still in a 'push' phase as a requirement through government regulation, and that interest from the business community is concerned with compliance rather than seeking to learn more about XBRL. The business stakeholders who responded to the questionnaire saw the time to be invested and the cost of software to be the greatest barriers.

From 2012 to 2013 ACRA (Singapore) conducted a series of studies and public consultation meetings to identify the needs of preparers and users. This was followed up in 2014 with meetings with Focus Groups to test a new preparation tool called BizFin^x. This resulted in the directive that from 3 March 2014, Incorporated Companies must lodge a full set of Financial Statements using XBRL through a special portal at www.bizfinx.gov.sg.[19] The BizFin^x tool provides data analysis reporting key indicators, trends and benchmarking against three competitor companies. It is available for free on the website and new releases are released through ACRA's website.

Overall support for the usage of XBRL was good but focus groups were concerned that there were insufficient skills within the workforce. Another concern was related to adherence to the taxonomy, where it was felt that this did not provide enough flexibility for companies with special needs.

ACRA's response has been to provide training through seminars and provision of help guides. ACRA also plans to engage software vendors keen to develop XBRL capabilities. Training sessions for BizFin^x are ongoing and help guides are freely available on ACRA's website.

## 30.7 What are the processes followed to adopt XBRL for outputting information?

There are four processes, supported by the appropriate software, to be completed to adopt XBRL. The processes are (a) taxonomy design, (b) mapping, (c) creating an instance document, and (d) selecting and applying a stylesheet.

### (a) The taxonomy needs to be designed

Taxonomy has two functions. It establishes relationships and defines elements acting like a dictionary. For example, the taxonomy for assets in the statement of financial position would be to show how total assets are derived by aggregating each asset and defining each asset as follows:

| | Relationship | definitions |
|---|---|---|
| Non-current assets | $a$ | Not expected to be converted into cash within one year |
| *Current assets* | | Expected to be turned into cash in less than one year |
| Inventory | $v$ | Finished goods ready for sale, goods in course of production and raw materials |
| Trade receivables | $w$ | Amounts owed by customers |
| Cash | $x$ | Cash and cash equivalents |
| Subtotal | $v + w + x$ | |
| Total assets | $a + v + w + x$ | |

The IFRS Taxonomy 2016[20] edition translates International Financial Reporting Standards (IFRSs) into eXtensible Business Reporting Language (XBRL) with separate modules now for full Standards, IFRS for SMEs and IFRS Practice Management Commentary.

The taxonomy also contains **linkbases** which provide additional information. For example:

- a means to cross-reference with the paragraph in the relevant IFRS;
- an indication of the language used in the financial report, e.g. English, French;
- prompts when a note to the accounts is required for a particular element.

### (b) Mapping

The term 'mapping' relates to equating the terminology used in the financial statements to 'names' used in the taxonomy. For example, if the taxonomy refers to 'Inventory' as being products held for sale, but the organisation refers to this as 'Stock in Trade' in the financial statements, then this needs to be 'mapped' to the taxonomy. All the names used in the financial statements, or any other reports, need thus to be compared and mapped to (identified with) the taxonomy. This 'mapping' is done the first time the taxonomy is used.

### (c) Instance documents

The instance document holds the data which are to be reported. For example, if preparing the statement of financial position at 30 September 2015, entries of individual asset values would be made in this document. This data would then be input to a stylesheet to produce the required report.

| | Values | Date |
|---|---|---|
| Non-current assets | 1,250 | 30.9.2015 |
| Inventory | 650 | 30.9.2015 |
| Trade receivables | 310 | 30.9.2015 |
| Cash | 129 | 30.9.2015 |

There is an American case study where the software from Altova Map Force is used to capture accounting into XBRL to produce the instance document – this software also has the capabilities to transform data from the General Ledger into XBRL.[21]

### (d) Stylesheets

The format of a required report is specified in a template referred to as a 'stylesheet' where the display is pre-designed. A stylesheet can be used repeatedly as, for example, for an annual report, or new stylesheets can be designed if reports are more variable as in interim reports. The annual report would be displayed in the correct format with appropriate headings, currency and scale. For example:

Statement of financial position as at 30 September 2015

|  | 000 | 000 |
|---|---|---|
| Non-current assets |  | 1,250 |
| *Current assets* |  |  |
| Inventory | 650 |  |
| Trade receivables | 310 |  |
| Cash | 129 |  |
|  |  | 1,089 |
| Total assets |  | 2,339 |

The taxonomy and stylesheets do not need to be changed every time a report is produced. The only changes that are made are those in the instance documents regarding data entries.

### Summary of the four processes

A summary is set out in Figure 30.4.

**Figure 30.4  Summary of the four processes**

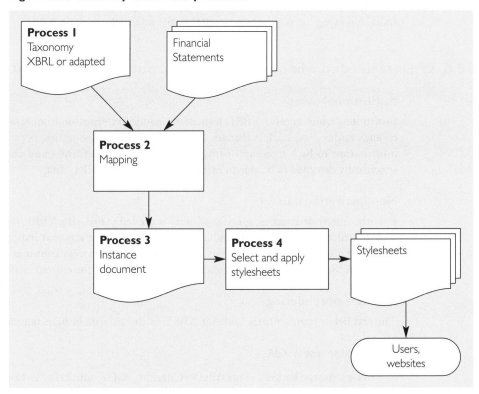

### 30.7.1 XBRL certification and other Educational resources

The XBRL Foundation Certificate Program[22] is an intensive training and examination process that will prepare stakeholders at all levels to understand the ramifications of using XBRL to meet their business objectives. It includes coverage of the relation between taxonomies and instance documents, linkbases and the content of XBRL instance documents.

For those interested in extending their knowledge of XBRL it is often a 'self-learning' path. However, this can bring rewards for career prospects, as can be seen in the article 'The future is now: XBRL emerges as career niche',[23] where a student discusses the advice given to her as how to gain the knowledge and experience needed. At the end of there are more suggestions.

Another excellent resource is Charles Hoffman's website.[24] He is often referred to as 'The father of XBRL' for his early involvement in XBRL and his push to advance XBRL. Chapters of his 'Financial Reporting using XBRL' book can be downloaded and there are many other postings and links to educational resources on the website.

For more information on learning about XBRL, consult the XBRL website for your jurisdiction. There are also private training operators located in various countries in the UK, Europe and internationally.

In the US the AICPA and XBRL US have developed for CPAs a comprehensive interactive online learning programme, the *XBRL U.S. GAAP Certificate Program,* to provide a sound understanding of XBRL financials.

Internationally companies are accessing training from the accounting profession, as in India[9] following the requirement in 2011 to file financial reports in XBRL.

## 30.8 What is needed when receiving XBRL output information?

#### Institutional users

Institutions which receive XBRL formatted financial information from companies, such as revenue authorities, stock exchanges, banks and insurance companies, normally require the information to be lodged according to a predetermined format and their software is specifically designed to be able to extract and display the XBRL data.

#### Non-institutional users

For other interested parties, specific software is needed to make the XBRL format data readable. In order for the text to be understood by a human in a way that indicates that we are looking at a financial report, it needs to be 'translated', a process known as **rendering,** by computer. 'Rendering' the items contained within XBRL is the current challenge.

#### Example of rendering

The text below represents the code for XBRL formatted data in an instance document.

*Instance document in XBRL*

```
<ifrs-gp:AssetsHeldSale contextRef=vCurrent_AsOf" unitRef="U-Euros"
    decimals="0">100000</ifrs-gp:AssetsHeldSale>

<ifrs-gp:ConstructionProgressCurrent contextRef="Current_AsOf" unitRBf="U-
    Euros" decimals="0">100000</ifrs-gp:ConstructionProgressCurrent>
```

```
<ifrs-gp:Inventories contextRef="Current_AsOf" unitRef="U-Euros"
    decimals="0">100000</ifrs-gp:Inventories>
<ifrs-gp:OtherFinancialAssetsCurrent contextRef="Current_AsOf" unitRef="U-
    Euros" decimals="0">100000</ifrs-gp:OtherFinancialAssetsCurrent>
<ifrs-gp:HedgingInstrumentsCurrentAsset contextRef="Current_AsOf"
    unitRef="U-Euros" decimals="0">100000</ifrs-gp:HedgingInstrumentsCurrent
    Asset>
<ifrs-gp:CurrentTaxReceivables contextRef="Current_AsOf" unitRef="U-Euros"
    decimals="0">100000</ifrs-gp:CurrentTaxReceivables>
<ifrs-gp:TradeOtherReceivablesNetCurrent contextRef="Current_AsOf"
    unitRef="U-Euros" decimals="0">100000</ifrs-gp:TradeOtherReceivablesNetCu
    rrent>
<ifrs-gp:PrepaymentsCurrent contextRef="Current_AsOf" unitRef="U-Euros"
    decimals="0">100000</ifrs-gp:PrepaymentsCurrent>
<ifrs-gp:CashCashEquivalents contextRef="Current_AsOf" unitRef="U-Euros"
    decimals="0">100000</ifrs-gp:CashCashEquivalents>
<ifrs-gp:OtherAssetsCurrent contextRef="Current_AsOf" unitRef="U-Euros"
    decimals="0">100000</ifrs-gp:OtherAssetsCurrent>
<ifrs-gp:AssetsCurrentTotal contextRef="Current_AsOf" unitRef="U-Euros"
    decimals="0">1000000</ifrs-gp:AssetsCurrentTotal>
```

Looking at the first two lines of code, it is possible to see that the data contain financial information about assets held for sale, that these are 'Current' and that the unit of measurement is in euros and has zero decimals with a value of 100,000. This is possible for a few lines but it would not be feasible to do this for a complex financial statement. Rendering translates the code into readable format as follows.

Rendered XBRL data

| CURRENT ASSETS | € |
|---|---|
| Assets held for sale | 100,000 |
| Construction in progress, current | 100,000 |
| Inventories | 100,000 |
| Other financial assets, current | 100,000 |
| Hedging instruments, current [asset] | 100,000 |
| Current tax receivables | 100,000 |
| Trade and other receivables, net, current | 100,000 |
| Prepayments, current | 100,000 |
| Cash and cash equivalents | 100,000 |
| Other assets, current | 100,000 |
| **Current assets, total** | 1,000,000 |

The data can now be recognised as belonging to that part of the financial statement where the current assets are listed.

The rendering process is of particular interest to investors and other third parties who may want to access financial data in XBRL format for evaluation purposes and who may not have software capable of rendering the instance document into human readable format. The ability to render an XBRL document becomes even more important for an investor or analyst seeking to carry out trend or inter-firm comparison analysis. To enable the information to be read in human-readable format, the UK has elected to use iXBRL (inline XBRL).[25]

### 30.8.1 How might XBRL assist the user?

If we take the revenue authorities as an example, they have had their own in-house-developed software for carrying out a risk analysis in an attempt to identify those that look as though they should be investigated. Such risk analysis was routine before XBRL but XBRL has allowed the existing analysis software to be refined – this allows obviously compliant companies to be identified and investigation to be targeted where there is possible or probable non-compliance. However, it is still not possible to present the data in human-readable form unless the data has been constructed using iXBRL.

However, there are now companies who will collect the XBRL data and present it in a readable format. These companies may also provide evaluation services where the data is presented with calculations such as percentage change from the previous period to the current period. Alternatively, the investor can download the data for the company they wish to evaluate or for a series of companies within a specific industry without the calculations to their own spreadsheet and then insert their own formulas. The companies often offer services at different levels and the fees reflect this. Universities can often obtain access to these companies for a fee; some fees are quite reasonable. For more on how XBRL can help companies and users and a review of the software mentioned here, see www.accountingweb.com/technology/accounting-software/calcbench-named-the-grand-prize-winner-of-the-xbrl-challenge. AccountingWeb also has more information and brief articles discussing the use of XBRL.

**Example of data services provided by www.calcbench.com**

Screen capture from Calcbench.com obtained through the two-week free service facility

| Export Export All Statements Using Excel? Download our Excel Add-in | Y 2015 X 1/1/2015 to 12/31/2015 SEC | %chg | Y 2014 X 1/1/2014 to 12/31/2014 SEC |
|---|---|---|---|
| **Revenue** | | | |
| Services | $49,911,000,000 | (10.35%) | $55,673,000,000 |
| Sales | $29,967,000,000 | (14.53%) | $35,063,000,000 |
| Financing | $1,864,000,000 | (9.38%) | $2,057,000,000 |
| **Total revenue (Note T)** detail+ | **$81,741,000,000** | (11.91%) | **$92,793,000,000** |
| **Cost** | | | |
| Services tag chart | $33,126,000,000 | (8.07%) | $36,034,000,000 |
| Sales | $6,920,000,000 | (25.69%) | $9,312,000,000 |
| Financing | $1,011,000,000 | (2.79%) | $1,040,000,000 |
| **Total cost** | **$41,057,000,000** | (11.49%) | **$46,386,000,000** |
| **Gross profit** | **$40,684,000,000** | (12.33%) | **$46,407,000,000** |
| *Gross Margin %* | *49.77%* | | *50.01%* |

As can be seen, there are comparative percentages for the two years 2014 and 2015. This is from the premium service the company provides. In the top-left corner there are facilities to choose additional parameters (more than there is space to show here). What is visible is the buttons enabling the user to download the data accessed to Excel and the Excel add-in provides the user with more (and easier) ways to perform calculations. Peer groups from the industry under review can also be added.

The above example was from a USA company, data sourced from the SEC. Company data in the UK can be accessed through Companies House but, as most of that is still in PDF format, it is better to access the company data through http://download.companieshouse. gov.uk/en_accountsdata.html.

The table below was constructed by downloading company data from one of the daily files to Excel. The comparative percentages were then constructed by the author using Excel formulas. This example demonstrates that it is possible for stakeholders to download data and apply their own evaluation techniques.

The downloaded data displayed in the example still shows the terminology used in iXBRL, but this could also be 'translated' to more conventional accounting terminology should this be preferred. (Note that the labels in column 2 are in XBRL/iXBRL format.)

**Example from a UK company. Data downloaded from one of the daily data files from Companies House**

| Fiscal Period<br>Period Start<br>Period End | | Y 2015<br>1/01/2015<br>31/12/2015 | % change | Y 2014<br>1/01/2014<br>31/12/2014 |
|---|---|---|---|---|
| Revenue | Electric Domestic Regulated Revenue | $277,864,000 | 3.49% | $268,488,000 |
| **Operating expenses:** | Operating Expenses Abstract | | | |
| Fuel and purchased power | Fuel And Purchased Power | $83,339,000 | −11.32% | $93,976,000 |
| Operations and maintenance | Utilities Operating Expense Maintenance And Operations | $68,088,000 | −3.22% | $70,356,000 |
| Depreciation and amortization | Depreciation Depletion And Amortization | $32,552,000 | 11.86% | $29,100,000 |
| Taxes – property | Taxes Excluding Income And Excise Taxes | $5,971,000 | 0.49% | $5,942,000 |
| Total operating expenses | Operating Expenses | $189,950,000 | −4.73% | $199,374,000 |
| Operating income | Operating Income Loss | $87,914,000 | 27.20% | $69,114,000 |
| **Other income (expense):** | Nonoperating Income Expense Abstract | | | |
| Interest expense | Interest Costs Incurred | ($22,337,000) | 8.60% | ($20,569,000) |
| AFUDC – borrowed | Public Utilities Allowance For Funds Used During Construction Borrowed Interest Costs Capitalized | $506,000 | 104.03% | $248,000 |
| Interest income | Investment Income Interest | $657,000 | 6.14% | $619,000 |
| AFUDC – equity | Public Utilities Allowance For Funds Used During Construction Capitalized Cost Of Equity | $918,000 | 76.88% | $519,000 |

(continued)

| Other expense | Other Nonoperating Expense | ($117,000) | 11.43% | ($105,000) |
|---|---|---|---|---|
| Other income | Other Nonoperating Income | $233,000 | −6.05% | $248,000 |
| **Total other income (expense)** | Non-operating Income Expense | ($20,140,000) | 5.78% | ($19,040,000) |
| Income from continuing operations before income taxes | Income Loss From Continuing Operations Before Income Taxes Minority Interest And Income Loss From Equity Method Investments | $67,774,000 | 35.35% | $50,074,000 |
| Income tax (expense) benefit | Income Tax Expense Benefit | ($22,600,000) | 36.87% | ($16,512,000) |
| Net income | Net Income Loss Available To Common Stockholders Basic | $45,174,000 | 34.60% | $33,562,000 |

Access to company data is also available through the database service providers mentioned earlier in this chapter and in Section 30.8.2. These data providers have access to UK, European and International company data and offer various levels of services.

Auditors also gain advantages, such as there being reduced risk of manual re-entry errors and, with XBRL GL, they can extract information in a single standardised form and review more data in greater detail, potentially in real time.

Society might benefit if it becomes possible to evaluate a company holistically by tagging, for instance, environmental and social information such as carbon disclosures (see www.cimaglobal.com/Documents/Thought_leadership_docs/Tomorrow's-Corporate-Reporting.pdf [26]).

### 30.8.2 Development of iXBRL

Inline XBRL (known as iXBRL) has been developed so that the XBRL data are capable of being read by the user. It achieves this by embedding the XBRL coding in an HTML document so that it is similar to reading a web page. iXBRL takes a report, say a company's published accounts, in Excel, MS Word or PDF and then 'translates' this to iXBRL. It is then still able to be viewed in human-readable format. This would be an advantage for smaller businesses where there may not be accountants with XBRL skills, or where the cost would be prohibitive and they also do not need more advanced software. Corefiling's software [27] is a good example where both XBRL and iXBRL are accommodated.

To see how a company would use their Seahorse® product to create iXBRL from existing financial information look at the flowchart at www.corefiling.com/products/seahorse/shworksireland.html. There are quite a number of software companies who have products available.

HRMC also has a page that lists software companies for taxation submissions; see www.gov.uk/government/publications/corporation-tax-commercial-software-suppliers (the list is updated regularly). The page also lists companies who will perform tagging services and providers of XBRL software for in-house development of tagging.

The advantage of the UK approach is that there is no need for the design of a taxonomy as iXBRL takes the already available data and constructs or renders the existing data into XBRL code. For a detailed report on this see *Company Reporting in the UK – an XBRL Success Story*.[28]

### How has iXBRL assisted the user?

iXBRL has provided a more streamlined process of distributing data to either government or users as the data is presented in human-readable format. The tagging is still being able to be investigated as it is 'underneath' the data. A simple right-click, when the arrow is in the document on the screen, will reveal the tags.

We have discussed the use of XBRL and iXBRL for submitting reports to statutory authorities. There have also been interesting developments in their use for internal accounting.

## 30.9 Progress of XBRL development for internal accounting

Development in the general ledger area is continuing and will probably be one of the most important developments for companies with consolidation requirements when multiple general ledgers are involved. The general ledger specification has the advantage that organisational data are classified at source and the classification decision with respect to XBRL names will have been made at the Chart of Accounts level.

This is quite a task as the financial statements usually report aggregated data. For example, the total for administration expenses in the Income Statement is usually made up by aggregating a number of different account classifications in the General Ledger. A further consideration is the effect of IFRSs when aggregating expense accounts. For example, the Chart of Account structures for the disclosure of segmentation by product class and by geographical areas are distinctly different. The XBRL code also needs to reflect this.

The XBRL for the General Ledger may also bring great cost savings as data collection at source is automated and the extraction and processing of data into reports can be achieved in a much shorter time. A company such as General Electric has more than 150 general ledgers which are not compatible in use. XBRL has the potential to streamline consolidation processes considerably.

XBRL GL prefers to use GL to mean 'Global Ledger' not 'General Ledger' so as to indicate that *any* transactional information can be dealt with, and that it provides a generic and system-independent way to record all the details in any kind of ledger.[29] The latest Global Ledger specifications (2015) are available at http://specifications.xbrl.org/spec-group-index-xbrl-gl.html.

In the US the American Institute of Certified Public Accountants has developed a voluntary data standard for the general ledger and accounts receivable ledger which can assist the analytical work of both the internal and external audit. One of the formats developed is in XBRL.

## 30.10 Real-time reporting

We know that investors are not a homogeneous group. It will include investors who have a long-term interest in a company and investors who have a short-term interest.

This influences their view on the timeliness of financial reporting – its reliability and relevance.

### Long-term view

For those with a long-term view the Annual Report is valued because it has been audited and is regarded as reliable as a means of assessing management's stewardship. Regulators have been taking steps to require companies to reduce the time between the end of the financial period and the publication of the report and companies themselves see that there could be a competitive advantage in doing this, with some taking only 10 days after the period end. There are indications that investors associate the speed of reporting with robust corporate governance and enhanced investment returns. The speed is also affected, of course, by the complexity of a company's operations and structure.

Regulators have also been addressing the need for investors to be aware of a company's business model and its procedures for dealing with risk through Management Commentaries and Strategic Reports.

Whilst there is an interest in receiving information during the year, it is not clear that investors would be happy for the company to incur the extra cost of auditing interim data – it is of interest but perhaps not of major significance.

### Short-term view

Investors looking to buy and sell shares during the financial year would welcome real-time reporting. There is a preparedness to accept that the data will be less reliable and might result in greater volatility in share price movements, which for some investors provides in itself an opportunity. The short-term investors are also not a homogeneous group. Some will have access to company briefings, others will need to rely on company reports.

### The form of interim reporting

There are practical problems involved with real-time reporting. Data may be less reliable and there is a problem auditing moving data. At present there is a requirement by some regulators to produce quarterly reports, but even with these reports there are critics who question their value.

A practical solution at present would seem to be for a company to provide warnings if there is an unexpected change in performance such as with profit warnings and qualitative interim reports with assurance rather than audit.

### Survey results

A survey carried out in 2013 on behalf of the ACCA[30] found that there was a genuine demand for 'real-time' reporting among investors and this would increase investor returns and enhance the level of confidence in corporate reporting. For example, 85% said that real-time data would improve their ability to react quickly and 71% said it would increase their understanding of corporate performance. However, almost two-thirds believed real-time reporting would create further financial instability and lead to an increased tendency to short-termism in financial markets, which raised the question as to whether what investors were asking for would be positive for the market as a whole.

Real time reporting is also seen as an important issue in sustainability reporting and performance control.[31] The use of XBRL is also seen as an important factor for sustainability reporting by many other authors.

## Stakeholder interaction with XBRL data

The XBRL International website (www.xbrl.org) has an extensive listing of companies and authorities currently using XBRL. The reader is encouraged to investigate further any of the resources available on the XBRL and other websites such as learn.vubiz.com/ChAccess/XBRL/, where there is an introductory course 'Advances in Business and Financial Reporting' (2016). A number of the links provided will lead to good discussions of the projects and demonstrate how XBRL is applied. Some of the links will also bring the reader to websites in languages other than English (Google translation toolbar may be helpful) and may be of particular interest to readers of this text living in non-English-speaking countries.

In the UK the FRC announced a major project starting in 2014, *Corporate Reporting in a Digital World,* conducted through the Financial Reporting Lab to investigate how companies do, and might in the future, use digital media in their corporate reporting to improve investors' access to information. The Lab will initially review how companies currently use a wide range of digital media, including websites, videos, apps, social media platforms and blogs in their external communications to investors, and how investors use what is produced. It will then progress to considering barriers to the use of digital media in reporting and how companies might make the most of technological opportunities. The Lab is inviting listed companies, investors and analysts to express their interest in taking part in the project.

A subsequent project report issued as part of the 2014 project found that investors still prefer PDF reports which are searchable and they wished reports to be kept 'simple' and 'optimized' for searching.[32]

## Summary

XBRL is still a developing area relating to organisational reporting. In the coming years this will continue and extend beyond the current focus on published financial statements. The general ledger area is developing and this will benefit the organisational information supply chain. Accounting software suppliers are also adopting XBRL in their developments and this will increase accessibility to XBRL. Accounting software companies are also using XBRL in their new developments aimed at smaller organisations. Software development is ongoing and the list provided by HMRC contains companies providing software services or XBRL design,[33] with a guide also available.[34]

Financial statements presented in XBRL format are capable of being downloaded into an analyst's/investor's own spreadsheet (such as Microsoft Excel). As we saw in the discussion on the use of iXBRL, this format is the easiest to directly download into a spreadsheet program. The advantage of this is that the analyst/investor does not need to retype the information. The commercial databases which compile specific information for analysts/investors are usually only concerned with public companies listed on the Stock Exchange. XBRL allows any type of financial information to be transferred to a statistical package without having to retype the information.

XBRL could thus also benefit not-for-profit organisations[35] and trusts. Professional accounting consultants are also able to use XBRL to transfer information from a client's accounting package into an analytical tool to prepare information to evaluate business efficiency. This information is often more extensive than the end-of-year financial information.

The large software developer SAP announced in February 2009 that 'SAP® BusinessObjects™' is now available for financial publications in XBRL. SAP has since developed what it calls 'Business Intelligence Solutions' providing data mining for different computer operating platforms.[36]

Accountants and students wishing to keep up to date with these developments are gaining a competitive advantage by creating and developing a 'niche' skill which can only add value to an organisation employing these professionals.

## REVIEW QUESTIONS

1   Discuss how an investor might benefit from annual reports being made available in XBRL.

2   Explain how a body such as a tax authority might benefit from XBRL.

3   Explain what you understand by taxonomy and mapping.

4   Explain the use of instance documents.

5   Explain the use of stylesheets.

6   Explain iXBRL and where it is used.

7   XBRL will make it easier to prepare quicker quarterly reports. Discuss the suggestion that this encourages short-termism and that companies should not therefore be required to produce on a quarterly basis.

8   'Interim assessment of performance is important but should only be discursive.' Discuss.

9   Investor demand for assurance takes precedence over their demand for speed when it comes to general financial information and liquidity. Access www.accaglobal.com/reporting and identify from its report *Understanding Investors: The Road to Real Time Reporting* three situations where a company seeks real-time reporting and whether this should be made available to investors at the same time.

10   Discuss the implications of using IFRS and NON-IFRS in financial reports when using XBRL.

11   Access the Lab project report *Digital Present: Current Use of Digital Media in Corporate Reporting*

   (www.frc.org.uk/Our-Work/Publications/Financial-Reporting-Lab/Lab-Project-Report-Digital-Present.pdf).

   Discuss how financial information might be most effectively made available to stakeholders over the next five years.

## EXERCISES

### Question 1

Visit http://xbrl.squarespace.com/journal/2008/12/18/hello-world-xbrl-example.html to view the 'Hello World' example of XBRL code and exercise. Download the Zip file and follow the instructions on the web page.

Write a one-page summary of your experience of evaluating this source.

### Question 2

Find the financial reports for a company of your own choice. List the company and describe the format of the Annual Report. See if you can also find information on the *company's own* website about its use of XBRL.

## Question 3

*Digital Reporting: A Progress Report,*[37] was an initiative from the Institute of Chartered Accountants in England & Wales commenting in 2004 on possible barriers to the development of increased digital reporting.

The report discusses two levels of reporting and a possible third level.

**Required:**
**Read the executive Summary or the whole report and then evaluate the two excerpts below:**

> A widely accepted digital reporting standard at Level 2 is capable of delivering real benefits. In general terms, an effective digital reporting standard is relevant to people throughout the business reporting supply chain: producers of business reports, software vendors, accountants, auditors, financial analysts, investors and creditors.

In contrast to this the report further states:

> Level 2 standards may be of less use to markets and analysts than originally supposed, because:

> ● they are at the end of the digital reporting value chain and the benefits do not arise for them until digital reporting standards are in wide use; and

> ● a lot of their activity is based on forms of probabilistic logic that do not necessarily or readily lend themselves to deterministic processing with reference to standardised data storage structures.'

**Comment on the above two excerpts and in particular the statement and reasons that level 2 standard may be of less use.**

**In addition you may want to discuss the possibility of there being a level 3 in Digital reporting (think of the Global General Ledger).**

## Question 4

Find out more about any of the following topics and write a one-page summary on:

(a) the XBRL Global general ledger work;

(b) use of XBRL by stock exchanges;

(c) the commitment by the IFRS to the XBRL project;

(d) accounting software companies involved in providing XBRL capabilities;

(e) public utilities that are using XBRL;

(f) government involvement in XBRL.

## Notes

1  http://ec.europa.eu/internal_market/securities/transparency/index_en.htm
2  www.keller.co.uk/N/media/Files/K/Keller/storage/pdfs/2014/interim-report-2014.pdf
3  www.bvdinfo.com/en-gb/our-products/company-information/national-products/fame
4  University of Sheffield www.sheffield.ac.uk/library/cdfiles/fame
5  For an extensive discussion on these Apps see www.businessinsider.com.au/17-must-have-mobile-apps-for-investors-2012-8?r=US&IR=T
6  www.w3.org/Consortium

7 www.xbrl.org/the-standard/what/financial-statement-data/

8 www.sec.gov/rules/final/2009/33-9002.pdf

9 www.acra.gov.sg/

10 www.xbrl.org/sbr-in-australia-by-the-numbers/

11 http://asic.gov.au/about-asic/media-centre/find-a-media-release/2015-releases/15-104mr-asic-introduces-format-for-improved-communication-of-financial-information/

12 www.apra.gov.au/CrossIndustry/Pages/D2A-and-XBRL.aspx

13 www.apra.gov.au/CrossIndustry/Pages/D2A.aspx

14 www.xbrl.org/performance-reporting-and-non-gaap-measures/

15 www.sec.gov/news/speech/schnurr-remarks-12th-life-sciences-accounting-congress.html

16 www.iasplus.com/en-gb/news/2015/07/uk-study

17 T. Dunne, C. Helliar, A. Lymer and R. Mousa, *XBRL: The Views of Stakeholders*, ACCA Research report 111, 2009

18 T. Dunne, C. Helliar, A. Lymer and R. Mousa, 'Stakeholder engagement in internet financial reporting: the diffusion of XBRL in the UK', *The British Accounting Review*, vol. 45, 2013, pp. 167–182.

19 www.acra.gov.sg/uploadedFiles/Content/How_To_Guides/XBRL_and_the_Value_of_Business_Data/Fact%20sheet.pdf

20 www.ifrs.org/XBRL/IFRS-Taxonomy/2016/Pages/default.aspx

21 www.altova.com/documents/MACPA_casestudy_followup3.pdf

22 www.xbrl.org/the-consortium/get-involved/individual-certification/

23 Sheriden, B. and Drew, J., 'The future is now: XBRL emerges as career niche', *Journal of Accountancy*, June 2012, www.journalofaccountancy.com/Issues/2012/Jun/20124962.htm

24 http://xbrl.squarespace.com/financial-reporting-using-xbrl/

25 www.xbrl.org.uk/techguidance/inlinexbrl.html

26 *Tomorrow's Corporate Reporting: A Critical System at Risk*, Tomorrow's Company, April 2011, www.cimaglobal.com/Documents/Thought_leadership_docs/Tomorrow's-Corporate-Reporting.pdf

27 www.corefiling.com/solutions/xbrl-ixbrl-for-companies/

28 www.esma.europa.eu/file/14623/download?token=Yg5r2jxm

29 www.xbrl.org/the-standard/what/global-ledger/

30 www.accaglobal.com/content/dam/acca/global/PDF-technical/financial-reporting/pol-afb-ui03.pdf

31 www.sciencedirect.com/science/article/pii/S0959652616001931

32 www.frc.org.uk/News-and-Events/FRC-Press/Press/2015/May/Investors-welcome-relevant-use-of-digital-reportin.aspx

33 www.gov.uk/government/publications/corporation-tax-commercial-software-suppliers

34 www.gov.uk/government/uploads/system/uploads/attachment_data/file/366133/xbrl-guide.pdf

35 www.xbrl.org.uk/techguidance/taxonomies.html\#combined

36 http://go.sap.com/solution/platform-technology/analytics/business-intelligence-bi.html

37 http://www.icaew.com/-/media/corporate/files/technical/financial-reporting/information-for-better-markets/ifbm/digital-reporting-a-progress-report.ashx

## Bibliography

H. Ashbaugh, K.M. Johnstone and T.D. Warfeld, 'Corporate reporting on the Internet', *Accounting Horizons*, vol. 13(3), 1999, pp. 241–257.

R. Debreceny and G. Gray, 'Financial reporting on the Internet and the external audit', *European Accounting Review*, vol. 8(2), 1999, pp. 335–350.

R. Debreceny and G. Gray, 'The production and use of semantically rich accounting reports on the Internet: XML and XBRL', *International Journal of Accounting Information Systems*, vol. 1(3), 2000.

D. Deller, M. Stubenrath and C. Weber, 'A survey of the use of the Internet for investor relations in the USA, UK and Germany', *European Accounting Review*, vol. 8(2), pp. 351–364.

Ernst & Young, *Web Enabled Business Reporting. De invloed van XBRL op het verslaggevingsprocess*, Kluwer, 2004.

M. Ettredge, V.J. Richardson and S. Scholz, *Accounting Information at Corporate Web Sites: Does the Auditor's Opinion Matter?*, University of Kansas, February 1999.

M. Ettredge, V.J. Richardson and S. Scholz, 'Going concern auditor reports at corporate web sites', *Research in Accounting Regulation*, vol. 14, 2000, pp. 3–21.

Neil Hannon, 'XBRL grows fast in Europe', *Strategic Finance*, October 2004, pp. 55–56.

Mark Huckelsby and Josef Macdonald, 'The three tenets of XBRL – adoption, adoption, adoption!', *Chartered Accountants Journal of New Zealand*, March 2004, pp. 46–47.

V. Richardson and S. Scholz, 'Corporate reporting and the Internet: vision reality and intervening obstacles', *Pacifc Accounting Review*, vol. 11(2), 2000, pp. 153–160.

Mike Rondel, 'XBRL – do I need to know more?', *Chartered Accountants Journal of New Zealand*, vol. 83(5), June 2004, pp. 37–40.

G. Trites, *The Impact of Technology on Financial and Business Reporting*, Toronto: Canadian Institute of Chartered Accountants, 1999.

**The following websites were accessed:**

www.adobe.com

www.xbrl.org/FRTaxonomies/

www.xbrl.org

www.ubmatrix.com/home/

www.semansys.com

www.edgar.com

PART **8**

# Accountability

# CHAPTER 31

# Corporate governance

## 31.1 Introduction

The main aim of this chapter is to create an awareness of what constitutes good corporate governance – how to achieve it, the threats to achieving it and the role of accountants and auditors.

### Objectives

By the end of this chapter, you should be able to:

- understand the concept of corporate governance;
- have an awareness of how and why governance mechanisms may differ from jurisdiction to jurisdiction;
- have an appreciation of the role which accounting and auditing play in the governance process;
- have a greater sensitivity to areas of potential conflicts of interest.

## 31.2 A systems perspective

Corporations do not act in a vacuum. They are corporate citizens of society with rights and responsibilities. The way in which they exercise these rights and responsibilities is influenced by the history, institutions and cultural expectations of society. A systems perspective recognises that an entity is not independent but is interdependent with its environment. This has given rise to the need for corporate governance.

Corporate governance is defined by C. Oman[1] as:

> private and public institutions, including laws, regulations and accepted business practices, which together govern the relationship, in a market economy, between corporate managers and entrepreneurs ('corporate insiders') on the one hand, and those who invest resources in corporations on the other.

### 31.2.1 Good corporate governance – investor perspective

When we pause to contemplate the contribution of corporations to our standard of living, we are reminded how important their contribution is to most aspects of our existence. It is therefore vital that they operate as good citizens in their treatment of the investors who provide their funds and of other stakeholders. This includes actions by management when dealing with investors such as:

- complying with the laws and norms of society;
- striving to achieve the company objectives in a manner which does not involve taking risks which are greater than expected or acceptable to investors;
- balancing short- and long-term performance;
- establishing mechanisms to ensure that managers are acting in the interests of shareholders and are not directly or indirectly using their knowledge or positions to gain inappropriate benefits at the expense of shareholders;
- providing investors with relevant, reliable and timely information that allows them to assess the performance, solvency and financial stability of the business; and
- providing investors with an independent opinion that the financial statements are a fair representation.

This list does not cover all eventualities but is intended to indicate what could be expected from corporate governance – good being determined by the degree that the actions and information flows achieve fair outcomes.

### 31.2.2 Good corporate governance – other stakeholder perspective

A stakeholder perspective addresses all the other parties whose continued support is necessary to ensure the satisfactory performance of the business. The parties are normally seen as belonging to one of the following categories: loan creditors, employees, trade unions representing employees, customers, governments and suppliers.

Good corporate governance might include actions by management such as:

- fair treatment of employees, avoiding discrimination;
- establishing mechanisms for resolving conflicts of interests;
- establishing mechanisms for whistle-blowing so that if inappropriate behaviour is taking place it is highlighted as quickly as possible so as to minimise the cost to the organisation and society;
- paying suppliers, particularly small businesses, promptly within the agreed credit period; and
- providing suppliers with relevant, reliable and timely information that allows them to assess the solvency of the business.

### 31.2.3 Good corporate governance – stakeholder pressure on Boards of Directors

It is often difficult for stakeholders to exert effective influence in practice.

First, this is because shareholders are not a homogeneous group – some wish to invest for the long term others have a more speculative interest. This puts some capital intensive companies in a quandary – if they invest in research for the long term, current profits available for paying dividends are hit which is less attractive to investors relying on dividends for their income.

Second, because as well as there being conflicting interests, there are also differences in the influence that a stakeholder can exert. Ideally, for example, dominant shareholders, institutional investors and major customers should have a greater ability to hold management to account and achieve good corporate governance outcomes. However, when we look at the makeup of shareholdings in the UK stock market we see that the fragmentation calls into question just how much influence any single group has – for example, over 50% is held by the rest of the world and only 6% held by insurance companies and 3% by pension funds.

Even accepting the existence of an ability to influence does not necessarily mean that it is put into effect, since the individual stakeholder's private interest might not be advanced by taking action – it might, for example, divert their management's attention away from their own business.

### 31.2.4 Good corporate governance – all sectors

The objective is to influence behaviour so that all parties act within the spirit of good governance. The actions and information flows above have been oriented towards business entities but we should expect all organisations to behave in the same way. For example, in the case of a not-for-profit enterprise such as a charity it is important that the methods by which money are raised are ethical and the manner in which the money used is consistent with the uses envisaged by the donors, and that an appropriate balance be achieved between administrative costs and the money devoted to assisting the beneficiaries of the charity.

Good governance requires constant vigilance, and in the UK fundraising has been the subject of a government report, House of Commons Public Administration and Constitutional Affairs Committee *The 2015 Charity Fundraising Controversy: Lessons for Trustees, the Charity Commission, and Regulators,* Third Report of Session 2015–16.[2]

The approach to enforcement of good corporate governance by charities varies internationally.

## 31.3 Different jurisdictions have different governance priorities

The predominant conflicts of interest will vary from country to country depending on each country's history, economic and legal developments, norms and religion.

In the UK and the United States, with their similar considerable reliance on stock exchanges for the financing of public companies, there is a need for an active, efficient capital market. This leads to their focus being on potential conflicts between management and shareholders.

In Germany, where companies have a board of directors made up of investors as well as an advisory board representing both management and employees, there is a recognition that there is a need to reconcile both management and employee long-term interests and to ensure that both groups are motivated to achieve the organisation's long-term goals.

In south-east Asia, with many of the large corporations having substantial shareholdings owned by members of a single family, the emphasis has been on avoiding conflicts between family and minority shareholders.

In Muslim countries companies should not be involved in activities related to alcohol and gambling; they cannot pay or charge interest and they have religious obligations to make a minimum level of donations. This means there is a need for corporate governance mechanisms to ensure that there is no conflict between commercial activity and religious obligations.

From the above we can see how the governance priorities differ from country to country. They result from the role of the political institutions, the stage of economic development, the diversity of stakeholder perspectives and a country's heritage in so far as it shapes the law, the religion and the social norms.

The large number of multinational companies means that these companies have to be sensitive to the approaches taken in all countries in which they have subsidiary companies and joint ventures. They also have to be aware of the provisions of the US Foreign Corrupt Practices Act 1977 and the UK Bribery Act 2010, particularly as the Bribery Act creates a corporate offence and personal liability for failing to prevent bribery by persons associated with a corporation.

### Companies identifying bribery and corruption risk management in their Annual Reports

The following is an extract from the Centrica 2012 Annual Report:

Anti-bribery and corruption is a business priority. Centrica shall regularly and systematically identify bribery and corruption risks in its business and implement adequate risk-based procedures aimed at preventing bribery and corruption occurring including:

- Audit – Our internal control systems will be subject to regular internal and independent audit to provide assurance that they are effective in countering bribery and corruption . . .

- Business relationships – We will ensure that our business partners – including contractors, suppliers, agents, brokers and joint venture partners – are fit to do business with . . .

- Conflicts of interest – Gifts and hospitality – We will address conflicts of interest and the risks created by gifts and hospitality through the implementation of our internal policies.

- Government officials – We will implement procedures applicable to our (or our agents', or those suppliers in our supply chains') dealings with government officials, political parties and related persons or organisations.

Just as governance priorities differ, so do the institutions and methods for controlling corporate governance. The institutions include statutory bodies enforcing detailed prescriptive requirements and statutory bodies that encourage voluntary adoption of good practices with disclosure, through voluntary organisations such as Transparency International UK to professional accounting bodies that have built the awareness of good corporate governance into their examination syllabi.

### 31.3.1 Corporate governance culture

In China, Russia and the former communist countries in Eastern Europe, the economies are being changed from state-controlled businesses to privately owned companies. The 'model' of these companies is similar to those in the US and UK. So, the trend is towards the US and UK model of companies' shares being listed on their national stock exchange. This trend to wider share ownership will encourage the development of corporate governance criteria similar to those in the US and the UK. For some countries this is a real cultural shift and it will take time for the concept of good corporate governance to be applied. The following is an extract from an OECD Note of a meeting on Corporate Governance Development in State-owned Enterprises in Russia:[3]

Finally, as stressed by investors, the OECD, and government officials at this expert's meeting, the emergence of a true corporate governance culture is vital. Such a culture-based approach should involve the understanding of the principles and values behind corporate governance, and replace the 'box-ticking' mechanistic approach in which superficial institutions fulfill certain criteria but do not bring real benefits in terms of effective achievement of corporate goals. This would complement the creation of specific incentives intended to guide the behaviour of economic actors.

## 31.4 Pressures on good governance behaviour vary over time

History shows that business behaviour is influenced by where we are in the economic cycle, whether it's a time of boom or bust.

### 31.4.1 Behaviour in boom times

During the booms there has always been a tendency to be over-optimistic and to expect the good times to continue indefinitely. In such periods there is a tendency for everyone to focus on making profits. The safeguards that are in the system to prevent conflicts of interest and to limit undesirable behaviour are seen as slowing down the business and causing genuine opportunities to be missed. Over-optimism leads to a business taking risks that the shareholders had not sanctioned and is, to that extent, excessive.

This is accompanied by a tendency to water down the controls or to simply ignore them. When that happens there will always be some unethical individuals who will exploit some of the opportunities for themselves rather than for the business.

### 31.4.2 Behaviour in bust times

We see a repetitive reaction from bust to bust. When it occurs some of the malpractices will come to light, there will be a public outcry and governance procedures will be tightened up. Although controls are weakly enforced during boom times, it is a fact of life that vigilance is required at all times. Fraud, misrepresentation, misappropriation and anti-social behaviour will be constantly with us and robust corporate governance systems need to be in place and monitored.

The ideal would be that the controls in place develop a culture that makes individuals constrain their own behaviour to that which is ethical, having previously sensitised themselves to recognise the potential conflicts of interest. It is interesting to see the approach taken by the professional accounting bodies which are concentrating on sensitising students and members to ethical issues.

## 31.5 Types of past unethical behaviour

Some of the unethical behaviour that has been identified in earlier periods and which our governance systems should attempt to prevent are listed below:

- Inflating profits by overstating revenues and understating expenses. For example, in 2016 the US Securities and Exchange Commission (SEC)[4] announced financial fraud cases against two companies, Logiteck and Ener1, and their executives. The SEC alleged deficiencies in Ener1's failure to properly impair assets on its balance sheet and Logitech's failure to write down the value of its inventory to avoid the financial consequences of disappointing sales.

In the Ener1 case, the SEC also found that Robert D. Hesselgesser, the engagement partner for PricewaterhouseCoopers LLP's audit of Ener1's 2010 financial statements, violated professional auditing standards when he failed to perform sufficient procedures to support his audit conclusions that Ener1 management had appropriately accounted for its assets and revenues. He was suspended from participating in the financial reporting or audits of public companies for two years.

'Auditors play a critical role regarding the accuracy of financial statements relied upon by investors, and they must be held accountable when they fail to do everything required under professional auditing standards,' said Michael Maloney, Chief Accountant of the SEC's Division of Enforcement.

- Insider trading, particularly around major events such as a forthcoming company buyout, takeover or development of a new product. Detection is actively pursued by the SEC in the US and penalties are exacted. For example, the SEC charged a former major league baseball player and three others with insider trading ahead of a company buyout and obtaining more than $1.7 million in illegal profits. $2.5 million was paid to settle the SEC's charges.

- Excessive remuneration so that the rewards flow disproportionately to management compared to other stakeholders and often with the major risks being borne by the other stakeholders.

- Excessive risk taking which is hidden from shareholders and stakeholders until after the catastrophe has struck.

- Unsuccessful managers being given 'golden handshakes' to leave and thus being rewarded for poor performance. For example, in Denmark it was reported that 'Banks are facing criticism for giving their CEOs million-kroner "golden handshakes", despite poor performances'.[5]

- Auditors, bankers, lawyers, credit rating agencies, and stock analysts, who might put their fees before the interests of the public for honest reporting.

- Directors who do not stand up to authoritarian managing directors or seriously question their ill-advised plans. For example, it was reported in 2010 that 'A dominant CEO and a weak board of directors was a recipe for disaster at Orion Bank of Naples [Florida]. Orion failed last November because Chief Executive Jerry Williams and his inexperienced board could not handle the bank's overly aggressive growth strategy, according to a new report by the Federal Reserve's Office of Inspector General'.[6]

- Management setting incentives for employees which encourage action that is not in the firm's interests.

## 31.6 The effect on capital markets of good corporate governance

Good governance is important to facilitate large-scale commerce. The mechanism of legal structures such as limited liability of companies exists because it allows the capital of many investors to be combined in the pursuit of economic activities which need large quantities of capital to be economically viable. There are also statutory provisions relating to directors' duties and shareholders' rights. This is a good backcloth which is necessary but not sufficient to ensure the effective working of the capital market.

In addition there has to be a high level of trust by shareholders in their relationship with management. Firstly, they need to believe the company will deal with them in an honest and prudent manner and act diligently. This means that shareholders need to be confident that:

- their money will be invested in ventures of an appropriate degree of risk;
- efforts will be made to achieve a competitive return on equity;
- management will not take personal advantage of their greater knowledge of events in the business; and
- the company will provide a flow of information that will contribute to the market fairly valuing shares at the times of purchase and sale.

Failure to achieve appropriate levels of trust will lead to the risk of the loss of potential investors or the provision of lesser amounts of funds at higher costs. Similarly if other stakeholders, such as the bank, do not trust the management, there will be fewer participants and the terms will be less favourable. Another way of addressing this is to say that people have a strong sense of what is or is not fair. Whilst economic necessity may lead to participation, the level of commitment is influenced by the perceived fairness of the transaction.

Also from a macro perspective, the more efficient and effective the individual firms, the better allocation of resources and the higher the average standard of living. If management as a group is not diligent in its activities and fair in its treatment of stakeholders, there will be lower standards of living both economically and socially.

In addition the current focus on corporate social responsibility could be seen as a response to governance failures by some companies. For example, some managers ignored externalities such as the costs to society of rectifying pollution because management was only judged on the financial results of the firm, and not the net benefit to society.

## 31.7 Risk management

We have seen with the issue by the IASB of its *Practice Statement Management Commentary* and the UK with its *Strategic Report* that there is a growing pressure internationally for a company to disclose its risk management policy. In any company there is a range of risks that have to be managed. It is not a matter of just avoiding risks but rather of systematically analysing the risks and then deciding how to decide what risks should be borne, which to avoid, and how to minimise the possible adverse consequences of those which it is not economic to shift. A good governance system will ensure that (a) comprehensive risk management occurs as a normal course of events (b) action taken is proportional and (c) there is transparent disclosure to shareholders and regulators of the nature, extent and management of these risks.

There is a variety of approaches which could be adopted to the process of identifying the types of risks associated with a company. In this chapter we will discuss briefly strategic, operational and legal/regulatory risks.

### 31.7.1 Strategic risks

Strategic risk is associated with maintaining the attractiveness and economic viability of the product and service offerings. In other words, current product decisions have to be made with a strong sense of their probable future consequences. To do that the business has to be constantly monitoring trends in the current markets, potential merging of markets,[7] shifting demographics and consumer tastes, technological developments, political developments and regulations so as to capitalise on opportunities and to counter threats. It must be remembered that to do nothing may involve as much or more risk as entering into new ventures. When entering into new projects there needs to be a thorough risk analysis to ensure that there are no false assumptions in the projections, there has been pilot testing, and the question of the exit strategy if the project fails has been seriously considered and costed.

### 31.7.2 Operational risks

Operational risks include (a) insurable risks, (b) transferable risks and (c) potential hazards.

#### Insurable risks

These include such risks as physical damage from fire, flood or accident and reputational damage from quality and public liability issues. The question then is 'If this event should happen could we comfortably bear the cost?' If the answer is no, then we should insure at least for the amount we couldn't afford to bear.

#### Transferable risks

These include such risks as difficulty recruiting skilled staff to meet orders or dependence on a key supplier.

On staffing, the question may be 'Could work be outsourced?' However, that in itself creates risks such as dependence, quality control, reliability of delivery, lack of involvement in technological developments, and financial risks associated with the subcontractor.

On supply policy, the question may be 'Should the company opt for multiple suppliers?' This would protect against normal hazards such as strikes at the supplier, adverse weather conditions blocking supply, or threats to supply caused by political factors but at a probable increase in cost.

#### Hazards

In relation to risks like occupational health and safety, the steps involve identification of potential hazards, identifying the best physical process for handling them, and developing standard ways of operating, then training personnel in those standard operating procedures, and regularly checking to ensure those procedures are being followed.

### 31.7.3 Legal and regulatory risks

This refers to the possibility that the firm will breach its legal or regulatory requirements and thus expose the company to fines and injury to its reputation. This involves being aware of the requirements of each country in which it operates or in which its products and services are used. Further, the staff of the company need to know of the relevant requirements which apply to their activities. They should also have access to advice in order to avoid problems or to address issues that do arise. Once again, standard operating procedures and standard documentation can help reduce the risks. Many businesses now have a Compliance Officer responsible for making sure outside regulatory requirements are being followed. Many of these now have a degree in accountancy, business or finance. In some companies the protection of intellectual property should be of considerable relevance.

### 31.7.4 IASB *Practice Statement Management Commentary*

Adequate disclosure of risk is now being addressed in the UK by the *Strategic Report* and by the IASB *Practice Statement Management Commentary,* which states:

> Management should disclose an entity's principal risk exposures and changes in those risks, together with its plans and strategies for bearing or mitigating those risks, as well as disclosure of the effectiveness of its risk management strategies.

## 31.8 The role of internal control, internal audit and audit committees in corporate governance

Good governance is supported by (a) adequate internal controls, (b) effective internal audit and (c) effective audit committees.

### 31.8.1 Adequate internal control

In some jurisdictions the company and the external auditors have to explicitly state that the company has adequate internal controls and the accounts present a fair view. In other jurisdictions it is implied that if the company receives a clean audit report then the internal controls are adequate.

In the US when the explicit requirement was introduced many companies spent considerable sums after the introduction of the Sarbanes–Oxley Act 2002 in upgrading their systems, particularly as the CEO and CFO were made personally liable for the effectiveness of the internal controls. For example, in 2016 the SEC settled charges against Magnum Hunter Resources Corporation and two of its officers for deficient oversight of the company's internal controls over financial reporting, resulting in fines of US$250,000 for the Company and US$25,000 and US$15,000 for the Company's CFO and CAO, respectively.

There is an opportunity cost in CEOs focusing on compliance issues rather than on strategic issues and an actual cost in upgrading systems. This led to some arguing that the costs were unjustified.

Whilst the need to consider cost–benefit considerations in relation to all corporate governance measures is a valid concern, it is also important to remember the costs of bad corporate governance. Good governance will not stop all fraud and excessive risk taking but it will stop them from being so widespread. The internal control systems should limit the ability of management to misdirect resources to their personal use or to publish financial statements with material misrepresentation.

### 31.8.2 Effective internal audit

Sound internal controls combined with an effective internal audit unit should make it more difficult for senior managers to misappropriate resources or misrepresent the financial position. Naturally we know that the more senior the managers the more likely it is that they can override the internal controls or pressure others to do so. It can be argued that such a situation justifies the requirement that the internal audit unit (if one exists) should report direct to the Audit Committee.

### 31.8.3 Effective audit committees

#### The UK Listing Authority

The UK Listing Authority requires in its *Disclosure Transparency Rules* that a listed company must have a body (the Audit Committee) with at least one independent member and one member who has competence in accounting and/or auditing. The role of the Committee is to:

1 monitor the financial reporting process;
2 monitor the effectiveness of the issuer's internal control, internal audit where applicable, and risk management systems;

**3** monitor the statutory audit of the annual and consolidated accounts;

**4** review and monitor the independence of the statutory auditor, and in particular the provision of additional services to the issuer.

### The Institute of Internal Auditors Model Audit Committee Charter

The Charter[8] states that the Audit Committee should:

**Approve** the risk-based internal audit annual plan.

**Review** with management and the chief audit executive the activities, staffing, and organisational structure of the internal audit function and, at least once per year, the performance of the chief audit executive, the effectiveness of the internal audit function, and significant accounting and reporting issues.

**Ensure** there are no unjustified restrictions or limitations, and review and concur in the appointment, replacement, or dismissal of the chief audit executive.

## 31.9 External audits in corporate governance

External audits are intended to increase participation in financial investing and to lower the cost of funds. They may be *ad hoc* reports or audit reports giving an opinion on the fair view of annual financial statements.

### Ad hoc reports

In the case of lending to companies it is not uncommon for lenders to impose restrictions to protect the interests of the lenders. Such restrictions or covenants include compliance with certain ratios such as liquidity and leverage or gearing ratios. Auditors then report to lenders or trustees for groups of lenders on the level of compliance. In this way auditors facilitate the flows of funds at good rates.

### Statutory audit reports

Similarly for shareholders the audit report is intended to create confidence that the financial statements are presenting a fair view of financial performance and position. If that confidence is undermined by examples of auditors failing to detect misrepresentation or material misstatement, the public becomes wary of holding shares, share prices in the market tend to fall and the availability of new funds shrinks.

### Enhanced audit reports

The IAASB responded to the need to improve investor confidence and communications between investors and the auditor by requiring[9] the auditor to discuss in the audit report matters such as audit risks, materiality used in the conduct of the audit and scope of audit work undertaken, including responses to audit risks.

One of the new ISAs, ISA 701 *Communicating Key Audit Matters in the Independent Auditor's Report,* requires the auditor to describe each key audit matter with an explanation of why the auditor considered the matter to be one of most significance in the audit and, to the extent the auditor considers it necessary as part of this explanation, its effect on the audit.

### Investor confidence

Confidence depends on shareholders accepting that:

(a) the auditors:

- are independent;
- approach the audit with a degree of scepticism;
- are professionally competent;
- have industry knowledge;
- carry out a quality audit;
- report the results of the audit in a clear manner; and

(b) the profession enforces audit standards.

### 31.9.1 Auditor independence

The external auditors should keep in mind that their main responsibility is to shareholders. However, there is a potential governance conflict in that for all practical purposes they are appointed by the board, their remuneration is agreed with the board and their day-to-day dealings are with the management. Appointments and remuneration have to be approved by the shareholders but this is normally a rubber-stamping exercise.

It is not uncommon for auditors to talk of the management as the customer, which is of course the wrong mindset. To reduce the identification with management and loss of independence arising from a personal interest in the financial performance of the client, a number of controls are often put in place, for example:

- Financial threats to independence:
  - Auditors and close relatives should not have shares or options in the company, particularly if the value of their financial interest could be directly affected by their decisions.
  - Auditors must not accept contingency fees or gifts, nor should relatives or close associates receive benefits.
  - Undertaking non-audit work the loss of which, if a significant amount, might be perceived as affecting the auditor's independence. This is a contentious issue with some advocating that auditors should not undertake non-audit work, whereas the client might consider it to be cost-effective. All the indications are that current practice will continue with disclosure of the amounts involved.

- Familiarity threats:
  - Appointments, terminations and the remuneration of auditors should be handled by the audit committee.
  - Auditors should not have worked for the company or its associates.
  - Audit partners should be rotated periodically so the audit is looked at with fresh eyes.
  - Audit tests should vary so that employees cannot anticipate what will be audited.
  - It is not desirable that audit staff be transferred to senior positions in a client company. This happens but it does mean that they will continue to have close relations with the auditors and knowledge of their audit procedures. Clients might regard this as a benefit.

However, the above are indications and not to be seen as taking a rule-based approach. Good governance is not just a matter of compliance with rules as ways can always be found to comply with rules whilst not complying with their spirit. It is really a question of behaviour – good governance depends on the auditors behaving independently, with professional competence, and identifying with shareholders and other stakeholders whose interests they are supposed to be protecting. Failing to do this leads to what is described as the expectation gap.

### 31.9.2 Lack of independence – Enron

The following is an extract from the United Nations Conference on Trade and Development G-24 Discussion Paper Series illustrating the dangers when there is a lack of independence:[10]

> Regarding auditing good corporate governance requires high-quality standards for preparation and disclosure, and independence for the external auditor. Enron's external auditor was Arthur Andersen, which also provided the firm with extensive internal auditing and consulting services . . . lack of independence linked to its multiple consultancy roles was a crucial factor in Andersen's failure to fulfill its obligations as Enron's external auditor.

### 31.9.3 Professional scepticism

Professional scepticism is defined[11] as 'an attitude that includes a questioning mind, being alert to conditions which may indicate possible misstatement due to error or fraud, and a critical assessment of audit evidence'. The auditor is explicitly required to plan and perform an audit with professional scepticism recognising that circumstances may exist that cause the financial statements to be materially misstated.

In the UK Audit Quality Inspections are carried out and consider all aspects of an audit. For example, it produced a report[12] on BDO LLP in 2015, where one of the findings was:

> On six audits we identified concerns regarding the level of professional scepticism applied in key audit areas. Whilst the firm has developed a number of initiatives intended to embed professional scepticism in the culture of the firm, including improved training, our file review findings continue to suggest that more needs to be done to achieve changes on individual audits.

#### Warning flags

The individual circumstances will vary but there are indicators such as the following that should be considered:

- Internal conditions:
  - Lack of personnel with appropriate accounting and financial reporting skills.
  - Changes in key personnel including departure of key executives.
  - Deficiencies in internal control, especially those not addressed by management.
  - Changes in the IT environment.
- Trading conditions:
  - Operations in regions that are economically unstable, for example countries with significant currency devaluation or highly inflationary economies.
  - Changes in the industry in which the entity operates.

- Developing or offering new products or services, or moving into new lines of business.
- Changes in the supply chain.

- Scale of operations:
  - Expanding into new locations.
  - Changes in the entity such as large acquisitions or reorganisations or other unusual events.
  - Entities or business segments likely to be sold.
  - The existence of complex alliances and joint ventures.

- Financial conditions:
  - Going concern and liquidity issues including loss of significant customers.
  - Constraints on the availability of capital and credit.
  - Use of off-balance-sheet finance, special-purpose entities, and other complex financing arrangements.
  - Significant transactions with related parties.
  - Excessive reliance on management representations

### 31.9.4 Example of where there was excessive reliance on management representations

In the normal course of an audit it is usual to obtain a letter of representation from management, for example providing information regarding a subsequent event occurring after year-end and the existence of off-balance-sheet contingencies. It is confirmation to the auditor that management has made full disclosure of all material activities and transactions in its financial records and statements.

However, the representations do not absolve the auditor from obtaining sufficient and appropriate audit evidence. The following is an extract[13] from an SEC finding relating to two Certified Public Accountants who were auditing a company (Structural Dynamics Research Corporation) which had improperly recorded sales and then written them off in the following accounting period:

> Despite the fact that the language in purchase orders clearly stated the orders were conditional and subject to cancellation, the auditors accepted the controller's explanation and did not take exception to the recognition of revenue on these orders. This undue reliance on management's representations constitutes insufficient professional skepticism by Present [the engagement partner].
>
> Moreover, Present failed to corroborate management's representations regarding conditional purchase orders with sufficient additional evidence that these sales were properly recorded . . . Overall, Present failed to exercise due professional care in the performance of the audit.

### 31.9.5 Developing and enforcing audit standards

#### The IAASB

There are international audit standards set by the International Auditing and Assurance Standards Board (IAASB). The IAASB in developing standards has to have regard to developments in financial reporting which has grown more complex with a greater variety of disclosures than those traditionally disclosed and the need for greater transparency in the audit work that has been carried out. As with the development of IFRSs, the IAASB follows a process of Discussion Papers, Exposure Drafts and IASs.

In 2014 it published a *Framework for Audit Quality: Key Elements that Create an Environment for Audit Quality* and in 2015 published revised IASs.

### The International Forum of Independent Audit Regulators (IFIAR)

The IFIAR is composed of 51 independent audit regulators from jurisdictions in Africa, the Americas, Asia, Europe, the Middle East and Oceania. It was formed in 2006 to provide a forum for regulators to share knowledge of the audit market environment and the practical experience gained from their independent audit regulatory activity.

IFIAR publishes the results of its surveys to inform investors, regulators, the financial community, auditors and the public about the current state of inspections of audits of public companies.

IFIAR's *2015 Survey of Inspection Findings*[14] found the highest number of audit inspection deficiencies in the areas of fair value measurement, internal control, and revenue. The rate of deficiencies in these audited areas, measured as the percentage of all inspected audits for these areas, was high:

| Total | Number of findings | Frequency of findings |
|---|---|---|
| Internal control testing | 173 | 23% |
| Fair value measurement | 158 | 18% |
| Risk assessment | 131 | 14% |
| Revenue recognition | 116 | 15% |

Whilst the standards are international, the enforcement of the standards is carried out nationally. National practice varies. In the UK, the Financial Reporting Council (FRC) is the independent regulator for corporate reporting and corporate governance. Through its Codes and Standards Committee the FRC has primary responsibility for setting, monitoring and enforcement of auditing standards in the UK.

## 31.9.6 Governance within audit firms

Within the audit practices there is also the need to apply systems to ensure that there are adequate reviews of the performance of individual auditors and that the individual partners do not take advantage of their positions of trust.

The greatest control mechanism within an audit firm is the culture of the firm. Arthur Wyatt made the following observation:[15]

> The leadership of the various firms needs to understand that the internal culture of firms needs a substantial amount of attention if the reputation of the firms is to be restored. No piece of legislation is likely to solve the behavioural changes that have evolved within the past thirty years.

### Impact of consultancy on audit attitudes

Wyatt, drawing on his experience in Arthur Andersen and his observation of competitors, indicated that in earlier times there was a culture of placing the maintenance of standards ahead of retention of clients; the smaller size of firms meant there was more informal monitoring of compliance with firm rules and ethical standards. Promotion was more likely to flow to those with the greatest technical expertise and compliance with ethical standards, rather than an ability to bring in more fees. The values of conservative accountants predominated over the risk-taking orientation of consultants.

Wyatt's view was that the growth and risk orientations of consulting are incompatible with the values needed to perform auditing in a manner which is independent in attitude.

### 31.9.7 The expectation gap

Another area of corporate governance and auditing relates to the expectation gap. The gap is between the stakeholders' expectation of the outcomes that can be expected from the auditors' performance and the outcomes that could reasonably be expected given the audit work that should have been performed.

The stakeholders' expectation is that the auditor guarantees that the financial statements are accurate, that every transaction has been 100% checked and any fraud would have been detected. The auditors' expectation is that the audit work carried out should identify material errors and misstatements based on a judgemental or statistical sampling approach.

#### Loss of confidence following corporate scandals

There have been a number of high-profile corporate failures and irregularities; for example, in the US, Enron failed, having inflated its earnings and hidden liabilities in SPEs (special-purpose entities). In 2008 the same problem of hiding liabilities appears to have occurred with Lehman Brothers where according to the Examiner's report[16] Lehman used what amounted to financial engineering to temporarily shuffle $50 billion of troubled assets off its books in the months before its collapse in September 2008 to conceal its dependence on borrowed money, and senior Lehman executives as well as the bank's accountants at Ernst & Young were aware of the moves. In Italy, Parmalat created a false paper trail and created assets where none existed; and in the US, the senior management of Tyco looted the company.

This raises questions such as (a) Were the auditors independent? (b) Did they carry out the work with due professional competence? and (c) Did they rely unduly on management representations?

### 31.9.8 Action by auditors to limit liability

In each of the above there is good reason for the expectation gap in that the audit had not been conducted in accordance with generally accepted audit standards and there was a lack of due professional care. If the auditors have been negligent then they are liable to be sued in a civil action. In the UK the profession has sought to obtain a statutory limit on their liability and, failing that, some have registered as limited liability partnerships – the path taken by Ernst & Young in 1996 and KPMG in 2002. In Australia some accountants operate under a statutory limit on their liability and in return ensure they have a minimum level of professional indemnity insurance.

### 31.9.9 Detection of fraud

An audit is designed to obtain evidence that the financial statements present a fair view and do not contain material misstatements. It is not a forensic investigation commissioned to detect fraud. Such an investigation would be expensive and in the majority of cases not be cost-effective. It has been argued that auditors should be required to carry out a fraud and detection role to avoid public concerns that arise when hearing about the high-profile corporate failures. However, it would appear that it is not so much a question of making every audit a forensic investigation to detect fraud but rather enforcing the exercise of due professional care in the conduct of all audits. The audit standards reinforce this when they emphasise the importance of scepticism.

### 31.9.10 Educating users

Many surveys have shown that there has been a considerable difference between auditors and audit report users regarding auditors' responsibilities for discovering fraud and predicting failure. Users of published financial statements need to be made aware that auditors rely on systems reviews and *sample testing* to evaluate the company's annual report. Based on those evaluations they form an opinion on the *likelihood* that the accounts provide a true and fair view or fairly present the accounts. However, they cannot guarantee the accounts are 100% accurate.

A number of major companies have collapsed without warning signs and the public have criticised the auditors. It is difficult when there are such high-profile corporate failures to persuade the public that lack of due professional care is not endemic. In response to these pressures auditors have modified their audit standards to place more emphasis on scepticism.

## 31.10 Executive remuneration in the UK

It is worth reinforcing the fact that the objective of corporate governance is to focus management on achieving the objectives of the company whilst keeping risks to appropriate levels and positioning the firm for a prosperous future. At the same time, sufficient safeguards must be in place to reduce the risks of resources being inappropriately diverted to any group at the expense of other groups involved.

### 31.10.1 The problem

The following is an extract[17] from a speech by Vince Cable, UK Secretary of State for business and industry, in 2012:

> The issue is **partly** about 'rewards for failure'. But it is not just that.
>
> There is also a ratchet in executive pay with everyone believing that they should be paid well above average and that they should be benchmarked against US peers when they live and work in the UK. It is of course a logical absurdity for everyone to be paid above the average, let alone in the top quartile. Imagine if this happened with workers' pay awards. There would be galloping wage inflation and loud business objections about our loss of competitiveness.
>
> While it is true that rising executive pay is a global phenomenon, trends in inequality at the very top are very divergent between countries, despite them all operating in the same global economy. There are world class companies in the Nordic countries, Japan, Holland and Germany who take a very different approach to the UK and US.
> But let me be clear. There is a legitimate role for high pay for exceptional talent and performance – quite apart from high returns to successful entrepreneurs – and I will defend that.

Since management is the group with the most discretion and power, it is important to ensure they do not obtain excessive remuneration or perks, or be allowed to shirk, or to gamble with company resources by taking excessive risks.

### 31.10.2 UK government response

In the UK there are new requirements[18] for directors remuneration reports from 2014. The report is split into three parts – a statement from the Chairman of the Remuneration Committee, a Policy Report and an Annual Report on remuneration. The Policy Report contains details of the performance measures (not the actual targets which are commercially sensitive) and is subject to a shareholder binding vote. The Annual Report includes a single figure for each director and the link between pay and performance. This follows the approach that disclosure should gradually result in change. This is supported when looking, for example, at the Kingfisher Remuneration Report[19] 2016, which comments positively on shareholder involvement:

> We were pleased by the level and quality of engagement and with the support received for our principles and proposed design. We welcomed the constructive feedback provided through the consultation process and this has been taken on board in our final proposals. To align incentives with the creation of long-term value, our proposed remuneration arrangements are a departure from the traditional UK executive pay model in some respects.
>
> Shareholders appreciated:
>
> - the reduced focus on annual bonus;
> - the increased five year performance period for the long-term incentive (Transformation Incentive); and
> - the balance between the short-term strategic objectives on the annual bonus, and the long-term business and financial measures on the equity elements of pay.

### 31.10.3 What is fair?

In the UK the statistics show[20] that in recent years the remuneration of executives relative to the average employee has been considerably higher than it was 20 years ago, and the remuneration of the top executive compared to the average of the next four executives is also higher than in the past.

From 1 January 2017 the Securities and Exchange Commission in the US requires public companies to disclose the ratio of the compensation of the chief executive officer (CEO) to the median compensation of its employees. The intention is that the disclosure of this information can be used to evaluate a CEO's compensation.

Just how this will play out is far from certain – the optimists hope that it will act as a restraint to ever increasing pay ratios, others might be inclined to see this as yet another ratio that CEOs will use to ratchet up their remuneration.

In the UK it is left to private organisations like the High Pay Centre[21] to calculate pay ratios. It reported in 2014 that average FTSE 100 CEO pay in 2014 was 183 times the earnings of the average full-time UK worker, up from 182 times in 2013 and 160 times in 2010.

Such high ratios seem intuitively unfair – but what is fair? Perhaps the question should be whether this higher relative remuneration reflects a greater contribution to performance, whether it reflects that as businesses increase in size the remuneration of the chief executive tends to increase to reflect the higher responsibilities, or whether it has been achieved simply because directors have been effectively able to set their own remuneration.

### 31.10.4 How to set criteria – in principle

There are a number of issues that will require a judgement to be made:

- What is the right balance between short-term performance and long-term performance? It is interesting to note that one of the measures[22] proposed in the European parliament is that:

    The remuneration policy for company directors should also contribute to the long-term growth of the company so that it corresponds to a more effective practice of corporate governance and is not linked entirely or largely to short-term investment objectives.

- What if there are revenues and costs that are beyond the control or influence of management? Should these be excluded from the measure?

- Also, to the extent that performance may be influenced by general economic conditions, should managers be assessed on absolute performance or relative performance?

Relative performance means that if the performance fell from 10% to minus 3% during an economic downturn, and competitors' performance fell to minus 5%, managers would qualify for a bonus recognising that their performance had been relatively better. This may be resented by shareholders who have seen the share price fall.

Often companies resort to outside consultants, but the observation has been made that one doesn't hear of outside consultants recommending a pay cut and they are in part responsible for ratcheting up the levels of remuneration.

### 31.10.5 Where do accountants feature in setting directors' remuneration?

The equity of the remuneration is not normally seen as an accounting matter, but accountants should ensure transparent disclosure of the performance criteria and of the payments. In some jurisdictions there is legislation setting out in some detail what has to be disclosed.

For example, in the UK The Large and Medium-sized Companies and Groups (Accounts and Reports) (Amendment) Regulations 2013 requires the annual report to contain a single total figure table comprising six columns, reporting for each director (with certain conditions):

- the total amount of salary and fees;
- all taxable benefits;
- money or other assets received or receivable for the relevant financial year as a result of the achievement of performance measures and targets relating to a period ending in that financial year;
- money or other assets received or receivable for periods of more than one financial year where final vesting is determined as a result of the achievement of performance measures or targets relating to a period ending in the relevant financial year;
- all pension-related benefits including payments (whether in cash or otherwise) in lieu of retirement benefits and all benefits in year from participating in pension schemes; and
- the total amount of the sums set out in the previous five columns.

It is interesting to see companies carrying out sensitivity tests to show the maximum that is achievable if all targets are met. For example, the following is an extract from the IMI Annual Report and Accounts 2014:[23]

To illustrate the opportunity available to our executive directors, and the *sensitivity* of pay to performance, the adjacent graphs set out pay outcomes for three performance scenarios:

- minimum, where pay is limited to fixed, non-performance related components;
- 'on-target', where bonus vests at target levels for each executive, and long-term incentives vest at threshold; and
- maximum, where all variable pay components vest in full.

### 31.10.6 Performance criteria

Directors are expected to produce increases in the share price and dividends. Traditional measures have been largely based on growth in earnings per share (EPS), which has encouraged companies to seek to increase short-term earnings at the expense of long-term earnings, e.g. by cutting back capital programmes. Even worse, concentrating on growth in earnings per share can result in a reduction in shareholder value, e.g. by companies borrowing and investing in projects that produce a return in excess of the interest charge, but less than the return expected by equity investors.

### 31.10.7 Institutional investor guidelines

One of the problems is the innovative nature of the remuneration packages that companies might adopt and the fact that there is no uniquely correct scheme. The following are examples of the various criteria which have evolved and which have been adopted:

**Absolute Measures or Targets**
Normalised earnings per share measured by reference to a percentage margin, for example 2% per annum growth, in excess of inflation over a 3 year period. It is important that the figures for earnings be smoothed where appropriate to avoid distortions arising from one-off extraordinary or exceptional items included within the FRS 3 definition of earnings per share.

**Comparative Measures**
Outperformance of an index or of the median or weighted average of a pre-defined peer group in the case of basic options: or the achievement of top quartile performance in the case of super-options:

(i) *Normalised earnings per share*
Outperformance of the median or weighted average rate of increase in normalised earnings of a peer group.

(ii) *Net Asset Value per Share*
Net asset value per share measured, for example against a predefined peer group or index.

(iii) *Total Shareholder Return (i.e. share price performance plus gross dividend per share)*
Where total shareholder return is used this should be based on exceeding the relevant benchmark within a predefined peer group but, as this formula relies substantially on share price, attainment of the criterion should also be supported by

a defined secondary criterion validating sustained and significant improvement in the underlying financial performance.

**(iv)** *Comparative Share Price*

Comparative share price relative to a peer group would be an acceptable alternative to total shareholder return, conditional in the same way on a secondary performance criterion validating sustained and significant improvement in underlying financial performance over the same period.

### 31.10.8 Institutional investors' statements of principles

In the UK, in response to The Large and Medium-sized Companies and Groups (Accounts and Reports) (Amendment) Regulations 2013, the Association of British Insurers (ABI)[24] and the National Association of Pension Funds (NAPF)[25] have issued statements of principles that they expect companies to consider when setting remuneration policies.

These include proactive proposals that schemes should ensure that executive rewards reflect long-term returns to shareholders by expecting executive management to make a material long-term investment in shares of the businesses they manage. There are also proposals to address the criticisms that have been made that poor performance has still been rewarded by proposing that there should be provisions that allow a company to forfeit all or part of a bonus or long-term incentive award before it has vested and been paid and claw back moneys already paid.

## 31.11 Corporate governance, legislation and codes

Investors looking to the safety and adequacy of the return on their investment are influenced by their level of confidence in the ability of the directors to achieve this. Good governance has not been fully defined and various reports have attempted to set out principles and practices which they perceive to be helpful in making directors accountable. These principles and practices are set out in a variety of Acts, e.g. Sarbanes–Oxley in the US and the Companies Act and regulations in the UK, and codes such as the Singapore Code of Corporate Governance 2012 and the UK Corporate Governance Code (formerly the Combined Code).

The various laws and codes that have been published set out principles and recommended best practice relating to the board of directors, directors' remuneration, relations with shareholders, accountability and audit.

### The European Corporate Governance Institute[26]

This is an excellent resource that covers pretty well all the corporate governance codes in the world. It is interesting to refer to the Institute's website to observe the number of new and amended codes since 2010 which reflects the growing importance attached to corporate governance in terms of investor confidence.

### 31.11.1 Codes as a partial solution

As the nature of business and expectations of society change, the governance requirements evolve to reflect the new laws and regulations. By anticipating changing requirements, companies can prepare for the future. At the same time they should identify the special areas of potential conflict in their own operations and develop policies to manage those relationships.

Good governance is a question of having the right attitudes. All the corporate governance codes will not achieve much if they focus on form rather than substance. Codes work because people want to achieve good governance. People can always find ways around rules.

The FRC has taken the view in 2014 that more effective application of, and reporting on, existing code principles may often have a greater impact on actual standards of governance and stewardship than managing further change.

Furthermore, rules cannot cover all cases, so good governance needs a commitment to the fundamental idea of fairness.

The research on whether good governance leads to lower cost of capital is very mixed, reflecting both the difficulty of identifying the impact of good governance and the fact that some engage with the spirit of the concept and some do not. There are those who question the impact of good corporate governance, and supporting the case of those who doubt that there is a positive impact on performance is an Australian research project[27] looking at companies in the S&P/ASX 200 index which found that companies which the researcher classified as having poor corporate governance outperformed companies classified as having good corporate governance over a range of measures including EBITDA growth and return on assets. There is an ongoing need for further research, particularly as to the effect on smaller listed companies, and it will be interesting to await the outcome.

## 31.12 Corporate governance – the UK experience

In the UK there have been a number of initiatives in attempting to achieve good corporate governance through (a) legislation, (b) the UK Corporate Governance Code, (c) non-executive directors (NEDs), (d) shareholder activism and (e) audit. We discuss each of these briefly below.

### 31.12.1 Legislation

Legislation is in place that attempts to ensure that investors receive sufficient information to make informed judgements. For example, there are requirements for the audit of financial statements, majority voting on directors' remuneration policy and disclosure of directors' remuneration. There could be a case for increased statutory involvement in the affairs of a company by, for example, putting a limit on benefits and specifying how share options should be structured. However, the government has gone down the road of disclosure and transparency to encourage and empower shareholder activism.

### 31.12.2 The UK Corporate Governance Code[28]

The Code is routinely reviewed every two years. The current code was published by the Financial Reporting Council (FRC) in 2012. It sets out standards of good practice in relation to board leadership and effectiveness, remuneration, accountability and relations with shareholders. It is not a rule book but is principles-based and sets out best practice. It relies for its effectiveness on disclosure by requiring companies listed on a stock exchange to explain if they do not comply with its provisions.

The original code made an interesting development by separating its proposals into two parts:

- Part 1 containing Principles of Good Governance (Main and Supplementary) relating to:
  - A: directors;
  - B: directors' remuneration;
  - C: relations with shareholders;
  - D: accountability and audit.
- Part 2 containing Codes of Best Practice with procedures to make the Principles operational.

The current updated Code continues to set out broad principles from which companies are largely free to choose their own method of implementation. The detailed code provisions are those which companies are required to say whether they have complied with and, where they have not complied, to explain why not. The intention is to combine flexibility over detailed implementation with clarity where there was non-compliance.

The principles and code provisions relating to the board of directors are set out below to illustrate the code's approach. The six principles that relate to directors cover:

- **A1** the board
- **A2** chairman and chief executive
- **A3** board balance and independence
- **A4** appointments to the board
- **A5** information and professional development
- **A6** performance evaluation.

As an illustration of the level of detail, the Principles (A1) and Provisions (A1.3 and A1.4) relating to the board are set out below.

### *A1 The Board*
### Main Principle
Every company should be headed by an effective board, which is collectively responsible for the success of the company.
### Supporting Principles include:

- The board should
  - set the company's values and standards; and
  - ensure that its obligations to its shareholders and others are understood and met.
- As part of their role as members of a unitary board, non-executive directors should
  - constructively challenge and help develop proposals on strategy;
  - scrutinise the performance of management in meeting agreed goals and objectives and monitor the reporting of performance;
  - satisfy themselves on the integrity of financial information and that financial controls and systems of risk management are robust and defensible.
- As non-executive directors they
  - are responsible for determining appropriate levels of remuneration of executive directors; and
  - have a prime role in appointing, and where necessary removing, executive directors, and in succession planning.

### Code Provisions (*relating to NEDs*)

A.1.3 The chairman should hold meetings with the non-executive directors without the executives present. Led by the senior independent director, the non-executive directors should meet without the chairman present at least annually to appraise the chairman's performance (as described in A.6.1) and on such other occasions as are deemed appropriate.

A.1.4 Where directors have concerns which cannot be resolved about the running of the company or a proposed action, they should ensure that their concerns are recorded in the board minutes. On resignation, a non-executive director should provide a written statement to the chairman, for circulation to the board, if they have any such concerns.

### Revisions to the code in 2012

The revisions included:

- Boards will be expected to confirm that the report and accounts, taken as a whole, is fair, balanced and understandable and provides the information needed for shareholders to assess the company's performance, business model and strategy.

- A description of the board's policy on diversity, including gender, any measurable objectives that it has set for implementing the policy, and progress on achieving the objectives.

- Evaluation of the board should consider the balance of skills, experience, independence and knowledge of the company on the board, its diversity, including gender, how the board works together as a unit, and other factors relevant to its effectiveness.

### Revisions to the code in 2014

The key changes to the code included:

*Going concern, risk management and internal control*
- Companies should state whether they consider it appropriate to adopt the going concern basis of accounting and identify any material uncertainties to their ability to continue to do so.

- Companies should robustly assess their principal risks and explain how they are being managed or mitigated.

- Companies should state whether they believe they will be able to continue in operation and meet their liabilities taking account of their current position and principal risks, and specify the period covered by this statement and why they consider it appropriate. It is expected that the period assessed will be significantly longer than 12 months.

- Companies should monitor their risk management and internal control systems and, at least annually, carry out a review of their effectiveness, and report on that review in the annual report.

*Remuneration*
- Greater emphasis be placed on ensuring that remuneration policies are designed with the long-term success of the company in mind, and that the lead responsibility for doing so rests with the remuneration committee.

- Companies should put in place arrangements that will enable them to recover or withhold variable pay when appropriate to do so, and should consider appropriate vesting and holding periods for deferred remuneration.

### 31.12.3 Non-executive directors (NEDs)

The main function of non-executive directors is to ensure that the executive directors are pursuing policies consistent with shareholders' interests.[29]

#### Review of their contribution

Considering the qualities that are required, the Cadbury Report recommended that the board should include non-executive directors of sufficient calibre and number for their views to carry significant weight in the board's decisions. Research[30] indicated that they are concerned to maintain their reputation in the external market in order to maintain their marketability.

NEDs on many boards bring added or essential commercial and financial expertise, for example on a routine basis as members of the audit committee, or on an *ad hoc* basis providing experience when a company is preparing to float or having specific industry knowledge. They are also valued as having a role in questioning investment decisions and entering into unduly risky projects.

#### Limitations

However, NEDs are not and never can be a universal panacea. It has to be recognised that there may be constraints such as:

- They might have divided loyalties, having been nominated by the chairman, the CEO or another board member.

- This has been addressed by the Code which states 'An explanation should be given if neither an external search consultancy nor open advertising has been used in the appointment of a nonexecutive director. Where an external search consultancy has been used, it should be identified in the report and a statement should be made as to whether it has any other connection with the company.'

- They might have other NED appointments and/or executive appointments which limit the time they can give to the company's affairs.

- This is addressed by some companies such as BUPA[31] which requires non-executive directors to disclose their other significant commitments to the board before appointment, with a broad indication of the time involved; and inform the board of any subsequent changes.

- They might not be able to restrain an overbearing CEO, particularly if the CEO is also the chairman.

- A 2009 survey[32] indicated that a third of non-executive directors feel they are unable to control their chairmen and chief executives, and almost 40% feel they would be unable to sack underperforming board colleagues.

With so many caveats, it would be reasonable to assume that NEDs could not easily divert a dominant CEO or executive directors from a planned course of action. In such cases, their influence on good corporate governance is reduced unless the interest of directors and shareholders already happen to coincide. However, if the issue is serious enough for one or more independent director to resign it is likely that the market will certainly take note.

### Independent NEDs and risk – a negative view

Research[33] commented that the view that outside directors brought experience and strategic expertise, together with vigilance in monitoring management decisions, to prevent strategic mistakes and/or opportunistic behaviour by management was not supported by much evidence that governance reduces risks. The researchers found little evidence that governance was effective in reducing the volatility of share prices or the chance of large adverse share price movements. As with the financial sector in the credit crunch, independent directors seem not to be a protection against companies adopting risky strategies.

### Independent NEDs and risk – a positive view

However, on a more positive note, the presence of NEDs is perceived to be indicative of good corporate governance, and a research report[34] indicated that good governance has a positive impact on investor confidence. The research examined 654 UK FTSE All-Share companies from 2003 to 2007 using unique governance data from the ABI's Institutional Voting and Information Service (IVIS). An extract from the ABI research is as follows:

> New research from the ABI (Association of British Insurers) shows that companies with the best corporate governance records have produced returns 18% higher than those with poor governance. It was also revealed that a breach of governance best practice (known as a red top in the ABI's guidance) reduces a company's industry-adjusted return on assets (ROA) by an average of 1 percentage point a year. For even the best performing companies (those within the top quartile of ROA performance), that equates to an actual fall of 8.6% in returns per year.
>
> The research also shows that shareholders investing in a poorly governed company suffer from low returns. £100 invested in a company with no corporate governance problems leads to an average return of £120 but if invested in the worst governed companies the return would have been just £102.

There are many highly talented, well-experienced NEDs but their ability to influence good governance should not be overestimated. Their effectiveness might be reduced if they have limited time, limited access to documents, limited respect from full-time executive directors and limited expertise within the remuneration and/or audit committees. When a company is prospering their influence could be extremely beneficial; when there are problems they may not have the authority to ensure good governance.

## 31.12.4 Shareholder activism

In the UK the need for good corporate governance is affected by how widely shares are held.

In the US and the UK, a large number of financial institutions and individuals hold shares in listed companies, so there is a greater need for corporate governance requirements. In Japan and most European countries (except the UK) shares in listed companies tend to be held by a small number of banks, financial institutions and individuals. Where there are few shareholders in a company, they can question the directors directly, so there is less need for corporate governance requirements.

The following table is an extract from the UK Office for National Statistics[35] showing the holdings in UK shares:

**Beneficial ownership of UK shares in 2014**

| | Percentages | |
| --- | --- | --- |
| | *2010* | *2014* |
| Rest of the world | 41.2 | 53.8 |
| Insurance companies | 8.6 | 5.9 |
| Pensions funds | 5.1 | 3.0 |
| Individuals | 11.5 | 11.9 |
| Unit trusts | 6.7 | 9.0 |
| Investment trusts | 2.1 | 1.8 |
| Other financial institutions | 16.0 | 7.1 |
| Charities | 0.9 | 1.2 |
| Private non-financial companies | 2.3 | 2.0 |
| Public sector | 3.1 | 2.9 |
| Banks | 2.5 | 1.4 |
| Total | 100.0 | 100 |

Figures show that at the end of 2010 the UK stock market was valued at £1,777.5 billion falling to £726.8 billion by 2014.

## Individual shareholder influence on corporate governance

With the rest of the world holding 53.8% and individual shareholders holding only 11.9% it is difficult for the latter group to exercise any significant group influence on management behaviour. In passing legislation, there is an implicit view that individual shareholders have a responsibility to achieve good corporate governance. Statutes can provide for disclosure and be fine-tuned in response to changing needs but they are not intended to replace shareholder activism. When the economy is booming there is a temptation to sit back, collect the dividends and capital gains, bin the annual report and post in proxy forms.

Shareholder influence has to rely on that exercised by the institutional investors.

## Large-block investors' influence on corporate governance

There is mixed evidence about the influence of large-block shareholders. The following is an extract from a Department of Trade and Industry report:[36]

> The report observed from a review of economics, corporate finance and 'law and economics' research literature that there was no unambiguous evidence that presence of large-block and institutional investors among the firm's shareholders performed monitoring and resource functions of 'good' corporate governance. However, management and business strategy research suggests that it does have a significant effect on *critical* organisational decisions, such as executive turnover, value-enhancing business strategy, and limitations on anti-takeover defences.

Feedback from the experts' evaluation of the governance roles of various types of shareholders provided the following pattern:[36]

| | Mean | Standard deviation |
|---|---|---|
| Pension funds, mutual funds, foundations | 4.58 | 1.50 |
| Private equity funds | 4.52 | 1.76 |
| Individual (non-family) blockholders | 4.36 | 1.70 |
| Family blockholders | 4.20 | 1.63 |
| Corporate pension funds | 3.85 | 1.55 |
| Insurance companies | 3.69 | 1.69 |
| Banks | 3.31 | 1.49 |
| Dispersed individual shareholders | 2.18 | 1.41 |

The highest scores were assigned to the governance roles of pension funds, mutual funds, foundations and private equity investors:

> Some respondents also suggested that various associations of institutional investors such as NAPF, ABI, etc., play strong governance roles, as do individual blockholders and family owners. At the other end of the spectrum are dispersed individual shareholders whose governance roles received the lowest score. However, it must be kept in mind that none of the individual scores is above 5 indicating that, on average, our experts were rather sceptical about the effectiveness of large blockholders from the 'good' governance perspective.[36]

A further related factor is that US and UK companies have tended to have a low gearing with most of the finance provided by shareholders. However, in other countries the gearing of companies is much higher, which indicates that most finance for companies comes from banks. If the majority of the finance is provided by shareholders, then there is a greater need for corporate governance requirements than if finance is in the form of loans where the lenders are able to stipulate conditions and loan covenants, e.g. the maximum level of gearing and action available to them if interest payments or capital repayments are missed.

However, institutional investors do not represent a majority in any company. Their role is to achieve the best return on the funds under their management consistent with their attitude to environmental and social issues. Their expertise has been largely directed towards the strategic management and performance of the company with, perhaps, an excessive concern with short-term gains. Issues such as directors' remuneration might well be of far less significance than the return on their investment.

## The Stewardship Code[37]

The **Stewardship Code** is a set of principles or guidelines issued by the FRC in 2010. Its principal aim is to make institutional investors take an active role to protect the interests of the people who have placed their money with them to invest.

The code consists of seven principles which, if followed, should benefit corporate governance. The principles are:

1 **Institutional investors should publicly disclose their policy on how they will discharge their stewardship responsibilities.** Such a policy should include how investee companies will be monitored with an active dialogue on the board and its policy on voting and the use made of proxy voting.

2 **Institutional investors should have a robust policy on managing conflicts of interest in relation to stewardship and this policy should be publicly disclosed.** Such a policy should include how to manage conflicts of interest when, for example, voting on matters affecting a parent company or client.

3 **Institutional investors should monitor when it is necessary to enter into an active dialogue with their boards.** Such monitoring should include satisfying themselves that the board and sub-committee structures are effective, and that independent directors provide adequate oversight and maintain a clear audit trail of the institution's decisions. The objective is to identify problems at an early stage to minimise any loss of shareholder value.

4 **Institutional investors should establish clear guidelines on when and how they will escalate their activities as a method of protecting and enhancing shareholder value.** Such guidelines should say the circumstances when they will actively intervene. Instances when institutional investors may want to intervene include when they have concerns about the company's strategy and performance, its governance or its approach to the risks arising from social and environmental matters. If there are concerns, then any action could escalate from meetings with management specifically to discuss the concerns through to requisitioning an EGM, possibly to change the board.

5 **Institutional investors should be willing to act collectively with other investors where appropriate.** Such action is proposed in extreme cases when the risks posed threaten the ability of the company to continue.

6 **Institutional investors should have a clear policy on voting and disclosure of voting activity.** Institutional investors should seek to vote all shares held. They should not automatically support the board and if they have been unable to reach a satisfactory outcome through active dialogue then they should register an abstention or vote against the resolution.

7 **Institutional investors should report periodically on their stewardship and voting activities.** Such reports should be made regularly and explain how they have discharged their responsibilities. However, it is recognised that confidentiality in specific situations may well be crucial to achieving a positive outcome.

The FRC proposes to extend these principles to all listed companies.

### The Kay Review[38]

The Kay Review of UK Equity Markets and Long-term Decision Making was published in 2012. It recommended that the Stewardship Code should be developed to incorporate a more expansive form of stewardship, focusing on strategic issues as well as questions of corporate governance. This is in keeping with the increasing pressure for companies to report risks and how they are addressing them. It also recommended that an investors' forum should be established to facilitate collective engagement by investors in UK companies. This recommendation has been acted on[39] and the 'Investors Forum' has been launched by the Collective Engagement Working Group.

● There has been recognition that a cultural change is needed with investors and companies developing a shared sense of partnership to promote long-term strategies that can generate sustainable wealth creation for all stakeholders. One way forward is for all major listed companies to hold an annual strategy meeting for institutional investors, outside the results cycle, where investors and company executives can link governance to the company's long-term strategy without the focus on short-term results. Where there are shared concerns about a particular company it is proposed that an Engagement Action Group should operate.

- An investors' forum should be established to facilitate collective engagement by investors in UK companies.

- Companies should consult their major long-term investors over major board appointments.

- High-quality, succinct narrative reporting should be strongly encouraged.

- Companies should structure directors' remuneration to relate incentives to sustainable long-term business performance. Long-term performance incentives should be provided only in the form of company shares to be held at least until after the executive has retired from the business.

- Asset management firms should similarly structure managers' remuneration so as to align the interests of asset managers with the interests and timescales of their clients. Pay should therefore not be related to short-term performance of the investment fund or asset management firm. Rather a long-term performance incentive should be provided in the form of an interest in the fund (either directly or via the firm) to be held at least until the manager is no longer responsible for that fund.

### Legal safeguards

Corporate governance has to react to changing circumstances and threats. It evolves and will continue to need to be revised and updated. The law provides minimum safeguards but in the ever-changing complexities of global trade and finance, good governance is dependent on the behaviour of directors and their commitment to principles and values. The UK system is heavily dependent on codes which set out principles and the requirement for directors to explain if they fail to comply. The UK Corporate Governance Code and Stewardship Code will rely for their effectiveness on investor engagement. This recognises that investors cannot delegate all responsibility to their agents, the directors, accept their dividends and be dormant principals.

### UK experience and international initiatives

It is interesting to note that what constitutes good corporate governance is evolving with new initiatives being taken globally. For example, the OECD is responding to weaknesses in corporate governance that became apparent in the financial crisis by developing recommendations for improvements in board practices, the remuneration process and how shareholders should actively exercise their rights. It is also reviewing governance in relation to risk management which featured as such a threat in the way financial institutions conducted their business. However, there is some concern that measures that might be essential for the control of the financial sector should not be imposed arbitrarily on non-financial sector organisations.

## 31.12.5 Audit

There has been audit reform in the EU[40] with a Directive setting out new rules which addresses independence, the expectation gap and competition.

### Independence
These include the mandatory rotation of auditors every 10 years (or 20 years subject to tendering), the prohibition on the provision of certain non-audit services to audit and the introduction of a cap on fees that can be earned from the provision of permitted non-audit services.

The *expectation* gap

This is to be improved by ensuring increased audit quality and more detailed and informative audit reports with meaningful data for investors and better accountability with a provision for 5% of the shareholders in a company to initiate actions to dismiss the auditors.

*Competition*

Medium sized audit practices have been precluded from obtaining audit work with some major companies that have had a 'Big Four only' policy. This restrictive practice is now prohibited. In addition there will be the impact of the prohibition of certain non-audit services to audit clients.

Auditors are subject to professional oversight to ensure that they are independent, up-to-date and competent. However, where there is a determined effort to mislead the auditors, for example by creating false paper trails and misstatement at the highest level, then there is the risk that fraud will be missed.

There have been allegations of audit negligence in some high-profile corporate failures, in some of which auditors have been found liable. In part, the financial crisis arising from issues such as the use of special-purpose entities and complex financial instruments has made life more difficult for auditors. This is because pressure groups, such as the investment banks, have influenced the regulators to allow, or not question, practices that have since been found to be highly risky and undisclosed in group accounts.

In general, whilst the audit appears to be a reliable mechanism for ensuring that the financial statements give a true and fair view, there is a need for audit staff to acquire a detailed understanding of the industry being audited and the risks attaching to financial instruments.

## Summary

Good governance is achieved when all parties feel that they have been fairly treated. It is achieved when behaviour is prompted by the idea of fairness to all parties. Independent behaviour is expected of the NEDs and auditors and they are expected to have the strength of character to act professionally with proper regard for the interest of the shareholders. The shareholders in turn should be exercising their rights and not be inert. They have a role to play and it is not fair of them to sit on their hands and complain.

Good corporate governance cannot be achieved by rules alone. The principle-based approach such as that of the FRC with the UK Corporate Governance Code recognises that it is behaviour that is the key – it sets out broad principles and a recommended set of provisions/rules which are indicative of good practice, and disclosure is required if there is a reason why they are not appropriate in a specific situation.

Good corporate governance depends on directors behaving in the best interest of shareholders. Corporate governance mechanisms to achieve this include legislation, corporate governance codes, appointment of NEDs, shareholder activism and audit. Such mechanisms are necessary when companies are financed largely by equity capital. It is noticeable that they are being developed in many countries in response to wider share ownership.

Corporate governance best practice is being regularly reviewed and improved internationally.

# REVIEW QUESTIONS

1 Explain in your own words what you understand corporate governance to mean.

2 Explain why governance procedures may vary from country to country.

3 What are the implications of governance for audit practices?

4 Auditors should take a more combative position and start with presumptive doubt and a more sceptical frame of mind, even though past experience of the FD and client staff has never revealed any cause for suspicion. Discuss the extent to which the requirement to adopt a different approach will increase the auditor's responsibility for detecting fraud.

5 The Association of British Insurers held the view that options should be exercised only if the company's earnings per share growth exceeded that of the Retail Price Index. The National Association of Pension Funds preferred the criterion to be a company's outperformance of the FTA All-Share Index.

   (a) Discuss the reasons for the differences in approach.

   (b) Discuss the implication of each approach to the financial reporting regulators and the auditors.

6 Research[41] suggests that companies whose managers own a significant proportion of the voting share capital tend to violate the UK Corporate Governance Code recommendations on board composition far more frequently than other companies. Discuss the advantages and disadvantages of enforcing greater compliance.

7 'Good corporate governance is a myth – just look at these frauds and irregularities:

   ● Enron www.sec.gov/litigation/litreleases/lr18582.htm

   ● WorldCom www.sec.gov/litigation/litreleases/lr17588.htm

   ● Xerox Corporation www.sec.gov/litigation/complaints/complr17465.htm

   ● Dell www.sec.gov/news/press/2010/2010-131.htm

   ● Lehman http://lehmanreport.jenner.com/VOLUME%201.pdf'

   How realistic is it to expect good governance to combat similar future behaviour?

8 'Stronger corporate governance legislation is emerging globally but true success will only come from self-regulation, increased internal controls and the strong ethical corporate culture that organisations create.' Discuss.

9 In the modern commercial world, auditors provide numerous other services to complement their audit work. These services include the following:

   (a) Accountancy and book-keeping assistance, e.g. in the maintenance of ledgers and in the preparation of monthly and annual accounts.

   (b) Consultancy services, e.g. advice on the design of information systems and organisational structures, advice on the choice of computer equipment and software packages, and advice on the recruitment of new executives.

   (c) Investigation work, e.g. appraisals of companies that might be taken over.

   (d) Taxation work, e.g. tax planning advice and preparation of tax returns to HM Revenue and Customs for both the company and the company's senior management.

Discuss:

(i) Whether any of these activities is unacceptable as a separate activity because it might weaken an auditor's independence.

(ii) The advantages and disadvantages to the shareholders of the audit firm providing this range of service.

10 The following is an extract from the *Sunday Times* of 8 March 2009:

Marc Jobling, the ABI's assistant director of investment affairs, said: 'Pay consultants are a big contributor to the problems around executive pay. We have heard of some who admit that they work for both management and independent directors – which is a clear conflict of interest and not acceptable. We believe that remuneration consultants, whose livelihood appears to depend on pushing an ever-upward spiral in executive pay, should be obliged to develop a code of ethics.'

Discuss the types of issues which should be included in such a code of ethics and how effective they would be in achieving good corporate governance.

11 There has been much criticism of the effectiveness of non-executive directors following failures such as Enron. Some consider that their interests are too close to those of the executive directors and they have neither the time nor the professional support to allow them to be effective monitors of the executive directors. Draft a job specification and personal criteria that you think would allay these criticisms.

12 In 2000, the chairman of the US Securities and Exchange Commission (SEC), Arthur Levitt, proposed that other services provided by audit firms to their audit clients should be severely restricted, probably solely to audit and tax work.[42] Discuss why this has still not happened.

13 Discuss how remuneration policies may adversely affect good corporate governance and how these effects may be reduced or prevented.

14 Discuss the major risks which will need to be managed by a pharmaceutical company and the extent to which these should be disclosed.

15 Egypt is a country in which many of the public companies have substantial shareholders in the form of founding families or government shareholders. How do you think that would affect corporate governance?

16 'Management will become accountable only when shareholders receive information on corporate strategy, future-based plans and budgets, and actual results with explanations of variances.' Discuss whether this is necessary, feasible and in the company's interest.

17 The Chartered Institute of Management Accountants (CIMA) has warned that linking directors' pay to EPS or return on assets is open to abuse, since these are not the objective measures they might appear.

(a) Identify four ways in which the directors might manipulate the EPS and return on assets without breaching existing standards.

(b) Suggest two alternative bases for setting criteria for bonuses.

18 Review reporting requirements in relation to disclosure of related party transactions and discuss their adequacy in relation to the avoidance of conflicts of interest.

19 Discuss in what situations audit independence could be compromised.

20 It has been suggested that an Investors Forum will make management more accountable to the shareholders. Discuss how this might be achieved when shareholdings are so widely held.

21 It has been suggested that there would be less of an expectation gap if there were to be a note to the accounts giving in relation to those assets and liabilities which involved estimates the range of values and confidence level in the reported figure – for example, land, inventory, trade receivables.

Discuss the pros and cons of this suggestion from the viewpoint of the shareholder and the auditor.

22 Access the FRC Guidance on the Strategic Report issued in June 2014 and refer to section 7 'The strategic report: content elements'. Then select a set of published accounts and review the extent to which the company has satisfied the guidance. (www.frc.org.uk/Our-Work/Publications/Accounting-and-Reporting-Policy/Guidance-on-the-Strategic-Report.pdf)

23 The IASB should issue a Practice Statement giving detailed guidance on the calculation of an alternative EPS figure if used to set targets for executive bonus.

Discuss.

24 It is proposed in France that long-term investors in a company should have double-voting rights unless they opt out.

Discuss the advantages and disadvantages of adopting this as requirement in all companies reporting under IFRSs.

## EXERCISES

### Question 1

Manufacturing Co. has been negotiating with Fred Paris regarding the sale of some property that represented an old manufacturing site which is now surplus to requirements. Because part of the site was used for manufacturing, it has to be decontaminated before it can be subdivided as a new housing development. This has complicated negotiations. Fred is a property developer and has a private company (Paris Property Development Pty Ltd) and is also a major (15%) shareholder of FP Development of which he is chairman. The negotiators for Manufacturing Co. note that the documents keep switching between Paris Property Development and FP Development and they use that as feedback as to how well they are negotiating.

**Required:**
**Is there a corporate governance failure? Discuss.**

### Question 2

Harvey Storm is chief executive of West Wing Savings and Loans. Harvey authorises a loan to Middleman Properties secured on the land it is about to purchase. Middleman Properties has little money of its own. Middleman Properties subdivides the land and builds houses on them. It offers buyers a house and finance package under which West Wing provides the house loans up to 97% of the house price even to couples with poor credit ratings. This allows Middleman Properties to ask for higher prices for the houses.

Middleman Properties appoints Frontman Homes as the selling agent who kindly provides buyers with the free services of a solicitor to handle all the legal aspects including the conveyancing. Most of the profits from the developments are paid to Frontman Homes as commissions. Harvey Storm's wife has a 20% interest in Frontman Homes.

**Required:**
**Are these corporate governance failures? Discuss.**

## Question 3

Conglomerate plc was a family company which was so successful that the founding Alexander family could not fully finance its expansion. So the company was floated on the Stock Exchange with the Alexander family holding 'A' class shares and the public holding 'B' class shares. 'A' class shares held the right to appoint six of the eleven directors. 'B' class shares could appoint five directors and had the same dividend rights as the 'A' class shares. The company could not be wound up unless a resolution was passed by 75% or more of 'A' class shareholders.

**Required:**
**Is there any risk of a governance failure? Discuss.**

## Question 4

The board of White plc is discussing the filling of a vacant position arising from the death of Lord White. A list of possible candidates is as follows:

(a) Lord Sperring, who is a well-known company director and who was the managing director of Sperring Manufacturers before he switched to being a professional director.

(b) John Spate, B.Eng., PhD, who is managing director of a successful, innovative high-technology company and will be taking retirement in four months' time.

(c) Gerald Stewart, B. Com, who is the retired managing director of Spry and Montgomery advertising agency which operates in six countries, being the UK and five other Commonwealth countries.

The managing director leads the discussion and focuses on the likelihood of the three candidates being able to work in harmony with other members of the board. He suggests that John Spate is too radical to be a member of the board of White plc. The other members of the board agree that he has a history of looking at things differently and would tend to distract the board.

The chairman of the board suggests that Lord Sperring is very well connected in the business community and would be able to open many doors for the managing director. It was unanimously agreed that the chairman should approach Lord Sperring to see if he would be willing to join the board.

**Required:**
**Critically discuss the appointment process.**

## Question 5

(a) Describe the value to the audit client of the audit firm providing consultancy services.

(b) Why is it undesirable for audit firms to provide consultancy services to audit clients?

(c) Why do audit firms want to continue to provide consultancy services to audit clients?

## Question 6

How is the relationship between the audit firm and the audit client different for:

(a) the provision of statutory audit when the auditor reports to the shareholders;

(b) the provision of consultancy services by audit firms?

## Question 7

Why is there a prohibition of auditors owning shares in client companies? Is this prohibition reasonable? Discuss.

## Notes

1 C. Oman (ed.), *Corporate Governance in Development: The Experiences of Brazil, Chile, India and South Africa*, OECD Development Centre and Center for International Private Enterprise, Paris and Washington, DC, 2003, cited in N. Meisel, *Governance Culture and Development*, Development Centre, OECD, Paris, 2004, p. 16.

2 http://www.publications.parliament.uk/pa/cm201516/cmselect/cmpubadm/980/980.pdf

3 www.oecd.org/dataoecd/28/62/38699164.pdf

4 www.sec.gov/news/pressrelease/2016-74.html4

5 http://cphpost.dk/business/ruin-bank-and-earn-ten-million-kroner

6 www.heraldtribune.com/article/20100719/COLUMNIST/7191018

7 An example of this is the convergence of computing, telephone, television and entertainment markets as new devices impinge on all fields compared to ten years ago when they were quite distinct fields.

8 https://na.theiia.org/standards-guidance/Public%20Documents/MODEL_AUDIT_COMMITTEE_CHARTER.pdf

9 *The New Auditor's Report: Enhancing Auditor Communications*, January 2015, Greater Transparency into the Financial Statement Audit. IAASB, www.ifac.org/system/files/uploads/IAASB/Auditor-Reporting-Fact-Sheet.pdf

10 A. Cornford, 'Enron and internationally agreed principles for corporate governance and the financial sector', G-24 Discussion Paper Series, United Nations.

11 ISA 200, *Overall Objectives of the Independent Auditor and the Conduct of an Audit in Accordance with International Standards on Auditing*, paragraph 13(l).

12 www.frc.org.uk/Our-Work/Publications/Audit-Quality-Review/Audit-Quality-Inspection-Report-May-2016-BDO-LLP.pdf

13 www.sec.gov/litigation/admin/3438494.txt

14 www.ifiar.org/IFIAR/media/Documents/General/About%20Us/IFIAR-2015-Survey-of-Inspection-Findings.pdf

15 A.R. Wyatt (2003), 'Accounting professionalism – they just don't get it!', http://aaahq.orgAM2003/WyattSpeech.pdf

16 http://lehmanreport.jenner.com/

17 www.bis.gov.uk/news/speeches/vince-cable-executive-pay-remuneration-2012

18 The Large and Medium-sized Companies and Groups (Accounts and Reports) (Amendment) Regulations 2013 www.legislation.gov.uk/uksi/2013/1981/schedule/made

19 www.kingfisher.com/files/pdf/directors_remuneration_report_2016.pdf

20 L. Bebchuk, M. Cremers and U. Peyer, 'Higher CEO salaries don't always pay off', *The Australian Financial Review*, 12 February 2010, p. 59.

21 http://highpaycentre.org/pubs/new-high-pay-centre-report-executive-pay-continues-to-climb-at-expense-of-o

22 www.europarl.europa.eu/sides/getDoc.do?pubRef=-//EP//TEXT+TA+P8-TA-2015-0257+0+DOC+XML+V0//EN

23 www.imiplc.com/~/media/Files/I/IMI/annual-reports/directors-remuneration-policy.pdf

24 www.ivis.co.uk/guidelines

25 www.napf.co.uk/PolicyandResearch/DocumentLibrary/~/media/Policy/Documents/0351_3_remuneration_principles_for_building_and_reinforcing%20_longterm_business_success_nov2013.pdf

26 www.ecgi.org

27 M. Gold, 'Corporate governance reform in Australia: the intersection of investment fiduciaries and issuers', in P. Ali and G. Gregoriou (eds), *International Corporate Governance after Sarbanes–Oxley*, John Wiley and Sons, New York, 2006.

28 www.frc.org.uk/Our-Work/Codes-Standards/Corporate-governance/UK-Corporate-Governance-Code.aspx

29 E. Fama, 'Agency problems and the theory of the firms', *Journal of Political Economy,* vol. 88, 1980, pp. 288–307.

30 E. Fama and M. Jensen, 'Separation of ownership and control', *Journal of Law and Economics,* vol. 26, 1983, pp. 301–25.

31 www.bupa.com/investor-relations/our-status-and-governance/our-corporate-governance/role-of-the-sid

32 www.guardian.co.uk/business/2009/feb/01/ftse-royal-bank-scotland-group

33 A. Abdullah and M. Page, *Corporate Governance and Corporate Performance: UK FTSE 350 Companies,* The Institute of Chartered Accountants of Scotland, Edinburgh, 2009.

34 ABI Research, *Corporate Governance 'Pays' for Shareholders and Company Performance,* ABI, 27 February 2008, Ref: 12/08.

35 www.ons.gov.uk/ons/rel/pnfc1/share-ownership---share-register-survey-report/2010/stb-share-ownership-2010.html

36 G. Igor Filatochev, H.G. Jackson and D. Allcock, *Key Drivers to Good Corporate Governance and Appropriateness of UK Policy Responses,* DTI, 2007, www.berr.gov.uk/files/file36671.pdf

37 www/frc.org.uk/Our-Work/Codes-Standards/Corporate-governance/UK-Corporate-Governance-Code.aspx

38 www.bis.gov.uk/assets/biscore/business-law/docs/k/12-917-kay-review-of-equity-markets-final-report.pdf

39 file:///C:/Users/Barry/Downloads/20131203-cewginvestorforum%20(1).pdf

40 http://europa.eu/rapid/press-release_STATEMENT-14-104_en.htm

41 K. Peasnell, P. Pope and S. Young, 'A new model board', *Accountancy,* July 1998, p. 115.

42 'PwC and E&Y in favour of rules to restrict services', *Accountancy,* October 2000, p. 7.

# CHAPTER 32

# Integrated reporting: sustainability, environmental and social

## 32.1 Introduction

Previous chapters have introduced the techniques involved in financial accounting and financial statement analysis. However, annual reporting to shareholders and other interested parties also involves management explaining past performance and indicating future opportunities, challenges and risks. To truly understand the performance of a company one needs to understand the strategies adopted by management, the business environment in which they operate and what they have done to prepare the company to meet the challenges of the future. Part of that involves choices about the level of risk the company wants to take.

Integrated reporting is an attempt to provide a systematic way of addressing the reporting of the performance of the company which incorporates awareness of the broad strategic approach of the company and links that strategy to performances in economic, environmental and social spheres.

In other words, a company should spell out how the company is going to achieve in a competitive environment and what that approach necessitates in terms of both its economic operations and its environmental and social activities.

The chapter objectives will be achieved by illustrating the way in which a company manages and integrates environmental and social information in its annual report. This requires greater attention by management to social and environmental issues as well as to traditional economic operations – it stresses the linkages between economic, environmental and social activities and measures performance in all those areas.

However, the extent to which environmental and social performance are considered key aspects of performance is likely to vary across companies and countries, being influenced by management views as to:

- how critical they are perceived to be in terms of achieving the economic strategy of the organisation;
- the appropriate roles and responsibility of business for environmental and social issues;
- how appropriate it is felt for environmental and social dimensions to be embedded in day-to-day management decisions and actions;
- how much the evaluation of an individual manager's performance is based on environmental and social performance.

Integrated reporting is important not only because it allows a better evaluation of the company's performance but also because it allows for a better evaluation of potential serious economic consequences if such issues are mismanaged.

## Objectives

By the end of this chapter, you should be able to:

- understand the objectives and frameworks of integrated reporting;
- be sensitised to the broad range of factors that companies need to address to reduce the future strategic risks;
- understand the historical context of the development of integrated reporting;
- be familiar with the major organisations who have contributed to the development of integrated reporting and the resources that they provide to report preparers;
- be able to explain the accountant's and auditor's roles in integrated reporting;
- be able to formulate well-thought-out views on the possible implications and future developments of the above.

## 32.2 Environmental and social disasters and the adverse consequences that can follow

The objective of this section is to bring home the magnitude of the economic consequences, and the level of social disruption, which can flow from inadequate management of such risks particularly in the areas of environmental risks, health and safety, resource protection, intellectual knowledge and protection, and supply chain management. Four examples will be briefly discussed to stress the significance of these to both economic success and the type of world in which we would like to live.

### 32.2.1 BP plc and its group

In April 2010 an oil rig in the Gulf of Mexico experienced a high-pressure methane gas surge from its well. It ignited and the explosion engulfed the drilling platform and oil flowed into the ocean for 87 days before the well was closed off. This had major adverse consequences:

**Social** – 11 workers were never found and their families were affected.

**Environmental** – the beaches which were spoilt by the oil or other chemicals took a substantial period to rectify, substantial numbers of wildlife were killed and many of the wildlife survivors had their habitats rendered unliveable.

**Economic** – the oil spill caused major disruption to companies operating in fishing and tourism in the area and of course there was a knock-on effect for all their suppliers.

For BP and the two other companies involved this was the start of major stress in trying to contain the oil flows, reducing the impact of the oil flows that couldn't be stopped, responding to government departments, trying to directly or indirectly help those suffering as a consequence of the disaster, defending court cases and trying to minimise the damage to the reputation of the company. Also some employees were subjected to criminal legal cases, which irrespective of the outcome would be very stressful.

According to the BP Group 2014 Strategic Report:

As at the end of 2014, the cumulative charge since the incident amounted to $43.5 billion. This does not include amounts that BP does not consider possible to measure reliably at this time. The magnitude and timing of all possible obligations continue to be subject to significant uncertainty.

It has also been reported[1] that in December 2015 a Mexican non-government organisation Sinaloa stated that it was bringing a class action as US parties had all been compensated for disruption, clean-ups and losses, but the Mexican government had not brought a case on behalf of affected Mexican people and businesses.

Our objective is not to focus on BP. It is rather to stress that environmental and safety issues are major management problems and require continued vigilance by management. Furthermore, if precautions fail to prevent such events then considerable time, energy and money will be consumed in handling the physical problems, business interruption, social and reputational aspects of such disasters. For investors the costs of managing environmental aspects (both prevention and rectification) are significant costs which they would like to think management has given the attention it deserves.

### 32.2.2 BHPBilliton

Failures place considerable pressure on management to rectify the situation, including handling legal issues and the direct and indirect losses which are incurred. However, it is wrong to think these issues are simple when viewed in terms of the complex economic, environmental, political and social issues involved.

For example, another company that faced similar problems was BHPBilliton when it invested in the Ok Tedi mine in Papua New Guinea and provided management personnel.[2] The mine polluted the area around the mine. Although BHPBilliton wanted to close the mine early it didn't have the power to enforce its wishes. It had to recognise the importance of the mine to Papua New Guinea in economic, political and social terms as the mine was a major source of foreign exchange for the country and an important source of employment in that developing country.

BHPBilliton took action to rectify or to compensate for past pollution, set in place future environmental safeguards, and in 2002 surrendered its shareholdings in order to extract itself from the situation.

What this example illustrates is the importance of environmental management for companies in terms of the consequences of failure to adequately manage environmental issues. Companies in mining and chemical industries often have to devote considerable efforts and investments in order to try to manage these issues without any guarantees of complete success or that future knowledge will not demonstrate that they missed some issues.

### 32.2.3 VW

Another example in this section is VW, whose employees were under pressure to reduce the pollution levels of diesel cars so that the company could get a larger market share, particularly in the USA. Being unable to satisfy US requirements, and also apparently unwilling to tell top management of their failure, they resorted to using software in the cars which reduced pollution levels (from the car's exhaust) when tested in the laboratory but did not reduce the pollution under normal driving conditions.

The result was that in normal operation the pollution level was in excess of US mandatory limits and sometimes considerably in excess. When the situation was uncovered VW was exposed to costs to fix 600,000 cars so they have lower pollution levels, compensation to car owners, and fines.[3] The chief executive took responsibility for the disaster and resigned. From 6 October 2015, VW was 'removed from the Dow Jones Sustainability Indices',[4] which meant it was no longer deemed a leader of its Industry Group in terms of environmental, social and governance factors and unattractive to ethical investors.

This case viewed from the outside would seem to suggest that the culture in the organisation (i.e. do employees feel they can share bad news with their superiors) was a major factor. It also highlights that the cost of failure can be high, particularly where companies use environmental credentials as a marketing tool. (Another industry which has been criticised for inappropriate cultures is the finance industry, where it has been argued that reward systems have encouraged some employees to ignore their moral and legal obligations to customers when giving financial advice or manipulating interest rates.)

### 32.2.4 Social dimensions

It would be wrong to think that other industries do not face their own challenges in terms of the possibility of disasters which could reflect badly on their businesses and affect customer attitudes to their products. We have become used to cheap clothing, but often that is supplied by countries with working conditions that would be condemned in developed countries. It takes a disaster or action by activists to bring these conditions to the attention of customers in developed countries.

One example of such a disaster occurred in 2013 at Rana Plaza in Bangladesh, where 1,129 people died because 'shoddy construction turned a building in Dhaka into a death trap when a garment manufacturing complex collapsed'.[5] To be fair, the UK retailers were more likely to have been assessing the factories for fire risks than for structural problems. Primark acted quickly to provide food parcels and financial support to the families affected but they were only one of many well-known brands linked to the factory.[6]

The disaster led to campaigners for garment workers' rights brokering a significant breakthrough, with 31 brands signing the Bangladesh Safety Accord. The Accord will sound dry to many fashion lovers. It is a contract between brands, retailers and trade unions in Bangladesh, and is a legally binding, five-year pact that makes independent safety inspections of 1,000 factories and public reporting on them mandatory. It is also the first-ever multi-buyer collective agreement. This was a historic moment for the campaign to clean up fashion.

Once again this demonstrates the need for and the difficulty of anticipating and eliminating potential problems. When such events do occur management has to decide what it is going to do both in terms of ethical responsibilities and in terms of protecting their brand image.

### 32.2.5 The lessons

The objective of this section is to use a few examples to demonstrate that managing corporate social responsibility is a major task of management. It is not easy but it can have a major impact on the company's brand and reputation, not to mention the financial impacts in the short and medium term. These in turn can affect access to resources such as loans, share capital, mineral reserves, rights to operate in a location, recruitment of quality employees and customer loyalty.

All industries face these corporate social responsibility problems which are not restricted just to the industries discussed above. Obviously the form they take will vary from industry to industry but the underlying issues will be similar. Further it is no longer a separate activity over and above profit making. It is main stream as it has to be integrated into day-to-day activities. Thus, when a product is being designed, trade-offs might have to be made between costs and safety (e.g. toy designs), efficiency and health and safety (e.g. building construction or paramedic well-being), and pressure for financial results versus risk mitigation.

## 32.3 Management accountability for environmental and social responsibility

This section will address the issue of the normative views on the role(s) of business. As pointed out earlier, the subjective views held by managers as to *the appropriate roles and responsibility of business will influence their day-to-day actions*. As these views become more widely held they will also influence the *legislation* of a country.

We set out below a discussion of competing views as to those responsibilities. Whilst we spell out a few possibilities, the reality is that a wide range of views are held and the discussion is designed to highlight some of those views. Subsequently there will be a discussion of the legal responsibility of directors of companies in the United Kingdom for the management and reporting on economic, environmental and social issues. We will also highlight in a subsequent section how South Africa has become a leader in integrated reporting and the influence of normative views which have been shaped by their history.

### 32.3.1 Shareholder primacy

#### Maximising profits

Sometimes the question is raised whether management's role should actually include environmental and social responsibility. Such discussions normally start with a quotation from Milton Friedman, a famous American economist, who said that management is responsible for providing maximum returns to shareholders (shareholder primacy theory), and social and environmental applications of funds by companies are normally inappropriate. According to that approach the shareholders themselves should be the ones who decide whether to donate to environmental or social activities out of their dividends or capital gains.

#### Difficulties with this approach

Friedman himself did not rule out expenditures on environmental and social activities if it increased shareholder returns. It is interesting to note, for example, that many companies which have undertaken initiatives to reduce energy costs purely based on environmental concerns have found that the cost savings have generated very attractive returns on investments.

Shareholder primacy is difficult, however, to apply in a complex world. How to decide, for example, over what period are profits to be maximised; how to determine whether the use of management resources for environmental and social purposes contributes to maximising earnings and share prices? Certainly as demonstrated above, if insufficient weight is given to the social and environmental activities then the costs of not doing so may be substantially greater than would have been incurred to avoid the environmental and social malpractices in the first place.

#### Economic and societal pressures that operate against profit maximising

##### Direct investment

Companies that give insufficient attention to environmental and social issues may find that direct investment into the company incurs an increase in the cost of capital, i.e. the cost of borrowing and the rate of return that is required by shareholders to justify the increased risks that they bear.

Further it is not just in relation to existing activities in which these responsibilities loom large. If a company is contemplating future investments there is a need to consider what future expectations of customers and the public will be in terms of good social and environmental practices. For example, future projections of revenue will depend on the corporate image at those future dates and the cost projections will need to reflect the environmental avoidance and environmental rectification costs which will be adopted by or imposed on the company.

### Shareholder activity

An increasing number of investment funds are avoiding companies which are deemed to be involved in anti-social activities such as being contributors to pollution (e.g. coal companies) or financing anti-social organisations (e.g. banks supporting companies which are contributing to anti-social activities) or producing unhealthy products (e.g. cigarettes). These decisions not to invest in certain companies may be based on social attitudes to the companies' activities or on assessments of higher risks – such as possible future liabilities for rectification, class actions for injury caused by products or threats to future rights to operate.

### Cost and risk trade-offs

It must be stressed that in a large corporation many executives will make decisions which make cost and risk trade-offs as part of normal operations. The way in which they are rewarded and achievements recognised will influence their priorities and the trade-offs they make. Individuals at lower levels may experience different pressures from those impinging on senior management and as a result they may make choices which are inappropriate from the perspective of senior management. This means that senior management, even under shareholder primacy, has to ensure that at all levels of the organisation decisions are made which give sufficient weight to environmental and social issues in line with top management priorities, and must avoid giving unintended messages that short-term profitability takes total priority.

### Move to the opposite profit-maximising shareholder primacy

Companies in the past have been able to disregard of the impact of externalities. Externalities are the costs borne by society, and not the company, as a result of the actions or the inactions of the company. Thus if a company discharges inadequately treated effluent from its manufacturing activities into the adjacent river the costs they impose on others are the externalities.

Mandatory regulations have gradually been imposed to make companies responsible for externalities, and voluntary initiatives have been encouraged to allow management more discretion in focusing on social and environmental issues. For example, in some US states it is possible to establish Benefit Corporations, which are a new type of company that uses the power of business to solve social and environmental problems, and where being good corporate citizens is one of the legal objectives of the company.

However, the widespread US view is that normal businesses should exercise shareholder primacy, but one legal authority[7] suggests that shareholders are just another party with a contract with the corporation, much the same as a supplier of raw materials. As such, the corporation as a separate legal entity manages its shareholder relations (the suppliers of finance) in the same way as it manages other supplier relations.

Given the dominant culture in the USA, and the heavy reliance on stock market financing, it is likely that in the main environmental and social action and reporting is likely to be less extensive than in continental Europe. (Obviously this is a generalisation and many US companies are very environmentally oriented, but in the main one would expect more environmental and social accounting in more 'socialistic cultures' such as Europe.)

In summary, the shareholder primacy view is that company management has a responsibility to maximise shareholder returns, which implies that environmental and social costs are incurred if, and only if, they contribute to the level of shareholder returns or are required under the law.

### 32.3.2 Stakeholder theory

Another normative view of the corporation is what is called stakeholder theory. Under such an approach, incorporation with limited liability is a privilege granted by the state because it is of benefit to the whole community. Thus the company should respect the need to contribute back to the state/community in generating employment, taxes and a good community environment if it is to retain its privileges.

Under stakeholder theory, management has a range of contributors to the operation whose continued contribution is of benefit or essential if the corporation is to achieve its aims. Thus the company is dependent on satisfying customers and suppliers of finance (shareholders and lenders); developing skills and knowledge (employees, professional firms, and suppliers); securing reliable sources of raw materials; and enjoying a productive environment.

A productive environment can be said to exist where the state supplies a transparent legal environment in which to operate and there are efficient transport links, sound exchange rate management, educated employees and protection of property and property-rights such as patents, etc. Under this view it is management's task to keep all stakeholders committed to the well-being of the company. It has to set strategic directions for the company so as to ensure the continued success of the business, and this includes the attraction and retention of satisfied stakeholders.[8]

Thus, under stakeholder theory, management has to keep stakeholders committed to supporting the operation of the company. One way of doing this is to use the Annual Report to communicate to the major stakeholders how the company will continue to satisfy their needs into the future.

### 32.3.3 Management obligations

Irrespective of which framework is adopted (shareholder primacy or stakeholder theory or just a sense of moral responsibilities or some other view of the world) management has considerable discretion and with that comes responsibility to communicate clearly the results of their actions and priorities.

It is the challenge of the current time to identify what and how the reporting should be extended to show how the management have positioned the company to deal with the risks inherent in an uncertain future. Part of the issue is how to focus on the important issues and provide greater insights without over-burdening the business and the readers of the Report.

There are certain statutory requirements relating to the environmental and social issues that need to be addressed in a Report, but it has to be recognised that management has considerable discretion in deciding what issues are important to the major community strategies, which may well vary from country to country. In South Africa, for example, the community is very concerned with the development of the skills of the black community and the improvement of health including reducing and treating Aids.

### UK statutory position

In the United Kingdom the law states that the company is primarily accountable to shareholders. However, section 172 of the Companies Act 2006 qualifies this to some extent when it says that the duty of a director is to act:[9]

> in the way [s]he considers, in good faith, would be most likely to promote the success of the company for the benefit of its members as a whole, and in doing so have regard (amongst other matters) to:
>
> (a) the likely consequences of any decision in the long term;
>
> (b) the interests of the company's employees;
>
> (c) the need to foster the company's business relationships with suppliers, customers and others;
>
> (d) the impact of the company's operations on the community and the environment;
>
> (e) the desirability of the company maintaining a reputation for high standards of business conduct; and
>
> (f) the need to act fairly as between members of the company.

Thus it takes a shareholder primacy approach but also requires selective stakeholder activities.

From October 2014 new regulations became operational which require companies to produce a Strategic Report, and the Financial Reporting Council produced a report, *Guidance on the Strategic Report*,[10] giving non-binding guidance on the content of the report. A quoted company must provide a description of its strategy and its business model. The FRC expanded on this when it recommended that the Strategic Report stress linkages between the items discussed in the strategic report and the annual report (paragraphs 6.15 to 7.26) and in paragraph 7.29 it says:

> To the extent necessary for an understanding of the development, performance or position of the entity's business, the Strategic Report should include information about:
>
> (a) environmental matters (including the impact of the business of the entity on the environment);
>
> (b) the entity's employees; and
>
> (c) social, community and human rights issues.

The information should include a description of any relevant policies in respect of those matters and the effectiveness of those policies.

Thus the Financial Reporting Council has adopted a set of policies which are reflected in the principles of integrated reporting covering economic, environmental, social and human rights issues, and governance. In this context, governance refers to developing appropriate corporate policies and decisions supported by a system which provides reasonable assurance that those are being implemented as intended.

### Monitoring performance

Stakeholders need to know whether the firm has governance systems to ensure management strategies and policies are implemented correctly and ethically, and that reporting systems capture accurate information and report fairly on those activities.

Given the emphasis on clear reporting and the focus on key issues there is still room for considerable discretion, which has both advantages and disadvantages. The major advantages include a better understanding of management's strategies and the risks they may be exposing the business to; the disadvantages include a lack of comparability, and possible selective reporting in not showing unsatisfactory areas of performance.

### Decisions taken by companies shape the future

Therefore business needs to be conscious that its actions and those of other businesses will shape the future environment in which they have to operate, which includes future laws and the economic conditions that they will be faced with. Businesses in general, especially large businesses, have such a major impact on the future of the world, and those in it, that they must take responsibility for their major impacts. Thus the Stern Review[11] suggests that inadequate attention to the environmental impacts of human and business activities means that business is potentially facing large reductions in gross domestic product (i.e. reduced business revenue).

There is much discussion of climate change, and the Report says there is evidence that climate change is already creating more extreme weather conditions with the resulting destruction of property and thus additional costs to business. On the other hand, the challenge of reducing environmental impacts potentially provides new business opportunities. Unilever in their 2015 Strategic Report[12] reports that since 2008 it has saved €600m by adopting eco-production.

The above discussions have highlighted the fact that different countries are likely to view the appropriate level of regulation differently, reflecting cultural norms.

## 32.4 Integrated reporting concepts

The International Integrated Reporting Council (IIRC) has been established to foster and guide the development of integrated reporting. Its activities include establishing principles to guide those wishing to adopt integrated reporting.[13] It has a wide range of businesses using their principles and providing feedback on their experiences. Presently integrated reporting is most widely reported by listed companies, particularly those in South Africa where it is a legal requirement, and to a lesser extent in Europe.

The expectation is that management should convey how they expect the business or organisation to achieve its goals and to keep its major stakeholders satisfied over the short term, medium term and long term. How the various components of that strategy support each other needs to be explained.

### Reporting to the suppliers of financial capital is seen as the primary role

Reporting on financial performance has traditionally focused on the maintenance of financial capital concept. In other words, *progress has not been made until the financial base has been increased.* Profit (or loss) represents the increase (decrease) in the financial capital invested in the business. However, an organisation is more than simply a financial investment. It involves the coordinated use of people, knowledge, legal privileges, reputations and customer relationships, supply chains, production facilities and natural resources.

As stated earlier, to understand the organisation and its potential for future success one needs to understand the resources it has at its disposal and how it intends to combine those resources to achieve its aims. The approach adopted is to get businesses to also report on progress in terms of improving key non-financial resources. The International <IR> Framework suggests a number of resources (called capitals), which most (but not all) organisations will be dependent on, as a starting framework to guide management in selecting the items to report upon. These capitals are financial, manufactured, intellectual, human, social and relationships, and natural.

**Manufactured capital** is the manufactured physical objects used in the production of goods and services.[14] Being manufactured items they exclude natural resources. Note that production is used in a very broad sense. It includes plant and machinery, goods manufactured for sale, roads and port facilities used in say a stevedoring firm or a mining operation, office equipment, etc. Thus a call centre would have office equipment as part of its production facilities. In summary it would include all tangible non-current assets and finished goods inventory. But the perspective is not the financial amount but the ability to service a given level of business activity at the required quality of performance.

**Intellectual capital** includes both the knowledge base of the organisation which supports its operations and the legal rights which protect specific items of knowledge (e.g. patents, copyright), or provide access to use of specific knowledge (e.g. licenses). Once again it is very broad in application. It would cover the intangible assets in the statement of financial position and would also include internally generated intangibles and systems knowledge which enable the company to provide high-quality services. Note also that some firms do not patent new inventions either because patenting is expensive to enforce or because it discloses confidential information to competitors. Thus if intellectual knowledge evolves rapidly it may not be worth patenting but rather the competitive advantage is dependent on continuous improvement and rapid incorporation of new ideas into the products. The degree to which the company is at the forefront of intellectual knowledge may be important to the competitive advantage which the company wants to exploit. If it is at the centre of the company's strategy then it is important to know whether it is likely that the company has maintained its intellectual advantage.

**Human capital** includes the skill levels of employees, their level of commitment to their jobs, and their ability to contribute to improvements in operations in all areas. The level of staff commitment may, of course, depend on things such as the opportunity for enhancing their skills and knowledge, opportunities for promotion without unfair discrimination and the provision of a safe working environment.

It also includes their identification and conformity with the governance strategies and corporate strategy, particularly in relation to the level of risk that management consider acceptable. An illustration of the latter is in a financial organisation where traders are given specific limits, and it is their willingness to comply not only with those limits but also the spirit of those limits that is key to management being able to control the firm.

Thus what is required is an organisational culture that supports fair and ethical values and compliance with company governance processes. Insights into whether a company has improved human capital could be captured by independent surveys of staff morale,[15] staff injury and death statistics, health issues including those resulting from work situations (e.g. exposure to chemicals) and the external environments (in some countries aids and malaria are major issues), and staff turnover rates.

**Social and relationship capital** relates to maintaining good relationships with all major stakeholders. For example, the perceptions of customers that the company will treat them appropriately in providing safe products, honouring commitments (delivery performance, replacing damaged goods), providing products sourced ethically, etc. Similarly relations with employees, suppliers, industry associations, and the communities in which they are located are all important in ensuring the ongoing level of support which the firm is dependent upon for current and future operations.

**Natural capital,** as the name implies, are the environmental resources that the organisation needs and uses in its operations. These environmental resources include those that can be renewed, such as forests which can be replaced by systematic replanting and husbandry.

Resources that cannot be renewed include oil, gas and minerals. If it is in the oil industry the firm needs to find new oil deposits or to develop new technology to make it economically viable to extract at least the same quantity of oil at the end of the period as at the beginning. Resource companies are already required to report on the level of their reserves as it is vital to making an assessment of the future prospects of such companies. Below are two extracts. The first is an extract from the accounts of Shell to illustrate the type of information provided:[16]

| | *2015* | *2014* | *2013* |
|---|---|---|---|
| **Oil and gas production available for sale (thousand boe/d)** | 2,954 | 3,080 | 3,199 |
| **Equity sales of LNG (million tonnes)** | 22.6 | 24.0 | 19.6 |
| **Proved oil and gas reserves at December 31 (million boe)** | 11,747 | 13,081 | 13,944 |

Note: boe/d = barrels of oil equivalent per day

The second is Marks and Spencer's 'Our Sustainable Value Creation Model' diagram:

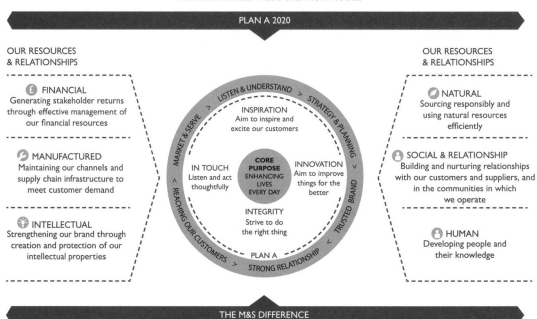

OUR SUSTAINABLE VALUE CREATION MODEL

### 32.4.1 The benefits of integrated reporting

Integrated reporting:

- should help us judge the quality of earnings and the level of associated risks;
- will force management to more clearly articulate their strategies and pay attention to performance of all capitals and to ensure the work in the various areas is coordinated; and
- is an attempt to get management to focus on the sustainability of their business.[17]

#### What integrated accounting is not

The International <IR> Framework does not provide standard reporting formats. Reporting according to a generic format would make it more difficult to fully appreciate the thinking and motivation of management. However, where the companies have chosen to report on specific elements of social and environmental accounting then common definitions would be an advantage for comparative purposes.

It also does not say that every capital should be reported upon. After all we don't want a company to spend valuable resources collecting information that may be important for other firms but is relatively unimportant for it, nor to overwhelm the reader with unimportant information.

#### Integrated reporting is not new

It is important to know that some companies have been reporting on the triple bottom line (financial, environmental and social issues[18]), and multiple bottom line, for some time and professional organisations with that expertise already exist. Some of those bodies will be discussed in this chapter. However, the important point is that since the reporting is tied into the strategy of the firm the coverage and emphasis must reflect the nature and approach of each specific firm.

## 32.5 The historical context of the evolution of integrated reporting[19] including the drivers of this movement

The evolution of integrated accounting can be seen as:

- attempts to tackle limitations in financial reporting by academics and the profession;
- driven by socially aware management in business; and
- a reaction to growing public awareness of the effect of pollution.

#### Attempts to tackle limitations in financial reporting by academics and the profession

In 1976 a new academic journal was started called *Accounting, Organization and Society*, reflecting the interest in these broader issues. Since that time these issues have become more mainstream in the accounting and management literature. In 1975 the profession published 'The Corporate Report', which essentially took a stakeholder approach and advocated producing a value added statement and an employment report. It took the view at that date that social accounting could not be adopted as there were no generally agreed measures.[20]

#### The value added statement

The value added statement flourished for a period of time and is still reported by some companies. The business is seen as buying in inputs (say materials and services like electricity) and processing them to sell at a higher price. The increase in value (the value added) is then shared amongst four groups:

- investors in the form of dividends and interest;
- the company as reinvestment in the business;
- payments to employees; and
- taxes to various levels of government.

The statement focuses on the split of the 'value added' between the various parties. Management used the statement to demonstrate that shareholders were not getting an excessive share of the value created. However, it did not address the split between different classifications of employees. It was not possible to assess whether management was receiving a fair share compared to other employees and shareholders and there was little incentive to provide this breakdown. The content of the report will be explained in a separate section below.

### 32.5.1 Failure to report human assets

It has been noted that in annual reports there are often statements like: 'We would like to thank our employees for their efforts during the year. Our employees are our greatest asset.' But the accounts do not directly reflect this. Human resources were reflected in some accounts during the period of the slave trade but since then they have generally not been treated as assets because they are not bound to the firm and can leave at any time.

Attempts have been made to develop methods of accounting for human resources such as:

- reflecting their replacement costs, recruitment costs, relocation costs paid to new employees, sign on bonuses, costs of lower productivity until they become familiar with company operations; or
- capitalising and amortising training costs; or
- valuing the assets based on future earning potential multiplied by the probabilities that they would continue with the firm for each year of the projections.

Such suggestions have not gained acceptance, however, partly due to cost considerations and ethical concerns about treating humans as assets, but mainly due to the failure to satisfy the IASB's conceptual definition of an asset.

This discussion is intended to highlight the fact that there has been serious concern about the completeness of accounting reports that do not include information about resources that are important if the business is to operate successfully in the future.

Another argument in favour of accounting for human resources in the statement of financial position is that management might be less willing to downsize during hard economic times if they had to recognise the cost of earlier financial investment in staff that they are discarding.

### 32.5.2 Drive by more socially aware management

In business initially the drive for reporting on environmental issues came altruistically from a small group of environmentally and socially aware individuals who did not want current generations to jeopardise the ability of future generations to have an equally rewarding existence. This was remarked on in the Brundtland Report.[21]

This was followed by other organisations acting from self-interest when becoming aware that they could face a possible community backlash from damaging environmental impacts they caused. Their interest was to manage public relations by reporting on the action they were taking to rectify environmental damage and to improve their production processes.

The difference between these two groups is that the former were interested in giving a comprehensive insight into the environmental impacts of their businesses and were seriously working to improve processes wherever possible. The second group were more interested in public relations and were selective in their disclosures, for example, deciding whether to include fines in their reported expenditures on environmental matters.

### 32.5.3 Reaction to the growing public awareness of the effect of pollution

Pollution of the environment has always been with us but until it reaches a level that impacts on most of us it tends to be ignored. Thus while it occurs out of sight or out of mind, then little is done. Further there needs to be potential for reducing it in terms of having the resources and knowledge to do so. Thus at the time of the industrial revolution there were chronic living and working conditions for the poor but they had little power to influence decision making.

Since those times, however, rising living standards, greater political power for the working classes, expanding cities making it more difficult to hide pollution and increases in knowledge have made it more important and feasible to tackle pollution.

#### Example of China's recent experience

China provides a good example. In the last 30 years China has focused on providing higher standards of living by acting as a cheap supplier to developed countries. However, there was a cost in that cheap forms of production often created high levels of pollution. As an economic solution it was extremely effective. The pollution impacted on the quality of life and the health of inhabitants so political pressure built for improved air quality and safer agricultural products. Government is now seeking to reduce the level of pollution by closing down old polluting factories, limiting expansion of motor cycle and car fleets, and installing more pollution controls in new factories. Similar changes in practices have also been seen in many countries, China only being different in that the cycle was condensed into a much shorter period.

Over time the proportion of the population placing importance on economic, environmental and social conditions has increased and they have placed pressure on companies to reflect these changing values.

### 32.5.4 Other limitations of traditional financial reporting

The growing awareness of the limitations of traditional accounting formed another driver for more comprehensive reporting. We discussed accounting for human resources above and the varying suggested treatment for goodwill in Chapter 19.

We saw that how to account for goodwill has been debated over a long period of time without a satisfactory resolution. Approaches that have been used include:

- an immediate write off (either to retained earnings or the profit statement);
- capitalisation of the amount paid which is retained until there is evidence of significant impairment; and
- initial treatment of the cost as an asset but with annual amortisation.

The assessment of whether the asset has decreased in value is very subjective in the absence of a sale.

The accounting for trademarks, patents, software, research and development, and other intangibles have similar problems. In particular, the increased importance of information technology highlights the problems of accounting for intangibles, especially as such items are notoriously associated with rapid and unexpected obsolescence.

Rapid changes in technology are disrupting industries and causing industries to converge leading to major changes to competition, manufacturing processes, and distribution systems and hence knowledge of these potential impacts and the company's preparedness are important in valuing the organisation.

Finally, technology is making knowledge of what is happening in the supply chain more quickly and more widely known with the possibility of boycotts being more easily coordinated. Thus greater management of supply chains is necessary to maintain earning capacity.

The fact that *financial accounting has inherent limitations* has given added impetus to integrated accounting. As mentioned previously this has evolved from environmental accounting to triple bottom line accounting (financial, environmental and social accounting).

The first country to incorporate integrated reporting into its regulatory requirements was South Africa in 2011. The requirement was that listed companies had to provide an integrated report or explain why not. The motivation is thought to have been *to increase trust in South African companies* following the removal of apartheid. It was hoped that with increased trust the South African companies would find it easier to attract foreign investments in companies and in joint ventures.[22]

## 32.5.5 The South African experience in more detail

This country will be examined because it highlights the interaction of social and historical forces in shaping the move to integrated reporting and the emphasis placed upon it. Obviously countries such as the USA with different history and culture are likely to approach sustainability and social dimensions slightly differently.

Under the apartheid regime in South Africa there was a concentration of wealth, managerial positions, educational opportunities and pleasant life styles in the hands of parts of the white minority. This was viewed by international groups as unfair, and boycotts occurred in athletics from the 1960s onwards followed by a wide range of boycotts of other sports including football, rugby, golf and cricket. By 1980 the pressure was widespread.

What may be less well known is that businesses were under pressure to stop dealing with South Africa and those multinationals with investments in South Africa felt they had to withdraw. When Nelson Mandela became the first black president in 1994 he was faced with improving the lot of black and coloured South Africans. Part of this was to improve living conditions, access to education and training, and employment opportunities. To increase employment he needed to attract more investment to South Africa.

Investment activities require confidence in the governance of companies in the country. To improve investment inflows there was a need for confidence that business would be conducted:

● appropriately according to fair laws;

● that conflicts of interest would be dealt with appropriately and ethically; and

● that companies would have good systems to ensure operations follow strategies in an orderly fashion.

In other words, there needed be confidence in good corporate governance. To create the necessary environment that would attract more investment, the Institute of Directors of Southern Africa in 1993 appointed a committee under the chairmanship of Mervyn King, a retired Supreme Court judge, to look at governance and that committee reported in 1994.

By 2002 it was time to update the code and this occurred in an environment in which environmental issues were attracting attention worldwide. So the second version of the corporate code, called King 2, recommended the use of triple bottom line reporting (reporting on financial, environmental and social performance). In particular, there is specific mention of policies and strategies in relation to HIV (Aids), procurement and black empowerment, and policies on disclosure of non-financial matters.[23] Aids was at that time a major issue in South Africa and obviously impinged both on the well-being of employees and on the performance of the business. Similarly by focusing on black sources of inputs firms could contribute to their living standards.

This highlights how the circumstances of the businesses and the country influence the emphasis in non-financial reporting. This occurs in other countries as well. In Papua New Guinea, for example, companies stress that the prevention and treatment of malaria and Aids, and the development of employees are issues of concern for both the country and the success of the business.

In 2009 the South African code was updated again, to King 3, and emphasises the integration of strategies, environmental and social issues. This was a deliberate attempt to make the environmental and social issues more relevant by linking them into strategic issues and to stress the long-term drivers of performance. Further elements were the need to overcome distrust of business, to realise that an increasing proportion of shareholders represent individuals either investing directly or through pension schemes, and to recognise that the acceptability of business is driven by assessments of fairness in the system.[24]

The code was clearly wedded to a stakeholder approach. It saw the additional environmental and social and governance information as an integral part of financial reporting as it relates to the sustainability of the reported earnings and as such was not non-financial information. It anticipated that companies would want to provide 'forward-looking' information as that would facilitate more accurate valuation of the business. (*Note*: It needs to be recognised that forward-looking information is easier to provide in some legal environments than others depending on director liability laws and whether there are safe harbours for honest forecasts based on reasonable assumptions at that time. Hence in some countries there has been a reluctance to provide such projections.)

As would be expected in a stakeholder approach, King 3 placed emphasis on the information being provided in very clear non-technical language with substance dominating over form. Further the additional information and issues need to be an essential part of operational management and reporting. Thus new systems need to be established to collect and verify the information. The internal audit needs to have the skills, with support of outside expertise if necessary, to include such systems in their normal checking and evaluation.

The code was initially aimed at companies listed on the Johannesburg Stock Exchange and large corporations. However, over time it was recognised the principles were applicable to a much wider range of organisations[25] including not-for-profit organisations. The codes (King 1, 2, 3) were intended to provide guidance but left it to the organisation to modify it where it was not a good fit. Thus it adopted an approach which said 'apply or explain' the reasons for deviation from the guidance in the code. A new version King 4 was being discussed in 2016 where the approach will no longer be 'apply or explain' but 'apply AND explain'.

## 32.6 The efforts on which integrated reporting builds

Readers should realise that integrated reporting is in its infancy and is building on the experience with previous forms of 'non-financial reporting' including triple bottom line reporting (financial, environmental and social reporting), sustainability reporting, and multiple bottom line reporting which often includes good governance as an additional item of focus. These earlier initiatives were developed by far-sighted individuals who wanted to contribute to a better world. As such, a number of organisations were founded to provide guidance and encourage companies to broaden the coverage of their reporting and, more importantly, to reflect these important issues in everyday management decision making.

A number of the organisations that created the momentum and knowledge base on which integrated reporting draws will be discussed next. They include Ceres, the Global Reporting Institute, The Sustainability Accounting Standards Board (SASB), the United Nations Global Compact, CDP Worldwide, AccountAbility, The Eco-Management and Audit Scheme, The Association of British Insurers, DJSI (the Dow Jones Sustainability Index), and the FTSE4 Good index series. Whilst the list may seem long they all cover different elements of environmental, social and governance achievement and reporting. Thus they range from guidelines on the matters to be reported, databases for comparisons across companies, guidelines on responsible investment disclosure with emphasis on the management of the risks, a range of audit possibilities, identification of high-performing organisations in terms of economic, social and governance factors and scoring of such performance. Amongst other things this highlights both the number of dimensions involved in improving sustainability and in its measurement and reporting. Further it shows the upsurge in focus on this, particularly over the last 25 years.

### 32.6.1 Ceres

Ceres was formed as a non-profit organisation advocating sustainability in response to a major disaster in 1989 when the *Exxon Valdez* oil tanker ran aground on a reef and spilt oil in Alaska's Prince William Sound, causing major destruction of wild life. Ceres set out to achieve a situation whereby businesses committed to operating for the well-being of humanity and protecting the Earth's environment.[26] As part of its efforts to shift the priorities of business and creating increased awareness of environmental issues, human rights and social accounting, Ceres supported the formation of the Global Reporting Initiative.

### 32.6.2 The Global Reporting Initiative (GRI)[27]

The GRI has a mission to develop global sustainability reporting guidelines for voluntary use by organisations reporting on the three linked elements of sustainability, namely the economic, environmental and social dimensions of their activities, products and services.

- The economic dimension recognises that performance is not just economic performance from a shareholder perspective but also covers economic impacts on all significant stakeholders. An example would be to disclose the impact on the local community as a result of the expansion of a facility or the closure of a factory. It also includes disclosures of specific expenditures such as those on research and development and training.
- The environmental dimension covers air, water, land, biodiversity, pollution, and health impacts.
- The social dimension covers human rights, corruption/anti-corruption, compliance with laws and regulations, impacts on supply chains, responsible products and marketing.

The Global Reporting Initiative means that parties contemplating a relationship such as assessing investment risk and obtaining goods or services will have available to them a clear picture of the human and ecological impacts of the business. Its influence has been growing and there are jurisdictions, such as Sweden, that require a GRI report.

### How useful are the GRI disclosures?

The usefulness of the disclosures depends on their credibility. Credibility is addressed in three ways:

- firstly there is a governance requirement that the level and extent of management involvement in sustainability policy setting, reporting, and compliance with those policies, have to be clearly identified;
- principles for defining report content and principles for defining report quality have to be specified; and finally
- it encourages reports to be 'verified' by an independent expert.

Its reports are based on the concept that they should disclose material factors and not be cluttered with insignificant material. The important negative messages are not to be buried in the fine print. They are based on disclosing both the areas of good performance and of bad performance.

Typical disclosures would include, for example, benefits obtained from government subsidies, tax breaks, and special privileges and, on the other side, information on fines or other sanctions for environmental and regulatory breaches. Where significant spills have occurred, the number of events, the volumes released and their impacts have to be given. If the company identifies instances of corruption these need to be reported on as well. If you want to use their framework you cannot cherry pick. Nor can you exclude information that makes management uncomfortable unless it is truly not material.

The company also has to outline its plans for the short, medium and long terms and how those will impact on sustainability.

### What if a company outsources?

It also recognises that companies might outsource task which create adverse consequences if a narrow coverage is chosen. Hence the emphasis on the group of companies' impacts irrespective of whether they are internal or external. As an example of these principles, the company or group of companies is required to report on employees and supervised workers, and in addition where a substantial portion of its work is conducted by 'outsiders' such as self-employed workers or subcontractors then that has to be reported on as well. In addition it requires the company to report on the supply chains and their impacts.

It is interesting to note that GRI does not see its application restricted to large corporations but sees it as also applicable to small and even micro businesses.[28]

### Increasing disclosures – Diageo plc

An interesting case study is Diageo plc in so far as it started with a Sustainability and Responsibility Report. It then decided to start the journey to integrated reporting beginning with the 2014 annual report. At the same time they continued to support the Global Reporting Initiative and the United Nations Global Compact (see below for a discussion of this). They realised that the new report did not include all the items previously covered so they published a Sustainability and Responsibility Performance Addendum.[29]

## 32.6.3 The Sustainability Accounting Standards Board[30]

This is a US non-profit organisation dedicated to encouraging business to undertake sustainability accounting. To improve the quality of reporting they have developed standards for a number of industries with particular emphasis on the need for comparability to improve investor decision making and to reduce the hurdles and costs facing analysts. As this is not a government entity its standards are not binding. However, they rely on the quality of the research and the resulting standards to attract companies to use their standards and metrics where applicable to the companies' strategies. At the time of preparing this chapter they had a 'full set of provisional standards for 79 industries in 10 sectors'.[31]

### 32.6.4 United Nations Global Compact

The United Nations has since 2000 been engaged in an attempt to influence society in adopting sustainability principles. As part of that initiative it has sought to get business and communities to sign up to a set of 10 principles covering human rights, labour, the environment, and anti-corruption.[32]

A business can sign up to being a signatory to the compact. So far businesses employing 58,600,000 employees have joined. Joining involves an undertaking to implement the principles in their strategies and operations, and to report annually on achievements to date in incorporating the sustainability principles, and plans to overcome current gaps. These annual reports are called Communications of Progress (COP). Those COPs have to include a statement by the chief executive officer of continuing commitment to the Global Compact and its principles, a description of practical action taken supported by quantitative and qualitative measures of outcomes. The COPs are filed on the Global Compact website. Companies which do not match commitment with adequate action can be removed from the Compact scheme.

The intention is to get companies to incorporate sustainability as an integral part of their activities including strategic planning and operations. Rather than being a burden these should be viewed as significant contributors to the success of the business including providing competitive advantages and in assisting in the identification of opportunities for growth and innovation. Whilst the Global Compact believes that the adoption of sustainability involves very fundamental values and obligations and not merely a question of risk containment, there is no doubt that if they do not become embedded in the core values and become significant drivers of the business then considerable risks are being taken.

The Global Compact endorses the GRI and <IR> approaches. In addition it recognises the possibility of resistance by some investors who adopt a narrowly interpreted shareholder primacy view. There is, therefore, a requirement that Global Compact signatories provide their investors with metrics describing gains in terms of extra revenue, cost savings and risk reductions flowing from a sustainability approach.

### 32.6.5 CDP Worldwide

CDP Worldwide is a UK charity which collects environmental information including emissions, water usage and forestry data. It also collects information on companies' environmental strategies and plans and drivers of changes in environmental performance both past and planned. Where companies agree the data is publicly available. Its data collection is designed to be compatible with GRI requirements. The information is claimed to be the largest self-reporting world wide database on the issues covered.[33] Companies can use this information to self-assess how they are performing relative to their peers.

### 32.6.6 AccountAbility[34]

This organisation follows a stakeholder approach to corporate social reporting and, based on such an approach, spells out both reporting principles and assurance standards.

Essentially its principles require an organisation to take responsibility for its material impacts on stakeholders, which in turn implies knowledge of those impacts gained through ongoing and systematic engagement with its stakeholders.

Its approach to assurance is interesting in that it has two types of assurance, both of which evaluate the information reported and systems used in terms of adherence to the principles developed by AccountAbility. Whereas Type 1 assurance assumes that the information is reliable and reports on adherence to AccountAbility principles, Type 2 assurance verifies compliance with Accountability principles and that the reported information is reliable.

This approach reflects the desire to have some assurance that the information is not selective and has some degree of credibility. However, at the same time there is a need to reflect the different stages of development of the environmental and social reporting in corporations, and the cost of providing comprehensive assurance.

### 32.6.7 The Eco-Management and Audit Scheme (EMAS)[35]

The Eco-Management and Audit Scheme was adopted as a voluntary environmental management scheme by the European Union (EU) in 1993 and has been upgraded over time. As such the scheme can now be used by organisations outside the EU. This scheme incorporates ISO 14001, the non-government international standards relating to systematic assessment of environmental impacts and the audit of compliance with those. ISO 14001 is endeavouring to apply the principles of quality management to environmental management and as such make eco-management an integral part of main stream management tasks. Companies may also apply additional ISO standards. Alternatively, some companies may follow the British standard 7750, which has similar objectives.

EMAS requires registered users of this system to report on energy efficiency, material efficiency, waste, biodiversity (land use and to start considering the impact of such land use on the eco-system or on habitats), and emissions. The objectives of EMAS include acting as a catalyst for innovation which improves both environmental and financial outcomes including identifying new business opportunities related to environmental performance.

The European Union has legislation on Corporate Social Responsibility Reporting coming into effect in 2017 and those who are complaint with EMAS will also be compliant with the new legislation.

#### Return on investment

In regard to this system it is interesting to contemplate why we have traditionally placed emphasis on return on investment. It is suggested that one reason for placing such emphasis is a recognition that as economic resources are in scarce supply it is desirable to optimise their use, i.e. look for good returns relative to the risks taken. In a world where more resources are going to be in scarce supply (e.g. water, clean air, liveable places, rare earth metals) it is also important for stakeholders to bear in mind that increased scarcity will force up prices, which will affect profitability if production systems have not found ways of minimising their use.

### 32.6.8 The Association of British Insurers (ABI)

The Association of British Insurers, being an industry association which represents companies who have major investment portfolios, is well placed to establish guidelines for reporting companies. In those guidelines the stress is on limited disclosure which is focused on the significant risks and opportunities in relation to ESG (environmental, social and governance) in the context of other risk factors, the mitigation of those risks, and their future plans. Thus if companies want to attract these insurance companies to invest in their shares it would be prudent to follow these guidelines.

### 32.6.9 FTSE ESG ratings

Based on public information, summarised information is provided about ESG performance based on the three pillars (economic, social and governance), and within those categories various themes are explored in more detail. Overall ratings are calculated not on a simple addition of the scores on the three pillars, but rather the score weights the factors according to their importance and the likely impact of performances in those areas: 'The criteria have been designed to help investors minimise ESG risks'.[36]

### 32.6.10 S & P Dow Jones Sustainability Index and RobcoSam Analyses

Companies are analysed by RobcoSam (a company with expertise in sustainability assessment) according to the three dimensions and are compared to the industry average and the best company within the industry on the individual dimensions (economic, environmental, and social) and overall.[37] Then the S & P Dow Jones Sustainability Index is calculated plotting the performance of leading sustainability driven companies worldwide (i.e. from 'the top 10% per industry of the 2,500 largest companies in the S & P Global Broad Market Index that lead their field in terms of financially material ESG factors'[38]).

## 32.7 The contribution of accountants

As pointed out previously, accounting professional bodies have been early advocates of broadening reporting to encompass environmental and social and governance dimensions. Thus in 1975 The Accounting Standards Steering Committee tried to get recognition for a broader scope of accountability when it published 'The Corporate Report'.

Various accountants argued for environmental and social accounting both before and after that report where the topics were sustainability, environmental accounting, corporate social responsibility, and triple bottom line. As momentum increased ACCA and Ceres established a Sustainability Reporting Award in 2002 and since that date such awards have been established by ACCA national bodies in 20 countries. Similar to other professional accounting bodies ACCA has embedded corporate social responsibility into its educational requirements. When in 2009 Mervyn King and the Prince of Wales ('Accounting 4 Sustainability') called a meeting to discuss the future of reporting, the accounting profession was represented by IASB and FASB, IFAC as well as the big four accounting firms. This initiative led to the formation of the International Integrated Reporting Council.

Whilst sustainability normally involves technical, scientific, legal, and social issues there are still roles for accountants in terms of strategic planning, control systems, external reporting and auditing.

### Strategic planning

As people intimately involved in all aspects of the business they should have a good overview of the business and its plans for the future. This means they are in a good position to identify what environmental, social, and human rights issues are important in the organisation, or are likely to be in the near future.[39]

As accountants are normally involved in strategic planning they can ensure that the environmental, social, human rights, ethical and governance, supply management, resource maintenance issues are adequately addressed. Whilst others may have more expertise in the technical issues it is the accountant who can relate these issues to the potential costs of not adequately addressing the issue. In project evaluations such as net present value assessments, for example, they can ask searching questions in relation to relevant costs or benefits which have not been included in the analysis.

### Control systems

In relation to controls systems, accountants can have important input into the items to be collected. They should monitor what other companies are reporting in terms of disclosures in annual reports and strategic reports with a view to ensuring their own systems cover all elements which are likely to be the focus of community demands in the future.

They should also be intimately familiar with the recommended measures established by the organisations discussed previously. Having identified the critical issues the information system can be designed to capture the relevant information. Accountants have a lot of experience in capturing information and what can go wrong in such a process. They should, therefore, be involved in identifying the most important information, the units of measure, how it is to be captured, designing the controls necessary to ensure its integrity, advising on key performance measures and how these are to be used when carrying out performance evaluations and attempting to predict any undesirable consequences from their use for evaluation.

### Management accountants

Management accountants have the challenge of how to collect and present information so as to capture management attention. For example, in relation to waste, it might be possible to extract costs from a range of accounts such as the costs paid to store, process or dispose of waste internally; the costs of transporting and disposing at commercial dumps; waste management salaries and estimated costs incurred by customers to dispose of discarded products and packaging, etc.

Highlighting such costs could lead to the identification of alternative strategies such as use of alternative materials in the product itself and in packaging or the need to invest in new processes to process waste.

### Financial accountants

Financial accountants can focus on how to communicate the environmental and social information so as to show trends and its relation to the strategy and value proposition of the company.

They take a positive proactive role, raising questions such as:

- Are there any issues of comparability of information across an industry which may need to be addressed?

- Is any information missing which is necessary to really understand the current position of the organisation and the future prospects of the company?

- Is there a need for strategies to address different audiences with different levels of information in different reports?

- Is there a need to revise any of the figures in the draft accounts?

- Is there a need to recognise impairments of intangible assets?

- Has there been any increase in pollution that warrants the inclusion in the accounts of provisions or liabilities for rectification?

- Is there a need to recognise environmental liabilities (IAS 37) and environmental assets or to report contingent assets and liabilities?

- Will there be pressure to reduce financial accounting disclosures to reduce information overload?

- Are the disclosures limited to the key facts and communicated in a clear, easy to understand manner?

- How should any Notes to the accounts be worded?

The following example of wording is taken from the BHPBilliton 2015 Annual Report:[40]

### Provision for closure and rehabilitation

The Group's accounting policy for the recognition of closure and rehabilitation provisions requires significant estimates and assumptions such as: requirements of the relevant legal and regulatory framework; the magnitude of possible contamination; and the timing, extent and costs of required closure and rehabilitation activity. These uncertainties may result in future actual expenditure differing from the amounts currently provided.

The provision recognised for each site is periodically reviewed and updated based on the facts and circumstances available at the time. Changes to the estimated future costs for operating sites are recognised in the balance sheet by adjusting both the closure and rehabilitation asset and provision. For closed sites, changes to estimated costs are recognised immediately in the income statement.

A further example taken from the Royal Dutch Shell 2015 Annual Report makes a similar statement:[41]

Of the decommissioning and restoration provision at December 31, 2015, an estimated $6,165 million is expected to be utilised within one to five years, $6,199 million within six to 10 years, and the remainder in later periods.

Reviews of estimated decommissioning and restoration costs and the discount rate applied are carried out annually. The review of cost estimates and a decrease in the discount rate applied resulted in an increase of $3,620 million (2014: $4,827 million increase) in both the provision, reported within remeasurements and other movements, and the corresponding property, plant and equipment assets reported within sales, retirements and other movements in Note 8.

Other provisions principally comprise amounts recognised in respect of environmental costs ($1,545 million at December 31, 2015; 2014 $1,364 million), litigation costs, employee in- and end-of-service benefits, onerous contracts related to the cessation of certain activities and redundancy costs.

This statement is interesting in that it highlights the subjective nature of the decisions as to the issues of timing, appropriate discount rates and estimation of future costs.

### Auditors

Internal auditors and external auditors need to consider which of the environmental and social disclosures need to be certified and who has the skill to perform the certification. If they are not accountants what supervision and training is desirable to ensure they apply the appropriate audit skills (as opposed to the technical skills)?

Although the certification does not have to be performed by an accountant or an accounting firm, the skills developed in traditional audits are a possible competitive advantage as could be the reputation of an established auditor.

There may be other areas which accountants may want to monitor and bring to the attention of management. One such is the vulnerability of the company to climate change. Again, practice questions are raised, such as:

- Are any of the assets vulnerable?
- Which products and customers are sensitive to climate variability?
- What are the implications for inventory levels?
- Is there a concentration of supply chains in areas which could be affected?
- Is there a need to diversify the locations of suppliers?

### Value added statements

An earlier attempt to address social accounting was the adoption of the value added statement as mentioned earlier. Of particular interest is that accountants perceived the need for this item of social accounting well before social accounting became more widely acknowledged.

Events of 2011 showed that the issue of fairness (which is one elements underlying the issue of the value added statement) is perceived by many as being a major factor in whether to support the current version of the economic system. Following the crash covering 2007 and 2008, governments around the world were required to borrow to support the financial institutions (banks were supported including the British government taking an 81% interest in RBS, and the USA government supported non-bank lenders, such as General Electric and insurer AIG, to preserve the overall economic system).

This support was perceived by many as the rich being the beneficiaries in the good times prior to the crash and then getting subsidies when the investments performed badly. Irrespective of who were the ultimate beneficiaries, the perception of many was that the top 1% of society were getting excessive benefits from the system whereas the remaining 99% were being unfairly treated.

A movement called Occupy Wall Street staged protests around the Western world in September 2011 to show their displeasure with the system. Whilst the protests have faded away the perceptions have not. Thus the value added statement was an early attempt by accountants to address the equity issue. However, questions may be asked as to whether the presentation is the best way to address the issue.

The statement of value added also illustrates how the perspectives adopted can determine the content of the social report and that social reporting is not always self-evident. Before discussing those issues a real example is provided.

### Example: Barloworld Integrated Report 2015[42]

A measure of the value created by the group is the amount of value added by its diverse trading, distribution and other activities to the cost of products and services purchased. The statement below shows the total value created and how it was distributed.

## Statement of total value added for the year ended 30 September

| | 2015 Rm | % | 2014 Rm | % | 2013 Rm | % |
|---|---|---|---|---|---|---|
| Revenue from continuing operations | 62,720 | | 62,101 | | 59,498 | |
| Revenue from discontinued operation | | | 2,783 | | 5,508 | |
| Paid to suppliers for materials and services | 47,554 | | 49,389 | | 51,019 | |
| Value added | 15,166 | | 15,494 | | 13,987 | |
| Income from investments[a] | 382 | | 297 | | 263 | |
| **Total value created** | 15,548 | | 15,791 | | 14,250 | |
| **Value distribution** | | | | | | |
| Employees (note 1) | 8,955 | 58 | 9,103 | 58 | 8,605 | 60 |
| Capital providers: | 2,259 | 15 | 1,856 | 12 | 1,630 | 12 |
| Finance costs | 1,252 | | 1,125 | | 1,022 | |
| Dividends to Barloworld Limited shareholders | 699 | | 639 | | 522 | |
| Dividends to non-controlling interest in subsidiaries | 109 | | 92 | | 86 | |
| Strategic black partners and community groups | 199 | | | | | |
| Government (note 2) | 948 | 6 | 1,103 | 7 | 952 | 7 |
| Communities (corporate social investment) | 17 | | 17 | | 17 | |
| Reinvested in the group to maintain and develop operations | 3,369 | 21 | 3,712 | 23 | 3,047 | 21 |
| Depreciation | 2,355 | | 2,208 | | 1,960 | |
| Retained profit | 1,142 | | 1,556 | | 1,080 | |
| Deferred taxation | (128) | | (52) | | 7 | |
| | 15,548 | 100 | 15,791 | 100 | 14,250 | 100 |
| **Value added ratios** | | | | | | |
| Number of employees (30 September) | 19,745 | | 19,616 | | 19,692 | |
| Revenue per employee (rand)[b] | 3,186,911 | | 3,301,297 | | 3,339,631 | |
| Value created per employee (rand)[b] | 790,010 | | 803,474 | | 732,083 | |
| Corporate social investment – % of profit after taxation | 1 | | 1 | | 1 | |

*Notes:*

**1. Employees**

| | | | | | | |
|---|---|---|---|---|---|---|
| Salaries, wages, overtime payments, commissions, bonuses and allowances[c] | 7,780 | | 7,673 | | 7,068 | |
| Employer contributions[d] | 1,175 | | 1,204 | | 1,071 | |
| **Total continuing operations** | 8,955 | | 8,877 | | 8,140 | |
| Discontinued operation | | | 226 | | 465 | |
| **Total group** | 8,955 | | 9,103 | | 8,605 | |

(continued)

|  | 2015 Rm | % | 2014 Rm | % | 2013 Rm | % |
|---|---|---|---|---|---|---|
| **2. Central and local government** | | | | | | |
| Current taxation | 770 | | 947 | | 821 | |
| Rates and taxes paid to local authorities | 63 | | 59 | | 54 | |
| Customs duties, import surcharges and excise taxes | 69 | | 49 | | 38 | |
| Skills development levy | 46 | | 48 | | 39 | |
| | 948 | | 1,103 | | 952 | |

[a]Includes interest received, dividend income and share of associate companies' and joint ventures' retained profit.
[b]Based on average number of employees.
[c]Represents the gross amounts paid to employees including taxes payable by the employees.
[d]In respect of pension funds, retirement annuities, provident funds, medical aid and insurance.

If this report is confusing the following should help. The report views the company as a mechanism for both creating products and services out of external inputs and then deciding how the economic gain is distributed to the various stakeholders who helped generate those benefits. So the above statement says the company sold goods and services for Rm62,720. These goods and services were only possible because the company paid Rm47,554 to external suppliers. Therefore the work performed within the company generated additional economic benefits of 62,720 minus 47,554, or Rm15,166. In addition the company earned Rm382 from investments so that is added on to the 15,166 to give total additional economic benefits generated (or the value added) of Rm15,548. That money was then divided up as follows amongst stakeholders as follows:

| | |
|---|---|
| Employee benefits including wages, pensions and healthcare | 8,955 |
| Rewards to financiers in the form of interest and dividends | 2,259 |
| Payments to government departments | 948 |
| Payment to a community group | 17 |
| Reinvestment into the business | 3,369 |
| Total of the amount shared up | 15,548 (which equals the amount of the value added calculated above) |

How is this information actually used? Can one draw accurate conclusions regarding the fairness of the division of the benefits generated?

*Note*: Barloworld has followed the traditional methods of preparing the value added statement and the comments below are not in any way related to their circumstances or business activities.

However, there are questions which could be raised about such calculations in general.

### What are the rewards to the financiers?

It could be argued that they get interest and dividends as shown above. But shareholders get both dividends and capital gains from the increase in the value of shares. So it could be argued that, although part of the reinvestment into the business is to cover wear and tear and obsolescence of equipment, the remaining part enhances the value of the shares.

### What is the category 'payments to government departments'?

This may in some circumstances be ambiguous. For example, is a payment of a royalty by a mining company based on the sales value of the ore which was shipped a payment of a tax or is it an agreed method of pricing the ore body sold to the mining company? If it is a fair cost of the raw ore then should it be a payment for goods and services in the calculation of the value added?

Where a government department provides services such as water, electricity or use of a motorway is that a payment to suppliers or is it an allocation to the government?

### Employee benefits

Whilst the total allocation to employees is interesting it might be more informative to know payments to different categories of employees, as the rewards for top-level employees may be considerably different from those to other employees. In the USA from 1 January 2017 a pay ratio will be filed under Item 402 of Regulation S-K. The ratio compares the total compensation of the chief executive officer to the median compensation of all other employees. Note the reference to median compensation rather than average compensation, which is to avoid the possibility of averages being skewed by atypical employees. The reported ratio will tell readers the number of times greater the chief executive's remuneration is compared to the typical (median) employee. It will be interesting to see if this information will be required by other countries.

## 32.8 Integrated reporting – its impact on the future development of financial reporting and accounting

As the world becomes more aware of the need to modify industry behaviour to reflect the challenges posed by the impact of their actions on the sustainability of our lifestyle, and the social and environmental systems which make that lifestyle achievable, there is pressure to adopt different mindsets.

The implication for accounting is to encourage integrated reporting. Instead of the previous focus primarily on financial capital and its changes, the integrated approach requires reporting on six types of capital, as illustrated in Figure 32.1.

This is not to suggest companies don't have to perform well on financial dimensions but rather that good financial performance is not sufficient on its own. It is integrated in the sense that it recognises that the achievement of the organisation's strategy probably requires support from all six areas and that the interaction with the other five capitals varies across organisations and hence the reporting should reflect that.

Further to understand the reports one needs a clear idea of the linkages between the strategy which builds on a sustainable competitive advantage and the various capitals. As the range of areas on which the organisation reports grows, the need to avoid information overload becomes much more important. Thus the focus is on the critical factors only. There is a need to communicate a coherent story of the organisation's current achievements and what it has done to position it to take advantage of the types of opportunities which are likely to arise in the future.

By reporting on multiple capitals it is hoped that the quality of external reporting will improve due to a more comprehensive analysis and that the limitations inherent in current reporting will be partly compensated for by the additional information. This is particularly relevant in businesses where the major assets are intangible (technology breakthroughs, systems, images and brand connotations, integrity, and governance systems), and where it is difficult to assess a value.

**Figure 32.1**

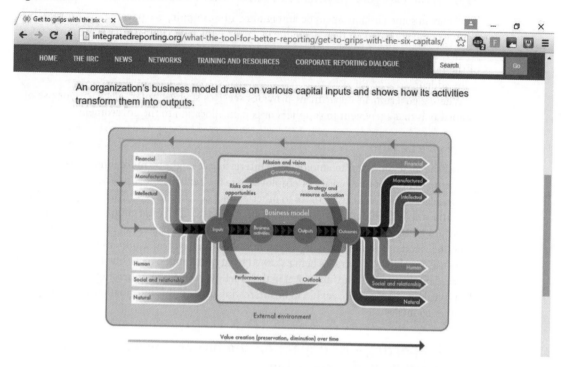

Also the looming risks associated with achieving sustainability often revolve around environmental issues and levels of social support, as well as legal frameworks and infrastructure. It is hoped that better reporting will lead to better and more reliable valuations and subsequently to better allocations of resources in society.

There is an expectation that, as reporting changes, the pressures on management to achieve on all capitals will lead to greater alignment of business decision making with the needs of society as a whole. In other words, the incorporation of corporate social responsibility into the integrated reporting system will reduce the number and size of externalities. Some companies will use integrated reports as public relations statements but it is a matter of the degree of puffery. Obviously companies like to promote their achievements. To the extent that major issues are avoided and not reported exposes the company to major risks such as litigation risks, reputational risks, and exposure of top management to career risks. Hopefully this will constrain the use of public relations to manageable proportions. Auditors have an opportunity to show their value by ensuring reporting is not misleading.

Ultimately, integrated reporting is only successful if it changes business behaviour to align more closely with what is good for society as a whole. This means reward systems must support the broader objectives. Accountants can contribute to the debate by providing feedback on practicalities and effectiveness.

## REVIEW QUESTIONS

1 GRI has Principles for Defining Report Content. Included in those is the principle of stakeholder inclusiveness, which says 'The organization should identify its stakeholders, and explain how it has

responded to their reasonable expectations and interest.' Using your university as the case study, identify its stakeholders and what would constitute reasonable expectations.

2 GRI has Principles for Defining Report Quality, which states that 'The report should reflect positive and negative aspects of the organization's performance to enable a reasoned assessment of overall performance.' Further they go on to say 'The overall presentation of the report's content should provide an unbiased picture of the organization's performance. The report should avoid selections, omissions, or presentation formats that are reasonably likely to unduly or inappropriately influence a decision or judgement by the report reader.' Obtain either an integrated accounting report, or a sustainability report, or an annual report and examine two graphs or diagrams and explain whether or not these criteria are met.

3 Identify an organisation that undertakes corporate social reporting and has an independent party provide assurance on such reporting. Explain in your own words what the assurance covers and does not cover, who it is addressed to, whether the assurance follows any particular standard(s).

4 Identify a South African company that applies integrated reporting and comment on the following: (i) the extent to which it deviates from the governance code and the quality of the justification for not complying; (ii) the quality of the communication; (iii) the extent to which choice of environmental and social reporting links to the corporate strategy; (iv) the extent to which the environmental and social information is audited.

5 Identify a company that is registered under the EMAS and discuss their disclosures under that scheme and what it indicates in terms of progress in achieving significant improvement in environmental achievements.

6 In linear programming the computer program allocates resources so as to maximise the profit function given the constraints imposed on the system. Such constraints may reflect limited markets, labour or material or production capacity scarcity. Discuss how such a technique could be used in relation to corporate social responsibility management.

7 Linda Midgley[43] suggested that the major deficiency with current integrated reports is that they do not provide a story which shows the linkage between the reporting on the various capitals. Explain in your own words why the story is important and why you think companies are not performing better on that aspect.

8 The Prince's Accounting for Sustainability Project was responsible for bringing together the sponsors of the International Integrated Reporting Council. The project is a co-sponsor of the Finance for the Future Awards to bring to the attention of the financial community the skills required for accounting in the twenty-first century. Identify one of the latest recipients (there are multiple categories so just choose one) of the award and explain in your own words the innovation in financial applications which they have been responsible for and discuss whether it has broader applications.

9 In 2016 the UK Financial Reporting Council objected to the proposed European Union directive on integrated reporting for large companies.[44] The discussion seems to revolve around disclosure of specific items of information versus discretionary disclosure based on the perceived relevance or importance of the information in relation to the reporting company's strategy. Discuss the pros and cons of discretion in relation to the disclosures in integrated reporting.

10 Aviva plc provided in relation to 2015 three relevant reports. Those reports are the Strategic Report 2015, Corporate Social Responsibility Summary 2015, and Aviva Environmental, Social and Governance Data Summary 2015. Read those reports and rank them in terms of usefulness to you and justify your ranking.

11 Obtain copies of three integrated accounting reports (including at least one which has been certified) and identify whether or not they have been certified. On any that has been certified review the 'statement' by the certifier and identify what they have actually done as part of the review, what

guidelines (if any) they have followed, and whether they have confidence in the report. (Note: ACCA and CPA Australia have produced integrated reports.)

12 From the IIRC website identify a company producing an integrated report. Read the report from an investor perspective and then from an employee perspective. Then provide two evaluations with reasons for your comments.

13 The Integrated Reporting Framework stresses the need for linkages to the business strategy to be clear and the reporting to be restricted to significant items. However, other parties stress the need for comparability. Discuss whether or not these two views are compatible.

14 Should integrated reports address allocation of value added? Justify your conclusions.

15 Select an industry and explain the best approach to conveying to readers the state of human resources.

16 Whenever a new system of metrics is used for performance evaluation smart people try to game the system. Identify a metric in the G4 system and identify how the system might be gamed.

(By to game the system we mean to beat the system by undertaking actions which are not desirable under the system but which get a good score on the evaluation system. An example might be an academic who is being evaluated on the number of publications in academic journals. The academic is going to publish a long article and then changes their mind and decides to split the research into two parts to get two publications without doing much extra work. The amount of research undertaken is not increased but the academic appears to be a better researcher.)

17 Nissan, the Japanese car company, decided that 'any environmentalism should pay for itself and for every penny you spend you must save a penny. You can spend as many pennies as you like as long as other environmental actions save an equal number.'[45] Discuss the significance of this for each of the major stakeholders.

18 Consumer-oriented models are more likely to be influenced by ethical principles. Discuss.

19 Look up the S & P Dow Jones Indices and then discuss:

(a) what you think the index can be used for;

(b) the number of high-performing companies by country;

(c) the comparative performance of two of those high performers.

## EXERCISES

### Question 1

Geoworld Enterprises plc has the following information extracted from its statement of income and payroll systems:

|  | £ |
|---|---|
| Revenue | 411,000,000 |
| Compensation expenses | 158,000,000 |
| Raw materials used | 100,000,000 |
| Payments to subcontractors | 51,000,000 |
| Energy expenses | 1,000,000 |
| Depreciation expenses | 1,000,000 |
| Interest expenses | 2,000,000 |
| Taxation expenses | 16,000,000 |

| Employment statistics | | Full time | | Part time | |
| --- | --- | --- | --- | --- | --- |
| | Number | Total payment to the group £ | Number | Total payment to the group £ | |
| CEO | 1x | 1,000,000 | | | |
| Senior executives | 5x | 3,000,000 | | | |
| Other executives | 10x | 4,000,000 | | | |
| Local employees | 2,000x | 80,000,000 | 1000x | 10,000,000 | |
| International employees | 2000x | 40,000,000 | 4,000x | 20,000,000 | |
| Subcontractors | 2,000x | 35,000,000 | 2,000x | 16,000,000 | |

Each fulltime employees works double the hours of part time staff.

Dividends paid to shareholders          3,000,000

**Required:**

(a) Prepare a value added statement.

(b) Prepare your version of the ratio of the chief executive salary to the median income of other employees. (Note the objective is not to get you to look up the standard form of the calculation but rather to get you to think about the complexities of the calculation and the need for standardisation of the system.) Justify your calculation(s).

(c) Would the required information be readily available in the typical information system? If not could such systems be easily modified?

(d) Look at the calculation in (b) above and consider how the CEO could improve their score in the future and whether all those possibilities would be in the interests of shareholders.

## Question 2

Wonder Kid Enterprises Company has produced the following results over the last three years:

| | 20XX | 20XY | 20XZ |
| --- | --- | --- | --- |
| Profit before interest and taxes | 1,000,000 | 1,600,000 | 3,000,000 |
| Interest | 160,000 | 320,000 | 900,000 |
| Taxes | 252,000 | 384,000 | 630,000 |
| Profit after interest and taxes | 588,000 | 896,000 | 1,470,000 |
| Financing using debt | 40% | 40% | 40% |
| Funds employed (debt + equity) | 4,000,000 | 8,000,000 | 20,000,000 |
| Shareholders' before tax required rate of return on investment | 20% | 20% | 25% |

Management has just issued its annual report for 20XZ and a fair reading of their commentary is that the company has done very well because the trend in profit after interest and taxes have shown a high level of growth. In addition it is disclosed that the development of its latest technological breakthrough is taking longer to get regulatory approval than earlier thought. A review of the financial press ascertains that interest rates have remained steady over the three years.

**Required:**
Discuss the results showing calculations where appropriate.

## Question 3

(a) Prepare a value added statement to be included in the corporate report of Hythe plc for the year ended 31 December 20X6, including the comparatives for 20X5, using the information given below:

|  | 20X6<br>£000 | 20X5<br>£000 |
|---|---|---|
| Non-current assets (net book value) | 3,725 | 3,594 |
| Trade receivables | 870 | 769 |
| Trade payables | 530 | 448 |
| 14% debentures | 1,200 | 1,080 |
| 6% preference shares | 400 | 400 |
| Ordinary shares (£1 each) | 3,200 | 3,200 |
| Sales | 5,124 | 4,604 |
| Materials consumed | 2,934 | 2,482 |
| Wages | 607 | 598 |
| Depreciation | 155 | 144 |
| Fuel consumed | 290 | 242 |
| Hire of plant and machinery | 41 | 38 |
| Salaries | 203 | 198 |
| Auditors' remuneration | 10 | 8 |
| Corporation tax provision | 402 | 393 |
| Ordinary share dividend | 9p | 8p |
| Number of employees | 40 | 42 |

(b) Although value added statements were recommended by The Corporate Report in 1975, as yet there is no accounting standard related to them. Explain what a value added statement is and provide reasons as to why you think it has not yet become mandatory to produce such a statement as a component of current financial statements through either a Financial Reporting Standard or company law.

## Question 4

The following items have been extracted from the accounts:

|  | 2005 (€m) | 2004 (€m) |
|---|---|---|
| Other income | 844 | 980 |
| Cost of materials | 25,694 | 24,467 |
| Financial income | −188 | 54 |
| Depreciation/amortisation | 4,207 | 3,589 |
| Providers of finance | 1,351 | 1,059 |
| Retained | 1,815 | 1,823 |
| Revenues | 46,656 | 44,335 |
| Government | 1,590 | 1,794 |
| Other expenses | 4,925 | 5,093 |
| Shareholders | 424 | 419 |
| Employees | 7,306 | 7,125 |

Required:

(a) Prepare a value added statement showing % for each year and % change.

(b) Draft a note for inclusion in the annual report commenting on the statement you have prepared.

## Question 5

David Mark is a sole trader who owns and operates supermarkets in each of three villages near Ousby. He has drafted his own accounts for the year ended 31 May 20X4 for each of the branches. They are as follows:

| | Arton | | Blendale | | Clifearn | |
|---|---|---|---|---|---|---|
| | £ | £ | £ | £ | £ | £ |
| Sales | | 910,800 | | 673,200 | | 382,800 |
| Cost of sales | | 633,100 | | 504,900 | | 287,100 |
| Gross profit | | 277,700 | | 168,300 | | 95,700 |
| Less: Expenses: | | | | | | |
| David Mark's salary | 10,560 | | 10,560 | | 10,560 | |
| Other salaries and wages | 143,220 | | 97,020 | | 78,540 | |
| Rent | | | 19,800 | | | |
| Rates | 8,920 | | 5,780 | | 2,865 | |
| Advertising | 2,640 | | 2,640 | | 2,640 | |
| Delivery van expenses | 5,280 | | 5,280 | | 5,280 | |
| General expenses | 11,220 | | 3,300 | | 1,188 | |
| Telephone | 2,640 | | 1,980 | | 1,584 | |
| Wrapping materials | 7,920 | | 3,960 | | 2,640 | |
| Depreciation: | | | | | | |
| Fixtures | 8,220 | | 4,260 | | 2,940 | |
| Vehicle | 3,000 | 203,620 | 3,000 | 157,580 | 3,000 | 111,237 |
| Net profit/(loss) | | 74,080 | | 10,720 | | (15,537) |

The figures for the year ended 31 May 20X4 follow the pattern of recent years. Because of this, David Mark is proposing to close the Clifearn supermarket immediately.

David Mark employs 12 full-time and 20 part-time staff. His recruitment policy is based on employing one extra part-time assistant for every £30,000 increase in branch sales. His staff deployment at the moment is as follows:

| | Arton | Blendale | Clifearn |
|---|---|---|---|
| Full-time staff (including managers) | 6 | 4 | 2 |
| Part-time staff | 8 | 6 | 6 |

Peter Gaskin, the manager of the Clifearn supermarket, asks David to give him another year to make the supermarket profitable. Peter has calculated that he must cover £125,500 expenses out of his gross profit in the year ended 31 May 20X5 in order to move into profitability. His calculations include extra staff costs and all other extra costs.

Additional information:

(i) General advertising for the business as a whole is controlled by David Mark. This costs £3,960 per annum. Each manager spends a further £1,320 advertising his own supermarket locally.

(ii) The delivery vehicle is used for deliveries from the Arton supermarket only.

(iii) David Mark has a central telephone switchboard which costs £1,584 rental per annum. Each super-market is charged for all calls actually made. For the year ended 31 May 20X4 these amounted to:

| Arton | £2,112 |
|---|---|
| Blendale | £1,452 |
| Clifearn | £1,056 |

Required:

(a) A report addressed to David Mark advising him whether to close the Clifearn supermarket. Your report should include a detailed financial statement based on the results for the year ended 31 May 20X4 relating to the Clifearn branch.

(b) Calculate the increased turnover and extra staff needed if Peter's suggestion is implemented.

(c) Comment on the social implications for the residents of Clifearn if (i) David Mark closes the supermarket, (ii) Peter Gaskin's recommendation is undertaken.

## * Question 6

Gettry Doffit plc is an international company with worldwide turnover of £26 million. The activities of the company include the breaking down and disposal of noxious chemicals at a specialised plant in the remote Scottish countryside. During the preparation of the financial statements for the year ended 31 March 20X5, it was discovered that:

1 Quantities of chemicals for disposals on site at the year-end included:

| (A) | Axylotl peroxide | 40,000 gallons |
| (B) | Pterodactyl chlorate | 35 tons |

Chemical A is disposed of for a South Korean company, which was invoiced for 170 million won on 30 January 20X5, for payment in 120 days. It is estimated that the costs of disposal will not exceed £75,000. £60,000 of costs have been incurred at the year-end.

Chemical B is disposed of for a British company on a standard contract for 'cost of disposal plus 35%', one month after processing. At the year-end the chemical has been broken down into harmless by-products at a cost of £77,000. The by-products, which belong to Gettry Doffit plc, are worth £2,500.

2 To cover against exchange risks, the company entered into two forward contracts on 30 January 20X5:

| No. 03067 | Sell 170 million won at 1,950 won | = £1: | 31 May 20X5 |
| No. 03068 | Buy $70,000 at $1.60 | = £1: | 31 May 20X5 |

Actual sterling exchange rates were:

| | won | $ |
|---|---|---|
| 30 January 20X5 | 1,900 | 1.70 |
| 31 March 20X5 | 2,000 | 1.38 |
| 30 April 20X5 (today) | 2,100 | 1.80 |

The company often **purchases** a standard chemical used in processing from a North American company, and the dollars will be applied towards this purpose.

3 The company entered into a contract to import a specialised chemical used in the breaking down of magnesium perambulate from a Nigerian company which demanded the raising of an irrevocable letter of credit for £65,000 to cover 130 tons of the chemical. By 31 March 20X5 bills of lading for 60 tons had been received and paid for under the letter of credit. It now appears that the total needed for the requirements of Gettry Doffit plc for the foreseeable future is only 90 tons.

4 On 16 October 20X4 Gettry Doffit plc entered into a joint venture as partners with Dumpet Andrunn plc to process perfidious recalcitrant (PR) at the Gettry Doffit plc site using Dumpet Andrunn plc's technology. Unfortunately, a spillage at the site on 15 April 20X5 has led to claims being filed against the two companies for £12 million. A public inquiry has been set up, to assess the cause of the accident and to determine liability, which the finance director of Gettry Doffit plc fears will be, at the very least, £3 million.

Required:

Discuss how these matters should be reflected in the financial statements of Gettry Doffit plc as on and for the year ended 31 March 20X5.

## Notes

1 www.theguardian.com/environment/2015/dec/11/bp-gulf-oil-spil

2 'BHP Billiton withdraws from Ok Tedi Copper Mine and establishes development fund for benefit of Papua New Guinea People', www.bhp/documents/investors/reports/2001/oktedimineexit-briefingpaper.pdf

3 J. Plungis, 'VW may have to clean the air its cars polluted', *The Australian Financial Review*, 24 February 2016, p. 10.

4 www.sustainability-indices.com/images/150929-statement-vw-exclusion_vdef.pdf

5 www.theguardian.com/world/2013/june23/rana-plaza-factory-disaster-bangladesh-primark

6 Ibid.

7 L. Stout, *The Shareholder Value Myth*, San Francisco, Berrett-Koehler, 2012.

8 Stakeholder theory has much in common with agency theory, which views the company as a network of contracts of which shareholder contracts are essentially no different from other contracts. A residual interest is not the same as ownership. See Stout (2012), op cit.

9 Financial Reporting Council, *Guidance on the Strategic Report*, June 2014, www.frc.org.uk/Our-Work/Publications/Accounting-and-Reporting-Policy/Guidance-on-the-Strategic-Report.pdf, p. 14.

10 https://frc.org.uk/Our-Work/Publications/Accounting-and-Reporting-Policy/Guidance-on-the-Strategic-Report.pdf

11 *The Stern Review: The Economics of Climate Change*, 30 October, 2006, HM Treasury.

12 The strategic report is extracted from the Unilever 2015 Annual Report.

13 The International <IR> Framework, www.theiirc.org

14 These descriptions are in 2.15 of the International <IR> Framework.

15 'During the process of preparing his bank ratings, Lafferty's team went back and analysed the 2007 annual report of HBOS, a British bank which blew itself up in the financial crisis. The report showed staff gave management a rating of 76 per cent. At the time, this number surprised industry pundits because the average was 50 per cent. Later, an HBOS whistle blower Paul Moore revealed that management had bullied staff into answering questions in the staff survey in the "correct" way.' Chanticleer, 'Banking on cultural change', *The Australian Financial Review*, 12-13 March 2016, p. 56.

16 www.shell.com/investors/financial-reporting/annual-publications/and entire_shell_ar15.pdf, p. 25.

17 http://drcaroladams.net/the-international-integrated-reporting-council-a-call-to-action/

18 With the extension of the range of reporting the term multiple bottom line covering economic, governance, social, ethical, and environmental (EGSEE) performance. See Z. Rezaee, *Business Sustainability*, Sheffield, Greenleaf Publishing, 2015, who says over 6000 public companies issue comprehensive reports compared to 50 companies ten years ago.

19 The history is outlined in J. Gleeson-White, *Six Capitals,* Sydney, Allen & Unwin, 2014.

20 'The Corporate Report', a discussion paper published by the Accounting Standards Steering Committee.

21 Based on information reported in Z. Rezaee, *Business Sustainability*, Sheffield, Greenleaf Publishing, 2015. The reference to the Brundtland Report is to the United Nations World Commission on Environment and Development, *Our Common Future*, Oxford University Press, 1987.

22 R.G. Eccles and M.P. Krzus with S.Ribot, *The Integrated Reporting Movement*, Hoboken, NJ, Wiley, 2015.

23 www.mervynking.co.za/downloads/CD_King2.pdf

24 www.ru.ac.za/media/rhodesuniversity/content/erm/documents/xx.%20King%203%20-%20King%20Report.pdf

25 www.prconversations.com/2009/09/difference-between-king-ii-and-king-iii-reports-on-governance/

26 www.ceres.org

27 www.globalreporting.org

28 www.globalreporting.org/resourcelibrary/Ready-to-Report-SME-booklet-online.pdf

29 www.diageo.com/en-row/csr/building-thriving-communities/sustainable-supply-chains/Pages/default.aspx

30 For more information, go to www.sasb.org

31 A letter from Jean Rogers, SASB CEO, 6 April 2016.

32 www.unglobalcompact.org/docs/publications/UN_Global_Compact_Guide_to_Corporate_Sustainability.pdf

33 www.cdp.net/CDP%20Questionaire%20Documents/CDP-Climate-Change-Information-request-2016.pdf

34 www.accountability.com

35 http://ec.europa.eu/environment/emas/news/index_en.htm#138

36 www.ftse.com/products/indices/f4g-esg-ratings

37 www.sustainability-indices.com/review/industry-group-leaders-2015.jsp

38 Ibid.

39 Rezaee, op. cit., suggests that 'about a third of the US GDP is sensitive to weather changes' and relies on J.K. Lazo, M. Lawson, P.H. Larsen and D.M. Waldman, 'United States economic sensitivity to weather variability', *Bulletin of the American Meteorological Society*, vol. 92, 2012, pp. 709–20.

40 www.bhpbilliton.com/~/media/bhp/documents/investors/annual-reports/2015/bhpbillitonannualreport2015_interactive.pdf?la=en

41 http://reports.shell.com/annual-report/2015/consolidated-financial-statements/notes/18-decommissioning-and-other-provisions.php

42 www.barloworld-reports.co.za/integrated-reports/ir-2015/bar-value-highlights.php

43 http://pwc.blogs.com/corporatereporting/2016/03/why-does-integrated-reporting-so-often-leaves-us-dissatisfied.html

44 www.iasplus.com/en/news/2016/04/frc

45 M. Brown, 'Greening the bottom line', *Management Today*, July, 1995, p. 73.

# Index

A & J Muklow plc 431
A M Castle & Co 499
A-scores 735–6
Aaronson, Graham 390
ABI *see* Association of British Insurers
absences, compensated 371
ACCA *see* Association of Chartered
    Certified Accountants
accountability 557, 821–5
AccountAbility 833, 835–6
Accountancy Development, International
    Forum on (IFAD) 156
accountants
  in business 177–8
  commercial awareness 4
  ethical behaviour *see* ethics
  executive remuneration and 798–9
  external reporting 3–4
  integrated reporting contributions
    837–43
  internal reporting 3, 4–8
  money laundering implications for 190
  in practice 176–7
  problems, ethics and 176–8
  reporting roles 5
  technical expertise 4
  view of income, capital and value
    204–6
  work environments, ethics and 181–3
  *see also* accounting profession; auditors
Accounting 4 Sustainability 837
accounting capital 205–6
Accounting Corporate Regulatory
    Authority (ACRA), Singapore
    761, 763
Accounting Council, FRC 136–7
Accounting Directive 139–41, 142, 146,
    476
accounting income 205
accounting numbers, role in defining
    contractual entitlements 131–2
*Accounting, Organization and Society* 828
accounting policies 45–6, 73, 140, 259–
    60, 433–5
accounting profession
  credibility 134
  cultural differences and 181
  ethical behaviour and 175–8
  public view of 133
  status of 149

accounting ratios *see* ratios
accounting standards
  arguments against 135
  arguments for 134
  conceptual framework 150–1, 155–69
  consensus-seeking 135
  enforcement
    co-operative approach 138
    Europe 141–2
    risk-based proactive approach 137
    UK 135–8
    USA 142–4
  ethics and 178–81
  global, advantages and disadvantages
    for publicly accountable entities
    144–5
  harmonisation 253–4
  macro-economic effects 175
  mandatory 132–4
  micro-economic effects 175
  need for 131–2
  overload 135
  setting 135–8
    European Union 139–41
    process, ethics and 174–5
    USA 142–4
  *see also* Financial Reporting Standards;
    International Accounting
    Standards; International Financial
    Reporting Standards; Statements
    of Financial Accounting
    Standards; Statements of
    Standard Accounting Practice
Accounting Standards Board (ASB) 135
  accrual accounting 27
  ethics and neutrality (Position Paper
    2012) 175
  *see also* Financial Reporting Standards;
    Statements of Standard
    Accounting Practice
Accounting Standards Committee (ASC)
    51, 151
Accounting Standards Steering
    Committee (ASSC)
  The Corporate Report 828, 837
accounting system differences 50
accounting theory 150, 156–8
accrual accounting 16, 17, 21–2
  Accounting Directive 140
  basis 22–3, 140

cash flow statements and 27–8
cash payments adjustments 23–4
cash receipts adjustments 23–4
deferred taxation 403
historical cost convention 22
income 205
non-current assets 24–7
statements of financial position 23–6
summary 28
views on 27
accrual data, failure predictions
    and 736
accruals 163
acid test ratios 502, 691–2
acquisitions
  cash 553–4
  fair value 547–8, 549, 551, 555–6
  foreign currencies and 633–7
  goodwill 472
  non-adjusting events 72
  share issues 282
  standards 132–4
  *see also* business combinations;
    consolidated accounts; groups
ACRA (Accounting Corporate
    Regulatory Authority), Singapore
    761, 763
actual performance 202
Actuarial Council, FRC 136
actuarial gains and losses, pension
    schemes 367
ad hoc reports by auditors 790
additional items reporting, FRC
    reminder on 43
adjusting events 71
adjustments 37, 231–3
administration overheads 499, 500
administrative expenses 37–8
administrative expenses ratios 685
Adobe® 756
advocacy threats 178
AEI, takeover by GEC 132–3
Aer Lingus 740
affirmative covenants 722
agency costs 8
aggressive earnings management 723–4
AGM (Annual General Meetings) 282
Agrana Group 500–1
agricultural activities 510–12
Ahold 133–4, 506

AIA (Association of International
    Accountants) 191
AICPA (American Institute of Certified
    Public Accountants) 766, 771
Aids, South Africa 832
AIG 840
AIM see Alternative Investment Market
AkzoNobel 414, 424
Alternative Investment Market (AIM)
    co-operative approach to enforcement
    138
Altman's Z-score 732–3
Amadeus 757
American Institute of Certified Public
    Accountants (AICPA) 766, 771
AML (anti-money laundering) standard
    190
amortisation 37, 132, 415, 467–8, 473–5
amortised costs 328, 339–40, 453
analysis
    cash flow statements 110–16
    financial statements see financial
        statements
    techniques
        A-scores 735–6
        golden rule 678
        H-scores 734–5, 741
        overview 678–9
        predicting corporate failure 732–6
        Z-scores 732–4, 741
    see also ratios
Annual General Meetings (AGM) 282
annual refunds, revenue recognition 260
annual reports 70
    accounting policy changes 73
    directors' reports 55
    discontinued operations 82–3
    errors 73–4
    events after reporting periods 70–3
    fraud 73–4
    held for sale 83–5
    intellectual capital disclosures in 480–1
    narrative information 716
    related party disclosures 85–9
    segment reporting 75–9
    Strategic Reports 54–5, 112
    see also financial statements; published
        accounts
annuity method, depreciation 419–20
anonymous whistle-blowing 188–9
Anti-Abuse Rule, General (GAAR)
    389–90
anti-avoidance rules, targeted (TAAR)
    389–90
anti-money laundering (AML)
    standard 190
anti-social behaviour 785
apartheid regime, South Africa 831
APB see Auditing Practices Board
Apple 477
appointments, ethics and 176
appropriate overheads 499–501, 503–4
arm's length transactions 85
Arthur Andersen 185, 189, 191, 792
artistic-related intangible assets 466

ASB see Accounting Standards Board
ASC (Accounting Standards Committee)
    51, 151
Aspen Pharmacare Holdings Ltd 332
assets
    biological 510–12
    capital maintenance and 285–6
    consolidated accounts 548–9, 550, 566
    contingent 311–12, 315
    current values 227
    deferred tax 400–1
    definitions 24, 165
    disaggregation 269
    held for sale 83–5
    human 829
    identified, leases 449
    inflation accounting 226, 227, 228
    loss or decline in value 72
    measurement 166
    mining 415
    non-monetary 205–6, 233–4, 629, 638,
        639
    pension schemes 365–9
    recognition 164
    related parties 89
    return on (ROA) 805
    revaluation 205, 400–1, 433, 556
    right of use, leases 452–3
    self-constructed 412
    turnover ratios 687–9, 695–6
    unconsumed costs, values of 206
    use of, leases 449–51
    see also current assets; financial assets;
        intangible assets; net assets; non-
        current assets; property, plant and
        equipment
associates
    acquired during the year 607–8
    consolidated accounts 601–8, 613
    definition 601–2
    disclosures 613
    equity method 602
    unrealised profits 605
Association of British Insurers (ABI)
    corporate governance research 805
    integrated reporting 833, 836–7
    Principles of Executive Remuneration
        800
Association of Chartered Certified
    Accountants (ACCA)
    corporate social responsibility 837
    credit agencies regulation 737
    ethics
        codes, assistance in designing 187–8
        examinations 191
    narrative reporting survey 56
    real-time reporting survey 772
    Sustainability Reporting Award 837
Association of International Accountants
    (AIA) 191
assurance 836
AstraZeneca 49, 282, 362, 556
Audit and Assurance Council, FRC 136
Audit and Assurance Faculty 723
audit committees 789–90

Auditing and Assurance Standards
    Board, International (IAASB)
    793–4
Auditing Practices Board (APB)
    Aggressive Earnings Management
        (Consultation Paper 2001) 723
    Practice Note 12 Money Laundering 190
auditors
    competition 810
    confidentiality breaches 190
    ethics and 185
    expectation gap 810
    governance within audit firms 794–5
    independence 791–2, 809
    integrated reporting 839–40
    liabilities 795
    limited liability partnerships 795
    negligence 810
    professional oversight 810
    scepticism 724, 792–3
    unethical behaviour and 184, 786
    work carried out by 716
    XBRL and 770
audits 507–8, 724, 742–3, 789–90, 809–10
Australia
    accounting profession 149
    accounting theory 150
    agricultural accounting 512
    auditor liability 795
    corporate governance 801
    legal system 147
    tax imputation system 388
    XBRL use 761–2
Autonomy Systems 253
available-for-sale financial assets 346
available-for-sale instruments 336
average cost (AVCO) 48–9, 496–7
avoidance of tax 389–92

badwill 476–7
BAE Systems 187
Baker Tilly 135
balance sheets see statements of financial
    position
Balfour Beatty plc 331, 522, 523
Bangladesh Safety Accord 820
bankers 786
banks 148–9, 328, 806, 807
Barloworld 840–2
BAS (Business Activity Statements) 761
Base Erosion Profit Shifting 392
basic earnings per share (BEPS) 652–3,
    655, 656–63
Baumol, William 180
Bayer Group 401, 467
BDO LLP 792
Beder, S. 186
behaviour
    corporate 785–6
    ethical see ethics
    professional 176
    unethical 183–8, 785–6
behavioural entity, economy as 210
Belgium, XBRL use 762
Benefit Corporations, USA 822

BEPS (basic earnings per share) 652–3, 655, 656–63
BFCF (business free cash flows) 114
BHP Billiton 720, 819, 839
binomial option pricing model 374
biological assets 510–12
Black–Scholes option pricing model 374
BMW 546–7, 552, 714, 756
boards of directors *see* directors
Boeing 715
Bolton Wanderers 111
bonds 663, 664
bonus element, rights issues 658–9, 660–1
bonus issues 655, 661–2
bonus plans, employees 371
bonuses
    directors 131–2
    for performance, revenue recognition 261
book values, subsidiaries 552–3
boom times, corporate behaviour in 785
borrowings
    costs, capitalisation 412–13
    inflation accounting 236–7
    powers 478
    *see also* loans
BP 185–6, 295, 720, 756, 818–19
brands 477–9
Brazil, IFRS adoption 139
Brexit 142, 742–3
bribery 187, 190, 784
BRICS countries 139
British Airways 189–90, 367
British Telecommunications plc (BT) 182, 202, 203, 282
Brundtland Report 829
BS 7750: 836
BUPA 804
business activities, environmental impacts 825
Business Activity Statements (BAS) 761
business combinations
    brands 479
    fair values 242–4, 555–6
    goodwill 472–7, 479
    non-controlling interests 549–50
    review of implementation of IFRS 3: 481
    *see also* acquisitions; consolidated accounts
business free cash flows (BFCF) 114
business risks disclosures 714–15
bust times, corporate behaviour in 785
buyback of shares 295–6, 657

Cable, Vince 796
Cadbury Report 804
Calcbench.com 768
Canada
    accounting profession 149
    accounting theory 150
    legal system 147
    tax imputation system 388
capacity to adapt concept 225
CAPEX (capital expenditure) 113, 114

capital
    accountants' views 204–6
    costs of 183
    definitions 214–15
    economists' view 208–14
    financial concept 164
    human 826
    intellectual 480–1, 826
    invested 202
    manufactured 826
    money 214, 215
    natural 827
    operating capacity 214
    physical concept 164
    potential consumption 214, 215
    real 215
    reconstructions 289–94
    reduction 288–96
    restructuring 280
    shareholders, inflation accounting 227
    social and relationship 826–7
    stakeholder approach 832
    weighted average cost (WACC) 728–9
    writing off part 288–94
    *see also* share capital; working capital
capital allowances 387
capital employed 729
capital expenditure (CAPEX) 113, 114
capital grants 430–2
capital investment incentive effect, deferred taxation 395
capital maintenance 214–15
    creditor protection 284–5
    depreciation 414
    financial 27, 223–5, 239–40
    IASB *Conceptual Framework* 167
    operating 225, 229–40
    share capital reduction 280
Capital Market Association, International (ICMA) 184
capital markets 138, 253, 786–7
capital profits 207
capital reconstructions 289–94
capital transactions with owners 44
capitalisation 469–71, 655
carrying amounts 423, 428, 453
CAS (Chinese Accounting Standards) 139
case-based approach to tax avoidance 392
Case Management Committee, FRC 136, 137
cash conversion cycle 689–90
cash conversion ratios (CCR) 114–15
cash cycle 689–90
cash debt coverage ratio 112
cash dividend coverage ratio (CDCR) 112, 114–15
cash equivalents 106, 109, 110
cash flow accounting 3–18, 23–4, 120
cash flow hedges 343
cash flow ratios 692–3, 694
cash flow statements 102
    accrual accounting 27–8
    analysing 110–16
    consolidated accounts 587–8

    development of 102–3
    direct method 103–4, 105
    disclosures 116
    examination question answering with time constraints 116–20
    financing activities 104, 109, 115
    IAS 7: 102–20
    indirect method 103, 104–6, 106–9, 588
    information needs 160
    investing activities 104, 106, 109, 113
    notes to 109–10, 115
    operating activities 103–10
    operations 104, 109, 111–12
    preparation when statements of income not available 118–20
    summary 120
cash flows 8–12
    discounted (DCF) 210–14
    failure predictions and 736
    free (FCF) 114–15, 720
    future 47, 112–13, 203
    private finance initiative 533–4
cash generating units (CGU) 423–4
cash ratios 693
cash-settled share-based payments 376–7
CCA (current cost accounting) 229–40
CCR (cash conversion ratios) 114–15
CDCR (cash dividend coverage ratio) 112, 114–15
CDP Worldwide 833, 835
Cello Group 667
Centrica 784
Ceres 833, 837
Certified Public Accountants (CPA), USA 191
Certified Public Accountants, American Institute of (AICPA) 766, 771
CGU (cash generating units) 423–4
chairmen's statements 55, 112
changes in equity statements (SOCE) 43–4, 582
charities 391
    corporate governance 783
chief operating decision makers (CODM) 75, 76, 77, 82
China
    Chinese Accounting Standards (CAS) 139
    corporate governance 784
    IFRS adoption 139
    pollution 830
class obligations 306
classical corporation tax system 387–8
classification
    current assets 44–5, 132
    errors 74
    financial assets 337
    financial instruments 337–41
    financial liabilities 337–9
    held for sale 83–5
    income 37–40
    non-current assets 44–5, 132, 428
    operating expenses 37–40
climate change 825, 840

Coca-Cola 477, 720
CoCoA (Continuous Contemporary Accounting) 222
Codes and Standards Committee, FRC 136–7
codes of corporate governance 800–10
CODM (chief operating decision makers) 75, 76, 77, 82
Coil SA 422
Colgate 756
Collective Engagement Working Group 808
Collins, D. 253
Colt SA 114
commercial awareness 4
commercial benefit of XBRL 762–3
commercial databases, ratio analysis 757
commissions, ethics and 177
Committee of Sponsoring Organizations of the Treadway Commission (COSO)
*Fraudulent Financial Reporting: 1987–1997 — An Analysis of U.S. Public Companies* 505
commodity contracts 330
common law legal systems 147
common size statements 681–2
Communications of Progress (COP) 835
community issues
key performance indicators 55
companies *see* limited liability companies; private companies; public companies; small and medium-sized enterprises; unquoted companies
Companies Act 1929: 201
Companies Act 1981: 147
Companies Act 2006: 54, 139, 280, 285, 286–7, 296, 800
Companies House, XBRL use 761, 769–70
Company Watch 734
comparability 134, 163
comparative share prices 800
compensated absences 371
compensation of key management personnel 88
competence 175–6
competition, auditors 810
competitive pressures, unquoted companies, share valuations 741
completed contracts method 520–1
completeness 15, 16
complexity 144
compliance
creative 147
with fundamental principles, threats to 178
components, construction contracts 526
compound instruments 331–2
compound interest 209
comprehensive income 40–1, 44
*see also* statements of comprehensive income
Compustat 757
conceptual framework 155

approaches 157–8
financial accounting theory historical overview 156–8
IASB *Conceptual Framework for Financial Reporting 2010 see* International Accounting Standards Board
IASC *Framework for the Presentation and Preparation of Financial Statements see* International Accounting Standards Committee
move towards 150–1
national differences 155–6
concessions, construction contracts 532–3
Conduct Committee, FRC 136, 137
confidentiality 176, 190
confirmatory values 12, 161
consideration, acquisitions 547
consistency 12, 43, 163
consolidated accounts
Accounting Directive 141
accounting for groups at date of acquisition 545–57
associates 601–8
cash flow statements 587–8
depreciation 583
excluded subsidiaries 555
foreign currency transactions 633–7
goodwill 584
IFRS 10: 545–7
inter-company transactions 568–71, 579–80
joint operations 609–10
joint ventures 610
non-current assets acquired from subsidiaries 583
partly owned subsidiaries 549–51
post-acquisition profits and losses 566
pre-acquisition profits and losses 565–6
preparation not required 554–5
profits 565–6, 580, 583–4
statements of changes in equity 582
statements of comprehensive income 580–9, 604–5, 607, 634, 635
statements of financial position 565–71, 602–4, 606
subsidiaries acquired during the year 584–6, 587–8
uniform policies 565
wholly owned subsidiaries 545, 548–9
constant purchasing power measurement of financial capital maintenance 27
construction contracts 519–34
constructive obligations 316
consultancies, auditors 794–5
consumer price index 222
contingent assets 311–12, 315
contingent liabilities 311, 312, 314–15, 316, 556
Continuous Contemporary Accounting (CoCoA) 222
contracts
construction 519–34
equally unperformed, revenue recognition 267
leases 450–1

modification of terms of, revenue recognition 268–9
non-adjusting events 72
onerous *see* onerous contracts
revenue recognition 259–60, 262–4
control
changes, unquoted companies, share valuations 740
construction contracts 524–5
definition 546–7
income as means of 202–3
intangible assets 466
internal 789–4
inventories 504–5
joint 609, 610
systems 838
convertible bonds 663, 664
convertible loans 331
convertible preference shares 283, 663–4
co-operative approach
accounting standards enforcement 138
COP (Communications of Progress) 835
Corefiling 770
corporate failure, prediction 732–6
corporate behaviour 785–6
corporate governance 781
audits 809–10
boards of directors 800, 802–5
capital markets 786–7
charities 783
codes 800–10
corporate behaviour and 785–6
culture 784–5
definition 781
executive remuneration 796–800
external audits 790–6
good 781–3
internal controls and internal audits 789–90
investor perspective 781–2
legal safeguards 809
legislation 800, 801
national differences 783–5
organisational cultures 784–5
risk management 787–8
shareholder activism 805–9
South Africa 831–2
stakeholder perspective 782
systems perspective 781–3
UK experience 801–10
The Corporate Report 828, 837
corporate social responsibility (CSR) 175, 820, 835–6, 837
corporation tax 386–403
corruption 784
COSA (cost of sales adjustment) 231–2
COSO *see* Committee of Sponsoring Organizations of the Treadway Commission
cost approach to valuation of intangibles 481
cost-plus contracts 520
costs
agency costs 8
amortised 328, 340–1, 453
of assets, unconsumed 206

of borrowing, capitalisation 412–13
Brexit possible effects 742
of capital 183
construction contracts 521–3
current service 366
decommissioning 310
development 470–1
direct *see* direct costs
discretionary 112
distribution 37
finance 38, 332–4
interest *see* interest
inventories, ascertainment 499–501
opportunity 228
overheads 499–501
past service, pension schemes 366–7
pension schemes 364–7
post retirement 364–7
promotion 37
property, plant and equipment
  412–13
redundancy 317
research *see* research costs
risks and, trade-offs 822
of sales 37, 231–2
selling 37
structures 682
termination 317
transport 37
warehousing 37
*see also* expenses; overheads
counter-terrorism financing (CTF)
  standard 190
covenants, loans 721–4
CPA (Certified Public Accountants),
  USA 191
CPPA (current purchasing power
  accounting) 221–2, 223–7
creative accounting 137, 505–7
creative compliance 147
credibility 134, 834
credit losses 342
credit ratings 736–7, 786
creditors 279
  protection of 284–6
  share capital reduction 291–4
  unincorporated businesses 285
  *see also* loan creditors
CSR *see* corporate social responsibility
CTF (counter-terrorism financing)
  standard 190
culture
  corporate governance 784–5
  differences, ethics and 180–1
  ethical influences of 174
  *see also* organisational cultures
cumulative preference shares 283
currency *see* foreign currency
current assets
  classification 44–5, 132
  held for sale 83–5
current cash debt coverage ratio 112
current cost accounting (CCA) 229–40
current cost reserves 231–9
current entry cost accounting *see*
  replacement cost: accounting

current exit cost accounting *see* net
  realisable value accounting
current purchasing power accounting
  (CPPA) 221–2, 223–7
current ratios 690–1, 695–6
current service costs 366
current taxation 38–9, 393–4
current value accounting (CVA) 221
curtailments, pension schemes 366–7
customer-related intangible
  assets 466
customers
  key performance indicators 55
cut-off dates, inventories 505
CVA (current value accounting) 221

damaged inventory items 508
Datastream 757
DCF (discounted cash flow) 210–14
debenture holders
  capital reconstruction schemes,
    reaction to 293–4
debentures 291–2
debt
  covenants 721–4
  coverage 112
  debt/equity ratios 693–5
  future, servicing 692–3
  perpetual 332
  service coverage ratios 718, 720
decision-usefulness, financial reporting
  756–7
decisions
  by companies, shaping future 825
  financial decision models 5–6
  investors' needs 52–6
  makers, chief operating (CODM) 75,
    76, 77, 82
  management, brands and 478–9
decline in value of assets 72
decommissioning costs 310
deductive approach, financial reporting
  157–8
Deere and Company 498
deferral method, deferred tax provisions
  395
deferred income, grants as 430–1
deferred taxation 394–403
defined benefit schemes *see* pension
  schemes
defined contribution schemes *see* pension
  schemes
Delaware, USA 392
Dell 756
Denmark
  unethical behaviour 786
  XBRL use 762
depreciation 37
  accrual accounting 25
  annuity method 419–20
  calculations 417–20
  choice of method 50, 420, 433–4
  consolidated accounts 583
  corporation tax 387
  current cost accounting 231, 232
  deferred tax and 395, 398–9

definitions 414–15
diminishing balance method 417, 418,
  420
formula 415–16
leases 452, 453
machine-hour method 418–19, 420
net realisable value accounting 228
residual values 415–16, 417
straight-line method 417–18, 420
sum of the units method 418
derecognition
  financial assets 337
  financial instruments 337
  IASB *Conceptual Framework* 166
  non-financial liabilities 316
derivatives 335, 340
detail, lack of, published account
  limitations 716–17
deterioration, inventories 502
Deutz 72
development
  costs 470–1
  key performance indicators 55
Diageo 477, 834
diesel cars pollution levels 819–20
digital financial reporting 755–73
diluted earnings per share 653, 662–6
dilutive potential ordinary shares 653
diminishing balance method, depreciation
  417, 418, 420
direct costs 37
  initial, leases 452, 455
direct investment 821–2
direct labour 499, 503
direct materials 499, 503
direct method, cash flow statements
  103–4, 105
direct overheads 499, 500
directors
  boards
    corporate governance 782–3, 800,
      802–5
    bonuses 131–2
    discipline 134
    independent 803, 805
    non-executive (NED) 803–5
    performance 799
    remuneration 796–800
    reports 55
disaggregation 269
disasters, environmental and social 818,
  820
discipline 134
disclosures
  Accounting Directive 141
  associates 613
  business risks 714–15
  cash flow statements 116
  compensation of key management
    personnel 88
  construction contracts 525–6
  controlling relationships 87
  discontinued operations 82–3
  earnings per share (EPS) 666–8
  financial instruments 345–51
  future profitability 116

disclosures (*continued*)
  government-related entities,
    exemptions 87–8
  hyperinflation 639
  IASB *Conceptual Framework* 167, 168
  intangible assets 468
  intellectual capital 480–1
  inventories 509–10
  joint ventures and joint operations 613
  liquidity 116
  mandatory 53
  non-financial liabilities 317–18
  pension schemes 369, 379–80
  property, plant and equipment (PPE)
    429–30
  provisions 310–11
  related parties 85–9
  research and development 470, 471
  revenue recognition 269
  risk 116
  segment information 77–9
  subsidiaries 612–13
  tax expense 393
  voluntary 116
discontinued operations 72, 82–3
discount rates 425
discounted cash flow (DCF) 210–14
discounting 208–9, 307
discretionary costs 112
discretionary expenditure, deferring 132
disposal groups 83–5
distributable profits 286–8
distributable reserves 280, 281, 285
distribution costs 37
distribution costs ratios 686
distribution overheads 500
dividends
  adjustment factors, Shariah principles
    721
  cash dividend coverage ratio (CDCR)
    112, 114–15
  consolidated accounts 580, 583–4
  cover 112, 726–7
  events after reporting dates 71–2
  inflation accounting and 226
  inter-company 569
  interim 72
  ordinary 281
  policies 203
  preference 281
  purification, Shariah principles 721
  revenue recognition 255
  taxation 387–9
  yield 727
DJSI (Dow Jones Sustainability Index)
  819, 833, 837
donations, charitable 391
Dow Jones Islamic Market Indices 720
Dow Jones Sustainability Index (DJSI)
  819, 833, 837
Du Pont pyramid approach, ratios 684
due care 175–6

EACC (earnings after cost of capital
  employed) 729
earnings

aggressive management 723–4
  construction contracts 524–5
  headline 667
  maintainable post-tax 653–4
  normalised 179
  quality of 41–2
  sustainable 179
  yields 726
  *see also* gains; income; profits
earnings after cost of capital employed
  (EACC) 729
earnings before interest, tax, depreciation
  and amortisation (EBITDA) 114–
  15, 473 717–20, 801
earnings before interest, tax, depreciation,
  amortisation and rental expense
  (EBITDAR) 719
earnings before interest, tax, depreciation,
  amortisation, rental expense and
  management fees (EBITDARM)
  719
earnings per share (EPS) 651, 726
  basic (BEPS) 652–3, 655, 656–63
  calculations 652–3, 654–7
  consolidated accounts 556
  conversion rights exercised 666
  diluted 653, 662–6
  disclosures 666–8
  importance 651–2
  income measurement and 202
  inventories and 494, 509–10
  non-current assets and 435
  normalised 799
  rights issues 657–62
  share prices 281
  shareholders and 653–4
Eastern Europe
  accounting profession 149
  corporate governance 784
Ebbers, Bernard 735
EBITDA (earnings before interest, tax,
  depreciation and amortisation)
  114–15, 473, 717–20, 801
EBITDA-based ratios 718–19
EBITDA/interest ratios 719, 720
EBITDAR (earnings before interest, tax,
  depreciation, amortisation and
  rental expense) 719
EBITDARM (earnings before interest,
  tax, depreciation, amortisation,
  rental expense and management
  fees) 719
ECGI (European Corporate Governance
  Institute) 800
Eco-Management and Audit Scheme
  (EMAS) 833, 836
economic benefits 306
  from use of assets, leases 449
  *see also* future economic benefits
economic consequences 818–19
economic dimension of sustainability
  833
economic income 208–14
economic lives 414–16, 433–4, 467–8
economic measures of ability to create
  value 55

economic pressures operating against
  profit maximisation 821–3
economic value added (EVA) 727–9,
  730–1
economic value of businesses 203,
  212–13
economists, view of income measurement
  208–14
economy as behavioural entity 210
effective yield 340–1
EFRAG *see* European Financial
  Reporting Advisory Group
EGM (Extraordinary General Meetings)
  282
Eighth Directive 139
elements of financial statements 165
EMAS (Eco-Management and Audit
  Scheme) 833, 836
embedded derivatives 340
empirical inductive approach, financial
  reporting 157
employees
  benefits 359–80, 843
  key performance indicators 55
  revenue restatement effects 253
EnBW 552
Ener1 785–6
enforcement, accounting standards *see*
  accounting standards
enhanced audit reports 790
enjoyment 210
Enron 133, 136, 142, 143, 189, 715, 723,
  792, 795
enterprise value/EBITDA ratios 718
entity-wide cash-based performance
  measures 717–20
environmental accounting 837
environmental activities, expenditure on
  821
environmental consequences 818–19
environmental dimension of sustainability
  833
environmental disasters 818–20
environmental impacts 825
environmental information 817
environmental liabilities 310
environmental issues
  key performance indicators 55
environmental management 819
environmental responsibilities
  management accountability for 821–5
environmental, social and governance
  (ESC) 836–7
EPEC (European PPP Expertise Centre)
  531
EPS *see* earnings per share
equally unperformed contracts, revenue
  recognition 267
equipment *see* property, plant and
  equipment
equitable exchanges 178–9
equity 280
  definition 165
  depletion 478
  impact on IFRS adoption 144–5
  investors 279–80

liabilities and 330–1
statements of changes in (SOCE) 43–4, 582
equity accounting method 602, 613–14
equity compensation plans 362
equity instruments 329–30
equity market capitalisation 148
equity-settled share-based payments 373–6, 377
Ernst & Young 795
errors
  adjusting events 71
  freedom from 162
  IASB *Conceptual Framework* 168
  inventories 505, 508
  prior-period 73–4
  strategic 735
ESMA *see* European Securities and Markets Authority
estimates 50, 74, 205, 210, 244, 305, 433–4, 738
ethics 173
  in accountants' work environments, research report 181–3
  accounting standards setting process and 174–5
  advice 182–3
  collapse in organisations, effects of 184
  company codes 185–7
  fundamental principles 176, 178
  guidelines 173–4
  IFAC *Code of Ethics for Professional Accountants* 175–8
  individual guidelines 173–4
  meaning of ethical behaviour 173–4
  neutrality and 175
  personal 173–4
  policies 182–3
  professional guidelines 174
  seniors' perspectives 182
  students and 182, 191–2
  trainees' perspectives 182
  unethical behaviour 183–8, 785–6
  values, implications for principles versus rules-based approaches to accounting standards 178–81
  whistleblowing 188–9
EU *see* European Union
European Corporate Governance Institute (ECGI) 800
European Federation of Accountants (FEE) 141
European Financial Reporting Advisory Group (EFRAG)
  ethics and neutrality (Position Paper 2012) 175
  IFRS endorsements 142
  *Towards a Disclosure Framework for the Notes* (Discussion Paper 2012) 135
European Parliament
  IFRS 8 reservations 80–1
European PPP Expertise Centre (EPEC) 531
European Securities and Markets Authority (ESMA)

*Considerations of materiality in financial reporting* (consultation paper 2011) 162
*Guidelines: Enforcement of Financial Information* (2014) 141–2
*Guidelines on Alternative Performance Measures* (draft) 717
European Union
  Accounting Directive 139–41, 142, 146, 476
  Base Erosion Profit Shifting 392
  Brexit *see* Brexit
  *Building a Capital Markets Union* (Commission Green Paper 2015) 138
  Corporate Social Responsibility Reporting 836
  credit rating agency regulation 737
  Eco-Management and Audit Scheme (EMAS) 833, 836
  Eighth Directive 139
  financial instruments concerns 328
  Fourth Directive 139, 147, 150
  IFRS endorsement 142
  Member State Options (MSO) 139–40
  regulatory burden on SMEs and micro-undertakings 141
  Seventh Directive 139
  standard setting and enforcement 139–41
  tax avoidance 392
EV (enterprise value)/EBITDA ratios 718
EVA (economic value added) 727–9, 730–1
EVA Momentum 729
evasion of tax 389–92
events after reporting periods 70–3
evidence, contract identification 259
Excel 756
exceptional items 41–3, 53
exchange differences, accounting for 627–40
excluded subsidiaries 555
Executive Committee, FRC 136, 137
executive remuneration 796–800
exempt traders, VAT 404
exercise dates, share-based payments 374
expectation gap, audits 795, 810
expected credit losses 342–3
expected income 211
expected losses 342–3
expenditure, capital (CAPEX) 113, 114
expenses
  accrual accounting 22–3
  analyses by function 38
  definition 165
  recognition 164
  share-based payments 372
  *see also* costs; operating expenses; overheads
explanatory notes to financial statements 45–8
exposure drafts *see* International Accounting Standards Board
eXtensible Business Reporting Language (XBRL) 756, 757–73

eXtensible Mark-up Language (XML) 758, 759
external audits 790–6
externalities 822
Extraordinary General Meetings (EGM) 282
Exxon Mobil 720
*Exxon Valdez* 833

failure prediction 732–6
fair exchanges 178–9
fair override 51–2
fair presentation 51–2
  *see also* true and fair view
fair values
  acquisitions 547–8, 549, 551, 555–6
  agricultural produce 510–12
  biological assets 510–12
  consideration, acquisitions 547
  consolidation depreciation adjustments 583
  definition 242
  distribution decisions and 288
  estimates 244
  financial assets 328, 337
  financial instruments 288, 328
  financial liabilities 328, 337–9
  financial statements, effects on 244
  hedging 343–4
  hierarchy 243
  impact of changes 339
  increasing use 242–3
  intangible assets 481–2
  judgement 243–4
  measurement 166
    IFRS 13 *see* International Financial Reporting Standards
  net assets, acquisitions 547–8
  pension schemes 365, 379
  share-based payments 373–80
  subsidiaries 552–3
fair view 45
  *see also* true and fair view
fairness 174–5, 797, 840
faithful representation 15, 16, 162, 166
Fame 757
familiarity threats 178, 791
families, ethical influences of 174
farming 510–12
FASB *see* Financial Accounting Standards Board
fashion clean-up campaign 820
FATF (Financial Action Task Force) 190
FCF (free cash flow) 114–15, 720
FEB *see* future economic benefits
Federation of Accountants, International (IFAC) *see* International Federation of Accountants
FEE (European Federation of Accountants) 141
fictitious transfers 506
FIFO (first-in-first-out) 48–9, 495, 496
Finance Acts 386, 387, 390
finance costs 38, 332–4
finance overheads 500

finance industry
  inappropriate cultures 820
finance leases *see* leases
financial accountants 838–9
financial accounting
  inherent limitations 831
  integrated reporting impact on future
    development of 843–5
  theory historical overview 156–8
Financial Accounting Standards Board
  (FASB)
  accounting standards 144
  *Accounting Standards Codification* 143
  accrual accounting 27
  Convergence Project 668
  fair values 242
  Framework joint project with IASB
    159
  lease accounting joint project with
    IASB 448
  Norwalk Agreement 144
  revenue recognition 254, 256
  standard setting 142–3
  *see also* Statements of Financial
    Accounting Standards
Financial Action Task Force (FATF) 190
financial assets 328, 329–30, 337, 341–3
financial capital 215
  maintenance 27, 223–5, 239–40
  suppliers 825–7
financial concept of capital 164
financial conditions 793
financial crisis (2008) 327–8
financial databases, ratio analysis 757
financial decision model 5–6
financial information
  qualitative characteristics 161–3, 165
  reliability improvement 715–16
  understandability improvement 714
  useful 161–3, 165
financial instruments 326
  amortised costs 340–1
  definitions 329–30
  derecognition 335–6
  disclosures 345–51
  EU concerns 328
  fair values 288, 328
  financial crisis (2008) 327–8
  hedging 343–5
  IAS 32: 327, 329–35, 346
  IAS 39: 327–9, 346, 347
  IASB problems 326–9
  IFRS 7: 326, 345–51
  IFRS 9: 326, 346–8
  measurement 337–41
  offsetting 334–5
  presentation 330–2
  recognition 335–6
  risk disclosures 348–51
  rules versus principles 327
  US GAAP 328
financial liabilities 328, 329–30, 337–9,
  452, 459
financial performance 683–90
financial ratios *see* ratios
financial reporting 713

analysis of published financial
  statements 713–43
Brexit impact 142
conceptual framework 150–1, 155–69
decision-usefulness 756–7
deductive approach 157–8
digital 755–73
empirical inductive approach 157
general purpose, objective of 165
global standards evolution 131–51
hard copy 755–6
history of 156–8
information flows post-XBRL 759–60
information flows pre-XBRL 757–8
integrated reporting impact on future
  development of 843–5
interim 772
international standards 138–51
materiality in 161–2
national differences 146–50
objectives 165, 755–7
pension schemes 360
shareholder information 714–16
real-time 771–2
small and medium-sized enterprises
  146
stewardship 755–6
traditional, limitations 830–1
*see also* published accounts
Financial Reporting Council (FRC)
  Accounting Council 136–7
  Actuarial Council 136
  additional items reporting, reminder
    on 43
  Audit and Assurance Council 136
  Board 136–7, 155
  Case Management Committee
    136, 137
  *Clear & Concise Initiative* 56
  Codes and Standards Committee
    136–7, 794
  Conduct Committee 136, 137
  corporate governance 801
  *Corporate Reporting in a Digital World*
    (project) 773
  exceptional items
    note on (PN 108) 42
    reminder on 43
  Executive Committee 136, 137
  Financial Reporting Review Panel *see*
    Financial Reporting Review Panel
  financial statements, consistency in
    preparation 43
  function 135–6
  going concern 16–17
  *Improving the Quality of Reporting by
    Smaller Listed and AIM Quoted
    Companies* (Discussion Paper
    2015) 138
  Monitoring Committee 136, 137
  narrative reporting review 56, 717
  Stewardship Code 807–8
  Strategic Reports, guidance 55, 56,
    824
  structure 136
  true and fair view 51–2

UK Corporate Governance
  Code 801
Financial Reporting Lab (FRL)
  *Corporate Reporting in a Digital World*
    (project) 773
Financial Reporting Review Panel
  (FRRP) 43, 52, 81, 135, 137–8,
    402, 479
Financial Reporting Standard for Smaller
  Entities (FRSSE) 145–6
Financial Reporting Standards (FRS)
  100 *Application of financial reporting
    requirements* 386
  101 *Reduced disclosure framework* 386
  102 *The financial reporting standard
    applicable in the UK and Republic
    of Ireland* 386
financial reports
  ethics and 179–80
  unethical behaviour, implications for
    stakeholders using 183–8
  *see also* financial reporting
financial risks 788
financial securities, revenue recognition
  267
financial statements
  analysis
    financial performance 683–90
    financing 693–5
    liquidity 690–3
    peer comparisons 695–6
    published financial statements
      713–43
    reports based on 696–7
  Brexit possible effects on 742–3
  comparability 134
  Conceptual Framework 160–1
  consistency in preparation 43
  current tax accounting 38–9
  elements 165
  explanatory notes 45–8
  for external users, contents 22
  fair presentation 51–2
  fair values effects on 244
  formats of statements for publication
    36–40, 48–50
  hyperinflation 638–9
  joint operations 609–10
  joint ventures 610
  internal statements of income from
    trial balances 33–6
  investors' needs other than 52–6
  leases *see* leases
  misstatements 74
  narrative reporting survey 56
  notes to 42–3, 45–8, 135, 509
  objectives 21–2, 160–1, 677
  omissions 74
  other comprehensive income 40–1
  preparation
    under cash flow concept 8–12
    published statements 33–57
  property, plant and equipment 433–5
  prospective changes 73, 74
  reporting entities and 165
  retrospective changes 73

reviews for management purposes 677–99
separate 612, 613–14
statements of changes in equity 43–4
statements of financial position 44–5
UK preparation choices following Brexit
XBRL 756, 757–73
*see also* annual reports; cash flow statements; financial reporting; published accounts; statements of comprehensive income; statements of financial position
financial structures of companies 681–2
financial threats to auditor independence 791
financiers, rewards to 842
financing
  activities, cash flows 104, 109, 115
  financial statement analysis, ratios 693–5
Findel 55, 289, 348–51
finite lives, intangible assets 467–8
first-in-first-out (FIFO) 48–9, 495, 496
Fiscal Studies, Institute for *see* Institute for Fiscal Studies
Fisher, Irving 210–11
fixed assets *see* non-current assets
fixed-price contracts 520
flexibility, XBRL 759
football clubs, money laundering and 190
Foreign Corrupt Practices Act 1977, USA 784
foreign currency
  definitions 628
  exchange differences, accounting for 627–40
formats
  financial statements for publication 36–40, 48–50
Fourth Directive 139, 147, 150
France
  agricultural accounting 512
  legal system 147
  tax and reporting systems 149
fraud
  adjusting events 71
  detection 795–6
  ethical collapse and 184
  governance behaviour and 785–6
  inventories 502, 504, 505–7
  prevention, USA 143
  prior period errors 73–4
  *see also* creative accounting
*fraus legis* 392
FRC *see* Financial Reporting Council
free cash flow (FCF) 114–15, 720
freehold land 415
Friedman, Daniel 180
Friedman, Milton 178, 821
FRL *see* Financial Reporting Lab
FRRP *see* Financial Reporting Review Panel
FRS *see* Financial Reporting Standards
FRSSE (Financial Reporting Standard for Smaller Entities) 145–6

FTSE ESG ratings 837
FTSE Shariah indices 720
FTSE4Good index series 833
functional currencies 627, 631–2
fundamental principles 176, 178
future cash flows *see* cash flows
future economic benefits (FEB) 465, 466, 467, 469, 475
future liabilities 556
future losses 556
future performance 3, 203
future profitability disclosures 116
future values 209

GAAP
  UK 142
  US *see* United States
GAAR (General Anti-Abuse Rule) 389–90
gains
  actuarial, pension schemes 367
  holding 227, 233–4, 239–40
  inflation accounting 227
  unrealised 40, 482
  *see also* earnings; income; profits
garment workers' rights campaigners 820
GDP (gross domestic product) 148
gearing
  current cost accounting 236
  leases impact 445
  ratios 478, 693–5
  revaluation and 433
General Anti-Abuse Rule (GAAR) 389–90
General Electric 132–3, 771, 840
general price indices (GPI) 222, 225, 226, 239
general purchasing power (GPP) *see* current purchasing power accounting
Generally Accepted Accounting Principles (GAAP)
  United Kingdom 142
  United States *see* United States
Germany
  corporate governance 783
  finance of industry 148
  legal system 147
  tax and reporting systems 149
  XBRL use 762
Getronics 283
Geveke nv Amsterdam 728
GlaxoSmithKline 720
global accounting standards 144–5
Global Reporting Initiative (GRI) 833–4, 835
Global Reporting Institute 833
global use of XBRL 762
Go-Ahead 430–1
going concern 16–17, 24–6, 72–3, 140, 207–8, 228, 163
golden handshakes 786
Goldfields 415
good corporate governance 781–3
goodwill
  accounting treatment 472–6

amortisation 473–7
consolidated accounts 548, 550, 552–3, 554, 567, 570, 584, 636
definition 472
IAS 38: 473, 476
IFRS 3: 472–7, 479, 554
impairment 473, 475–6, 584
intangible assets identifying to reduce amount of 473–4
internally generated 472
limitations of traditional financial reporting 830
negative 476–7, 554
purchased 472, 478, 548–9
reporting at cost in statements of financial position 472, 474
review of implementation of IFRS 3: 481
statements of financial position approach 475
writing off to reserves 472, 474, 478
Google 477, 720
governance
  in audit firms 794–5
  corporate *see* corporate governance
  departments, payments to 843
government-related entities 87–8
governments
  ethics actions 185, 187
  grants 430–2, 512
  whistleblowing and 189
GPI *see* general price indices
GPP (general purchasing power) *see* current purchasing power accounting
grant dates, share-based payments 373
grants 430–2, 512
GRI (Global Reporting Initiative) 833–4, 835
Grontmij N.V. 208
gross domestic product (GDP) 148
gross profit margin ratios 685
groups
  accounting at the date of acquisition 545–57
  definition 546
  *see also* acquisitions; business combinations; consolidated accounts
Gulf of Mexico oil rig disaster 818–19

H-scores 734–5, 741
Halfords 741
hard copy financial reporting 755–6
hazards 788
HCA (historical cost accounting) *see* historical costs
headline earnings 667
hedge funds 148–9
hedging 327, 343–5, 630
held for sale 83–5
held-to-maturity investments 337, 346, 347
Hesselgesser, Robert D. 786
Hewlett-Packard 253, 259–60
Hicks income model 211–13
hidden liabilities, unethical behaviour and 183–4

High Pay Centre 797
historical costs
  accounting (HCA) 204–5
    acceptance 156
    illustrations 223–7
    problems 220–1
    profits 240–1
  convention 22
  measurement 166
  principles 207
  valuations, agricultural activities 512
HIV, South Africa 832
HM Revenue and Customs 203, 761
HMV 208
Hoffman, Charles 766
holding gains 227, 233–4, 239–40
Holmen AB 510
horizontal analysis 681–2
HSBC 725
HTML (Hyper Text Mark-up
  Language) 758–9
Hugo Boss 478
human activities, environmental impacts
  825
human assets 829
human capital 826
human resources valuation 482
Hyper Text Mark-up Language
  (HTML) 758–9
hyperinflation 241–2, 638–9

IAASB (International Auditing and
  Assurance Standards Board) 793–4
IAS see International Accounting
  Standards
IASB see International Accounting
  Standards Board
IASC see International Accounting
  Standards Committee
IBM 720
ICAEW see Institute of Chartered
  Accountants in England and
  Wales
ICAS see Institute of Chartered
  Accountants of Scotland
ICD (intellectual capital disclosures)
  480–1
ICMA (International Capital Market
  Association) 184
identified assets, leases 449
IFAC see International Federation of
  Accountants
IFAD (International Forum on
  Accountancy Development) 156
IFIAR (International Forum of
  Independent Audit Regulators)
  794
IFRIC (International Financial Reporting
  Interpretations Committee) 135
IFRS see International Financial
  Reporting Standards
IFS see Institute for Fiscal Studies
IIA see Institute of Internal Auditors
IIRC (International Integrated Reporting
  Council) 825, 837
IMI 798–9

immaterial information 168
impairment 85, 341–3, 423–8, 474,
  475–6, 584, 605–7
Improvement Project, IASB 668
imputation system, corporation tax 388–9
Imtech 74
inappropriate organisational cultures 820
incentives 786
  construction contracts payments 521
income
  accountants' view 204–6
  classification 37–40
  comprehensive 40–1, 44
  concept of 204
  deferred, grants as 430–1
  definition 165
  economic 208–14
  economists' view 208–14
  expected 211
  grants as 430–1
  information 202
  as means of control 202–3
  as means of prediction 203
  measurement 201–16
  operating 41–3, 227
  recognition 164
  replacement cost 214–15
  smoothing, inventories 494, 495
  statements see statements of
    comprehensive income
  streams 423, 424–5
  see also earnings; gains; profits
income approach to valuation of
  intangibles 481
income tax 386
incurred losses 342
indefinite lives, intangible assets 468
independence
  auditors 809
  ethics and 177
Independent Audit Regulators,
  International Forum of (IFIAR)
  794
independent directors 803, 805
India, IFRS adoption 139
indirect method see cash flow statements
indirect overheads 499, 500
individual ethical guidelines 173–4
Indonesia, XBRL use 762
inflation 241–2, 433, 638–9, 741
inflation accounting 220–44
influence, significant 601–2
information
  environmental 817
  financial see financial information
  flows
    financial reporting post-XBRL
      759–60
    financial reporting pre-XBRL 757–8
  immaterial 168
  needs
    financial statements 160–1
    of internal users 3, 5–8
    of managers 3, 4–5
    of shareholders 3–4, 714–16
  social 817

unaudited, published account
  limitations 717
XBRL processes for outputting 763–6
Infosys Technologies 482
initial direct costs, leases 452, 455
Inline XBRL (iXBRL) 761, 770–1
Inman, M.L. 732
input method, construction contract
  earnings 525
insider trading 786
instance documents, XBRL 764, 765,
  766–7
Institute for Fiscal Studies (IFS) 391
  Countering Tax Avoidance in the UK:
    Which Way Forward? (discussion
    paper 2009) 392
Institute of Chartered Accountants in
  England and Wales (ICAEW)
  Ethics Advisory Service 184
  The Future Shape of Financial Reports
    102
  intellectual capital disclosures research
    report 480
  risk reporting 714
  Support Members Scheme 188
  Technical Release 02/10 Determination
    of realised profits and losses in the
    context of distributions under the
    Companies Act 2006: 288
Institute of Chartered Accountants of
  Scotland (ICAS)
  ethics 191
  'Taking Ethics to Heart' (discussion
    paper report) 181–3, 184
  The Future Shape of Financial Reports
    102
  The implementation of IFRS in the UK,
    Italy and Ireland (research report
    2008) 145
Institute of Directors of Southern Africa
  (IoDSA) 831
Institute of Internal Auditors (IIA)
  Model Audit Committee Charter 790
institutional investors 148–9, 799–800,
  806–8
institutional users of XBRL 766
Institutional Voting and Information
  Service (IVIS) 805
insurable risks 788
insurance companies 148–9
intangible assets 465
  accounting treatment 467–8
  acquisitions 556
  amortisation 467–8
  brands 477–9
  definition 465
  disclosures 468
  examples of 466
  fair values 481–2
  finite lives 467–8
  goodwill see goodwill
  human resources valuation 482
  identifying to reduce amount of
    goodwill 473–4
  IFRS for SMEs 471–2
  impairment 476, 468

identified under IAS 38, review of
    implementation 481–2
indefinite lives 468
intellectual capital 480–1
internally generated 471, 480–1
measurement 466
recognition criteria 466–71
research and development 468–71
useful economic lives 467–8
valuation 481–2
integrated reporting 817
    accountants' contributions 837–43
    benefits 828
    concepts 825–8
    drivers 828–32
    evolution historical context 828–32
    to financial capital suppliers 825–7
    impact on future development of
        financial reporting and accounting
        843–5
    South Africa 825, 831–2
Integrated Reporting Council,
    International (IIRC) 825, 837
integrity 175
Intel 473–4, 481
intellectual capital 826
    disclosures (ICD) 480–1
intellectual property
    transfers, revenue recognition 267
inter-company performance 757
inter-company transactions 568–71,
    579–80
inter-period performance 757
InterContinental Hotels Group 41–2, 72
interest
    compound 209
    consolidated accounts 580, 583–4
    costs, pension schemes 366
    cover 111, 692
    present values and 210
    rates 694
    revenue recognition 255
interests
    in associates 613
    non-controlling see non-controlling
        interests
    in joint operations and joint ventures
        613
    in subsidiaries 612–13
    vested 132
interim dividends 72
interim financial reporting 772
internal accounting, XBRL 771
internal auditors 839–40
Internal Auditors, Institute of (IIA) see
    Institute of Internal Auditors
internal audits 789–90, 832
internal conditions 792
internal control 789–90
internal rate of return (IRR) 7–8, 730
internal reporting 4–8
internal statements of income from trial
    balances 33–6
internally generated goodwill 472
internally generated intangible assets 471,
    480–1

International Accounting Standards
    (IAS)
    1 *Presentation of Financial Statements*
        cash and cash equivalents 106
        exceptional items 53
        fair presentation 51–2
        formats of statements of income
            36–40
        other comprehensive income 40–1
        statements of comprehensive income
            40–1
        statements of financial position 44–7
        tax rules and 387
    2 *Inventories*
        agricultural produce 510, 511
        definition 493–4
        development expenditure 470
        disclosure requirements 509–10
        properties held for sale 432
        self-constructed assets 412
        valuations 495–502
        work in progress 502
    7 *Statement of cash flows* 27–8,
        102–20
    8 *Accounting Policies, Changes in*
        *Accounting Estimates and Errors*
        46, 51, 73–4, 161, 393, 547
    10 *Events After the Reporting Period*
        70–3, 569
    11 *Construction Contracts* 519–23
    12 *Income Taxes* 386, 393–402, 430
    14 *Segment Reporting* 81
    16 *Property, Plant and Equipment* 395,
        411–23, 432, 475, 510, 511–12,
        566
    17 *Leases* 432, 447, 448
    18 *Revenue* 254–5, 256–7, 519
    19 *Employee Benefits* 317, 359–80, 377
    20 *Accounting for Government Grants*
        *and Disclosure of Government*
        *Assistance* 411, 432, 512
    21 *The Effects of Changes in Foreign*
        *Exchange Rates* 627, 628, 631–4
    23 *Borrowing Costs* 411, 412–13
    24 *Related Party Disclosures* 85–9
    26 *Accounting and Reporting by*
        *Retirement Benefit Plans* 359,
        377–80
    27 *Separate Financial Statements* 612,
        613–14
    28 *Investments in Associates* 602, 603,
        610, 611–12, 613, 614
    29 *Financial Reporting in*
        *Hyperinflationary Economies* 241,
        638–9
    30 *Disclosures in the Financial*
        *Statements of Banks* 346
    31 *Interests in Joint Ventures* 609
    32 *Financial Instruments: Disclosure a*
        *Presentation* 329–35, 346
    32 *Financial Instruments: Presentatio*
        327
    33 *Earnings per Share* 146, 652–3,
        666–8
    34 *Interim financial reporting* 146
    35 *Discontinuing Operations* 428

36 *Impairment of assets* 85, 411, 423–8,
    468, 554, 605
37 *Provisions, Contingent Liabilities and*
    *Contingent Assets* 303
    constructive obligations 316
    contingent assets 312, 315
    contingent consideration 547
    contingent liabilities 311, 312,
        314–15
    disclosures for non-financial
        liabilities 317–18
    disclosures for provisions 310–11
    ED/2010/1 *Measurement of*
        *Liabilities in IAS 37:* 319
    ED (exposure draft) *Non-financial*
        *Liabilities* 305, 312–18
    environmental assets and liabilities
        839
    *ex gratia* pension arrangements 360
    leases, lessee accounting 452
    legal obligations 316
    measurement of provisions 306–7
    onerous contracts 268, 317
    present values 316
    property, plant and equipment 412
    recognition of provisions 305–6
    restructuring 317, 556
    subsequent measurement and
        derecognition 316
    warranties 265
38 *Intangible Assets* 315, 465–71, 476,
    479
    review of implementation of
        identified intangibles under 481–2
39 *Financial Instruments: Recognition*
    *and Measurement* 327–9, 346–8
    fair values 288
40 *Investment property* 411, 432–3
41 *Agriculture* 432, 510–12
harmonisation 253–4
list 140
*see also* International Financial
    Reporting Standards
International Accounting Standards
    Board (IASB)
    accrual accounting 27
    *Conceptual Framework for Financial*
        *Reporting* 138, 159

International Accounting Standards
    Board (*continued*)
    objective of financial statements
        21–2, 160–1
    objective of general purpose
        financial reporting 165
    omissions 168
    presentation 167, 168
    qualitative characteristics of useful
        financial information 165
    recognition 164, 166
    relevance 166
    qualitative characteristics of useful
        financial information 161–3
    summary of approach 164
    taxation 387, 403
Convergence Project 668
*Disclosure Initiative project* 717
exposure drafts
    ED/2010/1 *Measurement of
        Liabilities in IAS 37:* 319
    ED/2013/10 *Equity Method in
        Separate Financial Statements*
        613–14
    ED/2015/3 *Conceptual Framework
        for Financial Reporting*
        164, 168
    ED *Non-financial Liabilities* 305,
        312–18
fair values 242
financial crisis (2008) and 327–8
financial statements composition 22
governance 328
hyperinflation accounting approach
    241–2
IAS 37 Research Project (2015 staff
    paper) 319
IFRS 8 post-implementation review
    81–2
Improvement Project 668
lease accounting joint project with
    FASB 448
*Management Commentary* (IFRS
    Practice Statement) 54, 112, 787,
    788
Norwalk Agreement 144
objective of financial statements 21–2
political pressures 328–9
*Practice Statement* 168
revenue recognition 253–4
small and medium-sized entities 146
work of 138–9
International Accounting Standards
    Committee (IASC)
*Framework for the Presentation and
    Preparation of Financial
    Statements* 138–9, 158–9, 163
    ⸻s 315
    ⸻l capital maintenance 27
    ⸻13, 315
    ⸻bases 499
    ⸻ture 469
    ⸻s 163
    ⸻rance
    ⸻793–4

International Capital Market Association
    (ICMA) 184
International Federation of Accountants
    (IFAC)
    *Code of Ethics for Professional
        Accountants* 175–8
    *Developing and Reporting
        Supplementary Financial Measures
        – Definition, Principles, and
        Disclosures* 717
International Financial Reporting
    Interpretations Committee
    (IFRIC) 135
International Financial Reporting
    Standards (IFRS)
    1 *First-time Adoption of International
        Financial Reporting Standards* 144
    2 *Share-Based Payments* 359, 372–7
    3 *Business Combinations*
        brands 479
        fair values 242, 547, 555–6
        goodwill 472–7, 479, 554
        non-controlling interests 549
        review of implementation of 481
    4 *Insurance contracts* 146
    5 *Non-current Assets Held for Sale and
        Discontinued Operations* 82–5, 146,
        411, 428, 602
    6 *Exploration for and Evaluation of
        Mineral Resources* 415, 432
    7 *Financial Instruments: Disclosures* 326,
        345–51, 614
    8 *Operating Segments* 75–9, 110, 146,
        555
    9 *Financial Instruments* 326, 335, 337–
        41, 459, 610, 613, 630
    10 *Consolidated Financial Statements*
        545–7, 565, 611
    11 *Joint Arrangements* 608, 609–10,
        612, 613, 614
    12 *Disclosure of Interests in Other
        Entities* 612
    13 *Fair Value Measurement* 243–4, 421,
        481, 555–6
    15 *Revenue from Contracts with
        Customers* 254, 256–69, 404, 457
        construction contracts 520, 524–6
    16 *Leases* 447, 448, 449–60
    adoption by countries 138–9
    EU adoption 142
    EU endorsement 142
    harmonisation 253–4
    IFRS for SMEs
        government grants 432
        intangible assets 471–2
        investment properties 434
        issue 135, 145
        measurement 423
        non-current assets held for sale 429
        property, plant and equipment 413,
            423, 429, 432, 434
    impact of adoption by countries 138–9
    *The implementation of IFRS in the UK,
        Italy and Ireland* (ICAS research
        report 2008) 145
    list 140

    production of 138–9
    United States and 144
    XBRL and 764
    *see also* International Accounting
        Standards
International Forum of Independent
    Audit Regulators (IFIAR) 794
International Forum on Accountancy
    Development (IFAD) 156
International Integrated Reporting
    Council (IIRC) 825, 837
International <IR> Framework 826, 828,
    835
International Standards on Auditing
    (ISA)
    540 *Auditing Accounting Estimates,
        including Fair Value Accounting
        Estimates, and Related Disclosures*
        724
    701 *Communicating Key Audit Matters
        in the Independent Auditor's Report*
        790
International Valuation Standards
    Council (IVSC) 479
intimidation threats 178
introductory reviews, ratio analysis 680–2
inventories 493
    adjusting events 71
    agricultural activities 510–12
    control 504–5
    costs ascertainment 499–501
    creative accounting 505–7
    current cost accounting 231
    cut-off dates 505
    definition 493–4
    disclosures 509–10
    deterioration 502
    errors 505, 508
    foreign exchange differences 629
    identification of items 508
    inaccurate records 506
    income smoothing 494, 495
    obsolescence 502, 507
    physical condition 508
    profits, valuation impact on 494–5
    shrinkage 504
    turnover ratios 688, 695
    unmarketable 507
    valuation 45, 48–9, 204–5, 494–502
    work-in-progress 502–4
    year-end count 507–8
investing activities, cash flows 104, 106,
    109, 113
investment companies, distributable
    profits 287
investment, direct 821–2
investment funds 822
investment property 432–3
investments held-to-maturity 337
investor-specific ratios 724–7
investors
    corporate governance perspective
        781–2
    decision-making needs 52–6
    IFRS 8, views on 81–2
    institutional 148–9, 799–800, 806–8

protection 557
Sarbanes-Oxley Act, USA 143–4
Investors Forum 808
IoDSA (Institute of Directors of
    Southern Africa) 831
Ireland
    *The implementation of IFRS in the UK,
    Italy and Ireland* (ICAS research
    report 2008) 145
    legal system 147
IRR (internal rate of return) 7–8, 730
ISA *see* International Standards on
    Auditing
Islamic Indices 720
ISO 14001: 836
Italy
    *The implementation of IFRS in the UK,
    Italy and Ireland* (ICAS research
    report 2008) 145
IVIS (Institutional Voting and
    Information Service) 805
IVSC (International Valuation Standards
    Council) 479
iXBRL (Inline XBRL) 761, 770–1

James Hardie Group 183–4
Japan
    finance of industry 148
    legal system 147
    XBRL use 762
Jennings, M.M. 184
Johannesburg Stock Exchange 832
John Lewis 42, 48
Johnson Matthey 131–2, 522
joint operations 608–14
joint ventures 608–14
journal adjustments 506

Kay Review 808–9
key management personnel compensation
    88
key performance indicators (KPI) 54–5,
    56, 717
King, Mervyn A. (Baron King of
    Rothbury)) 837
King, Mervyn E. (King Committee on
    Corporate Governance, South
    Africa) 831–2
Kingfisher 114, 797
KPI (key performance indicators) 54–5,
    56, 717
KPMG 145, 177, 795

labour, direct 499, 503
land
    agricultural 511
    freehold 415
language, and accounting systems 150
Large and Medium-sized Companies and
    Groups (Accounts and Reports)
    (Amendment) Regulations 2013:
    798, 800
large-block investors *see* institutional
    investors
last-in-first-out (LIFO) 495, 498–9
lawyers 786

leases 443
    amortised cost principles 453
    carrying amounts 453
    contract terms 450–1
    definition 449
    depreciation 452, 453
    extension options 454
    identified assets 449
    initial direct costs 452, 455
    finance leases 447–8, 451–2, 455–6
    financial liabilities 452
    financial statements 446
        lessees 451–5
        lessors 455–7
    gearing impact 445
    IAS 17: 447, 448
    IFRS 16: 447, 449–60
    liabilities 452–3
    low-value 455
    manufacture of leased assets by lessors
        456
    modifications 453–4
    need for accounting standard 444–7
    operating leases 447–8, 451–2, 457
    purchase and leasing compared 444–7
    purchase of leased assets by lessors 456
    return on capital employed impact
        446–7
    revenue recognition 266
    right of use assets 452–3
    short-term 455
    statements of financial performance
        445
    statements of financial position 445, 446
    statements of profit or loss 446
    substance over form 448
    substitution rights 449
    use of assets 449–51
legal obligations 316
legal risks 788
legal systems, national 147
Lehman Bros 257, 795
Lend Lease Group 523
Lenovo 477
lessees and lessors *see* leases
Lev & Schwartz model 482
leverage *see* gearing
Lexmark 507
liabilities 303
    adjusting events 71
    auditors 795
    capital maintenance and 285–6
    changes in 110
    consolidated accounts 548–9,
        550, 567
    contingent *see* contingent liabilities
    definitions 24, 165, 312
    equity and 330–1
    financial *see* financial liabilities
    future 556
    hidden, unethical behaviour and
        183–4
    leases 452–3
    non-financial 312–18
    pension scheme changes 365–9
    recognition 164

liability method, deferred tax provisions
    396–7
LIFO (last-in-first-out) 495, 498–9
limitations
    published accounts *see* published
        accounts
    traditional financial reporting 830–1
limited liability companies
    creditor protection 285
limited liability partnerships (LLP),
    auditors 795
Linde AG 546, 555
liquidity
    disclosures 116
    ratios 690–3
listed companies *see* public companies
Listing Authority, UK
    *Disclosure Transparency Rules* 789
Lloyds TSB 756
LLP (limited liability partnerships),
    auditors 795
loan creditors 279, 291
loans
    convertible 331
    covenants 721–4
    financial assets 346, 347
    related parties 89
    *see also* borrowings
local currencies 638
Logitech 785
long-service benefits 370
    *see also* pension schemes
long-term contracts, revenue recognition
    266, 522
Lonmin 723, 724
looting 795
losses
    actuarial, pension schemes 367
    associates 605
    consolidated accounts 565–6
    eliminating capital reduction
        288–94
    expected 342–3
    future 556
    impairment 425–6
    incurred 342
    inflation accounting 227
    operating 309
    statements of *see* statements of profit or
        loss
    tax losses 393–4
        unused 401–2
    unrealised 40
    in value of assets 72
low-value leases 455
Lufthansa 729

machine-hour method, depreciation
    418–19, 420
macroeconomic concept 202–3
macroeconomic effects, accounting
    standards 175
Magnum Hunter Resources Corporation
    789
maintainable post-tax earnings 653–4
Maloney, Michael 786

management
  accountability for environmental and
    social responsibility 821–5
  attitudes 50
  changes, unquoted companies, share
    valuations 741
  commentaries 54
  compensation of key management
    personnel 88
  decisions, brands and 478–9
  defects 735
  environmental 819
  EVA use attitudes 729
  by objectives 186
  obligations, environmental and social
    823–5
  orientation 226
  performance 730–1
  reporting to 3, 4–5
  representations 793
  reviews of financial statements for
    purposes of 677–99
  socially aware 829–30
  USA 143
management accountants 838
Management Commentaries 772
managers see management
Manchester City Football Club 311
mandatory standards 132–4
Mandela, Nelson 831
manufacture of leased assets by lessors
  456
manufactured capital 826
manufacturers' warranties 265–6
mapping, XBRL 764, 765
margin ratios 684–6
market approach to valuation of
  intangibles 481
market positioning 55
market-related vesting conditions 376
market share, key performance indicators
  55
marketing, ethics and 177
marketing-related intangible assets 466
markets
  morals and, realignment 180
Marks and Spencer 731, 827
matching concept 414
materiality 73, 141, 161–2, 167–8, 555
measurement
  Accounting Directive 140–1
  agricultural produce 510–11
  assets 166
  bases, inflation accounting 241
  biological assets 510–11
  conceptual framework 164
  contingent liabilities 315
  expected credit losses 342
  fair values 166, 243–4
  financial assets 337
  financial capital maintenance 27
  financial instruments 337–41
  financial liabilities 337
  historical costs 166
  IASB Conceptual Framework 164,
    166–7

income 201–16
  intangible assets 466
  non-controlling interests 549–51
  non-current assets held for sale 428–9
  non-financial liabilities 315, 316, 319
  pension assets or liabilities 366
  property, plant and equipment 421–3
  provisions 306–7
  segment information 77
  share-based payments 373
  statements of financial position 166
  termination benefits 371
  trade receivables 337
  value in use 166
medium-sized companies see small and
  medium-sized enterprises
Member State Options (MSO), EU
  139–40
Merck 114
mergers see acquisitions; business
  combinations; consolidated
  accounts
Metrogroup 72
Mexico
  Gulf of Mexico oil rig disaster 819
micro-economic effects, accounting
  standards 175
micro-undertakings
  regulatory burden on 141
Microsoft 477
Minefinders Corporation 307
minerals 415, 511
minimum share capital 286
mining assets 415
Miniscribe Corporation 506
minority interests see non-controlling
  interests
misappropriation 785
misrepresentation 785
misstatements 74, 168
mistakes see errors
Mitsubishi Logistics Corporation 555
Model Audit Committee Charter 790
modification
  leases 453–4
  terms of contracts, revenue recognition
    268–9
monetary items 227, 629, 639
monetary working capital adjustment
  (MWCA) 232–3, 235–9
money capital 214, 215
money laundering 190
Monitoring Committee, FRC 136, 137
monitoring performance 731, 824–5
Moody's 736
morals 180
  see also ethics
Morrisons 727
Mothercare 72
MSCI Barra 721
MSO (Member State Options), EU
  139–40
multinational companies
  ethics 181, 187
  tax avoidance and 392
multiple capitals 843–5

Munksjo AB 565, 569
Muslim countries
  corporate governance 783
  shariah compliance 720–1
MWCA (monetary working capital
  adjustment) 232–3, 235–9

NAPF see National Association of
  Pension Funds
narrative reporting
  Brexit possible effects 743
National Association of Pension Funds
  (NAPF)
  remuneration principles 800
national differences
  conceptual framework 155–6
  financial reporting 146–50
  legal systems 147
natural capital 827
NED (non-executive directors) 803–5
negative covenants 722
negative goodwill 476–7, 554
negligence, auditors 810
Nemetschek AG 628, 633
Nestlé 46, 720
net asset value per share 799
net assets 206, 547–8, 556, 566, 567
net cash positions 16
net debt/EBITDA ratios 718
net investment hedges 344–5
net operating profit after tax (NOPAT)
  728, 729
net present value (NPV) 7, 9, 333–4
net profits
  earnings per share 652
  impact on IFRS adoption 144–5
  margin ratios 684–5
net realisable value accounting (NRVA)
  222, 223–6, 228, 244
net realisable values (NRV) 494–5, 496,
  501–2, 506
Netherlands
  accounting profession 149
  accounting standards 145
  accounting theory 150
  tax and reporting systems 149
  tax avoidance 392
neutrality 15–16, 162, 175
New York v Ernst & Young (2010) 256
New Zealand
  legal system 147
  tax imputation system 388
Next 294, 501
Nike 186
Nixon, B. 470
nominal monetary units measurement of
  financial capital maintenance 27
nominal values, shares 283
non-adjusting events 71–2
non-cash transactions 109–10
non-controlling interests 549–51, 553,
  555, 566–8, 571, 636
non-cumulative preference shares 283
non-current assets
  accrual accounting 24–7
  adjusting events 71

capital reductions and 290–4
cash flow model 14–15
classification 44–5, 132
consolidated accounts 553, 583
held for sale 428–9
impairment 423–8
turnover ratios 687
*see also* intangible assets
non-distributable reserves 280, 281, 283–4, 285
non-executive directors (NED) 803–5
non-financial liabilities 312–18
non-institutional users of XBRL 766
non-monetary assets 205–6, 233–4, 638
non-monetary items 227, 230–1, 629, 639
non-recurring items 41–3
non-registered traders, VAT 404
non-voting shares 282
NOPAT (net operating profit after tax) 728, 729
Noranda Aluminium Holding Corp 497
normal activity model, inventory valuation 501
normalised earnings 179
normalised earnings per share 799
normative statements 157
norms, societal 178
Norwalk agreement 144
Norway, accounting system 150
notes to cash flow statements 109–10, 115
notes to financial statements 42–3, 45–8, 135, 509
Novartis 720
NPV (net present value) 7, 9, 333–4
NRV *see* net realisable values
NRVA *see* net realisable value accounting

objectives
    financial reporting 165, 755–7
    financial statements 21–2, 160–1, 677
    management by 186
objectivity 12, 175, 204, 205, 226
obligating events 306, 308
obligations
    contingent liabilities 314, 316
    management, environmental and social 823–5
    pension funds 365
    performance, revenue recognition 260, 262–4
    provisions 305–6, 308, 316
obsolescence, inventories 502, 507
Occupy Wall Street 840
OCI (other comprehensive income) 40–1
OECD *see* Organization for Economic Co-operation and Development
offers for subscription of shares 282
offsetting financial instruments 334–5
Oftel 203
Ofwat 203
Ok Tedi mine, Papua New Guinea 819
Oman, C. 781
omissions 74, 168
onerous contracts 268, 309, 317, 525
operating activities, cash flows 103–10
operating capacity capital 214

operating capital maintenance 225, 229–40
operating expenses
    classification 37–40
    ratios 685–6
operating income 41–3, 227
operating leases *see* leases
operating losses 309
operational risks 788
operations
    cash flows 104, 109, 111–12
    scale of 793
opportunity costs 228
options
    share-based payments 372–7
    shares 663, 666, 799, 801
ordinary shares 280, 281–2, 653
organisational cultures
    corporate governance 784–5
    inappropriate 820
Organization for Economic Cooperation and Development (OECD)
    corporate governance 784, 809
    *Report on Abuse of Charities for Money-laundering and Tax Evasion* (2009) 391
    small and medium-sized companies 138
Orion Bank of Naples 786
other comprehensive income (OCI) 40–1
other operating income or expense 38
output method, construction contract earnings 525
outsourcing 834
over-optimism 785
overheads 37, 499–501, 503–4, 506–7
    *see also* costs; expenses
overstated quantities 507
own shares, purchase of 294–6
owners
    capital transactions with 44

P/E ratios *see* price/earnings ratios
Papua New Guinea 819, 832
par values, shares 283
parent companies
    equity method use in separate financial statements 613–14
parents, ethical influences of 173
Parmalat 795
partial imputation system, corporation tax 388–9
partially exempt traders, VAT 404
participating preference shares 280, 283
partly owned subsidiaries 549–51
partnerships, capital maintenance 284–5
PAS-score (performance analysis score) 734
past events 306, 308, 314
past service costs, pension schemes 366–7
patents
    limitations of traditional financial reporting 831
pay ratio, USA 843
payables *see* trade payables
payments
    deferred, revenue recognition 261–2

PBIT (profit before interest and tax) 683–4, 695
PCaW (Public Concern at Work) 188
PDF files 756, 757
PE ratios *see* price/earnings ratios
peer comparisons, financial statement analysis 695–6
peer groups, ethical influences of 174
penalty clauses, construction contracts 521
pension funds 148–9
pension schemes
    assets
        actual and expected returns 367
        changes 365–9
    current service costs 366
    curtailments 366–7
    deferred tax 399–400
    defined benefit schemes 361–2, 363–4, 378–9
    defined contribution schemes 361, 363, 378, 379–80
    disclosures 369, 379–80
    employee interest 359–60
    equity compensation plans 362
    *ex gratia* arrangements 360
    fund obligations 365
    illustrations 363, 365, 368–9
    interest costs 366
    liability for costs 364–7
    multi-employer plans 369
    settlements 366–7
percentage of completion method 520–1
performance
    actual 202
    bonuses, revenue recognition 261
    directors 799
    entity-wide cash-based measures 717–20
    future 3, 203
    inter-company 757
    inter-period 757
    key performance indicators 54–5, 56, 717
    monitoring 731, 824–5
    obligations, revenue recognition 260, 262–4
    poor, rewards for 786
    predicted 202
    remuneration related to 730–1
    stewardship 202
performance analysis score (PAS-score) 734
Pergamon Press 132, 133
permanent differences, deferred taxation 394
perpetual debt 332
personal ethics 173–4
Petroleo Brasileiro 720
PFI (private finance initiative) 531–4
Pfizer 282
physical concept of capital 164
PI NAVIGATOR 757
placings of shares 282
planned activity model, inventory valuation 501

planning, strategic 837–8
plant *see* property, plant and equipment
policies
  accounting *see* accounting policies
  depreciation 434
  dividends 203
  ethics 182–3
  uniform, consolidated accounts 565
pollution 830
poor performance, rewards for 786
Portsmouth FC 111
position, key performance indicators 55
positive NPV 9
possible obligations 314
post retirement costs 364–7
potential consumption capital 214, 215
potential ordinary shares 653
PPE *see* property, plant and equipment
PPP (public–private partnerships) 531–4
pre-acquisition losses 565–6
pre-acquisition profits 565–6, 583–4
pre-contract bid costs 522
predicted performance 202
prediction
  consolidated accounts 557
  income as means of 203
  orientation 16
  ratios for, caution when using 697–9
predictive values 12, 161
preference shares *see* shares
Premier Foods 83
premiums, shares 283–4, 553–4
present obligations 305–6, 308, 314
present values (PV) 206, 208–10, 214,
    307, 316
  *see also* net present value
presentation
  Accounting Directive 141
  exceptional items 43
  financial instruments 330–2
  IASB *Conceptual Framework* 167, 168
  non-current assets held for sale 428–9
presentation currencies 627, 631, 632–3,
    638
price/earnings (PE) ratios 202, 281, 494,
    651–2, 725–6
price index systems 221–2, 226
  *see also* general price indices
price-level changes, accounting for
    220–44
prices
  changing 215, 156
    *see also* inflation; inflation accounting
  shares 724
PricewaterhouseCoopers (PwC) 145, 786
pricing transactions, revenue recognition
    260–2
Primark 820
Prince of Wales 837
principles-based approaches 178–81, 327
prior period adjustments 43
prior period errors 73–4
private companies 280–1
  distributable profits 286–7
  share capital reductions 288
private finance initiative (PFI) 531–4

produce, agricultural 510–12
professional behaviour 176
professional bodies
  ethics 174, 184–5, 187–8
  *see also* accounting profession
professional competence 175–6
professional oversight, auditors 810
professional scepticism, auditors 724,
    792–3
profit and loss accounts *see* statements of
    comprehensive income;
    statements of profit or loss
profit before interest and tax (PBIT)
    683–4, 695
profit-sharing 371
profitability, future 116
profits
  capital profits 207
  concept of 204
  consolidated accounts 565–6, 583–4,
    580
  current purchasing power 227
  distributable 286–8
  gross, margin ratios 685
  inflation accounting 231–3
  inter-company sales 568
  inventories valuation impact on 494–5
  maximisation 178, 821–3
  net *see* net profits
  post-acquisition 566
  pre-acquisition 565–6, 583–4
  private finance initiative 533
  realisation 207
  retained 205–6
  statements of *see* statements of profit or
    loss
  unrealised 207, 482, 605
  *see also* earnings; gains; income
projected unit credit method 365
promotion costs 37
property, plant and equipment (PPE)
    410–11
  cost of 412–13
  current cost accounting 230
  definition 411
  depreciation *see* depreciation
  disclosures 429–30
  financial statements interpretation
    433–5
  government grants 430–2
  impairment of assets 423–8
  investment properties 432–3
  measurement subsequent to initial
    recognition 421–3
  operating leases in books of lessors 457
  revaluations 421–3
  statements of financial position
    explanatory notes 46–7
  subsequent expenditure 413–16
  *see also* land; leases
proportionate consolidation 615
proportionate share method 549–51
prospective changes to financial
    statements 73, 74
provisions
  creation, decision tree 304–5

decommissioning costs 310
decreases 310
deferred tax 395–7
definition 305, 313
ED IAS 37 approach 313
environmental liabilities 310
increases 310
measurement 306–7
onerous contracts 309
operating losses 309
recognition 305–6
restructuring 309–10
treatment 305
unrealised profits 605
prudence 15, 141, 207, 501–2
public companies 280–1
  distributable profits 287
  share capital reductions 288
Public Concern at Work (PCaW) 188
public interest 176
Public Interest Disclosure Act 1999:
    188–9
public–private partnerships (PPP) 531–4
published accounts
  additional entity-wide cash-based
      performance measures 717–20
  analysis 713–43
  formats for 36–40, 48–50
  inventories 509–10
  limitations for interpretation purposes
    lack of detail 716–17
    unaudited information 717
  preparation 33–57
  reliability of financial information
    715–16
  users, educating 796
  *see also* annual reports; financial
      reporting; financial statements
purchase and leasing compared 444–7
purchase of leased assets by lessors 456
purchased goodwill 472, 478, 548–9
purchasing power 222, 225
PV *see* present values
PwC (PricewaterhouseCoopers) 145, 786
pyramid approach, ratios 684

qualitative characteristics 159, 161–3, 165
quality of earnings 41–2
quick ratios 691–2, 695–6

R&D (research and development)
    468–71, 831
R&R Ice Cream plc 50
ratios
  acid test 502, 691–2
  administrative expenses 685
  analysis
    benefits 678
    case study 679–80
    cautionary notes 678–9
    commercial databases 757
    cost structures of companies 682
    financial databases 757
    financial structures of companies
      681–2
    horizontal 681–2

introductory reviews 680–2
  vertical 681, 682
asset turnover 687–9, 695–6
brand effects on 478
cash 693
cash conversion (CCR) 114–15
cash dividend coverage (CDCR) 112,
  114–15
cash flow 692–3
current 690–1, 695–6
debt covenants 721–4
debt/equity 693–5
debt service coverage 718, 720
distribution costs 686
EBITDA-based 718–19
EBITDA/interest 719, 720
ED/2010/1 potential impact on 319
EV (enterprise value)/EBITDA 718
external factors 697–8
financing 693–5
gearing 693–5
gross profit margin 685
hedge 345
financial performance 683–90
interest cover 692
internal factors 698
inventory turnover 688, 695
investor-specific 724–7
liquidity 690–3
margin 684–6
net debt/EBITDA 718
net profit margin 684–5
non-current assets
  revaluation effects on 433
  turnover 687
operating expenses 685–6
peer comparisons 695–6
predictive use 697–9, 732–4
price/earnings see price/earnings
  ratios
profit before interest and tax (PBIT)
  683–4, 695
pyramid approach 684
quick 691–2, 695–6
reports based on 696–7
restrictive loan covenants 721–4
return on capital employed (ROCE) see
  return on capital employed
return on equity (ROE) 683, 724–5
return on investment (ROI) 683, 836
revaluation effects 433
scepticism 699
shariah compliance 720–1
trade payables 689
trade receivables 688–9
volume analysis 687–90
working capital 688–90
raw materials, inflation accounting 226
RBS 840
RCA (replacement cost accounting) 222,
  223–6, 227–8, 498–9
real capital 215
real terms system, inflation accounting
  239–40
real-time financial reporting 771–2
receivables

financial assets 346, 347
trade see trade receivables
recognition
  Accounting Directive 141
  agricultural produce 510–11
  assets 164
  biological assets 510–11
  expenses 164
  financial instruments 335–6
  foreign currency transactions 628
  IASB Conceptual Framework 164, 166
  income 164
  intangible assets 466–71
  liabilities 164
  pension assets or liabilities 366
  property, plant and equipment
    measurement subsequent to
    421–3
  provisions 305–6
  revenue see revenue
  share-based payments 372, 373
  termination benefits 371
  see also derecognition
reconstructions 289–94
redeemable preference shares 283
redemption of shares 72
redundancy costs 317
refunds, annual, revenue recognition 260
registered traders, VAT 404
Registrar of Companies (Companies
  House), XBRL use 761, 769–70
regulatory risks 788
reimbursements 316
related party disclosures 85–9
relevance 161, 166
relevant accounts 288
reliability 15–16, 715–16
religions, ethical influences of 174
remuneration
  directors 796–800
  ethics and 177
  excessive 786
  executive 796–800
  performance criteria 730–1
rendering, XBRL 766–7
replacement cost 203
  accounting (RCA) 222, 223–6, 227–8,
    498–9
  income 214–15
  inventory valuation 498–9
reporting
  accountants' roles 5
  entities, conceptual framework 161
  internal 4–8
  see also annual reports; financial
    reporting; integrated reporting;
    published accounts
research and development (R&D)
  468–71, 831
research costs 469–70
  deferred tax 400
reservation of title
  revenue recognition 266
reserves
  consolidated accounts 549, 551, 567,
    571

current cost 231–9
distributable 280, 281, 285
goodwill, writing off to 472, 474, 478
non-distributable see non-distributable
  reserves
revaluation 44, 433
share premiums 283–4, 553–4
residual values 415–16, 417
restrictive loan covenants 721–4
restructuring 72, 309–10, 317, 556
retail inventory valuation method 497–8
retail price index (RPI) 222, 226
retained profits 205–6
retention of title see reservation of title
retirement benefits see pension schemes
retirement funds 148–9
retrospective changes to financial
  statements 73
return on assets (ROA) 805
return on capital employed (ROCE) 435,
  446–7, 509, 557, 683–5
return on equity (ROE) 683, 724–5
return on investment (ROI) 683, 836
revaluations
  assets 205, 400–1, 433, 556
  property, plant and equipment 421–3
  reserves 44, 433
revenue
  accrual accounting 22–3
  assets disaggregation 269
  Brexit possible effects 742
  construction contracts 521
  definition 255, 257
  disaggregation 269
  grants 430–2
  investment, unquoted companies,
    share valuations 741
  recognition 253–4
    accounting standard development
      issues 255–6
    amounts identification 258–69
    annual refunds 260
    challenges 256–7
    construction contracts 524–5
    contracts 259–60, 262–4
    disclosures 269
    dividends 255
    equally unperformed contracts 267
    financial securities 267
    IAS 18 Revenue 254–5, 256–7
    identifying contracts with customers
      259–60
    IFRS 15 Revenue from Contracts with
      Customers 254, 256–69
    intellectual property transfers 267
    interest 255
    judgements 269
    leases 266
    long-term contracts 266, 522
    modification of terms of contracts
      268–9
    onerous contracts 268
    payments deferred 261–2
    performance bonuses 261
    performance obligations 260, 262–4
    pricing transactions 260–2

revenue (*continued*)
    reservation of title 266
    royalties 255
    sale of goods 254, 265
    sales and repurchases 267
    services 255, 265
    time value of money 261–2
    timing 256, 258–69
    transaction price allocation 262–4
    uncertainties 258
    warranties 265–6
    terms and conditions 269
reversal, deferred tax 395
reviews of financial statements for
        management purposes 677–99
Revsine, L. 203, 214
reward systems 820
rewards to financiers 842
rights issues 282, 657–62
Rio Tinto 631
risk-based proactive approach
    accounting standards enforcement 137
risks
    analysis using XBRL 768
    assessment 736–7
    business, disclosures 714–15
    costs and, trade-offs 822
    disclosures 116
    financial 788
    financial instruments disclosures
        348–51
    legal 788
    management, corporate governance
        787–8
    operational 788
    regulatory 788
    strategic 787–8
    taking, excessive 786
ROA (return on assets) 805
RobcoSam Analyses 837
ROCE *see* return on capital employed
Roche Holdings, Inc. 425, 720
ROE (return on equity) 683, 724–5
Rohan plc 331–2
ROI (return on investment) 683, 836
Rolls-Royce 187, 327, 471, 494, 714–15
Romalpa clauses *see* reservation of title
Roman law legal systems 147
Roosevelt, Franklin D. 390
Royal Bank of Scotland 840
Royal Dutch Shell 839
Royal Liverpool Hospital 531
royalties, revenue recognition 255
RPI (retail price index) 222, 226
rules-based approaches 178–81, 327
Russia
    corporate governance 784
    IFRS adoption 139
Ryanair 740

S&P *see* Standard & Poor's
SABMiller 468
Sainsbury's 361, 362, 429, 496, 719
Sajjad, Afra 56
salaries *see* remuneration
sale and leaseback transactions 457–60

sales
    cost of 37, 231–2
    of goods, revenue recognition 254, 265
    inter-company 568, 579, 580–1
    and repurchases, revenue recognition
        267
Samsung Electronics 720
Sarbanes-Oxley Act 2002, USA 143–4,
        185, 789, 800
SASB (Sustainability Accounting
        Standards Board) 833, 834–5
satisfaction 210
scale of operations 793
scepticism
    auditors 724, 792–3
    ratios 699
screening, Shariah principles 720–1
second opinions, ethics and 177
Securities and Exchange Commission
        (SEC)
    compensation disclosures 797
    enforcement by 143
    fraud cases 785–6
    reason for establishment 150, 155
    XBRL and 761
securities, financial, revenue recognition
        267
segment performance 718
segment reporting 75–9, 110
self-interest threats 178
self-review threats 178
selling
    costs 37
    overheads 500
seniors' perspectives of ethics 182
separate financial statements 612, 613–14
Serious Fraud Office (SFO) 187
services, revenue recognition 255, 265
set-off of inter-company balances 570–1
settlements, pension schemes 366–7
Seventh Directive 139
SFAS *see* Statements of Financial
        Accounting Standards
SFO (Serious Fraud Office) 187
share-based payments 372–7
share capital
    consolidated accounts 549, 551, 566–7,
        571
    minimum 286
    paid-in, repayment of part 294
    reduction 288–96
    unpaid, cancellation 294
    *see also* capital maintenance
shareholders
    activism 805–9
    activity 822
    capital, inflation accounting 227
    capital reduction and 290–4
    earnings per share and 653–4
    funds 237, 281–3, 478
    information needs 3–4, 714–16
    non-voting 282
    preference, capital reductions and 291
    primacy 821–3, 824
    private finance initiative 533–4
    returns 730–1

total funds 281–3
total return (TSR) *see* total shareholder
        return
    value (SV) 730
shares
    accounting entries 283–4
    beneficial ownership statistics 806
    bonus issues 655, 661–2
    buybacks 295–6, 657
    exchanges 553–4
    issuing 44, 72, 280–1, 282–4
    new issues at full market value 656
    nominal values 283
    non-voting 282
    offers for subscription 282
    options 663, 666, 799, 801
    ordinary 280, 281–2, 653
    own, purchase of 294–6
    par values 283
    placings 282
    preference 280, 281, 283, 292, 294,
        330–1, 663–4
    premiums 283–4, 553–4
    prices 724, 800
    redemption 72
    rights issues 282, 657–62
    splits 655–6
    treasury shares 295–6
    warrants 663
    *see also* earnings per share; share capital
shariah compliance 720–1
Shaw, D. 509
Shell 827
Shoprite Holdings 497
short-term employee benefits 370–1
short-term leases 455
shrinkage, inventories 504
Siemens 720, 729
significant influence 601–2
Sinaloa 819
Singapore
    Accounting Corporate Regulatory
        Authority (ACRA) 761, 763
    annual report disclosures 470
    Code of Corporate Governance 800
    XBRL 761, 763
single obligations 306
small and medium-sized enterprises
        (SME)
    borrowing costs 413
    definition 146
    failure prediction and 734
    IFRS for *see* International Financial
        Reporting Standards: IFRS for
        SMEs
    regulatory burden on 141
    reporting requirements 145
    Valuation Index 738
small companies *see* small and medium-
        sized enterprises
smaller listed companies
    co-operative approach to enforcement
        138
SME *see* small and medium-sized
        enterprises
Smith, Adam 178–9

SOCE (statements of changes in equity)
43–4, 160, 582
social accounting 837
social activities, expenditure on 821
social and relationship capital 826–7
social consequences 818–19
social dimension of sustainability 833
social disasters 818, 820
social groups, ethical influences of 174
social information 817
social issues, key performance indicators
55
social responsibilities
management accountability for
821–5
see also corporate social responsibility
socially aware management 829–30
societal norms 178
societal pressures operating against profit
maximisation 821–3
software
limitations of traditional financial
reporting 831
sole traders, capital maintenance 284–5
solvency 103
South Africa
apartheid regime 831
corporate governance 831–2
HIV (Aids) 832
IFRS adoption 139
integrated reporting 825, 831–2
sovereign wealth funds 148–9
SOX see Sarbanes-Oxley Act 2002
Spacek, Leonard 175
Special Purpose Entities (SPE) 795
Spirit Pub Company plc 309
splits, shares 655–6
SSAP see Statements of Standard
Accounting Practice
SSL International 431
stakeholders
corporate governance 782–3
corporate social reporting approach
835–6
theory 823
using financial reports, unethical
behaviour implications for
183–8
XBRL views 760, 763
Standard & Poor's 736
Global Broad Market Index 837
Why inconsistent reporting of exceptional
items can cloud underlying
profitability (2014 study) 53
standard cost, inventory valuation 497
standards see accounting standards;
Financial Reporting Standards;
International Accounting
Standards; International Financial
Reporting Standards; Statements
of Financial Accounting
Standards; Statements of
Standard Accounting Practice
Starbucks 655–6
statements of cash flows see cash flow
statements

statements of changes in equity (SOCE)
43–4, 160, 582
statements of comprehensive income
accrual accounting 23
Brexit possible effects 742
cash flow statements preparation when
not available 118–20
consolidated accounts 580–9, 604–5,
607, 634, 635
construction contracts 527, 529, 530
current cost accounting 237, 240
current taxation 393
decision-usefulness 43
deferred taxation 396
discontinued operations 82–3
foreign currencies and 634, 635
formats 586
hyperinflation 639
inflation accounting 231–3
information needs 160
internal 33–6
as linking statements 206
pension schemes 366, 368
real terms system 240
as statements of financial performance
167
tax expense 393–402
Statements of Financial Accounting
Standards (SFAS) (USA)
109 Accounting for Income Taxes 398
128 Earnings per Share 668
131 Disclosures about Segments of an
Enterprise and Related Information
80–1
statements of financial position 44–5
accrual accounting 23–6
brands 478
Brexit possible effects 743
cash flow accounting 13–14
consolidated accounts 565–71, 602–4,
606
construction contracts 522–3, 527, 529,
530
current cost accounting 229–31, 234–5,
238–9
current purchasing power 227
current taxation 393
depreciation effects 434
foreign currencies and 634, 636
goodwill, keeping in unchanged 472,
474
hyperinflation 639
inflation accounting 229–31, 234–5,
238–9
information needs 160
inventories 509
leases 445, 446
measurement 166
opening, restating to current cost
229–31
pension schemes 369
tax expense 393
statements of income see statements of
comprehensive income
statements of profit or loss 167
leases 446

Statements of Standard Accounting
Practice (SSAP)
5 Accounting for Value Added Tax 404
statutory audit reports 790
Stein Mart 497
Stern Review 825
stewardship 13–14, 15, 16, 21–2, 134,
202, 244, 755–6, 807–8, 809
stock see inventories; shares
stock analysts 786
Stohl, C. 186
straight-line methods
amortisation of goodwill 475
depreciation 417–18, 421
strategic mistakes 735
strategic planning 837–8
Strategic Reports 54–5, 112, 714, 772,
787, 788, 824
strategic risks 787–8
Structural Dynamics Research
Corporation 793
students, ethics and 182, 191–2
stylesheets, XBRL 764–5
subjectivity 228
subsidiaries
acquired during year 584–6, 587–8
book values 552–3
disclosures 612–13
excluded 555
fair values 552–3
foreign currencies 632, 633, 637
partly owned 549–51
wholly owned 545, 548–9
see also acquisitions; business
combinations; consolidated
accounts
substance of transactions 179
substance over form 15, 16, 330, 403, 448,
832
substitution rights, leases 449
sum of the units method, depreciation
418
Sunshine Holdings 3 Ltd 723
superfairness 180
supplier-related intangible assets 466
suppliers
key performance indicators 55
sustainability 833–5, 837, 843, 844
Sustainability Accounting Standards
Board (SASB) 833, 834–5
sustainable earnings 179
SV (shareholder value) 730
Sweden, GRI report 833
symptoms of failure 735–6

T J Hughes 505
TAAR (targeted anti-avoidance rules)
389–90
Taffler's Z-score 732, 733–4
tags, HTML, XML and XBRL 758–9
takeovers see acquisitions; business
combinations; consolidated
accounts
Tanzania 187
targeted anti-avoidance rules (TAAR)
389–90

targets, ethical codes and, conflicts between 186–7
tax havens 391
tax losses *see* losses
taxation
  accounting basis required 17
  avoidance 389–92
  corporation tax 386–403
  current 38–9, 393–4
  deferred 394–403
  evasion 389–92
  income measurement 203–4
  national differences 149
  value added tax 404
taxonomies, XBRL 763–4, 765
technical circulars 157
technical expertise 4
technology 831
technology-related intangible assets 466
Technotrans 310–11
temporary differences, deferred taxation 395–8
tendering, construction contracts 522
termination benefits 371
termination costs 317
Tesco 48, 80, 106, 134, 162, 719
Thameslink 531
theoretical ex-rights calculations, rights issues 658–9
third party evidence (TPE) 259
threats to compliance with fundamental principles 178
ThyssenKrupp 731
time value of money 261–2
timeliness 10, 163
timing differences, deferred taxation 394–8
timing of revenue recognition 256, 258–69
title, reservation of *see* reservation of title
total owners' equity 280–1
TOTAL SA 720
total shareholder return (TSR) 727, 730–1, 799–800
total shareholders' funds 281–3
TPE (third party evidence) 259
trade creditors *see* creditors
trade payables 280
  capital reductions and 291–4
  ratios 689
trade receivables
  measurement 337
  ratios 688–9
trademarks
  limitations of traditional financial reporting 831
trading
  conditions 792–3
  losses, capital reduction 288–94
  related parties 89
trainees' perspectives on ethics 182
training, ethics and 191–2
transactions
  foreign currencies 627–40
  related parties 89
  substance of 179

transferable risks 788
translation, foreign currencies 627, 628–31, 633, 637–8
transparency
  ED/2010/1 potential impact on 319
transport costs 37
Treadway Commission *see* Committee of Sponsoring Organizations of the Treadway Commission
treasury shares 295–6
trial balances 33–6
triple bottom line 828, 831, 837
true and fair view 51–2, 179, 180
TSR *see* total shareholder return
Tullow Oil 632
turnover
  asset turnover ratios 687–9, 695
  non–current asset turnover ratios 687
Tweedie, Sir David 305
Tyco 795

UK Corporate Governance Code 800, 801–10
unaudited information, published account limitations 717
uncertainties
  Brexit possible effects 742
  revenue recognition 258
  *see also* provisions
unconsumed costs of assets, values of 206
understandability 163
understated quantities 507
unethical behaviour 183–8, 785–6
Unilever 84, 89, 731
unincorporated businesses, capital maintenance 284–5
United Arab Emirates, XBRL use 762
United Kingdom
  accounting profession 149
  accounting theory 150
  agricultural accounting 512
  Brexit 142, 742–3
  Bribery Act 2010: 784
  corporate governance 783, 784
  executive remuneration 796–800
  GAAP 142
  *The implementation of IFRS in the UK, Italy and Ireland* (ICAS research report 2008) 145
  legal system 147
  Listing Authority *see* Listing Authority, UK
  management obligations 824
  mandatory standards 132–4
  own shares, buyback 296
  regulatory framework 135–8
  shareholder primacy 824
  tax and reporting systems 149
  treasury shares 296
  UK Corporate Governance Code 800, 801–10
  XBRL 761, 762
United Nations Global Compact 833, 834, 835
United States
  accounting profession 149

accounting standards 150, 476
accounting theory 150
American Institute of Certified Public Accountants (AICPA) 766, 771
Benefit Corporations 822
Certified Public Accountants (CPA) 191
corporate governance 783, 784
Delaware 392
Department of Justice 187
diesel cars pollution levels 819–20
finance of industry 148
Foreign Corrupt Practices Act 1977: 784
GAAP 143, 144, 155, 181, 328, 761, 766
Gulf of Mexico oil rig disaster 819
IFRS and 144
international standards, progress towards adoption 144
legal system 147
own shares, buyback 295
pay ratio 843
shareholder primacy 822
standard setting and enforcement 142–4
tax and reporting systems 149
XBRL 761, 762
*see also* Financial Accounting Standards Board; Securities and Exchange Commission; Statements of Financial Accounting Standards
unquoted companies
  share valuations 737–42
  *see also* private companies
unrealised gains 40, 482
unrealised losses 40
unrealised profits 207, 482, 605
unused tax losses 401–2
URL 756
useful economic lives 414–16, 433–4, 467–8
users of financial statements
  education 796
  needs 161

valuation accounting 242
Valuation Index, SMEs 738
Valuation Standards Council, International (IVSC) 479
valuations
  agricultural produce 512
  errors 74
  historical cost, agricultural activities 512
  intangible assets 481–2
  inventories *see* inventories
  pension schemes 379
  *see also* revaluations
value added statements 828–9, 840–2
value added tax (VAT) 404
value in use, measurement 166
values
  accountants' view 204–6
  capital 214–15

carrying 332–4
current value accounting (CVA) 221
determining value 727–31
economists' view 208–14
ethical, implications for principles
    versus rules-based approaches to
    accounting standards 178–81
future 209
residual 415–16, 417
shareholder value (SV) 730
of unconsumed costs of assets 206
in use 424–5, 427
see also fair values; net realisable values;
    present values
VAT (value added tax) 404
vendor specific objective evidence
    (VSOE) 259
verifiability 163
vertical analysis 681, 682
vested interests 132
vesting dates, share-based payments 374
Virgin Atlantic 190
Vodacom 756
Vodafone 473, 657
volatility 145, 714
Volkswagen 411, 819–20

volume analysis, ratios 687–90
voluntary disclosures 116
VSOE (vendor specific objective
    evidence) 259

WACC (weighted average cost of capital)
    728–9
warehousing costs 37
warning flags 792–3
warranties, revenue recognition 265–6
warrants, shares 663
Wassenan 145
Watford Association Football Club 312
wealth distribution 132
weighted average cost of capital (WACC)
    728–9
weighted average number of ordinary
    shares 653, 659–60
Westwick, C. 509
whistleblowing 188–9
wholly owned subsidiaries 545, 548–9
wider markets initiative (WMI) 531
Williams, Jerry 786
WIP (work-in-progress) 502–4
WMI (wider markets initiative) 531
work-in-progress (WIP) 502–4

working capital 14, 103, 104–5, 106, 109,
    111, 113, 232–3, 688–90
WorldCom 735
WPP 479
writing off part capital 288–94
Wyatt, Arthur 794–5

XBRL (eXtensible Business Reporting
    Language) 756, 757–73
XBRL Foundation Certificate Program
    766
XBRL International 759, 772–3
XML (eXtensible Mark-up Language)
    758, 759

year-end adjustments 35–6
year-end manipulations 505–6
yields
    dividends 727
    earnings 726
    effective 340–1
    unquoted companies, share valuations
        738

Z-scores 732–4, 741
Zeta model 733